# Lecture Notes in Computer Science 6466

Commenced Publication in 1973
Founding and Former Series Edit
Gerhard Goos, Juris Hartmanis, a

T0073979

Bijaya Ketan Panigrahi
Swagatam Das
Ponnuthurai Nagaratnam Suganthan
Subhransu Sekhar Dash (Eds.)

# Swarm, Evolutionary, and Memetic Computing

First International Conference on Swarm, Evolutionary,
and Memetic Computing, SEMCCO 2010
Chennai, India, December 16-18, 2010
Proceedings

 Springer

Volume Editors

Bijaya Ketan Panigrahi
Indian Institute of Technology
Department of Electrical Engineering
New Delhi, India
E-mail: bijayaketan.panigrahi@gmail.com

Swagatam Das
Jadavpur University
Department of Electronics and Communication Engineering
Kolkata, India
E-mail: swagatamdas19@yahoo.co.in

Ponnuthurai Nagaratnam Suganthan
Nanyang Technological University
School of Electrical and Electronic Engineering
Singapore
E-mail: epnsugan@ntu.edu.sg

Subhransu Sekhar Dash
SRM University
Department of Electrical and Electronics Engineering
Chennai, India
E-mail: munu_dash_2k@yahoo.com

Library of Congress Control Number: 2010939937


CR Subject Classification (1998): F.1, I.2, J.3, F.2, I.5, I.4

LNCS Sublibrary: SL 1 – Theoretical Computer Science and General Issues

ISSN      0302-9743
ISBN-10   3-642-17562-7 Springer Berlin Heidelberg New York
ISBN-13   978-3-642-17562-6 Springer Berlin Heidelberg New York

springer.com

© Springer-Verlag Berlin Heidelberg 2010
Printed in Germany

Typesetting: Camera-ready by author, data conversion by Scientific Publishing Services, Chennai, India
Printed on acid-free paper      06/3180

# Preface

This LNCS volume contains the papers presented at the First Swarm, Evolutionary and Memetic Computing Conference (SEMCCO 2010) held during December 16—18, 2010 at SRM University, Chennai, in India. SEMCCO 2010 marked the beginning of a prestigious international conference series that aims at bringing together researchers from academia and industry to report and review the latest progress in the cutting-edge research on swarm, evolutionary, and memetic computing, to explore new application areas, to design new bio-inspired algorithms for solving specific hard optimization problems, and finally to create awareness on these domains to a wider audience of practitioners.

SEMCCO 2010 received 225 paper submissions from 20 countries across the globe. After a rigorous peer-review process involving 610 reviews in total, 90 full-length articles were accepted for oral presentation at the conference. This corresponds to an acceptance rate of 40% and is intended for maintaining the high standards of the conference proceedings. The papers included in this LNCS volume cover a wide range of topics in swarm, evolutionary, and memetic computing algorithms and their real-world applications in problems selected from diverse domains of science and engineering.

The conference featured four distinguished keynote speakers. Kalyanmoy Deb's talk on 'Preference-Based Evolutionary Multiobjective Optimization' focused on three different possibilities of integrating multiple criteria decision-making (MCDM) techniques with an evolutionary multi-objective optimization (EMO) procedure and presented some recent research results. The lecture generated great interest among the participants of SEMCCO in paying more attention to this important and overlooked K.C. Tan's talk on 'Handling Uncertainties in Evolutionary Multi-objective Optimization' featured the challenges faced in handling uncertainties in EMO. Specifically, the impact of these uncertainties on multi-objective optimization was described along with a focus on the approaches/modifications to basic algorithm design for better and robust EMO performance. P.N. Suganthan, in his lecture on 'Evolutionary Algorithms with Diversity and Local Search Enhancements,' first addressed the issue of diversity management in populated evolutionary algorithms. He introduced some commonly used diversity measurement methods and subsequently presented a few different ways of enhancing the diversity of populations and demonstrated the benefits of diversity enhancement operations. He also demonstrated the integration of diversity enhancement and local search methods as two complementary operations to enhance the overall performance of evolutionary algorithms. Yew Soon Ong's lecture on 'Towards Memetic Computing' provided insight into the multi faceted view of meme in memetic computation. He reviewed the design issues anchoring on hybridization aspects of memetic computation. Subsequently, his talk focused on the algorithmic aspects and properties of a recently proposed probabilistic memetic framework that formalizes the design of adaptive hybrids or adaptive memetic algorithms as opposed to the typical ad-hoc means of design. Finally he took a peek into the journey toward memetic computing and uncovered some key aspects of the agent computing framework as an important means for enriching memetic computation research.

SEMCCO 2010 also included two tutorials, which were free to all conference participants. The tutorial delivered jointly by Swagatam Das and Rammohan Mallipeddi on 'Differential Evolution: Foundations, Perspectives, and Engineering Applications' systematically introduced the main features of one of the most powerful real parameter optimization algorithms of current interest – differential evolution (DE). DE is a very simple algorithm, requiring only a few lines of code in most of the existing programming languages. Nonetheless, DE exhibits remarkable performance in optimizing a wide variety of optimization problems in terms of final accuracy, convergence speed, and robustness as evidenced by the consistently excellent performance in all of the competitions organized under the IEEE Congress on Evolutionary Computation (CEC, http://www3.ntu.edu.sg/home/epnsugan/). This tutorial inspired both novices and experts of DE to a greater understanding of the very fundamentals of its working principles. The other tutorial by B.K. Panigrahi and S. Paramsivam was on "Applied Swarm Intelligence: A Power System Perspective" and included the application of swarm algorithms to power systems, power electronics and drives area. The tutorial made an excellent start to the three-day conference.

We take this opportunity to thank the authors of all submitted papers for their hard work, adherence to the deadlines and patience with the review process. The quality of a refereed volume depends mainly on the expertise and dedication of the reviewers. We are indebted to the Program Committee members who not only produced excellent reviews but also did these in the short timeframes that they were given.

We would also like to thank our sponsors for providing all the support and financial assistance. First, we are indebted to SRM University administration (The Chancellor, the Vice Chancellor, Pro Vice-Chancellor, Registrar, Director of Engineering and Technology, and faculty colleagues and administrative personnel) for supporting our cause and encouraging us to organize the conference at SRM University, Chennai. We would like to express our heartfelt thanks to Meng Hiot Lim and Yuhui Shi for providing valuable guidelines and inspiration to overcome various difficulties in the process of organizing this conference. The financial assistance from SRM University and the Department of Science and Technology (DST), Government of India, and several others in meeting a major portion of the expenses is highly appreciated. We would also like to thank the participants of this conference, who have considered the conference above all hardships. Finally, we would like to thank all the volunteers whose tireless efforts in meeting the deadlines and arranging every detail made sure that the conference could run smoothly. We hope the readers of these proceedings find the papers inspiring and enjoyable.

December 2010                                          Bijaya Ketan Panigrahi
                                                                 Swagatam Das
                                                                 P.N. Suganthan
                                                                 S.S. Dash

# Organization

## Chief Patrons

Shri T.R. Pachamuthu       Chancellor, SRM University
P. Sathayanarayanan       Vice-Chancellor, SRM University

## Patrons

M. Ponnavaikko       Provost, SRM University
T.P. Ganesan       Pro Vice-Chancellor, SRM University
N. Sethuraman       Registrar
C. Muthamizhchelvan       Director (E&T)

## Organizing Secretaries

S.S. Dash       SRM University, Chennai, India
K. Vijayakumar       SRM University, Chennai, India

## General Chairs

Meng-Hiot Lim       Nanyang Technological University, Singapore
Yuhui Shi       Xi'an Jiaotong-Liverpool University (XJTLU),
                             Suzhou, China

## Program Chairs

B.K. Panigrahi       Indian Institute of Technology (IIT), Delhi, India
Swagatam Das       Jadavpur University, Kolkata, India
S.S. Dash       SRM University, Chennai, India

## Steering Committee Chair

P.N. Suganthan, Singapore

## Proceedings Chair

Cao Qi, Singapore

## Special Session Chair

Sanjoy Das, Kansas State University, USA
Zhihua Cui, China

## Publicity Chairs

Simon Y Foo, Florida State University, USA
M. Arun Bhaskar, India
Chuan-Kang Ting, National Chung Cheng University, Taiwan

## International Advisory Committee

Maurice Clerc, France
Lakhmi C. Jain, Australia
Tao Ban, NICT, Japan
Roderich Gross, UK
Rajkumar Roy, UK
Jim Smith, UK
Carlos A. Coello Coello, Mexico
P.N. Suganthan, Singapore
Kalyanmoy Deb, India
Peng Shi, UK
N.R. Pal, India
Jeng-Shyang Pan, Taiwan
X.Z. Gao, Finland
Juan Luis Fernández Martínez, California, USA
Oscar Castillo, Mexico
Leandro Dos Santos Coelho, Brazil
Wei-Chiang Samuelson Hong, Taiwan
Zhihua Cui, China
Heitor Silvério Lopes, Brazil
Zong Woo Geem, USA
Rafael Stubs Parpinelli, Brazil
S.K. Udgata, India
S.S. Pattanaik, India
Rajendra Akerkar, India
Gerardo Beni, USA
S. Paramasivam, India
John L. Vian, USA
Sanjoy Das, USA
M.K. Tiwari, India
Shu-Heng Chen, Taiwan
S. Sundaram, Singapore
B.K. Dass, India
Dipankar Dasgupta, USA

K.E. Parsopoulos, Greece
M.A. Abido, Saudi Arabia
G.K. Venayagamoorthy, USA
Mohammed Alrashidi, Kuwait
Namrata Khemka, USA

## Local Organizing Committee

P.K.A. Muniswaran
S.V. Kasmir Raja
T.V. Gopal
C. Muthamizhchelvan
Narayana Rao
R. Ramaswami
R. Jagadeesan
S. Malarvizhi
T. Rama Rao
A. Vimala Juliet
C. Malathy
S. Rajendran
S.S. Sridhar
A. Rathinam
N. Chellamal
R. Sridhar

# Table of Contents

Self-adaptive Differential Evolution with Modified Multi-Trajectory
Search for CEC 2010 Large Scale Optimization ...................... 1
   *Shi-Zheng Zhao, Ponnuthurai Nagaratnam Suganthan, and
   Swagatam Das*

Differential Evolution Based Ascent Phase Trajectory Optimization for
a Hypersonic Vehicle .............................................. 11
   *Ritwik Giri and D. Ghose*

Dynamic Grouping Crowding Differential Evolution with Ensemble of
Parameters for Multi-modal Optimization ........................... 19
   *Bo Yang Qu, Pushpan Gouthanan, and
   Ponnuthurai Nagaratnam Suganthan*

Empirical Study on Migration Topologies and Migration Policies for
Island Based Distributed Differential Evolution Variants .............. 29
   *G. Jeyakumar and C. Shunmuga Velayutham*

Differential Evolution Based Fuzzy Clustering ....................... 38
   *V. Ravi, Nupur Aggarwal, and Nikunj Chauhan*

A Population Adaptive Differential Evolution Strategy to Light
Configuration Optimization of Photometric Stereo ................... 46
   *B. Sathyabama, V. Divya, S. Raju, and V. Abhaikumar*

Solving Multi Objective Stochastic Programming Problems Using
Differential Evolution ............................................. 54
   *Radha Thangaraj, Millie Pant, Pascal Bouvry, and Ajith Abraham*

Multi Sensor Fusion Using Fitness Adaptive Differential Evolution ..... 62
   *Ritwik Giri, Arnob Ghosh, Aritra Chowdhury, and Swagatam Das*

Differential Evolution Algorithm with Ensemble of Parameters and
Mutation and Crossover Strategies ................................. 71
   *Rammohan Mallipeddi and Ponnuthurai Nagaratnam Suganthan*

Design of Robust Optimal Fixed Structure Controller Using Self
Adaptive Differential Evolution .................................... 79
   *S. Miruna Joe Amali and S. Baskar*

Electromagnetic Antenna Configuration Optimization Using Fitness
Adaptive Differential Evolution .................................... 87
   *Aritra Chowdhury, Arnob Ghosh, Ritwik Giri, and Swagatam Das*

Analyzing the Explorative Power of Differential Evolution Variants on
Different Classes of Problems . . . . . . . . . . . . . . . . . . . . . . . . . . . . . . . . . . . . . . .    95
    *G. Jeyakumar and C. Shanmugavelayutham*

A Self Adaptive Differential Evolution Algorithm for Global
Optimization . . . . . . . . . . . . . . . . . . . . . . . . . . . . . . . . . . . . . . . . . . . . . . . . . . . . . . .   103
    *Pravesh Kumar and Millie Pant*

Optimization for Workspace Volume of 3R Robot Manipulator Using
Modified Differential Evolution . . . . . . . . . . . . . . . . . . . . . . . . . . . . . . . . . . . . .   111
    *Bibhuti Bhusan Biswal, Sumanta Panda, and Debadutta Mishra*

Adaptive Differential Evolution with $p$-Best Crossover for Continuous
Global Optimization . . . . . . . . . . . . . . . . . . . . . . . . . . . . . . . . . . . . . . . . . . . . . . . .   119
    *Sk. Minhazul Islam, Saurav Ghosh, Subhrajit Roy, and Swagatam Das*

A New Particle Swarm Optimization Algorithm for Dynamic
Environments . . . . . . . . . . . . . . . . . . . . . . . . . . . . . . . . . . . . . . . . . . . . . . . . . . . . . .   129
    *Masoud Kamosi, Ali B. Hashemi, and M.R. Meybodi*

Power Mutation Embedded Modified PSO for Global Optimization
Problems . . . . . . . . . . . . . . . . . . . . . . . . . . . . . . . . . . . . . . . . . . . . . . . . . . . . . . . . . .   139
    *Pinkey Chauhan, Kusum Deep, and Millie Pant*

PSO Advances and Application to Inverse Problems . . . . . . . . . . . . . . . . . . .   147
    *Juan Luis Fernández-Martínez and Esperanza García-Gonzalo*

Adaptive and Accelerated Exploration Particle Swarm Optimizer
(AAEPSO) for Solving Constrained Multiobjective Optimization
Problems . . . . . . . . . . . . . . . . . . . . . . . . . . . . . . . . . . . . . . . . . . . . . . . . . . . . . . . . . .   155
    *Layak Ali, Samrat L. Sabat, and Siba K. Udgata*

Expedite Particle Swarm Optimization Algorithm (EPSO) for
Optimization of MSA . . . . . . . . . . . . . . . . . . . . . . . . . . . . . . . . . . . . . . . . . . . . . .   163
    *Amit Rathi and Ritu Vijay*

Covariance Matrix Adapted Evolution Strategy Based Design of Mixed
$H_2/H_\infty$ PID Controller . . . . . . . . . . . . . . . . . . . . . . . . . . . . . . . . . . . . . . . . .   171
    *M. Willjuice Iruthayarajan and S. Baskar*

Towards a Link between Knee Solutions and Preferred Solution
Methodologies . . . . . . . . . . . . . . . . . . . . . . . . . . . . . . . . . . . . . . . . . . . . . . . . . . . . .   182
    *Kalyanmoy Deb and Shivam Gupta*

A Relation-Based Model for Convergence Analysis of Evolutionary
Algorithm . . . . . . . . . . . . . . . . . . . . . . . . . . . . . . . . . . . . . . . . . . . . . . . . . . . . . . . . . .   190
    *Zhi-Feng Hao, Han Huang, Haozhe Li, Shaohu Ling, and Benqing Li*

Neural Meta-Memes Framework for Combinatorial Optimization . . . . . . .   198
    *Li Qin Song, Meng Hiot Lim, and Yew Soon Ong*

An Improved Evolutionary Programming with Voting and Elitist
Dispersal Scheme ............................................... 206
    *Sayan Maity, Kumar Gunjan, and Swagatam Das*

Heuristic Algorithms for the $L(2,1)$-Labeling Problem ............... 214
    *B.S. Panda and Preeti Goel*

Runtime Analysis of Evolutionary Programming Based on Cauchy
Mutation ....................................................... 222
    *Han Huang, Zhifeng Hao, Zhaoquan Cai, and Yifan Zhu*

Best Hiding Capacity Scheme for Variable Length Messages Using
Particle Swarm Optimization .................................... 230
    *Ruchika Bajaj, Punam Bedi, and S.K. Pal*

Ant Colony Optimization for Markowitz Mean-Variance Portfolio
Model .......................................................... 238
    *Guang-Feng Deng and Woo-Tsong Lin*

Hybrid PSO Based Integration of Multiple Representations of Thermal
Hand Vein Patterns ............................................. 246
    *Amioy Kumar, Madasu Hanmandlu, and H.M. Gupta*

Detection and Length Estimation of Linear Scratch on Solid Surfaces
Using an Angle Constrained Ant Colony Technique................... 254
    *Siddharth Pal, Aniruddha Basak, and Swagatam Das*

An Intelligence Model with Max-Min Strategy for Constrained
Evolutionary Optimization ...................................... 262
    *Xueqiang Li, Zhifeng Hao, and Han Huang*

Parallel Ant-Miner (PAM) on High Performance Clusters ............. 270
    *Janaki Chintalapati, M. Arvind, S. Priyanka, N. Mangala, and
    Jayaraman Valadi*

A Software Tool for Data Clustering Using Particle Swarm
Optimization ................................................... 278
    *Kalyani Manda, A. Sai Hanuman, Suresh Chandra Satapathy,
    Vinaykumar Chaganti, and A. Vinaya Babu*

An ACO Approach to Job Scheduling in Grid Environment ........... 286
    *Ajay Kant, Arnesh Sharma, Sanchit Agarwal, and Satish Chandra*

Runtime Analysis of (1+1) Evolutionary Algorithm for a TSP
Instance ....................................................... 296
    *Yu Shan Zhang and Zhi Feng Hao*

An Evolutionary Approach to Intelligent Planning .................. 305
    *Shikha Mehta, Bhuvan Sachdeva, Rohit Bhargava, and Hema Banati*

Substitute Domination Relation for High Objective Number
Optimization .................................................. 314
  *Sofiene Kachroudi*

Discrete Variables Function Optimization Using Accelerated
Biogeography-Based Optimization.............................. 322
  *M.R. Lohokare, S.S. Pattnaik, S. Devi, B.K. Panigrahi, S. Das, and*
  *D.G. Jadhav*

A Genetic Algorithm Based Augmented Lagrangian Method for
Computationally Fast Constrained Optimization .................... 330
  *Soumil Srivastava and Kalyanmoy Deb*

Evolutionary Programming Improved by an Individual Random
Difference Mutation ............................................. 338
  *Zhaoquan Cai, Han Huang, Zhifeng Hao, and Xueqiang Li*

Taguchi Method Based Parametric Study of Generalized Generation
Gap Genetic Algorithm Model .................................... 344
  *S. Thangavelu and C. Shunmuga Velayutham*

EBFS-ICA: An Efficient Algorithm for CT-MRI Image Fusion ......... 351
  *Rutuparna Panda and Sanjay Agrawal*

Adaptive Nonlinear Signal Approximation Using Bacterial Foraging
Strategy ........................................................ 362
  *Naik Manoj Kumar and Panda Rutuparna*

Swarm Intelligence for Optimizing Hybridized Smoothing Filter in
Image Edge Enhancement ........................................ 370
  *B. Tirumala Rao, S. Dehuri, M. Dileep, and A. Vindhya*

A Hybrid GA-Adaptive Particle Swarm Optimization Based Tuning of
Unscented Kalman Filter for Harmonic Estimation .................. 380
  *Ravi Kumar Jatoth and Gogulamudi Anudeep Reddy*

Using Social Emotional Optimization Algorithm to Direct Orbits of
Chaotic Systems ................................................ 389
  *Zhihua Cui, Zhongzhi Shi, and Jianchao Zeng*

A Hybrid ANN-BFOA Approach for Optimization of FDM Process
Parameters...................................................... 396
  *Anoop Kumar Sood, R.K. Ohdar, and S.S. Mahapatra*

Bio Inspired Swarm Algorithm for Tumor Detection in Digital
Mammogram ..................................................... 404
  *J. Dheeba and Tamil Selvi*

A Hybrid Particle Swarm with Differential Evolution Operator
Approach (DEPSO) for Linear Array Synthesis ...................... 416
   *Soham Sarkar and Swagatam Das*

Sensor Deployment in 3-D Terrain Using Artificial Bee Colony
Algorithm...................................................... 424
   *S. Mini, Siba K. Udgata, and Samrat L. Sabat*

Novel Particle Swarm Optimization Based Synthesis of Concentric
Circular Antenna Array for Broadside Radiation ..................... 432
   *Durbadal Mandal, Sakti Prasad Ghoshal, and*
   *Anup Kumar Bhattacharjee*

A Particle Swarm Optimization Algorithm for Optimal Operating
Parameters of VMI Systems in a Two-Echelon Supply Chain .......... 440
   *Goh Sue-Ann and S.G. Ponnambalam*

Enhanced Memetic Algorithm for Task Scheduling ................... 448
   *S. Padmavathi, S. Mercy Shalinie, B.C. Someshwar, and*
   *T. Sasikumar*

Quadratic Approximation PSO for Economic Dispatch Problems with
Valve-Point Effects ...................................... ............ 460
   *Jagdish Chand Bansal and Kusum Deep*

Fuzzified PSO Algorithm for OPF with FACTS Devices in
Interconnected Power Systems .................................... 468
   *N.M. Jothi Swaroopan and P. Somasundaram*

Co-ordinated Design of AVR-PSS Using Multi Objective Genetic
Algorithm..................................................... 481
   *B. Selvabala and D. Devaraj*

A Genetic Algorithm Approach for the Multi-commodity, Multi-period
Distribution Planning in a Supply Chain Network Design .............. 494
   *G. Reza Nasiri, Hamid Davoudpouri, and Yaser Movahedi*

Particle Swarm Optimization with Watts-Strogatz Model ............. 506
   *Zhuanghua Zhu*

Multi-objective Evolutionary Algorithms to Solve Coverage and
Lifetime Optimization Problem in Wireless Sensor Networks........... 514
   *Koyel Chaudhuri and Dipankar Dasgupta*

Offline Parameter Estimation of Induction Motor Using a Meta
Heuristic Algorithm ......................................... 523
   *Ritwik Giri, Aritra Chowdhury, Arnob Ghosh, B.K. Panigrahi, and*
   *Swagatam Das*

Performance Evaluation of Particle Swarm Optimization Based Active
Noise Control Algorithm ........................................... 531
   *Nirmal Kumar Rout, Debi Prasad Das, and Ganapati Panda*

Solution to Non-convex Electric Power Dispatch Problem Using Seeker
Optimization Algorithm ............................................ 537
   *K.R. Krishnanand, P.K. Rout, B.K. Panigrahi, and
   Ankita Mohapatra*

Swarm Intelligence Algorithm for Induction Motor Field Efficiency
Evaluation ........................................................ 545
   *V.P. Sakthivel and S. Subramanian*

Artificial Bee Colony Algorithm for Transient Performance
Augmentation of Grid Connected Distributed Generation .............. 559
   *A. Chatterjee, S.P. Ghoshal, and V. Mukherjee*

Performance Comparison of Attribute Set Reduction Algorithms in
Stock Price Prediction - A Case Study on Indian Stock Data .......... 567
   *P. Bagavathi Sivakumar and V.P. Mohandas*

Dimensionality Reduction and Optimum Feature Selection in Designing
Efficient Classifiers .............................................. 575
   *A.K. Das and J. Sil*

Social Emotional Optimization Algorithm for Nonlinear Constrained
Optimization Problems ............................................. 583
   *Yuechun Xu, Zhihua Cui, and Jianchao Zeng*

Multi-objective Optimal Design of Switch Reluctance Motors Using
Adaptive Genetic Algorithm......................................... 591
   *Mehran Rashidi and Farzan Rashidi*

Genetic Algorithm Approaches to Solve RWA Problem in WDM
Optical Networks .................................................. 599
   *Ravi Sankar Barpanda, Ashok Kumar Turuk,
   Bibhudatta Sahoo, and Banshidhar Majhi*

Multi-objective Performance Optimization of Thermo-Electric Coolers
Using Dimensional Structural Parameters ........................... 607
   *P.K.S. Nain, J.M. Giri, S. Sharma, and K. Deb*

An Artificial Physics Optimization Algorithm for Multi-objective
Problems Based on Virtual Force Sorting Proceedings ................ 615
   *Yan Wang, Jian-chao Zeng, and Ying Tan*

Effective Document Clustering with Particle Swarm Optimization ...... 623
   *Ramanji Killani, K. Srinivasa Rao, Suresh Chandra Satapathy,
   Gunanidhi Pradhan, and K.R. Chandran*

A Hybrid Differential Invasive Weed Algorithm for Congestion
Management .................................................... 630
*Aniruddha Basak, Siddharth Pal, V. Ravikumar Pandi,
B.K. Panigrahi, and Swagatam Das*

Security Constrained Optimal Power Flow with FACTS Devices Using
Modified Particle Swarm Optimization............................. 639
*P. Somasundaram and N.B. Muthuselvan*

Tuning of PID Controller Using Internal Model Control with the Filter
Constant Optimized Using Bee Colony Optimization Technique ........ 648
*U. Sabura Banu and G. Uma*

An Efficient Estimation of Distribution Algorithm for Job Shop
Scheduling Problem ............................................. 656
*Xiao-juan He, Jian-chao Zeng, Song-dong Xue, and Li-fang Wang*

Semantic Web Service Discovery Algorithm Based on Swarm System ... 664
*Qiu Jian-ping and Chen Lichao*

Stochastic Ranking Particle Swarm Optimization for Constrained
Engineering Design Problems .................................... 672
*Samrat L. Sabat, Layak Ali, and Siba K. Udgata*

A New Improved Particle Swarm Optimization Technique for Daily
Economic Generation Scheduling of Cascaded Hydrothermal Systems ... 680
*K.K. Mandal, B. Tudu, and N. Chakraborty*

Improved Real Quantum Evolutionary Algorithm for Optimum
Economic Load Dispatch with Non-convex Loads .................... 689
*Nidul Sinha, Kaustabh Moni Hazarika, Shantanu Paul,
Himanshu Shekhar, and Amrita Karmakar*

Linear Array Geometry Synthesis with Minimum Side Lobe Level and
Null Control Using Dynamic Multi-Swarm Particle Swarm Optimizer
with Local Search .............................................. 701
*Pradipta Ghosh and Hamim Zafar*

Constraint Handling in Transmission Network Expansion Planning ..... 709
*R. Mallipeddi, Ashu Verma, P.N. Suganthan, B.K. Panigrahi, and
P.R. Bijwe*

A Novel Multi-objective Formulation for Hydrothermal Power
Scheduling Based on Reservoir End Volume Relaxation ............... 718
*Aniruddha Basak, Siddharth Pal, V. Ravikumar Pandi,
B.K. Panigrahi, M.K. Mallick, and Ankita Mohapatra*

Particle Swarm Optimization and Varying Chemotactic Step-Size
Bacterial Foraging Optimization Algorithms Based Dynamic Economic
Dispatch with Non-smooth Fuel Cost Functions ...................... 727
    P. Praveena, K. Vaisakh, and S. Rama Mohana Rao

Hydro-thermal Commitment Scheduling by Tabu Search Method with
Cooling-Banking Constraints ..................................... 739
    Nimain Charan Nayak and C. Christober Asir Rajan

**Author Index** ................................................. 753

# Self-adaptive Differential Evolution with Modified Multi-Trajectory Search for CEC'2010 Large Scale Optimization

Shi-Zheng Zhao[1], Ponnuthurai Nagaratnam Suganthan[1], and Swagatam Das[2]

[1] School of Electrical and Electronic Engineering,
Nanyang Technological University,
Singapore 639798, Singapore
ZH0047NG@e.ntu.edu.sg, epnsugan@ntu.edu.sg
[2] Dept. of Electronics and Telecommunication Engg,
Jadavpur University,
Kolkata 700 032, India
swagatamdas19@yahoo.co.in

**Abstract.** In order to solve large scale continuous optimization problems, Self-adaptive DE (SaDE) is enhanced by incorporating the JADE mutation strategy and hybridized with modified multi-trajectory search (MMTS) algorithm (SaDE-MMTS). The JADE mutation strategy, the "DE/current-to-pbest" which is a variation of the classic "DE/current-to best", is used for generating mutant vectors. After the mutation phase, the binomial (uniform) crossover, the exponential crossover as well as no crossover option are used to generate each pair of target and trial vectors. By utilizing the self-adaptation in SaDE, both trial vector generation strategies and their associated control parameter values are gradually self-adapted by learning from their previous experiences in generating promising solutions. Consequently, suitable offspring generation strategy along with associated parameter settings will be determined adaptively to match different phases of the search process. MMTS is applied frequently to refine several diversely distributed solutions at different search stages satisfying both the global and the local search requirement. The initialization of step sizes is also defined by a self-adaption during every MMTS step. The success rates of both SaDE and the MMTS are determined and compared, consequently, future function evaluations for both search algorithms are assigned proportionally to their recent past performance. The proposed SaDE-MMTS is employed to solve the 20 numerical optimization problems for the CEC'2010 Special Session and Competition on Large Scale Global Optimization and competitive results are presented.

**Keywords:** Evolutionary algorithm, Large Scale Global Optimization, Differential Evolution, Self-adaptive, modified multi-trajectory search.

## 1 Introduction

Differential Evolution (DE) algorithm, proposed by Storn and Price [11][1] [2][5][6][10], is a simple yet powerful population-based stochastic search technique

B.K. Panigrahi et al. (Eds.): SEMCCO 2010, LNCS 6466, pp. 1–10, 2010.

for solving global optimization problems in continuous search domain. In DE, there exist many trial vector generation strategies and crucial control parameters that significantly influence the optimization performance of the DE. Therefore, in order to successfully solve a specific optimization problem, it is generally required to perform a time-consuming and computationally demanding trial-and-error search for the most appropriate strategy and to tune the associated parameter values. Moreover, during the search process, the DE population may evolve through different regions in the search space thereby requiring different strategies and parameter settings. Hence, it is desirable to adaptively determine appropriate strategies and associated parameter values at different stages of evolution. In this paper, we apply the Self-adaptive DE (SaDE) [8][9][4] to make both crossover strategies and their associated parameters self-adaptive by learning from their previous experiences in generating improved solutions. Consequently, suitable generation strategies along with parameter settings can be determined adaptively to match different search phases. At each generation, a strategy together with associated parameter values will be assigned to each parent according to the selection probabilities learnt from the previous generations.

The JADE [15] introduces a new mutation strategy, "DE/current-to-pbest" with optional external archive. As a generalization of DE/current-to-best, DE/current-to-pbest utilizes not only the best solution information but also the information of other good solutions of the current population. To be specific, any of the top $p\%$, $p \in (0, 100]$ solutions will be randomly chosen in DE/current-to-pbest to play the role designed exclusively for the single best solution in DE/current-to-best. In addition, the difference between the archived solutions and a member in the current population can be incorporated into the mutation operation. This strategy is able to diversify the population and provides approximate direction of evolution.

The original MTS [12][13] employs search agents, which search for better solutions by moving with different step sizes in the parameter space from the original positions in each dimension. The step size was defined within a search range to fit the requirement of global and local search.

In this paper, the SaDE is enhanced by utilizing Modified MTS (MMTS), JADE mutation strategy (SaDE-MMTS) [18] and the binomial (uniform) crossover, the exponential crossover and without crossover to test the 20 numerical optimization problems for the CEC'2010 Special Session and Competition on Large Scale Global Optimization. The step sizes are also self-adapted during every MMTS step. The success rates of both SaDE and the MMTS are computed and consequently, future function evaluations for both search algorithms are assigned according to their recent past performance. The rest of the paper is organized as follows: Section 2 presents the details of the proposed SaDE-MMTS. Section 3 presents experimental results with analysis. The paper is concluded in Section 4 with a brief statement on future research directions.

## 2   SaDE with MMTS

Optimization algorithms perform differently when solving different optimization problems due to their distinct characteristics. But, some of them often lose their efficacy when solving complex problem instances with high dimensions. There are two main difficulties for those optimization methods whose performance deteriorates quickly as the dimensionality of the search space increases. First one is the high demand on exploration capabilities of the optimization methods. When the solution space of a problem increases exponentially with the number of problem dimensions, more efficient search strategies are required to explore all promising regions within a given time budget. Second, the complexity of a problem characteristics may increase with increasing dimensionality, e.g. uni-modality in lower dimensions may become multi-modality in higher dimensions for some problems. Due to these reasons, a successful search strategy in lower dimensions may no longer be capable of finding the optimal solution in higher dimension [14][3][16][17][26]. In this section, how to combine them to form the SaDE with Modified MTS (SaDE-MMTS) for solving large scale optimization problems is explained [18].

The JADE mutation strategy with small sized archive is coupled with two basic crossover operators (binomial crossover and exponential crossover) as well as no crossover option. The mutation strategies with exponential crossover and without any crossover are appropriate for solving linked problems. The binomial crossover is effective for solving separable problems when the *CR* is low while it is also effective for solving non-separable problems when *CR* is large. SaDE-MMTS also benefits from the self-adaptation of trial vector generation strategies and control parameter adaptation schemes in the SaDE by learning from their previous experiences to fit different characteristic of the problems and different search requirements of evolution phases. In the SaDE-MMTS [18], with respect to each target vector in the current population, one trial vector generation strategy is selected from the candidate pool according to the probability learned from its success rate in generating improved solutions within a certain number of previous generations. These probabilities are gradually adapted during evolution in the following manner. Assume that the probability of applying the kth strategy in the candidate pool to a target vector in the current population is $p_k$, $k = 1, 2, ..., K$, where $K$ is the total number of strategies in the pool. At the beginning, the probabilities with respect to each strategy are initialized as *1/K*, i.e. all strategies have the equal probability to be chosen. At the generation *G*, after evaluating all the generated trial vectors, the number of trial vectors generated by the $k^{th}$ strategy that can successfully enter the population is recorded as $ns_{k,G}$ while the number of trial vectors generated by the $k^{th}$ strategy that are discarded is recorded as $nf_{k,G}$. Success and Failure Memories are introduced to store these numbers within a fixed number of previous generations hereby named Learning Period (LP). Once two memories overflow after LP generations, the earliest records stored in the memories, i.e. $ns_{G-LP}$ or $nf_{G-LP}$ will be removed so that those numbers calculated in the current generation can be stored in the memories.

After the initial LP generations, the probabilities of choosing different strategies will be updated at each subsequent generation based on the Success and Failure Memories. For example, at the generation G, the probability of choosing the $k^{th}$ (k = 1, 2, ..., K) strategy is updated by:

$$p_{k,G} = \frac{S_{k,G}}{\sum_{k=1}^{K} S_{k,G}} , \quad S_{k,G} = \frac{\sum_{g=G-LP}^{G-1} ns_{k,g}}{\sum_{g=G-LP}^{G-1} ns_{k,g} + \sum_{g=G-LP}^{G-1} nf_{k,g}} + \varepsilon , \quad (k=1,2,..,K; \ G > LP) \quad (1)$$

where $S_{k,G}$ represents the success rate of the trial vectors generated by the $k^{th}$ strategy and successfully entering the next generation within the previous LP generations with respect to generation $G$. The small constant value $\varepsilon = 0.01$ is used to avoid the possible null success rates. To ensure that the probabilities of choosing strategies are always summed to 1, $S_{k,G}$ are further divided by $\sum_{k=1}^{K} S_k$ to obtain $p_{k,G}$. Obviously, the larger the success rate for the $k^{th}$ strategy within the previous LP generations is, the larger the probability of applying it to generate trial vectors in the current generation will be. The JADE mutation strategy contributes *pbest* as well as the evolution path to the SaDE-MMTS.

The MMTS is used periodically for a certain number of function evaluations, which is also determined by an adaptation procedure. At the beginning of optimization procedure, the SaDE and the MMTS are firstly conducted sequentially within one search cycle by using same number of function evaluations. Then the success rates of both SaDE and MMTS are calculated similarly as in equation 1. Subsequently, function evaluations are assigned to SaDE and MMTS in each search cycle proportional to the success rates of both search methods.

An adaptation approach is proposed in the paper to adaptively determine the initial step size parameter used in the MMTS every time the MMTS is applied. In each MMTS phase, we calculate the average of all mutual dimension-wise distances between current population members (AveDis), select one of the five linearly reducing factors (LRF) from 1 to 0.1, 5 to 0.1, 10 to 0.1, 20 to 0.1 and 40 to 0.1, and apply this LRF to scale AveDis over the evolution. After that, the step size will be further reduced when a better solution is found along a particular dimension.

The search agents in each MMTS step are selected from the current DE population by using a Clearing procedure [7]. The number of the search agents in each MMTS step is linearly reduced from 4 to 1, which associates the variation of search requirement from "global" to "local". The SaDE-MMTS is presented in Table 1.

**Table 1.** The algorithmic description of SaDE-MMTS

---

**INITIALIZATION**: Set the generation counter $G = 0$, and randomly initialize a population (*pops*) of $NP$ individuals $\mathbf{P}_G = \{\mathbf{X}_{1,G},...,\mathbf{X}_{NP,G}\}$ with $\mathbf{X}_{i,G} = \{x_{i,G}^1, ...,x_{i,G}^D\}$, $i = 1,...,NP$ uniformly distributed in the range $[\mathbf{X}_{min}, \mathbf{X}_{max}]$, where $\mathbf{X}_{min} = \{x_{min}^1,...,x_{min}^D\}$ and $\mathbf{X}_{max} = \{x_{max}^1,...,x_{max}^D\}$. Initialize the mean value of $CR$ ($CRm_k$), strategy probability ($p_{k,G}, k = 1,...,K$, $K$ is the no. of available strategies), learning period (*LP*). Evaluate the initial population.

**INTIAL OPTIMIZATION STEP**
Conduct both SaDE and MMTS in one search cycle for a certain number of function evaluations, determine the success rates for both approaches. Assign updated number of function evaluations proportionally according to the success rates of SaDE and MMTS in the next search cycle for both search methods.

**OPTIMIZATION LOOP**
**WHILE** stopping criterion is not satisfied.
Conduct both SaDE and MMTS in one search cycle, update the success rates for both approaches. Reassign updated number of function evaluations proportionally according to the success rates of SaDE and MMTS for the next search cycle for both search methods.

**Table 1.** (*continued*)

Step1.  Calculate strategy probability $P_{k,G}$ and update the *Success* and *Failure Memory*
   IF $G>LP$
   For $k=1$ to $K$

   Update the $P_{k,G}$ by equation 1

   Remove $ns_{k,G-LP}$ and $nf_{k,G-LP}$ out of the *Success* and *Failure Memory* respectively.
   END
   END
Step2.  Assign trial vector generation strategy by using stochastic universal sampling to target vector $\mathbf{X}_{i,G}$.

Assign control parameters to each target vector $\mathbf{X}_{i,G}$. Assign $\mathbf{X}_{pbest,G}$, $\mathbf{X}_{r_1^i,G}$ and $\overset{h}{\mathbf{X}}_{r_2^i,G}$ for each target

vector $\mathbf{X}_{i,G}$.
   /* Assign trial vector generation strategy */
         Using stochastic universal sampling to select one strategy $k$ for each target vector $\mathbf{X}_{i,G}$
   /* Assign control parameter $F$ */
         FOR $i=1$ to $NP$, $F_i = Normrnd(0.5, 0.3)$, END FOR
   /* Assign control parameter $CR$ */
         IF $G>= LP$
               FOR $k = 1$ to $K$, $CRm_k = median(CRMemory_k)$, END FOR
         END IF
         FOR $k = 1$ to $K$
            FOR $i=1$ to $NP$

               $CR_{k,i} = Normrnd(CRm_k, 0.1)$

               WHILE $CR_{m,i} < 0$ or $CR_{m,i} > 1$, $CR_{k,i} = Normrnd(CRm_k, 0.1)$, END
            END FOR
         END FOR
   /* Assign pbest vector and the other two distinct parameter vectors for each target vector */
         FOR $i=1$ to $NP$
         Randomly select the $\mathbf{X}_{pbest,G}$ for the target vector $\mathbf{X}_{i,G}$ from the top $p\%$ out of the *pops*.

         Randomly select the $\overset{h}{\mathbf{X}}_{r_1^i,G}$ for the target vector $\mathbf{X}_{i,G}$ from the *pops*.

         Randomly select the $\overset{h}{\mathbf{X}}_{r_2^i,G}$ for the target vector $\mathbf{X}_{i,G}$ from the *pops* $\square$ *arch*.
         END FOR
Step3.  Generate a new population where each trial vector $\mathbf{U}_{i,G}^k$ is generated according to associated trial

vector generation strategy $k$ out of the following listed three combinations and generated parameters $F_i$ and

$CR_{k,i}$.
Generation Strategy 1.  JADE mutation with exponential crossover;
Generation Strategy 2.  JADE mutation with binomial crossover;
Generation Strategy 3.  JADE mutation with no crossover;
Reassign the variable of trial vector $\mathbf{U}_{i,G}^k$ within the search space with its reflected value when it is outside

of the bounds.
Step4.  Selection and updating
   FOR $i=1$ to $NP$, Evaluate the trial vector $\mathbf{U}_{i,G}^k$

   IF $f(U_{i,G}^k) \leq f(X_{i,G})$

   $X_{i,G+1} = U_{i,G}^k$, $f(X_{i,G+1}) = f(U_{i,G}^k)$, $ns_{k,G} = ns_{k,G} +1$
   Store $CR_{k,i}$ into $CRMemory_k$, store $X_{i,G}$ into JADE archive, if the archive size is full, truncate the

   archive by removing a randomly selected archived member.

**Table 1.** (*continued*)

IF $f(U_{i,G}) < f(X_{best,G})$ , $X_{best,G} = U_{i,G}$ , $f(X_{best,G}) = f(U_{i,G})$ , END IF

ELSE     $nf_{k,G} = nf_{k,G} + 1$

END IF

END FOR

Store $ns_{k,G}$ and $nf_{k,G}$ ( $k = 1,..., K$ ) into the *Success* and *Failure Memory* respectively.

Increment the generation count $G = G+1$
Step5. IF search cycle of SaDE is completed
    FOR each search agent selected by Clearing
        Apply *MMTS* along each dimension with initial step size as *LRF\*AveDis*.
    ENDFOR
    ENDIF
**END WHILE**

## 3   Experiments Results

The 20 CEC'10 Test Functions [16] are considered in the simulation. Experiments were conducted on all 20 minimization problems with 1000 Dimensions. To solve these problems, the population size of SaDE-MMTS is set as 60. The maximum number of fitness evaluations is 3,000,000. Each run stops when the maximal number of evaluations is exhausted. The size of JADE archive is the same as the population size and the *pbest* selection ratio from the population is set as 0.5 [15], i.e. $p$=50% or top 30 of DE population is used as the *pbest*s. The initial control parameters for binomial crossover and exponential crossover are set as ($F$=0.5, $CR$=0.2) and ($F$=0.5, $CR$=0.9) respectively. Furthermore, the parameter $F$ is approximated by a normal distribution with mean value 0.5 and standard deviation 0.3, denoted by $N(0.5, 0.3)$ and $CR$ obeys a normal distribution with mean value $CRm$ obtained by self-adaptation and standard deviation 0.1, denoted by $N(CRm, 0.1)$ [8]. The learning period (LP) is set as 50 generations [8].

On each function, the SaDE-MMTS is tested. Solution quality for each function when the FEs counter reaches $FEs1 = 1.2e5$, $FEs2 = 6.0e5$ and $FEs3 = 3.0e6$. The 1st(best), 13th(median) and 25th(worst) function values, mean and standard deviation of the 25 runs are recorded in Table 2. In addition, for the comparison purpose, we include all the results reported in all the 9 published papers of the CEC2010 Special Session and Competition on Large Scale Global Optimization 1[19]; 2[20]; 3[21]; 4[22]; 5[23]; 6[24]; 7[17]; 8[25]; 9[26] and 10[18]. As we compare the results of 10 algothms for 20 benchmark functions in 3 search stages ($FEs = 1.2e5$, $FEs2 = 6.0e5$ and $FEs3 = 3.0e6$); 5 reporting values (best, median and worst, mean and standard deviation), hence, totally 20\*3\*5=300 competition categories have been conducted. For each of the 300 categories, we apply the Formula 1 point system (http://en.wikipedia.org/wiki/Formula_One_regulations). The participant with the highest score sum wins. In all categories holds, the smaller the measured value, the better performance. (small standard deviations, e.g., mean more reliable performance).

All the competition categories are showing in Fig. 1 (*y-axis*: scores; *x-axis*: algorithm index). It can be clearly observed that, overall, the SaDE-MMTS performs better than all the other algorithms included in this competition.

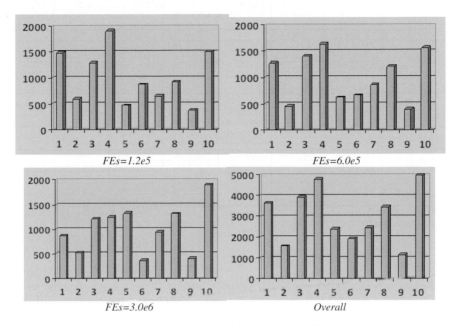

**Fig. 1.** Scores for all the 10 algorithms in 4 competition categories

**Table 2.** Experimental Results

| | | F1 | F2 | F3 | F4 | F5 | F6 | F7 |
|---|---|---|---|---|---|---|---|---|
| P1 | Best | 9.8021e+07 | 2.2354e+03 | 6.4858e+00 | 7.5961e+12 | 2.2056e+08 | 4.8465e+01 | 1.5649e+09 |
| | Median | 1.8507e+08 | 3.6989e+03 | 6.5519e+00 | 1.4583e+13 | 2.3110e+08 | 5.6584e+01 | 2.0611e+09 |
| | Worst | 2.2800e+08 | 3.9302e+03 | 6.9892e+00 | 2.7048e+13 | 3.1442e+08 | 5.8941e+01 | 2.3261e+09 |
| | Mean | 1.9615e+08 | 3.7152e+03 | 6.6420e+00 | 1.5163e+13 | 2.4941e+08 | 5.6800e+01 | 2.1846e+09 |
| | Std | 1.1021e+09 | 3.6451e+02 | 8.1611e-01 | 3.0021e+12 | 3.0165e+07 | 2.0850e+00 | 3.0051e+08 |
| P2 | Best | 1.0464e-08 | 4.4393e+02 | 1.4594e-02 | 8.9324e+11 | 7.0055e+07 | 1.1501e+01 | 4.3460e+07 |
| | Median | 1.8979e-07 | 9.2395e+02 | 2.8461e-01 | 1.9185e+12 | 1.2039e+08 | 1.4825e+01 | 7.4221e+07 |
| | Worst | 4.0082e-07 | 9.8530e+02 | 5.7461e-01 | 2.0170e+12 | 1.5820e+08 | 1.5820e+01 | 9.4817e+07 |
| | Mean | 1.9265e-07 | 9.4081e+02 | 3.6253e-01 | 1.9984e+12 | 1.2250e+08 | 1.5002e+01 | 7.7804e+07 |
| | Std | 2.0645e-08 | 9.6156e+01 | 3.2005e-02 | 2.0611e+11 | 2.5614e+07 | 1.6354e+00 | 8.0599e+06 |
| P3 | Best | 4.6165e-25 | 1.2546e+01 | 8.2656e-15 | 1.7850e+10 | 6.5621e+07 | 5.6554e-12 | 3.8187e-14 |
| | Median | 8.3997e-23 | 6.8461e+01 | 1.0316e-12 | 1.8414e+10 | 1.1892e+08 | 1.2039e+01 | 1.7473e-13 |
| | Worst | 4.2762e-21 | 1.0125e+02 | 4.4615e-10 | 3.0416e+10 | 1.4616e+08 | 1.3124e+01 | 2.0113e-12 |
| | Mean | 1.3697e-21 | 6.9410e+01 | 4.6116e-11 | 1.8865e+10 | 1.2004e+08 | 1.2254e+01 | 5.4885e-13 |
| | Std | 2.0514e-22 | 2.0035e+01 | 2.0616e-10 | 2.5610e+09 | 1.9516e+07 | 2.4515e+00 | 1.2256e-13 |
| | | F8 | F9 | F10 | F11 | F12 | F13 | F14 |
| P1 | Best | 1.2236e+08 | 3.5621e+08 | 7.4497e+03 | 2.0838e+02 | 1.5258e+05 | 1.4448e+06 | 1.3366e+09 |
| | Median | 2.1419e+08 | 4.6372e+08 | 8.4987e+03 | 2.1430e+02 | 1.6380e+05 | 1.5906e+06 | 1.3756e+09 |
| | Worst | 2.4403e+08 | 6.3641e+08 | 9.0497e+03 | 2.1598e+02 | 2.3205e+05 | 1.8899e+06 | 1.5167e+09 |
| | Mean | 2.1906e+08 | 4.8550e+08 | 8.8135e+03 | 2.1451e+02 | 1.7511e+05 | 1.6051e+06 | 1.4008e+09 |
| | Std | 2.9541e+07 | 5.3354e+07 | 9.2550e+02 | 2.5381e+01 | 2.1022e+04 | 1.9411e+05 | 2.8561e+08 |
| P2 | Best | 2.3350e+07 | 4.8042e+07 | 1.1052e+03 | 1.8139e+02 | 4.0553e+03 | 2.2406e+03 | 1.4422e+08 |
| | Median | 4.6766e+07 | 5.8029e+07 | 1.3067e+03 | 1.9089e+02 | 5.5037e+03 | 2.7911e+03 | 1.6803e+08 |
| | Worst | 9.9489e+07 | 7.0256e+07 | 4.3067e+03 | 1.9359e+02 | 7.1401e+03 | 2.9941e+03 | 1.7438e+08 |
| | Mean | 4.7841e+07 | 5.9950e+07 | 1.6532e+03 | 1.9197e+02 | 5.6151e+03 | 2.8000e+03 | 1.6945e+08 |
| | Std | 4.0052e+06 | 6.5614e+06 | 2.2612e+02 | 3.0420e+01 | 5.8115e+02 | 3.4561e+02 | 2.5611e+07 |

**Table 2.** (*continued*)

| | | | | | | | | |
|---|---|---|---|---|---|---|---|---|
| P3 | Best | 3.2413e-19 | 6.0192e+05 | 8.4611e+02 | 1.8139e+02 | 1.5728e-06 | 7.9732e+00 | 1.4144e+06 |
| | Median | 2.5616e+06 | 7.5705e+05 | 9.8494e+02 | 1.9089e+02 | 2.3172e-06 | 1.1959e+01 | 2.0463e+06 |
| | Worst | 3.9866e+06 | 1.1925e+06 | 1.0251e+03 | 1.9189e+02 | 4.0247e-04 | 1.3279e+01 | 3.7577e+06 |
| | Mean | 2.6177e+06 | 7.7561e+05 | 9.9945e+02 | 1.9099e+02 | 2.9612e-06 | 1.2056e+01 | 2.2456e+06 |
| | Std | 2.5510e+05 | 8.5611e+04 | 1.0288e+02 | 2.5610e+01 | 3.6894e-05 | 2.5614e+00 | 2.6562e+05 |

| | | F15 | F16 | F17 | F18 | F19 | F20 | |
|---|---|---|---|---|---|---|---|---|
| P1 | Best | 6.5641e+03 | 4.0605e+02 | 1.1246e+05 | 1.0265e+05 | 5.0386e+06 | 1.3637e+05 | |
| | Median | 8.8894e+03 | 4.0720e+02 | 1.1329e+05 | 1.0606e+05 | 5.2084e+06 | 2.5263e+05 | |
| | Worst | 1.2902e+04 | 4.1091e+02 | 1.2710e+05 | 1.6163e+05 | 5.7924e+06 | 2.7852e+05 | |
| | Mean | 8.9556e+04 | 4.0845e+02 | 1.2052e+05 | 1.1212e+05 | 5.3641e+06 | 2.5913e+05 | |
| | Std | 1.0025e+03 | 5.5612e+01 | 2.4540e+04 | 2.9561e+04 | 7.6121e+05 | 3.8461e+05 | |
| P2 | Best | 1.9654e+03 | 9.8941e+01 | 7.5470e+04 | 7.0390e+03 | 1.1866e+06 | 2.0365e+03 | |
| | Median | 6.5611e+03 | 2.7755e+02 | 7.9181e+04 | 1.1962e+04 | 1.3117e+06 | 2.0424e+03 | |
| | Worst | 7.3805e+03 | 3.0609e+02 | 8.0608e+04 | 1.9527e+04 | 1.4337e+06 | 2.2325e+03 | |
| | Mean | 6.9154e+03 | 2.8917e+02 | 8.0452e+04 | 1.3615e+04 | 1.3254e+06 | 2.1005e+03 | |
| | Std | 7.8911e+02 | 4.0236e+02 | 9.5533e+03 | 2.3521e+03 | 3.0544e+05 | 4.5611e+02 | |
| P3 | Best | 1.8556e+03 | 9.5613e+01 | 7.9870e-03 | 5.5000e+02 | 2.6273e+04 | 4.7148e+00 | |
| | Median | 5.2540e+03 | 2.6755e+02 | 1.2983e-02 | 6.3585e+02 | 2.9658e+04 | 8.4162e+00 | |
| | Worst | 7.3805e+03 | 3.0609e+02 | 1.5109e-02 | 1.3980e+03 | 3.0569e+04 | 7.0718e+01 | |
| | Mean | 5.5840e+03 | 2.8120e+02 | 1.3242e-02 | 7.5610e+02 | 2.9995e+04 | 9.1610e+00 | |
| | Std | 7.0561e+02 | 3.3021e+01 | 2.5641e-03 | 1.0051e+02 | 4.0050e+03 | 3.2460e+00 | |

P1, P2 AND P3 ARE THREE RECORDING SEARCH PHASES, $FEs1 = 1.2e5$, $FEs2 = 6.0e5$ and $FEs3 = 3E6$.

# 4   Conclusions

In order to solve complex problem instances especially with high dimensions, this paper applied SaDE-MMTS incorporating the JADE mutation strategy with small sized archive and two crossover operators (binomial crossover and exponential crossover) as well as no crossover option. Moreover, SaDE-MMTS employs adaptation of trial vector generation strategies and control parameters by learning from their previous experiences to suit different characteristics of the problems and different requirements of evolution phases. Furthermore, a Modified Multiple Trajectory Search (MMTS, i.e. line search) is used to improve the solutions generated by the SaDE. The SaDE-MMTS hybridization benefits from SaDE, JADE mutation strategy, different crossover operators and line search to solve large scale continuous optimization problems with diverse characteristics. Exploration as well as exploitation capabilities are also enhanced simultaneously by combining these schemes. In our future work, we will investigate more stable parameter settings, integrate additional DE-mutation strategies, and modification on this current framework to improve further the scalability of the SaDE-MMTS.

# References

1. Brest, J., Greiner, S., Boskovic, B., Mernik, M., Zumer, V.: Self-adapting control parameters in differential evolution: A comparative study on numerical benchmark problems. IEEE Transactions on Evolutionary Computation 10(6), 646–657 (2006)
2. Das, S., Abraham, A., Chakraborty, U.K., Konar, A.: Differential evolution using a neighborhood based mutation operator. IEEE Trans. on Evolutionary Computation 13(3), 526–553 (2009)

3.  Herrera, F., Lozano, M., Molina, D.: Test Suite for the Special Issue of Soft Computing on Scalability of Evolutionary Algorithms and other Metaheuristics for Large Scale Continuous Optimization Problems, http://sci2s.ugr.es/eamhco/CFP.php
4.  Huang, V.L., Qin, A.K., Suganthan, P.N.: Self-adaptive differential evolution algorithm for constrained real-parameter optimization. In: Proc. IEEE Congr. Evol. Comput. (CEC 2006), pp. 17–24 (July 2006)
5.  Price, K.V.: An Introduction to Differential Evolution. In: Corne, D., Dorigo, M., Glover, F. (eds.) New Ideas in Optimization, pp. 79–108. McGraw-Hill, London (1999)
6.  Price, K., Storn, R., Lampinen, J.: Differential Evolution - A Practical Approach to Global Optimization. Springer, Berlin (2005)
7.  Pétrowski, A.: A clearing procedure as a niching method for genetic algorithms. In: Proc. of the IEEE Int. Conf. on Evolutionary Computation, New York, USA, pp. 798–803 (1996)
8.  Qin, A.K., Huang, V.L., Suganthan, P.N.: Differential evolution algorithm with strategy adaptation for global numerical optimization. IEEE Trans on Evolutionary Computation 13(2), 398–417 (2009)
9.  Qin, A.K., Suganthan, P.N.: Self-adaptive differential evolution algorithm for numerical optimization. In: Proc. IEEE Congr. Evol. Comput. (CEC 2005), Edinburgh, Scotland, pp. 1785–1791. IEEE Press, Los Alamitos (2005)
10. Rahnamayan, S., Tizhoosh, H.R., Salama, M.M.A.: Opposition-Based Differential Evolution. IEEE Trans. on Evolutionary Computation 12(1), 64–79 (2008)
11. Storn, R., Price, K.V.: Differential evolution-A simple and efficient heuristic for global optimization over continuous Spaces. Journal of Global Optimization 11, 341 359 (1997)
12. Tseng, L.Y., Chen, C.: Multiple trajectory search for multiobjective optimization. In: Proc. IEEE Congr. Evol. Comput (CEC 2007), pp. 3609–3616 (2007)
13. Tseng, L.Y., Chen, C.: Multiple trajectory search for large scale global optimization. In: Proc. IEEE Congr. Evol. Comput. (CEC 2008), pp. 3052–3059 (2008)
14. Tang, K., Yao, X., Suganthan, P.N., MacNish, C., Chen, Y.P., Chen, C.M., Yang, Z.: Benchmark Functions for the CEC 2008 Special Session and Competition on Large Scale Global Optimization, Technical Report, Nature Inspired Computation and Applications Laboratory, USTC, China, & Nanyang Technological University, Singapore (November 2007)
15. Zhang, J.Q., Sanderson, A.C.: JADE: Adaptive Differential Evolution with Optional External Archive. IEEE Trans on Evolutionary Computation 13(5), 945–958 (2009)
16. Tang, K., Li, X.D., Suganthan, P.N., Yang, Z.Y., Weise, T.: Benchmark Functions for the CEC 2010 Special Session and Competition on Large-Scale Global Optimization (2010), http://nical.ustc.edu.cn/cec10ss.php, http://www3.ntu.edu.sg/home/EPNSugan/
17. Zhao, S.Z., Liang, J.J., Suganthan, P.N., Tasgetiren, M.F.: Dynamic Multi-swarm Particle Swarm Optimizer with Local Search for Large Scale Global Optimization. In: Proc. IEEE Congr. Evol. Comput (CEC 2010), Hong Kong, pp. 3845–3852 (June 2008)
18. Zhao, S.Z., Suganthan, P.N., Das, S.: Self-adaptive Differential Evolution with Multi-trajectory Search for Large Scale Optimization. Soft Computing (accepted)
19. Korosec, P., Tashkova, K., Silc, J.: The Differential Ant-Stigmergy Algorithm for Large-Scale Global Optimization. In: Proc. IEEE Congr. Evol. Comput. (CEC 2010), pp. 4288–4295 (2010)
20. Wang, H., Wu, Z., Rahnamayan, S., Jiang, D.: Sequential DE Enhanced by Neighborhood Search for Large Scale Global Optimization. In: Proc. IEEE Congr. Evol. Comput. (CEC 2010), pp. 4056–4062 (2010)

21. Wang, Y., Li, B.: Two-stage based Ensemble Optimization for Large-Scale Global Optimization. In: Proc. IEEE Congr. Evol. Comput. (CEC 2010), pp. 4488–4495 (2010)
22. Molina, D., Lozano, M., Herrera, F.: MA-SW-Chains: Memetic Algorithm Based on Local Search Chains for Large Scale Continuous Global Optimization. In: Proc. IEEE Congr. Evol. Comput. (CEC 2010), pp. 3153–3160 (2010)
23. Brest, J., Zamuda, A., Fister, I., Maucec, M.S.: Large Scale Global Optimization using Self-adaptive Differential Evolution Algorithm. In: Proc. IEEE Congr. Evol. Comput. (CEC 2010), pp. 3097–3104 (2010)
24. Omidvar, M.N., Li, X., Yao, X.: Cooperative Co-evolution with Delta Grouping for Large Scale Non-separable Function Optimization. In: Proc. IEEE Congr. Evol. Comput. (CEC 2010), pp. 1762–1769 (2010)
25. Chen, S.: Locust Swarms for Large Scale Global Optimization of Nonseparable Problems. Kukkonen, Benchmarking the Classic Differential Evolution Algorithm on Large-Scale Global Optimization
26. Yang, Z., Tang, K., Yao, X.: Large Scale Evolutionary Optimization Using Cooperative Coevolution. Information Sciences 178(15), 2985–2999 (2008)

# Differential Evolution Based Ascent Phase Trajectory Optimization for a Hypersonic Vehicle

Ritwik Giri[1] and D. Ghose[2]

[1] Dept. of Electronics and Telecommunication Engineering.
Jadavpur University, Kolkata 700 032, India
[2] Guidance, Control, and Decision Systems laboratory (GCDSL),
Department of Aerospace Engineering,
Indian Institute of Science,
Bangalore 560 012, India
ritwikgiri@gmail.com, dghose@aero.iisc.ernet.in

**Abstract.** In this paper, a new method for the numerical computation of optimal, or nearly optimal, solutions to aerospace trajectory problems is presented. Differential Evolution (DE), a powerful stochastic real-parameter optimization algorithm is used to optimize the ascent phase of a hypersonic vehicle. The vehicle has to undergo large changes in altitude and associated aerodynamic conditions. As a result, its aerodynamic characteristics, as well as its propulsion parameters, undergo drastic changes. Such trajectory optimization problems can be solved by converting it to a non-linear programming (NLP) problem. One of the issues in the NLP method is that it requires a fairly large number of grid points to arrive at an optimal solution. Differential Evolution based algorithm, proposed in this paper, is shown to perform equally well with lesser number of grid points. This is supported by extensive simulation results.

**Keywords:** Trajectory Optimization, Differential Evolution, angle of attack.

## 1 Introduction

Trajectory optimization is an important and challenging real-life optimization problem in aerospace research [1-3]. Numerical algorithms for these problems are difficult to design due to complicated trajectory constraints [4]. In aerospace vehicle trajectory optimization problems, flight paths that optimize a given cost function or performance index are sought. The cost function can be, for example, the flight time, the amount of burned fuel, or the deviation from a prescribed trajectory. Optimal control theory provides a framework for optimal trajectory design. However, solving an optimal control problem is a laborious and time-consuming task. The problem considered here is concerned with optimization of the ascent phase trajectory of a hypersonic vehicle. The cost function for the problem discussed here is the amount of burned fuel. This is because, the vehicle, after attaining the required altitude, needs to fly in a cruise phase using the remaining fuel. Maximization of the range of this flight is of importance in achieving the final mission. Thus the problem is posed one of minimization of the amount of burned fuel or maximization of the remaining fuel. Note that the complete

B.K. Panigrahi et al. (Eds.): SEMCCO 2010, LNCS 6466, pp. 11–18, 2010.

optimization problem should include both the ascent phase and the cruise phase. However, in this paper we address only the ascent phase and minimize the fuel utilized. These kinds of optimal control problems are usually solved using the Hamiltonian approach, which results in two point boundary value (TPBV) problems which are known to be notoriously sensitive to initial conditions on the co-state variables, especially for realistic aerospace vehicles subject to various trajectory constraints[1],[5],[6]. Alternatively, a non-linear programming problem (NLP) formulation has been proposed [1] in which the infinite dimensional optimal control problem is approximated as a finite dimensional problem by selecting discrete values of the control variable. The model is further simplified by using a propagation function based on standard extrapolation methods used in numerical integration. However, the solution process involves a large number of grid points for the final solution to be satisfactory.

In this paper a powerful Differential Evolution (DE) based algorithm has been proposed for the trajectory optimization problem. Use of DE for dynamical problems is rare in the literature. An exception is its use in missile guidance problem [7]. The ascent phase trajectory optimization problem using NLP has been earlier addressed in [8].

## 2  Problem Formulation

The experimental hypersonic vehicle is air dropped from a carrier aircraft and boosted to an initial Mach number at a specified altitude using solid rocket motors. The boosters are separated upon achieving this condition, which forms the initial condition for the problem. Then, the ascent phase commences and the final condition given in terms of the final Mach number and altitude is achieved (see Fig. 1(a)). The problem is to optimize the ascent phase trajectory so that the least fuel is expended (and maximum remaining fuel can be utilized during the subsequent cruise phase). Thus, the optimization problem is formulated as,

max  $m_f$

subject to,

$$\dot{h} = v \sin\gamma \, , \qquad \dot{x} = v \cos\gamma \, , \qquad \dot{m} = -\frac{T}{(I_{sp} \, g)} \, ,$$

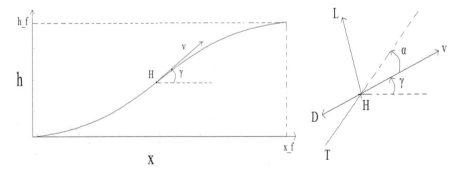

**Fig. 1.** (a) The ascent phase trajectory of the hypersonic vehicle H (b) The state variables

$$\dot{v} = a_{long} = \frac{T\cos\alpha - D}{m} - \frac{\mu\sin\gamma}{(R_e+h)^2},$$ (1)

$$\dot{\gamma} = \frac{a_{lat}}{v} = \frac{T\sin\alpha + L}{mv} + \cos\gamma\left[\frac{v}{(R_e+h)} - \frac{\mu}{v(R_e+h)^2}\right]$$

where, $h$ is the altitude (m), $v$ is the velocity (m/sec), $I_{sp}$ is the specific impulse (sec), $\alpha$ is the angle of attack (rad), $\gamma$ is the flight path angle (rad), $m$ is the mass (kg), $\mu$ is the gravitational constant, $g$ is the gravitational acceleration (m/$sec^2$), $T$ is the thrust (Newtons), $a_{lat}$ is the lateral acceleration on the vehicle (m/$sec^2$), $a_{long}$ is the longitudinal acceleration on the vehicle (m/$sec^2$), and $Re$ is the radius of the earth (m). The lift ($L$) and drag ($D$) forces are defined by,

$$D = 0.5\rho Sv^2 c_D \quad L = 0.5\rho Sv^2 c_L$$ (2)

where, $S$ is the aerodynamic reference area of the vehicle, $\rho$ is the atmospheric density, and $c_L$ and $c_D$ are the lift and drag coefficients, which are functions of the mach number and angle of attack. Moreover, the mass flow rate is also a function of mach number and angle of attack. The specific impulse is a function of mach number and altitude. The atmospheric density is a function of altitude. It should be noted that these dependencies are not easily expressed by standard formulas but have to be extracted from actual wind tunnel experiments and sophisticated numerical algorithms have to be used to create smooth function profiles. This adds to the complexity of the problem considerably when compared to standard static optimization problems. The data corresponding to the trajectory and vehicle parameters has been taken from [8].

The ascent phase trajectory optimization problem is defined through its initial conditions on the states and some desirable terminal conditions on some of the states such as altitude ($h_f$), velocity ($v_f$) and flight path angle ($\gamma_f$). In addition, the total time of flight ($t_f$), the horizontal range achieved during the ascent phase ($x_f$), the control variable angle of attack ($\alpha$), the lateral acceleration ($a_{lat}$), and the longitudinal acceleration($a_{long}$), are constrained to be within specified limits.

The problem has been taken from [8] where it has been solved using NLP. The main challenge of solving these kinds of problems lies in the function evaluation part. This is not a simple static optimization task, as it can be seen from the problem formulation. As in the NLP formulation [8], the problem is discretized by selecting $n$ temporal grid points and by defining the value of the control ($\alpha$) at those grid points. Note that the time of flight ($t_f$) is also unknown and is selected as a decision variable. The intermediate values of the control $\alpha$ are interpolated between the grid points using either step or linear interpolation. Thus, the decision vector has dimension $n + 1$ ($\alpha$ at $n$ grid points and $t_f$). Since there are terminal equality constraints in this problem, the fitness function for DE has been chosen appropriately as,

$$J = m_f - c_1[h(t_f) - h_f]^2 - c_2[v(t_f) - v_f]^2 - c_3[\gamma(t_f) - \gamma_f]^2$$

If the inequality constraints are violated then $J$ is given a large negative value. In the fitness function the constants $c_1$, $c_2$, $c_3$ have to be carefully chosen. The DE algorithm is implemented as given in the block diagram (Fig. 2).

## 3   Differential Evolution (DE) Algorithm

Differential Evolution (DE) [9-16], like Genetic Algorithms (GA), is a simple real-coded evolutionary algorithm and uses the concept of fitness in the same sense as in genetic algorithms .The major difference between DE and GA is that in DE some of the parents are generated through a mutation process before performing crossover, whereas GA usually selects parents from current population, performs crossover, and then mutates the offspring [7]. In the mutation process of a DE algorithm, the weighted difference between two randomly selected population members is added to a third member to generate a mutated solution. Then, the crossover operator is introduced to combine the mutated solution with the target solution so as to generate a trial solution. Though GA methods have been employed successfully to solve complex non-linear optimization problems, recent research has identified some deficiencies in GA performance. This degradation in efficiency is apparent when the parameters being optimized are highly correlated and the premature convergence of the GA degrades its performance in terms of reducing the search capability of GA. For all these reasons GA cannot be implemented to solve this problem. Thus, DE has been used for solving this problem. DE works through a simple cycle of stages, given in Figure 2.

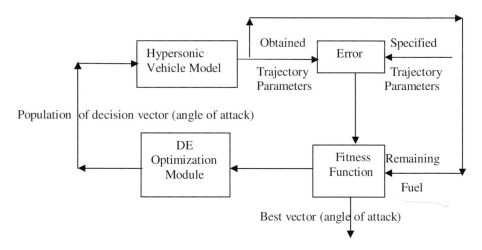

**Fig. 2.** Trajectory Optimization using DE

### 3.1  Initialization of the Parameter Vectors

DE searches for a global optimum point in a $D$-dimensional continuous hyperspace. It begins with a randomly initiated population of $NP$ $D$ dimensional real-valued parameter vectors. Each vector, also known as *genome/chromosome*, forms a candidate solution to the multi-dimensional optimization problem. We shall denote subsequent generations in DE by $G = 0,1...,G_{max}$. Since the parameter vectors are likely to be changed over different generations, we may adopt the following notation for representing the $i$-th vector of the population at the current generation:

$$\vec{X}_{i,G} = [x_{1,i,G}, x_{2,i,G}, x_{3,i,G}, ......, x_{D,i,G}]. = [\alpha_1, \alpha_2, \alpha_3, ....., \alpha_n, t_f]$$

Here the vector is chosen as the angle of attack ($\alpha$), which, along with the final time are the control variables. Thus the dimension of the problem is D=$n+1$ for $n$ grid points. The initial population (at $G = 0$) should cover the entire search space as much as possible by uniformly randomizing individuals within the search space constrained by the prescribed minimum and maximum bounds. The bounds of the components of the control vector are pre-specified. We can initialize the $j$-th component of the $i$-th vector as:

$$x_{j,i,0} = x_{j,\min} + rand_{i,j}[0,1) \cdot (x_{j,\max} - x_{j,\min}),$$

where rand is a uniformly distributed random number between 0 and 1 ($0 \le rand_{i,j}[0,1) < 1$) and is instantiated independently for each component of the $i$-th vector.

### 3.2 Mutation with Difference Vectors

After initialization, DE creates a *donor* control vector $\vec{V}_{i,n}$ corresponding to each population member or *target* control vector $\vec{X}_{i,G}$ in the current generation through mutation. It is the method of creating this donor vector, which differentiates between the various DE schemes. Here we have used the DE/best/1 scheme [11] which is given below.

$$\vec{V}_{i,G} = \vec{X}_{best,G} + F \cdot (\vec{X}_{r_1^i,G} - \vec{X}_{r_2^i,G}).$$

The indices $r_1^i, r_2^i$ are mutually exclusive integers randomly chosen from the range [1, NP], and all are different from the index $i$. These indices are randomly generated once for each donor vector. The scaling factor $F$ is a positive control parameter for scaling the difference vectors. Here in this problem we have chosen the value of $F$ as 0.8. $\vec{X}_{best,G}$ is the best individual vector with the best fitness (that is, maximum objective function value given above as $J$) in the population at generation $G$.

### 3.3 Crossover

To enhance the potential diversity of the population, a crossover operation comes into play after generating the donor control vector through mutation. The donor control vector exchanges its components with the target control vector $\vec{X}_{i,G}$ under this operation to form the *trial* control vector $\vec{U}_{i,G} = [u_{1,i,G}, u_{2,i,G}, u_{3,i,G} ...., u_{D,i,G}]$. In our algorithm we use binomial crossover that is performed on each of the $D$ variables whenever a randomly generated number between 0 and 1 is less than or equal to the $Cr$, the crossover rate value. In this case, the number of parameters inherited from the donor has a (nearly) binomial distribution. The scheme may be outlined as:

$$u_{j,i,G} = \begin{cases} v_{j,i,G}, & \text{if } (rand_{i,j}[0,1) \le Cr \text{ or } j = j_{rand} \\ x_{j,i,G}, & \text{otherwise}, \end{cases}$$

where, as before, $rand_{i,j}[0,1)$ is a uniformly distributed random number, which is called anew for each $j$-th component of the $i$-th parameter vector. $j_{rand} \in [1, 2, ...., D]$

Is a randomly chosen index, which ensures that $U_{i,G}$ gets at least one component from $V_{i,G}$ . Here $Cr$=0.9 has been used.

## 3.4 Selection

The next step of the algorithm calls for *selection* to determine whether the target or the trial control vector survives to the next generation and is described as:

$$\vec{X}_{i,G+1} = \vec{U}_{i,G}, \qquad \text{if } f(\vec{U}_{i,G}) \geq f(\vec{X}_{i,G})$$
$$= \vec{X}_{i,G}, \qquad \text{if } f(\vec{U}_{i,G}) < f(\vec{X}_{i,G})$$

where, $f(\vec{X})$ is the objective function, which is the fitness function $J(.)$ given above. For this problem we have chosen a population size of 50 and the number of maximum iterations is 100.

## 4   Computational Results

The initial and final conditions, the constraints and the constants used in the formulation have been taken from [8]. They are as follows:

$h(0) = 16000.0$ m,      $h(t_f) = 32000.0$ m,     $v(0) = 989.77$ m/s   $v(t_f) = 1847.0$ m/s,
$\gamma(0) = 0.0698$ rad,       $\gamma(t_f) = 0$ rad          $m(0) = 3600.0$ kg,     $x(0) = 0$ m,
$\mu = 3.9853 \times 1014\ m^3/s^2$  $g = 9.8$ m/$s^2$, $R_e = 6.378388 \times 106$ m, $S = 1\ m^2$

The trajectory related constraints are as follows: $t_f \leq 250$ s,   $x_f \leq 250000$ m,   $0° \leq \alpha \leq 8°$,   $a_{long} \leq 4g$,   $a_{lat} \leq 5g$ .

For evaluating the fitness function $J$, the constants used are, $c_1 = 100$, $c_2 = 10^4$, $c_3 = 10^6$. The simulation results are reported in Table 1(a) using DE and are compared with the results produced by NLP [8]. Here we have used two types of interpolation in case of angle of attack, one is step and the other one is linear. From the results it is evident that for same number of grid points DE outperforms NLP. As

**Table 1(a).** Results of ascent phase trajectory optimization

| Grid points | Method | $h(t_f)$ (m) | $v(t_f)$ (m/s) | $\gamma(t_f)$ (degree) | $m(t_f)$ (kg) | $m(t_f)$ (fuel) (kg) | $x(t_f)$ (X10$^5$ m) | $t_f$ (sec) |
|---|---|---|---|---|---|---|---|---|
| 5 | NLP(step) | 38431 | 1937 | 0.3553 | 2764.3 | 764.3 | 2.3341 | 143.13 |
|   | DE(step) | 32759 | 1901.9 | 0.5840 | 2824.0 | 824.0 | 2.3506 | 152.23 |
|   | NLP(linear) | 32305 | 1768 | -3.4665 | 2907.4 | 907.4 | 2.1672 | 143.13 |
|   | DE(linear) | 32001 | 1847.2 | 0.0447 | 2864.2 | 864.2 | 2.3024 | 152.23 |
| 9 | NLP(step) | 34701 | 1888.4 | -0.8626 | 2816.4 | 816.4 | 2.2623 | 142.02 |
|   | DE(step) | 32029 | 1849.9 | -0.3429 | 2857.8 | 857.8 | 2.3202 | 153.39 |
|   | NLP(linear) | 31730 | 1824.2 | -1.0466 | 2871.8 | 871.8 | 2.1743 | 142.02 |
|   | DE(linear) | 32000 | 1846.5 | -0.0679 | 2865.0 | 865.0 | 2.2935 | 153.39 |

Table 1(b). **Table 1(b).** NLP results for 33 and 65 grid points

| Grid points | Method | $h(t_f)$ (m) | $v(t_f)$ (m/s) | $\gamma(t_f)$ (degree) | $m(t_f)$ (kg) | $m(t_f)$ (fuel) (kg) | $x(t_f)$ ($\times10^5$ m) | $t_f$ (sec) |
|---|---|---|---|---|---|---|---|---|
| 33 | NLP(step) | 32509 | 1861 | -0.0954 | 2843.6 | 843.6 | 2.1747 | 139.92 |
|  | NLP(linear) | 31961 | 1846.9 | -0.0100 | 2855.4 | 855.4 | 2.1548 | 139.92 |
| 65 | NLP(step) | 32267 | 1854.0 | -0.0475 | 2849.5 | 849.5 | 2.1652 | 139.93 |
|  | NLP(linear) | 31994 | 1846.9 | -0.0033 | 2855.3 | 855.3 | 2.1552 | 139.93 |

expected, the integration using step interpolation has large error when compared to linear interpolation. We have also reported the results of NLP for 33 and 65 grid points in Table 1(b). It can be seen that only for such high number of grid points in NLP the result is comparable with DE with only 9 grid points.

Figure 3 shows variation of altitude, velocity, flight path angle, mass, and range with time using linearly interpolated control for 9 grid points.

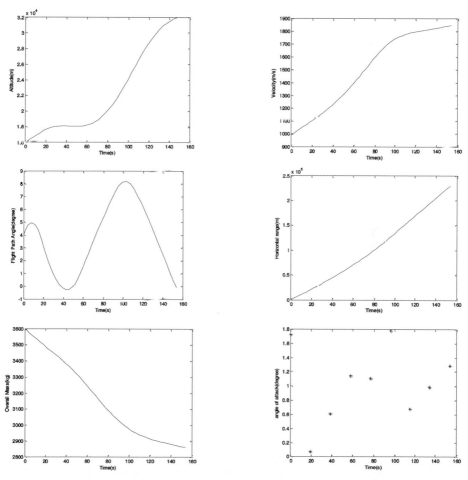

**Fig. 3.** State histories (for linearly interpolated control from 9 grid points) and angle of attack for 9 grid points

# 5 Conclusions

In this paper a DE based trajectory optimization method is proposed. DE gives better convergence characteristics with smaller number of grid points. We have also found that the linear interpolation of the control works much better than the step interpolation. This trajectory optimization problem can be extended to include the cruise phase also and future research will evaluate the performances of other improved recent DE variants.

# References

1. Betts, J.T.: Practical Methods for Optimal Control Using Nonlinear Programming. SIAM Publications, Philadelphia (2001)
2. Gath, P.F., Calise, A.J.: Optimization of launch vehicle ascent trajectories with path constraints and coast arcs. Journal of Guidance, Control, and Dynamics 24, 296–304 (2001)
3. Chenglong, H., Xin, C., Leni, W.: Optimizing RLV ascent trajectory using PSO algorithms. In: 2nd International Symposium on Systems and Control in Aerospace and Astronautics, December 2008, pp. 1–4 (2008)
4. Betts, J.T.: Survey of numerical methods for trajectory optimization. Journal of Guidance, Control, and Dynamics 21, 193–207 (1998)
5. Bryson, A.C., Ho, Y.C.: Applied Optimal Control: Optimization, Estimation, and Control, Blaisdel (1969)
6. Anderson, J.D.: Introduction to Flight. McGraw-Hill, Singapore (2000)
7. Raghunathan, T., Ghose, D.: An online-implementable differential evolution tuned all-aspect guidance law, Control Engineering Practice (2010), doi:10.1016/j.conengprac.2010.05.13
8. Prasanna, H.M., Ghose, D., Bhat, M.S., Bhattacharyya, C., Umakant, J.: Ascent phase trajectory optimization for a hypersonic vehicle using nonlinear programming. In: Gervasi, O., Gavrilova, M.L., Kumar, V., Laganá, A., Lee, H.P., Mun, Y., Taniar, D., Tan, C.J.K. (eds.) ICCSA 2005. LNCS, vol. 3483, pp. 548–557. Springer, Heidelberg (2005)
9. Storn, R., Price, K.: Differential evolution – A simple and efficient heuristic for global optimization over continuous spaces. Journal of Global Optimization 11(4), 341–359 (1997)
10. Price, K., Storn, R., Lampinen, J.: Differential evolution – A Practical Approach to Global Optimization. Springer, Berlin (2005)
11. Qin, A.K., Huang, V.L., Suganthan, P.N.: Differential evolution algorithm with strategy adaptation for global numerical optimization. IEEE Trans. on Evolutionary Computations, 398–417 (2009), doi:10.1109/TEVC.2008.927706
12. Mallipeddi, R., Suganthan, P.N., Pan, Q.K., Tasgetiren, M.F.: Differential evolution algorithm with ensemble of parameters and mutation strategies. Applied Soft Computing (in press), doi:10.1016/j.asoc.2010.04.024
13. Zhang, J., Sanderson, A.C.: JADE: adaptive differential evolution with optional external archive. IEEE Transactions on Evolutionary Computation 13(5), 945–958 (2009)
14. Das, S., Suganthan, P.N.: Differential evolution – a survey of the state-of-the-art. IEEE Transactions on Evolutionary Computation, doi:10.1109/TEVC.2010.2059031
15. Brest, J., Greiner, S., Boskovic, B., Mernik, M., Zumer, V.: Self-Adapting Control Parameters in Differential Evolution: A Comparative Study on Numerical Benchmark Problems. IEEE Transactions on Evolutionary Computation 10(6), 646–657 (2006)
16. Das, S., Abraham, A., Chakraborty, U.K., Konar, A.: Differential evolution using a neighborhood based mutation operator. IEEE Transactions on Evolutionary Computation 13(3), 526–553 (2009)

# Dynamic Grouping Crowding Differential Evolution with Ensemble of Parameters for Multi-modal Optimization

Bo Yang Qu[1], Pushpan Gouthanan[2], and Ponnuthurai Nagaratnam Suganthan[1]

[1] School of Electrical and Electronic Engineering,
Nanyang Technological University,
Singapore 639798, Singapore
E070088@e.ntu.edu.sg, epnsugan@ntu.edu.sg
[2] National Institute of technology-trichy, India
gouthapg7@gmail.com

**Abstract.** In recent years, multi-modal optimization has become an important area of active research. Many algorithms have been developed in literature to tackle multi-modal optimization problems. In this work, a dynamic grouping crowding differential evolution (DGCDE) with ensemble of parameter is proposed. In this algorithm, the population is dynamically regrouped into 3 equal subpopulations every few generations. Each of the subpopulations is assigned a set of parameters. The algorithms is tested on 12 classical benchmark multi-modal optimization problems and compared with the crowding differential evolution (Crowding DE) in literature. As shown in the experimental results, the proposed algorithm outperforms the Crowding DE with all three different parameter settings on the benchmark problems.

**Keywords:** Evolutionary algorithm, multi-modal optimization, Differential Evolution, niching.

## 1 Introduction

Evolutionary algorithms (EAs) have been shown to be effective in solving difficult optimization problems. The original forms of most EAs are designed for locating single global solution, which is not effective for multi-modal optimization. However, in real world optimization, the problems always fall into the multi-modal category, such as classification problems in machine learning [1] and inversion of teleseismic waves [2]. Multi-modal optimization refers to locate multiple optima (global or local) in one single run.

In literature, various techniques that known as "niching" methods are used and incorporated in EAs to enhance the algorithm with the ability of maintaining multiple stable subpopulation which target on locating different optima. Generally, the probability of getting trapped in a local optimum for niching EA is lower compared to conventional EA, as a niching EA searches for multiple optima in parallel. However, niching EA takes more function evaluations in order to reach the single global optima. The earliest niching approach was proposed by Cavicchio [3]. Other representative

B.K. Panigrahi et al. (Eds.): SEMCCO 2010, LNCS 6466, pp. 19–28, 2010.
© Springer-Verlag Berlin Heidelberg 2010

methods are crowding [4], [5], restricted tournament selection [6], clearing [7], fitness sharing [8], speciation [9] and ensemble of niching algorithms [24].

Differential evolution is a very effective global optimization technique. Niching techniques have also been incorporated into DE variants to enhance the ability of handling multimodal optimization [10], [11], [12]. Thomsen proposed a Crowding DE [13] and showed that Crowding DE outperform a DE based fitness sharing algorithm. In this paper, a dynamic grouping crowding differential evolution (DGCDE) with ensemble of parameter is proposed and compared to the Crowding DE with different parameter setting on a set of commonly used multi-modal optimization problems.

The remainder of this paper is organized as follows. Section 2 gives a brief overview of differential evolution, and Crowding DE. In Section 3, the proposed DGCDE algorithm is introduced. The problems definition and the results of the experiments are presented in sections 4. Finally, the paper is concluded in sections 5.

## 2   Differential Evolution and Crowding DE

### 2.1   Differential Evolution

The differential evolution (DE) algorithm was first introduced by Storn and Price [14]. Although the idea of DE is simple, it is very powerful in solving global optimization problem. Similar to other EAs, DE is also a population based searching algorithm. The individuals will compete with others inside the population. Four major steps are involved in DE known as, initialization, mutation, recombination and selection. In the mutation operation one of the following strategies are commonly used [15-16][22-23]:

DE/rand/1: $v_p = x_{r1} + F \cdot (x_{r2} - x_{r3})$

DE/best/1: $v_p = x_{best} + F \cdot (x_{r1} - x_{r2})$

DE/current-to-best/2: $v_p = x_p + F \cdot (x_{best} - x_p + x_{r1} - x_{r2})$

DE/best/2: $v_p = x_{best} + F \cdot (x_{r1} - x_{r2} + x_{r3} - x_{r4})$

DE/rand/2: $v_p = x_{r1} + F \cdot (x_{r2} - x_{r3} + x_{r4} - x_{r5})$

where $r_1$, $r_2$, $r_3$, $r_4$, $r_5$ are mutually different integers randomly generated in the range [1, $NP$ (population size)], $F$ is the scale factor used to scale difference vectors. $x_{best}$ is the solution with the best fitness value in the current population.

The crossover operation is applied to each pair of the generated mutant vector and its corresponding parent vector using the following equations:

$$u_{p,i} = \begin{cases} v_{p,i} & if \ rand_i \leq CR \ or \ i = i_{rand} \\ x_{p,i} & otherwise \end{cases}$$

where $u_p$ is the offspring vector. $CR$ is the crossover rate which is a user-specified constant.

## 2.2  Crowding DE

Crowding DE was first introduced by Thomsen to handle multi-modal optimization [13]. It modifies the selection phase of the original DE. In Crowding DE, the fitness value of a newly generated offspring is compared with that the nearest individual/neighbor from the current population. The Crowding DE algorithm is shown in the following Table:

**Table 1.** Crowding DE algorithm

| | |
|---|---|
| Step 1 | Use the basic DE to produce *NP* (population size) offspring.<br>For *i*=1:*NP* |
| Step 2 | Calculate the Euclidean distance vales of the offspring(*i*) to the other individuals in the DE Population. |
| Step 3 | Compare the fitness value of offspring(*i*) and the fitness value of the individual that has the smallest Euclidean distance . The offspring will replace the individual if it is fitter than that individual.<br>Endfor |
| Step 4 | Stop if the termination criteria are met otherwise go to step 1. |

# 3  DGCDE with Ensemble of Parameter

Although CDE has been shown to be effective in solving multimodal optimization problems, the original CDE only uses one single set of DE parameters. As we know, the performance of DE is closely related to the control parameters. According to "No free lunch" theorem [17], it is unlikely to find one parameter that can outperform all other parameters, since different parameter is suitable for different problems. Motivated by this observation, a dynamic grouping crowding differential evolution with ensemble of parameter is proposed.

In DGCDE, the algorithm starts with a single population (same as CDE). This population will be randomly divided into three subpopulations, while each of the subpopulation is assigned with a set of control parameters. The subpopulation runs as a speared DE for $m$ generation. After every $m$ generation, the subpopulation is combined and randomly regrouped again. The algorithm and flowchart are shown in Table 2 and Fig. 1 respectively. Note that the three sets of control parameters for three different subpopulations are chosen as $F_1 =0.9$, $CR_1 =0.3$; $F_2 =0.5$, $CR_2 =0.1$; $F_2 =0.5$, $CR_2 =0.3$.

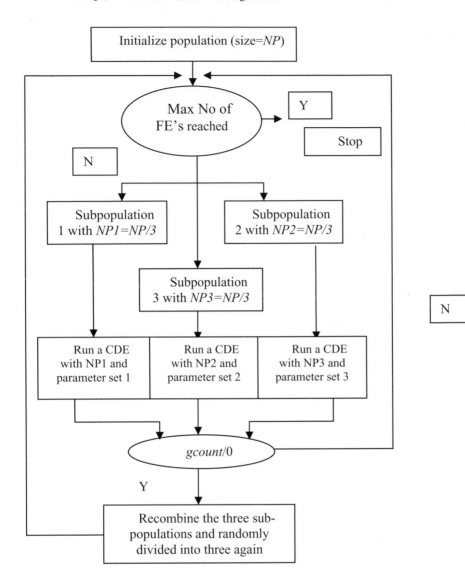

**Fig. 1.** The flowchart of DGCDE

**Table 2.** DGCDE algorithm

| | |
|---|---|
| Step 1 | Randomly initialize $NP$ (population size) solutions. Set generation counter $gcount=1$. |
| Step 2 | Randomly divided the $NP$ solution into three groups ($NP/3$ members for each group). Each group is assigned a different set of control parameter ($F$, $CR$). |

**Table 2.** (*continued*)

| | |
|---|---|
| Step 3 | If *gcount*/m=0 |
| | Combine the subgroups and Goes to step2 to regroup the population. |
| | Else |
| | Run each group as a separated CDE. |
| | Endif |
| Step 4 | Stop if the termination criteria are met otherwise go to step 3. |

## 4 Experiment Preparation

To assess the niching ability of the proposed algorithm, some frequently used multimodal optimization benchmark test functions with different characteristics are used. The following four DE variants were used in the experiments.

1.  DGCDE: dynamic grouping Crowding DE with ensemble of parameters.
2.  CDE1: Crowding DE with $F$ set to 0.9, $CR$ set to 0.3.
3.  CDE2: Crowding DE with $F$ set to 0.5, $CR$ set to 0.1.
4.  CDE3: Crowding DE with $F$ set to 0.5, $CR$ set to 0.3.

### 4.1 Test Function

The test functions that used in this paper are shown in Table 3.

**Table 3.** Test Functions

| Name | Test Function | Range ; Peaks Global/local |
|---|---|---|
| F1: Two Peak Trap [18] | $f_1(x) = \begin{cases} \dfrac{160}{15}(15-x), & \text{for } 0 \le x \le 15 \\ \dfrac{200}{5}(x-15), & \text{for } 15 \le x \le 20 \end{cases}$ | $0 \le x \le 20$ ; 1/1 |
| F2:Central Two-Peak Trap [18] | $f_2(x) = \begin{cases} \dfrac{160}{10}x, & \text{for } 0 \le x \le 10 \\ \dfrac{160}{5}(15-x) & \text{for } 10 \le x \le 15 \\ \dfrac{200}{5}(x-15), & \text{for } 15 \le x \le 20 \end{cases}$ | $0 \le x \le 20$ ; 1 |

**Table 3.** (*continued*)

| | | |
|---|---|---|
| F3:Five-Uneven-Peak Trap [9] | $f_3(x) = \begin{cases} 80(2.5 - x) & \text{for } 0 \le x < 2.5 \\ 64(x - 2.5) & \text{for } 2.5 \le x < 5 \\ 64(7.5 - x) & \text{for } 5 \le x < 7.5 \\ 28(x - 7.5) & \text{for } 7.5 \le x < 12.5 \\ 28(17.5 - x) & \text{for } 12.5 \le x < 17.5 \\ 32(x - 17.5) & \text{for } 17.5 \le x < 22.5 \\ 32(27.5 - x) & \text{for } 22.5 \le x < 27.5 \\ 80(x - 27.5) & \text{for } 27.5 \le x \le 30 \end{cases}$ | $0 \le x \le 20$ ; 2/3 |
| F4:Equal Maxima [19] | $f_4(x) = \sin^6(5\pi x)$ | $0 \le x \le 1$; 5/0 |
| F5:Decreasing Maxima [19] | $f_5(x) = \exp[-2\log(2) \cdot (\frac{x - 0.1}{0.8})^2] \cdot \sin^6(5\pi x)$ | $0 \le x \le 1$ ; 1/4 |
| F6: Uneven Maxima [19] | $f_6(x) = \sin^6(5\pi(x^{3/4} - 0.05))$ | $0 \le x \le 1$ ; 5/0 |
| F7: Uneven Decreasing Maxima [18] | $f_7(x) = \exp[-2\log(2) \cdot (\frac{x - 0.08}{0.854})^2] \cdot \sin^6(5\pi(x^{3/4} - 0.05))$ | $0 \le x \le 1$ ; 1/4 |
| F8: Himmelblau's function [18] | $f_8(x, y) = 200 - (x^2 + y - 11)^2 - (x + y^2 - 7)^2$ | $-6 \le x, y \le 6$ ; 4/0 |
| F9: Six-Hump Camel Back [20] | $f_9(x, y) = -4[(4 - 2.1x^2 + \frac{x^4}{3})x^2 + xy + (-4 + 4y^2)y^2]$ | $-1.9 \le x \le 1.9$; $-1.1 \le y \le 1.1$ 2/2 |
| F10: Shekel's foxholes [4] | $f_{10}(x, y) = 500 - \dfrac{1}{0.002 + \sum_{i=0}^{24} \dfrac{1}{1 + i + (x - a(i))^6 + (y - b(i))^6}}$ where $a(i) = 16(i \bmod 5) - 2)$, and $b(i) = 16(\lfloor (i/5) \rfloor - 2)$ | $-65.536 \le x, y \le 65.535$ ; 1/24 |
| F11:2D Inverted Shubert [9] | $f_{11}(\vec{x}) = -\prod_{i=1}^{2} \sum_{j=1}^{5} j \cos[(j+1)x_i + j]$ | $-10 \le x_1, x_2 \le 10$ ; 18/many |
| F12: Inverted Vincent [21] | $f(\vec{x}) = \frac{1}{n} \sum_{i=1}^{n} \sin(10.\log(x_i))$ where $n$ is the dimesnion of the problem | $0.25 \le x_i \le 10$ ; $6^n$ |

## 4.2 Experimental Setup

For the simulations, Matlab 7.1 is used as the programming language. The configurations of the computer are Intel Pentium® 4 CPU, 2 GB of RAM. The population size is set 60 for all test function and test variants. The maximum number of function evaluations is set to 10000 for all the test function. Therefore, the maximum number of generation will be 167. 20 independent runs are conducted for each of the algorithms.

To assess the performance of different algorithms, a level of accuracy (typically in the range of [0, 1]) need to be specified. This parameter used to measure how close the obtained solutions to the known global peaks are. An optimum is considered to be found if there exists a solution in the population within the tolerated distance to that optimum.

When doing the comparison, following to criteria are used:

1. Success Rate
2. Average number of optima found.

## 5   Experiments and Results

### 5.1  Success Rate

The success rate for all the four DE variants are recorded and presented in Table 4. The rank of each algorithm is presented in the bracket. As can be revealed from the table, the proposed DGCDE always ranks number one among all the tested algorithms. Therefore, we can conclude that DGCDE with ensemble of parameters can outperform all the three CDE with different parameter sets on the tested benchmark problems. Note that the success rate obtained is highly related to the user defined parameter level of accuracy.

**Table 4.** The success rate

| Test Function | Level of accuracy | CDE1 | CDE2 | CDE3 | DGCDE |
|---|---|---|---|---|---|
| F1 | 0.05 | 1 (1) | 1 (1) | 1 (1) | **1 (1)** |
| F2 | 0.05 | 1 (1) | 1 (1) | 1 (1) | **1 (1)** |
| F3 | 0.05 | 1 (1) | 1 (1) | 1 (1) | **1 (1)** |
| F4 | 0.000001 | 0.1 (4) | 0.95 (2) | 0.95 (2) | **1 (1)** |
| F5 | 0.000001 | 0.7 (4) | 1 (1) | 1 (1) | **1 (1)** |
| F6 | 0.000001 | 0.2 (2) | 0.15 (4) | 0.2 (2) | **0.9 (1)** |
| F7 | 0.000001 | 0.55 (3) | 0.65 (2) | 0.35 (4) | **0.85 (1)** |
| F8 | 0.0005 | 0 (1) | 0 (1) | 0 (1) | **0 (1)** |
| F9 | 0.000001 | 0 (1) | 0 (1) | 0 (1) | **0 (1)** |
| F10 | 0.00001 | 0.2 (4) | 0.95 (2) | 0.95 (2) | **1 (1)** |
| F11 | 0.05 | 0 (1) | 0 (1) | 0 (1) | **0 (1)** |
| F12 | 0.0001 | 0.1 (4) | 0.3 (3) | 0.4 (2) | **0.65 (1)** |
| Total Rank | | 27 | 20 | 19 | **12** |

### 5.2  Locate Both Global and Local Optima

A good niching algorithm should locate not only the global optima but also the local optima. To test the ability of locating both global and local optima, test function 5 and 10 are used. The results show in Table 5, which also indicate the DGCDE perform the best out of the four variants.

**Table 5.** Locating global and local optima

| Test Function | | CDE1 | CDE2 | CDE3 | DGCDE |
|---|---|---|---|---|---|
| | Mean | 3.8 | 5 | 5 | 5 |
| | Max | 5 | 5 | 5 | 5 |
| F5 | Min | 2 | 5 | 5 | 5 |
| | Std | 1.15 | 0 | 0 | 0 |
| | SR | 0.35 | 1 | 1 | 1 |
| | Mean | 6.25 | 11.55 | 13.7 | 14.05 |
| | Max | 12 | 15 | 17 | 17 |
| F10 | Min | 2 | 9 | 11 | 10 |
| | Std | 2.84 | 1.39 | 1.89 | 1.67 |
| | SR | 0 | 0 | 0 | 0 |

### 5.3 Locate Both Global and Local Optima

As mentioned in previous section, the parameter *level of accuracy* can affect the results of the algorithm. To demonstrate this more clearly, the plot (Fig. 2) on level of accuracy vs success rate is generated based on test function 12 (Inverted Vincent function). From the plot we can see, the success rate is increased by decreasing the level of accuracy.

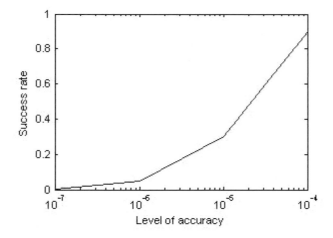

**Fig. 2.** The effect of varying level of accuracy

## 6   Conclusion

In this paper, a dynamic grouping crowding differential evolution (DGCDE) with ensemble of parameter algorithm for multi-modal optimization is introduced to overcome the difficulty of choosing DE parameter set. The proposed algorithm is compared with the original Crowding DE with different parameter setting on a set of commonly used multi-modal benchmark test problems. As we can see from the result, the proposed algorithm outperforms the Crowding DE for all the test problems.

# References

1. Mahfoud, S.W.: Niching methods for genetic algorithms. Ph.D. dissertation, Urbana, IL, USA, http://citeseer.ist.psu.edu/mahfoud95niching.html (1995)
2. Koper, K., Wysession, M.: Multimodal function optimization with a niching genetic algorithm: A seis-mological example. Bulletin of Seismological Society of America 89, 978–988 (1999)
3. Cavicchio, D.J.: Adaptive search using simulated evolution, Ph.D. dissertation, University of Michigan, Ann Arbor (1970)
4. De Jong, K.A.: An analysis of the behavior of a class of genetic adaptive systems, Ph.D. dissertation, University of Michigan (1975)
5. Mahfoud, S.W.: Crowding and preselection revisited. In: Manner, R., Manderick, B. (eds.) Parallel problem solving from nature, vol. 2, pp. 27–36
6. Harik, G.R.: Finding multimodal solutions using restricted tournament selection. In: Proceedings of the sixth International Conference on Genetic Algorithms. Morgan Kaufmann, San Francisco
7. Pétrowski, A.: A clearing procedure as a niching method for genetic algorithms. In: Proc. of the IEEE Int. Conf. on Evolutionary Computation, New York, USA, pp. 798–803 (1996)
8. Goldberg, D.E., Richardson, J.: Genetic algorithms with sharing for multimodal function optimization. In: Grefenstette, J. (ed.) Proceedings of the Second International Conference on Genetic Algorithms, pp. 41–49 (1987)
9. Li, J.P., Balazs, M.E., Parks, G.T., Clarkson, P.J.: A species conserving genetic algorithm for multimodal function optimization. Evol. Comput. 10(3), 207–234 (2002)
10. Zaharie, D.: Extensions of differential evolution algorithms for multimodal optimization. In: Proc. of 6th Int. Symposium of Symbolic and Numeric Algorithms for Scientific Computing, pp. 523–534 (2004)
11. Hendershot, Z.: A differential evolution algorithm for automatically discovering multiple global optima in multidimensional, discontinues spaces. In: Proceedings of MAICS 2004, Fifteenth Midwest Artificial Intelligence and Cognitive Sciences Conference, pp. 92–97 (2004)
12. Qu, B.Y., Suganthan, P.N.: Novel Multimodal Problems and Differential Evolution with Ensemble of Restricted Tournament Selection. In: IEEE Congress on Evolutionary Computation, Barcelona, Spain, pp. 3480–3486 (July 2010)
13. Thomsen, R.: Multi-modal optimization using crowding-based differential evolution. In: Proceedings of the 2004 Congress on Evolutionary Computation, vol. 2, pp. 1382–1389 (2004)
14. Storn, R., Price, K.V.: Differential evolution-A simple and efficient heuristic for global optimization over continuous spaces. J. of Global Optimization 11, 341–359 (1995)
15. Price, K.: An introduction to differential evolution. New Ideas in Optimization, 79–108 (1999)
16. Das, S., Suganthan, P.N.: Differential Evolution: A Survey of the State-of-the-art. IEEE Trans. on Evolutionary Computation, doi:10.1109/TEVC.2010.2059031

17. Wolpert, D.H., Macready, W.G.: No free lunch theorems for optimization. IEEE Transactions on Evolutionary Computation 1, 67–82 (1997)
18. Ackley, D.: An empirical study of bit vector function optimization. In: Genetic Algorithms Simulated Annealing, pp. 170–204. Pitman, London (1987)
19. Deb, K.: Genetic algorithms in multimodal function optimization, the Clearinghouse for Genetic Algorithms. M.S Thsis and Rep. 89002, Univ. Alabama, Tuscaloosa (1989)
20. Michalewicz, Z.: Genetic Algorithms + Data Structures = Evolution Programs. Springer, New York (1996)
21. Shir, O., Back, T.: Niche radius adaptation in the CMA-ES niching algorithms. In: Runarsson, T.P., Beyer, H.-G., Burke, E.K., Merelo-Guervós, J.J., Whitley, L.D., Yao, X. (eds.) PPSN 2006. LNCS, vol. 4193, pp. 142–151. Springer, Heidelberg (2006)
22. Mallipeddi, R., Suganthan, P.N., Pan, Q.K., Tasgetiren, M.F.: Differential evolution algorithm with ensemble of parameters and mutation strategies. Applied Soft Computing (accepted) doi:10.1016/j.asoc.2010.04.024
23. Qin, A.K., Huang, V.L., Suganthan, P.N.: Differential evolution algorithm with strategy adaptation for global numerical optimization. IEEE Trans. on Evolutionary Computations, 398–417 (April 2009), doi:10.1109/TEVC.2008.927706
24. Yu, E.L., Suganthan, P.N.: Ensemble of niching algorithms. Information Sciences 180(15), 2815–2833 (2010)

# Empirical Study on Migration Topologies and Migration Policies for Island Based Distributed Differential Evolution Variants

G. Jeyakumar and C. Shunmuga Velayutham

Amrita School of Engineering
Amrita Vishwa Vidyapeetham, Coimbatore
Tamil Nadu, India
g_jeyakumar@cb.amrita.edu,
cs_velayutham@cb.amrita.edu

**Abstract.** In this paper we present an empirical performance analysis of fourteen variants of Differential Evolution (DE) on a set of unconstrained global optimization problems. The island based distributed differential evolution counterparts of the above said 14 variants have been implemented with mesh and ring migration topologies and their superior performance over the serial implementation has been demonstrated. The competitive performance of ring topology based distributed differential evolution variants on the chosen problem has also been demonstrated. Six different migration policies are experimented for ring topology, and their performances are reported.

**Keywords:** Differential Evolution; Island Based Distributed Differential Evolution; Migration Policies; Unconstrained Global Optimization.

## 1 Introduction

Differential Evolution (DE), proposed by Storn and Price [1, 2], is a simple yet powerful Evolutionary Algorithm (EA) for global optimization in the continuous search domain [3]. DE has shown superior performance in both widely used test functions and real-world problems [4, 5]. DE employs mutation, recombination and selection operators like other EAs. However, it has some characteristics that makes it different from other members of the EA family. The major differences are in the way the offsprings (trial vectors) are generated and in the selection mechanism employed to transit to the next generation. In fact, DE uses a *differential mutation* operation, based on the distribution of parent solutions in the current population, coupled with recombination with a predetermined target vector to generate a trial vector followed by a *one-to-one greedy* selection between the trial vector and the target vector. Depending on the way the parent solutions are perturbed, there exists many trial vector generation strategies and consequently many DE variants.

In this paper, an empirical analysis of the performance of fourteen DE variants on six benchmark problems, with different features, has been carried out. The island based distributed population model of the above said fourteen DE variants has been

B.K. Panigrahi et al. (Eds.): SEMCCO 2010, LNCS 6466, pp. 29–37, 2010.

implemented with ring and mesh topologies and their performance comparison against the sequential variants on the chosen problems has also been carried out. The analyses demonstrate improvement in both performance efficacy and execution time in the case of the distributed DE (*dDE*) variants. Six different migration policies are experimented for ring topology, and their comparative performance analysis is presented.

The remainder of the paper is organized as follows. Section 2 describes the DE algorithm and the island based distributed DE. Section 3 reviews related works and Section 4 details the design of experiments. Section 5 discusses the results and finally Section 6 concludes the paper.

## 2   Distributed Differential Evolution (*dDE*)

DE algorithm explores the search space by sampling at multiple randomly chosen NP-D dimensional vectors (individuals) which encode the candidate solutions $X_{i,G}$. At each generation, DE employs *differential mutation* operation to produce a mutant vector $V_{i,G}$ (using the weighted difference of parent solutions i.e., $V_{i,G}=X_{r1,G}+F(X_{r2,G}-X_{r3,G})$) with respect to each individual $X_{i,G}$, the so called target vector, in the current population. This is followed by a crossover (binomial or exponential) between the mutant vector $V_{i,G}$ and the target vector $X_{i,G}$ to create a trial vector $U_{i,G}$. Further, a one-to-one knock out competition between the target vector $X_{i,G}$ and its corresponding trial vector $U_{i,G}$ decides the survivor for the next generation.

With seven commonly used mutation strategies and two crossover schemes, the 14 possible variants of DE are: *DE/rand/1/bin, DE/rand/1/exp, DE/best/1/bin, DE/best/1/exp, DE/rand/2/bin, DE/rand/2/exp, DE/best/2/bin, DE/best/2/exp, DE/current-to-rand/1/bin, DE/current-to-rand/1/exp, DE/current-to-best/1/bin, DE/current-to-best/1/exp, DE/rand-to-best/1/bin* and *DE/rand-to-best/1/exp.*

Owing to the fact that, unlike the other EAs, the crossover and selection operations in DE are local in nature, island based distributed versions of DE algorithm becomes a natural extension in parallel framework. For 14 DE variants we implemented their equivalent island based *dDE* counterpart whereby the population is partitioned into small subsets (known as islands) each evolving independently but also exchanging (migrating) information among them to co-operatively enhance the efficacy of the DE variants. The island based *dDE* is characterized by the following parameters – number of islands *ni*, migration frequency *mf*, number of migrants *nm*, selection policy *sp* that decides what individual migrate, replacement policy *rp* that determines which individual(s) the migrant(s) replace and the migration topology *mt* that decides which islands can send (or receive) the migrants.

## 3   Related Works

Efren Menzura-Montes et. al. [6] empirically compared the performance of eight DE variants. They concluded *rand/1/bin, best/1/bin, current-to-rand/1/bin* and *rand/2/dir* as the most competitive variants. However, the potential variants like *best/2/\*, rand-to-best/1/\** and *rand/2/\** were not considered in their study.

Babu and Munawar [7] compared the performance of ten variants of DE (excluding the *current-to-rand/1/\** and *current-to-best/1/\** variants of our variants suite) to solve the optimal design problem of shell-and-tube heat exchangers. They concluded *best/\*/\** strategies to be better than *rand/\*/\** strategies.

Kozlov K.N, Samsonov A.M [8] proposed a new migration scheme for parallel differential evolution. The new scheme replaces the oldest members of the population than the random one, in the migration process. D.K.Tasoulis et. al [9] implemented DE in parallel and experimentally shown that the extent of information exchange among subpopulation assigned to different processor nodes bears a significant impact on the performance of the algorithm.

Marina S. Ntipteni et. al [10] implemented a parallel asynchronous differential evolution algorithm. The algorithm uses a panmictic approach – a unique population is distributed among a cluster of PCs, with master-slave architecture. Different executable programs realize the evolution of the population; the exchange of information between different individuals is performed through shared text files.

Matthieu Weber et. al [11] proposed a novel distributed differential evolution algorithm named Distributed Differential Evolution with Explorative-Exploitative Population Families (DDE-EEPF). In DDE-EEPF the sub-populations are grouped into two families. This first family of sub-population has the role of exploration and the second family is for exploitation. The results show that the proposed algorithm is efficient for most of the analyzed problems. Daniela Zaharie and Dana Petcu [12] describe coarse-grained parallelization of an adaptive differential evolution algorithm. The parallelization is based on the multi-population model, a random connection topology being used, the results showed speedup in execution time and higher probability of convergence.

## 4   Design of Experiments

In this paper, we investigate the performance of fourteen DE variants and compare them against their island based distributed implementation with two different migration topologies, on a set of benchmark problems with high dimensionality and different features. We have chosen six test functions [6, 13], of dimensionality 30, grouped by features - unimodal separable, unimodal nonseparable, multimodal separable and multimodal nonseparable. All the test functions have an optimum value at zero, except for $f_3$. The details of the benchmark functions are described in Table 1. In order to show the similar results, the description of $f_3$ was adjusted to have its optimum value at zero by just adding the optimal value (12569.486618164879) [6].

The parameters for all the DE variants are: population size NP = 60 and maximum number of generations = 3000 (consequently, the maximum number of function evaluations calculate to 180,000). The moderate population size and number of generations were chosen to demonstrate the efficacy of DE variants in solving the chosen problems. The variants will stop before the number of generations is reached only if the tolerance error (which has been fixed as an error value of $1 \times 10^{-12}$) with respect to the global optimum is obtained. Following [6, 14], we defined a range for the scaling factor, $F \in [0.3, 0.9]$ and this value is generated anew at each generation for all variants. We use the same value for K as F.

**Table 1.** Description of the benchmark functions

| | |
|---|---|
| $f_1$ - Schwefel's Problem 2.21 <br> $f_{sch}(x) = max_i\{\|x_i\|, 1 \leq i \leq 30\}; -100 \leq x_i \leq 100$ | $f_4$ – Generalized Restrigin's Function <br> $f_{Ras}(x) = \sum_{i=1}^{30}[x_i^2 - 10 \cos(2\pi x_i) + 10]$; <br> $-5.12 \leq x_i \leq 5.12$ |
| $f_2$ – Schwefel's Problem 1.2 <br> $f_{schDS}(x) = \sum_{i=1}^{30}(\sum_{j=1}^{i} x_j)^2; -100 \leq x_i \leq 100$ | $f_5$ - Generalized Rosenbrock's Function <br> $f_{Ros}(x) = \sum_{i=1}^{29} \|100(x_{i+1} - x_i^2)^2 + (x_i - 1)^2\|$; <br> $-30 \leq x_i \leq 30$ |
| $f_3$ – Generalized Schwefel's Problem 2.26 <br> $f_{sch}(x) = \sum_{i=1}^{30}(x_i \sin(\sqrt{\|x_i\|})); -500 \leq x_i \leq 500$ | $f_6$ - Generalized Griewank's Function <br> $f_{Gri}(x) = \frac{1}{4000}\sum_{i=1}^{30} x_i^2 - \prod_{i=1}^{30} \cos\left(\frac{x_i}{\sqrt{i}}\right) + 1$; <br> $-600 \leq x_i \leq 600$ |

The crossover rate, CR, was tuned for each variant-test function combination. Eleven different values for the CR viz. {0.0, 0.1, 0.2, 0.3, 0.4, 0.5, 0.6, 0.7, 0.8, 0.9 and 1.0} were tested for each variant-test function combination for DE, with 50 independent runs. A bootstrap test was conducted in order to determine the confidence interval for the mean objective function value. The CR value corresponding to the best confidence interval (95%) was used in our experiment. In case of DE , the CR values are: for $f_1$\{0.5, 0.9, 0.2, 0.9, 0.2, 0.9, 0.2, 0.9, 0.2, 0.9, 0.2, 0.9, 0.4, 0.9\}, for $f_2$\{0.9, 0.9, 0.5, 0.9, 0.9, 0.9, 0.7, 0.9, 0.9, 0.9, 0.9, 0.9, 0.9, 0.9\} for $f_3$\{0.5, 0.0, 0.1, 0.7, 0.2, 0.3, 0.7, 0.3, 0.4, 0.3, 0.8, 0.2, 0.8, 0.4\} for $f_4$\{0.1, 0.9, 0.1, 0.9, 0.1, 0.9, 0.1, 0.9, 0.1, 0.9, 0.1, 0.9, 0.1, 0.9\} for $f_5$\{0.9, 0.9, 0.8, 0.8, 0.9, 0.9, 0.6, 0.9, 0.1, 0.9, 0.1, 0.9, 0.8, 0.9\} and for $f_6$\{0.1, 0.9, 0.1, 0.8, 0.1, 0.9, 0.1, 0.9, 0.1, 0.9, 0.2, 0.9, 0.1, 0.9 \}. The same CR values are used for *dDE* variants also.

The parameter for all *dDE* variants are: *ni* = 4 (the initial population of size 60 is divided into four subpopulations of size 15), *mf* = 45 (empirically decided based on previous experiments), *nm* = 1, *sp* = migrant is the best solution, *rp* = random solution (except the best solution) in the receiving population is replaced by the migrant and *mt* = ring topology/mesh topology. Henceforth, we call the *dDE* variants implemented with ring topology as *dDE-Ring* variants, and variants with mesh topology as *dDE-Mesh* variants. Being a preliminary study, the *dDE* have been implemented as multi-process MPI (Message Passing Interface) applications on a single machine.

As EA's are stochastic in nature, 100 independent runs were performed per variant per test function (by initializing the population for every run with uniform random initialization within the search space). For the sake of performance analysis among the variants, we present the mean objective function value (MOV), the probability of convergence $(P_c)$ [15] and Average Execution Time for each variant-test function combination.

## 5   Results and Discussion

The simulation results for the 14 DE variants and their island based *dDE-Mesh* and *dDE-Ring* counterparts are presented in Table 2 and Table 3. For the classical DE variants, the most competitive variants are *DE/rand-to-best/1/bin, DE/best/2/bin* and *DE/rand/1/bin*. The variants *DE/rand/2/bin* and *DE/best/2/exp* also showed good performance consistently. On the other hand the worst overall performances were consistently displayed by variants *DE/current-to-best/1/exp* and *DE/current-to-rand/1/exp*.

The variants *DE/best/1/exp* and *DE/current-to-rand/1/bin* were also displaying poor performance. Function $f_5$ was not solved by any variant.

**Table 2.** MOV obtained for DE and *dDE* variants for $f_1$, $f_2$ and $f_3$

| Variant | $f_1$ | | | $f_2$ | | | $f_3$ | | |
|---|---|---|---|---|---|---|---|---|---|
| | DE | dDE | | DE | dDE | | DE | dDE | |
| | | Mesh | Ring | | Mesh | Ring | | Mesh | Ring |
| *rand/1/bin* | **0.00** | **0.00** | **0.00** | **0.07** | 2.58 | 2.55 | 0.13 | 0.23 | **0.09** |
| *rand/1/exp* | 3.76 | 8.10 | **3.23** | 0.31 | 0.02 | **0.01** | 0.10 | 51.45 | **0.08** |
| *best/1/bin* | 1.96 | 0.14 | **0.04** | 13.27 | **0.00** | **0.00** | **0.00** | 0.03 | 0.01 |
| *best/1/exp* | 37.36 | 12.85 | **9.68** | 57.39 | **0.00** | **0.00** | 0.01 | 0.03 | **0.00** |
| *rand/2/bin* | 0.06 | **0.00** | 0.01 | 1.64 | 0.06 | **0.05** | 0.22 | 0.02 | **0.01** |
| *rand/2/exp* | 32.90 | 14.50 | **7.56** | 269.86 | **0.05** | 0.26 | 0.27 | 0.20 | **0.09** |
| *best/2/bin* | **0.00** | **0.00** | **0.00** | **0.00** | **0.00** | **0.00** | 0.17 | 0.10 | **0.04** |
| *best/2/exp* | **0.05** | 1.45 | 0.89 | **0.00** | **0.00** | **0.00** | 0.08 | 0.26 | **0.05** |
| *current-to-rand/1/bin* | 3.68 | **0.06** | 0.64 | 3210.36 | **0.09** | 13.79 | **0.14** | 0.48 | 0.22 |
| *current-to-rand/1/exp* | 57.52 | 24.26 | **20.57** | 3110.90 | **15.51** | 22.20 | **0.12** | 0.50 | 0.23 |
| *current-to-best/1/bin* | 3.71 | **0.06** | 0.66 | 3444.00 | **0.09** | 13.63 | 0.19 | 1.05 | **0.31** |
| *current-to-best/1/exp* | 56.67 | 24.10 | **20.02** | 2972.62 | 4.77 | 28.08 | **0.10** | 0.62 | 0.22 |
| *rand-to-best/1/bin* | **0.00** | **0.00** | **0.00** | **0.07** | 9.03 | 0.22 | **0.22** | 0.55 | 0.24 |
| *rand-to-best/1/exp* | 3.38 | 8.73 | **2.85** | 0.20 | **0.00** | 0.02 | 0.12 | 0.25 | **0.05** |

**Table 3.** MOV obtained for DE and *dDE* variants for $f_4$, $f_5$ and $f_6$

| Variant | $f_4$ | | | $f_5$ | | | $f_6$ | | |
|---|---|---|---|---|---|---|---|---|---|
| | DE | dDE | | DE | dDE | | DE | dDE | |
| | | Mesh | Ring | | Mesh | Ring | | Mesh | Ring |
| *rand/1/bin* | **0.00** | 0.25 | **0.00** | **21.99** | 37.54 | 38.82 | **0.00** | **0.00** | **0.00** |
| *rand/1/exp* | 47.93 | 25.41 | **10.54** | 25.48 | **23.42** | 34.32 | 0.05 | 0.03 | **0.01** |
| *best/1/bin* | 4.33 | 3.52 | **0.90** | 585899.88 | 215.22 | **35.48** | 3.72 | **0.00** | **0.00** |
| *best/1/exp* | 50.74 | 43.27 | **36.39** | 64543.84 | 16665.31 | **169.97** | 5.91 | 1.08 | **0.41** |
| *rand/2/bin* | **0.00** | 1.08 | 0.01 | **19.01** | 20.76 | 21.34 | **0.00** | **0.00** | **0.00** |
| *rand/2/exp* | 101.38 | 49.90 | **17.73** | 2741.32 | **16.79** | 25.82 | 0.21 | 0.03 | **0.01** |
| *best/2/bin* | 0.69 | 3.90 | **0.63** | **2.32** | 2.83 | 4.06 | **0.00** | 0.03 | **0.00** |
| *best/2/exp* | 80.63 | 44.89 | **29.52** | **1.12** | 2.10 | 6.19 | 0.03 | 0.02 | **0.01** |
| *current-to-rand/1/bin* | 37.75 | 44.89 | **9.02** | 52.81 | 59.92 | **41.18** | **0.00** | 0.01 | **0.00** |
| *current-to-rand/1/exp* | 235.14 | 152.13 | **134.49** | 199243.32 | 1291.28 | **433.25** | 1.21 | **0.10** | 0.18 |
| *current-to-best/1/bin* | 37.04 | 21.87 | **9.50** | 56.91 | 61.36 | **40.57** | **0.00** | **0.00** | **0.00** |
| *current-to-best/1/exp* | 232.80 | 155.25 | **131.13** | 119685.68 | **124.96** | 276.23 | 1.21 | **0.11** | 0.19 |
| *rand-to-best/1/bin* | **0.00** | 0.36 | **0.00** | **17.37** | 30.85 | 27.49 | **0.00** | **0.00** | **0.00** |
| *rand-to-best/1/exp* | 48.09 | 29.63 | 9.98 | 24.54 | 20.09 | 31.52 | 0.05 | 0.03 | 0.01 |

Table 2 and Table 3 also shows the performance of island based *dDE-Ring* and *dDE-Mesh* variants on the chosen six benchmark functions. As is clearly evident from the table, in most of the cases *dDE* variants outperformed their serial counterparts. This is evident in the case of worst performing variants also. Among the *dDE* variants, *dDE-Ring* variants perform relatively better than their *dDE-Mesh* counter-parts, in most of the cases. This is more evident in the cases $f_1, f_3, f_4$ and $f_6$.

The probability of convergence ($P_c$), the percentage of successful runs to total runs, is calculated for each variant-function combination. This measure identifies variants having higher convergence capability to global optimum. It is calculated as the mean percentage of number of successful runs out of total runs i.e $P_c = (nc\ /\ nt)\%$ where *nc* is total number of successful runs made by each variant for all the functions and *nt* is total number of runs, in our experiment $nt = 6 * 100 = 600$. Table 4 shows, in all the cases *dDE* variants display increased probability of convergence, except for the variants *DE/rand/1/bin, DE/current-to-rand/1/bin* and *DE/rand-to-best/1/bin*. Overall, *dDE-Ring* variants have acheived more number of successful runs than *dDE-Mesh* variants.

Despite the fact that *dDE* variants have been implemented as multi-process MPI applications on a single machine, we have observed improvement in average execution time as well as shown in Table 5.

**Table 4.** Number of successful runs and probability of convergence ($P_c$) for DE variants

| Sno | Variant | DE | | dDE- Mesh | | dDE-Ring | |
|---|---|---|---|---|---|---|---|
| | | *nc* | *Pc(%)* | *nc* | *Pc(%)* | *nc* | *Pc(%)* |
| 1 | *rand/1/bin* | 377 | **62.83** | 329 | 54.83 | 312 | 52.00 |
| 2 | *rand/1/exp* | 79 | 13.17 | 197 | **32.83** | 194 | 32.33 |
| 3 | *best/1/bin* | 257 | 42.83 | 284 | 47.33 | 326 | **54.33** |
| 4 | *best/1/exp* | 143 | 23.83 | 160 | 26.67 | 184 | **30.67** |
| 5 | *rand/2/bin* | 201 | 33.50 | 411 | **68.50** | 389 | 64.83 |
| 6 | *rand/2/exp* | 5 | 0.83 | 163 | **27.17** | 147 | 24.50 |
| 7 | *best/2/bin* | 386 | 64.33 | 356 | 59.33 | 459 | **76.50** |
| 8 | *best/2/exp* | 191 | 31.83 | 222 | 37.00 | 232 | **38.67** |
| 9 | *current-to-rand/1/bin* | 98 | **16.33** | 43 | 7.17 | 95 | 15.83 |
| 10 | *current-to-rand/1/exp* | 3 | 0.50 | 43 | **7.17** | 37 | 6.17 |
| 11 | *current-to-best/1/bin* | 99 | 16.50 | 61 | 10.17 | 101 | **16.83** |
| 12 | *current-to-best/1/exp* | 5 | 0.83 | 51 | **8.50** | 39 | 6.50 |
| 13 | *rand-to-best/1/bin* | 379 | **63.17** | 329 | 54.83 | 311 | 51.83 |
| 14 | *rand-to-best/1/exp* | 85 | 14.17 | 178 | 29.67 | 209 | **34.83** |
| | *Total* | 2308 | | 2827 | | **3035** | |

Next in our study, we experimented with 6 different migration policies (two different selection policies and three different replacement policies), for the *dDE-Ring* variants on two of the six benchmark functions viz. $f_1$ and $f_2$. The various migration policies are: 1) best migrant solution replaces a random solution (*b-r-r*). 2) best migrant solution replaces a random solution (except the best solution) (*b-r-r#b*). 3) best migrant solution replaces the worst solution (*b-r-w*). 4) random migrant solution replaces a random solution (*r-r-r*). 5) random migrant solution replaces a random solution (except the best solution) (*r-r-r#b*). 6) random migrant solution replaces the worst solution (*r-r-w*).

The MOV obtained for comparing the migration policies are shown in Table 6 and 7, for $f_1$ and $f_2$ respectively It is observed from the results that, comparatively, *b-r-w* policy gives competitive results in most of the cases. Overall, the *b-r-\** policies achieve better convergence than that of *r-r-\** polices.

**Table 5.** Speedup Measurement

| Function | DE | dDE-Mesh | | dDE-Ring | |
|---|---|---|---|---|---|
| | ExecTime | ExecTime | Speedup(%) | ExecTime | SpeedUp (%) |
| $f_1$ | 0.56 | 0.18 | 67.33 | 0.20 | 64.75 |
| $f_2$ | 1.22 | 0.30 | 75.21 | 0.35 | 71.76 |
| $f_3$ | 1.20 | 0.27 | 77.49 | 0.32 | 73.68 |
| $f_4$ | 1.32 | 0.30 | 77.44 | 0.29 | 77.85 |
| $f_5$ | 0.60 | 0.20 | 67.16 | 0.20 | 66.77 |
| $f_6$ | 1.37 | 0.29 | 78.77 | 0.32 | 76.82 |

**Table 6.** MOV Comparison of Various Migration Policies for $f_1$

| Variant | b-r-r | b-r-r#b | b-r-w | r-r-r | r-r-r#b | r-r-w |
|---|---|---|---|---|---|---|
| rand/1/bin | 0.09 | 0.06 | **0.05** | 0.25 | 0.89 | 3.28 |
| rand/1/exp | **0.00** | **0.00** | 0.01 | 0.11 | 0.05 | 0.02 |
| best/1/bin | **0.00** | **0.00** | **0.00** | **0.00** | **0.00** | **0.00** |
| best/1/exp | **0.00** | **0.00** | **0.00** | **0.00** | **0.00** | **0.00** |
| rand/2/bin | **0.00** | **0.00** | **0.00** | 0.03 | 0.08 | 0.32 |
| rand/2/exp | **0.11** | 0.13 | 0.17 | 1.89 | 1.43 | 0.70 |
| best/2/bin | **0.00** | **0.00** | **0.00** | **0.00** | **0.00** | **0.00** |
| best/2/exp | **0.00** | **0.00** | **0.00** | **0.00** | **0.00** | **0.00** |
| current-to-rand/1/bin | 16.57 | 14.01 | **3.87** | 3982.89 | 2687.72 | 725.55 |
| current-to-rand/1/exp | 31.84 | 17.18 | **7.26** | 1765.50 | 1465.18 | 281.33 |
| current-to-best/1/bin | 16.42 | 13.74 | **3.20** | 3661.85 | 2732.68 | 683.12 |
| current-to-best/1/exp | 37.42 | 20.95 | **7.76** | 1715.01 | 1347.27 | 311.39 |
| rand-to-best/1/bin | **0.07** | 0.37 | 0.10 | 0.18 | 7.57 | 3.74 |
| rand-to-best/1/exp | **0.00** | 0.01 | 0.01 | 0.03 | 0.04 | 0.03 |

**Table 7.** MOV Comparison of Various Migration Policies for $f_2$

| Variant | b-r-r | b-r-r#b | b-r-w | r-r-r | r-r-r#b | r-r-w |
|---|---|---|---|---|---|---|
| rand/1/bin | **0.00** | **0.00** | **0.00** | **0.00** | **0.00** | **0.00** |
| rand/1/exp | 2.86 | 2.55 | 3.73 | 1.72 | **1.35** | 2.65 |
| best/1/bin | **0.03** | 0.04 | 0.04 | **0.03** | **0.03** | **0.03** |
| best/1/exp | 8.67 | 8.98 | 9.29 | 8.70 | **8.43** | 9.62 |
| rand/2/bin | **0.01** | **0.01** | **0.01** | 0.02 | 0.02 | **0.01** |
| rand/2/exp | 8.12 | **7.63** | 7.80 | 11.71 | 9.69 | 7.79 |
| best/2/bin | **0.00** | **0.00** | **0.00** | **0.00** | **0.00** | **0.00** |
| best/2/exp | 0.71 | 0.78 | 0.98 | 0.76 | **0.67** | 0.96 |
| current-to-rand/1/bin | 0.72 | 0.63 | **0.36** | 3.87 | 3.42 | 1.83 |
| current-to-rand/1/exp | 21.94 | **20.61** | 21.18 | 50.13 | 44.22 | 32.00 |
| current-to-best/1/bin | 0.72 | 0.63 | **0.37** | 3.74 | 3.43 | 1.85 |
| current-to-best/1/exp | 21.38 | **21.37** | 23.58 | 50.73 | 43.07 | 33.32 |
| rand-to-best/1/bin | **0.00** | **0.00** | **0.00** | **0.00** | **0.00** | **0.00** |
| rand-to-best/1/exp | 2.83 | 3.32 | 3.98 | 1.83 | **1.54** | 2.93 |

# 6 Conclusion

In this paper, we presented an empirical comparative performance analysis of DE and distribute DE variants on a set of unconstrained global optimization problems. The *dDE* was implemented with Mesh and Ring topologies. The variants were tested on 6 test functions of dimension 30, grouped by their modality and decomposability. The best and worst performing DE variants were identified. The *dDE-Ring* variants were observed to perform relatively better than their serial and *dDE-Mesh* counterparts, in most of the cases. In fact the calculation of probability of convergence reiterated the observation about the performance of above said variants. Six different migration policies were experimented for *dDE-Ring* variants, with the migration policy *b-r-w*, displaying competitive performance against their counterparts.

# References

1. Storn, R., Price, K.: Differential Evolution – A Simple and Efficient Adaptive Scheme for Global Optimization over Continuous Spaces. Technical Report TR-95-012, ICSI (1995)
2. Storn, R., Price, K.: Differential Evolution – A Simple and Efficient Heuristic Strategy for Global Optimization and Continuous Spaces. Journal of Global Optimization 11(4), 341–359 (1997)
3. Price, K.V.: An Introduction to Differential Evolution. In: Corne, D., Dorigo, M., Glover, F. (eds.) New Ideas in Optimization, pp. 79–108. Mc Graw-Hill, UK (1999)
4. Price, K., Storn, R.M., Lampinen, J.A.: Differential Evolution: A Practical Approach to Global Optimization. Springer, Heidelberg (2005)
5. Chakraborty, U.K. (ed.): Advances in Differential Evolution. Studies in Computational Intelligence, vol. 143. Springer, Heidelberg (2008)
6. Mezura-Montes., E., Velazquez-Reyes., J., Coello, C.A.C.: A Comparative Study on Differential Evolution Variants for Global Optimization. In: Genetic and Evolutionary Computation Conference, GECCO 2006, July 8-12 (2006)
7. Babu. B. V., Munawar, S. A.: Optimal Design of Shell-and-Tube Heat Exchanges by Different Strategies of Differential Evolution. Technical Report, PILANI -333 031, Department of Chemical Engineering, Birla Institute of Technology and Science, Rajasthan, India (2001)
8. Kozlov, K.N., Samsonov, A.M.: New Migration Scheme for Parallel Differential Evolution. In: Proceedings of Fifth International Conference on Bioinformatics of Genome Regulation and Structure, pp. 141–144 (2006)
9. Tasoulis, D.K., Pavliis, N.G., Plagianakos, V.P., Vrahatis, M.N.: Parallel Differential Evolution. In: Congress on Evolutionary Computation (CEC 2004), Portland (2004)
10. Ntipteni, M.S., Valakos, I.M., Nikolos, I.K.: An Asynchronous Parallel Differential Evolution Algorithms. In: International Conference on Design Optimization and Application, Spain (2006)
11. Weber, M., Neri, F., Tirronen, V.: Distributed Differential Evolution with Explorative-Exploitative Population Families. In: Proceedings of Genetic Programming and Evolvable Machine, vol. 10, pp. 343–371 (2009)

12. Zaharie, D., Petcu, D.: Parallel Implementation of Multi-Population Differential Evolution. In: Grigoras, S.D., et al. (eds.) Concurrent Information Processing and Computing (CIPC 2003). Nato Advanced Research Workshop, pp. 262–269. A.I.Cuza University Press (2003)
13. Yao, X., Liu, Y., Liang, K.H., Lin, G.: Fast Evolutionary Algorithms. In: Rozenberg, G., Back, T., Eiben, A. (eds.) Advances in Evolutionary Computing: Theory and Applications, pp. 45–94. Springer, New York (2003)
14. Mezura-Montes, E.: Personal Communication (unpublished)
15. Feoktistov, V.: Differential Evolution in Search of Solutions. Springer, Heidelberg (2006)

# Differential Evolution Based Fuzzy Clustering

V. Ravi*, Nupur Aggarwal, and Nikunj Chauhan

Institute for Development and Research in Banking Technology, Castle Hills Road #1,
Masab Tank, Hyderabad – 500 057 A P, India
Tel.: +91-40-2353 4981
rav_padma@yahoo.com, nupur.wal@gmail.com,
nikunj.chauhan@gmail.com

**Abstract.** In this work, two new fuzzy clustering (FC) algorithms based on Differential Evolution (DE) are proposed. Five well-known data sets viz. Iris, Wine, Glass, E. Coli and Olive Oil are used to demonstrate the effectiveness of DEFC-1 and DEFC-2. They are compared with Fuzzy C-Means (FCM) algorithm and Threshold Accepting Based Fuzzy Clustering algorithms proposed by Ravi et al., [1]. Xie-Beni index is used to arrive at the 'optimal' number of clusters. Based on the numerical experiments, we infer that, in terms of least objective function value, these variants can be used as viable alternatives to FCM algorithm.

**Keywords:** Differential Evolution, Fuzzy Clustering, Xie-Beni Index, Objective Function, Global Optimization, Evolutionary Algorithm.

## Notation

$v_i$ is $i^{th}$ Cluster Center, $x_k$ is the $k^{th}$ data sample, m is the degree of fuzziness, $\mu_{ik}$ is them membership value of the $k^{th}$ sample in the $i^{th}$ cluster, U is the membership matrix, z is objective function, genmax is the maximum number of DE generations, gen is the generation counter, n is the number of samples, k is the number of features, $C_c$ is the number of clusters, Np is population size, F is the scale factor, CR is Crossover Factor and Eps is the accuracy used the convergence criteria.

## 1 Introduction

Fuzzy Clustering [2] plays a very important role in the fields of statistics and pattern recognition. In fuzzy C-means (FCM) algorithm, to account for the fuzziness present in a data set, each data sample belongs to every cluster to a certain degree, with the constraint that the sum of its membership degrees in all the clusters is 1. In a nutshell, the FCM performs Picard iteration between successive estimates of membership function matrix and the cluster centers. This process is called "alternating optimization" and is the basis of the "hill climbing" nature of the FCM. Consequently, FCM can get trapped in local minima when started with poor initialization. To solve this problem,

---

* Corresponding author.

B.K. Panigrahi et al. (Eds.): SEMCCO 2010, LNCS 6466, pp. 38–45, 2010.
© Springer-Verlag Berlin Heidelberg 2010

researchers employed several global optimization metaheuristics to it. This paper proposes two variants of DE based fuzzy clustering algorithms, DEFC-1 where the membership values matrix is taken as the set of decision variables and DEFC-2, where the vector of cluster centers is considered as the set of decision variables.

The main drawback of FCM is that, if started with poor initialization, it can get trapped in local minima. Generally the procedure is run with multiple initializations with the hope that some runs will lead to the global optimal solution [3]. Hence, several researchers formulated the entire clustering task of FCM explicitly as an optimization problem and solved it by using various metaheuristics viz., simulated annealing [4, 5], variable neighborhood search [6], genetic algorithms [3, 7], tabu search [8] and threshold accepting [1] were suggested. Recently, Yucheng et. al. [9] applied DE after FC so that it can lead to a global optimum. DE was also used with FCM in several different ways. Maulik and Saha [10] presented a real-coded modified DE based automatic fuzzy clustering algorithm which automatically evolves the number of clusters as well as the proper partitioning from a data set. Das and Konar [11] proposed an evolutionary-fuzzy clustering algorithm for automatically grouping the pixels of an image into different homogeneous regions. An improved variant of the DE was used to determine the number of naturally occurring clusters in the image as well as to refine the cluster centers. Zhang et. al. [12] used DE to optimize the coordinates of the samples distributed randomly on a plane. Kernel methods are used here to map the data in the original space into a high-dimensional feature space in which a fuzzy dissimilarity matrix is constructed. These studies reported better objective function values compared to the FCM.

## 2   Differential Evolution Algorithm

Originally proposed by Price and Storn [13], DE is a stochastic, population based optimization method. Because of the simple, fast and robust nature of DE, it has found widespread application. DE has been successfully applied to solve many real optimization problems such as aerodynamic shape optimization [14], optimization of radial active magnetic bearings [15], automated mirror design [16], optimization of fermentation using a high ethanol tolerance yeast [17], mechanical engineering design [18], neural network training [19 - 24] and parameter estimation in biofilter modeling [25]. Selection of Control Parameters in DE is very crucial. Brest et. al. [26] discusses an efficient technique for adapting control parameters associated with DE. JADE [27] implements a new mutation strategy "DE/current-to-pbest" with optional external archive and updating control parameters in an adaptive manner. The DE/current-to-pbest in JADE is a generalization of the classic "DE/current-to-best". Here, the optional archive operation utilizes historical data to provide information of progress direction. In Self-adaptive DE (SaDE) [28], both trial vector generation strategies and their associated control parameter values are gradually self-adapted by learning from their previous experiences in generating promising solutions.

## 3   Threshold Accepting Based Fuzzy Clustering Algorithms

Ravi et. al. [1] proposed two variants of threshold accepting based fuzzy clustering viz., TAFC-1 and TAFC-2. In TAFC-1, the solution matrix is the membership matrix) and the cluster centers are updated by using FCM. However, in TAFC-2, the solution vector contains the cluster centers, whereas the membership matrix is updated by using FCM. Further, in both variants, FCM is invoked to replace the current solution if the neighborhood solution is not acceptable. The Xie-Beni *measure* [29] was used to determine the optimal number of clusters. For more details, the reader can refer [1].

## 4   Differential Evolution Based Fuzzy Clustering Algorithms

Fuzzy clustering is formulated as a non-linear optimization problem as follows:

$$minimize \ z(U,v) = \sum_{i=1}^{cc}\sum_{k=1}^{n}(\mu_{ik})^{m}\|x_k - v_i\|^2 \tag{1}$$

$$Subject \ to \ \sum_{i=1}^{cc}\mu_{ik} = 1, \ 1 \le k \le n, \ 0 \le \mu_{ik} \le 1, for \ i=1,...,cc; \ k=1,...,n$$

DE is invoked here to find the global optimal solution to this problem. The "alternating optimization" feature of fuzzy C-means permits us to develop two distinct variants of the current algorithm. To determine the 'optimal' number of clusters the Xie-Beni cluster validity measure is used and is given by:

$$V_{XB} = \frac{\sum_{k=1}^{n}\sum_{i=1}^{cc}(\mu_{ik})^2\|x_k - v_i\|^2}{n\left\{\min\|v_i - v_j\|^2\right\}} \tag{2}$$

where $v_i$ and $v_j$ are cluster centers.

The number of clusters corresponding to the minimum value of the Xie-Beni index indicates the "optimal" number of clusters.

### 4.1   The DEFC-1 Algorithm

In DEFC-1, the membership matrix is considered to be the solution matrix and the cluster centers are updated using the equation of FCM. Because of this, DEFC-1 will have numerous decision variables as the number of patterns of any data exceeds the number of features. Thus, each element of the membership matrix of order $cc$ x $n$, is a decision variable. The steps for the algorithm are given below.

**Step 0:** *Data Normalization:* The input data is passed through the following transformation:

$$x_{ij} = \frac{x_{ij} - x\min_j}{x\max_j - x\min_j}, \ i = 1,2,...,n \ and \ j = 1,2,...,k \tag{3}$$

where $xmin_j$ and $xmax_j$ are the minimum and maximum of the $j^{th}$ feature and $n$, $k$ are respectively the number of samples and features.

**Step 1:** Initialize the number of clusters, $cc = 2$, generation counter $gen = 0$, maximum number of generations *genmax*, scale factor $F$, crossover factor $CR$, convergence criteria *eps* and population size $Np$.

**Step 2:** Generate randomly the initial population of feasible $Np$ solution matrices, in the range $(0,1)$. So the initial population is a $Np$ x $2$ x $n$ structure (starting with 2 clusters).

**Step 3:** The cluster centers are computed first and then the objective function value is computed for each of the $Np$ membership matrices by using the following expressions. Store the objective function value in an array of solutions $f^0$.

$$v_i = \frac{1}{\sum_{k=1}^{n} (\mu_{ik})^m} \sum_{k=1}^{n} (\mu_{ik})^m x_k, m \in (1,\infty), i = 1,...,cc \tag{4}$$

$$z(U, v) = \sum_{i=1}^{cc} \sum_{k=1}^{n} (\mu_{ik})^m \|x_k - v_i\|^2 \tag{5}$$

where $\|x_i - v_j\|^2$ denotes the Euclidean distance between vectors $x_k$ and $v_i$.

**Step 4:** Start while loop and repeat till generation counter $gen < genmax$

**Step 5:** For each member of population find three random integers $a, b, c$ between 0 to $Np$ - 1 and find noisy membership matrices in the usual way as found in differential evolution.

**Step 6:** Recombine each target membership matrices with corresponding noisy membership matrices to give trial membership matrices.

**Step 7:** Check whether each decision variable in each of the $Np$ trial membership matrices are within bound and that the "probability constraint" holds for each of the matrices. If bounds are violated or constraint is not satisfied, then bring the matrices arbitrarily back to bounds.

**Step 8:** For each of the trial membership matrix, calculate objective function value and cluster centers using equation 5 and 4 respectively. Store the value of objective function values in array $f^t$.

**Step 9:** For the entire $Np$ trial membership matrix, compare their corresponding objective function value with that of corresponding target membership matrix. If the former is less than the latter, replace target membership matrix with trial membership matrix and corresponding target cluster centers and target objective function value with that of trial cluster centers and target objective function value.

**Step 10:** Find the best or the minimum objective function value and the worst or the maximum objective function value from the newly generated population. If the absolute difference between the two is less than *eps*, go to step 12; else go to step 5.

**Step 11:** Check if maximum number of generations have been completed. If yes, go to step 12; else increase generation counter $gen$ by 1 and go to step 5.

**Step 12:** if($cc = 2$) {Compute the Xie-Beni measure. $cc = cc + 1$ and go to step 2.}
   else
   {Compute the Xie-Beni measure and compare it across the two successive values of $cc$. If the Xie-Beni measure for the current value of $cc$ is smaller than that of the previous value of $cc$ then stop. Else $cc = cc + 1$ and go to step 2.}
*End of DEFC – 1 algorithm.*

DEFC-2 is a dual algorithm to DEFC-1. Here, the cluster centers are the solution vectors and the membership matrix is updated using FCM. So, DEFC-2 will have a fewer number of decision variables. For the sake of brevity, the algorithm is not presented.

## 5   Results and Discussions

The algorithms DEFC-1, DEFC-2, TAFC-1, TAFC-2 and FCM were implemented in VC++ 6.0 on a Pentium IV machine with 2.39 Ghz and 256 MB RAM under Windows XP environment. Performance of the algorithms was compared on datasets: *Iris, Wine, Glass, E. Coli and Olive Oil.* The first four are from the UCI repository of machine learning [30], while *Olive Oil* data is from Forina and Armanino [31].

A concept of '*dominant clusters*' is used here to compare the performance of the algorithms. The number of *dominant clusters* is usually equal to the number of distinct classes present in a data set, if there are a few classes, say 3. However, in data sets such as *Olive oil, Glass, E. Coli,* there is a huge imbalance in that a large number of data samples belonged to only a few classes. So, in such cases, the number of dominant clusters is less than that of the distinct classes in the data. The concept of '*dominant clusters*' is invoked only in *Olive oil, Glass* and *E. Coli* datasets.

Parameters for DEFC-1 and DEFC-2 are scale factor *F*, crossover parameter *CR*, population size *Np* and degree of fuzziness *m*. The degree of fuzziness *m* was fixed at 3. Population size *Np* was taken in the range of $n*5$ to $n*10$. *F* was taken in the range 0.4 to 0.9. *CR* was taken in the range 0.4 to 0.9. Here, 20 experiments were conducted for both DEFC-1 and DEFC-2 for each data set and each algorithm by varying crucial parameters such as *F, CR* and *Np*. The results of FCM are presented in Table 1; the results of DEFC-1, TAFC-1, DEFC-2 and TAFC-2 are presented in Tables 2, 3,4 and 5 respectively. The algorithms are compared against: (i) *the number of clusters* (ii) *the optimal objective function value obtained* and (iii) *the number of function evaluations.*

As regards the number of clusters obtained, DEFC-1, DEFC-2, TAFC-1 and TAFC-2 outperformed FCM except for olive oil dataset in DEFC-2 where it gave 4 clusters. For all other datasets we obtained the number of clusters same as the '*dominant clusters*' in the datasets.

As regards the objective function value, TAFC-1 outperformed others in *Iris* and *Glass* datasets. However, in *Olive oil* dataset DEFC-2 yielded the least objective function value. FCM outperformed others in *Wine* and *E. Coli* datasets. Both DEFC-1 and DEFC-2 outperformed TAFC-2 in all datasets except *Wine*. Also, between DEFC-1 and DEFC-2, DEFC-2 outperformed DEFC-1 in all datasets.

Here we highlight the fact that DEFC-1 and DEFC-2 are driven purely by DE while the TAFC-1 and TAFC-2 use a hybrid approach wherein TA does the bulk of the job while the wisdom of FCM is also used occasionally. Given this fact, the performance of DEFC-1 and DEFC-2 is really commendable.

As regards the number of function evaluations, FCM outperformed others. Finally, we recommend the use of DEFC-1 and DEFC-2 to any data set where FCM can be used. We infer that the two algorithms are robust in obtaining the 'optimal' number of clusters and thus when stability and accuracy are the important criteria they can be used as an alternative to FCM. However, when number of function evaluations is the criterion, then FCM should be preferred.

**Table 1.** Results of FCM

| Data Set | Objective Function Value | #Clusters | #Function Evaluations | Xie-Beni Index value |
|---|---|---|---|---|
| Iris | 6.2327 | 2 | 62 | 0.0491 |
| Wine | 10.4796 | 3 | 333 | 0.4046 |
| E.coli | 7.7 | 3 | 245 | 0.1579 |
| Glass | 13.4493 | 2 | 94 | 0.1694 |
| Olive Oil | 43.9253 | 2 | 164 | 0.3033 |

**Table 2.** Results of DEFC-1

| Data Set | Objective Function Value | | | #Clusters | # Function Evaluations | | Xie-Beni Index value | |
| | Min | Max | Avg | | | | | |
|---|---|---|---|---|---|---|---|---|
| Iris | 8.217 | 9.01 | 8.66 | 3 | 84033 | 84020 | 7.288 | 4.749 |
| Wine | 14.61 | 19.35 | 16.122 | 3 | 236118 | 260130 | 9.022 | 3.997 |
| E.coli | 17.373 | 20.364 | 18.754 | 3 | 140770 | 132066 | 11.99 | 5.25 |
| Glass | 10.738 | 14.99 | 11.59 | 3 | 364182 | 348174 | 12.218 | 6.135 |
| Olive Oil | 35.928 | 45.043 | 39.919 | 3 | 156078 | 154222 | 15.79 | 9.484 |

**Table 3.** Results of TAFC-1

| Data Set | Objective Function Value | | | #Clusters | # Function Evaluations | | Xie-Beni Index value | |
| | Min | Max | Avg | | | | | |
|---|---|---|---|---|---|---|---|---|
| Iris | 2.3745 | 2.3886 | 2.3816 | 3 | 14266 | 7093 | 0.1015 | 0.1176 |
| Wine | 10.6056 | 10.6068 | 10.6062 | 3 | 4847 | 4995 | 9.9614 | 6.6879 |
| E.coli | 8.1692 | 33.1153 | 20.6423 | 3 | 4221 | 738 | 2.5322 | 0.6721 |
| Glass | 5.9155 | 6.0006 | 5.958 | 3 | 1951 | 1794 | 1.1772 | 1.5531 |
| Olive Oil | 32.805 | 34.806 | 33.805 | 3 | 10684 | 7749 | 32.805 | 22.524 |

**Table 4.** Results of DEFC-2

| Data Set | Objective Function Value | | | #Clusters | # Function Evaluations | | Xie-Beni Index value | |
| | Min | Max | Avg | | | | | |
|---|---|---|---|---|---|---|---|---|
| Iris | 6.5703 | 6.5710 | 6.5708 | 3 | 117513 | 175560 | 0.591 | 0.628 |
| Wine | 14.1455 | 14.579 | 14.214 | 3 | 93765 | 306102 | 56.14 | 0.834 |
| E.coli | 16.167 | 17.335 | 16.25 | 3 | 50666 | 180090 | 56.67 | 0.836 |
| Glass | 10.179 | 10.225 | 10.213 | 3 | 63420 | 240120 | 36.90 | 2.56 |
| Olive Oil | 19.124 | 20.46 | 19.45 | 4 | 227160 | 282141 | 6.51 | 0.714 |

**Table 5.** Results of TAFC-2

| Data Set | Objective Function Value | | | #Clusters | # Function Evaluations | | Xie-Beni Index value | |
| | Min | Max | Avg | | | | | |
|---|---|---|---|---|---|---|---|---|
| Iris | 9.9583 | 9.9583 | 9.9583 | 3 | 14625 | 12420 | 0.2988 | 0.2988 |
| Wine | 10.6061 | 10.6378 | 10.6224 | 3 | 6039 | 5653 | 4.389 | 12.604 |
| E.coli | 8.0352 | 36.9423 | 22.4887 | 3 | 15000 | 992 | 3.2064 | 0.7501 |
| Glass | 22.5367 | 22.7822 | 22.4611 | 3 | 876 | 17 | 1.107 | 1.1654 |
| Olive Oil | 20.1399 | 78.9517 | 49.5458 | 3 | 3780 | 2223 | 2.5971 | 4.7308 |

## 6   Conclusions

Here, we developed two novel DE based fuzzy clustering algorithms. Two variants viz. DEFC-1 and DEFC-2 are tested on a range of datasets. Results of DEFC-1 and DEFC-2 are compared against the original FCM as well as TAFC-1 and TAFC-2. Results show that both DEFC-1 and DEFC-2 are robust in obtaining the optimal number of clusters.. We infer that both DEFC-1 and DEFC-2 can be used as efficient and viable alternatives to the FCM when stability and accuracy are important criteria.

## References

1. Ravi, V., Bin, M., Ravi Kumar, P.: Threshold Accepting based fuzzy clustering algorithms. International Journal of Uncertainty, Fuzziness and Knowledge-based Systems 14(5), 617–632 (2006)
2. Bezdek, J.C.: Fuzzy Mathematics in Pattern Classification, Ph. D. thesis, Center for applied mathematics, Cornell University (1973)
3. Kuncheva, L.I., Bezdek, J.C.: Selection of cluster prototypes from data by a genetic algorithm. In: Proc. 5th European Congress on Intelligent Techniques and Soft Computing (EUFIT), Aachen, Germany, vol. 18, pp. 1683–1688 (1997)
4. Sun, L.-X., Danzer, K.: Fuzzy cluster analysis by simulate annealing. Journal of Chemometrics 10, 325–342 (1996)
5. Lukashin, V., Fuchs, R.: Analysis of temporal gene expression profiles: clustering by simulated annealing and determining the optimal number of clusters. Bioinformatics 17, 405–414 (2001)
6. Belacel, N., Hansen, P., Mladenovic, N.: Fuzzy J-Means: A new heuristic for fuzzy clustering. Pattern Recognition 35, 2193–2200 (2000)
7. Hall, L.O., Ozyurt, I.B., Bezdek, J.C.: Clustering with a genetically optimized approach. IEEE Transactions on Evolutionary Computation 3, 103–112 (1999)
8. Al-Sultan, K.S., Fedjki, C.A.: A tabu search-based algorithm for the fuzzy clustering problem. Pattern Recognition 30, 2023–2030 (1997)
9. Kao, Y., Lin, J.-C., Huang, S.-C.: Fuzzy Clustering by Differential Evolution. In: Eight International Conference on Intelligent System Designs and Applications (2008)
10. Maulik, U., Saha, I.: Automatic fuzzy clustering using modified Differential Evolution for Image Classification. IEEE transactions on Geoscience and Remote sensing 48(9) (September 2010)
11. Das, S., Konar, A.: Automatic Image Pixel Clustering with an Improved Differential Evolution. Applied Soft Computing, doi:10.1016/j.asoc.2007.12.008
12. Zhang, L., Ma, M., Liu, X., Sun, C., Liu, M., Zho, C.: Differential Evolution Fuzzy Clustering Algorithm based on Kernel methods. In: Wang, G.-Y., Peters, J.F., Skowron, A., Yao, Y. (eds.) RSKT 2006. LNCS (LNAI), vol. 4062, pp. 430–435. Springer, Heidelberg (2006)
13. Storn, R., Price, K.: Differential Evolution – A Simple and Efficient Heuristic for Global Optimization over Continuous Spaces. Journal of Global Optimization 11, 341–359 (1997)
14. Rogalsky, T., Kocabiyik, S., Derksen, R.: Differential evolution in aerodynamic optimization. Canadian Aeronautics and Space Journal 46(4), 183–190 (2000)
15. Stumberger, G., Dolinar, D., Pahner, U., Hameyer, K.: Optimization of radial active magnetic bearings using the finite element technique and differential evolution algorithm. IEEE Transactions on Magnetics 36(4), 1009–1013 (2000)

16. Doyle, S., Corcoran, D., Connell, J.: Automated mirror design using an evolution strategy. Optical Engineering 38(2), 323–333 (1999)
17. Wang, F.S., Sheu, J.W.: Multiobjective parameter estimation problems of fermentation processes using a high ethanol tolerance yeast. Chemical Engineering Science 55(18), 3685–3695 (2000)
18. Lampinen, J., Zelinka, I.: Mechanical Engineering Design Optimization by Differential Evolution. In: New Ideas in Optimization, pp. 127–146. McGraw-Hill, New York (1999)
19. Masters, T., Land, W.: A new training algorithm for the general regression neural network. In: IEEE International Conference on Systems, Man and Cybernetics, Computational Cybernetics and Simulation, vol. 3, pp. 1990–1994 (1997)
20. Zelinka, I., Lampinen, J.: An evolutionary learning algorithms for neural networks. In: 5th International Conference on Soft Computing MENDEL 1999, pp. 410–414 (1999)
21. Fischer, M.M., Hlavackova-Schindler, K., Reismann, M.: A global search procedure for parameter estimation in neural spatial interaction modelling. Regional Science 78(2), 119–134 (1999)
22. Gang, L., Yiqing, T., Fu, T.: A fast evolutionary algorithm for neural network training using differential evolution. In: ICYCS 1999 Fifth International Conference for Young Computer Scientists, vol. 1, pp. 507–511 (1999)
23. Schmitz, G.P., Aldrich, C.: Combinatorial Evolution of Regression Nodes in Feedforward Neural Networks. Neural Networks 12(1), 175–189 (1999)
24. Ilonen, J., Kamarainen, J.-K., Lampinen, J.: Differential Evolution Training Algorithm for Feedforward Neural Networks. Neural Processing Letters 17, 93–105 (2003)
25. Bhat, T.R., Venkataramani, D., Ravi, V., Murty, C.V.S.: Improved differential evolution method for efficient parameter estimation in biofilter modeling. Biochemical Engineering Journal 28, 167–176 (2006)
26. Brest, J., Greiner, S., Boskovic, B., Mernik, M., Zumer, V.: Self-Adapting Control Prameters in Differential Evolution: A Comparative Study on numerical benchmark problems. IEEE transactions on Evolutionary Computation 10(6), 646–657 (2006)
27. Zhang, J., Sanderson Arthur, C.: JADE: Adaptive Differential Evolution with Optional External Archive. IEEE transactions on Evolutionary Computation 13(5), 945–958 (2009)
28. Qin, A.K., Huang, V.L., Suganthan, P.N.: Differential Evolution Algorithm with strategy adaptation for Global Numerical Optimization. IEEE transactions on Evolutionary Computation 13(2) (April 2009)
29. Xie, X.L., Beni, G.: A Validity Measure for Fuzzy Clustering. IEEE Transactions on Pattern Analysis and Machine Intelligence 13(8), 841–847
30. Blake, C.L., Merz, C.J.: UCI repository of machine learning databases. University of California, Department of Information and Computer Science, Irvine (1998), http://www.ics.uci.edu/mlearn/MLRepository.html
31. Forina, M., Armanino, C.: Eigenvector projection and simplified nonlinear mapping of fatty acid content of Italian olive oils. Annali di Chimica 72, 127–141 (1982), ftp://ftp.clarkson.edu/pub/hopkepk/Chemdata/Original/oliveoil.dat

# A Population Adaptive Differential Evolution Strategy to Light Configuration Optimization of Photometric Stereo

B. Sathyabama, V. Divya, S. Raju, and V. Abhaikumar

Department of Electronics and communication Engineering,
Thiagarajar College of Engineering, Madurai
sbece@tce.edu, divya@tce.edu

**Abstract.** Differential Evolution is an optimization technique that has been successfully employed in various applications. In this paper we propose a novel Population Adaptive Differential Evolution strategy to the problem of generating an optimal light configuration for photometric stereo. For 'n' lights, any $2\pi/n$ of orthogonal light directions minimizes the uncertainty in scaled normal computation. The assumption is that the camera noise is additive and normally distributed. Uncertainty is defined as the expectation of squared distance of scaled normal to the ground truth. This metric is optimized with respect to the illumination angles at constant slant angle. Superiority of the new method is demonstrated by comparing it with sensitivity analysis and classical DE.

**Keywords:** Population Adaptive Differential Evolution (PADE), Photometric Stereo, Scaled Surface Normal.

## 1 Introduction

Photometric stereo is a method which computes local surface orientations and reflectance at each pixel using images captured under different illumination conditions with a fixed camera. It uses three or more images captured from a single viewpoint of a surface illuminated from different directions to obtain descriptions of reflectance and relief. In recent times photometric stereo is applied to different tasks, largely as a consequence of the inherent simplicity of the reflectance model used and the relative ease of practical implementation [1]. When applying the method, the surface of the object under observation is generally assumed to obey the Lambertian diffuse reflection model. In real time a dense array of surface orientations is determined using several images, acquired from a fixed viewpoint but under different illumination conditions. During the recovery of the surface under static conditions, it is not necessary to identify corresponding points among the different images and no constraint requirement on the continuity of the surface is necessary. The recovered surface normal can be used to generate a 3D surface relief or to render new images under different virtual lighting conditions. The method is object-centered rather than image-centered, as classification of the surface characteristics is based on the recovered reflectance and orientation. As it is related to the object's physical features,

B.K. Panigrahi et al. (Eds.): SEMCCO 2010, LNCS 6466, pp. 46–53, 2010.
© Springer-Verlag Berlin Heidelberg 2010

which are independent from the effects of illumination and viewing configuration, the method is more effective than other methods. Although photometric stereo is a reasonable and effective technique to implement, especially when the illumination is easily controlled, it is however subjected to a number of systemic errors. These concern all of the factors associated with an image formation procedure and follow as a consequence of the idealized assumptions of the reflectance model and lighting conditions. The effect of variation in lighting conditions has a significant bearing on the accuracy of photometric stereo. Thus, there is a need for estimating the optimal placement of photometric stereo lighting. This paper presents a simple and efficient Evolutionary algorithm to optimize the location of the light sources to analyze the uncertainty of the recovered scaled surface normal with respect to irradiance variance which directly affects the stability of the photometric stereo. A population Adaptive Differential Evolution algorithm is proposed to optimize uncertainty expression with less computation. Hence, the work is of significance for the development of practical applications of photometric stereo.

Differential evolution (DE) [2] is a population-based search strategy very similar to standard evolutionary algorithms. DE is defined for floating-point representations of individuals. The main difference is in the reproduction step where an offspring is created from three parents using an differential mutation and uniform discrete crossover .Population based algorithms have been successfully applied to a wide range of optimization problems, for example, image processing, pattern recognition , scheduling, engineering design amongst others [3,4].In connection with this DE is utilized in various imaging applications including clustering[5,6], denoising, Classification and thresholding. A review of the current literature reveals that DE  has not been employed for light configuration optimization problem to date.In the present work, we determine the optimal placement of lights for efficient photometric stereo by using an improved version of DE. DE is easy to implement and requires a negligible amount of parameter tuning to achieve considerably good search results. In DE, the user has to find the best values for the problem dependent control parameters. Finding the best values for the control parameters is a time consuming task. Several version of DE were proposed wherein the control parameters were modified according to the application. This paper provides a modification to the conventional DE algorithm from its classical form to improve its convergence properties at the same time to reduce the complexity of the conventional approaches to light configuration optimization.

The objective of this paper is dual. First, it aims at the automatic determination of the optimal healthy individuals.  This paper proposes a novel selection scheme for the search variables to determine the optimal individuals for next generation. Second, it attempts to show that differential evolution with a modification of the reduced population representation scheme, can give very promising results if applied to the automatic light configuration optimization problem by minimizing the camera noise which gives fast convergence with less computation. The proposed approach identifies optimal configurations both for the case of three light sources, and for the more complex case involving 'n' lights.

## 2  Scientific Background

### 2.1  Photometric Stereo

Photometric stereo gives us the ability to estimate local surface orientation by using several images of the same surface taken from the same viewpoint but under illumination from different directions. The light sources are ideally point sources some distance away in different directions, so that in each case there is a well-defined light source direction from which we measure surface orientation. Therefore, the change of the intensities in the images depends on both local surface orientation and illumination direction.

Assuming a Lambertian surface illuminated by a single distant light source, the observed image intensity $i$ at each pixel can be written as the product of the composite albedo (a combination of light source intensity  and intrinsic reflectance of surface material ) and the cosine value of the incidence angle between the incidence light direction, expressed as a unit column vector $i$, and the surface normal, expressed as a unit column vector N. Lambertian surface model is first transformed into matrix format. Therefore the intensity of pixel in the first image can be expressed as given below

$$i_1(x,y) = \rho \, k \cos\theta_i \qquad (1)$$

where $\rho$ is the albedo representing the amount of light reflected back from the surface, $k$ is the light source intensity, and $\theta_i$ is the angle of incidence. This can be further rewritten as

$$i_1(x,y) = \rho \, k(l.N) \qquad (2)$$

Further $l$ and N are the unit light and normal vectors, respectively, and vectors n= $\rho N$ and L =$kl$ are the scaled normal and the scaled light, respectively. Scaled normals and scaled lights are the basic entities of Lambertian photometric stereo. It is obvious that having the intensities $i_1$, $i_2$ and $i_3$ observed for three scaled light sources $L^1$, $L^2$ and $L^3$, there holds

$$i = [i_1, i_2, i_3] = L.n = [L^1, L^2, L^3].n \qquad (3)$$

Where the vector i = [$i_1$, $i_2$, $i_3$] stacks the intensity measurements and the matrix L, called the light matrix, stacks the scaled light vectors, Therefore, provided that L is invertible, it is possible to compute the scaled normal 'n' as

$$n = L^{-1}i \qquad (4)$$

In principle, there are several sources of errors which affect the accuracy with which the scaled surface normal is determined.

### 2.2  Light Configuration Parameters

Fig .1 describes the Slant and tilt of a light source l: The experiments are confined to the variation of illuminant direction where the viewer's position being fixed vertically

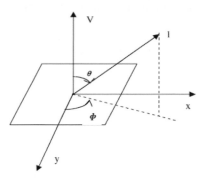

**Fig. 1.** Illustration of Slant and Tilt angle of a Light Source

above the physical object which lies upon a horizontal plane (as depicted in fig.1). The direction of a light is parameterized by slant and tilt. Slant $\theta$ is the angle between the light source and the vector v pointing towards the camera. As the angle the illuminant vector makes with the vertical is increased, the whole magnitude spectrum is uniformly amplified by a factor equal to the sine of that angle.Tilt $\phi$ is the angle which the projection of light source onto the camera plane (x–y) makes with axis x. The viewing vector v is assumed to be vertical for notational convenience. Thus it implies that an image forming process using directed illumination acts as a directional filter of texture. Such an effect is likely to have important implications for texture classification schemes. The directional properties of image texture are not intrinsic to the surface, but they are considerably affected by variation in illuminant tilt.Assuming that the light sources are of equal intensities optimal configuration is obtained. To fix the intensity, set $k=1$ for all light sources. To stress this assumption, use $L$ to denote the light matrix. Having n lights, the light matrix $L$ is thus formed by columns $L^k$ of unit $L^2$ norm.

### 2.3 Scaled Surface Normal

The deviations [7] due to variation in light source direction result in errors $\Delta n$ occurring in the scaled normal estimates ( $\Delta n = n - n'$ where $n'$ is the ground truth of the scaled normal). The camera sensor is noisy, with the additive and normally distributed noise. Therefore, if the camera sensor output intensity is $i$, it is the result of $i = i' + \Delta i$ with $i'$ being the true (noiseless) value and $\Delta i$ being from N(0, $\sigma^2$) where $N(\mu, \sigma^2)$ denotes the normal distribution with the mean $\mu$ and variance $\sigma^2$.The uncertainty $E(L)$ in scaled normal computation for a given light matrix L is defined as

$$E(L) = E[\Delta n^T \Delta n],  \tag{5}$$

where E [·] is expectation.

For three light sources and with the assumptions formulated above, equation (4) is linear and it follows that $\Delta n = L^{-1} \Delta i$ and for the uncertainty there holds:

$$E(L) = E\left[\Delta i^T L^{-1} L^{-T} \Delta i\right]  \tag{6}$$

as $E\,[(\Delta\,i_k)^2] = \sigma^2$ and as the noise in individual components of i is independent, this can be further rewritten to give:

$$E(L) = \sigma^2 trace\left[L^{-1}L^{-T}\right] = \sigma^2 trace\left[(L^T L)^{-1}\right] \qquad (7)$$

Thus, now the task is to minimize the above, subject to constraints given below:

$$L^* = \min \sigma^2 trace\left[(L^T L)^{-1}\right]$$
$$L \in GL(3) \qquad (8)$$
$$subject\ to\ L^T L = \begin{bmatrix} 1 & . & . \\ . & 1 & . \\ . & . & 1 \end{bmatrix} or\ trace\left[L^T L\right] = 3$$

where GL (3) is the group of 3x3 invertible matrices.

In this formulation, Equation (8) reveals the structure of the problem.

## 3  Proposed Population Adaptive Differential Evolution

In population adaptive DE instead of randomly selecting the individuals the best individuals among the given population are selected. The methodology is given below:

*Step1:* Initialize the population size Np, dimension size d, and range $[x_j^{(l)}, x_j^{(u)}]$. Randomly select the individuals for the given population size.

$$X_{j,i} = rand_{j,i}[0,1](x_j^{(u)} - x_j^{(l)}) . \qquad (9)$$

*Step 2:*   Perform mutation for each individual with its donors and form the new individual for the next generation after performing crossover and selection.

$$v_{i,G} = x_{r1,G} + F.(x_{r2,G} - x_{r3,G}) \qquad (10)$$

*Step 3:* After mutation, a "binomial" crossover operation forms the final trial vector; according to the $i^{th}$ population vector and its corresponding mutant vector

$$u_{i,j,G} = \begin{cases} v_{i,j,G}\ if\ rand(0,1) \le C_R\ or\ j = j_{rand} \\ x_{i,j,G}\ otherwise \end{cases} \quad i = 1,2,..N_p \quad and\ j = 1,2,..D \qquad (11)$$

*Step 4:* The selection operation selects according to the fitness value of the population vector and its corresponding trial vector, which vector will survive to be a member of the next generation.

$$X_{i,G+1} = \begin{cases} v_{i,G} & if\ f(u_{i,G}) < f(x_{i,G}) \\ x_{i,j,G} & otherwise \end{cases} \qquad (12)$$

*Step 5:* From the newly formed individual find the worst individuals among the current population. Assuming minimization

$$X_{worst,G+1} = X_{i,G+1} \quad if\ f(X_{i,G+1}) = f_{max} \qquad (13)$$

*Step 6:* Remove the worst individual and find the current population size.

*Step 7:* Repeat steps 2 to 6 until population size is reduced to 4.

*Step 8:* For the 4 individuals obtained in the previous step as individuals apply differential evolution outlined in steps 2-4 to find the optimized results.

### 3.1 Fitness Function

The fitness function used in this paper is $L^*$. The minimized value of $L^*$ shows that the light configuration is optimized

$$L^* = \min\ \sigma^2 trace\ \left[\left(L^T L^{-1}\right)\right] \tag{15}$$

where L is the light matrix.

### 3.2 Prime Individual Selection

In our proposed approach, at the initial stage we will randomly select the donors for each individual from the population. There is a possibility that the donor for an individual may be the donor itself .So we make sure that the population size is always greater than 3 or 4, when it is equal to 3or 4 (according to the problem) we will stop and take those  4 as individuals for next DE process . Since DE is a process in which the optimization is obtained using distinct individuals we need a minimum of three distinct individuals for each parent as basic criteria. In the proposed approach we will eliminate the weak individuals from our current population at end of each iteration. So the best formed individual is taken for further improvement. Thus at the end we get the most best individual out of  the  whole initial population.

## 4   Experimental Results

In this section, we compare performance of the Proposed PADE algorithm with Classical DE and a theoretical derivation for the optimal light configuration in conventional photometric stereo systems proposed by Drbohlav and Chantler [7]. Previously we applied the traditional DE algorithm for optimal placement of light configuration. To investigate the effects of the changes made in the classical DE algorithm, we have compared the PADE with an ordinary DE-based Optimization method, which uses the same representation scheme and fitness function as the PADE. For the PADE and classical DE algorithm, we randomly initialize the individuals as tilt angles and slant angle. Tilt angle is initialized in the range [0,360] and the slant angle is in the range [40,60].The angle difference is observed to be $120^0$ which is the expected difference between the tilt angles [7]. From the table1 it is observed that the slant angle is optimized to $54.74^0$ for various size of population and this optimization satisfies the theoretical result obtained from  Drbohlav and Chantler [7]. But the number of comparisons required to obtain that result is more in classical DE when compared to the proposed PADE. For $N$ population to be iterated over G generations the number of comparisons made is $N*G$ in classical DE whereas in the proposed method the N population is first reduced to 4 till that the number of

**Table 1.** Mean and Standard deviation of Slant angle optimization over 25 runs for classical DE and PADE (Mean± (standard deviation))

| Population size | DE | PADE |
|---|---|---|
| 100 | 54.7357± ( 0.000308) | 54.7345± (0.0838) |
| 200 | 54.7356± (0.0012) | 54.7394± ( 0.0118) |
| 300 | 54.7357± (1.7493e-004) | 54.7359± (0.0049) |
| 400 | 54.7370± (0.0043) | 54.7360± (0.0016) |

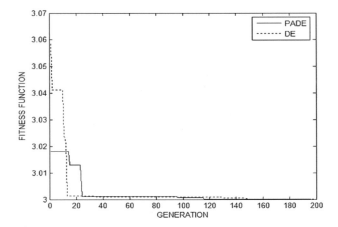

**Fig. 2.** Error function optimization for proposed method and DE with population size of 100

comparisons is $(N^2 +N-20)/2$ from that step Classical DE is adopted for which the number of comparisons made will be $4(G-N+4)$ so at the last the total no of comparisons made will be $(N^2 -7N+8G+12)/2$ .For example if we take $N=30$ and $G=50$ the number of comparisons made by classical DE will be 1500 and the proposed method involves only 551 comparisons .So the time complexity of the proposed method is about 3 times lesser than classical DE .From the table 1 it is seen that both PADE and DE converge to the same optimized value when iterated over equal number of generations with same population size and Fig.2 gives the convergence of the error function ,these results show that the proposed PADE doesn't converge to a premature value it searches only for the global optima in the given search space. The mutation factor and crossover probability for both classical DE and PADE is chosen to be 0.8and 0.5 respectively.

## 5   Conclusion

This paper has presented a new PADE-based strategy for light configuration optimization of photometric stereo. An important feature of the proposed technique is that it is able to automatically reduce the population size by finding the healthy individual and by discarding the weak individuals. In classical DE the population size remains constant consequently the number of computations for all generation is equal. In Population Adaptive DE the population size gets reduced as the generation increases. So the number of computations gets reduced as generation increases. Also in classical DE the individual with worst chromosomes remains in the population. This may affect some other individual's improvement in next generation. Conversely in PADE the worst individuals in a generation are neglected for next generation. So there is always enhancement of chromosomes as the generation increases. This improves efficiency and reduces computation time of PADE. The proposed PADE algorithm is able to outperform two other optimization algorithms in a statistically meaningful way discussed here.

# References

1. Woodham, R.J.: Photometric stereo: a reflectance map technique for determining surface orientation from image intensity. In: Proc. SPIE. Image Understanding System and Industrial Applications, vol. 155, pp. 136–143 (1978)
2. Storn, R., Price, K.: Differential evolution – a simple and efficient adaptive scheme for global optimization over continuous spaces, Technical Report TR-95-012, ICSI (1995)
3. Engelbrecht, A.: Fundamentals of Computational Swarm Intelligence. Wiley & Sons, Chichester (2005)
4. Price, K., Storn, R., Lampinen, J.: Differential Evolution: A Practical Approach to Global Optimization. Springer, Heidelberg (2005)
5. Das, S., Abraham, A., Konar, A.: Automatic Clustering Using an Improved Differential Evolution Algorithm. IEEE Transactions On Systems, Man, And Cybernetics—Part A: Systems And Humans 38(1) (January 2008)
6. Das, S., Konar, A.: Automatic image pixel clustering with an improved differential evolution. Applied Soft Computing Journal 9(1), 226–236 (2009)
7. Drbohlav, O., Chantler, M.: On optimal light configurations in photometric stereo. In: Proceedings of the 10th IEEE International Conference on Computer Vision, vol. II, pp. 1707–1712 (2005)

# Solving Multi Objective Stochastic Programming Problems Using Differential Evolution

Radha Thangaraj[1], Millie Pant[2], Pascal Bouvry[1], and Ajith Abraham[3]

[1] Faculty of Science, Technology and Communications, University of Luxembourg
[2] Department of Paper Technology, Indian Institute of Technology Roorkee, India
[3] Machine Intelligent Research Labs (MIR Labs), Scientific Network for Innovation
and Research Excellence, USA
t.radha@ieee.org, millifpt@iitr.ernet.in, pascal.bouvry@uni.lu,
ajith.abraham@ieee.org

**Abstract.** Stochastic (or probabilistic) programming is an optimization technique in which the constraints and/or the objective function of an optimization problem contains random variables. The mathematical models of these problems may follow any particular probability distribution for model coefficients. The objective here is to determine the proper values for model parameters influenced by random events. In this study, Differential Evolution (DE) and its two recent variants LDE1 and LDE2 are presented for solving multi objective linear stochastic programming (MOSLP) problems, having several conflicting objectives. The numerical results obtained by DE and its variants are compared with the available results from where it is observed that the DE and its variants significantly improve the quality of solution of the given considered problem in comparison with the quoted results in the literature.

**Keywords:** Differential Evolution, stochastic programming, multiobjective optimization.

## 1 Introduction

Stochastic programming (SP) is a mathematical programming where stochastic element is present in the data. In contrast to deterministic mathematical programming where the data (coefficients) are known numbers in stochastic programming these numbers follow a probability distribution. Thus we can say that SP is a framework for modeling optimization problems that involve uncertainty. The goal here is to find some policy that is feasible for all (or almost all) the possible data instances and maximizes the expectation of some function of the decisions and the random variables. More generally, such models are formulated, solved analytically or numerically, and analyzed in order to provide useful information to a decision-maker.

In the recent past, SP has been applied to the problems having multiple, conflicting and non-commensurable objectives where generally there does not exist a single solution which can optimize all the objectives. Several methods for solving Multi-Objective Stochastic Linear Programming (MOSLP) problems and their applications to various fields are available in literature [1] – [7]. Most of the probabilistic models

B.K. Panigrahi et al. (Eds.): SEMCCO 2010, LNCS 6466, pp. 54–61, 2010.

assume normal distribution for model coefficients. Sahoo and Biswal [8] presented some deterministic equivalents for the probabilistic problem involving normal and log-normal random variables for joint constraints. Charles et al. [9] addressed different forms of distributions like Power Function distribution, Pareto distribution, Beta distribution of first kind, Weibull distribution and Burr type XII distribution. In the present study we have followed the models proposed by Charles et al. [9] and have solved them using Differential Evolution algorithm.

The rest of the paper is organized as follows: Section 2 briefly describes the classical DE, LDE1 and LDE2 algorithms. The problem definition is given in section 3. In section 4; the experimental settings and numerical results are discussed. Finally the paper concludes with section 5.

## 2  Differential Evolution Algorithms

### 2.1  Classical Differential Evolution (DE)

Differential Evolution [10] is a population based metaheuristics that has been consistently ranked as one of the best search algorithm for solving benchmark as well as real life problems in several case studies.

A general DE variant may be denoted as *DE/X/Y/Z*, where *X* denotes the vector to be mutated, *Y* specifies the number of difference vectors used and *Z* specifies the crossover scheme which may be binomial (bin) or exponential (exp). Throughout the study we shall consider the mutation strategy *DE/rand/1/bin* [10] which is perhaps the most frequently used version of DE.

For a D-dimensional search space, each target vector $x_{i,g}$, a mutant vector is generated by

$$v_{i,g+1} = x_{r_1,g} + F*(x_{r_2,g} - x_{r_3,g})$$ (1)

where $r_1, r_2, r_3 \in \{1,2,....,NP\}$ are randomly chosen integers, must be different from each other and also different from the running index *i*. *F* (>0) is a scaling factor which controls the amplification of the differential evolution $(x_{r_2,g} - x_{r_3,g})$. In order to increase the diversity of the perturbed parameter vectors, crossover is introduced. The parent vector is mixed with the mutated vector to produce a trial vector $u_{ji,g+1}$,

$$u_{j,i,g+1} = \begin{cases} v_{j,i,g+1} & \text{if} \quad rand_j \leq C_r \vee j = k \\ x_{j,i,g+1} & \text{otherwise} \end{cases}$$ (2)

where j = 1, 2,......, D; $rand_j \in [0,1]$; CR is the crossover constant takes values in the range [0, 1] and $j_{rand} \in (1,2,.....,D)$ is the randomly chosen index.

The final phase of DE algorithm is selection. Here the population for the next generation is selected from the individual in current population and its corresponding trial vector according to the following rule:

$$x_{i,g+1} = \begin{cases} u_{i,g+1} & if \quad f(u_{i,g+1}) \le f(x_{i,g}) \\ x_{i,g} & otherwise \end{cases} \tag{3}$$

Thus, each individual of the advance (trial) population is compared with its counterpart in the current population. The one with the lower objective function value will survive from the tournament selection to the population of the next generation. As a result, all the individuals of the next generation are as good as or better than their counterparts in the current generation.

## 2.2 Laplace Differential Evolution (LDE)

The LDE algorithms are proposed by Thangaraj et al. [11]. These algorithms differ from the classical DE in the mutation phase in a twofold manner. These schemes make use the absolute weighted difference between the two vector points in place of the usual vector difference as in classical DE and secondly, in LDE schemes amplification factor, F (of the usual DE), is replaced by L, a random variable following Laplace distribution.

The mutation schemes of LDE1 and LDE2 algorithms are defined as follows:

### 2.2.1 LDE1 Scheme

$$v_{i,g+1} = x_{best,g} + L * | x_{r_1,g} - x_{r_2,g} | \tag{4}$$

In LDE1 scheme, the base vector is the one having the best fitness function value; whereas the other two individuals are randomly selected.

### 2.2.2 LDE2 Scheme

$$If\ (U(0,1) < 0.5)\ then\ v_{i,g+1} = x_{best,g} + L * | x_{r_1,g} - x_{r_2,g} |$$

$$Else\ \ v_{i,g+1} = x_{r_1,g} + F * (x_{r_2,g} - x_{r_3,g})$$

In LDE2 scheme, mutant vector using equation (4) and the basic mutant vector equation are applied probabilistically using a predefined value. A random variable following normal distribution U(0,1) is generated. If it is less than 0.5 then LDE1 scheme is applied otherwise Eqn. (1) is applied.

Both the modified versions, LDE1 and LDE2 have reportedly given good performances for solving benchmark as well as real life problems [11].

## 3 Problem Definition

Mathematical model of a constrained MOSLP may be given as [9]:

$$Maximize\ z_k = \sum_{j=1}^{n} c_j^k x_j\ ,\ k = 1,2,...,K$$

$$Subject\ to\ P\left(\sum_{j=1}^{n} a_{1j}x_j \le b_1, \sum_{j=1}^{n} a_{2j}x_j \le b_2,..., \sum_{j=1}^{n} a_{mj}x_j \le b_m\right) \ge p\ ,\ x_j \ge 0, j = 1,2,...,n$$

Where $0 < p < 1$ is usually close to 1. It has been assumed that the parameters $a_{ij}$ and $c_j$ are deterministic constants and $b_i$ are random variables. For more details the interested reader may please refer to [9]. In the present study, we have considered the two test problems which are used in [9]. These problems are multi-objective stochastic linear programming problems involving random variables following different distributions.

**Test problem 1: MOSLP1:**

*Maximize* $z_1 = 5x_1 + 6x_2 + 3x_3$, *Maximize* $z_2 = 6x_1 + 3x_2 + 5x_3$,

*Maximize* $z_3 = 2x_1 + 5x_2 + 8x_3$

Subject to

$P(3x_1 + 2x_2 + 2x_3 \leq b_1) \geq 0.90$, $P(2x_1 + 8x_2 + 5x_3 \leq b_2) \geq 0.98$

$P(5x_1 + 3x_2 + 2x_3 \leq b_3) \geq 0.95$, $P(0.5x_1 + 0.5x_2 + 0.25x_3 \leq b_4) \geq 0.90$

$P(8x_1 + 3x_2 + 4x_3 \leq b_5) \geq 0.99$, $x_1, x_2, x_3 \geq 0$

Here, $b_1$ follow Power Function distribution, $b_2$ follow Pareto distribution, $b_3$ follow Beta distribution, $b_4$ follow Weibull distribution; $b_5$ follow Burr type XII distribution. The problem is converted to deterministic model as follows:

*Maximize* $z = \lambda_1(5x_1 + 6x_2 + 3x_3) + \lambda_2(6x_1 + 3x_2 + 5x_3) + \lambda_3(2x_1 + 5x_2 + 8x_3)$

Subject to

$3x_1 + 2x_2 + 2x_3 \leq 6.3096$, $2x_1 + 8x_2 + 5x_3 \leq 8.0812$, $5x_1 + 3x_2 + 2x_3 \leq 4.7115$,

$0.5x_1 + 0.5x_2 + 0.25x_3 \leq 0.9379$, $8x_1 + 3x_2 + 4x_3 \leq 10.0321$, $\lambda_1 + \lambda_2 + \lambda_3 = 1$

$x_1, x_2, x_3, \lambda_1, \lambda_2, \lambda_3 \geq 0$

**Test problem 2: MOSLP2:**

*Maximize* $z_1 = 3x_1 + 8x_2 + 5x_3$, *Maximize* $z_2 = 7x_1 + 4x_2 + 3x_3$

*Maximize* $z_3 = 6x_1 + 7x_2 + 10.5x_3$

Subject to

$P(5x_1 + 4x_2 + 2x_3 \leq b_1) \geq 0.95$, $P(7x_1 + 3x_2 + x_3 \leq b_2) \geq 0.95$

$P(2x_1 + 7x_2 + 3x_3 \leq b_3) \geq 0.95$, $P(2x_1 + 3x_2 + 2.5x_3 \leq b_4) \geq 0.95$

$P(5x_1 + 2x_2 + 1.5x_3 \leq b_5) \geq 0.95$, $x_1, x_2, x_3 \geq 0$

Here $b_1$ follow Power Function distribution; $b_2$ follow Pareto distribution; $b_3$ follow Beta distribution of first kind; $b_4$ follow Weibull distribution and $b_5$ follow Burr type XII distribution. The deterministic model of the problem is given as:

*Maximize* $z = \lambda_1(3x_1 + 8x_2 + 5x_3) + \lambda_2(7x_1 + 4x_2 + 3x_3) + \lambda_3(6x_1 + 7x_2 + 10.5x_3)$

Subject to

$$\left[\frac{y_1^2}{9}\right]\left[\frac{y_2^2 - 100}{y_2^2}\right]\left[\frac{y_3 - 5}{10}\right]\left[\frac{e^{2y_4} - 1}{e^{2y_4}}\right]\left[\frac{3y_5^2}{1 + 3y_5^2}\right] \geq 0.95$$

$5x_1 + 4x_2 + 2x_3 = y_1$, $7x_1 + 3x_2 + x_3 = y_2$, $2x_1 + 7x_2 + 3x_3 = y_3$,

$2x_1 + 3x_2 + 2.5x_3 = y_4$, $5x_1 + 2x_2 + 1.5x_3 = y_5$, $\lambda_1 + \lambda_2 + \lambda_3 = 1$

$x_1, x_2, x_3, y_1, y_2, y_3, y_4, y_5, \lambda_1, \lambda_2, \lambda_3 \geq 0$.

## 4   Experimental Settings and Numerical Results

### 4.1   Parameter Settings

DE has three main control parameters; population size, crossover rate Cr and Scaling factor F which are fixed as 50, 0. 5 and 0.5 respectively. For LDE schemes the scaling factor is a random variable, L, following Laplace distribution. For each algorithm, the stopping criterion is to terminate the search process when the maximum number of generations is reached (assumed 1000 generations). Constraints are handled according to the approach based on repair methods suggested in [12]. A total of 50 runs for each experimental setting were conducted and the best solution throughout the run was recorded as global optimum. Results obtained by basic DE and LDE versions are also compared with previously quoted results [9].

### 4.2   Numerical Results

We have considered four test cases in each of the test problems. Since, $\lambda_1 + \lambda_2 + \lambda_3 = 1$, one of $\lambda_i$, $i$ = 1, 2, 3 could be eliminated to reduce the number of dependent variables from the expression of objective function. So, we assigned equal weights to two terms at a time in the objective expression. The resultant test cases are as follows:

(i) $\lambda_1 = W, \lambda_2 = \lambda_3 = \dfrac{1-W}{2}, 0 \leq W \leq 1$   (ii) $\lambda_2 = W, \lambda_1 = \lambda_3 = \dfrac{1-W}{2}, 0 \leq W \leq 1$

(iii) $\lambda_3 = W, \lambda_1 = \lambda_2 = \dfrac{1-W}{2}, 0 \leq W \leq 1$   (iv) $\lambda_1$, $\lambda_2$, and $\lambda_3$ are dependent variables.

The numerical results of the given two test problems MOSLP1 and MOSLP2 are recorded in Tables 1 and 2 respectively. The best solution obtained by DE and LDE algorithms for MOSLP1 in terms of optimal decision variable values and objective function value are given in Table 1. For the test case (i), the performance of LDE1 is better than all the other algorithms. For the remaining 3 test cases, LDE2 performs better than other compared algorithms. If we compare the LDE algorithms with classical DE algorithm then from the numerical results we can see that LDE algorithms are superior with classical DE algorithm. There is an improvement of 52% in objective function value when the problem is solved by LDE2 in comparison with the quoted result [9], where the problem is solved by Genetic Algorithm. The results of test problem MOSLP2 are given in Table 2. From this table also we can see that LDE2 algorithm is superior with others in all the test cases. The improvement of LDE2 algorithm in comparison with the results in the literature is 141%. Figure 1 shows the performance of DE and LDE algorithms in terms of objective function value.

**Table 1.** Results of MOSLP1

| | DE | LDE1 | LDE2 | GA [9] |
|---|---|---|---|---|
| $\lambda_1 = W, \lambda_1 = \lambda_2 = (1\text{-}W)/2, 0 \leq W \leq 1$ | | | | |
| z | 10.9905 | **10.997** | 10.996 | |
| $x_1$ | 0.349128 | 0.351905 | 0.35171 | --NA-- |
| $x_2$ | 0 | 0 | 0 | |
| $x_3$ | 1.47618 | 1.47538 | 1.47539 | |
| $\lambda_2 = W, \lambda_1 = \lambda_3 = (1\text{-}W)/2, 0 \leq W \leq 1$ | | | | |
| z | 9.48974 | **9.48975** | **9.48975** | |
| $x_1$ | 0.35214 | 0.35215 | 0.352142 | --NA-- |
| $x_2$ | 0 | 0 | 0 | |
| $x_3$ | 1.47538 | 1.47537 | 1.47538 | |
| $\lambda_3 = W, \lambda_1 = \lambda_2 = (1\text{-}W)/2, 0 \leq W \leq 1$ | | | | |
| z | 12.9277 | 12.9288 | **12.9292** | |
| $x_1$ | 0 | 0 | 0 | --NA-- |
| $x_2$ | 0 | 0 | 0 | |
| $x_3$ | 1.61611 | 1.61612 | 1.61617 | |
| **Problem described as in [9]** | | | | |
| z | 9.48978 | 11.3988 | **12.9299** | 8.5089 |
| $x_1$ | 0.352147 | 0.334378 | 0 | 0.3727 |
| $x_2$ | 2.12479e-007 | 0.00514505 | 0 | 0.2319 |
| $x_3$ | 1.47538 | 1.47426 | 1.61624 | 1.0761 |

**Table 2.** Results of MOSLP2

| | DE | LDE1 | LDE2 | GA [9] |
|---|---|---|---|---|
| $\lambda_1 = W, \lambda_1 = \lambda_2 = (1\text{-}W)/2, 0 \leq W \leq 1$ | | | | |
| z | 5.5452 | 6.3844 | **6.86328** | |
| $x_1$ | 0.170342 | 0.275175 | 0.297729 | |
| $x_2$ | 0.0367932 | 0.0654974 | 0.00485206 | |
| $x_3$ | 0.759151 | 0.627495 | 0.726168 | |
| $y_1$ | 2.5158 | 2.89285 | 2.96039 | --NA-- |
| $y_2$ | 2.06291 | 2.7502 | 2.82483 | |
| $y_3$ | 2.862 | 2.89131 | 2.80793 | |
| $y_4$ | 2.36484 | 2.31558 | 2.42544 | |
| $y_5$ | 2.06754 | 2.44811 | 2.5876 | |
| $\lambda_2 = W, \lambda_1 = \lambda_3 = (1\text{-}W)/2, 0 \leq W \leq 1$ | | | | |
| z | 5.3215 | 7.01255 | **7.72732** | |
| $x_1$ | 0.170342 | 0.12258 | 0 | |
| $x_2$ | 0.0367932 | 0.0575791 | 0.00166162 | |
| $x_3$ | 0.759151 | 0.777962 | 0.995503 | --NA-- |
| $y_1$ | 2.5158 | 2.39914 | 1.99765 | |
| $y_2$ | 2.06291 | 1.80875 | 1.00048 | |
| $y_3$ | 2.862 | 2.98209 | 2.99814 | |
| $y_4$ | 2.36484 | 2.36281 | 2.49374 | |
| $y_5$ | 2.06754 | 1.895 | 1.49658 | |
| $\lambda_3 = W, \lambda_1 = \lambda_2 = (1\text{-}W)/2, 0 \leq W \leq 1$ | | | | |
| z | 6.60213 | 9.3271 | **10.4638** | |
| $x_1$ | 0.170342 | 0.126015 | 0 | |
| $x_2$ | 0.0367932 | 0 | 0.00166304 | |
| $x_3$ | 0.759151 | 0.816303 | 0.995504 | --NA-- |
| $y_1$ | 2.5158 | 2.26268 | 1.99765 | |
| $y_2$ | 2.06291 | 1.69841 | 1.00049 | |
| $y_3$ | 2.862 | 2.70093 | 2.99815 | |

**Table 2.** (*continued*)

| | | | | |
|---|---|---|---|---|
| $y_4$ | 2.36484 | 2.29278 | 2.49374 | |
| $y_5$ | 2.06754 | 1.85453 | 1.49659 | |
| **Problem described as in [9]** | | | | |
| $z$ | 6.87235 | 7.13425 | **7.73912** | 3.2081 |
| $x_1$ | 2.65138e-006 | 0.000944931 | 0.000308158 | 0.1939 |
| $x_2$ | 0.000127494 | 0.061029 | 0.127573 | 0.2810 |
| $x_3$ | 0.664552 | 0.738963 | 0.688939 | 0.1968 |
| $y_1$ | 1.32963 | 1.72678 | 1.88971 | 2.4872 |
| $y_2$ | 0.664947 | 0.928675 | 1.07383 | 2.3971 |
| $y_3$ | 1.99454 | 2.64598 | 2.96046 | 2.9454 |
| $y_4$ | 1.66177 | 2.03239 | 2.10569 | 1.7229 |
| $y_5$ | 0.9971 | 1.0 | 1.0 | 1.8267 |

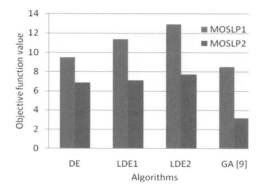

**Fig. 1.** Performance of DE and LDE algorithms in terms of objective function value

# 5   Conclusion

The Stochastic Programming is an optimization technique in which the constraints and/or the objective function of an optimization problem contains certain random variables following different probability distributions. In the present study DE and two of its recent variants LDE1 and LDE2 are used to solve two constrained multiobjective stochastic linear programming problems. Four test cases were considered with respect to the weighing factors and the results were produced in terms of objective function value and decision variable values. From the experimental results it was observed that the DE algorithm and its variants significantly improve the quality of solution of the considered problems in comparison with the quoted results in the literature. As expected the modified versions LDE1 and LDE2 performed better than the basic version of DE because of the presence of the Laplace mutation operator. In conclusion we can say that DE's present an attractive option for solving stochastic programming problems.

## Acknowledgement

This work was carried out during the tenure of an ERCIM "Alain Bensoussan" Fellowship Programme.

## References

1. Abdelaziz, F.B., Aouni, B., Rimeh, F.E.: Multi-objective programming for portfolio selection. European Journal Operational Research 177(3), 1811–1823 (2007)
2. Baba, N., Morimoto, A.: Stochastic approximations methods for solving the stochastic multi-objective programming problem. International Journal of Systems Sciences 24, 789–796 (1993)
3. Caballero, R., Cerdá, E., Munoz, M.M., Rey, L., Stancu-Minasian, I.M.: Efficient solution concepts and their relations in stochastic multi-objective programming. Journal of Optimization Theory and Applications 110, 53–74 (2001)
4. Charles, V., Dutta, D.: Bi-weighted multi-objective stochastic fractional programming problem with mixed constraints. In: Natarajan, R., Arulmozhi, G. (eds.) Second National Conference on Mathematical and Computational Models. Allied Publishers, Chennai (2003)
5. Goicoechea, A., Hansen, D.R., Duckstein, L.: Multi-objective Decision Analysis with Engineering and Business Application. John Wiley, New York (1982)
6. Leclercq, J.P.: Stochastic Programming: An Interactive Multiple Approach. European Journal of Operations Research 10, 33–41 (1982)
7. Suwarna, H., Biswal, M.P., Sinha, S.B.: Fuzzy programming approach to multiobjective stochastic linear programming problems. Fuzzy Sets and Systems 88, 173–181 (1997)
8. Sahoo, N.P., Biswal, M.P.: Computation of Probabilistic linear programming problems involving normal and log-normal random variables with a joint constraint. International Journal of Computer Mathematics 82(11), 1323–1338 (2005)
9. Charles, V., Ansari, S.I., Khalid, M.M.: Multi-Objective Stochastic Linear Programming with General form of Distributions,
   http://www.optimization-online.org/DB_FILE/2009/11/2448.pdf
10. Storn, R., Price, K.: Differential Evolution – a simple and efficient adaptive scheme for global optimization over continuous spaces, Technical Report, International Computer Science Institute, Berkley (1995)
11. Thangaraj, R., Pant, M., Abraham, A.: New Mutation Schemes for Differential Evolution Algorithm and their application to the Optimization of Directional Overcurrent Relay Settings. Applied Mathematics and Computation 216(2), 532–544 (2010)
12. Pant, M., Thangaraj, R., Singh, V.P.: Optimization of Mechanical Design Problems using Improved Differential Evolution Algorithm. Int. Journal of Recent Trends in Engineering 1(5), 21–25 (2009)

# Multi Sensor Fusion Using Fitness Adaptive Differential Evolution

Ritwik Giri, Arnob Ghosh, Aritra Chowdhury, and Swagatam Das

Dept. of Electronics and Telecommunication Engg.
Jadavpur University, Kolkata 700 032, India
ritwikgiri@gmail.com, arnob008@gmail.com,
aritra131288@gmail.com, swagatamdas19@yahoo.co.in

**Abstract.** The rising popularity of multi-source, multi-sensor networks supports real-life applications calls for an efficient and intelligent approach to information fusion. Traditional optimization techniques often fail to meet the demands. The evolutionary approach provides a valuable alternative due to its inherent parallel nature and its ability to deal with difficult problems. We present a new evolutionary approach based on a modified version of Differential Evolution (DE), called Fitness Adaptive Differential Evolution (FiADE). FiADE treats sensors in the network as distributed intelligent agents with various degrees of autonomy. Existing approaches based on intelligent agents cannot completely answer the question of how their agents could coordinate their decisions in a complex environment. The proposed approach is formulated to produce good result for the problems that are high-dimensional, highly nonlinear, and random. The proposed approach gives better result in case of optimal allocation of sensors. The performance of the proposed approach is compared with an evolutionary algorithm coordination generalized particle model (C-GPM).

**Keywords:** Multi-sensor fusion, Sensor behavior, Evolutionary algorithm, Dynamic sensor resource allocation problem, Differential Evolution (DE).

## 1 Introduction

Sensor fusion is a method of integrating signals from multiple sources into a single signal or piece of information. These sources are sensors or devices that allow for perception or measurement of the changing environment. As sensor nodes operate in harsh environment they are prone to failure. The method uses ''sensor fusion'' or ''data fusion'' algorithms which can be classified into different groups, including 1) fusion based on probabilistic models, 2) fusion based on least-squares techniques, and 3) intelligent fusion.

This paper presents an evolutionary approach to intelligent information fusion. Many applications in multi-sensor information fusion can be stated as optimization problems. Among the many different optimization techniques, evolutionary algorithms (EA) are a heuristic-based global search and optimization methods that have found their way into almost every area of real world optimization problems. EA

B.K. Panigrahi et al. (Eds.): SEMCCO 2010, LNCS 6466, pp. 62–70, 2010.
© Springer-Verlag Berlin Heidelberg 2010

provide a valuable alternative to traditional methods because of their inherent parallelism and their ability to deal with difficult problems that feature non-homogeneous, noisy, incomplete and/or obscured information, constrained resources, and massive processing of large amounts of data. Traditional methods based on correlation, mutual information, local optimization, and sequential processing may perform poorly. EA are inspired by the principles of natural evolution and genetics. Popular EA include genetic algorithm (GA) [1], simulated annealing algorithm (SA) [2] , ant colony optimization (ACO) [3] , particle swarm optimization (PSO) [4] , etc.

Recently, Differential Evolution (DE) [5,6] has emerged as a powerful and robust tool for solving the linear and non-linear equations. The performance of DE is severely dependent on two of its most important control parameters: The crossover rate ($Cr$) and scale factor ($F$) [5]. Some objective functions are very sensitive to the proper choice of the parameter settings in DE [7]. Therefore, researchers naturally started to consider some techniques to automatically find an optimal set of control parameters for DE [8,9]. Most recent trend in this direction is the use of self-adaptive strategies like the ones reported in [8] and [9]. This article suggests a novel automatic tuning method for the scale factor and crossover rate of population members in DE, based on their individual objective function values. This proposed variant of DE called Fitness Adaptive Differentia Evolution (FiADE) has been used to solve a dynamic multiple sensor resource allocation problem and the performance of the proposed is compared with another EA known as Coordination-Generalized Particle Model (C-GPM) [10].

The rest of the paper is organized as follows. In Section 2, we discuss and formulate the problem model for the typical multi-sensor system. In Section 3, we outline the basic steps of DE and it's proposed modification in FiADE. In Section 4, we describe an experiment to apply the proposed approach and to verify the claimed properties of the approach.

## 2   Dynamic Sensor Resource Allocation

In a sensor-based application with command and control, a major prerequisite to the success of the command and control process is the effective use of the scarce and costly sensing resources. These resources represent an important source of information on which the command and control process bases most of its reasoning. Whenever there are insufficient resources to perform all the desired tasks, the sensor management must allocate the available sensors to those tasks that could maximize the effectiveness of the sensing process.

The dynamic sensor allocation problem consists of selecting sensors of a multi-sensor system to be applied to various objects of interest using feedback strategies. Consider the problem of $n$ sensors $A = \{A_1, A_2, ..., A_n\}$, and $m$ objects, $T = \{T_1, T_2, ..., T_m\}$. In order to obtain useful information about the state of each object, appropriate sensors should be assigned to various objects at the time intervals $t \in \{0,1,2,...,T^{'} - 1\}$, where $T^{'}$ is the lifetime of the each sensor. The collections of sensors applied to object $k$ during interval $t$ is represented by a vector $X_k(t) = \{x_{1k}, x_{2k}, ..., x_{nk}\}$, where $x_{ik}$ =1 if sensor $i$ is used on object $k$ at interval $t$, otherwise $x_{ik} = 0$.

Because of the limited resources sustaining the whole system, the planned sensor distributions must satisfy the following constraint for every $t \in \{0,1,2,...,T'-1\}$

$$\sum_{k=1}^{m} r_{ik}(t)x_{ik}(t) = 1 \tag{1}$$

where $r_{ik}$ denotes that quantity of resources consumed by sensor $i$ on object $k$ being bounded within the limits as $0 \le r_{ik} \le 1$.

The goal of sensor allocation is to try to achieve an optimal allocation of all sensors to all the objects after T stages. Let $C = (c_{ik})_{n*m}$ be a two-dimensional weight vector. Sensor allocation can be defined as a problem to find a two-dimensional allocation vector $R = (r_{ik})_{n*m}$, which maximizes the objective in (2), subject to the constraint (1)

$$z(R) = \sum_{i=1}^{n} \sum_{k=1}^{m} c_{ik} r_{ik} \tag{2}$$

For convenience both $r_{ik}$ and $c_{ik}$ are normalized such that $0 \le c_{ik} \le 1$ and $0 \le r_{ik} \le 1$.

## 3   Classical Differential Evolution and It's Fitness Based Adaption

### 3.1   Classical DE

Classical DE was originally proposed by Storn and Price. Due to space crunch we do not discuss about the Classical DE here. Details of classical DE [5] and [6] can be referred.

### 3.2   Fitness Based Adaptive DE

The two most important control parameters of DE are the scale factor ($F$) and the crossover rate $Cr$. The performance of DE severely depends on the proper choice of these two parameters. Though the number of populations $NP$ is also a parameter, it does not need to be fine tuned and in many case it is a user defined parameter. It depends only on the complexity of the problem.

In this article we propose a scheme of reducing $F$ when the objective function value of any vector nears the maximum objective function value found so far in the population. In this case the vector is expected to suffer lesser perturbation so that it may undergo a fine search within a small neighborhood of he suspected optima. Equations (8) and (9) show two different schemes for updating the value of $F$ for the $i'th$ target vector.

$$\text{Scheme 1: } F_i = F_C * \left( \frac{\Delta f_i}{\lambda + \Delta f_i} \right), \tag{3}$$

Where, $\lambda = \varepsilon + \Delta f_i / Factor$ and $\Delta f_i = |f(\vec{X}_i) - f(\vec{X}_{best})|$ and $F_C$ = a constant value within the range [0,1], $\varepsilon$ being a very small quantity added to avoid the zero division error when $\Delta f_i = 0$ and $Factor$ being a scaling parameter greater than 1.

$$\text{Scheme 2: } F_i = F_C * \left(1 - e^{-\Delta f_i}\right) \tag{4}$$

Clearly, for both of scheme 1 & 2 as $\Delta f_i \to 0$, $F_i \to 0$ and as $\Delta f_i \to \infty$, $F_i \to F_C$.. Thus (8) & (9) exhibits the scale factor adaptation criteria illustrated above. Figures 1 shows the variation of $F$ with $\Delta f$ for a range between 0 and 10. But it is true for higher value also. As can be seen from Figure1, the two plots intersect at approximately $\Delta f = 2.4$.So from Figure 1, it is evident that as long as $\Delta f > 2.4$ scheme 2 results greater values of $F$. Vectors that are distributed away from the current best vector in fitness-space have their $F$ values large and keeps on exploring the fitness landscape maintain adequate population diversity. But as soon as $\Delta f$ falls below 2.4, scheme2 starts reducing $F$ drastically which decreases the explorative power of the vector, consequently resulting into premature termination of the algorithm. So, scheme 1 is used for scale factor adaptation in this region, thus minimizing the probability of premature termination. These two schemes as a whole help the vector to finely search the surroundings of some suspected optima. Thus the adaptation of the scale factor for the $i$-th target vector takes place in the following way:

$$if \quad \Delta f_i > 2.4,$$

$$F_i = F_C * \left(1 - e^{-\Delta f_i}\right), \tag{5}$$

$$else \quad F_i = F_C * \left(\frac{\Delta f_i}{\lambda + \Delta f_i}\right),$$

Similarly we adapt the values of crossover rate $Cr$ associated with each target vector according to the fitness of the donor vector produced. We know that, if $Cr$ is higher, then more genetic information will be passed to the trial vector from the donor vector, whereas if $Cr$ is lower then more genetic information will be transferred to the trial vector from the parent vector. Let, $\Delta f_{donor\_i} = (f(\vec{V_i}) - f(\vec{X}_{best}))$.

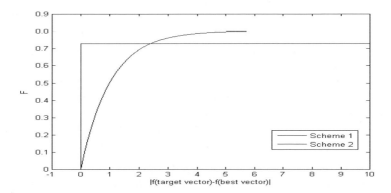

**Fig. 1.** Variation of F with $\Delta f$ varying in scale of 0 to10 according to the schemes outlined in (8) & (9)

Donor vectors having low positive value of $\Delta f_{donor\_i}$ are located close to the best particle obtained so far in the current population, hence their features are good enough to be transferred to the trial vector, hence for them Cr should be higher .Similarly for donor vectors having higher positive values of $\Delta f_{donor\_i}$ should have lower value of $Cr$. Now for donor vectors having objective function value lower than even the best particle of the current population (in case of minimization) $Cr$ (i.e. $\Delta f_{donor\_i}$ having a negative value) should have very high value, so that most of it's features are transmitted in the trial vector. So, we conclude that, the scheme for determining the value of $Cr$ for i'th donor vector $\vec{V}_i$ should be obtained as follows:

$$If \qquad f(\vec{V}_i) \leq f(\vec{X}_{best}), \qquad Cr_i = Cr_{const;} \qquad (6a)$$

$$else, \quad Cr_i = Cr_{min} + \frac{(Cr_{max} - Cr_{min})}{1 + \Delta f_{donor\_i}}; \qquad (6b)$$

where, $Cr_{max} > Cr_{min}$ and $Cr_{const}$ has a high value all being in the range [0,1]. Eqn (6 b) has been designed in such a way, because, for $f(\vec{V}_i) \geq f(\vec{X}_{best})$ we require that for $\Delta f_{donor\_i} \rightarrow 0$, $Cr_i$ should have high value and vice versa. Now this adaptation scheme of $F$ and $Cr$ has been applied on the DE/best/1/bin algorithm and in what follows, we shall refer to this new variant of DE as FiADE (Fitness Adaptive Differential Evolution).

## 4   Experimental Set Up and Results

In this section we demonstrate the utility of the proposed algorithm FiADE with an example of a robot which represents a multi-sensor fusion problem.

The robot has seven sensors: eye, nose, ear, arm, hand, leg and foot. The robot has a repertoire of three actions: open a door, take dictation, find food and take back. Now we describe in detail how to solve the multi-sensor fusion problem, namely, how to allocate sensors to objects.

Let sensors $A_i, i = 1, 2, ....., 7$ represent the eye, nose, ear, arm, hand, leg and foot of the robot, respectively. Let objects $T_k, k = 1, 2, 3$ represent the robot's actions of opening a door, taking dictation, and finding food and taking them back, respectively.

The input matrixes are $X$ and $C$. These are chosen as follows:

$x_{ik}$:
First, we establish the relations between sensors and objects (actions). If sensor $A_i$ is related to object $T_k$, then $x_{ik} = 1$, otherwise 0. For example, the eye, arm, hand, leg and foot are related to the object of opening a door; the eye, ear, arm and hand are related to the object of taking dictation. We can form the matrix $X$, as shown in Table 1A.

$c_{ik}$:
Based on the different effects of the sensors $A_1 - A_7$ on the objects $T_1 - T_3$ we can choose different weights $c_{ik}$. If sensor is more important to object $T_k$ than $T_l$

$(k, l = 1,2,3)$ then $c_{ik}$ will be larger than $c_{il}$. The following must be observed when choosing the weights: if $x_{ik} = 0$ then $c_{ik} = 0$ to ensure that the object $T_k$ which is not related to sensor $A_i$ is not allocated any sensor resource, $0 \leq c_{ik} \leq 1$ and $\sum_{k=1}^{3} c_{ik} = 1$ for $i = 1,2,...7$ to ensure that senor resources are fully allocated.

Following these conditions the $C$ matrix used for this particular problem is as shown in Table 1B.

Now we elaborate the construction of the $R$ matrix which is evolved through the proposed FiADE algorithm to maximize $z(R)$ as defined by (2).

## $R = [r_{ik}]$:

In this problem such an $R$ matrix has to be found so that (2) is maximized. So FiADE algorithm has to be applied to find that particular $R$ matrix which maximizes $z(R)$. Each entry of $R$ is initialized between 0 and 1 in a random manner obeying the following constraints.

a)  $r_{ik} = 0 | \forall x_{ik} = 0$. If $x_{ik} = 0$, then $r_{ik} = 0$, to ensure that an object $T_k$ which is not related to the sensor $A_i$ is not allocated any sensor resource.

b)  Non-Negativity: $0 \leq r_{ik} \leq 1$. If $min_{i,k} r_{ik} < 0$ then $r_{ik}$ is transformed into $r_{ik} = r_{ik} - min_{i,k} r_{ik}$.

c)  Normalization: Let $r_{ik} = r_{ik} / \sum_{k=1}^{3} r_{ik}$, in order that the sensor resources are fully allocated i.e. $\sum_{k=1}^{3} r_{ik} = 1, i = 1,2 .....7$

**Table 1.** The $X$ (1A) and $C$ (1B) matrices for the multi-sensor fusion problem

1A

| $X = [x_{ik}]$ | $T_1$, open the door | $T_2$, take the dictation | $T_3$, find food, take back |
|---|---|---|---|
| $A_1$ , eye | 1 | 1 | 1 |
| $A_2$ , nose | 0 | 0 | 1 |
| $A_3$ , ear | 0 | 1 | 0 |
| $A_4$ , arm | 1 | 1 | 1 |
| $A_5$ , hand | 1 | 1 | 1 |
| $A_6$ , leg | 1 | 0 | 1 |
| $A_7$ , foot | 1 | 0 | 1 |

1B

| $C = [c_{ik}]$ | $T_1$, open the door | $T_2$, take the dictation | $T_3$, find food, take back |
|---|---|---|---|
| $A_1$ , eye | 0.5 | 0.25 | 0.25 |
| $A_2$ , nose | 0 | 0 | 1 |
| $A_3$ , ear | 0 | 1 | 0 |
| $A_4$ , arm | 0.4 | 0.3 | 0.3 |
| $A_5$ , hand | 0.33 | 0.34 | 0.33 |
| $A_6$ , leg | 0.35 | 0 | 0.65 |
| $A_7$ , foot | 0.35 | 0 | 0.65 |

Thus from the above discussion it is evident that the various population individuals in FiADE should actually contain the $R$ matrix as their parameters. FiADE generally deals with the minimization problem. But (2) is the maximization problem. So for the sake of solving it through FiADE, it can be converted to minimization problem by making $-z(R)$ as the objective function of FiADE instead of $z(R)$.

Next, we delineate how FiADE has been used to solve the dynamic sensor allocation problem through the following outline of the algorithm.

**Outline of FiADE Algorithm to Multi sensor allocation Problem**
For FiADE, population size $NP$ is taken as 50 and the maximum number of generations ($G_{max}$ is kept at 100). Various parameters for the FiADE algorithm used in this paper are $F_c = 0.5, \epsilon = 10^{-14}, Cr_{max} = 0.7, Cr_{min} = 0.3, Cr_{const} = 0.95$. The steps through which FiADE proceeds to solve this particular problem are described below:-

### Step1: Initialization
a) *Input: C matrix and X matrix are the inputs.*
b) *Generate an initial population $\{r'_1, r'_2, \dots \dots, r'_N\}$ where $r'_i = R$, a two dimensional array having 7 rows and 3 columns i.e. each $r'_i$ is an R matrix described above. The components of each matrix are initialized randomly from [0, 1] i.e. $r_{ik} \in [0,1]$ for $i = 1,2,...7$ and $k = 1,2,3$ following the constraints for R matrix discussed above.*
c) *The fitness function is then evaluated for each individual.*

### Step2: Update
*For $G = 1,2,....,G_{max}$ do*

*For $j=1, 2... N$ do*
a) *Denote the best individual structure with the best fitness (i.e. lowest objective function value for minimization problem) as $r'_{best}$ in the population at generation G.*
b) *Mutation: Mutation step applied is DE/best/1 with the scaling factor F chosen according to (10). For each generation donor matrix is generated using the following method-*
   *For $i=1,2,...7$ do*
      *For $k=1,2,3$ do*
$$v_{j\,ik} = r'_{best,G_{ik}} + F(r'_{p_1^j,G} - r'_{p_2^j,G})$$
   *End For*
   *End For*
   *After mutation donor matrix is generated this is dealt in the same way as the individual R matrix is dealt during initialization*
c) *Crossover: The crossover rate Cr is chosen according to the (6a) and (6b) to generate the trial matrix. The trial matrix is also dealt in the same way as the donor matrix is dealt in the mutation step. Let the trial matrix generated is $U_j = u_{j_{ik}}$ for $i=1,2,....7$ and $k=1,2,3$.*
d) *Selection: If $f(U_j) \leq f(r'_j)$ then*
$$r'_{j,G+1} = U_j$$
$$\text{Otherwise, } r'_{j,G+1} = r'_j.$$
e) *Store the fitness function value of each individual.*
*End For*
   *The best fitness function value at each generation is displayed after each generation.*
*End For*

The best fitness obtained after the maximum number of generations is the optimum value and the corresponding matrix is the desired *optimum R* matrix. The optimum R matrix obtained running FiADE through 100 generations is shown in left column. The corresponding value of optimized $z(R)$ is **5.1366**. The corresponding matrix $R$ obtained by C-GPM method [10] after 100 generations is shown in right column, with the value of optimized $z(R)$ as 4.5.

$$R = \begin{pmatrix} 0.9975 & 0.0017 & 0.0008 \\ 0 & 0 & 1 \\ 0 & 1 & 0 \\ 0.9989 & 0.0007 & 0.0004 \\ 0.0040 & 0.9920 & 0.0040 \\ 0.0002 & 0 & 0.9998 \\ 0.0010 & 0 & 0.9990 \end{pmatrix} \qquad R = \begin{pmatrix} 0.8852 & 0.0277 & 0.0871 \\ 0 & 0 & 1 \\ 0 & 1 & 0 \\ 0.1041 & 0.0426 & 0.8533 \\ 0.1037 & 0.0565 & 0.8398 \\ 0.0723 & 0 & 0.9277 \\ 0.0723 & 0 & 0.9277 \end{pmatrix}$$

Thus the performance of the proposed algorithm in optimally allocating sensor resources is better than the previous attempts i.e. with the C-GPM algorithm in this problem. It clearly establishes the superiority of the proposed algorithm. The way the fitness function value i.e. the value of $z(R)$ approaches the maximum as the proposed algorithm FiADE progresses through the iterations is shown in the Fitness Value vs. Generation Counter plot as shown in Fig 2.

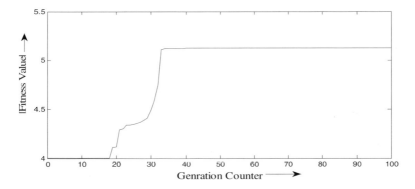

**Fig. 2.** Fitness vs Generation Counter plot for FiADE algorithm

## 5    Conclusion

In this paper, we describe a new evolutionary approach to multi-sensor fusion based on the Fitness Adaptive Differential Evolution (FiADE). We present the FiADE approach as a new branch of evolutionary algorithms, which can overcome the limitations of other existing evolutionary algorithms in capturing the entire dynamics inherent in the problem, especially those that are high-dimensional, highly nonlinear, and random. Hence, the FiADE approach can describe the complex behaviors and dynamics of multiple sensors. The validity of the proposed method is confirmed with the comparison of another robust evolutionary algorithm coordination generalized particle model (C-GPM). FiADE produces better result compared to C-GPM. Moreover FiADE is fast compared to C-GPM. Proposed FiADE algorithm can work out the optimum solution of any multisensory fusion problem.

# References

[1] Forrest, S.: Genetic algorithms—principles of natural-selection applied to computation. Science 261(5123), 872–878 (1993)
[2] Kirkpatrick, S., Gelatt, C.D., Vecchi, M.P.: Optimization by simulated annealing. Science 220(4598), 671–680 (1983)
[3] Bonabeau, E., Dorigo, M., Theraulaz, G.: Inspiration for optimization from social insect behaviour. Nature 406(6791), 39–42 (2000)
[4] Kennedy, J., Eberhart, R.C.: Particle swarm optimization. In: Proc. IEEE Conf. Neural Networks, Piscataway, NJ, vol. IV, pp. 1942–1948 (1995)
[5] Price, K., Storn, R., Lampinen, J.: Differential Evolution - A Practical Approach to Global Optimization. Springer, Berlin (2005)
[6] Storn, R., Price, K.: Differential evolution – A simple and efficient heuristic for global optimization over continuous spaces. Journal of Global Optimization 11(4), 341–359 (1997)
[7] Liu, J., Lampinen, J.: On setting the control parameters of the differential evolution method. In: Matoušek, R., Ošmera, P. (eds.) Proc. of Mendel 2002, 8th International Conference on Soft Computing, pp. 11–18 (2002)
[8] Qin, A.K., Huang, V.L., Suganthan, P.N.: Differential evolution algorithm with strategy adaptation for global numerical optimization". IEEE Transactions on Evolutionary Computation 13(2), 398–417 (2009)
[9] Brest, J., Greiner, S., Bošković, B., Mernik, M., Žumer, V.: Self-adapting Control parameters in differential evolution: a comparative study on numerical benchmark problems. IEEE Transaction on Evolutionary Computation 10(6), 646–657 (2006)
[10] Feng, X., Lau, F.C.M., Shuai, D.: The Coordination generalized Particle Model-An evolutionary approach to multi sensor fusion. Information Fusion 9(4), 450–464 (2008)

# Differential Evolution Algorithm with Ensemble of Parameters and Mutation and Crossover Strategies

Rammohan Mallipeddi and Ponnuthurai Nagaratnam Suganthan

Nanyang Technological university, Singapore, 639798
{mall0004,epnsugan}@ntu.edu.sg

**Abstract.** Differential Evolution (DE) has attracted much attention recently as an effective approach for solving numerical optimization problems. However, the performance of DE is sensitive to the choice of the mutation and crossover strategies and their associated control parameters. Thus, to obtain optimal performance, time consuming parameter tuning is necessary. Different mutation and crossover strategies with different parameter settings can be appropriate during different stages of the evolution. In this paper, we propose a DE with an ensemble of mutation and crossover strategies and their associated control parameters known as EPSDE. In EPSDE, a pool of distinct mutation and crossover strategies along with a pool of values for each control parameter coexists throughout the evolution process and competes to produce offspring. The performance of EPSDE is evaluated on a set of 25 bound-constrained problems designed for Conference on Evolutionary Computation (CEC) 2005 and is compared with state-of-the-art algorithm.

**Keywords:** Differential Evolution, Global optimization, Parameter adaptation, Ensemble, Mutation strategy adaptation.

## 1 Introduction

DE proposed by Storn and Price [1] is a fast and simple technique which performs well on a wide variety of problems. DE is a population based stochastic search technique, which is inherently parallel. DE has been successfully applied in diverse fields of engineering [2, 3, 4, 5, 6, 7, 8, 9, 10]. The performance [11, 12] of the DE algorithm is sensitive to the mutation strategy, crossover strategy and control parameters such as the population size ($NP$), crossover rate ($CR$) and the scale factor ($F$). The best settings for the control parameters can be different for different optimization problems and the same functions with different requirements for consumption time and accuracy. Therefore, to successfully solve a specific optimization problem, it is generally necessary to perform a time-consuming trial-and-error search for the most appropriate combination of strategies and their associated parameter values. However, such a trial-and-error search process suffers from high computational costs. The population of DE may evolve through different regions in the search space, within which different strategies [13] with different parameter settings may be more effective than others. Although different partial

B.K. Panigrahi et al. (Eds.): SEMCCO 2010, LNCS 6466, pp. 71–78, 2010.
© Springer-Verlag Berlin Heidelberg 2010

adaptation schemes have been proposed [14, 15, 13, 16, 17] to overcome the time consuming trial-and-error procedure, we demonstrate the superior performance of the ensemble strategy proposed [18].

The reminder of this paper is organized as follows: Section 2 presents a literature survey on different mutation and crossover strategies and parameter settings used in DE. Section 3 presents the proposed ensemble of mutation and crossover strategies and parameters in DE (EPSDE) algorithm. Section 4 presents the experimental results and discussions while Section 5 concludes the paper.

## 2   Literature Review

Differential Evolution (DE) algorithm is a floating-point encoded evolutionary algorithm for global optimization over continuous spaces [19]. The performance of DE becomes more sensitive to the strategy and the associated parameter values when the problem is complex [20]. Inappropriate choice of mutation and crossover strategies and the associated parameters may lead to premature convergence, stagnation or wastage of computational resources [21, 20, 22, 23, 16] . Initially it was thought that [19, 24] the control parameters of DE are not difficult to choose. But due to the complex interaction of control parameters with the DE's performance on hard optimization problems [14], choosing an appropriate mutation strategy and control parameters require some expertise. Since DE was proposed various empirical guidelines were suggested for choosing a mutation strategy and its associated control parameter settings.

In DE, the larger the population size ($NP$), the higher the probability of finding a global optimum. But, a larger population implies a slower convergence rate requiring a larger number of function evaluations. Initially $NP=10D$ was considered as a good choice [4] for DE to find a global optimum. However, to balance the speed and reliability different ranges of $NP$ values such as $5D$ to $10D$ [19], $3D$ to $8D$ [20] and $2D$ to $40D$ [25] were suggested.

The classical DE proposed by Price and Storn uses DE/rand/1/bin, which is most widely used. Later, various DE mutation strategies were proposed [26, 4]. In [20, 19] it was stated that a 2 difference vector strategies such as DE/rand/2/bin are better than DE/rand/1/bin due to their ability to improve diversity by producing more trial vectors [22]. DE/best/1/bin and DE/rand-to-best/1/bin are faster on easier optimization problems, but become unreliable when solving highly multi-modal problems. To balance the exploration and exploitation abilities of DE, and adaptive mutation strategy with optional external archive (JADE) was proposed [27]. DE/current-to-rand/1 being a rotation-invariant strategy can solve rotated problems better than other strategies [28].

The main difference between binomial and exponential crossover is the fact that while in the binomial case the components inherited from the mutant vector are arbitrarily selected in the case of exponential crossover they form one or two compact subsequences [29].

The crossover rate ($CR$) controls which and how many components are mutated in each element of the current population. The crossover rate $CR$ is a probability $0 \leq CR \leq 1$ of mixing between trial and target vectors. A large $CR$ speeds up convergence

[20, 4, 19]. In [19], it is said that $CR = 0.1$ is a good initial choice while $CR = 0.9$ or 1.0 can be tried to increase the convergence speed. For separable problems, $CR$ from the range (0, 0.2) is the best while for multi-modal, parameter dependant problems $CR$ in the range (0.9,1.0) is best [23, 25]. Based on these observations, $CR$ with non-continuous ranges are also used [30].

Scaling factor, $F$ is usually chosen in [0.5, 1] [4]. In [19], it is said that values of $F$ smaller than 0.4 and greater than 1.0 are occasionally effective. The scale factor $F$, is strictly greater than zero. A larger $F$ increases the probability of escaping from a local optimum [20, 25]. $F$ must be above a certain critical value to avoid premature convergence to a sub-optimal solution [20, 25], but if $F$ becomes too large, the number of function evaluations to find the optimum grows very quickly. In [20, 19], it is said that $F = 0.6$ or 0.5 would be a good initial choice while in [25] it is said that $F = 0.9$ would be a good initial choice. Typical values of $F$ are 0.4 to 0.95 according to [25].

Even though the above guidelines are useful for choosing the individual parameters of DE to some extent, the performance of DE is more sensitive to the combination of the mutation strategy and its associated parameters. To improve the performance of DE various adaptation techniques have been proposed [14, 26, 31, 32, 33, 16, 34, 13, 35, 36, 37, 38].

## 3 Ensemble of Mutation and Crossover Strategies and Parameters in DE (EPSDE)

The effectiveness of conventional DE in solving a numerical optimization problem depends on the selected mutation and crossover strategy and its associated parameter values. However, different optimization problems require different mutation strategies with different parameter values depending on the nature of problem (uni-modal and multi-modal) and available computation resources. In addition, to solve a specific problem, different mutation strategies with different parameter settings may be better during different stages of the evolution than a single mutation strategy with unique parameter settings as in the conventional DE. Motivated by these observations, we propose an ensemble of mutation and crossover strategies and parameter values for DE (EPSDE) in which a pool of mutation strategies, along with a pool of values corresponding to each associated parameter competes to produce successful offspring population. The candidate pool of mutation and mutation strategies and parameters should be restrictive to avoid the unfavorable influences of less effective mutation strategies and parameters [13]. The mutation strategies or the parameters present in a pool should have diverse characteristics, so that they can exhibit distinct performance characteristics during different stages of the evolution, when dealing with a particular problem.

EPSDE consists of a pool of mutation and crossover strategies along with a pool of values for each of the associated control parameters. Each member in the initial population is randomly assigned with a mutation strategy and associated parameter values taken from the respective pools. The population members (target vectors) produce offspring (trial vectors) using the assigned mutation strategy and parameter values. If the generated trial vector produced is better than the target vector, the mutation strategy and parameter values are retained with trial vector which becomes the parent (target vector) in the next generation. The combination of the mutation strategy and the parameter values that produced a better offspring than the parent are stored. If the target vector is better than the trial vector, then the target vector is randomly reinitialized with a new mutation strategy and associated parameter values from the respective pools or from the successful combinations stored with equal probability. This leads to an increased probability of production of offspring by the better combination of mutation strategy and the associated control parameters in the future generations.

In this paper the EPSDE formed uses the following mutation and crossover strategies and parameter values:

1) Mutation strategies: JADE [27] and DE/current-to-rand/1 [28]
2) Crossover strategies: Binomial crossover and exponential crossover [**39**]

In the proposed EPSDE, the population size ($NP = 50$) is maintained constant throughout the evolution process. $F \in \{0.5,0.9\}$ and $CR \in \{0.1,0.5,0.9\}$

**Table 1.** Ensemble of Parameters and Mutation and Crossover Strategies in DE (EPSDE)

---

**Step 1**   Set the generation number $G = 0$, and randomly initialize a population of $NP$ individuals $P_G = \{X_{i,G},...,X_{NP,G}\}$ with $X_{i,G} = \{x^1_{i,G},...,x^D_{i,G}\}, i = 1,...,NP$ uniformly distributed in the range $[X_{min}, X_{max}]$, where $X_{min} = \{x^1_{min},...,x^D_{min}\}$ and $X_{max} = \{x^1_{max},...,x^D_{max}\}$

**Step 2**   Select a pool of mutation strategies and a pool of values for each associated parameters corresponding to each mutation strategy.

**Step 3**   Each population member is randomly assigned with one of the mutation strategy from the pool and the associated parameter values are chosen randomly from the corresponding pool of values.

**Step 4**   WHILE stopping criterion is not satisfied
             DO

**Step 4.1 *Mutation step***
   /*Generate a mutated vector $V_{i,G} = \{v^1_{i,G}, v^2_{i,G},...,v^D_{i,G}\}$ for each target vector $\mathbf{X}_{i,G}$ */

      FOR $i = 1$ to $NP$
         Generate a mutated vector $V_{i,G} = \{v^1_{i,G}, v^2_{i,G},...,v^D_{i,G}\}$ corresponding to the target vector $\mathbf{X}_{i,G}$ using the mutation strategy and $F$ value associated with the target vector.
      END FOR

**Step 4.2 *Crossover step***
   /*Generate a trial vector $U_{i,G} = \{u^1_{i,G}, u^2_{i,G},...,u^D_{i,G}\}$ for each target vector $\mathbf{X}_{i,G}$ */

      FOR $i = 1$ to $NP$
         Generate a trial vector $U_{i,G} = \{u^1_{i,G}, u^2_{i,G},...,u^D_{i,G}\}$ corresponding to the target vector $\mathbf{X}_{i,G}$ using the crossover strategy and $CR$ value associated with the target vector.
      END FOR

**Table 1.** (*continued*)

**Step 4.3** *Selection step*
  /* Selection by competition between target (parent) and trial (offspring) vectors */
        FOR $i = 1$ to $NP$
        /* Evaluate the trial vector $U_{i,G}$ */
          IF $f(U_{i,G}) \leq f(X_{i,G})$, THEN $X_{i,G+1} = U_{i,G}$, $f(X_{i,G+1}) \leq f(U_{i,G})$
             IF $f(U_{i,G}) < f(X_{best,G})$, THEN $X_{best,G} = U_{i,G}$, $f(X_{best,G}) \leq f(U_{i,G})$
             /* $X_{best,G}$ is the best individual in generation $G$ */
             ELSE $X_{i,G+1} = X_{i,G}$
          END IF
        END IF
        END FOR

**Step 4.4** *Updating Step*
        FOR $i = 1$ to $NP$
        IF $f(U_{i,G}) > f(X_{i,G})$ THEN
            Randomly select a new mutation strategy and parameter values from the pools or from the stored successful combinations.
        END IF
        END FOR
**Step 4.5** *Increment the generation count* $G = G + 1$

**Step 5   END WHILE**

# 4 Experimental Results

To evaluate the performance of the algorithms the test problems of CEC 2005 are used. The maximum numbers of function evaluations used are 100000 and 300000 for 10D and 30D problems respectively. The results of the algorithms are presented in Table 2. In Table 2, for a particular problem the results are highlighted if the performance of the algorithm is statistically significant.

**Table 2.** Results for 10D and 30D benchmark problems of CEC 2005

| Fcn | 10D | | | | 30D | | | |
|---|---|---|---|---|---|---|---|---|
| | JADE | | EPSDE | | JADE | | EPSDE | |
| | Mean | Std | Mean | Std | Mean | Std | Mean | Std |
| $f_1$ | 0 | 0 | 0 | 0 | 0 | 0 | 0 | 0 |
| $f_2$ | 0 | 0 | 0 | 0 | 8.59E-28 | 4.19E-28 | 3.37E-27 | 4.73E-27 |
| $f_3$ | 1.11E-25 | 4.03E-26 | 6.96E-25 | 1.73E-26 | **7.96E+03** | **3.88E+03** | 7.74E+04 | 3.77E+04 |
| $f_4$ | 0 | 0 | 0 | 0 | 2.45E-02 | 8.40E-02 | **1.76E-12** | **2.97E-12** |
| $f_5$ | 2.42E-13 | 6.28E-13 | **0** | **0** | 7.53E+02 | 3.68E+02 | **2.26E+02** | **2.61E+02** |
| $f_6$ | 8.13E-01 | 1.67E+00 | **0** | **0** | 1.03E+01 | 2.72E+01 | **2.12E-20** | **1.13E-19** |
| $f_7$ | **7.51E-03** | **6.61E-03** | 3.94E-02 | 3.48E-02 | 1.56E-02 | 1.51E-02 | **5.60E-03** | **6.11E-03** |

**Table 2.** (*continued*)

| $f_8$ | 2.02E+01 | 1.54E-01 | 2.04E+01 | 5.00E-03 | 2.08E+01 | 2.46E-01 | 2.08E+01 | 1.31E-01 |
|---|---|---|---|---|---|---|---|---|
| $f_9$ | 0 | 0 | 0 | 0 | 0 | 0 | 0 | 0 |
| $f_{10}$ | 4.39E+00 | 1.09E+00 | **3.30E+00** | **9.59E-01** | **2.73E+01** | **5.70E+00** | 4.71E+01 | 1.52E+01 |
| $f_{11}$ | 4.42E+00 | 1.03E+00 | **4.16E+00** | **3.21E+00** | 2.68E+01 | 2.03E+00 | 2.86E+01 | 9.61E-01 |
| $f_{12}$ | 8.89E+01 | 2.89E+02 | **5.00E+00** | **7.07E+00** | 4.92E+03 | 3.97E+03 | 1.32E+04 | 1.35E+04 |
| $f_{13}$ | **2.48E-01** | **5.43E-02** | 4.13E-01 | 1.08E-01 | 1.67E+00 | 3.04E-02 | **1.19E+00** | **1.24E-01** |
| $f_{14}$ | **2.75E+00** | **3.00E-01** | 3.08E+00 | 8.31E-02 | 1.24E+01 | 3.27E-01 | 1.25E+01 | 1.64E-01 |
| $f_{15}$ | 1.16E+02 | 1.67E+02 | **8.53E+01** | **1.49E+02** | 3.20E+02 | 1.18E+02 | **2.12E+02** | **1.98E+01** |
| $f_{16}$ | 1.21E+02 | 6.78E+00 | **9.76E+01** | **4.40E+00** | 1.45E+02 | 1.55E+02 | **9.08E+01** | **2.98E+01** |
| $f_{17}$ | 1.31E+02 | 5.05E+00 | **1.21E+02** | **6.28E+00** | 1.34E+02 | 1.44E+02 | **1.04E+02** | **7.27E+01** |
| $f_{18}$ | 7.55E+02 | 1.86E+02 | **6.37E+02** | **3.03E+02** | 9.05E+02 | 1.82E+00 | **8.20E+02** | **3.35E+00** |
| $f_{19}$ | 7.40E+02 | 2.04E+02 | **5.82E+02** | **3.11E+02** | 8.98E+02 | 2.68E+01 | **8.21E+02** | **3.35E+00** |
| $f_{20}$ | 7.18E+02 | 2.15E+02 | **5.62E+02** | **2.96E+02** | 9.05E+02 | 1.51E+00 | **8.22E+02** | **4.17E+00** |
| $f_{21}$ | 5.30E+02 | 1.98E+02 | **4.80E+02** | **6.10E+00** | 5.10E+02 | 5.47E+01 | **5.00E+02** | **6.64E-14** |
| $f_{22}$ | **7.53E+02** | **1.94E+01** | 7.70E+02 | 1.90E+01 | 8.85E+02 | 1.84E+01 | 8.85E+02 | 6.82E+01 |
| $f_{23}$ | 2.15E+02 | 5.01E+01 | 2.13E+02 | 6.01E+01 | 5.50E+02 | 8.05E+01 | **5.07E+02** | **7.26E+00** |
| $f_{24}$ | 2.00E+02 | 2.90E-14 | 2.00E+02 | 2.90E-14 | **2.00E+02** | **2.90E-14** | 2.13E+02 | 1.52E+00 |
| $f_{25}$ | 5.22E+02 | 1.11E+02 | **4.41E+02** | **2.05E+02** | 2.11E+02 | 7.27E-01 | 2.13E+02 | 2.55E+00 |

From the results, it can be observed that EPSDE is significantly worse than, similar to and better than JADE in 4, 8 and 13 cases respectively in 10D problems. Similarly in 30D problems, EPSDE is significantly worse than, similar to and better than JADE in 3, 9 and 13 cases respectively.

## 5   Conclusions

The performance of DE depends on the selected mutation and crossover strategy and its associated parameter values. Different optimization problems require different mutation strategies with different parameter values depending on the nature of problem and available computation resources. For a problem at hand different mutation strategies with different parameter settings may be more effective during different stages of the evolution than a single mutation strategy with unique parameter settings as in the conventional DE. Based on these observations, we propose an ensemble of mutation and crossover strategies and parameter values in which a pool of mutation and crossover strategies, along with a pool of values corresponding to each associated parameter compete to produce offspring population. The performance of EPSDE is evaluated on set of benchmark problems and is favorably compared with the state-of-the-art DE methods in the literature.

# References

1. Storn, R., Price, K.: Differential evolution - a simple and efficient adaptive scheme for global optimization over continuous spaces, Technical Report TR-95-012, ICSI (1995), http://http.icsi.berkeley.edu/~storn/litera.html
2. Joshi, R., Sanderson, A.C.: Minimal representation multisensor fusion using differential evolution. IEEE Transactions on Systems, Man, and Cybernetics Part A:Systems and Humans 29(1), 63–76 (1999)
3. Rogalsky, T., Derksen, R.W., Kocabiyik, S.: Differential evolution in aerodynamic optimization. In: Proc. of 46th Annual Conference of Canadian Aeronautics and Space Institute, pp. 29–36 (1999)
4. Storn, R.: On the usage of differential evolution for function optimization. In: Biennial Conference of the North American Fuzzy Information Processing Society (NAFIPS), pp. 519–523. IEEE, Berkeley (1996)
5. Venu, M.K., Mallipeddi, R., Suganthan, P.N.: Fiber bragg grating sensor array interrogation using differential evolution. Optoelectronics and Advanced Materials - Rapid Communications 2(11), 682–685 (2008)
6. Ilonen, J., Kamarainen, J.K., Lampinen, J.: Differential evolution training algorithm for feed-forward neural networks. Neural Processing Letters 17(1), 93–105 (2003)
7. Das, S., Konar, A.: Automatic image pixel clustering with an improved differential evolution. Applied Soft Computing 9(1), 226–236 (2009)
8. Maulik, U., Saha, I.: Modified differential evolution based fuzzy clustering for pixel classification in remote sensing imagery. Pattern Recognition 42, 2135–2149 (2009)
9. Storn, R.: Differential evolution design of an iir-filter. In: IEEE International Conference on Evolutionary Computation, pp. 268–273. IEEE, Los Alamitos (1996)
10. Varadarajan, M., Swarup, K.S.: Differential evolution approach for optimal reactive power dispatch. Applied Soft Computing 8(4), 1549–1561 (2008)
11. Liu, J., Lampinen, J.: On setting the control parameter of the differential evolution method. In: Proc. 8th Int., Conf. Soft Computing (MENDEL 2002), pp. 11–18 (2002)
12. Das, S., Suganthan, P.N.: Differential evolution: A survey of the state-of-the-art. IEEE Trans. on Evolutionary Computation
13. Qin, A.K., Huang, V.L., Suganthan, P.N.: Differential evolution algorithm with strategy adaptation for global numerical optimization. IEEE Transactions on Evolutionary Computation 13(2), 398–417 (2009)
14. Brest, J., Greiner, S., Boscovic, B., Mernik, M., Zumer, V.: Self-adapting control parameters in differential evolution: A comparative study on numerical benchmark problems. IEEE Transactions on Evolutionary Computation 10(8), 646–657 (2006)
15. Omran, M.G.H., Salman, A., Engelbrecht, A.P.: Self-adaptive differential evolution. In: Hao, Y., Liu, J., Wang, Y.-P., Cheung, Y.-m., Yin, H., Jiao, L., Ma, J., Jiao, Y.-C. (eds.) CIS 2005. LNCS (LNAI), vol. 3801, pp. 192–199. Springer, Heidelberg (2005)
16. Zaharie, D.: Control of population diversity and adaptation in differential evolution algorithms. In: Proceedings of the 9th International Conference on Soft Computing, Brno, pp. 41–46 (2003)
17. Tvrdik, J.: Adaptation in differential evolution: A numerical comparison. Applied Soft Computing 9(3), 1149–1155 (2009)
18. Mallipeddi, R., Suganthan, P.N., Pan, Q.K., Tasgetiren, M.F.: Differential evolution algorithm with ensemble of parameters and mutation strategies. Applied Soft Computing
19. Storn, R., Price, K.: Differential evolution - a simple and efficient heuristic for global optimization over continuous spaces. Journal of Global Optimization 11(4), 341–359 (1997)

20. Gämperle, R., Müller, S.D., Koumoutsakos, P.: A parameter study for differential evolution. In: Advances in Intelligent Systems, Fuzzy Systems, Evolutionary Computation, pp. 293–298. WSEAS Press, Interlaken (2002)
21. Das, S., Konar, A., Chakraborty, U.K.: Two improved differential evolution schemes for faster global search. In: Proceedings of the 2005 conference on Genetic and evolutionary computation, pp. 991–998 (2005)
22. Lampinen, J., Zelinka, I.: On stagnation of the differential evolution algorithm. In: Proceedings of MENDEL 2000, 6th International Mendel Conference on Soft Computing, pp. 76–83 (2000)
23. Price, K.V., Storn, R.M., Lampinen, J.A. (eds.): Differential evolution: A practical approach to global optimization. Springer, Berlin (2005)
24. Storn, R., Price, K.: Differential evolution: A simple evolution strategy for fast optimization. Dr. Dobb's Journal 22(4), 18–24 (1997)
25. Rönkkönen, J., Kukkonen, S., Price, K.V.: Real-parameter optimization with differential evolution. In: IEEE Congress on Evolutionary Computation, pp. 506–513 (2005)
26. Price, K.V. (ed.): An introduction to differential evolution, pp. 79–108. McGraw-Hill, London (1999)
27. Zhang, J.: Jade: Adaptive differential evolution with optional external archive. IEEE Transactions on Evolutionary Computation 13(5), 945–958 (2009)
28. Iorio, A., Li, X.: Solving rotated multi-objective optimization problems using differential evolution. In: Australian Conference on Artificial Intelligence, Cairns, Australia, pp. 861–872 (2004)
29. Zaharie, D.: Influence of crossover on the behavior of differential evolution algorithms. Applied Soft Computing 9(3), 1126–1138 (2009)
30. Mezura-Montes, E., Velazquez-Reyes, J., Coello Coello, C.A.: Modified differential evolution for constrained optimization. In: IEEE Congress on Evolutionary Computation, pp. 25–32 (2006)
31. Chakraborthy, U.K., Das, S., Konar, A.: Differentail evolution with local neighborhood. In: Proceedings of Congress on Evolutionary Computation, pp. 2042–2049. IEEE press, Los Alamitos (2006)
32. Abbass, H.A.: The self-adaptive pareto differential evolution algorithm. In: Proceedings of the IEEE Congress on Evolutionary Computation, vol. 1, pp. 831–836 (2002)
33. Liu, J., Lampinen, J.: A fuzzy adaptive differential evolution algorithm. Soft Computing 9(6), 448–462 (2005)
34. Zaharie, D., Petcu, D.: Adaptive pareto differential evolution and its parallelization. In: Proc. of 5th International Conference on Parallel Processing and Applied Mathematics, pp. 261–268 (2003)
35. Teo, J.: Exploring dynamic self-adaptive populations in differential evolution. Soft Computing 10(8), 673–686 (2006)
36. Yang, Z., Tang, K., Yao, X.: Self-adaptive differential evolution with neighborhood search. In: Proceedings of the 2008 IEEE Congress on Evolutionary Computation (CEC 2008), Hong Kong, pp. 1110–1116 (2008)
37. Zhao, S.Z., Suganthan, P.N., Das, S.: Self-adaptive differential evolution with multi-trajectory search for large scale optimization. Soft Computing (accepted 2010)
38. Das, S., Abraham, A., Uday, K.C., Konar, A.: Differential evolution using a neighborhood-based mutation operator. IEEE Trans. on Evolutionary Computation 13(3), 526–553 (2009)
39. Zaharie, D.: Influence of crossover on the behavior of differential evolution algorithms. Applied Soft Computing 9(3), 1126–1138 (2009)

# Design of Robust Optimal Fixed Structure Controller Using Self Adaptive Differential Evolution

S. Miruna Joe Amali[1] and S. Baskar[2]

[1] Research Scholar, Thiagarajar College of Engineering, Madurai 625015, India
[2] Professor, Thiagarajar College of Engineering, Madurai 625015, India
smiruna@tce.edu, sbeee@tce.edu

**Abstract.** This paper presents a design of robust optimal fixed structure controller for systems with uncertainties and disturbance using Self Adaptive Differential Evolution (SaDE) algorithm. PID controller and second order polynomial structure are considered for fixed structure controller. The design problem is formulated as minimization of maximum value of real part of the poles subject to the robust stability criteria and load disturbance attenuation criteria. The performance of the proposed method is demonstrated with a test system. SaDE self adapts the trial vector generation strategy and crossover rate ($CR$) value during evolution. Self adaptive Penalty (SP) method is used for constraint handling. The results are compared with constrained PSO and mixed Deterministic/Randomized algorithms. It is shown experimentally that the SaDE adapts automatically to the best strategy and $CR$ value. Performance of the SaDE-based controller is superior to other methods in terms of success rate, robust stability, and disturbance attenuation.

**Keywords:** Control system synthesis, Fixed-order control, H∞ performance, robust control, structured synthesis, Self adaptive Differential Evolution.

## 1 Introduction

In practical control engineering, it is crucial to obtain reduced order /fixed structure controllers due to limitations of available computer resource and necessity of on-site controller tuning. Most of the real systems are vulnerable to external disturbances, measurement noise and model uncertainties. Robust controller designs are quite useful in dealing with systems under parameter perturbation, model uncertainties and uncertain disturbance [1]. There are two approaches dealing with robust optimal controller design problems. One is the structure-specified controller and the other is the output-feedback controller. The conventional output feedback design of optimal control are very complicated and not easily implemented for practical industrial applications as the order of the controller would not be lower than that of the plant. To overcome this difficulty, the structure-specified approach was used to solve the robust optimal control problem from suboptimal perspective [2].

For controllers with very special structure such as for proportional-integral-derivative (PID) or lead-lag compensators, various design methods are now available

B.K. Panigrahi et al. (Eds.): SEMCCO 2010, LNCS 6466, pp. 79–86, 2010.

for control engineers [3]. In particular, in the last few years various innovative techniques for designing controllers satisfying not only stability but also $H_\infty$ specifications have been proposed [4]. However, it will be difficult to extend these methods directly applicable to fixed-structure controller design problems, as they strongly depend on the specific structure.

As far as conventional $H_\infty$ controller design subject to fixed-order/fixed-structure is concerned, most approaches utilize linear matrix inequality (LMI) formulae. Apkarian, P., et al. [5], considered the design problem as optimization programs with a linear cost subject to LMI constraints along with nonlinear equality constraints representing a matrix inversion condition. Further, Saeki, M., [6] keep the controller variables directly in LMI to cope with the fixed-structure constraints. However, it will be difficult for any of these methods to treat both the controller structure and the multiple specifications simultaneously. More importantly application of these methods requires deep understanding of robust control theory.

Contrary to the deterministic approaches discussed above a probabilistic method based on randomized algorithms was proposed in [7]. In this method, a full order controller is randomly generated using a finite dimensional parameterization, and then model order reduction is utilized. Later Fujisaki, Y., et al. [8], proposed a mixed probabilistic/deterministic approach to aim at computational efficiency. These approaches can be utilized when we cannot obtain any solution within reasonable time by the existing deterministic approach. But these methods require thorough knowledge of both randomization and robust control theory. This justifies the search for new approaches to industrial controller design.

During past decades great attention has been paid to optimization methods for controller design. The controller design is formulated as a constrained optimization problem, more exactly as a highly non-linear minimization problem subject to a non-linear constraint for which no close solution can be obtained by conventional optimization techniques. Evolutionary algorithms (EAs) are global, parallel search techniques which emulate natural genetic operations. Because EAs simultaneously evaluate many points in the search space, it is more probable that it converges to an optimal solution.

Maruta, I., et al. [9] developed a constrained PSO algorithm to synthesis fixed structure robust controller by minimization of maximum value of real part of the poles subject to multiple H∞ specifications. Recently, Differential evolution (DE) [10] has been shown to be a simple yet efficient evolutionary algorithm for many optimization problems in real-world applications. Its performance, however, is still quite dependent on the setting of control parameters such as the mutation factor and the crossover probability and trial vector generation strategy.

Qin, A.K., et al. [11] proposed the Self adaptive Differential Evolution (SaDE) algorithm which adapts the trial vector generation strategy and the crossover probability as per the needs of the application avoiding the time consuming trial and error method. SaDE algorithm is applied to the design of fixed structure robust controller considering minimization of maximum value of real part of the poles subject to the robust stability criteria and load disturbance attenuation criteria.

## 2  Problem Description

Consider a control system with $n_i$ inputs and $n_o$ outputs, as shown below,

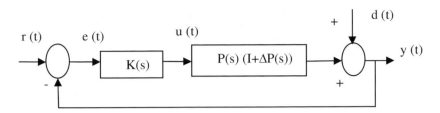

**Fig. 1.** Control System with plant perturbation and external disturbance

where $P(s)$ is the nominal plant, $\Delta P(s)$ is the plant perturbation, $K(s)$ is the controller, $r(t)$ is the reference input, $u(t)$ is the control input, $e(t)$ is the tracking error, $d(t)$ is the external disturbance, and $y(t)$ is the output of the system . Without loss of generality, the plant perturbation $\Delta P(s)$ is assumed to be bounded by a known stable function matrix $W_1(s)$.

$$\overline{\sigma}\left(\Delta P(j\omega)\right) \leq \overline{\sigma}\left(W_1(j\omega)\right), \quad \forall \omega \in [0,\alpha). \tag{1}$$

Where $\overline{\sigma}(A)$ denotes the maximum singular value of a matrix A.

If a controller $K(s)$ is designed such that the nominal closed loop system $\Delta P(s)=0$ and $dt=0$ is asymptotically stable, the robust stability performance satisfies the following inequality

$$f_1 = \left\| W_1(s) T(s) \right\|_\infty < 1. \tag{2}$$

and the disturbance attenuation performance satisfies the following inequality

$$f_2 = \left\| W_2(s) S(s) \right\|_\infty < 1. \tag{3}$$

Then the closed loop system is also asymptotically stable with $\Delta P(s)$ and $dt$ , where $W_2(s)$ is a stable weighting function matrix. $S(s)$ and $T(s)=I-S(s)$ are the sensitivity and complimentary sensitivity functions of the system, respectively

$$S(s)=\left(I+P(s)K(s)\right)^{-1}. \tag{4}$$

$$T(s)=P(s)K(s)\left(I+P(s)K(s)\right)^{-1}. \tag{5}$$

Robust stability and disturbance attenuation are often insufficient in the control system design for advancing the system performance. Therefore minimization of real part of the closed loop pole, minimization of balanced criteria, and minimization of closed loop norm are considered.

Let $\alpha_i$ denote the $i^{th}$ pole of the closed-loop system $T(s)$ and $\alpha_{max}$ be the pole, whose real part is greater than that of any other pole; i.e. $\text{Re}\left[\alpha_{max}\right] = \max_i \left(\text{Re}\,\alpha_i \; \forall_i\right)$ the minimization of $\text{Re}\left[\alpha_{max}\right]$ is also considered. In the proposed method, the objective function considered for the investigated problem of designing robust optimal controller is as given below,

$$\min J = \text{Re}\left[\alpha_{max}\right] . \tag{6}$$

## 3   SaDE Algorithm

Differential Evolution (DE) [10] is an efficient and powerful population-based stochastic search technique that has been used for global optimization in many real problems. But, the efficiency of DE crucially depends on choosing an appropriate trial vector generation strategy and their associated control parameter values. This is usually done by a trial-and-error scheme which requires high computational costs. The performance of the original DE algorithm is highly dependent on the strategies and parameter settings. Self-adaptation has been found to be highly beneficial for adjusting control parameters during evolutionary process, especially when done without any user interaction. In this paper we use SaDE algorithm [11] where four DE strategies and control parameter $CR$ are self-adapted.

The SaDE algorithm gives a promising path to self-adapt both the trial vector generation strategies and their associated control parameters according to their previous experiences of generating better solutions. The algorithm automatically adapts the learning strategies and the control parameter $CR$ during evolution.

### 3.1   Initialization

The initial population is initialized randomly and it should better cover the entire search space as much as possible by uniformly randomizing individuals within the search space constrained by the prescribed minimum and maximum parameter bounds.

### 3.2   Trial Vector Generation Strategy Adaptation

The mutation operator is applied to each individual or target vector $X_{i,G}$ at the generation $G$ to produce the mutant vector $V_{i,G}$. After the mutation phase, crossover operation is applied to each pair of the target vector $X_{i,G}$ and its corresponding mutant vector $V_{i,G}$ to generate a trial vector $U_{i,G}$. Instead of employing the computationally expensive trial-and-error search for the most suitable strategy and its associated parameter values, the SaDE algorithm maintains a strategy candidate pool, which includes four effective trial vector generation strategies with diverse characteristics [11]. For each individual in the current population, one strategy will be chosen according to a probability learnt from its previous experience of generating promising solutions and applied to perform the mutation operation. The strategy candidate pool consists of the following four strategies,

1) DE/rand/1/bin
2) DE/rand-to-best/2/bin
3) DE/rand/2/bin
4) DE/current-to-rand/1

The binomial-type crossover operator is utilized in the first three strategies. The crossover rate $CR$ will also be adapted along with the strategy. $j_{rand}$ is a randomly chosen integer in the range [1,D]. The binomial crossover operator copies the $j^{th}$ parameter of the mutant vector to the corresponding element in the trial vector $U_{i,G}$ if $rand_j[0,1) \leq CR$ or $j = j_{rand}$ .Otherwise, it is copied from the corresponding target vector $X_{i,G}$ . The probabilities of the strategies are updated only after an initial learning period (LP) generation which is set by the user. The probabilities are initialized to $\frac{1}{k}$, i.e., all strategies have the equal probability to be chosen. After the initial LP generations, the probabilities of choosing different strategies will be updated at each subsequent generation by,

$$ p_{k,G} = \frac{S'_{k,G}}{\sum_{k=1}^{K} S_{k,G}} . \tag{7} $$

Where, $S_{k,G} = \dfrac{\sum_{g=G-LP}^{G-1} ns_{k,g}}{\sum_{g=G-LP}^{G-1} ns_{k,g} + \sum_{g=G-LP}^{G-1} nf_{k,g}} + \varepsilon,$

$$ k = 1, 2, ......, K; \ G > LP . $$

$ns_{k,g}$ is the number of trial vectors successfully entering the next generation, generated by $k^{th}$ strategy, $nf_{k,g}$ is the number of trial vectors discarded while generated by $k^{th}$ strategy and $\varepsilon = 0.01$.

## 3.3 Parameter Adaptation

In the SaDE algorithm the population size *(NP)* is set by the user. The $F$ parameter is approximated by a normal distribution with mean value 0.5 and standard deviation 0.3. A set of values are randomly sampled from such normal distribution and applied to each target vector in the current population. $CR$ is normally distributed in a range with mean $CRm_k$ with respect to the $k^{th}$ strategy and standard deviation 0.1. Initially, $CRm_k$ is set at 0.5 for all the strategies. A set of $CR$ values conforming to the normal distribution $N(CRm_k, 0.1)$ are generated and applied to those target vectors to which the $k^{th}$ strategy is assigned. After the initial LP generations, the $CRm_k$ value is adapted with median of the successful $CR$ values (those $CR$ values that have generated trial vectors successfully entering the next generation) over the past LP generations for every subsequent generations. The control parameter $K$ in the strategy "DE/current-to-rand/1" is randomly generated within [0, 1] so as to eliminate one additional parameter. The Self adaptive Penalty method is employed for handling constraints [12].

## 4   Test System

In order to validate the performance of the proposed SaDE based robust fixed structure optimal controller, a simple SISO plant is considered. In order to show the effectiveness of the proposed method over mixed probabilistic/deterministic approach by [5], the example presented in their paper is considered. Consider the unity feedback system $\Sigma[x]$ consisting of

$$P(s) = \frac{17\left(1+s\right)\left(1+16s\right)\left(1-s+s^2\right)}{s\left(1-s\right)\left(90-s\right)\left(1+s+4s^2\right)} . \tag{8}$$

$$K(s) = \frac{\theta_0 + \alpha_0 s + \theta_2 s^2}{1 + \mu_0 s + \beta_2 s^2} . \tag{9}$$

To treat the robust $H_\infty$ disturbance attenuation problem, the weighting function is chosen as $W(s) = \frac{55\left(1+3s\right)}{1+800\,s}$. Let $x = (\theta_0, \alpha_0, \theta_2, \mu_0, \beta_2)^T$ denote the design parameter vector for the fixed order SISO plant controller. Its initial search space is taken as $x \in R^5$; $-5 \le x_i \le 5$, $i = 1,2,...,5$ based on the problem setting in [5]. Then our aim is to find an optimal controller which minimizes $\mathrm{Re}\left[\alpha_{max}\right]$ and the disturbance attenuation constraint given in (3). Also the pole placement condition of $\mathrm{Re}\,[\,\alpha_{max}\,(\,\Sigma\,[s;x]\,)\,] < -0.2$ should be satisfied.

For the SaDE algorithm, the population size is set as 300 and the generation count as 200. The algorithm was executed 40 times and feasible solutions were obtained in all the trials giving a 100% success rate. An increase in the $CRm$ values from the initial setting of 0.5 is observed. "DE/current-to-rand/1" performs better than the other strategies. The best controller obtained using SaDE algorithm and reported results using Constrained PSO and mixed deterministic/randomized method is given in Table 1. The corresponding pole location criterion is given in Table 2.

**Table 1.** Optimum controller for the Test System

| Method | Optimum Controller |
|---|---|
| Mixed Deterministic/Randomized Method | $K(s) = \dfrac{-0.532 - 0.5407\,s - 2.0868\;s^2}{1 - 0.3645 - 1.2592\;s^2} .$ |
| Constrained PSO | $K(s) = \dfrac{-0.5891 - 0.7339s - 2.5918s^2}{1 - 0.5578 - 1.555s^2} .$ |
| SaDE | $K(s) = \dfrac{-0.5854 - 0.7232\;s - 2.5793\;s^2}{1 - 0.5542\;s - 1.5516\;s^2} .$ |

**Table 2.** Comparison of performance for the Test System in terms of pole location

| Method | Re $\left[\alpha_{max}\right]$ |
|---|---|
| Mixed Deterministic/Randomized Method | -0.1132 |
| Constrained PSO | -0.5780 |
| SaDE | **-0.5905** |

## 5  Conclusion

This paper discusses application of SaDE algorithm for designing robust optimal fixed structure controllers for systems with uncertainties and disturbance. Minimization of maximum value of real part of the poles is considered as objective subject to the robust stability criteria and load disturbance attenuation constraints. The performance and validity of the proposed method are demonstrated with the SISO unity feedback system. For comparing the performance of the SaDE algorithm constrained PSO and mixed Deterministic/Randomized algorithm are considered. It is shown experimentally that the performance of the SaDE algorithm is better than the previous methods. In future, other improved DE algorithms [13, 14 15] will be used to solve this problem.

**Acknowledgments.** Authors thank UGC, New Delhi for financially supporting this work under the major project (38-248/2009(SR)) and Thiagarajar college of Engineering for providing necessary facilities for carrying this work. We also thank Dr. P. N. Suganthan, Associate Professor, School of Electrical and Electronics Engineering, Nanyang Technological University, Singapore, for providing support regarding the implementation of the SaDE algorithm.

## References

1. Doyle, J., Francis, B., Tennenbaum, A.: Feedback Control Theory. Macmillan Publishing co., Basingstoke (1990)
2. Ho, S.-J., Ho, S.-Y., Hung, M.-H., Shu, L.-S., Huang, H.-L.: Designing Structure-Specified Mixed $H_2/H\infty$ Optimal Controllers Using an Intelligent Genetic Algorithm IGA. IEEE Trans. Contr. Syst. Technol. 13(6), 1119–1124 (2005)
3. Astrom, K.J., Augglund, T.: PID Control-Theory, Design and Tuning, 2nd edn. Instrument Society of America, Research Triangle Park (1995)
4. Ho, M., Lin, C.: PID controller design for robust performance. IEEE Transactions on Automatic Control 48(8), 1404–1409 (2003)
5. Apkarian, P., Noll, D., Tuan, H.D.: Fixed-order $H_\infty$ control design via a partially augmented Lagrangian method. International Journal of Robust and Nonlinear control 13(12), 1137–1148 (2003)
6. Saeki, M.: Fixed structure PID controller design for standard $H_\infty$ control problem. Automatica 42(1), 93–100 (2006a)
7. Calafiore, G., Dabbene, F., Tempo, R.: Randomized algorithms for reduced order $H_\infty$ controller design. In: Proceedings of the American Control Conference, pp. 3837–3839 (2000)

8.  Fujisaki, Y., Oishi, Y., Tempo, R.: Mixed deterministic/randomized methods for fixed order controller design. IEEE Transactions on Automatic Control 53(9), 2033–2047 (2008)
9.  Maruta, I., Kim, T.H., Sugie, T.: Fixed-structure $H_\infty$ controller synthesis: A meta-heuristic approach using simple constrained particle swarm optimization. Automatica 45(2), 553–559 (2009)
10. Storn, R., Price, K.V.: Differential evolution-A simple and efficient heuristic for global optimization over continuous Spaces. J. Global Optim. 11, 341–359 (1997)
11. Qin, A.K., Huang, V.L., Suganthan, P.N.: Differential Evolution Algorithm With strategy Adaptation for Global Numerical Optimization. IEEE Trans. on Evolutionary Computation 13(2) (2009)
12. Tessema, B., Yen, G.G.: A self adaptive penalty function based algorithm for constrained optimization. In: IEEE Congress on Evolutionary Computation, pp. 246–253 (2006)
13. Das, S., Abraham, A., Chakraborty, U.K., Konar, A.: Differential evolution using a neighborhood based mutation operator. IEEE Transactions on Evolutionary Computation 13(3), 526–553 (2009)
14. Das, S., Suganthan, P.N.: Differential evolution – a survey of the state-of-the-art. IEEE Transactions on Evolutionary Computation, doi:10.1109/TEVC.2010.2059031
15. Mallipeddi, R., Suganthan, P.N., Pan, Q.K., Tasgetiren, M.F.: Differential evolution algorithm with ensemble of parameters and mutation strategies. Applied Soft Computing (in press), doi:DOI:10.1016/j.asoc.2010.04.024

# Electromagnetic Antenna Configuration Optimization Using Fitness Adaptive Differential Evolution

Aritra Chowdhury[1], Arnob Ghosh[1], Ritwik Giri[1], and Swagatam Das[1]

[1] Dept. of Electronics and Telecommunication Engg.
Jadavpur University, Kolkata 700 032, India
[2] Machine Intelligence Resarch Labs (MIR Labs) Global, USA
aritra131288@gmail.com, arnob008@gmail.com,
ritwikgiri@gmail.com, swagatandas19@yahoo.co.in

**Abstract.** In this article a novel numerical technique, called Fitness Adaptive Differential Evolution (FiADE) for optimizing certain pre-defined antenna configuration is represented. Differential Evolution (DE), inspired by the natural phenomenon of theory of evolution of life on earth, employs the similar computational steps as by any other Evolutionary Algorithm (EA). Scale Factor and Crossover Probability are two very important control parameter of DE since the former regulates the step size taken while mutating a population member in DE. This article describes a very competitive yet very simple form of adaptation technique for tuning the scale factor, on the run, without any user intervention. The adaptation strategy is based on the fitness function value of individuals in DE population. The feasibility, efficiency and effectiveness of the proposed algorithm for optimization of antenna problems are examined by a set of well-known antenna configurations.

**Keywords:** Optimization, directivity, Particle Swarm Optimization, Differential Evolution, Invasive Weed Optimization.

## 1 Introduction

Antenna design problems and applications always involve optimization processes that must be solved efficiently and effectively. To solve an antenna design problem, an engineer must envisage a proper view of the problem in his/her hand. So, the design is the struggle of the designer for finding a solution which best suits the sketched view. In support of this need, there have been various optimization techniques proposed by antenna designers. Among these, the so-called evolutionary algorithms (EAs) (e.g., genetic algorithms (GAs) [1], simulated annealing [2], particle-swarm optimizers [3]) have become widely used in electromagnetics [4]–[ 5] due to their simplicity, versatility, and robustness. However, these methods present certain drawbacks usually related to the intensive computational effort they demand  and the possibility of premature convergence.

To overcome these difficulties of the commonly used EAs, in this paper we use a variant, Fitness Adaptive Differential Evolution (FiADE) of another vastly used EA called Differential Evolution. The Differential Evolution (DE) [6,7] algorithm

B.K. Panigrahi et al. (Eds.): SEMCCO 2010, LNCS 6466, pp. 87–94, 2010.
© Springer-Verlag Berlin Heidelberg 2010

emerged as a very competitive form of evolutionary computing more than a decade ago.The performance of DE is severely dependent on two of its most important control parameters: The crossover rate ($Cr$) and scale factor ($F$) . Over the past decade many claims and counter-claims have been reported regarding the tuning and adaptation strategies of these control parameters. Some objective functions are very sensitive to the proper choice of the parameter settings in DE [8]. Therefore, researchers naturally started to consider some techniques to automatically find an optimal set of control parameters for DE [9-10]. Most recent trend in this direction is the use of self-adaptive strategies like the ones reported in [9] and [10]. However, self-adaptation schemes usually make the programming fairly complex and run the risk of increasing the number of function evaluations. This article suggests a novel automatic tuning method for the scale factor and crossover rate of population members in DE, based on their individual objective function values.

In this paper, the proposed algorithm and all it's competing algorithms have been used to optimize certain electromagnetic antenna configurations in a recently proposed [11] electromagnetic benchmark test-suite. The rest of the paper is organized as follows. Section 2 outlines the the proposed fitness based control parameter adaptation scheme of DE. Section 3 describes the two antenna configuration optimization problems and also establishes the expressions of the objective functions to be optimized by the evolutionary algorithms. Section 4 then reports the experimental results.

## 2   Classical Differential Evolution and It's fitness Based Adaption

Here we have used a novel fitness adaptive version of classical DE. For the details of classical DE  [6] and [7] can be referred.

### 2.1   Fitness Based Adaptive DE

In this article we aim at reducing $F$ when the objective function value of any vector nears the maximum objective function value found so far in the population. In this case the vector is expected to suffer lesser perturbation so that it may undergo a fine search within a small neighborhood of he suspected optima. Equations (1) and (2) show two different schemes for updating the value of $F$ for the $i'th$ target vector and these schemes have been used alternatively to determine the scale factor for each individual population member according to a certain criterion to be discussed next.

$$\text{Scheme 1:}\quad F_i = F_C * \left( \frac{\Delta f_i}{\lambda + \Delta f_i} \right), \tag{1}$$

Where, $\lambda = \varepsilon + \Delta f_i * K$   and $\Delta f_i = \left| f(\overset{n}{X_i}) - f(\overset{n}{X_{best}}) \right|$ & $F_C$ = a constant value within the range [0,1], $\varepsilon$ is a very small number tending to zero and $K$ (<1) is scaling factor. In this paper we have used $F_c$=0.8, $\varepsilon$ =0.001 and $K$=0.1.

$$\text{Scheme 2:}\quad F_i = F_C * \left(1 - e^{-\Delta f_i}\right) \tag{2}$$

Clearly, for both of scheme 1 & 2 as $\Delta f_i \to 0$, $F_i \to 0$ and as $\Delta f_i \to \infty$, $F_i \to F_C$. Thus (1) & (2) exhibits the scale factor adaptation criteria illustrated above. Figure 1 shows  the variation of $F$ with $\Delta f$ following both the schemes.. As can be seen from

Figure 1, the two plots intersect at approximately $\Delta f = 2.4$. The figure also implies that as long as $\Delta f > 2.4$ scheme 2 results greater values of $F$, which helps the vector to explore larger search volume. But as soon as $\Delta f$ falls below 2.4, scheme2 starts reducing $F$ drastically which decreases the explorative power of the vector, consequently resulting into premature termination of the algorithm. So, scheme 1 is used for scale factor adaptation in this region, thus minimizing the probability of premature termination.

Thus the adaptation of the scale factor for the $i$-th target vector takes place in the following way:

$if \ \Delta f_i > 2.4$,

$$F_i = F_C * \left(1 - e^{-\Delta f_i}\right),$$

$else \ \ F_i = F_C * \left(\frac{\Delta f_i}{\lambda + \Delta f_i}\right),$

Vectors that are distributed away from the current best vector in fitness-space have their $F$ values large (due to scheme 2) and keeps on exploring the fitness landscape thus maintaining adequate population diversity.

Similarly we adapt the values of crossover rate $Cr$ associated with each target vector. We know that, if $Cr$ is higher, then more genetic information will be passed to the trial vector from the donor vector, whereas if $Cr$ is lower then more genetic information will be transferred to the trial vector from the parent vector. So, we propose that, for maximization problems, as the objective function value of the donor vector gets higher, value of $Cr$ should be higher and vice-versa. As a measuring parameter of whether Cr should be increased for a donor vector, we define a variable $\Delta f_{donor\_i} = f(\overset{..}{X}_{best}) - f(\overset{..}{V}_i)$. Donor vectors having low positive values of $\Delta f_{donor\_i}$ are located close to the best particle obtained so far in the current population, hence their features are good enough to be transferred to the trial vector, hence for them $Cr$ should be higher. Similarly for donor vectors having high positive values of $\Delta f_{donor\_i}$ should have lower value of $Cr$. Now for donor vectors having objective function value higher than even the best particle of the current population i.e having negative $\Delta f_{donor\_i}$, $Cr$ should have very high value, so that most of it's features are transmitted in the trial vector. So, we conclude that, the scheme for determining the value of Cr for $i'th$ donor vector $\overset{..}{V}_i$ should be obtained as follows:

$if \ \ \Delta f_{donor\_i} < 0$
$Cr_i = Cr_{const;}$                                                                                    (3a)
$else$

$Cr_i = Cr_{min} + \dfrac{(Cr_{max} - Cr_{min})}{1 + \Delta f_{donor\_i}};$                                          (3b)

where, $Cr_{max} > Cr_{min}$ and $Cr_{const}$ has a high value all being in the range [0,1]. It can be easily verified that scheme outlined in eqn (3) exactly follows the $Cr$ adaptation criteria discussed above.

Now this adaptation scheme of $F$ and $Cr$ has been applied on the DE/best/1/bin algorithm and in what follows, we shall refer to this new variant of DE as FiADE (Fitness Adaptive Differential Evolution).

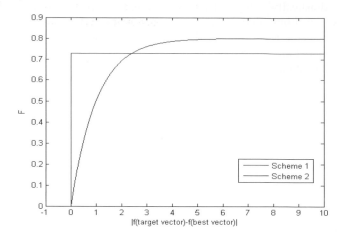

**Fig. 1.** Variation of F with $\Delta f$ varying in scale of 0 to 10 according to the schemes outlined in (1) & (2)

## 3   Electromagnetic Antenna Configuration Test-Suite Formulation

In this section two antenna configurations [11] are discussed in detail which have been used as a problem suite over which the proposed FiADE algorithm have been tested and compared with some other state-of-the-art metaheuristics.

### 3.1   Problem 1: Maximization of the Directivity of a Length Varying Dipole

The first problem is based on the maximization of the radiation characteristics of a finite-length thin wire dipole (Figure 2). As the length of the dipole increases, its radiation pattern becomes more directional, but when the length is greater than

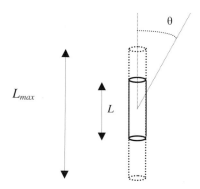

**Fig. 2.** Antenna configuration of Problem 1

approximately one wavelength, the directional properties are lost, due mainly to the grating lobes and increasing side lobe level. The ideal parameter measuring the directional properties of the dipole is it's directivity defined by (4).

$$D(\theta,\phi) = \frac{4\pi * U(\theta,\phi)}{P_{rad}}$$ (4)

Where,

$U(\theta,\phi)$=radiation intensity in the $(\theta,\phi)$ direction and $P_{rad}$ = total radiated power by the antenna

Again, $P_{rad} = \oiint_{\Omega} U(\theta,\phi)d\Omega = \int_{0}^{2\pi}\int_{0}^{\pi} U(\theta,\phi)\sin\theta d\theta d\phi$ (5)

Now, the radiation intensity $U(\theta,\phi)$ of a finite length dipole of length $l$, located at the origin of the three-dimensional co-ordinate system (considered for simplicity) and excited by a current of amplitude $I_0$ is given by (6) [ 12].

$$U(\theta,\phi) = \eta \frac{|I_0|^2}{8\pi^2}\left[\frac{\cos\left(\frac{kl}{2}\cos\theta\right) - \cos\left(\frac{kl}{2}\right)}{\sin\theta}\right]^2 \quad [k = \frac{2\pi}{\lambda} = \text{wave number}]$$

$$= B_0 F(\theta,\phi)$$ (6)

Where $B_0 = \eta\frac{|I_0|^2}{8\pi^2}$ & $F(\theta,\phi) = \left[\frac{\cos\left(\frac{kl}{2}\cos\theta\right) - \cos\left(\frac{kl}{2}\right)}{\sin\theta}\right]^2$

Therefore, $D(\theta,\phi) = \dfrac{4\pi * F(\theta,\phi)}{\int_{0}^{2\pi}\int_{0}^{\pi} F(\theta,\phi)\sin\theta d\theta d\phi}$ (7)

Hence (7) constructs the objective function of the FiADE algorithm for problem 1. Here $D(\theta,\phi)$ as defined by (12) is maximized by FiADE with respect to $l$ & $\theta$. Hence this problem is a 2-D unimodal optimization problem. The search space ranges for l and θ are [0.5λ ,3λ ] and $\left[0, \frac{\pi}{2}\right]$ respectively.

### 3.2   Problem 2: Maximization of the Directivity of a Uniform Linear Array of Half Wave Length Dipoles

The second problem proposed is based on the radiation characteristics of an array of 10 half-wavelength long dipoles contained in the XZ plane of the conventional three-dimensional coordinate system as shown in Fig 3. All the dipoles are fed at their centre with current distribution of same amplitude $I_0$ and zero progressive phase difference. Here also, the pertinent *"figure-of-merit"* of the directional property of the radiation pattern of the array is it's directivity as defined by (4). The following mathematical analysis establishes the expression of the radiation intensity $U(\theta,\phi)$ of the radiator array in Fig 3.

Since the array dipoles are identical, we can assume that the principle of *pattern multiplication* [12] is applicable here.

Now, the electric field component $E_\theta$ due to a single half-wavelength long dipole located at the origin is given by,

$$E_\theta = j\eta \frac{I_0 e^{-jkr}}{2\pi r} \left[ \frac{\cos\left(\frac{\pi}{2}\cos\theta\right)}{\sin\theta} \right] \qquad (8)$$

The *array factor AF* of the dipole array under consideration is given by [12],

$$(AF)_n = \frac{1}{N}\left[ \frac{\sin\left(\frac{N}{2}\Psi\right)}{\sin\left(\frac{1}{2}\Psi\right)} \right] \qquad (9)$$

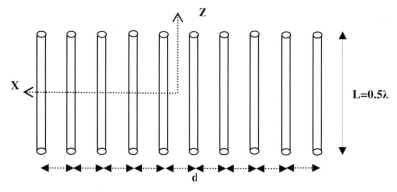

**Fig. 3.** Antenna Configuration of Problem 2

Where $\Psi = kd\cos\gamma + \beta$, $d$ being the separation and $\beta$ being the progressive phase difference between the successive array elements.

Therefore, the total electric field $E_{\theta t}$ according to principle of *pattern multiplication* is given by is given by , $E_{\theta t} = E_\theta * (AF)_n$

So, now the radiation intensity $U(\theta,\phi)$ is given by [12] ,

$$U(\theta,\phi) = \frac{\eta}{2}\frac{I_0^2}{4\pi^2}\left[ \frac{\cos\left(\frac{\pi}{2}\cos\theta\right)}{\sin\theta} \right]^2 \frac{1}{N^2}\left[ \frac{\sin\left(\frac{N}{2}\Psi\right)}{\sin\left(\frac{1}{2}\Psi\right)} \right]^2$$

$$= B_0 F(\theta,\phi) \qquad (10)$$

So, the directivity $D(\theta,\phi)$ is given by,   $D(\theta,\phi) = \dfrac{4\pi * F(\theta,\phi)}{\displaystyle\int_0^{2\pi}\int_0^{\pi} F(\theta,\phi)\sin\theta\, d\theta\, d\phi}$    (11)

Now for this particular problem directivity at $\theta = \dfrac{\pi}{2}$, $\phi = \dfrac{\pi}{2}$ direction is maximized.

Now (11) is modified by adding a randomly generated values from a normal distribution function of 0 mean and 0.2 variance . Then this modified function constructs the objective function of the FiADE algorithm for Benchmark problem 2. So, in this problem $D(\theta,\phi)$ with noise is maximized by FiADE by varying only $d$. Hence this problem is a 1-D noisy optimization problem . The search space range for $d$ is $[5\lambda,15\lambda]$ .

## 4  Experimental Set-Up and Results

In this section the results obtained by applying FiADE over the discussed two antenna configuration optimization problem and a comparison with other four state-of-the-art metaheuristics DE/rand/1/bin, DE/best/1/bin, PSO [13] & IWO [14]  have been reported.

### 4.1  Results

Table 1 shows the mean and standard deviation along with the best and worst fitness function value of 50 independent runs for each of the problem in the electromagnetic test-suite for each of the five algorithms. We have also performed a statistical test called *Wilcoxon's Rank Sum* test to check the statistical validity of the obtained results and have accordingly reported the corresponding P-values.Here N.A. denotes *Not Applicable*.

Among all the entries in Table 1, the best values are shown as bold-faced. From Table 1 it is clearly understood that the proposed algorithm FiADE has produced better results compared to all of it's competitors even in a statistically significant manner.  It clearly demonstrates the superiority of the proposed algorithm in solving the electromagnetic test suite problems.

**Table 1.** Mean and standard deviation along with the best and worst fitness function value tested on electromagnetic test-suite by different algorithms

| Algorithms | Problem 1 | | | | | | Problem 2 | | | | |
|---|---|---|---|---|---|---|---|---|---|---|---|
| | Best Fitness | Worst Fitness | Mean Fitness (std_dev) | $l$ | $\theta$ | P-value | Best Fitness | Worst Fitness | Mean Fitness (std_dev) | $d$ | P-value |
| FiADE | **3.2989** | **3.2956** | **3.2986 (0.0023)** | 2.5919 | 0.6135 | N.A. | **19.2035** | **19.0072** | **19.1942 (0.0007)** | 5.8705 | N.A. |
| DE/rand/1/bin | 3.2942 | 3.2659 | 3.2863 (0.0134) | 2.5554 | 0.5847 | 1.2120e-17 | 18.0250 | 17.5098 | 18.0028 (0.0081) | 14.5122 | 1.1417e-17 |
| DE/best/1/bin | 3.2941 | 3.2923 | 3.2937 (0.0059) | 2.5891 | 0.6013 | 2.7844e-17 | 19.1632 | 19.0039 | 19.1257 (0.0009) | 14.7016 | 2.9218e-12 |
| IWO | 3.2957 | 3.2943 | 3.2952 (0.0004) | 1.2681 | 1.5708 | 5.6428e-16 | 16.9751 | 15.3871 | 15.8760 (0.0123) | 5.9999 | 7.0661e-18 |
| PSO | 3.2926 | 3.2791 | 3.2845 (0.0038) | 1.2638 | 0.7357 | 7.0661e-18 | 17.9914 | 17.1875 | 17.7729 (0.0002) | 5.6089 | 7.0661e-18 |

## 5  Conclusions

Thus throughout this paper we have demonstrated how antenna configuration can be optimized to obtain the best possible directivity from it with the help of evolutionary algorithms. The proposed modification of DE  has also outperformed all of it's wisely chosen competing algorithms. So, the future research work will focus on more application of this algorithm in optimizing the antenna geometry configuration specially involving higher dimensional problems.

## References

[1] Goldberg, D.E.: Genetic Algorithms in Search, Optimization and Machine Learning. Addison-Wesley, Reading (1989)
[2] Kirkpatrick, S., Gellat Jr., C.D., Vecchi, M.P.: Optimization by simulated annealing. Science 220, 671–679 (1983)
[3] Kennedy, J., Eberhart, R.C.: Swarm Intelligence. Morgan Kauffman, San Francisco (2001)
[4] Rahmat-Samii, Y., Michielssen, E. (eds.): Electromagnetic Optimization by Genetic Algorithms. Wiley, New York (1999)
[5] Coleman, C., Rothwell, E., Ross, J.: Investigation of simulated annealing, ant-colony optimization, and genetic algorithms for self-structuring antennas. IEEE Trans. Antennas Propag. 52, 1007–1014 (2004)
[6] Storn, R., Price, K.: Differential evolution – A simple and efficient heuristic for global optimization over continuous spaces. Journal of Global Optimization 11(4), 341–359 (1997)
[7] Storn, R., Price, K.V.: Differential Evolution - a simple and efficient adaptive scheme for global optimization over continuous spaces, Technical Report TR-95-012,ICSI (1995), http://http.icsi.berkeley.edu/~storn/litera.html
[8] Liu, J., Lampinen, J.: On setting the control parameters of the differential evolution method. In: Matoušek, R., Ošmera, P. (eds.) Proc. of Mendel 2002, 8th International Conference on Soft Computing, pp. 11–18 (2002)
[9] Qin, A.K., Huang, V.L., Suganthan, P.N.: Differential evolution algorithm with strategy adaptation for global numerical optimization". IEEE Transactions on Evolutionary Computation 13(2), 398–417 (2009)
[10] Brest, J., Greiner, S., Bošković, B., Mernik, M., Žumer, V.: Self-adapting Control parameters in differential evolution: a comparative study on numerical benchmark problems. IEEE Transactions on Evolutionary Computation 10(6), 646–657 (2006)
[11] Pantoja, M.F., Bretones, A.R., Martin, R.G.: Benchmark Antenna Problems for Evolutionary Optimization Algorithms. IEEE Transaction on Antennas and Propagation 55(4), 1111–1121 (2007)
[12] Balanis, C.A.: Antenna Theory. Analysis and Design, 2nd edn. Wiley, New York (1997)
[13] Kennedy, J., Eberhart, R.: Particle Swarm Optimization. In: Proceedings of IEEE International Conference on Neural Networks, vol. IV, pp. 1942–1948 (1995)
[14] Mehrabian, A.R., Lucas, C.: A novel numerical optimization algorithm inspired from weed colonization. Ecological Informatics 1, 355–366 (2006)

# Analyzing the Explorative Power of Differential Evolution Variants on Different Classes of Problems

G. Jeyakumar[1] and C. Shanmugavelayutham[2]

[1,2] Assistant Professor
Department of Computer Science and Engineering
Amrita School of Engineering, Amrita Vishwa VidyaPeetham
Coimbatore, Tamil Nadu, India
g_jeyakumar@cb.amrita.edu,
cs_velayutham@cb.amrita.edu

**Abstract.** This paper is focusing on comparing the performance of Differential Evolution (DE) variants, in the light of analyzing their Explorative power on a set of benchmark function. We have chosen fourteen different variants of DE and fourteen benchmark functions grouped by feature: Unimodal Separable, Unimodal NonSeparable, Multimodal Separable and Multimodal NonSeparable. Fourteen variants of DE were implemented and tested on these fourteen functions for the dimension of 30. The explorative power of the variants is evaluated and analyzed by measuring the evolution of population variance, at each generation. This analysis provides insight about the competitiveness of DE variants in solving the problem at hand.

**Keywords:** Differential Evolution, Population Variance, Exploration, Diversity in Population, Convergence.

## 1 Introduction

Differential Evolution (DE), proposed by Storn and Price in 1995 [1], is a simple yet powerful evolutionary algorithm (EA) for global optimization in the continuous search domain [2]. The conceptual and algorithmic simplicity, high convergence characteristics and robustness of DE has made it an efficient and popular technique for real-valued parameter optimization [3,4]. By virtue of these characteristics, DE has shown superior performance in both widely used benchmark functions and real-world problems [5]. DE has some unique characteristics that make it different from other members of the EA family. The major difference are in the way the offspring (trial vectors) are generated and in the selection mechanism employed to transit to the next generation.

The remainder of the paper is organized as follows. In section 2, the review of DE algorithm is presented. Section 3 details the related works followed by the design of experiments in Section 4. Section 5 presents the results and Section 6 concludes the work.

B.K. Panigrahi et al. (Eds.): SEMCCO 2010, LNCS 6466, pp. 95–102, 2010.

## 2   DE Algorithm

DE algorithm aims at exploring the search space by sampling at multiple, randomly chosen NP D-dimensional parameter vectors (population of initial points). After population initialization an iterative process is started and at each iteration (generation) a new population is produced until a stopping criterion is satisfied. The general structure of DE algorithm is depicted in Figure 1.

```
Population Initialization
X(0) ← {x₁(0),...,x_NP(0)}
g ←0
Compute { f(x₁(g)),...,f(x_NP(g)) }
while the stopping condition is false do
  for i = 1 to NP do
    MutantVctor:yᵢ ← generatemutant(X(g))
    TrialVector:zᵢ←crossover(xᵢ(g),yᵢ)
    if f(zᵢ) < f(xᵢ(g)) then
        xᵢ(g+1) ← zᵢ
    else
        xᵢ(g+1) ← xᵢ(g)
    end if
  end for
  g ← g+1
  Compute{ f(x₁(g)),...,f(x_NP(g))}
  end while
```

**Fig. 1.** Description of DE algorithm

With seven commonly used mutation strategies and two crossover schemes, there are fourteen possible variants of DE viz. *rand/1/bin, rand/1/exp, best/1/bin, best/1/exp, rand/2/bin, rand/2/exp, best/2/bin, best/2/exp, current-to-rand/1/bin, current-to-rand/1/exp, current-to-best/1/bin, current-to-best/1/exp, rand-to-best/1/bin and rand-to-best/1/exp.*

Exploitation means the ability of an algorithm to use the information collected so far such that the search is oriented to the goal, while exploration is the process that allows introducing new information into the population. Rapid decreasing of the population diversity induces premature convergence and too slow decreasing (or even increasing) of population diversity induces a slow convergence. In many population-based algorithms the explorative power is influenced by the population diversity (a population consisting of almost identical elements has a low exploration power).

## 3   Related Work

Daniela Zaharie [6], provides theoretical insights on explorative power of Differential Evolutional algorithms, she describes an expression as a measure of the explorative power of population-based optimization methods. In her results, she analyzed the evolution of population variance for *rand/1/bin* variant for two test functions (Rastrigin and Ackley).

Daniela Zaharie [7], studied the relationship between the control parameters and the evolution of population variance of DE. It was shown that with proper selection of control parameters, the diversity in the population could be maintained.

Daniela Zaharie [8], analyzed the equilibrium between the exploration and exploitation in EAs, suggested that it could be achieved by controlling the population diversity, by parameter adaptation. Angela A.R.Sa et al., [9] proposed a modification to the standard mechanisms in DE algorithm in order to change the exploration Vs exploitation balance to improve its behavior. They suggested a modification to the selection scheme.

Hans-Georg Beyer [10], analyzed how the ES/EP-like algorithms perform the evolutionary search in the real-valued N-dimensional spaces. He described the search behavior as the antagonism of exploitation and exploration.

## 4   Design of Experiment

In our experiment, we investigated the explorative performance of fourteen variants on a set of benchmark functions, with high dimensionality and different features. We have chosen fourteen test functions [11, 12]. The details of the functions are: *f01* – Sphere Function, *f02* – Schwefel's Function 2.22, *f03* – Schwefel's Function 1.2, *f04* - Schwefel's Function 2.21, *f05* - Generalized Rosenbrock's Function, *f06* – Step Function, *f07* – Quartic Function with Noise, *f08* – Generalized Schwefel's Function 2.26, *f09* – Generalized Restrigin's Function, *f10* – Ackley's Function, *f11*- Generalized Griewank's Function, *f12&f13* – Generalized Penalized functions and *f14*-Bohachevsky Functions. We selected this set of functions because it is a well-known benchmark set in the literature to test EAs for global optimization. All the test functions have an optimum value of zero except of *f08*. In order to show the similar results, the description of *f08* was adjusted to have its optimum value at zero by just adding the optimal value 12569.5[12].

Classical DE has three control parameters: NP, F and CR. We fixed moderate population size (NP) of 60 in all our experiment. Based on [12, 13], we fixed a range for the mutation step size, F, as [0.3, 0.9], and it was generated anew at each generation. We use the same value for K as F. The crossover rate, CR, is tuned for each Variant-Function combination by conducting a bootstrap test with 11 different CR values {0.0, 0.1, 0.2, 0.3, 0.4, 0.5, 0.6, 0.7, 0.8, 0.9 and 1.0} and confidence interval of 95%.

As EA's are stochastic in nature, 100 independent runs were performed per variant per test function. For the sake of performance analysis among the variants, we present the mean objective function values (MOV) and average empirical population variance. Since, in DE algorithm the transformation are made independently for each component of the population elements, the empirical variance has been computed for all *n* components and for all the 100 independent runs i.e. we computed the variance at the component level of the population elements.

## 5   Results and Discussion

The simulation results for the unimodal separable functions: *f01, f02, f04, f06* and *f07*, and the unimodal nonseparable function *f03* are presented in Table 1. Table 2 displays the simulation results for the multimodal separable functions: *f08, f09* and *f14*, and for the multimodal non-separable functions *f05, f10, f11, f12* and *f13*.

Based on the overall results in Table 1 and 2, the most competitive variants were *rand-to-best/1/bin, best/2/bin* and *rand/1/bin*. And the worst performance was consistently displayed by *current-to-best/1/exp* and *current-to-rand/1/exp*. It is worth noting that binomial recombination showed a better performance over the exponential recombination.

**Table 1.** MOV Obtained for Unimodal functions

| Variant | f01 | f02 | f04 | f06 | f07 | f03 |
|---|---|---|---|---|---|---|
| rand/1/bin | 0.00 | 0.00 | 0.00 | 0.02 | 0.00 | 0.07 |
| rand/1/exp | 0.00 | 0.00 | 3.76 | 0.00 | 0.02 | 0.31 |
| best/1/bin | 457.25 | 0.14 | 1.96 | 437.25 | 0.09 | 13.27 |
| best/1/exp | 583.79 | 4.05 | 37.36 | 591.85 | 0.06 | 57.39 |
| rand/2/bin | 0.00 | 0.00 | 0.06 | 0.00 | 0.01 | 1.64 |
| rand/2/exp | 0.00 | 0.02 | 32.90 | 0.00 | 0.05 | 269.86 |
| best/2/bin | 0.00 | 0.00 | 0.00 | 0.07 | 0.00 | 0.00 |
| best/2/exp | 0.00 | 0.00 | 0.05 | 0.39 | 0.01 | 0.00 |
| current-to-rand/1/bin | 0.00 | 0.02 | 3.68 | 0.03 | 0.04 | 3210.36 |
| current-to-rand/1/exp | 24.29 | 44.22 | 57.52 | 43.07 | 0.27 | 3110.90 |
| current-to-best/1/bin | 0.00 | 0.02 | 3.71 | 0.00 | 0.04 | 3444.00 |
| current-to-best/1/exp | 24.37 | 45.04 | 56.67 | 41.95 | 0.26 | 2972.62 |
| rand-to-best/1/bin | 0.00 | 0.00 | 0.00 | 0.00 | 0.00 | 0.07 |
| rand-to-best/1/exp | 0.00 | 0.00 | 3.38 | 0.00 | 0.01 | 0.20 |

**Table 2.** MOV Obtained for Multimodal functions

| Variant | f08 | f09 | f14 | f05 | f10 | f11 | f12 | f13 |
|---|---|---|---|---|---|---|---|---|
| rand/1/bin | 0.13 | 0.00 | 0.00 | 21.99 | 0.09 | 0.00 | 0.00 | 0.00 |
| rand/1/exp | 0.10 | 47.93 | 0.00 | 25.48 | 0.09 | 0.05 | 0.00 | 0.00 |
| best/1/bin | 0.00 | 4.33 | 12.93 | 585899.88 | 3.58 | 3.72 | 15.78 | 973097.03 |
| best/1/exp | 0.01 | 50.74 | 32.18 | 64543.84 | 6.09 | 5.91 | 131448.66 | 154434.94 |
| rand/2/bin | 0.22 | 0.00 | 0.00 | 19.01 | 0.09 | 0.00 | 0.00 | 0.00 |
| rand/2/exp | 0.27 | 101.38 | 0.01 | 2741.32 | 0.01 | 0.21 | 0.00 | 0.01 |
| best/2/bin | 0.17 | 0.69 | 0.12 | 2.32 | 0.09 | 0.00 | 0.00 | 0.00 |
| best/2/exp | 0.08 | 80.63 | 2.53 | 1.12 | 0.83 | 0.03 | 0.14 | 0.00 |
| current-to-rand/1/bin | 0.14 | 37.75 | 0.00 | 52.81 | 0.01 | 0.00 | 0.00 | 0.00 |
| current-to-rand/1/exp | 0.12 | 235.14 | 18.35 | 199243.32 | 13.83 | 1.21 | 10.89 | 24.11 |
| current-to-best/1/bin | 0.19 | 37.04 | 0.00 | 56.91 | 0.01 | 0.00 | 0.00 | 0.00 |
| current-to-best/1/exp | 0.10 | 232.80 | 18.21 | 119685.68 | 13.69 | 1.21 | 10.37 | 23.04 |
| rand-to-best/1/bin | 0.22 | 0.00 | 0.00 | 17.37 | 0.09 | 0.00 | 0.00 | 0.00 |
| rand-to-best/1/exp | 0.12 | 48.09 | 0.00 | 24.54 | 0.09 | 0.05 | 0.00 | 0.00 |

Next in our experiment, the population variance is calculated for each variant-function combination, for each generation. This measure identifies exploration capability of the variants, in maintaining the population diversity. It is measured for each variant-function combination at each generation for 100 runs, the average value at each generation for 100 runs is calculated. The results for the variants *rand/1bin, best/1/bin, rand/2/bin, best/2/bin, rand-to-best/1/bin, rand/1/exp, rand/2/exp, best/2/exp and rand-to-best/1/exp* are presented in Table 3 for the functions *f05*. In general, it is noticed that the "bin" variants maintained the population diversity and they reached the global optimum, most of the "exp" variants are suffering with stagnation problem and the other worst performing variants are falling in premature convergence.

**Table 3.** Empirical Evolution of Population Variance measured for *f05*

| G | rand/1/ bin | best/1/ bin | rand/2/ bin | best/2/ bin | r-t-b/ 1/ bin | rand/1/ exp | rand/2/ exp | best/2/ exp | r-t-b/ 1/exp |
|---|---|---|---|---|---|---|---|---|---|
| 0 | 294.30 | 293.95 | 295.22 | 295.14 | 294.36 | 294.02 | 294.34 | 294.98 | 294.1 |
| 72 | 42.14 | 0.00 | 176.47 | 18.50 | 76.10 | 147.73 | 266.66 | 88.83 | 173.8 |
| 300 | 0.14 | 0.00 | 33.16 | 0.06 | 0.74 | 93.89 | 1075.20 | 7.53 | 363.7 |
| 502 | 0.00 | 0.00 | 3.36 | 0.01 | 0.02 | 109.66 | 4246.51 | 2.68 | 753.3 |
| 564 | 0.00 | 0.00 | 1.65 | 0.00 | 0.01 | 71.14 | 4690.43 | 2.10 | 701.6 |
| 592 | 0.00 | 0.00 | 1.28 | 0.00 | 0.00 | 104.58 | 5195.36 | 0.53 | 642.2 |
| 900 | 0.00 | 0.00 | 0.06 | 0.00 | 0.00 | 116.76 | 7168.32 | 0.03 | 173.5 |
| 1180 | 0.00 | 0.00 | 0.00 | 0.00 | 0.00 | 58.75 | 9214.48 | 0.01 | 4.81 |
| 1206 | 0.00 | 0.00 | 0.00 | 0.00 | 0.00 | 38.10 | 9499.41 | 0.01 | 5.14 |
| 1316 | 0.00 | 0.00 | 0.00 | 0.00 | 0.00 | 23.22 | 10836.24 | 0.00 | 0.95 |
| 1500 | 0.00 | 0.00 | 0.00 | 0.00 | 0.00 | 16.20 | 10378.97 | 0.01 | 0.15 |
| 1800 | 0.00 | 0.00 | 0.00 | 0.00 | 0.00 | 9.13 | 6144.02 | 0.00 | 0.04 |
| 2100 | 0.00 | 0.00 | 0.00 | 0.00 | 0.00 | 8.14 | 4369.85 | 0.00 | 0.01 |
| 2141 | 0.00 | 0.00 | 0.00 | 0.00 | 0.00 | 8.49 | 4438.36 | 0.00 | 0.00 |
| 2400 | 0.00 | 0.00 | 0.00 | 0.00 | 0.00 | 4.01 | 2935.45 | 0.00 | 0.00 |
| 2700 | 0.00 | 0.00 | 0.00 | 0.00 | 0.00 | 0.33 | 2352.16 | 0.00 | 0.00 |
| 2999 | 0.00 | 0.00 | 0.00 | 0.00 | 0.00 | 0.29 | 1645.25 | 0.00 | 0.00 |

We compared the performance of the variants at three different situations : best run - at which a variant provides least objective function value, best successful run - successful run with less number of function evaluations and worst run - at which the variant provides highest objective function value and/or taking more number of function evaluations.

Table 4 shows the performance of *rand/1/bin* and *best/1/bin* at their best run for *f05*. The result shows that the *rand/1/bin* maintains the population diversity and reaches the global optimum. *best/1/bin* gives rapid decrease in population diversity, and soon falling in local optimum, at the generation of 800 itself. Table 5 shows that performance of these variants at their best successful run, it shows they maintained the population diversity till they reach the global optimum.

**Table 4.** Evolution of population variance by *rand/1/bin* and *best/1/bin* in their best run, for *f05*

| | | DE/rand/1/bin | | | | | | DE/best/1/bin | | |
|---|---|---|---|---|---|---|---|---|---|---|
| Run | G | ObjValue | Mean | Stddev | Variance | Run | G | ObjValue | Mean | Stddev | Variance |
| 77 | 0 | 220828146 | 467552539.29 | 118880410.66 | 298.46 | 85 | 0 | 164735406.97 | 452016366.39 | 120419762.95 | 288.37 |
| 77 | 100 | 1038759.89 | 3331062.3 | 1019135.04 | 28.35 | 85 | 72 | 3399 | 3495.02 | 54.76 | 0 |
| 77 | 200 | 34613.23 | 74892.74 | 20094.11 | 4.04 | 85 | 100 | 2993.95 | 2996.83 | 1.54 | 0 |
| 77 | 300 | 1419.04 | 2192.18 | 397.06 | 0.47 | 85 | 200 | 2384.2 | 2384.72 | 0.4 | 0 |
| 77 | 400 | 343.37 | 394.53 | 28.32 | 0.15 | 85 | 300 | 2347.39 | 2347.46 | 0.03 | 0 |
| 77 | 500 | 181.63 | 216.17 | 14.03 | 0.05 | 85 | 400 | 2248.47 | 2248.52 | 0.03 | 0 |
| 77 | 600 | 105.51 | 118 | 5.41 | 0.02 | 85 | 500 | 2195.43 | 2197.84 | 1.15 | 0 |
| 77 | 677 | 83.71 | 88.58 | 1.95 | 0 | 85 | 600 | 2166.18 | 2166.18 | 0 | 0 |
| 77 | 800 | 74.61 | 75.03 | 0.18 | 0 | 85 | 700 | 2166.06 | 2166.07 | 0.01 | 0 |
| 77 | 1000 | 72.43 | 72.55 | 0.04 | 0 | 85 | 800 | 2037.24 | 2037.24 | 0 | 0 |
| 77 | 1500 | 68.93 | 69.02 | 0.04 | 0 | 85 | 1000 | 2037.24 | 2037.24 | 0 | 0 |
| 77 | 2000 | 2.32 | 2.99 | 0.3 | 0 | 85 | 1500 | 2037.24 | 2037.24 | 0 | 0 |
| 77 | 2416 | 0 | 0.01 | 0 | 0 | 85 | 2000 | 2037.24 | 2037.24 | 0 | 0 |
| 77 | 2750 | 0 | 0 | 0 | 0 | 85 | 2500 | 2037.24 | 2037.24 | 0 | 0 |

Performance in worst runs for *f05* and *f06* are presented in the Table 6 and Table 7, respectively. For both *f05* and *f06*, *best/1/bin* falls in premature convergence, *rand/1/bin* converges well. For *f06*, *rand/1/bin* reaches the optimum at the earliest.

**Table 5.** Population variance evolution by *rand/1/bin* and *best/1/bin* in best successful run for *f06*

| | | DE/rand/1/bin | | | | | | DE/best/1/bin | | | |
|---|---|---|---|---|---|---|---|---|---|---|---|
| Run | G | ObjValue | Mean | Stddev | Variance | Run | G | ObjValue | Mean | Stddev | Variance |
| 40 | 0 | 65183 | 99249.92 | 15013.5 | 3268.78 | 54 | 0 | 71086 | 94734.1 | 13535.91 | 3212.77 |
| 40 | 100 | 1924 | 3929.85 | 947.31 | 129.27 | 54 | 100 | 615 | 1231.15 | 488.71 | 37.17 |
| 40 | 200 | 62 | 109.57 | 22.44 | 3.53 | 54 | 200 | 6 | 12.53 | 4.24 | 0.36 |
| 40 | 296 | 0 | 5.32 | 1.91 | 0.19 | 54 | 224 | 0 | 4.37 | 1.78 | 0.15 |

**Table 6.** Evolution of population variance by *rand/1/bin* and *best/1/bin* in their worst run, for *f05*

| | | DE/rand/1/bin | | | | | | DE/best/1/bin | | | |
|---|---|---|---|---|---|---|---|---|---|---|---|
| Run | G | ObjValue | Mean | Stddev | Variance | Run | G | ObjValue | Mean | Stddev | Variance |
| 29 | 0 | 181144284.61 | 457672791.46 | 125086337.24 | 287.59 | 88 | 0 | 256740044.11 | 478817311.65 | 123838344.95 | 301.02 |
| 29 | 300 | 41035.48 | 44042.8 | 1332.01 | 0.61 | 88 | 51 | 5649634.18 | 5674033.2 | 11351.7 | 0 |
| 29 | 600 | 6407.75 | 6885.99 | 214.14 | 0.15 | 88 | 250 | 5190703.43 | 5191499.2 | 383.79 | 0 |
| 29 | 900 | 172.22 | 182.92 | 5.12 | 0.02 | 88 | 500 | 5171928.84 | 5173090.6 | 724.78 | 0 |
| 29 | 1200 | 105.76 | 106.84 | 0.39 | 0 | 88 | 900 | 4960999.16 | 4960999.21 | 0.02 | 0 |
| 29 | 1500 | 91.51 | 91.87 | 0.14 | 0 | 88 | 1200 | 4960560.05 | 4960560.05 | 0 | 0 |
| 29 | 1800 | 84.18 | 84.49 | 0.13 | 0 | 88 | 1500 | 4960560.05 | 4960560.05 | 0 | 0 |
| 29 | 2100 | 80.3 | 80.55 | 0.09 | 0 | 88 | 1800 | 4960560.05 | 4960560.05 | 0 | 0 |
| 29 | 2400 | 78.37 | 78.39 | 0.01 | 0 | 88 | 2000 | 4960560.05 | 4960560.05 | 0 | 0 |
| 29 | 2700 | 76.9 | 76.97 | 0.02 | 0 | 88 | 2500 | 4960560.05 | 4960560.05 | 0 | 0 |
| 29 | 2999 | 75.7 | 75.79 | 0.04 | 0 | 88 | 2999 | 4960560.05 | 4960560.05 | 0 | 0 |

The results suggest that the variant *rand/1/bin* is most competitive at all the three situations. *best/1/bin* behaves similar to *rand/1/bin* only in its best successful run(if any), otherwise suffering with premature convergence. This is due to the reason that the *best/1/bin* variant exploring the search space only in the region near to the best candidate of the population, this makes the variation operators to lose their power and the exploitation becomes dominant. Since selection operation usually decreases the population variance, the variant with too high convergence rate with poor search coverage, typically results in a premature convergence.

Next, we analyzed the convergence nature of the */*/*exp* variants, Table 8 shows the result for *f04*. It shows that even though these variants could maintain diversity in population and did not fall in any local optimum, they could not reach the global optimum, within the specified number of generations. This shows that the "exp" variants are slow in convergence due to the spread of population on uninteresting regions of the search space ie., exploration process becomes dominant, and this leads to stagnation in convergence.

**Table 7.** Evolution of population variance by *rand/1/bin* and *best/1/bin* in their worst run, for *f06*

| | | DE/rand/1/bin | | | | | | DE/best/1/bin | | | |
|---|---|---|---|---|---|---|---|---|---|---|---|
| Run | G | ObjValue | Mean | Stddev | Variance | Run | G | ObjValue | Mean | Stddev | Variance |
| 98 | 0 | 64382 | 102933.3 | 15742.62 | 3408.2 | 22 | 0 | 72697 | 95531.15 | 15164.99 | 3299.37 |
| 98 | 100 | 2944 | 5190.92 | 1366.67 | 172.5 | 22 | 100 | 3099 | 4060.53 | 707.61 | 55.43 |
| 98 | 200 | 134 | 256.08 | 47.62 | 8.5 | 22 | 200 | 2222 | 2236.38 | 10.27 | 0.86 |
| 98 | 300 | 6 | 11.63 | 2.63 | 0.41 | 22 | 300 | 2209 | 2209.22 | 0.42 | 0.04 |
| 98 | 346 | 0 | 2.4 | 1.24 | 0.11 | 22 | 338 | 2209 | 2209 | 0 | 0.01 |
| | | | | | | 22 | 388 | 2209 | 2209 | 0 | 0 |
| | | | | | | 22 | 650 | 2209 | 2209 | 0 | 0 |
| | | | | | | 22 | 1000 | 2209 | 2209 | 0 | 0 |
| | | | | | | 22 | 2000 | 2209 | 2209 | 0 | 0 |
| | | | | | | 22 | 2500 | 2209 | 2209 | 0 | 0 |
| | | | | | | 22 | 2999 | 2209 | 2209 | 0 | 0 |

**Table 8.** Results for "exp" variants

| | DE/rand/1/exp | | | | DE/rand/2exp | | | | DE/best/2/exp | | | | DE/rand-to-best/1/exp | | |
|---|---|---|---|---|---|---|---|---|---|---|---|---|---|---|---|
| G | ObjValue | Mean | Stddev | G | ObjValue | Mean | Stddev | G | ObjValue | Mean | Stddev | G | ObjValue | Mean | Stddev |
| 0 | 84.4 | 97.07 | 3.13 | 0 | 74.31 | 96.12 | 4.4 | 0 | 87.18 | 97.16 | 2.65 | 0 | 87.35 | 97.24 | 2.93 |
| 300 | 45.71 | 75.59 | 12.14 | 300 | 70.5 | 90.42 | 6.97 | 300 | 36.52 | 46.76 | 7.54 | 300 | 54.2 | 82.74 | 9.71 |
| 600 | 42.46 | 57.43 | 7.79 | 600 | 57.79 | 86.1 | 8.41 | 600 | 15.28 | 18.09 | 2.1 | 600 | 41.78 | 55.06 | 8.09 |
| 900 | 22.4 | 32.33 | 4.82 | 900 | 51.48 | 80.09 | 8.64 | 900 | 7.79 | 9.48 | 1.18 | 900 | 22.06 | 35.95 | 6.11 |
| 1200 | 17.56 | 22.88 | 2.59 | 1200 | 50.64 | 76.03 | 8.13 | 1200 | 3.1 | 3.62 | 0.52 | 1200 | 17.83 | 24.3 | 3.34 |
| 1500 | 12.22 | 16.69 | 2.2 | 1500 | 48.23 | 69.34 | 9.11 | 1500 | 1.32 | 1.61 | 0.21 | 1500 | 12.33 | 17.89 | 2.22 |
| 1800 | 8.96 | 13.06 | 1.61 | 1800 | 45.03 | 63.63 | 8.4 | 1800 | 0.78 | 0.87 | 0.07 | 1800 | 9.68 | 13.82 | 1.61 |
| 2100 | 5.65 | 8.32 | 1.33 | 2100 | 45.03 | 58.65 | 7.33 | 2100 | 0.5 | 0.56 | 0.04 | 2100 | 6.59 | 9.2 | 1.35 |
| 2400 | 4.05 | 5.71 | 0.69 | 2400 | 34.86 | 53.12 | 6.11 | 2400 | 0.29 | 0.34 | 0.03 | 2400 | 4.56 | 6.84 | 1.04 |
| 2700 | 2.65 | 3.98 | 0.59 | 2700 | 33.38 | 46.27 | 6.85 | 2724 | 0.18 | 0.2 | 0.02 | 2700 | 3.37 | 4.74 | 0.63 |
| 2999 | 2.03 | 2.71 | 0.32 | 2999 | 29.02 | 40.11 | 5.14 | 2999 | 0.13 | 0.13 | 0 | 2999 | 2.39 | 3.16 | 0.4 |

Based on the overall results in Tables 3 to 8, it is observed that the "exp" variants and "bin" variants generate different exploration patterns, because the binomial cross-over mutating arbitrary components and the exponential crossover mutating a sequence of components. In binomial recombination the parameter CR determines explicitly the probability for a component to be replaced with a mutated one. In the case of exponential crossover, CR is used to decide how many components will be mutated. Because of these differences, they have different mutation probabilities and different distributions of the number of the mutated components for the same value of CR.

# 6 Conclusion

An empirical comparison of 14 DE variants to solve global optimization problems is presented. The results identified, */*/bin variants are clearly much better than */*/exp variants. This behavior is seems to be due to the fact that the "exp" variants are falling in stagnation problem, but not the "bin" variants, and it is evident in our results. The identified most competitive variant were rand/1/bin, rand-to-best/1/bin, rand/2/bin and best/2/bin, and worst performing variants were current-to-rand/1/exp, current-to-best/1/exp and best/1/*. The convergence property of the variants is analyzed by measuring their explorative power through population variance, it is observed that best performing variants show good convergence speed and exploration power, others are suffering with premature convergence or stagnation.

# References

1. Storn, R., Price, K.: Differential Evolution – A Simple and Efficient Adaptive Scheme for Global Optimization over Continuous Spaces. Technical Report TR-95-012, ICSI (1995)
2. Storn, R., Price, K.: Differential Evolution – A Simple and Efficient Heuristic Strategy for Global Optimization and Continuous Spaces. Journal of Global Optimization 11, 341–359 (1997)
3. Price, K.V.: An Introduction to Differential Evolution. In: Corne, D., Dorigo, M., Glover, F. (eds.) New Ideas in Optimization, pp. 79–108. Mc Graw-Hill, UK (1999)
4. Price, K., Storn, R.M., Lampinen, J.A.: Differential Evolution: A practical Approach to Global Optimzation. Springer, Heidelberg (2005)

5. Vesterstrom, J., Thomsen, R.: A Comparative Study of Differential Evolution Particle Swarm Optimization and Evolutionary Algorithm on Numerical Benchmark Problems. In: Proceedings of the IEEE Congress on Evolutionary Computation (CEC 2004), vol. 3, pp. 1980–1987 (2004)
6. Zaharie, D.: On the Explorative Power of Differential Evolution Algorithms. In: 3rd Int. Workshop Symbolic and Numeric Algorithms of Scientific Computing SYNASC 2001, Romania (2001)
7. Zaharie, D.: Critical values for the control parameters of Differential Evolution algorithms. In: Proc. of the 8th International Conference of Soft Computing, pp. 62–67 (2002)
8. Zaharie, D.: Control of Population Diversity and Adaptation in Differential Evolution Algorithms. In: Matouek, R., Omera, P. (eds.) Proceedings of Mendel Ninth International Conference on Soft Computing, pp. 41–46 (2003)
9. Angela, A.R.S., Andrade, A.O., Soares, A.B.: Exploration vs Exploitation in Differential Evolution. Convention in Communication, Interaction and Social Intelligence, Scotland (2008)
10. Beyer, H.-G.: On the Explorative Power of ES/EP-like Algorithms. In: Porto, V.W., Waagen, D. (eds.) EP 1998. LNCS, vol. 1447, pp. 323–334. Springer, Heidelberg (1998)
11. Yao, H., Liu, Y., Lian, K.H., Lin, G.: Fast Evolutionary Algorithms. In: Rozenberg, G., Back, T., Eiben, A. (eds.) Advances in Evolutionary Computing Theory and Applications, pp. 45–94. Springer, New York (2003)
12. Mezura-Montes, E., Velazquez-Reyes, J., Coello Coello, A.C.: A Comparative Study on Differential Evolution Variants for Global Optimization. In: GECCO 2006 (2006)
13. Mezura-Montes, E.: Personal Communication (unpublished)

# A Self Adaptive Differential Evolution Algorithm for Global Optimization

Pravesh Kumar and Millie Pant

Indian Institute of Technology Roorkee, India
tomardpt@iitr.ernet.in, millifpt@iitr.ernet.in

**Abstract.** This paper presents a new Differential Evolution algorithm based on hybridization of adaptive control parameters and trigonometric mutation. First we propose a self adaptive DE named ADE where choice of control parameter F and Cr is not fixed at some constant value but is taken iteratively. The proposed algorithm is further modified by applying trigonometric mutation in it and the corresponding algorithm is named as ATDE. The performance of ATDE is evaluated on the set of 8 benchmark functions and the results are compared with the classical DE algorithm in terms of average fitness function value, number of function evaluations, convergence time and success rate. The numerical result shows the competence of the proposed algorithm.

**Keywords:** Differential evolution, Control parameters, Trigonometric mutation, Global optimization.

## 1 Introduction

Differential Evolution (DE) algorithm was proposed by Price and Storn in 1995 [1], [2]. It is a population based, direct-search algorithm used for optimisation in continuous domains. Its effectiveness and efficiency have been successfully demonstrated in many application fields such as pattern recognition, communication, mechanical engineering and so on[1] [3], [4]. DE outperforms many other optimization algorithms in terms of convergence speed and robustness over common benchmark problems and real world applications.

One of the major problem faced by the users while using a population based search technique like DE is the setting/ tuning of control parameters associated with it. This is a fairly a time consuming task but is also the most crucial task for the success of the algorithm. This trouble can be minimized by the application of self adaptive parameters. Some recent modification dealing with the development of adaptive/self adaptive control parameters are discussed in [5]–[12].

In this paper we introduce a new Differential Evolution algorithm with adaptive control parameters for Crossover (Cr) and amplitude factor (F). The proposed algorithm, initially named Adaptive DE or ADE is further modified by using trigonometric mutation in it and is called ATDE. Numerical results show that the proposed modifications in DE can provide a measure to tune the balance between the convergence rate and the robustness of the algorithm [14], [15].

B.K. Panigrahi et al. (Eds.): SEMCCO 2010, LNCS 6466, pp. 103–110, 2010.

The rest of the paper is organized as follows: The basic DE is given in Section 2. Section 3 discusses the proposed ADE and ATDE algorithms. In section 4 experimental settings are given. In section 5, numerical results are discussed; finally the paper concludes with section 6.

## 2   The Basic DE

Basic DE algorithm is a kind of evolutionary algorithm, which is used to optimize the minima of functions. In this paper the term basic DE refers to the DE/rand/1/bin scheme. DE starts with an initial population vector, which is randomly generated when no preliminary knowledge about the solution space is available. Let $X_{i, G}$, $i=1$, 2…., $NP$; are the solution vector, where $i$ denote the population and $G$ denote the generation to which the population belongs. For basic DE (DE/rand/1/bin), the mutation, crossover, and selection operators are defined as follows:

**Mutation:** For each target vector $X_{i, G}$ mutant vector $V_{i, G+1}$ is defined by:

$$V_{i, G+1} = X_{r1, G} + F (X_{r2, G} - X_{r3, G})$$

Where $r_1$, $r_2$, $r_3 \in 1, 2, …, NP$; are randomly chosen integers, distinct from each other and also different from the running index $i$. $F$ is a real and constant factor having value between [0, 2] and controls the amplification of differential variation $(X_{r2, G} - X_{r3, G})$.

**Crossover:** Crossover is introduced to increase the diversity of perturbed parameter vectors $V_{i,G+1} = \{V_{1,i,G+1}, V_{2,i,G+1} … V_{D,i,G+1}\}$.
Let $U_{i,G+1} = \{U_{1,i,G+1}, U_{2,i,G+1} … U_{D,i,G+1}\}$ be the trial vector then $U_{i,G}$ is defined as:

$$U_{j,i,G+1} = \begin{cases} V_{j,i,G+1} \ if \ rand_j \ (0,1) \leq Cr \ \forall \ j = k \\ X_{j,i,G} \qquad\qquad\qquad otherwise \end{cases}$$

Where $j = 1, 2, … D$ ($D$=dimension of problem), $rand_j \in [0, 1]$; $Cr$ is the crossover constant takes values in the range [0, 1] and $k \in 1, 2,..., D$; is the randomly chosen index.

**Selection:** It is an approach to decide which vector ($X_{i,G}$ or $U_{i,G+1}$) should be a member of next generation $G+1$. If vector $U_{i,G+1}$ yields a smaller cost function value than $X_{i,G}$ then $X_{i,G+1}$ is set to $U_{i,G+1}$; otherwise, the old value $X_{i,G}$ is retained.

## 3   Proposed Algorithm

In this Section, we describe the adaptive Differential Evolution algorithm using Trigonometric mutation (ATDE). First we developed a new differential evolution algorithm by taking control parameters in a new manner. We call this algorithm as Adaptive DE or ADE. After that we hybrid ADE with trigonometric DE (TDE) and propose a new algorithm named as ATDE. The structural difference between the proposed ATDE algorithm and the basic DE is the selection of control parameters $Cr$ and $F$ and then embedding trigonometric mutation in it.

Varying the values of control parameters in successive generations provides more randomness to the algorithm which in turn may help in improving the working of algorithm in terms of exploration and exploitation.

Although we need to fix the values for some parameters in the proposed ATDE algorithm, it can be called adaptive in the sense that in every generation the values of control parameters $F$ and $Cr$ change according to some simple rules which are defined as follows:

$$F_{G+1} = \begin{cases} F_l + rand_1\sqrt{rand_2^2 + rand_3^2} & if \ P_F < rand_4 \\ F_u & otherwise; \end{cases} \quad (1)$$

$$Cr_{G+1} = \begin{cases} Cr_l * rand_5 & if \ P_{Cr} < rand_6 \\ Cr_u & otherwise; \end{cases} \quad (2)$$

Here $rand_j, j \in \{1, 2, 3, 4, 5, 6\}$ are uniform random number between $[0, 1]$. $P_F$ and $P_{Cr}$ are the probabilities to adjust the factors $F$ and $Cr$ respectively. In the present study we have taken $P_F = P_{Cr} = 0.5$. Values of $F_l$ and $Cr_l$ are taken as 0.1 while $F_u$ and $Cr_l$ are taken as 0.5. To keep $F$ and $Cr$ within the range $[0.1, 0.5]$, we have used the following bounds:

$$F_{G+1} = \begin{cases} 2 * F_l - F_{G+1} & if \ F_{G+1} < F_l \\ 2 * F_u - F_{G+1} & if \ F_{G+1} > F_u \end{cases} \quad (3)$$

$$Cr_{G+1} = \begin{cases} 2 * Cr_l - Cr_{G+1} & if \ Cr_{G+1} < Cr_l \\ 2 * Cr_u - Cr_{G+1} & if \ Cr_{G+1} > Cr_u \end{cases} \quad (4)$$

$F_{G+1}$ and $Cr_{G+1}$ are obtained for each iteration. So, they influence the mutation, crossover, and selection operations of every new particle.

The mutation operation is performed according to the following formulation:

$$V_{i,G+1} = (X_{r1,G} + X_{r2,G} + X_{r3,G})/3 + (p_2 - p_1)(X_{r1,G} - X_{r2,G}) + (p_3 - p_2)(X_{r2,G} - X_{r3,G}) + (p_1 - p_3)(X_{r3,G} - X_{r1,G}) \quad (5)$$

where:

$$p_1 = |f(X_{r1,G})|/p.$$
$$p_2 = |f(X_{r2,G})|/p.$$
$$p_3 = |f(X_{r3,G})|/p.$$

and

$$p = |f(X_{r1,G})| + |f(X_{r2,G})| + |f(X_{r3,G})|.$$

### 3.1  Computational Steps of ATDE Algorithm

1. Initialize the population
2. Set the control parameters by equation (1) and (2).
3. Perform Mutation as follows:
   3.1 Perform trigonometric mutation with Equation (5) with a probability $P_t$, or
   3.2 Perform original mutation as used in DE (with a probability $1-P_t$).

4.  Crossover operation.
5.  Evaluate the population with the objective function.
6.  Perform Selection.
7.  Repeat from step 2 to 5.

## 4  Experimental Setting

We used DEVC++ to implement our algorithm and generated initial population by using inbuilt random number generator *rand ( ) function* available in DEV-C++. The population size is taken as $3*D$ for all the test problems, where '*D*' is dimension of function.

The control parameters, crossover rate and scaling factor $F$, for classical DE and TDE are both fixed at 0.5. Maximum number of iteration is fixed at 5000.

For TDE and ATDE we fixed "trigonometric mutation probability constant" $P_t$ at 0.01.

Overall acceleration rate AR, which is taken for the purpose of comparison is defined as:

$$AR = \left(1 - \frac{\sum_{i=0}^{i=\mu} NFE \ by \ one \ algorithm}{\sum_{i=0}^{i=\mu} NFE \ by \ another \ algorithm}\right) * 100$$

Where $\mu$ is number of function. In every case, a run was terminated when the best function value obtained is less than a threshold for the given function or when the maximum number of function evaluation (NFE=$10^6$) was reached.

## 5  Numerical Results

In this section we analyze the proposed ATDE algorithm by comparing it with basic DE and TDE. We also observe the performance of the proposed algorithm without using trigonometric mutation in it i.e. by just using adaptive control parameters in it i.e. for algorithm ADE.

Comparisons are done in terms of average fitness function value, average number of function evaluations and the average time in execution taken by every algorithm to solve a particular problem. In every case, a run was terminated When an accuracy of $10^{-04}$ i.e. $|f_{max} - f_{min}| < 10^{-4}$ was reached or when the maximum number of function evaluation (NFE=$10^6$) was reached.

Table-1 provides total number of function evaluation (NFE), percentage improvement in terms of NFE and average time taken for the execution of each algorithm for 8 benchmarks function. In Table-2 comparison of mean fitness values by each algorithm are listed. As it is clear from the Table 1 that in terms of NFE and time taken by ATDE is less than all other algorithm that shows ATDE give the better performance in comparison to all others algorithms.

For solving 8 problems the average NFE taken by ATDE are 311139 while NFE taken by DE, TDE and ADE are 603995, 512555, and 333130 respectively. This implies that acceleration rate for ATDE around DE is 48.4% while acceleration rate for

TDE and ADE around DE is only 15.13% and 44.8% respectively. The same performance can be observed from the average execution time. The total average execution time taken by ATDE is 7.2 second while for DE, TDE, and ADE it is 12.6, 10.6 and 7.8. This implies the acceleration rate of ATDE is 42.8% while acceleration rate of TDE and ADE are 15.8% and 38.09% respectively around DE.

Figure 1 -3 show convergence graphs and Figure 4 and Figure 5 present bar graphs for NFE and execution time by each algorithm.

**Table 1.** Average time and Average number of function evaluation (NFE) in 10 runs

| Fun | Dim | Average time (sec) | | | | NFE | | | |
|-----|-----|------|------|------|------|--------|--------|--------|--------|
| | | DE | TDE | ADE | ATDE | DE | TDE | ADE | ATDE |
| F1 | 30 | 2.3 | 1.9 | 1.6 | *1.5* | 85401 | 69849 | 58761 | *53973* |
| F2 | 30 | 1 | 0.9 | 0.7 | *0.7* | 54810 | 45486 | 37917 | *35640* |
| F3 | 30 | 2.5 | 1.9 | 1.7 | *1.5* | 72486 | 56727 | 47412 | *44469* |
| F4 | 30 | 0.6 | 0.5 | 0.5 | *0.4* | 36000 | 30456 | 25236 | *23670* |
| F5 | 15 | 1.9 | 1.8 | 0.4 | *0.3* | 159152 | 145571 | 30370 | *28566* |
| F6 | 30 | 0.7 | 0.6 | 0.5 | *0.5* | 80937 | 68409 | 54009 | *51012* |
| F7 | 30 | 0.9 | 0.7 | 0.6 | *0.6* | 47808 | 39411 | 33021 | *31032* |
| F8 | 30 | 2.7 | 2.3 | 1.8 | *1.7* | 67401 | 56646 | 46404 | *42777* |
| Total | | 12.6 | 10.6 | 7.8 | *7.2* | 603995 | 512555 | 333130 | *311139* |
| AR(%) | | | 15.8 | 38.09 | *42.8* | | 15.13 | 44.8 | *48.4* |

**Table 2.** Mean fitness of functions in 10 runs

| Fun | Dim | Mean Fitness | | | |
|-----|-----|------|------|------|------|
| | | DE | Trig DE | Adapt DE | Adapt Trig DE |
| F1 | 30 | 1.78948e-005 | *1.30994e-005* | 1.43686e-005 | 1.36096e-005 |
| F2 | 30 | 6.50938e-006 | 5.33965e-006 | 5.31857e-006 | *4.47427e-006* |
| F3 | 30 | 6.74221e-006 | 4.90212e-006 | 5.03811e-006 | *4.21794e-006* |
| F4 | 15 | -0.999994 | -0.999995 | -0.999995 | *-0.999995* |
| F5 | 15 | 3.6472e-006 | 3.37852e-006 | 3.15338e-006 | *2.82888e-006* |
| F6 | 30 | 1.61349e-005 | *1.0456e-005* | 1.21634e-005 | 1.09391e-005 |
| F7 | 30 | 5.79941e-006 | 5.22825e-006 | 5.07326e-006 | *4.48877e-006* |
| F8 | 30 | 6.99783e-006 | *4.69566e-006* | 5.05867e-006 | 4.82615e-006 |

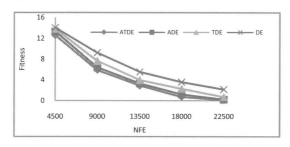

**Fig. 1.** Ackley Function (F1)

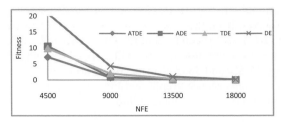

**Fig. 2.** Sphere Function (F6)

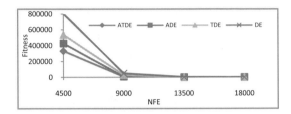

**Fig. 3.** Zakharov Function (F8)

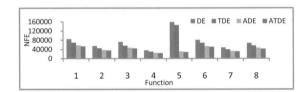

**Fig. 4.** NFE taken by DE, TDE, ADE, and ATDE for 8 benchmark problems

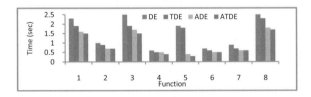

**Fig. 5.** Execution time taken by DE, TDE, ADE, and ATDE for 8 benchmark problems

## 6  Conclusions

In the present study we proposed a modified DE framework called ATDE having adaptive control parameters for F and Cr and using trigonometric mutation adaptively. The numerical results show that the proposed modifications help in improving the performance of DE in terms of convergence rate without compromising with the quality of solution. The DE variant having the adaptive control parameters (ADE) is 44% faster while ATDE is 48% faster than the basic DE on the problems considered in the present study. These algorithms are also better than TDE which is only 15% faster than the basic DE. The present work can be extended in several directions. We can modify it for an adaptive population size to make it fully adaptive in nature. Also it can be extended for constrained and real life optimization problems.

# References

1. Storn, R., Price, K.: Differential evolution—A simple and efficient adaptive scheme for global optimization over continuous spaces. Berkeley, CA, Tech. Rep., TR-95-012 (1995)
2. Storn, R., Price, K.: Differential Evolution - A Simple and Efficient Heuristic for Global Optimization over Continuous Spaces. Journal of Global Optimization 11, 341–359 (1997)
3. Price, K.: An introduction to DE. In: Corne, D., Marco, D., Glover, F. (eds.) New Ideas in Optimization, pp. 78–108. McGraw-Hill, London (1999)
4. Storn, R., Price, K.: Minimizing the real function of the ICEC 1996 contest by DE. In: IEEE International Conference on Evolutionary Computation, Nagoya, pp. 842–844 (1996)
5. Storn, R., Price, K.: DE-a simple evolution strategy for fast optimization. Dr. Dobb's Journal, 18–24 and 78 (April 1997)
6. Thangaraj, R., Pant, M., Abraham, A.: A Simple Adaptive Differential Evolution Algorithm. In: IEEE World Congress on Nature and Biologically Inspired Computing & 8th International Conference on Computer Information Systems and Industrial Management Applications (2009)
7. Das, S., Konar, A., Chakraborty, U.K.: Two improved differential evolution schemes for faster global search. In: ACMSIGEVO Proceedings of GECCO, Washington D.C., pp. 991–998 (2005)
8. Teo, J.: Exploring Dynamic Self-adaptive Populations in Differential Evolution. Soft Computing - A Fusion of Foundations, Methodologies and Applications 10(8), 673–686 (2006)
9. Brest, J., Boskovic, B., Greiner, S., Zumer, V., Maucec, M.S.: Performance Comparison of Self-Adaptive and Adaptive Differential Evolution Algorithms. Technical Report #2006-1-LABRAJ, University of Maribor, Faculty of Electrical Engineering and Computer Science, Slovenia. (2006), http://marcel.unimbsi/janez/brest-TR1.html
10. Brest, J., Greiner, S., Boskovic, B., Mernik, M., Zumer, V.: Self- Adapting Control Parameters in Differential Evolution; A Comparative Study on Numerical Benchmark Problems. IEEE Transactions on Evolutionary Computation 10(6), 646–657 (2006)
11. Ali, M.M.: Differential Evolution with Preferential Crossover. European Journal of Operational Research 181, 1137–1147 (2007)
12. Yang, Z., Tang, K., Yao, X.: Self-adaptive Differential Evolution with Neighborhood Search. In: Proc. IEEE Congress on Evolutionary Computation, Hong Kong, pp. 1110–1116 (2008)
13. Qin, A.K., Huang, V.L., Suganthan, P.N.: Differential Evolution Algorithm with Strategy Adaptation for Global Numerical Optimization. IEEE Transactions on Evolutionary Computations 13(2), 398–417 (2009)
14. Fan, H., Lampinen, J.: A Trigonometric Mutation Operation to Differential Evolution. Journal of Global Optimization 27, 105–112 (2003)
15. Pant, M., Ali, M., Abraham, A.: Mixed Mutation Strategy Embedded Differential Evolution. In: Proc. IEEE XI$^{th}$ Conference on Congress on Evolutionary Computation, pp. 1240–1246 (2009)

# Appendix

1. Ackley Function:

$$F_1 = -20 * \exp\left(-0.2\sqrt{1/n \sum_{i=0}^{n} x_i^2}\right) - \exp\left(\sqrt{1/n \sum_{i=0}^{n} \cos(2\pi x_i)}\right) + 20 + e;$$

With $-32 \leq xi \leq 32$ and min F1 $(0, 0..., 0) = 0$.

2. Axis Parallel hyper-ellipsoid: $F_2 = \sum_{i=1}^{n} i x_i^2$;   With $-5.12 \leq x_i \leq 5.12$, min $F_2$ $(0, 0..., 0) = 0$.

3. Griewenk Function: $F_3 = \frac{1}{4000} \sum_{i=0}^{n} x_i^2 - \prod_{i=1}^{n} \cos\left(\frac{x_i}{\sqrt{i}}\right) + 1$; With $-600 \leq x_i \leq 600$ and min $F_3$ $(0, 0..., 0) = 0$.

4. Exponential Function: $F_4 = \exp(-0.5 \sum_{i=1}^{n} x_i^2)$; With $-1 \leq x_i \leq 1$ and min $F_4$ $(0, 0..., 0) = -1$.

5. Restrigin's Function: $F_5 = 10n + \sum_{i=1}^{n} (x_i^2 - 10\cos(2\pi x_i))$; With $-5.12 \leq x_i \leq 5.12$ and min $F_5$ $(0, 0..., 0) = 0$.

6. Schawefel Function: $F_6 = \sum_{i=1}^{n} |x_i| + \prod_{i=1}^{n} |x_i|$; With $-10 \leq x_i \leq 10$ and min $F_6$ $(0, 0..., 0) = 0$.

7. Sphere Function: $F_7 = \sum_{i=1}^{n} x_i^2$; With $-5.12 \leq x_i \leq 5.12$ and min $F_7 (0, 0... 0) = 0$.

8. Zakharov Function: $F_8 = \sum_{i=1}^{n} x_i^2 + \left(\sum_{i=1}^{n} 0.5 i x_i^2\right)^4$; With $-5 \leq x_i \leq 10$ and min $F_8$ $(0, 0..., 0) = 0$.

# Optimization for Workspace Volume of 3R Robot Manipulator Using Modified Differential Evolution

Bibhuti Bhusan Biswal[1], Sumanta Panda[2], and Debadutta Mishra[2]

[1] National Institute of Technology,Rourkela, 769008, Orissa, India
[2] Veer Surendra Sai University of Technology, Burla, 768018,Orissa, India
Bibhuti Bhusan Biswal, bibhuti.biswal@gmail.com,
Sumanta Panda,sumanta.panda@gmail.com,
Debadutta Mishra,dmvssut@gmail.com

**Abstract.** Robotic manipulators with three-revolute (3R) family of positional configurations are very common in the industrial robots (IRs). The manipulator capability of a robot largely depends on the workspace (WS) of the manipulator apart from other parameters. With the constraints in mind, the optimization of the workspace is of prime importance in designing the manipulator. The workspace of manipulator is formulated as a constrained optimization problem with workspace volume as objective function. It is observed that the previous literature is confined to use of conventional soft computing algorithms only, while a new search modified algorithm is conceptualized and proposed here to improve the computational time. The proposed algorithm gives a good set of geometric parameters of manipulator within the applied constrained limits. The availability of such an algorithm for optimizing the workspace is important, especially for highly constrained environments. The efficiency of the proposed approach to optimize the workspace of 3R manipulators is exhibited through two cases.

**Keywords:** Industrial robot; Manipulators; Workspace; Constraints.

## 1 Introduction

The manipulator workspace is defined as the region of reachable points by a reference point H on the extremity of a manipulator chain,Gupta and Roth [1]. Generally speaking, a robot manipulator structure can be subdivided into a regional structure and orientation structure. The regional structure consists of the arm, which moves the end-effectors to a desired position in the workspace of the robot manipulator. The orientation structure comprised of the links that, rotates the end effectors to the desired orientation in the workspace. In this study, the regional structure of the robot manipulators is examined rather than the orientation structure. The workspace volume should be computed with high accuracy as it influences the manipulator's dimensional design, its positioning in the work environment, and its dexterity to execute tasks. In this approach the design of manipulators with three-revolute joints (3R) is reformulated as an optimization problem that takes into account the characteristics of the workspace. This research proposes an algebraic formulation to estimate the cross section area, and workspace volume.

B.K. Panigrahi et al. (Eds.): SEMCCO 2010, LNCS 6466, pp. 111–118, 2010.

Several investigators have focused on the properties of the workspace of open chain robotics with the purpose of emphasizing its geometric and kinematic characteristics. Ceccarelli [3] presented an algebraic formulation to determine the workspace of revolution manipulators. The formulation is a function of the dimensional parameters in the manipulator chain and specifically of the last revolute joint angle, only through mathematical model of workspace developed by Ceccarelli [3] is of crucial importance, however the manipulators optimal design is not considered. Lanni et al. [4] investigated and solved the design of manipulators modeled as an optimization problem that takes into account the characteristics of the workspace. Wenger [5] demonstrated that it is possible to consider a manipulator's execution of nonsingular changing posture motions in the design stage. Ceccarelli and Lanni [6] presented a suitable formulation for the workspace that can be used in the design of manipulators, which was formulated as a multi-objective optimization problem using the workspace volume and robot dimensions as objective functions. Bergamaschi et al.[7] presented the condition for the regularity and parameterization of the envelop, penalties are imposed to minimize the voids and control the total area. The present work aims at developing a novel search methodology based on differential evolutionary algorithm, where the initialization and selection stages are modified to optimize the workspace volume. Finally the workspace volume for diverse cases obtained by the proposed algorithm are reported and the results are compared in terms of computational time with the results of Bergamaschi et al. [2] to show the superiority of the  proposed algorithm over the conventional differential evolutionary algorithm.

## 2   Formulation for Workspace Volume

One of the most commonly used methods to geometrically describe a general open chain 3R manipulator with three-revolute joints is the one which uses the Hartenberg and Denavit (H–D) notation, whose scheme is exhibited in Fig. 1 and the transformation matrix is as given in Eq.(1). The design parameters for the link size are represented as $a_1, a_2, a_3, d_2,$ $d_3, a_1, a_2$ ($d_1$ is not meaningful, since it shifts the workspace up and down).

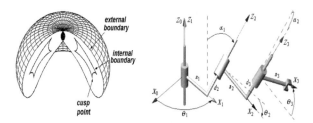

**Fig. 1.** The workspace for 3 revolute manipulators and design parameters. [Bergamaschi et al.(2008)]

Here, $1$and reference $0$ have the same origin, the transformation matrices of a reference on the former are:

$$T_{i-1}^{i} = Rot(\alpha_{i-1,}X_{i-1})Trans(a_{i-1,}0,0)Trans(0,0,d_i)Rot(\theta_{i,}Z_i)$$

$$= \begin{pmatrix} C\theta_i & -S\theta_i & 0 & a_{i-1} \\ S\theta_iC\alpha_{i-1} & C\theta_iC\alpha_{i-1} & S\alpha_{i-1} & d_iS\alpha_{i-1} \\ -S\theta_iS\alpha_{i-1} & C\theta_iC\alpha_{i-1} & C\alpha_{i-1} & d_iC\alpha_{i-1} \\ 0 & 0 & 0 & 1 \end{pmatrix} \tag{1}$$

where, $a_0 = \alpha_0 = 0$, $d_1 = 0$, $C\alpha_{i-1} = cos\alpha_{i-1}$, $S\alpha_{i-1} = sin\alpha_{i-1}$, $C\theta_i = cos\ \theta_i$, and $S\theta_i = sin\ \theta_i$, for $i = 1, 2, 3$.

According to Gupta and Roth [1], the workspace $W(H)$ of a point $H$ of the end-effectors of a manipulator is the set of all points which H occupies as the joint variables are varied throughout their entire ranges. Point H is usually chosen as the center of the end-effectors, or the tip of a finger, or even the end of the manipulator itself. The position of this point with respect to reference $X_3Y_3Z_3$ can be represented by the vector

$$H_3 = \begin{bmatrix} a_3 & 0 & 0 & 1 \end{bmatrix}^T \tag{2}$$

where $H_3$ denotes the point $H$ in the reference $X_3Y_3Z_3$, the superscripts $T$ means transposed vector and $a_3$ is the distance from the end-effector to the last joint. The workspace of a three-revolute open chain manipulator can be given in the form of the radial reach $r$ and axial reach $z$ with respect to the base frame, according to Ceccarelli and Lani [6]. The axial $z$ and radial $r$ coordinates of the boundary points are given as the solution for the system Eq.(3), assuming that $sin\alpha_1 \neq 0$, $C \neq 0$, and $E \neq 0$. After some algebraic manipulation we can see that

$$\left. \begin{array}{l} z = [-FG \pm (-E^2Q)^{1/2}]/C(E^2+G^2) - D/C \\ r = \{[(Cz+D)G+F]/(E+A-z^2)\}^{1/2} \end{array} \right\} \quad \text{where, } Q = B\ (E^2+G^2) + F^2 \tag{3}$$

Eq.(3) that represents an envelope is a only function of the parameter $\theta_3$. This research proposes numerical formulation to approximate the cross-sectional area, through its discretization within a rectangular mesh. Initially, the extreme values of vectors r and z should be obtained as

$$r_{min} = min(r); \ r_{max} = max(r); \ z_{min} = min(z); \ z_{max} = max(z); \tag{4}$$

$$\Delta r = (r_{max} - r_{min})/n_r \ and \ \Delta z = (z_{max} - z_{min})/n_z \tag{5}$$

The $n_r$ and $n_z$ values must be adopted so that the sizes of the elementary areas ($\Delta$r or $\Delta$z) are at least 1% of the total distances considered in the discretization ($r_{max} - r_{min}$ or $z_{max} - z_{min}$). Given a certain point $(r, z)$, its position inside the discretization mesh is determined through the following index control:

$$i = int\{(r-r_{min})/\Delta r\} + 1 \ and \ j = int\{(z-z_{min})/\Delta z\} + 1 \tag{6}$$

where $i$ and $j$ are computed as integer numbers. The points that belongs to the workspace is identified by $P_{ij} = 1$, otherwise $P_{ij} = 0$, which means:

$$P_{ij} = \begin{cases} P_{ij} = 1, if, P_{ij} \in W(H) \\ P_{ij} = 0, if, P_{ij} \notin W(H) \end{cases} \tag{7}$$

where $W(H)$ indicates workspace region. In this way, the total area is obtained by the sum of every elementary area of the mesh that are totally or partially contained in the cross section. In Eq. (7), it is observed that only the points that belong to the workspace contribute to the calculation of the area:

$$A_{r,z} = \sum_{i=1}^{i_{max}} \sum_{j=1}^{j_{max}} (P_{ij} \Delta r \Delta z) \tag{8}$$

The coordinates of the center of the mass is calculated considering the sum of the center of the mass of each elementary area, divided by the total area, using the following equation:

$$r_g = \frac{\sum\limits_{i=1}^{i_{max}} \sum\limits_{j=1}^{j_{max}} (p_{ij} \Delta r \Delta z)((i-1)\Delta r + \dfrac{\Delta r}{2} + r_{min})}{A_T} \tag{9}$$

Finally, after the calculation of the cross sectional area and the coordinates of the center of the mass, given by Eqs. (8) and (9), the workspace volume of the manipulator can be evaluated as presented by Beer and Johnston [9] is formulated as

$$V = 2\pi r_g A_T \tag{10}$$

The different limiting constraints are as follows

$$\left. \begin{array}{l} 0.01 < a_i < a_i^u \ for \ i = 1, 2, 3, \ldots \ldots \\[2mm] 0.01 < d_i < d_i^u \ for \ j = 1, 2, 3, \ldots \ldots \\[2mm] 0.05^0 < \alpha_k < 90^0 \ for \ k = 2, 3 \ldots \ldots \end{array} \right\} \tag{11}$$

The regularity and inequality constraints are given as follows:

$$g_1 = \frac{\partial^2 f}{\partial \theta^2} \neq 0 \quad (12); \qquad g_2 = z > 0 \quad (13); \qquad g_3 = r < 0.7 * L_{max} \quad (14)$$

where

$$L_{max} = \sqrt{(a_1^u)^2 + (d_1^u)^2} + \sqrt{(a_2^u)^2 + (d_2^u)^2} + a_3^u \tag{15}$$

The values $a_i^u$ and $d_i^u$ are the maximum values that the respective parameters $a_i$ and $d_j$ can assume during the optimization process, for $i = 1, 2, 3$ and $j = 2, 3$. In this technique, the problems with constraints are transformed into unconstrained problems by adding a penalty function $p(x)$ to the original objective function to limit constraint violations. This new objective function is called as pseudo-objective function. The pseudo-objective function is given by the form:

$$\phi(x) = F_c(x) + r_p * p(x) \qquad r_p \text{ is the penalty factor} \qquad (16)$$

$$p(x) = [\sum_{i=1}^{m} \{\max[0, g_i(x)]\}^2 + \sum_{i=1}^{p} [h_i(x)]^2] \qquad (17)$$

where $F_c(x)$ is the original objective function given in Eq. (16), $P(x)$ is an imposed penalty function given by Eq. (17), $g_i$ are the inequality constraints, $h_i$ are the equality constraints. The scalar $r_p$ is a multiplier that quantifies the magnitude of the penalty.

# 3 Proposed Algorithm

Evolutionary Algorithms (EAs) are optimization techniques based on the concept of a population of individuals that evolve and improve their fitness through probabilistic operators like recombination and mutation. The field of evolutionary computation has experienced significant growth in the optimization area. There are ten different mutation strategies used in DE. Price and Storn [10] gave the working principle of DE with ten strategies. A strategy that works out to be the best for a given problem may not work well when applied for a different problem. Evolutionary algorithms have been successfully applied to optimization problems within robotic systems area and to the optimization of manipulator workspace problem in particular [2]. In [2], the authors have not taken into considerations the limiting constraints of link size, only the regularity and inequality constraints are considered during the initialization and mutation stage. The DE algorithm is modified so as to expedite the optimization. The modifications are discussed below. The proposed algorithm uses the mean zero and standard deviation one normal distribution for initializing the population and 50% of the better individuals are selected from the parents for mutation.

The details of the proposed algorithm is discussed below:

**Step 1.** Initialize the population using normal distribution with mean zero and standard deviation one.
**Step 2.** For all particles evaluate the objective function. Choose the better 50% individuals (the fitness higher individuals) to attend population evaluation.
**Step 3.** While stopping criterion is not satisfied
Do;   **Step 3.1.** Mutation; For all particles
Generate a mutated vector $V_{i,g}$ corresponding to the target vector $X_{i,g}$ using various strategies.   End for
**Step 3.2.** Crossover // Generate trial vector $U_{i,g}$
For all particle ;   Select j $_{rand}$ ∈ { $1,....D$} ; For j=1 to $D$
If (rand(0,1) ≤ CR or j =j $_{rand}$) ;   Then $U_{i,g} = V_{i,g}$ ; Else  $U_{i,g} = X_{i,g}$
End if;   End for;   End for; Step **3.3.** Selection
For all particles Better 50% individuals were selected from the offspring and parents.
End for;   **Step 3.4.** Go to next generation; **Step 4.** End while

## 4  Simulations and Results

The optimization problem is investigated using the proposed DE algorithm. The algorithm code was developed in MATLAB by the authors. The results of the final parameters, final volume and time of execution which are the best value obtained after 20 trials for each mutation strategies are represented. The optimal radial cross section for each case is as illustrated. In this case NP= 30 and $i_{max}$ =100 is assumed. The cost function, given by Eq. (24) was optimized by the algorithm in each run. The penalty factor of Eq. (16) is assumed as $r_p = 100$. The cross over probability CR= 0.8 and mutation step size F= 0.4.

Case-1: Optimization problem given by Eq. (10), Considering $a_i^u = d_i^u < 1.0$ Eq.(11) and the regularity constraint Eq. (12). The radial cross section is as shown in Fig.2. The simulation results shown in table-1 reveal that the proposed algorithm with DE/rand/1/bin strategy gives best workspace volume and less computational time. The standard deviation is less for this strategy as compared to other. The radial cross section is as shown in Fig. 2. The workspace volume obtained is117.02 unit of volume (u.v.) and computational time is 55.44 min. The neighborhood and skip search algorithm gives less computational time i.e. faster convergence.

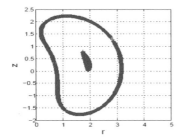    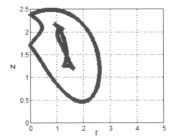

**Fig. 2.** Optimal radial section for Case-1    **Fig. 3.** Optimal radial  section for Case-3

**Table 1.** Result obtained for case-1,best value after 20 trials

| DE Strategy | Optimum DH Parameters | | | | | | | Volume [u.v.] | Time (min) | S/D |
|---|---|---|---|---|---|---|---|---|---|---|
| | $a_1$ [u.m] | $a_2$ [u.m] | $a_3$ [u.m] | $d_2$ [u.m] | $d_3$ [u.m] | $\alpha_1$ (deg.) | $\alpha_2$ (deg.) | | | |
| DE/best/1/exp | 0.92 | 0.90 | 0.96 | 0.59 | 0.95 | 74.92 | 45.24 | 114.90 | 60.22 | 65.73 |
| DE/rand/1/exp | 0.91 | 0.95 | 0.93 | 0.47 | 0.92 | 75.35 | 48.56 | 116.65 | 56.24 | 80.60 |
| DE/rand-to-best/1/exp | 0.97 | 0.97 | 0.92 | 0.51 | 0.98 | 73.96 | 47.74 | 115.45 | 60.11 | 87.95 |
| DE/best/2//exp | 0.96 | 0.92 | 0.95 | 0.55 | 0.97 | 77.86 | 49.65 | 115.98 | 58.65 | 74.44 |
| DE/rand/2//exp | 0.95 | 0.95 | 0.92 | 0.59 | 0.95 | 73.76 | 44.15 | 115.43 | 57.90 | 84.32 |
| DE/best/1/bin | 0.91 | 0.92 | 0.97 | 0.58 | 0.95 | 73.56 | 47.55 | 116.65 | 58.21 | 70.21 |
| **DE/rand/1/bin** | **0.93** | **0.97** | **0.92** | **0.56** | **0.93** | **76.45** | **46.46** | **117.02** | **55.44** | **61.23** |
| DE/rand-to-best/1/bin | 0.95 | 0.92 | 0.92 | 0.47 | 0.94 | 71.49 | 41.57 | 116.23 | 56.98 | 78.32 |
| DE/best/2//bin | 0.92 | 0.93 | 0.95 | 0.45 | 0.92 | 72.31 | 42.54 | 114.78 | 58.21 | 89.65 |
| DE/rand/2/bin | 0.97 | 0.94 | 0.95 | 0.44 | 0.94 | 71.45 | 44.67 | 116.57 | 58.98 | 93.11 |

Case-2: Optimization problem given by Eq. (10). Considering, $a_i^u = d_i^u \leq 1.0$, the regularity constraint Eq.(12), $z > 0$ and $r < 0.7 \ L_{max} = 0.7 \ x \ (2 \ \sqrt{2} + 1) \approx 2.68.$ . The simulation results are shown in table-2. The radial cross section is presented in Fig.3. The workspace volume obtained is 44.25 unit of volume (u.v.) and computational time is 65.89 min. This shows that even though the problem is highly constrained the neighborhood and skip search algorithm gives less computational time i.e. faster convergence.

**Table 2.** Results obtained for case 2, best value after 20 trials

| DE Strategy | Optimum DH Parameters | | | | | | | Volume [u.v.] | Time (min) | S/D |
|---|---|---|---|---|---|---|---|---|---|---|
| | $a_1$ [u.m] | $a_2$ [u.m] | $a3$ [u.m] | $d2$ [u.m] | $d3$ [u.m] | $\alpha1$ (deg.) | $\alpha2$ (deg.) | | | |
| DE/best/1/exp | 0.44 | 0.87 | 0.94 | 0.93 | 0.95 | 22.09 | 42.51 | 41.21 | 68.45 | 84.25 |
| DE/rand/1/exp | 0.43 | 0.92 | 0.95 | 0.95 | 0.87 | 22.31 | 47.81 | 42.26 | 66.94 | 93.81 |
| DE/rand-to-best/1/exp | 0.41 | 0.96 | 0.92 | 0.94 | 0.96 | 16.32 | 63.65 | 43.71 | 66.79 | 96.92 |
| DE/best/2/exp | 0.55 | 0.93 | 0.98 | 0.89 | 0.96 | 11.92 | 42.24 | 39.27 | 70.73 | 72.53 |
| DE/rand/2/exp | 0.49 | 0.87 | 0.96 | 0.95 | 0.86 | 15.16 | 43.21 | 36.33 | 68.97 | 88.21 |
| DE/best/1/bin | 0.56 | 0.93 | 0.93 | 0.92 | 0.99 | 11.32 | 46.81 | 42.43 | 66.72 | 75.85 |
| **DE/rand/1/bin** | **0.52** | **0.85** | **0.97** | **0.92** | **0.98** | **14.21** | **46.23** | **44.25** | **65.89** | **64.10** |
| DE/rand-to-best/1/bin | 0.46 | 0.92 | 0.93 | 0.94 | 0. 90 | 11.21 | 60.28 | 43.88 | 68.20 | 81.92 |
| DE/best/2/bin | 0.51 | 0.94 | 0.86 | 0.97 | 0.88 | 12.32 | 52.35 | 41.66 | 67.35 | 96.45 |
| DE/rand/2/bin | 0.39 | 0.99 | 0.93 | 0.99 | 0.83 | 15.45 | 61.24 | 42.76 | 66.39 | 52.82 |

**Table 3.** Comparisions of Results

| Bergamaschi et al. (2008) Case-1 | | | | | | | | | | | |
|---|---|---|---|---|---|---|---|---|---|---|---|
| Algorithm | a1 [u.m] | a2 [u.m] | a3 [u.m] | d2 [u.m] | d3 [u.m] | $\alpha1$ (deg.) | $\alpha2$ (deg.) | Volume [u.v.] | Time [Min] | % increase volume w.r.t.DE | % Improvement in time |
| SQP | 1.00 | 0.97 | 1.00 | 0.49 | 1.00 | 84.45 | 52.41 | 101.55 | 8.80 | - | - |
| GA | 1.00 | 1.00 | 1.00 | 0.48 | 1.00 | 86.50 | 56.09 | 105.28 | 87.24 | - | - |
| DE | 1.00 | 1.00 | 1.00 | 0.45 | 1.00 | 83.73 | 57.17 | 105.23 | 57.84 | - | - |
| PSO | 1.00 | 1.00 | 1.00 | 0.50 | 1.00 | 89.58 | 57.48 | 104.81 | 104.0 | - | - |
| **Proposed** | **0.93** | **0.97** | **0.92** | **0.56** | **0.93** | **76.45** | **46.46** | **117.02** | **55.44** | **11.20** | **4.14** |
| Bergamaschi et al. (2008) Case-2 | | | | | | | | | | | |
| Algorithm | a1 [u.m] | a2 [u.m] | a3 [u.m] | d2 [u.m] | d3 [u.m] | $\alpha1$ (deg.) | $\alpha2$ (deg.) | Volume [u.v.] | Time [Min] | % increase volume w.r.t.DE | % Improvemet in time |
| SQP | 0.48 | 0.88 | 1.00 | 1.00 | 0.98 | 16.91 | 65.80 | 39.64 | 3.86 | - | - |
| GA | 0.82 | 0.60 | 0.84 | 1.00 | 1.00 | 26.59 | 61.12 | 37.27 | 170.8 | - | - |
| DE | 0.46 | 0.96 | 1.00 | 1.00 | 1.00 | 16.45 | 66.11 | 39.27 | 66.72 | - | - |
| PSO | 0.44 | 0.91 | 0.99 | 1.00 | 1.00 | 17.70 | 63.69 | 39.29 | 76.30 | - | - |
| **Proposed** | **0.52** | **0.85** | **0.97** | **0.92** | **0.98** | **14.21** | **46.23** | **44.25** | **65.89** | **12.68** | **1.24** |

## 5  Conclusions

Diverse cases are presented imposing different constraints to demonstrate the efficiency of the proposed algorithm. It may be noted that the optimum workspace volume depends mainly on angles $\alpha_1$ and $\alpha_2$. Our empirical studies with the diverse cases show that DE/rand/1/bin strategy is more effective as compared to other strategies. Table-3 shows that the workspace volume in case-1 and that in case-2 is increased by 11.20%,    and 12.68%, where as the computational time are decreased by 4.14%, and 1.24% respectively. It is further realized that even in case of highly constrained problem as in case-2, the computational time is not very high though the workspace volume is less as compared to other cases. These results as shown in Table-3 encourage researchers in this particular area to develop hybrid techniques which will further reduce the computational time for this problem.

# References

[1] Gupta, K.C., Roth, B.: Design considerations for manipulator workspace. Journal of Mechanical Design 104, 704–711 (1982)
[2] Bergamaschi, P.R., Nogueira, A.C., Saramago, S.F.P.: Design and optimization of 3R manipulators using the workspace features. Applied Mathematics and Computation 172(1), 439–463 (2006)
[3] Ceccarelli, M.: A formulation for the workspace boundary of general Nrevolute manipulators. Mechanism and Machine Theory 31(5), 637–646 (1996)
[4] Lanni, C., Saramago, S.F.P., Ceccarelli, M.: Optimal design of 3R manipulators using classical techniques and simulated annealing. Revista Brasileira de Ciências Mecânicas 24(4), 293–301 (2002)
[5] Wenger: Some guidelines for the kinematic design of new manipulators. Mechanism and Machine Theory 35, 437–449 (2000)
[6] Ceccarelli, M., Lanni, C.: A multi-objective optimum design of general 3R manipulators for prescribed workspace limits. Mechanism and Machine Theory 39, 119–132 (2004)
[7] Bergamaschi, P.R., Nogueira, A.C., Saramago, S.F.P.: Design and optimization of 3R manipulators using the workspace features. Applied Mathematics and Computation 172(1), 439–463 (2006)
[8] Beer, F.P., Johnston Jr., E.R.: Vector Mechanics for Engineers: Statics and Dynamics, 3rd edn. Mc Graw Hill, New York (1977)
[9] Price, K., Storn, R.: Differential Evolution – A simple evolution strategy for fast optimization. Bob's Journal 22(4), 18–24 (1997)

# Adaptive Differential Evolution with *p*-Best Crossover for Continuous Global Optimization

Sk Minhazul Islam, Saurav Ghosh, Subhrajit Roy, and Swagatam Das

Dept. of Electronics and Telecommunication Engg.,
Jadavpur University, Kolkata 700 032, India
skminha.isl@gmail.com, saurav_online@yahoo.in,
roy.subhrajit20@gmail.com, swagatamdas19@yahoo.co.in

**Abstract.** Differential Evolution (DE) is arguably one of the most powerful stochastic real parameter optimization algorithms in current use. DE operates through the similar computational steps as employed by a standard Evolutionary Algorithm (EA). However, unlike the traditional EAs, the DE-variants perturb the current-generation population members with the scaled differences of randomly selected and distinct population members. Therefore, no separate probability distribution has to be used, which makes the scheme self-organizing in this respect. Its performance, however, is still quite dependent on the setting of control parameters such as the mutation factor and the crossover probability according to both experimental studies and theoretical analyses. Our aim is to design a DE algorithm with control parameters such as the scale factor and the crossover constants adapting themselves to different problem landscapes avoiding any user intervention. Further to improve the convergence performance an innovative crossover mechanism is proposed here.

**Keywords:** Differential Evolution, Numerical Optimization, Parameter Adaptation, *p*-best Crossover.

## 1 Introduction

Scientists and engineers from all disciplines often have to deal with the classical problem of global optimization where the main target is to determine a set of model parameters or state-variables that provide the globally minimum or maximum value of a predefined cost or objective function, or a set of optimal tradeoff values in the case of two or more conflicting objectives. In this article we consider bound-constrained single-objective optimization problems that involve $D$ decision variables represented in a vector like $\vec{X} = [x_1, x_2, x_3, ..., x_D]^T$ and a scalar objective function (or fitness function) to judge the quality of the solution that we have achieved. Locating the global optimal solutions becomes very challenging for single-objective problems arising in many practical situations, due to the presence of high dimensionality, strong epitasis, ill-conditioning, and multimodality of the objective function. Differential Evolution [1]-[5],[8] has emerged as a very competitive optimizer for continuous search spaces, exhibiting remarkable performances in several competitions held under the IEEE Congress on Evolutionary Computation (CEC). A detail survey of the DE

B.K. Panigrahi et al. (Eds.): SEMCCO 2010, LNCS 6466, pp. 119–128, 2010.
© Springer-Verlag Berlin Heidelberg 2010

family of algorithms can be found in [25].In this paper we propose a simple yet very powerful adaptive DE variant depicted as ADEpBX which implements a modified version of the mutation scheme "DE/target-to-best/1/bin" along with an innovative type of crossover scheme named as *p*-best crossover. The detailed description of the algorithm is discussed in section 3.

## 2   Classical DE

DE is a simple real-coded evolutionary algorithm. In this section we describe the basic operations of DE and introduce necessary notations and terminologies which facilitate the explanation of our adaptive DE algorithm later.

### 2.1   Initialization of the Parameter Vectors

DE searches for a global optimum point in a $D$-dimensional continuous hyperspace. It begins with a randomly initiated population of $Np$ (population number) $D$ dimensional real-valued parameter vectors. Each vector, also known as *genome/chromosome*, forms a candidate solution to the multi-dimensional optimization problem. We shall denote subsequent generations in DE by $G = 0,1...,G_{\max}$.Here we adopt the following notation for representing the $i$-th vector of the population at the current generation:

$$\vec{X}_{i,G} = [x_{1,i,G}, x_{2,i,G}, x_{3,i,G},......, x_{D,i,G}].\tag{1}$$

For each parameter of the problem, there may be a certain range within which the value of the parameter should lie for better search results. The initial population (at $G = 0$) should cover the entire search space as much as possible by uniformly randomizing individuals within the search space constrained by the prescribed minimum and maximum bounds:

$$\vec{X}_{\min} = \{x_{1,\min}, x_{2,\min},...., x_{D,\min}\} \text{ and } \vec{X}_{\max} = \{x_{1,\max}, x_{2,\max},...., x_{D,\max}\}.$$

Hence we may initialize the $j$-th component of the $i$-th vector as:

$$x_{j,i,0} = x_{j,\min} + rand_{i,j}(0,1) \cdot (x_{j,\max} - x_{j,\min})\tag{2}$$

Here rand is a uniformly distributed random number lying between 0 and 1 (actually $0 \le rand_{i,j}(0,1) < 1$) and is instantiated independently for each component of the $i$-th vector.

### 2.2   Mutation with Difference Vectors

After initialization, DE creates a *donor* vector $\vec{V}_{i,G}$ corresponding to each population member or target vector $\vec{X}_{i,G}$ in the current generation through mutation. It is the method of creating this donor vector, which differentiates between the various DE schemes. The following are the two most frequent mutation strategies used in the literature:

1)"DE/rand/1"

$$\vec{V}_{i,G} = \vec{X}_{r_1^i,G} + F \cdot (\vec{X}_{r_2^i,G} - \vec{X}_{r_3^i,G}) \qquad (3)$$

2) "DE/target-to-best/1"

$$\vec{V}_{i,G} = \vec{X}_{i,G} + F \cdot (\vec{X}_{best,G} - \vec{X}_{i,G}) + F \cdot (\vec{X}_{r_1^i,G} - \vec{X}_{r_2^i,G}) \qquad (4)$$

The indices $r_1^i, r_2^i, r_3^i, r_4^i$, and $r_5^i$ are distinct integers uniformly chosen from the set $\{1, 2, \ldots, Np\}/\{i\}$. These indices are randomly generated once for each donor vector. The scaling factor $F$ is a positive control parameter for scaling the difference vectors. $\vec{X}_{best,G}$ is the best individual vector with the best fitness (i.e. lowest objective function value for minimization problem) in the population at generation $G$.

## 2.3 Crossover

To enhance the potential diversity of the population, a crossover operation comes into play after generating the donor vector through mutation. The donor vector exchanges its components with the target vector $\vec{X}_{i,G}$ under this operation to form the *trial* vector $\vec{U}_{i,G} = [u_{1,i,G}, u_{2,i,G}, u_{3,i,G}, \ldots, u_{D,i,G}]$. The scheme may be outlined as.

$$u_{j,i,G} = \begin{cases} v_{j,i,G}, & \text{if } (rand_{i,j}(0,1) \le Cr \text{ or } j = j_{rand} \\ x_{j,i,G}, & \text{otherwise}, \end{cases} \qquad (5)$$

Here, $rand_{i,j}(0,1)$ is a uniformly distributed random number, for each $j$-th component of the $i$-th parameter vector. $j_{rand} \in \{1,2,\ldots,D\}$ is a randomly chosen index, which ensures that $\vec{U}_{i,G}$ gets at least one component from $\vec{V}_{i,G}$. These $F$, $Cr$ and population number are the control parameters of the basic DE.

## 2.4 Selection

The next step of the algorithm calls for *selection* to determine whether the target or the trial vector survives to the next generation i.e. at $G = G+1$. The selection operation is described as:

$$\vec{X}_{i,G+1} = \begin{cases} \vec{U}_{i,G}, & \text{if } f(\vec{U}_{i,G}) \le f(\vec{X}_{i,G}) \\ \vec{X}_{i,G}, & \text{if } f(\vec{U}_{i,G}) \ge f(\vec{X}_{i,G}) \end{cases} \qquad (6)$$

where $f(\vec{X})$ is the objective function to be minimized.

# 3 ADEpBX

In this section, we propose a new DE algorithm, ADEpBX, which implements an innovative mutation strategy and controls $F$ and $Cr$ in an adaptive [9]-[20] manner. This algorithm also proposes an innovative type of crossover scheme.

## 3.1 New Mutation Strategy: -DE/target-to-poprandbest /bin/1

DE/target-to-best/1 is one of the widely used mutation strategies in DE where the new donor vector used to perturb each population member, is created using any two randomly selected member of the population as well as the best vector of the current generation. The notation of this strategy has been shown earlier.

ADEpBX uses a newly proposed mutation strategy named as *DE/target-to-poprandbest /bin/1*. *DE/target-to-poprandbest/1* is actually a modified version of DE/target-to-best/1.

$$\vec{V}_{i,G} = \vec{X}_{i,G} + F \cdot (\vec{X}_{poprandbest,G} - \vec{X}_{i,G} + \vec{X}_{r_1^i,G} - \vec{X}_{r_2^i,G}). \tag{7}$$

$X_{(poprandbest)}$ is the best of q % vectors randomly chosen from the current population. $X_{(r1,g)}$ and $X_{(r2,g)}$ are vectors chosen randomly from the current population.

The main problem with DE/target-to-best/1/bin scheme is that this scheme uses the best vector to generate the mutated vectors. It promotes exploitation as all the population vectors are attracted towards the best position. As a result of such exploitative tendency the population can lose its global exploration abilities and can get trapped to some locally optimal point on the search space. In ADEpBX it has been aimed to maintain a balance between the two contradictory aspects of DE-exploration and exploitation. So some modifications have been introduced to overcome the limitations of fast but less reliable convergence performance of target-to-best scheme. Instead of using the best vector, the best of a dynamic group of q% vectors randomly chosen from the current population has been used to generate the donor vector. As a result the strategy proposed somewhat diminishes the greediness nature of the target-to-best scheme enhancing the population diversity and a proper trade-off between exploration and exploitation has been achieved to some extent.

## 3.2 Parameter Adaptation

**Scale Factor adaptation:** At every generation the scale factor $F_i$ *of* each individual target vector   is   independently generated according to a Cauchy distribution with location parameter $F_m$ and scale parameter 0.1i.e.

$$F_i = randci(F_m,0.1) \tag{8}$$

The Cauchy distribution is implemented in the algorithm in such a way that the values of $F_i$ for all target vectors lie between 0 and 1. Denote $F_{success}$ as the set of all successful scale factors of the current  population generating better trial vectors that are likely to advance to the next generation and *mean(F)* as the mean of  all the scale factors associated with the target vectors of the current population. $F_m$ of the Cauchy distribution is initialized to be 0.5 and then updated at the end of each generation in the following manner:-

**Case 1:** *mean (F) < 0.85*

$$F_m = (0.9 + 0.01 \cdot abs(randn)) \cdot F_m + 0.1 \cdot (1 + 0.01 \cdot abs(randn)) \cdot powermean(F_{success}) \quad (9)$$

**Case 2:** *mean (F) > 0.85*

$$F_m = (0.85 + 0.01 \cdot abs(randn)) \cdot F_m + 0.1 \cdot (1 + 0.01 \cdot abs(randn)) \cdot powermean(F_{success}) \quad (10)$$

$$powermean(F_{success}) = \sum x \in F_{success} (x^n / length(F_{success}))^{1/n} \quad (11)$$

Here the argument n is taken as 1.5.

**Crossover probability adaptation:** At every generation the crossover probability $Cr_i$ of each individual vector *is* independently generated according to a normal distribution of mean $Cr_m$ and standard deviation 0.1i.e.

$$Cr_i = randn_i(Cr_m, 0.1) \quad (12)$$

And then kept in   [0, 1]. Denote $Cr_{success}$ as the set of all successful crossover probabilities $Cr_i$'s at the current generation. The mean $Cr_m$ is initialized to be 0.7 and then updated at the end of each generation as

$$Cr_m = (0.9 + 0.001 \cdot abs(randn)) \cdot Cr_m + 0.1 \cdot (1 + 0.001 \cdot abs(randn)) \cdot powermean(Cr_{success}) \quad (13)$$

$$powermean(Cr_{success}) = \sum x \in Cr_{success} (x^n / length(Cr_{success}))^{1/n} \quad (14)$$

Here the argument n is taken as 1.5.

**Explanation of parameter adaptation:** In DE three most important parameters [6], [21] that affect the algorithm performance are the *Np, F* and *Cr*. Here *Np* has been kept fixed. The scale factor, *F*, actually improves the convergence speed while the crossover probability, *Cr*, is associated with the property and complexity of the problem. During the adaptation of $F_m$ the usage of Power mean leads to higher value of $F_m$ that accounts for larger perturbation to the target vectors, thus avoiding premature convergence at local optima. The essence of $F_{success}$ is that it memorizes the successful scale factors thus glorifying the chance of creating better donor vectors by extending it to the following generations. $F_m$ is used as a location parameter of Cauchy distribution which rather diversifies the values of *F* as compared to the traditional normal distribution [7].For the adaption of $Cr_m$ the usage of $Cr_{success}$ again records the successful *Cr* values, thus generates better individuals as offsprings which are more likely to survive. A normal distribution with mean $Cr_m$ and standard deviation of 0.1 is used to generate the *Cr* values. The usage of power mean instead of arithmetic mean in adaptation of $Cr_m$ leads to higher values of *Cr* which eliminates the implicit bias of   *Cr* towards small values.

### 3.3  *p*-Best Crossover Operation

The crossover operation used in ADEpBX named as *p*-best crossover where for each donor vector, a vector is randomly selected from the *p* top-ranking vectors (according to their objective function values) in the current population and then normal binomial crossover is performed as per eqn. (5) between the donor vector and the randomly selected *p*-best vector to generate the trial vector at the same index. Thus the offspring achieve a much high probability to advance to the subsequent generation due to injection of information of the *p*-best vector. The *p*-best crossover operation has served a splendid purpose in enhancing the convergence speed of the algorithm which is inevitable in single objective optimization as the number of function evaluations is limited.

## 4   Experimental Setup and Results

### 4.1  Benchmark Functions Used

We have used a test - bed of twenty-five well - known boundary-constrained benchmark functions to evaluate the performance of the new adaptive DE variant. These functions constituted the benchmark of CEC-2005 competition on single objective optimization.

### 4.2  Algorithms Compared

The results of ADEpBX on the above test bed have been compared to the following algorithms:

- DE/rand/1/bin [22]
- JADE with $c = 0.1$, $p = 0.05$ and optional external archive.[20]
- jDE with $F_l$=0.1,$F_u$=0.9 and $\tau_1=\tau_2=0.1$[16]
- Self Adaptive DE(SaDE)[23]
- DMS-PSO [24].

### 4.3  Simulation Strategies and Parameter Settings

Functions $f_1$ to $f_{25}$ were tested in 30 dimensions (30D). The maximum number of function evaluations (FEs) was set to 3e+05. Two important parameters in ADEpBX are: q controls the greediness of the mutation strategy target-to-poprandbest and *p* determines the *p*-best crossover operation. Both these parameters are insensitive to different objective functions as evident from their roles. ADEpBX usually executes best with q set to $1/4^{th}$ of the population size which is kept as 100 for all the assigned problems and *p* is dynamically updated with generation (or iteration) according to the equation shown below.

$$p = \left\lceil \frac{Np}{2}\left(1 - \frac{iter}{iter\_\max}\right) \right\rceil + 1 \tag{15}$$

Here $Np$ represents the population size and $iter\_$max represents the maximum number of iterations allotted. The reduction routine of $p$ favors exploration at the beginning of the search and exploitation during the later stages by gradually downsizing the elitist portion of the population, with a randomly selected member from where the component mixing of the donor vector is allowed for formation of the trial vector. For the contestant algorithms, we employ the best suited parametric set-up, chosen with guidelines from their respective literatures. All the algorithms are tested on a Pentium core 2 duo machine with 2 GB RAM and 2.23 GHz speed.

## 4.4 Results on Numerical Benchmarks

Tables 1 to 5 show the mean and the standard deviation of the best-of-run errors for 50 independent runs of each of the nine algorithms on twenty-five numerical benchmarks for $D = 30$ respectively. Note that the best-of-the-run error corresponds to absolute difference between the best-of-the-run value $f(\vec{x}_{best})$ and the actual optimum $f*$ of a particular objective function i.e. $\left| f(\vec{x}_{best}) - f* \right|$.

**Table 1.** Mean and standard deviation of error values for function1-5

| Algorithms | $f_1$ | $f_2$ | $f_3$ | $f_4$ | $f_5$ |
|---|---|---|---|---|---|
| | Mean(Std) | Mean(Std) | Mean(Std) | Mean(Std) | Mean(Std) |
| DE/rand/1/bin | 2.4536e-28 (3.4756e-28) | 5.49e-08 (1.2e-07) | 2.89e+05 (1.93e+05) | 5.04e-01 (8.58e-01) | 1.2719e+03 (2.83e+02) |
| JADE | 1.3258se-54 (9.2436e-54) | 2.5146e-26 (3.4269e-26) | 4.7421e+04 (1.6213e+04) | 5.1159e-07 (4.0194e-07) | 3.2792e+02 (1.8494e+02) |
| jDE | 3.8652e-29 (4.5732e-29) | 7.5064e-06 (7.3804e-06) | 2.2663e+05 (1.6085e+05) | 2.7305e-01 (2.7305e-01) | 1.1108e+03 (3.7238e+02) |
| SaDE | 6.7843e-30 (2.3879e-30) | 9.7191e-08 (4.8596e-07) | 5.0521e+04 (1.5754e+05) | 5.8160e-06 (1.4479e-05) | 7.8803e+02 (1.2439e+03) |
| DMS-L-PSO | 2.3462e-20 (5.6234e-20) | 1.1757e-07 (6.5592e-08) | 1.6343e-06 (3.9247e-06) | 2.5487e+03 (3.0638e+02) | 2.1858e+03 (8.2641e+02) |
| ADEpBX | **1.3429e-62 (2.4352e-61)** | **1.9981e-26 (2.4429e-26)** | 4.0977e+04 (3.2699e+04) | **6.9268e-08 (8.9742e-08)** | 2.2057e+02 (1.6754e+02) |

**Table 2.** Mean and standard deviation of error values for function 6-10

| Algorithms | $f_6$ | $f_7$ | $f_8$ | $f_9$ | $f_{10}$ |
|---|---|---|---|---|---|
| | Mean(Std) | Mean(Std) | Mean(Std) | Mean(Std) | Mean(Std) |
| DE/rand/1/bin | 3.7764e+00 (2.71e+00) | 9.6575e-01 (9.14e-02) | 2.0941e+01 (6.25e-02) | 5.3742e-14 (6.7342e-14) | 6.1643e+01 (4.56e+01) |
| JADE | 5.6094e+00 (1.9445e+01) | 6.9598e-03 (4.4845e-03) | 2.0929e+01 (2.6628e-02) | 5.9272e-22 (8.9543e-22) | 3.0313e+01 (8.3551e+00) |
| jDE | 1.1196e+01 (1.3987e+00) | 9.8597e-03 (3.4824e-03) | 2.093`e+01 (2.5067e-02) | 8.3264e-16 (2.3645e-15) | 5.2547e+01 (4.4660e+00) |
| SaDE | 2.1248e+001 (1.3413e+01) | 8.2727e-03 (1.1445e-02) | 2.0140e+01 (5.7258e-02) | 2.2737e-15 (1.1369e-14) | 3.5758e+01 (6.0809e+00) |
| DMS-L-PSO | 4.7840e-01 (1.3222e+00) | 6.9990e-03 (4.5371e-03) | **2.0000e+01 (2.3029e-04)** | 1.7591e+01 (3.0222e+00) | 3.7410e+01 (5.2883e+00) |
| ADEpBX | **3.9873e-01 (1.0815e+00)** | **6.6472e-03 (9.0313e-03)** | **2.0000e+01 (6.7185e-06)** | 1.0342e+01 (3.2346e+00) | **2.8890e+01 (8.9159e+00)** |

**Table 3.** Mean and standard deviation of error values for function 11-15

| Algorithms | $f_{11}$ | $f_{12}$ | $f_{13}$ | $f_{14}$ | $f_{15}$ |
|---|---|---|---|---|---|
| | Mean(Std) | Mean(Std) | Mean(Std) | Mean(Std) | Mean(Std) |
| DE/rand/1/bin | 3.2648e+01 (1.0954e+01) | 8.4331e+04 (6.2535e+04 | 4.5130e+00 (2.2662e+00 | 1.3347e+01 (3.4764e-01) | 4.8432e+02 (2.1467e+0 |
| JADE | 2.6456e+01 (1.9169e+01) | 2.6978e+04 (6.8003e+03 | 1.6285e+00 (4.8739e-02) | 1.2771e+01 (2.2057e-01) | 2.8884e+02 (9.0503e+00 |
| jDE | 3.1370e+01 (2.3952e+00) | 3.8376e+04 (6.5374e+03) | 1.8568e+00 (1.0313e-01) | 1.3545e+01 (9.9402e-02) | 2.9642e+02 (1.8711e+0 |
| SaDE | 2.6562e+01 (1.1275e+00) | 8.7345e+02 (9.3383e+02) | 1.2070e+00 (1.3420e-01) | 1.2760e+01 (2.5936e-01) | 3.2775e+02 (9.6450e+0 |
| DMS-L-PSO | 2.7278e+01 (1.5739e+00) | 2.5359e+02 (2.8883e+02) | 2.3595e+00 (5.2823e-01) | 1.2961e+01 (4.1146e-01) | 3.4400e+02 (5.0662e+01) |
| ADEpBX | **1.7590e+01** **(6.0615e+00)** | 9.5793e+04 (8.133e+03) | **1.1051e+00** **(5.6060e-02)** | **1.2429e+01** **(3.4320e-01)** | **2.8553e+02** **(9.7542e+0** |

**Table 4.** Mean and standard deviation of error values for function 16-20

| Algorithms | $f_{16}$ | $f_{17}$ | $f_{18}$ | $f_{19}$ | $f_{20}$ |
|---|---|---|---|---|---|
| | Mean(Std) | Mean(Std) | Mean(Std) | Mean(Std) | Mean(Std) |
| DE/rand/1/bin | 2.8228e+02 (1.1328e+01) | 3.0942e+02 (1.5698e+01) | 9.1342e+02 (8.4336e-01) | 9.1984e+02 (1.2190e+00) | 9.1317e+02 (1.1642e+00) |
| JADE | 7.4383e+01 (3.9432e+01) | 8.4619e+01 (3.5763e+01) | 8.1679e+02 (1.6523e-01) | 8.1644e+02 (1.5419e-01) | 8.1697e+02 (1.7231e-01) |
| jDE | 1.2854e+02 (4.0730e+01) | 1.6189e+02 (4.7251e+01) | 8.6111e+02 (1.8705e+00) | 8.4801e+02 (3.1790e+00) | 8.5466e+02 (9.54e-01) |
| SaDE | 1.379e+02 (1.702e+01) | 1.509e+03 (9.363e+02) | 9.544e+02 (3.438e+01) | 8.458e+02 (6.215e+01) | 2.040e+03 (8.768e+02) |
| DMS-L-PSO | 1.1950e+02 (1.2068e+02) | 1.4519e+02 (7.3247e+01) | 9.1053e+02 (1.5761e+00) | 9.1060e+02 (1.3383e+00) | 9.0189e+02 (3.0719e+01) |
| ADEpBX | **7.2307e+01** **(3.8872e+01)** | **8.2328e+01** **(3.9757e+01)** | **8.1626e+02** **(1.5209e-01)** | **8.1625e+02** **(1.5340e-01)** | **8.1642e+02** **(1.6990e-01)** |

**Table 5.** Mean and standard deviation of error values for function 21-25

| Algorithms | $f_{21}$ | $f_{22}$ | $f_{23}$ | $f_{24}$ | $f_{25}$ |
|---|---|---|---|---|---|
| | Mean(Std) | Mean(Std) | Mean(Std) | Mean(Std) | Mean(Std) |
| DE/rand/1/bin | 5.8135e+02 (2.6247e+01) | 9.6425e+02 (1.1439e+01) | 6.2131e+02 (3.0647e+01) | 3.14e34+02 (3.3249e+01) | 9.8643e+02 (2.1775e+01) |
| JADE | 8.5838e+02 (1.1013e+00) | 5.0762e+02 (1.6550e+00) | 8.6558e+02 (6.6102e-01) | 2.1141e+02 (1.5664e+01) | 2.1135e+02 (3.5588e+00) |
| jDE | 8.6002e+02 (1.1361e+00) | 5.0340e+02 (2.9115e+00) | 6.1835e+02 (4.5481e+00) | 2.1081e+02 (2.8842e+00) | 9.761e+02 (2.409e+01) |
| SaDE | 1.730e+03 (5.118e+02) | 1.582e+03 (4.252e+02) | 5.506e+02 (2.489e+01) | **2.0000e+02** **(1.2455e-04)** | 5.0012e+02 (5.683e-02) |
| DMS-L-PSO | 5.0134e+02 (1.0132e-04) | 9.2154e+02 (9.841e+01) | 5.344e+02 (4.001e-01) | **2.0000e+02** **(5.0123e-04)** | 9.889e+02 (3.015e+01) |
| ADEpBX | **5.0000e+02** **(0)** | **5.0021e+02** **(4.5755e-01)** | **5.3416e+02** **(7.8384e-04)** | 2.0985e+02 (3.5882e+00) | **2.0962e+002** **(3.6271e+00)** |

## 4.5   Analysis of Results

Tables 1-5 indicate that out of 25 in 19 cases ADEpBX ranked first considering the mean error. It is to be noted that ADEpBX has shown superiority in case of rotated, hybrid as well as functions with noise in fitness. So function rotation, incorporating multiplicative noise in them as well as composition of functions does not hamper the performance of the proposed algorithm significantly. SADE, JADE and DMS-PSO remained as the toughest competitors for ADEpBX though the latter has yielded better results in majority of the cases.

## 5 Conclusion

Over past one decade of research DE has reached an impressive state. Nowadays an extensive research work is going on in designing various DE algorithms to optimize large-scale high-dimensional problems (D=1000, D=500). ADEpBX has been tested in the CEC 2010 high dimensional benchmark functions where it has been observed to give promising results in case of non-separable functions. The parameter adaptation and the mutation scheme which are the main features in ADEpBX can be quite useful in constraint, multi-objective, multi-modal, large-scale and dynamic optimization where our initial studies have shown exciting results, there are still many open questions in incorporating parameter adaptation schemes to evolutionary optimization.

## References

[1] Storn, R., Price, K.: Differential evolution a simple and efficient heuristic for global optimization over continuous spaces. J. Global Optimization 11(4), 341–359 (1997)

[2] Price, K.V., Storn, R.M., Lampinen, J.A.: Differential Evolution: A Practical Approach to Global Optimization, 1st edn. Springer, New York (2005)

[3] Joshi, R., Sanderson, A.C.: Minimal representation multisensory fusion using differential evolution. IEEE Trans. Syst., Man Cybern. 29(1), 63–76 (1999)

[4] Zhang, J., Avasarala, V., Subbu, R.: Evolutionary optimization of transition probability matrices for credit decision-making. Eur. J. Oper. Res. (to be published)

[5] Zhang, J., Avasarala, V., Sanderson, A.C., Mullen, T.: Differential evolution for discrete optimization: An experimental study on combinatorial auction problems. In: Proc. IEEE World Congr. Comput. Intell., Hong Kong, China, pp. 2794–2800 (June 2008)

[6] Gamperle, R., Muller, S.D., Koumoutsakos, P.: A parameter study for differential evolution. In: Proc. Advances Intell. Syst., Fuzzy Syst., Evol. Comput., Crete, Greece, pp. 293–298 (2002)

[7] Zhang, J., Sanderson, A.C.: An approximate Gaussian model of differential evolution with spherical fitness functions. In: Proc. IEEE Congr. Evol. Comput., Singapore, pp. 2220–2228 (September 2007)

[8] Mezura-Montes, E., Velázquez-Reyes, J., Coello Coello, C.A.: A comparative study of differential evolution variants for global optimization. In: Proc. Genetic Evol. Comput. Conf., Seattle, WA, pp. 485–492 (July 2006)

[9] Abbass, H.A.: The self-adaptive pareto differential evolution algorithm. In: Proc. IEEE Congr. Evol. Comput., Honolulu, HI, vol. 1, pp. 831–836 (May 2002)

[10] Teo, J.: Exploring dynamic self-adaptive populations in differential evolution. Soft Comput.: Fusion Found., Methodologies Applicat. 10(8), 673–686 (2006)

[11] Liu, J., Lampinen, J.: A fuzzy adaptive differential evolution algorithm. Soft Comput.: Fusion Found., Methodologies Applicat. 9(6), 448–462 (2005)

[12] Xue, F., Sanderson, A.C., Bonissone, P.P., Graves, R.J.: Fuzzy logic controlled multiobjective differential evolution. In: Proc. IEEE Int. Conf. Fuzzy Syst., Reno, NV, pp. 720–725 (June 2005)

[13] Qin, A.K., Suganthan, P.N.: Self-adaptive differential evolution algorithm for numerical optimization. In: Proc. IEEE Congr. Evol. Comput., vol. 2, pp. 1785–1791 (September 2005)

[14] Huang, V.L., Qin, A.K., Suganthan, P.N.: Self-adaptive differential evolution algorithm for constrained real-parameter optimization. In: Proc. IEEE Congr. Evol. Comput., pp. 17–24 (July 2006)

[15] Brest, J., Greiner, S., Boskovic, B., Mernik, M., Zumer, V.: Self-adapting control parameters in differential evolution: A comparative study on numerical benchmark problems. IEEE Trans. Evol. Comput. 10(6), 646–657 (2006)

[16] Brest, J., Zumer, V., Maucec, M.S.: Self-adaptive differential evolution algorithm in constrained real-parameter optimization. In: Proc. IEEE Congr. Evol. Comput., Vancouver, BC, pp. 215–222 (July 2006)

[17] Brest, J., Boskovic, B., Greiner, S., Zumer, V., Maucec, M.S.: Performance comparison of self-adaptive and adaptive differential evolution algorithms. Soft Comput.: Fusion Found., Methodologies Applicat. 11(7), 617–629 (2007)

[18] Yang, Z., Tang, K., Yao, X.: Self-adaptive differential evolution with neighborhood search. In: Proc. IEEE Congr. Evol. Comput., Hong Kong, China, pp. 1110–1116 (June 2008)

[19] Angeline, P.J.: Adaptive and self-adaptive evolutionary computations. In: Computational Intelligence: A Dynamic Systems Perspective, pp. 152–163 (1995)

[20] Zhang, J., Sanderson, A.C.: JADE: Self-adaptive differential evolution with fast and reliable convergence performance. In: Proc. IEEE Congr. Evol. Comput., Singapore, pp. 2251–2258 (September 2007)

[21] Eiben, A.E., Hinterding, R., Michalewicz, Z.: Parameter control in evolutionary algorithms. IEEE Trans. Evol. Comput. 3(2), 124–141 (1999)

[22] Ronkkonen, J., Kukkonen, S., Price, K.: Real-parameter optimization using Differential Evolution. In: IEEE CEC 2005 (2005)

[23] Qin, A.K., Suganthan, P.N.: Self-adaptive Differential Evolution for numerical optimization. In: IEEE CEC 2005 (2005)

[24] Liang, J.J., Suganthan, P.N.: Dynamic Multi-Swarm Particle Swarm Optimizer with Local Search. In: IEEE CEC 2005 (2005)

[25] Das, S., Suganthan, P.N.: Differential Evolution: A Survey of the State-of-the-art. IEEE Trans. Evol. Comput. (2010)

# A New Particle Swarm Optimization Algorithm for Dynamic Environments

Masoud Kamosi[1], Ali B. Hashemi[2], and M.R. Meybodi[2]

[1] Department of Computer Engineering, Science and Research Branch,
Islamic Azad University, Tehran, Iran
[2] Department of Computer Engineering and Information Technology,
Amirkabir University of Technology, Tehran, Iran
masoud.kamosi@gmail.com, {a_hashemi,mmeybodi}@aut.ac.ir

**Abstract.** Many real world optimization problems are dynamic in which global optimum and local optima change over time. Particle swarm optimization has performed well to find and track optima in dynamic environments. In this paper, we propose a new particle swarm optimization algorithm for dynamic environments. The proposed algorithm utilizes a parent swarm to explore the search space and some child swarms to exploit promising areas found by the parent swarm. To improve the search performance, when the search areas of two child swarms overlap, the worse child swarms will be removed. Moreover, in order to quickly track the changes in the environment, all particles in a child swarm perform a random local search around the best position found by the child swarm after a change in the environment is detected. Experimental results on different dynamic environments modelled by moving peaks benchmark show that the proposed algorithm outperforms other PSO algorithms, including FMSO, a similar particle swarm algorithm for dynamic environments, for all tested environments.

**Keywords:** Particle Swarm Optimization, Dynamic Environments.

## 1 Introduction

The particle swarm optimization algorithm (PSO) is introduced by Kennedy and Eberhart [1]. In PSO, a potential solution for a problem is considered as a bird, which is called a particle, flies through a D-dimensional space and adjusts its position according to its own experience and other particles'. In PSO, a particle is represented by its position vector $p$ and its velocity vector $v$. In time step $t$, particle $i$ calculates its new velocity then updates its position according to Equation (1) and Equation (2), respectively.

$$v_i(t+1) = wv_i(t) + c_1 r_1 (pbest_i - p_i(t)) + c_2 r_2 (gbest - p_i(t)) \tag{1}$$

$$p_i(t+1) = p_i(t) + v_i(t+1) \tag{2}$$

where $w$ is the inertial weight, and $c_1$ and $c_2$ are positive acceleration coefficients used to scale the contribution of cognitive and social components, respectively. $pbest_i$ is the best position that particle $i$ has been visited. $gbest$ is the best position found by all particles in the swarm. $r_1$ and $r_2$ are uniform random variables in range [0,1].

B.K. Panigrahi et al. (Eds.): SEMCCO 2010, LNCS 6466, pp. 129–138, 2010.

The standard particle swarm optimization algorithms and its variants [2, 3] have been performed well for static environment. Yet, it is shown that PSO, like evolutionary algorithms, must be modified to not only find the optimal solution in a short time but also to be capable of tracking the solution after a change in the environment occurred. In order to have these capabilities, two important problems should be addressed for designing a particle swarm optimization algorithm for dynamic environments: outdated memory and diversity loss[4]. Outdated memory refers to the condition in which memory of the particles, that is the best location visited in the past and its corresponding fitness, may no longer be valid after a change in the environment [5]. Outdated memory problem is usually solved in one of these two ways: re-evaluating the memory [6] or forgetting the memory [7]. Diversity loss occurs when the swarm converges on a few peaks in the landscape and loses its ability to find new peaks, which is required after the environment changes. There are two approaches to deal with diversity loss problem. In the first approach, a diversity maintenance mechanism runs periodically (or when a change is detected) and re-distributes the particles if the diversity falls below a threshold[8]. In the second approach, diversity is always monitored and as soon as it falls below a threshold, the swarm will be re-diversified.

In this paper, we propose a new multi-swarm algorithm for dynamic environments which address the diversity loss problem by introducing two types of swarm: a parent swarm, which explores the search space to find promising area containing local optima and several non-overlapping child swarms, each of which is responsible for exploiting a promising area found by the parent swarm. In the proposed algorithm, both parent and child swarms use the standard PSO[9] with the local neighborhood [10], in which a particle is affected by the best experience of its swarm rather than the best experience of all particles in the environment. Moreover, in order to track the changing local optima, after a change is detected in the environment particles in each child swarms perform a random search around the best position of that child swarm. Extensive experiments show that for all tested dynamic environments the proposed algorithm outperforms all tested PSO algorithms, including FMSO[11], with which shares the idea of utilizing a parent swarms and child swarms.

The rest of this paper is organized as follows: Section 2 briefly reviews particle swarm optimization algorithms for dynamic environments introduced in the literature. The proposed algorithm is presented in section 3. Section 4 presents the experimental results of the proposed algorithm along with comparison with alternative approaches from the literature. Finally, section 5 concludes this paper.

## 2    PSO in Dynamic Environments

Hu and Eberhart proposed re-randomization PSO for optimization in dynamic environments[8] in which some particles randomly are relocated after a change is detected or when the diversity is lost, to prevent losing the diversity. Li and Dam [12] showed that a grid-like neighborhood structure used in FGPSO[13] can perform better than RPSO in high dimensional dynamic environments by restricting the information sharing and preventing the convergence of particles to the global best position, thereby enhancing population diversity. Janson and Middendorf proposed HPSO, a tree-like structure hierarchical PSO [14], and reported improvements over standard PSO for dynamic environments. They also suggested Partitioned Hierarchical PSO in which a hierarchy of particles is partitioned into several sub-swarms for a limited number of generations after a change in the environment is detected [15]. Lung and Dumitresc [16] used two collaborating populations of equal size, one swarm is responsible for preserving the diversity of the particles by using a crowding differential evolutionary algorithm [17] while the other keeps track of global optimum with a PSO algorithm.

Blackwell and Bentley presented a repulsion mechanism in using the analogy of atom particles [18, 19]. In their model, a swarm is comprised of charged and neutral particles. The charged particles repel each other, leading to a cloud of charged particles orbiting a contracting, neutral, PSO nucleus. Moreover, Blackwell et al. extended the idea of charged particles to a quantum model and presented a multi-swarm method [4, 20, 21].

Du and Li [22] suggested an algorithm which divides particles into two parts. The first part uses a standard PSO enhanced by a Gaussian local search to find the global optimum quickly and the second part extends the searching area of the algorithm and patrols around the first part to track the changed global optimum which possibly escaped from the coverage of the first part. Although their algorithm performs well in the environments with one or two local optima, it cannot find the global optimum when the environment has more local optima.

Li and Yang proposed a fast multi-swarm method (FMSO) which maintains the diversity through the run [11]. To meet this end two type of swarms are used: a parent swarm which maintains the diversity and detects the promising search area in the whole search space using a fast evolutionary programming algorithm, and a group of child swarms which explore the local area for the local optima found by the parent using a fast PSO algorithm. This mechanism makes the child swarms spread out over the highest multiple peaks, as many as possible, and guarantees to converge to a local optimum in a short time. Moreover, In [23], the authors introduced a clustering particle swarm optimizer in which a clustering algorithm partitions the swarm into several sub-swarms each searching for a local optimum.

Liu et al. [24] introduced compound particle swarm optimization (CPSO) utilizing a new type of particles which helps explore the search space more comprehensively after a change occurred in the environment. In another work, they used composite particles which help quickly find the promising optima in the search space while maintaining the diversity by a scattering operator[25].

Hashemi and Meybodi introduced cellular PSO, a hybrid model of cellular automata and PSO [26]. In cellular PSO, a cellular automaton partitions the search space into cells. At any time, in some cells of the cellular automaton a group of particles search for a local optimum using their best personal experiences and the best solution found in their neighborhood cells. To prevent losing the diversity, a limit on the number of particles in each cell is imposed. Furthermore, to track the changes in the environment, in [27] particles in cellular PSO change their role to quantum particles and perform a random search around the previously found optima for a few iterations after a change is detected in the environment.

## 3   The Proposed Algorithm

The proposed multi-swarm algorithm consists of a parent swarm and some child swarms. The parent swarm is responsible for finding promising area in the search space upon which a child swarm is created to exploit the new found promising area. The proposed algorithm works as follows.

After initializing the parent swarm, the particles in the parent swarm begin searching in the search space. At each iteration, velocity and position of a particle $i$ in the parent swarm is updated using its best personal position ($pbest_i$) and the best position found by the parent swarm ($cbest_{parent}$) according to (1) and (2), respectively. If the fitness of the new position of particle $i$ is better than its best personal position ($pbest_i$), $pbest_i$ will be updated to the new position. Likewise, the best position found in the parent swarm ($cbest_{parent}$) will be updated. Afterwards, the distance between particle $i$ and the attractor of each child swarm $c$, i.e. the best position found by a child swarm $c$ ($cbest_c$), is calculated. If the distance between particle $i$ and the attractor of a child swarm $c$ is less than $r$, the attractor of the child swarm $c$ will be updated to the position of particle $i$. Then, particle $i$ will be reinitialized. When all particles in the parent swarm are updated, if the best position found in the parent swarm ($cbest_{parent}$) is improved, a new child swarm will be created with $cbest_{parent}$ as its attractor. If there are $m$ particles in the parent swarm whose distances to the attractor of the newly created child swarm are less than $r$, these particles will be moved to the new child swarm, at the same time $m$ new particles will be created and initialized in the parent swarm. If the number of particles moved to the newly created child swarm ($m$) is less than the number of particles determined for a child swarm ($\pi$), $\pi$-$m$ particles for the child swarm will be created and initialized in a hypersphere with radius $r/3$ centered at the child swarm's attractor. Afterwards, all particles in every child swarm $c$ update their velocity and position according to (3) and (2), respectively. Then, the personal best position ($pbest$) for all child particles and the child swarms' best position ($cbest_j$) will be updated.

$$v_i(t+1) = wv_i(t) + c_1 r_1 \left( pbest_i - p_i(t) \right) + c_2 r_2 \left( cbest_c - p_i(t) \right) \tag{3}$$

Since searching an area with more than one child swarm is not very useful, at the end of each iteration every two child swarms are checked whether they are searching in the same area or not. Two child swarms are searching in the same area or they are colliding, if the Euclidian distance between their attractors is less than a specified threshold $r_{excl}$. If a collision between two child swarms is detected, the worse child swarm whose attractor is less fit than the other's, will be destroyed.

In the proposed algorithm, when an environment change is detected, particles in the parent swarm re-evaluate their positions and reset their best personal position ($pbest$) to their current position. However, the particles in the child swarms change their behaviors in the following iteration after a change is detected in the environment. They will set their new positions to a random location in a hypersphere with radius $r_s$ centered at their swarm's attractor. Then they will reset their best personal positions ($pbest$) to their new position and update the child swarms attractor.

## 4   Experimental Study

In this section, we first describe moving peaks benchmark [28] on which the proposed algorithms is evaluated. Then, experimental settings are described. Finally, experimental results of the proposed algorithm are presented and compared with alternative approaches from the literature.

**Algorithm 1.** Proposed multi-swarm optimization algorithm

```
Initialization the parent swarm
repeat
  if a change is detected in the environment then
    for each particle i in the parent swarm do
        pbest_i = p_i
    end-for
    Set cbest_parent to the best position found by the particles in the parent swarm
    for each child swarm c  do
      for each particle i in the child swarm c  do
          p_i=a random position in a hypersphere with radius r_s centered at cbest_c
          pbest_i = p_i
      end-for
      Set cbest_c to the best position found by the particles in child swarm c
    end-for
    continue
  end-if

  for each particle i in the parent swarm do
    Update position of particle i according to eq. 1 and eq. 2.
    Update pbest_i
    for each swarm c do
      if distance(p_i, cbest_c) < r  then
        if  f(p_i) > f(cbest_c)  then
          cbest_c = p_i
        end-if
        Reinitialize particle i
      end-if
    end-for
  end-for
  Set cbest_parent to the best position found by the particles in the parent swarm
  if cbest_parent is updated then
    // create a new child swarm v around the new position found by the parent swarm
    cbest_v = cbest_parent
    for each particle i in parent swarm do
      if distance(p_i, cbest_v) < r then
        if  |v| < π   then
          copy particle i to the child swarm v
        end-if
        Initialize particle i
      end-if
    end-for
    while |v| < π
      Create a new particle in the child swarm v within a radius r/3 centered at
          cbest_v
    end-while
  end-if

  for child swarm c  do
    for each particle i in the child swarm c  do
      Update position of particle i according to eq. (3) and eq. (2)
      Update pbest_i
    end-for
    Set cbest_c to the best position found by the particles in child swarm c
  end-for
  for each pair of child swarms (k, l), k≠l do
    if  distance(cbest_k, cbest_l) < r_excl then
        Destroy the child swarm whose cbest has a less fitness value.
    end-if
  end-for
until a maximum number of fitness evaluations is reached
```

Moving peaks benchmark (Fig. 1) [28] is widely used in the literature to evaluate the performance of optimization algorithms in dynamic environments [29]. In this benchmark, there are some peaks in a multi-dimensional space, where the height, width, and position of each peak alter when the environment changes. Unless stated otherwise, the parameters of the moving peaks benchmark are set to the values presented in Table 1.

In order to measure the efficiency of the algorithms, offline error that is the average fitness of the best position found by the swarm at every point in time is used [30].

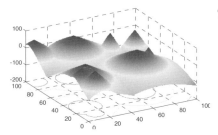

**Fig. 1.** Moving peaks benchmark

**Table 1.** Default settings of moving peaks benchmark

| Parameter | Value |
|---|---|
| number of peaks $m$ | 10 |
| frequency of change $f$ | every 5000 FEs |
| height severity | 7.0 |
| width severity | 1.0 |
| peak shape | cone |
| shift length $s$ | 1.0 |
| number of dimensions $D$ | 5 |
| cone height range $H$ | [30.0, 70.0] |
| cone width range $W$ | [1, 12] |
| cone standard height $I$ | 50.0 |
| search space range $A$ | [0, 100] |

## 4.1  Experimental Settings

For the proposed algorithms the acceleration coefficients $c_1$ and $c_2$ are set to 1.496180 and the inertial weight $w$ is set to 0.729844 [31]. The number of particles in the parent swarm and the child swarms ($\pi$) are set to 5 and 10 particles, respectively. The radius of the child swarms ($r$), the minimum allowed distance between two child swarm ($r_{excl}$) and the radius of quantum particles ($r_s$) are set to 30.0, 30.0, and 0.5, respectively. The proposed algorithm is compared with mQSO[4] and FMSO [11], and cellular PSO [26, 27]. For mQSO we adapted a configuration 10(5+5$^q$) which creates 10 swarms with 5 neutral (standard) particles and 5 quantum particles with $r_{cloud}$=0.5 and $r_{excl}= r_{conv}$ =31.5, as suggested in [4, 21]. For FMSO, there are at most 10 child swarms each has a radius of 25.0. The size of the parent and the child swarms are set to 100 and 10 particles, respectively[11]. For cellular PSO, a 5-Dimensional cellular automaton with $10^5$ cells and Moore neighborhood with radius of two cells is embedded into the search space. The maximum velocity of particles is set to the neighborhood radius of the cellular automaton and the radius for the random local search ($r$) is set to 0.5 for all experiments. The cell capacity $\theta$ is set to 10 particles for every cell[26, 27].

## 4.2  Experimental Results

For all algorithms we reported the average offline error and 95% confidence interval for 100 runs. Offline error of the proposed algorithm, mQSO10(5+5$^q$) [4], FMSO [11], and cellular PSO[26, 27] for different dynamic environment is presented in table 2 to table 5. For each environment, result of the best performing algorithm(s) with 95% confidence is printed in bold. When the offline errors of the best two (or more) algorithms are not statistically different, all are printed in bold.

As depicted in the table 2 to table 5, the proposed algorithm outperforms other tested PSO algorithms, including FMSO, for all environments. Moreover, the difference between offline error of the proposed algorithm and the next best algorithm decreases as the environment changes less frequently from $f$=500 (table 2) to $f$=10000 (table 5). This is because the proposed algorithm quickly finds better solutions than other algorithms after a change occurs in the environment, especially at the early iterations (Fig. 2).

Furthermore, in the proposed algorithm the number of child swarms converges to the number of peaks in the environment (Fig. 3). This will help the proposed algorithm to track the changes more effectively since there will be a child swarm on each peak.

**Table 2.** Offline error ±Standard Error for f =500

| m | Proposed algorithm | mQSO10 | FMSO | CellularPSO |
|---|---|---|---|---|
| 1 | **5.46**±0.30 | 33.67±3.4 | 27.58±0.9 | 13.4±0.74 |
| 5 | **5.48**±0.19 | 11.91±0.7 | 19.45±0.4 | 9.63±0.49 |
| 10 | **5.95**±0.09 | 9.62±0.34 | 18.26±0.3 | 9.42±0.21 |
| 20 | **6.45**±0.16 | 9.07±0.25 | 17.34±0.3 | 8.84±0.28 |
| 30 | **6.60**±0.14 | 8.80±0.21 | 16.39±0.4 | 8.81±0.24 |
| 40 | **6.85**±0.13 | 8.55±0.21 | 15.34±0.4 | 8.94±0.24 |
| 50 | **7.04**±0.10 | 8.72±0.20 | 15.54±0.2 | 8.62±0.23 |
| 100 | **7.39**±0.13 | 8.54±0.16 | 12.87±0.6 | 8.54±0.21 |
| 200 | **7.52**±0.12 | 8.19±0.17 | 11.52±0.6 | 8.28±0.18 |

**Table 3.** Offline error ±Standard Error for f =1000

| m | Proposed algorithm | mQSO10 | FMSO | CellularPSO |
|---|---|---|---|---|
| 1 | **2.90**±0.18 | 18.6±1.6 | 14.42±0.4 | 6.77±0.38 |
| 5 | **3.35**±0.18 | 6.56±0.38 | 10.59±0.2 | 5.30±0.32 |
| 10 | **3.94**±0.08 | 5.71±0.22 | 10.40±0.1 | 5.15±0.13 |
| 20 | **4.33**±0.12 | 5.85±0.15 | 10.33±0.1 | 5.23±0.18 |
| 30 | **4.41**±0.11 | 5.81±0.15 | 10.06±0.1 | 5.33±0.16 |
| 40 | **4.52**±0.09 | 5.70±0.14 | 9.85±0.11 | 5.61±0.16 |
| 50 | **4.57**±0.08 | 5.87±0.13 | 9.54±0.11 | 5.55±0.14 |
| 100 | **4.77**±0.08 | 5.83±0.13 | 8.77±0.09 | 5.57±0.12 |
| 200 | **4.76**±0.07 | 5.54±0.11 | 8.06±0.07 | 5.50±0.12 |

**Table 4.** Offline error ±Standard Error for $f$=5000

| m | Proposed algorithm | mQSO10 | FMSO | CellularPSO |
|---|---|---|---|---|
| 1 | **0.56**±0.04 | 3.82±0.35 | 3.44±0.11 | 2.55±0.12 |
| 5 | **1.06**±0.06 | 1.90±0.08 | 2.94±0.07 | 1.68±0.11 |
| 10 | **1.51**±0.04 | 1.91±0.08 | 3.11±0.06 | 1.78±0.05 |
| 20 | **1.89**±0.04 | 2.56±0.10 | 3.36±0.06 | 2.61±0.07 |
| 30 | **2.03**±0.06 | 2.68±0.10 | 3.28±0.05 | 2.93±0.08 |
| 40 | **2.04**±0.06 | 2.65±0.08 | 3.26±0.04 | 3.14±0.08 |
| 50 | **2.08**±0.02 | 2.63±0.08 | 3.22±0.05 | 3.26±0.08 |
| 100 | **2.14**±0.02 | 2.52±0.06 | 3.06±0.04 | 3.41±0.07 |
| 200 | **2.11**±0.03 | 2.36±0.05 | 2.84±0.03 | 3.40±0.06 |

**Table 5.** Offline error ±Standard Error for $f$=10000

| m | Proposed algorithm | mQSO10 | FMSO | CellularPSO |
|---|---|---|---|---|
| 1 | **0.27**±0.02 | 1.90±0.18 | 1.90±0.06 | 1.53±0.12 |
| 5 | **0.70**±0.10 | 1.03±0.06 | 1.75±0.06 | 0.92±0.10 |
| 10 | **0.97**±0.04 | 1.10±0.07 | 1.91±0.04 | 1.19±0.07 |
| 20 | **1.34**±0.08 | 1.84±0.08 | 2.16±0.04 | 2.20±0.10 |
| 30 | **1.43**±0.05 | 2.00±0.09 | 2.18±0.04 | 2.60±0.13 |
| 40 | **1.47**±0.06 | 1.99±0.07 | 2.21±0.03 | 2.73±0.11 |
| 50 | **1.47**±0.04 | 1.99±0.07 | 2.60±0.08 | 2.84±0.12 |
| 100 | **1.50**±0.03 | 1.85±0.05 | 2.20±0.03 | 2.93±0.09 |
| 200 | **1.48**±0.02 | 1.71±0.04 | 2.00±0.02 | 2.88±0.07 |

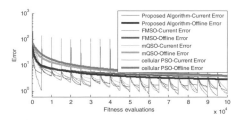

**Fig. 2.** Convergence of the offline error

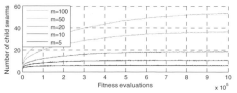

**Fig. 3.** Convergence of the number of child swarms

### 4.3 Effect of Varying the Size of the Parent Swarm

This experiment examines the effect of the size of the parent swarm, i.e. the number of particles in the parent swarm, on offline error. The visualized results in Fig. 4 and Fig. 5 depicts that when there are many peaks in the environment ($m=50$ or $m=100$) or when the environment changes slowly ($f=5000$ or $f=10000$) the size of the parent swarm does not affect offline error significantly. For other environments, offline error escalates by increasing the size of the parent swarm. The less peaks exist in the environment or the more frequently the changes occur, the more offline error will be affected by increasing the size of the parent swarm. However, if there are 5 peaks in the environment and $f=500$ (Fig. 5), the offline error slightly decreases when the size of the parent swarm increases from 1 particle to 5 particles.

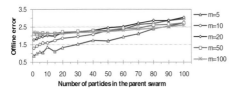

**Fig. 4.** The effect of the size of the parent swarm on the offline error

**Fig. 5.** The effect of the size of the parent swarm on the offline error

### 4.4 Effect of Varying the Size of the Child Swarms

This experiment examines the effect of the size of the child swarms ($\pi$), i.e. the number of particles in each child swarm, on offline error. As depicted in Fig. 6 and Fig. 7, the optimal value for the number of particles in the child swarms for different environments is 10 particles. In addition, either increasing or decreasing the number of particles in the child swarms from its optimal value ($\pi=10$) increases offline error monotonically. The reason is that existence of many particles in the child swarms not only does not help finding better solutions but also consumes precious function evaluations. Conversely, when there are too few particles in the child swarms, they cannot find the peaks quickly enough thereby increasing offline error.

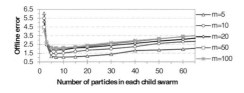
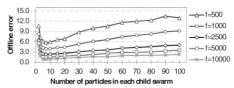
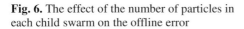

**Fig. 6.** The effect of the number of particles in each child swarm on the offline error

**Fig. 7.** The effect of the number of particles in each child swarm on the offline error

# 5 Conclusion

In this paper, we proposed a new multi-swarm PSO algorithm for dynamic environment environments. The proposed PSO consists of a parent swarm and some child swarms. The parent swarm is responsible for exploring the search space and finding promising regions containing a local optimum. Child swarms exploit the promising regions found by the parent swarm. To prevent redundant search in the same area, two mechanisms have been adapted. If a parent particle collides with a child swarm, it will be reinitialized. If two child swarms collide the one with the least fitness will be removed. In addition, to track the local optima after detecting a change in the environment, particles in each child swarm temporarily change their behavior to quantum particles and perform a random search around the child swarm's attractor. Results of the experiments show that for all tested environments the proposed algorithm outperforms all tested PSO algorithms, including FMSO, a previously presented multi-swarm algorithm with the similar approach.

# References

1. Kennedy, J., Eberhart, R.C.: Particle swarm optimization. In: IEEE International conference on neural networks, Piscataway, NJ, USA, vol. IV, pp. 1942–1948 (1995)
2. del Valle, Y., Venayagamoorthy, G.K., Mohagheghi, S., Hernandez, J.C., Harley, R.G.: Particle Swarm Optimization: Basic Concepts, Variants and Applications in Power Systems. IEEE Transactions on Evolutionary Computation 12, 171–195 (2008)
3. Hashemi, A.B., Meybodi, M.R.: A note on the learning automata based algorithms for adaptive parameter selection in PSO. Applied Soft Computing 11, 689–705 (2011)
4. Blackwell, T., Branke, J.: Multiswarms, exclusion, and anti-convergence in dynamic environments. IEEE Transactions on Evolutionary Computation 10, 459–472 (2006)
5. Blackwell, T.: Particle swarm optimization in dynamic environments. In: Evolutionary Computation in Dynamic and Uncertain Environments, pp. 29–49 (2007)
6. Eberhart, R.C., Shi, Y.: Tracking and optimizing dynamic systems with particle swarms. In: IEEE Congress on Evolutionary Computation, Seoul, Korea, vol. 1, pp. 94–100 (2001)
7. Carlisle, A., Dozier, G.: Adapting particle swarm optimization to dynamic environments. In: International Conference on Artificial Intelligence, Las Vegas, NV, USA, vol. 1, pp. 429–434 (2000)
8. Hu, X., Eberhart, R.C.: Adaptive particle swarm optimization: detection and response to dynamic systems. In: IEEE Congress on Evolutionary Computation, Honolulu, HI, USA, vol. 2, pp. 1666–1670 (2002)
9. Bratton, D., Kennedy, J.: Defining a standard for particle swarm optimization. In: IEEE Swarm Intelligence Symposium, Honolulu, Hawaii, USA, pp. 120–127 (2007)
10. Eberhart, R.C., Dobbins, R., Simpson, P. (eds.): Evolutionary Computation Implementations. Computational Intelligence PC Tools, pp. 212–226. Morgan Kaufmann, San Francisco (1996)
11. Li, C., Yang, S.: Fast Multi-Swarm Optimization for Dynamic Optimization Problems. In: Fourth International Conference on Natural Computation, Jinan, Shandong, China, vol. 7, pp. 624–628 (2008)

12. Li, X., Dam, K.H.: Comparing particle swarms for tracking extrema in dynamic environments. In: IEEE Congress on Evolutionary Computation, Canberra, Australia, pp. 1772–1779 (2003)
13. Kennedy, J., Mendes, R.: Population structure and particle swarm performance. In: Evolutionary Computation Congress, Honolulu, Hawaii, USA, pp. 1671–1676 (2002)
14. Janson, S., Middendorf, M.: A Hierarchical Particle Swarm Optimizer for Dynamic Optimization Problems. Applications of Evolutionary Computing, 513–524 (2004)
15. Janson, S., Middendorf, M.: A hierarchical particle swarm optimizer for noisy and dynamic environments. Genetic Programming and Evolvable Machines 7, 329–354 (2006)
16. Lung, R.I., Dumitrescu, D.: A collaborative model for tracking optima in dynamic environments. In: IEEE Congress on Evolutionary Computation, Singapore, pp. 564–567 (2007)
17. Thomsen, R.: Multimodal optimization using crowding-based differential evolution. In: IEEE Congress on Evolutionary Computation, Portland, Oregon, USA, pp. 1382–1389 (2004)
18. Blackwell, T.: Swarms in Dynamic Environments. In: Cantú-Paz, E., Foster, J.A., Deb, K., Davis, L., Roy, R., O'Reilly, U.-M., Beyer, H.-G., Kendall, G., Wilson, S.W., Harman, M., Wegener, J., Dasgupta, D., Potter, M.A., Schultz, A., Dowsland, K.A., Jonoska, N., Miller, J., Standish, R.K. (eds.) GECCO 2003. LNCS, vol. 2723, p. 200. Springer, Heidelberg (2003)
19. Blackwell, T.M., Bentley, P.J.: Dynamic search with charged swarms. In: Genetic and evolutionary computation conference, pp. 19–26. Morgan Kaufmann Publishers Inc., New York (2002)
20. Blackwell, T., Branke, J.: Multi-swarm Optimization in Dynamic Environments. In: Applications of Evolutionary Computing, pp. 489–500. Springer, Heidelberg (2004)
21. Blackwell, T., Branke, J., Li, X.: Particle Swarms for Dynamic Optimization Problems. Swarm Intelligence, 193–217 (2008)
22. Du, W., Li, B.: Multi-strategy ensemble particle swarm optimization for dynamic optimization. Information Sciences 178, 3096–3109 (2008)
23. Li, C., Yang, S.: A clustering particle swarm optimizer for dynamic optimization. In: IEEE Congress on Evolutionary Computation, pp. 439–446 (2009)
24. Liu, L., Wang, D., Yang, S.: Compound Particle Swarm Optimization in Dynamic Environments. Applications of Evolutionary Computing, 616–625 (2008)
25. Liu, L., Yang, S., Wang, D.: Particle Swarm Optimization With Composite Particles in Dynamic Environments. IEEE Transactions on Systems, Man, and Cybernetics, Part B: Cybernetics, 1–15 (2010)
26. Hashemi, A.B., Meybodi, M.R.: Cellular PSO: A PSO for Dynamic Environments. Advances in Computation and Intelligence, 422–433 (2009)
27. Hashemi, A.B., Meybodi, M.R.: A multi-role cellular PSO for dynamic environments. In: 14th International CSI Computer Conference, Tehran, Iran, pp. 412–417 (2009)
28. Branke, J.: Memory enhanced evolutionary algorithms for changing optimization problem. In: 1999 Congress on Evolutionary Computation, Washington D.C., USA, vol. 3, pp. 1875–1882 (1999)
29. Moser, I.: All Currently Known Publications On Approaches Which Solve the Moving Peaks Problem. Swinburne University of Technology, Melbourne, Australia (2007)
30. Branke, J., Schmeck, H.: Designing evolutionary algorithms for dynamic optimization problems. Advances in evolutionary computing: theory and applications, 239–262 (2003)
31. van den Bergh, F.: An Analysis of Particle Swarm Optimizers, Ph.D. dissertation, Department of Computer Science, University of Pretoria, Pretoria, South Africa (2002)

# Power Mutation Embedded Modified PSO for Global Optimization Problems

Pinkey Chauhan[1], Kusum Deep[1], and Millie Pant[2]

[1] Department of Mathematics, Indian Institute of Technology Roorkee
[2] Department of Paper and Pulp Technology, Indian Institute of Technology Roorkee,
Roorkee - 247667, India
`pinkeychauhan030@gmail.com,`
`{kusumfma,millifpt}@iitr.ernet.in`

**Abstract.** In the present study we propose a simple and modified framework for Particle Swarm Optimization (PSO) algorithm by incorporating in it a newly defined operator based on Power Mutation (PM). The resulting PSO variants are named as (Modified Power Mutation PSO) MPMPSO and MPMPSO 1 which differs from each other in the manner of implementation of mutation operator. In MPMPSO, PM is applied stochastically in conjugation with basic position update equation of PSO and in MPMPSO 1, PM is applied on the worst particle of swarm at each iteration. A suite of ten standard benchmark problems is employed to evaluate the performance of the proposed variations. Experimental results show that the proposed MPMPSO outperforms the existing method on most of the test functions in terms of convergence and solution quality.

**Keywords:** Power Mutation, Particle Swarm Optimization.

## 1 Introduction

PSO, a popular algorithm for solving global optimization problems, is a member of the wide category of swarm intelligence methods, which are based on the simulation of the social behaviour displayed by various species. The main idea behind the particle swarm concept was to graphically simulate the coordinated and unpredictable behaviour of a bird flock [2], with the aim of discovering patterns that govern the ability of birds to fly synchronously, and to suddenly change direction with a regrouping in an optimal formation. From this initial objective, the concept evolved into a simple and efficient optimization algorithm. This innovative idea was introduced by Kennedy and Eberhart in 1995[2] that contribute a lot in solving complex and nonlinear global optimization problems. In PSO, individuals, referred to as particles, are "flown" through hyper dimensional search space. Changes to the position of particles within the search space are based on personal and social behaviour of particles. The changes to a particle within the swarm are therefore influenced by factors like particle's personal and its neighbours experience/ knowledge. The most advantageous fact with PSO is that it can be easily implemented as compared to other population based algorithms and is efficient in solving many real world complex optimization problems. PSO has a more global searching ability at the beginning of the run and has greater local search ability

B.K. Panigrahi et al. (Eds.): SEMCCO 2010, LNCS 6466, pp. 139–146, 2010.
© Springer-Verlag Berlin Heidelberg 2010

near the end of the run. Several researchers have analysed the performance of PSO with different settings [3, 9, 10, 11, 14]. However, like other population based algorithms, PSO also faces the problem of premature convergence with the increase in complexity of the problems. This mainly happens due to the loss of diversity as a consequence of fast information flow among the particles. To overcome this drawback many ideas borrowed from other metaheuristic methods has been implemented in PSO by researchers. Concept of Mutation in Evolutionary algorithms maintains diversity in search space and helps the algorithm to come out of local optima. The notion of implementing mutation in PSO was also found effective to deal with the problem of 'trapping in local optima'. So far many mutation operators like Gaussian, Cauchy, uniform and Levy mutation etc. has been implemented in PSO to improve its performance. [6] proposed the implementation of Gaussian mutation in PSO. Cauchy mutation operators with different modifications were implemented in PSO by [1, 7] to enhance the searching ability and prevent premature convergence. [8] proposed the idea of mutation in PSO based on Levy distribution that employs a larger capability of the global exploration by providing a large velocity scale for each particle.

In this paper we propose the idea of implementing power mutation (PM) [4] in PSO using two strategies different from each other in the manner in which mutation is applied. We compared our results with PSO, Cauchy mutation [1], FDR-PSO [5], CEP [12], FEP [12] and PMPSO [13] on ten well known benchmark functions. The remaining of this paper is organised as follows. Section 2 gives a brief view of Standard PSO. Section 3 presents the detailed description of proposed variants of PSO. Ten benchmark problems are taken to evaluate the performance of proposed variants which are described in section 4. Analysis of results is done in Section 5. Section 6 concludes the paper.

## 2   Basic Particle Swarm Optimization

For a D-dimensional space, the i-th particle of the swarm can be represented as a D-dimensional vector, $X_i = (x_{i1}, x_{i2}, ..., x_{iD})^T$. The velocity (position change) of this particle can be represented by another D- dimensional vector $V_i = (v_{i1},... ,v_{iD})^T$. The best previously visited position of the $i$-th particle is denoted as $P_i = (p_{i1}, p_{i2}, ..., p_{iD})^T$. Defining $g$ as the index of the best particle in the swarm, the swarm is manipulated according to velocity update equation and position update equation which are given by (1) and (2) respectively as below:

$$v_{id} = w * v_{id} + c_1 r_1 (p_{id} - x_{id}) + c_2 r_2 (p_{gd} - x_{id})$$

(1)

$$x_{id} = x_{id} + v_{id}$$

(2)

Where $d = 1, 2... D; i = 1, 2... S$, where $S$ is the size of the swarm. $w$ is the weighting factor, for large value of "$w$" particle tends to keep its current direction for a longer time that prevents premature convergence. "$c_1$" and "$c_2$" are constants, called cognitive and social scaling parameters respectively used to measure the contribution of personal and social components. The parameters "$r_1$" and "$r_2$" are used to maintain diversity of the population and are uniformly distributed in the range [0,1]. Equations (1) and (2) define the initial version of PSO algorithm. A constant, $Vmax$, is used to arbitrarily limit the velocities of the particles and improve the resolution of the search.

## 3  The Modified Power Mutation PSO

The modified Power mutation PSO is based on the implementation of Power Mutation (PM) in PSO with different strategies. In a previous study [13] implementation of PM in PSO is done over the gbest particle that guides the whole swarm and pushes the swarm towards better positions. Here in this paper we have proposed two types of implementations of Power mutation, which is a mutation operator for Real coded GA proposed by [4]. The first implementation is performed at the movement of particles with a predefined probability 0.5 as an alternative to basic position update equation. The basic position update equation is mainly governed by the velocity update equation, and works as an implicit mutation operator that maintains the diversity within the search space. Therefore in the present variant we have proposed the implementation of an explicit mutation operator to update particle positions as an alternative, so as to increase the diversity and performance of PSO. This modified PSO algorithm is named as MPMPSO. Another variant of PSO proposed in this paper is based on the implementation of Power mutation on the worst particle within the search space. This worst particle is traced on the basis of fitness evaluation of particle's personal best positions. Particle with the lowest personal best fitness value is considered as the worst particle of the swarm. Although this strategy may led to decrease in the diversity of the search space but on the other hand increases the convergence of the algorithm. This implementation of Power mutation in PSO is named as MPMPSO 1.

For the second Variant (MPMPSO 1) the Standard PSO procedure is same but with an additional step of searching the worst particle of swarm at each iteration and mutate it using power mutation and then replace the worst particle with the mutated one, if it has better fitness value. The Mutation operator considered in this study is described in subsection with parameter settings taken in proposed PSO variants. The basic steps for proposed variant MPMPSO are briefly shown below.

---
***Algorithm for MPMPSO***

*begin*
    *t→0    // iteration*
    *Initialize a D – dimensional swarm, S*
    *Evaluate fitness of each particle of swarm*
  *For t=1 to Max iteration*
  *For i=1 to S*
    *For d=1 to D*
      *Update velocity using basic velocity update equation (1)*
      *Update Position as*
      *If(rand() ≤ 0.5)*
        *Apply basic position update equation(2)*
     *end*
     *else*
      *Perform power mutation with prob $P_m = 1/d$*
     *end*
    *End –for-d;*
   *Evaluate fitness of updated positions*
   *Update Pbest and Gbest*
   *End-for-i;*
  *Iteration (t)++;*
  *End-for-t;*
 *End*
---

### 3.1 Power Mutation

Let $\bar{x}$ be a parent solution then a mutated solution, $x$ is created in the following manner. First, a uniform random     number $t \in [0, 1]$ and a random number $s$ which follows the power distribution, $s = (s_1)^p$, where "$s_1$" is a uniform random number between 0 and 1, are created and "$p$" is called the index of mutation. It governs the strength of perturbation of power mutation. Having determined "$s$" a mutated solution is created as:

$$x = \begin{cases} \bar{x} - s(\bar{x} - x^l), & t < r; \\ \bar{x} + s(x^u - \bar{x}), & t \geq r. \end{cases}$$

Where, $t = \dfrac{\bar{x} - x^l}{x^u - \bar{x}}$ and $x^l$, $x^u$ being the lower and upper bounds on the value of the

decision variable and r a uniformly distributed random number between 0 and 1. Here in MPMPSO and MPMPSO 1, we decrease the perturbation parameter $p$ iteration wise from 25 to 1.0. In early iteration for large value of $p$, mutated   particle will be far from parent particle that increase the explorative property of PSO, while in later iterations of PSO the small value of "$p$" led to the convergence of particle of PSO to global optimal solutions as the mutated particle will we near to the parent particles in later stage.

## 4   Test Problems: Parameter Settings and Results

In order to test the proposed improved variants of PSO, ten test problems are taken that are listed in Table 4. The test suite consists of unimodal as well as multimodal functions to evaluate the performance of proposed algorithms. Functions from f1 to f6 are unimodal while functions from f7 to f10 are multimodal with the aim to minimize each function.

### 4.1   Parameter Settings

A choice of suitable parameters contributes a lot to improve the performance of PSO. In this study, we have taken the same parameter settings as in previous studies [13]. The parameter settings for proposed variants are given as below in Table 1. Other then these parameters described in Table 1. We have   chosen the value of $V_{max}$ as the half of the search space on each dimension as we observed experimentally that it worked better than a fixed $V_{max}$ value.

- Acceleration Coefficients, $C_1 = C_2 = 1.49618$
- Swarm Size = 50 and Numbers of Simulations = 30
- $V_{max} = 0.5 (x_{max} - x_{min})$ and Inertia  weight (w) = 0.72984
- Maximum no of generations are set as: For functions from $f_1$ to $f_4$, Max No. Of Generations is set to 1000, for $f_5$, Max.  No of Generations are set to 10000, for $f_6$ Max Generations are set to 3000, for $f_7$ and $f_8$ it is set to 5000 and for $f_9$ and $f_{10}$ Max Generations are set to 1000.

**Table 1.** Results obtained using PSO, HPSO, and FDR-PSO for Functions from f1-f4

|        | PSO [1]  |          | HPSO[1]  |          | FDR-PSO[5] |
|--------|----------|----------|----------|----------|----------|
| Fun.   | Mean     | SD       | Mean     | SD       | Mean     |
| $f_1$  | 1.57e-06 | 5.11e-06 | 1.79e-07 | 3.51e-07 | 2.63e-07 |
| $f_2$  | 3.53e-06 | 1.55e-05 | 6.38e-07 | 1.98e-06 | 1.07e-05 |
| $f_3$  | 17.5646  | 36.4659  | 0.398    | 0.3082   | 0.9080   |
| $f_4$  | 1.84e-19 | 6.14e-19 | 2.53e-19 | 9.38e-19 | 5.3e-19  |

**Table 2.** Results obtained using PSO, HPSO, CEP, and FEP for Functions $f_5 - f_9$

|         | PSO[1]   |          | HPSO[1]  |          | CEP[12]  |          | FEP[12]  |          |
|---------|----------|----------|----------|----------|----------|----------|----------|----------|
| Fun.    | Mean     | SD       | Mean     | SD       | Mean     | SD       | Mean     | SD       |
| $f_5$   | 1.8016   | 2.8389   | 1.419    | 1.4256   | 6.17     | 13.61    | 5.06     | 5.87     |
| $f_6$   | 4.57e-03 | 1.69e-03 | 4.37e-03 | 1.51e-03 | 1.8e-02  | 6.4e-03  | 7.6e-03  | 2.6e-03  |
| $f_7$   | -6726.5  | 544.5    | -12558.9 | 6.2373   | -7917.5  | 634.5    | -12554.5 | 52.6     |
| $f_8$   | 37.0721  | 9.7295   | 31.8005  | 9.1618   | 89.0     | 23.1     | 4.6e-02  | 2.1e-03  |
| $f_9$   | 8.96e-02 | 0.2882   | 3.66e-02 | 3.19e-02 | 8.6e-02  | 0.12     | 1.6e-02  | 2.2e-02  |
| $f_{10}$| 1.1289   | 1.1298   | 8.86e-06 | 8.58e-02 | 9.2      | 2.8      | 1.8e-02  | 2.1e-03  |

## 4.2   Experimental Results

In this section, computational results for testing of MPMPSO and MPMPSO 1 on ten benchmark problems described above are reported. The algorithms are coded in visual C++. Table 1 gives the results as quoted in literature for PSO, HPSO, and FDR-PSO on functions $f_1$ to $f_4$ over. Table 2 contains results for PSO, HPSO, CEP, and FEP on functions $f_5$ to $f_{10}$ as recorded in literature. Table 3 shows results for both proposed modified versions of PSO and PMPSO [13] on functions $f_1$ to $f_{10}$ over 30 runs and 100 runs respectively. The Mean and SD stands for the mean best function values found over the max no of generations taken and standard deviation respectively.

**Table 3.** Results obtained using PMPSO and MPMPSO and MPMPSO 1 for Functions $f_1 - f_{10}$

| | PMPSO[13] | | MPMPSO | | MPMPSO 1 | |
|---|---|---|---|---|---|---|
| Fun. | Mean | SD | Mean | SD | Mean | SD |
| f1 | 1.02e-11 | 5.37e-13 | 0.0 | 0.0 | 2.19e-05 | 1.75e-05 |
| f2 | 5.99e-09 | 2.31e-10 | 1.05 | 5.14 | 4.15e-04 | 8.55e-03 |
| f3 | 1.56e-10 | 9.63e-11 | 1.92e-05 | 7.13e-01 | 7.81e-02 | 3.67e-02 |
| f4 | 2.45e-31 | 6.21e-32 | 3.87e-48 | 3.81e-47 | 2.56e-15 | 1.11e-12 |
| f5 | 0.158 | 0.246 | 2.51e-03 | 1.61e-02 | 8.46e-02 | 1.55e-02 |
| f6 | 2.42e-03 | 3.14e-03 | 1.17e-04 | 1.08e-04 | 5.03e-03 | 1.20e-02 |
| f7 | -8305.5 | 357.6 | -10357.988 | 707.01 | -10697.786 | 770.21 |
| f8 | 38.8 | 11.3 | 0.0 | 0.0 | 1.89 | 1.33 |
| f9 | 4.43e-02 | 1.48e-02 | 0.0 | 0.0 | 0.33921 | 0.196 |
| f10 | 1.16 | 1.52 | 4.44e-16 | 4.41e-16 | 8.85e-002 | 0.905 |

## 5   Analysis of Results

In this Section, we discuss the results obtained by the proposed versions and other algorithms. Computational results clearly show that the proposed MPMPSO outperforms other algorithms on functions $f_1$ and $f_4$ - $f_{10}$ except $f_7$, but for $f_7$ results are still better from PMPSO, PSO and CEP. While for functions $f_2$ and $f_3$ results are not as good as compared to other algorithms, but for MPMPSO it is observed experimentally that results for these functions improved with great degree by changing swarm size and number of generations. On the other hand, implementation of PM on worst particle of the swarm (MPMPSO 1) works very well on functions like $f_3$, $f_5$, $f_6$, $f_7$ and $f_{10}$. For function $f_7$, MPMPSO 1 worked better then PSO, CEP, PMPSO and MPMPSO and on fun $f_5$ it outperformed all other algorithms except MPMPSO. Hence MPMPSO 1 is also efficient for solving multimodal functions and also works well on unimodal function. Hence from above discussion of results we observed that the two proposed variants produces good results on considered test problems and could be recommend to solve other test problems and real life based applications.

**Table 4.** Unimodal (f1-f6) and Multimodal (f7-f10) test functions used in the present study

| Function | Range & Dimension | Minima |
|---|---|---|
| $f_1(x) = \sum_{i=1}^{n} x_i^2$ | $[-5.12, 5.12]^{20}$ | 0 |
| $f_2(x) = \sum_{i=1}^{n} i * x_i^2$ | $[-5.12, 5.12]^{20}$ | 0 |
| $f_3(x) = \sum_{i=1}^{n} \left( \sum_{j=1}^{i} x_j \right)^2$ | $[-65.536, 65.636]^{20}$ | 0 |
| $f_4(x) = \sum_{i=1}^{n} |x_i|^{i+1}$ | $[-1, 1]^{20}$ | 0 |
| $f_5(x) = \sum_{i=1}^{n-1} \left( 100 * (x_{i+1} - x_i^2)^2 + (x_i - 1)^2 \right)$ | $[-30, 30]^{30}$ | 0 |
| $f_6(x) = \sum_{i=1}^{n} i * x_i^4 + random\, [0,1)$ | $[-1.28, 1.28]^{30}$ | 0 |
| $f_7(x) = \sum_{i=1}^{n} - x_i * \sin\left( -\sqrt{|x_i|} \right)$ | $[-500, 500]^{30}$ | -12569.5 |
| $f_8(x) = 10n + \sum_{i=1}^{n} \left( x_i^2 - 10\cos(2\pi x_i) \right)$ | $[-5.12, 5.12]^{30}$ | 0 |
| $f_9(x) = \sum_{i=1}^{n} \frac{x_i^2}{4000} - \prod_{i=1}^{n} \cos\left( \frac{x_i}{\sqrt{i}} \right) + 1$ | $[-600, 600]^{30}$ | 0 |
| $f_{10}(x) = 20 + e - 20\exp\left( 0.02\sum_{i=1}^{n} \sqrt{\frac{1}{n}\sum_{i=1}^{n} x_i^2} \right) - \exp\left( \frac{1}{n}\sum_{i=1}^{n}\cos(2\pi x_i) \right)$ | $[-30, 30]^{30}$ | 0 |

## 6  Conclusion

This paper presents two modified variants of PSO by incorporating power mutation at different points in standard PSO. These versions are proposed with the aim of solving premature convergence problem in PSO. The experimental results shows that the proposed version MPMPSO outperforms the previous PM based version of PSO [13] and most of the other algorithms taken for comparison for multimodal as well as unimodal functions. The other variant MPMPSO 1 is also efficient for solving multimodal functions as compared to PMPSO and other algorithms and performs very well on unimodal functions. The experimental results show that the new variant MPMPSO is efficient for solving multimodal as well as unimodal function. Here the results are taken for restricted number of generations and swarm size. It is observed that by changing these parameters we can find the better optimal solutions for functions like $f_2$ and $f_3$, although it will result in increase of computation and function evaluations. Hence the proposed variants are efficient and reliable algorithms for solving various optimization problems.

**Acknowledgement.** The second author, acknowledges Ministry of Human Resources, New Delhi, India, for providing the financial support.

# References

1. Wang, H., Liu, Y., Li, C.H., Zeng, S.Y.: A hybrid particle swarm algorithm with Cauchy mutation. In: Proceedings of IEEE Swarm Intelligence Symposium, pp. 356–360 (2007)
2. Kennedy, J., Eberhart, R.C.: Particle Swarm Optimization. In: Proceedings of the IEEE International Joint Conference on Neural Networks, pp. 1942–1948 (1995)
3. Kennedy, J.: Small Worlds and Mega-Minds: Effects of Neighbourhood Topology on Particle Swarm Performance. In: Proceedings of the 1999 Congress of Evolutionary Computation, vol. 3, pp. 1931–1938. IEEE Press, Los Alamitos (1999)
4. Deep, K., Thakur, M.: A new mutation operator for real coded genetic algorithms. Applied mathematics and Computation 193, 211–230 (2007)
5. Veeramachaneni, K., Peram, T., Mohan, C., Osadciw, L.A.: Optimization using particle swarms with near neighbour interactions. In: Cantú-Paz, E., Foster, J.A., Deb, K., Davis, L., Roy, R., O'Reilly, U.-M., Beyer, H.-G., Kendall, G., Wilson, S.W., Harman, M., Wegener, J., Dasgupta, D., Potter, M.A., Schultz, A., Dowsland, K.A., Jonoska, N., Miller, J., Standish, R.K. (eds.) GECCO 2003. LNCS, vol. 2723, pp. 110–121. Springer, Heidelberg (2003)
6. Higashi, N., Iba, H.: Particle Swarm Optimization with Gaussian Mutation. In: IEEE Swarm Intelligence Symposium, Indianapolis, pp. 72–79 (2003)
7. Kang, L., Liu, Y., Zeng, S.: Fast Multi-swarm Optimization with Cauchy Mutation and Crossover Operation. In: Kang, L., Liu, Y., Zeng, S. (eds.) ISICA 2007. LNCS, vol. 4683, pp. 344–352. Springer, Heidelberg (2007)
8. Cai, X., Zeng, J.C., Cui, Z., Tan, Y.: Particle Swarm Optimization Using Lévy Probability Distribution. In: Kang, L., Liu, Y., Zeng, S. (eds.) ISICA 2007. LNCS, vol. 4683, pp. 353–361. Springer, Heidelberg (2007)
9. Clerc, M.: The Swarm and the Queen, Towards a Deterministic and Adaptive Particle Swarm Optimization. In: Proceedings 1999 Congress on Evolutionary computation, Washington DC, pp. 1951–1957 (1999)
10. Suganthan, P.N.: Particle Swarm Optimiser with Neighbourhood Operator. In: Proceedings of the 1999 Congress of Evolutionary Computation, vol. 3, pp. 1958–1962. IEEE Press, Los Alamitos (1999)
11. Shi, Y.H., Eberhart, R.C.: A Modified Particle Swarm Optimizer. In: Proceedings IEEE International Conference on Evolutionary Computation, Anchorage, Alaska (1998)
12. Yao, X., Liu, Y., Lin, G.: Evolutionary programming made faster. IEEE Transactions on Evolutionary Computation 3, 82–102 (1999)
13. Xiaoling, W., Zhong, M.: Particle swarm Optimization Based on Power Mutation. In: International Colloquium on Computing, Communication, Control, and Management (ISECS), pp. 464–467 (2009)
14. Shi, Y., Eberhart, R.C.: Parameter Selection in Particle Swarm Optimization. In: Porto, V.W., Waagen, D. (eds.) EP 1998. LNCS, vol. 1447, pp. 591–600. Springer, Heidelberg (1998)

# PSO Advances and Application to Inverse Problems

Juan Luis Fernández-Martínez[1,2,3] and Esperanza García-Gonzalo[1]

[1] Department of Mathematics, University of Oviedo, Oviedo, Spain
[2] Energy Resources Department, Stanford University, Palo Alto, California, USA
[3] Department of Civil and Environmental Engineering,
University of California Berkeley, Berkeley, USA

**Abstract.** Particle swarm optimization (PSO) is a Swarm Intelligence technique used for optimization motivated by the social behavior of individuals in large groups in nature. The damped mass-spring analogy known as the PSO continuous model allowed us to derive a whole family of particle swarm optimizers with different properties with regard to their exploitation/exploration balance. Using the theory of stochastic differential and difference equations, we fully characterize the stability behavior of these algorithms. PSO and RR-PSO are the most performant algorithms of this family in terms of rate of convergence. Other family members have better exploration capabilities. The so called four point algorithms use more information of previous iterations to update the particles positions and trajectories and seem to be more exploratory than most of the 3 points versions. Finally, based on the done analysis, we can affirm that the PSO optimizers are not heuristic algorithms since there exist mathematical results that can be used to explain their consistency/convergence.

**Keywords:** Particle Swarm Optimization, Stochastic Stability Analysis, Convergence, Inverse Problems.

## 1 The Generalized PSO (GPSO)

The particle swarm algorithm [6] applied to optimization problems is very simple: individuals, or particles, are represented by vectors whose length is the number of degrees of freedom of the optimization problem. First, a population of particles is initialized with random positions $(\mathbf{x}_i^0)$ and velocities $(\mathbf{v}_i^0)$. An objective function is used to compute the objective value for each particle. As time advances, the position and velocity of each particle is updated taking in account its objective function value and of the objective function values of its neighbors. At time-step $k+1$, the algorithm updates positions $\left(\mathbf{x}_i^{k+1}\right)$ and velocities $\left(\mathbf{v}_i^{k+1}\right)$ of the individuals as follows:

$$\mathbf{v}_i^{k+1} = \omega \mathbf{v}_i^k + \phi_1(\mathbf{g}^k - \mathbf{x}_i^k) + \phi_2(\mathbf{l}_i^k - \mathbf{x}_i^k),$$
$$\mathbf{x}_i^{k+1} = \mathbf{x}_i^k + \mathbf{v}_i^{k+1},$$

B.K. Panigrahi et al. (Eds.): SEMCCO 2010, LNCS 6466, pp. 147–154, 2010.

with

$$\phi_1 = r_1 a_g, \; \phi_2 = r_2 a_l, \; r_1, r_2 \in U(0,1) \; \omega, a_l, a_g \in \mathbb{R},$$

where $\mathbf{l}_i^k$ is the $i$−th particle's best position, $\mathbf{g}^k$ the global best position on the whole swarm, $\phi_1$, $\phi_2$ are the random global and local accelerations, and $\omega$ is a real constant called inertia weight. Finally, $r_1$ and $r_2$ are random numbers uniformly distributed in $(0,1)$, to weight the global and local acceleration constants, $a_g$ and $a_l$.

PSO can be seen as the particular case for $\Delta t = 1$ of the generalized PSO (GPSO) algorithm [2]:

$$v(t + \Delta t) = (1 - (1 - \omega)\,\Delta t)\,v(t) + \phi_1 \Delta t \,(g(t) - x(t)) + \phi_2 \Delta t\,(l(t) - x(t)),$$
$$x(t + \Delta t) = x(t) + v(t + \Delta t)\Delta t.$$

This algorithm can be spelled only in terms of position using a three point $(t + \Delta t, t$ and $t - \Delta t)$ difference equation:

$$x(t + \Delta t) + Ax(t) + Bx(t - \Delta t) = (\phi_1 g(t) + \phi_2 l(t))\Delta t^2 \tag{1}$$

with

$$A = \Delta t(1 - w)\Delta t - 2 + \Delta t^2 \phi \qquad B = 1 - (1 - w)\Delta t$$

This model was derived using a mechanical analogy: a damped mass-spring system with unit mass, damping factor, $1 - \omega$, and total stiffness constant, $\phi = \phi_1 + \phi_2$, the so-called PSO continuous model:

$$\begin{cases} x''(t) + (1 - \omega)\,x'(t) + \phi x(t) = \phi_1 g\,(t - t_0) + \phi_2 l\,(t - t_0), \; t \in R, \\ x(0) = x_0, \\ x'(0) = v_0. \end{cases}$$

In this case $x(t)$ stands for the coordinate trajectory of any particle in the swarm. It interacts with other particles through the local and global attractors, $l(t)$, $g(t)$. In this model, mean particle trajectories oscillate around the point:

$$o(t) = \frac{a_g g\,(t - t_0) + a_l l\,(t - t_0)}{a_g + a_l}.$$

and the attractors might be delayed a time $t_0$ with respect to the particle trajectories [3]. The first and second order moment stability regions for the GPSO are:

$$S_{gpso}^1 = \left\{ (\omega, \overline{\phi}) : 1 - \frac{2}{\Delta t} < \omega < 1, \; 0 < \overline{\phi} < \frac{1}{\Delta t^2}(2\omega\Delta t - 2\Delta t + 4) \right\},$$

$$S_{gpso}^2 = \left\{ (\omega, \overline{\phi}) : 1 - \frac{2}{\Delta t} < \omega < 1, \; 0 < \overline{\phi} < \phi_{gpso}\,(w, \alpha, \Delta t) \right\},$$

where $\overline{\phi} = \frac{a_g + a_l}{2}$ is the total mean acceleration and $\phi_{gpso}\,(\omega, \alpha, \Delta t)$ is the analytic expression for the limit hyperbola of second order stability:

$$\phi_{gpso}\,(\omega, \alpha, \Delta t) = \frac{12}{\Delta t}\frac{(1 - \omega)\,(2 + (\omega - 1)\,\Delta t)}{4 - 4(\omega - 1)\Delta t + (\alpha^2 - 2\alpha)\,(2 + (\omega - 1)\Delta t)}.$$

$\alpha = \frac{a_g}{\overline{\phi}} = \frac{2a_g}{a_g + a_l}$ is the ratio between the global acceleration and the total mean acceleration, and varies in the interval $[0, 2]$. Low values of $\alpha$ imply that for the same value of $\overline{\phi}$ the local acceleration is bigger than the global one, and thus, the algorithm is more exploratory. These stability regions do coincide for $\Delta t = 1$ with those shown in previous analyses for the PSO case [1], [8], [7].

Figure 1a-b shows, for the PSO case, the first and second order stability regions and their corresponding spectral radii. The spectral radii are related to the attenuation of the first and second order trajectories. In the PSO case, the first order spectral radius is zero in $(\omega, \overline{\phi}) = (0, 1)$. The first order stability zone $(S^1_{gpso})$ only depends on $(w, \overline{\phi})$, while the second order stability region $(S^2_{gpso})$ depends on $(w, a_g, a_l)$. Also, the second order stability region is embedded in the first order stability region, and depends symmetrically on $\alpha$, reaching its maximum size when $\alpha = 1$ $(a_l = a_g)$.

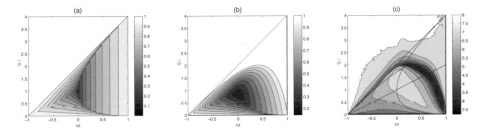

**Fig. 1.** PSO: (a) First and (b) second order stability region and corresponding spectral radii. (c) Logarithmic median misfit errors for the Rosenbrock function in 50 simulations after 300 iterations.

## 2  Other PSO Family Members

Beginning with the mechanical analogy and the PSO continuous model, a family of PSO members with different properties with regard to their exploitation/exploration balance has been constructed. We can have progressive, centered and regressive discretizations both for acceleration and velocity. The result can be a three point difference equation as in PSO (1), CC-PSO, CP-PSO, RR-PSO and PP-PSO; or a four point difference equation as in RC-PSO, RP-PSO, PR-PSO and PC-PSO. The different discretizations and the resulting algorithms are shown in Table 1. The consistency of the different PSO family members has been related to the stability of their first and second order trajectories [5], [3]. The type of mean trajectories depend on the character of the eigenvalues of the first order difference equation. Basically there are four kind of trajectories: damped oscillatory in the complex eigenvalue region, symmetrically and asymmetrically zigzagging in the regions of negative real eigenvalues and almost monotonous decreasing character in the region of positive real eigenvalues. Maximum exploration in reached in the complex region. The second order trajectories show a

**Table 1.** Different schema for the discretization of the mass-spring equation and the resulting algorithms

|  |  | Acceleration discretization | | |
|---|---|---|---|---|
|  |  | *Regressive* | *Centered* | *Progressive* |
|  | *Regressive* | RR-PSO | PSO | **PR-PSO** |
| **Velocity discretization** | *Centered* | **RC-PSO** | CC-PSO | **PC-PSO** |
|  | *Progressive* | **RP-PSO** | CP-PSO | PP-PSO |

similar kind of behavior. The second order spectral radius controls the rate of attenuation of the second order moments of the particle trajectories (variance and temporal covariance between $x(t)$ and $x(t + \Delta t)$). These results have been confirmed by numerical experiments with different benchmark functions in several dimensions. Figure 1c shows for PSO the contour plots of the misfit error (in logarithmic scale) after a certain number of iterations (300) for the Rosenbrock function. This numerical analysis is done for a lattice of $(\omega, \overline{\phi})$ points located in the corresponding first order stability regions over 50 different simulations. For GPSO, CC-PSO and CP-PSO better parameter sets $\omega, a_g, a_l$ are located on the first order complex region, close to the upper border of the second order stability region where the attraction from the particle oscillation center is lost, i.e. the variance becomes unbounded; and around the intersection to the median lines of the first stability regions where the temporal covariance between trajectories is close to zero. The PP-PSO [4] does not converge for $\omega < 0$, and the good parameter sets are in the complex region close to the limit of second order stability and to $\overline{\phi} = 0$. The good parameters sets for the RR-PSO are concentrated around the line of equation $\overline{\phi} = 3\left(\omega - \frac{3}{2}\right)$, mainly for inertia values greater than two. This line is located in a zone of medium attenuation and high frequency of trajectories.

Figure 2 shows, for the different members of the PSO family, the second order spectral radii, related to the most interesting points $(\omega, \overline{\phi})$ from both the point of view of the convergence and exploration. These points are located inside or close to the border. Figures 3 and 4 show some numerical results for two benchmark functions. These same experiments have been made for 10 and 30 dimensions, and with Rastrigin and Sphere benchmark functions.

## 3   Selection of the PSO Member: Application to Inverse Problems

Most of the inverse problems can be written in discrete form as:

$$\mathbf{d} = \mathbf{F}(\mathbf{m})$$

where $\mathbf{d} \in \mathbf{R}^s$ is the observed data, $\mathbf{m} \in \mathbf{R}^n$ is the vector containing the model parameters, and $\mathbf{F} : \mathbf{R}^n \to \mathbf{R}^s$ is the physical model, that typically involves the

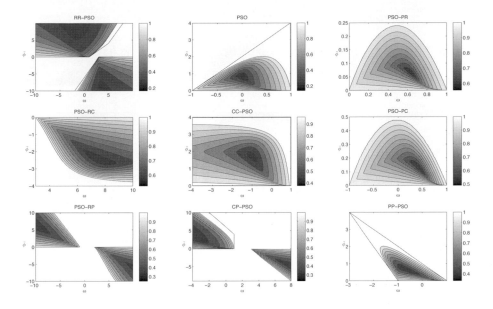

**Fig. 2.** Second order spectral radius for all the members of the family

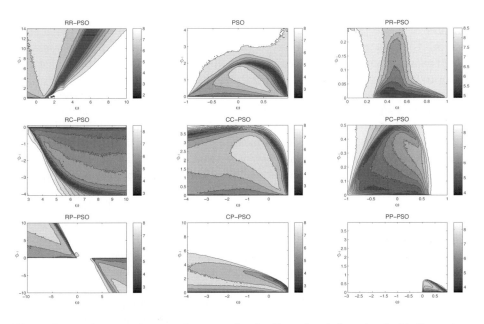

**Fig. 3.** Logarithmic median misfit errors for the Rosenbrock function in 50 dimensions after 300 iterations with 100 particles using 50 runs for each point for all the members of the family

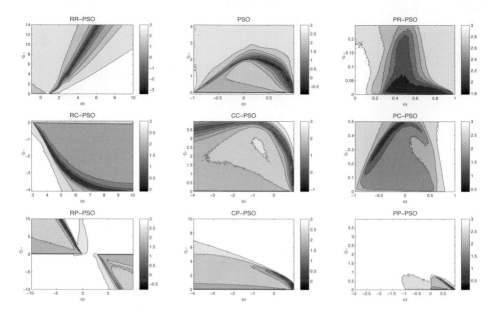

**Fig. 4.** Logarithmic median misfit errors for the Griewank function with the same parameters as in Figure 3

solution of a set partial differential equations, integral equations or algebraic system. Given a particular observed data set $\mathbf{d}$, the inverse problem is then solved as an optimization problem, that is, finding the model that minimizes the data prediction error expressed in a certain norm $\|\mathbf{d} - \mathbf{F}(\mathbf{m})\|_p$.

The above optimization problem turns out to be ill-posed because the forward model $\mathbf{F}$ is a simplification of reality (numerical approximations included); the data are noisy and discrete in number, that is, there is not a sufficient number of data to uniquely determine one solution. These three points cause an inverse problem to be very different from any other kind of optimization problem since physics and data are involved on the cost function. In addition, the topography of the prediction error function usually corresponds to functions having the global minimum located in a very flat and elongated valley or surrounded by many local minima, as the Rosenbrock and Griewank functions. The type of the numerical difficulty found depends mainly on the forward functional $\mathbf{F}$, that is, the problem physics. The effect of data noise is to increase the presence of local minima and/or the size of the valley topography. Combinations of both pathologies are also possible in real problems.

Local optimization methods are not able to discriminate among the multiple choices consistent with the end criteria and may land quite unpredictably at any point on that area. These pathologies are treated through regularization techniques and the use of "good" prior information and/or initial guesses. Global optimization methods, such as genetic algorithms, simulated annealing, particle swarm, differential evolution, etc, are very interesting because instead of solving the inverse problem as an optimization problem, they are able to sample the region of the model space containing the models that fit the observed data within a given tolerance, that is, they are able to provide an idea of the posterior distribution of the inverse model parameters. To perform this task they do not need in principle any prior model to stabilize the inversion and are able to avoid the strong dependence of the solution upon noisy data.

Particle swarm optimization and its variants are interesting global methods since they are able to quickly approximate the posterior distribution of the model parameters. To correctly perform this task a good balance between exploration and exploitation, and the CP-PSO version seems to be a good option. Conversely when only a good model (the candidate to global minimum) is needed and no uncertainty analysis is performed, the RR-PSO and GPSO versions have better convergence rates to locate this solution. The RC-GPSO has worse convergence for some functions but better, for example, for the Rastrigin function, and so it can be an option to try instead of the PSO. This facts can be taken into account to select the appropriate PSO version when facing a real problem.

# 4   Conclusions

Particle swarm optimization (PSO) is an evolutionary computational technique used for optimization motivated by the social behavior of individuals in large groups in nature. Different approaches have been used to understand how this algorithm works and trying to improve its convergence properties for different kind of problems. These approaches go from heuristic to mathematical analysis, passing through numerical experimentation. Although the scientific community has been able to solve a big variety of engineering problems, the tuning of the PSO parameters still remains one of its major drawbacks. By trying to avoid heuristics, it can be proved that PSO can be physically interpreted as a particular discretization of a stochastic damped mass-spring system. Knowledge of this analogy has been crucial in deriving the PSO continuous model and to deduce a family of PSO members with different properties with regard to their exploitation/exploration balance. At first, we derived a family of PSO-like versions algorithms wich can be written as three point difference finite equation (CC-PSO, CP-PSO, PP-PSO, and RR-PSO). Using the theory of stochastic differential and difference equations, we fully characterize the stability behavior of these algorithms. For well posed problems, a sufficient condition to achieve convergence is to select the PSO parameters close to the upper limit of second order stability. This result is also confirmed by numerical experimentation for different benchmark functions having an increasing degree of numerical difficulties. Although the first and second order trajectories of these algorithms are isomorphic, they are very different from GPSO. All these algorithms can be written as three point difference finite equation. If we consider the four discretizations left, they can be written as a four point difference finite equation. This members of the family of PSO-like versions are: the RC-PSO (regressive-centered PSO), the RP-PSO (regressive-progressive PSO), the PR-PSO (progressive-regressive

PSO) and the PC-PSO (progressive-centered PSO). In the context of inverse problems, we address the question of how to select the appropriate PSO version: the four points algorithms, CP-PSO and PP-PSO are the most exploratory versions and should be selected when we want to perform sampling of the posterior distribution of the inverse model parameters. Conversely, RR-PSO, CC-PSO and GPSO provide higher convergence rates. The RC-GPSO has worse convergence for some functions but better for example, the Rastrigin function, and so it can be an option to try instead of the PSO.

**Acknowledgments.** This work benefited from a one-year sabbatical grant at the University of California Berkeley (Department of Civil and Environmental Engineering), given by the University of Oviedo (Spain) and by the "Secretaría de Estado de Universidades y de Investigación" of the Spanish Ministry of Science and Innovation. We also acknowledge the financial support for the present academic year coming from the University of California Berkeley, the Lawrence Berkeley National Laboratory (Earth Science Division) and the Energy Resources Engineering Department at Stanford University, that is allowing us to apply this methodology to several geophysical and reservoir inverse problems (Stanford Center for Reservoir Forecasting and Smart Field Consortiums).

# References

1. Clerc, M., Kennedy, J.: The particle swarm - explosion, stability, and convergence in a multidimensional complex space. IEEE Trans. on Evol. Comp. 6, 58–73 (2002)
2. Fernández-Martínez, J.L., García-Gonzalo, E.: The generalized PSO: a new door to PSO evolution. J. of Artif. Evol. and Appl. Article ID 861275, 15 pages (2008)
3. Fernández-Martínez, J.L., García-Gonzalo, E.: The PSO family: deduction, stochastic analysis and comparison. Swarm Int. 3, 245–273 (2009)
4. Fernández-Martínez, J.L., García-Gonzalo, E.: The PP-GPSO and RR-GPSO. Tech. rep., University of Oviedo (2010)
5. Fernández-Martínez, J.L., García-Gonzalo, E., Fernández-Álvarez, J.: Theoretical analysis of particle swarm trajectories through a mechanical analogy. Int. J. of Comp. Int. Res. 4, 93–104 (2008)
6. Kennedy, J., Eberhart, R.: Particle swarm optimization. In: Proceedings IEEE International Conference on Neural Networks, Perth, WA, Australia, vol. 4, pp. 1942–1948 (1995)
7. Poli, R.: Dynamics and stability of the sampling distribution of particle swarm optimisers via moment analysis. J. of Artif. Evol. and Appl. Article ID 761459, 10 pages (2008)
8. Zheng, Y.L., Ma, L.H., Zhang, L.Y., Qian, J.X.: On the convergence analysis and parameter selection in particle swarm optimization. In: International Conference on Machine Learning and Cybernetics, Xi'an, China, vol. 3, pp. 1802–1807 (2003)

# Adaptive and Accelerated Exploration Particle Swarm Optimizer (AAEPSO) for Solving Constrained Multiobjective Optimization Problems

Layak Ali[1], Samrat L. Sabat[1,*], and Siba K. Udgata[2]

[1] School of Physics University of Hyderabad, Hyderabad -500046, India
`informlayak@gmail.com, slssp@gmail.com`
[2] Department of Computer & Information Sciences, University of Hyderabad,
Hyderabad 500046, India
`udgatacs@uohyd.ernet.in`

**Abstract.** Many science and engineering design problems are modeled as constrained multiobjective optimization problem. The major challenges in solving these problems are (i) conflicting objectives and (ii) non linear constraints. These conflicts are responsible for diverging the solution from true Pareto-front. This paper presents a variation of particle swarm optimization algorithm integrated with accelerated exploration technique that adapts to iteration for solving constrained multiobjective optimization problems. Performance of the proposed algorithm is evaluated on standard constrained multiobjective benchmark functions (CEC 2009) and compared with recently proposed DECMOSA algorithm. The comprehensive experimental results show the effectiveness of the proposed algorithm in terms of generation distance, diversity and convergence metric.

## 1 Introduction

Constrained Multiobjective Optimization (CMO) is an important research area in science and engineering domain [6]. The CMO usually involve, optimization of conflicting objectives subject to certain constraints. Many techniques have been proposed for solving unconstrained multiobjective optimization problems in the literature [1,3]. Similarly few techniques have also been proposed for solving CMO [7].

Particle Swarm Optimization (PSO) is a population-based Swarm Intelligence (SI), first introduced by Eberhart and Kennedy [2] used for solving optimization problems. It simulates the social behavior of a group of simple individuals i.e. bird flock or fish school [2]. Based on the collective intelligence, the swarm adjusts its flying direction to search for a global optimum. In PSO, each individual (particle) in the swarm represents a potential solution. Every particle remembers

---

* Corresponding author.

B.K. Panigrahi et al. (Eds.): SEMCCO 2010, LNCS 6466, pp. 155–162, 2010.

its current position and the best position found so far called personal best (*pbest*). The best solution among the whole swarm is called global best (*gbest*). The location of this member is communicated to all the particles and hence the flying trajectory of the particles is altered in the direction of the swarm's *gbest* and it's own *pbest* as

$$V = V + c_1 * \varepsilon_1 * (pbest - X) + c_2 * \varepsilon_2 * (gbest - X)$$
$$X = X + V$$

The basic PSO described by above equation is not able to find global solutions for multimodal functions. This is because, the solutions are trapped in local minima. To overcome this difficulty, many variants of PSO have been proposed and shown good performance in solving nonlinear unconstrained optimization problems [4,5]. However the standard versions of PSO, like the other evolutionary algorithms, lacks an explicit mechanisms to handle multiobjective and constraints that are often found in science and engineering optimization problems. In order to solve complex constrained multiobjective problems, this paper presents Adaptive and Accelerated Exploration Particle Swarm Optimizer (AAEPSO) [5] hybridized with and Pareto-optimality.

This paper is organized as follows. Section 2 describes Constrained Multiobjective Optimization. Section 3 describes the proposed algorithm for CMO using Particle Swarm Optimization. Section 4 reports simulation results and performance evaluation followed by conclusions in Section 5.

## 2   Constrained Multiobjective Optimization

Constrained Multiobjective Optimization (CMO) problems are being used for either to minimize or maximize a set of objective functions with some equality and/or inequality constraints. In the general form, it can be defined as

$$\begin{aligned} Minimize f_j(\overrightarrow{x}) &= f_j(x_1, x_2, \dots, x_n), j = 1, 2, \dots, k \\ subject\ to: \qquad g_i(\overrightarrow{x}) &\geq 0, i = 1, 2, \dots, q \\ h_i(\overrightarrow{x}) &= 0, i = q+1, q+2, \dots, m \\ l_i &\leq x_i \leq u_i, i = 1, 2, \dots, D \end{aligned} \qquad (1)$$

where each $f_j$ , $j \in [1, d]$ is the objective function to be minimized or maximized. $g_i$, and $h_i$ are the inequality and equality constraints respectively. The values $l_i$ and $u_i$ for $1 \leq i \leq D$ are the lower and upper bounds defining the search space. Since multiple objectives in CMO are usually consists of conflicting objectives, hence single solution does not describe the optimal decision. There can be a set of optimal solution to a given problem. The tradeoffs among them is defined in terms of Pareto optimality.

**Pareto optimality**
A feasible decision vector $\overrightarrow{x_p}$ is said to dominate another feasible vector $\overrightarrow{x_q}$ (denoted by $\overrightarrow{x_p} \prec \overrightarrow{x_q}$ ), if & iff $\forall i \in 1, 2 \dots k : f_i(\mathbf{u}) \leq f_i(\mathbf{v})$ and $\exists j \in 1, 2 \dots k :$

$f_j(\mathbf{u}) < f_j(\mathbf{v})$. If there is no solution $\vec{x_p}$ that dominates $\vec{x_q}$ , then $\vec{x_q}$ is a Pareto optimal solution. The set of all Pareto optimal solutions in the decision space is termed as Pareto optimal set and the corresponding set of objective vector is termed as Pareto optimal front. The aim of multiobjective optimization algorithm is to obtain the Pareto optimal front accurately.

# 3   Proposed Algorithm for Constrained Multiobjective Optimization

The detail implementation steps for the proposed algorithm is presented in Algorithm 1. The objective functions $f_k(x)$ and constrained functions $g(x)$ and $h(x)$ for all $NP$ particles are evaluated. Based on constraint violations, all the particles are categorized as either feasible or infeasible. Using Pareto optimal concept nondominated particles are selected from the set of feasible particles. Now, these selected particles have the Nondominated feasible solution for the CMO under consideration. The infeasible and dominated particles are termed as diverged particles. Proposed algorithm presents a novel strategy to identify the diverged particles and accelerate them towards the best solution with a greater exploration power. The search process is carried out in the neighborhood of best particle. To preserve the diversity among the swarm and to avoid the swarm from collapsing, the following strategies are implemented. The diverged particles in the population are forced to search in the neighborhood of best particle, but are not re-initialized to the position of best particle. The acceleration and exploration power are imparted to the diverged particles based on their Euclidean distance from best particle and their fitness values. The choice between these two are altered after a random iteration number between 20% to 60 % of total number of iteration. The number of diverged particles are randomly selected between 10 to 90 percent of the total number of diverged particles in the swarm. The exploration power imparted to the diverged particle decreases exponentially with iteration as $AE_f^t = R_{max} * e^{\frac{-t}{u}}$ . Where $u$ is a constant used to control the exponential distribution. We have conducted many experiments to estimate the value of $u$ and is found to be 10 so that the exploration factor starts decreasing exponentially from $R_{max}$ to zero. $R_{max}$ is the initial search range of the problem in all dimensions. Thus, this strategy gives complete freedom to diverged particles for exploring the solution available around the best particle [4,5]. A diverged particle is selected randomly and the value of all dimensions of the selected particles are guided by the corresponding dimensional value of a randomly selected Nondominated feasible particle. We have used the guiding principle as explained above [5]. A bounded external archive is maintained for nondominated feasible solutions. The best Nondominated feasible particle for the current iteration is selected and is compared with previous $gbest$, the one with minimum objective will be treated as $gbest$ for the next generation, similarly the personal best $pbest$ of the particles are updated.

---

**Algorithm 1.** AAEPSO

---

**Initialization**

Initialize the swarm of size NP:

Initialize position $'X'$ and velocity $'V'$ randomly in the search range $(X_{max}, X_{min})$.

Initialize Selection $(S_f)$ and Acceleration Exploration $(AE_f)$ factor as in[5] .

Evaluate the fitness values of all particles.

Set the current position as *pbest* and the particle with the best fitness value as *gbest*.

Initialize the bounded Archive to the size of population

**Optimize**

**for** $t \leftarrow 1, Maxgen$ **do**

$w^t, c_1^t, c_2^t = w_{max} - ((w_{max} - w_{min})/Maxgen) * t$  $Where$  $w_{max} = 0.9, w_{min} = 0.2$

Decrease $AE_f$ exponentially as in [5]

Update velocity and position of each particle as

$$V_{i,d}^{t+1} = w^t V_{i,d}^t + c_1^t * rand_1 * (pbest_{i,d}^t - X_{i,d}^t) + c_2^t * rand_2 * (gbest_d^t - X_{i,d}^t)\ (2)$$
$$X_{i,d}^{t+1} = X_{i,d}^t + V_{i,d}^{t+1} \tag{3}$$

Evaluate fitness and constraints violations for each particle.

Find the Feasible solutions.

Find the Pareto-optimal of feasible solutions.

Update *pbest*: If current fitness dominates the previous then set current position as *pbest* else retain *pbest*.

Update *gbest*: If best of all the current *pbest* dominates the previous *gbest* then set best *pbest* as *gbest* else retain *gbest*.

Check the dominating status of new solution (X) with the solutions in the archive.

    **if** X dominates any member of Archive **then**

        Delete the dominated member and insert X in the Archive

    **else if** X is neither dominated by the members of Archive or the members by X **then**

        Insert X in the Archive

    **else if** X is dominated by the members of Archive **then**

        reject X

    **end if**

    **if** Size of Archive exceeds maximum size **then**

        use crowding distance to eliminate less dominated particles.

    **end if**

Apply Accelerated Exploration to Nonfeasible and Dominated particles as in [5].

**end for**  $t$

continue optimizing until stopping criteria or exceeding maximum iteration

**Report results**

**Terminate**

---

## 4   Simulation and Results

The simulations are carried on a desktop PC with specifications as Pentium Core2Duo, 2GHz and 2GB RAM. Algorithm is coded in Matlab 7.2 and executed in Windows-XP platform. The simulation parameters of the proposed algorithm are; population size = 100 and number of runs = 30 for each benchmark function. The performance of proposed AAEPSO algorithm is compared on standard benchmark functions CF1 to CF10 from CEC 2009 [8]. These functions have different characteristics in terms of convexity, discontinuity and non uniformity in objective and constrained functions. A set of performance metrics such as a) Inverted Generational Distance (IGD) [8], b) Convergence Metric (CM) [3], c) Diversity Metric (DM) [3], d) Robustness and f) Pareto fronts are used to measure the performance of the algorithm.

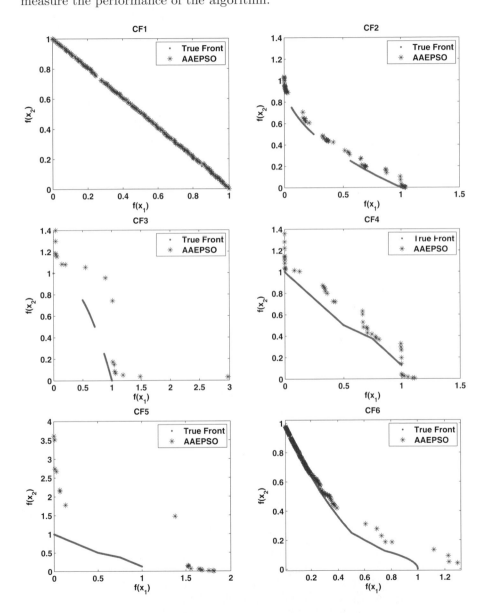

**Fig. 1.** Pareto fronts obtained by AAEPSO

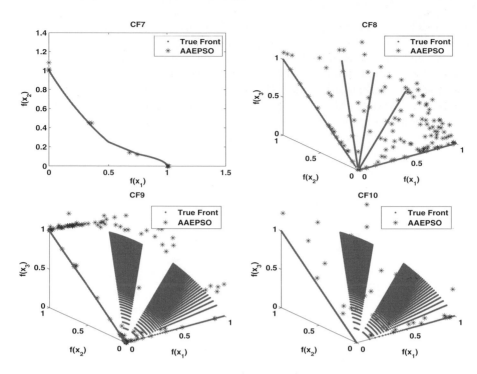

**Fig. 1.** (*continued*)

**Table 1.** IGD values obtained on each test problem

| Fun | Alg | mean | std | best | worst |
|---|---|---|---|---|---|
| CF1 | AAEPSO | **7.5492e-3** | **1.1009e-3** | 5.9495e-3 | 9.9889e-3 |
| | DECMOSA | 1.0774e-1 | 1.9592e-1 | 5.8125e-2 | 1.8625e-1 |
| CF2 | AAEPSO | **5.5236e-2** | **1.0786e-2** | 3.9789e-2 | 7.5663e-2 |
| | DECMOSA | 9.4608e-2 | 2.9428e-1 | 3.7197e-2 | 2.5701e-1 |
| CF3 | AAEPSO | **4.1226e-1** | 2.0861e-1 | 1.1075e-1 | 7.7062e-1 |
| | DECMOSA | 1.0000e+6 | **0** | 1.0000e+6 | 1.0000e+6 |
| CF4 | AAEPSO | **1.0438e-1** | **1.5358e-2** | 8.1998e-2 | 1.4665e-1 |
| | DECMOSA | 1.5266e-1 | 4.6660e-1 | 5.3345e-2 | 3.0168e-1 |
| CF5 | AAEPSO | 7.0260e-1 | **1.5458e-1** | 4.6857e-1 | 1.2210 |
| | DECMOSA | **4.1276e-1** | 5.9078e-1 | 9.6384e-2 | 5.3776e-1 |
| CF6 | AAEPSO | **6.7704e-2** | **1.1566e-2** | 4.7178e-2 | 7.4715e-2 |
| | DECMOSA | 1.4782e-1 | 1.2472e-1 | 8.2309e-2 | 1.8700e-1 |
| CF7 | AAEPSO | 5.5005e-1 | 3.0453e-1 | 1.1398e-1 | 9.7807e-1 |
| | DECMOSA | **2.6049e-1** | **2.5994e-1** | 1.7050e-1 | 3.7381e-1 |
| CF8 | AAEPSO | **2.4903e-1** | **1.4302e-1** | 1.4055e-1 | 6.7565e-1 |
| | DECMOSA | 1.7634e-1 | 6.2578e-1 | 9.7747e-2 | 4.2067e-1 |
| CF9 | AAEPSO | **1.2388e-1** | **6.3178e-2** | 1.8461e-1 | 3.9548e-1 |
| | DECMOSA | 1.2713e-1 | 1.4579e-1 | 1.0837e-1 | 2.6525e-1 |
| CF10 | AAEPSO | **4.8241e-1** | **1.4726e-1** | 3.1764e-1 | 8.1108e-1 |
| | DECMOSA | 5.0705e-1 | 1.1989 | 2.8477e-1 | 8.1108e-1 |

Figure 1 shows the Pareto fronts obtained by proposed AAEPSO algorithm for 10 benchmark functions CF1 to CF10 [8]. From the Figure 1, it is evident that the proposed algorithm gives best front for functions CF1, CF2, CF4, CF6 and CF7, where as it gives competitive fronts for other functions except CF5 and CF3. Table 1 compares the statistical values of IGD of proposed AAEPSO algorithm with DECMOSA [7] algorithm. It clearly show that the mean IGD value of proposed AAEPSO algorithm is better than DECMOSA for CF1, CF3,CF4, CF6,CF8, CF9 and CF10 functions where as comparable for other functions. Similar trend is also found for IGD standard deviation. Table 2 and Table 3 show the statistical values of diversity and convergence metric of proposed AAEPSO respectively. The stability of the AAEPSO is proved to be well again on almost all the functions except CF3 and CF7 as evident from Table 1.

**Table 2.** Diversity Metric obtained on each test problem

| Fun | mean | std | best | worst |
| --- | --- | --- | --- | --- |
| CF1 | 3.12 | 5.36e-2 | 3.05 | 3.27 |
| CF2 | 9.16e-1 | 1.51e-2 | 9.05e-1 | 9.63e-1 |
| CF3 | 1.07 | 2.07e-2 | 1.03 | 1.14 |
| CF4 | 2.19e-1 | 6.24e-2 | 1.63e-1 | 3.42e-1 |
| CF5 | 6.76e-1 | 1.38e-1 | 5.40e-1 | 8.96e-1 |
| CF6 | 5.40e-1 | 1.78e-1 | 2.80e-1 | 8.72e-1 |
| CF7 | 5.46e-1 | 1.93e-1 | 2.47e-1 | 9.67e-1 |
| CF8 | 9.88e-1 | 4.77e-3 | 9.77e-1 | 9.94e-1 |
| CF9 | 1.11 | 2.09e-3 | 1.10 | 1.11 |
| CF10 | 1.11 | 1.37e-2 | 1.05 | 1.11 |

**Table 3.** Convergence Metric obtained on each test problem

| Fun | mean | std | best | worst |
| --- | --- | --- | --- | --- |
| CF1 | 7.54e-3 | 1.10e-3 | 5.94e-3 | 9.98e-3 |
| CF2 | 5.52e-2 | 1.07e-2 | 3.97e-2 | 7.56e-2 |
| CF3 | 4.12e-1 | 2.08e-1 | 1.10e-1 | 7.70e-1 |
| CF4 | 1.04e-1 | 1.53e-2 | 8.19e-2 | 1.46e-1 |
| CF5 | 7.02e-1 | 1.54e-1 | 4.68e-1 | 1.22 |
| CF6 | 6.77e-2 | 1.15e-2 | 4.71e-2 | 9.47e-2 |
| CF7 | 5.50e-1 | 3.04e-1 | 1.13e-1 | 9.78e-1 |
| CF8 | 2.49e-1 | 1.43e-1 | 1.40e-1 | 6.75e-1 |
| CF9 | 2.23e-1 | 6.31e-2 | 1.84e-1 | 3.95e-1 |
| CF10 | 4.82e-1 | 1.47e-1 | 3.17e-1 | 8.11e-1 |

# 5   Conclusions

In this paper, we have proposed a constrained multiobjective optimization algorithm based on Adaptive and Accelerated Exploration Particle Swarm algorithm for constrained multiobjective optimization problems. The performance of the proposed algorithm is evaluated on standard constrained multiobjective benchmark function proposed in CEC 2009. Initial results show that the AAEPSO algorithm can also be used for solving constrained multiobjective optimization problem up to a certain degree of satisfaction. We propose to explore other variations of the proposed algorithm for standard benchmark function to improve the performance. The proved suitability of the AAEPSO has motivated the authors to apply it on real world engineering design problems.

# References

1. Deb, K., Pratap, A., Agarwal, S., Meyarivan, T.: A fast and elitist multiobjective genetic algorithm: NSGA-II. IEEE Transactions on Evolutionary Computation 6(2), 182–197 (2002)
2. Eberhart, R., Kenedy, J.: Particle swarm optimization. In: Proceedings of IEEE Int. Conference on Neural Networks, Piscataway, NJ, pp. 1114–1121 (November 1995)
3. Huang, V., Suganthan, P., Liang, J.: Comprehensive Learning Particle Swarm Optimizer for Solving Multi-Objective Optimization Problems. International Journal of Intelligent Systems 21(2), 209–211 (2006)
4. Sabat S.L., Ali, L.: The hyperspherical acceleration effect particle swarm optimizer. Appl. Soft. Computing 9(13), 906–917 (2008)
5. Sabat, S.L., Ali, L., Udgata, S.K.: Adaptive accelerated exploration particle swarm optimizer for global multimodal functions. In: World Congress on Nature and Biologically Inspired Computing, Coimbatore, India, pp. 654–659 (December 2009)
6. Sarker, R., Abbass, H., Karim, S.: An evolutionary algorithm for constrained multiobjective optimization problems. In: The Fifth Australasia Japan Joint Workshop, pp. 19–21. University of Otago, Dunedin (November 2001)
7. Zamuda, A., Brest, J., Boškovic, B., Žumer, V.: Differential evolution with self-adaptation and local search for constrained multiobjective optimization. In: CEC 2009: Proceedings of the Eleventh conference on Congress on Evolutionary Computation, pp. 195–202. IEEE Press, Piscataway (2009)
8. Zhang, Q., Zhou, A., Zhao, S., Suganthan, P.N., Liu, W., Tiwari, S.: Multiobjective optimization Test Instances for the CEC 2009 Special Session and Competition. Tech. rep., Nanyang Technological University, Singapore (2009)

# Expedite Particle Swarm Optimization Algorithm (EPSO) for Optimization of MSA

Amit Rathi and Ritu Vijay

Department of Electronics, Banasthali University, Banasthali, Tonk, Rajasthan, India

**Abstract.** This paper presents a new designing method of Rectangular patch Microstrip Antenna using an Artificial searches Algorithm with some constraints. It requires two stages for designing. In first stage, bandwidth of MSA is modeled using bench Mark function. In second stage, output of first stage give to modified Artificial search Algorithm which is Particle Swarm Algorithm (PSO) as input and get output in the form of five parameter-dimensions width, frequency range, dielectric loss tangent, length over a ground plane with a substrate thickness and electrical thickness. In PSO Cognition, factor and Social learning Factor give very important effect on balancing the local search and global search in PSO. Basing the modification of cognition factor and social learning factor, this paper presents the strategy that at the starting process cognition-learning factor has more effect then social learning factor. Gradually social learning factor has more impact after learning cognition factor for find out global best. The aim is to find out under above circumstances these modifications in PSO can give better result for optimization of microstrip Antenna (MSA).

**Keywords:** Artificial Search Algorithm, inverse modeling, Particle Swarm Optimization, Cognition Factor, Social Learning Factor, Local Search and Global Search.

## 1   Introduction

In MSA designing procedure, first modeling is performed then inverse modeling is done. For this it require a system (H), which have some input parameter like $P_1$, $P_2$, $P_3$ ... $P_n$ for giving a desired output (Q) of the system (Fig. 1). Above step for calculating output $Q_d$, require inverse modeling procedure.

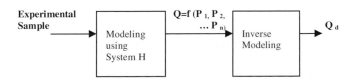

**Fig. 1.** Modeling and Inverse Modeling of Samples

B.K. Panigrahi et al. (Eds.): SEMCCO 2010, LNCS 6466, pp. 163–170, 2010.
© Springer-Verlag Berlin Heidelberg 2010

Main aim of this paper is designing of a Rectangular patch MSA antenna after its modeling. After mathematical modeling of five input parameter frequency range , dimension width, ground plane length with substrate thickness, electrical thickness and dielectric loss tangent , it give output as a Bandwidth of MSA. After getting bandwidth then an artificial search algorithm is used as an inverse model to find bandwidth is as input for desire frequency range, dimension width, ground plane length with substrate thickness, electrical thickness and dielectric loss tangent as output, which is show in fig. 2.

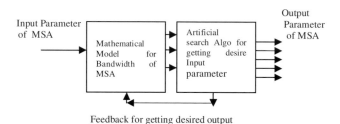

**Fig. 2.** Desired input parameter searching for a fixed Bandwidth Antenna MSA

Here Particle swarm optimization (PSO) algorithm is used as an artificial search algorithm. PSO is to be efficient for any application optimization developed by Kennedy and Eberhart is based on the analogy of bird flocks or fish school movements. The Cognition factor and Social learning Factor coefficient ($C_1$ and $C_2$) are one of the parameter in PSO [1] [2]. This have important effect on balancing the local search and global search in PSO, $C_1$ is cognitive coefficient has greater value then $C_2$ this particle goes to self-learning .It controls the pull to the personal best position. The main goal of our work is investigation of the efficiency of new PSO, which is Expedite PSO (EPSO) in MSA by taking $C_1$ and $C_2$ varying quantities for each iteration (K).

A Rectangular patch antenna [4] [5] with single coaxial feed is constructed by low cost FR-4 substrate. Aim of this paper best particle error, physical thickness, operating frequency, electrical thickness, dimensions width, dielectric loss tangent and bandwidth are investigated between rectangular patch antennas using standard PSO and rectangular patch antenna using modified PSO.

The remaining part of this paper is organized as follow. Section 2 briefly outlines the basics of the PSO algorithms and modification of PSO (EPSO) in term of dynamics $C_1$ and $C_2$ for each iteration. Section 3 shows the improved PSO algorithm. In section 4 introduction and structure of rectangular patch MSA antenna is described. Experimental setting and results are described in section 5 and finally section 6 described conclusion of this paper.

## 2  Standard PSO Algorithm and Modification

The Particle Swarm Optimization algorithm (PSO) [1] [2] [3] searches for the global minimum of the cost-function, i.e., minimizes the cost-function of a problem by simulating movement and interaction of particles in a swarm. The position of a particle corresponds to one possible solution of the problem, i.e., it represents one point in the optimization space. Since we assume that there is no a priori knowledge of the optimization problem, there is equal possibility of choosing any point in the optimization space at the beginning of the optimization. Therefore, PSO starts with randomly chosen positions and velocities of particles. Each agent has information about the best position found by itself, $P_{best}$ (which is the position vector in the optimization space), and the best position found by whole swarm, $G_{best}$. The velocity vector for the calculation of the particle position in the next iteration is calculated as:

$$V_n = w * V_{n-1} + C_1 * rand\ (\ ) * (\ P_{best} - X_{n-1}) + C_2\ rand\ (\ )(G_{best} - X_{n-1}) \tag{1}$$

Where $V_{n-1}$ is the particle velocity in the previous iteration, $w$ is inertia coefficient, rand ( ) is the function that generates uniformly distributed random numbers in the interval from 0.0 to 1.0, $C_1$ is the cognitive coefficient (it controls the pull to the personal best position), and $C_2$ is the social-rate coefficient (it controls the pull to the global best position). The next position of the particle in the optimization space is calculated as:

$$X_n = X_{n-1} + V_n\ \Delta t \tag{2}$$

Where $\Delta t$ is most often considered to be of a unit value. It is found that particles might fly-out from the given optimization space if there are no limits for the velocity. Therefore, the maximal velocity $V_{max}$ is introduced as another parameter of the PSO. The maximal velocity, $V_{max,}$ represents the maximal percentage of the dynamic range of the optimization variable for which the velocity can change in successive movements of the particle.

Expedite coefficients Cognition factor and Social Learning Factor for improving PSO derived from standard PSO. The authors modified cognitive factor ($C_1$) and Social learning factor ($C_2$) for getting better efficiency. Which show that cognitive factor required first to search best position. After searching local best and knowing the information about local best then search for the global best.

Expedite coefficients Cognition factor ($C_1$) and Social Learning Factor ($C_2$) for improving PSO is expressed as:

$$C_1 = (1 - (K_i - K_{min}) / K_{max}) \tag{3}$$

$$C_2 = (K_i - K_{min}) / K_{max}) \tag{4}$$

Where-

| | |
|---|---|
| $K_i$ | = $i^{th}$ iteration |
| $K_{min}$ | = predefined first iteration |
| $K_{max}$ | = last or final iteration |
| $K_i \geq K_{max}$ | |

## 3   Improved PSO (EPSO) Algorithm

Step-1-Intialize Parameter w, Swarm size, L best, G best and iteration
Step-2 Set $C_1$ and C2 (equation 3, 4)
Step-3- Set the function by which take the optimum value f($x_n$)

Step-4- Update the local best/ Global Best
Step-5- Update velocity V $_n$ for all Particles
Step-6- Update position x $_n$ for all particle
Step-7-If the total no. of iteration > Iteration Number
Step-8- Yes then store result and compare if no then go to step three (3)
Step 9- Stop.

## 4   Structure of Rectangular Microstrip Patch Antenna

The simplest patch antenna uses a patch, which is one half-wavelength-long with the dielectric loading included over a larger ground plane separated by a constant thickness. This type of configuration showing in fig 4, where w and L are width and height of the Rectangular patch antenna [4][5][6]. The antenna pattern becomes the combination of the two sets of radiators [2][13][14].

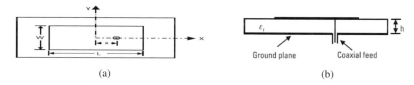

(a)                                             (b)

**Fig. 3.** (a) Top view (b) Side View of Rectangular Microstrip Antenna

A Rectangular patch of 18 mm width having permittivity $\varepsilon_r = 4.4$, substrate height h = 0.16 cm, frequency range = 4.8 GHz, Electrical Thickness =0.038, Dielectric Loss Tangent =0.001 and Bandwidth (percentage) =4.9. (Appendix) [4][5] [8] [10].

## 5   Experiment Setting and Result

For experiment setting, test the new strategies to verify their performance. Using Benchmark functions to experiment, the swarm's size is 5 in all experiment, every function experiments 100 times independently, w=0.4, $c_1$ and $c_2$ according to the equation [2].

Benchmark functions are given as follows:

Sphere:
$$f1(x) = \sum_{i=1}^{n} xi^2$$

Rosenrock:
$$f_2(x) = \sum_{i=1}^{n-1} [100(x_{(i+1)} - x_i)^2 + (x_i - 1)^2]$$

Rastrigin:
$$f_3(x) = \sum_{i=1}^{n} [(x_i^2 - 10\cos(2\Pi x) + 10]$$

Girewank:

$$f_4(x) = \frac{1}{4000} \sum_{i=1}^{n} [(x_i^2 - \prod_{i=1}^{n} \cos(\frac{x_i}{\sqrt{i}}) + 1$$

Schaffer:

$$f_5(x) = 0.5 + \frac{(\sin \sqrt{x_1^2 + x_2^2})^2 - 0.5}{[1 + 0.001(x_1^2 + x_2^2)]^2}$$

Benchmark functions' dimensions, the initial range, the criterion and the global optimum result is shown at Table 1.

**Table 1.** Benchmark functions

| Function | Dimension | Initial range | Criterion | The global optimum result |
|---|---|---|---|---|
| Sphere | 30 | [−100, 100] | 0.01 | 0 |
| Rosenbrock | 30 | [−30, 30] | 100 | 0 |
| Rastrigin | 30 | [−5.12, 5.12] | 50 | 0 |
| Girewank | 30 | [−600, 600] | 0.05 | 0 |
| Schaffer f6 | 2 | [−100, 100] | 0.00001 | 0 |

## 5.1 Results

Different parameter and their limitation range of MSA show in table 2.

**Table 2.** Parameter and their limitation ranges of MSA

| MSA parameters | Range |
|---|---|
| Frequency (f$_r$) | [1.5,10.5] |
| Physical Thickness (h) | [0.1,5.12] |
| Electrical thickness (h/$_d$) | [0.0075,0.3248] |
| Dimension Width (w) | [10.76,24.64] |
| Dielectric Loss Tangent (tan ï ) | [0.0009,0.003] |

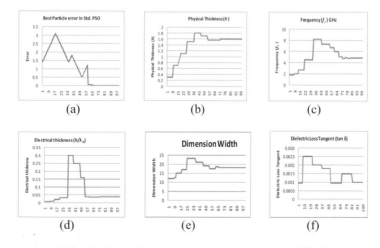

(a)        (b)        (c)

(d)        (e)        (f)

**Fig. 4.** (a) Error (b)Physical Thickness (c) Frequency (d) Electrical Thickness (e) Dimension width (f) Dielectric Loss Tangent

Here Particle of PSO has five different dimensions so they search space region with different velocities. For fine searching, it is necessary to search with high velocity and terminated with low value.

Figure 4 show each iteration errors of best particle and five variable obtained valves. For evolution of performance, each iteration of PSO are performed by bench mark function for getting bandwidth and then this bandwidth is compared to desired bandwidth 4.9.Above comparisons are shows by figure 5.

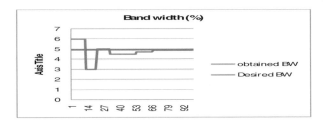

**Fig. 5.** Desired Bandwidth and obtained Bandwidth comparison

## 5.2 Modified PSO (EPSO) Effect

Applying modified PSO (EPSO) in above case figure 6 show each iteration error of the best Particle and obtained value of five variable .Table 3 show different parameter of modified PSO algorithm. Table 4 shows the results of standard PSO and modified PSO. For evolution of performance, each iteration of PSO are performed by bench mark function for getting bandwidth and then this bandwidth is compared to desired bandwidth 4.9. Above comparison show by figure 7.

**Table 3.** Parameter of standard and Modified PSO

| Algorithm→ <br> Parameter ↓ | Standard PSO | New Modified PSO |
|---|---|---|
| w | 0.4 | 0.4 |
| Swarm Size | 5 | 5 |
| Iteration | 100 | 100 |
| C1 | 1.4 | $(1- ( K_i - K_{min} ) / K_{max})$ |
| C2 | 1.4 | $(K_i - K_{min} ) / K_{max}$ |

**Table 4.** Results

| Parameter | Iteration required for standard PSO | Iteration required for modify PSO |
|---|---|---|
| Best Particle error | 69 | 43 |
| Frequency ($f_r$) | 82 | 70 |
| Physical Thickness ($h$) | 73 | 68 |
| Electrical thickness (h/$\lambda_d$) | 94 | 79 |
| Dimension Width | 67 | 57 |
| Dielectric Loss Tangent (tan $\delta$) | 84 | 70 |
| Band width (%) | 68 | 52 |

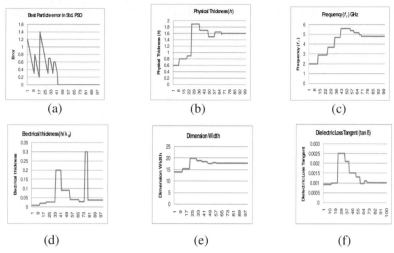

(a)                                       (b)                                       (c)

(d)                                       (e)                                       (f)

**Fig. 6.** (a) Error (b)Physical Thickness (c) Frequency (d) Electrical Thickness (e) Dimension width (f) Dielectric Loss Tangent (g) Bandwidth obtained in Modified PSO

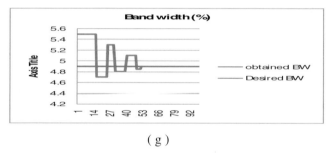

( g )

**Fig. 7.** Desired Bandwidth and Optimized Bandwidth comparison in Modified PSO

# 6   Conclusion

A Particle Swarm Optimization (PSO) based approach is proposed for designing microstrip antenna using some benchmark function. The author have proposed to take first cognitive factor large as compared to social factor then for next step gradually decreased C1 and increased C2 give better result as compare to existing algorithm. The proposed method is new and computationally efficient and accurate. This give better result and required less computational time by maintaining good quality of solution as compared to original Particle Swarm Optimization algorithm (PSO). The proposed method is new and computationally efficient and accurate which show in table 3.

# References

1. Kennedy, J., Eberhart, R.C.: Particle swarm optimization. In: Proc. IEEE Int. Conf. Neural Networks, pp. 1942–1948 (1995)
2. Bakwad, K.M., Patnayak, S.S., Sohi, B.S., Devi, S., Gollapudi, S.V.R.S., Vidya Sagar, C., Patra, P.K.: Small population Based Modified Parallel Particle swarm Optimization for Motion Estimation. In: Proc. IEEE Int. (2008)

3. Liang, J.J., Qin, A.K., Suganthan, P.N., Baskar, S.: Comprehensive learning particle swarm optimizer for global optimization of multimodal functions. IEEE Trans. Evol. Comput. 10(3), 281–296 (2006)
4. Yazdi, H.S., Yazdi, M.S.: Particle swarm optimization –Based Rectangular Microstrip Antenna Designing. International Journal of Computer and Electrical Engineering 1(4), 1793–8163 (2009)
5. Kara, M.: A simple technique for the calculation of bandwidth of rectangular microstrip antenna elements with various substratethicknesse, Microw. Microw. Opt. Technol. Lett. 12, 16–20 (1996)
6. Pozar, Schaubert: Microstrip Antennas. Proceedings of the IEEE 80 (1992)
7. Kara, M.: A novel technique to calculate the bandwidth of rectangular microstrip antenna elements with thick substrates. Microw. Opt. Technol. Lett. 12, 59–64 (1996)
8. Sagiroglu, S., Guney, K., Erler, M.: Calculation of bandwidth for electrically thin and thick rectangular microstrip antennas with the use of multilayered perceptrons. Int. J. Microw Comput. Aided Eng. 9, 277–286 (1999)
9. Kaplan, A., Guney, K., Ozer, S.: Fuzzy associative memories for the computation of the bandwidth of rectangular microstrip antennas with thin and thick substrates. Int. J. Electron. 88, 189–195 (2001)
10. Bahl, I.J., Bhartia, P.: Microstrip antennas. Artech House, Canton (1980)
11. Pozar, D.M.: Considerations for millimeter wave printed antennas. IEEE Trans. Antennas Propagat. 31, 740–747 (1983)
12. Wi, S.-H., Lee, Y.-S., Yook, J.G.: Wideband Microstrip Patch Antenna With U Shaped Parasitic Elements. IEEE Transaction On Antenna and Propagation 55(4) (April 2007)
13. Liang, J.J., Suganthan, P.N.: Dynamic Multi-Swarm Particle Swarm Optimizer. In: IEEE Swarm Intelligence Symposium, Pasadena, CA, USA, pp. 124–129 (2005)
14. Liang, J.J., Qin, A.K., Suganthan, P.N., Baskar, S.: Comprehensive Learning Particle Swarm Optimizer for Global Optimization of Multimodal Functions. IEEE Trans. on Evolutionary Computation 10(3), 281–295 (2006)

## Appendix

The test data sets used in this paper have been obtained from previous experimental works [17, 19], which are given in Table 5. The 7 data sets in Table 5 is used to see result.

**Table 5.** Measured Bandwidth of RMSA (Electrically Thin and Thick)

| Patch No. | h (mm) | F (GHz) | h/$\lambda_d$ | W (mm) | tan θ | Measured [5] [7][9][11][12] BW (%) |
|---|---|---|---|---|---|---|
| 1 | 0.17 | 7.74 | 0.0065 | 8.5 | 0.001 | 1.070 |
| 2 | 0.79 | 3.970 | 0.0155 | 20.00 | 0.001 | 2.200 |
| 3 | 0.79 | 7.730 | .0326 | 10.63 | 0.001 | 3.850 |
| 4 | 0.79 | 3.545 | 0.0149 | 20.74 | 0.002 | 1.950 |
| 5 | 1.27 | 4.600 | 0.0622 | 9.10 | 0.001 | 2.050 |
| 6 | 1.57 | 5.060 | 0.0404 | 17.20 | 0.001 | 5.100 |
| 7* | 1.57 | 4.805 | 0.0384 | 18.10 | 0.001 | 4.900 |
| 8 | 1.63 | 6.560 | 0.0569 | 12.70 | 0.002 | 6.800 |

* Test data set.

# Covariance Matrix Adapted Evolution Strategy Based Design of Mixed $H_2/H_\infty$ PID Controller

M. Willjuice Iruthayarajan[1] and S. Baskar[2]

[1] Department of Electrical and Electronic Engineering, National Engineering College,
Kovilpatti 628503, India
m_willjuice@yahoo.com
[2] Department of Electrical and Electronic Engineering, Thiagarajar College of Engineering,
Madurai, 625015, India
sbeee@tce.edu

**Abstract.** This paper discusses the application of the covariance matrix adapted evolution strategy (CMAES) technique to the design of the mixed $H_2/H_\infty$ PID controller. The optimal robust PID controller is designed by minimizing the weighted sum of integral squared error (ISE) and balanced robust performance criterion involving robust stability and disturbance attenuation performance subjected to robust stability and disturbance attenuation constraints. In CMAES algorithm, these constraints are effectively handled by penalty parameter-less scheme. In order to test the performance of CMAES algorithm, MIMO distillation column model is considered. For the purpose of comparison, reported intelligent genetic algorithm (IGA) method is used. The statistical performances of combined ISE and balanced robust performance criterion in ten independent simulation runs show that a performance of CMAES is better than IGA method. Robustness test conducted on the system also shows that the robust performance of CMAES designed controller is better than IGA based controller under model uncertainty and external disturbances.

**Keywords:** PID, CMAES, MIMO system, Robustness.

## 1 Introduction

Robustness is an important criterion in controller design because most of the real systems are vulnerable to external disturbances, measurement noise and model uncertainties [1-2]. There are two approaches dealing with robust optimal controller design problems. One is the structure-specified controller and the other is the output-feedback controller. Since the order of the robust output-feedback controller is much higher than that of the system, it is not easy to implement the controller for higher order systems in practical engineering applications. To overcome this difficulty, the structure-specified approach solves the robust optimal control problem from suboptimal perspective [3-8]. Optimal robust PID controller design for systems with uncertainties and disturbance is an active area of research.

More than 90% of industrial controllers are still implemented based on PID control algorithms, as no other controller matches the simplicity, clear functionality, applicability

B.K. Panigrahi et al. (Eds.): SEMCCO 2010, LNCS 6466, pp. 171–181, 2010.

and ease of use offered by the PID controllers [9]. The PID controllers perform several important functions, such as elimination of steady-state offset, anticipation of deviation and generation of adequate corrective signals through the derivative action.

To achieve required system performance specifications, PID controller design of industrial systems is complicated due to the fact that the system has non-linear plant and actuator dynamics and various uncertainties such as modeling error and external disturbances involved in the system. As a result of these difficulties, the PID controllers are rarely tuned optimally and the engineers will need to settle for a compromise in system performance. Thus, poor tuning can lead to poor control performance and even poor quality products.

The robust PID control is a powerful method to overcome this problem. These design procedures maintain the stability and performance level in spite of uncertainties in system dynamics and uncertain disturbances [10]. Many researches have employed mixed $H_2/H_\infty$ optimal design strategy for robust optimal PID controller. Chen *et al.* [3] have proposed the design of simple genetic algorithm (GA) based mixed $H_2/H_\infty$ PID controller for SISO system by minimizing ISE ($H_2$ Norm) subjected to robust stability and disturbance attenuation constraints.

Chen *et al.* [4] have also presented GA based optimal $H_\infty$ PID controller for MIMO system subjected to minimization of combined robust stability and disturbance attenuation performance criterion for a specified parameter range determined by Routh criterion. Krohling *et al.* [5] have suggested design of two-stage GA based optimal disturbance rejection PID controller for a servo motor system. Tan *et al.* [6] have proposed the optimal PID tuning procedure for multivariable process making use of Riccati equations and $H_\infty$ loop-shaping approach. Ho *et al.* [7] have applied orthogonal simulated annealing algorithm (OSA) for the design of optimal PID controller for MIMO system by minimizing combined ISE and balanced performance criterion involving disturbance attenuation and robust stability. Recently, Ho *et al.* [8] have also presented the mixed $H_2/H_\infty$ MIMO optimal PID controller design using intelligent genetic algorithm (IGA). They compared the performance of the IGA-based $H_2/H_\infty$ MIMO optimal PID controller with all previous results [8].

Recently, in order to alleviate difficulties of genetic algorithm while optimizing a deceptive and non-separable function, estimation of distribution algorithm (EDA) is introduced. EDAs use probability distributions derived from the function to be optimized to generate search points instead of crossover and mutation as done by genetic algorithms. The other parts of the EDA algorithms are identical. A popular EDA method namely Covariance Matrix Adapted Evolution Strategy (CMAES) has been successfully applied in varieties of engineering optimization problems [11]. This algorithm outperforms all other similar classes of learning algorithms on the benchmark multimodal functions [12]. In [13], application of CMAES algorithm is demonstrated for the design of centralized PID controller as an unconstrained optimization problem by minimizing IAE only without considering robust stability constraint.

In this paper, CMAES based robust optimal PID controller design scheme is presented. It focuses mainly on designing the optimal robust PID controller by minimizing the weighted sum of ISE and balanced robust performance criterion involving robust stability performance and disturbance attenuation performance using CMAES algorithm. The performances of CMAES are evaluated on MIMO distillation column model For the purpose of comparison, the result of previous reported IGA based controller is considered.

The remaining part of the paper is organized as follows. Section 2 introduces the concept of robust PID controller design. Section 3 describes the algorithmic steps of CMAES method. Section 4 introduces MIMO systems considered for robust optimal PID controller design. Section 5 presents the implementation details the simulation results of CMAES based robust optimal PID controller design. Conclusions are given in Section 6.

## 2  Robust Controller

Consider a control system with $q_i$ inputs and $q_o$ outputs, as shown in Fig. 1, where $P(s)$ is the nominal plant, $\Delta P(s)$ is the plant perturbation, $G_c(s)$ is the controller, $r(t)$ is the reference input, $u(t)$ is the control input, $e(t)$ is the tracking error, $d(t)$ is the external disturbance, and $y(t)$ is the output of the system [8].

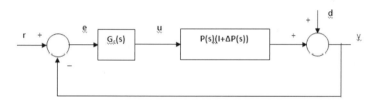

**Fig. 1.** Control system with plant perturbation and external disturbance

The plant perturbation $\Delta P(s)$ is assumed to be bounded by a known stable function matrix $W_1(s)$

$$\bar{\sigma}(\Delta P(j\omega)) \le \bar{\sigma}(W_1(j\omega)), \forall_\omega \in [0, \infty) \tag{1}$$

where $\bar{\sigma}(A)$ denotes the maximum singular value of a matrix $A$.

### 2.1  Robust PID Controller

If a controller $G_c(s)$ is designed such that the nominal closed loop system ($\Delta P(s) = 0$ and $d(t) = 0$) is asymptotically stable, the robust stability performance satisfies the following inequality

$$J_a = \left\|W_1(s)T(s)\right\|_\infty < 1 \tag{2}$$

and the disturbance attenuation performance satisfies the following inequality

$$J_b = \left\|W_2(s)S(s)\right\|_\infty < 1 \tag{3}$$

then the closed loop system is also asymptotically stable with $\Delta P(s)$ and $d(t)$, where $W_2(s)$ is a stable weighting function matrix specified by designers. $S(s)$ and $T(s) = I - S(s)$ are the sensitivity and complementary sensitivity functions of the system, respectively

$$S(s) = (I + P(s)G_c(s))^{-1} \tag{4}$$

$$T(s) = P(s)G_c(s)(I + P(s)G_c(s))^{-1} \tag{5}$$

$H_\infty$-norm in (2) and (3) is defined as

$$\|A(s)\|_\infty \equiv \max_\omega \overline{\sigma}(A(j\omega)) \tag{6}$$

Minimization of balanced performance criterion $J_\infty = (J_a^2 + J_b^2)^{1/2}$ [8] is considered to minimize both $J_a$ and $J_b$ simultaneously. For improving the system performance, robust stability and disturbance attenuation are often not enough for the control system design. The minimization of tracking error $J_2$ (i.e., $H_2$ norm) should be taken into account

$$J_2 = \int_0^\infty e^T(t)e(t)dt \tag{7}$$

where $e(t) = r(t) - y(t)$ is the error determined with $\Delta P(s) = 0$ and $d(t) = 0$.

Objective function involving $J_2$ and $J_\infty$ is modified from in [8], because the values of $J_2$ and $J_\infty$ are not in the same range. Here the following weighted sum of $J_2$ and $J_\infty$ is considered for designing robust optimal controller.

$$J = w_1 J_2 + w_2 J_\infty \tag{8}$$

where $w_1$ and $w_2$ are constants used for normalizing $J_2$ and $J_\infty$ respectively.

Hence, the robust optimal controller design problem is stated as minimization of $J$ subjected to robust stability and disturbance attenuation constraints as defined in (2) and (3).

## 2.2  Robust PID Controller Structure

In general, transfer function of a structure-specified controller can be expressed as follows:

$$G_c(s) = \frac{N_c(s)}{D_c(s)} = \frac{B_m s^m + B_{m-1} s^{m-1} + \cdots + B_0}{s^n + a_{n-1} s^{n-1} + \cdots + a_0} \tag{9}$$

where $m$ and $n$ fixed orders of $N_c(s)$ and $D_c(s)$ respectively. Also $B_k$ is defined in (10).

$$\boldsymbol{B}_k = \begin{bmatrix} b_{k11} & \cdots & b_{k1n_i} \\ \vdots & \ddots & \vdots \\ b_{kn_01} & \cdots & b_{kn_0n_i} \end{bmatrix} \quad \text{for } k = 0,1,\cdots m. \tag{10}$$

where $n_i$ and $n_o$ are the no of inputs and outputs respectively.

Most of the conventional controllers used in industrial control systems have fundamental structures such as PID and lead/lag configurations. Such controllers are special cases of the structure-specified controllers. For the PID controller, we have $n = 1, m = 2$ and $a_0 = 0$, i.e.

$$G_c(s) = \frac{\boldsymbol{B}_2 s^2 + \boldsymbol{B}_1 s + \boldsymbol{B}_0}{s} \tag{11}$$

In case of the system with complicated plant and a single simple-structure controller, one seems to have less freedom of controller parameters to tune the system to achieve the H$_\infty$ optimal design objectives. In this situation, we must increase the order $m$ and $n$ of the controller in (9).

## 3 Covariance Matrix Adapted Evolution Strategy

CMAES is a class of continuous EA that generates new population members by sampling from a probability distribution that is constructed during the optimization process. One of the key concepts of this algorithm involves the learning of correlations between parameters and the use of the correlations to accelerate the convergence of the algorithm. The adaptation mechanism of CMAES consists of two parts, 1) the adaptation of the covariance matrix **CM** and 2) the adaptation of the global step size $\sigma$. The covariance matrix **CM** is adapted by the evolution path and difference vectors between the $\mu$ best individuals in the current and previous generation. The CMAES algorithm is presented below.

### 3.1 CMAES Algorithm

**Step 1:** Generate an initial random solution which is a column vector.

**Step 2:** The offspring at $(g+1)^{\text{th}}$ generation $x_k^{g+1}$ are sampled from a Gaussian distribution using covariance matrix and global step size at $g^{\text{th}}$ generation.

$$x_k^{(g+1)} = z_k, \qquad z_k = N\left(\langle x\rangle_\mu^{(g)}, \sigma^{(g)^2} \mathbf{CM}^{(g)}\right) \quad k = 1,...,\lambda \tag{12}$$

where $\langle x\rangle_\mu^{(g)} = \sum_{i=1}^{\mu} x_i^{(g)}$ with $\mu$, number of the best individuals selected from the population.

The parameters $c_c, c_{\text{cov}}, c_\sigma$ and $d$ required for further computations are given by default in terms of the number of decision variables $(n)$ and $\mu$, as follows:

$$c_c = \frac{4}{n+4}, \quad c_\sigma = \frac{10}{n+20}, \quad d = \max\left(1, \frac{3\mu}{n+10}\right) + c_\sigma,$$

$$c_{cov} = \frac{1}{\mu} \frac{2}{(n+\sqrt{2})^2} + \left(1 - \frac{1}{\mu}\right) \min\left(1, \frac{2\mu-1}{(n+2)^2 + \mu}\right) \tag{13}$$

The parameters $c_\sigma$ and $c_{cov}$ control independently the adaptation time scales for the global step size and the covariance matrix.

The initial values are $\mathbf{P}_\sigma^{(0)} = \mathbf{P}_c^{(0)} = \mathbf{0}$, $\sigma^{(0)} = 0.25(\mathbf{x}_u - x_l)$ and $\mathbf{CM}^{(0)} = \mathbf{I}$.

where $x_u, x_l$ are upper and lower bound of decision variables.

**Step 3:** The evolution path $\mathbf{P}_c^{(g+1)}$ is computed as follows:

$$\mathbf{P}_c^{(g+1)} = (1-c_c) \cdot \mathbf{P}_c^{(g)} + \sqrt{c_c(2-c_c)} \cdot \frac{\sqrt{\mu}}{\sigma^{(g)}} \left(\langle x \rangle_\mu^{(g+1)} - \langle x \rangle_\mu^g\right) \tag{14}$$

$$\mathbf{CM}^{(g+1)} = (1-c_{cov}) \cdot \mathbf{CM}^{(g)} + c_{cov} \cdot \left( \begin{array}{l} \frac{1}{\mu} \mathbf{P}_c^{(g+1)} (\mathbf{P}_c^{(g+1)})^\mathrm{T} + \\ (1-\frac{1}{\mu}) \frac{1}{\mu} \sum_{i=1}^{\mu} \frac{1}{\sigma^{(g)^2}} (x_i^{(g+1)} - \langle x \rangle_\mu^{(g)})(x_i^{(g+1)} - \langle x \rangle_\mu^{(g)})^\mathrm{T} \end{array} \right) \tag{15}$$

The strategy parameter $c_{cov} \in [0,1]$ determines the rate of change of the covariance matrix $\mathbf{CM}$.

**Step 4:** Adaptation of global step size $\sigma^{(g+1)}$ is based on a conjugate evolution path $\mathbf{P}_\sigma^{(g+1)}$

$$\mathbf{P}_\sigma^{(g+1)} = (1-c_\sigma) \cdot \mathbf{P}_\sigma^{(g)} + \sqrt{c_\sigma(2-c_\sigma)} \cdot \mathbf{BB}^{(g)}(\mathbf{DD}^{(g)})^{-1}(\mathbf{BB}^{(g)})^{-1} \frac{\sqrt{\mu}}{\sigma^{(g)}} \left(\langle x \rangle_\mu^{(g+2)} - \langle x \rangle_\mu^g\right) \tag{16}$$

the matrices $\mathbf{BB}^{(g)}$ and $\mathbf{DD}^{(g)}$ are obtained through a principal component analysis:

$$\mathbf{CM}^{(g)} = \mathbf{BB}^{(g)}(\mathbf{DD}^{(g)})^2(\mathbf{BB}^{(g)})^\mathrm{T} \tag{17}$$

where the columns of $\mathbf{BB}^{(g)}$ are the normalized Eigen vectors of $\mathbf{CM}^{(g)}$ and $\mathbf{DD}^{(g)}$ is the diagonal matrix of the square roots of the given Eigen values of $\mathbf{CM}^{(g)}$ The global step size $\sigma^{(g+1)}$ is determined by

$$\sigma^{(g+1)} = \sigma^{(g)} \exp\left(\frac{c_\sigma}{d}\left(\frac{\|\mathbf{P}_\sigma^{(g+1)}\|}{E(\|N(0,\mathbf{I})\|)} - 1\right)\right) \tag{18}$$

**Step 5:** Repeat Steps 2-4 until the stopping criteria are satisfied.

## 3.2 Penalty Parameter-Less Constraint Handling Scheme

Usually, penalty parameter approach is used for constraint handling in Evolutionary Algorithms. The difficulty of this approach is the selection of an appropriate penalty parameter for the given problem. In this paper, penalty parameter-less constraint-handling scheme is employed, in which all feasible solutions have zero constraint violation and all infeasible solutions are evaluated according to their constraint violations alone. Hence, both the objective function value and constraint violation are not combined in any solution to the population. Thus there is no need to have any penalty parameter for this approach. The fitness function is calculated using (19) [14-15].

$$F(\overline{x}) = \begin{cases} f(\overline{x}) & if \ g_j(\overline{x}) \le 0 \quad \forall j = 1,2\cdots,m \\ \\ f_{max} + \sum_{j=1}^{m}(g_j(\overline{x})) & otherwise \end{cases} \qquad (19)$$

where $F(\overline{x})$ is fitness function, $f(\overline{x})$ the objective function, $g_j(\overline{x})$ the $j^{th}$ normalized absolute constraint violations and $f_{max}$ the objective function value of the worst feasible solution in the population.

## 4  Test System

In order to validate the performance of the proposed CMAES based robust PID optimal controller, MIMO distillation column model is considered and the details are given below.

Consider a highly coupled distillation column model [6, 8], where

$$P(s) = \begin{bmatrix} \dfrac{-33.98}{(98.02s+1)(0.42s+1)} & \dfrac{32.63}{(99.6s+1)(0.35s+1)} \\ \dfrac{-18.85}{(75.43s+1)(0.30s+1)} & \dfrac{34.84}{(110.5s+1)(0.03s+1)} \end{bmatrix} \qquad (20)$$

where the outputs 1 and 2 are temperatures of tray 21 and tray 7 and inputs 1 and 2 are the liquid reflux and vapor boil-up rates, respectively.

The bound $W_1(s)$ of the plant uncertainties $\Delta P(s)$

$$W_1(s) = \frac{100s+1}{s+1000} I_{2\times2} \qquad (21)$$

and for attenuate disturbance, a weighting function $W_2(s)$ consisting of low-pass filter

$$W_2(s) = \frac{s+1000}{1000s+1} I_{2\times2} \qquad (22)$$

are considered.

## 5  Simulation Results

All the simulations are carried on Pentium Core2duo PC operating @2.2 GHz with 2 GB RAM. In order to validate the performance of the proposed CMAES based robust PID controller MIMO distillation column model is considered. The test system is simulated using MATLAB-Control System Toolbox. The MATLAB code available for CMAES algorithm at N. Hansen's website [16] is suitably modified to incorporate penalty parameter-less strategy for constraint handling. Owing to the randomness of the evolutionary algorithms, 10 independent trials are conducted and the best, mean, standard deviation (STD) of $J_2$, $J_\infty$ and $J$ are reported and also Average Functional Evaluation (AFE) obtained is used to compare the performances of the algorithms. For the purpose of comparison, already reported results of IGA method [8] are taken.

Maximum number of functional evaluations (Fevalmax) with tolerance on design variables (Tolx) or objective function (Tolf) is used as stopping criteria. In simulations, Fevalmax is set at 20,000. The Tolx and Tolf are fixed at $10^{-4}$ and previous 10 generations are considered for calculating these parameters.

The PID controller structure is given in (11), where

$$B_2 = \begin{bmatrix} b_{2_{11}} & b_{2_{12}} \\ b_{2_{21}} & b_{2_{22}} \end{bmatrix}, \ B_1 = \begin{bmatrix} b_{1_{11}} & b_{1_{12}} \\ b_{1_{21}} & b_{1_{22}} \end{bmatrix}, \ B_0 = \begin{bmatrix} b_{0_{11}} & b_{0_{12}} \\ b_{0_{21}} & b_{0_{22}} \end{bmatrix} \quad (23)$$

The design variables for this system are

$$x = [b_{2_{11}}, b_{2_{12}}, b_{2_{21}}, b_{2_{22}}, b_{1_{11}}, b_{1_{12}}, b_{1_{21}}, b_{1_{22}}, b_{0_{11}}, b_{0_{12}}, b_{0_{21}}, b_{0_{22}}]^T \quad (24)$$

The lower and upper bounds of the design variables are taken as given in (25).

$$-200 \le x_i \le +200 \quad \text{for} \quad i = 1, \ 2, \ 3, \ \dots, \ 12 \quad (25)$$

CMAES algorithm is used to design a robust PID controller for distillation column plant by minimizing ISE for unit step reference input and balanced robust performance criterion. The population size is fixed at 15. For simulations, sampling interval is set at 0.01 sec. From the reported results [8], it is clear that the $J_2$ is much higher than $J_\infty$. If we add both the objectives without normalization, then the algorithm will tend to minimize $J_2$ and relatively less importance is given to the minimization of $J_\infty$. In order to give equal importance to both the objectives, the objectives should be normalized by choosing proper weights as given in (8). In this problem, using the reported result [8], 17 and 0.85 are taken for $w_1$ and $w_2$ respectively. The best optimal robust PID controller $G_c(s)$ obtained using CMAES for the distillation column is reported in (26). The performances such as $J_2$, $J_\infty$, $J$ of the system with both controllers are reported in Table 1 and also the number of functional evaluations ($N_{eval}$) used for getting this solution is reported.

The best controller obtained using CMAES algorithm is given in (26).

$$G_c(s) = \frac{\begin{bmatrix} -8.9166 & 0.8319 \\ -0.6851 & 0.7122 \end{bmatrix} s^2 + \begin{bmatrix} -70.1597 & 28.5600 \\ -26.8627 & 26.7152 \end{bmatrix} s + \begin{bmatrix} -119.0114 & 159.6830 \\ -98.0529 & 131.8109 \end{bmatrix}}{s} \quad (26)$$

The ISE combined with balanced robust performance criterion ( $J$ ) for the best controller designed using CMAES algorithm is 18 % lesser than IGA based controller. Because of the normalization of $J_2$ and $J_\infty$ , both ISE and balanced robust performance criterion are also lesser than IGA method. Also, CMAES algorithm takes approximately 14% less $N_{eval}$.

**Table 1.** Performance Comparison

| Method | $J_2$ | $J_\infty$ | $J$ | $N_{eval}$ |
|--------|-------|------------|-----|------------|
| IGA [8] | 16.7777 | 0.8520 | 17.6297 | 16211 |
| CMAES | 13.7493 | 0.6882 | 14.4375 | 13967 |

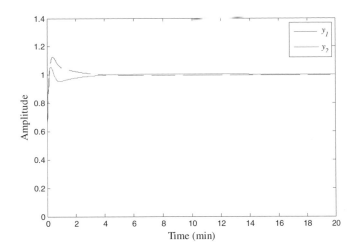

**Fig. 2.** Step response of distillation column with plant perturbation using IGA controller

The step responses of the system with plant perturbation $\Delta P(s)$ in (21) using IGA-based and CMAES-based controllers are shown in Figs. 2 and 3 respectively. From the step response characteristics, it is clear that the step responses ($y_1$ and $y_2$) for the best optimal controller designed using CMAES is better than IGA method in terms of less overshoot and quick settling time.

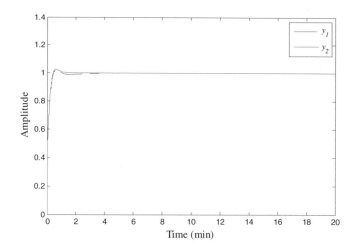

**Fig. 3.** Step response of distillation column with plant perturbation using CMAES controller

The statistical performances like best, mean and standard deviation (STD) in ISE combined with the balanced performance criterion involving disturbance attenuation and robust stability and average functional evaluation (AFE) in 10 trials are reported in Table 2.

From Table 2, it is very clear that CMAES algorithm is more consistent as STD of all the measures is less. AFE of CMAES is 27% lesser than $N_{eval}$ reported for the best result of IGA method.

**Table 2.** Statistical Performance

| Performance | Best | Mean | STD |
|---|---|---|---|
| $J_2$ | 13.7493 | 13.9730 | 0.1417 |
| $J_\infty$ | 0.6730 | 0.6834 | 0.0059 |
| $J$ | 14.4375 | 14.6564 | 0.1370 |
| AFE | | 11816 | |

## 6  Conclusion

In this paper, CMAES algorithm based design of robust optimal PID controllers for system with model uncertainties and disturbance is discussed. Minimization of weighted sum of ISE and balanced robust performance criterion is considered as the objective. The performance and validity of the proposed method are demonstrated on distillation column MIMO systems. The results of CMAES method are compared with already reported IGA method. It is shown empirically that the performance of the CMAES based method is better than the IGA method with respect to the best result and consistency. The robust test conducted on the optimal controller designed with

CMAES method gives better robust performance against model uncertainty and external disturbances than the IGA based controller. The better performance of the CMAES algorithm is mainly due to the learning of the correlations between the design parameters and the objective function in terms of covariance matrix and using this information for generating new individuals. This simulation studies clearly indicate that CMAES method is more suitable for designing robust optimal controllers.

# References

1. Doyle, J.C., Francis, B., Tennenbaum, A.: Feedback Control Theory. Macmillan Publishing Co., Basingstoke (1990)
2. Zhou, K., Doyle, J.C., Glover, K.: Robust and Optimal Control. Prentice Hall, Englewood Cliffs (1996)
3. Chen, B.-S., Cheng, Y.-M., Lee, C.-H.: A genetic approach to mixed H2/H∞ optimal PID control. IEEE Control Syst. Mag. 15(5), 51–60 (1995)
4. Chen, B.-S., Cheng, Y.-M.: A structure-specified H∞ optimal control design for practical applications: a genetic approach. IEEE Trans. Contr. Syst. Technol. 6(6), 707–718 (1998)
5. Krohling, R.A., Rey, J.P.: Design of optimal disturbance rejection PID controllers using genetic algorithms. IEEE Trans. Evol. Comput. 5(2), 78–82 (2001)
6. Tan, W., Chen, T., Marquez, H.J.: Robust controller design and PID tuning for multivariable processes. Asian J. Control 4, 439–451 (2002)
7. Ho, S.-J., Ho, S.-Y., Shu, L.-S.: OSA: orthogonal simulated annealing algorithm and its application to designing mixed H2/H∞ optimal controllers. IEEE Trans. Syst. Man, Cybern. A, Syst. Humans 34(5), 588–600 (2004)
8. Ho, S.-J., Ho, S.-Y., Hung, M.-H., Shu, L.-S., Huang, H.-L.: Designing Structure-Specified Mixed H2/H∞ Optimal Controllers Using an Intelligent Genetic Algorithm IGA. IEEE Trans. Contr. Syst. Technol. 13(6), 1119–1124 (2005)
9. Ang, K.H., Chang, G., Li, Y.: PID control system Analysis, Design and Technology. IEEE trans. Contr. Syst. Technol. 13(4), 559–577 (2005)
10. Jamshidi, M., Coelho, L.D.S., Krohling, R.A., Fleming, P.J.: Robust Control Systems with Genetic Algorithms, 1st edn. CRC Press, Boca Raton (2002)
11. Baskar, S., Alphones, A., Suganthan, P.N., Ngo, N.Q., Zheng, R.T.: Design of Optimal Length Low-Dispersion FBG Filter Using Covariance Matrix Adapted Evolution. IEEE Photonics Technology Letters 17(10), 2119–2121 (2005)
12. Kern, S., Muller, S.D., Hansen, N., Büche, D., Ocenasek, J., Koumoutsakos, P.: Learning probability distributions in continuous evolutionary algorithms—A comparative review. Natural Comput. 3(1), 77–112 (2004)
13. Willjuice Iruthayarajan, M., Baskar, S.: Covariance matrix adaptation evolution strategy based design of centralized PID controller. Expert systems with application 37, 5775–5781 (2010)
14. Deb, K.: An efficient constraint handling method for genetic algorithms. Comput. Methods Appl. Mech. Engg. 186(2-4), 311–338 (2000)
15. Manoharan, P.S., Kannan, P.S., Baskar, S., Iruthayarajan, M.W.: Penalty parameter-less constraint handling scheme based evolutionary algorithm solutions to economic dispatch. IET Gener. Transm. Distrib. 2(4), 478–490 (2008)
16. http://lautaro.bionik.tu-berlin.de/user/niko/cmaes_inmatlab. html version 3 (June 2008)

# Towards a Link between Knee Solutions and Preferred Solution Methodologies

Kalyanmoy Deb and Shivam Gupta

Kanpur Genetic Algorithm Laboratory
Indian Institute of Technology Kanpur
Kanpur, U.P. 208016, India
{deb,sgupta}@iitk.ac.in

**Abstract.** In a bi-criteria optimization problem, often the user is interested in a subset of solutions lying in the knee region. On the other hand in many problem-solving tasks, often one or a few methodologies are commonly used. In this paper, we argue that there is a link between the knee solutions in bi-criteria problems and the preferred methodologies when viewed from a conflicting bi-criterion standpoint. We illustrate our argument with the help of a number of popularly used problem-solving tasks. Each task, when perceived as a bicriteria problem, seems to exhibit a knee or a knee-region and the commonly-used methodology seems to lie within the knee-region. This linking is certainly an interesting finding and may have a long-term implication in the development of efficient solution methodologies for different scientific and other problem-solving tasks.

**Keywords:** Multi-objective optimization, knee point, preferred solutions, bicriteria problems, evolutionary algorithms, NSGA-II.

## 1 Introduction

Multi-objective optimization involves a number of conflicting objectives. Such problems give rise to a set of solutions non-dominant to each other known as Pareto-optimal solutions (collectively forming a Pareto-optimal front). There exists certain multi-objective optimization problems which exhibit a *knee* point on their Pareto-optimal front. A lot of research has been done on finding representative solutions in knee region [1,2,4,5,7,11,12,14]. A knee point is almost always the most preferred solution, since it requires an unfavorably large sacrifice in one objective to gain a small amount in the other objective.

In this paper, we make an interesting connection between knee points in bi-objective problems and preferred solution methodologies often used in certain problem-solving tasks in practice. Problem-solving tasks such as finding a mathematical regression, clustering a set of two or three-dimensional data, sorting a set of numbers, finding root of an equation numerically, and others are encountered frequently in scientific research or engineering application. Usually one or two methods are commonly preferred in practice while solving such problems. We argue that a plausible reason for why some methodologies are preferred over other

B.K. Panigrahi et al. (Eds.): SEMCCO 2010, LNCS 6466, pp. 182–189, 2010.

methods may come from this connection and realizing that the knee-region of the trade-off front may correspond to the preferred method. A number of generic and engineering problem-solving tasks are chosen and demonstrate that commonly-used solution principles lie near the knee-region of the associated bi-objective Pareto-optimal set.

## 2    A Knee Solution in a Bi-objective Optimization Problem

We restrict ourselves for minimization of two conflicting objectives only ($f_i$ : $\mathcal{S} \to \mathbf{R}$, $i = 1, 2$) as functions of decision variables $\mathbf{x}$:

$$\begin{aligned} \text{minimize } &\{f_1(\mathbf{x}), f_2(\mathbf{x})\}, \\ \text{subject to } &\mathbf{x} \in \mathcal{S}, \end{aligned} \qquad (1)$$

where $\mathcal{S} \subset \mathbf{R}^n$ denotes the set of feasible solutions. A vector of objective function values calculated at a point $\mathbf{x} \in \mathcal{S}$ is called an objective vector $\mathbf{f}(\mathbf{x}) = (f_1(\mathbf{x}), f_2(\mathbf{x}))^T$. The knee solution to a bi-objective optimization problem is found using the *Bend-Angle* approach [6], where the angle between the lines joining a point $\mathbf{f}(\mathbf{x})$ to its two extremes is maximum in the normalized objective space.

## 3    Problem-Solving Tasks

In this section, we take two different generic problem-solving tasks and two engineering design problems to understand and analyze the reasons for popularity of common solution methodologies from a bi-objective point of view.

### 3.1    Bucket Sorting Procedure

Sorting algorithms differ in terms of computational complexity, memory usage, and stability. We consider the bucket sorting algorithm since its performance can be controlled by using a parameter, called the bucket size $d$. The data-set is divided into $d$ buckets, where each bucket can take entries within a specified range of values. Each bucket is sorted using *Insertion Sort*. The space and time complexities are calculated in orders of the data-set size, $n$ and bucket size, $d$.

-  *Space Complexity* is $O(2n + d)$: output takes $O(n)$, bucket takes $O(\sum d_i)$ ($= O(n)$), and the vector that stores the size of each bucket takes $O(d)$.
-  *Time Complexity* is $O(n + 2)$: $O(n)$ is required to allocate the data entries to their corresponding bucket, $O(1)$ is required for each call made to insertion sort which sorts the numbers in a bucket, and $O(1)$ time is required for each swap made in the insertion sort.

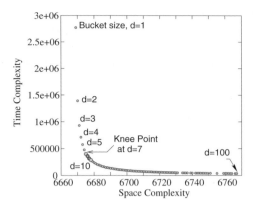

**Fig. 1.** The bucket sort algorithm exhibits a knee-region with bucket size close to 10

A data-set consisting of 3,334 randomly generated numbers ranging from 3 to 9999 is chosen for sorting. It is sorted using the bucket sort procedure, each time with a different number of buckets ($d$ varying from 1 to 100). In some sense, each bucket size plays as a different sorting strategy and we are interested in knowing if there exists a strategy that could give a good trade-off between time and memory. Figure 1 shows the variation of time and space complexities and presence of knee point at $d = 7$ (close to $d = 10$). A similar study is performed on other data-sets and they also exhibit a knee point close to $d = 10$. This drives us to question why $d = 10$ (in the entire range from 1 to 100) is a good trade-off strategy for computational time and computer memory usage! This can be explained with the help of another sorting procedure called the *radix sort*, where the data-set is sorted starting from the least significant digit (rightmost), followed by the second-least significant digit and so on till the most significant digit (leftmost). Since the elements of the data-set that we choose belongs to the decimal number system, the bucket size $d$ required will be equal to 10 (corresponding to digits 0 to 9). Therefore in some sense radix sort and the bucket sort ($d = 10$) follow similar principle to sort a data-set with natural numbers and a consideration of 10 buckets seem to have a connotation with the radix sort algorithm.

## 3.2   Curve Fitting

Different curve fitting models have have different ideologies which mark them apart from one another and produce different kinds of approximations. Polynomial regression is seen as the most preferred curve fitting technique due to its ease of use and tangible approximation. We investigate its importance in comparison to other curve fitting models by considering two conflicting goals of a curve fitting task – the *degree-of-freedom* (DOF) and the *residual sum of squares* (RSS). A general curve fitting model can be expressed using Equation 2. Given a regression model, one can obtain an estimate of parameters, $\hat{\beta}$. This is used to calculate the DOF and RSS from Equation 3. The DOF measures the complexity of the fitted curve and RSS measures the error of approximation. We have used four curve fitting models, namely Polynomial Regression, Splines, Penalized Linear Spline Regression and Quadratic Local Regression (refer [13] for details).

$$\boldsymbol{y} = \boldsymbol{X\beta} + \varepsilon,$$
$$\hat{\boldsymbol{y}} = \boldsymbol{X\hat{\beta}}, \tag{2}$$
$$= \boldsymbol{Hy}.$$

$$DOF = trace(\boldsymbol{H}).$$
$$RSS = \|\boldsymbol{y} - \hat{\boldsymbol{y}}\|_2. \tag{3}$$

1. *Polynomial Regression*:

$$\hat{\beta} = \boldsymbol{X}(\boldsymbol{X}^T\boldsymbol{X})^{-1}\boldsymbol{X}^T\boldsymbol{y}. \tag{4}$$

2. *Splines*: Here $\kappa$ represents the 'knots' which define the curve segment for the splines.

$$\text{Linear}: y = \beta_0 + \beta_1 x + \sum_{k=1}^{K} b_k(x - \kappa_k)_+, \tag{5}$$

$$\text{Quadratic}: y = \beta_0 + \beta_1 x + \beta_2 x^2 + \sum_{k=1}^{K} b_k(x - \kappa_k)_+^2. \tag{6}$$

3. *Penalized Linear Spline Regression*: Here $\lambda$ is smoothing parameter and varied in $[0.01\text{-}200]$.

$$\hat{\beta}_\lambda = (\boldsymbol{X}^T\boldsymbol{X} + \lambda^2\boldsymbol{D})^{-1}\boldsymbol{X}^T\boldsymbol{y}.$$
$$\boldsymbol{D} = \begin{bmatrix} \boldsymbol{0}_{2\times2} & \boldsymbol{0}_{2\times K} \\ \boldsymbol{0}_{K\times2} & \boldsymbol{I}_{K\times K} \end{bmatrix} \tag{7}$$

4. *Quadratic Local Regression*: The kernel function $K(x)$ is taken as $e^{-x^2}$. Here $h$ is the smoothing parameter (varied in range $[0.01\text{-}1]$).

$$\hat{\beta} = (\boldsymbol{X}_x^T\boldsymbol{W}_x\boldsymbol{X}_x)^{-1}\boldsymbol{X}_x^T\boldsymbol{W}_x\boldsymbol{y} \tag{8}$$

$$\boldsymbol{X}_x = \begin{bmatrix} 1 & (x_1 - x) & (x_1 - x)^2 \\ \vdots & \vdots & \vdots \\ 1 & (x_n - x) & (x_n - x)^2 \end{bmatrix} \tag{9}$$

$$\boldsymbol{W}_x = diag\left\{ K\left(\frac{x_1 - x}{h}\right), \cdots, K\left(\frac{x_n - x}{h}\right)\right\}. \tag{10}$$

Four data-sets[1], namely *lidar, fossil, electrical usage* and *simulated* are used. These data-sets are fitted with different approximation models with variation in

---

[1] Source: http://www.stat.tamu.edu/~carroll/semiregbook

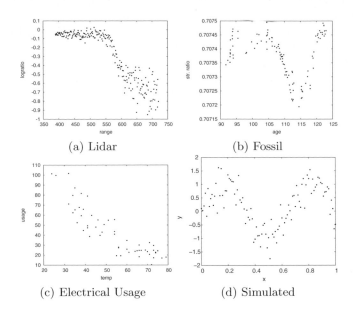

**Fig. 2.** Four different data-sets used for Regression Analysis

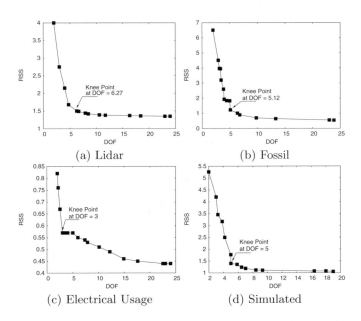

**Fig. 3.** Plot of RSS-DOF for different curve fitting models applied on the given data-sets

their parameters. Figure 2 gives the plot of different data-sets. Figure 3 gives the variation of RSS with DOF for these four data-sets using different modeling techniques discussed above. It is clear from the plots that (DOF,RSS) obtained using polynomial regression models are falling close to the knee point of the corresponding Pareto-optimal front, indicating that polynomial regression with $DOF \in [3, 6]$, in general, provides a good trade-off between computational complexity and obtained error of regression. Based on this finding, we argue that a favourable trade-off between computation and error can be one of the reasons why researchers prefer polynomial regression with a small DOF.

### 3.3  Signalized Intersection Design

In design of signalized intersection, a traffic engineer aims to minimize the time spent by a vehicle on the intersection (*delay*) and desires that the intersection operates close to its capacity thus utilizing the resources efficiently. The delay at a signalized intersection can be given by [9,10]:

$$D = D_1 + \sigma_{D_1} + D_2 + \sigma_{D_2},$$

$$D_1 = 0.5C\frac{(1 - \lambda)^2}{1 - \lambda \cdot x_1},$$

$$D_2 = 900T\left((X - 1) + \sqrt{(X - 1)^2 + \frac{8kX}{cT}}\right),$$

$$\sigma_{D_1} = \frac{C^2(1 - \lambda)^3(1 + 3\lambda - 4\lambda x_1)}{12(1 - \lambda x_1)^2},$$

$$\sigma_{D_2} = \frac{TX}{2c} + \frac{T^2(1 - X)^2}{12}, \tag{11}$$

where $D$ is the *total delay*, $C$ ($= 60$ s) is cycle length, $\lambda$ ($= 0.5$) is $\frac{\text{Green time}}{\text{Cycle time}}$, $T$ ($= 15$ min) is time of evaluation, $X \in [0.1, 1.6]$ is *volume-capacity-ratio*, $x_1$ is $\min(X, 1)$, $c$ ($= 900$ veh/hr) is capacity flow rate, and $k = 0.5$.

Figure 4 shows the variation between delay and capacity-volume-ratio for a single approach single lane signalized intersection. Considering delay and capacity-volume-ratio as the objectives to be minimized for the bi-objective signalized intersection design problem, the Pareto-optimal front shown in Figure 4 exhibits a knee point at (cap/vol=1.25, delay=60.04 s). It is worthwhile to note that at this solution the intersection is operating near capacity (cap/vol=1.0) though undersaturated, as an over-saturation would lead to very high delays. Such a design is preferred by a traffic engineer [3] and this specific desired solution corresponds to a knee solution to the underlying bi-objective optimization problem.

### 3.4  Leg Mechanism Design

Here we discuss the two-objective scenario of a robotic leg-mechanism in which minimization of force applied to the ground and energy required to execute the walking motion are considered. Among other constraints, there were two

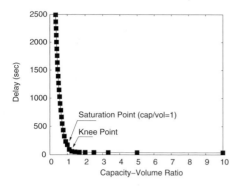 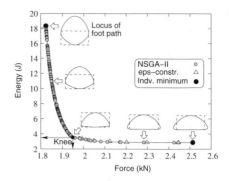

**Fig. 4.** Trade-off frontier and knee point for the Signalized Intersection Problem

**Fig. 5.** Trade-off front and knee point for the Leg Mechanism Design Problem

constraints which restrict the lower bound on horizontal and vertical strides (for details refer [8]). Figure 5 shows the trade-off front and the presence of a knee point. The knee point is: (Force=1.948 kN, Energy=3.535 J). Interestingly, the Pareto-optimal solutions that require smaller force requires a larger vertical leg movement violating its specified lower bound, and the solutions that require lesser energy requires a larger horizontal stride thereby violating its specified lower bound. It is the knee solution which satisfies the horizontal as well as the vertical bound. The energy needed to lift the leg to gain on the actuating force is quite high and the gain in energy needed for making larger horizontal stride requires a much larger actuating force. Due to these requirements, a designer would not be inclined to choose any design other than the knee solution.

This problem illustrates a generic phenomenon. If constraints are absent, the solution is a trivial – no walking at all, i.e, zero actuating force and zero required energy. Since a minimum horizontal stride is recommended as a hard constraint, some amount of force is needed to be applied. On the other hand, since a lower bound on the vertical leg movement is specified, some energy is also required. The Pareto-optimal solutions are divided around a specific point where the constraints are satisfied. Additionally if the trade-off on either side of the specific point is sharp enough that it renders other points as insignificant, then the specific point becomes a knee point and stands as an obvious preferred solution.

## 4   Conclusions

In this paper we have reviewed a number of bi-objective optimization problems with conflicting objectives showing a knee-like Pareto-optimal front. We have argued the existence of some commonly used methodologies in certain problem-solving tasks based on their equivalence with the knee point in an underlying bi-criteria problem. We have chosen a number of generic problem-solving tasks, such as sorting and regression and a few engineering design problems to illustrate this aspect. The results indicate that such a relationship exists and provides motivation to explore further with the help of other problem-solving tasks or engineering problems and to improve our understanding of knee points.

# References

1. Bechikh, S., Ben Said, L., Ghédira, K.: Searching for knee regions in multi-objective optimization using mobile reference points. In: Proceedings of the 2010 ACM Symposium on Applied Computing, pp. 1118–1125. ACM, New York (2010)
2. Branke, J., Deb, K., Dierolf, H., Osswald, M.: Finding knees in multi-objective optimization. In: Yao, X., Burke, E.K., Lozano, J.A., Smith, J., Merelo-Guervós, J.J., Bullinaria, J.A., Rowe, J.E., Tiño, P., Kabán, A., Schwefel, H.-P. (eds.) PPSN 2004. LNCS, vol. 3242, pp. 722–731. Springer, Heidelberg (2004)
3. Chakroborty, P., Das, A.: Principles of Transportation Engineering. PHI Learning Pvt. Ltd. (2004)
4. Das, I.: On characterizing the knee of the Pareto curve based on Normal-Boundary Intersection. Structural and Multidisciplinary Optimization 18(2), 107–115 (1999)
5. Deb, K.: Multi-objective optimization using evolutionary algorithms. Wiley, Chichester (2001)
6. Deb, K., Gupta, S.: Understanding Knee Points in Bicriteria Problems and Their Implications as Preferred Solution Principles. Tech. Rep. 2010005, KanGAL, Indian Institute of Technology Kanpur (2010)
7. Deb, K., Sundar, J.: Reference point based multi-objective optimization using evolutionary algorithms. In: Proceedings of the 8th annual conference on Genetic and evolutionary computation, p. 642. ACM, New York (2006)
8. Deb, K., Tiwari, S.: Multi-objective optimization of a leg mechanism using genetic algorithms. Engineering Optimization 37(4), 325–350 (2005)
9. Dion, F., Rakha, H., Kang, Y.: Comparison of delay estimates at under-saturated and over-saturated pre-timed signalized intersections. Transportation Research Part B: Methodological 38(2), 99–122 (2004)
10. Fu, L., Hellinga, B.: Delay variability at signalized intersections. Transportation Research Record: Journal of the Transportation Research Board 1710, 215–221 (2000)
11. Rachmawati, L., Srinivasan, D.: A multi-objective evolutionary algorithm with weighted-sum niching for convergence on knee regions. In: Proceedings of the 8th annual conference on Genetic and evolutionary computation, p. 750. ACM, New York (2006)
12. Rachmawati, L., Srinivasan, D.: Multiobjective evolutionary algorithm with controllable focus on the knees of the Pareto front. IEEE Transactions on Evolutionary Computation 13(4), 810–824 (2009)
13. Ruppert, D., Wand, M., Carroll, R.: Semiparametric regression. Cambridge Univ. Pr., Cambridge (2003)
14. Schütze, O., Laumanns, M., Coello Coello, C.: Approximating the Knee of an MOP with Stochastic Search Algorithms. In: Rudolph, G., Jansen, T., Lucas, S., Poloni, C., Beume, N. (eds.) PPSN 2008. LNCS, vol. 5199, pp. 795–804. Springer, Heidelberg (2008)

# A Relation-Based Model for Convergence Analysis of Evolutionary Algorithm

Zhi-Feng Hao[1], Han Huang[2,3,4], Haozhe Li[2], Shaohu Ling[2], and Benqing Li[2]

[1] The Faculty of computer, Guangdong University of Technology,
Guangzhou 510006, P.R. China
mazfhao@scut.edu.cn
[2] School of Software Engineering, South China University of Technology,
Guangzhou, 510006, P.R. China
[3] State Key Lab. for Novel Software Technology, Nanjing University 210093, P.R. China
[4] Dept of Management Sciences, College of Business,
City University of Hong Kong, Hong Kong
hhan@scut.edu.cn

**Abstract.** There have been many results on convergence of evolutionary algorithm (EA) since it was proposed, but few result focused on convergence analysis based on relation theory. This paper proposed a relation-based model to study the equivalence and ordering of EA in convergence. The equivalence relation named equivalence in status (EIS) can be used to divide a given set of EAs into equivalence classes in which the EAs have the same capacity of convergence. EAs belonging to different EIS classes have different capacities of convergence based on the absorbing Markov chain model, which is described as an ordering relation named superiority in status. The performance of an EA can be improved if it is modified to be superior in status to its original version.

## 1 Introduction

Recently, evolutionary computation has been divided into the following four areas: evolutionary optimization, evolutionary learning, evolutionary design and theoretical foundation [1]. Among them, theoretical foundation research is important and helpful for us to study the function and behavior of EAs. As part of the theoretical foundation research, convergence analysis is necessary to confirm the correctness of EAs. Thus, we need a model or method for convergence contrast to evaluate and improve the convergence capacity of EAs, on which this paper focuses.

Since genetic algorithm [2] was first proposed, several studies have been published on the convergence analysis of EAs. Some preliminary results like pattern theorem [2], Walsh analysis [3-4], and blocking assumption [5-6], were devoted to the idiographic performance of genetic algorithms (GAs). Later, Markov chain analysis was done on the convergence of EAs, which mentions whether an evolutionary algorithm can converge to the global optimal solution. Goldberg and Segrest [7] used homogeneous Markov chain to analyze the convergence of genetic algorithm. Eiben [8] proved the global convergence of GA with elitist selection. Rudolph [9] verified that

B.K. Panigrahi et al. (Eds.): SEMCCO 2010, LNCS 6466, pp. 190–197, 2010.

the standard GA with crossover, mutation and selection operators cannot converge to the global optimum based on homogeneous Markov chain. He [10] presents a theoretical analysis of convergence conditions for evolutionary algorithms.

However, few studies have touched upon the theory for the convergence performance comparison of EA. Most of the research on the topic was done and verified experimentally without a strictly-defined theoretical framework or model. Therefore, the present paper proposes a relation model for analyzing the convergence capacity of evolutionary algorithm.

Relation including equivalence and ordering is one of the most important theories in discrete mathematics, and was used in the following application of evolutionary algorithms. Pareto comparison is an ordering for selection operator of multi-objective evolutionary algorithm. Except these, there is less result on convergence analysis of EA with relation model. Differently, a kind of EAs is the tackled objects of the proposed relation model which contains the equivalence and ordering of EAs in the property of convergence capacity.

## 2 Theoretical Preparation

There are several kinds of evolutionary algorithms, of which the framework can be described abstractly as follows.

---

1.  Discrete encoding.
2.  Initialization. t=0.
3.  Evaluation and Selection. t=t+1.
4.  If the stop criterion is satisfied then
        Output the best-so-far solution.
    Else
        Go to step 5.
    Endif
5. Recombination of the solutions at t-th iteration. Go to step 3.

---

**Fig. 1.** The framework of evolutionary algorithm

We only consider the EA following the framework of fig.1 as the analyzed objects by the proposed model. Some definitions are given for the modeling of EA.

**Definition 1.** $\{\xi_t\}_{t=0}^{+\infty}$ is said to be the stochastic process of EA, where $\xi_t$ is the t-th population of an evolutionary algorithm, $\xi_0$ is the initial one, $\forall \xi_t \in Y$, and $Y$ is the status space.

Lemma 1 indicates an important property of the stochastic process.

**Lemma 1.** The stochastic process for EA is a Markov process.

**Proof.** Because an EA generates a new population of solutions only based on the current population, for $\forall Y_1 \subset Y$, $P\{\xi_{t+1} \in Y_1 | \xi_0, ..., \xi_t\} = P\{\xi_{t+1} \in Y_1 | \xi_t\}$ where

$\{\xi_t\}_{t=0}^{+\infty}$ is the stochastic process of EA and $Y$ is the status space of $\xi_t$. Thus, $\{\xi_t\}_{t=0}^{+\infty}$ is a Markov process.

$\{\xi_t\}_{t=0}^{+\infty}$ is a Markov chain [11] when $Y$ is a discrete status space. For example, EA of discrete individual can be modeled as a Markov chain. In fact, most of the EAs belong to this type because the encoding of solution must be discrete when the algorithm is programmed on the computer. This paper mainly studies the EAs modeled as a Markov chain. Besides the Markov property of EAs, we need a set of optimal status as the objective status of the stochastic process of EAs.

**Definition 2.** $Y^* \subset Y$ is an optimal status set if $\forall \xi^* \in Y^*$ contains at least one optimal solution, where $\{\xi_t\}_{t=0}^{+\infty}$ is a Markov chain of EA and $Y$ is the status space.

According to Lemma 1, EA can be modeled as a Markov chain. In other words, $Y^*$ is the set of populations in which there is at least an optimal individual. As definition 2 indicates, EA attains an optimal solution at the t-th iteration when $\xi_t \in Y^*$. $Y^*$ may change in the same status space $Y$ when the evaluation function is different. Furthermore, EA can converge to an optimal solution if $\lim_{t \to +\infty} P\{\xi_t \in Y^*\} = 1$, which is the following definition.

**Definition 3.** EA converges if $\lim_{t \to +\infty} P\{\xi_t \in Y^*\} = 1$.

In the framework shown by Fig. 1, EA can keep the best-so-far solution during running. Therefore, we will introduce another definition with $Y^*$ and Markov chain.

**Definition 4.** $\{\xi_t\}_{t=0}^{+\infty}$ is an absorbing Markov chain if $P\{\xi_{t+1} \notin Y^* | \xi_t \in Y^*\} = 0$ ($\forall t = 0, 1, \ldots$).

The concept of absorbing Markov chain was proposed to analyze the running time of EAs [12-13]. We also use it to model the EA that follows the framework of Fig. 1.

**Lemma 2.** The stochastic process $\{\xi_t\}_{t=0}^{+\infty}$ of EA following the framework of Fig. 1 is an absorbing Markov process.

**Proof.** Because of the best-so-far solution, EA will never lose the optimal solution once found. Thus, $\{\xi_t\}_{t=0}^{+\infty}$ satisfies that $P\{\xi_{t+1} \notin Y^* | \xi_t \in Y^*\} = 0$ ($\forall t = 0, 1, \ldots$). $\{\xi_t\}_{t=0}^{+\infty}$ is an absorbing Markov chain.

Many EAs for real problems can be modeled by an absorbing Markov chain because an EA will keep the best-so-far solution per iteration.

## 3   Equivalence in Status

Based on the theoretical preparation, we will propose the relation models including an equivalence relation and an ordering for the convergence comparison of EAs. This subsection will introduce the first relation named equivalence in status (EIS).

First, we need an item to describe the attaining status of EA.

**Definition 5.** Given a Markov chain $\{\xi_t^a\}_{t=0}^{+\infty}$ for the EA $a$, $\Xi_t^a$ is the set of possible attaining status of EA $a$ in the $t$-th iteration such that

$$\Xi_t^a = \{\xi^x \mid P\{\xi_t^a = \xi^x \in Y \mid \xi_{t-1}^a \notin Y^*\} \geq \delta_t\}, \quad \text{where} \quad \delta_t > 0 \quad \text{and}$$

$$\prod_{t=0}^{+\infty}(1-\delta_t) = 0 \ (t = 1, 2, \dots ).$$

$\Xi_t^a$ can be considered as the set of feasible status of EA $a$ in the $t$-th iteration. It can evaluate the searching scope of EA. The definition of $\Xi_t^a$ only applies the EAs of discrete code. Based on $\Xi_t^a$, we can present the definition of relation as follows.

**Definition 6.** Given a set of EAs signed as $S_{EA}$ and the Markov chains $\{\xi_t^a\}_{t=0}^{+\infty}, \{\xi_t^b\}_{t=0}^{+\infty}$ for $a, b \in S_{EA}$, it is said that $a$ is equivalent in status (EIS) to $b$ if $\Xi_t^a \cap Y^* = \Xi_t^b \cap Y^*$ ($t = 1, 2, \dots$), signed as $a \hat{=} b$.

If two EAs are equivalent in status to each other, their sets of possible attaining status are the same, intersected with the optimal status set. EA $a$ and $b$ can attain the same optimal status in the $t$-th iteration when $a \hat{=} b$. EIS has an important property for the classification of EAs, which is shown by theorem 1.

**Theorem 1.** Equivalence in status ($\hat{=} \subseteq S_{EA} \times S_{EA}$) is an equivalence relation, where $S_{EA}$ is a given set of EAs.

**Proof.** Because $a \hat{=} a$ for $\forall a \in S_{EA}$, $a \hat{=} b \Leftrightarrow b \hat{=} a$ for $\forall a, b \in S_{EA}$ and $a \hat{=} b \wedge b \hat{=} c \Leftrightarrow a \hat{=} c$ for $\forall a, b, c \in S_{EA}$. Therefore, $\hat{=}$ is an equivalence relation.

According to the property of equivalence relation, the given set $S_{EA}$ can be divided into equivalence classes which have no shared elements. $\forall x \in S_{EA}$ can generate an equivalence class signed as $[x]_{\hat{=}}$. Furthermore, $S_{EA} / \hat{=}$ is a mapping: $S_{EA} \rightarrow \Re$, where for $\forall Y^{\hat{=}} \in \Re$, $Y^{\hat{=}}$ is the possible subset of $Y^*$.

## 4 Equivalence in Status and Convergence

The goal of introducing EIS relation is to analyzing the convergence of EA. This subsection will introduce the relation between EIS and the convergence of evolutionary algorithm. First, Lemma is given as a preparation.

**Lemma 3.** EA $a$ converges if $P\{\xi_t^a \in Y^* \mid \xi_{t-1}^a \notin Y^*\} \geq \delta_t$ when $\exists t' \geq 0$, $t > t'$ and $\prod_{t=0}^{+\infty}(1-\delta_t) = 0$, where $\{\xi_t^a\}_{t=0}^{+\infty}$ is an absorbing Markov chain for the EA $a$.

**Proof.**   Because   $P\{\xi_t^a \in Y^* | \xi_{t-1}^a \notin Y^*\} \geq \delta_t$   when   $\exists t' \geq 0$   and   $t > t'$ ,

$P\{\xi_t^a \notin Y^* | \xi_{t-1}^a \notin Y^*\} \leq 1 - \delta_t$ .   Given   $P_{not}^a(t) = \prod_{i=0}^{t-1} P\{\xi_{i+1}^a \notin Y^* | \xi_i^a \notin Y^*\}$ ,

we   have   $\lim_{t \to \infty} P_{not}^a(t) \leq \prod_{t=0}^{+\infty} (1 - \delta_t)$ .   Because   $\prod_{t=0}^{+\infty} (1 - \delta_t) = 0$ ,

$\lim_{t \to \infty} P_{not}^a(t) = 0$ . Therefore, evolutionary algorithm $a$ can attain the optimal status at

least once when the iteration time is infinite.

Because $\{\xi_t^a\}_{t=0}^{+\infty}$ is an absorbing Markov chain, $P\{\xi_t^a \notin Y^* | \xi_{t-1}^a \in Y^*\} = 0$ ac-

cording to definition 4, i.e. $P\{\xi_t^a \in Y^* | \xi_{t-1}^a \in Y^*\} = 1$ for $t = 1, 2, \ldots$ . Thus,

$$P\{\xi_t^a \notin Y^*\} = P\{\xi_t^a \notin Y^* | \xi_{t-1}^a \notin Y^*\} \cdot P\{\xi_{t-1}^a \notin Y^*\}$$

$$+ P\{\xi_t^a \notin Y^* | \xi_{t-1}^a \in Y^*\} \cdot P\{\xi_{t-1}^a \in Y^*\} = P\{\xi_0^a \notin Y^*\} \cdot P_{not}^a(t)$$

Because $P\{\xi_t^a \in Y^*\} = 1 - P\{\xi_t^a \notin Y^*\}$ ,

$$\lim_{t \to \infty} P\{\xi_t^a \in Y^*\} = 1 - \lim_{t \to \infty} P\{\xi_t^a \notin Y^*\} = 1 - P\{\xi_0^a \notin Y^*\} \cdot \lim_{t \to \infty} P_{not}^a(t) = 1$$

Therefore, $a$ converges according to definition 3.   □

We can use Lemma 3 to propose a theorem for the convergence of EA with EIS.

**Theorem 2.** Given a set of EAs signed as $S_{EA}$ and an equivalence class $[x]_{\hat{=}}$

$(\forall x \in S_{EA})$, $\forall x_2 \in [x]_{\hat{=}}$ converges, if the stochastic process of $x_2$ is an absorbing

Markov chain and $\exists x_1 \in [x]_{\hat{=}}$ converges.

**Proof.** According to definition 3, $\lim_{t \to +\infty} P\{\xi_t^{x_1} \in Y^*\} = 1$ because $x_1 \in [x]_{\hat{=}}$ con-

verges. Thus, for $\forall \varepsilon = 1/t > 0$ , $\exists t' > 0$ , $P\{\xi_t^{x_1} \in Y^*\} > 1 - \varepsilon = 1 - 1/t$

when $t > t'$. If $\delta_t = 1 - 1/t > 0$ , $\prod_{t=0}^{+\infty} (1 - \delta_t) = 0$, so $\xi_t^{x_1} \in \Xi_t^{x_1}$ (Definition 5)

i.e.   $\Xi_t^{x_1} \cap Y^* \neq \varnothing$   when   $t > t'$ .   $x_1 \hat{=} x_2$   for   $\forall x_2 \in [x]_{\hat{=}}$ ,   so

$\Xi_t^{x_2} \cap Y^* = \Xi_t^{x_1} \cap Y^* \neq \varnothing$ when $t > t'$ according to definition 6. Thus,

$P\{\Xi_t^{x_2} \cap Y^* \neq \varnothing\} \geq \delta_t$   when   $t > t'$   based   on   definition   5,   so

$P\{\xi_t^{x_2} \in Y^* | \xi_{t-1}^{x_2} \notin Y^*\} \geq \delta_t$ where $\prod_{t=0}^{+\infty} (1 - \delta_t) = 0$. Therefore, $x_2$ converges.

Theorem 2 indicates that an equivalence ($\hat{=}$) class of EAs modeled as absorbing
Markov chains converge as long as an EA in the class converges. EAs of the same
EIS class have the same convergence capacity with the property of absorbing Markov
chain. The theorem also reveals useful information that we can study the convergence

of other EAs of the EIS class of $a$ when having difficulty in proving the convergence of EA $a$ of the considered framework (Fig. 1). The following corollary indicates this property in the negative direction.

**Corollary 1.** Given a set of EAs signed as $S_{EA}$ and an equivalence class $[x]_{\triangleq}$ ( $\forall x \in S_{EA}$ ), $\forall x \in [x]_{\triangleq}$ cannot converge if $\exists x_2 \in [x]_{\triangleq}$ cannot converge and the stochastic process of $x_2$ is an absorbing Markov chain.

**Proof.** Using reduction to absurdity, it is supposed that $\exists x_1 \in [x]_{\triangleq}$ converges if $\exists x_2 \in [x]_{\triangleq}$ cannot converge and the stochastic process of $x_2$ is an absorbing Markov chain. According to theorem 2, $\forall x' \in [x]_{\triangleq}$ converge if the stochastic process of $x'$ is an absorbing Markov chain. $x_2$ can also converge, which is contradictory to the precondition that $x_2 \in [x]_{\triangleq}$ cannot converge, i.e. $\forall x \in [x]_{\triangleq}$ cannot converge.      □

Corollary 1 indicates that an equivalence ( $\triangleq$ ) class of EAs modeled as absorbing Markov chains cannot converge as long as one EA in the class cannot. In another word, if EA $a$ of the considered framework (Fig. 1) does not converge, other EAs of the EIS class of $a$ are all unable to converge.

## 5   Superior in Status and Convergence

Based on the relation of equivalence in status, the section proposes an ordering relation to compare the given EAs in convergence capacity.

**Definition 7.** Given a set of EAs signed as $S_{EA}$ and two Markov chains $\{\xi_t^a\}_{t=0}^{+\infty}, \{\xi_t^b\}_{t=0}^{+\infty}$ for $\forall a, b \in S_{EA}$, it is said that $b$ is superior in status to $a$ if $\Xi_t^a \cap Y^* \subseteq \Xi_t^b \cap Y^*$ for $t = 1, 2, \dots$, signed as $b \succ a$ or $a \prec b$.

$b \succ a$ means that EA $b$ can attain all of the solutions found by EA $a$, and some of the solutions are not found by EA $a$. The following theorem and corollary indicates the convergence relation between $a$ and $b$ if $b \succ a$.

**Theorem 3.** Given a set of EAs signed as $S_{EA}$ and $\forall a, b \in S_{EA}$, $b$ converges, if $b \succ a$, the stochastic process of $b$ is an absorbing Markov chain and $a$ converges.

**Proof.** According to definition 3, $\lim_{t \to +\infty} P\{\xi_t^a \in Y^*\} = 1$ for $a$ converges. Thus, for $\forall \varepsilon = 1/t > 0$ and $\exists t' > 0$, $P\{\xi_t^a \in Y^*\} > 1 - \varepsilon = 1 - 1/t$ when $t > t'$.

If $\delta_t = 1 - 1/t > 0$ , $\prod_{t=0}^{+\infty}(1-\delta_t) = 0$ . Thus, $\xi_t^a \in \Xi_t^a$ i.e. $\Xi_t^a \cap Y^* = \varnothing$ when $t > t'$. $x_1 \triangleq x_2$ for $\exists x_2 \in [x]_{\triangleq}$, so $\Xi_t^{x_2} \cap Y^* = \Xi_t^{x_1} \cap Y^* \neq \varnothing$ when $b \succ a$

according to definition 7. Therefore, $\Xi_t^b \cap Y^* \supseteq \Xi_t^a \cap Y^* \neq \varnothing$ when $t > t'$ based

on definition 5, so $P\{\xi_t^b \in Y^* \big| \xi_{t-1}^b \notin Y^*\} \geq \delta_t$ where $\prod_{t=0}^{+\infty}(1-\delta_t)=0$. $b$ con-

verges for Lemma 3.                                                                                     □

Theorem 3 displays that the EA $b$ modeled as an absorbing Markov chain converges as long as $a \prec b$ and $a$ converges, which is another method to prove the convergence of an EA. The following corollary also indicates this property in the negative direction.

**Corollary 2.** Given a set of EAs signed as $S_{EA}$ and $\forall a, b \in S_{EA}$, $a$ cannot converge if (1) $b \succ a$, (2) the stochastic process of $b$ is an absorbing Markov chain and (3) $b$ cannot converge.

**Proof.** Using the method of proof by contradiction, it is supposed that $a$ converges, so $b$ also converges based on theorem 3, which is contradictory to the precondition that $b$ cannot converge. Thus, $a$ cannot converge.                                         □

Given two evolutionary algorithms $a$ and $b$ meeting that $b \succ a$ and their stochastic processes are absorbing Markov chain, the convergence capacity of $b$ is not worse than that of $a$ if $\exists \beta \in Y^* \wedge \beta \in \Xi_t^a$ ( $t = 1, 2, ...$ ). Moreover, the performance of $b$ can be better than that of $a$ if $\forall \alpha \in Y^* \wedge \alpha \notin \Xi_t^a$ and $\exists \gamma \in Y^* \wedge \gamma \in \Xi_t^b$ ( $t = 1, 2, ...$ ). Therefore, the convergence capacity of an EA can be improved by designing a novel one superior in status to it.

## 6  Conclusion and Discussion

The present paper proposes a relation-based model for analyzing the convergence capacity of evolutionary algorithm based on absorbing Markov chain. The model contains an equivalence relation named equivalence in status (EIS) and ordering relation named superiority in status (SIS). Any given set of evolutionary algorithms can be divided into several equivalence classes with EIS. It has been revealed that the EAs belonging to the same class have the same convergence properties, which is indicated as theorems. Another relation SIS can be used to rank the given EAs in terms of convergence capacity. The idea of improving the convergence capacity of EAs roots in the theory that the EA-I can perform better than EA-II in global convergence if EA-I EA-II. The proposed model can be only used to the EAs that have the property of absorbing Markov chain. Equivalence in status seems to be more significant in theory than in practical. Superior in status can be used to improve the convergence capacity of evolutionary algorithm. However, the improvement depends on a condition that the inferior EA cannot attain the optimal status which belongs to the possible status set of the superior one. In general, the improved EA is not worse than the original one. Thus, it is a weak improvement.

Furthermore, the SIS-based improvement may raise additional computational effort. In the future study, the improved relation model will be studied to discuss the convergence and computational time in order to make more fundamental improvement of EAs.

## Acknowledgement

National Natural Science Foundation of China (61003066,61070033,60873078), Doctoral Program of the Ministry of Education (20090172120035) and Fundamental Research Funds for the Central Universities, SCUT(2009ZM0052).

## References

1. Yao, X., Xu, Y.: Recent Advances in Evolutionary Computation. Journal of Computer Science & Technology 21(1), 1–18 (2006)
2. Holland, J.H.: Adaptation in Natural and Artificial Systems, 1st edn. (1975), 2nd edn. MIT press, Cambridge (1992)
3. Goldberg, D.E.: Simple Genetic Algorithms and the Minimal Deceptive Problem. In: Davis, L. (ed.) Genetic Algorithms and Simulated Annealing, London Pitman, pp. 74–78 (1987)
4. Bethke, A.D.: Comparison of Genetic Algorithms and Gradient-Vased Optimizers on Parallel Processors: Efficiency of Use of Processing Capacity Technical Report No.197, University of Michigen, Login of Computers Group, Ann Arbor (1976)
5. Grefenstette, J.J.: Deception considered harmful. In: Whitley, L.D. (ed.) Foundations of Genetic Algorithms, vol. 2, pp. 75–91. Morgan Kaufmann, San Mateo (1993)
6. Rudolph, G.: Convergence Properties of Evolutionary Algorithms. Verlag Dr. KovaYc, Hamburg (1997)
7. Goldberg, D.E., Segrest, P.: Finite Markov Chain Analysis of Genetic Algorithm. In: Genetic Algorithms and Their pplication: Proceeding of the Second International Conference on Genetic Algorithms, pp. 7–8 (1987)
8. Eiben, A.E., Aarts, E.H., Van Hee, K.M.: Global Convergence of Genetic Algorithms: An infinite Markov Chain Analysis. In: Schwefel, H.P. (ed.) Parallel Problem Solving from Nature, pp. 4–12. Springer, Heidelberg (1991)
9. Rudolph, G.: Convergence Properties of Canonical Genetic Algorithms. IEEE Transaction on Neural Networks 5(1), 96–101 (1994)
10. He, J., Yu, X.H.: Conditions for the convergence of evolutionary algorithms. Journal of System Architecture 47, 601–612 (2001)
11. Iosifescu, M.: Finite Markov Processes and Their Applications. Willey, Chichester (1980)
12. He, J., Yao, X.: Drift analysis and average time complexity of evolutionary algorithms. Artificial Intelligence 127(1), 57–85 (2001)
13. Yu, Y., Zhou, Z.H.: A new approach to estimating the expected first hitting time of evolutionary algorithms. Artificial Intelligence 172, 1809–1832 (2008)

# Neural Meta-Memes Framework for Combinatorial Optimization

Li Qin Song[1], Meng Hiot Lim[1], and Yew Soon Ong[2]

[1] School of Electrical & Electronic Engineering, Nanyang Technological University,
Singapore 639798
[2] School of Computer Engineering, Nanyang Technological University,
Singapore 639798

**Abstract.** In this paper, we present a Neural Meta-Memes Framework (NMMF) for combinatorial optimization. NMMF is a framework which models basic optimization algorithms as memes and manages them dynamically when solving combinatorial problems. NMMF encompasses neural networks which serve as the overall planner/coordinator to balance the workload between memes. We show the efficacy of the proposed NMMF through empirical study on a class of combinatorial problem, the quadratic assignment problem (QAP).

## 1 Introduction

Combinatorial optimization deals with maximization or minimization of discrete problems. Examples of combinatorial problems include job-shop scheduling problem, vehicle routing problem, travelling salesman problem, graph partitioning, etc. The objective is to find the optimum from a large but finite number of solutions. Since the number of solutions is finite, it is theoretically possible to find the optimum by enumerating all solutions of the problem. But in practice the number of solutions increases exponentially with the problem size and this makes the exact methods impractical for large scale problems.

For most of the large scale combinatorial problems, stochastic methods are the only viable methods to achieve good feasible solutions. Numerous stochastic techniques for combinatorial optimization have been reported in recent decades, such as tabu search [9], simulating annealing [4], hybrid genetic algorithm [5], [6], memetic algorithm [7], [10], particle swarm optimization [2], and so on [11], [12]. Among all the combinatorial problems in computer science, quadratic assignment problem (QAP) is arguably one of the hardest. It was formulated by Koopmans and Beckmann to solve the cost minimizing problem of assigning a number of plants to the same number of locations [3]. A QAP of size $n$ may be stated as assigning $n$ facilities to $n$ locations. The objective for the QAP is to minimize the following equation:

$$C(\pi) = \sum_{i=1}^{n} \sum_{j=1}^{n} a_{ij} b_{\pi(i)\pi(j)} \tag{1}$$

where $a_{ij}$ represents the distance between locations $i$ and $j$; $b_{rs}$ represents the flow between facilities $r$ and $s$. Here $\pi$ is a permutation of the set $M = \{1, 2, ..., n\}$ and $\pi(i)$ denotes that facility $\pi(i)$ is assigned to location $i$.

B.K. Panigrahi et al. (Eds.): SEMCCO 2010, LNCS 6466, pp. 198–205, 2010.

Accordingly the "*no free lunch theorem*" [14] has been generally accepted as a stipulation that there is no single algorithm which can consistently solve any type of combinatorial problems. However, by combining multiple algorithms or techniques and managing them accordingly, it is possible that a framework which consistently provides good results for different types of combinatorial problems can be configured. Our focus in this article is on a neural meta-memes framework (NMMF) for combinatorial optimization. The original definition of a meme is a unit of cultural information inheritable between individuals. In [8] the meme's definition is extended as a mechanism that captures the essence of knowledge in the form of procedures that affect the transition of solutions during a search. A basic algorithm's unique search procedure(s) bring special improvement to the search and provide predictable search results. Such an algorithm can be modeled as a reliable knowledge system, in other words, a meme. In the proposed NMMF, single algorithms are modeled as memes. Here the neural meta-memes refers to the neural networks within NMMF acting as manager which manipulates the memes with intention to configure a balanced problem-solving mechanism so as to achieve good solutions for different combinatorial problems. In the next section, details of NMMF are presented. Experimental results and analysis are reported in Section 3. Finally in Section 4, we conclude this paper.

## 2   Neural Meta-Memes Framework (NMMF)

NMMF is an optimization framework for managing memes and utilizing each of the meme's best traits. The NMMF manages memes to form a unique optimized balanced mechanism specifically for the problem under test. In this section, more details are elaborated on the main components of NMMF: the meme pool, the mechanism refining center and the neural networks.

### 2.1   Meme Pool

The three algorithms used to compose the meme pool are tabu search, simulated annealing and genetic algorithm. Within a typical *tabu search* (TS) method, a tabu list is equipped with a solution to record its recent moves. All neighbors of the solution are examined every generation and the best one replaces that solution. The move from that solution to its best neighbor is recorded in the tabu list with a preset tenure. The tabu list increases the search efficiency by forbidding the moves recorded in the list unless an aspiration criterion is met which usually refers to a notable improvement by the move. A simplified version of robust tabu search [9] is adopted in NMMF. *Simulated annealing* (SA) is carried on by randomly generating a fixed number of candidate moves every generation for a solution. The outcomes by these candidate moves are checked. Those moves which bring improvements to this solution are performed, and others are given a chance which the probability value is derived from a probability function related to the solution value and a temperature value which is updated (usually reduced) every generation. *Genetic algorithm* (GA) is an evolutionary algorithm including different genetic operators. The parent selection operator is used to select parent individuals from the population based on techniques such as roulette wheel selection, tournament selection, etc. The crossover operator helps to generate

offspring individuals from the parent individuals with different techniques. The mutation operator is used to maintain the population diversity by applying a fixed range of
randomly swaps to the solutions with a preset mutation rate.

## 2.2 Mechanism Refining Center

This component functions as a learning center. A unique mechanism is produced for a
problem through a greedy learning process. The generated optimized mechanism
(consists of optimized parameters) and the problem data is archived into a database.
The database is used to train the neural networks. The parameters defining a mechanism are the numbers of continuous iterations without improvement for the three
memes, that is, $Num_{GA}$ for GA, $Num_{SA}$ for SA and $Num_{TS}$ for TS. The learning process
starts with a preset values set which has been proved efficient on solving combinatorial problems. In each generation, every parameter is searched for its neighbors with
other parameters unchanged and the corresponding values sets are tested. The search
stops when the best result found is not improved for a certain number of generations.
The values set which produces the best result will be the optimized parameters. The
ranges of variations for the three parameters are [0, 10] for $Num_{GA}$, [0, 10] for $Num_{SA}$
and [90, 110] for $Num_{TS}$. Our experience shows that mechanisms with parameters out
of these ranges produce significantly worse solutions.

## 2.3 Neural Networks

For evaluation purpose, the QAP benchmarks are tested with NMMF. The inputs of
the neural networks are designed to be adapted to the QAP. In [13], Vollmann and
Buffa introduced the flow dominance (fd) as shown in equation 2 as a measure of the
characteristics of QAPs:

$$ fd(c) = \frac{a}{b}; \quad a = \sqrt{\frac{\sum_{i=1}^{n}\sum_{j=1}^{n}(c_{ij}-b)^2}{n^2}}; \quad b = \frac{\sum_{i=1}^{n}\sum_{j=1}^{n}c_{ij}}{n^2} \tag{2} $$

where $c_{ij}$ is the entry number in position $ij$ in the flow matrix, $n$ is the problem size.
The distance dominance for distance matrix is defined similarly. Higher value of flow
dominance indicates fewer facilities contribute much more to the overall flow than
others. Another coefficient is the sparsity which is calculated by equation 3:

$$ sp = n_0/n^2 \tag{3} $$

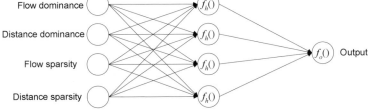

Fig. 1. Three-layer neural network used in NMMF

where $n_0$ is the total number of zero entries in a matrix, $n$ is the problem size. The sparsity gives the proportion of zero entries with reference to the total number of entries. Real-life QAPs usually have large sparsity values. Flow dominance, distance dominance, flow sparsity and distance sparsity are the input parameters for the neural networks. To adapt with other types of combinatorial problems, the inputs of neural networks can be easily modified according to the problems characteristics.

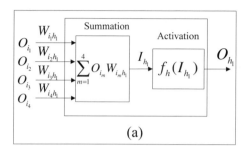 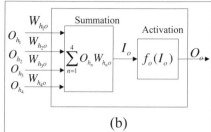

(a)                                           (b)

**Fig. 2.** Structures of the neurons: (a) hidden neuron 1; (b) output neuron

Three isolated neural networks are used in NMMF. Each one is responsible for generating one of the three parameters: $Num_{GA}$, $Num_{SA}$ and $Num_{TS}$. In the following we only elaborate one neural network which can be any of the three used in NMMF by replacing "*Output*" with one of the three parameters. As shown in Fig. 1, the neural network includes 3 layers: input layer including 4 input neurons, hidden layer including 4 hidden neurons and output layer including one output neuron. This neural network adopts the back propagation update rule to train its weights. The back propagation rule was introduced by Werbos [15] and further enriched and popularized by Rumehart *et al.* [16]. The following derivation is also available in [17], [18]. The difference between the output "*Out*" produced from neural network and the expected output "*Exp*" is given in equation 4:

$$E = Out - Exp .$$

(4)

The back propagation update rule is designed to provide a gradient descent minimization for $E^2$. To minimize $E^2$ value through adjusting weights, we have to know the effect of changing each of the weights. The back propagation update rule utilizes the error $E^2$ as feedback signal to direct the directions of adjusting weights. The partial derivative $\partial E^2 / \partial W$ gives the direction of modifying weight $W$. Equation 5 is the update formula for weight $W$:

$$W(new) = W(old) - \eta \frac{\partial E^2}{\partial W(old)}$$

(5)

where $\eta$ is learning rate which ranges between 0 and 1.

Fig. 2(a) shows the details of hidden neuron 1 and Fig. 2(b) gives the details of the only output neuron. In the following some details analysis is given on the update rule for weight $W_{h_1 o}$ between output and hidden neuron 1. With the definition in equation 5, we continue by expanding $\partial E^2 / \partial W$:

$$\frac{\partial E^2}{\partial W_{h_1 o}} = \frac{\partial E^2}{\partial I_o}\frac{\partial I_o}{\partial W_{h_1 o}}; \tag{6}$$

$$\frac{\partial I_o}{\partial W_{h_1 o}} = \frac{\partial \sum_{n=1}^{4} O_{h_n} W_{h_n o}}{\partial W_{h_1 o}} = \frac{\partial O_{h_1} W_{h_1 o}}{\partial W_{h_1 o}} + \frac{\partial \sum_{n=2}^{4} O_{h_n} W_{h_n o}}{\partial W_{h_1 o}}. \tag{7}$$

Because only hidden neuron 1 has dependence on $W_{h_1 o}$, the last item on right side of equation 7 equals to 0. Equation 7 is further simplified to:

$$\frac{\partial I_o}{\partial W_{h_1 o}} = \frac{\partial O_{h_1} W_{h_1 o}}{\partial W_{h_1 o}} = O_{h_1}. \tag{8}$$

Insert equation 4 into $\frac{\partial E^2}{\partial I_o}$:

$$\frac{\partial E^2}{\partial I_o} = \frac{\partial (Out - Exp)^2}{\partial I_o} = 2(Out - Exp)\frac{\partial Out}{\partial I_o} = 2E\frac{\partial f_o(I_o)}{\partial I_o} = 2E f_o'(I_o). \tag{9}$$

With equations 5, 6, 8 and 9, we get the update formula for $W_{h_1 o}$:

$$W_{h_1 o}(new) = W_{h_1 o}(old) - \eta 2 O_{h_1} E f_o'(I_o). \tag{10}$$

Replace the hidden neuron index "1" by $n$ ($n = 1, 2, ..., 4$):

$$W_{h_n o}(new) = W_{h_n o}(old) - \eta 2 O_{h_n} E f_o'(I_o). \tag{11}$$

Equation 11 denotes the update rule for weights between hidden neuron $n$ and the output neuron. Similarly we can derive the update rule for weights between input neurons and hidden neurons:

$$W_{i_m h_n}(new) = W_{i_m h_n}(old) - \eta 2 E f_o'(I_o) W_{h_n o} f_h'(I_{h_n}) O_{i_m}. \tag{12}$$

Equation 12 denotes the update rule for weights between input neuron $m$ and hidden neuron $n$. In NMMF, we choose linear function for $f_o(I_o)$ and *tanh* function for $f_h(I_h)$:

$$f_o(I_o) = I_o; \quad f_h(I_h) = \tanh(I_h) \tag{13}$$

and their corresponding derivatives are:

$$f_o(I_o) = 1; \quad f_h(I_h) = 1 - \tanh^2(I_h). \tag{14}$$

Insert the two derivatives in equation 14 into equations 11 and 12 respectively, with identity functions $O_{i_m} = I_{i_m}$ ($m = 1,2,...4$) used in input neurons, the update rules are as follow:

$$W_{h_n o}(new) = W_{h_n o}(old) - \eta 2 E O_{h_n} \tag{15}$$

$$W_{i_m h_n}(new) = W_{i_m h_n}(old) - \eta 2 E W_{h_n o}(1 - O_{h_n}^2) I_{i_m} \tag{16}$$

where $m=(1,2,...,4)$ and $n=(1,2,...,4)$. With the weights update rules defined by equations 15 and 16 and the training patterns provided by mechanism refining center, the neural networks in NMMF can be trained with relatively simple steps.

# 3   Experimental Results and Analysis

A suite of small size QAP benchmarks were chosen from different groups to generate training patterns with the mechanism refining center. These benchmarks were chosen because they are easy to be solved to optima in relatively short computational time. With these training patterns, the three neural networks were trained for 100000 generations. The experiments were carried on 16 large scale QAP benchmarks; 20 separate runs were carried out for each scenario. For each run, we allocate a computation time budget of 1000 seconds (for *tho150*, this limit extends to 1010 seconds). The parametric settings of the 3 memes are: *Tabu Search*: tabu length = problem size; *Simulated Annealing*: starting temperature = 30.0, temperature annealing factor $\alpha$= 0.9998, number of neighbors searched in one generation = 200; *Genetic Algorithm*: crossover rate = 0.5, mutation rate = 0.05, mutation range = 0.01; Population size = 60. The computing platform is Intel Core 2 DUO 2.66Ghz CPU with 2GB memory in Windows XP operating system. In Table 1, the experimental results are listed.

The *Problem* column refers to the benchmark name, the digits embedded in each name indicates its problem size. *Mechanism* refers to the optimized mechanism ($Num_{GA}$, $Num_{SA}$, $Num_{TS}$) generated by NMMF for each benchmark. *Optimum solution* refers to the cost value of the optimum solution. *Ave time* refers to the average CPU time cost for all 20 runs. *Max time* refers to the longest CPU time cost within all 20 runs. *Success rate* refers to the percentage of finding the optimum solution. *Best gap* refers to the percentage difference between the best solution found and the optimum. *Average gap* refers to the percentage difference between the average solution cost and the optimum. *Worst gap* refers to the percentage difference between the worst search result and the optimum in 20 runs.

**Table 1.** Experimental results on QAP benchmarks by NMMF

| Problem | Mechanism | Optimum solution | Success rate(%) | Best gap(%) | Average gap(%) | Worst gap(%) | Ave time(s) | Max time(s) |
|---------|-----------|------------------|-----------------|-------------|----------------|--------------|-------------|-------------|
| lipa80a | (0,5,101) | 253195 | 100 | 0 | 0 | 0 | 141.39 | 222.41 |
| lipa90a | (0,5,102) | 360630 | 100 | 0 | 0 | 0 | 285.71 | 587.11 |
| sko72 | (1,3,107) | 66256 | 100 | 0 | 0 | 0 | 97.19 | 201.00 |
| sko81 | (1,3,107) | 90998 | 100 | 0 | 0 | 0 | 276.61 | 978.51 |
| sko90 | (1,3,108) | 115534 | 90 | 0 | 0.0038 | 0.038 | 281.44 | 862.13 |
| sko100a | (1,3,108) | 152002 | 75 | 0 | 0.0088 | 0.058 | 309.73 | 849.69 |
| sko100b | (1,3,108) | 153890 | 100 | 0 | 0 | 0 | 276.87 | 744.86 |
| sko100c | (1,3,108) | 147862 | 95 | 0 | 0.00007 | 0.0014 | 406.94 | 858.81 |
| tai50a | (5,3,101) | 4938796 | 5 | 0 | 0.35 | 0.58 | 378.83 | 831.50 |
| tai60a | (5,3,101) | 7205962 | 0 | 0.16 | 0.33 | 0.54 | 513.96 | 949.39 |
| tai80a | (5,3,101) | 13511780 | 0 | 0.32 | 0.47 | 0.68 | 546.86 | 925.06 |
| tai100a | (5,4,100) | 21052466 | 0 | 0.26 | 0.43 | 0.68 | 644.63 | 991.33 |
| tai80b | (1,3,106) | 818415043 | 100 | 0 | 0 | 0 | 150.06 | 649.84 |
| tai100b | (1,3,101) | 1185996137 | 80 | 0 | 0.025 | 0.14 | 261.15 | 625.75 |
| tho150 | (1,3,103) | 8133398 | 5 | 0 | 0.039 | 0.069 | 893.01 | 1002.3 |
| wil100 | (2,3,101) | 273038 | 25 | 0 | 0.0036 | 0.039 | 259.99 | 761.66 |

In Table 2, we list the results of 13 instances by both NMMF and the evolutionary strategy iterative local search method (ES-ILS) [11]. The better success rate, best gap and average gap are highlighted in bold for each benchmark. Since older versions of the three optimum solutions are adopted in [11], the results on *tai50a*, *tai80a* and *tai100a* for NMMF are recalculated for comparison purpose. Table 2 shows that NMMF outperforms ES-ILS for 12 out of the 13 cases. NMMF presents better average values and higher success rates on most of the cases than ES-ILS. For example, NMMF gives success rate of 100% on *sko81*, *sko100b* while ES-ILS only gives the success rates of 52% and 50% correspondingly. NMMF manages to solve *tai50a*, *tai100a*, and *tho150* to optima within 20 runs while ES-ILS fails to solve any of the 3 instances to optima in all its trails. The 16 problems were also tested with "non-optimized" mechanisms, the results are obviously worse than the results by the optimized mechanisms generated by NMMF. This further proves that NMMF is a reliable method for solving combinatorial problems.

**Table 2.** Comparison of experimental results for NMMF and ES-ILS [11]

| Problem | Optimum Solution | Neural Meta-Memes Framework (NMMF) | | | Evolution Strategy-Iterated Local Search (ES-ILS) | | |
|---|---|---|---|---|---|---|---|
| | | Success rate(%) | Best gap(%) | Average gap(%) | Success rate(%) | Best gap(%) | Average gap(%) |
| tai50a | 4941410 | **15** | **-0.053** | **0.30** | 0 | 0.34 | 0.61 |
| tai60a | 7205962 | 0 | **0.16** | **0.33** | 0 | 0.68 | 0.82 |
| tai80a | 13540420 | 0 | **0.11** | **0.26** | 0 | 0.46 | 0.62 |
| tai100a | 21123042 | **25** | **-0.077** | **0.097** | 0 | 0.54 | 0.69 |
| sko72 | 66256 | **100** | **0** | **0** | 88 | **0** | 0.0012 |
| sko81 | 90998 | **100** | **0** | **0** | 52 | **0** | 0.0074 |
| sko90 | 115534 | **90** | **0** | **0.0038** | 40 | **0** | 0.0057 |
| sko100a | 152002 | **75** | **0** | **0.0088** | 30 | **0** | 0.012 |
| sko100b | 153890 | **100** | **0** | **0** | 50 | **0** | 0.0068 |
| sko100c | 147862 | **95** | **0** | **0.00007** | 60 | **0** | 0.0023 |
| wil100 | 273038 | **25** | **0** | **0.0036** | 10 | **0** | 0.0041 |
| tho150 | 8133398 | **5** | **0** | **0.039** | 0 | 0.041 | 0.068 |
| tai100b | 1185996137 | 80 | 0 | 0.025 | **100** | **0** | **0** |

# 4   Conclusions

NMMF is designed for solving combinatorial problems in a flexible way through the collaboration of different memes. The mechanism refining center acts as a pattern supplier for the neural networks. Through the training processes, the experience gained from solving small size problems is stored in the form of fully trained neural networks. With the neural networks NMMF is capable of generating optimized mechanisms for different combinatorial problems. The NMMF with fully trained neural networks were tested with 16 large scale QAP benchmarks. The results analysis shows the robustness and effectiveness of NMMF for combinatorial optimization.

In future, NMMF can be extended by including more memes, for example, the ant colony and particle swarming. More memes will introduce more diversity and variety, which will lead to a more robust framework for combinatorial optimization.

# References

1. Burkard, R.E., Karisch, S.E., Rendl, F.: QAPLB A quadratic assignment problem i-brary. Journal of Global Optimization 10, 391–403 (1997),
   http://www.opt.math.tu-graz.ac.at/qaplib/,
   http://qaplib.uwaterloo.ca/inst.html
2. Kennedy, J., Eberhart, R.: Particle swarm optimization. In: Proc. of the IEEE Int. Conf. on Neural Networks, Piscataway, NJ, pp. 1942–1948 (1995)
3. Koopmans, T.C., Beckmann, M.J.: Assignment problems and the location of economic activities. Econometrica 25, 53–76 (1957)
4. Laursen, P.S.: Simulated annealing for the QAP—Optimal tradeoff between simulation time and solution quality. European Journal of Operational Research 69, 238–243 (1993)
5. Lim, M.H., Yuan, Y., Omatu, S.: Efficient genetic algorithms using simple genes exchange local search policy for the quadratic assignment problem. Computational Optimization and Applications 15, 249–268 (2000)
6. Lim, M.H., Yuan, Y., Omatu, S.: Extensive testing of a hybrid genetic algorithm for quadratic assignment problem. Computational Optimization and Applications 23, 47–64 (2002)
7. Lim, M.H., Gustafson, S., Krasnogor, N., Ong, Y.S.: Editorial to the first issue. Memetic Computing 1, 1–2 (2009)
8. Meuth, R., Lim, M.H., Ong, Y.S., Wunsh, D.C.: A proposition on memes and meta-memes in computing for higher-order learning. Memetic Computing 1(2), 85–100 (2009)
9. Taillard, E.D.: Robust taboo search for the quadratic assignment problem. Parallel Computing 17, 443–455 (1991)
10. Tang, J., Lim, M.H., Ong, Y.S., Er, M.J.: Parallel memetic algorithm with selective local search for large scale quadratic assignment problems. Int'l Journal of Innovative Computing, Information and Control 2(6), 1399–1416 (2006)
11. Stützle, T.: Iterated local search for the quadratic assignment problem. European Journal of Operational Research 174(3), 1519–1539 (2006)
12. Song, L.Q., Lim, M.H., Suganthan, P.N.: Ensemble of optimization algorithms for solv-ing quadratic assignment problems. International Journal of Innovative Computing, Information and Control 6(9) (2010)
13. Vollmann, T.E., Buffa, E.S.: The facilities layout problem in perspective. Management Science 12(10), 450–468 (1966)
14. Wolpert, D.H., Macready, W.G.: No free lunch theorems for optimization. IEEE Transactions on Evolutionary Computation 1(1), 67–82 (1997)
15. Werbos, P.J.: Beyond regression: New tools for prediction and analysis in the behavioural sciences, Ph.D. Thesis, Harvard University, Cambridge, MA (1974)
16. Rumelhart, D.E., Hinton, G.E., Williams, R.J.: Learning internal representation by error propagation. In: Parallel Distributed Processing: Exploration in the Microstructure of Cognition, vol. 1, ch. 8. MIT Press, Cambridge (1986)
17. Brierley, P.: Appendix A in Some practical applications of neural networks in the electricity industry, Eng. D. Thesis, Cranfield University, UK (1998)
18. Brierley, P., Batty, B.: Data mining with neural networks - an applied example in understanding electricity consumption patterns. Knowledge Discovery and Data Mining ch. 12, 240–303 (1999)

# An Improved Evolutionary Programming with Voting and Elitist Dispersal Scheme

Sayan Maity, Kumar Gunjan, and Swagatam Das

Dept. of Electronics and Telecommunication Engg.,
Jadavpur University, Kolkata 700032, India
sayanmaity.10@gmail.com,
{mailstogunjan,swagatamdas19}@yahoo.co.in

**Abstract.** Although initially conceived for evolving finite state machines, Evolutionary Programming (EP), in its present form, is largely used as a powerful real parameter optimizer. For function optimization, EP mainly relies on its mutation operators. Over past few years several mutation operators have been proposed to improve the performance of EP on a wide variety of numerical benchmarks. However, unlike real-coded GAs, there has been no fitness-induced bias in parent selection for mutation in EP. That means the i-th population member is selected deterministically for mutation and creation of the i-th offspring in each generation. In this article we present an improved EP variant called Evolutionary Programming with Voting and Elitist Dispersal (EPVE). The scheme encompasses a voting process which not only gives importance to best solutions but also consider those solutions which are converging fast. By introducing Elitist Dispersal Scheme we maintain the elitism by keeping the potential solutions intact and other solutions are perturbed accordingly, so that those come out of the local minima. By applying these two techniques we can be able to explore those regions which have not been explored so far that may contain optima. Comparison with the recent and best-known versions of EP over 25 benchmark functions from the CEC (Congress on Evolutionary Computation) 2005 test-suite for real parameter optimization reflects the superiority of the new scheme in terms of final accuracy, speed, and robustness.

**Keywords:** Evolutionary Programming, Optimization, Tournament Selection Elitism.

## 1 Introduction

Evolutionary programming (EP) was introduced by Lawrence J. Fogel and his colleagues in the USA during the early 1960s [1], [2] in order to use simulated evolution as a learning process capable of generating artificial intelligence. EP is a stochastic optimization technique similar to the Genetic Algorithms (GAs), however unlike conventional GAs, it emphasizes on the behavioral linkage between parents and their offspring, rather than seeking to emulate specific genetic operators as observed in nature. A lot of variants of EP have been developed so far while research

B.K. Panigrahi et al. (Eds.): SEMCCO 2010, LNCS 6466, pp. 206–213, 2010.

works carried on the improvement of EP considering the mutation operator. To mutate an individual, various mutation operators such as Gaussian (CEP) [3], Cauchy (FEP) [4] and Lévy [5] are used. However each mutation operator has its advantages and disadvantages, largely performance of the EP can be improved by using different mutation operators simultaneously or by integrating several mutation operators into one algorithm or by adaptively controlled usage of mutation operators. In [6], an ensemble approach has been taken where each mutation operator has its related population and every population benefits from different mutation operators with different parameter values whenever they are effective during different phases of the search process.

Apart from experimenting with the mutation operator, a few attempts have been made to modify the survivor selection strategy by facilitating proper coordination among the candidate solutions of EP to improve its performance. Instead of following the conventional tournament selection, recently Chen *et al.* [7] incorporated three survivor selection rules in Fast EP (FEP) [4] in order to encourage both fitness diversity and solution diversity in MEP [7]. The tournament selection process is biased towards the better solution as the probability of selection of best fit member is higher and the members which belong to regions which may be global optima, and are less fit, is neglected just because enough exploitation has not been carried out there. In this paper we have proposed a *voting selection* process to overcome this shortcoming. A way to enhance the exploration and exploitation capability and to maintain a tradeoff between exploration and exploitation in EP is also proposed here. Further to reduce the chance of convergence at local optima is reduced with the help of proposed *Elitist Dispersal Scheme* (EDS) and Elitist Learning Scheme (ELS) [8].

Rest of the paper is organized in the following way. The proposed variant of EP i.e. EPVE is described in sufficient details in Section 2. Section 3 describes the experimental set-up, comparison results, and discusses their implications. Finally Section 4 concludes the paper and unfolds a few important future research issues.

## 2 Evolutionary Programming with Voting and Elitist Dispersal Scheme (EPVE)

The aspect of proposing the new EPVE variant has been discussed in the introduction section. The main incorporation of ideas over the existing variants is mainly the *voting selection* process and the implementation of *Elitist dispersal scheme* (EDS).

### 2.1 Mutation Scheme: Infection with Best Process

The mutation scheme has a significant role in the performance of Evolutionary Programming. Mutation with other member helps in information exchange among the population. So the performance can be improved if the members are mutated with self or other member in a controlled way with time. To improve exploitation some members are mutated with the best member (i.e. best in terms of absolute fitness) of the parent population at initial stage of optimization. If the number of members being mutated with best one is small, good exploration is expected and if large, good exploitation is expected. To maintain proper balance between exploration and exploitation at different stages of optimization the number of members mutated with best one is kept increasing with time. The best member for mutation is chosen randomly from the best $R_1$ members of the parent solution. So initially the exploration is emphasized and latter exploitation is emphasized as most of the members are searching around the best one. The number of members to be mutated with best solutions $R_2$ is increasing with time i.e. with the no. of generation is increasing the tendency of the particles to mutate with best solutions is increasing that reflects exploitation is occurring that decided by following function at time $t$, is evaluated by

$$R_2 = 2.0 \times ceil\left(\mu \times (t-1)^{0.85/MaxGen}\right),$$ (1)

and     $$R_1 = \mu - R_2,$$ (2)

where $MaxGen = Fe\_Max / 2 / \mu$, $Fe\_Max =$ maximum number of function evaluation allowed, $\mu$ is the population size and $ceil$ round-off the floating point number to nearest higher integer. The variation in $R_1$ and $R_2$ Vs time $t$ for 10 dimensional problem is shown in Fig. 1.

## 2.2 Offspring Adaptation

A method to exchange information among the members is adapted, which is proposed by Chen *et al.* [7]. The first set of offspring $(\vec{x}_i', \vec{\eta}_i'), \forall i \in \{1,...,\mu\}$, where components of $\vec{x}_i'$ are the decision variables and those of $\vec{\eta}_i'$ are the strategy parameters, are generated using mutation scheme as in CEP or FEP depending on the strategy. The combined offspring is adapted at position $i$ with a probability $Pc$, otherwise copy of a randomly selected parent member is adapted as second offspring at that position.

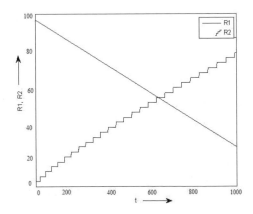

**Fig. 1.** $(R_1, R_2)$ Vs time $t$ i.e. generation for 10 Dimensional problem with $\mu=100$ and $Max\_Gen=500$

Thus, the second offspring ($\vec{x}_i'', \vec{\eta}_i''$) at position $i$ is adapted as follows: where $r$ is a random integer,

$$\vec{x}_i'' = \begin{cases} (\vec{x}_i''', \vec{\eta}_i''') & \text{if } rand(0,1) \le Pc \\ (\vec{x}_r, \vec{\eta}_r) & \text{otherwise} \end{cases}, \tag{3}$$

such that $r \in \{1, ..., \mu\}$. The combined offspring $(\vec{x}_i''', \vec{\eta}_i''')$ is generated using the offspring adaptation strategy of Differential Evolution . Now, at every position '$i$' there are three members, one parent and two offspring. Exactly one member from each position is to survive after applying selection procedure.

## 2.3 Voting Process

In EP members are selected with respect to a score gathered by competitors using tournament process. Here, a new process to score the contending members has been proposed. The process has been named as '*voting process*' for its similarity with voting process in general election. The first step is to define a union of competitors consists of parent population and offspring population produced as discussed in section 2. $\vec{C}(t) = \vec{P}(t) \cup \vec{X}'(t) \cup \vec{X}''(t)$. Here $\vec{P}(t)$ is the parent population, $\vec{X}'(t)$ and $\vec{X}''(t)$ are the two sets of offspring. Then a subset of this union $\vec{V}(t)$ is created by randomly selecting $q$ different members out of $sizeof(\vec{C}(t))$ contenders.

$$\vec{V}(t) = \left\{ vtr_i(t) \mid vtr_i \in \vec{C}(t), i = 1, ..., q \right\} \tag{4}$$

where $1 \le q < (3 \times \mu)$ is number of voters belongs to the set $\vec{C}(t)$ that has been generated by combining the parent, and two sets of offspring solutions. This set of voters remains same for a certain generation and for each and every competing member. Every voter can cast two votes at most. A voter chooses to cast a single vote for a member if the voter is inferior in terms of fitness and double votes if the member is better than their respective parents also. Inclusion of facility to cast second vote increases the probability of selection of inferior though improving member. In case of tournament selection the best fit member has got highest probability of selection and hence the selection is biased towards the best one neglecting the fact that other members which are currently inferior but converging fast can provide potential solution. In proposed voting process the probability of selection of the members which are improving is increased. Initially parent members are randomly assumed to be best or worse than their parents but, after the completion of first voting process and at the time of selection, selected members have to remember their quality of being better or worse than their respective parents.

## 2.4 Elitist Dispersal Scheme and Elitist Learning Strategy for Best Members

At the beginning of search process good exploration is observed but, after some iterations, most of the solutions starts getting attracted towards pitfalls and get stagnated and potential search operation is carried out by better members only. An attempt to eliminate such kind of stagnation, the current set of solutions is needed to be dispersed with elitism. Dispersal should be done in such a manner that the new set does not loose potential solutions of parent set (Elitism) and other solutions are repositioned to enhance further search, coming out of local traps. Because of elitism and dispersal process in repositioning the solution set, it is called Elitist Dispersal Scheme (EDS). Application of EDS is useful after some iteration when a solution starts to stagnate. For proposed EPVE; we apply EDS after every 45 iterations. In EDS top 11 percent of the current populations according to their vote's count are assumed to be potential carried in the next set of solution. Other members are dispersed to new positions in order to either come out of local trap or sample new position to restart the search. Thus next 74 percent of the members are generated using equation (5) with Cauchy distribution and mutation scale factor $rn$ which ensures bigger mutation around the worst population to jump out of the current position which may be local optima. Rest 15 percent of members are re-initiated randomly within the search space.

$$\vec{x}_i'(j) = \vec{x}_i(j) + \vec{\eta}_i(j).D_i^j(0,1).rn, \quad j=1,...,n, \ i=19,...,\mu \qquad (5)$$

where $D_i^j(0,1)$ is a sample from Cauchy distribution, $\vec{\eta}_i$ is the strategy parameter and, $rn$ is varied with iteration such that bigger perturbation is ensured throughout the iterations.

As, even the best members, might have converged to or be converging towards the local optima, to overcome from this trapping in local minima ELS is implemented. For top 11 percent there is a way implemented to jump out of the current optima if it is local. Elitist Learning Strategy (ELS) [8] randomly chooses one dimension of the member and move it around based on the current iteration/generation count 't' using Gaussian distribution.

---

**Pseudo-code:** Evolutionary Programming with **Voting** and **Elitist Dispersal Scheme**

---

Set the generation counter $t = 0$.
Initialize the strategy parameters like CEP;

Create and initialize a population of trial solutions $\vec{P}(0)$ of $\mu$ individuals;

*for* each individual $\vec{X}_i(t) \in \vec{P}(t)$ *do*

   Evaluate the fitness $f(\vec{X}_i(t))$;

*end for*
*while* stopping conditions are not true *do*
*for* each individual $\vec{X}_i(t) \in \vec{P}(t)$ *do*

   Apply mutation operator to generate first offspring ( $\vec{X}_i'(t)$ ).

   Apply offspring adaptation technique to generate other offspring ( $\vec{X}_i''(t)$ ).

Evaluate the fitness $f(\vec{X}_i^{\,\prime}(t))$, $f(\vec{X}_i^{\,\prime}(t))$;

Add $\vec{X}_i^{\,\prime}(t)$ and $\vec{X}_i^{\,\prime\prime}(t)$ to the set of offspring population $\vec{P}^{\,\prime}(t)$;

*end for*

Allot a score to each and every member of combined parent and offspring population $\vec{P}(t) \cup \vec{P}^{\,\prime}(t)$ using voting process;

Select the new population $\vec{P}(t+1)$ from the combined parent and offspring population by applying a position based selection operator [6];

*if* $t$ is divisible by 45

Implement Elitist Dispersal Scheme (EDS) to generate the new population $\vec{P}^{\,\prime}(t+1)$ from the current population $\vec{P}(t+1)$;

Obtain the new population $\vec{P}^{\,\prime\prime}(t+1)$ by implementing ELS to top 11percent of $\vec{P}^{\,\prime}(t+1)$, while carrying forward other members intact;

*end if*

Increase generation counter as $t = t+1$;

*end while*

---

## 3   Experiments and Results: Numerical Benchmarks

The EPVE algorithm is tested using a selected set of standard test functions from the special session on real-parameter optimization of the IEEE Congress on Evolutionary Computations, CEC 2005 [9]. These functions span a diverse set of problem features, including multimodality, ruggedness, noise in fitness, ill-conditioning, nonseparability, interdependence (rotation), and high-dimensionality, and are based on classical benchmark functions such as Rosenbrock's, Rastrigin's, Swefel's, Griewank's and Ackley's function. In summary, functions 1–5 are unimodal, functions 6–12 are multimodal, and functions 13–25 are hybrid composition functions, implementing a combination of several well-known benchmark functions. All the functions are tested in 10 and 30 dimensions. Here for space inadequacy we are only giving the mean of the best-of-run errors for 30 dimension problems.

### 3.1   Algorithms Compared and Parametric Set-Up

Performance of the EPVE algorithm is compared with the following EP variants: 1) Classical EP (CEP), 2) Fast EP (FEP), 3) EP with Adaptive Lévy Mutation (ALEP), 4) Modified EP (MEP), 5) Adaptive FEP (AFEP) 6) EP based on Reinforcement Learning (RLEP). For the contestant algorithms, we employ the best-suited parametric set-up, chosen with guidelines from their respective literatures and also through a series of hand-tuning experiments.

### 3.2   Results on Benchmark Functions

Twenty-five independent runs of each algorithm on each problem are taken. Each run is continued up to 1,00,000 Function Evaluations (FEs) for 10-D problems and

**Table 1.** Average Error of the best-of-run solutions for 25 independent runs tested on benchmark functions $f_1 - f_{25}$, each in $n = 30$ dimensions. Each run of each algorithm was continued up to $10^5$ FEs.

| Function / Algorithms | $f_1$ | $f_2$ | $f_3$ | $f_4$ | $f_5$ |
|---|---|---|---|---|---|
| EPVE | **6.0000e-08** | 2.2904e+02 | **1.4688e+05** | **1.9373e+02** | **4.5580e+02** |
| CEP | 5.3726e-04 | 2.4112e+03 | 2.6176e+07 | 5.3721e+04 | 9.8362e+03 |
| FEP | 3.8298e-04 | 7.2315e+02 | 1.4182e+06 | 3.8867e+04 | 9.7451e+03 |
| ALEP | 2.9182e-04 | 1.8921e+01 | 3.7287e+06 | 3.1132e+03 | 9.6512e+03 |
| MEP | 3.5840e-07 | 6.8363e+02 | 3.6010e+06 | 1.2010e+04 | 9.5934e+03 |
| AFEP | 2.8273e-05 | **1.6721e+00** | 8.0828e+05 | 2.0372e+02 | 8.6624e+02 |
| RLEP | 2.8372e-05 | 2.7872e+00 | 2.7187e+06 | 7.7121e+03 | 9.6013e+03 |

| Function / Algorithms | $f_6$ | $f_7$ | $f_8$ | $f_9$ | $f_{10}$ |
|---|---|---|---|---|---|
| EPVE | **3.4930e+02** | **4.7500e-03** | **2.0431e+01** | 3.0820e+01 | **7.0880e+01** |
| CEP | 8.5465e+02 | 2.8984e-01 | 2.1003e+01 | 3.2173e+00 | 5.7873e+02 |
| FEP | 5.8937e+02 | 9.5340e-01 | 2.0674e+01 | 5.9021e-01 | 3.1721e+02 |
| ALEP | 6.5637e+02 | 2.8804e-02 | 2.0672e+01 | 3.2718e+00 | 2.7712e+02 |
| MEP | 4.3450e+02 | 4.6963e+03 | 2.0481e+01 | **3.426e-05** | 2.6315e+02 |
| AFEP | 3.5200e+02 | 2.8892e-01 | 2.0581e+01 | 6.2712e+00 | 7.8213e+01 |
| RLEP | 4.7302e+02 | 2.9437e-01 | 2.0663e+01 | 1.0115e+01 | 1.0251e+02 |

| Function / Algorithms | $f_{11}$ | $f_{12}$ | $f_{13}$ | $f_{14}$ | $f_{15}$ |
|---|---|---|---|---|---|
| EPVE | **1.0198e+01** | 1.0792e+05 | 3.1920e+00 | **1.2279e+01** | **2.5544e+02** |
| CEP | 4.7372e+01 | 1.2461e+04 | 1.6729e+00 | 1.2315e+01 | 4.1529e+02 |
| FEP | 3.4501e+01 | 6.3678e+03 | 1.7294e+00 | 1.3631e+01 | 3.1872e+02 |
| ALEP | 3.2526e+01 | 1.9825e+04 | 1.6973e+00 | 1.3747e+01 | 2.8784e+02 |
| MEP | 3.0473e+01 | **1.0780e+04** | **1.0080e+00** | 1.3556e+01 | 3.0089e+02 |
| AFEP | 1.0245e+01 | 5.6728e+04 | 1.7133e+00 | 1.2662e+01 | 4.02215e+02 |
| RLEP | 1.5321e+01 | 1.9342e+04 | 1.7282e+00 | 1.2889e+01 | 3.3722e+02 |

| Function / Algorithms | $f_{16}$ | $f_{17}$ | $f_{18}$ | $f_{19}$ | $f_{20}$ |
|---|---|---|---|---|---|
| EPVE | **9.3063e+01** | **1.0637e+02** | **3.0000e+02** | 8.0000e+02 | 8.0032e+02 |
| CEP | 4.7361e+02 | 4.5628e+02 | 8.0937e+02 | 9.2836e+02 | 1.0352e+03 |
| FEP | 4.4035e+02 | 4.4763e+02 | 9.7284e+02 | 9.7952e+02 | 9.8241e+02 |
| ALEP | 2.1463e+02 | 4.0723e+02 | 9.0352e+02 | 9.8723e+02 | 7.5341e+02 |
| MEP | 3.3753e+02 | 2.8188e+02 | 9.6993e+02 | 9.3589e+02 | 9.4135e+02 |
| AFEP | 1.3722e+02 | 1.2468e+02 | 3.2613e+02 | **3.0000e+02** | **3.0729e+02** |
| RLEP | 1.1354e+02 | 3.4409e+02 | 3.1074e+02 | 7.5462e+02 | 6.4532e+02 |

| Function / Algorithms | $f_{21}$ | $f_{22}$ | $f_{23}$ | $f_{24}$ | $f_{25}$ |
|---|---|---|---|---|---|
| EPVE | **5.0000e+02** | 9.2551e+02 | **5.3976e+02** | **2.0000e+02** | **1.1664e+02** |
| CEP | 8.9238e+02 | 8.4819e+02 | 7.4672e+02 | 1.0536e+03 | 4.7287e+02 |
| FEP | 5.9728e+02 | 8.2314e+02 | 5.9281e+02 | 8.5654e+02 | 3.6762e+02 |
| ALEP | 6.0609e+02 | 8.0155e+02 | 5.6663e+02 | 8.3512e+02 | 3.2831e+02 |
| MEP | 7.5579e+02 | 1.1645e+03 | 8.9416e+02 | 2.7367e+02 | 3.4307e+02 |
| AFEP | 5.2361e+02 | 7.8468e+02 | 5.9283e+02 | 3.6733e+02 | 2.8987e+02 |
| RLEP | 7.0333e+02 | **7.5463e+02** | 5.7982e+02 | 3.0827e+02 | 3.9787e+02 |

3,00,000 FEs for 30-D problems. Here for space inadequacy we are only giving the mean of the best-of-run errors for 30 dimension problems. The mean of the best-of-run errors for 30D problems are reported in Table 1. Note that the best-of-the-run error corresponds to absolute difference between the best-of-the-run value $f(\vec{x}_{best})$ and the actual optimum $f^*$ of a particular objective function i.e. $\left| f(\vec{x}_{best}) - f^* \right|$. Best entries have been marked in bold in Table. A close observation of Tables 1 reveals that on the 30-dimensional problems, *EPVE* alone achieves best final accuracy in 18 out of 25 test cases.

## 4 Conclusion

In this article we propose a new selection process known as voting process which gives an emphasis to the quick converging solutions keeping the best solutions intact. The proposed elitist dispersal scheme is used to perturbed the solution fruitfully those are trapped in the local minima. We demonstrated how the *Evolutionary Programming with Voting and Elitist Dispersal Scheme*, explored the unexplored search space which may contain the optima. The proposed schemes are very simple to implement, adds no extra control parameters, and does not impose any serious computational burden in terms FEs on the main EP algorithm. We compare EPVE with the six state-of-the-art EP-variants over 25 numerical benchmarks of 30 dimensions to prove its superiority among the other EP variants.

## References

1. Fogel, L.J.: Autonomous automata. Industrial Research 4, 14–19 (1962)
2. Fogel, L.J.: On the Organization of Intellect, Ph. D. thesis. University of California, Los Angeles (1964)
3. Fogel, L.J., Owens, A.J., Walsh, M.J.: Artificial Intelligence through Simulated Evolution. John Wiley, New York (1966)
4. Yao, X., Liu, Y., Liu, G.: Evolutionary programming made faster. IEEE Transactions on Evolutionary Computation 3(2), 82–102 (1999)
5. Lee, C.Y., Yao, X.: Evolutionary programming using mutations based on the Lévy probability distribution. IEEE Transactions on Evolutionary Computation 8(1), 1–13 (2004)
6. Mallipeddi, R., Mallipeddi, S., Suganthan, P.N.: Ensemble strategies with adaptive evolutionary programming. Information Sciences 180(9), 1571–1581
7. Chen, G., Low, C.P., Yang, Z.: Preserving and Exploiting Genetic Diversity in Evolutionary Programming Algorithms. IEEE Transactions on Evolutionary Computation 13(3), 661–673 (2009)
8. Zhan, Z.-H., Zhang, J., Li, Y., Chung, H.S.-H.: Adaptive Particle Swarm Optimization, Systems, Man, and Cybernetics. IEEE Transactions on Part B: Cybernetics 39(6), 1362–1381 (2009)
9. Suganthan, P.N., Hansen, N., Liang, J.J., Deb, K., Chen, Y.-P., Auger, A., Tiwari, S.: Problem definitions and evaluation criteria for the CEC 2005 special session on real-parameter optimization, Technical Report, Nanyang Technological University, Singapore, KanGAL Report #2005005, IIT Kanpur, India (May 2005)

# Heuristic Algorithms for the $L(2,1)$-Labeling Problem

B.S. Panda[*] and Preeti Goel[**]

Computer Science and Application Group,
Department of Mathematics,
Indian Institute of Technology Delhi,
Hauz Khas, New Delhi 110 016, India
bspanda@maths.iitd.ac.in, preeti039@gmail.com

**Abstract.** An $L(2,1)$-labeling of a graph $G$ is an assignment $f$ from the vertex set $V(G)$ to the set of nonnegative integers such that $|f(x) - f(y)| \geq 2$ if $x$ and $y$ are adjacent and $|f(x) - f(y)| \geq 1$ if $x$ and $y$ are at distance two for all $x$ and $y$ in $V(G)$. The span of an $L(2,1)$-labeling $f$ is the maximum value of $f(x)$ over all vertices $x$ of $G$. The $L(2,1)$-labeling number of a graph $G$, denoted as $\lambda(G)$, is the least integer $k$ such that $G$ has an $L(2,1)$-labeling with span $k$.

Since the decision version of the $L(2,1)$-labeling problem is NP-complete, it is important to investigate heuristic approaches. In this paper, we first implement some heuristic algorithms and then perform an analysis of the obtained results.

## 1 Introduction

The well-known Frequency Assignment Problem (introduced by Hale [8]) deals with the task of assigning frequencies to radio transmitters located at different locations such that interference is avoided or minimized. It can be modeled as graph coloring problem where the vertices represent the transmitters and two vertices are adjacent if there is possible interference between the corresponding two transmitters.

$L(2,1)$-labeling problem was introduced by Griggs and Yeh [7], initially proposed by Roberts, as a variation of the frequency assignment problem. An $L(2,1)$-labeling of a graph $G$ is an assignment of nonnegative integer $f(x)$ to each vertex $x$ of $G$ such that $|f(x) - f(y)| \geq 2$ if the $x$ and $y$ are adjacent and $|f(x) - f(y)| \geq 1$ if the distance between $x$ and $y$ is 2. The span of this labeling, denoted by $SP_2(f, G)$, is the maximum value of $f(x)$ over all vertices $x$ of $G$. The $L(2,1)$-labeling number $\lambda(G)$ of a graph $G$ is the minimum value of $SP_2(f, G)$ over all $L(2,1)$-labeling $f$ of $G$.

Due to its practical importance, the $L(2,1)$-labeling problem has been widely studied [4,7,12]. On the other hand, this problem is also attractive from the

---

[*] Corresponding author.
[**] This author was supported by Council of Scientific & Industrial Research, India.

B.K. Panigrahi et al. (Eds.): SEMCCO 2010, LNCS 6466, pp. 214–221, 2010.

graph theoretical point of view since it is a kind of vertex coloring problem. The decision version of the vertex coloring problem is NP-complete in general [5], and it remains so for most of its variations and generalizations.

The $L(2,1)$-labeling problem is a well-known NP-complete problem that has been studied extensively in recent years. So it is unlikely that a polynomial time optimal $L(2,1)$-labeling algorithm exists for general graphs. However efficient $L(2,1)$-labeling algorithms have been developed by various researchers for many special graph classes by exploiting the special properties exhibited by these graph classes. For a survey of recent results we refer the interested reader to [15,3]. This motivated us to look for heuristic algorithms for $L(2,1)$-labeling of general graphs. In this paper we propose some heuristic algorithms to tackle with $L(2,1)$-labeling of an arbitrary graph.

## 2    Greedy Based Heuristics

The Greedy $L(2,1)$-labeling algorithm described in Fig. 1 always produces an $L(2,1)$-labeling of a graph $G$. This algorithm has been used extensively by researchers to obtain upper bound for $\lambda(G)$ of a graph $G$ by producing an $L(2,1)$-labeling of $G$. The algorithm takes an ordering $\alpha = v_1, v_2, \ldots, v_n$ of $V(G)$ and assigns labels to vertices in this order. Algorithm 1 can be implemented as follows. Each vertex maintains the labels that have been assigned to its neighbors. When a vertex is labeled with a label, this label is added to label list of each of its neighbors. To select the least integer satisfying the condition given in Line 3 of the Algorithm 1 for a vertex $v_i$, one has to examine the label list maintained by $v_i$ and the label lists maintained by each neighbor of $v_i$. This takes $O(d_i + \sum_{x \in N(v_i)} d(x))$ time which is at most $O(d_i \Delta)$, where $d_i = d(v_i)$. Thus we have the following theorem.

---

**Algorithm 1.** Greedy-$L(2,1)$-labeling$(\alpha)$

1  $S = \emptyset$;
2  **foreach** $i = 1$ **to**  $n$ **do**
3      Let $j$ be the smallest non-negative integer such that
        $j \notin \{f(v), f(v) - 1, f(v) + 1 | v \in N_G(v_i) \cap S\} \bigcup \{f(w) | w \in S \text{ and } d(v_i, w) = 2\}$;
4      $f(v_i) := j$;
5      $S := S \cup \{v_i\}$
6  **end**

---

**Fig. 1.** A greedy algorithm for $L(2,1)$-labeling

**Theorem 1.** *Algorithm 1 can be implemented in $O(\Delta(n + m))$ time.*

An ordering $\alpha$ of vertices of $V(G)$ of a graph $G$ can be obtained as follows. Randomly select a vertex which has not been selected so far and assign it to

$v_1$. Select another vertex which has not been selected so far and assign it to $v_2$. Continue this process till $v_n$ has been assigned. Such a vertex ordering is called **Random Order**.

The Greedy-$L(2,1)$-labeling$(\alpha)$ algorithm has the potential to produce an optimal $L(2,1)$-labeling of $G$ if $\alpha$ is an appropriate vertex ordering. For example, let $k = \lambda(G)$ and let $f$ be an optimal $L(2,1)$-labeling of $G$. Let $V_i = \{x \in V(G)|f(x) = i\}, 0 \leq i \leq k$. Let $\alpha_i$ be any ordering of $V_i$, $0 \leq i \leq k$. Consider the ordering $\alpha = \alpha_0, \alpha_1, \ldots, \alpha_k$, i.e., $\alpha$ is obtained by concatenating $\alpha_0, \alpha_1, \ldots, \alpha_k$ in this order. It is easy to see that Greedy-$L(2,1)$-labeling$(\alpha)$ will produce $f$. Hence Greedy-$L(2,1)$-labeling$(\alpha)$ can produce optimal $L(2,1)$-labeling if suitable $\alpha$ is given as input. In this section we propose two heuristics to generate a vertex ordering $\alpha$ of $V(G)$ of an arbitrary graph $G = (V, E)$ so as to minimize the span of the $L(2,1)$-labeling $f$, where $f =$ Greedy-$L(2,1)$-labeling$(\alpha)$.

Our heuristics are based on the analysis of the span of $f$ where $f$ is Greedy-$L(2,1)$-labeling$(\alpha)$ for an arbitrary vertex ordering $\alpha$. Let $\alpha = v_1, v_2, \ldots, v_n$. Consider the vertex $v_i$. The number of labels forbidden for $v_i$ in Greedy-$L(2,1)$-labeling$(\alpha)$ is at most $3d_{G_i}(v_i) + |N_2(v_i) \cap V_i|$, where $V_i = \{v_1, v_2, \ldots, v_i\}, G_i = G[V_i], N_2(v_i) = \{x|d_G(x, v_i) = 2\}$. So to minimize the number of forbidden labels for $v_i$, we need to minimize the sum of the two terms as seen above. However, minimizing these two terms simultaneously is difficult. So we focus on the first term. The first term is the degree of $v_i$ in $G_i$. So $v_n$ is chosen to be the vertex having the lowest degree. After deleting the vertex $v_n$ from the graph $G$, $v_{n-1}$ is selected to be the vertex having the smallest degree in $G - v_n$. This process is continued to get an ordering. The vertex ordering so generated is called **"Smallest-Last" order**. The details of the ordering is given below.

*Smallest-last order:* In this heuristic, vertices are ordered so that the degree of $v_j$ in the graph induced by the set $\{v_1, v_2 \ldots v_j\}$ is (one of) the smallest. Mainly, smallest-last order assigns the vertex of smallest degree in $V$ to be $v_n$. This vertex is then deleted from the graph and next smallest degree vertex is found, and is assigned to $v_{n-1}$ and then it is deleted. The algorithm proceeds until all vertices have been deleted from $G$. The vertex ordering $\sigma_1 : v_1, v_2, \ldots, v_n$ thus obtained is such that $d(v_i)$ is minimum in the induced graph $G_i[\{v_1, v_2, \ldots, v_i\}]$. Such a vertex ordering can be computed in linear time, i.e., in $O(n + m)$ time as shown by Matula et al. [11].

This heuristic will label trees with at most $\Delta + 2$ labels. However, for general graph a vertex $v_i$ can have at most $\Delta$ neighbors, each of which further can have $\Delta - 1$ neighbors at most, whose label cannot be assigned to $v_i$. Therefore at most $3\Delta + \Delta(\Delta - 1) = \Delta^2 + 2\Delta$ labels will be avoided for $v_i$. Hence $\Delta^2 + 2\Delta$ labels will be sufficient by the Greedy-$L(2,1)$-labeling$(\alpha)$ if $\alpha$ is a smallest-last order.

*Largest-first order:* In the smallest-last order, we try to minimize $d_{G_i}(v_i)$ so that the total number of labels are minimized. Another way to achieve this is to choose an ordering $\alpha = v_1, v_2, \ldots, v_n$ such that $|N_G(v_i) \cap \{v_{i+1}, v_{i+2}, \ldots, v_n\}|$ is maximum so that the number of labeled neighbors of $v_i$ is minimum. Largest-first order can be obtained by simply sorting the vertices of a graph in non-increasing order of their degrees. Using bucket sort, such an ordering can be computed in $O(n + m)$ time.

## 2.1  Experimental Results

We have analyzed random order, smallest-last order and largest-first order on random graphs. Both smallest-last order and largest-first order are better heuristics than random order. There are many random graphs for which largest-first gives better results than smallest-last. We compare one heuristic over another in a fixed number of cases and count the number of cases the first heuristic is better than the second one and compute the percentage. This percentage is called the efficiency of one heuristic over the other.

The efficiency comparison of both the order on tress and chordal graphs is given in Fig. 2. The efficiency comparison of both order on random graphs with $n = 100$ for small values of $\Delta$ is shown in Fig. 3. For each $\Delta$ given in the bar graph shown in Fig. 3 and Fig. 2(b), efficiency of an ordering gives the percentage of the cases in which it performs better than the other one. For trees, largest-first gives better results than smallest-last as shown in Fig. 2(a), whereas for chordal graphs the efficiency of smallest-last order is much smaller than efficiency of largest-first order (see Fig. 2(b)). The efficiency comparison of both orderings on random graphs is shown in Fig. 3.

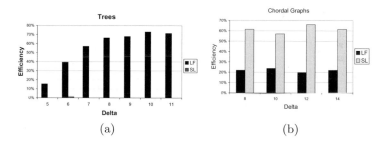

(a)                                                          (b)

**Fig. 2.** Efficiency comparison of the span generated by largest-first (LF) order and smallest-last (SL) order of (a) Trees and, (b) Random Chordal Graphs

So Greedy-$L(2,1)$-labeling$(\alpha)$ gives better result in some cases when $\alpha$ is generated using largest-first order than smallest-last order. Similarly, in some other cases Greedy-$L(2,1)$-labeling$(\alpha)$ gives better result when $\alpha$ is generated using smallest-last order than largest-first order.

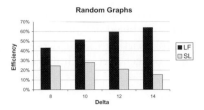

**Fig. 3.** Efficiency comparison of span generated by largest-first (LF)order and smallest-last (SL) order of Random graphs with $n = 100$

# 3    Genetic Algorithm

The *Genetic Algorithms (GA's)* are heuristic search algorithms that imitates the natural process of evolution.

They were developed by Holland [10] to study the adaptive process of natural systems and to develop artificial systems that combine the notion of survival of the fittest, random and yet structured search, and parallel evaluation of nodes in the search space. Genetic algorithms have the ability to create an initial population of feasible solutions, and then recombine them in a way to guide their search to only the most promising areas of the search space. Genetic algorithms have been successfully applied to many applications in various domains such as scheduling [1], robotics [2], machine learning [6], signal processing [14,9], combinatorial optimization [13].

## 3.1    Genetic Algorithm for $L(2, 1)$-Labeling Problem

We now define a genetic encoding of the $L(2, 1)$-labeling problem. A gene corresponds to a vertex of the graph and a chromosome corresponds to an ordering of vertices. Each individual is made up of one chromosome which is a permutation of vertices. An individual is represented by a vector $\sigma(I) = (v_1, \ldots, v_n)$ where $n$ is the number of vertices in the graph. The fitness of a chromosome $\alpha = v_1, v_2, \ldots, v_n$ is the span of the $L(2, 1)$-labeling produced by Greedy-$L(2, 1)$-labeling($\alpha$). Let $f(I)$ denote the span of Greedy-$L(2, 1)$-labeling($I$). We have used three methods to initialize the population of $k$ chromosomes. The first method generates all of the $k$ chromosomes randomly. In the second method we generate $k - 1$ chromosome randomly and add a chromosome produced by a largest-first order. In the third method we generate $k - 1$ chromosome randomly and add a chromosome produced by smallest-last order. The GA which uses the population generated by the first method is called GA(rand), the GA which uses the population generated by the second method is called GA(LF), and the GA which uses the population generated by the third method is called GA(SL).

The selection of parents for reproduction is done by *roulette wheel selection*[6]. It consists of assigning a portion of the wheel to each individual according to their performance relative to the entire population. The higher the

| **Algorithm 2.** Procedure GA-$L(2,1)$-Labeling |
|---|
| 1  Generate a population $S$ of $k$ chromosomes; |
| 2  Evaluate and assign the fitness for each individual $\alpha$ to be the span of the labeling produced by Greedy-$L(2,1)$-labeling($\alpha$); |
| 3  Store the *best-So-Far* fitness value ; |
| 4  **while** *Stopping condition not satisfied* **do** |
| 5      select two chromosomes $P_1$ and $P_2$ from $S$ using roulette wheel selector; |
| 6      Apply cycle crossover with probability 0.9 to produce offsprings $C_1$ and $C_2$ ; |
| 7      Apply mutation with probability 0.1 to $P_1$ to get $C_3$; |
| 8      Evaluate fitness of the offsprings generated ; |
| 9      Replace weaker chromosomes in $S$ if any with the offsprings to obtain $S'$ such that $|S'| = |S|$; |
| 10     Update bestSoFar; |
| 11 **end** |
| 12 Select the ordering representing the *best-So-Far* individual ; |
| 13 Assign labels to it using Greedy-$L(2,1)$-labeling Algorithm.; |

**Fig. 4.** A genetic algorithm for $L(2,1)$-labeling of graphs

performance of an individual, the higher area it gets assigned on the wheel. Therefore the probability of an individual to be picked is: $P_i(x) = \dfrac{f(x)}{\sum_{i=1}^{n} f_i}$. The higher the fitness value, the individual has a higher chance to pass its genes to the next generation.

The ***Crossover operator*** takes two chromosomes from the population and combines them to generate offspring that may be better than the parents. We use a specialized crossover operator called ***cycle crossover(CX)***. The idea of cycle crossover is to preserve relative order that elements occur. Let $P_1$ and $P_2$ be two parent chromosomes. The cycle crossover is applied on $P_1$ and $P_2$ as follows.

1. Construct an offspring $C_1$ from $(P_1, P_2)$ in the following way.
   (a) Start the cycle with the first vertex $P_1[1]$ of $P_1$.
   (b) Let $i_1$ be such that $P_2[1] = P_1[i_1]$.
   (c) Let $i_2$ be such that $P_2[i_1] = P_1[i_2]$.
   (d) Repeat steps $b$ and $c$ to get the first index $i_k$ such that $P_2[i_k] = P_1[1]$.
2. Put the vertices of the cycle in the first child $C_1$ on the positions they have in the first parent. Fill the remaining position of $C_1$ from $P_2$ in the order they appear in $P_2$.
3. Similarly $C_2$ is constructed from $(P_2, P_1)$.

*Example 1.* Consider the following two parent chromosomes, $P_1 = (v_1, v_2, v_3, v_4, v_5, v_6, v_7, v_8, v_9)$ and $P_2 = (v_4, v_1, v_2, v_8, v_7, v_6, v_9, v_3, v_5)$. Then each vertex and its position comes from one of the parents. Start by taking the first vertex from $P_1$ so that $C_1 = (v_1 \times \times \times \times \times \times \times \times)$. The next vertex must be from $P_2$ and from the same position. This gives vertex $v_4$, which is at position 4 in $P_1$ so that $C_1 = (v_1 \times \times v_4 \times \times \times \times \times)$. In $P_2$, the vertex $v_8$ has same position $v_4$ in $P_1$, so that $C_1 = (v_1 \times \times v_4 \times \times \times v_8 \times)$. We continue with $C_1 = (v_1 \times v_3, v_4 \times \times \times v_8 \times)$, $C_1 = (v_1, v_2, v_3, v_4, \times \times \times v_8 \times)$. Note that the selection of $v_2$ now forces the selection of $v_1$ and this gives a cycle. So we have, $C_1 = (v_1, v_2, v_3, v_4, v_7, v_6, v_9, v_8, v_5)$.

If we now start form $P_2$ then $C_2 = (v_4, v_1, v_2, v_8 \times \times \times v_3 \times)$ completes the first cycle. Filling in from $P_1$ we get, $C_2 = (v_4, v_1, v_2, v_8, v_5, v_6, v_7, v_3, v_9)$.

We have used the probability of crossover to be 0.9. The **mutation** chosen was to select two vertices at random from a chromosome and swap them. The **mutation probability** $(P_m)$ we have used is 0.1. The termination or convergence criterion used in our algorithm is **Maximum number of generations** that finally brings the search to a halt. The Pseudo code of our implementation is given in Fig. 4.

## 3.2   Experimental Results

We have used our all the three genetic algorithms on random graphs with 50, 80 and 100 vertices, respectively. The initial population is chosen to be (i) random, (ii) contain smallest-last order, and (iii) largest-first order. A comparison of the spans generated by our genetic algorithms with the spans generated

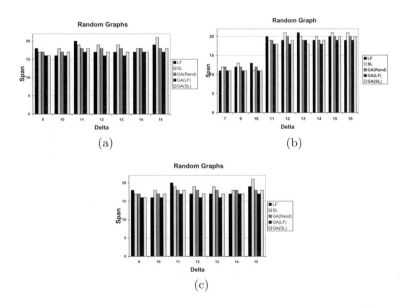

**Fig. 5.** Span produced by greedy heuristics largest-first (LF) order, smallest-last (SL) order, and span produced by GA initialized with largest-first (LF) order, smallest-last (SL) order and random order, for random graphs with (a) $n = 50$, $m = 150$, (b) $n = 80$, $m = 250$ and, (c) $n = 100$, $m = 350$, population size = 20, no. of generations = 150

by the greedy heuristics, discussed in Section 2, for random graphs is given in Fig(s). 5(a), 5(b) and 5(c). It can be seen that all the three genetic algorithms performed better than the two heuristics, largest-first order and smallest-last order. Also we observed that the GA(LF) and GA(SL) are better heuristics than the GA(Rand).

# References

1. Abraham, A., Buyya, R., Nath, B.: Nature's heuristics for scheduling jobs on computational grids. In: 8th IEEE International Conference on Advanced Computing and Communications, Cochin, India, pp. 45–52 (2000)
2. Ahuactzin, J.M., Talbi, E.-G., Bessiere, P., Mazer, E.: Using genetic algorithms for robot motion planning. In: Selected Papers from the Workshop on Geometric Reasoning for Perception and Action, London, pp. 84–93. Springer, Heidelberg (1993)
3. Calamoneri, T.: The $L(h, k)$-labelling problem: a survey and annotated bibliography. Comput. J. 49(5), 585–608 (2006)
4. Chang, G.J., Kuo, D.: The $L(2, 1)$-labeling problem on graphs. SIAM J. Discret. Math. 9(2), 309–316 (1996)
5. Garey, M.R., Johnson, D.S.: Computers and intractibility. W. H. Freeman and Co. Ltd., New York (1979)
6. Goldberg, D.E.: Genetic algorithms in search, optimization and machine learning. Addison-Wesley Longman Publishing Co., Inc., Boston (1989)
7. Griggs, J.R., Yeh, R.K.: Labelling graphs with a condition at distance 2. SIAM J. Discret. Math. 5(4), 586–595 (1992)
8. Hale, W.K.: Frequency assignment: theory and applications. Proceedings of the IEEE 68, 1497–1514 (1980)
9. Holladay, K.L., Robbins, K.A.: Evolution of signal processing algorithms using vector based genetic programming. In: 15th International Conference on Digital Signal Processing, pp. 503–506. IEEE, Los Alamitos (2007)
10. Holland, J.H.: Adaptation in natural and artificial systems. MIT Press, Cambridge (1992)
11. Matula, D.W., Beck, L.L.: Smallest-last ordering and clustering and graph coloring algorithms. J. ACM 30(3), 417–427 (1983)
12. Sakai, D.: Labeling chordal graphs: distance two condition. SIAM J. Discret. Math. 7(1), 133–140 (1994)
13. Sakuma, J., Kobayashi, S.: A genetic algorithm for privacy preserving combinatorial optimization. In: GECCO 2007: Proceedings of the 9th annual conference on Genetic and evolutionary computation, pp. 1372–1379. ACM, New York (2007)
14. White, M.S., Flockton, S.J.: Genetic algorithms for digital signal processing. In: Fogarty, T.C. (ed.) AISB-WS 1994. LNCS, vol. 865, pp. 291–303. Springer, Heidelberg (1994)
15. Yeh, R.K.: A survey on labeling graphs with a condition at distance two. Discrete Math 306(12), 1217–1231 (2006)

# Runtime Analysis of Evolutionary Programming Based on Cauchy Mutation

Han Huang[1,2,3], Zhifeng Hao[4], Zhaoquan Cai[5], and Yifan Zhu[1]

[1] School of Software Engineering, South China University of Technology,
Guangzhou, P.R. China, 510006
[2] State Key Lab. for Novel Software Technology, Nanjing University, P.R. China
[3] Dept of Management Sciences, College of Business,
City University of Hong Kong, Hong Kong
hhan@scut.edu.cn, bssthh@163.com
[4] The Faculty of computer, Guangdong University of Technology, Guangzhou, P.R. China
[5] Education Technology Center, Huizhou University, Huizhou, P.R. China

**Abstract.** This paper puts forward a brief runtime analysis of an evolutionary programming (EP) which is one of the most important continuous optimization evolutionary algorithms. A theoretical framework of runtime analysis is proposed by modeling EP as an absorbing Markov process. The framework is used to study the runtime of a classical EP algorithm named as EP with Cauchy mutation (FEP). It is proved that the runtime of FEP can be less than a polynomial of n if the Lebesgue measure of optimal solution set is more than an exponential form of 2. Moreover, the runtime analysis result can be used to explain the performance of EP based on Cauchy mutation.

## 1 Introduction

EP was first proposed as a finite state machine technique [1], and then widespread in continuous optimization and combinatorial optimization problems [2]. Later, the study of EP mainly focused on the influence of its parameters and the design of adaptive strategy. There have been several EP versions with different probability-distribution-based mutations.

The first successful EP algorithm is EP with Gauss mutation (CEP). Fogel [1], Bäck [3] and Schwefel [4] did a lot of work on CEP, and proposed an adaptive EP with Gauss-distribution mutation to improve the function of non-adaptive CEP. Yao [5] pointed out that CEP is only good at solving unimodal function and close-peak function optimization problems. Hence, Yao introduced Cauchy distribution to the mutation and proposed a fast EP algorithm (FEP) [5]. FEP improved the performance of CEP in solving multimodal function and dispersed peak function problems.

Theoretical foundation of EP has been studied as an open research topic since it was proposed [3-4]. The informed work mainly focused on convergence of EP algorithm. Bäck [3] and Schwefel [4] proposed this topic in their survey of evolutionary algorithms. Fogel [2] first presented the convergence of EP and proved EP can converge to the optimal solution by making the solution space discrete. Rudolph [7-9] put forward the proof of the convergence of CEP [4] and FEP [5] of arbitrary initial

B.K. Panigrahi et al. (Eds.): SEMCCO 2010, LNCS 6466, pp. 222–229, 2010.

population. Rudolph's [9] work mainly directed towards the continuous solution space, so the result is more general than Fogel's.

The study of convergence only tell us whether an EP algorithm can find the optimal solution with infinite iteration time, but it cannot reveal how fast the EP algorithm can converge. There are few results about computational time complexity of EP such as the runtime analysis results of EA [10-11] and ACO [12]. Therefore, this paper presents an EP runtime analysis framework and the case studies of FEP [5].

## 2   Evolutionary Programming Based on Cauchy Mutation

This section introduces two considered EP algorithms FEP [5]. A definition of minimum optimization continuous problem is given first.

**Definition 1.** A minimization problem is defined as $(\mathbf{S}, f)$. $\mathbf{S} \subseteq \mathbf{R}^n$ is a finite subspace of $n$-dimension real domain $\mathbf{R}^n$. $f : \mathbf{S} \to \mathbf{R}$ is a $n$-dimension real function, called objective function. The problem is to find a n-dimension vector $x_{\min} \in \mathbf{S}$ such that $\forall x \in \mathbf{S}: f(x_{\min}) \le f(x)$. Without loss of generality, it can be supposed that $\exists b_i > 0$ $\mathbf{S} = \prod_{i=1}^{n} [-b_i, b_i]$.

According to the idea of Ref. [5], $f$ is not required to be continuous but necessary to be bounded. We only consider the unconstrained continuous minimization as the theoretical object.

Based on the definition, EP based on Cauchy mutation can be described as follow.

1) Arbitrarily generate $m_p$ individuals which is signed as a couple of real vectors $(x_i, \sigma_i)$, where $x_i$ is the optimized variable, $\sigma_i$ is the variation variable and $i = 1, ..., m_p$. Iteration time $t = 0$ and the initial $\sigma_i \le 2$ referred to Ref. [5].

2) Calculate the fitness of each individual $(x_i, \sigma_i)$ according to the objective function for $i = 1, ..., m_p$.

3) For each $(x_i, \sigma_i)$ and $i = 1, ..., m_p$, run the following formulas to generate the offspring $(x'_i, \sigma'_i)$ of $(x_i, \sigma_i)$.

**FEP**: create the offspring as follows for $j = 1, ..., n$

$$\sigma'_i(j) = \sigma_i(j) \cdot \exp\{\tau' N(0,1) + \tau N_j(0,1)\} \qquad (1)$$

$$x'_i(j) = x_i(j) + \sigma'_i(j)\delta_j \qquad (2)$$

where $\delta(j)$ is a random number generated anew for each $j$ from Cauchy distribution, of which the density function is

$$k_{\phi=1}(y) = \pi^{-1} \cdot (1 + y^2)^{-1} \qquad -\infty < y < \infty \qquad (3)$$

Moreover, $N(0,1)$ is a standard Gaussian random variable for the given $i$ and $N_j(0,1)$ is a newly generated Gaussian random variable for each $j$. The parameters $\tau$ and $\tau'$ are defined as

$$\tau = 1/\sqrt{2\sqrt{m_p}} \quad \text{and} \quad \tau' = 1/\sqrt{2m_p} \qquad (4)$$

4) Evaluate the fitness of the offspring $(x'_i, \sigma'_i)$ for $i = 1, ..., m_p$.

5) For i-th individual $\chi_i$ from the parents and offspring, select $q$ different individuals for comparison. If the fitness of $\chi_i$ is less than the selected one, $\chi_i$ obtain a "win".

6) Select $m_p$ individuals who have the most time of "win" as the parents in the next iteration. Select individuals of least function value if the number of individuals with 100% wins is greater than m_p.

7) If the terminal condition is satisfied, output the best-s0-far solution and exit, otherwise, $t = t + 1$ and go back to 3-rd step.

## 3   Theoretical Framework of Evolutionary Programming

A Markov process model of EP is built in this section since EP algorithm is used to tackle continuous optimization problems. According to Def.1, we can suppose that $f$ satisfies the following properties for the theoretical study. 1) $f$ is a bounded function defined on $S$. 2) The subspace of the optimal solutions of $S$ is no empty. 3) For $\forall \varepsilon > 0$, $M_\varepsilon = \{x \in S \mid f(x) > f^* - \varepsilon\}$ where $f^* = \min\{f(x) \mid x \in S\}$. The Lebesgue measure of $M_\varepsilon$ is larger than zero, signed as $m(M_\varepsilon) > 0$. The first supposed condition is dependent on considered problems. The second one is necessary for every optimization problems. Moreover, the problem cannot be solved by any methods if the last hypothetical point.

**Definition 2.** The stochastic process is defined as $\{\xi_t^{EP}\}_{t=0}^{+\infty}$. $\xi_t^{EP} = \bigcup_{i=1}^{m_p} \{(x_{i,t}, \sigma_{i,t})\}$ where $x_{i,t}$ the individual of t-th iteration and $\sigma_{i,t}$ is the variation variable of t-th iteration.

**Definition 3.** The states space of EP is $Y_{EP}$, $\xi_t^{EP} \in Y_{EP}$ for $t = 0, 1, 2, ...$.

**Definition 4.** The optimal state space of EP is $Y_{EP}^* \subseteq Y_{EP}$. $\forall \xi_{EP}^* \in Y_{EP}^*$ such that for

$\forall \varepsilon > 0 \ \exists (x_i^*, \sigma_i) \in \xi_{EP}^*$ and $x_i^* \in M_\varepsilon$ where $M_\varepsilon = \{x \in \mathbf{S} \mid f(x) > f^* - \varepsilon\}$.

**Lemma 1.** The stochastic process $\{\xi_t^{EP}\}_{t=0}^{+\infty}$ of EP is a Markov process of discrete time $t$.

**Proof.** $\xi_t^{EP} = \bigcup_{i=1}^{m_p} \{(x_{i,t}, \sigma_{i,t})\}$ is a real vector  because of Def. 1, the optimal space $Y_{EP}$ of EP is continuous. Furthermore, $\xi_t^{EP}$ is only dependent on $\xi_{t-1}^{EP}$ for $t = 1, 2, \dots$ no matter what the initial $\xi_0^{EP}$ according to Eqs.(1)-(4) and the $5^{\text{th}}$-$6^{\text{th}}$ steps. Hence, $\{\xi_t^{EP}\}_{t=0}^{+\infty}$ is a Markov process of discrete $t$, which is called Markov process for short in this paper.

**Lemma 2.** The stochastic process $\{\xi_t^{EP}\}_{t=0}^{+\infty}$ of EP is an absorbing Markov process.

**Proof.** $\xi_t^{EP} = \bigcup_{i=1}^{m_p} \{(x_{i,t}, \sigma_{i,t})\}$ is a Markov process according to Lemma 1. $\xi_t^{EP} \in Y_{EP}^*$ when $\exists (x_{i,t}^*, \sigma_{i,t})$ and $x_{i,t}^*$ is the optimal solution. Considering the $5^{\text{th}}$ - $6^{\text{th}}$ steps of EP, $x_{i,t}^*$ obtain the most times of "win", so $x_{i,t}^*$ can be selected as the individual of the next iteration by probability one for $t = 1, 2, \dots$ . Therefore, $P\{\xi_{t+1}^{EP} \notin Y_{EP}^* \mid \xi_t^{EP} \in Y_{EP}^*\} = 0$. $\{\xi_t^{EP}\}_{t=0}^{+\infty}$ is an absorbing Markov process.

The convergence time is used as a measurement to analyze the runtime of EP algorithms in this paper. First, some definitions of convergence time are introduced.

**Definition 5.** $\lambda_t^{EP} = P\{\xi_t^{EP} \in Y_{EP}^*\}$ is the probability that EP attains the optimal state space at t-th iteration.

**Definition 6.** $\mu_{EP}$ is the first hitting time and $E\mu_{EP}$ is the expected first hitting time, such that $\xi_t^{EP} \in Y_{EP}^*$ if and $\xi_t^{EP} \notin Y_{EP}^*$ if $0 \le t < \mu_{EP}$.

The expected first hitting time $E\mu_{EP}$ is used to study the computational complexity of evolutionary algorithm [10-11]. According to the definitions, we can draw a conclusion as theorem 1.

**Theorem 1.** $E\mu_{EP} = \sum_{i=0}^{+\infty} (1 - \lambda_i^{EP})$ is held, if $\lim_{t \to +\infty} \lambda_t^{EP} = 1$ , $\{\xi_t^{EP}\}_{t=0}^{+\infty}$ and $\lambda_t^{EP} = P\{\xi_t^{EP} \in Y_{EP}^*\}$  is the stochastic process of EP.

**Proof.** According to Lemma 2, $\{\xi_t^{EP}\}_{t=0}^{+\infty}$ is an absorbing Markov process. $P\{\mu_{EP} = t\} = \lambda_t^{EP} - \lambda_{t-1}^{EP}$ is held, since $\lambda_t^{EP} = P\{\xi_t^{EP} \in Y_{EP}^*\} = P\{\mu_{EP} \leq t\}$ is true. It follows that $\lambda_t^{EP} - \lambda_{t-1}^{EP} = P\{\mu_{EP} \leq t\} - P\{\mu_{EP} \leq t-1\} = P\{\mu_{EP} = t\}$. Therefore, we have $E\mu_{EP} = \sum_{t=1}^{+\infty} t \cdot (\lambda_t^{EP} - \lambda_{t-1}^{EP}) = \sum_{t=0}^{+\infty} [\lim_{N \to +\infty} \lambda_N^{EP} - \lambda_t^{EP}] = \sum_{i=0}^{+\infty} (1 - \lambda_i^{EP})$.

Theorem 2 makes an improvement of theorem 1.

**Theorem 2.** If the stochastic process of EP is $\{\xi_t^{EP}\}_{t=0}^{+\infty}$ and $p_t = P\{\xi_t^{EP} \in Y^* \mid \xi_{t-1}^{EP} \notin Y^*\}$ for $t = 1, 2, \ldots$, $E\mu_{EP} = \sum_{i=0}^{+\infty} [(1 - \lambda_0^{EP}) \prod_{i=1}^{t} (1 - p_i)]$.

**Proof.** According to Lemma 2, $\{\xi_t^{EP}\}_{t=0}^{+\infty}$ is an absorbing Markov process. $\lambda_t^{EP} = P\{\xi_t^{EP} \in Y_{EP}^*\} = P\{\mu_{EP} \leq t\}$, so

$$\lambda_t^{EP} = (1 - \lambda_{t-1}^{EP})P\{\xi_t^{EP} \in Y_{EP}^* \mid \xi_{t-1}^{EP} \notin Y_{EP}^*\} + \lambda_{t-1}^{EP}P\{\xi_t^{EP} \in Y_{EP}^* \mid \xi_{t-1}^{EP} \in Y_{EP}^*\} \quad (5)$$

Thus, $\lambda_t^{EP} = (1 - \lambda_{t-1}^{EP})P_t + \lambda_{t-1}^{EP}$, so

$$1 - \lambda_t^{EP} = (1 - \lambda_0^{EP}) \prod_{i=1}^{t} (1 - p_i) \quad (6)$$

Following the results of theorem 1,

$$E\mu_{EP} = \sum_{i=0}^{+\infty} [(1 - \lambda_0^{EP}) \prod_{i=1}^{t} (1 - p_i)] \quad (7)$$

The following section will make use of the theorems to analyze the runtime of FEP.

## 4 Running Time Analysis of EP Based on Cauchy Mutation

FEP is an EP with Cauchy distribution mutation, proposed by Yao [10], to improve the performance of CEP [1] in solving multimodal function problems. The process of FEP is given in Section 2, and the main contribution is using the Eqs. (1)-(3).

**Theorem 3.** Given the stochastic process $\{\xi_t^{FEP}\}_{t=0}^{+\infty}$ of FEP, we have $P\{\xi_t^{FEP} \notin Y_{FEP}^* \mid \xi_{t-1}^{FEP} \in Y_{FEP}^*\} \geq 1 - (1 - \frac{m(M_\varepsilon)}{(\pi + \pi b_{max}^2)^n})^{m_p}$ where $m(M_\varepsilon)$ is the Lebesgue measure of $M_\varepsilon$ (Def.4), $m_p$ is the population size and $b_{max} = \max_{j=1,\ldots,n} \{b_j\}$ (Def. 1).

**Proof.** According to Equation 2, Cauchy mutation of FEP will generate a random vector $\delta = (\delta_1(1), \delta_2(1), ..., \delta_n(1))$, where $\delta_j(1)$ is a random variable of independent identity distribution following Equation (3).

Based on Def. 4, $\exists t$ , $\xi_t^{FEP} \in Y_{FEP}^*$ such that For $\forall \varepsilon > 0$ , $\exists (x_i^*, \sigma_i) \in \xi_t^{FEP}$, $x_i^* \in M_\varepsilon$ and $M_\varepsilon = \{x \in S \mid f(x) > f^* - \varepsilon\}$. According to Equation (2), $P\{x_i' \in M_\varepsilon\} = P\{\delta \in M'_\varepsilon\}$ , where $M'_\varepsilon = \{x \mid x \in \prod_{j=1}^{n}[l_j, h_j]\}$ , $M'_\varepsilon \supseteq S$ , $S = \prod_{i=1}^{n}[-b_i, b_i]$ , $h_j = 2b_j / \sigma'_i(j)$ and $l_j = -h_j$ . Thus, $M'_\varepsilon \supseteq M_\varepsilon$, then we have

$$P\{x_i' \in M_\varepsilon\} = \int_{M'_\varepsilon} k_{\phi=1}(y)dm \geq \int_{M_\varepsilon} k_{\phi=1}(y)dm \tag{8}$$

and

$$P\{x_i' \in M_\varepsilon\} \geq m(M_\varepsilon) \cdot (\pi + \pi \cdot b_{max}^2)^{-n} \tag{9}$$

where $b_{max} = \max_{j=1,...,n}\{b_j\}$ .

Therefore, $P\{\xi_t^{FEP} \in Y_{FEP}^* \mid \xi_{t-1}^{FEP} \notin Y_{FEP}^*\} = 1 - \prod_{i=1}^{m_p}(1 - P\{x_i' \in M_\varepsilon\})$. Hence,

$$P\{\xi_t^{FEP} \notin Y_{FEP}^* \mid \xi_{t-1}^{FEP} \in Y_{FEP}^*\} \geq 1 - (1 - \frac{m(M_\varepsilon)}{(\pi + \pi b_{max}^2)^n})^{m_p} \tag{10}$$

The conclusion of Theorem 3 indicates that the measure of $m(M_\varepsilon)$ influences possibility that a FEP can attain the optimal solution at t-th iteration but not (t-1)-th iteration. Meanwhile, big $b_{max}$ raises the difficult of the solution.

**Corollary 1.** Given the stochastic process $\{\xi_t^{FEP}\}_{t=0}^{+\infty}$ of FEP, we have: 1) $\lim_{t \to +\infty} \lambda_t^{FEP} = P\{\xi_t^{FEP} \in Y_{FEP}^*\} = 1$ and 2) the convergence time of FEP is

$$E\mu_{FEP} \leq (1 - \lambda_0^{FEP}) / (1 - (1 - \frac{m(M_\varepsilon)}{(\pi + \pi b_{max}^2)^n})^{m_p}) \tag{11}$$

where $m(M_\varepsilon)$ is the Lebesgue measure of $M_\varepsilon$ (Def. 4), $m_p$ is the population size and $b_{max} = \max_{j=1,...,n}\{b_j\}$ (Def. 1).

**Proof.** 1) According to Theorem 3,

$$P\{\xi_t^{FEP} \notin Y_{FEP}^* \mid \xi_{t-1}^{FEP} \in Y_{FEP}^*\} \geq 1-(1-\frac{m(M_\varepsilon)}{(\pi+\pi b_{max}^2)^n})^{m_p} \text{ and } 0 < \frac{m(M_\varepsilon)}{(\pi+\pi b_{max}^2)^n} < 1$$

for the third hypothetical condition in Section 3. We can sign
$\theta_{t-1}^1 = 1-(1-m(M_\varepsilon)/(\pi+\pi b_{max}^2)^n)^{m_p}$ for $t=1,2,\ldots$ , then $0 < \theta_t^1 < 1$ and

$$\lim_{t\to+\infty} \prod_{i=0}^{t} (1-\theta_i^1) = 0 \quad . \quad \lim_{t\to+\infty} \lambda_t^{FEP} \geq 1-(1-\lambda_0^{FEP})\lim_{t\to+\infty}\prod_{i=0}^{t}(1-\theta_i^1) = 1 \quad .$$

$$\lim_{t\to+\infty} \lambda_t^{FEP} = P\{\xi_t^{FEP} \in Y_{FEP}^*\} = 1 \text{ since } \lambda_t^{FEP} \leq 1.$$

2) Since $\lim_{t\to+\infty} \lambda_t^{FEP} = 1$ and the conclusion of Theorem 2 and 3,

$$E\mu_{FEP} \leq (1-\lambda_0^{FEP})/(1-(1-m(M_\varepsilon)/(\pi+\pi b_{max}^2)^n)^{m_p}) .$$

The first result of Corollary 1 proves the convergence of FEP, and that larger $m(M_\varepsilon)$ can make the convergence faster. Considering the assumption that

$$(1-\frac{m(M_\varepsilon)}{(\pi+\pi \cdot b_{max}^2)^n})^{m_p} \approx 1-m_p \cdot \frac{m(M_\varepsilon)}{(\pi+\pi \cdot b_{max}^2)^n} \tag{12}$$

we can have $E\mu_{FEP} \leq \dfrac{1-\lambda_0^{FEP}}{m_p m(M_\varepsilon)}(\pi+\pi b_{max}^2)^n$ . Hence, the runtime of FEP is

nearly $O(\beta_1^n)$ when $m(M_\varepsilon)$ is a constant greater than zero, where $\beta_1 = \pi+\pi b_{max}^2$ . Moreover, given $c_1 = (1-\lambda_0^{FEP})/m_p > 0$ and $k=1,2,\ldots$ , $m(M_\varepsilon)c^{-1} \geq 2^{n\log\beta_1 - k\log n} \Leftrightarrow E\mu_{FEP} = c\beta_1^n/m(M_\varepsilon) \leq n^k$ . Thus, the runtime of FEP can be $O(n^k)$ if $m(M_\varepsilon)c^{-1} \geq 2^{n\log\beta_1 - k\log n}$ .

## 5   Discussion and Conclusion

Evolutionary programming (EP) is a classical continuous evolutionary algorithm. Gaussian mutation EP (CEP), Cauchy mutation EP (FEP) played an important role in evolutionary computation. The convergence of EP has been proved, but there have been few recent studies of runtime analysis for EP. The contributions of this paper include 1) presenting a theoretical framework of EP to evaluate its runtime generally, and 2) proposing a runtime theorem of FEP containing the conditions for exponential and polynomial time complexity. Future study is suggested to extend the results into other kinds of continuous evolutionary algorithms like Differential evolution (DE).

Moreover, the theoretical results of CEP, FEP and LEP should be improved by giving the analysis examples of exponential and polynomial time complexity.

## Acknowledgement

National Natural Science Foundation of China (61003066,61070033), Doctoral Program of the Ministry of Education (20090172120035), Natural Science Foundation of Guangdong Province (9151008901000165, 10151601501000015), Key Technology Research and Development Programs of Guangdong Province (2009B010800026) and Fundamental Research Funds for the Central Universities, SCUT(2009ZM0052), Key Technology Research and Development Programs of Huizhou (2009G024) and Special Fund Project of Huizhou Modern Information Services.

## References

1. Fogel, L.J., Owens, A.J., Walsh, M.J.: Artificial Intelligence through Simulated Evolution. Wiley, New York (1996)
2. Fogel, D.B.: Applying evolutionary programming to selected traveling sales-man problems. Cybernetics System 24, 27–36 (1993)
3. Bäck, T., Schwefel, H.P.: An overview of evolutionary algorithms for parameter optimization. Evolutionary Computation 1(1), 1  23 (1993)
4. Schwefel, H.P.: Evolution and Optimum Seeking. Wiley, New York (1995)
5. Yao, X., Liu, Y., Lin, G.: Evolutionary programming made faster. IEEE Transactions on Evolutionary Computation 3(2), 82–103 (1999)
6. Brest, J., Greiner, S., Boskovic, B., Mernik, M., Zumer, V.: Self-Adaptive Control Parameters in Differential Evolution: A Comparative Study on Numerical Benchmark Problems. IEEE Transactions on Evolutionary Computation 10(6), 646–657 (2006)
7. Rudolph, G.: Self-Adaptation and global convergence: A Counter-Example. In: Proceedings of the Congress on Evolutionary Computation, vol. 1, pp. 646–651. IEEE Press, Piscataway (1999)
8. Rudolph, G.: Convergence of non-elitist strategies. In: Proceedings of the First IEEE Conference on Evolutionary Computation, vol. 1, pp. 63–66. IEEE Press, Piscataway (1994)
9. Rudolph, G.: Convergence of evolutionary algorithms in general search spaces. In: Proceedings of the Third IEEE Conference on Evolutionary Computation, pp. 50–54. IEEE Press, Piscateway (1996)
10. He, J., Yao, X.: Drift analysis and average time complexity of evolutionary algorithms. Artificial Intelligence 127(1), 57–85 (2001)
11. Yu, Y., Zhou, Z.H.: A new approach to estimating the expected first hitting time of evolutionary algorithms. Artificial Intelligence 172, 1809–1832 (2008)
12. Huang, H., Wu, C.G., Hao, Z.F.: A Pheromone-rate-based Analysis on the Convergence Time of ACO Algorithm. IEEE Transaction on System, Man and Cybernetics – Part B 39(4), 910–923 (2009)

# Best Hiding Capacity Scheme for Variable Length Messages Using Particle Swarm Optimization

Ruchika Bajaj[1], Punam Bedi[1], and S.K. Pal[2]

[1] Department of Computer Science, University of Delhi,
Delhi, India
[2] Scientific Analysis Group, DRDO, Delhi, India
ruchikabajaj.bsc@gmail.com, pbedi@cs.du.ac.in, skptech@yahoo.com

**Abstract.** Steganography is an art of hiding information in such a way that prevents the detection of hidden messages. Besides security of data, the quantity of data that can be hidden in a single cover medium, is also very important. We present a secure data hiding scheme with high embedding capacity for messages of variable length based on Particle Swarm Optimization. This technique gives the best pixel positions in the cover image, which can be used to hide the secret data. In the proposed scheme, k bits of the secret message are substituted into k least significant bits of the image pixel, where k varies from 1 to 4 depending on the message length. The proposed scheme is tested and results compared with simple LSB substitution, uniform 4-bit LSB hiding (with PSO) for the test images Nature, Baboon, Lena and Kitty. The experimental study confirms that the proposed method achieves high data hiding capacity and maintains imperceptibility and minimizes the distortion between the cover image and the obtained stego image.

**Keywords:** Information Hiding, Steganography, Hiding Capacity, Particle Swarm Optimization, Variable Length Message.

## 1 Introduction

Information assets are critical to any business and of supreme concern to the survival of any organization in today's globalised digital economy. To protect this highly confidential information from being intercepted, modified, or used by unauthorized entities, we need to have methods for achieving information security [6].

Information security is the process of protecting information against unauthorized access, use, disclosure, disruption, modification or destruction [9]. The most well-known method for information security is using Information Hiding, which is the process of hiding details of an object or function [10]. An important subdiscipline of information hiding is *steganography*. It is the science of hiding information. It hides the secret message within the host data set and makes its presence imperceptible [3]. The main goal of steganography is to avoid drawing suspicion to the existence of a hidden message. The following formula provides a very generic description of the steganographic process:

cover_medium + hidden_data + stego_key = stego_medium

B.K. Panigrahi et al. (Eds.): SEMCCO 2010, LNCS 6466, pp. 230–237, 2010.

In this context, the cover_medium is the file in which we will hide the hidden_data, which may also be dispersed using the stego_key. The resultant file is the stego_medium. The cover_medium are typically image or audio files.

*Least Significant Bit (LSB)* substitution technique of steganography is by far the most popular and simplest way of embedding secret messages. The basic idea here is to embed the secret message in the least significant bits of images. In this technique, the message is stored in the LSB of the pixels which could be considered as random noise [5]. Therefore altering them does not significantly affect the quality of the cover image. The procedure for such technique is to convert the desired hidden message into binary form and then encrypt each digit into a least significant bit of the data image.

There are several issues to be considered when studying steganographic systems. One among the key performance measures used to compare different message embedding algorithms is *steganography capacity*. In a general sense, it is the maximum message size that can be embedded, subject to certain constraints [4]. Steganalysis is a new branch of research and not much work is done in literature on increasing steganography capacity without being detected. In [8], PSO is used for hiding messages using 1-bit LSB.

This paper proposes a variation of simple LSB substitution technique in which k bits of the secret message are embedded into the k least significant bits of an image pixel where k varies from 1 to 4. But, embedding any number of bits in any randomly selected column of image pixels does not satisfy both the goals of achieving less image distortion and high embedding capacity at the same time. Thus, to achieve both these goals, an optimization technique known as Particle Swarm Optimization has been used, which gives us the best pixel positions in the cover image, so that the stego image obtained after using these pixel positions has less distortion and greater similarity with the original cover image.

## 2   Particle Swarm Optimization

Particle Swarm Optimization (PSO) is an artificial intelligence technique based on the study of collective behavior in decentralized, self-organized systems. It applies the concept of social interaction to problem solving. A PSO algorithm maintains a swarm of particles, where each particle represents a potential solution. A *swarm* is similar to a population, while a *particle* is similar to an individual. The particles are "flown" through a multidimensional search space, where the position of each particle is adjusted according to its own experience and that of its neighbors [1]. Let $x_i(t)$ denote the position of particle $i$ in the search space at time step $t$. The position of the particle is changed by adding a velocity $v_i(t)$ to the current position, i.e.

$$x_i(t+1) = x_i(t) + v_i(t+1). \qquad (1)$$

It is the velocity vector that drives the optimization process, and reflects both the experiential knowledge of the particle (referred as the *cognitive component*), and socially exchanged information from the particle's neighborhood (referred as the *social component*) [1]. When a particle takes all the population as its topological neighbors, the best value is a global best and is called gbest. For gbest PSO, the velocity of particle i is calculated as:

$$v_{ij}(t+1) = v_{ij}(t) + c_1 r_{1j}(t)[y_{ij}(t) - x_{ij}(t)] + c_2 r_{2j}(t)[Y_j(t) - x_{ij}(t)] \qquad (2)$$

where $v_{ij}(t)$ is the velocity of the particle $i$ in dimension $j = 1,....,n_x$ at time step t. $x_{ij}(t)$ is the position of particle $i$ in dimension $j$ at time step $t$. $c_1$, $c_2$ are positive acceleration constants used to scale the contribution of cognitive and social components respectively. $r_{1j}(t)$, $r_{2j}(t) \sim U(0,1)$ are random values in the range [0,1] sampled from a uniform distribution. The personal best position $y_i$ associated with particle $i$ is the best position the particle has visited since the first time step. Considering minimization problems, the personal best position at the next time step t+1 is calculated as:

$$y_i(t+1) = \begin{cases} y_i(t) \text{ if } f(x_i(t+1)) \geq f(y_i(t)) \\ x_i(t+1) \text{ if } f(x_i(t+1)) < f(y_i(t)) \end{cases} \qquad (3)$$

where $f$ is the fitness function which measures how close the corresponding solution is to the optimum. The global best position $Y(t)$ at time step t, is defined as

$$Y(t) \; \varepsilon \; \{y_0(t),...,y_{ns}(t)\} \mid f((Y(t)) = \min\{f(y_0(t)),...,f(y_{ns}(t))\} \qquad (4)$$

where $n_s$ is the total number of particles in the swarm.

The particle swarm optimization process is iterative. Repeated iterations are executed until a stopping condition is satisfied. Firstly an initial swarm is generated, and then within each iteration, value of fitness function is evaluated. Also the velocity and the position of each particle is updated. This algorithm can be terminated when a maximum number of iterations has been exceeded or an acceptable solution has been found or no improvement is observed over a number of iterations.

## 3   Finding Best Pixel Positions Using PSO

The objective of trying to search for an efficient and secure data hiding scheme with high embedding capacity and less distortion between the original cover image and the stego image can be achieved through our proposed method which is based on particle swarm optimization. The proposed technique adopts the following steps to achieve our objective:

**Step 1:** To establish the functioning of PSO toolbox in MATLAB. This PSO should attempt to solve the continuous optimization problem of the form:

$$\min(x) \; objective\_function(x)$$

**Step 2:** An image to be treated as cover image is taken, in which we want to embed the secret message.

**Step 3:** Firstly, simple LSB substitution method is applied on the cover image and the pixel values are chosen randomly to change their least significant bits according to the message bits to hide and resulting stego image is obtained.

**Step 4:** The divergence between the original cover image and the obtained stego image is calculated through the image quality measures such as Mean Square Error, Peak Signal to Noise Ratio and Structural Similarity index. These measures are calculated in MATLAB using the methods implemented for each of these image quality measures which takes as input the original cover image and the stego image.

**Step 5:** Now in order to improve the image quality as compared to the above scheme applied in Step 3 , we run PSO algorithm on the image in order to get the best optimized positions (in the form of 2D coordinates of the image pixel values) where we intend to hide the message bits. To do so, we first set the objective function.

**Step 5.1: Setting the objective function**

An ideal objective function should be able to correctly identify and minimize the three factors of the image quality: i) the amount of image distortion ii) the type of distortion, and iii) the distribution of error [2]. Thus, we set our objective function as the *Singular Value Decomposition (SVD) based image quality measure* which correctly identifies the above three factors. It can be used as a graphical or scalar measure to predict the distortion introduced by a wide range of noise sources.

Every grayscale image can be considered to be a matrix with an integer number corresponding to each pixel. Suppose we call this matrix as A. Then it could be decomposed into a product of 3 matrices, $A = USV^T$, where U and V are orthogonal matrices. $U^TU = I$, $V^TV = I$ and $S = diag(s_1, s_2, ...)$. I refers to identity matrix. The diagonal entries of S are called the singular values of A, and the columns of V are called the right singular vectors of A. This decomposition is known as the Singular Value Decomposition (SVD) of A. If the SVD is applied to the full images, we obtain a global measure whereas if a smaller block (e.g., 8 x 8) is used, we compute the local error in that block [2]. The SVD computes a *graphical measure* which is a bivariate measure that computes the distance between the singular values of the original image block and the singular values of the distorted image block. It is given as:

$$D_i = \sqrt{\sum_{i=1}^{n} (s_i - \hat{s}_i)^2} \tag{5}$$

where $s_i$ are the singular values of the original block, $\hat{s}_i$ are the singular values of the distorted block, and n is the block size. And a numerical or scalar measure which is derived from the graphical measure and computes the global error expressed as a single numerical value depending on the distortion type [2].

$$MSVD = \frac{\sum_{i=1}^{(k/n)\times(k/n)} |D_i - D_{mid}|}{(k/n)\times(k/n)} \tag{6}$$

where $D_{mid}$ represents the mid point of the sorted $D_i$'s . k is the image size, and n is the block size.

**Step 5.2: Setting the PSO parameters**

After setting the objective function, we need to set the various parameters in the PSO function such as:

- Specifying the number of iterations to be run (upto 1000 iterations were sufficient to converge to a solution).
- Specifying the number of particles in the swarm. The number of particles will be set to the message length in terms of bits. For example, if the message length is 64 bits, then the number of particles will be set to 64.
- Setting the initial population of the particles in the swarm. This initial population is a population within the cover image itself.

After setting all the parameters, PSO is run in order to minimize our objective function. The result so obtained gives the best value of the objective function for each iteration. Then, a 2D array is created which stores the XY indexes corresponding to the global best value for every iteration. The resulting pixel coordinates are then used to hide the given message and get the stego image after embedding the message bits with the help of proposed variable hiding schemes.

## 4   Embedding Scheme for Variable Length Messages

In order to embed secret messages of any given length and also to achieve high capacity i.e. embedding the long messages, we divide the cover image into different blocks based on the number of bits in the message to be hidden. Then we run PSO for each of these blocks individually, in order to obtain the pixel coordinates corresponding to these blocks of the image. Now, every block will be evaluated based on the objective function value. Thus a block which achieves a lower value of the objective function, results in more number of pixel values which can be used for hiding the secret message, and appears to be a more promising image portion for the embedding scheme. Whereas a block which achieves a relatively higher value for the objective function, results in less number of pixel values which can be used for hiding the secret information.

After obtaining the required image pixel coordinates for every image block, we use these coordinates in the LSB substitution method and hide the message bits in either 1, 2, 3 or 4 least significant bits of the image pixels, and thus obtain the required new stego image. This stego image can be obtained through either of the following embedding schemes:

- Applying *'uniform bit hiding'* for the entire image either use 1 bit, 2 bit, 3 bit or 4 bit LSB substitution scheme for embedding.
- Depending on the number of pixel coordinates obtained for each image block, we decide our embedding scheme, i.e. for a block with maximum number of pixels, we hide the secret message bits using 1 bit LSB substitution, using 2 bit LSB substitution in the block obtaining second most number of pixels and 3 bit and 4 bit LSB substitution in the blocks obtaining the least number of pixel coordinates; so that we minimize the number of changes occurring in the image. And thus results in less distortion as well as increases the data hiding capacity as compared to the uniform hiding scheme applied. This we call as the *'variable hiding scheme 1'*.
- We can hide the secret message bits using 4 bit LSB substitution in the block with maximum number of pixel coordinates, 3 bit LSB substitution in the block obtaining second most number of pixel coordinates and 2 bit and 1 bit LSB substitution in the blocks obtaining least number of pixel coordinates. This we call as the *'variable hiding scheme 2'*.This embedding scheme will considerably increase the data hiding capacity with a slight increase in the resulting image distortion, but still achieving far better results than the uniform hiding scheme.

## 5   Extraction of Secret Information

Secret information from the stego image can be extracted based on a *secret key* at the receiver end. The secret key can be send to the receiver separately in a secure manner. This secret key is a set of ordered pairs based on the combination of the image block number and the number of bits of the hiding scheme applied in that block. For example: if the secret key generated is [4 3;2 4;3 1;1 2], then it signifies that the fourth image block applies 3 bit LSB substitution, second image block applies 4 bit LSB substitution, and so on.

Using this secret key, receiver can move to the corresponding image blocks and compute the indexes where the secret message bits are embedded in that block. Then, those number of least significant bits can be extracted by the receiver as mentioned in the secret key combination from the binary equivalents of the intensity values present at the computed indexes. Concatenating these secret message bits obtained from various image blocks and converting them into the characters from their corresponding decimal values gives the secret message to be obtained.

## 6   Experimental Results

The proposed scheme is implemented in MATLAB. Four grayscale images of size 128 x 128 pixels are used in the simulations of the experiments. Two different messages of different lengths are used, one of length 704 bits and another of length 2112 bits. To observe the change in the values of different image quality measures, firstly the simple LSB hiding method is applied and the value of the various image quality measures are calculated. The results are then compared with our proposed methods of embedding, one with uniform hiding scheme and the other with the variable hiding schemes. The image quality measures used to measure the image quality of the obtained stego image from the different embedding schemes applied are – Mean Square Error (MSE), Peak Signal to Noise Ratio (PSNR) and Structural Similarity Index (SSIM). Figure1 shows the test images used.

| Nature | Baboon | Lena | Kitty |
|--------|--------|------|-------|
|  | 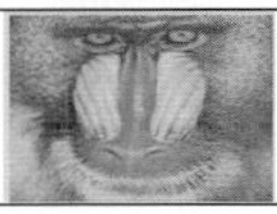 |  |  |

**Fig. 1.** Test Images

Table 1 shows the results obtained for the image 'Nature.jpg' and 'Baboon.jpg' respectively, where a secret message of size 704 bits is embedded. Table2 shows the results obtained for the image 'Lena.jpg' and 'Kitty.jpg' respectively, where a secret message of size 2112 bits is embedded.

**Table 1.**

| Embedding Scheme | Results for 'Nature.jpg' Performance Measures | | | Results for 'Baboon.jpg' Performance Measures | | |
|------------------|------|------|------|------|------|------|
| | MSE | PSNR | SSIM | MSE | PSNR | SSIM |
| Simple LSB Substitution (Without PSO) | 0.3796 | 52.3378 | 0.9965 | 0.4072 | 52.0324 | 0.9989 |
| Uniform 4-bit LSB hiding (With PSO) | 0.3691 | 52.4596 | 0.9989 | 0.3961 | 52.1526 | 0.9995 |
| Variable hiding Scheme 1 | 0.0325 | 63.0159 | 0.9998 | 0.0281 | 63.6380 | 0.9999 |
| Variable hiding Scheme 2 | 0.1097 | 57.7271 | 0.9991 | 0.1354 | 56.8134 | 0.9997 |

**Table 2.**

| Embedding Scheme | Results for 'Lena.jpg' Performance Measures | | | Results for 'Kitty.jpg' Performance Measures | | |
|---|---|---|---|---|---|---|
| | MSE | PSNR | SSIM | MSE | PSNR | SSIM |
| Simple LSB Substitution (Without PSO) | 1.5407 | 46.2536 | 0.9919 | 1.4350 | 46.5623 | 0.9901 |
| Uniform 4-bit LSB hiding (With PSO) | 1.1823 | 47.4037 | 0.9969 | 1.2000 | 47.3392 | 0.9909 |
| Variable hiding Scheme 1 | 0.3787 | 52.3483 | 0.9992 | 0.4268 | 51.8290 | 0.9966 |
| Variable hiding Scheme 2 | 0.5941 | 50.3921 | 0.9989 | 0.2913 | 53.4871 | 0.9976 |

The graphs obtained for the above results are shown in Figure 2. These graphs are plotted against the different image quality measures (i.e. MSE, PSNR and SSIM) and the embedding scheme applied, where embedding scheme 1, 2, 3 and 4 refers to the simple LSB substitution (without PSO), uniform 4-bit LSB hiding (with PSO), variable hiding scheme 1 and variable hiding scheme 2 (as explained in section 4) respectively.

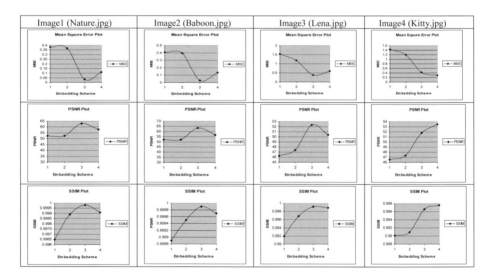

**Fig. 2.** Comparison Results in form of Graphs

From the above graphs obtained, we observe that the value for MSE decreases and the value for PSNR and SSIM increases significantly for the variable hiding schemes implemented using PSO as compared to the simple LSB substitution scheme without using PSO. This shows that the stego image obtained through our proposed schemes based on PSO has less divergence and greater similarity with the original cover image.

# 7  Conclusion

The main objective of the work carried out was to search for an efficient high capacity data hiding scheme to hide the secret data messages of variable length. An embedding scheme which uses Particle Swarm Optimization to give the best pixel positions in the cover image that were used to embed the secret message bits so that less image distortion occurs is presented in this paper. Data hiding through simple LSB technique was used for variable length messages where message bits were substituted in the 1, 2 3 or 4 least significant bits of the image pixels.

In this scheme, the cover image was divided into a specified number of blocks which varies in accordance with the length of message i.e. more number of blocks for large number of message bits and less number of blocks for lesser number of message bits, with each block of equal dimension. Then PSO method was applied on each block which evaluates the value of the objective function for each iteration, and calculates the best pixel positions for each block. These best positions were then used in the least significant bit substitution technique to hide the secret message bits. Each image block uses variable embedding scheme depending on the number of best pixel positions returned by applying PSO for that particular block.

The image quality measures were calculated to compare the results of simple LSB hiding in random pixels without using PSO algorithm with our proposed method based on PSO. Experimental results show that our proposed technique based on Particle Swarm Optimization achieves high data embedding capacity and minimizes distortion between cover image and the stego image.

# References

1. Engelbrecht, A.P.: Fundamentals of Computational Swarm Intelligence. John Wiley & Sons, Inc., Chichester (2005)
2. Shnayderman, A., Gusev, A., Eskicioglu, A.M.: An SVD-Based Gray-Scale Image Quality Measure for Local and Global Assessment, PSC- City University of New York (CUNY) Research Award (2003-2004)
3. Avcibas, I., Kharrazi, M., Memon, N., Sankur, B.: Image Steganalysis with Binary Similarity Measures. EURASIP Journal on Applied Signal Processing 17, 2749–2757 (2005)
4. ChandraMouli, R., Memon, N.D.: Steganography Capacity: A Steganalysis Perspective. Air Force Research Laboratory, U.S. Government (2006)
5. Katzenbeisser, S., Fabien, A., Petitcolas, P.: Information Hiding Techniques for Steganography and Digital Watermarking. Artech House, Inc., Boston (2000)
6. Kuo, W.C., Wuu, L.C., Shyi, C.N., Kuo, S.H.: A Data Hiding Scheme with High Embedding Capacity Based on General Improving Exploiting Modification Direction method. In: Ninth International Conference on Hybrid Intelligent Systems, vol. 3, pp. 69–72 (2009)
7. Guo, Y., Kong, X., You, X.: Secure Steganography Based on Binary Particle Swarm Optimization. Journal of Electronics 26(2) (2009)
8. Li, X., Wang, J.: A steganographic method based upon JPEG and particle swarm optimization algorithm. Information Sciences 177, 3099–3109 (2007)
9. Article on Information Security, from Wikipedia (accessed in May, 2010)
10. Article on Information Hiding, from Webopedia (accessed in May, 2010)

# Ant Colony Optimization for Markowitz Mean-Variance Portfolio Model

Guang-Feng Deng and Woo-Tsong Lin

Department of Management Information Systems, National Chengchi University,
64, Sec. 2, Chihnan Rd., Wenshan Dist, Taipei 116, Taiwan ROC Taiwan ROC
95356502@nccu.edu.tw, lin@mis.nccu.edu.tw

**Abstract.** This work presents Ant Colony Optimization (ACO), which was initially developed to be a meta-heuristic for combinatorial optimization, for solving the cardinality constraints Markowitz mean-variance portfolio model (nonlinear mixed quadratic programming problem). To our knowledge, an efficient algorithmic solution for this problem has not been proposed until now. Using heuristic algorithms in this case is imperative. Numerical solutions are obtained for five analyses of weekly price data for the following indices for the period March, 1992 to September, 1997: Hang Seng 31 in Hong Kong, DAX 100 in Germany, FTSE 100 in UK, S&P 100 in USA and Nikkei 225 in Japan. The test results indicate that the ACO is much more robust and effective than Particle swarm optimization (PSO), especially for low-risk investment portfolios.

**Keywords:** Ant Colony Optimization (ACO), Markowitz mean-variance portfolio model, cardinality constrained portfolio optimization problem, nonlinear mixed quadratic programming problem.

## 1 Introduction

Ant Colony Optimization (ACO), collaborative population-based swarm intelligent algorithm, introduced by Dorigo in 1992, has proven effective in many empirical studies[1]. The idea of ACO was inspired by the foraging behavior of ant colonies that find the shortest route between ant's nest and a source of food by exchanging information via pheromone deposited on the trips. This pheromone information is used to guide the route search and let ants cooperate with each other as a whole community to achieve robust behavior capable of finding high quality solutions in a large search space.

Portfolio optimization, which is the allocation of wealth among several assets, is an essential problem in modern risk management. Expected returns and risks are the most important criteria in portfolio optimization problems. Investors generally prefer to maximize returns and minimize risk. However, high returns generally involve increased risk. The Markowitz mean –variance portfolio model, which is among the best models for solving the portfolio selection problem, can be described in terms of the mean return of the assets and the variance of return (risk) between these assets [2]. The basic model obtains the "efficient frontier", which is the portfolio of assets that achieves a predetermined level of expected return at minimal risk. For every level of desired mean return, this efficiency frontier indicates the best investment strategy.

B.K. Panigrahi et al. (Eds.): SEMCCO 2010, LNCS 6466, pp. 238–245, 2010.

From a practical perspective, portfolio selection problem consider many constraints of real-world investments, including trading limitations, portfolio size, etc. However, the basic Markowitz mean-variance model does not include cardinality constraints to ensure the investment in a given number of different assets, nor does it include bounding constraints to limit the funds invested in each asset. Although portfolio optimization using the standard Markowitz model is NP-hard, the solution to this problem with a sufficiently small number of variables can be solved by using quadratic programming. The problem becomes much more difficult if the number of variables is increased or if additional constraints such as cardinality constraints are introduced [3]. Such constraints formed nonlinear mixed integer programming problems, which are considerably more difficult to solve than the original problem. Exact solution methods are inadequate. Therefore, heuristic solutions for the portfolio selection problem have been proposed such as evolutionary algorithms, tabu search (TS), simulated annealing (SA), neural networks and Particle swarm optimization (PSO) [2-10].

This study presents an extension of ACO to the Markowitz mean-variance portfolio model, which includes cardinality and bounding constraints, to solve Cardinality Constrained Markowitz mean-variance Portfolio Optimization problems (CCMPO problems).

The performance of the ACO was compared with Particle swarm optimization (PSO). Performance was compared using five problems, involving 31-255 dimensions corresponding to weekly data for March, 1992 to September, 1997. The test data were obtained from the following indices: Hang Seng 31 in Hong Kong, DAX 100 in Germany, FTSE 100 in UK, S&P 100 in USA and Nikkei 225 in Japan. Results show that the ACO is much more robust and effective than PSO algorithms in terms of tracing out the efficient frontier accurately, especially in risk-aversion CCMPO problems.

Following this introduction, Section 2 presents ACO for continuous domain and the model formulation for the Cardinality constrained Markowitz mean-variance portfolio optimization problems, and Section 3 describes the application of ACO for solving this problem. The computational experiment in Section 4 evaluates the ACO model and experimental results. Section 5 presents conclusions and proposes future works.

## 2   Ant Colony Optimization (ACO) and Markowitz Mean-Variance Portfolio Model

### 2.1   Ant Colony Optimization Algorithm for Continuous Domain

This section explains pheromone representation in ACO for continuous optimization problem. In the case of continuous optimization, the choice an ant makes is not restricted to a finite set. Hence, it is impossible to represent the pheromone in the form of a table. We adopt an approach that was proposed by Socha and Dorigo(2008)[11]. In Socha and Dorigo way, ACO adopt to keep track of a certain number of the solutions in a solution archive $T$ used to update the pheromone table. For each solution $s_l$ to an $n$-dimensional problem, ACO stores in $T$ the values of its $n$ variables and the value of the objective function $f(s_l)$. The $i$th variable of $l$th solution is hereby denoted by $s^i_l$.

We use a continuous probability density function based on Gaussian function ($g^i_l$) to represent $s^i_l$ that parameterized with three factor: $\omega_l$ is the weight associated with the individual Gaussian function, $\mu^i_l$ is the mean, and $\sigma^i_l$ is the standard deviations. Then we use components of the solutions to dynamically generate probability density function ($g^i_l$). The solutions in the archive are used to calculate the values of these parameters, and used to guide the ants in their search process.

The number of solutions memorized in the archive is set to $k$. For each dimension $i = 1,\ldots,n$ of the problem and each solution $l = 1,\ldots,k$ in the archive, the value $\mu^i_l = s^i_l$. The $l$th weight $\omega_l$ is created in the following way. Each solution that is added to the archive $T$ is evaluated and ranked. The solutions in the archive are sorted according to their rank—i.e., solution $s_l$ has rank $l$. The weight $\omega_l$ of the solution $s_l$ is calculated according to the following formula:

$$\omega_l = \frac{1}{qk\sqrt{2\pi}} e^{-\frac{(l-1)^2}{2q^2k^2}} \tag{1}$$

which essentially defines the weight to be a value of the Gaussian function with argument $l$, mean 1.0, and standard deviation $qk$, where $q$ is a parameter of the algorithm. When $q$ is small, the best-ranked solutions are strongly preferred, and when $q$ is large, the probability becomes more uniform. The influence of this parameter on ACO is similar to adjusting the balance between the iteration-best and the best-so-far pheromone updates used in ACO.

## 2.2 Markowitz Optimal Portfolio Optimization Model

The portfolio selection problem is a multi-objective optimization problem, and all non-dominated solutions can be used to produce the efficient frontier. To calculate cardinality constraints for the Markowitz Optimal Model, this study used the model formulation presented in [4, 5]. The notation used in this analysis is based on Markowitz mean-variance model for solving the portfolio selection problem. Let $N$ be the number of different assets, $r_i$ be the expected return of asset $i$ ($i=1,\ldots,N$), $c_{i,j}$ be the covariance between assets $i$ and $j$ ($i=1,\ldots,N$; $j=1,\ldots,N$), The decision variables $x_i$ represent the proportion ($0 \leq x_i \leq 1$) of the portfolio invested in asset $i$ ($i=1,\ldots,N$) and a weighting parameter $\lambda$. Using this notation, the cardinality constrained Markowitz mean-variance model for the portfolio selection problem can be presented as

$$Min \quad \lambda \left[ \sum_{i=1}^{N} \sum_{j=1}^{N} x_i \cdot x_j \cdot c_{ij} \right] - (1-\lambda) \left[ \sum_{i=1}^{N} x_i \cdot r_i \right] \tag{2}$$

subject to

$$\sum_{i=1}^{N} x_i = 1 \tag{3}$$

$$\sum_{i=1}^{N} z_i = K \tag{4}$$

$$\varepsilon_i z_i \leq x_i \leq \delta_i z_i \quad , \quad i = 1, ..., N \tag{5}$$

$$z_i \in [0, 1] \quad , \quad i = 1, ..., N \tag{6}$$

where $\lambda \in [0,1]$ is the risk aversion parameter. The case $\lambda=0$ represents the maximum expected return for the portfolio (disregarding risk), and the optimal portfolio is the single asset with the highest return. The case $\lambda=1$ represents the minimal total risk for the selected portfolio (disregarding return), and the optimal portfolio includes numerous assets. The two extremes $\lambda=0$ and $\lambda=1$, $\lambda$ represent the tradeoff between risk and return. Equation (3) ensures that the sum of the proportions is 1. The equation $\sum_{i=1}^{N} \sum_{j=1}^{N} x_i \cdot x_j \cdot c_{ij}$ obtains total variance (risk), which should be minimized and the equation $\sum_{i=1}^{N} x_i \cdot r_i$ obtains the total portfolio return, which should be maximized.

Let $K$ be the desired number of assets in the portfolio, let $\varepsilon_i$ be the minimum proportion of the portfolio allocated to asset $i$ ($i=1, ..., N$) if any of asset $i$ is held, and let $\delta_i$ be the maximum proportion allocated to asset $i$ ($i=1, ..., N$) if any of asset $i$ is held, where $0 \leq \varepsilon_i \leq \delta_i \leq 1$ ($i=1, ..., N$). In practice $\varepsilon_i$ represents a "min-buy" or "minimum transaction level" for asset $i$, and $\delta_i$ limits portfolio exposure to asset $i$. Equation (6) is the Zero-one integrality constraint.

## 3   ACO for CCMPO Problems

This section describes the three major algorithmic components of ACO approach to CCMPO problems.

**Solution Construction:** Given decision variable $x_i$, $i = 1, ..., n$, each representing the proportion of capital to be invested in the $j$th asset, an ant constructs a solution(portfolio) by performing $n$ construction steps. At construction step $i$ an ant choose a value for variable $x_i$. At construction step $i$, the choosing process is accomplished as follows. First, the weight of the Gaussian function of element is computed following Eq. (7). Second, depending on the $\omega$ of Gaussian function, an ant chooses a Gaussian function $g_l^i$. The probability $p_l$ of choosing the $l$th Gaussian function is given by:

$$p_l = \frac{\omega_l}{\sum_{r=1}^{k} \omega_r} \tag{7}$$

Third, from the chosen Gaussian function (i.e., at step $i$—function $g_l^i$). We use a random number generator that is able to generate random numbers according to a parametrized normal distribution, or by using a uniform random generator in conjunction with. The choice of the $l$th Gaussian function is done only once per ant, per iteration. This means that an ant uses the Gaussian functions associated with the single chosen solution $s_l$, that is, functions $g_l^i$, $i = 1 ..., n$, for constructing the whole solution in a given iteration.

In order to establish the value of the standard deviation $\sigma$ at construction step $i$, we calculate the average distance from the chosen solution $s_l$ to other solutions in the archive, and we multiply it by the parameter $\xi$:

$$\sigma_l^i = \xi \sum_{e=1}^{k} \frac{\left| s_e^i - s_l^i \right|}{k-1} \tag{8}$$

The parameter $\xi > 0$, which is the same for all the dimensions, has an effect similar to that of the pheromone evaporation rate in ACO. The higher the value of $\xi$, the lower the convergence speed of the algorithm. While the rate of pheromone evaporation in ACO influences the long term memory—i.e., worse solutions are forgotten faster— $\xi$ in ACO influences the way the long term memory is used—i.e., the search is less biased towards the points of the search space that have been already explored (and which are kept in the archive). This whole process is repeated for each dimension $i = 1,\ldots,n$, and each time the average distance $\sigma$ is calculated only with the use of the single dimension $i$.

**Constraints satisfaction:** For handling the cardinality constraints, $K$ is the desired number of assets in the portfolio. Given a set $Q$ of $K$ assets, Let $K^{new}$ represent the number of assets in portfolio (the numbers of the proportion $w_i$ greater than 0) after solution construction by ant. If $K^{new} < K$, some assets must be added to $Q$; if $K^{new} > K$, then some assets must be removed from $Q$ until $K^{new} = K$. Considering the removal of assets in the case $K^{new} > K$. This study deletes the smallest assets. If $K^{new} < K$ assets, assets remaining to be added must be identified. This study randomly adds an asset $i \notin Q$ and assigns the minimum proportional value $\varepsilon_i$ to the new asset.

According to Eq. (5), the value of $x_i$ must also satisfy $0 \leqq \varepsilon_i \leqq x_i \leqq \delta_i \leqq 1$ for $i \in Q$. Let $s_i$ represent the proportion of the new solution belonging to $Q$. If $s_i < \varepsilon_i$, the minimum proportional value of $\varepsilon_i$ replaces asset $s_i$. If $s_i > \varepsilon_i$, the proportional share of the free portfolio is calculated as follows :

$$x_i = \varepsilon_i + \frac{s_i}{\sum_{j \in Q, s_i > \varepsilon_i} s_i}(1 - \sum_{j \in Q} \varepsilon_i) \tag{9}$$

This minimizes the proportional value of $\varepsilon_i$ for the useless assets $i \in Q$ so that particles converge faster in the search process, especially in CCMPO problems involving low values for risk aversion parameter $\lambda$.

**Pheromone Update:** As mentioned earlier, in case of ACO, the pheromone information is stored as a solution archive. This implies that the pheromone update procedure has to perform some form of update on this archive.

The size $k$ of the archive $T$ is a parameter of the algorithm. However, $k$ may not be smaller than the number of dimensions of the problem being solved. At the start of the algorithm, the solution archive $T$ is initialized generating k solutions by uniform random sampling. Pheromone update is accomplished by adding the set of newly generated solutions to the solution archive $T$ and then removing the same number of worst solutions, so that the total size of the archive does not change. This process ensures that only the best solutions are kept in the archive, so that they effectively guide the ants in the search process.

# 4 Computational Experiments

To test the performance of the ACO for CCMPO problems, the computational experiments were performed. The experiment compared the performance of the ACO with PSO to CCMPO problems.

## 4.1 Definition of Experiments

The ACO searches for efficient frontiers by testing 50 different values for the risk aversion parameter $\lambda$ in the cardinality-constrained Markowitz portfolio model. The experiment employed the five benchmark datasets used earlier in [4, 5] These data correspond to weekly price data from March, 1992 to September, 1997 for the following indices: Hang Seng 31 in Hong Kong, DAX 100 in Germany, FTSE 100 in UK, S&P 100 in USA and Nikkei 225 in Japan. The number $N$ of different assets considered for each index was 31, 85, 89, 98 and 225, respectively. The sets of mean return of each asset, covariance between these assets and efficient frontier 2000 points are publicly available at http://people.brunel.ac.uk/mastjjb/jeb/orlib/ portinfo.html. The cardinality constraints used the values $K = 10$, $\varepsilon_i = 0.01$ and $\delta_i = 1$ for problem formulation.

The criteria used to quantify the performance of ACO for CCMPO problem solving were accuracy. Accuracy refers to the quality of the solution obtained. This analysis used the standard deviation (risk) and return of the best solution for each $\lambda$ to compare standard efficient frontiers and to measure percentage error respectively, and the lower value of standard deviation error and mean returns error was used as the percentage error associated with a portfolio. For example, let the pair $(s_i, r_i)$ represent the standard deviation(risk) and mean return of a point obtained by ACO. Additionally, let $s_i^*$ be the standard deviation corresponding to $r_i$ according to a linear interpolation in the standard efficient frontier. The standard deviation of return error $e_i$ for any point $(s_i, r_i)$ is defined as the value $100 (s_i^* - s_i)/ s_i^*$. Similarly, by using the return $r_i^*$ corresponding to $s_i$ according to a linear interpolation in the standard efficient frontier, mean return error $\eta_i$ can be defined as the quantity $100(r_i - r_i^*)/ r_i^*$. The error measure defined in [4] was calculated by averaging the minimums between the mean return errors $e_i$ and the standard deviation of return errors $\eta_i$.

## 4.2 Comparative Performance of the ACO with PSO

This section compares the ACO to PSO for CCMPO problems. This study applied the following parameters for all the test problems: For ACO, No. of ants: 100, speed of convergence ($\xi$): 0.85, Locality of the search process ($q$): $10^{-4}$ and archive size($k$): 50. For PSO, the value (*inertia weight, acceleration coefficient*($c_1$, $c_2$), *velocity*$_{max}$) set to (0.7298, 1.49618, 1.49618, 1) as suggested in[1, 5, 12]. Swarm size is set to 100. Both algorithms terminate when no improvement occurs over 100 iterations. In initialization phase, the individual in the swarm are randomly valued for each dimension between the bounds. Similarly, the velocity is initialized to zero in each dimension. The average value of twenty-five independent runs trials for each test was recorded. Both ACO and PSO algorithms presented in this paper were coded in MATLAB language and tested on a Pentium M processor with 1.6 GHz CPU speed and 1 GB RAM machine, running Windows.

Table 1 shows the minimum mean percentage error of portfolio for ACO and PSO. The best minimum mean percentage error for each problem is in boldface. Clearly, the ACO generally obtained a lower minimum mean percentage error than PSO did. Table 1 also exhibits the average CPU times and the number of iterations of convergence for each method. The comparison results indicate that the ACO required no more iterations than PSO did, and the CPU time required to solve the CCMPO problems was reasonable and practical. When solving complex CCMPO problems (number of assets>100) such as the last problem, the time required to run a trial was only slightly longer than simple CCMPO problems (number of assets<100).

**Table 1.** Experimental results for CCMPO problems

| Problem name/ assets($N$) | | PSO | ACO |
|---|---|---|---|
| Hang Seng 31 | Mean percentage error | 1.104717681 | **1.09430155** |
| | Best cost | 1.095717385 | 1.093296022 |
| | CPU time(s)/ Iterations of Stopping | 4.5/393 | 4.8/427 |
| DAX100 85 | Mean percentage error | 2.92051537 | **2.5414127** |
| | Best cost | 2.862105063 | 2.450878 |
| | CPU time(s)/ Iterations of Stopping | 24.0/492 | 26.8/511 |
| FTSE100 89 | Mean percentage error | 1.427812792 | **1.0622338** |
| | Best cost | 1.399256536 | 1.012178 |
| | CPU time(s)/ Iterations of Stopping | 30.4/487 | 31.4/515 |
| S&P100 98 | Mean percentage error | 2.555478598 | **1.6903454** |
| | Best cost | 2.399256536 | 1.622178 |
| | CPU time(s)/ Iterations of Stopping | 35.6/555 | 36.6/581 |
| Nikkei 225 | Mean percentage error | 0.964592 | **0.687015592** |
| | Best cost | 0.94530016 | 0.631875 |
| | CPU time(s)/ Iterations of Stopping | 78.2/565 | 75.8/545 |

For risk aversion parameter $\lambda$, when value $\lambda$ is low (e <40), the portfolio emphasizes to maximize return regardless of risk. The objective function of CCMPO problems according to equation (1) became almost linear. The portfolio in this case typically included significant investments less than the $K = 10$ assets (here, the term "significant investment" refers to any investment exceeding $1/K$.) When value $\lambda$ is high(e $\geq$40), the portfolio emphasizes to minimize risk regardless of return, the objective function becomes nonlinear. In the portfolio obtained in this case, the diversity of significant investments were close to $K$ assets.

When high value of $\lambda(e\geq40)$ was considered (emphasize risk), the ACO outperformed PSO except in the smallest benchmark problem (the first problem). This study found that PSO quickly stagnates to the local optimum when CCMPO problems consider high values for risk aversion parameter $\lambda$. Additionally, ACO and PSO performed comparably, when low value of $\lambda(e<40)$ was considered (regardless of the risk).

## 5 Conclusion

This work presents an extension of Ant Colony Optimization, which was initially developed for combinatorial optimization, for solving the cardinality constraints Markowitz mean-variance portfolio optimization model. The standard Markowitz mean-variance model was generalized to include cardinality and bounding constraints. Such constraints convert the portfolio selection problem into a mixed quadratic and integer programming problem, for which computationally efficient algorithms have not been developed. The ACO was tested on CCMPO problem set. Comparisons with PSO showed that ACO is much more robust and effective, especially for low-risk investments.

## References

1. Engelbrecht, A.P.: Fundamentals of Computational Swarm Intelligence. Wiley, Chichester (2005)
2. Markowitz, H.: Portfolio Selection. Journal of Finance, 77–91 (1952)
3. Maringer, D., Kellerer, H.: Optimization of Cardinality Constrained Portfolios with a Hybrid Local Search Algorithm. Or Spectrum 25(4), 481–495 (2003)
4. Chang, T.J., Meade, N., Beasley, J.E., Sharaiha, T.M.: Heuristics for Cardinality Constrained Portfolio Optimisation. Computers & Operations Research 27(13), 1271–1302 (2000)
5. Fernandez, A., Gomez, S.: Portfolio Selection using Neural Networks. Computers & Operations Research 34(4), 1177–1191 (2007)
6. Crama, Y., Schyns, M.: Simulated Annealing for Complex Portfolio Selection Problems. European Journal of Operational Research 150(3), 546–571 (2003)
7. Socha, K., Dorigo, M.: Ant Colony Optimization for Continuous Domains. European Journal of Operational Research 185(3), 1155–1173 (2008)
8. Pai, G.A.V., Michel, T.: Evolutionary Optimization of Constrained k-means Clustered Assets for Diversification in Small Portfolios. IEEE Transactions on Evolutionary Computation 13(5), 1030–1053 (2009)
9. Bertsimas, D., Shioda, R.: Algorithm for Cardinality-constrained Quadratic Optimization. Computational Optimization and Applications 43(1), 1–22 (2009)
10. Cura, T.: Particle Swarm Optimization Approach to Portfolio Optimization. Nonlinear Analysis: Real World Applications 10(4), 2396–2406 (2009)
11. Kennedy, J., Eberhart, R.C., Shi, Y.: Swarm Intelligence. The Morgan Kaufmann series in evolutionary computation, San Francisco (2001)
12. Clerc, M.: Particle Swarm Optimization, London (2006)

# Hybrid PSO Based Integration of Multiple Representations of Thermal Hand Vein Patterns

Amioy Kumar, Madasu Hanmandlu, and H.M. Gupta

Biometrics Research Laboratory, Department of Electrical Engineering,
Indian Institute of Technology Delhi, Hauz Khas, New Delhi, India-110016

**Abstract.** This paper outlines a novel personal authentication approach by integrating the multiple feature representations of thermal hand vein patterns. In the present work, vein patterns are regarded as comprising textures. Accordingly two types of texture features using Gabor wavelets and fuzzy logic are extracted from the acquired vein images. Since both the approaches have different domains of feature representation, their integration is accomplished at the decision level by incorporating individual decisions using the Euclidean distance based classifiers. The optimal decision parameters comprising individual decision thresholds and one fusion rule out of 16 rules for two features are estimated with the help of hybrid Particle Swarm Optimization (PSO) which can optimize the decisions taken by the individual classifiers. The experimental results carried out on 100 user database are promising thus confirming the usefulness of the proposed authentication system.

**Index Terms:** Hand veins, Gabor wavelets, Fuzzy Features, and Hybrid PSO.

## 1 Introduction

The gaining popularity of the vein patterns as a promising biometric trait is due to its reliability, uniqueness, and power to defy imposter attacks whenever deployed for personal authentication. Beneath the skin, vein patterns are too hard to intercept for an intruder, hence is a safer biometric trait. In this paper, our efforts are focused on developing an online biometric system using thermal hand vein patterns from palm dorsa. The vein patterns are represented using multiple features and integrated at the decision level. The proposed system is automatic and dynamically selects the optimal decision parameters, like individual thresholds and fusion rule [10] for online authentication tasks.

Hand based vein patterns is well researched for personal authentication and mainly pertain to the palmer part [5], the dorsal part [2] [3] and the finger veins [6]. Extraction of multiple features and their integration based on some fusion rules have been the subject matter of several researchers [1] [7]. A fine review of related works on vein authentication is presented in [8]. In most of the published work [1] [2] [3] [4], the veins patterns are represented by their skeletons. However, vein patterns are not perceivable sometimes during the acquisition due to acquisition complexities and lead to high False Acceptance Rates (FAR>1%) [1] [7]. We, therefore, opt for the texture

B.K. Panigrahi et al. (Eds.): SEMCCO 2010, LNCS 6466, pp. 246–253, 2010.

based approaches for multiple feature representation; which relies upon the arrangement of the acquired patterns. Further, the decision level integration approach that uses the binary fusion rule [10] in the proposed system allows a user to choose the best decision parameters according to the applications. Thus, designing an online authentication system by minimizing the error rates, especially FAR, is a prime motivation for the proposed work.

The block diagram of the complete system is shown in Fig. 1. It involves automatic extraction of vein patterns, multiple features, and selection of all the decision points for the final integrated decision for online authentication. The organization of the paper is as follows: The image acquisition system and the extraction of ROI (Region of Interest) are detailed in Section 2. Two types of texture representations by Gabor wavelets and fuzzy logic are described in Section 3. The decision level fusion accomplished through hybrid PSO is briefed in Section 4. Experimental results are relegated to Section 5. Finally conclusions are provided in Section 6.

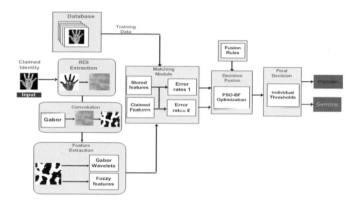

**Fig. 1.** Block diagram for online authentication using hand vein patterns

## 2   Image Acquisition and Roi Extraction

In the present work, infrared thermographic camera is used for the image acquisition. The camera is mounted on a wooden stand at a height of $1m$ above the base table. The users are allowed to freely put their hand in front of the camera inside the box in a place earmarked for the hand; lest it would be out of focus. The imaging setup and the acquired image are shown in Fig. 2.

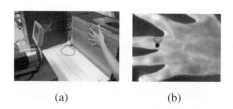

(a)                          (b)

**Fig. 2.** (a) Camera Setup. (b) Captured Image.

The ROI extraction method, somewhat similar to [1], involves the use of the web-bings between the fingers to define a coordinate system. The webbings are taken between the middle finger and the index finger, and between the little finger and the ring finger. The algorithm for extracting the ROI is same as in [8]. Fig. 3 show steps involved in ROI extraction of acquired vein images.

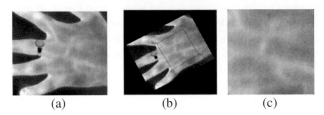

(a)                    (b)                    (c)

**Fig. 3.** (a) Vein image (b) Located square ROI area on Palm dorsa (c) Extracted ROI

## 3   Multiple Feature Extraction

Multiple feature representations help achieve better performance from biometric modalities in comparison to single feature representation. However, selecting the effective features is a precursor to getting better performance. A literature survey reveals that texture based feature extraction has rarely attempted on the vein patterns though it has already made inroads into fingerprint and Palmprint. However, many of these approaches suffer from the inability to bring forth the inner and coarse level information from the texture patterns. This pitfall substantiates our resolve to go for multiple feature representations, using Gabor wavelets [8] and fuzzy features by partitioning the ROIs into sliding windows.

### 3.1   Gabor Wavelets

In general a 1D wavelet transform decomposes an image $f(x, y)$ into a family of functions denoted by $\psi_{m,n}(x)$, through dilation and translation of the kernel function $\psi(x)$ expressed as:

$$\psi_{m,n}(x) = 2^{-\frac{m}{2}} \psi(2^{-m} x - n) \tag{1}$$

Where m is the dilation and n is the translation indices and the kernel $\psi(x)$ is called the mother wavelet. The mother wavelet is constructed using scaling functions made up of high pass and low pass filters at different levels of scaling. A family of functions can be generated by translating and scaling the mother wavelet. Similarly, a family of 2D Gabor wavelets is produced by choosing a Gabor based mother wavelet [8]. The Gabor wavelets are convolved with the partitioned windows and the overall standard deviation of this convolution is stored as a feature. The Gabor wavelet based feature extraction is the same as detailed in [8].

## 3.2  Fuzzy Based Features

The ambiguity in the spatial arrangement of the gray levels of the pixels in a window accounting for the spatial fuzziness cannot be dealt with the frequency domain transforms and requires a separate treatment. One way to represent this ambiguity is by providing a degree of association in the form of a membership function to the gray level property. The basic idea is to assign a membership function to each neighboring pixel with respect to the central pixel of the partitioned window so as to account for the random arrangement of gray levels in the neighborhood. The cumulative response of all the pixels in the window is calculated using their membership functions yielding a feature. The algorithm used to extract fuzzy based features is outlined below:

1.  Divide a ROI into a number of non-overlapping windows.
2.  Consider  the center pixel  in a window of size $WxW$ and calculate the average intensity $\bar{I}$ (i,j) in the window as :

$$\bar{I}(i, j) = \frac{1}{WxW - 1} \sum_{m,n \neq i,j}^{R} I(m,n) \tag{2}$$

3.  Find the maximum intensity, max I(i,j) in  the window.

4.  Replace the center pixel with $\bar{I}$ (i,j) and calculate $\mu_{ij}$  for every neighboring pixel from:

$$\mu_{i,j} = e^{-\left[\frac{\left|I(i,j)-\overline{I(i,j)}\right|}{\max I(i,j)}\right]} \tag{3}$$

Where N is varied from    1 to 2  with step size 0.1and the best performance is observed for N=2.

5.  For every window, calculate the cumulative response using:

$$FF = \frac{\sum\left(\mu_{ij} xI(i,j)\right)}{\sum \mu_{ij}} \tag{4}$$

The above is the fuzzy based feature and the dimension of the feature vectors equal to the number of windows in a ROI.

## 4  Decision Level Fusion

Camped with Gabor wavelet and fuzzy based features, we embark upon on their integration at the decision level fusion. The decision level fusion acts on the individual binary decisions [9] of the classifiers derived by applying the thresholds which are chosen to optimize the decisions. A notable work on the decision level fusion of two sensors using simulated data is traced to Ref. [10] which invokes (PSO) for the optimal selection of the decision threshold and fusion rules. This work was later validated on the database of palmprint and hand geometry in [9]. The present work follows the similar lines by adopting the same decision level fusion strategies but for integrating two feature representations of the vein patterns using a hybrid PSO.

## 4.1 Hybrid PSO Based Rule Selection

In PSO each particle is associated with some velocity according to which it moves in the multi-dimensional solution space and it also has memory to keep information of its previous visited space; hence its movement is influenced by two factors: the local best solution ($Pos_{id}$) due to itself and the global best solution ($Pos_{gd}$) due to all particles participating in the solution space [11]. The goal of the PSO is to optimally choose the decision parameters consisting of decision thresholds and a fusion rule out of 16 defined rules for two sensors [10]. The aim of choosing the decision parameters is to minimize the weighted sum of the overall errors; i.e. FAR and FRR. An objective function E is defined to optimize the error as:

$$\text{Minimize} \quad E = CFA * GFAR + CFR * GFRR. \tag{5}$$
$$CFR = 2 - CFA$$

Where CFA is the cost of falsely accepting an imposter, and CFR is the cost of falsely rejecting. GFAR and GFRR are the global error rates as derived in [10].

From the experiments carried out on the vein database it is observed that PSO sometimes gets stuck up in local minima causing premature convergence. This is because PSO lacks the direction to move in the solution space, which results in selecting some non-monotonic rules as the optimal one. Here the ability of choosing direction by Bacterial Foraging can be utilized. So the PSO is hybridized by incorporating the *tumble* and the *swim* operations of Bacteria Foraging (BF) to move in the direction of the hazardous and nutrient rich environments respectively [12]. A unit length random direction, say $\Delta(i)$, is generated for each swarm and this defines the direction of movement after a move. The hybrid PSO exploits the error resulting from the local and global best positions due to PSO and explores the solution space by the random direction due to BF. The convergence of the hybrid PSO is assured by the exploitation and exploration abilities bequeathed from PSO and BF.

Let us consider a *d*-dimensional solution space. The i$^{th}$ particle of the swarm can be represented as d-dimensional vector, $X_i = (x_{i1}, x_{i2}, ..., x_{id})$ where the first subscript denotes the particle number and the second subscript denotes the dimension. Coming to our problem we have d=2 with the first dimension denoting the FAR1 and the second dimension denoting the FAR2. The number of particles (swarms) is taken to be 15 after experimentation. The particle's own best position $Pos_{id}$ and the global best position $Pos_{gd}$ at $k^{th}$ iteration is updated by:

$$X_{id}^{K} = X_{id}^{K} + \left[ \frac{\Delta(i)}{\sqrt{\Delta(i)^{T}\Delta(i)}} \times \left\{ \alpha\left(Pos_{id} - X_{id}^{K+1}\right) + \beta\left(Pos_{gd} - X_{id}^{K+1}\right) \right\} \right] \tag{6}$$

Where i = 1,2,.....M; $\alpha$ and $\beta$ are the positive constants, called cognitive parameter and social parameter respectively and in our algorithm specified as 1 and 1.9 such that their sum is less than 4 [11]. If the move is a swim, Eq. (6) is updated in the generated direction and if the move is a tumble Eq. (5) is updated once in the reverse direction. Using the hybrid PSO, E (Eq. 5) is evaluated for the fixed cost CFA knowing fully well GFAR from FAR1and FAR2 for all the particles. The fusion rule corresponding to the minimum E gives GFAR and the threshold, which form our decision parameters [9].

## 5   Experimental Results

A database of 100 users with 10 images each is acquired at the Biometric research laboratory, IIT Delhi. Out of 10 enrolled images, five are randomly chosen for training and the remaining five for testing. The ROI of size $130 \times 130$ is extracted and enhanced by Gabor filter. The enhanced ROI is partitioned into 64 sliding windows of size $16 \times 16$ and Gabor wavelets at 0, 45, 90, and 135degrees are convolved to extract the first feature vector of size 256. Fuzzy feature vector of size 64 corresponding to 64 windows is the second one. The individual decisions are made using these two feature vectors based on the Euclidean distance. The ROC (Receiver operating characteristics) plot corresponding to each feature vector is shown in Fig. 4 (a).

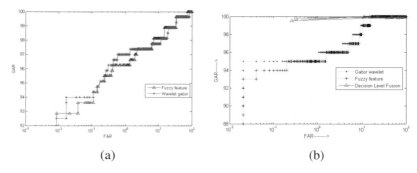

(a)                                (b)

**Fig. 4.** (a) ROC for Gabor wavelet and Fuzzy features (b) ROC curve for comparison of two features with decision level fusion

In the learning phase of the online authentication, the hybrid PSO helps learn the optimal decision parameters for the decision level fusion. Since the selection of decision parameters is largely dependent on the cost functions CFA, we vary CFA from 0.1 to 1.9 and the decision parameters which minimize E in (Eq. 5) corresponding to each CFA is chosen.

The vein database is divided into training and testing samples to validate the performance of the online verification. Out of 10 enrolled images, five are randomly chosen as training and the rest as testing. Each of the test vein images is matched with the training images by utilizing the decision parameters calculated at the training phase. With 100 users (10 samples each) the 500 genuine scores and 49500 imposter scores are generated using the Euclidean distance as the classifier. We find that no single user is rejected falsely while only one user accepted falsely; hence the classifier works with nearly 100% verification accuracy. The 5 enrolled training images of each user are compared with the test images of the rest 995 users and a correct match is noted down when two vein patterns belong to the same user. The GAR for the authentication system is found to be 99% at FAR of 0.1%. The ROC with regard to the identification using the decision level fusion of the two feature representations is shown in Fig. 4 (b).

The next set of experiments is performed at the score level using the averaged sum and product rule. The score level fusion gives GAR of 96% for FAR of 0.01%, whereas the decision level fusion with the selected fusion rules gives GAR of 99 % at FAR of 0.1% thus outperforming the score level fusion (Fig. 5 (a)).

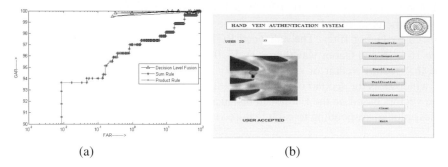

(a)                                    (b)

**Fig. 5.** (a) Comparison of averaged sum and product rules with decision level fusion (b) User Authentication using graphical user interface

The authentication system is implemented in MATLAB. The computational complexity is summarized in Table 1. The system runs on Intel dual core 2.1 GHz processor with 2 GB RAM and can operate at very fast processing speed (175ms). However, it may be noted that the time taken by the hybrid PSO for learning the decision parameters during training is not included in this processing time. This is because once the decision parameters are learned with hybrid PSO these are straightaway used in the online authentication. Fig. 5 (b) shows the online authentication system using GUI.

**Table 1.** Computational timings for key processes

| Process | Time (M. Sec) |
|---|---|
| Image Loading | 30 |
| ROI Extraction | 75 |
| Multiple Feature Extraction | 50 |
| Decision Fusion | 20 |

## 6   Conclusion

The infrared thermal vein patterns on the palm dorsa are investigated in the present work for online authentication. In order to minimize the errors incurred, particularly FAR, two texture feature representations are proposed, one using Gabor wavelets and the other using the fuzzy based features by partitioning the ROI into sliding windows of size 16 ×16 pixels. The decision level integration of the multiple features is facilitated through hybrid PSO. The main feature of the proposed online authentication is that it automatically decides the decision parameters based on the specific application yielding low FAR of 0.1% with high GAR of 99 %. The highpoint of the proposed authentication system is that it has a facility to trade off between FAR and FRR by switching among the fusion rules. The hybrid PSO is tested on 100 user database with 10 samples each and its performance found to be superior to other online biometric approaches.

The contributions of the work include the consideration of two texture representations based on Gabor wavelets and fuzzy features, integration of these two representations based on the decision level fusion, hybridization of PSO and lastly development of online authentication system.

# References

[1] Lin, C.-L., Fan, K.-C.: Biometric verification using thermal images of palm-dorsa vein patterns. IEEE transactions on circuits and systems for video technology 14, 199–213 (2004)

[2] Wang, L., Leedham, G.: A Thermal Hand Vein Pattern Verification System. In: Singh, S., Singh, M., Apte, C., Perner, P. (eds.) ICAPR 2005. LNCS, vol. 3687, pp. 58–65. Springer, Heidelberg (2005)

[3] Wang, L., Leedham, G., Cho, S.-Y.: Infrared imaging of hand vein patterns for biometric purposes. IET Compt. Vis. 1, 113–122 (2007)

[4] Wang, L., Leedham, G.: Near- and Far- Infrared Imaging for Vein Pattern Biometrics. In: IEEE Int. Conf. on Video Based Surveillance International Conference (2006)

[5] Malki, S., Spaanenburg, L.: Hand Veins Feature Extraction Using DT-CNNS. In: Proc. SPIE, vol. 6590 (2007)

[6] Miura, N., Nagasaka, A., Miyatake, T.: Feature Extraction of Finger-Vein Pattern Based on Repeated Line Tracking and its application to personal Identification. Machine Vision and Applications 15, 194–203 (2004)

[7] Wang, K., Zhang, Y., Yuan, Z., Zhuang, D.: Hand Vein Recognition Based on Multi Supplemental Features of Multi-Classifier Fusion Decision. In: Proceedings of the 2006 IEEE International Conference on Mechatronics and Automation, Luoyang, China (June 2006)

[8] Kumar, A., Hanmandlu, M., Gupta, H.M.: Online Biometric Authentication Using Hand Vein Patterns. In: IEEE Symposium: Computational Intelligence for Security and Defense Applications, Ottawa, Canada, July 8-10, (2009)

[9] Hanmandlu, M., Kumar, A., Madasu, V.K., Yarlagadda, P.: Fusion of Hand Based Biometrics using Particle Swarm optimization. In: Proc. of the Fifth Int. Conf. on Information Technology: New Generations, USA, pp. 783–788 (2008)

[10] Veeramachaneni, K., Osadciw, L.A., Varshney, P.K.: An Adaptive Multimodal Biometric Management Algorithm. IEEE Trans. On Systems, Man,and Cybernetics—Part C: Applications And Reviews 35(3) (August 2005)

[11] Eberhart, R.C., Kennedy, J.: A New Optimizer Using Particle Swarm Theory. In: Proceedings Sixth Symposium on Micro Machine and Human Science, pp. 39–43. IEEE Service Center, Piscataway (1995)

[12] Passino, K.M.: Biomimicry of Bacteria Foraging for Distributed Optimization and control. IEEE Control Systems Magazine (June 2002)

# Detection and Length Estimation of Linear Scratch on Solid Surfaces Using an Angle Constrained Ant Colony Technique

Siddharth Pal, Aniruddha Basak, and Swagatam Das

Department of Electronics and Telecommunications,
Jadavpur University, India
sidd_pal2002@yahoo.com, aniruddha_ju_etce@yahoo.com,
swagatamdas19@yahoo.co.in

**Abstract.** In many manufacturing areas the detection of surface defects is one of the most important processes in quality control. Currently in order to detect small scratches on solid surfaces most of the industries working on material manufacturing rely on visual inspection primarily. In this article we propose a hybrid computational intelligence technique to automatically detect a linear scratch from a solid surface and estimate its length (in pixel unit) simultaneously. The approach is based on a swarm intelligence algorithm called Ant Colony Optimization (ACO) and image preprocessing with Wiener and Sobel filters as well as the Canny edge detector. The ACO algorithm is mostly used to compensate for the broken parts of the scratch. Our experimental results confirm that the proposed technique can be used for detecting scratches from noisy and degraded images, even when it is very difficult for conventional image processing to distinguish the scratch area from its background.

**Keywords:** detection, quality control, image preprocessing, Canny edge detector, ant colony optimization.

## 1 Introduction

Image processing techniques are used for fault estimation and quality control in manufacturing industries with an objective of overcoming physical limitations and subjective judgment by humans. In [1] the authors propose to solve the complex problem of textile quality control by the means of computer vision using advanced digital signal and image processing tools. In [2], Qu *et al.* have used morphological gradient methods to detect wafer defects, a process that constitutes an important component of the quality control in IC production process.

There exists some interesting literature on scratch detection and removal from archival film sequences. Scratches can be detected using a 1-D signal obtained from local extreme of vertically sub-sampled image frames in [3]. The resultant 1-D signal is modeled as a damped-sinusoid to decide a scratch. A generalized form of the scratch model proposed in [3] is presented in [4]. This method extends Kokaram's scratch model and makes it work without any threshold adjustment. The generalized scratch detection method in [4] has better detection accuracy than [3], but still suffers from

B.K. Panigrahi et al. (Eds.): SEMCCO 2010, LNCS 6466, pp. 254–261, 2010.
© Springer-Verlag Berlin Heidelberg 2010

vertical edge features. Wavelet decomposition of image frames is employed to detect scratches in [5]. Approximation and vertical detail coefficients are employed in the detection step, and scratch restoration is also performed in the wavelet domain. Column variances of image frames are utilized with simple statistics in [6]. Scratch removal is handled as an optimization problem and solved using Genetic Algorithms (GAs) in this work. Temporal scratch detection is for the first time proposed in [7]. Scratch tracking is performed over vertically sub-sampled image frames employing Kalman filter in [7-9]. Recently, a Multiple Hypothesis Tracker (MHT) is utilized for scratch tracking in [10]. In the restoration stage low and high frequency components of the image frames are evaluated in different ways in [7-8]. Low frequency image parts are restored using polynomial interpolation while Fourier series are employed for high frequency components. In [10], the high frequency restoration process is performed using a MAP reconstruction approach. However, none of these techniques deal with the length estimation of scratch. Moreover these methods are mostly suitable for detecting prominent scratches from film sequences and usually fail in case of strong vertical image features and also if the brightness level of scratch pixels and background pixel have overlapping range. No wonder that none of these techniques commonly found in literature has so far been applied to the industry level problems of scratch finding and length estimation on flat solid surfaces.

For many solid material manufacturing industries detection and length estimation of small linear scratches on the surface of products form an essential part of fault diagnosis and quality control. Typically the scratches vary in width between 5 to 20 pixels and their length remains greater than or equal to 200 pixels.

The ant colony optimization algorithm (ACO) [14], introduced by Marco Dorigo, is a probabilistic technique for solving computational problems, which can be reduced to finding good paths through graphs. Ant colony optimization algorithms have been used to produce near-optimal solutions to the Travelling Salesman Problem (TSP) [15]. Some researchers have used ACO to solve specific image processing or machine vision problems, like imitation and reproduction of human vision perception and optical illusions[11], texture classification [12], and edge detection[12,13]. Inspired by the existing results here we employ an ACO module primarily to connect the broken pieces of a scratch from a preprocessed edge image.

## 2   The Proposed Method

We begin with a flowchart of the main modules of our method shown in Figure 1. Note that first in each loop the image is rotated through a certain angle and we preprocess the rotated image. The edge image is obtained in the final form after the preprocessing module of the flowchart. We expect that in this image the pixel value will be 1 if it had been present on an edge of the original image, otherwise it will be 0. The length of the longest scratch is obtained and if a scratch of significant length is found, it is forwarded to the Angle Constrained ACO(ACACO) module. The endpoints of the scratch, original image, and edge image is provided to that module. The scratch obtained might be in broken form and ACACO is applied to join the broken parts so that we can retrieve the original scratch in its entirety.

After having rotated the image from 0° to 180° and having got the endpoints of all the potential scratches, the endpoints of the scratch with the longest length is displayed.

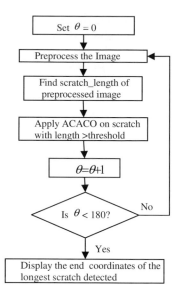

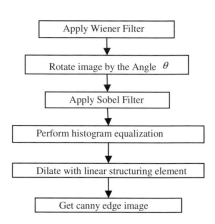

**Fig. 1.** Flow-chart of the scratch detection and length estimation method

**Fig. 2.** Flow-chart for the image preprocessing

## A. Image Preprocessing

In the preprocessing module of the image we apply three filters to the basic image and one morphological technique called *dilation*, with a linear structuring element. A flowchart of this module has been shown in Figure 2. Note that the Wiener filter is mainly used to remove noise in the original image. It filters the image adaptively, tailoring itself to the local image variance: where the variance is large it performs little smoothing and where the variance is more it performs more smoothing. This approach provides better results than linear filtering. It is more selective than a comparable linear filter, preserving edges and high frequency parts of an image. Experimentally Wiener filter gave much better results than the other filters in the present scenario.

In our algorithm we needed a horizontal edge emphasizing filter and the Sobel filter satisfies that requirement. Other edge filters would not give results as good as Sobel filter because they tend to catch edges in all directions. Results improve much more when we concentrate either in the horizontal or in the vertical direction. Finally having applied Sobel filter and dilated the image with the linear structuring element we find the scratches ending up as a few pixels wide in the processed image. For length calculations and for applying ACACO we take the Canny edge image so that now we have the boundary of the scratches.

Why vary angle during preprocessing of image? This would be the first question that would arise if someone reads the main flowchart. Say we are given a noisy image containing a scratch and we are required to obtain its length. The scratch might be detected as broken. We could use ACACO to join the broken scratches. For ACO or for any similar algorithm to work a proper edge image needs to be fed. Canny and

Sobel edge images alone are clearly unacceptable. Even in case of applying a combination of several filters, the Canny and Sobel edge images remain unhelpful. Here we rotate the Wiener filtered image by each degree and apply Sobel filter to it emphasizing the horizontal edges in the rotated image. Say we have a scratch at angle $\theta$. When the image is rotated by angle $\theta$, the scratch edges become prominent after applying Sobel filter.

The process of finding the length of a suspected scratch has been given below in the form of a pseudo-code:

## Module: Length Finding

```
Loop1:i=1 to no_rows
    Loop2:j =1 to no_columns
            If at i^{th} row and j^{th} column, 1 is detected in canny
            edge image
                    Proceed
            Else
                    Goto Loop2
            Find all the pixels on the scratch by recursion
            Find scratch length using the logic that the endpoints
            must be farthest away and the no other pair of pixels
            can be found which are separated by a greater distance
            If scratch_length>threshold
                    Send canny edge image,original image,
                    endpoints to ACACO module
    end(for loop2)
end(for loop1)
```

## B. Angle Constrained ACO (ACACO) Technique

The basic flowchart listing the various steps of the algorithm is shown in figure 3. The ants are initialized on the endpoints at the beginning of each run. In each run every ant completes one tour. In that tour it either finds endpoint to another scratch , finds the edge of a scratch or remains unsuccessful in finding anything significant. For the first two cases the ant will have a chance of depositing pheromone. Once endpoint of a scratch is detected then we will check whether the alignments of the two scratches are similar or not. If so, then we will join the two scratches virtually by updating the endpoint of the scratch.

We will first explain the rules governing ACO evolution and then move on to describe the modifications involved in Angle Constrained approach in ACACO module.

Suppose ant is at pixel $i$. In a single step it can move only to a neighboring pixel. Let the set of neighboring pixels maintaining angle constraints be $Y$. We will discuss the Angle constraints later in this section.

The next step of an ant is governed primarily by two factors, pheromone level and path visibility factor. The pheromone deposition level between pixel $i$ and pixel $j$ is

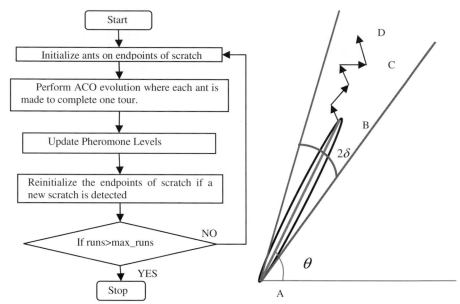

**Fig. 3.** Flowchart showing the basic Steps of ACACO module

**Fig. 4.** Image showing the angle constraints

expressed as $\tau_{i,j}$. The path visibility factor between pixel $i$ and pixel $j$ is given in equation 1.

$$\eta_{i,j} = \max\left(1/|image(i)-image(j)|,1\right) \quad (1)$$

The pixel to which the ant will travel next from pixel $i$ is given in equation 2.

$$pixel_{next} = \operatorname*{argmax}_{j\in Y}\left\{\left[\tau_{i,j}\right]^{\alpha}\left[\eta_{i,j}\right]^{\beta}\right\} \quad \text{if } r\le r_0 \left.\begin{array}{c} \\ \\ \end{array}\right\}$$
$$= J \qquad\qquad\qquad \text{otherwise} \qquad (2)$$

where,

$r$ denotes a random variable (0,1),J is a randomly determined neighboring pixel satisfying angle constraints.

In figure 4 ants are shown to be initialized at the endpoints of the scratch detected ie $A(x_1, y_1)$ and $B(x_2, y_2)$. Suppose the ant has traveled from pixel $B(x_2, y_2)$ to $C(x_3, y_3)$. Let us assume that the ant is considering to move to $D(x_4, y_4)$ from $C(x_3, y_3)$. We require that the line DA not make an angle greater than $\delta$ with line AB. Thus the angular field of view of the ants is restricted to $2\delta$. This is shown in equation 3.

$$\left|\tan^{-1}\left(\frac{y_4 - y_1}{x_4 - x_1}\right) - \theta\right| \le \delta \quad (3)$$

The canny edge image gives us the boundary of the scratches. If the image is very noisy such that the scratch is very hard to detect then the image processing techniques might read a single scratch as a series of broken scratches. We used ACO to join the broken scratches. To be joined the broken scratches need to be favorably aligned. Even path visibility factor must be taken into account to ensure that they were a part of a single scratch.

The pheromone level is updated using the formula:

$$\tau_{ij} = \tau_{ij} + \frac{1}{tour\_length} \qquad (4)$$

After the contribution of all successful ants has been considered the pheromone trail is evaporated by equation 5.

$$\tau_{ij} = (1 - \zeta)\tau_{ij} + \zeta\tau_0 \qquad (5)$$

where $\zeta$ is the pheromone evaporation rate, $0 \leq \zeta \leq 1$, $\tau_0$ is the initial pheromone level. It is evident that we have adapted the ants to search along the line so that iterations required is minimized. The ants deposit pheromone along the paths where they find edge pixels. Using this heuristic information they finally find the endpoint.

## 3   Experimental Results

The values of the various parameters of our algorithm are given below-

- Threshold for minimum scratchlength = 40 pixels
- Parameters pertaining to ACO evolution were chosen as $\alpha = 1, \beta = 2$.
- Initial value of pheromone trail $\tau_0 = .0001$.
- Local pheromone evaporation ratio $\xi = .1$
- Number of ants=7, max_runs=20.

The angle constrained ACO technique(ACACO) can be used to detect scratches from extremely noisy images after the preprocessing techniques are applied as described in section 3. Figure 5 is the first test image that we have considered which shows a than scratch on a solid metal surface. The image is a real life image and the scratch can barely be made out by the naked eye. Figure 6 shows the canny edge image of the test image. The edge images carry no information about the scratch present in original image. Figure 7 shows the preprocessed image. We see that the preprocessing technique specially adapted for linear scratches detects them when the image is rotated by $74^0$. This means that the scratch makes an angle of $74^0$ with the horizontal x-axis. However the figure detects the scratches in broken form. We need to run the ACACO module to join the broken scratches. Then we run the Length-finding module discussed in section 3.1 to estimate the length of scratch. The final detected image is shown in figure 8 and the scratch was found to be 117.4436 pixels long. In figure 8 the movement of ants is shown  clearly joining the two detected scratches of figure 7.

**Fig. 5.** 1st Test Image

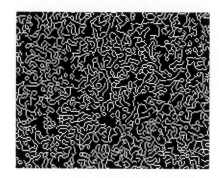

**Fig. 6.** Canny Edge Image of Figure 5

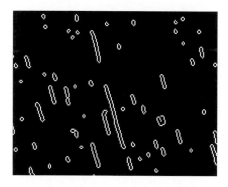

**Fig. 7.** Preprocessed Image

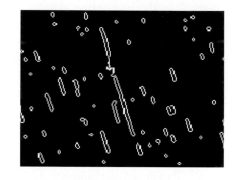

**Fig. 8.** Final Detected Image of Test Image 1

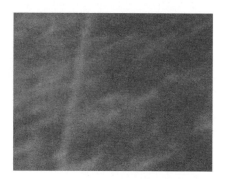

**Fig. 9.** 2nd Test Image

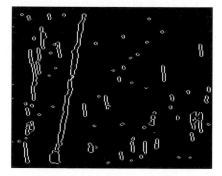

**Fig. 10.** Final Detected Image of Test Image 2

However a third linear scratch detected in the lower side of figure 7 could not be joined probably because they are not a part of a single scratch. This is where the path visibility factor of the ants comes into picture. In figure 9 we have considered a linear scratch on a wooden surface. Figure 10 shows the detected image. The image shows the ants joining the two broken parts detected by preprocessing algorithms. The scratch length was found to be 240.8755 pixels long.

# 4  Conclusion

The method of detecting linear scratches from extremely noisy images has been discussed in this paper. First we have discussed a preprocessing technique which effectively detects linear scratches. It must be remembered that the preprocessing technique has been specially designed for linear structures. This modification was important to reduce the complexity of our algorithm and make it viable for real time image processing.

# References

[1]  Cay, A., Vassiliadis, S., Rangoussi, M., Tarakçıoglu, I.: On the use of image processing techniques for the estimation of the porosity of textile fabrics. World Academy of Science, Engineering and Technology 2 (2005)

[2]  Qu, G., Wood, S.L., Teh, C.: Wafer Defect Detection Using Directional Morphological Gradient Techniques. EURASIP Journal on Applied Signal Processing 2002(7), 686–703 (2002)

[3]  Kokaram, A.: Detection and removal of line scratch in degraded motion picture sequences. In: VIII European Signal Processing Conference (EUSIPCO), Trieste, Italy, pp. 5–8 (September 1996)

[4]  Bruni, V., Vitulano, D.: A generalized model for scratch detection. IEEE Transactions on Image Processing 13(1), 44–50 (2004)

[5]  Bretschneider, T., Kao, O., Bones, P.J.: Removal of vertical scratches in digitised historical film sequences using wavelet decomposition. In: Image and Vision Computing New Zealand (IVCNZ), Dunedin, New Zealand, pp. 38 43 (November 2000)

[6]  Tegolo, D., Isgro, F.: Scratch detection and removal from static images using simple statistics and genetic algorithms. In: IEEE International Conference on Image Processing (ICIP), Thessaloniki Greece, pp. 265–286 (October 2001)

[7]  Joyeux, L., Buisson, O., Besserer, B., Boukir, S.: Detection and removal of line scratches in motion picture films. In: IEEE Conf. on Computer Vision and Pattern Recognition, pp. 548–553. Ft. Collins, Co., USA (1999)

[8]  Joyeux, L., Buisson, O., Besserer, B., Boukir, S.: Reconstruction of degraded image sequences. Application to film restoration, Image and Vision Computing 19(8), 503–516 (2001)

[9]  Joyeux, L., Besserer, B., Boukir, S.: Tracking and map reconstruction of line scratches in degraded motion pictures. Machine Vision and Application 13(3), 119–128 (2002)

[10]  Besserer, B., Thire, C.: Detection and tracking scheme for line scratch removal in an image sequence. In: Pajdla, T., Matas, J(G.) (eds.) ECCV 2004. LNCS, vol. 3023, pp. 264–275. Springer, Heidelberg (2004)

[11]  Vallone, U., Mérigot, A.: Imitating human visual attention and reproduction optical allusion by ant scan. Internat. J. Comput. Intell. Appl. 3, 157–166 (2003)

[12]  Zhuang, X., Mastorakis, N.E.: Image processing with the artificial swarm intelligence. WSEAS Trans. Comput. 4, 333–341 (2005)

[13]  Lu, D.-S., Chen, C.-C.: Edge detection improvement by ant colony optimization. Pattern Recognition Letters 29, 416–425 (2008)

[14]  Dorigo, M., Stutzle, T.: Ant Colony Optimization. MIT Press, Cambridge (2004)

[15]  Dorigo, M., Gambardella, L.M.: Ant Colony System : A Cooperative Learning Approach to the Traveling Salesman Problem. IEEE Transactions on Evolutionary Computation 1(1), 53–66 (1997)

# An Intelligence Model with Max-Min Strategy for Constrained Evolutionary Optimization

Xueqiang Li[1], Zhifeng Hao[2], and Han Huang[3]

[1] School of Computer Science and Engineering, South China University of Technology,
Guangzhou, 510006, China
[2] Faculty of Computer, Guangdong University of Technology, Guangzhou, 510006, China
[3] School of Software Engineering, South China University of Technology,
Guangzhou, 510006, P.R. China
lxqchn@163.com

**Abstract.** An intelligence model (IM) is proposed for constrained optimization in this paper. In this model, two main issues are considered: first, handling feasible and infeasible individuals in population, and second, recognizing the piecewise continuous Pareto front to avoid unnecessary search, it could reduce the amount of calculation and improve the efficiency of search. In addition, max-min strategy is used in selecting optimization. By integrating IM with evolutionary algorithm (EA), a generic constrained optimization evolutionary (IMEA) is derived. The new algorithm is applied to tackle 7 test instances on the CEC2009 MOEA competition, and the performance is assessed by IGD metric, the results suggest that it outperforms or performs similarly to other algorithms in CEC2009 competition.

**Keywords:** Constrained Optimization Problems, Max-min Strategy, Evolutionary Algorithm, Intelligence Model.

## 1 Introduction

Constrained optimization problems (COPs) are usual problems in the fields of management science, and evolutionary algorithms (EAs) have been successfully used to solve global optimization problems. K. Deb [1] proposed Pareto comparison in NSGA- II , H. Liu and Y. Wang [2] applied max-min strategy in MOEA, Q. Zhang and H. Li [3] search optima in each adjoining section based on decomposition method, H. Liu and X. Li [4, 5] used dynamical crossover and mutation probability, designed the uniformity weight on spherical space and searched optima in the sub-regional for multiobjective problems (MOPs). During the last decade, some EAs with different constraint handling methods have been proposed, Michalewicz and Schoenauer [6], Coello [7] provided a comprehensive survey of the most popular constraint-handling techniques currently used with EAs, grouping them into four and five categories respectively, Y. Wang and Z. Cai [8] proposed an tradeoff model to deal with feasible and infeasible solutions, they considered three main issues in the paper, and Y. Gebre. Woldesenbet, G.G. Yen, and B. G. Tessema [9] proposed a constraint handling technique for multiobjective evolutionary algorithms based on an adaptive penalty

B.K. Panigrahi et al. (Eds.): SEMCCO 2010, LNCS 6466, pp. 262–269, 2010.

function and a distance measure, B. Y. Qu and P. N. Suganthan [10] used an ensemble of constraint handling methods (ECHM) to tackle constrained multiobjective optimization problems.

How to balance the feasible and infeasible solutions in evolutionary processes, and how to improve the effectiveness when the decision variables dimension is high and constraints with complex Pareto front is also a great challenge.

In real world, a feasible solution is more useful than an infeasible solution, because some constraint violations can not be made up, but some infeasible individuals may carry more important information, it is more easy for algorithm to find the final solution than feasible individuals in some generations. So how to balance this contradiction, some methods [6-10] adopt the tradeoff between the constraint violations and the objective function, but they are difficult to suit for various problems. In this paper, we propose a new method to deal with this contradiction between feasible and infeasible individuals for COPs, the method can give consideration to both kinds of individuals: first, in order to get more feasible individuals, feasible individuals will be priority selected after reproduction, it ensures the population contains more feasible individuals; second, under the max-min strategy, each weight reselects optimal individuals from the current population wherever it is feasible to reproduce new individuals, by this way the search can be more efficient.

Also, when the Pareto front of a COP is piecewise continuous, then using max-min strategy to search optimum will waste much computation on piecewise region. In this paper, through assessing the sum of the distances between different Pareto solutions selected by corresponding weight vectors in different directions, if the sum is larger than the average distance, then we consider the region corresponding to weight vector is piecewise, and this region will not be searched in reproduction.

At last, for every new individual, the constraints of individuals are computed first, because some individuals will be deleted before computing their fitness, it can reduce the amount of calculation in this way.

We evaluate the efficiency of this algorithm on 7 hard test instances on the CEC2009 MOEA competition. The performance is assessed by using the IGD metric, and experimental results indicate that IMEA of this paper outperforms or performs similarly to other algorithms in CEC2009 competition [12].

The remainder of this paper is organized as follows, section2 gives the fitness function, section 3 presents a detail review of handling feasible and infeasible individual, section 4 gives the method how to recognize the piecewise continuous Pareto front, section 5 shows the framework. In section 6 the experimental results of the IGD metric are reported. Finally, section 7 concludes this paper.

## 2 Construction of the Fitness Function

Without loss of generality, the model of COPs can be formulated as follows:

$$\begin{cases} \min f(x) = \left( f_1(x), f_2(x), ..., f_m(x) \right) \\ s.t \ \ g_i(x) \geq 0 \qquad i = 1, 2, \cdots, k \\ \qquad x \in X \subseteq R^n \end{cases} \tag{1}$$

where $x = (x_1, x_2, \cdots, x_n)^{\mathrm{T}}$, and $l_i \le x_i \le u_i, (i = 1, 2, \cdots, n)$, $f(x)$ is the objective vector, $g_i(x)$ $(i = 1, 2, \cdots, k)$ is the constraint function.

In this paper, the fitness function utilizes max-min strategy as literature [5]:

$$F_i(x) = \max_{1 \le j \le m} \left\{ w_j^i \log_2 \left(1 + f_j(x) - f_j^* \right) \right\}, i = 1, 2, \cdots N \tag{2}$$

where weight vectors $w^i$ $(i = 1, 2, \cdots, N)$ are uniform designed on the space sphere, $N$ is population scale, $f_j^*$ is the minimum of the objective function $f_j(x)$, it is approximated by the minimum of $f_j(x)$ appearing in evolutionary process.

## 3   Handling Feasible and Infeasible Individuals in Updating and Reproduction

The degree of constraint violation of $x^i (i = 1, 2, \cdots, N)$ is $h^i = \left| \sum_{j=1}^{k} h_j^i(x^i) \right|$, where $h_j^i(x^i) = \min\{0, g_j^i(x^i)\}$, $(j = 1, 2, \cdots, k)$. $h^i = 0$, if $x^i$ is feasible, and $h^i > 0$ otherwise.

### 3.1   The Feasible Individuals Priority in Updating Population

Suppose the current population is $\{x^1, x^2, \cdots, x^N\}$, which reproduce $M$ new individuals $\{\tilde{x}^1, \tilde{x}^2, \cdots, \tilde{x}^M\}$, and their constraint violation degrees are $\{h^1, h^2, \cdots, h^N\}$, and $\{\tilde{h}^1, \tilde{h}^2, \cdots, \tilde{h}^M\}$ respectively. The feasible priority is applied as follows:

Step 1. Count the total number $S$ of $\tilde{h}^j (j = 1, 2, \cdots, M)$ that is greater than 0, if $S > S_1$, then delete the individuals whose $\tilde{h}^j > 0$; if $S < S_2$, then remain $S_2$ smaller individuals, and delete the other new individuals, set $S = S_2$, suppose the remained new individuals are $\{\tilde{x}^{i_1}, \tilde{x}^{i_2}, \tilde{x}^{i_s}\}$. $S_1$ and $S_2$ are predetermined certain value, and $0 < S_2 < S_1 < M$.

Step 2. For each $w^i (i = 1, 2, \cdots, N)$, Calculate the fitness $\{F_i(\tilde{x}^{i_1}), F_i(\tilde{x}^{i_2}), \cdots, F_i(\tilde{x}^{i_s})\}$ of $\{\tilde{x}^{i_1}, \tilde{x}^{i_2}, \cdots, \tilde{x}^{i_s}\}$. If there exist feasible solutions in $\{\tilde{x}^{i_1}, \tilde{x}^{i_2}, \cdots, \tilde{x}^{i_s}\}$, and the fitness of the minimum feasible solution is less than $F_i(x^i)$ or $h^i < 0$, then exchange this solution with $x^i$, and exchange its fitness with $F_i(x^i)$; if there are no feasible solutions in $\{\tilde{x}^{i_1}, \tilde{x}^{i_2}, \cdots, \tilde{x}^{i_s}\}$, meanwhile $h^i < 0$ and the fitness of the minimum feasible solution is less than $F_i(x^i)$, then exchange this solution with $x^i$, and exchange its fitness with $F_i(x^i)$.

## 3.2 The Optimal Individuals Priority in Reproduction

In order to improve the efficiency of the search, one of individuals participating in reproduction should be better, so we select the optimal individuals by each $w^i (i = 1,2,\cdots, N)$ in current population to take part in cross, no mater whether they are feasible or infeasible, meanwhile, to avoid falling in the local convergence, the external storage method are used in this paper as [5].

## 4  Recognizing the Piecewise Continuous Pareto Front

For weight $w^i (i = 1,2,\cdots, N)$, the solutions selection is used by the max-min strategy: $x^i = \arg \min_{j=1\cdot N} \max_{l=1\cdot m} \{w_l^i f_l^j\}$. While $m=2$, and the distribution of rounds respect Pareto solutions are showed in figure 1, for each $w^i (i = 1,2,\cdots, N)$, three cases are discussed:

(1)  if $(f_1^j, f_2^j)$  is  on  the  weight  ray,  then  $w_1^i f_1^j = w_2^i f_2^j$ ,  and $\max_{l=1:m}\{w_l^i f_l^j\} = w_1^i f_1^j$ or $w_2^i f_2^j$.

(2)   if $(f_1^j, f_2^j)$  is  over  the  weight  ray,  then  $w_1^i f_1^j < w_2^i f_2^j$ , $\max_{l=1:m} \{w_l^i f_l^j\} = w_2^i f_2^j$.

(3) if $(f_1^j, f_2^j)$ is under the weight ray, then $w_1^i f_1^j > w_2^i f_2^j$ , $\max_{l=1:m} \{w_l^i f_l^j\} = w_1^i f_1^j$.

Obviously, when points over the weight ray, the search is according to the value of $f_2$ and when points under the weight ray, otherwise the search is according to the value of $f_1$, so point $(\tilde{f}_1, \tilde{f}_2)$ will be selected over the $w^i$ ray, and point $(f_1^*, f_2^*)$ will be selected under the $w^i$ ray in the fig 1 for the minimum solution.

While $m>2$, Pareto solutions are divided into $m$ areas by each $w^i (i=1,2,\cdots,N)$, and Pareto points are selected by the value of $f_l$ in $l$-th $(l = 1,2,\cdots,m)$ areas by $w^i$, then $m$ optimal Pareto solutions will be selected by $w^i$.

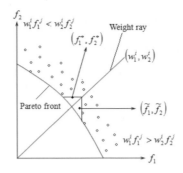

**Fig. 1.** The solutions selection through max-min strategy in two-dimensional space

If there are holes in Pareto front, some regions will be no intersection point between some weight rays with Pareto front as shown in fig 2, but $m$ optimal Pareto solutions will also be selected by each of this weight vectors, and the distance between this $m$ optimal Pareto solutions will be very large; if there exists an intersection point, the value will be small, so whether a region has hole or not can be judged by the distance of Pareto solutions selected by each weight ray $w^j (i = 1, 2, \cdots, N)$.

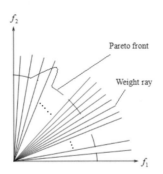

**Fig. 2.** The solutions selection when holes in Pareto space

Recognizing piecewise continuous Pareto front is as follows:

Step 1. For each $w^i (i = 1, 2 \cdots, N)$, $m$ Pareto solutions $\left\{ f^{i_1}, f^{i_2}, \cdots, f^{i_m} \right\}$ will be selected, where $f^{i_j} = (f_1^{i_j}, f_2^{i_j}, \cdots, f_m^{i_j})^T, j = 1, 2, \cdots, m.$

Step 2. Set $\bar{f}_l^i = \dfrac{\sum\limits_{j=1}^{m} f_l^{i_j}}{m}, l = 1, 2, \cdots, m$ , set $\bar{d} = \dfrac{d^i}{N}$ , where $d^i = \dfrac{\sum\limits_{j=1}^{m} d(\bar{f}^i, f^{i_j})}{m}$ ,

$\bar{f}^i = (\bar{f}_1^i, \bar{f}_2^i, \cdots, \bar{f}_m^i)^T.$

Step 3. For each $w^i (i = 1,2\cdots, N)$, if the $d^i$ is greater than $2\overline{d}$, the region of the corresponding weight $w^i$ ray is considered piecewise continuous.

## 5  The Main Framework of Algorithm

The framework of algorithm based on above chapters.

Step 1. Initialize the population $\{x^1, x^2, \cdots, x^N\}$ and external storage, design the weight vectors $w^i (i = 1,2\cdots, N)$, calculate the $f_j^* (j = 1,2,\cdots, m)$, set the maximum computation times $Mg$ and the mutation probability $P_m$.

Step 2. Reproduction: For $i$ = 1 to $N$

2.1 For each $w^i$, select an optimal individual $\overline{x}^i$ form population as subsection 3.2, and calculate $d^i$ and $2\overline{d}$ as section 4. If $d^i < 2\overline{d}$ and $r \le P$, then select another individual $\hat{x}^i$ from $i$ -th external storage to participate in reproduction; If $d^i < 2\overline{d}$ and $r > P$, then select another crossover individuals from population to participate in reproduction; otherwise reproduction will not be executed, where $r$ is a random number in $[0,1]$.

2.2  Crossover: $\tilde{x}^{ic} = \overline{x}^i + rc \cdot (\overline{x}^i - \hat{x}^i)$, where $rc = r_1 \cdot \left(1 - r_2^{-\left(1-\left(\frac{gen}{Mg}\right)^{0.5}\right)}\right)$,

$r_1$ is a random number in $[-1,1]$ and $r_2$ is a random number in $[0,1]$.

2.3  Mutation: $x_h^i = \tilde{x}_h^{ic} + rm * (ub(h) - lb(h))$ where $h \in \{1,2,3,\cdots, n\}$ with probability $P_m$, and $rm = r_1 \cdot \left(1 - r_2^{\left(1-\left(\frac{gen}{Mg}\right)^{0.5}\right)}\right)$, where $r_1$ and $r_2$ are got as above.

Step 3. Update the population performing as subsection 3.1, external storage and $f_j^* (j = 1,2,\cdots, m)$ are updated as in paper [5].

Step 4. If $gen \le Mg$, go to step2; otherwise, stop.

## 6  Computer Simulation

We simulate 7 constrained multiobjective test functions from the literature [12] by computer. The IGD metric has been defined in paper [11]. The parameters of algorithm are set as follows:

Set $P_m = 1/n$, the population size $N = 100$ for two objective problems, $N = 150$ for three objective problems, and $N = 762$ for five objective problems, set $Mg = 300000$.

The Configuration of computer in simulation is: System: Windows XP Professional sp3; RAM: 1G; CPU: T2050; CPU 1.60 GHz; Computer Language: Matlab 7.0.

**Table 1.** The average IGD metric by each algorithm in 30 runs for each test function

| Algorithms | CF1 | CF2 | CF3 | CF4 | CF5 | CF6 | CF7 |
|---|---|---|---|---|---|---|---|
| MOEADGM | 0.0108 | 0.008 | 0.5134 | 0.0707 | 0.5446 | 0.2071 | 0.5356 |
| LiuLi-Algorithm | 0.00085 | 0.0042 | 0.18291 | 0.01423 | 0.10973 | 0.01395 | 0.10446 |
| DMOEA-DD | 0.01131 | 0.0021 | 0.05631 | 0.00699 | 0.01577 | 0.01502 | 0.01905 |
| NSGAIILS | 0.00692 | 0.01183 | 0.23994 | 0.01576 | 0.1842 | 0.02013 | 0.23345 |
| MTS | 0.01918 | 0.02677 | 0.10446 | 0.01109 | 0.02077 | 0.01616 | 0.02469 |
| GDE3 | 0.0294 | 0.01597 | 0.12751 | 0.00799 | 0.06799 | 0.06199 | 0.04169 |
| DECMOSASQP | 0.10773 | 0.0946 | 100000 | 0.15265 | 0.41275 | 0.14782 | 0.26049 |
| IMEA | 0.000237 | 0.00302 | 0.18392 | 0.02002 | 0.31531 | 0.05041 | 0.09867 |

The simulation results of IGD metric in table1 indicate that the algorithm (IMEA) of this paper finds almost more optimal solutions of CF1, CF2, CF6 and CF7, and performs simulation with other algorithms in CF3-CF5, it shows this algorithm is effective. The test function is hard for algorithm to find the optimal solutions, so we will do more work on improving the search efficiency in future work.

## 7   Conclusions

This paper has proposed an intelligence model with max-min strategy for constrained evolutionary optimization, called IMEA. During the updating the feasible individuals are first selected to ensure the algorithm search more new feasible solutions, and in reproduction the optimal individuals are selected to participate in reproduction, which makes the algorithm search more optimal solutions. Also a method recognizing the piecewise continuous Pareto front method is executed to avoid unnecessary search, and the external storage is used to avoid local convergence. At last, the algorithm is applied to tackle 7 test instances on the CEC2009 MOEA competition, and the performance is assessed by using IGD metric, the results suggest that it outperforms or performs similarly to other algorithms in CEC2009 competition.

## Acknowledgment

This work is supported by National Natural Science Foundation of China (61003066, 61070033), Doctoral Program of the Ministry of Education (20090172120035), Natural Science Foundation of Guangdong Province (9151008901000165), Key Technology Research and Development Programs of Guangdong Province (2009B010800026) and Fundamental Research Funds for the Central Universities, SCUT(2009ZM0052). The authors are grateful to Mr. Zhang Yu Shan, Ms. Zhang Xiao Ling, the anonymous associate editor and anonymous referees.

## References

1. Deb, K., Pratap, A., Agarwal, S., Meyarivan, T.: A fast and elitist multiobjective genetic algorithm: NSGA-II. IEEE Transactions on Evolutionary Computation 6(2), 182–197 (2002)
2. Liu, H.-l., Wang, Y.: A novel multiobjective evolutionary algorithm based on minmax strategy. In: Liu, J., Cheung, Y.-m., Yin, H. (eds.) IDEAL 2003. LNCS, vol. 2690. Springer, Heidelberg (2003)
3. Zhang, Q., Li, H.: MOEA/D: A Multi-objective Evolutionary Algorithm Based on Decomposition. IEEE Trans. on Evolutionary Computation 11(6), 712–731 (2007)
4. Liu, H.-l., Li, X., Chen, Y.: Multi-Objective Evolutionary Algorithm Based on Dynamical Crossover and Mutation. In: Proceedings International Conference on Computational Intelligence and Security CIS 2008, vol. 1, pp. 150–155 (2008)
5. Liu, H.-l., Li, X.: The multiobjective evolutionary algorithm based on determined weights and sub-regional search. In: 2009 IEEE Congress on Evolutionary Computation, CEC 2009, pp. 1928–1934 (2009)
6. Michalewicz, Z., Schoenauer, M.: Evolutionary algorithm for constrained parameter optimization problems. Evolutionary Computation 4(1), 1–32 (1996)
7. Coello, C.A.C.: Theoretical and numerical constraint-handling techniques used with evolutionary algorithms: A survey of the state of the art. Comput. Meth. Appl. Mech. Eng. 191(11-12), 1245–1287 (2002)
8. Wang, Y., Cai, Z., Zhou, Y., Zeng, W.: An Adaptive Tradeoff Model for Constrained Evolutionary Optimization. IEEE Trans. on Evolutionary Computation 12(1), 80–92 (2008)
9. Woldesenbet, Y.G., Yen, G.G., Tessema, B.G.: Constraint Handling in Multiobjective Evolutionary Optimization. IEEE Trans. on Evolutionary Computation 13(3), 514–525 (2009)
10. Qu, B.Y., Suganthan, P.N.: Constrained multi-objective optimization algorithm with ensemble of constraint handling methods, Engineering Optimization (in press, 2010)
11. Zitzler, E., Thiele, L., Laumanns, M., Fonseca, C.M., da Fonseca, V.G.: Performance assessment of multiobjective optimizers: An analys is and review. IEEE Trans. Evol. Comput. 7(2), 117–132 (2003)
12. Zhang, Q., Suganthan, P.N.: Final Report on CEC'09 MOEA Competition, Working Report, CES-887, School of Computer Science and Electrical Engineering, University of Essex (2008),
    http://dces.essex.ac.uk/staff/qzhang/MOEAcompetition/
    cecmoeafinalreport.pdf

# Parallel Ant-Miner (PAM) on
# High Performance Clusters

Janaki Chintalapati[1], M. Arvind[2], S. Priyanka[1],
N. Mangala[1], and Jayaraman Valadi[3]

[1] Center for Development of Advanced Computing, Bangalore, India
[2] Currently working with Samsung, Bangalore
[3] Center for Development of Advanced Computing, Pune, India
{janaki,priyankas,mangala}@cdacb.ernet.in,
arvind.maan@gmail.com, jayaramanv@cdac.in

**Abstract.** This study implements parallelization of Ant-Miner for classification rules discovery. Ant-Miner code is parallelized and optimized in a cluster environment by employing master-slave model. The parallelization is achieved in two different operations of Ant-Miner viz. discretization of continuous attributes and rule construction by ants. For rule mining operation, ants are equally distributed into groups and sent across the different cluster nodes. The performance study of Parallel Ant-Miner (PAM) employs different publicly available datasets. The results indicate remarkable improvement in computational time without compromising on the classification accuracy and quality of discovered rules. Dermatology data having 33 features and musk data having 168 features were taken to study performance with respect to timings. Speedup almost equivalent to ideal speedup was obtained on 8 CPUs with increase in number of features and number of ants. Also performance with respect to accuracies was done using lung cancer data.

**Keywords:** Rule mining, ACO, Parallel Ant-miner, Discretization, Garuda Grid.

## 1 Introduction

Rule Mining may be defined as a technique to find out potentially useful patterns from data or a method for discovering interesting relations between variables in large databases. Ant-Miner is a rule mining method based on Ant colony algorithm (ACO). In the real world, ants (initially) wander randomly, and upon finding food return to their colony while laying down pheromone trails. ACO algorithm introduced by Marco Dorigo is inspired by the behavior of ants in finding paths from the colony to food (M. Dorigo et.al., 2006, Shelokar et al. 2004a) etc.

Recently, ACO has also shown application in rule mining for discovery of classification rules in a given dataset (Parpinelli et al. 2002; Allen & Alex 2006; and Shelokar et al. 2004b). In this rule mining algorithm called Ant-Miner, software ants generate rules by using heuristic information and pheromone communication. At each iteration, the rules constructed by different ants are evaluated and the rule with

B.K. Panigrahi et al. (Eds.): SEMCCO 2010, LNCS 6466, pp. 270–277, 2010.

highest prediction quality is denoted as a discovered rule, which represents information extracted from the dataset. Instances correctly covered by the discovered rule are removed from the training set, and another iteration is started. This process is repeated for as many iterations as necessary to find rules covering almost all cases in the training set.

In this study, we propose parallel implementation of Ant-Miner. This is achieved at two stages of Ant-Miner algorithm, viz. discretization of continuous attributes (the present version of Ant-Miner handles attributes with only categorical values) and rule construction process (ant starts with empty rule and incrementally builds the rule by adding terms). We have observed these two tasks demand more computational resources and their parallel implementation can substantially speed the rule mining operation by Ant-Miner. In parallel Ant-Miner, each processor (slave) applies Ant-Miner algorithm locally where certain number of ants generate rules using pheromone and heuristic information. Once all the processors submit their output to the master, best discovered rule is obtained and the global pheromone information is updated. The instances covered by the best rule are removed from the training set and the process is repeated till most of the instances in the training set are covered or the algorithm has discovered sufficient number of rules. Recently, Roozmand and Zamanifar (2008) proposed parallel implementation of Ant-Miner. In their approach, at each processor (slave) ants construct rules whose consequent is a given class label only. This approach is different in many ways than our proposed implementation. In our approach, at a processor ants essentially can construct rules having different class labels. Also, the master store all the discovered rules in a separate rule set in the order of discovery.

## 2 Parallel Ant-Miner Implementation

The current parallel implementation of Ant-Miner is done based on profiling where the serial code is profiled to see the most time consuming part.

### 2.1 Discretization

While profiling the serial code for Rule Mining, it was observed that approximately 50% of the time is used for discretizing the data (as shown in Fig 1). The task of extracting knowledge from databases is quite often performed by machine learning algorithms. The majority of these algorithms can be applied only to data described by discrete numerical or nominal attributes (features). In the case of continuous attributes, there is a need for a discretization algorithm that transforms continuous attributes into discrete ones (Fan Min et al, 2005). So to convert input data into discrete, we have used algorithm, called CAIM (class-attribute interdependence maximization), which is designed to work with supervised data (Lukas et al 2004). The goal of the CAIM algorithm is to maximize the class-attribute interdependence and to generate a minimal number of discrete intervals. The algorithm does not require the user to predefine the number of intervals, as opposed to some other discretization algorithms. The tests performed using CAIM and six other state-of-the-art discretization algorithms show that discrete attributes generated by the CAIM algorithm almost always have the lowest number of intervals and the highest class-attribute interdependency. As discretization is seen to be taking more time after profiling, parallel implementation was done to convert discretizing (CAIM) into parallel discretizing using Flynn's taxonomy (SIMD) (Flynn M, 1972). We realized that discretization works on single row of matrix at one time independently. So to get discretized result fast, we took advantage of row wise discretization process. The input data is splitted into same size in term of number of rows and has been allotted to available processes corresponding to number of processors.

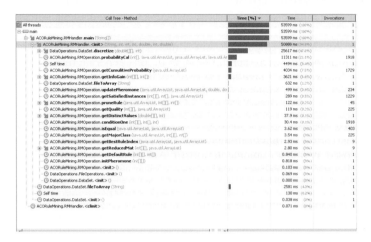

**Fig. 1.** Profiling shows Discretization to be taking maximum amount of time

The input file supplied to the code is read in the form of transpose matrix into a 2-D array. For each attribute, distinct values are checked, sorted and then stored in an array. Minimum and Maximum values are taken, and all possible intervals are stored in boundaryarray. Also, the original column values are maintained in currentAttr array. DScheme array holds minimum and maximum values and then gradually other interval values are added in the dScheme array from boundary list array.

## 2.2 Parallel Ant-Miner Algorithm (PAM) for Rule Mining

Parallel Ant-Miner Algorithm (PAM) is designed using Master Slave paradigm for rule mining, where master takes care of pheromone initialization and update, Attribute matrix reduction, best rule search. In PAM, each processor is assigned with a group of ants. Even master performs slave task to utilize resources efficiently. Each group of ants discovers its own local rules and sends back the data to the master process. A group of ants are allocated on the processor to search for the antecedent part of the rules.

As depicted in the Fig 2, Master process is responsible for pheromone updation, attribute matrix reduction and filtration of best rule. Discretized results from step1 become input to master process and it is the master process responsibility to broadcast input data to all other slave processes (other group of ants). Master process does pheromone initialization and hand pheromone matrix to slave processes, then slave makes use of pheromone values to generate local rules. Slave selects attributes based on probability calculation results and then forms new rule by judging its quality in terms of frequent usage of rule.  By use of efficient communication methods between ants, the algorithm become able to discover more high quality rules by reducing the speed of convergence and also avoid gathering irrelevant terms of the rule and decrease the time complexity of rule pruning. Rule pruning is done to find out best local rule. After rule pruning, new rule is added to local discovered rule list. If local discovered rules become more than covered rules or it doesn't get net attribute to traverse on the basis of probability calculation then all new local discovered rules are sent back to master process. Master process gathers local rules and their respective qualities from all groups of ants (different processes) and removes duplicate entries.

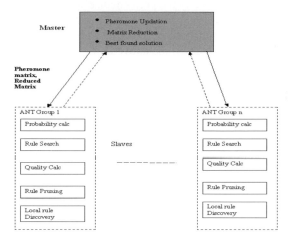

**Fig. 2.** Master-Slave Paradigm for Parallel Implementation of Ant-Miner

Master process calculates the best quality among different ant group local rules qualities. On the basis of quality, master search out for best rule. Once Master generates the best rule, it truncates the discrete attribute matrix and produce new reduced attribute matrix that is again broadcasted to all groups for further rule generation with updated pheromone value.

## 3   Implementation Details

Ant-Miner Code written in Java is parallelized using mpiJava 1.2.5 (http://www. hpjava.org/mpiJava.html) configured using MPICH-1.2.6 (http://www.mcs.anl.gov/ research/projects/mpich2/) and Java JDK1.6 (https://jdk6.dev.java.net/).

## 4   Performance Evaluation of Parallel Ant-Miner

The performance study of parallel Ant-Miner code has been done on an HPC Linux cluster. This cluster is one of the HPC resources of Garuda Grid. C-DAC's GARUDA

Grid is an initiative to make grid computing revolutionary to science and industry by aggregating High Performance Computing Systems and terabytes of storage over an ultra-high speed multi services network (Prahlada Rao et.al. 2009). The GARUDA grid is a federation of heterogeneous HPC clusters currently aggregating over 1500CPUs.

**Datasets:** Four different datasets were taken to study the performance with respect to time and accuracy. The four datasets are musk data (168 features and 476 instances), dermatology data (33 features and 358 instances), Iris data (4 features and 150 instances) and lung cancer data (32 instances and 56 features) downloaded from UCI Machine learning repository (http://archive.ics.uci.edu/ml/). Musk data and Dermatology data were taken to study the performance with respect to time whereas iris and lung cancer data was chosen to study the performance with respect to accuracy.

Parameters used for both musk data and dermatology data are: Maximum uncovered Cases (MUC) = 5, Minimum cases to be covered by a rule = 5, RHO = 0.5, Biasing (Q) = 0.8. PAM was executed on the above datasets using 1,2,4 and 8 CPUs and speedup was calculated.

$$\text{Speedup} = \frac{\text{Time taken on 1 CPU}}{\text{Time taken on 'n' CPUs}}$$

For dermatology data, speedup obtained was 2.07 on 8 CPUs (as shown in Table 1 and Fig 2) inspite of using 1600 ants. But for musk data, as the number of features were more, time taken on two CPUs was very high even for 32 ants and speedup obtained was 7.56 using 8CPUs (Table 2 & Fig 3). Speedup obtained on 2CPUs was more than ideal speedup may be because of execution on one node with two processors and inter processor communication could be very low.

As we increased the number of ants from 32 to 128ants, the time taken on 8 CPUs drastically reduced compared to single CPU giving a speedup 8.08, which is equivalent to ideal speedup. This performance improvement of parallel Ant-miner could be because of parallel discretization step.

**Table 1.** Performance of PAM using dermatology data

| Number of CPUs | Time (minutes) | Speedup | Ideal Speedup |
|---|---|---|---|
| 1 | 87 | 1 | 1 |
| 2 | 59 | 1.47 | 2 |
| 4 | 46 | 1.89 | 4 |
| 8 | 42 | 2.07 | 8 |

**Table 2.** Performance of PAM using Musk data

| Number of CPUs | Time (mts) for 32Ants | Speedup | Time (mts) for 128 Ants | Speedup | Ideal Speedup |
|---|---|---|---|---|---|
| 1 | 174 | 1 | 582 | 1 | 1 |
| 2 | 70 | 2.48 | 330 | 1.76 | 2 |
| 4 | 46 | 3.78 | 189 | 3.07 | 4 |
| 8 | 23 | 7.56 | 72 | 8.08 | 8 |

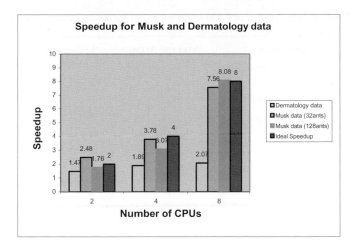

**Fig. 3.** Speedup gained using dermatology and musk data on 2, 4 and 8 CPUs

## 4.1 Study of PAM with Respect to Accuracy

We studied the performance of PAM with respect to accuracy using iris data and lung cancer data. For Iris data, we have got an accuracy of more than 92% for different combinations of parameters. Results of only lung cancer data are reported here in detail. Study was done for lung cancer data by changing the number of ants as 100,200,400, 800 and 1600. The parameters used for the study are: Maximum cases remained uncovered (MUC) = 5, Minimum cases to be covered by a rule (Min) = 5, RHO = 0.5, Biasing (Q) = 0.8. Average was taken over three runs for accuracy and time. The performance with respect to time and accuracy was found to be good with 800 ants and as we increased the number of ants to 1600, performance with respect to accuracy and time was found to be degraded (as shown in Table 3). We have found that for such small dataset, using more number of ants was not of use and 800 ants is the optimal number to get better accuracy.

We also studied the performance by changing the parameters of minimum cases to be covered by a rule (Min), maximum cases remained uncovered (MUC), RHO and Biasing (Q). We have found that accuracy obtained was good using MUC=5, Min=5, Rho =0.5 and Biasing (Q) = 0.8 (as shown in Table 4).

**Table 3.** Performance of PAM with respect to accuracy for Lung cancer data

| Total No of Ants | Average Accuracy | Average Time(mts) |
|---|---|---|
| 100 | 75.23 | 3.33 |
| 100 | 81.9 | 2 |
| 400 | 84.07 | 4.4 |
| 400 | 81.9 | 2.33 |
| 800 | 85.04 | 7.5 |
| 1600 | 80.23 | 15.33 |

**Table 4.** Performance of PAM with change in parameters using 800 ants

| Parameters | | | | Average Accuracy | Average Time (mts) |
|---|---|---|---|---|---|
| MUC | Min | Rho | Q | | |
| 5 | 5 | 0.5 | 0.7 | 63.57 | 9 |
| 5 | 5 | 0.5 | 0.9 | 73.57 | 3 |
| 5 | 5 | 0.5 | 0.6 | 78.57 | 10 |
| **5** | **5** | **0.5** | **0.8** | **85.04** | **7.5** |
| 10 | 10 | 0.5 | 0.8 | 73.57 | 4 |
| 10 | 10 | 0.6 | 0.8 | 63.57 | 5 |
| 10 | 10 | 0.7 | 0.8 | 73.57 | 4 |

## 5  Conclusion

The Ant-miner algorithm for rule mining was parallelized and enabled on HPC clusters of Garuda Grid. We have parallelized both discretization step and rule mining steps of Ant-Miner, which helped in improving the performance of PAM with respect to time. Performance obtained was good for data having more number of features than for the dataset having less number of features. For dermatology dataset having only 33 features, a speedup of only 2.07 was obtained on 8 CPUs though the ideal speedup is 8. But for musk data having 168 features, a speedup of 7.56 was obtained on 8 CPUs for 32 ants and speedup equivalent to ideal speedup was obtained for 128 ants. Performance of PAM increased with increase in number of features and number of ants. Also performance with respect to accuracy was found to be good using certain combination of parameters for lung cancer data. Accuracy could be improved by properly optimizing the parameters and the best accuracy was found to be higher when parameters of Minimum cases to be covered per rule and Maximum cases uncovered where set to 5.

**Acknowledgments.** Authors would like to acknowledge Department of Information Technology (DIT) and Department of Science and Technology (DST) for their financial support.

## References

Chan, A., Freitas, A.: A New Classification-Rule Pruning Procedure for an Ant Colony Algorithm. In: Talbi, E.-G., Liardet, P., Collet, P., Lutton, E., Schoenauer, M. (eds.) EA 2005. LNCS, vol. 3871, pp. 25–36. Springer, Heidelberg (2006)

Min, F., Xie, L., Liu, Q., Cai, H.: A Divide-and-Conquer Discretization Algorithm. In: Wang, L., Jin, Y. (eds.) FSKD 2005. LNCS (LNAI), vol. 3613, pp. 1277–1286. Springer, Heidelberg (2005)

Flynn, M.: Some Computer Organizations and Their Effectiveness. IEEE Trans. Comput. C-21, 948 (1972)

Kurgan, L.A., Cios, K.J.: CAIM Discretization Algorithm. IEEE Transactions on Knowledge And Data Engineering 16(2) (February 2004)

Parpinelli, R.S., Lopes, H.S., Freitas, A.A.: Data mining with an ant colony optimization algorithm. IEEE Transactions on Evolutionary Computation, special issue on Ant Colony Algorithms 6(4), 321–332 (2002)

Prahlada Rao, B.B., Ramakrishnan, S., RajaGopalan, M.R., Subrata, C., Mangala, N., Sridharan, R.: e-infrastructures in IT: A Case study on Indian National Grid Computing Initiative-GARUDA. In: A Case study on Indian National Grid Computing Initiative-GARUDA, International Supercomputing Conference ISC 2009, vol. 23(3-4), pp. 283–290 (June 2009)

Shelokar, P.S., Jayaraman, V.K., Kulkarni, B.D.: An ant colony approach for clustering. Analytica Chimica Acta 509, 187–195 (2004a)

Shelokar, P.S., Jayaraman, V.K., Kulkarni, B.D.: An ant colony classifier system: application to some process engineering problems. Computers & Chemical Engineering 28, 1577–1584 (2004b)

Roozmand, O., Zamanifar, K.: Parallel Ant Miner 2. In: Rutkowski, L., Tadeusiewicz, R., Zadeh, L.A., Zurada, J.M. (eds.) ICAISC 2008. LNCS (LNAI), vol. 5097, pp. 681–692. Springer, Heidelberg (2008)

# A Software Tool for Data Clustering Using Particle Swarm Optimization

Kalyani Manda[1], A. Sai Hanuman[2], Suresh Chandra Satapathy[3],
Vinaykumar Chaganti[4], and A. Vinaya Babu[5]

[1] Maharaj Vijayaram Gajapat Raj Engineering College, Vijayanagaram, India
[2] GRIET, Hyderabad, India
[3] Anil Neerukonda Institute of Technology and Science, Visakhapatnam, India
[4] GITAM, Vishakapatnam, India
[5] JNTU, Hyderabad, India

**Abstract.** Many universities all over the world have been offering courses on swarm intelligence from 1990s. Particle Swarm Optimization is a swarm intelligence technique. It is relatively young, with a pronounce need for a mature teaching method. This paper presents an educational software tool in MATLAB to aid the teaching of PSO fundamentals and its applications to data clustering. This software offers the advantage of running the classical K-Means clustering algorithm and also provides facility to simulate hybridization of K-Means with PSO to explore better clustering performances. The graphical user interfaces are user-friendly and offer good learning scope to aspiring learners of PSO.

**Keywords:** Particle swarm optimization, data clustering, learning tools.

## 1 Introduction

Computational techniques inspired by nature; such as artificial neural networks [1], fuzzy systems [2], evolutionary computation [3] and swarm intelligence [4] etc have found the interest of the scholarly. Particle Swarm Optimization is a unique approach to swarm intelligence based on simplified simulations of animal social behaviors such as fish schooling and bird flocking. It is first introduced by Kennedy and Eberhart as a self-adaptive search optimization. Its applications are generally found in solving complex engineering problems, mainly in non-linear function minimization, optimal capacitor placement in distributed systems, shape optimization, dynamic systems and game theory, constrained and unconstrained optimization, multi objective optimization problems, control systems and others.

Off late, the interest and scope for research in PSO seems to be on a high. It is therefore worthwhile to consider giving good quality learning to the beginners in the field. Simulation is one among the better teaching methods for sure. Through this paper, a software tutorial for PSO, developed to aid the teaching of PSO concepts and its applications to data clustering, is introduced. The software offers facilities to simulate classical K-means [6] clustering algorithm, PSO clustering, and hybridizations of K-Means and PSO. The software provides a scope of experimentation by allowing the learner to choose different tuning parameters for PSO along with suitable particle sizes

B.K. Panigrahi et al. (Eds.): SEMCCO 2010, LNCS 6466, pp. 278–285, 2010.

and iterations to obtain better clustering performances. The software is GUI based and supported by various plots and graphs for better presentation of the derived results. This work is done using MATLAB (Matrix LABoratory). MATLAB is a computational environment for modeling, analyzing and simulating a wide variety of intelligent systems. It also provides a very good access to the students by providing a numerous design and analysis tools in Fuzzy Systems, Neural Networks and Optimization tool boxes.

The remainder of this paper is organized as follows. In Section 2, the three clustering algorithms; K-Means, PSO, and hybrid algorithms on three numerical datasets – Iris, Wine, and Cancer (collected from UCI machine repository) are discussed. In Section 3, the software for PSO based data clustering is presented by taking a conventional K-Means clustering algorithm, PSO, and hybrid clustering algorithms. In Section 4, comparative analysis of all the clustering algorithms with experimental results is given based on their intra and inters cluster similarities and quantization error. Section 5 concludes the paper.

## 2   Data Clustering

Data clustering is a process of grouping a set of data vectors into a number of clusters or bins such that elements or data vectors within the same cluster are similar to one another and are dissimilar to the elements in other clusters. Broadly, there are two classes of clustering algorithms, *supervised* and *unsupervised*. With supervised clustering, the learning algorithm has an external teacher that indicates the target class to which the data vector should belong. For unsupervised clustering, a teacher does not exist, and data vectors are grouped based on distance from one another.

### 2.1   K-Means Clustering

K-Means algorithm falls under partitional based clustering technique. It was introduced by MacQueen [6]. K in K-Means signifies the number of clusters into which data is to be partitioned. This algorithm aims at assigning each pattern of a given dataset to the cluster having the nearest centroid. K-Means algorithm uses similarity measure to determine the closeness of two patterns. Similarity can be measured using Euclidean Distance or Manhattan Distance or Minkowski Distance. In this paper, Euclidean Distance is considered as the similarity measure. For more on K-Means clustering algorithm, refer to MacQueen [6].

### 2.2   PSO Clustering

The concept of Particle Swarm Optimization was discovered through simple social model simulation. It is related to bird flocking, fish schooling, and swarming theory. A "swarm" is an apparently disorganized population of moving particles that tend to cluster together while each particle seems to be moving in a random direction.

In the context of PSO clustering, a single particle represents $N_k$ cluster centroid vectors. Each particle xi is constructed as follows:

$$x_i = (a_{i1}, a_{i2}........a_{ij}.....a_{iN_k})  \tag{1}$$

Where $a_{ij}$= $j^{th}$ cluster centroid vector of $i^{th}$ particle in cluster $C_{ij}$.

The fitness of the particle is easily measured as the intracluster distance (the distance among the vectors of a given cluster) which needs to be minimized. It is given by

$$\frac{\sum_{j=1}^{N_k}\left[\sum_{\forall z_p \in C_{ij}} d(z_p, a_j)\right]}{N_k} \tag{2}$$

Here $z_p$ denotes the $p^{th}$ data vector, $C_{ij}$ is the $i^{th}$ particles $j^{th}$ cluster, $a_j$ denotes centroid vector of cluster j, $d(z_p, a_j) = \sqrt{\sum_{k=1}^{N_d} (z_{pk} - a_{jk})^2}$ denoting the Euclidean distance, and $N_k$ denotes number of cluster centroid vectors.

There are different versions of PSO models [5]. In the software we propose we stuck to the basic PSO model called gbest model wherein every particle will interact with every other particles to decide its optimum direction. This section now presents a standard gbest PSO clustering algorithm.

Data vectors can be clustered using standard gbest PSO as follows:

   i.    Randomly select $N_k$ cluster centroids to initialize each particle

   ii.   For $I = 1$ to $I_{max}$ do

       a)  For each particle i do

       b)  For each data vector $z_p$

           i.    calculate Euclidean distance $d(z_p, a_{ij})$ to all cluster centroids $C_{ij}$

           ii.   assign $z_p$ to the cluster $C_{ij}$ such that $d(z_p, a_{ij}) = \min_{\forall k=1.....N_k} \{d(z_p, a_{ik})\}$

           iii.  calculate the fitness using equation (2)

       c)  Update the pbest and gbest positions

       d)  Update the cluster centroids using the below equations

$$vel_{id}(I) = w * vel_{id}(I-1) + c1 * rand() * (p_{id} - x_{id}(I-1)) + c2 * rand() * (p_{gd} - x_{id}(I-1)) \tag{3}$$

$$x_{id}(I) = x_{id}(I-1) + vel_{id}(I) \tag{4}$$

Where $I_{max}$ is the maximum number of iterations.

## 2.3  Hybridized Clustering with K-Means and PSO

In the proposed software, we tried hybridization in two ways. The first one is K-Means + PSO technique, where in the K-Means clustering algorithm is executed, the resulting centroids of which are used to seed the initial swarm, while the rest of the swarm is initialized randomly. PSO algorithm is then executed (as in sec 2.2).

The second one is PSO + K-Means technique. In this, first PSO algorithm is executed once, whose resulting gbest is used as one of the centroids for K-Means, while the rest of the centroids are initialized randomly. K-Means algorithm is then executed.

Our software offers the facilities of exploring these possibilities with various options of choosing parameters and number of iterations to investigate the ideas.

## 3   Software Tutorial for PSO Based Data Clustering

The objective of this software is to let the users learn how PSO can be applied in the area of clustering. The idea is to involve the user for setting the parameters of PSO clustering algorithm. For this application, three data sets have been taken namely Iris, wine and breast cancer. As the data sets considered for this application are pre classified, the number of clusters taken is same as that of their number of classes.

**Table 1.** Results of K-Means Clustering

| Measures/datasets | Iris | Wine | Cancer |
|---|---|---|---|
| Intra cluster distance | 1.94212 | 293.617 | 671.53 |
| Inter cluster distance | 10.167 | 1474.22 | 1331.33 |
| Quantization error | 0.647374 | 97.0723 | 335.765 |
| Time ( in sec) | 24.3050 | 1.7562 | 6.75965 |

The results of clustering are shown in terms of intra class and inter class similarities and also quantization error [Table 1]. A confusion matrix is also given where an accuracy test can be made between the expected clusters and actual clusters. The time taken by the algorithm to cluster the data is also given. The results of K-Means clustering given in Table 1 are appended in the fig. 1 (as displayed by the software).

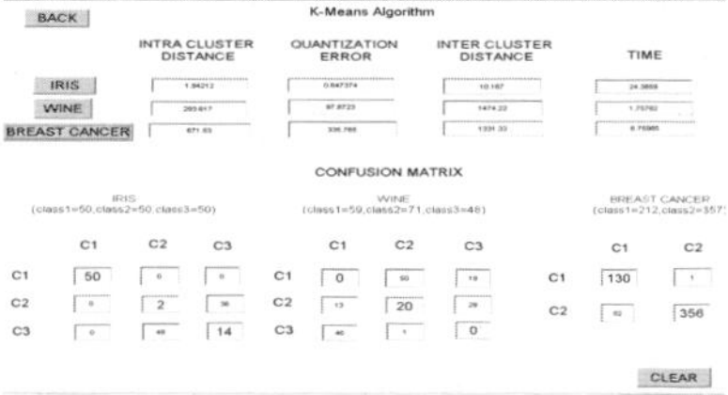

**Fig. 1.** Results of K-means clustering on three datasets

Fig. 2 displays the scope given for the user, to specify all the PSO parameters like swarm size, inertia of weight, and acceleration coefficients. The results of clustering are shown in the same way as in K-Means clustering [Table 2]. Sample results are computed taking swarm size as 3, inertia weight as 0.72, and c1 and c2 both 1. However, the user can play with this software giving any values to see how the PSO clustering algorithm performs.

282    K. Manda et al.

**Table 2.** Results of gbest PSO Clustering

| Swarm size = 3,  Inertia of weight=0.72 ,   c1=1      and        c2=1 | | | |
|---|---|---|---|
| *Measures/datasets* | *Iris* | *Wine* | *Cancer* |
| Intra cluster distance | 0.648096 | 145.849 | 222.833 |
| Inter cluster distance | 3.37355 | 749.14 | 432.382 |
| Quantization error | 0.216032 | 48.6163 | 111.416 |
| Time in sec | 19.9997 | 12.9741 | 76.1937 |

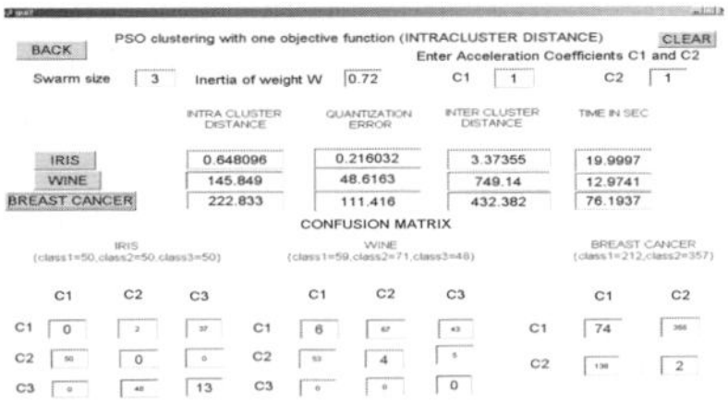

**Fig. 2.** Results of PSO based Clustering

On a similar note, the sample results and screen displays from the software for two proposed hybridization algorithms are also presented below: K-Means+PSO [Table 3, Fig. 3] and PSO+K-Means [Table 4, Fig. 4].

**Table 3.** Results of K-Means+PSO Clustering Algorithm

| Swarm size = 3,  Inertia of weight=0.72 ,   c1=1      and        c2=1 | | | |
|---|---|---|---|
| *Measures/datasets* | *Iris* | *Wine* | *Cancer* |
| Intra cluster distance | 0.986767 | 148.68 | 334.202 |
| Inter cluster distance | 4.95916 | 811.311 | 640.836 |
| Quantization error | 0.328922 | 49.5601 | 167.101 |
| Time in sec | 12.6541 | 14.3183 | 43.847 |

**Table 4.** Results of PSO+K-Means Clustering Algorithm

| Swarm size = 3,  Inertia of weight=0.72 ,   c1=1      and        c2=1 | | | |
|---|---|---|---|
| *Measures/datasets* | *Iris* | *Wine* | *Cancer* |
| Intra cluster distance | 0.621062 | 142.808 | 220.765 |
| Inter cluster distance | 5.08348 | 737.112 | 665.667 |
| Quantization error | 0.223687 | 47.9361 | 111.882 |
| Time in sec | 8.75372 | 10.8275 | 38.1585 |

**Fig. 3.** Results of K-Means+PSO          **Fig. 4.** Results of PSO+K-Means

## 4   Comparative Analysis with Experimental Results

This software tutorial gives a comparative study on all the four clustering algorithms, K-Means, PSO, K-Means+PSO and PSO+K-Means. According to the experimental results obtained, it is observed that the accuracy rate of PSO+K-Means is high. Table 5 shows the results, and Fig. 5 appends the display from the software.

**Table 5.** Comparative results of four clustering algorithms

| Results of K-Means Clustering | | | |
|---|---|---|---|
| *Measures/datasets* | *Iris* | *Wine* | *Cancer* |
| Intra cluster distance | 1.94212 | 293.617 | 671.53 |
| Inter cluster distance | 10.167 | 1474.22 | 1331.33 |
| Quantization error | 0.647374 | 97.0723 | 335.765 |
| Time in sec | 24.3050 | 1.7562 | 6.75965 |
| Results of gbest PSO clustering | | | |
| Swarm size = 3,  Inertia of weight=0.72 ,   c1=1      and        c2=1 | | | |
| *Measures/datasets* | *Iris* | *Wine* | *Cancer* |
| Intra cluster distance | 0.648096 | 145.849 | 222.833 |
| Inter cluster distance | 3.37355 | 749.14 | 432.382 |
| Quantization error | 0.216032 | 48.6163 | 111.416 |
| Time in sec | 19.9997 | 12.9741 | 76.1937 |
| Results of K-Means + PSO Clustering algorithm | | | |
| Swarm size = 3,  Inertia of weight=0.72 ,   c1=1      and        c2=1 | | | |

**Table 5.** (*continued*)

| Measures/datasets | Iris | Wine | Cancer |
|---|---|---|---|
| Intra cluster distance | 0.986767 | 148.68 | 334.202 |
| Inter cluster distance | 4.95916 | 811.311 | 640.836 |
| Quantization error | 0.328922 | 49.5601 | 167.101 |
| Time in sec | 12.6541 | 14.3183 | 43.847 |
| Results of PSO + K-Means Clustering algorithm | | | |
| Swarm size = 3,  Inertia of weight=0.72 ,   c1=1      and        c2=1 | | | |
| Measures/datasets | Iris | Wine | Cancer |
| Intra cluster distance | 0.621062 | 142.808 | 220.765 |
| Inter cluster distance | 5.08348 | 737.112 | 665.667 |
| Quantization error | 0.223687 | 47.9361 | 111.882 |
| Time in sec | 8.75372 | 10.8275 | 38.1585 |

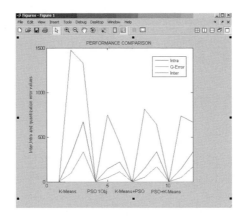

**Fig. 5.** Fitness Curves

Fig. 5 shows the intra and inter cluster distances, quantization error and the time as marked with blue, red, green, and black colors respectively, for all four algorithms.

## 5   Conclusion and Future Scope

The PSO is a stochastic algorithm based on sociometry of bird flocking behaviors. Each particle in PSO interacts with each other in finding the optimal destinations using its own cognitive decision component and social decision component. The simple mathematical equations to update the particles next velocity and position have made this algorithm very popular among researchers in various fields. This paper presented a learning software tool for using PSO for a very specific application in data mining called data clustering. Through the software presented in this paper learners can have first hand information about the PSO basics and also can proceed in investigating fundamentals in clustering algorithms. The entire software has been developed using MATLAB. The GUI generated using MATLAB are very convenient for users to use and experiment. Also, users have been provided various options to choose suitable parameters and check the effectiveness of those in clustering results. The fitness graph generated while comparing all four clustering algorithms discussed earlier can provide a better insight about the performances. The confusion matrices generated are the indications of the accuracies of the algorithm on investigated dataset. Authors note it here that no such comprehensive tools have been developed so far to explore PSO based clustering using MATLAB. It is envisioned that the presented software will offer a good learning environment to students keeping interest in this filed.

As further scope, the other PSO models are to be included with facilities to include more parameter setting environment. The variants of PSO also can be explored for the purpose and a complete package can be developed for clustering applications.

## References

1. Bishop, X.M.: Neural networks for pattern recognition. Oxford University Press, Oxford (1995)
2. Yurkiovich, S., Passino, K.M.: A laboratory course on fuzzy control. IEEE Trans. Educ. 42(1), 15–21 (1999)
3. Coelho, L.S., Coelho, A.A.R.: Computational intelligence in process control: fuzzy, evolutionary, neural, and hybrid approaches. Int. J. Knowl-Based Intell. Eng. Sys. 2(2), 80–94 (1998)
4. Bonabeau, E., Dorigo, M., Theraulaz, G.: Swarm intelligence: from natural to artificial systems. Oxford University Press, Oxford (1999)
5. Kennedy, J.F., Eberhart, R.C.: Particle swarm optimization. In: Proceedings of the IEEE International conference on neural networks, Perth, Australia, vol. 4, pp. 1942–1948 (1995)
6. MacQueen, J.B.: Some Methods for classification and Analysis of Multivariate Observations. In: Proceedings of 5th Berkeley Symposium on Mathematical Statistics and Probability, vol. 1, pp. 281–297. University of California Press (1967)

# An ACO Approach to Job Scheduling in Grid Environment

Ajay Kant, Arnesh Sharma, Sanchit Agarwal, and Satish Chandra

Department of CSE & IT, Jaypee University of Information Technology, Solan, India
{ajaykant,arnesh.89,agg.sanchit.cool}@gmail.com,
satish.chandra@juit.ac.in

**Abstract.** Due to recent advances in the wide-area network technologies and low cost of computing resources, grid computing has become an active research area. The efficiency of a grid environment largely depends on the scheduling method it follows. This paper proposes a framework for grid scheduling using dynamic information and an ant colony optimization algorithm to improve the decision of scheduling. A notion of two types of ants -'Red Ants' and 'Black Ants' have been introduced. The purpose of red and Black Ants has been explained and algorithms have been developed for optimizing the resource utilization. The proposed method does optimization at two levels and it is found to be more efficient than existing methods.

**Keywords:** Grid Computing, Job Scheduling, Ant Colony Optimization (ACO), Red Ants, Black Ants, Workload.

## 1 Introduction

Grid Computing consists of multiple computer systems, which work autonomously and also communicate through a network. A computational grid is essentially a hardware and software infrastructure that provides dependable, consistent, pervasive, and inexpensive access to high-end computational capabilities [1]. It is a shared environment implemented via the deployment of a persistent, standards-based service infrastructure that supports the creation of, and resource sharing within, distributed communities. Resources can be computers, storage space, instruments, software applications, and data, all connected through the Internet and a middleware software layer.

Grid computing environment uses a middleware to divide and distribute pieces of program among several computers, which are heterogeneous, loosely coupled and geographically dispersed. The aim of this paper is to develop a scheduling algorithm for a computational Grid system. This is achieved by a two stage approach based on Ant Colony Optimization (ACO) and the dynamics of Grid computing. The proposed model consists of two types of ants namely, *Red Ants* (for system resource estimation) and *Black Ants* (for decision of resource allocation). The motivation behind considering two types of ants is that it provides a more efficient solution to job scheduling which has been discussed later in this paper.

B.K. Panigrahi et al. (Eds.): SEMCCO 2010, LNCS 6466, pp. 286–295, 2010.

## 2  Problem Statement

The computation sites of an application or a job are usually selected by the grid scheduler according to resource status and certain performance models. Since at any time in a grid resources can connect and disconnect themselves according to their internal policies therefore grid has a dynamic environment.

In a dynamic environment task scheduling has two major components: system state estimation and decision making [2]. System state estimation involves collecting state information throughout the grid system and constructing an estimate. On the basis of the estimate, decisions are made to assign a task to a selected resource. The main challenge of the job scheduling in grid system is the selection of required resource types depending on their efficiency and workload and scheduling the jobs on the selected resources so that there is maximum resource utilization and minimum job completion time unlike previous scenarios in which all the resources were time and again scheduled for a required set of task which unnecessarily accounts for low efficiency and greater time complexity.

Job scheduling improves the overall system performance by utilizing the scattered resources. This paper proposes a framework based on ACO, for grid scheduling using dynamic information. The highly dynamic nature of the grid makes the scheduling problem more challenging, as several resources might disconnect or connect from the grid at any moment of time.

## 3  Existing Methods

The complexity of a general scheduling problem is NP-Complete [3]. One way of categorizing the scheduling algorithms in Grid Computing is static [4] and dynamic [5]. In static information regarding the tasks and the required resources are available by the time the application is scheduled whereas, in case of dynamic scheduling as the application executes, task allocation is performed on the fly.

One major breakthrough in grid scheduling was the work of Berman *et al* [6] who noted that via schedule adaptation, it is possible to use sophisticated scheduling heuristics, like list-scheduling approaches which are sensitive to performance prediction errors, for grid environments in which resource availabilities change over time. Some popular heuristic algorithms, which have been applied in grid, are min-min by Ke Liu *et al* [7] and the fast greedy by Stefka Fidanova *et al* [8]. Durchova *et al* proposed a model [9] based on multiple objective niched pareto genetic Algorithm (NPGA) that involves evolution during a comprehensive search and work on multiple solutions.

Another major landmark in the history of grid computing was the year 1999 when Dorigo, Di Caro and Gambardella [10][11] proposed the metaheuristic Ant Colony Optimization. Lorpunmanee [16] *et al* proposed a model based on ACO for dynamic job scheduling in a grid environment. Ruay-Shiung, Jih-Sheng and Po-Sheng Lin proposed a Balanced Ant Colony Optimization (BACO) algorithm [12] for job scheduling in the Grid environment.

## 4  ACO Basics

Ants in an ACO based approach are artificial intelligent agents which try to find a path in the network, which has the minimum cost. Ants are launched from a source node $s$ and move through neighbour repeater nodes $r_i$, to reach a final destination node $d$. To begin with an initial pheromone value $\tau_0$ is associated with each node. A node is described as a base node whenever data has to be transferred to the destination from it and thus launching of the ants is performed at the source. After launching, the choice of the next node $r$ is guided by a probabilistic decision rule [13]:

$$p_k(r,s) = \begin{cases} \frac{[\tau(r,s)]^\alpha \cdot [\eta(r,s)]^\beta}{\sum_{r\in R_s}[\tau(r,s)]^\alpha \cdot [\eta(r,s)]^\beta} , & if \ k \notin tabu^r \\ 0 & , \quad otherwise \end{cases} \tag{1}$$

Where $\tau(r, s)$ is the pheromone value, $\eta(r, s)$ is the value of the heuristic related to energy, Rs are the receiver nodes. For node $r$, $tabu^r$ is the list of identities of received data packages previously. $\alpha$, $\beta$ are two parameters that control the relative weight of the pheromone trail and heuristic value . Finally the most optimal and cost effective path is selected and globally updated.

## 5  Proposed Model

We propose a new model based on ACO for scheduling jobs in a computing grid. In this model two kinds of ants have been considered namely *Red Ants* and *Black Ants* for two stage optimization. Due to the short listing of the resources in the first stage of optimization by *Red Ants*, only the required resources of desired efficiency are selected on which scheduling is performed by the *Black Ants*. This avoids the selection of the entire resources associated with the grid which is computationally expensive.

Red Ants select the appropriate resources $S$ from the resource pool having $R$ resources, where $S<R$. In these S resources the arriving task are to be scheduled. From the set of resources $(S)$ finalized by the *Red Ants*, *Black Ants* attempts a tour to give an optimal path for mapping the arriving jobs ($J$ where $J > S$) on selected resources $(S)$. Fig. 1 outlines the grid model selected for this study.

A 'dynamic' computational grid has been taken into consideration in which users can register any time. After registration, they are able to submit jobs to the grid environment. The submitted jobs are received at the receiver side. The received jobs are put into a job pool.

The *Red Ants* take control of these jobs to find appropriate resources for their execution. The information regarding the appropriate type and the corresponding efficiency of the required resources is taken from the *Grid Resource Table* (GRT) (as described in Table 1) which is synonymous to the *Grid Information Service* (GIS) [14], which maintains and updates the status of the grid resources. The resources shortlisted by the *Red Ants* are kept into a *Target Resource Set* (TRS). Since the network topology is unknown, we shall be using Self Cloning Ants [15]. They are used to find appropriate resources from the resource pool.

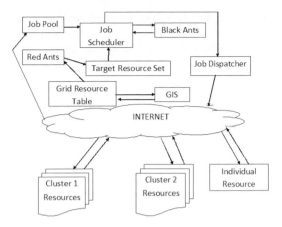

**Fig. 1.** An outline of the proposed grid model

The *Black Ants* are used to allocate the jobs to the resources selected by the *Red Ants*. The targeted resources are fed into a scheduling module i.e. *Job Scheduler* (JS). Here scheduling is performed by the *Black Ants* following heuristic algorithm. An optimal tour constructed by the *Black Ants* is submitted to the Job Dispatcher which delivers jobs to a selected resource and maintains these jobs in the grid queue.

### 5.1 Searching Algorithm for *Red Ants*

*Red Ants* are used for searching required type of the resources, which can solve the given tasks and have the minimum workload, the information of which can be gathered from the *Grid Resource Table* (GRT).The GRT is supposed to be having entries which contain the data regarding the following attributes –

- Resource Id – A unique identification number assigned to each resource.
- Resource Name $(R)$ – The generic name of the different resources like $M_1$, $M_2$, $R_1$, $R_2$ for different kinds of resources in the grid.
- Resource Type $(R\_Type)$ – The different type of resources depending on their functionalities and classification. Two resource types M and R are taken which denote the examples like file servers, printers and so on.
- *Workload (W)* – It is defined as the time after which the resources start processing an arrived task.
- *Priority standard (R_Eff)* - The *priority standard for jobs* is defined as High Priority (H) or Low Priority (L). A high priority job is processed by a resource of high efficiency (H) and low priority job by resource of low efficiency (L).
- Resource id of correlated resources *(Neighbours)*

The Target Resource Set is set of 'm' (m<t where t is number of task) resources which are required to solve the incoming task and have the minimum workload. An

290      A. Kant et al.

Optimized Self Cloning ACO algorithm is employed to determine the required resources from the network mesh consisting of multiple resources of different types.

In the self cloning algorithm, red ant shows one of the three basic behaviours. These are:

1. Moving from one row to another
2. Killing itself
3. Cloning itself if necessary.

The behaviour of the *Red Ants* is described by the following algorithm.

> *Procedure RedAnt*
> *begin*
>     *read the pheromone status flag ( PSF ) of the row*
>     *if ( PSF = visited )*
>     *ant destroys itself*
>     *else*
>     *if ( R_Type = Target_R_Type and*
>            *Task_priority = R_Eff and*
>               *W < Total_Processing _Time)*
>        *add R details to Target_Resource_Set*
>        *PSF ← visited*
>        *call RedAnt for each neighbouring nodes*
>     *end if*
>     *end if*
> *end*

**Table 1.** Grid resource Table

| R | R_Type | R_Eff | W | Neighbours |
|---|---|---|---|---|
| $M_1$ | M | H | 50 | $M_2,R_1,R_3$ |
| $R_1$ | R | H | 30 | $M_1,M_2,R_6$ |
| $R_2$ | R | L | 40 | $M_2,R_4,R_6$ |
| $R_3$ | R | H | 50 | $M_1,R_5$ |
| $R_4$ | R | H | 20 | $R_2,R_5$ |
| $M_2$ | M | L | 60 | $R_1,R_2$ |
| $R_5$ | R | L | 10 | $R_3,R_4,R_6$ |
| $R_6$ | R | H | 45 | $R_1,R_2,R_5$ |

Let $t_1$, $t_2$, $t_3$, $t_4$ be the four jobs with priority H and resource type R with processing time of 8, 13, 5, 17 respectively. Therefore total processing time is 43. From Grid Resource Table (Table 1) we select all the resources with efficiency H and workload less than total processing time i.e. 43.

Behaviour of the *Red Ant* in accordance with the proposed algorithm on the grid resource table (Table 1) can be shown in Fig 2.

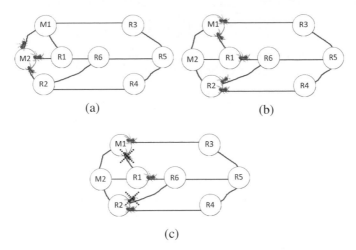

**Fig. 2.** (a): *Red Ants* start from $M_2$ to $M_1,R_1,R_2$ (b): $R_1$, $R_2$ added to TRS and ants self clonned from $M_1$, $R_1$, $R_2$ (c): Ants which reach $R_1$ and $R_6$ from $M_1$ and $R_2$ destroy themselves

**Table 2.** Target resource set

| R | R_Type | R_Eff | W |
|---|--------|-------|---|
| $R_1$ | R | H | 30 |
| $R_4$ | R | H | 20 |

Hence target resource set is constructed consisting of two resources $R_1$ and $R_2$ of efficiency H and workload less than total processing time as shown in Table 2.

### 5.2  Algorithm for *Black Ants*

After submission of the targeted resources by the *Red Ants*, the following heuristic algorithm is used by the *Black Ants* to find an efficient tour of the selected resources.

Implementation of ACO by *Black Ants* follows this sequence of steps:

1. *Pheromone Initialization:* For pheromone initialization a parameter known as *Completion Time* ($C_{i,j}$) i.e. completion time of $j^{th}$ job on $i^{th}$ machine with a due date $d_j$ has been defined as

$$C_{i,j} = a_j + r_j + w_{i,j} \qquad (2)$$

where $a_j$ is the arrival time, $r_j$ is the release time, and

$$w_{i,j} = w_i + p_j \qquad (3)$$

where $w_i$ is the load of machine $i$ and $p_j$ is the processing time of $j^{th}$ job.

The tardiness of the $j^{th}$ job in machine $i$ is given as

$$T_{i,j} = max(C_{i,j} - d_{i,j}, 0) \qquad (4)$$

The objective is to minimize the maximal total tardiness time of all the jobs within machine of grid environment [16]. This time is given by:

$$\sum_{i=0}^{n}\left(\sum_{j=1}^{n}T_{i,j}\right)$$

For a given set of m machines M ($m_1$, $m_2$, $m_3$....., $m_m$) and n jobs J ($j_1$, $j_2$, $j_3$.....,$j_n$), let the initial pheromone trail be given by equation (5)

$$\tau_0 = \frac{1}{m.\left(\sum_{i=1}^{m} T_{i_{Actual}} + \sum_{i=1}^{m}(\sum_{j=1}^{n} T_{i,j})_{Expected}\right)} \tag{5}$$

The actual tardiness time of jobs, which are already completed on machine $i$ is the expected tardiness time of jobs, which are scheduled on machine $i$ is given by

$$\sum_{i=1}^{m} T_i {}_{Actual}$$

2. *The State Transition Rule*: The movement of ant from node $i$ to node $j$ is driven by probability $p_{i,j}$ as described in equation (6)

$$p_{i,j} = \frac{(T_{i,j}^{\alpha})(\eta_{i,j}^{\beta})}{\Sigma(T_{i,j}^{\alpha})\left(\eta_{i,j}^{\beta}\right)} \tag{6}$$

Where,

$\tau_{i,j}$ is the amount of pheromone on edge $\alpha$ is the parameter which controls the influence of $\tau_{i,j}$.

$\eta_{i,j}$ is the desired of assignment of a job $j$ on machine $i$ which is inversely proportional to the completion time of job.

$\beta$ is a parameter to control the influence of $\eta_{i,j}$.

3. *Updation Rule* [16]: While ants build a tour, they visit the various nodes and edges and pheromone updation takes place by the equation:

$$\tau_{i,j}=(1-\rho)\,\tau_{i,j} + \Delta\tau_{i,j} \tag{7}$$

where $\rho(0<\rho\leq1)$ is the parameter which is the rate of pheromone evaporation.

$\tau_{i,j}$ is the amount of pheromone on a given edge $i,j$. The amount of pheromone deposited, typically given by

$$\Delta\tau_{i,j}^{k} = \begin{cases} {}^{1}/_{L_k} & if\ ant\ k\ travels\ on\ edge\ i,j \\ 0 & otherwise \end{cases}$$

where $L_k$ is the cost of the $k^{th}$ ant's tour (typically length).

## 6  Experiment and Results

The job scheduling technique is simulated in the grid environment as described in Section 5. Since a grid system consist of large number of computing and storing sites, the experiment was performed on  49 resources which include printers, file servers and different type of machines having varied configuration of processors ranging from Pentium IV processor to Dual core and RAM ranging from 512 MB to 2

GB. Different computational workloads were tested in the experiment. Table 3 lists the properties of different tasks used in the experimental setup. The tasks were assigned to different resource sets which were of 49 types and the observations were used to infer the results from it.

**Table 3.** Tasks and resources properties

| Fields | Numerical Value | Properties |
|---|---|---|
| Total number of tasks | 15,000 | |
| Completion time of tasks | 5,000-10,000 | Million Instructions (MI) |
| Arrival Time Distribution | 1-40,000 | Poisson Distribution |
| Number of Resources Requirement | 10-15 CPUs | Processing Elements (PE) |

Comparative study of proposed heuristic algorithm for *Black Ants* with Min-Min and FCFS scheduling algorithms on four jobs $T_1$, $T_2$, $T_3$, $T_4$ with Processing Time 8,13,5,17 respectively on the Target Resource Set $(R_1, R_2)$ with initial workload (30,20) constructed by *Red Ants* gives the total completion time of 48, 52 and 50 time units which are illustrated by the three Gantt Charts.

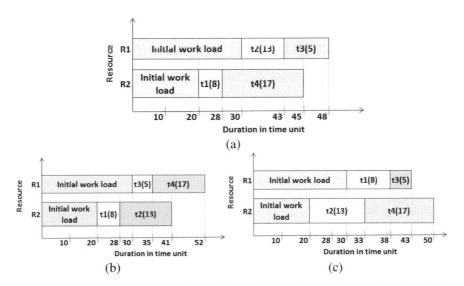

**Fig. 3.** a) Graph showing the completion of Job on ACO with completion time 48 units. b) MIN-MIN with completion time 52 units. **c)** FCFS with completion time 50 units.

Fig.4(a) shows the results of comparison of the proposed ACO algorithm with the Min-Min and FCFS algorithms. The results show that the tardiness time based on the number of available machines in the grid system. On the other hand as shown in Fig. 4b, an ACO algorithm performs much slower than the other scheduler algorithms. The reason for that is ACO calculates several times for searching the optimal resource that is assigned to process the job. Hence, the calculation time of scheduling consumes more resources.

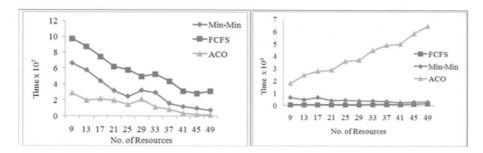

**Fig. 4.** (a): Total tardiness time of dynamic job scheduling in grid computing. (b): Total scheduling time of dynamic job scheduling in grid computing.

# 7 Conclusion

As evident from figure 4, total tardiness time of job scheduling decreases at the cost of an initial increase in total scheduling time. Comparisons with the existing state of the art methods have proven that an ACO based approach in Grid Environment is highly favourable for job scheduling. The success of the proposed algorithm is solely attributed to two stage optimization. Since the grid environment is highly heterogeneous and dynamic in nature the topology of the network cannot be determined, which has been taken care of by the self cloning *Red Ants*. The division in the population of ants helps in scheduling jobs such that minimum tardiness time for the jobs is taken. This approach can find a further use in the existing ACO based application.

# References

1. Foster, I., Kesselman, C.: The grid: blueprint for a future computing infrastructure. Morgan Kaufmann Publishers, USA (1999)
2. Dong, F., Akl, S.G.: " Scheduling algorithms for grid computing: state of the art and open problems", Technical Report No. 2006-504. School of Computing, Queen's University Kingston, Ontario (2006)
3. Foster, I., Roy, A., Sander, V.: A quality of service architecture that combines resource reservation and application adaptation. In: Proc. 8th Int. Workshop on Quality of Service, Pittsburgh, PA, USA, pp. 181–188 (2000)
4. You, S.Y., Kim, H.Y., Hwang, D.H., Kim, S.C.: Task scheduling algorithm in grid considering heterogeneous environment. In: Proc. of the International Conference on Parallel and Distributed Processing Techniques and Applications, PDPTA 2004, Nevada, USA, pp. 240–245 (June 2004)
5. Chen, H., Maheswaran, M.: Distributed dynamic scheduling of composite tasks on grid computing systems. In: Proc. of the 16th International Parallel and Distributed Processing Symposium (IPDPS 2002), Fort Lauderdale, Florida USA, pp. 88–97 (April 2002)
6. Berman, F., Wolski, R., Casanova, H., Cirne, W., Dail, H., Faerman, M., Figueira, S., Hayes, J., Obertelli, G., Schopf, J., Shao, G., Smallen, S., Spring, N., Su, A., Zagorodnov, D.: Adaptive computing on the grid using AppLeS. IEEE Trans. on Parallel and Distributed Systems (TPDS) 14(4), 369–382 (2003)

7. Liu, K., Chen, J., Jin, H., Yang, Y.: A Min-Min Average Algorithm for Scheduling Transaction-Intensive Grid Workflows. In: 7th Australasian Symposium on Grid Computing and e-Research, Wellington, New Zealand
8. Fidanova, S., Durchova, M.: Ant Algorithm for Grid Scheduling Problem. In: Lirkov, I., Margenov, S., Waśniewski, J. (eds.) LSSC 2005. LNCS, vol. 3743, pp. 405–412. Springer, Heidelberg (2006)
9. Benedict, S., Rejitha, R.S., Vasudevan, V.: An Evolutionary Hybrid Scheduling Algorithm for Computational Grids. Journal of Advanced Computational Intelligence and Intelligent Informatics 12(5), 479–484 (2008)
10. Dorigo, M., Stutzle, T.: Ant Colony Optimization. MIT Press, Cambridge (2004)
11. Dorigo, M., Gambardella, L.M.: Ant colony system: a cooperative learning approach to the traveling salesman problem. IEEE Transactions on Evolutionary Computation 1(1), 53–66 (1997)
12. Chang, R.-S., Chang, J.-S., Lin, P.-S.: An ant algorithm for balanced job scheduling in grids. Future Generation Computer Systems archive 25(1), 20–27 (2009)
13. Okdem, S., Karaboga, D.: Routing in Wireless Sensor Networks Using an Ant Colony Optimization (ACO) Router Chip. Sensors 2009 9(2), 909–921 (2009)
14. Czajkowski, K., Kesselman, C., Fitzgerald, S., Foster, I.: Grid Information Services for Distributed Resource Sharing, hpdc. In: 10th IEEE International Symposium on High Performance Distributed Computing (HPDC-10 2001), p. 181 (2001)
15. Murat Esin, E., Erdogan, S.Z.: Self cloning ant colony approach and optimal path finding. In: Proceedings of Euro American Association on Telematics and Information Systems, Colombia (2006)
16. Lorpunmanee, S., Sap, M.N., Abdullah, A.H., Chompoo-inwai, C.: An Ant Colony Optimization for Dynamic Job Scheduling in Grid Environment. World Academy of Science, Engineering and Technology 29, 314–321 (2007)

# Runtime Analysis of (1+1) Evolutionary Algorithm for a TSP Instance

Yu Shan Zhang[1,2] and Zhi Feng Hao[2,3]

[1] School of Mathematics & Computational Science,
Guangdong University of Business Studies, Guangzhou, 510320, P.R. China
[2] School of Computer Science & Engineering, South China University of Technology,
Guangzhou, 510006, P.R. China
[3] Faculty of Computer, Guangdong University of Technology,
Guangzhou, 510006, P.R. China
scuthill@163.com, mazfhao@scut.edu.cn

**Abstract.** Evolutionary Algorithms (EAs) have been used widely and successfully in solving a famous classical combinatorial optimization problem-the traveling salesman problem (TSP).There are lots of experimental results concerning the TSP. However, relatively few theoretical results on the runtime analysis of EAs on the TSP are available. This paper conducts a runtime analysis of a simple Evolutionary Algorithm called (1+1) EA on a TSP instance. We represent a tour as a string of integer, and randomly choose 2-opt and 3-opt operator as the mutation operator at each iteration. The expected runtime of (1+1) EA on this TSP instance is proved to be $O(n^4)$, which is tighter than $O(n^6 + (1/\rho)n\ln n)$ of (1+1) MMAA (Max-Min ant algorithms) . It is also shown that the selection of mutation operator is very important in (1+1) EA.

**Keywords:** Computational complexity, Evolutionary Algorithm (EA), Traveling salesman problem (TSP).

## 1 Introduction

Evolutionary Algorithms are a class of randomized search heuristics based on principles of biological evolution, which are often applied to solve optimization problems. There are a lot of different types of Evolutionary Algorithms, the best known are Genetic Algorithms (GAs) [1], Evolution Strategies (ES) [2], Evolutionary Programming (EP) [3]. There are lots of experimental results available concerning applications of EAs in various combinatorial optimization problems [4, 5, 6], but compared to that amount, the theoretical knowledge of how they perform lags behind. In the early days, attention was mainly paid to practical applications. However, since the 1980s when EAs started to become popular, there have been theoretical investigations about some properties of EAs, although few.

In 1990s, the theoretical research of EAs focused on the convergence properties. Using Markov Chains, Rudolph [7] proved that canonical GAs with mutation, crossover and proportional selection do not converge to the global optimum, while

B.K. Panigrahi et al. (Eds.): SEMCCO 2010, LNCS 6466, pp. 296–304, 2010.
© Springer-Verlag Berlin Heidelberg 2010

elitist variants can converge. He also discussed the condition of convergence of non-elitist ES using martingale theory [8]. Then he extended his analysis by defining general conditions that, if satisfied by an EA, guarantee its convergence [9]. However, it is insufficient to determine whether an algorithm converges or not, furthermore we should study the expected time for the solution to be found ,i.e. the average number of iterations that an algorithm needs to reach the global optimal solution.

Since the late 1990s, some theoretical results about the runtime analysis of EAs have emerged. A simple Evolutionary algorithm called (1+1)EA was first investigated for the classes of pseudo-Boolean functions such as OneMax, LeadingOnes, BinVal, Linear function, Trap function [10, 11].Afterward the runtime analyses of EAs were extended to many combinatorial optimization problem such as partition problem [12], graph coloring problem [13].But with regard to the runtime analysis of (1+1)EA on the Traveling Salesman Problem (TSP), few results are available. Recently Zhou [14] proposed the first rigorous runtime analysis of a simple ACO algorithm called (1+1) MMAA (Max-Min ant algorithms) on some TSP instances, which was illuminating to the investigation of the cases of (1+1) EA.

In this paper, we present a time complexity analysis of a simple Evolutionary Algorithm called (1+1) EA on a TSP instance. Through this preliminary work, we expect to obtain an insight of how (1+1) EA performs on this NP-hard combinatorial optimization problem. We construct a TSP instance of undirected complete graph, in which a tour is represented as a string of integer. At each iteration, a 2-opt and 3-opt operator [14] is randomly chosen as the mutation operator, subsequently the level-reaching estimation technique [15] is applied to estimate the upper bound of the expected runtime.

The organization of this paper is as follows. Section 2 introduces some basic knowledge of TSP, (1+1) Evolutionary Algorithm, the level-reaching estimation technique used to estimate the upper bound of expected running time. In section 3, a TSP instance of undirected complete graph was constructed for analysis. Aiming at this instance, we obtain an upper bound of $O(n^4)$. Finally, we draw a conclusion in section 4.

## 2   The TSP, (1+1) EA and Level-Reaching Estimation Technique

### 2.1   The Traveling Salesman Problem

Here we present a brief introduction to the Traveling Salesman Problem. The detailed description can be found in any standard textbook about discrete mathematics or graph theory.

A graph is an ordered pair $G = \langle V, E \rangle$ comprising of a set $V$ of vertices together with a set $E$ of edges, which satisfies $E \subseteq V \times V$ . We restrict our attention to undirected graph throughout the paper. A simple graph is an undirected graph that has no loops and no more than one edge between any two different vertices. A simple graph that contains exactly one edge between any two different vertices is called a complete graph.

A weighted graph is a graph in which each edge is given a numerical weight. Such weights might represent, for example, costs, lengths or capacities, etc. depending on the problem. The weight of the graph is sum of the weights given to all edges.

A sequence of edges denotes a path. Assume $V = \{1, 2, \cdots, n\}$ is the node set of a complete graph, a path is denoted by a permutation of the set $V$ , e.g. $P = (i_1, i_2, \cdots, i_n), (i_k \in V, k = 1, 2, \cdots, n)$ means a path starting at $i_1$ and ending at $i_n$: $i_1 \rightarrow i_2 \rightarrow \cdots \rightarrow i_n$. A path starting and ending at the same vertex is called a cycle or circuit. A cycle that visits each vertex exactly once and returns to the starting vertex is called a Hamilton cycle or a tour of the graph $G$ .In the following parts, we represent a tour by $\sigma = (\sigma_1, \sigma_2, \cdots, \sigma_n, \sigma_1)$, in which $(\sigma_1, \sigma_2, \cdots, \sigma_n)$ denotes a permutation of $\{1, 2, \cdots, n\}$ .

Given a weighted graph, the task for TSP is to find a Hamilton cycle of the minimum total weight. It is well-known that the traditional deterministic algorithms have to spend much time solving the TSP.

## 2.2  (1+1) Evolutionary Algorithm

The (1+1) EA is the most simple variant of an EA that is still of theoretical and practical interest. The usual (1+1) EA [11] uses a binary string as an individual assuming the objective function to have Boolean inputs, and uses a bitwise mutation operator that flips each bit independently with a probability $p_m$ . Nevertheless, the algorithm presented in this paper is a bit different. First, the objective function $f : S \rightarrow R$ to be minimized is the weight value of the tour, so the individual is not a binary string, instead we use a string of integer; Secondly, the mutation operator is not the bitwise mutation operator, instead, we choose a 2-opt and 3-opt operator randomly as a mutation operator. The algorithm can be formalized as follows.

---

**Algorithm 1**
  Begin
    Initialization: choose randomly a permutation of $\{1, 2, \cdots, n\}$ as
        an initial solution $\xi_0$ ;
    While (termination-condition is not met ) do
      Select 2-opt and 3-opt operator with probability 1/2 respectively
        as a mutation operator;
    Mutate $\xi_k$ and get $\xi_k{}'$ as an offspring;
      If $f(\xi_k) > f(\xi_k{}')$ then $\xi_{k+1} = \xi_k{}'$;
        Else $\xi_{k+1} = \xi_k$ ;
    End If
      $k \leftarrow k + 1$ ;
    End While
  End

---

## 2.3  The Level-Reaching Estimation Technique

The level-reaching estimation technique is a powerful mathematical tool in the runtime analysis of evolutionary algorithms [11, 15]. The technique has been even extended to the runtime analysis of ACO algorithms [14, 16] due to its simplicity and practicability.

**Definition 1.**  Let $f : S \rightarrow R$ be an objective function to be minimized, where $S$ is a finite search space. Let $f_0, f_1, \cdots, f_m$ be the possible different function values of $f$, and suppose these values to be sorted such that $f_0 < f_1 < f_2 < \cdots < f_m$. For any $i = 0, 1, \cdots, m$, let $A_i = \{x \in S \mid f(x) = f_i\}$. Then $\{A_0, A_1, \cdots, A_m\}$ is called an $f$-based partition.

**Lemma 1.**  Let $\{A_0, A_1, \cdots, A_m\}$ be an $f$-based partition, let $p(A_i)$ be the probability that a randomly chosen search point belongs to $A_i$, let $s(a)$ be the probability that a mutation of $a \in A_i$ belongs to $A_{i-1} \bigcup \cdots \bigcup A_0$, and let $s_i = \min\{s(a) \mid a \in A_i\}$, $X_f$ be the runtime of the algorithm on the function $f$. Then

$$E(X_f) \le \sum_{1 \le i \le m} p(A_i)(s_i^{-1} + s_{i-1}^{-1} + \cdots + s_1^{-1}) \le s_1^{-1} + s_2^{-1} + \cdots + s_m^{-1}. \tag{1}$$

**Proof.** Please see [15].  ∎

The lemma can give an upper bound of expected running time if we can calculate the transition probability bound $s_i, i = 1, 2, \cdots, m$.

# 3  Time Upper Bound for a TSP Instance

We first construct a TSP instance of undirected complete graph and then analyze the expected runtime of the above algorithm 1 with the level-reaching estimation technique.

Let $G = \langle V, E \rangle$ be a weighted complete undirected graph with a vertex set $V = \{1, 2, \cdots, n\}$, for each $1 \le i, j \le n$, define weight $w(i, j)$ of edge $(i, j)$ as below :

$$w(i, j) = \begin{cases} 1, & i = 1, \cdots, n-1, j = i+1, \\ 1, & i = n, j = 1, \\ n, & \text{otherwise} \end{cases}$$

Without loss of generality, we fix the starting and ending vertex of a tour of $G$ as vertex 1. The task is to find a shortest tour staring at vertex 1 and finally returns to vertex 1 in $G$. All the feasible solutions can be denoted as $(1, \sigma_2, \sigma_3, \cdots, \sigma_n, 1)$ in which $(\sigma_2, \sigma_3, \cdots, \sigma_n)$ is a permutation of $\{2, 3, \cdots, n\}$. If a tour $T = (1, \sigma_2, \sigma_3, \cdots, \sigma_n, 1)$ has $k$ edges of weight $n$, then the total weight

$w(T) = kn + (n - k)$, so there are altogether $n+1$ different weights of the tour in $G$ .The $w$ -based partition of the search space is $A_k = \{T \mid T = (1, \sigma_2, \cdots, \sigma_n, 1), w(T) = kn + (n-k)\}$, $k = 0, 1, 2, \cdots, n$. Obvio us-ly, the unique optimal solution is $(1, 2, 3, \cdots, n, 1)$ in $A_0$, whose total weight is $n$.

Denote the $t$ -th generation population of the Algorithm 1 by $\xi_t$, $t = 0, 1, 2, \cdots$.

Let $B_1 = \{$select the 2-opt operator as the mutation operator$\}$,

$B_2 = \{$select the 3-opt operator as the mutation operator$\}$,

For any given tour $T \in A_k$, $k = 1, 2, \cdots, n$. define $s(T) = P\{\xi_{t+1} \in A_{k-1} \bigcup A_{k-2} \bigcup \cdots \bigcup A_0 \mid \xi_t = T\}$. Let $s_k = \min\{s(T) \mid T \in A_k\}$.

**Theorem 1.** The upper bound of the expected runtime of (1+1) EA on the above TSP instance is $O(n^4)$.

**Proof.** We might as well assume that $n > 6$.

Suppose a tour $\sigma = (1, \sigma_2, \cdots, \sigma_n, 1) \in A_k, k > 0$ is given, where $(\sigma_2, \sigma_3, \cdots, \sigma_n)$ is a permutation of $(2, 3, \cdots, n)$. Since $\sigma$ is not the shortest tour, denote $\sigma_u$ as the first vertex in the tour $\sigma$ satisfying $w(\sigma_u, \sigma_{u+1}) = n$. Let $\sigma_v = \sigma_u + 1$, note that $w(\sigma_u, \sigma_v) = 1$ due to the construction of the graph $G$.

Then there are two cases for the tour $\sigma$ with respect to the weight $w(\sigma_v, \sigma_{v+1})$.

***Case 1.*** $w(\sigma_v, \sigma_{v+1}) = n$.
In this case, the 2-opt operator can be selected with probability 1/2 as the mutation operator, which removes two edges from the current tour $\sigma$, and replaces them with two other edges. Fig. 1 illustrates this transition.

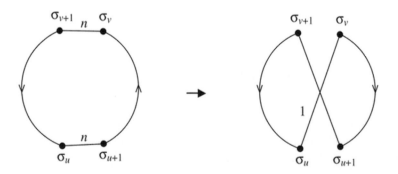

**Fig. 1.** 2-opt operator

Through the 2-opt operator, two links $\{(\sigma_u, \sigma_{u+1}), (\sigma_v, \sigma_{v+1})\}$ of the current tour $\sigma$ are replaced with two other links $\{(\sigma_u, \sigma_v), (\sigma_{u+1}, \sigma_{v+1})\}$. Thus, The current tour $\sigma = (1, \cdots, \sigma_u, \sigma_{u+1}, \cdots, \sigma_v, \sigma_{v+1}, \cdots, \sigma_n, 1)$ is transformed to $\sigma' = (1, \cdots, \sigma_u, \sigma_v, \sigma_{v-1} \cdots, \sigma_{u+1}, \sigma_{v+1}, \cdots, \sigma_n, 1)$.

Since $w(\sigma_u, \sigma_{u+1}) = w(\sigma_v, \sigma_{v+1}) = n$, and $w(\sigma_u, \sigma_v) = 1$, the total weight $w(\sigma')$ of $\sigma'$ is strictly smaller than that of $\sigma$. At each iteration, the 2-opt operator can be realized in this way: select randomly two vertices in $(\sigma_2, \sigma_3, \cdots, \sigma_n)$ and invert the substring between (and including) these two vertices. The number of total possible outcomes is $C_{n-1}^2$. Therefore, the transition probability at each step of iteration can be calculated as below.

$$
\begin{aligned}
s(\sigma) &= P\{\xi_{t+1} \in A_{k-1} \cup A_{k-2} \cup \cdots \cup A_0 \mid \xi_t = \sigma\} \\
&= \frac{P\{\xi_{t+1} \in A_{k-1} \cup A_{k-2} \cup \cdots \cup A_0 \mid B_1, \xi_t = \sigma\} P\{B_1, \xi_t = \sigma\}}{P\{\xi_t = \sigma\}} + \\
&\quad \frac{P\{\xi_{t+1} \in A_{k-1} \cup A_{k-2} \cup \cdots \cup A_0 \mid B_2, \xi_t = \sigma\} P\{B_2, \xi_t = \sigma\}}{P\{\xi_t - \sigma\}} \\
&\geq \frac{1}{C_{n-1}^2} P\{B_1 \mid \xi_t = \sigma\} = \frac{1}{2C_{n-1}^2} = \frac{1}{(n-1)(n-2).}
\end{aligned}
\tag{2}
$$

***Case 2.*** $w(\sigma_v, \sigma_{v+1}) = 1$.

In this case, it is obvious that $w(\sigma_{v-1}, \sigma_v) = n$, because $\sigma_v$ is adjacent to at most two weight 1 edges and $w(\sigma_u, \sigma_v) = 1$.

There must exist at least one weight $n$ edge in the path $(\sigma_v, \sigma_{v+1}, \cdots, \sigma_u)$, otherwise, there exists a cycle $(\sigma_v, \sigma_{v+1}, \cdots, \sigma_u, \sigma_v)$ whose weight is strictly smaller than $n$, which is in contradiction with the fact that the weight of any cycle of $G$ is no less than $n$.

Let $(\sigma_w, \sigma_{w+1})$ be the first edge of weight $n$ in path $(\sigma_v, \sigma_{v+1}, \cdots, \sigma_u)$, Fig. 2 is the illustration.

To get a shorter tour, the 3-opt operator instead of 2-opt operator need to be adopted. This can be done in this way: pick out two vertices in $(\sigma_2, \sigma_3, \cdots, \sigma_n)$ of $\sigma$, e.g. $\sigma_i, \sigma_j$, and insert the path $(\sigma_i, \sigma_{i+1}, \cdots, \sigma_j)$ between two adjacent vertices to form a new tour $\sigma'$.

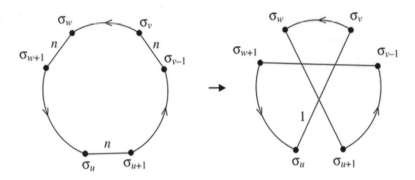

**Fig. 2.** 3-opt operator

As is shown in Fig.2, three links $\{(\sigma_u, \sigma_{u+1}), (\sigma_{v-1}, \sigma_v), (\sigma_w, \sigma_{w+1})\}$ of $\sigma$ are replaced with three other links $\{(\sigma_u, \sigma_v), (\sigma_w, \sigma_{u+1}), (\sigma_{v-1}, \sigma_{w+1})\}$ by inserting $(\sigma_v, \sigma_{v+1}, \cdots, \sigma_w)$ between $\sigma_u$ and $\sigma_{u+1}$, leading to a new tour $\sigma' = (1, \cdots, \sigma_u, \sigma_v, \sigma_{v+1} \cdots, \sigma_w, \sigma_{u+1}, \sigma_{u+2}, \cdots, \sigma_{v-1}, \sigma_{w+1}, \cdots, \sigma_n, 1)$ . Since $w(\sigma_u, \sigma_{u+1}) = w(\sigma_{v-1}, \sigma_v) = w(\sigma_w, \sigma_{w+1}) = n$ and $w(\sigma_u, \sigma_v) = 1$ , the total weight of $\sigma'$ is strictly smaller than that of $\sigma$. Similarly, the transition probability at each iteration can be calculated as below.

$$s(\sigma) = P\{\xi_{t+1} \in A_{k-1} \bigcup A_{k-2} \bigcup \cdots \bigcup A_0 \mid \xi_t = \sigma\}$$

$$= \frac{P\{\xi_{t+1} \in A_{k-1} \bigcup A_{k-2} \bigcup \cdots \bigcup A_0 \mid B_1, \xi_t = \sigma\} P\{B_1, \xi_t = \sigma\}}{P\{\xi_t = \sigma\}} +$$

$$\frac{P\{\xi_{t+1} \in A_{k-1} \bigcup A_{k-2} \bigcup \cdots \bigcup A_0 \mid B_2, \xi_t = \sigma\} P\{B_2, \xi_t = \sigma\}}{P\{\xi_t = \sigma\}} \qquad (3)$$

$$\geq \frac{1}{nC_{n-1}^2} P\{B_2 \mid \xi_t = \sigma\} = \frac{1}{2nC_{n-1}^2} = \frac{1}{n(n-1)(n-2)}.$$

Summing up case 1 and 2, we conclude $s_k = \min\{s(\sigma) \mid \sigma \in A_k\} \geq 1/n^3, k = 1, 2, \cdots, n$. Finally we obtain the upper bound of the expected runtime according to lemma 1

$$E(X_f) \leq s_1^{-1} + s_2^{-1} + \cdots + s_n^{-1} \leq n \cdot (1/n^3)^{-1} = O(n^4). \qquad \blacksquare$$

## 4   Conclusions

In this paper, we apply the level-reaching estimation technique to obtain an upper bound of expected runtime of (1+1) EA on a simple TSP instance. The result shows that although the (1+1) EA is a very simple variant of Evolutionary algorithms, its potential can not be underestimated. As far as the above instance is concerned, the (1+1) MMAA reported in [14] needs an upper bound of $O(n^6 + (1/\rho)n \ln n)$ while the (1+1) EA in this article needs $O(n^4)$, which is tighter. We can also see that the selection of mutation operator is very important in (1+1) EA, a well-chosen mutation operator can reduce the running time.

The proposed analysis approach can be extended to other combinatorial optimization problems, which we will discuss in another article. Moreover, we believe that the computational framework is also applicable to (1+1) ES and can be generalized for population based EAs, if we combine drift analysis[17,18]. All the issues will be studied in the next step.

**Acknowledgments.** This work was supported by the Natural Science Foundation of China (61070033), Natural Science Foundation of Guangdong Province (9251009001000005, 9151600301000001), Key Technology Research and Development Programs of Guangdong Province (2009B010800026). The authors would like to express thanks to Dr. Zhou Yu Ren, Dr. Huang Han and the anonymous reviewers.

# References

1. Goldberg, D.E.: Genetic Algorithms in Search, Optimization, and Machine Learning. Addison-Wesley, Reading (1989)
2. Schwefel, H.-P.: Evolution and Optimum Seeking. Wiley, New York( (1995)
3. Fogel, D.B.: Evolutionary Computation: Toward a New Philosophy of Machine Intelligence. IEEE Press, Piscataway (1995)
4. Karakoca, M., Kavakb, A.: Genetic Approach for Dynamic OVSF Code Allocation in 3G Wireless Networks. Applied Soft Computing 9(1), 348–361 (2009)
5. Liang, K.-H., Yao, X., Newton, C., Hoffman, D.: A New Evolutionary Approach to Cutting Stock Problems with and without Contiguity. Computers & Operations Research 29(12), 1641–1659 (2002)
6. Beligiannis, G.N., Moschopoulos, C.N., Kaperonisa, G.P., et al.: Applying Evolutionary Computation to the School Timetabling Problem: The Greek Case. Computers & Operations Research 35, 1265–1280 (2008)
7. Rudolph, G.: Convergence Analysis of Canonical Genetic Algorithms. IEEE Transactions on Neural Networks 5(1), 96–101 (1994)
8. Rudolph, G.: Convergence of Non-elitist Strategies. In: The First IEEE Conference on Evolutionary Computation, vol. 1, pp. 63–66. IEEE Press, Orlando (1994)
9. Rudolph, G.: Convergence Properties of Evolutionary Algorithms. Ph.D. Thesis. Verlag Dr. Kovac, Hamburg (1997)
10. Droste, S., Jansen, T., Wegener, I.: A Rigorous Complexity Analysis of the (1+1) Evolutionary Algorithm for Linear Functions with Boolean Inputs. In: IEEE International Conference on Evolutionary Computation, pp. 499–504. IEEE Press, NJ (1998)
11. Droste, S., Jansen, T., Wegener, I.: On the Analysis of the (1+1)Evolutionary Algorithm. Theoretical Computer Science 276, 51–81 (2002)

12. Witt, C.: Worst-case and Average-case Approximations by Simple Randomized Search Heuristic. In: Diekert, V., Durand, B. (eds.) STACS 2005. LNCS, vol. 3404, pp. 44–56. Springer, Heidelberg (2005)
13. Sudholt, D.: Crossover is Provably Essential for the Ising Model on Trees. In: Genetic and Evolutionary Computation Conference, Washington, DC, pp. 1161–1167 (2005)
14. Zhou, Y.R.: Runtime Analysis of Ant Colony Optimization Algorithm for TSP Instances. IEEE Transaction on Evolutionary Computation 13(5), 1083–1092 (2009)
15. Wegener, I.: Methods for the Analysis of Evolutionary Algorithms on Pseudo-boolean Functions. In: Sarker, R., Mohammadian, M., Yao, X. (eds.) Evolutionary Optimization. Kluwer Academic Publishers, Boston (2001)
16. Gutjahr, W.J.: Mathematical Runtime Analysis of ACO Algorithms: Survey on an Emerging Issue. Swarm Intelligence 1(1), 59–79 (2007)
17. Oliveto, P.S., He, J., Yao, X.: Analysis of the (1+1)-EA for Finding Approximate Solutions to Vertex Cover Problems. IEEE Transactions on Evolutionary Computation 13(5), 1006–1029 (2009)
18. Chen, T., He, J., Sun, G., et al.: A New Approach for Analyzing Average Time Complexity of Population-based Evolutionary Algorithms on Unimodal Problems. IEEE Transactions on Systems, Man and Cybernetics, Part B 39(5), 1092–1106 (2009)

# An Evolutionary Approach to Intelligent Planning

Shikha Mehta[1], Bhuvan Sachdeva[2], Rohit Bhargava[3], and Hema Banati[1]

[1] Department of Computer Science, Dyal Singh College, University of Delhi, Delhi
[2] Movico technologies, Gurgaon
[3] Accenture , Mumbai
{mehtshikha,bhuv.sac,bhargavarohit15}@gmail.com,
banatihema@hotmail.com

**Abstract.** With the explosion of information on WWW, planning and decision making has become a tedious task. The huge volume of distributed and heterogeneous information resources and the complexity involved in their coordination and scheduling leads to difficulties in the conception of optimal plans. This paper presents an intelligent planner which uses modified Genetic Algorithm assisted Case Based Reasoning (CBR) to solve the cold start problem faced by CBR systems and generates novel plans. This approach minimizes the need of populating preliminary cases in the CBR systems. The system is capable of generating synchronized optimal plans within the specified constraints. The effectiveness of the approach is demonstrated with the help of case study on e-Travel Planning. Rigorous experiments were performed to generate synchronized plans with one hop and two hops between train and flight modes of transport. Results proved that GA assisted CBR outperforms the traditional CBR significantly in providing the number of optimized plans and solving cold start problem.

**Keywords:** CBR-GA hybrid, Intelligent Planner, GA based cost optimization, Cold Start Problem, Synchronized Travel Plans.

## 1 Introduction

Since times immemorial, planning is ubiquitous in everyday life-from meal planning to Day Planning, Activity Planning, Travel Planning, Investment Planning, Tax Planning, Project Planning etc. With the world getting closer, man has more options to choose. However searching, retrieving and analyzing information from heterogeneous and distributed information resources for day-today planning is a wearisome task. This has motivated the researchers to explore the possibilities of automating the planning task using Artificial Intelligence techniques. One of the most successful AI technology applied in commercial and industrial applications is Case Based Reasoning (CBR).CBR [4] is a problem solving paradigm that emphasizes reasoning and planning from prior experience. Each case in CBR based systems may represent a plan or sub-plan to solve a particular problem. CBR retains every new experience in the memory, each time a problem is solved, making it immediately available for future problems. However CBR proves inefficient in a situation for

B.K. Panigrahi et al. (Eds.): SEMCCO 2010, LNCS 6466, pp. 305–313, 2010.
© Springer-Verlag Berlin Heidelberg 2010

which it has no past experience like system proposed by [1] [3] [10] may fail to provide any suggestions to the user if the initial cases are not populated manually. This problem is popularly known as Cold-Start problem and is more prevalent in the systems which depend upon past solutions to solve future queries. Thus various approaches have been integrated with the CBR to analyze the best algorithm or technique to improve the performance of CBR like Meta reasoning tried to improve the efficiency of a cased based reasoning approach but on few occasions it introduced unwanted changes that degraded the system performance [9]. In the current scenario integration of evolutionary approach like Genetic Algorithm (GA) with CBR has been observed as successful innovation over traditional CBR technique. Genetic algorithms (GAs) are a population-based Meta heuristics invented by John Holland in the 1960s [5].Genetic algorithms are evolutionary search and optimization algorithms based on the mechanics of natural genetics and natural selection. They are a family of computational models that use the notion of evolution to generate successively better solutions from previous generations of solutions. The hybrid (CBR-GA) model named SOCBR (Simultaneous Optimization of CBR) outperformed the other models namely COCBR (Conventional CBR), FWCBR (CBR with Feature Weighting), ISCBR (CBR with Instance Selection), and SOCBR (Simultaneous Optimization of CBR) in judging the status of bankrupt or non-bankrupt [7]. Besides the application of GA has also been exploited in different phases of CBR like CBR-GA hybrid for Case retrieval was demonstrated in travel and foodmart [3], tablet formulation problem [8] and Corporate Bond Rating [11]. The utility of GA in CBR revision phase was established in generating timetable solutions [2].The integration of CBR with GA approach has been proved to be better in comparison to other variations of CBR. Nevertheless the application of Genetic algorithms to solve the Cold Start problem occurring in CBR and to generate synchronized and optimized novel plans is still an unexplored research area.

In this respect the paper presents modified Genetic algorithm assisted Case Based Reasoning approach for solving Cold-Start problem faced by CBR based systems and generate novel plans. The effectiveness of the approach is established with the help of case study on e-Travel Planning. Proposed approach provides optimized solution plans with minimum duration, synchronized for train and Flight modes of transport within the budget specified by the user. The organization of the paper is as follows. Section 2 presents System architecture and Algorithm. Experiments and results are given in section 3 followed by conclusion and future work in section 4.

## 2   System Architecture and Algorithm

The architecture of the prototype system developed to demonstrate the capabilities of the evolutionary approach to intelligent planning is shown in the Fig 1. System employs agents to leverage the benefits of Agent architecture [6]. These agents perform the various activities to be carried out by the system. Team of agents include User Agent (UA), Planner Agent (PA), Case Based Reasoning Agent (CBRA), Genetic Algorithm Agent (GAA), Repository Agent (RA) and Verification Agent (VA).  The overall algorithm in phases as follows:-

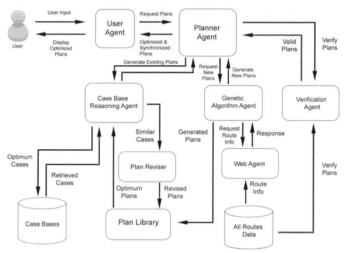

**Fig. 1.** System architecture

**Phase 1:** The User Agent (UA) accepts the query submitted by the user and forwards it to the Planner Agent (PA) for further processing. PA builds an abstract representation of the query received from UA, and processes it to compute solution plans. PA is assisted by two subordinate agents for query processing Case Based Reasoning Agent (CBRA) and Genetic Algorithm Agent (GAA). PA primarily invokes CBRA to find the similar cases based on preferences provided by the user.

**Phase 2:** CBRA predominantly refers the Case Based Reasoning system (CBRs) plan library to check if it has any prior plans stored, with respect to the user specified query. CBRA then tries to fit various modes of transport within the given budget for its optimization. The plans are finally adapted to the new adjusted modes and budget.

**Phase 3:** In this phase the reused plans from the previous phase are revised by changing the cities and budget for further optimization. CBRA passes these plans to PA. PA checks if the number of plans received after revising the cases are sufficient (that is if they are above threshold) to satisfy the user. In such a situation if there are no plans retrieved by CBRA e.g. user submits a new query for which CBR has no past experience, CBR based systems fail to provide any plans to the user. However in our system PA invokes GAA to generate novel plans. Simultaneously PA also invokes VA to verify the current availability status of the plans (if any) generated by CBRA, before communicating them to the UA. It helps in providing only the updated and valid plans to the user e.g. in travel planning domain existing plans may fail if the train or flight no more runs.

**Phase 4:** GAA firstly invokes Repository Agent (RA) to gather route information from the Repository. GAA uses proposed modified genetic algorithm to optimize the route information received from RA and evolve plans within the user specified budget. Steps of the modified Genetic algorithm are as follows:-

**Step 4.1.** Size of population determines the number of plans generated by the system. An initial population of 200 chromosomes is generated by GAA. Any change in population size leads to corresponding change in quantitative number of plans generated by the algorithm. The size and structure of chromosome depends on the user preference of the route. Route with one hop and two hops has Chromosome of size 3 and 4 respectively.

Chromosome Structure for size 3:

| Source | Budget | Hop | Budget | Destination |
|--------|--------|-----|--------|-------------|

Chromosome Structure for size 4:

| Source | Budget | Hop | Budget | Hop | Budget | Destination |
|--------|--------|-----|--------|-----|--------|-------------|

**Step 4.2:** Thereafter a maximum allowable cost is distributed between all two consecutive genes within the chromosome. The sum of all cost within a chromosome is equal to the budget given by the user.

**Step 4.3:** To compute the Fitness of a particular chromosome, the fitness function is as follows:-

$$F\,(Chr) = \sum (n) \tag{1}$$

Where Chr is an individual chromosome, n is the total number of ways one can reach the destination from the source.

**Step 4.4:** The chromosome with highest fitness value is considered most fit.

**Step 4.5:** GAA uses Elitism [7] mechanism for selecting the chromosomes for next generation and performs multipoint crossover with crossover probability of .7 and a mutation probability of 0.03.

**Step 4.6:** GAA employs an additional Evolve operator along with the conventional Crossover and Mutation operators, for optimizing the plans within specified number of generations. The functionality of evolve operator involves duplication of best fit genes with only a slight modification to the parameters. If the new genes are more fit, then the old genes are replaced with the new genes. Thus the genes evolve into better solutions, thereby improving the fitness of the chromosome. Afterwards GAA communicates optimized plans to the Planner Agent.

**Phase 5:** Thereafter GAA stores new plans and their sub-plans in CBRs plan library for solving future queries.

**Phase 6:** PA sends integrated plans (from VA and GAA) to UA to be presented to the user. UA presents the top N plans with minimum time within the budget preferred by the user.

# 3   Experiments and Results

Rigorous experiments were performed to assess the competence of proposed approach as compared to traditional CBR system. The prototype system was developed using JADE (Java Agent Development Environment), J2EE (Java 2 Enterprise Edition) and MySql database and executed on Core2 Duo 1.67 GHz processor and 2-GB RAM computer. Specialized programs were developed to retrieve the real datasets of Indian flight [12] and train [13] modes of transport for performing the experiments. The number of stops considered in each case (i.e. flight and train) was different, 162 cities were considered with respect to trains and 20 cities were taken for the flights. All the possible trains and flights between two stops were stored in the database and included in the dataset. On the whole dataset constituted 90000 tuples of various trains and 900 tuples for diverse flights between two stations. The various attributes of trains and flights database include source, destination, fares of different classes, arrival time and departure time.

**Experiment 1:** This experiment substantiates the ability of system to serve diverse requirements of the users. For example for a query like Source: Bangalore, Destination: Calcutta, Budget: Rs. 9000 and Mode: both (train and flight), algorithm generates varied kinds of plans like 1-hop plans, plans with 2-hops and direct plans as shown in Fig 2

| No. | Source | Date | Departure | Arrival | Mode | Number | Name | Destination | |
|---|---|---|---|---|---|---|---|---|---|
| 1 | Bangalore | 2-6-2010 | 06:40 | 09:05 | flight | 6E 341 | IndiGo | Calcutta | 5381.0 |
| Total :5381.0 | | | | | | | | | |
| 2 | Bangalore | 2-6-2010 | 09.55 | 12:20 | flight | SG 528 | SpiceJet | Calcutta | 4431.0 |
| Total :4431.0 | | | | | | | | | |
| 3 | Bangalore | 2-6-2010 | 06:20 | 09:50 | flight | IT 3431 | Kingfisher Red | Calcutta | 5700.0 |
| Total :5700.0 | | | | | | | | | |
| 4 | Bangalore | 2-6-2010 | 11:55 | 14:20 | flight | 6E 155 | IndiGo | Calcutta | 4431.0 |

D:\planning agents\intelligent travel planning\pp...

| 13 | Bangalore | 2-6-2010 | 20:15 | 22:55 | flight | SG 216 | SpiceJet | Delhi | 3581.0 |
|---|---|---|---|---|---|---|---|---|---|
| | Delhi | 3-6-2010 | 07:30 | 09:30 | flight | 6E 257 | IndiGo | Bhubaneswar | 3180.0 |
| | Bhubaneswar | 3-6-2010 | 23:50 | 07:05 | train | 2882 | Puri Hwh G Rath | Calcutta | 403.0 |
| Total:7164.0 | | | | | | | | | |
| 14 | Bangalore | 3-6-2010 | 10:10 | 12:10 | flight | 6E 154 | IndiGo | Ahmedabad | 3182.0 |
| | Ahmedabad | 3-6-2010 | 15:40 | 03:35 | train | 2905 | Pbr Howrah Exp | Calcutta | 2004.0 |
| Total:5186.0 | | | | | | | | | |
| 15 | Bangalore | 2-6-2010 | 08:45 | 11:40 | flight | SG 224 | SpiceJet | Delhi | 3752.0 |
| | Delhi | 2-6-2010 | 14:40 | 09:40 | train | 2368 | Vikramshila Exp | Kiul | 1427.0 |
| | Kiul | 3-6-2010 | 16:55 | 03:30 | train | 3106 | Bui Sdah Exp | Calcutta | 555.0 |
| Total:5734.0 | | | | | | | | | |

**Fig. 2.** Optimized and synchronized plans

All these plans are synchronized across train and flight modes of transport with different permutations and combinations as seen in Fig 2 like plans with 2-hops may be Flight-Flight-Train or Flight-Train-Train etc. The plans optimized within the budget provided by the user are depicted in the decreasing order of time for complete journey.

**Experiment 2:** To establish the capability of our approach in solving cold-start problem and generate novel plans, system was tested on 50 random queries with different source and destinations for both (train and flight) modes of transport and travel budget of around Rs.4000. Fig 3 shows the number of plans with 1-hop and Fig4 exhibits the number of plans with 2-hops between source and destination, generated by CBR alone and CBR-GA hybrid. These figures precisely illustrate that CBR-GA is able to generate plans even for the preliminary queries whereas CBR based system starts generating plans only after having some experience of the related queries. Thus the proposed system is competent in providing results irrespective of any past experience. Fig 5 portrays the total number of plans with zero hops, one hop and two hops between the source and destination retrieved by traditional CBR system and hybrid CBR-GA. These results establish the performance of the system in generating total number of indirect plans (1-hop and 2-hop) as compared to the number of available direct plans. However most of the existing commercial web based travel planning systems present only direct plans to the user which are very less as compared to the number of indirect plans. Together the direct and indirect plans may lead to an enhanced user experience.

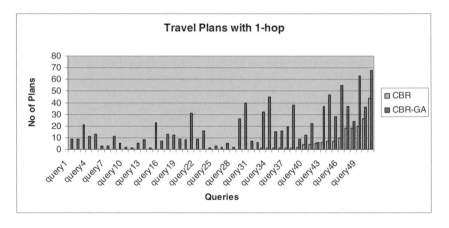

**Fig. 3.** Plans with 1-hop

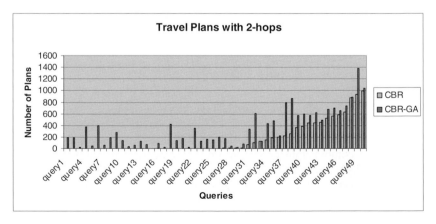

**Fig. 4.** Plans with 2-hop

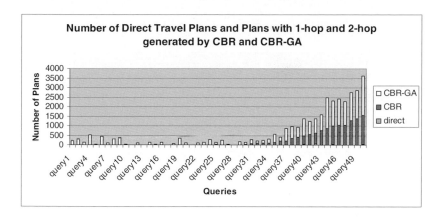

**Fig. 5.** Total indirect plans generated by CBR alone and by CBR-GA hybrid as compared to number of direct plans

**Experiment 3:** It was conducted to show the performance of modified GA as compared to conventional GA as shown in Fig 6. Since the fitness of the chromosome is computed using equation (1), behavior of GA was observed over the 50 different queries. The figure illustrates that over the generations additional evolve operator improves the performance of GA significantly as compared to traditional GA.

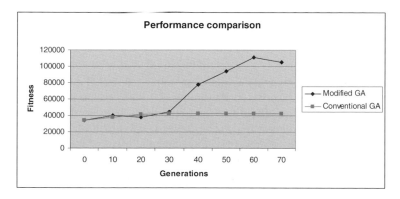

**Fig. 6.** Performance of Modified GA

**Experiment 4:** This experiment corroborates the ability of system in generating wide variety of optimized plans within a particular cost range. Fig 7 depicts the number of plans generated within a cost range after optimizing the user specified budget (Rs 9000 in this case) across different modes of transport. These plans may help in serving the wide variety of users in a better way.

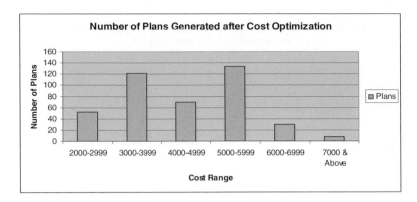

**Fig. 7.** Number of plans retrieved within a particular cost range

On the whole, contribution of proposed approach to the existing research is noteworthy. Results of the meticulous experiments evidently demonstrate that proposed approach to CBR-GA hybrid is considerably better than CBR alone. The competency of the system in solving Cold-Start problems and in generating novel plans has been well established through experiments. This approach also curtails the need of maintaining initial case base repository to handle preliminary queries. The ability of modified Genetic Algorithm in cost optimization reveals that large number of plans computed within various ranges may provide better experience to the user. The proposed approach to hybridization of GA with CBR for optimizing and synchronizing plans across multiple modes may be extended for Time Optimization also.

## 4   Conclusion

This paper presented an intelligent planning approach based on adapted Genetic algorithm (GA) assisted Case Based Reasoning (CBR) to tackle the problems posed in CBR based systems. The efficacy of the approach is demonstrated via case study on e-travel planning for generating the optimized and synchronized indirect travel plans across various modes of transport. Experimental results involving real datasets of Indian train and flight modes of transportation revealed that the algorithm designed using proposed hybrid approach is highly efficient in generating novel plans and in solving cold-start problem stirring in systems developed using CBR alone. Future work includes extending the work to other application domains.

## References

[1] Camacho, D., Aler, R., Borrajo, D., Molina, M.J.: Multi-agent plan based information gathering. Journal of Applied Intelligence 25, 59–71 (2006)
[2] Grech, A., Main, J.: A Case-Based Reasoning Approach to Formulating University Timetables Using Genetic Algorithms. In: Khosla, R., Howlett, R.J., Jain, L.C. (eds.) KES 2005. LNCS (LNAI), vol. 3681, pp. 76–83. Springer, Heidelberg (2005)

 [3] Yang, H.-L., Cheng-Shu, W.: Two stages of case-based reasoning - Integrating genetic algorithm with data mining mechanism. Expert Systems with Applications: An International Journal archive 35(1-2), 262–272 (2008)
 [4] Kolodner, J.: Case-Based Reasoning. Morgan and Kaufmann publishers, San Francisco
 [5] Mitchell, M.: An Introduction to Genetic Algorithm. MIT Press, Cambridge (1999)
 [6] Wooldridge, M.: An Introduction to Multi Agents. John Wiley & Sons, Chichester (2003)
 [7] Ahn, H., Kim, K., Han, I.: Hybrid Genetic Algorithms and Case-Based Reasoning Systems. In: International Symposium of Computational and Information Science, pp. 922–927. Springer, Heidelberg (2004)
 [8] Jarmulak, J., Craw, S., Rowe, R.: Genetic Algorithms to Optimise CBR Retrieval. In: Blanzieri, E., Portinale, L. (eds.) EWCBR 2000. LNCS (LNAI), vol. 1898, pp. 159–194. Springer, Heidelberg (2000)
 [9] Mehta, M., Ontañón, S., Ram, A.: Using Meta-reasoning to Improve the Performance of Case-Based Planning. In: McGinty, L., Wilson, D.C. (eds.) 8th International Conference on Case Based Reasoning. LNCS, vol. 5650, pp. 210–224. Springer, Heidelberg (2009)
[10] Niknafs, A.A., Shiri, M.E., Javidi, M.M.: A Case-Based Reasoning Approach in E-Tourism: Tour Itinerary Planning. In: Proceedings of the 14th International Workshop on Database and Expert Systems Applications. IEEE, Los Alamitos (2003)
[11] Shin, K., Han, I.: A Hybrid Approach Using CBR and GA for Corporate Bond Rating. In: International Conference on Case Based Reasoning. ACM, New York (2008)
[12] http://www.cleartrip.com
[13] http://www.indianrail.gov.in

# Substitute Domination Relation for High Objective Number Optimization

Sofiene Kachroudi

Applied Mathematics and Systems Department, Ecole Centrale de Paris,
Grande voie des vignes Chatenay Malabry, France
sofiane.kachroudi@ecp.fr

**Abstract.** In this paper, we introduce the average rank dominance relation which substitutes the Pareto domination relation for high objective number optimization. The substitute relation is based on the performances of the solutions in each objective and calculated as the average rank of the solutions on each objective. In addition, the paper studies substituting the Pareto domination relation by the new domination relation in the well known multi-objective algorithms NSGAII and SMPSO which are based respectively on the genetic and particle swarm optimization. The new algorithms are tested on the first four problems of DTLZ family and compared to the original algorithms via new performance indicators.

## 1 Introduction

The multi-objective optimization aims to estimate the true Pareto front in the multi-dimensional objective space. Besides some exact and gradient based multi-objective optimization algorithms, multi-objective metaheuristic algorithms have been largely studied and treated in the specialized literature. The NSGAII algorithm [1] is a genetic based multi-objective algorithm whose performances were widely proved and the algorithm is still considered as a reference multi-objective algorithm.

More recently, new multi-objective particle swarm based algorithms were proposed taking advantage of the success of the particle swarm intelligence to converge to optimal solutions. As examples, we can quote [2], [3]. A more recent multi-objective PSO algorithm is the Speed-constrained Multi-objective PSO algorithm (SMPSO [4]). Compared to the algorithm of [3], SMPSO uses to constraint the particle's velocity. Among these particle swarm based algorithms, comparative studies show that the SMPSO algorithm is the best one for many test problems.

All these algorithms were thought to handle many objectives. However in practice, their performances become more and more poor when the number of objectives increases. It is only recently that the difficulties of increasing the objective number were outlined accurately and algorithmic improvements were proposed in order to overcome these issues. As examples, in [5] new second distances were used to substitute the crowding distance in the NSGAII algorithm. In [6], the original objective space was partitioned randomly into many subspaces and the solutions were re-ranked with respect to these subspaces using substitute second distance as in [5]. As we know, for the particle swarm optimization algorithms, no significant works have been published to

B.K. Panigrahi et al. (Eds.): SEMCCO 2010, LNCS 6466, pp. 314–321, 2010.

deal with the case of many-objective optimization except a preliminary work in [7] by partitioning, in the first step, the objective space into smaller subspaces and the population into smaller subpopulations before using, in the second step, the SMPSO algorithm to resolve the initial optimization problem with all the particles of the subpopulations. In parallel of these specific algorithmic works, the question of the efficiency of the Pareto domination relation for many-objective optimization were outlined. The modification of this relation represents a possible way that may increase the selection pressure and hence improve the search ability of the algorithms. Another way consists of substituting the Pareto domination relation by introducing different ranks based on the performances of the solutions objective by objective( [10], [11]). A particular ranking method especially interesting is the simple average ranking [8] which is the basis of our domination relation.

In this paper, we propose a domination relation that substitutes the Pareto domination relation in the NSAGII and SMPSO algorithms. First, we propose the average rank domination relation. Then we present the modified versions of NSGAII and SMPSO algorithms in which some selection mechanisms use the substitute domination relation. In the next section, we describe the DTLZ problems and propose the performance indicators constructed in order to construe the experimentation results. The section 5 is dedicated to the numerical results of the first four problems of DTLZ family. In the section 6, we conclude the paper by a brief summary and suggestions for future works.

## 2   Average Rank Domination Relation

Before describing the details of the domination relation, let's take a simple example. We consider a multi-objective optimization problem consisting of minimizing 5 objectives. We suppose that, during the optimization iterations, we have the four following solutions in the objective space:

$$s_1 = [4; 0.5; 3; 2; 5]^T$$
$$s_2 = [1; 3; 2; 1.5; 4]^T$$
$$s_3 = [2; 1; 1.5; 1; 1]^T$$
$$s_4 = [1.5; 0.7; 1; 0.5; 2]^T$$

The four solutions are non dominated in the sense of the Pareto domination relation and thus equivalent. However, the solution $s_4$ is better than the others in 4 objectives. The solution $s_3$ is better than $s_1$ and $s_2$ in 4 objectives and $s_2$ is better than $s_1$ in also 4 objectives. Therefore, it appears obvious that for this example, the Pareto domination relation is insufficient to distinguish solutions and enhance selection. As a consequence, it becomes necessary to define new domination relations that enhance the selection pressure by relaxing the domination rule.

The substitute domination relation proposed here is based on the average ranking method defined as follows:

**Definition 1.** *Average Rank*
*Given a set of solutions $\{s_1,...,s_m\}$, the average rank $m\_rank(s_k)$ of the solution $s_k$ is defined as follows:*

$$m\_rank(s_k) - \frac{1}{n}\sum_{i=1}^{n} rank(s_k, i)$$

*where $rank(s_k, i)$ is the rank of the solution $s_k$ among the solution set, ranked increasingly, with respect to the objective i.*

With this last definition, we define the average rank domination relation.

**Definition 2.** *Average Rank Domination Relation*
*Given two solutions $s_1$ and $s_2$:*

- *$s_1$ is said to dominate $s_2$ if and only if $m\_rank(s_1) < m\_rank(s_2)$,*
- *$s_1$ is said to be dominated by $s_2$ if and only if $m\_rank(s_1) > m\_rank(s_2)$ and*
- *$s_1$ and $s_2$ is said to be non dominated if and only if $m\_rank(s_1) = m\_rank(s_2)$.*

The average rank domination relation have the very important property that it preserves the Pareto domination relation.

*Property 1.* if a solution $s_1$ dominates, in the sense of Pareto, a solution $s_2$, therefore $s_1$ dominates $s_2$ in the sense of the average rank.

In fact, if $s_1$ dominates $s_2$ in the sense of Pareto, we have $\forall i \in \{1, ..., n\}$, $rank(s_1, i) \leq rank(s_2, i)$ and $\exists j \in \{1, ..., n\}$ such that $rank(s_1, j) < rank(s_2, j)$. This leads to $\frac{1}{n}\sum_{i=1}^{n} rank(s_1, i) < \frac{1}{n}\sum_{i=1}^{n} rank(s_2, i)$ and thus $m\_rank(s_1) < m\_rank(s_2)$ that is the definition of $s_1$ dominating $s_2$ in the sense of the average rank.

## 3    NSGAII and SMPSO Algorithms with the Average Rank Dominance Relation

Two of the most powerful multi-objective optimization algorithms are the NSGAII and SMPSO algorithms which both use the Pareto dominance relation as a selection criteria. In the following subsections, we show how we substitute the Pareto dominance relation by the average rank domination one.

The selection mechanism in the NSGAII algorithm is achieved firstly by ranking the solutions with respect to successive fronts obtained by the Pareto dominance relation. Secondly and for solutions of the same fronts, the selection is achieved by re-ranking them with the crowding distance which is a density measure. As shown in [?], for many-objective optimization problems, the percentage of non dominated solutions may raise until 100% (all solutions are in the same front) sometimes since the initializing step for some problems. In such cases, the Pareto dominance has no longer effect on the selection mechanism and the selection is achieved only by the crowding distance.

By using the average rank domination relation instead of the Pareto domination one, the selection mechanism will be achieved almost exclusively by this first ranking. In fact, it is quasi-impossible to have the situation in which two solutions randomly chosen have the same average rank. With respect to the original NSGAII algorithm, the modifications are:

- Substituting the Pareto dominance relation by the average rank dominance relation.
- Re-ranking all the solutions by the crowding distance in one step and not in many steps in which re-ranking the solutions of successive fronts is achieved each one alone. The re-ranking operation, as said before, have minor consequences on the selection mechanism since very few solutions will have the same average rank.

The particle swarm optimization is based on the principle that every particle has a memory which let it to remember its best position in the past and the best position of its neighborhood (position in the decision space is a decision vector). In single objective optimization, the update of a particle's memory is simple contrary to the multi-objective case. In addition, during the optimization algorithm execution, a multi-objective particle swarm based algorithm must dispose of at least one external archive in which non dominated solutions have to be stocked. The SMPSO algorithm has the following features:

- The update of the best position is based on the Pareto domination relation. When the best past position and the new position are non dominated, the update is achieved randomly between the two positions.
- The selection of the best position of the neighborhood is also given thanks to the Pareto domination relation. When many neighbor particles are non dominated, the crowding distance is used to select the best position.
- There are one external archive to stock all non dominated solutions, along the algorithm execution. If the archive is full, the crowding distance is used to discard solutions with lower values.

The average rank domination relation substitutes the Pareto domination in the update of the particle's best position and the neighborhood's best position. The management of the external archive remains unchanged.

# 4   Experimentation

In this section, we present the problems 1 to 4 of DTLZ problems family and the performance indicators that will be used to compare the algorithms in the next section.

## 4.1   DTLZ Problems

The DTLZ problems family [9] is a scalable multi-objective optimization problems family. The systematic scalability of the DTLZ problems to any objective and decision variables numbers is a very useful property that let us to test simply the algorithms for different objective numbers. The DTLZ problems are designed so that they reproduce almost of the situations encountered in the real life. Many DTLZ problems have multiple local Pareto front and for some of them, it is too hard, for the algorithms, to find the global Pareto front. For some others, it is hard to obtain solutions well spread on the true Pareto front. In addition to these features, the problems 1 to 4 of the DTLZ family have the important property that their global Pareto fronts have simple continuous shapes with very simple analytical expressions. For all these reasons, we use the problems 1 to 4 of DTLZ family to test and study our approach. The particular features of these four problems are as follows:

- DTLZ1: have multiple local Pareto fronts and a linear global Pareto front that is an hyperplane given by the following equation:

$$\sum_{i=1}^{n} f_i = \frac{1}{2}$$

- DTLZ2, DTLZ3 and DTLZ4: are spheric problems and their global Pareto front is given by the following equation:

$$\sum_{i=1}^{n} f_i^2 = 1$$

## 4.2 Performance Indicators

In multi-objective optimization, the main goal of algorithms is to estimate the true global Pareto front. The accuracy of the estimation is measured by a convergence indicator which gives the closeness of the solutions to the true Pareto front and a spread indicator which verifies that the solutions cover the maximum of the Pareto front shape. The features of the first four DTLZ problems offer great possibilities to construct simple performance indicators even for the case of many objectives.

Given a solution set $S = \{s_1, ..., s_m\}$, the convergence indicator is as follows:

- For DTLZ1: as the Pareto front is an hyperplane of equation $\sum_{i=1}^{n} f_i = \frac{1}{2}$, the convergence indicator is

$$\frac{1}{m} \sum_{i=1}^{m} \left( \sum_{j=1}^{n} f_j^i - \frac{1}{2} \right)$$

where $f_j^i$ is the $j^{th}$ objective value of solution $i$.
- For DTLZ2, DTLZ3 and DTLZ4: they have the same Pareto front shape equation of the form $\sum_{i=1}^{n} f_i^2 = 1$. Therefore, the convergence indicator is given by:

$$\frac{1}{m} \sum_{i=1}^{m} \left( \sum_{j=1}^{n} (f_j^i)^2 - 1 \right)$$

One way to measure spread (and convergence) is to calculate some distance between the solution set found and a perfect solution set that maximize the spread. From our point of view, given a solution set of $m$ solutions, the values of the objective j of the perfect solutions set have to be:

- $f_j^{i*} = 0 + (i-1) \times \frac{\frac{1}{2}-0}{m-1}; i \in \{1, ..., m\}$ for DTLZ1 problem.
- $f_j^{i*} = 0 + (i-1) \times \frac{1-0}{m-1}; i \in \{1, ..., m\}$ for DTLZ2, DTLZ3 and DTLZ4 problems.

In fact, from our point of view and for the objective $j$, the perfect solutions must be separated by a regular distance between the minimum and the maximum of the objective of the true Pareto front. The average objective values difference between the solutions found and the perfect ones give the first spread measure:

$$\frac{1}{m} \sum_{i=1}^{m} \sum_{j=1}^{n} |f_j^i - f_j^{i*}|$$

## 5    Numerical Results

The tests are performed for the first four DTLZ problems with 20, 40 and 80 objectives. The algorithms run for 30 times independently. For the NSGAII algorithm and its modified version, the crossover probability is 0.9, the mutation probability is one divided by the decision variables number, the population has 100 individuals and the iteration number is 200. For the SMPSO algorithm and its modified version, the constriction factor is 0.1, the swarm has 100 particles and the iteration number is 200. The convergence and the first spread indicators are summarized respectively on table 1 and 2.

**Table 1.** Convergence and Spread indicator for DTLZ problems

**Convergence**

| Problem | Objective number | NSGAII | mod. NSGAII | SMPSO | mod. SMPSO |
|---------|------------------|--------|-------------|-------|------------|
| DTLZ1 | 20 | 1766.9236 | **472.88606** | **943.12388** | 998.2111 |
|  | 40 | 1825.0498 | **365.36258** | **908.96938** | 972.76465 |
|  | 80 | 1787.8256 | **717.25986** | **852.83625** | 905.61137 |
| DTLZ2 | 20 | 4.5478379 | **0.3290681** | **4.4867753** | 4.5292413 |
|  | 40 | 4.614103 | **0.9284698** | **4.4816829** | 4.4910533 |
|  | 80 | 4.2647145 | **1.2097324** | **3.9105593** | 4.3164842 |
| DTLZ3 | 20 | 3684.0946 | **643.39527** | **1691.9877** | 2019.566 |
|  | 40 | 3821.4805 | **1568.2155** | **1913.1853** | 1973.4509 |
|  | 80 | 3828.936 | **1731.4865** | 1870.2043 | **1709.2733** |
| DTLZ4 | 20 | 4.416096 | **0.0014388** | 4.2619014 | **4.1623968** |
|  | 40 | 4.2300806 | **0.1737628** | 4.3863182 | **4.2478095** |
|  | 80 | 3.7586969 | **0.5281895** | 4.1037263 | **4.0388898** |

**Spread**

| Problem | Objective number | NSGAII | mod. NSGAII | SMPSO | mod. SMPSO |
|---------|------------------|--------|-------------|-------|------------|
| DTLZ1 | 20 | 87.939837 | **12.285315** | **46.783929** | 49.531409 |
|  | 40 | 45.258509 | **5.1286157** | **22.554933** | 24.079481 |
|  | 80 | 22.141624 | **9.2885433** | **10.82289** | 11.432982 |
| DTLZ2 | 20 | **0.4581926** | 0.5181403 | **0.5242023** | 0.5097869 |
|  | 40 | **0.3824058** | 0.5229357 | **0.4728237** | 0.4515359 |
|  | 80 | **0.3468251** | 0.5150310 | **0.4725059** | 0.4494330 |
| DTLZ3 | 20 | 432.74618 | **34.984911** | **198.12915** | 269.6884 |
|  | 40 | 284.59636 | **39.19643** | **148.91623** | 159.46392 |
|  | 80 | 203.753 | **21.848936** | 73.097521 | **64.666036** |
| DTLZ4 | 20 | 0.5528908 | **0.3665240** | **0.5865524** | 0.5875006 |
|  | 40 | 0.5465345 | **0.5040552** | 0.5349946 | **0.529645** |
|  | 80 | 0.5142767 | **0.5066190** | 0.5297088 | **0.5275344** |

With respect to the convergence indicator, the NSGAII algorithm with the average rank domination relation is better than the original NSGAII in all the problems for all objective number. However for the SMPSO algorithm, the substitute domination relation has no real positive effect. From the point of view of the first spread indicator, the average rank domination relation enhances the spread of the solutions for the NSGAII algorithm for all DTLZ problems except the DTLZ2. For the SMPSO algorithm, it enhances the spread for the DTLZ2 and DTLZ4 problems.

# 6 Conclusion

The paper proposed a substitute domination relation based on the average rank method especially useful for many-objective optimization. This relation substitutes the classical Pareto domination relation in the NSGAII and SMPSO algorithms and their modified versions were tested on the first four DTLZ problems. The results with high number of objectives show a better convergence with the substitute domination relation for NSGAII algorithm. However for the SMPSO algorithm, no great improvements have to be highlighted. The future works will concern the enhancement of the solutions spread with this domination relation and the construction of more simple and reliable performance indicators.

# References

1. Deb, K., Pratap, A., Agarwal, S., Meyarivan, T.: A fast and elitist multi-objective genetic algorithm: NSGA-II. IEEE Trans. on Evolutionary Computation, 182–197 (April 2002)
2. Coello Coello, C.A., Lechuga, M.S.: MOPSO: a proposal for multiple objective particle swarm optimization. In: WCCI Proceedings of the 2002 World on Congress on Computational Intelligence, pp. 1051–1056 (2002)
3. Reyes Sierra, M., Coello Coello, C.A.: Improving PSO-Based Multiobjective Optimization Using Crowding, Mutation and ε-Dominance. In: Coello Coello, C.A., Hernández Aguirre, A., Zitzler, E. (eds.) EMO 2005. LNCS, vol. 3410, pp. 505–519. Springer, Heidelberg (2005)
4. Nebro, A.J., Durillo, J.J., García-Nieto, J., Coello Coello, C.A., Luna, F., Alba, E.: SMPSO: A New PSO-based Metaheuristic for Multi-objective Optimization. In: IEEE Symposium on Computational Intelligence in Multicriteria Decision-Making (MCDM 2009), pp. 66–73 (2009)
5. Singh, H.K., Isaacs, A., Ray, T., Smith, W.: A Study on the Performance of Substitute Distance Based Approaches for Evolutionary Many-Objective Optimization. In: Li, X., Kirley, M., Zhang, M., Green, D., Ciesielski, V., Abbass, H.A., Michalewicz, Z., Hendtlass, T., Deb, K., Tan, K.C., Branke, J., Shi, Y. (eds.) SEAL 2008. LNCS, vol. 5361, pp. 401–410. Springer, Heidelberg (2008)
6. Aguirre, H., Tanaka, K.: Space Partitioning with Adaptive ε-Ranking and Substitute Distance Assignments: A comparative Study on Many-Objective MNK-Landscapes. In: GECCO 2009 (2009)
7. Kachroudi, S.: Particle Swarm Optimization Algorithm with Space Partitioning for Many-Objective Optimization (2010) (to be published in META 2010)
8. Corne, D., Knowles, J.: Techniques for highly multi-objective optimization: Some non-dominated points are better than others. In: Proc. of 2007 Genetic and Evolutionary Computation Conference, pp. 773–780 (July 2007)

9. Deb, K., Thiele, L., Laumanns, M., Zitzler, E.: Scalable Multi-objective Optimization Test Problems. In: Proceedings of the Congress on Evolutionary Computation (CEC 2002), pp. 825–830 (2002)
10. Qu, B.Y., Suganthan, P.N.: Multi-Objective Evolutionary Algorithms based on the Summation of Normalized Objectives and Diversified Selection. Information Sciences 180(17), 3170–3181 (2010)
11. Bentley, P.J., Wakefield, J.P.: Finding acceptable solutions in the Pareto-optimal range using multiobjective genetic algorithms. Soft Computing in Engineering Design and Manufacturing, 231–240 (1997)

# Discrete Variables Function Optimization Using Accelerated Biogeography-Based Optimization

M.R. Lohokare[1], S.S. Pattnaik[1], S. Devi[1], B.K. Panigrahi[2], S. Das[3], and D.G. Jadhav[1]

[1] National Institute of Technical Teachers' Training and Research Chandigarh, India
shyampattnaik@yahoo.com
[2] Indian Institute of Technology, Delhi, India
bkpanigrahi@ee.iitd.ac.in
[3] Kansas State University, Rolla, USA
sdas@ksu.edu

**Abstract.** Biogeography-Based Optimization (BBO) is a bio-inspired and population based optimization algorithm. This is mainly formulated to optimize functions of discrete variables. But the convergence of BBO to the optimum value is slow as it lacks in exploration ability. The proposed Accelerated Biogeography-Based Optimization (ABBO) technique is an improved version of BBO. In this paper, authors accelerated the original BBO to enhance the exploitation and exploration ability by modified mutation operator and clear duplicate operator. This significantly improves the convergence characteristics of the original algorithm. To validate the performance of ABBO, experiments have been conducted on unimodal and multimodal benchmark functions of discrete variables. The results shows excellent performance when compared with other modified BBOs and other optimization techniques like stud genetic algorithm (SGA) and ant colony optimization (ACO). The results are also analyzed by using two paired t- test.

**Keywords:** Biogeography-Based Optimization (BBO), Accelerated Biogeography-Based Optimization (ABBO), Optimization, Exploration.

## 1 Introduction

Many evolutionary algorithms (EAs) like Genetic Algorithm (GA) [1], Stud GA (SGA) [2], ACO [3], Particle Swarm Optimization (PSO) [4], Differential Evolution (DE) [5], and Harmony Search (HS) [6] have been introduced to solve multidimensional and multivariable complex optimization problem. Biogeography-Based Optimization (BBO) [7] is a biology inspired optimization technique. BBO adopts migration operator to share information between solutions like GA, PSO and HS. In BBO poor solutions accept a lot of features from good ones which improve the quality of those solutions. This is the unique feature of BBO algorithm compared to other algorithms. This feature makes the exploitation ability of BBO good similar to HS. But this process creates the harmful similar solutions. Evolutionary algorithms like GA, DE utilizes the crossover operation. This operation sometimes degrades the quality of initially good solutions in later stage of the process. But BBO does not

B.K. Panigrahi et al. (Eds.): SEMCCO 2010, LNCS 6466, pp. 322–329, 2010.

utilize crossover like operation; thus solutions get fine tuned gradually as the process goes on through migration operation. BBO also clearly differs from ACO, because ACO generates a new set of solutions with each iteration, on the other hand BBO maintains its set of solutions from one iteration to the next, relying on migration to probabilistically adapt those solutions. Elitism operation has made the algorithm more efficient in this respect. This gives an edge to BBO over techniques mentioned above. Unlike PSO solutions, GA and BBO solutions do not have tendency to clump together in similar groups due to its new type of mutation operator. This is an added advantage of BBO in comparison to PSO.

In BBO, each individual solution is a vector of integers (discrete version) initialized randomly and is applied to the sensor selection problem for aircraft engine health estimation. After testing on many benchmarks, and comparing with many other widely used heuristic algorithms like GAs, Stud GAs, ACO, and others, BBO outperformed most of the other algorithms on most of the benchmark functions [7]. Biogeography is the study of distribution of species in nature. Each possible solution is an island and their features that characterize habitability are called suitability index variables (SIV). The goodness of each solution is called its habitat suitability index (HSI) [7]. In BBO, a habitat H is a vector of N (SIVs) integers initialized randomly. Before optimizing, each individual of population is evaluated and then follows migration and mutation step to reach global minima. In migration the information is shared between habitats that depend on emigration rates $\mu$ and immigration rates $\lambda$ of each solution. Each solution is modified depending on probability $P_{mod}$ that is a user-defined parameter. Each individual has its own $\lambda$ and $\mu$ and are functions of the number of species $K$ in the habitat BBO has shown its ability to solve optimization problem. Still there are several open search questions that should be addressed for BBO so that it gives better convergence.

The remainder of this paper is organized as follows the proposed Accelerated Biogeography-Based Optimization (ABBO) technique is discussed in section 2. Experimental results with unimodal and multimodal discrete functions are given in section 3 and conclusion is presented in section 4.

## 2   Accelerated BBO (ABBO)

ABBO, the same concept of migration is used as has been done in BBO to maintain its exploitation ability. Modified mutation and clear duplicate operators are used in mutation scheme of BBO to accelerate convergence characteristics, thus making ABBO different from BBO.

### 2.1   Modified Mutation Operator

Creating infeasible solutions is the problem of population based optimization algorithms. Creating too many infeasible solutions may slow down the algorithm. In BBO, the mutation is used to increase the diversity of the population. Mutation operator modifies a habitat's SIV randomly based on mutation rate $m$ for the case of E=I. The mutation rate m is expressed as (14) in [7] which is inversely proportional to species count probability. In BBO, if a solution is selected for mutation, then it is replaced by a randomly generated new solution set. This random mutation affects the exploration ability of BBO.

In ABBO, modified mutation operator creates new feasible solution by combing the parent individual with the scaled differences of parent individual and randomly selected other individual of the same population vectors. A mutated individual SIV (Hi(j))is generated according to the following equation.

$$Hi(j) = Hi(j) + F \times (Hr_1(j) - Hi(j)) .$$  (1)

where, $Hi(j)$ is the parent SIV to be mutated, $Hr_1(j)$ is the randomly select SIV ($r1 \in [1, P]$), and F is the scaling factor ( $F \in [0.1, 0.9]$) that controls the amplification of the difference vector ($Hr_1(j) - Hi(j)$). In ABBO, authors have selected habitat SIVs to be mutate only for the worst half ($j = P/2$ to $P$) of the solutions based on the $m$.

Modified mutation algorithm as proposed by authors is described as follows:

**For** i = P/2 to P
   **For** j = 1to N
      Use $\lambda_i$ and $\mu_i$ to compute the probability $P_i$
      Select SIV $H_i(j)$ with probability $\alpha P_i$
      **If** $Hi(j)$ is selected
      Select uniform randomly $r_1$
      Select $Hi(j) = Hi(j) + F \times (Hr_1(j) - Hi(j))$
      **end**
   **end**
**end**

This mutation scheme tends to increase the diversity among the population. It acts as a fine tuning unit and accelerates the convergence characteristics.

## 2.2 Modified Clear Duplicate Operator

In BBO, migration process creates the harmful similar habitats. In BBO, the similar habitat is modified to a new solution by simply replacing one of the SIV of similar habitat randomly within the feasible range, which leads to slow down the algorithm. But, in ABBO, the similar habitat is modified to a new solution $H_i$ by replacing one of the SIV ($Hi(j)$) with feasible solution generated by controlling the amount of diversity between maximum and minimum SIVs of the two similar habitats and is expressed as (2).

$$Hi(j) = (min(Hi) + (max(Hj)-min(Hi)) \times rand()) .$$  (2)

This modification maintains the diversity of newly generated solution from maximum and minimum SIVs of similar habitats. This helps to prevent similar solutions as well as maintains the diversity of the algorithm.

Modified clear duplicate operator algorithm as suggested by authors is described as follows.

**For** i = 1 to P
    **For** j = i+1 to P
        **If** Hi and Hj is equal
            $j_{rand}$ = rndint(1,N)
            Replace $H_i(j_{rand})$ as per equation (2)
        **end**
    **end**
**end**

ABBO also follows migration and mutation step to reach global minima. Pseudo code of ABBO is described as follows:

Step 1: Initialize the population P randomly.
Step 2: Evaluate the fitness and sort the population from best to worst.
Step 3: Initialize species count probability of each Habitat
Step 4: **While** The termination criteria is not met **do**
Step 5: Save the best habitats in a temporary array (Elitism)
Step 6: For each habitat, map the HSI to number of species S, λ and μ
Step 7: Probabilistically choose the immigration island based on $\mu$
Step 8: Migrate randomly selected SIVs based on the selected island in Step7.
Step 9: Mutate the population probabilistically as per equation (1)
Step 10: Evaluate the fitness and sort the population from best to worst.
Step 11: Replace worst with best habitat from temporary
Step 12: Check for feasibility and similar habitat (Replace it as per eq. (2))
Step 13: **end while**

## 3 Experimental Results

In BBO, each individual solution is a vector of integers (discrete version) initialized and tested on 14 benchmark functions [7], [8]. The results are compared with many other widely used heuristic algorithms like Gas, stud Gas, ACO, and others. BBO performs the best on 4 benchmark functions, SGA performs best on 7 benchmark functions and ACO performs best on 3 benchmark functions. The results are also compared with other modified BBO algorithms [9]. BBO/ES by incorporating features of ES, BBO/RE by addition of immigration refusal approach and BBO/ES/RE by incorporating features of ES and immigration refusal approach into BBO and their performance is compared with BBO. The control parameters for SGA and ACO are set same as given in [7], [8]. The control parameter for ABBO and BBO are set as follows: habitat modification probability=1, Mutation probability =0.005, Elitism parameter = 1. The experimentation is carried out for a set of fourteen benchmark functions as shown in Table 1 [9], where 'S' denotes the search range of the benchmark function. The parameters for experimentation are set as follows; number of Monte Carlo simulations=100, generations per Monte Carlo simulation =100, population size (islands) =100, number of variables of each function (SIVs) =20 The granularity or precision of each benchmark function is set as 0.1 and only for quartic function it is set as 0.01.

Following performance criteria's are selected for the comparison of algorithms.

1) Error [11] = f(x)-f(x*), where x* is global optimum of the solution. Best minimum error (Min) is recorded when the generations is reached in 100 runs. Mean and standard deviation of the error is also calculated.
2) Convergence Response [11] = Error (log) versus generations.

**Table 1.** Benchmark Functions

| F | Function name | S | $f_{min}$ | F | Function name | S | $f_{min}$ |
|---|---------------|---|-----------|---|---------------|---|-----------|
| $f_1$ | Ackley's | $[-30,30]^D$ | 0 | $f_8$ | Rosenbrock's | $[-2.048,2.048]^D$ | 0 |
| $f_2$ | Fletcher-Powell | $[\pi,-\pi]^D$ | 0 | $f_9$ | Schwefel's 1.2 | $[-65.536,65.536]^D$ | 0 |
| $f_3$ | Griwank | $[-600,600]^D$ | 0 | $f_{10}$ | Schwefel's 2.21 | $[-100,100]^D$ | 0 |
| $f_4$ | Penalised #1 | $[-50,50]^D$ | 0 | $f_{11}$ | Schwefel's 2.22 | $[-10,10]^D$ | 0 |
| $f_5$ | Penalised #2 | $[-50,50]^D$ | 0 | $f_{12}$ | Schwefel's 2.26 | $[-512,512]^D$ | -12569.5 |
| $f_6$ | Quartic | $[-1.28,1.28]^D$ | 0 | $f_{13}$ | Sphere | $[-5.12,5.12]^D$ | 0 |
| $f_7$ | Rastrigin's | $[-5.12,5.12]^D$ | 0 | $f_{14}$ | Step | $[-200,200]^D$ | 0 |

Table 2 show the results of best error values on all test factions after 100 Monte Carlo simulations, where "Mean" indicates the mean best error values and "Std. Dev." stands for the standard deviation. ABBO gives excellent performance than BBO and other algorithms for all the benchmark functions. The results are also analyzed with statistical two-tailed t-test. Based on the t-test results, it can be seen that the suggested integrations of modified mutation and clear duplicate operator have big effect on the BBO. Table 3 shows the result of best minimum error (Min) found after 100 Monte Carlo simulations of each algorithm for each benchmark function. The results show that ABBO is most effective in finding function minima ('Min') when multiple runs are made, performing the best on all benchmark functions when compared with BBO and other modified BBOs, namely BBO/ES, BBO/RE, and BBO/ES/RE except function $f_2$. Fig. 1 shows convergence graphs for selected functions, it shows that in the beginning of the evaluation process BBO converges faster than ABBO while ABBO is able to improve its solution steadily for a long run. This is due to integration of modified mutation and clear duplicate operator into original BBO, which balances the exploitation and exploration ability of the ABBO. It also shows that convergence characteristics of ABBO get accelerated as compared to SGA and ACO.

**Table 2.** Best error values on all test factions found after 100 Monte Carlo simulations. Where; "Mean" indicates the mean best error values, "Std. Dev." stands for the standard deviation. "1Vs 2", "1Vs 2", "1Vs 2" stands for ABBO Vs BBO, ABBO Vs SGA and ABBO Vs ACO respectively.

| F | ABBO Mean± Std Dev | BBO Mean± Std Dev | SGA Mean± Std Dev | ACO Mean ± Std Dev | 1Vs 2 t test | 1 Vs 3 t test | 1Vs 4 t test |
|---|---|---|---|---|---|---|---|
| $f_1$ | 2.57E-01±1.74E-01 | 3.96E+00±5.39E-01 | 3.94E+00±6.08E-01 | 1.33E+01±1.23E+00 | -67.28 | -57.65 | -105.2 |
| $f_2$ | 2.61E+04±1.42E+04 | 2.64E+04±1.23E+04 | 3.39E+04±1.65E+04 | 5.31E+05±1.27E+05 | -.151 | -3.47 | -39.33 |
| $f_3$ | 9.36E-01±1.36E-01 | 1.92E+00±4.33E-01 | 1.44E+00±1.80E-01 | 3.97E+00±1.43E+00 | -21.92 | -22.62 | -21.24 |
| $f_4$ | 8.15E-02±9.75E-02 | 1.98E+00±8.84E-01 | 3.44E-01±2.35E-01 | 6.23E+07±1.01E+08 | -21.38 | -10.54 | -6.16 |
| $f_5$ | 3.31E-01±2.60E-01 | 3.37E+01±1.98E+02 | 2.20E+00±9.56E-01 | 1.48E+08±2.20E+08 | -1.68 | -18.24 | -6.72 |
| $f_6$ | 1.45E-06±2.62E-06 | 1.40E-03±2.44E-03 | 1.30E-04±1.37E-04 | 5.62E-01±6.61E-01 | -5.72 | -9.37 | -8.49 |
| $f_7$ | 1.26E+00±1.29E+00 | 1.05E+01±3.28E+00 | 1.76E+01±4.34E+00 | 1.28E+02±1.63E+01 | -25.69 | -34.44 | -77.35 |
| $f_8$ | 3.80E+01±2.55E+01 | 5.36E+01±2.83E+01 | 5.93E+01±2.90E+01 | 1.68E+03±4.28E+02 | -3.89 | -5.74 | -38.20 |
| $f_9$ | 2.56E+01±5.73E+01 | 1.61E+02±6.56E+01 | 1.17E+02±6.08E+01 | 5.02E+02±1.65E+02 | -14.77 | -11.86 | -27.49 |
| $f_{10}$ | 1.78E+03±9.82E+02 | 1.80E+03±7.34E+02 | 4.00E+03±1.45E+03 | 5.93E+03±1.54E+03 | -.132 | -13.19 | -22.59 |
| $f_{11}$ | 0.00E+00±0.00E+00 | 1.74E+00±4.88E-01 | 2.97E+00±7.96E-01 | 4.11E+01±5.54E+00 | -35.61 | -37.34 | -74.13 |
| $f_{12}$ | 2.14E+01±9.61E+00 | 2.95E+01±8.72E+00 | 2.25E+01±1.29E+01 | 3.71E+01±6.23E+00 | -6.36 | -.67 | -13.57 |
| $f_{13}$ | 0.00E+00±0.00E+00 | 2.72E-01±1.03E-01 | 2.05E-01±8.10E-02 | 2.19E+01±5.33E+00 | -26.29 | -25.29 | -41.13 |
| $f_{14}$ | 3.60E-01±9.38E-01 | 1.04E+02±4.39E+01 | 4.20E+01±2.37E+01 | 5.03E+02±1.90E+02 | -23.64 | -17.54 | -26.48 |

**Table 3.** Best error values on all test factions, where "Min" indicates the best minimum error (Min) found after 100 Monte Carlo simulations

| F | ABBO | BBO | SGA | ACO | BBO/ES | BBO/RE | BBO/ES/RE |
|---|---|---|---|---|---|---|---|
| $f_1$ | 0.115077 | 2.91426 | 2.806245 | 9.855767 | 1.34 | 3.03 | 1.42 |
| $f_2$ | 6668.131 | 5622.112 | 9664.57 | 257244.2 | 4503.96 | 6216.63 | 2248.52 |
| $f_3$ | 0.280615 | 1.233452 | 1.084708 | 2.121222 | 1.04 | 1.42 | 1.07 |
| $f_4$ | 0.003134 | 0.368596 | 0.035431 | 0.073855 | 0.04 | 1.10 | 0.03 |
| $f_5$ | 0.053509 | 2.421646 | 0.276538 | 0.957975 | 0.46 | 4.56 | 0.51 |
| $f_6$ | 0 | 8.75E-05 | 7.64E-06 | 0.068517 | 4.81E-06 | 2.22E-04 | 6.33E-06 |
| $f_7$ | 0 | 4.043576 | 9.010674 | 95.81435 | 0.00 | 4.04 | 0.00 |
| $f_8$ | 12.01905 | 17.75205 | 16.31821 | 806.7435 | 12.80 | 21.41 | 13.44 |
| $f_9$ | 0.129412 | 47.90353 | 28.73949 | 171.7919 | 9.52 | 28.69 | 12.10 |
| $f_{10}$ | 347.4716 | 611.6718 | 1124.325 | 2717.325 | 654.65 | 866.16 | 889.69 |
| $f_{11}$ | 0 | 0.5 | 1.5 | 23.6 | 0.10 | 0.70 | 0.10 |
| $f_{12}$ | 6.1 | 9.7 | 8.3 | 21.2 | 8.40 | 10.50 | 9.30 |
| $f_{13}$ | 0 | 0.07055 | 0.040314 | 10.80424 | 0.00 | 0.12 | 0.01 |
| $f_{14}$ | 0 | 39 | 8 | 129 | 7.00 | 39.00 | 7.00 |

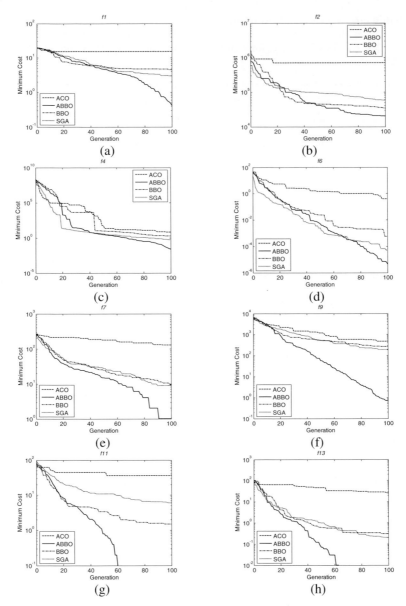

**Fig. 1.** Convergence response of ACO, ABBO, BBO and SGA for selected functions (a) $f_1$. (b) $f_2$. (c) $f_4$. (d) $f_6$. (e) $f_7$. (f) $f_9$. (g) $f_{11}$. (h) $f_{13}$.

# 4  Conclusion

In this paper, the authors present an improved optimization technique named as accelerated BBO 'ABBO'. Modified mutation and clear duplicate operators can improve the performance of BBO Performance of ABBO is demonstrated on integer initialized fourteen benchmark functions. Experimental analysis shows that ABBO can solve optimization problem of discrete variables with improved accuracy and with fast convergence rate than BBO, SGA and ACO. For future work, ABBO can be applied to discrete real world problems and its performance can be tested to optimize functions of continuous variables with more comprehensive set of benchmark functions.

# References

1. Michalewicz, Z.: Genetic Algorithms+ Data Structures= Evolution Programs. Springer, New York (1992)
2. Khatib, W., Fleming, P.: The stud GA: A mini revolution? In: Eiben, A. (ed.) Parallel problem solving from nature. Springer, New York (1998)
3. Dorigo, M., Gambardella, L., Middendorf, M., Stutzle, T.: Special section on 'ant colony optimization. IEEE Trans. Evol. Comput. 6(4), 317–365 (2002)
4. Kennedy, J., Eberhart, R.: Particle Swarm Optimization. In: Proceeding of IEEE International Conference on Neural Networks, pp. 1942–1948 (1995)
5. Storn, R., Price, K.: Differential evolution-a simple and efficient heuristic for global optimization over continuous spaces. J. Global Opt. 11(4), 341–359 (1997)
6. Gao, X.Z., Wang, X., Ovaska, S.J.: Uni-modal and multi-modal optimization using modified harmony search methods. International Journal of Innovative Computing, Information and Control 5(10A), 2985–2996 (2009)
7. Simon, D.: Biogeography-based optimization. IEEE Trans Evolutionary Computation 12(6), 702–713 (2008)
8. The Matlab code of biogeography-based optimization, http://academic.csuohio.edu/simond/bbo
9. Du, D., Simand, D., Ergezer, M.: Biogeography-Based Optimization combined with evolutionary strategy and immigration refusal. In: Proceeding of IEEE International Conference on Systems, Man, and Cybernetics, SMC 2009, USA, pp. 997–1002 (2009)
10. Yao, X., Liu, Y., Lin, G.: Evolutionary programming made faster. IEEE Trans Evolutionary Computation 3(2), 82–102 (1999)
11. Suganthan, P.N., Hansen, N., Liang, J.J., Deb, K., Chen, Y.P., Auger, A., Tiwari, S.: Problem Definations and Evaluation Criteria for the CEC 2005, Special Session on Real-Parameter Optimization (2005), http://www.ntu.edu.sg/home/EPNSSugan

# A Genetic Algorithm Based Augmented Lagrangian Method for Computationally Fast Constrained Optimization

Soumil Srivastava and Kalyanmoy Deb

Kanpur Genetic Algorithms Laboratory (KanGAL),
Department of Mechanical Engineering,
Indian Institute of Technology Kanpur,
Kanpur, UP, India - 208016
{soumil,deb}@iitk.ac.in
http://www.iitk.ac.in/kangal/

**Abstract.** Among the penalty based approaches for constrained optimization, Augmented Lagrangian (AL) methods are better in at least three ways: (i) they have theoretical convergence properties, (ii) they distort the original objective function minimally to allow a better search behavior, and (iii) they can find the optimal Lagrange multiplier for each constraint as a by-product of optimization. Instead of keeping a constant penalty parameter throughout the optimization process, these algorithms update the parameters adaptively so that the corresponding penalized function dynamically changes its optimum from the unconstrained minimum point to the constrained minimum point with iterations. However, the flip side of these algorithms is that the overall algorithm is a serial implementation of a number of optimization tasks, a process that is usually time-consuming. In this paper, we devise a genetic algorithm based parameter update strategy to a particular AL method. The strategy is self-adaptive in order to make the overall genetic algorithm based augmented Lagrangian (GAAL) method parameter-free. The GAAL method is applied to a number of constrained test problems taken from the EA literature. The function evaluations required by GAAL in many problems is an order or more lower than existing methods.

**Keywords:** Augmented Lagrangian method, evolutionary algorithms, self-adaptive algorithm, Lagrange multipliers.

## 1   Introduction

Constrained optimization problems are the most important and ubiquitous type of engineering optimization problems. Evolutionary Algorithms (EA) have been applied extensively for tackling these problems with various degrees of success. The penalty function approach is a relatively simple and remarkably easy to implement and therefore, is quite popular. But the approach also has several functional and operational drawbacks which limit its precision and speed. First,

B.K. Panigrahi et al. (Eds.): SEMCCO 2010, LNCS 6466, pp. 330–337, 2010.
© Springer-Verlag Berlin Heidelberg 2010

the penalty function approaches do not take into account the mathematical form (linear or non-linear, convex or non-convex, unimodal or multi-modal, etc.) of the constraints. Second, the addition of the penalty term on the objective function usually makes a distortion in the objective function, which may create artificial non-linearity and multi-modalities that may thwart the progress of an optimization algorithm to the true constrained minimum point. Third, most penalty function methods do not have a convergence proof and works under the assumption that at the constrained minimum point the penalized function has an absolute minimum value provided a sufficiently large penalty parameter value is chosen to penalize infeasible solutions. Various types of sophisticated penalty function methods have been devised in the past to overcome some of these drawbacks, such as multi-level penalty functions [2], dynamic penalty functions [3], and others. But according to a study by Michalewicz and Schoenauer [4], such sophisticated methods are less generic and work well on some problems but not on others.

The second author had proposed a parameter-less approach in 2000 [1], which eliminated the need for a penalty parameter and was received quite favorably. Some of these methods use a bi-objective approach [5], or a multiobjective approach [6] for handling constraints. Some methods use other evolutionary approaches, such as the particle swarm optimization (PSO) [10], differential evolution (DE) [11] and report excellent performance. In this paper, we revisit the use of a classical Augmented Lagrangian (AL) approach, but employ a genetic algorithm to update its parameters adaptively. For each constraint (equality and inequality), the particular AL method used in this study involves a dynamically changed parameter. The population approach of a GA maintains diversity of solutions and allows a more global search of the individual optimization tasks. Furthermore, the switching from one parameter setting to another is made completely self-adaptive based on population statistics so that once started the user does not have to control the switching from one optimization task to another. A classical optimization algorithm (`fmincon()` of MATLAB) is employed to terminate the run. The Augmented Lagrangian approaches are better than penalty function approaches in a number of ways:

1. The particular AL approach used in this study has a theoretical property of converging to a Karush-Kuhn-Tucker (KKT) point.
2. The AL approach does not distort the original objective function, instead it has an effect of *shifting* the objective function in a manner so that its optimum moves from the unconstrained minimum to the constrained minimum point. This does not change the complexity of the problem too much from start to finish and makes it easier to choose a single optimization algorithm for the entire problem-solving task.
3. As a by-product, AL methods provide the Lagrange multiplier value for each constraint. Lagrange multipliers are important for subsequent post-optimality analysis and for sensitivity analysis. The ability to compute Lagrange multipliers provides AL methods a definite edge over other optimization algorithms.

However, one of the criticisms of the AL methods is the requirement of a number of optimization tasks, which makes the overall approach computationally expensive. Also, subsequent optimization tasks depend on the accuracy of previous optimization tasks, thereby requiring to solve an optimization problem with an adequate accuracy. Another matter which is not adequately discussed in the literature, but is also an important factor is that in solving multi-modal problems, if an earlier optimization task did not converge to an appropriate optimum point, the value of the associated parameters computed at the *false* optimum will be different than that are required for the algorithm to converge to the true constrained minimum point.

## 2    Augmented Lagrangian Method and Proposed Algorithm

A general notation for a constrained optimization problem is:

$$
\begin{aligned}
&\text{Minimize } f(\mathbf{x}), \\
&\text{subject to } g_j(\mathbf{x}) \geq 0, \quad \forall\, j = 1, 2, \ldots, J, \\
&\qquad\qquad x_i^l \leq x_i \leq x_i^u, \quad \forall\, i = 1, 2, \ldots, n.
\end{aligned} \tag{1}
$$

For brevity, equality constraints are not considered here. In the classical Augmented Lagrangian method for constrained optimization, the objective function $f(\mathbf{x})$ is modified to

$$
P(\mathbf{x}, \sigma^t, \tau^t) = f(\mathbf{x}) + R \sum_{j=1}^{J} \left[ \left( \langle g_j(x) + \sigma_j^t \rangle \right)^2 - \left( \sigma_j^t \right)^2 \right], \tag{2}
$$

where $\langle g(x) \rangle = g(\mathbf{x})$ if $g(\mathbf{x}) < 0$ else it is zero. The superscript $t$ indicates the $t$-th optimization problem for which multipliers $\sigma_j^t$ are kept fixed. However, these multipliers are updated at the end of each optimization task. The initial values of multipliers are usually set as follows: $\sigma_j^0 = 0$. Multipliers $\sigma_j^t$ are updated after $t$-th optimization and kept fixed for the $(t+1)$-th iteration as follows:

$$
\sigma_j^{t+1} = \langle \sigma_j^t + g_j(\mathbf{x}^t) \rangle, \; j = 1, 2, \ldots, J, \tag{3}
$$

where $\mathbf{x}^t$ is the optimum solution of the $t$-th penalized function $P$. It is also important to mention that the starting solution of the initial optimization task can be chosen any arbitrary solution, whereas the initial solution to the $t$-th optimization problem is the optimum solution found at $(t - 1)$-th optimization task. This sequential optimization procedure continues till not much change in optimum solutions of the two consecutive optimization tasks is observed. It is also interesting to mention that the penalty parameter $R$ is usually kept constant throughout the entire optimization process.

A big result which can be obtained from a KKT analysis of the above penalized optimization problem is that at a theoretical termination of the algorithm (say, occurring at iteration $T$), the optimal Lagrangian multipliers for the original problem can be calculated forthwith by using the following relationship:

$$u_j = -2R\sigma_j^T, \tag{4}$$

Although the above description and its associated theoretical result are attractive, there are some practical implementation issues which we discuss next. First, since the value of $R$ is kept fixed throughout the optimization process, it may be apparent that its value can be fixed to any arbitrary value. Although it is fine theoretically, in practice the progress of the algorithm largely depends on the chosen value of $R$. Notice that all constraints are multiplied by the same penalty parameter $R$. Thus, there is a need for normalizing the constraint functions before using them in equation 2 to equalize their importance. Second, the value of $R$ makes a balance between the objective function $f$ and the constraint violation given by the second term in equation 2. Unless a proper balance is established, either the objective function is not emphasized enough or the constraint violation is not emphasized. The above will result in prematurely converging to an arbitrary feasible solution or to an infeasible solution, respectively. Importantly, for arriving at an computationally efficient approach, such a balance must be made adaptive with more emphasize to constraint violation in the beginning of the optimization process and then emphasizing the objective function.

Based on these discussions, we suggest a GA based AL method, which has the following properties:

1. GAAL self-adaptively determines the update of multiplier values $\sigma_j$.
2. GAAL self-adaptively alters the value of $R$ and its associate multiplier values
3. GAAL uses a termination condition based on solutions obtained for successive $R$ updates and its subsequent classical optimization run.
4. GAAL is seamless in that no user intervention is needed once the algorithm is started.

## 2.1   Proposed GAAL Method

In this study, we restrict ourselves with inequality constraints only. In the following, we first present the proposed procedure and then discuss its individual operators:

1. **Initialization**
   (a) Set $t = 0$. Initialize the GA population $\mathcal{P}^t$ with $N$ members randomly.
   (b) Set $\sigma_j^t = 0$ for all constraints.
   (c) Set the initial penalty parameter $R$ based on the statistics of the initial population as follows:

   $$R = 50 \left( \sum_N |f(\mathbf{x})| \Big/ \left| \sum_N \mathrm{CV}(\mathbf{x}) \right| \right), \tag{5}$$

   where $\mathrm{CV}(\mathbf{x}) = \sum_{j=1}^{J} (\langle \hat{g}_j(x) \rangle)^2$ and $\hat{g}_j$ is the normalized version of the constraint function $g_j$. Set $R_{\mathrm{old}} = R$.
   (d) Note the best population member $\mathbf{x}^t$. Increment $t$ by one.

2. For every generation $t$, perform the following steps:

    (a) Perform one generation of the GA using binary tournament selection using $P()$ as fitness measure to be minimized, the simulated binary crossover (SBX) operator [7] and an adaptive polynomial mutation operator [8] on population $\mathcal{P}^t$ to create a new offspring population $\mathcal{Q}^t$.

    (b) Choose the best population member $\mathbf{x}^t$ of $\mathcal{Q}^t$.

    (c) Compute $\rho = \left| \frac{P(\mathbf{x}^t, \sigma^t) - P(\mathbf{x}^{t-1}, \sigma^{t-1})}{P(\mathbf{x}^{t-1}, \sigma^{t-1})} \right|$. If $\rho \leq \delta_1$, update the multipliers using:

$$\sigma_j^{t+1} = \langle \sigma_j^t + g_j(\mathbf{x}^t) \rangle, \ j = 1, 2, \dots, J$$

    Else increment counter $t$ by one and go to Step 2.

    (d) If $(t \bmod \kappa) = 0$ and $\rho < \delta_2$, set penalty parameter $R$ as follows:

$$R = 10 * w \frac{\sum_N |f(\mathbf{x})|}{N} + (1 - w) R_{\text{old}}, \tag{6}$$

    and update multipliers as follows:

$$\sigma_j^t = \sigma_j^t \frac{R_{\text{old}}}{R}, \ j = 1, 2, \dots, J.$$

    Set $R_{\text{old}} = R$ and start a classical algorithm run with the current best population member $(\mathbf{x}^t)$.

    Else increment counter $t$ by one and go to Step 2.

3. **Termination check:** If $(($*difference between results of two subsequent* `fmincon()` *runs*$) < \epsilon)$, report the result of the last `fmincon()` run as the result. Otherwise, increment counter $t$ by one and go to Step 2.

The SBX operator is the same as that in [7]. However, we use an adaptive mutation operator in which mutation probability is changed with generation counter as follows:

$$p_m = \frac{0.1}{n} + \frac{0.1t}{t_{max}} \left( 1 - \frac{1}{n} \right), \tag{7}$$

where $n$ is the number of variables, $t$ is the number of generations and $t_{max}$ is the maximum number of generations set by the user during the run. This creates about 1% perturbance in the solutions in the first generation and subsequently decreases the perturbance in the later generations. The mutation index is not changed. We update the multipliers $\sigma_j^t$ and penalty parameter $R$ at two different levels in this method. If the improvement in the best population member is less than $\delta_1$ then we update the multipliers alone and continue. If this updation does not yield better results in the succeeding generations, we make a change in the value of $R$ for the algorithm to look for good solutions elsewhere in the search space. The numbers 50 and 10 used in equation 5 and 6 are found through experiments and give good results. At the beginning the penalty parameter $R$ tries to keep the penalty at about 50 times the function value and reduces it in subsequent updates gradually to about 10 times. The parameters used in this algorithm are:

1. Population size $N$: We recommend the use of $N = max(10n, 50)$, where $n$ is the number of variables in the problem.
2. Probability of crossover $p_c$ and SBX index $\eta_c$: We recommend $p_c = 0.9$ and $\eta_c = 2$. They are found to work well on all our test problems.
3. Mutation index $\eta_m$: We recommend $\eta_m = 100 + t$.
4. Update threshold $\delta_1$: Based on simulation studies, we recommend using $\delta_1 = 0.1$ or 10%. This parameter is used to decide on an update of the multipliers.
5. Update threshold $\delta_2$: Based on simulation studies, we recommend using $\delta_2 = 0.0001$ or 0.01%. This parameter is used to decide on an update of $R$ and start a classical method run.
6. $R$ update parameter $\kappa$: This parameter can be used to prevent too frequent changes in $R$. Based on parametric studies(not shown for brevity, we recommend using $\kappa=5$.
7. Weight parameter $\omega$: This parameter determines the extent of transition towards the newly determined penalty parameter. This is important as it directly affects the speed and nature of convergence. Based on parametric studies, we recommend using $\omega=0.5$.
8. Terminating parameter $\epsilon$: We take $\epsilon = 0.0001$.

# 3   Results and Discussion

In this section, we apply our method on different test problems studied commonly in literature. The details of these problems can be found in [9]. We have chosen $\kappa = 5$, $\omega = 0.5$ and $\epsilon = 0.0001$ in our studies. Twenty-five runs from different initial random populations are taken for each problem and results are compared to those reported in [10], [11] and [12] in Table 1.

**Table 1.** Comparison of function evals. of proposed method and other best knowns

| Prob | Zavala et al.[10] | | | Takahama & Sakai[11] | | | Brest[12] | | | Proposed Method | | |
|---|---|---|---|---|---|---|---|---|---|---|---|---|
| | Best | Median | Worst | Best | Median | Worst | Best | Median | Worst | Best | Median | Worst |
| g01 | 80776 | 90343 | 96669 | 18594 | 19502 | **19971** | 51685 | 55211 | 57151 | **12617** | **15870** | 34717 |
| g02 | 87419 | 93359 | 99654 | 108303 | 114347 | 129255 | 175090 | 226789 | 253197 | **15849** | **38937** | **66785** |
| g04 | 3147 | 103308 | 110915 | 12771 | 13719 | 14466 | 56730 | 62506 | 67383 | **1861** | **3611** | **4111** |
| g06 | 95944 | 109765 | 130293 | 5037 | 5733 | **6243** | 31410 | 34586 | 37033 | **1005** | **2755** | 12355 |
| g07 | 114709 | 138767 | 208751 | 60873 | 67946 | 75569 | 184927 | 197901 | 221866 | **10408** | **20219** | **30218** |
| g08 | 2270 | 4282 | 5433 | **621** | **881** | **1173** | 1905 | 4044 | 4777 | 4605 | 100606 | 100809 |
| g09 | 94593 | 103857 | 119718 | 19234 | 21080 | 21987 | 79296 | 89372 | 98062 | **2953** | **6450** | **8205** |
| g10 | 109243 | 135735 | 193426 | 87848 | 92807 | 107794 | 203851 | 220676 | 264575 | **9371** | **10578** | **16175** |
| g12 | 482 | 6158 | 9928 | 2901 | 4269 | 5620 | 364 | 6899 | 10424 | 1209 | **1705** | 1957 |
| g18 | 97157 | 107690 | 124217 | 46856 | 57910 | 60108 | 139131 | 169638 | 191345 | **11461** | **14161** | 26306 |
| g24 | 11081 | 18278 | 633378 | 1959 | 2451 | **2739** | 9359 | 12844 | 14827 | **1005** | **1505** | 3911 |

It can be seen that the algorithm is performing better than other renowned methods in many of the problems. Table 2 shows the detailed results of the proposed method. The methods performs very well except for g02 and g08. Both g02 and g08 have a multimodal objective function which makes them difficult problems. Details about the nature of these problems can be found in [9]. Methods

**Table 2.** Comparison of function evals. of proposed method and other best knowns. Successful run means result is within 0.1% of the known optimum and is feasible.

| Prob | Best known optimum | Proposed method | | | | | | | Succ. |
|---|---|---|---|---|---|---|---|---|---|
| | | $f^*$ | | | Function evaluations | | | | runs |
| | | Best | Median | Worst | Min | Median | Max | | |
| g01 | -15 | -15 | -15 | -12.453125 | 12617 | 15870 | 34717 | | 24 |
| g02 | -0.803619 | -0.803619 | -0.803619 | -0.744767 | 15849 | 38937 | 66785 | | 2 |
| g04 | -30665.538671 | -30665.538672 | -30665.538672 | -30665.538672 | 1861 | 3611 | 4111 | | 25 |
| g06 | -6961.813875 | -6961.813876 | -6961.813876 | -6961.813876 | 1005 | 2755 | 12355 | | 25 |
| g07 | 24.306209 | 24.306209 | 24.306209 | 24.306209 | 10408 | 20219 | 30218 | | 25 |
| g08 | -0.095825 | -0.095825 | -0.095825 | 0 | 4605 | 100606 | 100809 | | 8 |
| g09 | 680.630057 | 680.630057 | 680.630057 | 680.630057 | 2953 | 6450 | 8205 | | 25 |
| g10 | 7049.24802 | 7049.248021 | 7049.248021 | 7049.248021 | 9371 | 10578 | 16175 | | 25 |
| g12 | -1 | -0.999375 | -0.999375 | -0.999375 | 1209 | 1705 | 1957 | | 25 |
| g18 | -0.866025 | -0.866025 | -0.866025 | -0.674981 | 11461 | 14161 | 26306 | | 24 |
| g24 | -5.508013 | -5.508013 | -5.508013 | -5.508013 | 1005 | 1505 | 3911 | | 25 |

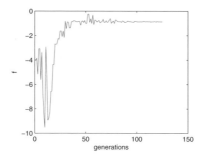

**Fig. 1.** Problem g18 : $f(\mathbf{x})$ vs. generations

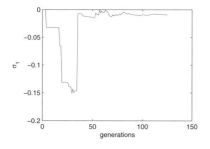 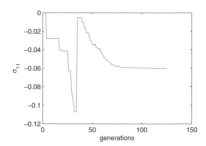

**Fig. 2.** Problem g18 : $\sigma_1$ vs. generations    **Fig. 3.** Problem g18 : $\sigma_{11}$ vs. generations

which use difference operators can use the periodicity of these problems as an advantage and give better performance. Figure 1 shows the evolution of the best function value for g18 over the generations and its stabilization to the optimum value. Figures 2 and 3 show the adaptive behaviour of $\sigma_1$ and $\sigma_{11}$ respectively.

# 4   Conclusions

In this paper, we have proposed a GA that follows the principle of augmented Lagrangian method in solving constrained optimization problems. The proposed algorithm has shown to work better than existing approaches in most of the standard test problems. The obtained solutions are found to be remarkably accurate (upto sixth decimal places) to the best-known results. This method takes advantage of the GA population methodology and amplifies the power of the classical method. Multiple parallel searches mean faster convergence and possibility of parallel-processing. This also tries to ensure that the algorithm does not get stuck onto some local optimum. A by-product of our methodology is that the Lagrange multipliers are also obtained without any additional effort, thereby giving us information about the influence of individual constraints on the solution and also help us identify which constraints are inactive on the optimum.

# References

1. Deb, K.: An efficient constraint handling method for genetic algorithms. Computer Methods in Applied Mechanics and Engineering 186, 311–338 (2000)
2. Homaifar, A., Lai, S.H.-V., Qi, X.: Constrained optimization via genetic algorithms. Simulation 62(4), 242–254 (1994)
3. Joines, J.A., Houck, C.R.: On the use of nonstationary penalty functions to solve nonlinear constrained optimization problems with GAs. In: Michalewicz, Z. (ed.) Proceedings of the International Conference on Evolutionary Computation, pp. 579–584. IEEE Press, Piscataway (1994)
4. Michalewicz, Z., Schoenauer, M.: Evolutionary algorithms for constrained parameter optimization problems. Evolutionary Computation 4(1), 1–32 (1996)
5. Zhou, Y., Li, Y., He, J., Kang, L.: Multi-objective and MGG evolutionary algorithm for constrained optimization. In: Proceedings of Congress on Evolutionary Computation, pp. 1–5 (2003)
6. Coello, C.A.C.: Treating objectives as constraints for single objective optimization. Engineering Optimization 32(3), 275–308 (2000)
7. Deb, K., Agrawal, R.B.: Simulated binary crossover for continuous search space. Complex Systems 9, 115–148 (1995)
8. Michalewicz, Z.: Genetic algorithms, numerical optimization and constraints. In: Eshelman, L. (ed.) Proceedings of the Sixth International Conference on Genetic Algorithms, pp. 151–158. Morgan Kaufmann, San Mateo (1995)
9. Deb, K., Datta, R.: A Fast and Accurate Solution of Constrained Optimization Problems Using a Hybrid Bi-Objective and Penalty Function Approach. In: Proceedings of the IEEE World Congress on Computational Intelligence (WCCI 2010). IEEE Press, Barcelona (2010)
10. Zavala, A.E.M., Aguirre, A.H., Diharce, E.R.V.: Continuous Constrained Optimization with Dynamic Tolerance Using the COPSO Algorithm, pp. 1–24. Springer, Heidelberg (2009)
11. Takahama, T., Sakai, S.: Solving Difficult Constrained Optimization Problems by the $\epsilon$ Constrained Differential Evolution with Gradient Based Mutation, pp. 51–72. Springer, Heidelberg (2009)
12. Brest, J.: Constrained Real-Parameter Optimization with $\epsilon$ Self- Adaptive Differential Evolution, pp. 73–94. Springer, Heidelberg (2009)

# Evolutionary Programming Improved by an Individual Random Difference Mutation

Zhaoquan Cai[1], Han Huang[2,3,4], Zhifeng Hao[5], and Xueqiang Li[2]

[1] Education Technology Center, Huizhou University, Huizhou 516007, P.R. China
cai@163.com
[2] School of Software Engineering, South China University of Technology,
Guangzhou, 510006, P.R. China
[3] State Key Lab. for Novel Software Technology, Nanjing University,
Nanjing 210093, P.R. China
[4] Dept of Management Sciences, College of Business,
City University of Hong Kong, Hong Kong
hhan@scut.edu.cn
[5] Faculty of Computer Science, Guangdong University of Technology,
510006 Guangzhou, P.R. China
zfhao@gdut.edu.cn

**Abstract.** Evolutionary programming (EP) is a classical evolutionary algorithm for continuous optimization. There have been several EP algorithms proposed based on different mutations strategies like Gaussian, Cauchy, Levy and other stochastic distributions. However, their convergence speed should be improved. An EP based on individual random difference (EP-IRD) was proposed to attain better solutions in a higher speed. The mutation of EP-IRD uses a random difference of individuals selected randomly to update the variance with which offspring are generated. The IRD-based mutation can make the better offspring according to the current population faster than the mathematical stochastic distribution. The numerical results of solving benchmark problems indicate that EP-IRD performs better than other four EP algorithms based on mathematical stochastic distribution in the items of convergence speed, optimal value on average and standard deviation.

## 1 Introduction

There were three kinds of evolutionary algorithms (EAs): genetic algorithm (GA) [1], evolutionary programming (EP) [2] and evolutionary strategy (ES) [3-4], in the classical filed of evolutionary computation. GA is usually used for discrete optimization problems, while EP and ES aim at continuous optimization. EP was first proposed as a finite state machine technique [2], and then widespread in continuous optimization and combinatorial optimization problems [5-7]. Later, the study of EP mainly focused on the influence of its parameters and the design of adaptive strategies. There have been several EP versions with different probability-distribution-based mutations.

The first successful EP algorithm is EP with Gauss mutation (CEP) [5]. Fogel [6-7], Bäck [8] and Schwefel [8-9] did a lot of work on CEP, and proposed an

B.K. Panigrahi et al. (Eds.): SEMCCO 2010, LNCS 6466, pp. 338–343, 2010.
© Springer-Verlag Berlin Heidelberg 2010

adaptive EP with Gauss-distribution mutation to improve the performing of non-adaptive CEP. Yao [10] pointed out that CEP is only efficient at solving unimodal function and close-peak function optimization problems. Hence, Yao introduced Cauchy distribution to the mutation and proposed a fast EP algorithm (FEP) [10]. FEP improved on the performance of CEP in solving multi-modal function and dispersed peak function problems. Inspired by Yao's work [10], Lee [11] added Lévy distribution into EP and designed an EP with Lévy-distribution mutation (LEP). LEP performs better than CEP and FEP in solving multi-modal function and very-dispersed peak function problems on average. Lee modified LEP to an adaptive LEP since there is a parameter necessary to set in Lévy distribution. Adaptive LEP is more efficient than LEP with 4 more times of evaluation.

Therefore, CEP [5], FEP [10] and LEP [11] can be considered as the classical evolutionary programming algorithms. Several modified EPs are designed based on them.

Differential evolution (DE) [12] is another continuous evolutionary algorithm, and outstanding to solve the benchmark problems of [10]. An evolutionary programming based on reinforcement learning (RLEP) [13] is proposed, and its performance is the same as or better than the best of the four basic mutation operators [5, 10-12]. Another EP algorithm (NEP) [14] is proposed based on a non-uniform mutation operator. NEP is faster and more robust for most multimodal benchmark functions tested. The results [15] show that the mixed strategy performs equally well or better than the best of the Gaussian, Cauchy, Lévy, and single-point mutation operators. A diversity-based selection strategy [16] improved the performance of EPs.

The mutations of most EPs [5, 10-11, 13-14] except DE [12] are based on stochastic-tic distributions which have nothing to do with individuals. Thus, there is no heuristic information leading the evolution of individuals so that the convergence speed of EP is not perfect or to be improved. An EP based on individual random difference was proposed in this paper to not accelerate the convergence to the optimal. The performance of EP was verified by numerical results of benchmark problems.

## 2   Process of IRD-Based Evolutionary Programming

The process of evolutionary programming is given as follows, where Step 3 is the sole different part among different EPs.

1) Arbitrarily generate $m_p$ individuals which is signed as a couple of real vectors $(x_i, \sigma_i)$, where $x_i$ is the optimized variable, $\sigma_i$ is the variation variable and $i = 1, ..., m_p$. Iteration time $t = 0$ and the initial $\sigma_i(j) \leq 2$ ( $j = 1, ..., n$ ) referred to [17].

2) Calculate the fitness of each individual $(x_i, \sigma_i)$ according to the objective function for $i = 1, ..., m_p$.

3) For each $(x_i, \sigma_i)$ and $i = 1, ..., m_p$, run the following equations to generate the offspring $(x'_i, \sigma'_i)$ of $(x_i, \sigma_i)$.

Create the offspring as follows for $j = 1, ..., n$

$$\sigma_i(j) = x_{r1}(j) - x_{r2}(j) \tag{1}$$

where $r_1$ and $r_2$ are random numbers of uniform distribution from the set of $\{i = 1, ..., m_p\}$ such that $r_1 \neq r_2 \neq i$.

$$x'_i(j) = mutation(x_i(j), \sigma_i(j)) \tag{2}$$

4) Evaluate the fitness of the offspring $(x'_i, \sigma'_i)$ for $i = 1, ..., m_p$.

5) For the i-th individual $\chi_i$ from the parents and offspring, select $q$ different individuals for comparison. If the fitness of $\chi_i$ is less than the selected one, $\chi_i$ obtain a "win". Run this step for $i = 1, ..., m_p$.

6) Select $m_p$ individuals who have the most time of "win" as the parents in the next iteration. Select $m_p$ individuals of least function value if the number of individuals with 100% wins is greater than $m_p$.

7) If the terminal condition is satisfied, output the best-so-far solution and exit, otherwise, $t = t + 1$ and go back to 3-rd step.

The next section will describe the IRD-based mutation as Eq. (2) shows in detail.

## 3   Mutation Based on Individual Random Difference

In the mutation of Eq. (2), the random difference of Eq. (1) is used to update the individuals. The offspring are generated by the following Eq. (3) according to $\sigma = \{\sigma_1, ..., \sigma_{m_p}\}$.

$$x'_i(j) = \begin{cases} (1 - \pi_i)x_i(j) + \pi_i\sigma'_i(j) & r(j) \leq CR_i \vee j = rn(i) \\ x_i(j) & r(j) > CR_i \wedge j \neq rn(i) \end{cases} \tag{3}$$

where real parameter $g_i \in (0,1]$, $\pi_i$ is a random number by uniform distribution in $(0,1]$ when $t = 0$ and renewed by random number in $(0,1]$ with probability 0.1 when $t > 0$. For $i = 1, ..., m_p$ and $j = 1, ..., n$, the $j$-th dimension of the $i$-th individual will be mutated when $r(j) \leq CR_i$, where $r(j)$ is a random number by uniform distribution in $(0,1]$ and the control parameter $CR_i \in (0,1]$. $rn(i)$ is random integer number from $\{1, ..., n\}$ to guarantee at least one dimension of the individual mutates. The $j$-th dimension of the $i$-th individual remain the same when $r(j) > CR_i$ and $j \neq rn(i)$. For $i = 1, ..., m_p$, $CR_i$ is renewed by probability 0.1.

The mutation of Eq. (3) can make some dimensions of the individual remain and others change, which is mainly different from other mutations [5, 10-11, 13-14]. The aim of IRD-based mutation is to keep the good dimensions for the next iteration, which can improve the performance of the mutations based on stochastic distributions.

The proposed EP-IRD algorithm has the same process of other EPs [5, 10-11, 13-14] except mutation step. The updating of parameters $CR_i$ and $\pi_i$ ($i = 1, ..., m_p$) will increase computational time which is not more than the generation time of stochastic distribution of other EPs. Thus, EP-IRD has less computational effort than CEP [5], FEP [10], LEP [11], ALEP [11] and others [13-14].

The mutation strategy of EP-IRD is a little similar to a DE algorithm [18], but there are still several different points. The DE selects three different individuals for mutation, but EP-IRD selects two individual to generate the variance. EP-IRD uses mutation to produce offspring without crossover which is the key operator of DE. EP-IRD uses tournament selection but DE uses greed selection.

## 4  Numerical Results

This section will present a comparison result of solving benchmark problems [10] by five EP algorithms to indicate the effectiveness of EP-IRD. The tested EPs include CEP [5], FEP [10], LEP [11], ALEP [11] and EP-IRD. In the experiment, the parameter of EP-IRD is set as $g_i \in [0.1, 1]$ and the population size of EPs is all $m_p = 100$.

**Table 1.** Comparison results among CEP, FEP and EP-IRD

| Prob-lem | Itera-tion | IDEP AVG | CEP AVG | FEP AVG | IDEP STD | CEP STD | FEP STD |
|---|---|---|---|---|---|---|---|
| f1 | 1500 | **5.69E-67** | 2.2E-04 | 5.7E-04 | 9.53E-67 | 5.9E-04 | 1.3E-04 |
| f2 | 2000 | **1.48E-45** | 2.6E-03 | 8.1E-03 | 1.49E-45 | 1.7E-04 | 7.7E-04 |
| f3 | 5000 | **3.51E-67** | 5.0E-02 | 1.6E-02 | 4.26E-67 | 6.6E-02 | 1.4E-02 |
| f4 | 5000 | **3.34E-65** | 2.0 | 0.3 | 3.12E-65 | 1.2 | 0.5 |
| f5 | 20000 | **0** | 6.17 | 5.06 | 0 | 13.61 | 5.87 |
| f6 | 1500 | **0** | 577.76 | 0 | 0 | 1125.76 | 0 |
| f7 | 3000 | **2.01E-24** | 1.8E-03 | 7.6E-3 | 4.93E-24 | 6.4E-03 | 2.6E-03 |
| f8 | 9000 | -12406.13 | -7917.1 | **-12554.5** | 264.57 | 634.5 | 52.6 |
| f9 | 5000 | **0** | 89.0 | 4.6E-02 | 0 | 23.1 | 1.2E-02 |
| f10 | 1500 | **4.14E-15** | 9.2 | 1.8E-02 | 8.31E-31 | 2.8 | 2.1E-03 |
| f11 | 2000 | **0** | 8.6E-02 | 1.6E-02 | 0 | 0.12 | 2.2E-02 |
| f12 | 1500 | **1.12E-11** | 1.76 | 9.2E-06 | 0 | 2.4 | 3.6E-06 |
| f13 | 1500 | **1.07E-11** | 1.4 | 1.6E-04 | 0 | 3.7 | 7.3E-05 |
| f14 | 100 | **-1.0316** | -1.03 | -1.03 | 9.48E-06 | 4.9E-07 | 4.9E-07 |
| f15 | 100 | **0.39789** | 0.398 | 0.398 | 5.17E-07 | 1.5E-07 | 1.5E-07 |
| f16 | 100 | **3.0** | **3.0** | 3.02 | 0 | 0 | 0.11 |

**Table 2.** Comparison results among EP-IRD, LEP and ALEP

| Problem | Iteration | IDEP AVG | LEP AVG | ALEP AVG | IDEP STD | LEP STD | ALEP STD |
|---------|-----------|----------|---------|----------|----------|---------|----------|
| f1 | 1500 | **5.69E-67** | 6.59E-04 | 6.32E-04 | 9.53E-67 | 6.4E-05 | 7.6E-05 |
| f3 | 1500 | **2.39E-18** | 30.629 | 0.0418 | 2.72E-18 | 22.113 | 0.0596 |
| f5 | 1500 | **28.56** | 57.75 | 43.40 | 0.091 | 41.60 | 31.52 |
| f8 | 1500 | -9515.80 | **-11898.9** | -11469.2 | 359.01 | 52.2 | 58.2 |
| f9 | 1500 | **2.51** | 12.50 | 5.87 | 0.338 | 2.29 | 2.07 |
| f10 | 1500 | **4.14E-15** | 3.1E-02 | 1.9E-02 | 8.31E-31 | 2.0E-03 | 1.0E-03 |
| f11 | 1500 | **0** | 1.8E-02 | 2.4E-02 | 0 | 1.7E-02 | 2.8E-02 |
| f12 | 1500 | **1.12E-11** | 3.0E-05 | 6.0E-06 | 0 | 4.0E-06 | 1.0E-06 |
| f13 | 1500 | **1.07E-11** | 2.6E-04 | 9.8E-05 | 0 | 3.0E-05 | 1.2E-05 |
| f14 | 30 | **-1.03156** | -1.031 | -1.031 | 4.85E-05 | 0 | 0 |
| f16 | 30 | 3.00003 | **3.0** | **3.0** | 3.86E-05 | 0 | 0 |

The maximum iteration of the EPs is the same shown in the second column of Table 1 and Table 2. All of the EPs run independently 50 times. The average value of the best-so-far is given in column 3-5 of Table 1-2 and the standard deviation is given in column 6-8.

Table 1 indicates EP-IRD performs better than FEP [10] and CEP [5] in solving all of the benchmark problems by the value of average and standard deviation. EP-IRD is obviously superior to CEP and FEP in the solution of unimodal functions and mul-ti-modal functions.

Table 2 shows that EP-IRD has better and more deviation results than LEP and ALEP in solving unimodal functions. EP-IRD performs the best among the three algorithms in f9-f13 except f8, f14 and f16 in which they have the same effectiveness, which proves EP-IRD is good at solving multi-modal functions.

Therefore, EP-IRD has faster convergence speed than other tested EPs according to the numerical results above.

# 5   Conclusion

Evolutionary programming was considered as the classical evolutional algorithm for solving continuous optimization because of its real-number coding and mutation. However, for the non-heuristic mutation abased on stochastic distribution, it is easy for EPs to fall into slow convergence to the optimal. In this paper, a random individual difference mutation is used to make the EP algorithm heuristic. An EP based on random individual difference (EP-IRD) is proposed to improve the convergence speed of EPs based on stochastic distribution. The results of the numerical experiments show that EP-IRD has a faster convergence speed than four EPs based on stochastic distribution in solving both unimodal functions and multi-modal functions.

## Acknowledgement

National Natural Science Foundation of China (61003066,61070033), Doctoral Program of the Ministry of Education (20090172120035), Natural Science Foundation of Guangdong Province (9151008901000165, 10151601501000015), Key Technology Research and Development Programs of Guangdong Province (2009B010800026) and Fundamental Research Funds for the Central Universities, SCUT(2009ZM0052), Key Technology Research and Development Programs of Huizhou (2009G024) and Special Fund Project of Huizhou Modern Information Services.

## References

1. Holland, J.H.: Adaptation in Natural and Artificial Systems, 1st edn. (1975), 2nd edn. MIT press, Cambridge (1992)
2. Fogel, L.J., Owens, A.J., Walsh, M.J.: Artificial Intelligence through Simulated Evolution. Wiley, New York (1996)
3. Rechenberg, I.: Evolutions strategies: Optimiering technischer Systeme nach Prinzipien der biologischen Evolution. Frommann-Holzboog, Stuttgart (1973)
4. Schwefel, H.P.: Numerische Optimierung von Computer-Modellen mittels der Evolutions strategies, vol. 26. Interdisciplinary Systems Research. Birkhauser, Basle (1977)
5. Fogel, D.B.: System Identification Through Simulated Evolution: A Machine Learning Approach to Modeling. Ginn, Needham Heights (1991)
6. Fogel, D.B.: Evolving artificial intelligence. Ph.D. dissertation, University of California, San Diego (1992)
7. Fogel, D.B.: Applying evolutionary programming to selected traveling sales-man problems. Cybernetics System 24, 27–36 (1993)
8. Bäck, T., Schwefel, H.P.: An overview of evolutionary algorithms for parameter optimization. Evolutionary Computation 1(1), 1–23 (1993)
9. Schwefel, H.P.: Evolution and Optimum Seeking. Wiley, New York (1995)
10. Yao, X., Liu, Y., Lin, G.: Evolutionary programming made faster. IEEE Transactions on Evolutionary Computation 3(2), 82–103 (1999)
11. Lee, C.Y., Yao, X.: Evolutionary programming using mutations based on Lévy probability distribution. IEEE Transactions on Evolutionary Computation 8(5), 1–13 (2004)
12. Abdel-Rahman, H., Masao, F.: Directed Evolutionary Programming: Towards an Improved Performance of Evolutionary Programming, pp. 1521–1528 (2006)
13. Zhang, H., Lu, J.: Adaptive evolutionary programming based on reinforcement learning. Information Sciences 178, 971–984 (2008)
14. Zhao, X., Gao, X.S., Hu, Z.C.: Evolutionary programming based on non-uniform mutation. Applied Mathematics and Computation 192, 1–11 (2007)
15. Dong, H., He, J., Huang, H., Hou, W.: Evolutionary programming using a mixed mutation strategy. Information Sciences 177, 312–327 (2007)
16. Chen, G., Low, C.P., Yang, Z.: Preserving and Exploiting Genetic Diversity in Evolutionary Programming Algorithms. IEEE Transactions on Evolutionary Computation 13(3), 661–673 (2009)
17. Liang, K.H., Yao, X.: Adapting Self-Adaptive Parameters in Evolutionary Algorithms. Applied Intelligence 15, 171–180 (2001)
18. Brest, J., Greiner, S., Boskovic, B., Mernik, M., Zumer, V.: Self-Adaptive Control Parameters in Differential Evolution: A Comparative Study on Numerical Benchmark Problems. IEEE Transactions on Evolutionary Computation 10(6), 646–657 (2006)

# Taguchi Method Based Parametric Study of Generalized Generation Gap Genetic Algorithm Model

S. Thangavelu and C. Shunmuga Velayutham

Amrita School of Engineering,
Amrita Vishwa Vidyapeetham, Coimbatore,
Tamil Nadu, India
s_thangavel@cb.amrita.edu, cs_velayutham@cb.amrita.edu

**Abstract.** In this paper, a parametric study of Generalized Generation Gap (G3) Genetic Algorithm (GA) model with Simplex crossover (SPX) using Taguchi method has been presented. Population size, number of parents and offspring pool size are considered as design factors with five levels. The analysis of mean factor is conducted to find the influence of design factors and their optimal combination for six benchmark functions. The experimental results suggest more experiments on granularity of design factor levels for better performance efficacy.

**Keywords:** Genetic Algorithm, Simplex Crossover, Generalized Generation Gap model, Taguchi method of analysis.

## 1 Introduction

There have been an increasing interest in the study and use of real-parameter Evolutionary Algorithms (EA's) to solve complex real life continuous optimization problems. Evolution Strategies (ES), Evolutionary Programming (EP) and Differential Evolution (DE) are popular instances of real-parameter EA's. Despite the fact that, Genetic Algorithms (GAs) traditionally use bit string representation, real-valued representation in GA's has attracted many researchers who are working on its various aspects like GA population-alteration models, recombination operators etc.

Over the past few years, numerous studies on real-parameter GA's have resulted in population-alteration models like MGG (Minimum Generation Gap model) [1], G3 (Generalized Generation Gap model) [2] and recombination operators like Blend Crossover (BLX), Simulated Binary Crossover (SBX) [9], Simplex Crossover (SPX) [4,10], Unimodal Normal Distribution Crossover (UNDX) [11] and Parent Centric Crossover (PCX) [2,5].

Despite the extensive study of the above said models and recombination operators in the past, there are very few parametric studies unlike in the case of other nature inspired algorithm [13],[14], to establish the best parameter settings for the various model-recombination operator combinations. In this paper we perform a preliminary parametric study of G3 model with SPX crossover by varying the population size, number of parents and number of offsprings. The parametric study employs an efficient experimental design using Taguchi method with the above said three genetic

B.K. Panigrahi et al. (Eds.): SEMCCO 2010, LNCS 6466, pp. 344–350, 2010.

parameters as the design factors. The study involves testing the GA (G3+SPX) on a set of six benchmark functions of high dimensionality and varying features like modality and decomposability.

This paper is organized as follows: Section 2 describes the G3 model and the SPX crossover operator, Section 3 explains the design of experiments while simulation results are discussed in Section 4. Finally, Section 5 concludes the paper.

## 2   Genetic Algorithm Model

Research interests towards population-alteration models different from a standard genetic algorithm for real-parameter optimization led to the proposal of Minimum generation gap (MGG) model by Satoh, Yamamura and Kobayashi [1]. The simple yet efficient MGG model was modified, to make it computationally more efficient by Deb et. al., to Generalized generation gap (G3) model [2]. In fact, both MGG and G3 are steady-state models, where recombination and selection operators are intertwined and can be used to study the behavior of host of recombination operators like SPX, UNDX, PCX, etc. The basic GA model used in this paper, for parametric study, is G3 model with SPX recombination operator.

The G3 model can be summarized as follows:

> *Initialize Population $P_G$; (G=0)*
> *Do*
> *{*
>     *Select the best parent and $\mu$-1 other parents randomly.*
>     *Generate $\lambda$ offsprings from $\mu$ parents using a recombination operator.*
>     *Choose two parents randomly from the $\mu$ parents.*
>     *Combine the chosen two parents with $\lambda$ offsprings and choose the best two*
>         *solutions from the combined subpopulation to replace the chosen*
>         *two parents (to form $P_{G+1}$)*
> *} while termination criterion is true;*

The Simplex crossover operator (SPX), proposed by Tsutsui, Yamamura and Higuchi [3], is a multi-parent recombination operator that assigns a uniform probability distribution for creating any solution in a restricted region called simplex. The SPX procedure [4,10] for generating an offspring from $(n+1)$ parents [3] is as follows:

1. *Choose $(n+1)$ parental vectors $X_k$ ($k=0,1,...n$) and calculate their center of mass O as*

$$O = \frac{1}{n+1}\sum_{k=0}^{n} X_k$$

2. *Generate random numbers r as*

$$r_k = u^{\left(\frac{1}{k+1}\right)} , k = 0,1,2,...,n$$

*where u is uniform random number $\epsilon$[0.0,1.0]*

3. *Calculate Y and C respectively, as*

$$Y_k = O + \varepsilon\,(X_k - O),$$

*where  k=0,1,2,...,n and ε is the*
*expansion rate, a control parameter*

$$C_k = \begin{cases} 0 & k = 0 \\ r_{k-1}(Y_{k-1} - Y_k + C_{k-1}), & k = 1,2,\dots,n \end{cases}$$

4. *Generate an offspring C as*

$$C = Y_n + C_n$$

# 3   Design of Experiments

The parametric study on the chosen GA model (G3 with SPX operator) and its performance has been investigated on six benchmark problems [6,7] with high dimensionality of 30, grouped by features – unimodal separable functions, unimodal nonseparable functions, multimodal separable functions and multimodal nonseparable functions. The description of the benchmark functions, used in this paper, are provided in Table 1.

All the test functions have an optimum value at zero except *f3*. In order to show the similar results, the description of *f3* was adjusted to have its optimum value at zero by just adding the optimal value for the function with 30 decision variables (12569.486618164879) [6].

**Table 1.** Description of the benchmark functions

| | |
|---|---|
| *f1*  - Schwefel's Problem 2.21<br>$f_{sch}(x) = max_i\{\lvert x_i \rvert, 1 \le i \le 30\};$<br>$-100 \le x_i \le 100$ | *f4* – Generalized Restrigin's Function<br>$f_{Ras}(x) = \sum_{i=1}^{30} [x_i^2 - 10\cos(2\pi x_i) + 10];$<br>$-5.12 \le x_i \le 5.12$ |
| *f2* – Schwefel's Problem 1.2<br>$f_{schDS}(x) = \sum_{i=1}^{30} \left( \sum_{j=1}^{i} x_j \right)^2 ;$<br>$-100 \le x_i \le 100$ | *f5* - Generalized Rosenbrock's Function<br>$f_{Ros}(x) = \sum_{i=1}^{29} \lvert 100(x_{i+1} - x_i^2)^2 + (x_i - 1)^2 \rvert;$<br>$-30 \le x_i \le 30$ |
| *f3* – Generalized Schwefel's Problem 2.26<br>$f_{Sch}(x) = \sum_{i=1}^{30} (x_i \sin(\sqrt{\lvert x_i \rvert}));$<br>$-500 \le x_i \le 500$ | *f6* - Generalized Griewank's Function<br>$f_{Gri}(x) = \frac{1}{4000} \sum_{i=1}^{30} x_i^2 - \prod_{i=1}^{30} \cos\left(\frac{x_i}{\sqrt{i}}\right) + 1;$<br>$-600 \le x_i \le 600$ |

In Taguchi's parameter design method [8,11,12], employed in this paper for parametric study, an orthogonal array depending on the number and levels of design factors is used to study parameter space. The population size (N), number of parents (μ) and number of offsprings (λ) have been chosen as three design factors with five levels as shown in table 2. The expansion rate parameter ε preserves covariance matrix of the population and works well if set as $\sqrt{\mu + 1}$ where μ is the number of parents. Twenty five experiments are required to determine the optimum combination of the levels of chosen design factors. Table 3 shows the standard Taguchi's orthogonal array *L-25* containing parameter combinations used in numerical experiments. The

**Table 2.** Design factors and their levels

| Design factors | Level 1 | Level 2 | Level 3 | Level 4 | Level 5 |
|---|---|---|---|---|---|
| Population size (N) | 100 | 200 | 300 | 400 | 500 |
| Parent size ($\mu$) | 2 | 10 | 17 | 24 | 31 |
| Children size ($\lambda$) | 10 | 30 | 50 | 70 | 100 |

Taguchi's robust design methodology determines design factors settings such that effects of noise factors on the performance characteristic, that is, smaller the better is minimized.

For each parametric combination in Table 3, the GA model is run to 400,000 function evaluations to optimize each benchmark function and the experiment is repeated 30 times for each function. The analysis of means is conducted to find the influence of each design factors and the best parameter combination. The GA model with thus found parameters is run on each function 100 times to calculate performance efficacy.

**Table 3.** Taguchi's *L25* orthogonal array containing parameter combinations

| Experiment | N | $\mu$ | $\lambda$ |
|---|---|---|---|
| 1 | 100 | 2 | 10 |
| 2 | 100 | 10 | 30 |
| 3 | 100 | 17 | 50 |
| 4 | 100 | 24 | 70 |
| 5 | 100 | 31 | 100 |
| 6 | 200 | 2 | 30 |
| 7 | 200 | 10 | 50 |
| 8 | 200 | 17 | 70 |
| 9 | 200 | 24 | 100 |
| 10 | 200 | 31 | 10 |
| 11 | 300 | 2 | 50 |
| 12 | 300 | 10 | 70 |
| 13 | 300 | 17 | 100 |
| 14 | 300 | 24 | 10 |
| 15 | 300 | 31 | 30 |
| 16 | 400 | 2 | 70 |
| 17 | 400 | 10 | 100 |
| 18 | 400 | 17 | 10 |
| 19 | 400 | 24 | 30 |
| 20 | 400 | 31 | 50 |
| 21 | 500 | 2 | 100 |
| 22 | 500 | 10 | 10 |
| 23 | 500 | 17 | 30 |
| 24 | 500 | 24 | 50 |
| 25 | 500 | 31 | 70 |

# 4   Simulation Results and Discussion

The results of the six bench marks functions are given below. The analysis was performed on mean factor. The response table for means obtained for the six benchmark functions $f1 - f6$ are shown respectively in Tables 4 – 9. It can be observed from the rank values that mostly the number of offsprings ($\lambda$) has the largest effect on the performance criterion. As can be seen from the tables, the optimum settings of parameters for functions $f1$, $f2$ and $f5$ calculates to $N_5$, $\mu_5$, $\lambda_5$ (ie. 500, 31, 100). This result, in fact, suggests that the levels of design factors could be increased for better insight. The optimum parameter settings for functions $f3$, $f4$ and $f6$ respectively calculates to $N_3$, $\mu_3$, $\lambda_5$ (ie. 300, 17, 100), $N_2$, $\mu_3$, $\lambda_5$ (ie. 200, 17, 100) and $N_4$, $\mu_4$, $\lambda_5$ (ie. 400, 24, 100).

The GA model is tested on each benchmark function with the calculated parameter combinations. Being stochastic in nature, each GA experiment is repeated 100 times and the mean objective function values, for each benchmark function, are reported in Table 10.

Although the results were not very impressive, more experiments on design factor selection and granularity of levels would provide better insight on parameter combinations and better performance efficacy. Taguchi robust parameter design method ensures that the obtained performance are better than the average performance of other parameter combinations with a far smaller experiment that full factorial.

**Table 4.** Response table for means obtained for function $f1$

| Level | $N$ | $\mu$ | $\lambda$ |
|---|---|---|---|
| 1 | 4.8858 | 7.8597 | 2.7448 |
| 2 | 2.2183 | 1.3691 | 2.7016 |
| 3 | 1.5440 | 0.6687 | 2.2717 |
| 4 | 1.3265 | 0.6046 | 1.9253 |
| 5 | 1.1068 | 0.5793 | 1.4380 |
| Delta | 3.7789 | 7.2804 | 1.3069 |
| Rank | 2 | 3 | 1 |

**Table 5.** Response table for means obtained for function $f2$

| Level | $N$ | $\mu$ | $\lambda$ |
|---|---|---|---|
| 1 | 324.103 | 283.740 | 227.775 |
| 2 | 41.596 | 44.044 | 81.107 |
| 3 | 14.861 | 29.601 | 45.397 |
| 4 | 4.214 | 19.272 | 23.429 |
| 5 | 1.339 | 9.457 | 8.406 |
| Delta | 322.764 | 274.283 | 219.370 |
| Rank | 3 | 2 | 1 |

**Table 6.** Response table for means obtained for function $f3$

| Level | $N$ | $\mu$ | $\lambda$ |
|---|---|---|---|
| 1 | -1226.4805 | 1979.7158 | -1606.8469 |
| 2 | -1667.3556 | -2559.9418 | -1403.6149 |
| 3 | -1730.8361 | -2627.7902 | -1206.1370 |
| 4 | -1523.1615 | -2061.1851 | -1218.0493 |
| 5 | -1137.3099 | -2015.9423 | -1850.4955 |
| Delta | 593.5262 | 4607.506 | 644.3585 |
| Rank | 1 | 3 | 2 |

**Table 7.** Response table for means obtained for function *f4*

| Level | N | μ | λ |
|---|---|---|---|
| 1 | 39.845 | 68.909 | 20.544 |
| 2 | 18.576 | 16.313 | 25.876 |
| 3 | 20.803 | 7.872 | 70.329 |
| 4 | 44.397 | 29.038 | 51.472 |
| 5 | 64.711 | 66.199 | 20.111 |
| Delta | 46.135 | 61.037 | 50.218 |
| Rank | 1 | 3 | 2 |

**Table 8.** Response table for means obtained for function *f5*

| Level | N | μ | λ |
|---|---|---|---|
| 1 | 1353.94 | 936.42 | 891.44 |
| 2 | 83.61 | 332.25 | 367.77 |
| 3 | 35.33 | 112.26 | 121.09 |
| 4 | 32.57 | 84.88 | 91.80 |
| 5 | 28.10 | 67.74 | 61.46 |
| Delta | 1325.83 | 868.68 | 829.98 |
| Rank | 3 | 2 | 1 |

**Table 9.** Response table for means obtained for function *f6*

| Level | N | μ | λ |
|---|---|---|---|
| 1 | 1.57108 | 0.64482 | 0.61454 |
| 2 | 0.39269 | 0.45691 | 0.58042 |
| 3 | 0.02843 | 0.27566 | 0.34016 |
| 4 | 0.00562 | 0.25818 | 0.25810 |
| 5 | 0.00663 | 0.36888 | 0.21121 |
| Delta | 1.56546 | 0.38664 | 0.40333 |
| Rank | 3 | 1 | 3 |

**Table 10.** Performance of GA model on benchmark functions with optimal parameter settings

| SNo | Function | N | μ | λ | Mean | Std.Dev |
|---|---|---|---|---|---|---|
| 1 | *f1* | 500 | 31 | 100 | 0.097881431131 | 0.012372186241 |
| 2 | *f2* | 500 | 31 | 100 | 0.036296946443 | 0.007952509856 |
| 3 | *f3* | 300 | 17 | 100 | -2507.522726 | 2375.401282 |
| 4 | *f4* | 200 | 17 | 100 | 5.757988 | 12.234992 |
| 5 | *f5* | 500 | 31 | 100 | 28.108220 | 0.439616 |
| 6 | *f6* | 400 | 24 | 100 | 0.000209 | 6.76147 |

## 5   Conclusion

In this paper a preliminary parametric study of generalized generation gap (G3) GA model with simplex crossover (SPX) operator has been carried out. An efficient experimental design using Taguchi's method has been employed for the parametric study. Population size, number of parents and offspring size have been considered as design factors with five levels. Twenty five experiments were required to identify the optimal parameter settings for each of the six benchmark functions considered in this study. The analysis of means is used to find the influence of each design factors and optimal parameter combinations. In most of the cases, the number of offspring is observed to have largest effect on performance criterion. The GA model was run with optimal parameter settings on all benchmark functions and the performance in terms of mean objective function values has been reported. The observation suggested more experiments on design factor selection and granularity of design factor levels. More experiments will be carried out, in future, to gain insight by adding more state-of-the-art benchmark functions of diverse characteristics like shifted, rotated, composite, multi-modal, etc. possible from the IEEE CEC 2005 problems and competition on real parameter optimization.

# References

1. Satoh, H., Yamamura, M., Kobayashi, S.: Minimal generation gap model for Gas considering both exploration and exploitation. In: Proceedings of the IIZUKA. Methodologies for the Conception, Design, and Application of Intelligent Systems, pp. 494–497 (1996)
2. Deb, K., Anand, A., Joshi, D.: A Computationally Efficient Evolutionary Algorithm for Real-Parameter Optimization: KanGAL Report Number 2002003 (April 11, 2002)
3. Tsutsui, S., Yamamura, M., Higuchi, T.: Multi-parent Recombination with Simplex Crossover in Real Coded Genetic Algorithms
4. Tsutsui, S.: David, E.G., K. Sastry.: Linkage Learning in Real-Coded Gas with Simplex Crossover
5. Deb, K., Joshi, D., Anand, A.: Real-Coded Evolutionary Algorithms with Parent-Centric Recombination
6. Mezura-Montes, E., Velazquez-Reyes, J., Coello Coello, C.A.: A Comparative Study on Differential Evolution Variants for Global Optimization. In: Genetic and Evolutionary Computation Conference, GECCO 2006, July 8-12 (2006)
7. Yao, X., Liu, Y., Liang, K.H., Lin, G.: Fast Evolutionary Algorithms. In: Rozenberg, G., Back, T., Eiben, A. (eds.) Advances in Evolutionary Computing: Theory and Applications, pp. 45–94. Springer, New York (2003)
8. Gopalsamy, B.M., Mondal, B., Ghosh, S.: Taguchi method and ANOVA: An approach for process parameters optimization of hard machining while machining hardened steel
9. Deb, K., Agrawal, R.B.: Simulated binary crossover for continuous search space. Complex Systems 9, 115–148 (1995)
10. Higuchi, T., Tsutsui, S., Yamamura, M.: Theoretical analysis of simpelx crossover for real-coded genetic algorithms. In: Deb, K., Rudolph, G., Lutton, E., Merelo, J.J., Schoenauer, M., Schwefel, H.-P., Yao, X. (eds.) PPSN 2000. LNCS, vol. 1917, pp. 365–374. Springer, Heidelberg (2000)
11. Ono, I., Kobayashi, S.: A real-coded genetic algorithm for function optimization using unimodal normal distribution crossover. In: Proceedings of the Seventh International Conference on Genetic Algorithms (ICGA-7), pp. 246–253 (1997)
12. Hwang, C.-C., Lyu, L.-Y., Liu, C.-T., Li, P.-L.: Optimal design of an SPM Motor Using Genetic Algorithms and Taguchi Method
13. Qin, A.K., Huang, V.L., Suganthan, P.N.: Differential evolution algorithm with strategy adaptation for global numerical optimization. IEEE Transactions on Evolutionary Computation 13(2), 398–417 (2009)
14. Zielinski, K., Laur, R.: Adaptive Parameter Setting for a Multi-Objective Particle Swarm Optimization Algorithm. In: Proc. CEC 2007 (2007)

# EBFS-ICA: An Efficient Algorithm for CT-MRI Image Fusion

Rutuparna Panda and Sanjay Agrawal

Department of Electronics and Telecommunication Engg.
VSS University of Technology, Burla-768018, India
Phone: 91-663-2431857; Fax: 91-663-2430204
r_ppanda@yahoo.co.in

**Abstract.** Analyzing the spatial and spectral properties of CT and MRI scan medical images; this article proposes a novel method for CT-MRI image fusion. Independent component analysis is used to analyze images for acquiring independent component. This paper addresses an efficient algorithm for ICA-based image fusion with selection of optimal independent components using *E-coli* Bacterial Foraging Optimization Technique. Different methods were suggested in the literature to select the largest eigenvalues and their corresponding eigenvectors for ICA based image fusion. But, there is no unified approach for selecting optimal ICA bases to improvise the performance. In this context, we propose a new algorithm called EBFS-ICA which uses a nutrient concentration function (cost function). Here the cost function is maximized through hill climbing via a type of biased random walk. The proposed EBFS-ICA algorithm offers two distinct additional advantages. First, the proposed algorithm can supplement the features of ICA. Second, the random bias incorporated in EBFS guide us to move in the direction of increasingly favorable environment. Finally, we use fusion rules to generate the fused image which contain more integrated accurate detail information of different soft tissue such as muscles and blood vessels. Experimental results presented here show the effectiveness of the proposed EBFS-ICA algorithm. Further, the efficiency of our method is better than FastICA method used in medical image fusion field.

**Keywords:** Biomedical image fusion, Bacteria Foraging, PCA, ICA.

## 1 Introduction

Developments in medical imaging field, as well as significant progress in computer hardware and software design, have led to improvements in the delineation and modeling of brain tumor volumes for radiation therapy. For accurate diagnoses, radiologists must integrate information from multiple image formats. Fused, anatomically-consistent images are especially beneficial in diagnosing and treating cancer. This depends on the clinical stage of the disease (prostate gland and a variable portion of the seminal vesicles). Computation and localization of these volumes are the basis upon which exact treatment plans are designed. CT and MRI scan images play an important role in this connection. CT scan image easily recognizes the upper

B.K. Panigrahi et al. (Eds.): SEMCCO 2010, LNCS 6466, pp. 351–361, 2010.

prostate and seminal vesicles. However, the lower extent of the gland is difficult to distinguish from adjacent normal structures, *i.e.* urogenital diaphragm, due to availability of small CT numbers. On the other hand, MRI image yields more contrast than CT scan image when differentiating the prostate gland from the periprostatic soft tissues, as well as allowing more precise delineation of normal critical structures and more accurate definition of treatment volumes. Interestingly, diagnostic information available from MRI image can be incorporated into that of CT scan image. The process of integrating such type of complementary information from the MRI image and CT scan image into a single medical image is called "image fusion". This method enables (in a complete manner) the radiation oncologist and medical physicist to design and execute a successful course of therapy.

The basic idea of PCA [1-5] is to construct a subspace that represents an input image with lower dimensional feature vectors. The principal components, derived from an ensemble image serving as feature vectors, span the significant variations among other images. The PCA algorithm finds an optimal linear transformation that maps the original $n-$dimensional data space into a $m-$dimensional feature space $(m < n)$ to achieve dimensionality reduction. Suppose the $N$ sample images are given as $\{x_1, x_2, ..., x_N\}$. Each image is modeled as a $n-$dimensional vector formed via lexicographic ordering of a 2D pixel array. The total scatter matrix can be represented as the correlation of the 'centered' images

$$S = \sum_{k=1}^{N} (x_k - \bar{x})(x_k - \bar{x})^T \tag{1}$$

where $\bar{x}$ denotes the mean of the $N$ sample vectors in the training set

$$\bar{x} = \frac{1}{N} \sum_{k=1}^{N} x_k . \tag{2}$$

Considered a linear transformation matrix: $E = [e_1, e_2, ..., e_m]$. The column vectors of $E$ are the eigenvectors $e_1, e_2, ..., e_m$ of $S$ associated with the first $m$ largest eigenvectors $\lambda_1 \geq \lambda_2 \geq .... \geq \lambda_m$. The $m$ eigenvectors $e_1, e_2, ..., e_m$ constitutes a $m-$dimensional feature space.

In practice, finding the eigenvectors of the scatter matrix $S = XX^T$, where the input matrix given by $-X = [x_1, x_2, ..., x_N]$, of size $n \times n$ is an intractable task for typical image sizes. As the size of $S$ is too large, a simplified method of calculation has to be adopted. The number of training image are usually much smaller then the pixel in an image $(N << n)$. The eigenvectors $e$ and associated eigenvalues of $\lambda$ of $XX^T$ can be found from the eigenvectors $\bar{e}$ and corresponding eigenvalues $\bar{\lambda}$ of $X^T X$, which are mathematically more tractable and easier to obtain. The eigenvectors are $e = X\bar{e}$ and the eigenvalues remain the same $(\lambda = \bar{\lambda})$. Given an image $x$

for testing, the PCA analysis expands the face in terms of $m$ vectors. The linear transformation $W^T$ produces a $m-$ dimensional feature vector $a = (a_1, a_2, ..., a_m)^T$

$$a = W^T (x - \bar{x}).\tag{3}$$

Each of the transform coefficients $a_i = e_i^T (x - \bar{x})$, $i = 1, ...., m$ describes the contribution of each vector to that image. Different metrics for evaluating image fusion results are reported in [7, 8].

In the recent past, a new distributed optimization technique called bacteria foraging optimization (BFO) technique was proposed in [6]. The algorithm emulates the chemotactic (foraging) behavior of E. *coli* bacteria that are living in human intestine. Chemotaxis behavior of E. *coli* bacteria can be used to solve non gradient optimization problems with the help of run and tumble mechanism to move the cell in right direction. Swarming is also a bacterial foraging behavior where cell released attractants is used for signaling other cells so that they swarm together. The motion patterns of bacteria are decided (in the presence of chemical attractants and repellents) using swarming behavior. Other important steps involved in bacterial foraging optimization method are reproduction, elimination and dispersal. These steps represent various activities of social bacterial foraging. In a reproduction step, the least healthy bacteria die as they could not search much nutrient during their lifetime of foraging and the healthiest bacteria can reproduce (each split into two bacteria). In an elimination-dispersal step, any bacteria can be eliminated from the population by dispersing it to a random location. Note that the frequency of chemotactic steps in BFO is greater than the frequency of reproduction steps. Many more characteristics of chemotactic and swarming behavior have been reported in [6]. However, we ignore some characteristics of chemotaxis and swarming strategies to make our computer simulation programs simple. Recently, different modifications to BFO are reported in [9-13].

Thus, we have been motivated to use BFO to search optimal principal components of the sample images and then to use them to develop an improved fusion algorithm. A new BFO-PCA is developed in this paper. The BFO-PCA is then used for dimension reduction. A new optimized ICA based algorithm called EBFS-ICA is developed here. To backup our statements, some experimental results are produced.

## 2 Bacteria Foraging Optimization

Bacteria foraging [6] is an optimization process, motivated from biological behavior of bacteria. Basic idea of foraging is to maximize the energy obtained per unit time spent for foraging. The foraging theory is based on search of nutrients in a way that maximizes their energy intake $E$ per unit time $T$ spent for foraging and tries to maximize a function like

$$\frac{E}{T}\tag{4}$$

Foraging involves finding such patches, deciding whether to enter a patch and search for food, and whether to continue searching for food in the current patch or to go find another patch that hopefully has a higher quality of nutrients than the current patch. The bacteria can move in two different ways; it can run (swim for a period of time) or it can tumble, and it alternates between these two modes in its entire lifetime. After a tumble, the cells are generally pointed in random direction, but slightly biased towards the previous traveling zone. Thus, it is a biased kind of random walk. A bacteria comes under three different stage in its life time, that are chemotaxes, reproduction and elimination & dispersal event.

*Chemotaxes*

The motion patterns that the bacteria generate in the presence of chemical attractants and repellents are called chemotaxes. This helps the other bacterium to follow the root. Nest, suppose that the bacterium happens to encounter a nutrient gradient. The change in the concentration of the nutrient triggers a reaction such that the bacterium will spend more time swimming and less time tumbling. As long as it travels on a positive concentration gradient, it will tend to lengthen the time spends swimming, up to a certain point. The swimming or tumbling is done by the decision-making mechanisms. Here, it performs a type of sampling and it remembers the concentration a moment ago, compares it with a current one, and makes decisions based on the difference.

To represent a tumble, a unit length random direction, say $\phi(j)$, is generated; this will be used to define the direction of movement after a tumble. In particular, we let

$$\theta^i(j+1,k,l) = \theta^i(j,k,l) + C(i)\phi(j) \tag{5}$$

Where $\theta^i(j,k,l)$ represent location of the $i^{th}$ bacterium and $C(i)$ denote a basic chemotactic step size.

When cell-to-cell signaling takes place via an attractant, then the bacteria swarm together, and it can be methodically treated as combined cell-to-cell attraction and repelling effects. That is

$$J_{cc}(\theta, P(j,k,l)) = \sum_{i=1}^{S} J_{cc}^i(\theta, \theta^i(j,k,l))$$

$$= \sum_{i=1}^{S}\left[-d_{attract}\exp\left(-w_{attract}\sum_{m=1}^{p}(\theta_m - \theta_m^i)^2\right)\right]$$

$$+ \sum_{i=1}^{S}\left[h_{repellent}\exp\left(-w_{repellent}\sum_{m=1}^{p}(\theta_m - \theta_m^i)^2\right)\right] \tag{6}$$

Where S is the total number of bacterium, p is the number parameter to be optimized, J is the cost function and $d_{attract}$, $w_{attract}$, $h_{repellent}$, $w_{repellent}$ are different coefficients should be properly choused.

*Reproduction*

After some chemotaxis step it compares all the nutrient concentration where bacteria are present. Where the higher nutrient concentration it found, at that place each bacteria reproduce an exact copy of its own. With low nutrient concentration, the bacteria will die.

*Elimination & Dispersal*
This is another important event, used to assist the chemotaxis step. It keep track on the bacteria, whether they are in appropriate place or not. If not, then it places bacteria in arbitrary food space for new beginning of search. From a broad prospective, elimination and dispersal are parts of the population-level long-distance motile behavior.

## Bacteria Foraging Optimization Algorithm

1.      *Initialization*

- Chose $S$ number of bacteria for the chemotaxis step as the number of population.
- Then determine the number of parameter to be optimized $p$.
- Then determine the number of chemotaxis step $N_c$, number of reproduction step, $N_{re}$ and the number of elimination & dispersal step as $N_{ed}$.
- Then determine the maximum length of swimming of a bacterium when hill climbing as $N_s$.
- Also determine the chemotactic step size for swimming $C(i)$ as $i = 1,2,....,S$.
- Then chose these $d_{attract}$, $w_{attract}$, $h_{repellent}$, $w_{repellent}$ parameter that helps in swarming with appropriate value.
- Initial value of $\theta^i$, $i = 1,2,....,S$ must be chosen, so that these are randomly distributed across the domain of the optimization problem.
- Initially $j = k = l = 0$, where $j, k, l$ parameter determine how many step it already move in chemotaxis, reproduction and elimination & dispersal event.
- Define elimination and dispersal probability $p_{ed}$.

For the algorithm, note that updates to the $\theta^i$ automatically result in updates to $P$, where $P$ represent the position of each member in the population of the $S$ bacteria at the respective step.

2.   *Iterative algorithm*

A.   Elimination-dispersal loop: $l = l + 1$

B.   Reproduction loop: $k = k + 1$

C.   Chemotaxis loop: $j = j + 1$

a. For $i = 1,2,...S$, take a chemotactic step for bacterium $i$ as follows.

b. Compute $J(i, j, k, l)$. Let

$$J(i, j, k, l) = J(i, j, k, l) + J_{cc}\left(\theta^i (j, k, l), P(j, k, l)\right)$$(i.e., add on the cell-to-cell attractant effect to the nutrient concentration).

c. Save the value $J(i, j, k, l)$ as $J_{last}$ for the next step, to get a better cost via a run.

d. Tumble:    Generate    a    random    vector $\Delta(i) \in \mathfrak{R}^p$ with    each    element $\Delta_m(i), m = 1,2,...p$ , a random number on [-1, 1].

e. Move: Let $\theta^i(j+1,k,l) = \theta^i(j,k,l) + C(i)\dfrac{\Delta(i)}{\sqrt{\Delta^T(i)\Delta(i)}}$ . This results in a

step of size $C(i)$ in the direction of the tumble for bacterium $i$.

f. Compute $J(i, j+1,k,l) = J(i, j,k,l) + J_{cc}\left(\theta^i(j+1,k,l), P(j+1,k,l)\right)$.

g. Swim:

   i. Let $m = 0$, as a counter for swim length.

   ii. While $m < N_s$

- Let $m = m+1$
- If $J(i, j+1.k.l) < J_{last}$ (if doing better),

    then $\qquad\qquad J_{last} = J(i, j+1,k,l) \qquad\qquad$ and $\qquad\qquad$ let

$$\theta^i(j+1,k,l) = \theta^i(j+1,k,l) + C(i)\dfrac{\Delta(i)}{\sqrt{\Delta^T(i)\Delta(i)}}$$

    and use this $\theta^i(j+1,k,l)$ to compute the new $J(i, j+1,k,l)$ as f.

- Else, let $m = N_s$. End of the while loop.

h. Move to the next bacterium $(i+1)$ if $i \neq S$, to step b. till $i == S$ .

D.   Verify the $j < N_c$ , if yes then go to C.

E.   Reproduction:

a. For the given $k$ and $l$, and each $i = 1,2,...S$ , let $J_{health}^i = \displaystyle\sum_{j=1}^{N_c+1} J(i, j,k,l)$ be the

health of bacterium $i$ . Sort    bacteria and chemotactic parameters $C(i)$ in order of ascending cost $J_{health}$ (higher cost means lower health).

b. The $S_r = \dfrac{S}{2}$ bacteria with higher cost will be die and other $S_r$ with best value

split, that means the exact replica of the lower cost will be generated and placed in the same location as there parents.

F.   If $k < N_{re}$ , go to step B.

G.   Elimination-dispersal: For $i = 1,2,...S$ , with probability $p_{ed}$, eliminate and dispersed each bacterium by keeping the population constants. This can be achieved by randomly placing the bacterium in search space.

H.   If $l < N_{ed}$ , then go to step A; otherwise end.

# 3   EBFS-ICA Algorithm

Central limit theorem provides us an idea that non-Gaussian is independent. Hence, non-Gaussianity is a strong measure of independence. The first quantitative measure of non-Gaussianity is kurtosis which is the fourth order moment of random data. Given some random data '$x$' the kurtosis of '$x$' denoted by $kurt(x)$ is defined as [5]

$$kurt(x) = E\{x^4\}-3E\{x^2\} \tag{7}$$

Where E $\{.\}$ is the expectation. For simplicity, if we assume $x$ to be normalized so that the variance is equal to unity, i.e. $E\{x^2\}$ =1, then $kurt(x)$ =E$\{x^4\}$-3. This implies kurtosis is the normalized version of the fourth moment $E\{x^4\}$.

For a Gaussian $x$, the fourth moment equals to $3(3E\{x^2\})^2$. So for Gaussian random variables, the kurtosis value is zero and for non-Gaussian random variables kurtosis value is non-zero. In fact, when kurtosis value is positive the random variables are called *super Gaussian* or *leptokurtic* and when negative called *sub Gaussian* or *platykurtic*. It is noteworthy to mention here that super Gaussian random variables have a "spiky" probability density function with heavy tails and sub Gaussian random variables have a flat probability density function. However, kurtosis is very sensitive to outliers in the given data set, which is a limitation of kurtosis as the contrast function considered for some applications. Here we use kurtosis defined in (7) as the contrast (nutrient) function to be maximized. The algorithm is made for minimization of the nutrient function, so we consider J

$$J= (1/\text{contrast function}) \tag{8}$$

Before presenting the observed mixed signal data for optimization the two preprocessing steps, centering and whitening, are performed on it.

### *Step-1: Preprocessing*
The mean $X_m = (x_{1m}, x_{2m},\ldots\ldots\ldots,x_{nm})^T$ of the observed mixed signal data $X$ $=(x_1,x_2,\ldots\ldots\ldots,x_n)^T$ is computed and the mean is subtracted from the observed data set to make it zero mean.

$$X_c=X-X_m \tag{9}$$

The covariance matrix $C_{ov}X_c$ of the centered data $X_c$ is computed. The eigenvalue decomposition of $C_{ov}X_c$ is performed. If D is the eigenvalue matrix and E is the eigenvector matrix then

$$Z = D^{-1/2} E*X_c \tag{10}$$

Where Z= $(z_1, z_2,\ldots\ldots\ldots, z_n)^T$ represents the whitened observed mixed signal data. The random column vector w which is represented as the position P of the bacteria is used to find the linear transformation $w^T z$. The bacteria foraging technique finds the value of w at which J $(w^T z)$ is minimized.

### *Step-2: Initialization as explained in Section 2*

### *Step-3 Iterative algorithm for optimization as explained in Section 2*

The position of the bacteria $w_1$ at which global minimum value is obtained yields the first independent component.

***Step-4: Evaluation of the Other Independent Components:*** To estimate the other ICs step 3 of the algorithm is repeated for getting weight vectors $w_2$............$w_n$. To prevent different vectors from converging to the same optimum and hence the same IC, the weight vectors are decorrelated using Gram-Schmidt like orthogonalization. When p vectors $w_1$............$w_p$ have been estimated, step 3 is run for $w_{p+1}$ and after every iteration step the following iteration steps are performed.

$$w_{p+1} = w_{p+1} - \sum_{j=1}^{p} (w^T_{p+1} w_j) w_j \tag{11}$$

$$w_{p+1} = \frac{w_{p+1}}{\sqrt{w^T_{p+1} w_{p+1}}} \tag{12}$$

Above equations constrain the Bacteria Foraging Optimization process.

The position of the bacteria $w_1$ at which global minimum value is obtained yields the first independent component.

## 4   Experimental Results

This section presents EBFS-ICA based fusion of CT and MRI images. Images of size 173x173 considered for this experiment are shown in Fig.1 (a) & (b). Fig.2 (a) display results obtained by FastICA method. Fig.1 (b) show results obtained by the proposed EBFS-ICA method. The algorithm is implemented in MATLAB. A non overlapping window of size 3x3 is used to extract the patches. Every NxN non-overlapping patches are isolated. It is transformed into a vector $I_k(t)$ using lexicographic ordering Each of these vectors $I_k(t)$ are arranged column wise in a matrix which is then transformed to the ICA domain representation $u_k(t)$. Assuming that $A$ is the estimated analysis (mixing) kernel, we have:

$$u_k(t) = T\{I_k(t)\} = AI_k(t) \tag{13}$$

Estimation of $A$ involves the following steps:-

1. At first the pre-processing steps for ICA are performed like centering and whitening.
2. Now ICA estimation is performed on the whitened data Z instead of original data '$x$'.
3. Dimensionality reduction by PCA is carried on by projecting the dimensional data to a lower dimensional space spanned by m (m<N) dominant eigenvectors (i.e. eigenvectors corresponding to large eigenvectors) of the correlation matrix $C_x$ . The eigenvectors matrix E and the diagonal matrix of eigenvectors D are of dimension $N$ x $m$ and $m$ x $m$ respectively.

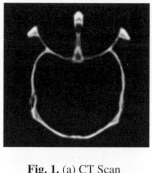

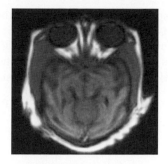

**Fig. 1.** (a) CT Scan                          **Fig. 1.** (b) MRI Scan

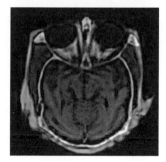

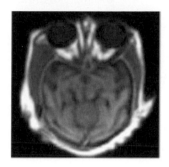

**Fig. 2.** (a) Fused image using FASTICA      **Fig. 2.** (b)Fused image using EBFS-ICA

If $V$ is the obtained $K \times N$ PCA matrix, the input image patches are transformed by:

$$Z(t) = Vp(t) \tag{14}$$

4. After the PCA preprocessing step we select the statistically independent basis vectors using the optimization of the negentropy. The following rule defines a
FastICA approach that optimizes negentropy, as proposed in [5]:

$$a_i^+ \leftarrow \varepsilon\{a_i\phi(a_i^T Z)\} - \varepsilon\{\phi'(a_i^T Z)\}a_i \quad 1 \le i \le k \tag{15}$$

$$A \leftarrow A(A^T A)^{-0.5} \tag{16}$$

Where $\Phi(x) = -\partial G(x)/\partial x$ defines the statistical properties

$$G(x) = \frac{1}{a1}\log(\cosh(a_1 y))$$ of the signals in the transform domain [4].

where $a_{1=}1$ such that $\Phi(x) = tanh(x)$

5. After the input image patches $p(t)$ are transformed to their ICA domain representations $vk(t)$, we can perform image fusion in the optimal ICA domain in the same manner as it is performed in e.g. the wavelet domain. The equivalent vectors $vk(t)$ from each image are combined in the ICA domain to obtain a new image $vf(t)$. The method that combines the coefficients in the ICA domain is called the "fusion rule". After the composite image $vf(t)$ is constructed in the optimal ICA domain, we can move back

to the spatial domain, using the synthesis kernel $A$, and synthesize the image *if* (*x; y*). Weight combination pixel based fusion rule [5] is used to obtain fused image.

Results are compared with FastICA algorithm [5] and are presented in Table-1. Metrics (RMSE, Entropy, SNR, Mutual information and standard deviation) proposed in [7, 8] are used here for comparison.

**Table 1.** Performance Evaluation

| Algorithm | RMSE | Entropy | SNR | Mutual Information | Standard Deviation |
|---|---|---|---|---|---|
| FastICA | 0.2502 | 6.1542 | 6.1458 e+004 | 2.0849 | 0.1299 |
| EBFS-ICA | 0.1542 | 6.3060 | 6.6402e+004 | 2.5491 | 0.1875 |

## 5 Conclusion

A new algorithm called EBFS-ICA is presented for biomedical signal processing applications. From Fig.2 and Table-1, it is seen that optimal ICA bases derived here outperform the Fast ICA algorithm proposed in [5]. The proposed algorithm may be useful for other fusion applications.

## References

1. Comon, P.: Independent Component Analysis-A new concept. Signal Processing 36, 287–314 (1994)
2. Cardoso, J.F.: Blind Signal Separation: Statistical Principles. Proc. of IEEE 9(10), 2009–2025 (1998)
3. Hyvarinen, A., Kahrunen, J., Oja, E.: Independent Component Analysis. John Wiley & Sons, Chichester (2001)
4. Hyvärinen, A., Oja, E.: Independent Component Analysis: Algorithms and Applications. Neural Networks 13(4), 411–430 (2000)
5. Mitianoudis, N., Stathaki, T.: Pixel-based and Region-based Image Fusion schemes using ICA bases. Information Fusion (2006)
6. Passino, K.M.: Biomimicry of Bacterial Foraging for distributed optimization and control. IEEE Control Syst. Mag. 22(3), 52–67 (2002)
7. Gupta, S., Ramesh, K.P., Blasch, E.P.: Mutual Information Metric Evaluation for PET/MRI Image Fusion. Wright State University, 978-14244-2616-4/08/$25.00 ©2008 IEEE (2008)
8. Malviya, A., Bhirud, S.G.: Objective Criterion for Performance Evaluation of Image Fusion Techniques. ©2010 International Journal of Computer applications (2010)
9. Panigrahi, B.K., Ravikumar Pandi, V.: Congestion management using adaptive bacterial foraging algorithm. International Journal on Energy Conversion and Management 50, 1202–1209 (2009)

10. Panigrahi, B.K., Ravikumar Pandi, V.: A Bacterial Foraging Optimization – Nelder Mead Hybrid Algorithm for Economic Load Dispatch. IET Proceedings of Gen Trans and Distribution 2(4), 556–565 (2008)
11. Dasgupta, S., Das, S., Abraham, A., Biswas, A.: Adaptive computational chemotaxis in bacterial foraging optimization: an analysis. IEEE Transactions on Evolutionary Computing 13(4), 919–941 (2009)
12. Das, S., Biswas, A., Dasgupta, S., Abraham, A.: The Bacterial Foraging Optimization – Algorithm, Analysis, and Applications. In: Foundations on Computational Intelligence. Studies in Computational Intelligence. Springer, Heidelberg (2008)
13. Dasgupta, S., Das, S., Abraham, A., Biswas, A.: Automatic circle detection on digital images using an adaptive bacterial foraging algorithm. In: Soft Computing: Soft Computing - A Fusion of Foundations, Methodologies and Applications, vol. 14(11), Springer, Heidelberg (2010)

# Adaptive Nonlinear Signal Approximation Using Bacterial Foraging Strategy

Naik Manoj Kumar[1] and Panda Rutuparna[2]

[1] Department of Electronics & Instrumentation Engg., Jagannath Institute For
Technology & Management, Paralakhemundi, Orissa, 761211, India
naik.manoj.kumar@gmail.com
[2] Department of Electronics and Telecommunication Engg.,
Veer Surendra Sai University of Technology, Burla-768018, India
r_pp2002@yahoo.co.in

**Abstract.** Uniform approximation of signals has been an area of interest for researchers working in different disciplines of science and engineering. This paper
presents an adaptive algorithm based on E. coli bacteria foraging strategy
(EBFS) for uniform approximation of signals by linear combinations of shifted
nonlinear basis functions. New class of nonlinear basis functions has been derived from a sigmoid function. The weight factor of the newly proposed nonlinear basis functions has been optimized by using the EBFS to minimize the mean
square error. Different test signals are considered for validation of the present
technique. Results are also compared with Genetic algorithm approach. The proposed technique could also be useful in fractional signal processing applications.

**Keywords:** Signal Approximation, Nonlinear Functions, Combinatorial Theory, Bacterial Foraging, GA.

## 1   Introduction

Since long, researchers of different disciplines of science and engineering have been
trying to investigate new class of basis functions for uniform approximation of signals.
Signal approximation is an important area of research in the field of digital signal and
image processing. Nonlinear signal approximation techniques are more useful in the
sense that they are more precise than linear approximation schemes and maintain equal
resolution throughout the entire signal support. This has motivated us to introduce an
adaptive nonlinear signal approximation scheme using nonlinear basis functions followed by an optimization strategy. The newly proposed class of nonlinear basis functions can provide minimum curvature. In this connection, these nonlinear basis set
warrant us a wide scope for nonlinear signal approximation. To the best of our knowledge, we do not have an adaptive nonlinear signal approximation technique using
nonlinear basis functions together with an optimization scheme till date.

   First part of the paper deals with the development of nonlinear basis functions localizing a sigmoid function. The new class of nonlinear basis functions have been
developed using the combinatorial theory. These basis set can be used to approximate
any signal with a greater accuracy by suitably choosing the value of weight factor '$w$'.

B.K. Panigrahi et al. (Eds.): SEMCCO 2010, LNCS 6466, pp. 362–369, 2010.
© Springer-Verlag Berlin Heidelberg 2010

The choice of the weight 'w' is important to reduce the error of approximation. In this context, the present paper focuses on the use of an optimization technique to find the optimum value of weight 'w'. It is believed that the proposed method of signal approximation may be useful for different signal and image processing applications.

Passino [1] has reported a new distributed optimization technique known as *E. coli* bacteria foraging strategy (EBFS). He has also explained the biology and physics underlying the foraging behavior of *E. coli* bacteria that are present in human intestines. These bacteria are also capable of aerotaxis, thermotaxis and phototaxis. Chemotaxis is a foraging behavior of these bacteria which can be used to solve non gradient optimization problems. A chemotactic step may be a tumble followed by a run or else a tumble followed by another tumble. This enables a cell to move in a right direction of increasingly nutrient gradient. Swarming is also a bacterial foraging strategy where cell released attractants is used for signaling other cells so that they swarm together. Other steps involved in bacterial foraging are reproduction, elimination and dispersal. In the reproduction step, the least healthy bacteria die because they could not get much nutrient during their lifetime of foraging and, thus, cannot reproduce. On the other hand, the healthiest bacteria each split into two bacteria and are stored in the same location. In an elimination-dispersal step, any bacteria can be eliminated from the population by dispersing it to a random location. It is interesting to note that the frequency of chemotactic steps is greater than the frequency of reproduction steps. For simplicity of our computer simulation programs, we ignore many more characteristics of chemotactic and swarming strategies.

This EBFS can be used for different engineering applications where we need optimization. Most of the researcher study the BFS algorithm characteristics and also apply in different applications [2-4]. In this paper, we have been motivated to use the EBFS for finding the optimum value of weight 'w' to minimize the error of approximation. Different test functions have been considered for validation of the proposed scheme. Results are also compared with the Genetic algorithm approach. Finally, it has been concluded that the proposed method of signal approximation together with the EBFS has shown better error convergence and tracking performance.

## 2   Development of Nonlinear Basis Functions

It has been seen from the literature [5-7] that the nonlinear sigmoid function act as activation functions in artificial neural networks. The sigmoid has been also extensively used in Bayesian estimation of classification of probabilities [6, 7]. Nonlinear characteristics and mono tonicity makes it attractive for use as an activation function in artificial neural networks. Its lower order derivatives exhibit simple forms and make them attractive for development of different learning algorithms. These learning algorithms are useful to solve pattern recognition problems. In this section, we introduce a class of nonlinear basis functions derived from the nonlinear sigmoid function. The sigmoid function in one dimension is defined as [5]

$$y = \frac{1}{1 + e^{-wx}} \tag{1}$$

Where $w \in \Re^p$ with $p = 1$ is the weight factor and $x \in \Re^p$ with $p=1$ is the independent variable. It is interesting to note that the sigmoid function possesses odd symmetry and the range $0 \le y \le 1$ corresponds to $-\infty \le x \le \infty$.

A bunch of sigmoid functions have been extensively used in the design and development of neural networks. Here, the motivation behind the use of one such simple sigmoid function is that the same function is also known as the logistic function. Interestingly, this logistic function has been extensively used for statistical modeling of data. The logistic function shown in Eq. (1) can also be called as the technical linking function, which may be used to estimate '$x$' by using the well known rela-

tion $x = \left( w^{-1} \right) \log_e \left( \dfrac{y}{1-y} \right)$.

*Definition 1*: The nonlinear basis function of degree '$n$' is defined as

$$B^{(n)}(x) = L_1 \sum_{k=1}^{n} C_k^{(n)} \, y^k \, q^{n+1-k}, \tag{2}$$

Where $L_1 = w^n$; $\quad C_k^{(n)} = 0 \;\; for\; all\; n \le 0, k < 1\; and\; k > n$ and $q = (1-y)$.

The values of $C_k^{(n)}$, *for all $n > 0, k \ge 1$ and $k \le n$*, are given below.

$$C_k^{(n)} = \;\; [1\; 0\; 0\; 0\; 0\; 0\; 0;$$
$$2\; 2\; 0\; 0\; 0\; 0\; 0;$$
$$6\; 24\; 6\; 0\; 0\; 0\; 0;$$
$$24\; 264\; 264\; 24\; 0\; 0\; 0;$$
$$120\; 3120\; 7920\; 3120\; 120\; 0\; 0;$$
$$720\; 41040\; 217440\; 217440\; 41040\; 720\; 0;$$
$$5040\; 604800\; 6002640\; 12176640\; 6002640\; 604800\; 5040];$$

Note that '$n$' and '$k$' corresponds to rows and columns, respectively. Here, the degree '$n$' decides the number of terms required to write the basis function locally as a polynomial. The $C_k^{(n)}$ coefficients have been derived using the combinatorial theory [8]. Thus, a new class of nonlinear basis functions has been generated by localizing the sigmoid function. Two different nonlinear basis functions have been shown in Fig.1.

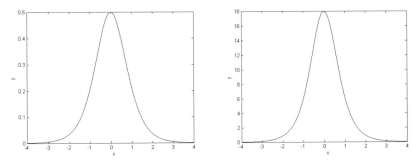

**Fig. 1.** Nonlinear basis functions (left to right (a) $n=1$, $w=2$ and (b) $n=3$, $w=2$)

The problem of uniform approximations to any continuous function $f(x)$ by using continuous approximating functions is intriguing. Readers are invited to further explore this topic. In this paper, we have presented explicit expressions for construction of such types of approximating functions. The proposed nonlinear basis functions may be useful for uniform approximation of signals. They can provide us uniform resolution throughout the entire signal support. Any continuous function on $\Re^n$ can be uniformly approximated by a finite series in terms of such basis set. This may be noted that uniform approximation can be achieved by approximating $f(x)$ by a function '$h$' on $\Re^n$ with continuous partials. Interestingly, '$h$' has a uniform convergent series in $\Re^n$ which may be truncated to approximate any continuous function $f(x)$. Thus, a continuous signal can be uniformly approximated by a finite sum of continuous un-invariant functions introduced in this paper. The proposed basis set may be useful for minimizing the mean square error (approximation error) to a larger extent by optimizing the weight factor '$w$' using an efficient optimization technique. It may be noted here that the number of terms in the linear combination is minimal for $n=1$.

The change in output, corresponding to a change in input $\delta x$, is approximated by

$$\delta y \cong \sum_{n=1}^{N} \frac{1}{n!} (\| w \| \| \delta x \| \cos\theta)^n \, B^n(y) \tag{3}$$

Where, $N$ is the order of approximation. Note that $\theta$ is the angle between $w$ and $\delta x$. When $f(x)$ has energy at high frequencies, then the proposed method of nonlinear signal approximation may be useful to include all energy terms optimally by evaluating the optimal weight factor '$w$'.

## 3   BFS: Selection of Weight Factor

### 3.1   Bacterial Representation

We generally chose the one variable to indicate the parameter to be optimized as $p$ and other variable for searching of the optimal weight '$w$'. We generally chose the number of bacteria $S$ for the optimal weight selection.

### 3.2   Cost Function

The approximation of a continuous signal $f(x)$ with a linear combination of the shifted nonlinear basis functions $B^{(n)}(x)$ of degree '$n$' has been considered in this section. The approximated signal is given by

$$\overline{f}(x) = \sum_{k=0}^{N-1} f(k) \, B^{(n)}(x-k). \tag{4}$$

The bacterium for which the cost function is minimal is the sorted corresponding value from the ordered locations. This is the optimum value for the weight factor '$w$'. The cost function '$J$' has been calculated as follows:

$$J = \sum_{k=1}^{NS} e^2(k) = \sum_{k}^{NS} [f(k) - \overline{f}(k)]^2 \qquad (5)$$

Where, $NS$ is number of samples. According to cost function, EBFS algorithm proposed by Passino [4] gives the weight parameter '$w$' for the best approximation.

# 4 Application

In this section, the proposed scheme has been considered for signal approximation applications. The proposed nonlinear functions can be used for approximation of polynomials of degree $< n$. The EBFS has been used to get the optimal value of the weight parameter '$w$' for the best approximation. This has been achieved by reducing the cost function.

Two different test functions have been considered for this experiment. First one is a monomial $f(x) = x$, the second one is a logarithmic chirp of 1 kHz to 2 kHz. Note that the sampling rate is 100 samples per second. These test signals are displayed in Fig. 2.

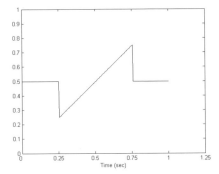 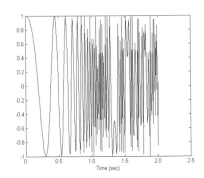

**Fig. 2.** Two test signals (Left to Right (a) Monomial $f(x) = x$ and (b) Logarithmic chirp 1 kHz to 2 kHz)

The proposed method has been implemented in MATLAB and used for approximation of these two test signals in terms of linear combinations of proposed shifted nonlinear basis functions. Note that these values are chosen while considering the nonlinear basis functions of degree '$n=3$'.

The different parameters chosen for the EBFS algorithm for the adaptive nonlinear signal approximation are as follows: $S=12$, $p=1$, $N_s=4$, $N_{re}=10$, $N_{ed}=10$, $P_{ed}=0.25$, $d_{attract}=0.01$, $h_{repelent}=0.01$, $w_{repelent}=10$ for both test signals. Some variant parameters are give in the Table 1 and the error signals have been plotted in Fig. 3.

**Table 1.** Parameter for EBFS

| Signals | $N_c$ | $w_{attract}$ | $C(i)$ |
|---------|-------|---------------|--------|
| Test # 1 | 5 | 0.1 | 0.068 |
| Test # 2 | 10 | 0.009 | 0.1 |

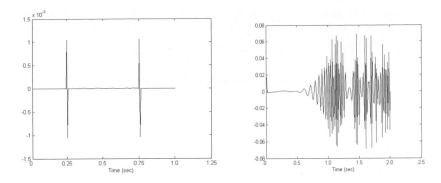

**Fig. 3.** Error signals (Left to right (a) and (b), corresponding to Fig. 2 (a) and (b))

It may be noted that the least number of evaluation of the cost function (the best result) has been obtained to achieve $10^{-5}$ as the minimum value of the cost function '$J$' with $C(i)=0.068$ for the test signal # 1 and $C(i)=0.1$ for other test signals. The convergence behavior of the proposed scheme in terms of cost function value vs. number of iterations has been plotted in Fig. 4. For the test signal # 1, 150 (30 iterations for a loop $\times$ 5 chemotaxis loops) iterations complete one reproduction loop and there is one elimination and dispersal of bacteria after each reproduction loop. For other test signals # 2, 300 (30 iterations for a loop $\times$ 10 chemotaxis loops) iterations complete one reproduction loop. From Fig. 4, it is seen that the proposed scheme has shown better convergence and tracking record.

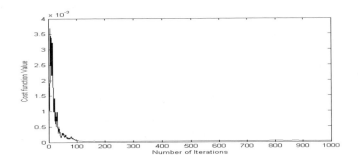

**Fig. 4.** Convergence characteristics of the EBFS algorithm

For the performance evaluation, *%error* has been taken as

$$\%error = \left\{ \left( \sum_{k=1}^{NS} e^2(k) \right) \middle/ \left( \sum_{k=1}^{NS} f^2(k) \right) \right\} \qquad (6)$$

For a comparison, genetic algorithm (GA) [9, 10] has also been used for optimization. In this simulation, maximum number of generations considered is 1000. Note that 20

chromosomes of 40 bits (base10 arithmetic) have been used with crossover and mutation probabilities of 80% and 1%, respectively. On the other hand, we have chosen
only 12 bacteria for EBFS. Results are tabulated in Table 2.

**Table 2.** Performance evaluation

| Signa ls | GA | | | | EBFS | | | |
|---|---|---|---|---|---|---|---|---|
| | %error | | | Time in sec | %error | | | Time in sec |
| | $n = 3$ | $n = 5$ | $n = 7$ | | $n = 3$ | $n = 5$ | $n = 7$ | |
| Test # 1 | 0.0059 | 0.0016 | 0.0021 | 0.14224 | 0.00002 | $< 10^{-5}$ | $< 10^{-5}$ | 0.10073 |
| Test # 2 | 0.2715 | 0.0579 | 0.0023 | 0.15802 | 0.1403 | 0.0480 | 0.0003 | 0.10978 |

## 5   Conclusion

We have introduced a set of nonlinear basis functions of any degree '$n$' by localizing
the sigmoid function. These basis functions have simple forms and may be useful for
different signal and image processing applications. The proposed idea may also be
extended for development of nonlinear basis functions of fractional order and may be
useful for fractional signal processing applications [11, 12]. The proposed adaptive
nonlinear signal approximation technique using bacterial foraging seems to be useful
than the conventional techniques. Two different types of test signals have been considered for validation of the algorithm. Results produced reveal the accuracy and
suitability of the proposed scheme. The accuracy can be improved by increasing the
degree '$n$'. Interestingly, the increase in degree does not add computational complexity. The EBFS is better than the GA technique for optimizing the value of weight
factor '$w$'. With a standard PC (Pentium-IV) with clock speed 2.4 GHz and
MATLAB 6.5, the convergence time is about 0.1 second starting with a random iteration to reach a *%error* of 0.1403, which is quite acceptable. Finally, we conclude that
the investigations carried out in the paper leaves wide scope for extensions and applications in different fields of science and engineering.

## References

[1]  Passino, K.M.: Biomimicry of Bacterial Foraging for Distributed Optimization and Con-
     trol. IEEE Control System Mag., 52–67 (2002)
[2]  Dasgupta, S., Das, S., Abraham, A., Biswas, A.: Adaptive computational chemotaxis in
     bacterial foraging optimization: an analysis. IEEE Transactions on Evolutionary Comput-
     ing 13(4), 919–941 (2009)
[3]  Das, S., Dasgupta, S., Biswas, A., Abraham, A., Konar, A.: On stability of chemotactic
     dynamics in bacterial foraging optimization algorithm. IEEE Transactions on SMC,
     part – A 39(3), 670–679 (2009)
[4]  Mishra, S.: A hybrid least square-fuzzy bacterial foraging strategy for harmonic estima-
     tion. IEEE Trans. on Evolutionary Comp. 9(1), 61–73 (2005)

[5]  Lippmann, R.: An introduction to computing with neural nets. IEEE ASSP magazine 4, 4–22 (1987)

[6]  Scarborough, J.B.: Numerical Mathematical Analysis. Oxford & IBH Pub. Co., New Delhi (1979)

[7]  Grossberg, S.: Neural Networks and Natural Intelligence. MIT Press, Cambridge (1988)

[8]  Krishnamurthy, V.: Combinatorics: Theory and applications. John Wiley and Sons, Chichester (1986)

[9]  Goldberg, D.E.: Genetic Algorithms in Search, Optimization, and Machine Learning. Pearson Education Asia (2000)

[10]  Bettayeba, M., Qidwai, U.: A hybrid least square-GA-based algorithm for harmonic estimation. IEEE Trans. On Power Delivery 18(2), 377–382 (2003)

[11]  Ortigueira, M.D.: Introduction to fractional signal processing. Part I: Continuous-Time Systems. In: IEE Proc. on Vision, Image and Signal Processing, vol. 1, pp. 62–70 (2000)

[12]  Panda, R., Dash, M.: Fractional generalized splines and signal processing. Signal Processing 86(9), 2340–2350 (2006)

# Swarm Intelligence for Optimizing Hybridized Smoothing Filter in Image Edge Enhancement

B. Tirumala Rao[1], S. Dehuri[2], M. Dileep[1], and A. Vindhya[1]

[1] Department of Computer Science and Engineering,
ANITS, Visakhapatnam, India
{b.tirimula,rajashankar0206,avvari.vindhya}@gmail.com
[2] Department of Information & Communication Technology
Fakir Mohan University, Vyasa Vihar, Balasore-756019, India
satchi.lapa@gmail.com

**Abstract.** In this modern era, image transmission and processing plays a major role. It would be impossible to retrieve information from satellite and medical images without the help of image processing techniques. Edge enhancement is an image processing step that enhances the edge contrast of an image or video in an attempt to improve its acutance. Edges are the representations of the discontinuities of image intensity functions. For processing these discontinuities in an image, a good edge enhancement technique is essential. The proposed work uses a new idea for edge enhancement using hybridized smoothening filters and we introduce a promising technique of obtaining best hybrid filter using swarm algorithms (Artificial Bee Colony (ABC), Particle Swarm Optimization (PSO) and Ant Colony Optimization (ACO)) to search for an optimal sequence of filters from among a set of rather simple, representative image processing filters. This paper deals with the analysis of the swarm intelligence techniques through the combination of hybrid filters generated by these algorithms for image edge enhancement.

**Keywords:** Image edge enhancement, hybridized smoothening filter, Swarm algorithms, PSO, ACO, ABC.

## 1 Introduction

In the modern information era, digital images have been widely used in an aggrandizing number of applications and the effort on edge enhancement has been focused mostly to improve visual perception of images that are unclear (blurred). Edges are the representations of the discontinuities of image intensity functions. For processing these discontinuities in an image a good edge enhancement technique is essential. These edge enhancement techniques fall under two categories: smoothening filters and sharpening filters [3]. Smoothing filters are used for blurring and noise reduction [1]. Noise reduction can be accomplished by blurring with linear filters (mean, median and mode) and nonlinear filters (circular, pyramidal and cone) [1]. Sharpening filters (Laplacian, Sobel, Prewitt and Robert filters) are used to highlight fine details

B.K. Panigrahi et al. (Eds.): SEMCCO 2010, LNCS 6466, pp. 370–379, 2010.

in an image or to enhance details that have been blurred but because of their results of complexity and image quality, smoothening filters are used which involves simple subtractive smoothened image concept which reduces complexity and makes the images look sharper than they really are.

In the paper [1], B.Tirimula Rao et al, 2009 developed a new approach to edge enhancement by using the smoothening filters which results in low complexity. This can also be done with the help of a new filter called the hybridized smoothening filter (a sequence of smoothening filter). The optimal magnitude (for different combinations of smoothening filters) of the hybrid filter is found by using Swarm algorithms(ABC, PSO and ACO) [8] which decreases the time complexity, space complexity, increases the probability of obtaining best hybrid filter, as well as increases the quality of the image that is it gives a perfect edge enhanced image. Swarm algorithms combine the utility and complexity of problem-solving computer programs with the power and simplicity of natural selection.

This edge enhancement technique leads to enhance all high spatial frequency detail in an image including edges, lines and points of high gradients. In this approach the details of edges in an image can be obtained by subtracting a smoothed image from the original. This subtractive smoothing method has been used as the simplest way to obtain high spatial frequency image and this method of edge enhancement makes the image brighter and real edges are detected.

Hybrid filter is defined as the series of existing filters (smoothening filters) to optimize the magnitude of the image [2]. It can efficiently remove large amounts of mixed Gaussian and impulsive noise besides preserving the image details. In this approach, hybrid filter is taken as combination of smoothening filters (e.g., 1-2-3-4-5-6 i.e., suppose 1-mean, 2-median, 3-mode, 4-circular, 5-pyramidal, 6-cone, the output of mean filter is taken as input for median filter and the output of median filter is given as input to the next and so on). This hybrid filter yields optimal threshold values using clustering algorithm mentioned in [10].

Hybrid filters, its optimization using swarm algorithms explained in Section 2. In Section 3, experimental results are discussed and in Section 4 conclusion and the future work in this domain are given.

## 2   Swarm Algorithms for Optimizing Hybridized Smoothing Filter in Edge Enhancement

In PSO [4, 5], a population of particles starts to move in search space by following the current optimum particles and changing the positions in order to find out the optima. The position of a particle refers to a possible solution of the function to be optimized. Evaluating the function by the particle's position provides the fitness of that solution. In every iteration, each particle is updated by following the best solution of current particle achieved so far (particle best) and the best of the population (global best). When a particle takes part of the population as its topological neighbours, the best value is a local best. The particles tend to move to good areas in the search space by

the information spreading to the swarm. The particle is moved to a new position calculated by the velocity updated at each time step t. The swarm in PSO is initialized by
assigning each particle to a uniformly and randomly chosen position in the search
space.

ACO [6, 7] has been recently developed as a population based Meta heuristic that
has been successfully applied to several NP-hard combinatorial problems. The ACO
is the one of the most recent techniques for approximate optimization methods. The
main idea is that it is indirect local communication among the individuals of a population of artificial ants. The core of ant's behaviour is the communication between the
ants by means of chemical pheromone trails, which enables them to find shortest
paths between their nest and food sources. The role of pheromone is to guide the other
ants towards the target points. This behaviour of real ant colonies exploited. The ACO
is consisted of three main phases; initialization, pheromone update and solution phase.
All of these phases build a complete search to the global optimum. At the beginning
of the first iteration, all ants search randomly to the best solution of a given problem
within the feasible solution space, and old ant colony is created at initialization phase.
After that, quantity of pheromone is updated. In the solution phase, new ant colony is
created based on the best solution from the old ant colony. Then, the best solutions of
two colonies are compared. At the end of the first iteration, feasible solution space is
reduced by a vector that guides the bounds of search space during the ACO application. Optimum solution is then searched in the reduced search space during the algorithm progress. The ACO reaches to the global optimum as ants find their routes in
the limited space.

In ABC [8,9] algorithm, the position of a food source represents a possible solution
to the optimization problem and the nectar amount of a food source corresponds to the
quality (fitness) of the associated solution. The number of the employed bees or the
onlooker bees is equal to the number of solutions in the population. At the first step,
the ABC generates a randomly distributed initial population $P(C=0)$ of SN solutions
(food source positions), where SN denotes the size of employed bees or onlooker
bees. Each solution $x_i(i= 1, 2, \ldots , SN)$ is a D-dimensional vector. Here, D is the
number of optimization parameters. After initialization, the population of the positions (solutions) is subject to repeated cycles, $C =1, 2, \ldots ,MCN$, of the search processes of the employed bees, the onlooker bees and the scout bees. An employed bee
produces a modification on the position (solution) in her memory depending on the
local information (visual information) and tests the nectar amount (fitness value) of
the new source (new solution). If the nectar amount of the new one is higher than that
of the previous one, the bee memorizes the new position and forgets the old one. Otherwise she keeps the position of the previous one in her memory. After all employed
bees complete the search process, they share the nectar information of the food
sources and their position information with the onlooker bees. An onlooker bee evaluates the nectar information taken from all employed bees and chooses a food source
with a probability related to its nectar amount. As in the case of the employed bee, she
produces a modification on the position in her memory and checks the nectar amount
of the candidate source. If the nectar is higher than that of the previous one, the bee
memorizes the new position and forgets the old one.

Table 1 demonstrates the working of the Swarm algorithms for Image Edge
Enhancement.

**Table 1.** Swarm algorithms for edge enhancement

| | PSO | ACO | ABC |
|---|---|---|---|
| **Initialize population** | As there are six filters, we consider our swarm as a six dimensional and we can have the maximum number of particles in the swarm as $6^6$. Initially n particles are randomly selected from available swarm in PSO and here the initial particle represents initial random combination. | An ant is a hybrid combination of filters. Ant colony of size n is randomly initialized. **Initialize Pheromone trail:** Pheromone trail is a group of hybrid filters combinations that equal the size of the ant colony. Phero-mone trail is also initialized randomly. | As there are six filters we consider our bee as six dimensional. An artificial bee colony with n scout bees is randomly initialized. |
| **Evaluation of fitness** | An individual's fitness is measured by the sum of intensities of edges in an enhanced image, because a gray image with a visual good contrast includes many intensive edges. The magnitude is evaluated for this sequence of filters using fitness function with initial velocity assumed as a vector that is derived from six dimensional space (i.e., the velocity represents a sequence that varies with the iterations) The sum of intensities of edges E(k)[11] included in the enhanced image is calculated by the following expression. $$E(k)=\sum_x\sum_y \sqrt{\delta h_k(x,y)^2+\delta v_k(x,y)^2}$$ $\delta h_k(x,y)=g_k(x+1,y-1)+g_k(x+1,y)+g_k(x+1,y+1)-g_k(x-1,y-1)-g_k(x-1,y)-g_k(x-1,y+1)$. $\delta v_k(x,y)=g_k(x-1,y+1)+g_k(x,y-1)+g_k(x+1,y+1)-g_k(x-1,y-1)-g_k(x,y-1)-g_k(x+1,y-1)$. The fitness of the individual 'n' is obtained by the following expression $F(x_n)=rand(x_n)/E(k)$, where rand ( $x_n$ ) contains all hybrid filter combinations that gives optimal magnitudes. | | |
| **Obtaining fittest individuals** | **Local & Global best values:** The best magnitude in each cycle is initialized to the local best value thus giving the local best hybrid filter combination till that iteration. The global best value is initialized to the local best value obtained in the first iteration. In the following iteration if the global best value is greater than the local best value is updated with the new global best value. | **Determining best ants in the colony:** Ants are compared on the basis of the fitness value. An ant having the best fitness value is being selected and stored for further updating of solution spaces. The search direction depends on the best ant. | **Determining fittest bees in the colony:** Here the hybrid filter combinations which gives the best fittest values are taken and stored for further updating of solution spaces |

**Table. 1.** (*continued*)

| Updating search direction | Updating Particle velocity & position:The particle is moved to a new position calculated by the velocity updated at each time step t. $x(t+1)=x(t)+v(t+1)$ The velocity update is performed as indicated in the equation below: $V(t+1)=\omega.v(t)+$ $\phi_1\,rand(0,1)(p(t)\text{-}x(t))$ $+\phi_2\,rand(0,1)(g(t)\text{-}(t))$ Where p(t),g(t) are local best and global best threshold magnitudes. x(t) is the present position vector.$\phi1,\phi2$ are constant threshold values (1-31) taken in random and $\omega$ is 1/(iteration number). The swarm in PSO is initialized by assigning each particle to a uniformly and randomly chosen position in the search space. Velocities are initialized randomly in the range $[v_{min},v_{max}]$ | Updating Pheromone trail: The pheromone trail is updated using a neighbourhood search done for each of the ant which is in the 10% range of the original ant's fitness value, represents one of the hybrid filter combination which was randomly selected. The pheromone trail is updated by selecting the best of these neighbours comparing with the original ant and best of these two is taken as the combination for the next iteration. The way for exploring the search space of solutions is being directed by the best solution and the pheromone trail. | Neighborhood Search: Neighbourhood solutions for the best solutions are generated. These neighbourhoods are generated by first generating random population and selecting the required combination in the given range (10%). The least of these neighbourhood fitness values is taken, compared and is updated with parent value. Now the best of hybrid filter combinations for which the neighbourhood search is done is made up for the next cycle and rest of the combinations are generated randomly for the next cycle. |
|---|---|---|---|
| **Rule of selection, extinction & multiplication** | Initially n random combinations are generated. Depending on the velocity vector the next particle in swarm is being generated as per the defined equations. The magnitude is being calculated using fitness function for the updated sequence and is being checked for the best value for that sequence (i.e., particle best value) and the best value explored so far for any sequence (i.e., global best particle).This process is being generated for all the particles in swarm till the maximum iterations or the global best value repeats for many times. | The new ant colony is being generated from the search direction determined and updated pheromone trail. Neighbourhood search is done for each of the ant which is in the 10% range of the original ant's fitness value. The pheromone trail is updated by selecting the best of these neighbours and original ant. The above process continues until we get repeated optimum values or the minimum error. | Search initially starts with the number of scout bees in the bee hive (n). Only those individuals that have lower fitness are selected from the population and are survived to the next generation. Individuals that have higher fitness are extinguished in the hive and are made Scout bees or Onlooker bees as they do not have qualifications to survive to the next cycle. Neighbours are found by taking the random population for first two best solutions. The remaining combinations are discarded and new bees are recruited in their place by random search. This process continues until we get repeated optimum values or the minimum error. |

**Table. 1.** (*continued*)

| Completion of evolution | As per our experimental results, the PSO algorithm converges to global optima in a maximum of 75 Fitness Function Evaluations (FFE). | As per our experimental results, the ACO algorithm converges to global optima in a maximum of 150 Fitness Function Evaluations (FFE). | As per our experimental results, the ABC algorithm converges to global optima in a maximum of 285 Fitness Function Evaluations (FFE). |
|---|---|---|---|

## 3 Experiments and Results

The images cameramen, skull, tower [3], original image and noisy image (Bin Wang et al.1993, original image corrupted by Gaussian noise with a mean of zero and a standard deviation (σ) of 8) are taken as references for our work. The number of gray levels of these images is 256 and the bit depth is 8. The following table gives the details of these images.

**Table 2.** Details of reference images

| Image | Size(pixels) | Resolution(ppi) |
|---|---|---|
| Cameraman | 256 × 256 | 72 × 72 |
| Skull | 374 × 452 | 72 × 72 |
| Tower | 370 × 457 | 200 × 200 |
| Original image | 306 × 341 | 72 × 72 |

Table 3 avers how the hybrid filter obtained by swarm algorithms excellently enhances the image's edges compared to other filters and figure 2 depicts these results. Table 4 and figure 2 compares the results of swarm algorithms on original image at various noise levels. Noise is the amount of disturbances that can be seen in the image. This noise is added to the image using GIMP software. Image is given as input to GIMP and a pick noise filter is applied with different random seed values as 10000,20000,30000,40000. This pick filter is a noise filter which randomly interchanges the pixel values with its neighbours.

**Comparison of Swarm Algorithms (ABC, PSO & ACO) Results:** Swarm algorithms are compared based on their results on Original image. The optimal threshold magnitude for this image by applying adaptive thresholding is 30271.The fitness is calculated by

$F(x_n)=rand(x_n)/E(k)$

Where $rand(x_n)$ contains all hybrid filter combinations that gives optimal magnitudes. $E(K)$ for the original image is 17300.

**ABC:** In this algorithm the food source represents the magnitude of the image, employed bees represents the initial random combinations of hybrid filters (7), onlooker bees as the best of the randomly generated combinations (2), the recruit bees which are the combinations that are in the 10% range of the onlooker bees (of 25). In each iteration, 5 new hybrid combinations (scout bees) are randomly generated while retaining the best 2 combinations from previous one. So the population size(7) remains constant. After 285 FFE the optimal threshold magnitude 30271 is obtained and the hybrid filter combination is 1 1 4 6 3 1.

**PSO:** Here position denotes the magnitude of the image. Initial positions and velocities are the hybrid filter combinations generated randomly (15). Depending on the velocity vector the next particle in swarm is being generated as per the defined equations, where $\omega$ is taken as 1/(iteration number) and $\phi_1, \phi_2$ are constant threshold values taken randomly in the range [1,2.5]. The population remains constant as 15 as the positions are only changed. Local best and the global best values are updated each iteration. After 75 FFE the optimal threshold magnitude 30271 is obtained and the hybrid filter combination is 6 1 3 3 3 6.

**ACO:** Here ants represent the hybrid filter combinations and the food source is magnitude of the image which has to be optimized. An initial population and pheromone trail of size 5 is randomly generated. The pheromone trail is updated based on a neighbourhood search done for each of the ant which is in the 10% range of the original ant's fitness value. The pheromone trail is updated by selecting the best among these neighbours (randomly 5 for each ant) and original ant. After 150 FFE the near optimal magnitude 30274 is obtained and the hybrid filter combination is 3 1 1 6 4 1. The above results substantiate that all these Swarm algorithms produce optimal results for this image.

**Table 3.** Comparison of results obtained by different filters for various images

| Optimal Threshold Magnitude Using | Images | | | | |
|---|---|---|---|---|---|
| | Camera Man | Skull | Tower | Original Image | Noisy Image |
| **Adaptive Clustering** | 2462 | 21676 | 133200 | 30271 | 23727 |
| **Mean Filter** | 1425 | 17126 | 133833 | 29620 | 26658 |
| **Median Filter** | 2553 | 15522 | 148998 | 19065 | 22267 |
| **Mode Filter** | 2386 | 13668 | 143792 | 17541 | 26229 |
| **Circular Filter** | 2071 | 28768 | 144141 | 37998 | 24523 |
| **Pyramidal Filter** | 2283 | 28273 | 124668 | 27951 | 21803 |
| **Cone Filter** | 2438 | 19272 | 146705 | 23464 | 25693 |
| **Hybrid Filter by PSO** | 2464 | 21795 | 133211 | 30271 | 23738 |
| **Hybrid Filter by ABC** | 2464 | 21682 | 133208 | 30271 | 23732 |
| **Hybrid Filter by ACO** | 2453 | 21775 | 133208 | 30274 | 23743 |

**Values Obtained through Different Filters:** Table 3 gives a remarkable view of all filters applied on different images and their respective optimal magnitudes. The first row in the table represents the original magnitude of the image. Relying on the values in the table one can ascertain that results obtained by hybrid filters are closer to original magnitudes of the images. It can be inferred from the table that the results obtained by PSO, ACO & ABC vary from image to image. Any one of the Swarm algorithms might give better results for a given image. But it doesn't hold for all images, the performance of Swarm algorithms varies with images. Albeit these Swarm algorithms always produce optimal results than other traditional approaches. Figure 1 depicts the results of original image after edge enhancement by various filters.

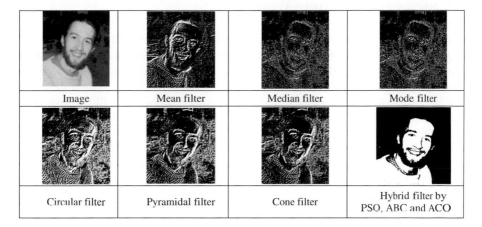

**Fig. 1.** Results after edge enhancement of original image using various filters

**Comparative Results of Swarm Algorithms by Applying Noise at Different Levels:** Original magnitudes of the image are computed at various noise levels by applying adaptive thresholding. It can be inferred from the table that Swarm algorithms are successful in attaining optimal threshold magnitudes.

**Original Image:** Table 3 emphasizes that ABC and PSO yields optimal results for original image. For noise levels 10000, 20000, 30000 & 40000 optimal results are induced by ABC, PSO, and ACO respectively. From these results it can be endorsed that even for a single image different algorithms produce best results at various noise levels.

**Table 4.** Results of Swarm algorithms for original image at different levels for noise

| Algorithm used | Original image | Pick noise 10000 | Pick noise 20000 | Pick noise 30000 | Pick noise 40000 |
|---|---|---|---|---|---|
| Adaptive thresholding | 30271 | 30330 | 30253 | 30375 | 30234 |
| ABC | 30271 | 30338 | 30269 | 30377 | 30243 |
| PSO | 30271 | 30340 | 30253 | 30376 | 30241 |
| ACO | 30274 | 30345 | 30271 | 30381 | 30240 |

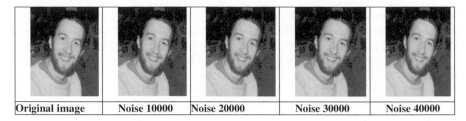

| Original image | Noise 10000 | Noise 20000 | Noise 30000 | Noise 40000 |

**Fig. 2.** Results of original image after edge enhancement at different noise levels

# 4   Conclusion and Future Work

By analyzing the experimental results of all the three swarm methods namely ABC, PSO, and ACO that are implemented for novel approach of image edge enhancement using smoothening hybrid filters, it is observed that these algorithms provide better image quality and enhanced information from the original image with a clear edge over traditional approach. Among the implemented algorithms, ABC is giving best approximate results when compared to PSO and ACO. But ABC algorithm takes more time for computing when compared to other two algorithms because of its neighbourhood generation. PSO and ACO algorithms are taking less computing time compared to ABC algorithm. Considering the fitness function evaluations PSO is more suitable. But if we consider edge enhancement performance ABC is best.

We have done our research in the direction of edge enhancement by hybrid filters as it has not been explored till date. There are numerous edge enhancement approaches have been proposed in different real-world applications, in order to examine the performance on edge enhancement against noise and several other factors of an image we extend connotations to our work with Artificial Immune System (AIS), Differential Evolution (DE), Bacterial foraging optimization algorithm, Neuro Fuzzy, Neuro Genetic, Simulated Annealing and fuzzy logic.

# References

1. Tirimula Rao, B., Venkat Rao, K., Kiran Swathi, G., Pruthvi Shanthi, G., Sree Durga, J.: A Novel Approach to Image Edge Enhancement Using Smoothing Filters. ICFAI Journal of Computer Sciences 3(2), 37–53 (2009)
2. Benela, T.R., Jampala, S.D., Villa, S.H., Konathala, B.: A novel approach to image edge enhancement using artificial bee colony algorithm for hybridized smoothening filters. In: BICA 2009, IEEE Conference, India (2009); ISBN 978-1-4244-5612-3/09
3. Gonzalez, Woods: Digital Image Processing, 2nd edn. Prentice Hall, Englewood Cliffs (2001)
4. Kennedy, J., Eberhart, R.C.: Particle swarm optimization. In: Proceedings of the IEEE International Conference on Neural Networks, Perth, Australia, pp. 1942–1948 (1995)
5. Braik, M., Sheta, A., Ayesh, A.: Image enhancement using particle swarm optimization. In: Proceedings of World Congress on Engineering, London, U.K., vol. 1 (2007)

6. Baskan, O., Haldenbilen, S., Ceylan, H., Ceylan, H.: A new solution algorithm for improving performance of ant colony optimization. Applied Mathematics and Computation 211, 75–84 (2009)
7. Dorigo, M., Stutzle, T.: A Brad Book. MIT Press, Cambridge
8. Baykaoglu, A., Ozbakir, L., Tpakan, P.: Artificial bee colony algorithm and its application to generalized assignment problem. In: Chan, F.T.S., Tiwari, M.K. (eds.) Swarm Intelligence: Focus on Ant and Particle Swarm Optimization, p. 532 (2007); ISBN 978-3-902613-09-7
9. Karaboga, D., Akay, B.: A comparative study of artificial bee colony algorithm. Applied Mathematics and Computation 214, 108–132 (2009)
10. Savakis, A.E.: Adaptive document image thresholding using foreground and background clustering. In: IEEE Proceedings of International Conference on Image Processing ICIP 1998, vol. 3, pp. 785–789 (1998)
11. Saitoh, F.: Image contrast enhancement using genetic algorithm. In: IEEE International Conference on System, Man, and Cybernetics, IEEE SMC 1999, vol. 4, pp. 899–904 (1999)

# A Hybrid GA-Adaptive Particle Swarm Optimization Based Tuning of Unscented Kalman Filter for Harmonic Estimation

Ravi Kumar Jatoth and Gogulamudi Anudeep Reddy

Department of ECE
National Institute of Technology-Warangal, India
ravikumar@nitw.ac.in, anudeep477@gmail.com

**Abstract.** This paper proposes Hybrid Genetic Algorithm (GA)-Adaptive Particle Swarm Optimization (APSO) aided Unscented Kalman Filter (UKF) to estimate the harmonic components present in power system voltage/current waveforms. The initial choice of the process and measurement error covariance matrices Q and R (called tuning of the filter) plays a vital role in removal of noise. Hence, hybrid GA-APSO algorithm is used to estimate the error covariance matrices by minimizing the Root Mean Square Error(RMSE) of the UKF. Simulation results are presented to demonstrate the estimation accuracy is significantly improved in comparison with that of conventional UKF.

**Keywords:** Unscented Kalman Filter, Genetic Algorithm, Adaptive Particle Swarm Optimization, Hybrid GA-APSO and Harmonic Estimation.

## 1 Introduction

Power quality has been an issue of growing concern amongst a broad spectrum of power customers over the past few years. The increasing use of power-electronic equipment, in power systems, harmonic pollution, produced by nonlinear electronically controlled equipment, has significantly deteriorated the power quality in electrical networks. Some of the major factors which contribute towards deteriorating power quality are voltage sags, swells and harmonics. The presence of harmonics can cause interference in communication circuits, over heating of magnetic portions of electrical systems, resonances of mechanical devices etc. Detection and subsequently elimination of harmonics using suitable harmonic filter has therefore been a major research concern of power engineers in recent years [1].

Several algorithms have been developed in the past few decades based on total least squares (TLS) [2], neural network [3] and orthogonal least squares (OLS) [4] to address the problem of Harmonic estimation . One of the alternate approaches for frequency estimation is the method based on Unscented Kalman filter, where the problem of harmonic estimation has been formulated as a state estimation. The main advantage of unscented transformation in UKF is that it does not use linearization for

B.K. Panigrahi et al. (Eds.): SEMCCO 2010, LNCS 6466, pp. 380–388, 2010.

computing the state and error covariance matrices resulting in a more accurate estima-
tionup to second order nonlinearity. However the initial choices of noise co variances
are crucial in noise rejection [5]. Thus for best signal tracking performance, it is proposed in this paper to use Hybrid GA-APSO, for the optimal choice of error covariance matrices Q and R.

Particle swarm optimization technique is a stochastic optimization technique developed by Eberhert and Kennedy that simulates the social behavior of birds or fish.
Genetic Algorithms are a family of computational models inspired by evolution. PSO
suffers from premature convergence and fast rate of information flow between particles, resulting in the creation of similar particles with a loss of diversity that increases
the possibility of being trapped in local minima [6]. Though Adaptive PSO can avoid
getting into local best solution efficiently and improve its searching ability than PSO,
it is not as efficient as global exploration like in GA. To overcome the limitations of
APSO, we use hybrid GA-APSO algorithm. In this model the initial population of
APSO is assigned by solution of GA.

## 2   Signal Model

Consider a signal consisting of N sinusoids which can be modeled as

$$y_k = \sum_{n=0}^{N} A_n \cos(\,2(n+1)\pi f_0 t_k + \varphi_n) + v_k, \quad k = 1, 2, \ldots M \tag{1}$$

Where $A_n$, $\varphi_n$ are amplitude and phase of the $n^{th}$ sinusoid respectively, $t_k = kT_s$ where
$T_s$ is the sampling time. $f_0$ is the fundamental frequency.

The white noise $v_k$ can be modelled as $v_k \sim N(0, R_k)$, and measured noise covariance
is given by

$$R_k = E(v_k v_k^T) \tag{2}$$

The discrete signal can be represented in state space as

$$x_{k+1} = F_k x_k + w_k \tag{3}$$

Process noise $w_k$ can be modeled as $w_k \sim N(0, Q_k)$, and process noise covariance is

$$Q_k = E(w_k w_k^T) \tag{4}$$

The observation model is given by

$$y_k = H x_k + v_k \tag{5}$$

Where, H is the observation matrix [5].

Suppose $a_1^{th}$, $a_2^{th}$ ......$a_n^{th}$ harmonics of amplitudes $A_1$, $A_2 \ldots A_n$ and phases $\varphi_1, \varphi_2 \ldots \varphi_n$
respectively are present in the signal of fundamental frequency $f_0$, having amplitude
$A_0$ and phase $\varphi_0$.

In this model the state variables are

$$\begin{bmatrix} x_{1k} \\ x_{2k} \\ x_{3k} \\ x_{4k} \\ \vdots \\ \vdots \\ \vdots \\ \vdots \\ x_{fk} \end{bmatrix} = \begin{bmatrix} A_0 \sin( x_{fk}.kT_s + \varphi_0) \\ A_0 \cos( x_{fk}.kT_s + \varphi_0) \\ A_1 \sin( a_1 x_{fk}.kT_s + \varphi_1) \\ A_1 \cos( a_1 x_{fk}.kT_s + \varphi_1) \\ \vdots \\ \vdots \\ A_n \sin( a_n x_{fk}.kT_s + \varphi_n) \\ A_n \cos( a_n x_{fk}.kT_s + \varphi_n) \\ 2\pi f_0 \end{bmatrix} \qquad (6)$$

Transition matrix $F_k=$

$$\begin{bmatrix} \cos( x_{fk}.T_s) & \sin( x_{fk}.T_s) \cdots & 0 & 0 & 0 \\ -\sin( x_{fk}.T_s) & \cos( x_{fk}.T_s) \cdots & 0 & 0 & 0 \\ 0 & 0 & \cdots & 0 & 0 & 0 \\ 0 & 0 & \cdots & 0 & 0 & 0 \\ \cdots & \cdots & \cdots & \cdots & \cdots & \cdots \\ 0 & 0 & \cdots \cos( a_n x_{fk}.T_s) & \sin( a_n x_{fk}.T_s) & 0 \\ 0 & 0 & \cdots -\sin( a_n x_{fk}.T_s) & \cos( a_n x_{fk}.T_s) & 0 \\ 0 & 0 & \cdots & 0 & 0 & 1 \end{bmatrix} \qquad (7)$$

The observation matrix $H = [0\ 1\ 0\ 1\ \ldots\ldots\ldots.0\ 1\ 0]$ \qquad (8)

The model noise covariance matrix $Q = \begin{bmatrix} q_1 & 0 & \cdots & 0 \\ 0 & q_2 & \cdots & 0 \\ \cdots & \cdots & \cdots & \cdots \\ 0 & 0 & \cdots & q_f \end{bmatrix}$ \qquad (9)

## 3 Unscented Kalman Filter (UKF)

The UKF is a recursive minimum-mean square error (MMSE) estimator. It is based on the unscented transform (UT). State distribution is approximated by Gaussian random vector and is represented by a set of deterministically chosen sample points called sigma points, which completely capture true mean and covariance of the distribution [7].

Let $n$-dimension state vector $\hat{x}_{k-1}$ with mean $\hat{x}_{k-1/k-1}$ and covariance $P_{k-1/k-1}$ is approximated by $2n+1$ sigma points. Then one cycle of the UKF is as follows.

**Sigma point Calculation:** Compute the $2n+1$ sigma points as follows:

$$\chi_{k-1/k-1}^{0} = \hat{x}_{k-1/k-1}$$
$$W_0 = k/(n+k) \qquad (10)$$

$$\chi_{k-1/k-1}^{i} = \hat{x}_{k-1/k-1} + (\sqrt{(n+k)P_{k-1/k-1}})_i$$
$$W_i = 1/2(n+k), \qquad i = 1,\ldots\ldots n \tag{11}$$

$$\chi_{k-1/k-1}^{i+n} = \hat{x}_{k-1/k-1} - (\sqrt{(n+k)P_{k-1/k-1}})_i$$
$$W_{i+n} = 1/2(n+k), \qquad i = 1,\ldots\ldots n \tag{12}$$

Where $k$ is a scaling factor and $(\sqrt{(n+k)P_{k-1/k-1}})_i$ is the $i^{th}$ row or column (depending on the matrix square root form, if $P = A^T A$ then rows of $A$ is used otherwise if $P = AA^T$, the columns of A is used) of the matrix square root of $(n+k)P_{k-1/k-1}$, and $W_i$ is the normalized weight of the $i^{th}$ point. Cholesky decomposition is used for finding the matrix square root.

**Propagation:** Propagate the sigma points and obtain the mean and covariance of the state by

$$\chi_{k/k-1}^{i} = f(\chi_{k-1/k-1}^{i}) \tag{13}$$

$$\hat{x}_{k/k-1} = \sum_{i=0}^{2n} W_i \chi_{k/k-1}^{i} \tag{14}$$

$$P_{k/k-1} = Q_{k-1} + \sum_{i=0}^{2n} W_i [\chi_{k/k-1}^{i} - \hat{x}_{k/k-1}] \times [\chi_{k/k-1}^{i} - \hat{x}_{k/k-1}]^T \tag{15}$$

**Update:** Calculate the measurement sigma points using h (.) and update the mean and Covariance by

$$Z_{k/k-1}^{i} = h(\chi_{k/k-1}^{i}) \tag{16}$$

$$\hat{z}_{k/k-1} = \sum_{i=0}^{2n} W_i Z_{k/k-1}^{i} \tag{17}$$

$$\tilde{v}_k = z_k - \hat{z}_{k/k-1} \tag{18}$$

$$\hat{x}_{k/k} = \hat{x}_{k/k-1} + K_k \tilde{v}_k \tag{19}$$

$$P_{k/k} = P_{k/k-1} - K_k P_{zz} K_k^T \tag{20}$$

where $$P_{zz} = R_k + \sum_{i=0}^{2n} W_i [Z_{k/k-1}^{i} - \hat{z}_{k/k-1}] \times [Z_{k/k-1}^{i} - \hat{z}_{k/k-1}]^T \tag{21}$$

$$P_{xz} = \sum_{i=0}^{2n} W_i [\chi_{k/k-1}^{i} - \hat{x}_{k/k-1}] \times [Z_{k/k-1}^{i} - \hat{z}_{k/k-1}]^T \tag{22}$$

and $$K_k = P_{xz} P_{zz}^{-1} \tag{23}$$

## 4   Evolutionary Algorithms for Tuning UKF

### 4.1   Genetic Algorithm (GA)

Genetic Algorithms are family of computational models inspired by evolution [9].These algorithms encode a potential solution to a specific problem on a simple chromosome-like data structure and apply recombination and mutation operators to these structures so as to preserve critical information [6].

### 4.2   Adaptive Particle Swarm Optimization(APSO)

Particle swarm optimization is a population based stochastic optimization technique inspired by the social behavior of the bird flocking or fish schooling etc.The values of the particles having the most fittest value is called gbest (global best value) and the fittest value of the particle in its entire search is called pbest (particle best value) [5].

The modified velocity and position of each particle at time (t+1) can be calculated as

$$v_i(t+1) = K[w.v_i(t) + c1.rand().(pbest_i - p_i(t)) + c2.rand().(gbest_i - p_i(t))]$$
$$p_i(t+1) = p_i(t) + v_i(t+1) \tag{24}$$

Where $v_i$(t+1) is the velocity of i$^{th}$ particle at time t+1, $p_i$ is the current position, $w$ is the inertial weight factor c1, c2 are acceleration constant, rand() is an uniform random value in the range [0,1], K is the constriction factor which is given by [5]

$$K = 1/\left(\left|2 - (c_1 + c_2) - \sqrt{(c_1 + c_2)^2 - 4(c_1 + c_2)}\right|\right) \tag{25}$$

The inertial weight $w$ is updated by finding the variance of the population fitness as

$$\sigma^2 = \sum_{i=1}^{N} \left((f_i - f_{avg})/f\right)^2 \tag{26}$$

Where $f_{avg}$ is the average fitness of the population of particles in a given generation, $f_i$ is the fitness of the i$^{th}$ particle in the population. N is the total number of particles.

$$f = \max\left(\left|f_i - f_{avg}\right|\right), \quad i = 1, 2, 3 \ldots N \tag{27}$$

In the equation given above $f$ is normalizing factor which is used to limit $\sigma$.

$$\Delta w = rand_1().\Delta\sigma.|\Delta\sigma| + rand_2().\Delta\sigma.(1 - |\Delta\sigma|)$$
$$\text{where} \quad \Delta\sigma = \sigma(k) - \sigma(k-1) \tag{28}$$

Thus the value of the new weight is obtained as

$$w(k) = w(k-1) + \Delta w; \quad 0.4 \le w(k) \le 0.9 \tag{29}$$

Thus inertial weight is adapted randomly depending on variance of the fitness which results in an optional coordination of local and global searching abilities of particles.

### 4.3  Hybrid GA-APSO

PSO suffers from premature convergence .The underlying principle behind this problem is that, for global best PSO, particles converge to a single point, which is on the line between the global best and the personal best positions. This point is not guaranteed for a local optimum. Another reason for this problem is fast rate of information flow between particles, resulting in the creation of similar particles with a loss of diversity that increases the possibility of being trapped in local minima [6].

One advantage of PSO over GA is its algorithmic simplicity. Another clear difference between PSO and GA is the ability to control convergence. Crossover and mutation rates can subtly affect the convergence of GA, but these cannot be analogous to the level of control achieved through manipulating of the inertial weight in APSO. In fact, the decrease of inertial weight dramatically increases the swarm's convergence. Thus to have merits of APSO with those of GA, Hybrid GA-APSO is used. In this model the initial population of APSO is assigned by solution of GA. The total numbers of iterations are equally shared by GA and APSO.

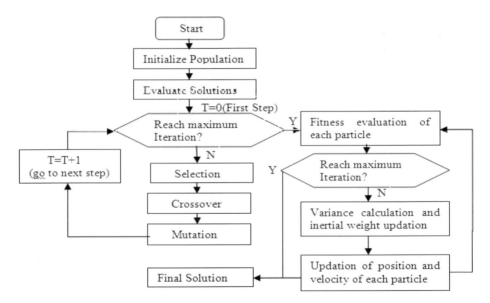

**Fig. 1.** Block diagram of GA-APSO

## 5  Simulations and Results

In this paper we are estimating harmonics in a Sample system shown in fig.1 [8].

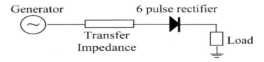

**Fig. 2.** A two-bus architecture with six-pulse full-wave bridge rectifier supplying load

**Table 1.** Frequency content of the test signal, voltage at the load bus

| Harmonic Order | Amplitude(P.U.) | Phase(Degree) |
|---|---|---|
| Fundamental (50Hz) | 0.95 | -2.02 |
| $5^{th}$ ( 250Hz ) | 0.09 | 82.1 |
| $7^{th}$ ( 350Hz ) | 0.043 | 7.9 |
| $11^{th}$ ( 550Hz ) | 0.03 | -147.1 |
| $13^{th}$ ( 650Hz ) | 0.033 | 162.6 |

From the above data when we simulated the following results are obtained.

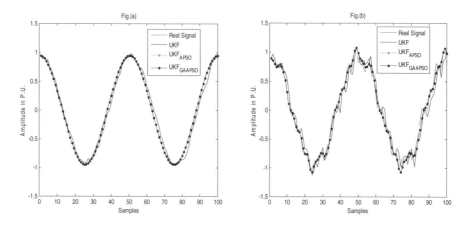

**Fig. 3.** Actual and Estimation waveforms (a)Fundamental (b) Harmonic with UKF, UKFAPSO and UKFGAAPSO for SNR=20dB

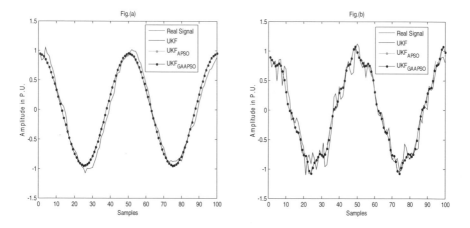

**Fig. 4.** Actual and Estimation waveforms (a)Fundamental (b) Harmonic with UKF, UKFAPSO and UKFGAAPSO for SNR=10dB

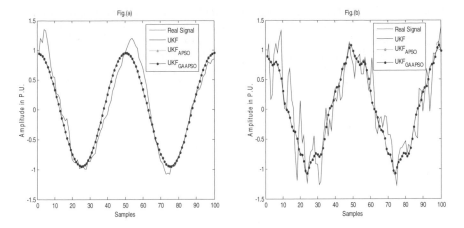

**Fig. 5.** Actual and Estimation waveforms (a)Fundamental (b) Harmonic with UKF, UKFAPSO and UKFGAAPSO for SNR=0dB

From the above figures we can observe that hybrid GA-APSO tuned UKF is performing better in various noise cases like 20dB, 10dB and 0dB, and the obtained RMSE is listed in the table2 below.

**Table 2.** Comparison of RMSE for fundamental and harmonic estimation

| SNR | Fundamental | | | Harmonic | | |
|---|---|---|---|---|---|---|
| | UKF | UKFAPSO | UKFGAAPSO | UKF | UKFAPSO | UKFGAAPSO |
| 20 dB | 0.0781 | 0.0138 | 0.0120 | 0.1284 | 0.0349 | 0.0317 |
| 10 dB | 0.1055 | 0.0261 | 0.0196 | 0.1997 | 0.0391 | 0.0385 |
| 0 dB | 0.3034 | 0.0274 | 0.0256 | 0.4089 | 0.0412 | 0.0411 |

## 6  Conclusion

The work presents tuning procedure for UKF. A comparison was made between UKF, PSO Tuned UKF and Hybrid GA-APSO Tuned UKF for Fundamental and Harmonic Signal estimation. Both large and small variations with noise are considered for fundamental and harmonic signal estimation. It is observed that Root Mean Square Error (RMSE) minimizes in Hybrid GA-APSOTuned UKF than conventional UKF.

## References

1. Zhang, J., Akshya, S., Nirmal-Kumar, C.N., Liu, J.J.: Estimation of Power Quality using an Unscented Kalman Filter. In: TENCON 2007-IEEE Region 10 Conference (2007)
2. Rahaman, M.D.A., Yu, K.B.: Total least squares approach for frequency estimation using linear prediction. IEEE Transactions on Acoustics, Speech and Signal Processing 35(10), 1440–1454 (1987)

3. Cichocki, A., Lobos, T.: Artificial neural networks for real time estimation of basic waveforms of voltages and currents. IEEE Transactions on Power Systems 9(2), 612–618 (1994)
4. Swain, A., Zhao, L., Patel, N.: Accurate estimation of harmonic components of power signa. In: Tencon 2005 IEEE Region 10 Conference, pp. 1–4 (2005)
5. Dash, P.K., Panigrahi, B.K., Hasan, S.: Hybrid Particle Swarm Optimization and Unscented Filtering Technique for Estimation of Non-stationary Signal Parameters. IETE Journal of Research 55(6) (November-December 2009)
6. Premalatha, K., Natarajan, A.M.: Hybrid PSO and GA for Global Maximization. Int. J. Open Problems Compt. Math. 2(4) (December 2009)
7. Michail, N.P., Emmanouil, G.A., Nikolaos, K.U.: Maneuvering target tracking using multiple bistatic range and range-rate measurements. In: Petsios, M.N., et al. (eds.) Signal Processing, vol. 87, pp. 665–686 (2007)
8. Mishra, S.: A Hybrid Least Square-Fuzzy Bacterial Foraging Strategy for Harmonic Estimation. IEEE Transactions on evolutionary computing 9(1) (February 2005)
9. Goldberg, D.E.: Genetic Algorithms in search, optimization, and machine learning. Addison-Wesley Publishing Corporation, Inc., Reading (1989)

# Using Social Emotional Optimization Algorithm to Direct Orbits of Chaotic Systems

Zhihua Cui[1,2,3], Zhongzhi Shi[2], and Jianchao Zeng[1]

[1] Complex System and Computational Intelligence Laboratory,
Taiyuan University of Science and Technology,
No. 66 Waliu Road, Wanbailin District, Taiyuan, Shanxi, 030024, P.R. China
cuizhihua@gmail.com
[2] The Key Laboratory of Intelligent Information Processing,
Institute of Computing Technology Chinese Academy of Sciences,
No. 6 Kexueyuan South Road, Zhongguancun,
Haidian District, Beijing, China, 100190
shizz@ics.ict.ac.cn
[3] State Key Laboratory for Novel Software Technology,
Nanjing University, Jiangsu, 210093, P.R. China
zengjianchao@263.net

**Abstract.** Social emotional optimization algorithm (SEOA) is a new novel population-based stochastic optimization algorithm. In SEOA, each individual simulates one natural person. All of them are communicated through cooperation and competition to increase social status. The winner with the highest status will be the final solution. In this paper, SEOA is employed to solve the directing orbits of chaotic systems, simulation results show this new variant increases the performance significantly when compared with particle swarm optimization algorithm.

## 1 Introduction

Swarm intelligence is a methodology by simulating the animal social behaviors, e.g. birds flocking, fish schooling and insect herding. Two classical examples are ant colony algorithm[1][2] and particle swarm optimization[?][?].

Ant colony algorithm is first proposed by Dorigo in 1991. It simulates the ant search pattern, each individual is called an ant, it will be search food by exploring new area or following other ants' track. Particle swarm optimization (PSO)is a novel population-based swarm intelligent methodology. In standard particle swarm optimization, each individual is called a particle, and flies around the search domain. Each particle manipulates four items: position, velocity, historical best positions found by itself and the entire swarm.

Social emotional optimization algorithm (SEOA) [?][?][?] is a novel swarm intelligent population-based optimization algorithm by simulating the human social behaviors. In SEOA methodology, each individual represents one person, while all points in the problem space constructs the social status society. In this virtual world, all individuals aim to seek the higher social status. Therefore, they

B.K. Panigrahi et al. (Eds.): SEMCCO 2010, LNCS 6466, pp. 389–395, 2010.

will communicated through cooperation and competition to increase personal status, while the one with highest score will win and output as the final solution. In this paper, SEOA is used to directing orbits of chaotic systems.

The rest of paper is organized as follows. Section 2 gives a brief description for social emotional optimization algorithm. Then, the details of directing orbits of chaotic systems is introduced in Section 3. Finally, the simulation results show the proposed algorithm can adjust the exploration and exploitation capabilities dynamically, and improve the convergence speed effectively.

## 2   Social Emotional Optimization Algorithm

In human society, all people do their work hardly to increase their society status. To obtain this object, people will try their bests to find the path so that higher rewards can be obtained from society. Inspired by this phenomenon, Cui et al. proposed a new methodology, social emotional optimization algorithm (SEOA) in which each individual aims to increase the society status.

In SEOA methodology, each individual represents a virtual person, in each iteration, he will choice the behavior according to the corresponding emotion index. After the behavior is done, a status value will be feedback from the society to confirm whether this behavior is right or not. If this choice is right, the emotion index of himself will increase, otherwise,emotion index will decrease.

In the first step, all individuals' emotion indexes are set to 1, with this value, all individuals' emotion indexes is the largest value, therefore, they will think their behavior in this iteration is right, and choice the next behavior as follows:

$$\vec{x_j}(1) = \vec{x_j}(0) \oplus Manner_1 \tag{1}$$

while $\vec{x_j}(0)$ represents the degree of $j's$ individual in the initialization period, the corresponding fitness value is denoted as the society status value. Symbol $\oplus$ meas the operation, in this paper, we only take it as addition operation $+$. Since the belief index of $j$ is 1, the next behavior motion $Manner_1$ is determined by:

$$Manner_1 = -k_1 \cdot rand_1 \cdot \sum_{s=1}^{L}(\vec{x_s}(0) - \vec{x_j}(0)) \tag{2}$$

while $k_1$ is a parameter used to control the size, $rand_1$ is one random number with uniform distribution. total $L$ individuals are selected whose status values are the worst to provide a reminder for individual $j$ to avoid the wrong behaviors.

In the $t$ generation, if individual $j$ do not obtain one better society status value than all previous values, the $j's$ emotional index is decreased as follows:

$$BI_j(t+1) = BI_j(t) - \Delta \tag{3}$$

while $\Delta$ is a predefined value. In this paper, this parameter is set to 0.05, this value is coming from experimental tests. If individual $j$ is rewarded a new status value which is the best one among all iterations, then

$$BI_j(t+1) = 1.0 \tag{4}$$

Remark: If $BI_j(t+1) < 0.0$ is occur according to Eq.(3), then $BI_j(t+1) = 0.0$.

In order to simulate the behavior of human, we define a behavior set which contains three kinds of manners $\{Manner_2, Manner_3, Manner_4\}$. Since the emotion affects the behavior behavior, the next behavior will be changed according to the following three rules:

If $BI_j(t+1) < TH_1$

$$\vec{x_j}(t+1) = \vec{x_j}(t) + Manner_2 \tag{5}$$

If $TH_1 \le BI_j(t+1) < TH_2$

$$\vec{x_j}(t+1) = \vec{x_j}(t) + Manner_3 \tag{6}$$

Otherwise

$$\vec{x_j}(t+1) = \vec{x_j}(t) + Manner_4 \tag{7}$$

Two parameters $TH_1$ and $TH_2$ are two thresholds aiming to restrict the different behavior manner. For Case 1, because the belief index is too small, individual $j$ prefers to simulate others' successful experiences. Therefore, the update equation is

$$Manner_2 = k_2 \cdot rand_2 \cdot (\overrightarrow{Status}_{best}(t) - \vec{x_j}(t)) \tag{8}$$

while $\overrightarrow{Status}_{best}(t)$ represents the best society status degree obtained from all people previously. In other words, it is

$$\overrightarrow{Status}_{best}(t) = \arg\min_s\{f(\vec{x_s}(h))|1 \le h \le t)\} \tag{9}$$

With the similar method, $Manner_3$ is defined

$$\begin{aligned} Manner_3 = {}& k_3 \cdot rand_3 \cdot (\vec{x}_{j\,best}(t) - \vec{x_j}(t)) \\ & + k_2 \cdot rand_2 \cdot (\overrightarrow{Status}_{best}(t) - \vec{x_j}(t)) \\ & - k_1 \cdot rand_1 \cdot \sum_{s=1}^{L}(\vec{x_s}(0) - \vec{x_j}(0)) \end{aligned} \tag{10}$$

while $\vec{x}_{j\,best}(t)$ denotes the best status value obtained by individual $j$ previously, and is defined by

$$\vec{x}_{j\,best}(t) = \arg\min\{f(\vec{x_j}(h))|1 \le h \le t)\} \tag{11}$$

For $Manner_4$, we have

$$\begin{aligned} Manner_4 = {}& k_3 \cdot rand_3 \cdot (\vec{x}_{j\,best}(t) - \vec{x_j}(t)) \\ & - k_1 \cdot rand_1 \cdot \sum_{s=1}^{L}(\vec{x_s}(0) - \vec{x_j}(0)) \end{aligned} \tag{12}$$

Because the phase "social cognitive optimization algorithm(SCOA)" has been used by Xie et al.[?] in 2002, we change this algorithm into social emotional optimization algorithm(SEOA) in order to avoid confusing, although they are two different algorithms.

The detail steps of social emotional optimization algorithm (SEOA) are listed as follows:

Step1. Initializing all individuals respectively, the initial position of individuals randomly distributed in the problem space;

Step2. Computing the fitness value of each individual according to objective function;

Step3. For $j'th$ individual, the behavior motion is selected according to its emotion index;

Step 4. For all population, the position is updated;

Step5. Determining the emotion index;

Step6. If the criteria is satisfied, output the best solution; otherwise, goto step 2.

## 3   Directing Orbits of Chaotic Systems

Directing orbits of chaotic systems is a multi-modal numerical optimization problem [?][?]. Consider the following discrete chaotic dynamical system:

$$\overrightarrow{x}(t+1) = \overrightarrow{f}(\overrightarrow{x}(t)), \quad t = 1, 2, ..., N \tag{13}$$

where state $\overrightarrow{x}(t) \in R^n$, $\overrightarrow{f} : R^n \rightarrow R^n$ is continuously differentiable.

Let $\overrightarrow{x}_0 \in R^n$ be an initial state of the system. If small perturbation $\overrightarrow{u}(t) \in R^n$ is added to the chaotic system, then

$$\overrightarrow{x}(t+1) = \overrightarrow{f}(\overrightarrow{x}(t)) + \overrightarrow{u}(t), \quad t = 0, 2, ..., N - 1 \tag{14}$$

where $||\overrightarrow{u}(t)|| \le \mu$, $\mu$ is a positive real constant.

The goal is to determine suitable $\overrightarrow{u}(t)$ so as to make $\overrightarrow{x}(N)$ in the $\epsilon$−neighborhood of the target $\overrightarrow{x}(t)$, i.e., $||\overrightarrow{x}(N) - \overrightarrow{x}(t)|| < \epsilon$, where a local controller is effective for chaos control.

Generally, assume that $\overrightarrow{u}(t)$ acts only on the first component of $\overrightarrow{f}$, then the problem can be re-formulated as follows:

min $||\overrightarrow{x}(N) - \overrightarrow{x}(t)||$ by choosing suitable $\overrightarrow{u}(t)$,   t=0,2,...,N-1

S.t.

$$\begin{cases} x_1(t+1) = f_1(\overrightarrow{x}(t)) + \overrightarrow{u}(t) \\ x_j(t+1) = \overrightarrow{f}_j(\overrightarrow{x}(t)) \qquad \text{j=2,3,...,n} \end{cases} \tag{15}$$

$$|u(t)| \le \mu \tag{16}$$

$$\overrightarrow{x}(0) = \overrightarrow{x}_0 \tag{17}$$

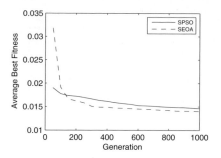

**Fig. 1.** Comparison with $N = 7$ with $Error = 0.01$

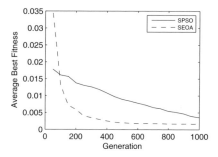

**Fig. 2.** Comparison with $N = 8$ with $Error = 0.01$

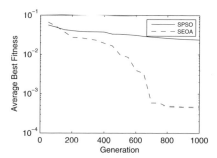

**Fig. 3.** Comparison with $N = 9$ with $Error = 0.01$

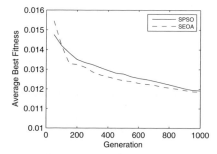

**Fig. 4.** Comparison with $N = 7$ with $Error = 0.02$

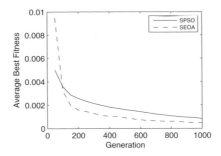

**Fig. 5.** Comparison with $N = 8$ with $Error = 0.02$

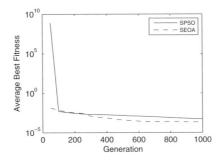

**Fig. 6.** Comparison with $N = 9$ with $Error = 0.02$

## 4    Simulation Results

As a typical discrete chaotic system, Hénon Map is employed as an example in this paper. Hénon May can be described as follows:

$$\begin{cases} x_1(t+1) = -px_1^2(t) + x_2(t) + 1 \\ x_2(t+1) = qx_1(t) \end{cases} \tag{18}$$

where $p = 1.4$, $q = 0.3$.

The target $\overrightarrow{x}(t)$ is set to be a fixed point of the system $(0.63135, 0.18941)^T$, $\overrightarrow{x}_0 = (0,0)^T$, and $\overrightarrow{u}(t)$ is only added to $\overrightarrow{x}_1$ with the bound $\mu = 0.01, 0.02$ and $0.03$. The population is 20, and the largest generation is 1000.

To test the performance of SEOA, the standard version of PSO (SPSO)[?] is used to compare. The coefficients of SPSO are set as follows:

The inertia weight $w$ is decreased linearly from 0.9 to 0.4. Accelerator coefficients $c_1$ and $c_2$ are set to 2.0.

It is obviously SEOA is superior to SPSO significantly.

## 5    Conclusion

This paper applied one newly proposed swarm intelligent technique, social emotional optimization algorithm to direct the orbits of chaotic systems, simulation results show it is effective. The further researches are to investigate the affections of the swarm size and other parameter settings.

## Acknowledgement

This paper is supported by the Key Project of Chinese Ministry of Education(No.209021).

## References

1. Dorigo, M., Dorigo, M., Maniezzo, V., Colorni, A.: The ant system: optimization by a colony of cooperating agents. IEEE Transactions on Systems, Man, and Cybernetics-Part B(S1083-4419) 26(1), 29–41 (1996)
2. Colorni, A., Dorigo, M., Maniezzo, V.: Distributed optimization by ant colonies. In: Proceedings of 1st European Conference Artificial Life, pp. 134–142. Elsevier, Pans (1991)
3. Eberhart, R.C., Kennedy, J.: A new optimizer using particle swarm theory. In: Proceedings of 6th International Symposium on Micro Machine and Human Science, pp. 39–43 (1995)
4. Kennedy, J., Eberhart, R.C.: Particle swarm optimization. In: Proceedings of ICNN 1995 - IEEE International Conference on Neural Networks, pp. 1942–1948. IEEE CS Press, Perth (1995)
5. Cui, Z.H., Cai, X.J.: Using Social Cognitive Optimization Algorithm to Solve Nonlinear Equations. In: Proceedings of 9th IEEE International Conference on Cognitive Informatics (ICCI 2010), July 7-9, pp. 199–203. Tsinghua University, Beijing (2010)
6. Chen, Y.J., Cui, Z.H., Zeng, J.C.: Structural Optimization of Lennard-Jones Clusters by Hybrid Social Cognitive Optimization Algorithm. In: Proceedings of 9th IEEE International Conference on Cognitive Informatics (ICCI 2010), July 7-9, pp. 204–208. Tsinghua University, Beijing (2010)
7. Wei, Z.H., Cui, Z.H., Zeng, J.C.: Social Cognitive Optimization Algorithm with Reactive Power Optimization of Power System. In: Proceedings of 2nd International Conference on Computational Aspects of Social Networks, TaiYuan, China, pp. 11–14 (2010)
8. Xie, X.F., Zhang, W.J., Yang, Z.L.: Social cognitive optimization for nonlinear programming problems. In: International Conference on Machine Learning and Cybernetics, Beijing, China, pp. 779–783 (2002)
9. Liu, B., Wang, L., Jin, Y.H., Tang, F., Huang, D.X.: Directing orbits of chaotic systems by particle swarm optimization. Chaos Solitons & Fractals 29, 454–461 (2006)
10. Wang, L., Li, L.L., Tang, F.: Directing orbits of chaotic dynamical systems using a hybrid optimization strategy. Physical Letters A 324, 22–25 (2004)
11. Shi, Y., Eberhart, R.C.: A modified particle swarm optimizer. In: Proceedings of the IEEE International Conference on Evolutionary Computation, Anchorage, Alaska, USA, pp. 69–73

# A Hybrid ANN-BFOA Approach for Optimization of FDM Process Parameters

Anoop Kumar Sood[1], R.K. Ohdar[2], and S.S. Mahapatra[3]

[1] Department of Manufacturing Engineering, National Institute of Foundry and Forge
Technology, Ranchi-834003, India
anoopkumarsood@gmail.com
[2] Department of Forge technology, National Institute of Foundry and Forge Technology,
Ranchi-834003, India
rkohdar@yahoo.com
[3] Department of Mechanical Engineering, National Institute of Technology,
Rourkela-769008, India
mahapatrass2003@yahoo.com

**Abstract.** This study proposes an integrated approach for effectively assisting the practitioners in prediction and optimization of process parameters of fused deposition modelling (FDM) process for improving the mechanical strength of fabricated part. The experimental data are used for efficiently training and testing artificial neural network (ANN) model that finely maps the relationship between the input process control factors and output responses. Bayesian regularization is adopted for selection of optimum network architecture because of its ability to fix number of network parameters irrespective of network size. ANN model is trained using Levenberg-Marquardt algorithm and the resulting network has good generalization capability that eliminates the chance of over fitting. Finally, ANN network is combined with bacterial-foraging optimization algorithm (BFOA) to suggest theoretical combination of parameter settings to improve strength related responses of processed parts.

## 1 Introduction

Fused deposition modelling (FDM) is one of the rapid prototyping (RP) processes that build part of any geometry by sequential deposition of material on a layer by layer basis. Unlike other RP systems which involve an array of lasers, powders, resins, this process uses heated thermoplastic filaments which are extruded from the tip of nozzle in a prescribed manner. Previous work on FDM has shown that process parameters such as layer thickness ($x_1$), part build orientation ($x_2$), raster angle ($x_3$), raster width ($x_4$) and air gap ($x_5$) significantly influence the part dimensional accuracy, roughness and strength [1-3] in a non linear manner. The exact determination of these parameters for part quality improvement, particularly mechanical strength, using traditional methodologies will be costly and time consuming for the required level of precision. To solve this problem, present study proposes use of back propagation algorithm (BPA) based artificial neural network (ANN) for modelling the relationship between

B.K. Panigrahi et al. (Eds.): SEMCCO 2010, LNCS 6466, pp. 396–403, 2010.

tensile strength ($F_T$), flexural strength ($F_F$), Impact strength ($F_s$) and compressive strength ($F_c$) of test specimen and above mention parameters. In order to achieve faster convergence, Levenberg-Marquardt algorithm (LMA) is used for training purpose. LMA is a virtual standard in nonlinear optimization which significantly outperforms gradient decent, conjugate gradient methods and quasi-Newton algorithms for medium sized problems [4]. Bayesian regularization is adopted to improve the generalization ability of trained network. It is particularly useful to problems that would suffer if a portion of the small available data is reserved to a validation set [4]. Finally, Bacterial-foraging optimization algorithm (BFOA) which attempts to model the individual and group behavior of Escherichia coli (E. coli) bacteria as a distributed optimization process is used to suggest theoretical combination of parameter settings to improve overall strength of part.

## 2  Data Collection

Specimens (Fig. 1) were fabricated using FDM Vantage SE machine setting the control factors (Table 1) of the process at the levels shown in Table 2 for each experimental run. The material used for part fabrication is acrylonitrile butadiene styrene (ABS P400). Tensile test, Flexural test and compression test were carried out in

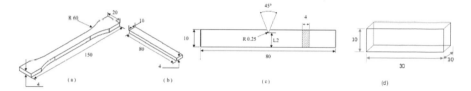

**Fig. 1.** Test specimens (all dimensions are in mm): (a) Tensile; (b) Flexural (L2=3.2); (c) Impact; (d) Compression test specimen

**Table 1.** Factors and their levels

| Fixed Factors | | Control Factors | | | | |
|---|---|---|---|---|---|---|
| Factor | Values | Factor | Levels | | | Unit |
| Fill Style | Perimeter/Raster | Layer thickness ($x_1$) | 0.127 | 0.178 | 0.254 | mm |
| Contour width | 0.4064mm | Orientation ($x_2$) | 0 | 15 | 30 | degree |
| Interior style | Solid normal | Raster angle ($x_3$) | 0 | 30 | 60 | degree |
| Visible surface | Normal Raster | Raster width ($x_4$) | 0.4064 | 0.4564 | 0.5064 | mm |
| X, Y, Z shrink factor | 1.0038mm | AirGap ($x_5$) | 0.000 | 0.004 | 0.008 | mm |
| Perimeter to raster gap | 0.000mm | | | | | |

Instron 1195 series IX automated material testing system as per ISO R527:1966, ISO
R178:1975 and ISO604-1973 standards. Charpy impact test was performed in Instron
Wolpert pendulum impact test machine in accordance with ISO 179:1982 standard.
The database (Table 2) is then divided into two categories, namely: (A) A training
category, which is exclusively used to adjust the network weights (B) A test category,
which corresponds to the set that validates the results of the training protocol.

**Table 2.** Experimental data

| $x_1$ | $x_2$ | $x_3$ | $x_4$ | $x_5$ | $F_T$ | $F_F$ | $F_I$ | $F_C$ |
|---|---|---|---|---|---|---|---|---|
| **A**: Training Data | | | | | | | | |
| 0.127 | 00 | 00 | 0.4064 | 0.008 | 15.6659 | 34.2989 | 0.367013 | 15.21 |
| 0.254 | 00 | 00 | 0.4064 | 0.000 | 16.1392 | 35.3593 | 0.429862 | 12.41 |
| 0.127 | 30 | 00 | 0.4064 | 0.000 | 9.1229 | 18.8296 | 0.363542 | 10.16 |
| 0.254 | 30 | 00 | 0.4064 | 0.008 | 13.2081 | 24.5193 | 0.426042 | 10.78 |
| 0.127 | 00 | 60 | 0.4064 | 0.000 | 16.701 | 36.5796 | 0.375695 | 14.28 |
| 0.254 | 00 | 60 | 0.4064 | 0.008 | 17.9122 | 38.0993 | 0.462153 | 15.83 |
| 0.127 | 30 | 60 | 0.4064 | 0.008 | 18.0913 | 39.2423 | 0.395833 | 7.448 |
| 0.254 | 30 | 60 | 0.4064 | 0.000 | 14.0295 | 22.2167 | 0.466667 | 16.98 |
| 0.127 | 00 | 00 | 0.5064 | 0.000 | 14.4981 | 27.604 | 0.342708 | 13.89 |
| 0.254 | 00 | 00 | 0.5064 | 0.008 | 14.8892 | 34.5569 | 0.429167 | 16.18 |
| 0.127 | 30 | 00 | 0.5064 | 0.008 | 11.0262 | 20.0259 | 0.379167 | 11.13 |
| 0.254 | 30 | 00 | 0.5064 | 0.000 | 14.7661 | 25.2563 | 0.450001 | 10.44 |
| 0.127 | 00 | 60 | 0.5064 | 0.008 | 15.451 | 36.2904 | 0.375 | 13.58 |
| 0.254 | 00 | 60 | 0.5064 | 0.000 | 15.9244 | 37.3507 | 0.437785 | 16.29 |
| 0.127 | 30 | 60 | 0.5064 | 0.000 | 11.8476 | 22.9759 | 0.419792 | 11.83 |
| 0.254 | 30 | 60 | 0.5064 | 0.008 | 15.9328 | 28.8362 | 0.482292 | 10.78 |
| **B**: Testing Data | | | | | | | | |
| 0.127 | 00 | 00 | 0.4064 | 0.004 | 15.16 | 32.564 | 0.3541 | 14.5953 |
| 0.254 | 30 | 60 | 0.5064 | 0.004 | 14.897 | 26.486 | 0.4734 | 11.6865 |
| 0.254 | 15 | 60 | 0.5064 | 0.008 | 18.4 | 35.1411 | 0.4713 | 11.7600 |
| 0.178 | 30 | 30 | 0.5064 | 0.004 | 12.4848 | 22.2463 | 0.419 | 11.0810 |
| 0.127 | 15 | 60 | 0.4564 | 0.000 | 15.0459 | 31.983 | 0.38 | 12.7572 |
| 0.254 | 15 | 30 | 0.4064 | 0.000 | 15.4011 | 28.6149 | 0.4354 | 14.8511 |
| 0.254 | 30 | 30 | 0.5064 | 0.008 | 14.3023 | 25.64 | 0.474 | 12.1000 |
| 0.178 | 30 | 30 | 0.5064 | 0.004 | 12.4848 | 22.2463 | 0.419 | 11.081 |
| 0.178 | 30 | 60 | 0.4564 | 0.004 | 15.2502 | 29.1473 | 0.4368 | 10.5800 |
| 0.127 | 15 | 60 | 0.5064 | 0.008 | 14.38 | 34.1966 | 0.3839 | 12.2100 |
| 0.127 | 00 | 00 | 0.4064 | 0.008 | 15.6659 | 34.2989 | 0.346 | 14.2100 |
| 0.254 | 00 | 00 | 0.4064 | 0.004 | 16.45 | 38.09 | 0.4185 | 12.3767 |
| 0.127 | 30 | 00 | 0.4064 | 0.004 | 11.0297 | 20.84 | 0.3757 | 9.2222 |
| 0.127 | 30 | 00 | 0.4064 | 0.008 | 13.9442 | 26.2342 | 0.3875 | 8.7400 |

# 3   ANN Training and Architecture

The training of neural network involves updating the weights of the connections in such a manner that the error between the outputs of the neural network and the actual output is minimized. To achieve faster convergence, the learning rate of an algorithm that defines the shift of the weight vector has to be dynamically varied in accordance with the region that the weight vector currently stands. The LMA comes under the faster BPA and was designed to approach second-order training speed but without having to compute the Hessian matrix directly. Typically, training aims to reduce the sum of squared errors $F=E_D$. Bayesian framework also considers the sum of squares of the network weight $E_W$ and the objective function becomes minimization of $F=\beta E_D+\alpha E_W$ $\alpha$, $\beta$ are objective function parameters. For the convergence the network should be train until the sum squared error, the sum squared weights, and the effective number of parameters reaches constant values. In present work the input layer had five neurons which correspond to $x_1$, $x_2$, $x_3$, $x_4$ and $x_5$ respectively. The output layer consists of four neurons, corresponding to $F_T$, $F_F$, $F_I$ and $F_C$ value respectively. To determine the number of neurons in hidden layer, various network configurations in which hidden layer neurons varies from five to the point were effective number of parameters almost become constant are used. The activation level of neuron is determined by tan-sigmoid transfer function except for output layer neurons for which linear output transfer function is used so that output is not limited to small values. For training, input-output data is first mapped into the range [-1, 1]. Training data set consisting of both the input parameters (factors) and the resulting output parameters (strength) is shown in Table 2.A. Once the network is trained testing data set (Table 2.B) of input and output vectors is used to confirm the generalized predictability of the network.

# 4   Fitness Function

For generating fitness-function concept of desirability is used. The more closely the response approaches the ideal intervals or ideal values, the closer the desirability is to 1. All the desirability can be combined to form a composite desirability, which converts a multi-response into a single-response [3]. For present problem it is desirable to maximize all the responses therefore for measuring the desirability higher the better quality characteristic is considered. For this desirability can be measured as:

$$d_{ij} = \begin{cases} 0 & if & y_{ij} \leq low_j \\ \dfrac{y_{ij}-low_j}{High_j\_low_j} & if & low_j \leq y_{ij} \leq High_j \\ 1 & if & y_{ij} \geq High_i \end{cases} \tag{1}$$

where $d_{ij}$ is the desirability of $i^{th}$ alternative of $j^{th}$ response. $y_{ij}$ is the found value of $i^{th}$ alternative of $j^{th}$ response. $low_j$ and $High_j$ are the minimum and the maximum values respectively of the experiment data for $j^{th}$ response. These desirability values are combined to single unit known as composite desirability as:

$$C_d^i = (\prod_{j=1}^{m} d_{ij}^{w_j})^{\frac{1}{\sum_{j=1}^{m} w_j}} \tag{2}$$

where $C_d^i$ is the composite desirability of $i^{th}$ alternative. $w_j$ is the weight or importance of $j^{th}$ response, usually decided by the designer. For present study $w_j = 1 \; \forall j$.
The fitness function is formulated as follows:

$$\text{Maximization of } F(X) = C_d(\eta(X)) \tag{3}$$

Subject to

$$
\begin{aligned}
0.127 &\leq x_1 \leq 0.254 \\
0 &\leq x_2 \leq 30 \\
0 &\leq x_3 \leq 60 \\
0.4064 &\leq x_4 \leq 0.5064 \\
0.000 &\leq x_5 \leq 0.008
\end{aligned}
\tag{4}
$$

where $X = [x_1, x_2, x_3, x_4, x_5]$ are the process variables, input to neural network $\eta$, whose
outputs are combined to form composite desirability $C_d$.

## 5   Bacteria Foraging Optimization Algorithm (BFOA)

As other swarm intelligence algorithms, BFOA is based on social and cooperative
behaviors found in nature. In fact, the way bacteria look for regions of high levels of
nutrients can be seen as an optimization process. Each bacterium tries to maximize its
obtained energy per each unit of time expended on the foraging process and avoiding
noxious substances. Besides, swarm search assumes communication among individuals [5,6]. BFOA algorithm involves two steps [5,6].

### 1-Initializtion
(i) Number of parameters (p) to be optimized, (ii) Number of bacteria (s) to be used
for searching the total region, (iii) Maximum swimming length ($SL_{max}$) after which
tumbling of bacteria will be undertaken in a chemotaxis step, (iv) Number of iteration
(Nc) to be undertaken in a chemotaxis loop, (v) Maximum number of reproduction
(NR) cycles, (vi) Maximum number of elimination-dispersal (Ne) events imposed on
bacteria, (vii) Probability (Ped) with which elimination-dispersal will continue (viii)
Location P(p, s, 1) of initial set of bacteria, (ix) Random swim direction (Ø(j)) and
step length (C(i)), (x) Swarming coefficients ($d_a$, $w_a$, $h_r$ and $w_r$).

### 2-Iterative Algorithm
The algorithm begins with evaluation of the cost function for the initial bacterial
population. Any $i^{th}$ bacteria and its corresponding cost function in the $j^{th}$ chemotactic,
$k^{th}$ reproduction and $l^{th}$ elimination stages is identified by, $\theta^i(j, k, l)$ and $F(i, k, l)$ respectively. The steps of algorithm can be established as follows [5].

1. Elimination-dispersal loop: $l=l+1$
2. Reproduction loop: $k=k+1$
3. Chemotaxis loop: $j=j+1$
    a.  $\forall i$ ,calculate $F(i, k, l)$
    b.  Find $\theta_g$ $(j, k, l)$ from all the cost functions evaluated till that point. $\theta_g$ is the global minima ($F$ is minimize). Calculate the penalty function $F_{cc}=F_{sa}+F$. Where swarm attachment cost is defined by the following equation

$$F_{sa} = \sum_{i=1}^{S}[-d_a \exp(-\ \omega_a \sum_{m=1}^{p}(\theta_{gm} - \theta_m^i)^2)] + \sum_{i=1}^{S}[\ h_r \exp(-\ \omega_r \sum_{m=1}^{p}(\theta_{gm} - \theta_m^i)^2)] \qquad (5)$$

where $m$ represent the $m^{th}$ parameter of bacteria position.
    c.  if j=1

$$\theta^i(j+1,k,l) = \theta^i(j,k,l) + C(i)\Phi(i) \qquad (6)$$

where $\Phi$ is unit random direction
    d.  For, $j>1$
        i.  If, $F_{cc}(i,j,k,l)<F_{cc}(i,j-1,k,l)\&SL<SL_{max}$
            swim, using Eq. 6, Increment $SL=SL+1$
        ii. else tumbel (generate direction randomly), Reset SL=0
    e.  Increment $j= j|1$, GOTO step 3, if $j<NC$
4. Start reproduction: Sort bacteria in order of ascending cost ($F_{cc}$), higher cost of any bacteria means lower health. Out of total s bacteria, the better half will sustain the evolution process and replace the other less healthy bacteria that are deemed to die. Increment $k=k+1$, GOTO step 2 if $k<NR$
5. Elimination-dispersal: With some probability the existing set of bacteria gets eliminated and dispersed in random direction. Increment $l=l+1$, GOTO step 1, if $l<Ne$
6. Loop to step 2 until a stop criteria is met.

In present study, adaptive step length as given in Eq. 7 is considered.

$$C(i) = \left.|F^i(\theta)|\middle/ 1+1/|F^i(\theta)|\right. \qquad (7)$$

Whenever a generated particle lies beyond each parameter low value ($l_v$) and high value ($h_v$), a repair rule is applied according to Eq. 8 and Eq. 9, respectively.

$$x_i = x_i + rand[0,1].\{h_v(x_i)\_l_v(x_i)\} \qquad (8)$$

$$x_i = x_i \_ rand[0,1].\{h_v(x_i)\_l_v(x_i)\} \qquad (9)$$

# 6  Results

After training, the topology 5-10-4 is selected as the optimum with training sum of square error as $8.202\times10^{-11}$ (goal is $10^{-10}$) in 172 epochs. In order to evaluate the competence of this trained network, the training data set was presented to the trained network. Fig. 2 shows the regression analysis results between the network response and the corresponding targets. High correlation coefficient (R-value) between the outputs and targets establish the performance of network. Bacteria foraging method find process parameter values for maximization of $C_d$. Parameters of swarming such as $d_a$, $w_a$, $h_r$ and $w_r$ are set at 1.9, 0.2, 1.9 and10 respectively, by trial and error method based on algoritn fastest convergence. In order to apply BFOA, initial parameters are set randomly as: number of bacteria s=10, chemotactic loop limit Nc =25, maximum swim length $SL_{max}$ =20, reproduction loop limit NR =10, elimination-dispersal loop limit Ne =20, and probability of elimination dispersal Ped =0.001. For composite desirability (fitness function) calculation, high and low values for each response are taken from experimental data (Table 2). Convergence curve (Fig. 3) shows that maximum $C_d$ =0.9052 is obtained at the factor level $x_1$= 0.2523mm, $x_2$=0.036degree, $x_3$=58.1013degree, $x_4$=0.4197mm, and $x_5$=0.0028mm. Strength values at this point is $F_T$=18.1180MPa, $F_F$=39.2303MPa, $F_I$=0.4548MJ/m$^2$ and $F_c$=16.0553MPa.

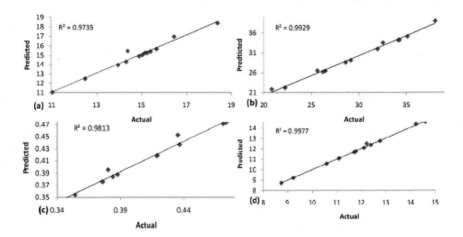

**Fig. 2.** Network prediction results (a) Tensile (b) Flexural (c) Impact (d) Compressive Strength

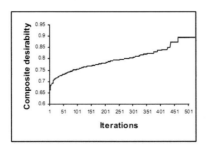

**Fig. 3.** Convergence curve

# 7 Conclusion

In this study hybrid ANN-BFOA approach is proposed and applied to optimize the FDM process for better mechanical strength. For faster training of ANN, LMA was used. Generally, method for improving network generalization is to use a network that is just large enough to provide an adequate fit. Unfortunately, it is difficult to know beforehand how large a network should be for a specific application. To overcome the problem Bayesian regularization that provides better generalization performance was adopted. A latest evolutionary approach known as bacterial foraging has been used to predict optimal parameter settings. Methodology adopted is general enough and can be relevant to other problems of function approximation and optimization, especially those related with multi input-multi output.

# References

[1] Sood, A.K., Ohdar, R.K., Mahapatra, S.S.: Improving Dimensional Accuracy of Fused Deposition Modelling Process using Grey Taguchi Method. Mater. and Des. 30(10), 4243–4252 (2009)

[2] Ahn, D., Kweon, J.H., Kwon, S., Song, J., Lee, S.: Representation of Surface Roughness in Fused Deposition Modelling. J. of Mater Process Technol. 209(15-16), 5593–5600 (2009)

[3] Sood, A.K., Ohdar, R.K., Mahapatra, S.S.: Parametric Appraisal of Mechanical Property of Fused Deposition Modelling Processed Parts. Mater. and Des. 31(1), 287–295 (2010)

[4] Torrecilla, J.S., Otero, L., Sanz, P.D.: Optimization of an Artificial Neural Network for Thermal/Pressure Food Processing: Evaluation of training algorithms. Comput. and Electron in Agric 56(2), 101–110 (2007)

[5] Biswas, A., Dasgupta, S., Das, S., Abraham, A.: Synergy of PSO and bacterial foraging optimization: a comparative study on numerical benchmarks. In: Corchado, E., et al. (eds.) Innovations in Hybrid Intelligent Systems, Germany. ASC, vol. 44, pp. 255–263. Springer, Germany (2007)

[6] Dasgupta, S., Das, S., Abraham, A., Biswas, A.: Adaptive Computational Chemotaxis in Bacterial Foraging Optimization: An Analysis. IEEE Trans. on Evolut. Comput. 13(4), 919–941 (2009)

# Bio Inspired Swarm Algorithm for Tumor Detection in Digital Mammogram

J. Dheeba[1] and Tamil Selvi[2]

[1] Research Scholar, Anna University, Tirunelveli
deeps_3u4@yahoo.com
[2] Professor, Department of Electronics and Communication Engineering
National Engineering College, kovilpatti
tamilgopal2004@yahoo.co.in

**Abstract.** Microcalcification clusters in mammograms is the significant early sign of breast cancer. Individual clusters are difficult to detect and hence an automatic computer aided mechanism will help the radiologist in detecting the microcalcification clusters in an easy and efficient way. This paper presents a new classification approach for detection of microcalcification in digital mammogram using particle swarm optimization algorithm (PSO) based clustering technique. Fuzzy C-means clustering technique, well defined for clustering data sets are used in combination with the PSO. We adopt the particle swarm optimization to search the cluster center in the arbitrary data set automatically. PSO can search the best solution from the probability option of the Social-only model and Cognition-only model. This method is quite simple and valid, and it can avoid the minimum local value. The proposed classification approach is applied to a database of 322 dense mammographic images, originating from the MIAS database. Results shows that the proposed PSO-FCM approach gives better detection performance compared to conventional approaches.

**Keywords:** Computer Aided Diagnosis, Microcalcification, Mammograms, Particle Swarm Optimisation, Fuzzy C-Means Gabor features, Integer wavelet transform (IWT).

## 1 Introduction

BREAST cancer is one of the frequent and leading causes of mortality amongst women between the ages of 40 to 69 in urban areas. World wide breast cancer comprises 10.4% of all cancer incidences with women [12]. In Western countries about 53% to 92% of the population has this disease. According to American Cancer Society (ACS) 2.4 million living in United States has been diagnosed with and treated for breast cancer [14]. There are various methods for breast cancer screening like clinical and self breast exams, genetic screening, ultrasound, magnetic resonance imaging and mammography. Mammography is the best and most efficient method for detecting breast cancer at the early stage. Mammography is a specific type of imaging that uses a low dose x-ray system to examine breast. In a phillipine study [1] a mammogram screening was done to 151,198 women, out of that 3479 women had this disease and

B.K. Panigrahi et al. (Eds.): SEMCCO 2010, LNCS 6466, pp. 404–415, 2010.
© Springer-Verlag Berlin Heidelberg 2010

was referred for diagnosis. Mammography can detect a growth as small as 0.5 cm in the depth of the breast that may not be palpable from surface. However mammography combined with breast self examination and clinical examinations is the most optimal method for detection of cancer [2]. Age is one of the risk factor for breast cancer. The ACS has recommended that the women should obtain her first baseline mammogram between the ages of 35 to 40 [14].

Microcalcificaitons (MC) are quiet tiny bits of calcium, and may show up in clusters or in patterns and are associated with extra cell activity in breast tissue. Scattered MC can indicate early breast cancer, which are usually a sign of benign breast cancer. MC in the breast show up as white speckles on breast x-rays. The calcifications are small; usually varying from 100 micrometer to 300 micrometer, but in reality may be as large as 2 mm. The Computer Aided Diagnosis (CAD) system will help the radiologist in detecting suspicious areas on the mammograms. According to ACS, some studies have shown that CAD can help find cancers that radiologist otherwise might have missed.

In the past two decades the detection and classification of MC clusters in the mammograms, using the CAD methods has been investigated by several researchers. Berman Sahiner et al. used a Convolution Neural Network (CNN) classifier to classify the masses and the normal breast tissue [4]. First, the Region of Interest (ROI) of the image is taken and it was subjected to averaging and subsampling. Second, gray level difference statistics (GLDS) and spatial gray level dependence (SGLD) features were computed from different subregions. The computed features were given as input to the CNN classifier. Ligang ei et al. [5] has investigated various machine learning methods for classification of MC clusters. As input eight image features were automatically extracted from the clustered MC. Cascio.D [6] developed an automatic CAD scheme for mammographic interpretations. The scheme makes use of the Artificial Neural Network to classify mass lesions using the geometric information and shape parameters as input to the classifier. Jong and Hyyun [7] proposed a three layer Backpropagation Neural Network (BPNN) for automatic detection of microcalcificaiton clusters. Texture features are extracted to classify the ROI containing clustered MC and ROI containing normal tissues.

Schemes based on wavelet transforms have been proposed for detecting microcalcifications in mammograms [8] [9]. Wavelet features are used to enhance the features in the mammograms because small sized calcifications are difficult to detect and segment. Brijesh verma and John Zakos [10] developed a CAD system based on neural network for MC detection. A combination of 14 features was extracted from the mammogram image. A BPNN was used for classification into benign and malignant cancer. Rianne and Nico [11], developed a set of context features for identifying the normal tissue with which a malignant masses are detected in the mammograms. The context features were taken from multiple views of the mammogram images in order to increase the performance significantly. Sung-Nien Yu [13] used a wavelet filter to detect all the suspicious regions using the mean pixel value. In the next stage textural features based on Markov random field (MRF) and fractal models together with statistical textural features were used and a three layer BPNN is used for classification. Subhash [30] proposed an algorithm by combining Markov random field and PSO.

Gath and Geva proposed an unsupervised clustering algorithm based on the combination of FCM and fuzzy maximum likelihood estimation [15]. Lorette et al. [16] proposed an algorithm based on fuzzy C-means (FCM) clustering to dynamically determine the number of clusters in a data set. This approach, however, requires a parameter to be specified, which a profound effect on the number of clusters has generated (i.e. not fully unsupervised). Similarly, Boujemaa [17] proposed an algorithm, based on a generalization of the competitive agglomeration clustering algorithm introduced by Frigui and Krishnapuram [18]. The algorithms found within the above paragraph try to modify the objective functions of FCM.

Particle swarm optimization (PSO) is a population based algorithm. This algorithm simulates bird flocking or fish schooling behavior to achieve a self-evolution system. In this paper a clustering method based on PSO based evolutionary computation is developed. It can search automatically the optimum solution space of the FCM clusters centers. The proposed PSO-FCM algorithm finds the cluster positions optimally and classifies the mammogram patterns.

The major objective of this paper is to take multiple texture features from the original image to discriminate between microcalcification and the normal tissue in the breast. As a first stage, the original image is decomposed using Integer Wavelet Transform (IWT) and features are extracted from the decomposed image using gabor features. In the second stage, the extracted features are compared by means of their ability in detecting microcalcification clusters using PSO optimized Fuzzy C-Means clustering. We use mammograms from the Mammographic Image Analysis Society (MIAS) database which contain 322 mammograms [19].

The paper is organized as follows. In Section 2 we summarize PSO-FCM mammogram screening CAD approach. Section 3 describes Classification results using MIAS database. Section 4 presents the conclusion.

## 2    PSO-FCM Based Mammogram Screening

### 2.1    Mammogram Database and Preprocessing

The UK research group has generated a MIAS database of digital mammograms[19]. The database contains left and right breast images of 161 patients. Its quantity consists of 322 images, which belongs to three types such as Normal, benign and malignant. The database has been reduced to 200 micron pixel edge, so that all images are 1024 x 1024. There are 208 normal, 63 benign and 51 malignant (abnormal) images. It also includes radiologists 'truth' marking on the locations of any abnormalities that may be present. The database is concluding of four different kinds of abnormalities namely: architectural distortions, stellate lesions, Circumscribed masses and calcifications.

As a preprocessing step, the breast area is separated from the background image. This saves the processing time and also the memory space.

### 2.2    Proposed Algorithm

We propose a novel approach to computer-aided diagnosis of breast cancer using mammographic findings. This is illustrated using the flowchart shown in Fig.1.

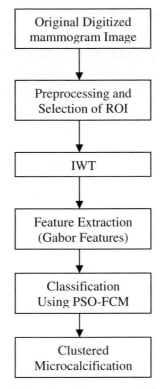

**Fig. 1.** Flowchart of our proposed CAD System

## 2.3   Integer Wavelet Transform

The wavelet transform is widely acknowledged to feature excellent decorrelation properties [22] and it exhibits excellent lossy compression performance, and has been selected for the new standard JPEG 2000 [20]. In fact, followed by efficient encoders which exploit the intra and interband residual correlation, and suitable rate-distortion optimization techniques, the DWT allows to form finely scalable bitstreams [23]. A more efficient approach to lossless compression is the use of integer transforms, such as the integer wavelet transform (IWT) [24]. The transform coefficients exhibit the feature of being exactly represented by finite precision numbers, and this allows for truly lossless encoding.

The lossless and lossy image compression performance of the IWT has already been reported in the literature [23]. Recently, the lifting scheme (LS) [24] has been introduced for efficient computation of the DWT. Its main advantage with respect to the classical filter bank structure lies in its better computational efficiency and in the fact that it enables a new method for filter design. Moreover, the IWT can be computed starting from any real valued wavelet filter by means of a straightforward modification of the LS [24]. Therefore, the LS represent a distinguished choice for the implementation of encoders with progressive lossy-to-lossless compression capabilities, providing a common core for computing both the DWT and the IWT.

## 2.4 Gabor Features Extraction

The word texture is in general regarded as surface appearance or tactile qualities. A texture can be regarded as a self-similar object. In image processing the texture of a region describes the pattern of spatial variation of gray tones (or in the different color bands in a color image) in a neighborhood that is small compared to the region. By definition, texture classification is to identify the texture class in a region, whereas texture segmentation means finding a boundary map between different textures regions of an image [25]. There is an ambiguity here since classification can be used for segmentation. We use the term texture classification in the following even though the goal of the classification is segmentation. Most texture classification algorithms start by finding a local feature vector which in turn is used for classification. Texture classification using learned (over complete) dictionaries and sparse representation is a relatively new area in texture classification.

The Gabor wavelet was first introduced by David Gabor in 1946. The use of features based on Gabor filters has been promoted for their useful properties in image processing. The most important properties are related to invariance, illumination, rotation, scale, and translation. These properties are based on the fact that they are all parameters of Gabor filters themselves. This is especially useful in feature extraction, where Gabor filters have succeeded in diverse applications, like texture analysis.

The Gabor wavelet is a sinusoidal plane wave with a particular frequency and orientation, modulated by a Gaussian envelope. It can characterize the spatial frequency structure in the image while preserving information of spatial relations and, thus, is suitable for extracting the orientation-dependent frequency contents of patterns.

Also, the use of Gabor filters in extracting textured image features is motivated by various factors. The Gabor representation has been shown to be optimal in the sense of minimizing the joint two-dimensional uncertainty in space and frequency. These filters can be considered as orientation and scale tunable edge and line (bar) detectors, and the statistics of these micro features in a given region are often used to characterize the underlying texture information.

A two dimensional Gabor function $g(x, y)$ and its Fourier transform $G(u, v)$ can be written as:

$$g(x, y) = \left( \frac{1}{2\pi\sigma_x\sigma_y} \right) \exp\left[ -\frac{1}{2}\left( \frac{x'^2}{\sigma_x^2} + \frac{y'^2}{\sigma_y^2} \right) + 2\pi j W_x \right]$$

$$G(u, v) = \exp\left\{ -\frac{1}{2}\left[ \frac{(u-W)}{\sigma_u^2} + \frac{v^2}{\sigma_v^2} \right] \right\}$$

where $\sigma_u = 1/2\pi\sigma_x$ and $\sigma_v = 1/2\pi\sigma_y$ gabor functions form a complete but nonorthogonal basis set. Expanding a signal using this basis provides a localized frequency description. A class of self-similar functions, referred to as Gabor wavelets in the following discussion, is now considered. Let $g(x, y)$ be the mother Gabor wavelet, then this self-similar filter dictionary can be obtained by appropriate dilations and rotations of $g(x, y)$ through the generating function:

$$g_{mn}(x, y) = a^{-m}G(x', y'), a > 1, \ m, \ n = \text{integer}$$

$$x' = a^{-m}(x\cos\theta + y\sin\theta), \text{ and } y' = a^{-m}(-x\sin\theta + y\cos\theta),$$

Where, $\theta = n\pi / K$ and K is the total number of orientations. The scale factor $a^{-m}$ is meant to ensure that the energy is independent of m.

The nonorthogonality of the gabor filters implies that there is redundant information in the filtered images, and the following strategy is used to reduce this redundancy. Let $U_l$ and $U_h$ denote the lower and upper center frequencies of interest. Let K be the number of orientations and S be the number of scaled in the multiresolution decomposition. The filter parameters $\sigma_u$ and $\sigma_v$ (and thus $\sigma_x$ and $\sigma_y$) are computed using the following formulas.

$$a = (U_h / U_l)^{-\frac{1}{S-1}}$$

$$\sigma_u = \frac{(a-1)U_h}{(a+1)\sqrt{2\ln 2}}$$

$$\sigma_v = \tan\left(\frac{\pi}{2k}\right)\left[U_h - 2\ln\left(\frac{\sigma_u^2}{U_h}\right)\right]\left[2\ln 2 - \frac{(2\ln 2)^2\sigma_u^2}{U_h^2}\right]^{-\frac{1}{2}}$$

Where $W = U_h$ and $m = 0,1,...., S-1$. In order to eliminate sensitivity of the filter response to absolute intensity values, the real components of the gabor filters are biased by adding a constant to make then zero mean.

## 2.5 PSO-FCM Classification

Particle swarm optimizers (PSO) are population-based optimization algorithms modeled after the simulation of social behavior of bird flocks [26],[27]. PSO is generally considered to be an evolutionary computation (EC) paradigm. Other EC paradigms include genetic algorithms (GA), genetic programming (GP), evolutionary strategies (ES), and evolutionary programming (EP) [28]. These approaches simulate biological evolution and are population-based. In a PSO system, a swarm of individuals (called *particles*) fly through the search space. Each particle represents a candidate solution to the optimization problem. The position of a particle is influenced by the best position visited by itself (i.e. its own experience) and the position of the best particle in its neighborhood (i.e. the experience of neighboring particles). When the neighborhood of a particle is the entire swarm, the best position in the neighborhood is referred to as the global best particle, and the resulting algorithm is referred to as a *gbest* PSO. When smaller neighborhoods are used, the algorithm is generally referred to as a *pbest* PSO [29]. The performance of each particle (i.e. how close the particle is from the global optimum) is measured using a fitness function that varies depending on the optimization problem.

410     J. Dheeba and T. Selvi

The working of PSO for Fuzzy C-means clustering is described as: for a D-dimensional search space the position of the $i^{th}$ particle is represented as $X_i = (x_{i1}, x_{i2}, ...., x_{iD})$. Each particle maintains a memory of its previous best position $P_{best} = (p_{i1}, p_{i2}, ..., p_{iD})$. The best one among all the particles in the population is represented as $P_{gbest} = (p_{g1}, p_{g2}, ..., p_{gD})$. The velocity of each particle is represented as $Vi = (v_{i1}, v_{i2}, ...., v_{iD})$. In each iteration, the $p$ vector of the particle with best fitness in the local neighbourhood, designated $g$, and the $p$ vector of the current particle are combined to adjust the velocity along each dimension and a new position of the particle is determined using that velocity. The two basic equations which govern the working of PSO are that of velocity vector and position vector given by:

$$v_{id}(t+1) = wv_{id}(t) + c_1 r_{id}(t)(p_{id}(t) - x_{id}(t)) +$$
$$c_2 r_{2d}(t)(p_{gd}(t) - x_{id}(t))$$

(1)

$$x_{id}(t+1) = x_{id}(t) + v_{id}(t+1)$$

(2)

The first part of equation (1) represents the inertia of the previous velocity, the second part is the cognition part and it tells us about the personal experience of the particle, the third part represents the cooperation among particles and is therefore named as the social component. Acceleration constants $c_1, c_2$ and inertia weight $w$ are the predefined by the user and $r_1, r_2$ are the uniformly generated random numbers in the range of $[0,1]$.

In the context of clustering, a single particle represents the FCM *membership matrix* vectors. That is, in swarm algorithm each particle $X_i$ represents a number of candidate membership matrix for the current data vectors.

Fig. 2 is an example of the encoding of the single particle in the PSO initial population. Let the number of clusters be two, mammogram with normal tissue and with cancer tissue, and the search space is two-dimension. The string of this particle represents two cluster centers [(-4.5, 9) and (23, 15)].

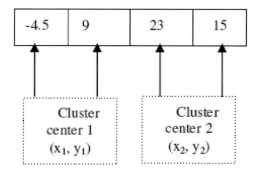

**Fig. 2.** An encoding of single particle in the initial population

Using the standard PSO, the image data vectors are clustered as,

**Step 1:** Initialize each particle to contain FCM membership matrix U with random values between 0 and 1 such that the following constraint is satisfied

$$\sum_{i=1}^{c} u_{ij} = 1 \quad \text{for} \quad j = 1,2,..,n$$

*where c is the no. of clusters*

**Step 2:** for $i = 1$ to $it_{max}$ do

1. For each particle $i$ calculate the $c$ fuzzy cluster center $c_i$, $i = 1,2$ using equation 3.

$$c_i = \frac{\sum_{j=1}^{n} u_{ij}^m x_j}{\sum_{j=1}^{n} u_{ij}^m} \tag{3}$$

2. Compute the fitness function by equation 4

$$J(U, c_1,...,c_c) = \sum_{i-1}^{c} J_i = \sum_{i=1}^{c} \sum_{j}^{n} u_{ij}^m d_{ij}^2 \tag{4}$$

where $u_{ij}$ is between 0 and 1; $c_i$ is the cluster centre of fuzzy group I; $d_{ij} = \|c_i - x_j\|$ is the Euclidean distance between i$^{th}$ cluster centre and j$^{th}$ data point; $m\varepsilon[1,\infty]$ is a weighting exponent.
3. Calculate the global best and personal best position using PSO as explained in 2.5.
4. Update the membership matrix $u$ by equation 5 using the global best/ personal best positions.

$$u_{ij} = \frac{1}{\sum_{k=1}^{c} \left(\frac{d_{ij}}{d_{kj}}\right)^{2/(m-1)}} \tag{5}$$

5. Update the cluster centroids using equation 3.

# 3  PSO-FCM Classification Results

## 3.1  MIAS Database

Our segmentation algorithm has been applied to 322 mammograms with masses of varying size and subtlety obtained from the UK (MIAS) database [19]. The images from this database have a resolution of 50 microns (0.05 mm/pixel), 8 bits per. pixel.

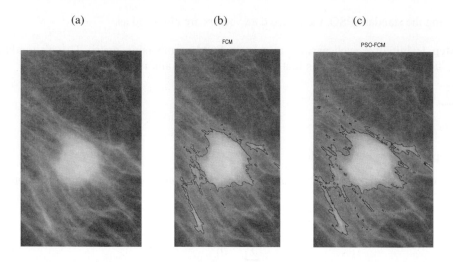

**Fig. 3.** Classification results (a) Mammogram pattern mdb015 of MIAS database. (b). FCM clustering results (c)PSO-FCM Clustering

The proposed method segments/classifies the input mammogram into suspicious and non-suspicious regions (i.e. normal breast tissue and malignant tissues). Our aim was that no case of malignancy-indicating microcalcification should escape radiological analysis. We therefore started from two basic assumptions: (i) the microcalcifications have an aspect that differentiates them from the other elements of the breast because of their different X-ray opacity; and (ii) since we are looking for microcalcifications that are in an incipient stage, they involve a very small proportion of the total area of the breast because they otherwise would be clearly visible to any radiologist and there would consequently be no point in using our system.

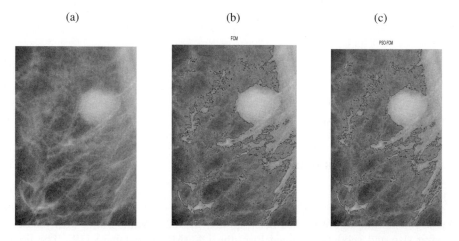

**Fig. 4.** Classification results (a) Mammogram pattern mdb025 of MIAS database. (b). FCM clustering results (c)PSO-FCM Clustering

The detection results for various mammogram patterns are illustrated in Fig. 3-4. Since those regions in a mammogram corresponding to tumor tissues have different texture patterns and gray levels than the normal ones, it is possible to classify these regions.

The results reported in this section are averages and standard deviations over 20 simulations. Furthermore, if the best solution has not been improved after a user-specified number of iterations (50 iterations was used for all the experiments conducted) then the algorithm will terminate. A classification accuracy true positive 88.5% is achieved for the database under study (i.e), MIAS Database which is high when compared to the classification accuracy of FCM clustering which is 83.4%. As a future enhancement a multi swarm PSO [31] can be used which takes interacting multiple swarms in a dynamic environment.

## 4   Conclusion

We present a novel approach to the problem of computer-aided analysis of digital mammograms for breast cancer detection. The algorithm developed here classifies mammograms into normal & abnormal. First, the structures in mammograms produced by normal glandular tissue of varying density are eliminated using a Integer Wavelet Transform (IWT) based local average subtraction. The gabor features are extracted and classification approaches using hybrid PSO-FCM shows good classification results. Using the mammographic data from the Mammographic Image Analysis Society (MIAS) database a recognition score of 88.5% was achieved using the proposed approach. In summary, we find that using the proposed CAD system can help radiologists to interpret mass lesions.

## References

1. Pisani, et al.: Outcome of Screening by clinical examination of the breast in a trial in the phillipines. Int. J. Cancer (2006)
2. Kopans, D.B.: Breast Imaging, pp. 81–95. J.B.Lippincoff, Philadelphia (1989)
3. Romans, M.C.: Report from the Jacobs Institute – American Cancer Society Workshop on Mammogram screening and primary care providers, current issue, "women's Health issues" Vol.2, pp. 169-172 (1992)
4. Sahiner, B., et al.: Classificaiton of Mass and Normal Breast Tissue: A convolution Neural Network classifier with spatial domain and Texture Images. IEEE trans. on Medical Imaging 15(5), 598–609 (1996)
5. Liangei, et al.: A Study on Several Machine-Learning Methods for Classification of Malignant and Benign Clustered Microcalcificaitons. IEEE Trans. on Medical Imaging 24(3), 371–380 (2005)
6. Cascio, D., et al.: Mammogram Segmentation by Contour Searching and Mass Lesions Classification with Neural Network. IEEE Trans. on Nuclear Science 53(5), 2827–2833 (2006)

7. Kim, J.K., Park, H.W.: Statistical Textural Features for Detection of MIcrocalcifications in Digitized Mammograms. IEEE Trans. on Medical Imaging 18(3), 231–238 (1999)
8. Strickland, R.N., Hahn: Wavelet Transforms for Detecting Microcalcificaitons in Mammograms. IEEE Trans. on Medical Imaging 15(2), 218–229 (1996)
9. Wang, T.C., et al.: Detection of Microcalcifications in Digital Mammograms Using Wavelets. IEEE Trans. on Medical Imaging 1(4), 498–509 (1998)
10. Verma, B., Zakos, J.: A computer Aided Diagnosis System for Digital Mammogram Based on Fuzzy Neural and Feature Extraction Techniques. IEEE Trans, on Informaiton Technology in Biomedicine 5(1), 46–54 (2001)
11. Hopse, R., Karssemeijer, N.: Use of Normal Tissue Context in Computer Aided Detection of masses in Mamograms. IEEE Trans. on Medical Imaging 28(12), 2033–2041 (2009)
12. Ferlay, J., et al.: cancer incidence, mortality and prevalence worldwide. In: GLOBOCAN 2002, IARC cancer base No.5 version 2.0, IARC press, Lyon (2004)
13. Yu, S.-N., Huang, Y.-K.: Detection of microcalcifications in digital mammograms using combined model-based and statistical textural features. Expert Systems with Applications 37, 5461–5469 (2010)
14. American Cancer Society. Breast cancer facts and figures 2009-2010. American Cancer Society, Inc., Atlanta (2009a)
15. Gath, I., Geva, A.: Unsupervised Optimal Fuzzy Clustering. IEEE Transactions on Pattern Analysis and Machine Intelligence 11(7), 773–781 (1989)
16. Lorette, A., Descombes, X., Zerubia, J.: Fully Unsupervised Fuzzy Clustering with Entropy Criterion. In: International Conference on Pattern Recognition (ICPR 2000), vol. 3, pp. 3998–4001 (2000)
17. Boujemaa: On Competitive Unsupervised Clustering. In: International Conference on Pattern Recognition (ICPR 2000), vol. 1, pp. 1631–1634 (2000)
18. Frigui, H., Krishnapuram, R.: Clustering by Competitive Agglomeration. Pattern Recognition Letters 30(7), 1109–1119 (1997)
19. Suckling, J., Parker, J., et al.: The mammographic images analysis society digital mammogram database. In: Proc. 2nd Int. Workshop Digital mammography, ork, U.K., pp. 375–380 (July 1994)
20. ISO/IEC FCD 15 444-1V1.0. (December 1999), http://www.jpeg.org/public/fcd15444-1.pdf
21. Ortega, A., Ramchandran, K.: Rate-distortion methods for image and video compression. IEEE Signal Processing Mag. 15, 23–50 (1998)
22. Antonini, M., Barlaud, M., Mathieu, P., Daubechies, I.: Image coding using wavelet transform. IEEE Trans. Image Processing 1, 205–220 (1992)
23. Said, A., Pearlman, W.A.: A new, fast, and efficient image codec based on set partitioning in hierarchical trees. IEEE Trans. Circuits, Syst. Video Technol. 6, 243–250 (1996)
24. Calderbank, R.C., Daubechies, I., Sweldens, W., Yeo, B.: Wavelet transforms that map integers to integers. Appl. Comput. Harmon. Anal. 5(3), 332–369 (1998)
25. Zhang, B.: Histogram of Gabor Phase Patterns (HGPP): A Novel Object Representation Approach for Face Recognition. IEEE Transactions on Image Processing 16(1), 57–68 (2007)
26. Kennedy, J., Eberhart, R.: Particle Swarm Optimization. In: Proceedings of IEEE International Conference on Neural Networks, Perth, Australia, vol. 4, pp. 1942–1948 (1995)
27. Kennedy, J., Eberhart, R.: Swarm Intelligence. Morgan Kaufmann, San Francisco (2001)

28. Engelbrecht, A.: Computational Intelligence: An Introduction. John Wiley and Sons, Chichester (2002)
29. Shi, Y., Eberhart, R.: Parameter Selection in Particle Swarm Optimization. In: Evolutionary Programming VII: Proceedings of EP 2008, pp. 591–600 (1998)
30. Subash, et al.: Detection of masses in Digital mammograms. International Journal of Computer and Network Security 2(2), 78–86 (2010)
31. Liang, J.J., Suganthan, P.N.: Dynamic Multi-Swarm Particle Swarm Optimizer. In: IEEE Swarm Intelligence Symposium, Pasadena, CA, USA, pp. 124–129 (2005)

# A Hybrid Particle Swarm with Differential Evolution Operator Approach (DEPSO) for Linear Array Synthesis

Soham Sarkar[1] and Swagatam Das[2]

[1] ECE Department, RCC Institute of Information Technology, Kolkata, India
`sarkar.soham@gmail.com`
[2] ETCE Department, Jadavpur University, Kolkata, India
`swagatamdas19@yahoo.co.in`

**Abstract.** In recent years particle swarm optimization emerges as one of the most efficient global optimization tools. In this paper, a hybrid particle swarm with differential evolution operator, termed DEPSO, is applied for the synthesis of linear array geometry. Here, the minimum side lobe level and null control, both are obtained by optimizing the spacing between the array elements by this technique. Moreover, a statistical comparison is also provided to establish its performance against the results obtained by Genetic Algorithm (GA), classical Particle Swarm Optimization (PSO), Tabu Search Algorithm (TSA), Differential Evolution (DE) and Memetic Algorithm (MA).

**Keywords:** Particle Swarm Optimization (PSO), Differential Evolution (DE), Antenna array, null control, Side Lobe Suppression.

## 1 Introduction

The main objective in antenna array geometry synthesis is to determine the physical layout of the array that produces the radiation pattern that is closest to the desired pattern. The shape of the desired pattern can vary widely depending on the application [1-3]. Most of the synthesis methods are concerned with suppressing the sidelobe level (SLL) while preserving the gain of the main beam, others deals with decreasing the effects of interference and jamming which can be achieved by controlling the null point [4]. For the linear array geometry, this can be achieved by controlling the spacing between the elements, while keeping a uniform excitation over the array aperture. Other techniques of controlling the array pattern employ nonuniform Excitation and phased arrays. Over the years design of antenna array involves state-of-the-art meta-heuristics like the Genetic Algorithm (GA), simulate annealing (SA) and Particle Swarm Optimization (PSO). PSO has proven to be the most effective one as compared to the others regarding this kind of optimization problem [5].

In this paper a hybrid evolutionary-swarm algorithms called differential evolution particle swarm optimization (DEPSO) applied array synthesis. DEPSO is inspired by Differential Evolution (DE) and PSO, the two most computational cost effective algorithms in recent years. This hybrid strategy restrains self-organized particle swarm dynamics and also provides the bell-shaped mutations with consensus on the population

B.K. Panigrahi et al. (Eds.): SEMCCO 2010, LNCS 646, pp. 416–423, 2010.

diversity by DE operator [6]. Experimental results establish that DEPSO achieves a faster convergence speed compared to PSO [6].

The rest of the paper is organized in the following way. Section 2 gives an overview about the formulation of the array pattern synthesis as an optimization task. In Section 3, the DEPSO algorithm is discussed with a brief introduction of DE and PSO algorithms. Experimental settings have been covered and the results have been presented in Section 4. Finally the paper is concluded in Section 5.

## 2   Formulation of the Design Problem

An antenna array is a configuration of individual radiating elements that are arranged in space and can be used to produce a directional radiation pattern. For a linear antenna array, let us assume that we have $2N$ isotropic radiators placed symmetrically along the $x$-axis. The array geometry is shown in Figure 1.

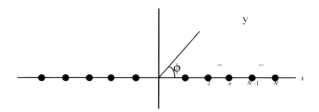

**Fig. 1.** Symmetrically placed linear array

The array factor in the azimuth plane can be written as,

$$AF(\phi) = 2.\sum_{n=1}^{N} I_n \cos[k.x_n.\cos(\phi) + \varphi_n] \tag{1}$$

Where k is the wave number, and $I_n$, $\varphi_n$ and $x_n$ are respectively excitation magnitude, phase and location of the $n$th element. The array factor can be further simplified by assuming a uniform excitation of amplitude and phase (*i.e.* $I_n = 1$ and $\varphi_n = 0$ for all elements).

$$AF(\phi) = 2.\sum_{n=1}^{N} \cos[k.x_n.\cos(\phi)] \tag{2}$$

Now the statement of the problem, addressed here, simply reduces to: apply the DEPSO algorithm to find the locations $x_n$ of the array elements that will result in an array beam with minimum SLL and, if desired, nulls at specific directions. The objective function used in this optimization problem is:

$$f = \sum_i \frac{1}{\Delta\phi_i} \int_{\phi_{li}}^{\phi_{ui}} \left| AF(\phi) \right|^2 .d\phi + \sum_k \left| AF(\phi_k) \right|^2 \tag{3}$$

Where $\Delta\phi_i$ represents the bandwidth to suppress and $\Delta\phi_i = \phi_{ui} - \phi_{li}$ and $\phi_k$ is the direction of the nulls. The left side ($f_{SLL}$) is used for the side lobe suppression while right side ($f_{NULL}$)) of the above equation symbolizes null control. The combined sum functioned as an objective function for the optimization algorithm for the minimization of both of them.

## 3   Hybrid DE-PSO Algorithm

### 3.1   Particle Swarm Optimization (PSO)

James Kennedy and Russel C. Eberhart introduced the concept of function-optimization by means of a particle swarm in 1995 [7]. In PSO a population of particles is initialized with random positions $X_i$ and velocities $V_i$ , and a fitness function, $f$, is evaluated, using the particle's positional coordinates as input values. In an n-dimensional search space, $X_i = (x_{i1}, x_{i2}, x_{i3},...., x_{im})$ and $V_i =(v_{i1}, v_{i2}, v_{i3},....,$                                    $v_{in}$                                    ).
Positions and velocities are adjusted, and the function is evaluated with the new coordinates at each time-step. The velocity and position update equations for the $d^{th}$ dimension of $i$-th particle in the swarm may be given as follows:

$$V_{id}(t+1)=w. \ V_{id}(t)+C_1.\varphi_1.(P_{id}-X_{id}(t))+C_2.\varphi_2.(P_{gd}-X_{id}(t)) \tag{4a}$$

$$X_{id}(t+1)= X_{id}(t)+ V_{id}(t+1) \tag{4b}$$

he variables $\varphi_1$ and $\varphi_2$ are random positive numbers, drawn from a uniform distribution, and with an upper limit $\varphi_{max}$ which is a parameter of the system. $C_1$ and $C_2$ are called acceleration constants, and $\omega$ is the inertia weight. $P_{id}$ is the best solution found so far by an individual particle, while $P_{gd}$ represents the fittest particle found so far in the entire community.

### 3.2   Hybrid Differential Evolution and Particle Swarm Optimization

Several analyses later on PSO revealed that sometimes it results in premature convergence especially with small $w$ or constriction coefficient. The performance can be improved by using a bell-shaped mutation, such as Gaussian distribution, but a function of consensus on the step-size along with the search process is preferable [6]. This can be achieved by using a DE mutation operator [8-11] along with classical PSO. The procedure for the implementation of DEPSO involves the following basic steps:

1.   In every odd iteration performs a classical PSO algorithm on each individuals of the population by using equation (4)

2.   For every even iteration executes the following steps
     a)        Calculate the difference vectors $\vec{\Delta}_1$ and $\vec{\Delta}_2$ by using equation (5) and (6)

$$\vec{\Delta}_1 = \vec{P}_{Ad} - \vec{P}_{Bd} \qquad A \neq B \tag{5}$$

$$\vec{\Delta}_2 = \vec{P}_{Cd} - \vec{P}_{Dd} \qquad C \neq D \tag{6}$$

Where $\vec{P}_{Ad}, \vec{P}_{Bd}, \vec{P}_{Cd}, \vec{P}_{Dd}$ are chosen from the local best, $P_{id}$ set.

b)      The mutation are provided by the DE operators on $\vec{P}_i$ ,with a trail point $\vec{T}_i = \vec{P}_i$, which for $d^{th}$ dimension:

$$\textbf{IF } (rand\ () < CR \textbf{ OR } d==k)$$
$$\textbf{THEN } T_{id} = P_{gd} + \delta_{id} \tag{7}$$

Where
$$\delta_{id} = (\vec{\Delta}_1 + \vec{\Delta}_2)/2 \tag{8}$$

c)      $\vec{T}_i$ will replace $\vec{P}_i$ only if it is better than $\vec{P}_i$

3.   The $\vec{P}_i$ and $\vec{P}_g$ of the new population are recalculated

4.   Repeat steps 1-3 until convergence.

$X_i$ is chosen for the mutation instead of $\vec{P}_i$ to protect the swarm from disorganizing. In addition to this, performing DE operator in the even generation will be helpful in order to achieve consensus mutation on $\vec{P}_i$ and diversity of the swarm.

# 4   Experimental Results

This paper illustrated the performance of DEPSO for synthesis of linear array geometry. The results have been compared with the state of the art algorithms like DE, GA, PSO, Tabu Search Algorithm (TSA), Memetic Algorithm (MA) [12-19].

**Table 1.** Geometry of the 12 element linear array normalized with respect to $\lambda/2$ (*median solution of 50 runs*)

| ALGORITHM | ELEMENT SPACING | | | | | |
|---|---|---|---|---|---|---|
| DE-PSO | ±0.4979 | ±1.2609 | ±2.2873 | ±3.2291 | ±4.6121 | ±6.0741 |
| DE/best/1/bin | ±0.1327 | ±1.3386 | ±1.8480 | ±2.9350 | ±3.8348 | ±5.1019 |
| GA | ±0.5068 | ±1.2611 | ±2.2885 | ±3.1910 | ±4.5611 | ±5.9998 |
| PSO | ±0.2470 | ±1.3109 | ±1.9367 | ±2.9717 | ±3.9272 | ±5.1808 |
| TSA | ±0.3881 | ±1.2588 | ±2.1076 | ±3.0525 | ±4.1881 | ±5.4507 |
| MA | ±0.4819 | ±1.2781 | ±2.2881 | ±3.2357 | ±4.6025 | ±5.9990 |

**Table 2.** Statistical values pertaining to example 1

| Algorithm | DEPSO | DE/best/1/bin | GA | PSO | TSA | MA |
|---|---|---|---|---|---|---|
| Mean | **0.008858** | 0.010395 | 0.009061 | 0.010843 | 0.011219 | 0.009196 |
| Standard deviation | **0.000021** | 0.000284 | 0.000681 | 0.000712 | 0.000319 | 0.000521 |
| P-Values | NA | 1.1894e-10 | 2.2917e-10 | 1.3493e-11 | 3.9034e-13 | 1.3493e-16 |

For DEPSO the following parametric setup is used for all the design examples considered here: $C_1 = 1.5$, $C_2 = 1.5$, $w=0.5$ and CR=0.3. For the competitor algorithms we used the best possible parametric setup as explained in the relevant literatures [20-26].In the first example metaheuristics were used to design 12 element array for minimum SLL in bands $[0^o, 82^o]$ and $[98^o, 180^o]$ and no null direction. Figure 2 shows the gain versus Azimuth Angle plot. Table 1 depicts the geometry of the linear array normalized to $\lambda / 2$.

Table 2 illustrates the mean objective function values and standard deviations as obtained for the proposed and above mentioned optimization technique. A nonparametric statistical test called Wilcoxon's rank sum test (with 5% significance level) for independent samples has been done to check the difference in final results in a statistically significant way.

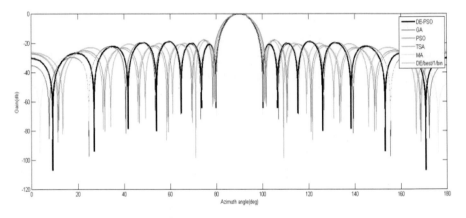

**Fig. 2.** Normalized patterns for 12 element array (*example 1*)

**Table 3.** Geometry of the 22 element linear array normalized with respect to $\lambda / 2$ (*median solution of 50 runs*)

| ALGORITHM | ELEMENT SPACING | | | | | | | | | | |
|---|---|---|---|---|---|---|---|---|---|---|---|
| DE-PSO | ±0.686 | ±0.686 | ±1.465 | ±2.585 | ±2.585 | ±3.797 | ±4.473 | ±5.498 | ±6.725 | ±8.331 | ±9.828 |
| DE/best/1/bin | ±0.077 | ±1.167 | ±1.788 | ±2.582 | ±3.389 | ±4.147 | ±5.233 | ±6.266 | ±7.647 | ±9.306 | ±10.831 |
| GA | ±0.0002 | ±1.061 | ±1.486 | ±2.419 | ±3.386 | ±4.285 | ±5.407 | ±6.846 | ±8.042 | ±9.136 | ±10.398 |
| PSO | ±0.3006 | ±1.177 | ±1.855 | ±2.685 | ±3.524 | ±4.428 | ±5.468 | ±6.580 | ±7.953 | ±9.552 | ±11.00 |
| TSA | ±0.6982 | ±1.071 | ±2.485 | ±2.541 | ±4.148 | ±5.479 | ±6.480 | ±7.573 | ±8.714 | ±10.211 | ±11.64 |
| MA | ±0.8113 | ±2.273 | ±3.157 | ±3.948 | ±4.770 | ±5.411 | ±6.432 | ±6.934 | ±7.896 | ±8.712 | ±10.124 |

The second example has minimum SLL in bands $[0^o, 82^o]$ and $[98^o, 180^o]$ and null direction in $81^o$ and $99^o$ .The array pattern obtained by various algorithms is described in Table 3. From Figure 3, which shows the Gain vs. Azimuth angle plot, it is established that DEPSO has minimized SLL to the greatest extent and has a low gain value at the null directions as well. Mean objective function values, standard deviation and p-value is listed in the Table 4. According to this table of DEPSO algorithm shows the lowest value.

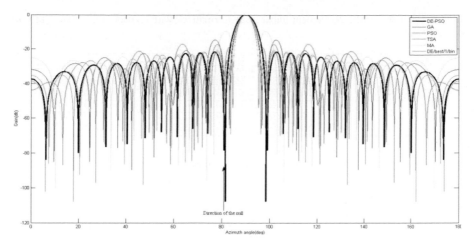

**Fig. 3.** Normalized patterns for 22 element array (*example 2*)

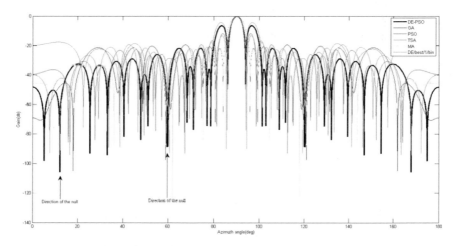

**Fig. 4.** Normalized patterns for 26 element array (example 3)

**Table 4.** Statistical values pertaining to example 2

| Algorithm | DEPSO | DE/best/1/bin | GA | PSO | TSA | MA |
|---|---|---|---|---|---|---|
| Mean | **0.010171** | 0.011593 | 0.023662 | 0.016755 | 0.021898 | 0.021630 |
| Standard deviation | **0.000118** | 0.001248 | 0.001201 | 0.001613 | 0.001109 | 0.001331 |
| P-Values | NA | 3.2547e-10 | 6.1304e-12 | 5.5647e-12 | 9.6808e-15 | 8.0040e-17 |

The third example describes design of a 26 elements array which has minimum side lobe level (SLL) in the bands $[0^o, 80^o]$ and $[100^o, 180^o]$ and having nulls at $12^o$, $60^o$, $120^o$, and $168^o$. Table 5 and 6 listed the elements spacing and comparative study of mean fitness function values, standard deviation and *p*-value as resulted from the different metaheuristics .The lowest mean value appeared in the case of DEPSO and also from Figure 3 it is evident that it results lowest side lobe level and maximum null depth in the desired direction of null.

**Table 5.** Geometry of the 26 element linear array normalized with respect to λ / 2 (*median solution of 50 runs*)

| ALGORITHM | ELEMENT SPACING | | | | | | | | | | | | |
|---|---|---|---|---|---|---|---|---|---|---|---|---|
| DE-PSO | ±2.095 | ±3.527 | ±4.408 | ±5.520 | ±5.847 | ±6.786 | ±7.519 | ±7.792 | ±9.063 | ±9.208 | ±10.43 | ±11.15 | ±12.45 |
| DE/best/1/bin | ±3.156 | ±4.462 | ±5.011 | ±5.834 | ±6.332 | ±6.836 | ±7.932 | ±8.053 | ±8.553 | ±9.106 | ±9.943 | ±10.44 | ±11.69 |
| GA | ±0.424 | ±0.847 | ±1.579 | ±2.468 | ±2.993 | ±4.391 | ±4.629 | ±5.640 | ±6.399 | ±7.791 | ±8.795 | ±9.974 | ±11.38 |
| PSO | ±0.579 | ±1.741 | ±2.806 | ±3.923 | ±4.885 | ±5.939 | ±7.100 | ±8.137 | ±9.171 | ±9.956 | ±10.75 | ±11.82 | ±13.00 |
| TSA | ±0.531 | ±1.491 | ±2.468 | ±3.445 | ±4.524 | ±5.501 | ±6.491 | ±7.268 | ±8.498 | ±9.514 | ±10.27 | ±11.44 | ±12.42 |
| MA | ±0.452 | ±0.851 | ±1.606 | ±2.497 | ±3.019 | ±4.397 | ±4.629 | ±5.687 | ±6.399 | ±7.792 | ±8.796 | ±9.976 | ±11.40 |

**Table 6.** Statistical values pertaining to example 3

| Algorithm | DEPSO | DE/best/1/bin | GA | PSO | TSA | MA |
|---|---|---|---|---|---|---|
| Mean | **0.009397** | 0.010556 | 0.050279 | 0.048131 | 0.061428 | 0.027195 |
| Standard deviation | **0.000949** | 0.000623 | 0.003163 | 0.003331 | 0.008221 | 0.001109 |
| P-Values | NA | 4.4826e-12 | 5.5647e-12 | 9.6808e-15 | 4.0040e-13 | 6.1304e-12 |

# 5 Conclusions

This paper elaborated the application of a Hybrid Particle Swarm with Differential Evolution Operator called DE-PSO in designing a non-uniform linear antenna.DEPSO efficiently find out optimal element spacing which resulting suppressed side lobe and null control in desire directions. Future research activities could be done to modify the existing algorithm to achieve more robustness. Optimization of excitation amplitude and phase of each element for array designing also could be carried out using DE-PSO in order to attain more control array pattern and exploring other array geometries.

# References

1. Godara, L.C. (ed.): Handbook of Antennas in Wireless Communications. CRC, Boca Raton (2002)
2. Bucci, O.M., D'Elia, D., Mazzarella, G., Panatiello, G.: Antenna pattern synthesis: A new general approach. Proc. IEEE 82, 358–371 (1994)
3. Rahmat-Samii, Y., Michielssen, E. (eds.): Electromagnetic Optimization by Genetic Algorithms. Wiley, New York (1999)
4. Lebret, H., Boyd, S.: Antenna array pattern synthesis via convex optimization. IEEE Transactions on Signal Processing 45(3) (March 1997)
5. Khodier, M.M., Christodoulou, C.G.: Linear array geometry synthesis with minimum side lobe level and null control using particle swarm optimization. IEEE Transactions on Antennas and Propagation 53(8) (August 2005)
6. Zhang, W.-J., Xie, X.-F.: DEPSO- Hybrid Particle Swarm with Differential Evolution Operator. In: IEEE International Conference on Systems, Man & Cybernetics (SMCC), Washington DC USA, pp. 3816–3821 (2003)
7. Kennedy, J., Eberhart, R.: Particle swarm optimization. In: Proc. IEEE Int. conf. Neural Networks, pp. 1942–1948 (1995)
8. Storn, R., Price, K.V.: Differential Evolution – a simple and efficient adaptive scheme for global optimization over continuous spaces. Technical Report TR-95-012,ICSI

9. Storn, R., Price, K.V.: Minimizing the real functions of the ICEC 1996 contest by differential evolution. In: Proceedings of the 1996 IEEE international conference on evolutionary computation, Nagoya, Japan, pp. 842–844. IEEE Press, New York (1996)
10. Storn, R., Price, K.: Differential evolution – A simple and efficient heuristic for global optimization over continuous spaces. Journal of Global Optimization 11(4), 341–359 (1997)
11. Price, K., Storn, R., Lampinen, J.: Differential evolution – A Practical Approach to Global Optimization. Springer, Berlin (2005)
12. Holland, J.H.: Adaptation in Natural and Artificial Systems. University of Michigan Press, Ann Harbor (1975)
13. Bäck, T., Fogel, D., Michalewicz, Z.: Handbook of Evolutionary Computation. Oxford Univ. Press, Oxford (1997)
14. Eiben, A.E., Smith, J.E.: Introduction to Evolutionary Computing. Springer, Heidelberg (2003)
15. Kirkpatrik, S., Gelatt, C., Vecchi, M.: Optimization by Simulated Annealing. Science 220, 671–680 (1983)
16. Glover, F., Laguna, M.: Tabu Search. Kluwer, Norwell (1997)
17. Taguchi, G., Chowdhury, S., Wu, Y.: Taguchi's Quality Engineering Handbook. Wiley, New York (2005)
18. Ong, Y.S., Keane, A.J.: Meta-lamarckian learning in memetic algorithms. IEEE Transactions on Evolutionary Computation 8(2), 99–110 (2004)
19. Kennedy, J., Eberhart, R.C., Shi, Y.: Swarm Intelligence. Morgan Kaufmann, San Francisco (2001)
20. Chowdhury, A., Giri, R., Ghosh, A., Das, S., Abraham, A.: Linear Antenna Array Synthesis using Fitness-Adaptive Differential Evolution Algorithm. In: IEEE Congress on Evolutionary Computation (CEC), WCCI 2010, Barcelona, Spain (2010)
21. Pal, S., Basak, A., Das, S., Abraham, A.: Linear antenna array synthesis with invasive weed optimization algorithm. In: International Conference on Soft Computing and Pattern Recognition (SoCPaR 2009), December 4-7, Malacca Malaysia (2009)
22. Udina, A., Martin, N.M., Jain, L.C.: Linear antenna array optimization by genetic means. In: Third International Conference on Knowledge-Based Intelligent Information Engineering Systems Adelaide, Australia (September 1999)
23. Cengiz, Y., Tokat, H.: Linear Antenna Array Design With use of Genetic, Memetic and Tabu Search Optimization Algorithms. Progress In Electromagnetics Research (PIER) C 1, 63–72 (2008)
24. Weng, W.-C., Yang, F., Elsherbeni, A.Z.: Linear Antenna Array Synthesis Using Taguchi's Method - A Novel Optimization Technique in Electromagnetics. IEEE Transactions on Antenna and Propagation 55(3), 723–730 (2007)
25. Ares-Pena, F.J., Rodriguez-Gonzalez, A., Villanueva-Lopez, E., Rengarajan, S.R.: Genetic algorithms in the design and optimization of antenna array patterns. IEEE Transactions on Antennas and Propagation 47, 506–510 (1999)
26. Tian, Y.B., Qian, J.: Improve the performance of a linear array by changing the spaces among array elements in terms of genetic algorithm. IEEE Transactions on Antennas and Propagation 53, 2226–2230 (2005)

# Sensor Deployment in 3-D Terrain Using Artificial Bee Colony Algorithm

S. Mini[1], Siba K. Udgata[1], and Samrat L. Sabat[2]

[1] Department of Computer and Information Sciences
University of Hyderabad, Hyderabad, 500046, India
`mini2min2002@yahoo.co.in`, `udgatacs@uohyd.ernet.in`
[2] School of Physics
University of Hyderabad, Hyderabad, 500046, India
`slssp@uohyd.ernet.in`

**Abstract.** The ability to determine the optimal deployment location of sensor nodes in a region to satisfy coverage requirement is a key component of establishing an efficient network. Random deployment of sensor nodes fails to be optimal when nodes are deployed where no targets need to be covered, resulting in wastage of energy. The objective of this paper is to place the given number of sensor nodes such that all targets are covered and the required sensing range is minimum. We model the sensor deployment problem as a clustering problem and the optimal locations for sensor deployment are obtained using Artificial Bee Colony (ABC) algorithm. We analyze how the sensing range varies with the number of sensor nodes and also carry out sensitivity analysis test to find the variation in sensing range if the sensor nodes are deployed in a near optimal position.

**Keywords:** Sensor Deployment, Target Coverage, ABC Algorithm.

## 1 Introduction

The emergence of Wireless Sensor Network(WSN) has paved the way for many advancements in the field of computer science and communication. But still there are many challenges that deserve lots of research work. Sensor deployment is one such problem that needs attention among many others. Deployment of sensor nodes needs to be cost effective and energy efficient. Dense deployment might incur significant deployment cost and maintenance cost. Placing minimum number of nodes for complete coverage will solve this problem. A target is said to be covered if it lies within the sensing range of at least one sensor node. A poor deployment strategy results in wastage of energy, which is the vital resource of sensor nodes. Deploying sensor nodes at a large area where the number of targets is less, requires an efficient scheme such that each node covers at least one target and the sensing range is minimum.

We aim at placing the sensor nodes at locations such that the sensing range is minimum. This problem of deploying sensor nodes can be solved using many

B.K. Panigrahi et al. (Eds.): SEMCCO 2010, LNCS 6466, pp. 424–431, 2010.

optimization techniques. To choose the optimal deployment locations, we use Artificial Bee Colony (ABC) algorithm, which is currently used to solve many combinatorial optimization problems [1].

## 2   Related Work

Clouqueur et al. [2] propose a method to determine the number of sensors to be deployed to carry out target detection in a region of interest. The minimum exposure is used as a measure of the goodness of deployment, the goal being to maximize the exposure of the least exposed path in the region. Watfa et al. [3] present a method to compute the minimum number of sensor nodes required for complete coverage of a 3D region. Andersen et al. [4] present an approach called discretization which modeled sensor deployment problem as a discrete optimization problem. The main drawback of discretization is that it is not possible to guarantee k-coverage of the complete region. Karaboga et al. [5] present a survey of algorithms based on bee swarm intelligence and their applications. Karaboga et al. [6] show that ABC algorithm can be efficiently used for solving constrained optimization problems. Karaboga et al. [7] compare the performance of ABC algorithm with the traditional back propagation algorithm and the genetic algorithm which is a well-known evolutionary algorithm. Karaboga et al. [8] compare the performance of ABC algorithm with that of DE (Differential Evolution) and PSO (Particle Swarm Optimization) algorithms, and EA (Evolutionary Algorithm) for a set of well-known bench mark functions. Simulation results show that ABC algorithm performs better and can be efficiently employed to solve the multimodal engineering problems with high dimensionality. Karaboga et al. [9] show that the Artificial Bee Colony algorithm can successfully be applied to clustering for the purpose of classification. Pan et al. [10] propose DABC (Discrete Artificial Bee Colony) algorithm which has the ability to obtain good results for the lot-streaming flow shop scheduling problems with total weighted earliness and tardiness criterion. Akay et al. [11] present some modifications to the standard ABC algorithm and the performance of the modified ABC algorithm is investigated for real-parameter optimization on both basic and composite functions. Udgata et al. [12] propose ABC based method for area coverage problem in wireless sensor network. The area under consideration is a two dimensional irregular terrain and the objective is to find the sensor node deployment positions in order to minimize the sensing range.

## 3   Problem Definition

### 3.1   Sensor Coverage

A sensor node located at $(x_1, y_1, z_1)$ can cover a target at $(x_2, y_2, z_2)$ if the euclidean distance between the sensor node and the target is less than or equal to the sensing range $r$.

$$\sqrt{(x_1 - x_2)^2 + (y_1 - y_2)^2 + (z_1 - z_2)^2} \leq r \qquad (1)$$

## 3.2  Mean of Location Points

The mean value of the location points $(x_q, y_q, z_q)$ for $q = 1, 2, \cdots N$, is represented by $(a_1, a_2, a_3)$, where

$$a_1 = \frac{\sum_{q=1}^{N}(x_q)}{N} \tag{2}$$

$$a_2 = \frac{\sum_{q=1}^{N}(y_q)}{N} \tag{3}$$

$$a_3 = \frac{\sum_{q=1}^{N}(z_q)}{N} \tag{4}$$

## 3.3  Sensor Deployment to Achieve Target Coverage

Given a set of $k$ targets $T = \{T_1, T_2, \ldots, T_k\}$ located in $u \times v \times w$ region and $n$ sensor nodes $S = \{S_1, S_2, \ldots, S_n\}$, place the nodes such that all targets are covered and sensing range is minimum. The objective is to cover all the targets and to minimize the function

$$F = \forall_j((max(distance(S_j, P_g)))) \tag{5}$$

where P is the set of all targets monitored by $S_j$, $j = 1, 2, \ldots, n$, $g = 1, 2, \ldots, h$, where h is the total number of targets $S_j$ monitors.

## 3.4  Cluster Formation

Partitioning the targets into clusters will be a key to identify the new position of sensors. Each sensor is associated to a cluster. Let the set of clusters to be formed be represented as $C = \{C_1, C_2, \ldots, C_n\}$. A target $T_i$ belongs to $C_j$ if and only if $distance(T_i, S_j) \leq distance(T_i, S_l) \forall_l$ where $l = 1, 2, \ldots, n$ ; $l \neq j$ and $i = 1, 2, \ldots, k$. After computing clusters, if any $C_j = \phi$, mark $C = C - \{C_j\}$ and it indicates that $S_j$ is not associated to any cluster.

# 4  Proposed Method

The target locations are stationary. A solution is a set of locations where the sensors can be deployed to cover all the targets and sensing range is optimal. Initial solutions are randomly generated. Let the solution population be $B$. Each solution $B_e = \{(x_1, y_1, z_1), (x_2, y_2, z_2), \ldots, (x_n, y_n, z_n)\}$ where $e = 1, 2, \ldots, m$, $m$ the total number of bees and $n$ the total number of nodes to be deployed, corresponds to a bee. The initial task is to form clusters according to their location. Each cluster has a sensor node associated to it. The Euclidean distances of the targets and the solutions are calculated. Clusters are formed based on this distance measure. Clusters are generated in such a way that no sensor location in a solution is left idle without forming a cluster. The number of targets in a cluster

```
 1: for each B_e do
 2:     var = 0
 3:     repeat
 4:        if var = 0 then
 5:           Calculate distance between each target and all the sensor locations
 6:           Form clusters by assigning targets to sensor nodes which is at min-
              imum distance (Sec. 3.4)
 7:           if number of clusters = number of sensor nodes then
 8:              Move the sensor location to each cluster centroid
 9:              var = 1
10:           else
11:              Move sensors without assigned targets to random target loca-
                 tions
12:           end if
13:        end if
14:     until var = 1
15: end for
```

**Fig. 1.** Pseudocode: Cluster Formation

will be less if sensor to which the cluster is associated is located at a remote place. The number of clusters is equal to the number of sensor nodes to be deployed. The employed bees return with the solution having the cluster centroids. All the deployment locations in a solution is replaced by the corresponding cluster centroid. The pseudocode for forming clusters is given in Fig. 1.

The Euclidean distance between each target and the sensor location to which it is associated is used as the fitness function to evaluate the solutions. Let $D_j = (D_{j1}, D_{j2}, D_{j3})$ be the cluster centroid of $j^{th}$ cluster. $F(D_j)$ refers to the nectar amount at food source located at $D_j$. After watching the waggle dance of employed bees, an onlooker goes to the region of $D_j$ with probability $p_j$ defined as,

$$p_j = \frac{F(D_j)}{\sum_{k=1}^{r} F(D_k)} \tag{6}$$

where r is the total number of food sources. The onlooker finds a neighborhood food source in the vicinity of $D_j$ by using,

$$D_j(t+1) = D_j(t) + \delta_{jm} \times v \tag{7}$$

where $\delta_{jm}$ is the neighborhood patch size for $m^{th}$ food source, $v$ is random uniform variate $\in [-1, 1]$ and calculates the fitness value. It should be noted that the solutions are not allowed to move beyond the edge of the region. The new solutions are also evaluated by the fitness function. If any new solution is better than the existing one, choose that solution and discard the old one. Scout bees search for a random feasible solution. The solution with the least sensing range is finally chosen as the best solution. The pseudocode of proposed scheme is given in Fig. 2.

```
 1: Initialize the solution population B
 2: Evaluate fitness
 3: Produce new solutions based on cluster centroids
 4: Choose the fittest bee
 5: cycle = 1
 6: repeat
 7:     Search for new solutions in the neighborhood
 8:     if new solution better than old solution then
 9:         Memorize new solution and discard old solution
10:     end if
11:     Replace the discarded solution with a newly randomly generated solu-
        tion
12:     Memorize the best solution
13:     cycle = cycle + 1
14: until cycle = maximumcycles
```

Fig. 2. Pseudocode: Proposed Scheme

## 5     Results and Discussion

We consider a $10000 \times 1000 \times 20$ region for our experiments. The number of bees is taken as 10, number of cycles is 5000, limit for neighborhood search is 50 and the number of runs is 10. The number of scout bees is half the colony size. MATLAB 7 is used for implementing the code.

### 5.1     Impact of Varying Number of Sensors

Initially, the sensors are randomly deployed in the region. Then we use the proposed scheme to find the minimum sensing range required to cover all targets when 10, 20, 30, 40, and 50 sensor nodes are to be deployed, for all instances. We also analyze how the sensing range requirement varies when these many nodes are deployed. The number of clusters increases as we increase the number of sensor nodes. As expected, when the number of sensor nodes to be deployed increases, the sensing range requirement decreases. Fig. 3(a) shows a region where 5 sensor nodes are randomly deployed to cover 100 targets. It is evident that random positioning of sensor nodes will lead to higher sensing range requirement. Fig. 3(b) shows the sensor positioning using proposed method.

### 5.2     Impact of Varying Number of Targets

We further experiment with 100, 150, 200, 250 and 300 targets required to be covered. The results reveal that for higher number of targets to be covered, the sensing range requirement need not essentially be high. Sensing range requirement is highly dependent on the location of the targets to be covered. The results can also be used to find the minimum number of sensor nodes required to cover specific number of targets in the 3-D region.

## 5.3   Sensitivity Analysis

It may be hard to deploy the sensors exactly at positions where sensing range is optimal. Sensitivity analysis is conducted to show that if the optimum sensing range is $r$, a minor variation in the deployment position will increase the sensing range by $r + \Delta r$. We have changed the optimum deployment positions by $\pm 0.05$ and calculated the new sensing range. $\Delta r$ in our experiments is found to be of less significance. With short variations in deployment locations, the sensing range is unlikely to change by a great deal.

**Table 1.** Experimental Results

| N.T[1] | Instance | N.S[2] | Sensing Range | | | |
| | | | Best | Mean | S.D[3] | S.A[4] |
|---|---|---|---|---|---|---|
| | | 10 | 186.98 | 188.13 | 0.64192 | 186.9811 |
| | | 20 | 114.3379 | 118.4548 | 2.1029 | 114.3384 |
| | 1 | 30 | 87.6874 | 90.0354 | 1.0400 | 87.6882 |
| | | 40 | 63.4054 | 65.3157 | 1.8324 | 63.4059 |
| | | 50 | 49.5816 | 50.9661 | 1.8140 | 49.5821 |
| | | 10 | 184.1918 | 184.7208 | 1.6730 | 184.1922 |
| | | 20 | 115.4610 | 119.3832 | 1.8695 | 115.4615 |
| 100 | 2 | 30 | 84.9064 | 87.0718 | 2.6032 | 84.9071 |
| | | 40 | 69.3854 | 71.6397 | 0.9229 | 69.3862 |
| | | 50 | 58.2466 | 58.4824 | 0.2932 | 58.2473 |
| | | 10 | 181.6067 | 182.1482 | 0.3771 | 181.6075 |
| | | 20 | 117.1343 | 119.0717 | 2.8190 | 117.1349 |
| | 3 | 30 | 77.1276 | 80.2721 | 2.1903 | 77.1282 |
| | | 40 | 63.3700 | 65.6508 | 2.3794 | 63.3709 |
| | | 50 | 47.1407 | 52.2644 | 3.5930 | 47.1413 |
| | | 10 | 191.7437 | 191.7967 | 0.1119 | 191.7451 |
| | | 20 | 128.0501 | 130.5561 | 2.0591 | 128.0512 |
| | 1 | 30 | 99.5088 | 101.5264 | 1.3337 | 99.5096 |
| | | 40 | 75.5250 | 80.8992 | 2.8299 | 75.5261 |
| | | 50 | 66.1258 | 69.5385 | 2.3705 | 66.1266 |
| | | 10 | 193.8134 | 195.6920 | 1.1346 | 193.8142 |
| | | 20 | 129.0478 | 131.6591 | 1.8178 | 129.0489 |
| 150 | 2 | 30 | 97.5421 | 99.9508 | 1.4614 | 97.5432 |
| | | 40 | 78.1811 | 81.8042 | 2.7662 | 78.1820 |
| | | 50 | 68.3036 | 69.8833 | 0.9382 | 68.3041 |
| | | 10 | 196.7644 | 198.9204 | 1.0617 | 196.7652 |
| | | 20 | 125.4089 | 127.3348 | 1.3931 | 125.4094 |
| | 3 | 30 | 96.5723 | 100.0147 | 3.1478 | 96.5733 |
| | | 40 | 81.4014 | 85.8361 | 2.4127 | 81.4021 |
| | | 50 | 63.7116 | 67.4450 | 1.7579 | 63.7124 |
| | | 10 | 202.7842 | 206.1761 | 2.4813 | 202.7851 |
| | | 20 | 133.5582 | 138.6081 | 2.3092 | 133.5594 |
| | 1 | 30 | 107.1941 | 111.3038 | 1.9069 | 107.1951 |
| | | 40 | 90.1866 | 90.5195 | 0.5383 | 90.1874 |
| | | 50 | 77.8637 | 80.5316 | 1.7654 | 77.8645 |
| | | 10 | 202.2031 | 205.2051 | 2.0391 | 202.2043 |
| | | 20 | 137.7456 | 138.2118 | 1.4743 | 137.7460 |
| 200 | 2 | 30 | 105.1987 | 107.9643 | 2.2147 | 105.1993 |
| | | 40 | 89.3053 | 92.0209 | 2.6471 | 89.3059 |
| | | 50 | 74.5064 | 79.0891 | 2.9762 | 74.5073 |
| | | 10 | 206.7405 | 209.8609 | 2.6877 | 206.7411 |
| | | 20 | 137.6746 | 140.7612 | 3.0012 | 137.6751 |
| | 3 | 30 | 108.8329 | 112.7664 | 3.3648 | 108.8334 |
| | | 40 | 88.5695 | 92.2584 | 2.5915 | 88.5699 |
| | | 50 | 76.1729 | 80.9785 | 2.0613 | 76.1736 |
| | | 10 | 201.2638 | 204.3816 | 2.8954 | 201.2685 |
| | | 20 | 141.5312 | 143.6458 | 1.7454 | 141.5344 |
| | 1 | 30 | 110.8853 | 114.1874 | 2.3604 | 110.8879 |

Continued on Next Page...

**Table 1.** (*continued*)

| N.T[1] | Instance | N.S[2] | Sensing Range | | | |
|---|---|---|---|---|---|---|
| | | | Best | Mean | S.D[3] | S.A[4] |
| | | 40 | 95.4957 | 98.9885 | 2.2606 | 95.4971 |
| | | 50 | 82.5617 | 86.0401 | 2.3175 | 82.5668 |
| | | 10 | 203.7413 | 206.7031 | 1.7217 | 203.7483 |
| | | 20 | 136.1346 | 140.1602 | 2.8649 | 136.1378 |
| 250 | 2 | 30 | 108.7985 | 113.2567 | 3.0677 | 108.7999 |
| | | 40 | 96.5735 | 98.4735 | 1.2601 | 96.5788 |
| | | 50 | 80.3470 | 85.5074 | 3.2465 | 80.3489 |
| | | 10 | 200.4533 | 203.1586 | 1.6736 | 200.4561 |
| | | 20 | 133.5535 | 140.1006 | 3.4084 | 133.5543 |
| | 3 | 30 | 112.4476 | 115.7390 | 3.0216 | 112.4487 |
| | | 40 | 92.9055 | 98.9916 | 3.9353 | 92.9066 |
| | | 50 | 83.7854 | 87.1102 | 1.8054 | 83.7869 |
| | | 10 | 205.6524 | 207.7388 | 2.5691 | 205.6539 |
| | | 20 | 140.6248 | 143.0383 | 2.2727 | 140.6250 |
| | 1 | 30 | 118.0386 | 121.1791 | 1.9145 | 118.0394 |
| | | 40 | 98.0940 | 101.7488 | 2.7508 | 98.0958 |
| | | 50 | 85.9487 | 88.8374 | 1.6634 | 85.9496 |
| | | 10 | 201.1333 | 203.3193 | 1.5883 | 201.1352 |
| | | 20 | 142.2615 | 145.7269 | 2.2225 | 142.2662 |
| 300 | 2 | 30 | 113.5598 | 117.4515 | 2.9796 | 113.5607 |
| | | 40 | 98.8548 | 102.5049 | 2.2987 | 98.8576 |
| | | 50 | 90.7467 | 93.2498 | 1.6390 | 90.7556 |
| | | 10 | 211.8635 | 213.2055 | 1.3112 | 211.8648 |
| | | 20 | 144.5674 | 148.0025 | 1.8398 | 144.5738 |
| | 3 | 30 | 112.9409 | 114.1154 | 1.3858 | 112.9415 |
| | | 40 | 97.4597 | 102.1549 | 2.5310 | 97.4641 |
| | | 50 | 87.9301 | 91.2699 | 2.5740 | 87.9302 |

[1] Number of targets, [2] Number of sensors, [3] Standard deviation, [4] Sensitivity analysis

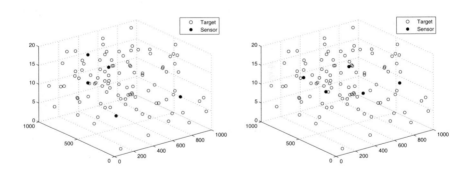

(a) Random placement of 5 sensor nodes  (b) Positioning using proposed scheme

**Fig. 3.** An example

## 6   Conclusion

We have introduced a scheme where sensor deployment locations in a 3D-region can be computed using ABC algorithm. It focuses on discovery of locations where the sensors can be deployed such that the sensing range is minimum. Simulation results show that a suitable solution can be obtained by using ABC algorithm. We experimented in a large region and for large number of sensor nodes to assess the performance of our proposed method. Deployment and maintenance cost can be minimized by using such a cost effective scheme. The sensitivity analysis shows the robustness of the scheme. It is found that slight change in the actual placement of nodes do not result in much change in the required sensing range. The method can also be used to find the minimum number of sensor nodes required for a specific sensing range to monitor targets in the region. In future, we propose to compare the performance of the ABC algorithm with other swarm intelligence algorithms. We also propose to extend this work for $k$-coverage and Q-coverage problems also.

# References

1. Karaboga, D., Basturk, B.: A powerful and efficient algorithm for numerical function optimization: artificial bee colony (ABC) algorithm. Journal of Global Optimization 39, 459–471 (2007)
2. Clouqueur, T., Phipatanasuphorn, V., Ramanathan, P., Saluja, K.: Sensor Deployment Strategy for Detection of Targets Traversing a Region. Mobile Networks and Applications 8, 453–461 (2003)
3. Watfa, M., Commuri, S.: Optimal 3-Dimensional Sensor Deployment Strategy. In: Proc. of IEEE CCNC 2006, pp. 892–896 (2006)
4. Andersen, T., Tirthapura, S.: Wireless Sensor Deployment for 3D Coverage with Constraints. In: Proc. of the 6th International Conference on Networked Sensing Systems, pp. 78–81 (2009)
5. Karaboga, D., Akay, B.: A survey: algorithms simulating bee swarm intelligence. Artificial Intelligence Review 31, 61–85 (2009)
6. Karaboga, D., Basturk, B.: Artificial Bee Colony (ABC) Optimization Algorithm for Solving Constrained Optimization Problems. In: Melin, P., Castillo, O., Aguilar, L.T., Kacprzyk, J., Pedrycz, W. (eds.) IFSA 2007. LNCS (LNAI), vol. 4529, pp. 789–798. Springer, Heidelberg (2007)
7. Karaboga, D., Akay, B., Ozturk, C.: Artificial Bee Colony (ABC) Optimization Algorithm for Training Feed-Forward Neural Networks. In: Torra, V., Narukawa, Y., Yoshida, Y. (eds.) MDAI 2007. LNCS (LNAI), vol. 4617, pp. 318–329. Springer, Heidelberg (2007)
8. Karaboga, D., Basturk, B.: On the performance of artificial bee colony (ABC) algorithm. Applied Soft Computing 8, 687–697 (2008)
9. Karaboga, D., Ozturk, C.: A novel clustering approach: Artificial Bee Colony (ABC) algorithm. Applied Soft Computing 11, 652–657 (2010)
10. Pan, Q.-K., Tasgetiren, M.F., Suganthan, P.N., Chua, T.J.: A discrete artificial bee colony algorithm for the lot-streaming flow shop scheduling problem. Information Sciences (2010), doi:10.1016/j.ins.2009.12.025
11. Akay, B., Karaboga, D.: A modified Artificial Bee Colony algorithm for real-parameter optimization. Information Sciences (2010), doi:10.1016/j.ins.2010.07.015
12. Udgata, S.K., Sabat, S.L., Mini, S.: Sensor Deployment in Irregular Terrain using ABC Algorithm. In: Proc. of IEEE BICA 2009, pp. 296–300 (2009)

# Novel Particle Swarm Optimization Based Synthesis of Concentric Circular Antenna Array for Broadside Radiation

Durbadal Mandal[1], Sakti Prasad Ghoshal[2], and Anup Kumar Bhattacharjee[1]

[1] Department of Electronics and Communication Engineering, National Institute of Technology, Durgapur, West Bengal, India
[2] Department of Electrical Engineering, National Institute of Technology, Durgapur, West Bengal, India
durbadal.bittu@gmail.com, spghoshalnitdgp@gmail.com, akbece12@yahoo.com

**Abstract.** In many applications it is desirable to have the maximum radiation of an array directed normal to the axis of the array. In this paper, the broadside radiation patterns of three-ring Concentric Circular Antenna Arrays (CCAA) with central element feeding have been reported. For each optimal synthesis, optimal current excitation weights and optimal radii of the rings are determined having the objective of maximum Sidelobe Level (SLL) reduction. The optimization technique adopted is Novel Particle Swarm Optimization (NPSO). Standard Particle Swarm Optimization (SPSO) is also employed for comparative optimization but it proves to be suboptimal. The extensive computational results show that the particular CCAA containing 4, 6 and 8 number of elements in three successive rings along with central element feeding yields grand minimum SLL (-56.58 dB) determined by NPSO.

**Keywords:** Concentric Circular Antenna Array; Non-uniform Excitation; Optimal Radii; Broadside Radiation; Sidelobe Level; Particle Swarm Optimization.

## 1 Introduction

Antenna arrays have been used widely in different applications including radar, sonar, biomedicine, communications, and imaging [1, 2]. Over the past few decades [3-12] many synthesis methods are concerned with suppressing the SLL while preserving the gain of the main beam. The array geometries that have been studied include mainly uniform linear arrays, uniform rectangular (URA), and circular arrays (UCA). A linear array has excellent directivity and it can form the narrowest mainlobe in a given direction, but it does not work equally well in all azimuthal directions. A major disadvantage of the URA is that an additional major lobe of the same intensity appears on the opposite side. Another popular type of antenna arrays is the circular array which has several advantages over other schemes such as all-azimuth scan capability (i.e., it can perform $360^0$ scan around its center) and the beam pattern can be kept invariant. For mitigating high sidelobe levels, Concentric Circular Array Antennas (CCAA) are

B.K. Panigrahi et al. (Eds.): SEMCCO 2010, LNCS 6466, pp. 432–439, 2010.

utilized, that contain many concentric circular rings of different radii and number of elements. It has several advantages including the flexibility in array pattern synthesis and design both in narrowband and broadband applications. CCAA are also favored in the direction of arrival (DOA) applications since these provide almost invariant azimuth angle coverage.

In this paper the authors study the uniform CCAA with central element feeding that have an equal inter-element spacing in a particular ring of the same array. The beam pattern, sidelobe level and beamwidth are examined with a design goal of optimum sidelobe level reduction. This involves nonlinear dependence between array factor and antenna element parameters, which becomes a highly complex optimization problem. The classical optimization methods cannot bear the demand of such complex optimization problem.

Classical optimization methods have several disadvantages such as: i) highly sensitive to starting points when the number of solution variables and hence the size of the solution space increase, ii) frequent convergence to local optimum solution or divergence or revisiting the same suboptimal solution, iii) requirement of continuous and differentiable objective cost function (gradient search methods), iv) requirement of the piecewise linear cost approximation (linear programming), and v) problem of convergence and algorithm complexity (non-linear programming). For the optimization of such complex, highly non-linear, discontinuous, and non-differentiable array factors of CCAA design, various heuristic search evolutionary techniques as GA and some variants of PSO [2, 13, 14] were adopted. In this paper, an optimal CCAA set is determined by optimizing both current excitation weights and radii of the rings with the help of a Novel Particle Swarm Optimization (NPSO) [15]. The array factors due to optimal radii and non-uniform excitations in various CCAA syntheses are examined to find the best possible design. Standard Particle Swarm Optimization (SPSO) is also employed for comparative optimization but it proves to be suboptimal.

## 2 Design Equation

Geometrical configuration is a key factor in the design process of an antenna array. For CCAA, the elements are arranged in such a way that all antenna elements are placed in multiple concentric circular rings, which differ in radii and in number of elements. Fig. 1 shows the general configuration of CCAA with M concentric circular rings, where the $m^{th}$ (m = 1, 2,..., M) ring has a radius $r_m$ and the corresponding number of elements is $N_m$. If all the elements (in all the rings) are assumed to be isotopic sources, the radiation pattern of this array can be written in terms of its array factor only.

Referring to Fig. 1, the array factor, $AF(\theta, I)$ for the CCAA in x-y plane may be written as [14]:

$$AF(\theta, I) = \sum_{m=1}^{M} \sum_{i=1}^{N_m} I_{mi} \exp\left[j\left(kr_m \sin\theta \cos(\phi - \phi_{mi}) + \alpha_{mi}\right)\right] \tag{1}$$

where $I_{mi}$ denotes current excitation of the $i^{th}$ element of the $m^{th}$ ring, $k = 2\pi / \lambda$; $\lambda$ being the signal wave-length. If the elevation angle, $\phi$ = constant, then (1) may be written as a periodic function of $\theta$ with a period of $2\pi$ radian i.e. the radiation pattern will be a broadside array pattern. The azimuth angle to the $i^{th}$ element of the $m^{th}$ ring is $\phi_{mi}$. The elements in each ring are assumed to be uniformly distributed. $\phi_{mi}$ and $\alpha_{mi}$ are also obtained from [14] as:

$$\phi_{mi} = 2\pi\left((i-1)/N_m\right) \qquad (2)$$

$$\alpha_{mi} = -Kr_m \sin\theta_0 \cos\left(\phi - \phi_{mi}\right) \qquad (3)$$

$\theta_0$ is the value of $\theta$ where peak of the main lobe is obtained. After defining the array factor, the next step in the design process is to formulate the objective function which is to be minimized. The objective function "Cost Function" $(CF)$ may be written as (4):

$$CF = W_{F1} \times \frac{\left|AF\left(\theta_{msl1}, I_{mi}\right) + AF\left(\theta_{msl2}, I_{mi}\right)\right|}{\left|AF\left(\theta_0, I_{mi}\right)\right|} + W_{F2} \times \left(BWFN_{computed} - BWFN\left(I_{mi} = 1\right)\right) (4)$$

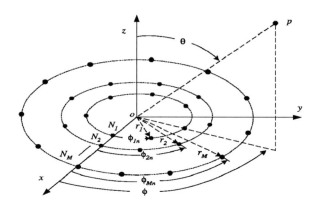

**Fig. 1.** Concentric circular antenna array (CCAA)

$BWFN$ is an abbreviated form of first null beamwidth, or, in simple terms, angular width between the first nulls on either side of the main beam. $CF$ is computed only if $BWFN_{computed} < BWFN\left(I_{mi} = 1\right)$ and corresponding solution of current excitation weights is retained in the active population otherwise not retained. $W_{F1}$ (*unitless*) and $W_{F2}$ (*radian$^{-1}$*) are the weighting factors. $\theta_0$ is the angle where the highest maximum of central lobe is attained in $\theta \in [-\pi, \pi]$. $\theta_{msl1}$ is the angle where the maximum sidelobe $\left(AF\left(\theta_{msl1}, I_{mi}\right)\right)$ is attained in the lower band and $\theta_{msl2}$ is the angle where the maximum sidelobe $\left(AF\left(\theta_{msl2}, I_{mi}\right)\right)$ is attained in the upper band. $W_{F1}$ and $W_{F2}$ are so chosen that optimization of SLL remains more dominant than optimization of $BWFN_{computed}$ and $CF$ never becomes negative. In (4) the two beamwidths, $BWFN_{computed}$ and $BWFN\left(I_{mi} = 1\right)$ basically refer to the computed first null beamwidths in radian for the non-uniform excitation case and for uniform excitation case respectively. Minimization of $CF$ means maximum reductions of SLL both in lower and upper sidebands and lesser $BWFN_{computed}$ as compared to $BWFN(I_{mi}=1)$. The evolutionary optimization techniques employed for optimizing the current excitation weights resulting in the minimization of $CF$ and hence reductions in both SLL and $BWFN$ are described in the next section.

# 3  Evolutionary Techniques Employed

SPSO and NPSO as implemented for the optimization of current excitation weights and radii of the rings of the CCAA are given in [14, 15]. So, the steps of SPSO and NPSO are not described due to limitation in space.

# 4  Experimental Results

This section gives the computational results for various CCAA synthesis obtained by SPSO and NPSO techniques. For each optimization technique eight three-ring (M= 3) CCAA structures are assumed. Each CCAA maintains a fixed optimal inter-element spacing between the elements in each ring. The limits of the radius of a particular ring of CCAA are decided by the product of number of elements in the ring and the ine-quality constraint for the inter-element spacing, $d$, $(d \in [\lambda/2, \lambda])$. For all sets of ex-periments, the number of elements for the inner most ring is $N_1$, for outermost ring is $N_3$, whereas the middle ring consists of $N_2$ number of elements. For all the cases, $\theta_0 =$ $0^0$ and $\phi = \Pi/4$ are considered so that the peak of the main lobe starts from the origin.

Since PSO techniques are sometimes quite sensitive to certain parameters, the simu-lation parameters should be carefully chosen. Best chosen maximum population pool size, $n_p = 120$, maximum iteration cycles, $N_m = 40$.

The SPSO and NPSO generate a set of optimal non-uniform current excitation weights and optimal radii for each synthesis set of CCAA. $I_{mi}=1$ corresponds to uni-form current excitation. Sets of three-ring CCAA ($N_1$, $N_2$, $N_3$) synthesis considered are (3,5,7), (4,6,8), (5,7,9), (6,8,10), (7,9,11), (8,10,12), (9,11,13), and (10,12,13) elements with central element feeding. Some of the optimal results are shown in Tables 2-3. Table 1 depicts SLL values and BWFN values for all corresponding uniformly excited ($I_{mi}=1$) CCAA synthesis sets.

## 4.1  Analysis of Radiation Patterns of CCAA

Figs. 2-3 depict the substantial reductions in SLL with optimal non-uniform current excitation weights and radii, as compared to the case of non-optimal uniform current excitation weights and radii (considering fixed inter-element spacing, d=λ/2). As seen from Tables 2, SLL reduces to -52.24 dB for Set II, -40.86 dB for Set IV, and -37.64 dB for Set VI; with respect to -15.90 dB, -12.16 dB and -10.78 dB respectively for SPSO technique. The improved SLL values shown in Table 3 are -56.58 dB, -42.72 dB and -40.58 dB with initial values of -15.90 dB, -12.16 dB and -10.78 dB for the CCAA Set II, Set IV and Set VI elements respectively for NPSO technique. Above results revels that the CCAA Set No. II along with central element feeding yields grand maximum SLL reduction among all the sets; so, this is the optimal set.

## 4.2  Convergence Profiles of SPSO and NPSO

The minimum $CF$ values are plotted against the number of iteration cycles to get the convergence profiles for the optimization techniques. Figs. 4(a)-(b) show the convergence profiles for SPSO and NPSO in case of non-uniformly excited CCAA Set No. II respectively. The grand minimum $CF$ values are 0.0892 and 0.0511 for SPSO and

**Table 1.** SLL and BWFN for uniformly excited ( $I_{mi}$=1) CCAA sets with central element feeding

| Set No. | No. of elements in each rings ($N_1$,$N_2$,$N_3$) | SLL (dB) | BWFN (deg) |
|---------|-----------------------------------------------------|----------|------------|
| I | 3, 5, 7 | -32.69 | 152.6 |
| II | 4, 6, 8 | -15.90 | 108.0 |
| III | 5, 7, 9 | -13.20 | 88.4 |
| IV | 6, 8, 10 | -12.16 | 75.2 |
| V | 7, 9, 11 | -11.34 | 65.5 |
| VI | 8, 10, 12 | -10.78 | 58.6 |
| VII | 9, 11, 13 | -10.34 | 52.9 |
| VIII | 10, 12, 14 | -10.00 | 47.7 |

**Table 2.** Current Excitation Weights, Radii, SLL and BWFN For Non-Uniformly Excited CCAA with Central Element Feeding Using SPSO

| Set No. | ( $I_{11}, I_{12}$ ,....., $I_{mi}$); ($r_1$, $r_2$, $r_3$) in $\lambda$ | SLL (dB) | BWFN (deg) |
|---------|---------------------------------------------------------------------------|----------|------------|
| II | 0     1.0000     0.3508     0.9772     0.3377     0<br>0.3742     0.2997     0.9960     0.5374     0.8504<br>0.1859   0.4974   0.2067     0   0.4706   0.5251<br>0.4553   0.4325;   0.3647   0.5970   1.1144 | -52.12 | 99.8 |
| IV | 0.1866     0     0     0     0.4641     0.1288<br>0.3985   1.0000   1.0000   1.0000   0.5982     0<br>0     1.0000     0     0.7102     0.4139     1.0000<br>1.0000   0.7140   0.2517     0   0.5849   0.7264<br>0.0071;   0.5444   0.7453   1.2602 | -40.86 | 77.0 |
| VI | 1.0000     1.0000     0.9074     0.7550     1.0000<br>0.9487     0   1.0000     0   0.1364   0.2756<br>0.6475   0.9540   0.6517   1.0000     0   1.0000<br>1.0000   0.3702     0   0.6115   0.8899     0<br>0.1866   0.4487   1.0000   0.1584   1.0000<br>0.9973   1.0000     0;   0.8385   0.9184<br>1.6350 | -37.64 | 59.7 |

NPSO respectively. Comparing the convergence profiles of both techniques, NPSO shows the minimum cost function (*CF*) value as compared to SPSO. So, NPSO has better optimization performance. All computations were done in MATLAB 7.5 on core (TM) 2 duo processor, 3.00 GHz with 2 GB RAM.

**Table 3.** Current excitation weights, radii, SLL and BWFN for non-uniformly excited CCAA with central element feeding using NPSO

| Set No. | $(I_{11}, I_{12}, ...., I_{mi})$; $(r_1, r_2, r_3)$ in $\lambda$ | SLL (dB) | BWFN (deg) |
|---|---|---|---|
| II | 1.0000    0    1.0000    1.0000    1.0000    0.4792<br>0.8311    0.7740    0.7482    0    1.0000    0.2231<br>0.4288    0.1811    0.1903    0.4197    0.9701<br>0.5448    0.4866;    0.4196    0.5978    1.1772 | -56.58 | 101.1 |
| IV | 0.2181    0.1979    0.6014    0.6522    0.5822<br>0.6475    1.0000    1.0000    0    0.9253    0.3164<br>0    0.6744    0    1.0000    0.7360    0    0<br>1.0000    1.0000    0.4316    0    0    1.0000<br>0.4119;    0.5617    0.7794    1.2598 | -42.72 | 77.2 |
| VI | 0    0.2342    0    1.0000    0.5326    0.0423<br>0    1.0000    1.0000    0.5188    0.7021    0.7418<br>0.8449    0.2925    0.3341    1.0000    0.3605<br>0.8883    0    0.4751    0.1944    0.7718    0<br>0.4892    0.3968    0.3215    0.2615    0.5273<br>1.0000    1.0000    0.1530;    0.8288    0.9033<br>1.5925 | -40.58 | 60.6 |

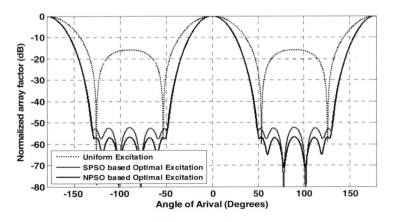

**Fig. 2.** Broadside Radiation for a uniformly excited CCAA and corresponding SPSO and NPSO based non-uniformly excited CCAA Set II with central element feeding

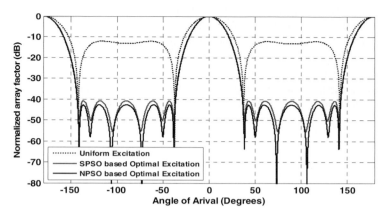

**Fig. 3.** Broadside Radiation for a uniformly excited CCAA and corresponding SPSO and NPSO based non-uniformly excited CCAA Set IV with central element feeding

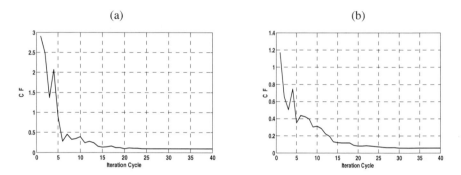

**Fig. 4.** Convergence profile for the (a) SPSO and (b) NPSO in case of non-uniformly excited CCAA Set No. II

## 5   Conclusions

This paper illustrates how to model the optimal synthesis of non-uniformly excitation in three-ring CCAA with optimal radii for maximum sidelobe level reduction of the broadside radiation patterns using the evolutionary optimization techniques as SPSO and NPSO. NPSO technique proves to be more robust technique; yields true optimal excitations and global minimum values of SLL for all sets of CCAA designs. SPSO is less robust and yield suboptimal results. Experimental results reveal that the design of non-uniformly excited CCAA offers a considerable SLL reduction along with the reduction of BWFN as compared to the corresponding uniformly excited CCAA. The main contribution of the paper is twofold: (i) The CCAA set II, with central element feeding gives the grand maximum SLL reduction (**-56.58dB**) as compared to all other sets, which one is thus the grand optimal set among all the three-ring structures, and ii) Comparing the performances of both techniques, NPSO shows the better optimization performance as compared to SPSO.

# References

1. Balanis, C.A.: Antenna Theory Analysis and Design. John Wiley & Sons, New York (1997)
2. Haupt, R.L., Werner, D.H.: Genetic Algorithms in Electromagnetics. IEEE Press Wiley-Interscience (2007)
3. Stearns, C., Stewart, A.: An investigation of concentric ring antennas with low sidelobes. IEEE Trans. Antennas Propag. 13(6), 856–863 (1995)
4. Das, R.: Concentric ring array. IEEE Trans. Antennas Propag. 14(3), 398–400 (1966)
5. Goto, N., Cheng, D.K.: On the synthesis of concentric-ring arrays. IEEE Proc. 58(5), 839–840 (1970)
6. Biller, L., Friedman, G.: Optimization of radiation patterns for an array of concentric ring sources. IEEE Trans. Audio Electroacoust. 21(1), 57–61 (1973)
7. Huebner, M.D.A.: Design and optimization of small concentric ring arrays. In: Proc. IEEE AP-S Symp., pp. 455–458 (1978)
8. Holtrup, M.G., Margulnaud, A., Citerns, J.: Synthesis of electronically steerable antenna arrays with element on concentric rings with reduced sidelobes. In: Proc. IEEE AP-S Symp., pp. 800–803 (2001)
9. Haupt, R.L.: Optimized element spacing for low sidelobe concentric ring arrays. IEEE Trans. Antennas Propag. 56(1), 266–268 (2008)
10. Dessouky, M., Sharshar, H., Albagory, Y.: Efficient sidelobe reduction technique for small-sized concentric circular arrays. In: Progress In Electromagnetics Research PIER 65, pp. 187–200 (2006)
11. Shihab, M., Najjar, Y., Dib, N., Khodier, M.: Design of non-uniform circular antenna arrays using particle swarm optimization. Journal of Electrical Engineering 59(4), 216–220 (2008)
12. Ho, S.L., Yang, S., Guangzheng, N., Edward, W.C.L., Wong, H.C.: A particle swarm optimization-based method for multiobjective design optimizations. IEEE Trans Magnetics 41(5), 1756–1759 (2005)
13. Eberhart, R.C., Shi, Y.: Particle swarm optimization: developments, applications and resources, evolutionary computation. In: Proceedings of the 2001 Congress on Evolutionary Computation, vol. 1, pp. 81–86 (2001)
14. Mandal, D., Ghoshal, S.P., Bhattacharjee, A.K.: Design of Concentric Circular Antenna Array With Central Element Feeding Using Particle Swarm Optimization With Constriction Factor and Inertia Weight Approach and Evolutionary Programing Technique. Journal of Infrared Milli Terahz Waves 31(6), 667–680 (2010)
15. Mandal, D., Ghoshal, S.P., Bhattacharjee, A.K.: A Novel Particle Swarm Optimization Based Optimal Design of Three-Ring Concentric Circular Antenna Array. In: IEEE International Conference on Advances in Computing, Control, and Telecommunication Technologies, ACT 2009, pp. 385–389 (2009)

# A Particle Swarm Optimization Algorithm for Optimal Operating Parameters of VMI Systems in a Two-Echelon Supply Chain

Goh Sue-Ann and S.G. Ponnambalam

Monash University, Sunway Campus, 46150 Bandar Sunway, Malaysia
sueanngoh@gmail.com,
sgponnambalam@eng.monash.edu.my

**Abstract.** This paper focuses on the operational issues of a Two-echelon Single-Vendor-Multiple-Buyers Supply chain (TSVMBSC) under vendor managed inventory (VMI) mode of operation. To determine the optimal sales quantity for each buyer in TSVMBC, a mathematical model is formulated. Based on the optimal sales quantity can be obtained and the optimal sales price that will determine the optimal channel profit and contract price between the vendor and buyer. All this parameters depends upon the understanding of the revenue sharing between the vendor and buyers. A Particle Swarm Optimization (PSO) is proposed for this problem. Solutions obtained from PSO is compared with the best known results reported in literature.

## 1 Introduction

Two-echelon Single-Vendor-Multiple-Buyers Supply chain (TSVMBSC) is the definition of an integrated inventory model of Vendor Managed Inventory (VMI) system in a two-echelon supply chain that comprises of a single vendor and multiple buyers [8]. In the recent years, many research work and practical application has been done in VMI system in many industries. In some occasions, VMI is also known as the consignment inventory and has been widely used in various industries [2]. Stocks are kept in the buyer's location and payments are not made to vendor until it has been sold until stocks are sold. The typical VMI system involves the supplier monitoring the stocks in the inventory located at the buyer's location and assumes full responsibility in replenishing it.

It is proven through survey that VMI achieved higher penetration than just-in-time and stock less methods [2]. Evidently, in the long run, VMI benefit both side of the party, the buying company and the supplier. This is because, with this merging, there is a clear decrease in inventory related cost, and final sales volume. With such decrease, the purchase price will increase, and finally, most importantly, the channel profit, which is the measure of the supply chain success, increases. Moreover, with the share ales information under VMI system, there are less distortion in information between vendor and buyer [1, 6]. With this, the inventory cost will be reduced and capacity will be fully utilized.

The scope of this paper is to determine the optimal sales quantity $y_{jopt}$ to maximize channel profit. Based on the optimal sales quantity, the sales price, $P_{yjopt}$ and contract

B.K. Panigrahi et al. (Eds.): SEMCCO 2010, LNCS 6466, pp. 440–447, 2010.

price $W_{jopt}$ are derived. This problem is a nonlinear integer programming (NIP) as it involves two different sets of linear constraints, one for the sales quantity of the buyers and also the capacity of the vendor and 'n' integer variables.

## 2  Literature Review

Many researches have been done on two-echelon supply chain integrated models. Lu [7] formulated a model with the objective of minimization of the vendor's total annual costs without considering the cost of buyers in order to analyze its importance in the following cases such as products critical to buyers, products with high switching costs and high supplier concentration.

The relative performances of 'Identical Delivery Quantity (IDQ)' and 'Deliver what is produced (DWP)' strategies for delivering quantities using various parameters were analyzed by Viswanathan [9]. This is done with the objective to obtain minimum joint average annual cost in an integrated vendor-buyer inventory model. Lu [7] proposed to first find the optimal solution for the one-vendor-one-buyer case before presenting a heuristic approach for the one-vendor-multi-buyer case. It is suggested by Goyal [4] that a joint economic lot size (JELS) model where its objective is to minimize the total relevant cost for both vendor and buyer. Lu also mentioned that an essential assumption must be made before implementing the models. This assumption is that the vendor must know the buyer's annual demand and the holding and ordering costs that governs the buyer's inventory policy.

Woo et al. [10] discussed and develop an analytical model to obtain the optimal investment amount and replenishment decisions for both vendor and buyers. Their work is considered a pioneer model in investigating the effects of ordering cost reduction on the integrated inventory system.

Yao and Chiou [11] proposed a search algorithm and their algorithm obtained a better result than Lu's search procedure. Lu's model was considered and identified that vendor's production setup interval will affect the vendor's optimal annual cost function. It is a piece-wise convex curve, and therefore, the search algorithm can be developed to yield an optimal solution for any sub-problem.LINGO is a NIP solution provider for smaller scale problems [3]. Dong and Xu [2] proposed a model for when the number of buyers reduced to a single buyer, thus reducing the TSVMBSC problem to a single-vendor-single-buyer model. Nachiappan [8] proposed a Genetic Algorithm approach for the TSVMBSC problem. The performance of PSO and GA-AIS heuristics are compared with that of LINGO, DX model and GA model. The mathematical model presented in [8] is adopted in this research. Channel profit is maximized and profit is shared among the members involved in the supply chain due to ever increasing competition. Therefore this paper deals with the price and quantity of product to increase the channel profit with relation to buyers. Table 1 lists the notations, Table 2 to Table 7 shows the buyer and vendor related data used in this paper.

## 3  Particle Swarm Optimization (PSO)

Particle swarm optimization (PSO) is a population based algorithm where each particle represents a potential solution. This algorithm is first invented by Russel Eberhart and

James Kennedy. According to Haupt and Haupt [5], the thought process behind the algorithm was inspired by the social behavior of animals such as bird flocking or fish schooling.

Particles are fired into a multidimensional solution search space. This is where the position of each particle is adjusted based on their own experiences and the neighbors. Each of these particles represents a possible solution in the search space. These particles move around to search for the optimum solution. They cooperate and exchange information about positions they have visited. The particles move to a new position by adjusting the velocity. Then, they update their respective velocities and positions based on the local and global best solution. The two main components of PSO algorithm are the position update and velocity update.

Velocity update:

$$V_{t+1} = V_t + C1(PB - P_t) + C2(GB - P_t) \tag{1}$$

Where C1 and C2 are the local and global fitness (C1 + C2 = 1), PB = Particle best and GB = Global best.

Position update:

$$S = t + 1 = \frac{1}{e^{-vt}} + 1 \tag{2}$$

if $S$ more than 0, set $p_t = 1$, if $S$ less than 0, set $p_t = 0$.

## 4    Objective Function

The objective function for this context is finding the maximum channel profit of the supply chain. The optimization problem that maximizes channel profit $P_c$ is discussed in this section.

$$Maximize\ P_c = \sum_{j=1}^{n} \left\{ a_j y_j - b_j y_j^2 - 0.5\theta_j y_j^2 - [2(H_s + H_{bj})(S_s + S_{bj})y_j]^{\frac{1}{2}} \right\} \tag{3}$$

Subjecting to: Buyer sales quantity constraints:

$$y_{jmin} \leq y_j \leq y_{jmax} \tag{4}$$

Vendor capacity constraints:

$$\sum_{j=1}^{n} y_{jmin} \leq C \leq \sum_{j=1}^{n} y_{jmin} \tag{5}$$

Nonnegative constraints and integer:

$$y_{jm} \geq 0 \tag{6}$$

In this paper, an optimal sales quantity $y_{jopt}$ for the maximum channel profit $P_c$ of the Two-echelon Single-Vendor-Multiple-Buyers Supply chain under vendor managed inventory mode of operation is determined. After the derivation of the channel profit,

**Table 1.** Nomenclature

| Notation | Description |
|---|---|
| $a_j$ | Intercept value of the demand pattern of $j^{th}$ buyer |
| $b_j$ | Cost slope of the demand pattern of the $j^{th}$ buyer |
| $C$ | Capacity of the vendor |
| $H_{bj}$ | Holding cost of the $j^{th}$ buyer in independent mode |
| $H_s$ | Holding cost of the vendor in independent mode |
| $j$ | Buyer identifier ($j$ = 1 to n) |
| $n$ | Number of buyers |
| $Pb_j$ | Profit of the $j^{th}$ buyer |
| $P_c$ | Channel profit |
| $P_{copt}$ | Optimal channel profit |
| $P_s$ | Vendor profit |
| $P_{sj}$ | Profit obtained by vendor when supplying products to the buyer $j$ |
| $PR_j$ | Revenue share ratio between vendor and the $j^{th}$ buyer |
| $P(y)$ | Sales Price |
| $P(y_{jopt})$ | Optimal sales price of the $j^{th}$ buyer |
| $S_{bj}$ | Setup cost of the jth buyer per order in independent mode |
| $S_s$ | Setup cost of the vendor per order in independent mode |
| $W$ | Contract price |
| $W_{jopt}$ | Contract price between vendor and buyer $j$ |
| $y_j$ | Optimal contract price between vendor and buyer $j$ |
| $y_j$ | Sales quantity of the $j^{th}$ buyer |
| $y_{jmin}$ | Minimum expected sales quantity of the $j^{th}$ buyer |
| $y_{jmax}$ | Maximum expected sales quantity of the $j^{th}$ buyer |
| $y_{jopt}$ | Optimal sales quantity of the $j^{th}$ buyer |
| $\vartheta_j$ | Flow cost per unit from vendor to buyer $j$ |
| $v_j$ | Transportation resource cost per unit from vendor to buyer $j$ |
| $\delta$ | Production cost per unit |

subsequently, the sales price $P_{yj}$ corresponding to $y_{jopt}$ and acceptable contract price $W_{jopt}$ is derived. The mathematical expressions for these parameters are:

By substituting the optimal sales quantity $y_{jopt}$, the optimal sales price $P_{yjopt}$, is furnished as below:

$$P_{jyopt} = a_j - b_j y_{jopt} \tag{7}$$

By substituting the optimal sales quantity $y_{jopt}$, the acceptable contract price $W_{jopt}$, is as below:

$$W_{jopt} = \frac{a_j y_{jopt} PR_j - b_j y_{jopt}^2 PR_j + \delta y_{jopt} + 0.5\theta_j y_{jopt}^2 + [2(H_s + H_{bj})(S_s + S_{bj})y_{jopt}]^{\frac{1}{2}}}{(1 + PR_j)y_{jopt}} \tag{8}$$

**Table 2.** Buyer related data (one buyer)

| $H_{bj}$ | $S_{bj}$ | $a_j$ | $b_j$ | $y_{jmin}$ | $y_{jmax}$ | $\theta_j$ | $PR_j$ |
|---|---|---|---|---|---|---|---|
| 9 | 300 | 80 | 0.01 | 1000 | 2000 | 0.005 | 1 |

**Table 3.** Vendor related data (one buyer)

| $H_s$ | $S_s$ | $C$ | $\delta$ |
|---|---|---|---|
| 9 | 150 | 6150 | 40 |

**Table 4.** Buyer related data (three buyer)

| $Y_j$ | $H_{bj}$ | $S_{bj}$ | $a_j$ | $b_j$ | $y_{jmin}$ | $y_{jmax}$ | $\theta_j$ | $PR_j$ |
|---|---|---|---|---|---|---|---|---|
| 1 | 7 | 10 | 20 | 0.004 | 2000 | 4000 | 0.004 | 1 |
| 2 | 2 | 20 | 19 | 0.005 | 500 | 3000 | 0.0057 | 1.2 |
| 3 | 9 | 30 | 18 | 0.008 | 500 | 1500 | 0.008 | 1.2 |

**Table 5.** Vendor related data (three buyer)

| $H_s$ | $S_s$ | $C$ | $\delta$ |
|---|---|---|---|
| 9 | 15 | 5750 | 7 |

**Table 6.** Buyer related data (five buyer)

| $Y_j$ | $H_{bj}$ | $S_{bj}$ | $a_j$ | $b_j$ | $y_{jmin}$ | $y_{jmax}$ | $\theta_j$ | $PR_j$ |
|---|---|---|---|---|---|---|---|---|
| 1 | 7 | 10 | 20 | 0.004 | 2000 | 4000 | 0.004 | 1 |
| 2 | 8 | 20 | 19 | 0.005 | 500 | 3000 | 0.0057 | 1.2 |
| 3 | 9 | 30 | 18 | 0.008 | 500 | 1500 | 0.008 | 1.2 |
| 4 | 7 | 15 | 21 | 0.003 | 1700 | 3500 | 0.005 | 1.3 |
| 5 | 9 | 25 | 18 | 0.006 | 500 | 2500 | 0.007 | 1.4 |

**Table 7.** Vendor related data (five buyer)

| $H_s$ | $S_s$ | $C$ | $\delta$ |
|---|---|---|---|
| 9 | 15 | 9850 | 7 |

## 5  Algorithm Flowchart

- **Step 1: Extract Initialize and generate initial variables**
  Population size is set to be double the number of buyers, that is $popsize = 2n$.
- **Step 2: Generate initial population and velocity**
  The initial velocity and position are randomly generated.
- **Step 3: Generate binary string for buyers**
  The $j^{th}$ particle in the notation $y_j$ indicates the sales quantity for buyer $j$. Each particle is represented by a set of 10 bits binary number.

**Table 8.** PSO compared with LINGO, DX and GA

| Heuristics | $Y_{jopt}$ | $P_{yopt}$ | $P_{copt}$ |
|---|---|---|---|
| LINGO | 1535 | 64.65 | 26960.49 |
| Dong and Xu | 1535 | 64.65 | 26960.49 |
| GA | 1532 | 64.68 | 26960.42 |
| PSO | 1536 | 64.64 | 26960.5 |

**Table 9.** Comparison of PSO with LINGO and GA

|  | LINGO | | | GA | | | PSO | | |
|---|---|---|---|---|---|---|---|---|---|
| J | 1 | 2 | 3 | 1 | 2 | 3 | 1 | 2 | 3 |
| $Y_{jopt}$ | 2000 | 657 | 500 | 2002 | 673 | 500 | 2000 | 729 | 500 |
| $P_{yopt}$ | 14 | 15.7 | 14 | 14 | 15.6 | 14 | 12 | 15.3514 | 14 |
| $P_{copt}$ |  | 5982.1 | |  | 5978.2 | |  | 5979.8 | |

- **Step 4: Convert string to decimal interpolate to fit the range.**
  These particles are interpolated to fit the range of $y_{min} < y_j < y_{max}$ using the following equation:

$$y_j - y_{jmin} + \left( \frac{169(correspondingdecimalvalueofbinarystring)}{y_{jmax}} \right) (y_{jmax} - y_{jmin})$$

$$(9)$$

- **Step 5: Evaluate with objective function, $P_c$**
  The objective function of this research is maximizing the channel profit, $P_c$. The feasible solution $y_j$ are decoded and substitute into the channel profit using (3).
- **Step 6: Update velocity and position**
  The program repeats from step 3 until stopping criterion is met. The global best parameter will be taken to be the best generated channel profit. Finally, using the optimal sales quantity the optimal sales price and acceptable contract price are calculated for each buyer.

# 6   Performance Analysis

The performances of the models are tested against the objective function. By obtaining the optimal sales quantity, $y_{jopt}$, the channel profit,$P_c$ can be evaluated using (3). The evaluated channel profit generated subject to its constraints noted in (4), (5) and (6). Subsequently, the optimal sales price, $Py_{opt}$ and acceptable contract price, $W_{jopt}$ will be derived using (7) and (8) respectively.

## 6.1   One-Vendor One-Buyer

When the model is reduced to a single-vendor single-buyer problem, the iterative heuristics of the DX model is proposed to obtain an optimal solution. Using the data obtained from Table 2 and Table 3, the best solution obtained by the proposed PSO is compared with the results reported in the literature. The comparative results are presented in Table 8. Based on Table 8, it is found that the proposed PSO generates a solution better than solutions generated by DX, GA and optimal solution of LINGO.

## 6.2   One-Vendor Three-Buyers

LINGO Optimization solver is a tool that can be used to obtain optimal parameters for a small sized TSVMBSC problem. Based on the data provided in Table 4 and Table 5, the optimal operating parameters are generated using PSO. Looking at Table 9, the channel profit generated by PSO is relatively closer to the optimal channel profit generated through LINGO and slightly higher than the value produced using GA.

## 7   Conclusion

In this paper a PSO is proposed to obtain optimal parameters for VMI system in a two echelon supply chain. The existing models LINGO, DX and GA are used as comparison. It is found that the proposed PSO algorithm performs better than GA and DX and providing values closer to the optimal solution provider, LINGO. The assumption made in this model are assuming that there is a linear relationship between the price and the sales quantity, zero lead time, allowing no backlog and stock out. Besides that, the holding cost and setup cost for this study are assumed to be the summation of both of the buyer and vendor. However, in reality, it is generally less than that.

## References

[1] Chen, F., Drezner, Z., Ryan, J.K., Simchi-Levi, D.: Quantifying the bullwhip effect in a simple supply chain: The impact of forecasting, lead times, and information. Management science 46(3), 436–443 (2000)
[2] Dong, Y., Xu, K.: A supply chain model of vendor managed inventory. Transportation Research Part E: Logistics and Transportation Review 38(2), 75–95 (2002)
[3] Fahimnia, B., Luong, L., Marian, R.: An integrated model for the optimisation of a two-echelon supply network. Journal of Achievements in Materials and Manufacturing Engineering 31(2) (2008)
[4] Goyal, S.K.: An integrated inventory model for a single supplier-single customer problem. International Journal of Production Research 15(1), 107–111 (1977)
[5] Haupt, R.L., Haupt, S.E.: Practical genetic algorithms. Wiley-Interscience, Hoboken (2004)
[6] Lee, H.L., Padmanabhan, V., Whang, S.: Information distortion in a supply chain: the bullwhip effect. Management science 43(4), 546–558 (1997)
[7] Lu, L.: A one-vendor multi-buyer integrated inventory model. European Journal of Operational Research 81(2), 312–323 (1995)
[8] Nachiappan, S., Jawahar, N.: A genetic algorithm for optimal operating parameters of VMI system in a two-echelon supply chain. European Journal of Operational Research 182(3), 1433–1452 (2007)

[9] Viswanathan, S.: Optimal strategy for the integrated vendor-buyer inventory model. European Journal of Operational Research 105(1), 38–42 (1998)

[10] Woo, Y., Hsu, S., Wu, S.: An integrated inventory model for a single vendor and multiple buyers with ordering cost reduction. International Journal of Production Economics 73(3), 203–215 (2001)

[11] Yao, M., Chiou, C.: On a replenishment coordination model in an integrated supply chain with one vendor and multiple buyers. European Journal of Operational Research 159(2), 406–419 (2004)

# Enhanced Memetic Algorithm for Task Scheduling

S. Padmavathi[1,*], S. Mercy Shalinie[2], B.C. Someshwar[3], and T. Sasikumar[4]

[1] Asst.Prof., Department of Computer Science & Engineering,
[2] Professor, Department of Computer Science & Engineering,
[3,4] Student, Department of Computer Science & Engineering,
Thiagarajar College of Engineering,
Madurai-625 015, Tamilnadu, India
spmcse@tce.edu,
shalinie@tce.edu,
somsekaran@tce.edu,
tmsasikumar@tce.edu

**Abstract.** Scheduling tasks onto the processors of a parallel system is a crucial part of program parallelization. Due to the NP-hardness of the task scheduling problem, scheduling algorithms are based on heuristics that try to produce good rather than optimal schedules. This paper proposes a Memetic algorithm with Tabu search and Simulated Annealing as local search for solving Task scheduling problem considering communication contention. This problem consists of finding a schedule for a general task graph to be executed on a cluster of workstations and hence the schedule length can be minimized. Our approach combines local search (by self experience) and global search (by neighboring experience) possessing high search efficiency. The proposed approach is compared with existing list scheduling heuristics. The numerical results clearly indicate that our proposed approach produces solutions which are closer to optimality and/or better quality than the existing list scheduling heuristics.

**Keywords:** Direct Acyclic Graph (DAG); Task scheduling; Genetic algorithm; Memetic algorithm (MA); Hill-climbing Algorithm; Tabu search; Local search.

## 1 Introduction

To run a parallel program on a parallel computer it must be parallelized. This includes the decomposition of the program into (sub) tasks, the analysis of the dependencies among the tasks and the scheduling of the tasks onto the processors of the parallel system. The scheduling is the crucial part of the performance of the program. There are numerous variants of this problem depending on whether we consider communication delays or not, whether the multiprocessor systems are heterogeneous or homogeneous and other considerations. The objective of the task scheduling problem is to minimize the makespan (schedule length) i.e., the overall computation time of any application represented as Directed Acyclic Graph (DAG). Optimal scheduling

---

[*] Corresponding author.

B.K. Panigrahi et al. (Eds.): SEMCCO 2010, LNCS 6466, pp. 448–459, 2010.

of tasks of a DAG onto a set of processors is a strong NP-Hard problem. It has been proven to be NP-Complete for which optimal solutions can be found only after an exhaustive search many scheduling heuristics for which near optimal solutions were proposed in the literature [1, 2]. Classical scheduling model assumes that each task is processed on one processor at a time. Early scheduling algorithms did not take communication cost into account, but due to the increasing importance for parallel performance, consideration of communication cost is included in the proposed approach which is significant to produce an accurate and efficient schedule length. Genetic Algorithm [21, 22] is one of the most widely studied guided random search techniques for the task scheduling problem. Although they provide good quality of schedules, their execution times are significantly higher than other alternatives. Extensive tests are required for the set of control parameters used in GA-based solution.

GA for static scheduling of m tasks to n processors based on k-way partitioning was developed in [14]. Successive improvements to the initial schedule were made through reproduction, mutation and one-point crossover operators. The traditional methods such as branch and bound divide and conquer and dynamic programming gives the global optimum, but it is often time consuming [15]. The researchers [16] have derived optimal task assignments to minimize the sum of the task execution and communication costs with the branch-bound method and evaluated the computational complexity of this method using simulation techniques. Modern heuristic [17] are general purpose optimization algorithms. Their efficiency or applicability is not tied to any specific problem-domain. To improve the efficiency of the heuristics based approach, there exist guided random search techniques like Simulated Annealing, Tabu Search, Particle Swarm Optimization, Genetic Algorithm etc.

GA is not well suited for fine-tuning structures which are close to optimal solution [18].Memetic algorithms are evolutionary algorithms (EAs) that apply a separate local search process to refine individual. (i.e.) improve their fitness by hill-climbing). MA [19]can be viewed as a marriage between a population-based global technique and a local search made by each of the individuals. It is a special kind of GA with a local hill climbing. MA yields faster convergence when compared to GA, because the balance between the exploration and exploitation in the search process. Hybrid heuristics combines the feature of different methods in a complementary fashion results in more robust and effective optimization tools. Particularly, it is well known that the performance of evolutionary algorithms can be improved by combining problem-dependent local searches. MAs [23] may be considered as a union of population–based global search and local improvements which are inspired by Darwin principles of natural evolution and Dawkins notion of meme, defined as a unit of cultural evolution that is capable of local refinements. In MAs, several studies [23], [27] have been focused on how to achieve a reasonable combination of global and local searches and how to make a good balance between exploration and exploitation. MA evolve a population of individuals in which genetic operators are used to create new individuals which are all brought (closer) to their local maximum using local search. This may provide us with much better candidate starting points for local search to improve. To test the performance of the proposed approach, highly communicating task graph like Gaussian elimination is generated and also tested with randomly generated DAGs. The proposed approach converges faster than the GA.

The paper is organized as follows: introduction is followed by the problem definition which is presented in Sect.2.Section 3 discusses the fundamentals of GA and
MA. Section 4 introduces the proposed algorithms and implementation aspects. Section 5 presents the experimental results and discussions. Finally the conclusions and
future research directions are presented in Section 6.

## 2  Task Scheduling Problem

The most popular graph model used for the scheduling of programs is DAG which is
a directed and acyclic graph, $G = (V, E, w, c)$ representing a program $P$. Here $V$ is a
set of nodes (vertices) and $E$ is a set of directed edges. The nodes $n_i \in V$ is associated
with one task 'i' of the modeled program and the edge $e_{ij} \in E$ (with $n_i$, $n_j \in V$) is
associated with the communication from task 'i' to task 'j'. The weight w ($n_i$) assigned to node $n_i$ represents its computation cost and the weight w ($e_{ij}$) assigned
to edge $e_{ij}$ represents its communication cost. The communication cost among two
nodes assigned to the same processor is assumed to be zero.

Priority is computed and assigned to each task based on the following attributes
namely, Average Computation Cost (ACC), Data transfer cost (DTC) and rank of the
predecessor task (RPT).The ACC of a task is the average Computation cost on all
the 'm' processors and it is computed by using (1).

$$ACC(v_i) = \sum_{j=1}^{m} \frac{w_{i,j}}{m} \tag{1}$$

The DTC of a task $v_i$ is the amount of communication cost incurred to transfer the
data from task $v_i$ to all its immediate successor task and it is computed at each level
l using (2)

$$DTC(v_i) = \sum_{j=1}^{n} C_{i,j} : i < j \tag{2}$$

$$= 0 \text{ for exit tasks}$$

Where 'n' is the number of nodes in the next level. The RPT of a task $v_i$ is the
highest rank of all its immediate predecessor task and it is computed in eqn (3)

$$RPT(v_i) = Max\{rank(v_1), rank(v_2),...rank(v_h)\} \tag{3}$$

$$= 0 \quad \text{for entry task}$$

Where $v_1, v_2, v_3....... v_h$ are the immediate predecessor of $v_i$. Rank is computed for each
task $v_i$ based on its ACC, DTC, RPT values. Here, the maximum rank of predecessor
tasks of task $v_i$ as one of the parameters to calculate the rank of the task $v_i$ and the
rank computation is given by (4).

$$rank(v_i) = round\{ACC(v_i) + DTC(v_i) + RPT(v_i)\} \tag{4}$$

Priority is assigned to all the tasks at each level l, based on its rank value. At
each level, the task with highest rank value receives the highest priority followed

by task with next highest rank value and so on. Tie, if any, is broken using ACC value. The task with minimum ACC value receives the higher priority.

If a node $n_i$ is scheduled to a processor P, then the starting time on this processor as ST($n_i$, P) and its finish time as FT($n_i$, P). After all the nodes of DAG have been scheduled to the target system the schedule length is defined as maxi {FT ($n_i$, P)} over all processors. The Data Ready Time DRT ($n_i$, P) of a node $n_i$ is defined as the time at which the last communication from its parent nodes finishes. For a valid schedule, (5) must be true for all nodes.

$$ST(ni, P) \geq DRT(n_i, P) \tag{5}$$

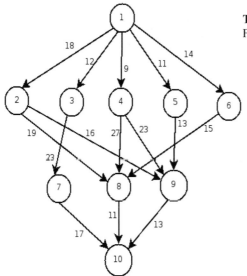

**Fig. 1.** Sample DAG

**Table 1.** Computational cost matrix (W) for Fig.1

| T | P1 | P2 | P3 |
|---|----|----|----|
| 1 | 14 | 16 | 9 |
| 2 | 13 | 19 | 18 |
| 3 | 11 | 13 | 19 |
| 4 | 13 | 8 | 17 |
| 5 | 12 | 13 | 10 |
| 6 | 13 | 16 | 9 |
| 7 | 7 | 15 | 11 |
| 8 | 5 | 11 | 14 |
| 9 | 18 | 12 | 20 |
| 10 | 21 | 7 | 16 |

A task graph is shown in Fig.1and its computation cost matrix is shown in Table 1. Let EST ($n_i$, $p_j$) and EFT ($n_i$, pj) are the Earliest Start Time and Earliest Finish Time of task $n_i$ on $p_j$, respectively. For the entry task $v_{entry}$, EST($v_{entry}$, $p_j$) = 0, and for the other tasks in the graph, the EST and EFT values are computed recursively, starting from the entry task, as shown in (6) and (7). In order to compute the EFT of a task $n_i$, all immediate predecessor tasks of $n_i$ must have been scheduled.

$$EST(n_i, p_j) = \max\{avail[j], \max(AFT(n_k + C_{i,k}))\} \tag{6}$$

Where $n_k \in pred(n_i)$

$$EFT(n_i, p_j) = w_{ij} + EST(n_i, p_j) \tag{7}$$

Where pred ($n_i$) is the set of immediate predecessor tasks of task $n_i$ and avail[j] is the earliest time at which processor pj is ready for task execution. If $n_k$ is the last assigned task on processor pj, then avail[j] is the time at which the processor pj completed the execution of the task $n_k$ and it is ready to execute another task. The inner max block in the EST equation returns the ready time, i.e., the time when all the data needed by $n_i$ has arrived at processor pj. After a task $n_k$ is scheduled on a processor pj, the earliest start time and the earliest finish time of $n_i$ on processor pj is equal to the actual start time AST($n_k$) and the actual finish time AFT($n_k$) of task $n_k$, respectively. After all tasks in a graph are scheduled, the schedule length (i.e. the overall completion time) will be the actual finish time of the exit task, $n_{exit}$. If there are multiple exit tasks and the convention of inserting a pseudo exit task is not applied, the schedule length (which is also called makespan) is defined as

$$makespan = \max\left[AFT\left(n_{exit}\right)\right] \tag{8}$$

The objective function of the task scheduling problem is to determine the assignment of tasks of a given application to processors such that its schedule length is minimized

# 3   Memetic Algorithm

The memetic algorithms [15] can be viewed as a marriage between a population-based global technique and a local search made by each of the individuals. They are a special kind of genetic algorithms with a local hill climbing. Like genetic algorithms, memetic Algorithms are a population-based approach. They have shown that they are orders of magnitude faster than traditional genetic Algorithms for some problem domains. In a memetic algorithm the population is initialized at random or using a heuristic. Then, each individual makes local search to improve its fitness. To form a new population for the next generation, higher quality individuals are selected. The selection phase is identical in form to that used in the classical genetic algorithm selection phase. Once two parents are selected, their chromosomes are combined and classical operators of crossover are applied to generate new individuals. The latter are enhanced using a local search technique. The role of local search in memetic algorithms is to locate the local optimum more efficiently then the genetic algorithm.

A. Local Search Algorithm
Local search can be thought of as the process of an individual improving its idea of the solution .The hill climbing search algorithm is the default local search algorithm. It is simply a loop that continuously moves in the direction of increasing quality value. It starts with the random solution and iteratively makes small changes to the solution each time improving it. If the algorithm cannot see any improvement anymore, it terminates.

Tabu search is a meta heuristic that guides a local heuristic search procedure to explore the solution space beyond local optimality. [Braun et al., 2001] also describe a tabu search (TS) approach to this problem. The approach described starts with a randomly generated initial solution. All possible swaps of any two jobs between all processors is then considered, the best swap is selected and the two jobs are reassigned to the corresponding processors. This local search is repeated until there is no further improvement. This, locally optimized, solution is then added to a tabu list to ensure that this region of the search space will not be needlessly visited again. The algorithm then makes a 'long hop' to another region of the search space by using another randomly generated solution that must differ from any solution in the tabu list by at least half the processor assignments. This solution is then locally optimized, and the entire process is repeated until the maximum number of iterations is met. This is a simple TS strategy that is effectively performing random re-start hill climbing but avoiding previously visited regions of the search space using the tabu list. Simulated Annealing is also a meta heuristic that differs from tabu search in the fact that swaps are made in a random way, rather than all possible combinations.

# 4   The Proposed Approach

The overall approach of memetic algorithm with Tabu search as local search enriches the searching behavior and avoids the premature convergence whose pseudo code is presented in Fig.2.

Generate Chromosomes based on the population size and calculate their fitness value
Find the best fitness value and have it as the initial solution
Perform Tabu search over the Chromosomes and find the best fit value
  Initial solution is updated with the best fit value
  While (! Stopping criteria) Crossover ()
    Mutation () Tabu Search ()
    If fitness value < best fit value then
      Update Best Fit Value
    End If
  End While

**Fig. 2.** The Proposed memetic algorithm

A. Genetic representation
For task scheduling, a chromosome represents a solution in other words a schedule. A schedule consists of the processor allocation and the start time of each node of the task graph. The representation of the chromosome holds the information that serves as an input for a heuristic to create a schedule. There are three basic elements to choose among. The first is the list of tasks to be scheduled. The second is the order in which these tasks should be executed on a given processor and the third is the list of processors on which these tasks should be assigned to

| 1 | 2 | 3 |
|---|---|---|
| (3,1) | (2,2) | (1,3) |

**Fig. 3.** Chromosomal representation

Each chromosome is represented as a group of genes i.e. ta-processor pair $(T_i, P_i)$ indicating that task $T_i$ is assigned to the processor $P_i$ shown in Fig 3. The position of genes in a chromosome represents the order in which tasks should be executed. For example the following chromosomal representation shows that task 1 should be executed on processor 3 and task 2 on processor 2 and task 1 on processor 3. It also indicates that task 2 is executed first followed by task 3 which in turn is followed by task 1. Fig.3 shows that task 3 is executed first followed by 2 which in turn is followed by task 2 and then 1.

## B. Initialization

There are two ways to generate the initial population namely; the random initialization and heuristic initialization. The initial chromosomes need not represent a legal solution. Population size is the one of the most important factors in MA problems. Small population size may cause the solutions to converge too quickly if the population size is too large.

Most of the scheduling heuristics generate the initial population randomly, with the necessary care on feasible solutions. The population is created randomly i.e. a predefined number of chromosomes are generated, the collection of which form the initial. Here the initial population is generated based on the priority calculation of the tasks at each level as shown in Table 2.

## Fitness function

GA mimics the survival of the fittest principle of nature to make the search process. This value is also known as the objective value. As the objective of the task scheduling problem is to find the shortest possible schedule, the fitness of a chromosome is directly related to the length of the associated schedule. Here the fitness value is determined by the earliest finish time of the last task.

## C. Selection

In this step, the chromosomes in the population are first ranked based on their fitness value for the best to the worst. Then they are selected to the pool.

## D. Reproduction

Reproduction process forms a new population of chromosomes by selecting the chromosome in the old population based on their fitness value through cross over and mutation. This is equivalent to assigning a subset of tasks to different processors. Single point and two point crossovers are alternatively performed and the crossover probability is also selected randomly.

## E. Mutation operator

Here the partial-gene mutation is employed. It takes each chromosome from the fittest ones and changes a randomly selected gene $(T_i, P_i)$ to $(T_i, P_j)$ which introduces diversity each time when it is applied, and consequently the population continues slowly to improve. Therefore the probability of crossover and partial-gene mutation is not fixed in the proposed algorithm.

## F. Local Search

Local search can be thought of as the process of an individual improving its idea of the solution. One of the most important characteristics of the local search is that it should be fast. Since the tabu search algorithm has been observed to be an efficient for this problem, it is used as a local search.

## G. Termination Criteria

When no improvement solution has been found over the last n iterations, the algorithm terminates. Typically this value is between 50 to 500 depending on the desired quality of the solution and the size of the problem. But for a large problem, improvement moves are likely to be found with lower frequency.

# 5   Results and Discussions

A number of experiments are carried out which outlines the effectiveness of the proposed algorithm. The purpose of these experiments is to compare the performance of memetic algorithm based approach with GA approach for the task scheduling problem. The proposed approach has been implemented on 32 nodes HP Proliant cluster. DAGs are generated randomly with different communication cost whose size varies from 10 to 50. Highly communication intensive application like Gaussian elimination task graph is also generated with matrix size varying from 3 to 15. The results are compared for varying population size, where the size ranges from 5 to 200. Although the memetic algorithm is a GA combined with the Tabu Search as a local search, it is not necessarily the case that the genetic parameters are the most ideal for a memetic algorithm. The tasks are selected for an initial pool according to the priority value as shown in Table 2 for the Gaussian Elimination task graph and are selected according to their fitness value. The proposed approach is also tested with etaillards benchmark for 15 jobs on 15 machines and noted that the proposed approach is better than the MA-LS approach.

**Table 2.** The DTC, ACC, RPT, rank and Priority values for the tasks in Fig.1

| Task | ACC | RPT | DTC | Level | Rank | Priority |
|------|-----|-----|-----|-------|------|----------|
| 1 | 14.5 | 0 | 64 | 1 | 78 | 1 |
| 2 | 12 | 78 | 35 | 2 | 125 | 2 |
| 3 | 13.5 | 78 | 23 | 2 | 114 | 3 |
| 4 | 16 | 78 | 50 | 2 | 144 | 1 |
| 5 | 16 | 78 | 13 | 2 | 107 | 5 |
| 6 | 16 | 78 | 15 | 2 | 109 | 4 |
| 7 | 16 | 114 | 17 | 3 | 147 | 3 |
| 8 | 16 | 144 | 11 | 3 | 171 | 2 |
| 9 | 16 | 144 | 13 | 3 | 173 | 1 |
| 10 | 16 | 173 | 0 | 4 | 189 | 1 |

The performance of both MA-TS and MA-SA for fine grained application whose CCR=0.1 by varying the no.of.iterations is shown in Fig. 4. From the graph, the performance of MA-SA is very poor upto 20 iterations and varies form 20 to 60 iterations. It reaches the optimum when the iteration value reaches 75. This shows that both MA-SA and MA-TS behaves same for fine grained application. The number of iterations are increased for a given population size.

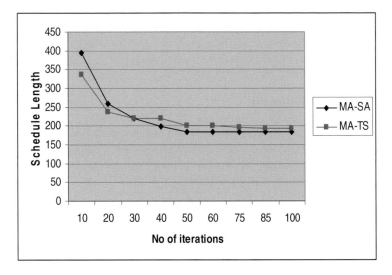

**Fig. 4.** Schedule length Vs No.of.Iteration

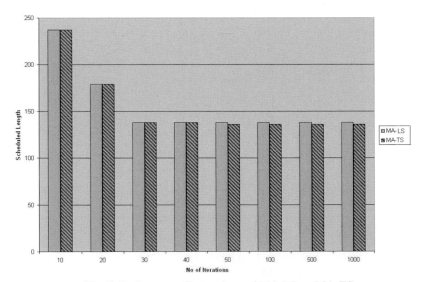

**Fig. 5.** Performance Comparison of MA-LS vs MA-TS

The performance of MA-TS is almost the same as that of MA-LS approach irrespective of the size of the Gaussian Elimination Task Graph. Fig. 5 shows the performance of low communication graph (CCR=0.1), the results are same initially but at the particular value of iteration, the behavior of MA-TS is very low compared to MA-LS. The main reason for the comparatively lesser scheduled length is due to the fact that Tabu search has identified a smaller working time processor sequence during its method of swap and relocate. The characteristic of tabu search is that it climbs rapidly to the nearest optima and then subject to the tabu list constraints searches for other optima in the region. Intuitively, the large neighborhood space directs the tabu search to search more of the neighborhood of the first local optima.

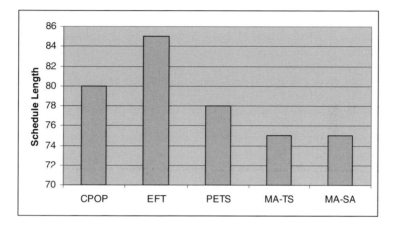

**Fig. 6.** Performance Comparison

The proposed memetic algorithm (MA- TS) performs well when compared to the classical list scheduling heuristics like EFT, CPOP and PETS algorithm in many aspects shown in shown in Fig 6. From the above results, the proposed memetic algorithm performs well when compared to other list scheduling heuristics.

## 6   Conclusion

In this paper, by hybridizing the population based evolutionary searching ability of GA with local improvement abilities of Tabu Search(TS) to balance exploration and exploitation, effective MA-TS has been proposed for Task Scheduling with an objective to minimize the makespan. It is appropriate for scheduling highly communication intensive applications on cluster of workstations considering communication contention. MA-TS experimental results show that the proposed approach gives better solution compared to other two. Since TS avoid premature convergence compared to HC as local search. MA-SA behaves same as MA-TS for fine grained application. The future enhancement of this work is to introduce processor involvement in task scheduling using this approach MA.

# References

[1] Gerasoulis, A., Yang, T.: A Comparison of clustering heuristics for scheduling DAGs on multiprocessors. Journal of Parallel and Distributed Computing 16(4), 276–291 (1992)

[2] Kwok, Y., Ahmad, I.: Benchmarking the task graph scheduling algorithms. In: Proc. Int. Par. Processing Symposium on Parallel and Distributed Processing (IPPS/SPDP 1998), USA, Florida, pp. 531–537 (April 1998)

[3] Macey, B.S., Zomaya, A.Y.: A Performance evaluation of CP list scheduling heuristics for communicating Intensive task graphs. In: Parallel Processing Symposium, pp. 538–541 (1998)

[4] Topcuoglu, H., Hariri, S., Wu, M.Y.: Performance Effective and Low Complexity task scheduling for heterogeneous computing. IEEE Transaction on Parallel and Distributed Systems 13(3) (2002)

[5] Illavarasan, E., Thambidurai, P.: Low complexity performance effective task Scheduling algorithm for Heterogeneous computing environments. Journal of Computer sciences 3(2), 94–103 (2007)

[6] Hou, E.S., Ansari, N., Ren, H.: A Genetic algorithm for Multiprocessor Scheduling. IEEE Transaction on Parallel and Distributed Systems 5(2) (1994)

[7] Singh, H., Youssef, A.: Mapping and scheduling heterogeneous Task Graphs using Genetic algorithms

[8] Vidakiazod, M.R., Bhattachariya, S.S.: A Modular Genetic algorithm for scheduling task graphs, Technical report UMIACS-TR- 2003-66, Institute of Advanced Computer Studies, University of Maryland at College park (June 2003)

[9] Wang, L., Siegel, H.J., Rowchoudhry, V.P., Maciejewski, A.A.: Task matching and scheduling in heterogeneous computing environments using a genetic algorithm-based approach. Journal of Parallel and Distributed Computing 4, 8–22 (1997)

[10] Dhodhi, M.K., Ahmad, I., Yatama, A.: An integrated technique for task matching and scheduling onto distributed heterogeneous computing systems. Journal of Parallel and Distributed Computing 62, 1338–1361 (2002)

[11] Kim, S.C., Lee, S.: Push-pull: Guided search DAG scheduling for Heterogeneous clusters. In: Proc. Intl. Conf. Parallel Processing (2005)

[12] Annie, S.W., Yu, H., Jin, S., Lin, K.C.: An incremental genetic algorithm approach to multiprocessor scheduling. IEEE Trans. on Parallel and Distributed Systems 15, 824–834 (2004)

[13] Braun, T.D., Siegel, H.J., Beck, N., Boloni, L.L.: A comparison study of static mapping heuristics for a class of meta-tasks on heterogeneous computing systems. In: Proc. 8th Workshop on Heterogeneous Processing, pp. 15–29 (1999)

[14] El-Gendy, S.M.: Task Allocation using Genetic algorithms, MS thesis, University of Louisville (1994)

[15] Chiang, T.-C., Chang, P.-Y., Huang, Y.-M.: Multi-Processor Tasks with Resource and Timing Constraints Using Particle Swarm Optimization. IJCSNS International Journal of Computer Science Network security 6(4), 71–77 (2006)

[16] Peng, D.-T., Shin, K.G., Abdelzaher, T.F.: Assignment and scheduling Communicating Periodic tasks in Distributed Real-Time Systems. IEEE Transaction on Software Engineering 23(12), 745–758 (1997)

[17] Abdelmaged Elsadek, A.: EARL Wells, A heuristic model for Task allocation in heterogeneous distributed computing systems. The International Journal of Computers and Their Applications 6(1), 1–36 (1999)

[18] Goldberg, D.E.: Genetic Algorithms in Search, Optimization and Machine Learning. Addison-Wesley, Reading (1989)

[19] Moscato, P.: On evolution, scorch, optimization. Genetic algorithms and Martial arts: toward memetic algorithms, Technical report, California (1989)

[20] Liu, D., Li, Y., Yu, M.: A Genetic algorithm for Task Scheduling in Network Computing Environment. In: Fifth International Conference on Algorithms & Architecture for Parallel Processing, ICA3PP 2002 (2002)

[21] Dhodhi, M.K., Ahmed, I., Yatama, A.: An Integrated Technique for Task Matching and Scheduling Onto distributed heterogeneous Computing Systems. Journal of parallel and distributed computing 62, 1338–1361 (2002)

[22] Bajaj, R., Agarwal, D.P.: Improving Scheduling of tasks in a Heterogeneous Environments. IEEE Trans.on Parallel and Distributed Systems 15(2) (February 2004)

[23] Hart, W.E., Krasnogor, N., Smith, J.E.: Recent Advances in Memtic Algorithms. Springer, Heidelberg (2004)

[24] Merz, P.: Memtic Algorithms for combinatorial Optimization problems: fitness landscape and effective search strategies, Ph.D. dissertation, univ.Siegean, Germany (2000)

[25] Quientero, A., Pierre, S.: Sequential and multi-population memetic algorithms for assigning cells to switches in mobile networks. Comput.Networks 43(3), 247–261 (2003)

[26] Franca, P.M., Mendes, A., Moscato, P.: A memetic algorithm for the total tardiness single machine scheduling problem, Eur. J.Oper.Res 132(1), 224–242 (2001)

[27] Ishibuchi, H., Yoshida, T., Murata, T.: Balance between genetic search and local search inmemetic algorithms for multiobjective permutation flowshop scheduling. IEEE Trans. Evol. Comput. 7(2), 925–941 (2004)

[28] Ong, Y.S., Lim, M.H., Zhu, N., Wong, K.W.: Classification of adaptive memetic algorithms:A comparative study. IEEE Trans. Syst., Man, Cybern. 36(1), 141–152 (2006)

[29] Maheswaran, R., Ponnambalam, S.G., Aravindan, C.: A Metaheuristic approach to single machine scheduling problems. International Journal of Advanced Manufacturing Technology 25, 772–776 (2005)

[30] Yeh, W.C.: A Memetic algorithm for the n/2/Flowshop/$\alpha$ F+BcMAX Scheduling problem. Intenrational Journal of Advanced Manufacturing Technology 20, 464–473 (2002)

[31] Burke, E.K., Smith, A.J.: A Memetic algorithm to schedule planned grid maintenance. In: Computational Intelligence for Modelling, Control and Automation, pp. 12–127. IOS Press, Amsterdam (1999)

[32] Burke, E., Clark, J., Smith, J.: Four Methods for maintenance scheduling, pp. 264–269. Springer, Heidelberg (1998)

# Quadratic Approximation PSO for Economic Dispatch Problems with Valve-Point Effects

Jagdish Chand Bansal[1] and Kusum Deep[2]

[1] ABV- Indian Institute of Information Technology and Management, Gwalior, India
jcbansal@iiitm.ac.in
[2] Department of Mathematics, Indian Institute of Technology Roorkee, India
kusumfma@iitr.ernet.in

**Abstract.** Quadratic Approximation Particle Swarm Optimization (qPSO) is a variant of Particle Swarm Optimization (PSO) which hybridize Quadratic Approximation Operator (QA) with PSO. qPSO is already proven to be cost effective and reliable for the test problems of continuous optimization. Economic dispatch (ED) problem is one of the fundamental issues in power system operations. The problem of economic dispatch turns out to be a continuous optimization problem which is solved using original PSO and its variant qPSO in expectation of better results. Results are also compared with the earlier published results.

**Keywords:** Particle Swarm Optimization; Economic Dispatch; Quadratic Approximation.

## 1 Introduction

Economic dispatch is one of the most important problems to be solved in the operation and planning of a power system. The primary objective of the ED problem is to determine the optimal combination of power outputs of all generating units so as to meet the required load demand at minimum operating cost while satisfying system equality and inequality constraints. The practical ED problem is represented as a non-smooth optimization problem with equality and inequality constraints, which cannot be solved by the traditional mathematical methods. Dynamic programming method [1] can solve such types of problems, but it suffers from so-called the curse of dimensionality. Over the past few years, in order to solve this problem, many efficient methods have been developed such as genetic algorithm [2], evolutionary programming [3], [4], tabu search [5], neural network approaches [6], and particle swarm optimization [7], [8], [9], [10].

This paper presents the solution of Economic Dispatch Problems with Valve-point Effects with data as given in [10] using PSO and qPSO [15]. Results obtained by these two algorithms are also compared with the earlier published results. Rest of the paper is organized as below: Section 2 presents the mathematical formulation of Economic Dispatch Problems with Valve-point Effects. In section 3 Particle Swarm Optimization and in section 4 Quadratic Approximation Particle Swarm Optimization (qPSO) is summarized. Numerical results are obtained and analyzed in section 5. Section 6 concludes the paper.

B.K. Panigrahi et al. (Eds.): SEMCCO 2010, LNCS 6466, pp. 460–467, 2010.

## 2   Problem Formulation

The main objective of ED problem is to minimize the total fuel cost of power plants subjected to the operating constraints of a power system. Generally, it can be formulated with an objective function and two constraints [10]:

$$F_T = \sum_{i=1}^{n} F_i(P_i) \tag{1}$$

$$F_i(P_i) = a_i + b_i P_i + c_i P_i^2 \qquad \forall\ i = 1, 2, \ldots, n \tag{2}$$

Where,

$F_T$ : Total generation cost; $F_i$ : Cost function of generator $I$; $a_i$, $b_i$, $c_i$: Cost coefficients of generator $I$; $P_i$: Power output of generator $I$; $n$: Number of generators.

*Constraints I*
*Active Power Balance Equation:* For power balance, an equality constraint should be satisfied. The total generated power should be the same as the total demand plus the total line loss. However, the transmission loss is not considered in this paper for simplicity.

*Constraints II*
*Minimum and Maximum Power Limits:* Generation output of each unit should be laid between its minimum and maximum limits. The corresponding inequality constraints for each generator are

$$P_{i,\min} \leq P_i \leq P_{i,\max} \tag{3}$$

where $P_{i,\min}$ and $P_{i,\max}$ are the minimum and maximum output of generator $i$, respectively.

The generating units with multi-valve steam turbines exhibit a greater variation in the fuel cost functions. Since the valve point results in the ripples, a cost function contains higher order nonlinearity. Therefore, the cost function (2) may be written as below to consider the valve point effects:

$$F_i(P_i) = a_i + b_i P_i + c_i P_i^2 + \left| e_i \times \sin\left(f_i \times \left(P_{i,\min} - P_i\right)\right)\right| \tag{4}$$
$$\forall\ i = 1, 2, \ldots, n$$

where $e_i$ and $f_i$ are the cost coefficients of generator $i$ reflecting valve-point effect.

## 3   Particle Swarm Optimization

The particle swarm optimization algorithm, originally introduced in terms of social and cognitive behavior by Kennedy and Eberhart in 1995 [11], solves problems in many fields, especially engineering and computer science. The power of the technique is its fairly simple computations and sharing of information within the algorithm as it derives its internal communications from the social behavior of individuals. The individuals, called particles henceforth, are flown through the multi-dimensional search space with each particle representing a possible solution to the multi-dimensional optimization problem. Each solution's fitness is based on a performance function related to the optimization problem being solved.

The movement of the particles is influenced by two factors using information from iteration-to-iteration as well as particle-to-particle. As a result of iteration-to-iteration information, the particle stores in its memory the best solution visited so far, called *pbest,* and experiences an attraction towards this solution as it traverses through the solution search space. As a result of the particle-to-particle information, the particle stores in its memory the best solution visited by any particle, and experiences an attraction towards this solution, called *gbest,* as well. The first and second factors are called cognitive and social components, respectively. After each iteration, the *pbest* and *gbest* are updated for each particle if a better or more dominating solution (in terms of fitness) is found. This process continues, iteratively, until either the desired result is converged upon, or it's determined that an acceptable solution cannot be found within computational limits.

For an n-dimensional search space, the *i-th* particle of the swarm is represented by a *n-* dimensional vector, $X_i = (x_{i1}, x_{i2}, ...,x_{in})^T$. The velocity of this particle is represented by another n-dimensional vector $V_i = (v_{i1}, v_{i2},...,v_{in})^T$. The previously best visited position of the *i-th* particle is denoted as $P_i = (p_{i1}, p_{i2}, ...,p_{in})^T$. 'g' is the index of the best particle in the swarm. The velocity of the *ith* particle is updated using the velocity update equation given by

$$v_{id} = v_{id} + c_1 r_1 (p_{id} - x_{id}) + c_2 r_2 (p_{gd} - x_{id}) \tag{5}$$

and the position is updated using

$$x_{id} = x_{id} + v_{id} \tag{6}$$

where $d = 1, 2... n$ represents the dimension and $i = 1, 2,..., S$ represents the particle index. $S$ is the size of the swarm and $c_1$ and $c_2$ are constants, called cognitive and social scaling parameters respectively (usually, $c_1 = c_2$; $r_1$, $r_2$ are random numbers drawn from a uniform distribution). Equations (5) and (6) define the classical version of PSO algorithm. A constant, *Vmax*, was introduced to arbitrarily limit the velocities of the particles and improve the resolution of the search. The maximum velocity *Vmax*, serves as a constraint to control the global exploration ability of particle swarm. Further, the concept of an inertia weight was developed to better control exploration and exploitation. The motivation was to be able to eliminate the need for *Vmax*. The inclusion of an inertia weight in the particle swarm optimization algorithm was first reported in the literature in 1998 [12].

The resulting velocity update equation becomes:

$$v_{id} = w * v_{id} + c_1 r_1 (p_{id} - x_{id}) + c_2 r_2 (p_{gd} - x_{id}) \tag{7}$$

Eberhart and Shi, [13] indicate that the optimal strategy is to initially set $w$ to 0.9 and reduce it linearly to 0.4, allowing initial exploration followed by acceleration toward an improved global optimum.

Clerc has introduced a constriction factor, $\chi$ [14], which improves PSO's ability to constrain and control velocities. $\chi$ is computed as:

$$\chi = \frac{2}{\left|2 - \phi - \sqrt{\phi(\phi - 4)}\right|} \tag{8}$$

where $\phi = c_1 + c_2, \phi > 4$, and the velocity update equation is then

$$v_{id} = \chi * \left(v_{id} + c_1 r_1 (p_{id} - x_{id}) + c_2 r_2 (p_{gd} - x_{id})\right) \tag{9}$$

Eberhart and Shi, [13] found that $\chi$, combined with constraints on *Vmax*, significantly improved the PSO performance.

## 4   Quadratic Approximation Particle Swarm Optimization (qPSO)

### 4.1   Motivation

Deep and Das [18], hybridized a binary GA by incorporating Quadratic Approximation (QA) operator as an additional operator for local search which showed a substantial improvement in the performance of GA. PSO has the efficiency to solve a wide variety of problems with a larger percentage of success. Mohan and Shankar [19] proved that Random Search technique (RST) which uses QA operator provides fast convergence rate but once stuck in a local optima, it is generally difficult to come out of it. Perhaps social knowledge concept of PSO could help RST in coming out of the local optima. As compared to GAs, the PSO has much more profound intelligent background and could be performed more easily. These two facts motivated to hybridize PSO and QA with the expectation of faster convergence (from QA) and improved results (from PSO) [15].

### 4.2   Quadratic Approximation Operator

QA is an operator which determines the point of minima of the quadratic hyper surface passing through three points in a D- dimensional space. It works as follows:

1. Select the particle $R_1$, with the best objective function value. Choose two random particles $R_2$ and $R_3$ such that out of $R_1$, $R_2$ and $R_3$, at least two are distinct.
2. Find the point of minima $R^*$ of the quadratic surface passing through $R_1$, $R_2$ and $R_3$, where

$$R^* = 0.5 \left( \frac{\left(R_2^2 - R_3^2\right)f(R_1) + \left(R_3^2 - R_1^2\right)f(R_2) + \left(R_1^2 - R_2^2\right)f(R_3)}{\left(R_2 - R_3\right)f(R_1) + \left(R_3 - R_1\right)f(R_2) + \left(R_1 - R_2\right)f(R_3)} \right) \tag{10}$$

where $f(R_1)$, $f(R_2)$ and $f(R_3)$ are the objective function values at $R_1$, $R_2$ and $R_3$ respectively. The calculations are to be done component wise using (10) to obtain $R^*$.

## 4.3 The Process of Hybridization

In each iteration, the whole swarm S is divided into two subswarms (say $S_1$ and $S_2$). From one generation to the next generation, $S_1$ is evolved using PSO, whereas $S_2$ is evolved using QA. Figure 1 shows the idea that stands behind qPSO and the way to integrate the two techniques. qPSO consists in a strong co-operation of QA and PSO, since it maintains the integration of the two techniques for the entire run. It should be noted that $R_1$ used in QA and gbest used in PSO both are the global best position of the entire swarm (let us call it GBEST) i.e $R_1$ = GBEST and gbest = GBEST. The strength of the qPSO lies in the facts that both PSO and QA use the GBEST simultaneously or in other words, subswarm $S_1$ and $S_2$ share their best positions with each other and for transition from one iteration to the next, both updating schemes use the entire swarm's information. However, in updating a particle's position by QA, no information about its current position is applied as in PSO but the presence of memory of the corresponding subswarm preserves the best performed particles. So in $(i+1)^{th}$ iteration QA will not produce worse solution than that in $i^{th}$ iteration. For more details of qPSO process refer [15].

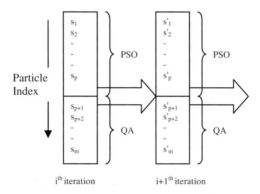

**Fig. 1.** Transition from $i^{th}$ iteration to $i+1^{th}$ iteration

We consider constriction version of PSO. Percentage of swarm to be updated by PSO or QA is an important parameter of qPSO. We call this parameter as *coefficient of hybridization (CH)*. *CH* is the percentage of swarm which is evolved using QA in each iteration. Thus, if *CH* = 0, then the algorithm is pure PSO (the whole swarm is updated by PSO operators), and if CH = 100 then the algorithm is pure QA (the whole swarm is updated by QA operator) while for 0<CH<100 the corresponding percentage of swarm is evolved by QA and the rest with PSO. The optimal value of CH is 30% [15].

## 5   Computational Experiments

In this paper, the power system of 40 generating units with valve-point effects is tested [10]. Refer [10], for the input data of the test system with 40 generating units and the total demand is considered as 10,500 MW.

## 5.1 Selection of Parameters

In the literature, different values of parameters are used. In this paper the selection of parameter is based on [15]. We set swarm size S = 100. Constriction version of PSO and qPSO are used. Constriction coefficient $\chi$ is calculated from equation (8). The

**Table 1.** Comparison of results obtained by PSO, qPSO, HPSO and IPSO based on mean objective function value (Mean OBJ), minimum objective function value (Min OBJ) and the standard deviation (SD)

| Method | Mon OBJ | Mean OBJ | SD |
|---|---|---|---|
| PSO | 121425.7989 | 121590.3289 | 92.8702 |
| HPSO [10] | 121452.6741 | 121537.1906 | - |
| IPSO [9] | 121432.177 | 121801.909 | 287.452 |
| qPSO | 121411.7764 | 121503.0048 | 57.6192 |

**Table 2.** Generation output of each generator in case of minimum total cost and the corresponding total cost in 40-unit system for PSO and qPSO

| Unit | PSO | qPSO | Unit | PSO | qPSO |
|---|---|---|---|---|---|
| 1 | 112.2629 | 111.776 | 21 | 523.3612 | 523.3405 |
| 2 | 111.9654 | 111.7013 | 22 | 523.337 | 523.2933 |
| 3 | 97.53544 | 97.41573 | 23 | 523.3437 | 523.3627 |
| 4 | 179.7479 | 179.7756 | 24 | 523.2956 | 523.3602 |
| 5 | 90.14323 | 88.315 | 25 | 523.3138 | 523.3191 |
| 6 | 139.9949 | 139.989 | 26 | 523.4079 | 523.287 |
| 7 | 259.7157 | 259.7313 | 27 | 10.0301 | 10.02257 |
| 8 | 284.8357 | 284.7436 | 28 | 10.02232 | 10.02202 |
| 9 | 284.7714 | 284.6194 | 29 | 10.01248 | 10.0232 |
| 10 | 130.017 | 130.0528 | 30 | 89.51979 | 88.62734 |
| 11 | 168.8275 | 168.8038 | 31 | 189.9937 | 189.9887 |
| 12 | 94.06347 | 168.801 | 32 | 189.9976 | 189.9908 |
| 13 | 214.7621 | 214.7706 | 33 | 189.998 | 189.9911 |
| 14 | 394.2736 | 304.5479 | 34 | 166.081 | 164.9038 |
| 15 | 304.5572 | 394.283 | 35 | 199.9889 | 165.0771 |
| 16 | 394.2549 | 394.2789 | 36 | 199.9752 | 165.3116 |
| 17 | 489.3522 | 489.2917 | 37 | 109.981 | 109.9916 |
| 18 | 489.3013 | 489.3259 | 38 | 109.9851 | 109.9878 |
| 19 | 511.2805 | 511.2811 | 39 | 109.9835 | 109.9741 |
| 20 | 511.3106 | 511.2862 | 40 | 511.3926 | 511.3359 |
| Total Power (MW) | PSO: 10,500 | | | qPSO: 10,500 | |
| Total Generation Cost | PSO: 121425.7989 | | | qPSO: **121411.7764** | |

cognitive and social scaling parameters $c_1$ and $c_2$ are set to 2.8 and 1.3 respectively [15]. Maximum velocity, Vmax is set equal to 0.5*(Xmax-Xmin), where Xmax and Xmin are the upper and lower bounds of the decision variable. The coefficient of hybridization (CH) is set to 30% [15]. The total number of simulations considered is 100. The criterion to terminate the simulation of the algorithms is reaching maximum number of iterations which was set 3000.

### 5.2  Computational Results

In Table 1, the mean objective function value (Mean OBJ), minimum objective function value (Min OBJ) and the standard deviation (SD) obtained by PSO and qPSO are tabulated. Table 1 also compares the results obtained by PSO, qPSO to the Hybrid PSO with crossover (HPSO) [10] and Improved Particle Swarm Optimization (IPSO) [9]. Table 2 summarizes the generation output of each generator and the corresponding cost in 40-unit system obtained by PSO and qPSO. It is observed that the generation output obtained by PSO and qPSO satisfy both the constraints. Also the minimum cost obtained by qPSO is the best over PSO and other methods applied earlier for this problem. Therefore, qPSO with the proposed parameter setting is strongly recommended for the solution of Economic Dispatch Problems with Valve-point Effects.

## 6  Conclusion

In this paper, Particle Swarm Optimization and Quadratic Approximation Particle Swarm Optimization are applied to solve the problem of Economic Dispatch with Valve-Point Effects. It is shown that qPSO provides the best results over all published results till date (to the best of authors' knowledge). However, a fine tuning of parameters of PSO and qPSO is not carried out in this study, an intensive study for selection of these parameters may produce even better results. Finally, qPSO is always recommended for the solution of the Economic Dispatch with Valve-Point Effects.

## References

1. Liang, Z.X., Glover, J.D.: A zoom feature for a dynamic programming solution to economic dispatch including transmission losses. IEEE Trans. on Power Systems 7(2), 544–550 (1992)
2. Walters, D.C., Sheble, G.B.: Genetic algorithm solution of economic dispatch with the valve point loading. IEEE Trans. on Power Systems 8(3), 1325–1332 (1993)
3. Yang, H.T., Yang, P.C., Huang, C.L.: Evolutionary programming based economic dispatch for units with non-smooth fuel cost functions. IEEE Trans. on Power Systems 11(1), 112–118 (1996)
4. Sinha, N., Chakrabarti, R., Chattopadhyay, P.K.: Evolutionary programming techniques for economic load dispatch. IEEE Trans. On Evolutionary Computations 7(1), 83–94 (2003)
5. Lin, W.M., Cheng, F.S., Tsay, M.T.: An improved Tabu search for economic dispatch with multiple minima. IEEE Trans. on Power Systems 17(1), 108–112 (2002)

6. Lee, K.Y., Sode-Yome, A., Park, J.H.: Adaptive Hopfield neural network for economic load dispatch. IEEE Trans. on Power Systems 13(2), 519–526 (1998)
7. Park, J.B., Lee, K.S., Shin, J.R., Lee, K.Y.: A particle swarm optimization for economic dispatch with nonsmooth cost functions. IEEE Trans. on Power Systems 20(1), 34–42 (2005)
8. Victoire, T.A.A., Jeyakumar, A.E.: Hybrid PSO-SQP for economic dispatch with valve-point effect. Electric Power Systems Research 71(1), 51–59 (2004)
9. Jong-Bae, P., Yun-Won, J., Hyun-Houng, K., Joong-Rin, S.: An Improved Particle Swarm Optimization for Economic Dispatch With Valve Point Effect. International Journal of Innovations in Energy Systems and Power 1(1) (November 2006)
10. Park, J.B., Jeong, Y.W., Shin, J.R., Lee, K.Y., Kim, J.H.: A Hybrid Particle Swarm Optimization Employing Crossover Operation for Economic Dispatch Problems with Valve-point Effects. In: International Conference Intelligent Systems Applications to Power Systems, ISAP 2007, pp. 281–286 (2007)
11. Kennedy, J., Eberhart, R.C.: Particle swarm optimization. In: Proceedings IEEE International Conference Neural Network, vol. 4, pp. 1942–1948 (1995)
12. Shi, Y., Eberhart, R.C.: A modified particle swarm optimizer. In: Proc. IEEE International Conference on Evolutionary Computation, Piscataway, NJ, pp. 69–73. IEEE Press, Los Alamitos (1998)
13. Eberhart, R.C., Shi, Y.: Comparing inertia weights and constriction factors in particle swarm optimization. In: 2000 Congress on Evolutionary Computing, vol. 1, pp. 84–88 (2000)
14. Clerc, M.: The swarm and the queen: towards a deterministic and adaptive particle swarm optimization. In: Proc. ICEC 1999, Washington, DC, pp. 1951–1957 (1999)
15. Deep, K., Bansal, J.C.: Hybridization of Particle Swarm Optimization with Quadratic Approximation. In: OPSEARCH, vol. 46(1), pp. 3–24. Springer, Heidelberg (2009)
16. Deep, K., Thakur, M.: A new crossover operator for real coded genetic algorithms. Applied Mathematics and Computation 188, 895–911 (2007)
17. Deb, K.: Multi-Objective Optimization using Evolutionary Algorithms, ch. 4. Wiley, Chichester (2001)
18. Deep, K., Das, K.N.: Quadratic approximation based hybrid genetic algorithm for function optimization. Applied Mathematics and Computation 203(1), 86–98 (2008)
19. Mohan, C., Shanker, K., (now Deep, K.): A random search technique for global optimization based on quadratic approximation. Asia Pacific Journal of Operations Research 11, 93–101 (1994)

# Fuzzified PSO Algorithm for OPF with FACTS Devices in Interconnected Power Systems

N.M. Jothi Swaroopan[1] and P. Somasundaram[2]

[1] Research Scholar, Department of Electrical and Electronics Engineering, CEG,
Anna University, India
[2] Asst Prof., Department of Electrical and Electronics Engineering, CEG,
Anna University, India-600025
nmjothi@yahoo.com, somauu77@gmail.com

**Abstract.** This paper presents a new computationally efficient improved stochastic algorithm for solving Optimal Power Flow (OPF) in interconnected power systems with FACTS devices. This proposed technique is based on the combined application of Fuzzy logic strategy incorporated in Particle Swarm Optimization (PSO) algorithm, hence named as Fuzzified PSO (FPSO). The FACTS devices considered here include Static Var Compensator (SVC), Static Synchronous Compensator (STATCOM), Thyristor Controlled Series Capacitor (TCSC) and Unified Power Flow Controller (UPFC). The proposed method is tested on single area IEEE 30-bus system and interconnected two area systems. The optimal solutions obtained using Evolutionary Programming (EP), PSO and FPSO are compared and analyzed. The analysis reveals that the proposed algorithm is relatively simple, efficient and reliable.

**Keywords:** Optimal Power Flow; OPF; Flexible AC Transmission Systems; FACTS; Particle Swarm Optimization; PSO; Fuzzy logic.

## 1 Introduction

Electric power systems are interconnected due to the fact that it is a better system to operate with more reliability, improved stability and less production cost than the isolated systems. Flexible AC transmission systems (FACTS) devices are integrated in power systems to control power flow, increase transmission line stability limit, and improve the security of transmission systems [6]. In interconnected power systems, Optimal Power Flow (OPF) problem is a large-scale non-linear optimization problem with both linear and non-linear constraints. In the last 30 year's many different solution approaches have been proposed such as, generalized reduced Gradient method, Successive Linear Programming (SLP), Quadratic Programming, Interior Point method to solve the OPF problems [9-10]. The most commonly used method is successive linear programming [3-5], the disadvantage of this algorithm is optimal solution depends on initial condition. It suffers from oscillations and also the model becomes inaccurate when wider variations are allowed in the control variables. For medium size power systems, the conventional methods for OPF calculations may be fast and efficient enough.

B.K. Panigrahi et al. (Eds.): SEMCCO 2010, LNCS 6466, pp. 468–480, 2010.

However, for large-scale interconnected power systems the higher dimension of possible solution space and increase of constraints result in excessive computational burden. With a view to reduce the computational burden some stochastic techniques [1,7] have been developed. In Evolutionary programming (EP) technique [7] uses floating point representation for decision variables, hence is applicable for large continuous domain optimizations. In EP, only mutation operator is used and by avoiding crossover between parents and the individuality of each parent is retained.

Particle Swarm Optimization (PSO) is a powerful optimization procedure that has been successfully applied to a number of combinatorial optimization problems. It has the ability to avoid entrapment in local minima by employing a flexible memory system. The optimal power flow (OPF) problem is effectively solved using PSO algorithm [11 –16]. The major drawback of PSO method is large number of iterations and very large computation time. In the present trend, there has been an increasing interest in the application of Fuzzy model. Fuzzy logic has been applied in PSO algorithm. This gives promising results especially in cases where the processes are too complex to be analyzed by conventional techniques or where the available information is inexact or uncertain. Hence in this paper an amendment based on fuzzy logic is incorporated in PSO technique for solving the OPF problem. The fuzzy logic is implemented in this effective stochastic algorithm (PSO) for obtaining a much better (faster) convergence.

## 2   Modeling of FACTS Devices

Broadly speaking, the existing steady state models of FACTS devices can be classified into two categories. One is decoupled model and the other is coupled model. In a decoupled model, the FACTS devices are usually replaced with a fictitious PQ and/or PV bus, which results in the modification of Jacobian matrix structure. Generally, a coupled model consists of two major models: Voltage Source Model (VSM) and Power Injection Model (PIM). The VSM is formulated as series and/or shunt inserted voltage source according to the device's operating principle therefore, it can represent the corresponding device in a more intuitive (insightful) way. However, it destroys the symmetric characteristics of admittance matrix. With the conversion of inserted voltage source to power injections to the related buses, the PIM retains the symmetry of admittance matrix. Due to this advantage, applications of this model are extended to nearly all FACTS devices and are widely used in the literature corresponding to operation and control of FACTS equipped power systems. SVC and STATCOM essentially control the voltage of a bus in a system. TCSC essentially controls power flow over a line and UPFC controls both the bus voltage and power flow over a line.

### 2.1  SVC

SVC at a bus is capable of controlling the corresponding bus voltage magnitude during steady state and dynamic state (during faults). It can exchange (with the connected bus) reactive power only. It consists of passive elements only. In power injection model, reactive power injected by the SVC at the connected bus $Q_{SVC}$ is the control variable. In fictitious generator bus model, bus voltage magnitude of the fictitious PV-bus $V_{SVC}$ is the control variable. Thus with the inclusion of SVC there is an additional control variable $Q_{SVC}$ or $V_{SVC}$ in the OPF problem[5].

## 2.2  STATCOM

STATCOM is a shunt-connected controller (connected at a bus). It is based on voltage source converters, hence, due to the absence of passive elements, the size and response time are lower than SVC. Moreover the exchange (with the connected bus) of reactive power is proportional to the bus voltage magnitude for STATCOM whereas it is proportional to the square of bus voltage magnitude for SVC. Thus voltage control of STATCOM is much better than SVC under low voltage conditions. In power injection model, reactive power injected by the STATCOM at the connected bus $Q_{STAT}$ is the control variable. Thus with the inclusion of STATCOM there is an additional control variable $Q_{STAT}$ in the OPF problem [5].

## 2.3  TCSC

TCSC is a series connected controller (connected in a line). Its major purpose is to increase power transfer during steady state. It can avoid sub-synchronous oscillations. It contributes mainly for rotor angle stability and indirectly controls the bus voltage. It consists of passive elements only. During steady state, TCSC can be considered as a static reactance $-jx_C$. The controllable reactance $x_C$ is directly used as the control variable in the power flow equations. Generally, up to 70% compensation is allowed. For OPF problem power injection model of TCSC is used. In power injection model, reactance offered by TCSC $x_C$ is the control variable. The change in the line flow due to TCSC can be represented as the line flow without TCSC with additional power (complex) injections at the receiving $(S_{jc})$ and sending $(S_{ic})$ ends [5].

## 2.4  UPFC

For OPF problem, power injection model of UPFC is used (between buses i and j). In power injection model [10], there are three control variables, i.e., the magnitude and angle of inserted voltage $(V_T, \Phi_T)$ and the magnitude of quadrature current $I_q$. The control variables are included in the power flow equation by calculating the real and reactive power injections using equations. Thus, with the inclusion of UPFC, there are three additional control variables $(V_T, \Phi_T)$ and $I_q$ in OPF problem.

# 3  Problem Formulation

The original multi-area OPF problem is decoupled to equivalent single area sub-problems where new variables namely the transmission line flows are considered. Thereby, the multi-area OPF problem has been decoupled into independent single area OPF sub-problems [2] (one for each area) with two more variables namely, $T_{ij}^A$ and $T_{ji}^{AA}$ ( *Tie* line flows).

The Objective function,

$$\text{Min} F_T^A = \sum_{i=1}^{cng} \left( a_{GCi}^A P_{GCi}^{A^2} + b_{GCi}^A P_{GCi}^A + c_{GCi}^A \right) + a_{GS}^A P_{GS}^{A^2} + b_{GS}^A P_{GS}^A + c_{GS}^A \qquad (1)$$

Subjected to
Power flow equations:

$$PF^A(X^A, U^A, C^{AA}) = 0 \qquad (2)$$

where $X^A$, $U^A$ and $C^A$, are state vector, control vector and parameter vector pertaining to area $A$ and $C^{AA}$ is the parameter vector comprising of a set of tie-line scheduled power flow from area $A$ to the adjacent area $AA$. Constraints on control variables are,
Generation active power limits:

$$P_{GCi}^{Amin} \le P_{GCi}^A \le P_{GCi}^{Amax} \; ; i= 1,2,3,...,cng \qquad (3)$$

Slack bus generation limit:

$$P_{GS}^{Amin} \le P_{GS}^A \le P_{GS}^{Amax} \qquad (4)$$

Controllable bus voltage magnitude limits:

$$V_{Ci}^{Amin} \le V_{Ci}^A \le V_{Ci}^{Amax} \; ; i= 1,2,3,...,cnv \qquad (5)$$

SVC MVAr limits:

$$Q_{SVCi}^{Amin} \le Q_{SVCi}^A \le Q_{SVCi}^{Amax} \; ; i= 1,2,3,...,nsvc \qquad (6)$$

STATCOM MVAr limits:

$$Q_{STATi}^{Amin} \le Q_{STATi}^A \le Q_{STATi}^{Amax} \; ; i= 1,2,3,...,nstat \qquad (7)$$

TCSC series capacitor limits:

$$x_{Ci}^{Amin} \le x_{Ci}^A \le x_{Ci}^{Amax} \; ; i= 1,2,3,...,ntcsc \qquad (8)$$

UPFC voltage magnitude, phase angle and quadrature current limits:

$$V_{Ti}^{Amin} \le V_{Ti}^A \le V_{Ti}^{Amax} \; ; i= 1,2,3,...,nupfc \qquad (9)$$

$$\Phi_{Ti}^{Amin} \le \Phi_{Ti}^A \le \Phi_{Ti}^{Amax} \; ; i= 1,2,3,...,nupfc \qquad (10)$$

$$I_{qi}^{Amin} \le I_{qi}^A \le I_{qi}^{Amax} \; ; i= 1,2,3,...,nupfc \qquad (11)$$

# 4   Methodology Using FPSO

The PSO method introduced in 1995 by Kennedy and Eberhart [11] is motivated by social behavior of organisms such as fish schooling and bird flocking. Here individuals called as particles change their positions with time. During flight, each particle adjusts its position according to its own experience, and the experience of neighbouring particles. Let $x$ and $v$ denote the particle position and its corresponding velocity in the search space. *pbest* is the best previous position of the particle and *gbest* is the best particle among all the particles in the group. The velocity and position for each element in the particle at $(t+1)^{th}$ iteration is calculated by using the following equations.

$$v_i^{t+1} = k*\{ w* v_i^t + \varphi_1.\ rand(pbest - x_i^t) + \varphi_2.\ rand(gbest - x_i^t)\} \tag{12}$$

$$x_i^{t+1} = x_{i+}^t v_i^{t+1} \tag{13}$$

where $x_i$ and $v_i$ are the current position and velocity of the $i^{th}$ particle, $w$ is the inertia weight factor, $\varphi_1$ and $\varphi_2$ are acceleration constants, rand() is the function that generates uniform random number in the range [0,1] and $k$ is the constriction factor introduced by Eberhart and Shi to avoid the swarm from premature convergence and to ensure stability of the system.

The selection of $w$ provides a balance between global and local explorations. In general, the inertia weight $w$ is set as

$$w = w_{max} - \{( w_{max} - w_{min}) / t_{max} \}\ t \tag{14}$$

where $t_{max}$ is the maximum number of iterations or generations and $w_{max}$ and $w_{min}$ are the upper and lower limit of the inertia weight. The inertia weight balances global and local explorations and it decreases linearly from 0.9 to 0.4 in each run. The constants $c_1$ and $c_2$ pulls each particle toward *pbest* and *gbest* positions. $V_{max}$ was set at 10 – 20 % of the dynamic range of variable on each dimension.

## 4.1  PSO Algorithm for Equivalent Single Area OPF Sub-problem with FACTS Devices

PSO, as an optimization tool, provides a population-based search procedure in which individuals called particles change their positions (states) with time. It is similar to the other evolutionary algorithms; each particle in the swarm is initialized randomly within the effective real power operating limits. The location of the $j^{th}$ particle is represented as $X_j = ( P_{11,\ j},\ldots\ldots P_{1n,\ j},\ldots\ldots P_{mn,\ j})$ for j = 1,2,..N$_p$ and, $P_{max,\ j}\ \in\ |\ P\ mn,min,$ $P\ mn,max|$ ,where $P_{mn,min}$ and $P_{mn,max}$ are the lower and upper bounds for the generation respectively. The best previous position (giving the best fitness value) of the $j^{th}$ particle is recorded and represented as, $X_j^P = ( P_{11,\ j}^P,\ldots\ldots P_{1n,\ j}^P,\ldots\ldots P_{mn,\ j}^P)$ for j = 1,2,..N$_p$ which is also called *pbest*. The index of the best particle among all the particles in the swarm is represented as $X_j^G = ( P_{11,\ j}^G,\ldots\ldots P_{1n,\ j}^G,\ldots\ldots P_{mn,\ j}^G)$ called as *gbest*. The velocity for the $j^{th}$ particle is represented as $V_j = ( V_{11,\ j},\ldots\ldots V_{1n,\ j},\ldots\ldots V_{mn,\ j})$, is clamped to a maximum velocity, $V_{max} = ( V\ max,_{11},\ldots\ldots V\ max,_{1m},\ldots\ldots, V_{max}_{,mn})$ which is specified by the user. In PSO, at each iteration $(t)$, the velocity and location of each particle is changed toward its *pbest* and *gbest* locations according to the equations (15) and (16), respectively.

$$V^{(t+1)}_{mn\ j} = w* v^{(t)}_{mn\ j} + c_1*rand()*(P^P_{mn\ j} - P^{(t)}_{mn\ j} + c_2*rand()*(P^g_{mn\ j} - P^{(t)}_{mn\ j}) \tag{15}$$

$$P^{(t+1)}_{mn\ j} = P^{(t)}_{mn\ j} + v^{(t+1)}_{mn\ j} \tag{16}$$

where $w$ is inertia weight, $c_1$ and $c_2$ are acceleration constants and rand() is a uniform random number in the range [0, 1]. In equation (15), the first part represents the inertia of pervious velocity; the second part is the "cognition" part, which represents the private thinking by itself; the third part is the "social" part, which represents the cooperation among the particles. If the sum of accelerations would cause the velocity $v_{mn, j}$ on that dimension to exceed $v_{max,mn}$ then $v_{mn, j}$ is limited to $v_{max,mn}$ . $v_{max}$ determines the resolution with which regions between the present position and the target position are searched.

The process for implementing PSO is as follows:

a) Initialization of particles: An initial swarm of size $N_p$ is generated randomly within the feasible range.

$$X^{(t)}{}_j = [\ P^{(t)}{}_{11,\ j},\ldots\ldots P^{(t)}{}_{In,\ j},\ldots\ldots P^{(t)}{}_{nm,\ j}] \tag{17}$$

he elements of each particle $X_j$ ; $j = 1,2, \ldots., N_p$ are the real power output of committed generating units.

b) The fitness function for each particle is computed as,

$$f_j = F_j + k_1|APBC_j| + k_2\sum P^{lim}{}_{t,\ j};\quad j = 1,2,\ldots.,Np\ and\ t = 1,2,\ldots, Nt \tag{18}$$

The values of penalty factors $k_1$ and $k_2$ are chosen such that if there is any constraint violations the fitness function value corresponding to that particle will be ineffective. The maximum fitness function value among the particles is stored as $f_{max..}$

c) Determination of *pbest* and *gbest* particles: Compare the evaluated fitness value of each particle with its *pbest*. If current value is better than *pbest*, then set the current location as the *pbest* location. If the best *pbest* is better than *best*, the value is set to *gbest*.

d) Modification of member velocity: Change the member velocity of the each individual particle $v_{mn,j}$ according to the equations (15).

e) Modification of member position: The member position in each particle is modified according to (16).

f) If $t = t_{max}$ then the individual that generates the latest *gbest* is the optimal solution. Otherwise repeat the process from step b.

## 4.2 Fuzzfied PSO Algorithm for Equivalent Single Area OPF Sub Problem Using FACTS Devices

In the classical PSO technique the value of inertia weight is computed based on the iteration ($t$ & $t_{max}$) alone which is independent of the problem being solved. However, for practical applications it may lead to slow and premature convergence. Hence there is a need for an adaptive inertia weight. The convergence depends on the relative fitness function value *fpi / fmax*. It is an essential factor, which has a major influence in the convergence process. If the relative fitness value *fpi / fmax* is low then the inertia weight is small and vice versa.

The other factor is the search range ($P_{mn,max}$ - $P_{mn,min}$) which is a constant throughout the whole search process. But actually the search range varies for each generation or iteration. Hence there is a need for an effective search range. Thus these factors need a certain control to obtain a better convergence. Moreover the relationship between them seems arbitrary, complex and ambiguous to determine, hence fuzzy logic strategy where the search criteria are not precisely bounded would be more appropriate than a crisp relation. Thus an adaptive inertia weight can be obtained from the fuzzy logic strategy thereby leading to an improved PSO technique termed as Fuzzy PSO (FPSO). The various sequential steps involved in the fuzzy implemented PSO based algorithm are as follows:

(i) The fuzzy logic inputs and output are decided and their feasible ranges are declared. The two fuzzy inputs are,

$$Input\ 1 = F_{pi} / F_{max} \tag{19}$$

$$Input\ 2 = Max\ \{\ (\ P_{mn,max} - P_{mn}{}^{pi});\ (\ P_{nm}{}^{pi} - P_{mn,min})\ \} \tag{20}$$

The *Input1* is the first essential factor and *Input 2* is an active search range determined as the maximum search distance or range pertaining to each element $P_{mn}$ of particle $I_{pi}$ in the present iteration from any of its corresponding limits (maximum or minimum). The output of the fuzzy logic strategy is the inertia weight w.

(ii) Fuzzification of inputs and output using triangular membership function. Five fuzzy linguistic sets have been used for each of the inputs and output as shown in Figure.1.

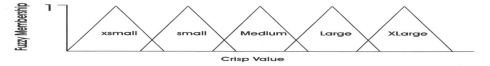

**Fig. 1.** Fuzzy Membership function

(iii) The fuzzy rule base is formulated for all combinations of fuzzy inputs based on their ranges.
(iv) Defuzzification of output using Centroid method.

$$C = \sum_{i=1}^{5} x_i y_i \Big/ \sum_{i=1}^{5} y_i \tag{21}$$

Where $x_i$ the mid-point of each fuzzy output set and $y_i$ is its corresponding membership function value.

The Centroid $C$ is scaled (multiplied by its range) to obtain inertia weight value of each element in the particle.

## 5   Sample System Studies and Results

The stochastic algorithm (EP, PSO and FPSO) for solving multi-area OPF problem with various FACTS controllers are tested on a standard IEEE 30-bus test system and an interconnected two area test system formed by interconnecting two identical standard IEEE 30-bus systems through a tie-line of scheduled interchange (from area 1 to area 2). The standard IEEE 30-bus test system consists of six generating units, 41 lines and a total demand of 283.4 MW. The interconnected two-area test system has a tie line of 20 MW scheduled interchange between buses 5 and 26 corresponding to area 1 and 2 respectively. The optimal parameters obtained for the stochastic algorithm are as follows, for IEEE 30-bus and interconnected two area test systems. The parameters used in the PSO approaches are as follows: $c_1 = c_2 = 2.05$, $w_{max} = 2.0$ and $w_{min} = 0.2$. In these case studies, the maximum number of iteration $t_{max}$, is fixed at 25. The optimum swarm size $N_p$ for the proposed models are 100. For each proposed models, 100 independent runs were made involving 100 different initial trial solutions. Convergence is tested for 100 trial runs. The simulations were carried out on Pentium IV, 2.5 GHz processor. The SVC is located at bus 21 of IEEE 30-bus test system. Its reactive power limits are 11.2 MVAr (capacitive) and -2.5 MVAr (inductive) with slope $X_{SL}$ as 0.02 p.u (2 %). The corresponding voltage limits are 0.9 and 1.1 p.u V. The optimal solution of IEEE 30-bus test system using the proposed algorithm with SVC is presented in Table 1.

**Table 1.** Optimal solution of IEEE 30-bus system with SVC at bus 21

| *Algorithm* | *EP* | PSO | *FPSO* |
|---|---|---|---|
| PG1 (MW) | 151.3 05 | 151.638 | 151.209 |
| PG2 (MW) | 56.9185 | 56.165 | 57.3439 |
| PG5 (MW) | 23.2179 | 22.4625 | 23.1848 |
| PG8 (MW) | 29.6407 | 30 | 28.8152 |
| PG11 (MW) | 15.8943 | 16.3184 | 15.0463 |
| PG13 (MW) | 14.5783 | 15.1184 | 15.9941 |
| V1 (p.u ) | 1.04992 | 1.04981 | 1.04989 |
| V2 (p.u ) | 1.03498 | 1.0322 | 1.03577 |
| V5 (p.u ) | 1.00673 | 0.995337 | 1.01371 |
| V8 (p.u ) | 1.02005 | 1.01799 | 1.02345 |
| V11 (p.u ) | 1.04956 | 0.986924 | 1.043 |
| V13 (p.u ) | 1.01122 | 1.03837 | 1.02019 |
| $Q_{SVC}$ (MVAr) | 7.77573 | 10.1482 | 6.03788 |
| Total PG (MW) | 291.555 | 291.703 | 291.593 |
| Total QG (MVAr) | 62.3722 | 60.3306 | 63.8308 |
| Loss (MW) | 8.18503 | 8.1814 | 8.1813 |
| Total fuel cost ($/hr) | 808.879 | 808.684 | 808.587 |
| Number of iterations | 310 | 250 | 170 |
| Computation time (sec) | 90 | 70 | 60 |

**Table 2.** Optimal solution of IEEE 30-bus system with STATCOM at bus 26

| Algorithm | EP | PSO | FPSO |
|---|---|---|---|
| PG1 (MW) | 151.466 | 151.942 | 151.451 |
| PG2 (MW) | 56.9536 | 57.4435 | 55.952 |
| PG5 (MW) | 23.772 | 23.2686 | 24.1523 |
| PG8 (MW) | 29.8479 | 28.4128 | 28.2243 |
| PG11 (MW) | 15.3667 | 15.227 | 17.3101 |
| PG13 (MW) | 14.26 | 15.477 | 14.5634 |
| V1 (p.u ) | 1.05 | 1.05 | 1.05 |
| V2 (p.u ) | 1.03315 | 1.03435 | 1.03263 |
| V5 (p.u ) | 1.00114 | 0.999314 | 0.998089 |
| V8 (p.u ) | 1.01402 | 1.02164 | 1.0154 |
| V11 (p.u ) | 1.01309 | 1.04067 | 1.00406 |
| V13 (p.u ) | 1.02178 | 1.03359 | 1.03068 |
| QSTATCOM (MVAr) | 5.27382 | 9.2121 | 3.8959 |
| Total PG (MW) | 291.667 | 291.77 | 291.653 |
| Total QG (MVAr) | 65.2271 | 61.0839 | 66.6168 |
| Loss (MW) | 8.26651 | 8.37043 | 8.2533 |
| Total fuel cost ($/hr) | 808.793 | 808.607 | 809.517 |
| Number of iterations | 310 | 250 | 170 |
| Computation time (sec) | 90 | 70 | 60 |

From Table 1 it is inferred that for the same optimum the number of iterations or generations are low for PSO and FPSO algorithm than EP technique. Moreover the FPSO algorithm has a faster convergence (less computation time and less number of iterations) than PSO algorithm. Hence the fuzzy implemented PSO algorithm is simple and efficient for single area OPF problem with SVC. From Table 1 it is inferred that with the inclusion of SVC at bus 21 the total reactive power generations, loss and total fuel cost are reduced. The voltage magnitude of bus 21 is 0.980311 p.u V, which is higher than the base case value 0.958252 p.u V, thus ensuring the voltage reliability of the entire system. The STATCOM is located at bus 26 of IEEE 30-bus test system. Its reactive power limits are 12.5 MVAr (injection) and −3.5 MVAr (absorption). The corresponding voltage limits are 0.9 and 1.1 p.u V. The optimal solutions of IEEE 30-bus test system using proposed algorithm with STATCOM at bus 26 is presented in Table 2. From Table 2 it is inferred that with the inclusion of STATCOM at bus 26 the total reactive power generations, loss and total fuel cost are reduced. It can be inferred that with the STATCOM at bus 26 the voltage profile of the system are well within its limits and moreover the voltage magnitude of bus 26 is 0.975366 p.u V, which is higher than the base case value 0.928088 p.u V. Thus both SVC and STATCOM have a similar effect on the voltage profile of the system. The TCSC is located in line 4 (connecting buses 3 and 4) of IEEE 30-bus test system. The range of compensation by TCSC is 0 to 70% of line reactance (line where TCSC is located). The optimal solution of IEEE 30-bus test system using the proposed algorithms with TCSC is presented in Table 3. From Table 3 it is inferred that with the inclusion of TCSC in line 4 the active power generation of generator 1 is increased and thus there is a reduction of total fuel cost and loss. With the inclusion of TCSC in line 4 the power transfer capability of the line has increased, thus ensuring the enhancement of steady state stability limit of the transmission line. The UPFC is located in line 4 (connecting buses 3 and 4) of IEEE 30-bus test system. Its quadrature current limits are −1 (injection) to 1 (absorption) p.u A. The magnitude limits of inserted voltage are 0 to 0.1 p.u V.

**Table 3.** Optimal solution of IEEE 30-bus system with TCSC in line 4

| Algorithm | EP | PSO | FPSO |
|---|---|---|---|
| PG1 (MW) | 156.38 | 155.831 | 156.444 |
| PG2 (MW) | 54.6929 | 54.5447 | 57.7051 |
| PG5 (MW) | 24.3593 | 23.0501 | 24.6535 |
| PG8 (MW) | 27.1947 | 27.3421 | 23.1717 |
| PG11 (MW) | 15.5184 | 16.7528 | 17.2476 |
| PG13 (MW) | 13.1385 | 13.6269 | 12.0512 |
| V1 (p.u ) | 1.02689 | 1.04786 | 1.04732 |
| V2 (p.u ) | 1.00969 | 1.02891 | 1.03176 |
| V5 (p.u ) | 0.976714 | 0.997721 | 1.00814 |
| V8 (p.u ) | 1.00423 | 1.01756 | 1.02524 |
| V11 (p.u ) | 1.03263 | 1.00024 | 1.02793 |
| V13 (p.u ) | 1.03803 | 1.05 | 0.978249 |
| Xc (p.u ohm) | 0.02653 | 0.0265285 | 0.02653 |
| Total PG (MW) | 291.209 | 291.147 | 291.348 |
| Total QG (MVAr) | 74.5706 | 72.121 | 73.1882 |
| Loss (MW) | 7.94769 | 7.74739 | 7.6512 |
| Total fuel cost ($/hr) | 805.031 | 804.393 | 804.114 |
| Number of iterations | 320 | 250 | 180 |
| Computation time (sec) | 95 | 75 | 65 |

The optimal solutions of IEEE 30-bus test system using the proposed algorithms based single area OPF problem with UPFC in line 4 is presented in Table 4. With the inclusion of UPFC in line 4 the power transfer capability of the line has increased, thus ensuring the enhancement of steady state stability limit of the transmission line. Moreover the voltage magnitudes of all buses are higher than the base case values, thus ensuring the voltage reliability of the entire power system. From Table 4 it is observed that there is a drastic reduction of total fuel cost and loss.

**Table 4.** Optimal solution of IEEE 30-bus system with UPFC in line 4

| Algorithm | EP | PSO | FPSO |
|---|---|---|---|
| PG1 (MW) | 168.9 | 167.129 | 167.15 |
| PG2 (MW) | 49.1754 | 46.141 | 45.13 |
| PG5 (MW) | 21.7279 | 20.0018 | 20.08 |
| PG8 (MW) | 20.035 | 21.714 | 24.075 |
| PG11 (MW) | 12.8859 | 13.171 | 11.7985 |
| PG13 (MW) | 13.9454 | 18.1891 | 18.18 |
| V1 (p.u ) | 1.04428 | 0.9819 | 0.97054 |
| V2 (p.u ) | 1.03515 | 0.9917 | 1.09013 |
| V5 (p.u ) | 1.00291 | 0.9971 | 0.99788 |
| V8 (p.u ) | 1.03407 | 1.0013 | 0.9875 |
| V11 (p.u ) | 1.00963 | 1.01 | 1.016 |
| V13 (p.u ) | 1.03012 | 1.041 | 1.0156 |
| $I_q$ (p.u A) | -0.158003 | -0.1921 | -0.1534 |
| $V_T$ (p.u V) | 0.0625549 | 0.06275 | 0.0767 |
| $\Phi_T$ (radian) | -2.2488 | -2.0012 | -2.023 |
| Total PG (MW) | 286.4135 | 286.3459 | 286.67 |
| Total QG (MVAr) | 55.5868 | 65.16 | 67.06 |
| Loss (MW) | 3.27011 | 3.01352 | 2.9459 |
| Total fuel cost ($/hr) | 782.457 | 782.449 | 782.39 |
| Number of iterations | 320 | 260 | 180 |
| Computation time (sec) | 95 | 78 | 65 |

For the interconnected two-area test system, TCSC is located in line 4 (connecting buses3 and 4) of area 1 and SVC at bus 21 of area 2. The TCSC and SVC ratings are the same as mentioned above.

The optimal solutions of interconnected two-area test system using the proposed algorithms based multi-area OPF problem with TCSC in area 1 and SVC at area 2 are presented in Table 5. From Table 5 it is inferred that FPSO algorithm has a faster convergence (less computation time and less number of iterations) than PSO algorithm. It is inferred that with the inclusion of TCSC in line 4 of area 1 and SVC at bus 21 of area 2 there is a reduction of total fuel cost of each area. With the inclusion of TCSC the power transfer capability of the line has increased moreover due to the inclusion of SVC the voltage profile of the system are well within its limits, thus ensuring the voltage reliability and the enhancement of steady state stability limit of the entire multi-area power system. Hence the fuzzy implemented PSO algorithm is simple and efficient for multi-area OPF problem with multiple FACTS controllers.

**Table 5.** Optimal solution of multi-area OPF with multiple FACTS controllers using PSO and FPSO based algorithms

| Area | Area 1 sub-problem | | Area 2 sub-problem | |
| Algorithm | PSO | FPSO | PSO | FPSO |
| --- | --- | --- | --- | --- |
| PG1 (MW) | 154.921 | 156.116 | 149.656 | 149.329 |
| PG2 (MW) | 62.10281 | 64.1889 | 52.3233 | 51.3532 |
| PG5 (MW) | 25.341 | 26.2598 | 22.2335 | 21.3352 |
| PG8 (MW) | 30.1 | 30 | 23.3816 | 24.5808 |
| PG11 (MW) | 21 | 17.0717 | 12.2549 | 13.4056 |
| PG13 (MW) | 19.001 | 18.3676 | 12.1786 | 12 |
| V1 (p.u ) | 1.0231 | 1.05 | 1.05 | 1.05 |
| V2 (p.u ) | 1.0091 | 1.03318 | 1.03429 | 1.03156 |
| V5 (p.u ) | 0.98001 | 0.998478 | 1.0051 | 1.00272 |
| V8 (p.u ) | 1.005 | 1.03607 | 1.01856 | 1.01789 |
| V11 (p.u ) | 1.00124 | 1.04257 | 1.02111 | 1.00734 |
| V13 (p.u ) | 1.00193 | 1.01593 | 0.997254 | 0.995546 |
| Xc (p.u ohm) | 0.02653 | 0.0263828 | - | - |
| QSVC (MVAr) | - | - | 7.18335 | 11.0407 |
| Total PG (MW) | 312.465 | 312.704 | 272.028 | 272.054 |
| Total QG (MVAr) | 78.091 | 74.4232 | 61.0733 | 56.9974 |
| Loss (MW) | 9.06511 | 8.6043 | 8.62819 | 8.60385 |
| Total fuel cost ($/hr) | 886.912 | 884.466 | 737.306 | 737.219 |
| Number of iterations | 270 | 190 | 270 | 190 |
| Computation time (sec) | 90 | 70 | 90 | 70 |

## 6  Conclusions

This paper presents an improved, simple, efficient and reliable FPSO for solving multi-area OPF problem with various FACTS devices. The proposed algorithm is developed from PSO technique by an amendment of fuzzy logic for obtaining a much better convergence. This paper demonstrates with clarity, chronological development and by successful application of the proposed algorithm on standard test systems for solving OPF problem for interconnected power system. The results obtained from these proposed algorithms are compared. The analysis reveals that PSO based algorithm converges faster than EP based algorithm and the fuzzy implemented algorithm FPSO is much faster in convergence than PSO algorithm. The proposed algorithm (FPSO) has the potential to be applied to other power engineering problems.

# References

1. Basu, M.: Optimal power flow with FACTS devices using differential evolution. Electrical Power and Energy Systems 30, 150–156 (2008)
2. Biskas, P.N., Bakirtzis, A.G.: 'Decentralized security constrained DC-OPF of interconnected power systems'. In: IEE Proceedings Generation, Transmission and Distribution, vol. 151(6), pp. 747–754 (2004)
3. Chung, T.S., Ge, S.: Optimal power flow incorporating FACTS devices and power flow control constraints. In: IEEE Conference, vol. 98, pp. 415–419 (1998)
4. Ge, S.Y., Chung, T.S.: Optimal active power flow incorporating power flow control needs in flexible AC transmission systems. IEEE Transactions on Power Systems 14(2), 738–744 (1998)
5. Ge, S.Y., Chung, T.S., Wong, Y.K.: A new method to incorporate FACTS devices in optimal power flow. In: IEEE Conference, vol. 98, pp. 122–127 (1998)
6. Hingorani, N.G., Gyugyi, L.: Understanding FACTS: Concepts and Technology of Flexible AC Transmission Systems, The institute of Electrical and Electronics Engineers, New York (2000)
7. Lai, L.L., Ma, J.T.: Power flow control in FACTS using evolutionary programming. IEEE Transactions on Power Systems 95, 109–113 (1995)
8. Li, N., Xu, Y., Chen, H.: FACTS-based power flow control in interconnected power systems. IEEE Transactions on Power Systems 15(1), 257–262 (2000)
9. Padhy, N.P., Abdel-Moamen, M.A.: Power flow control and solutions with multiple and multi-type FACTS devices. Electric Power Systems Research 74, 341–351 (2005)
10. Padhy, N.P., Abdel-Moamen, M.A.R., Trivedi, P.K., Das, H.: A hybrid model for optimal power flow incorporating FACTS devices. IEEE Transactions on Power Systems 1, 510–515 (2001)
11. Poli, R., Kennedy, J., Blackwell, T.: Particle swarm optimization: An overview. Swarm Intelligence 1(1), 33–57 (2007)
12. Fukuyama, Y., Tahyama, S., Yoshida, H., Kawata, K., Nahnishi, Y.: A particle swarm optimization for reactive power and voltage control considering voltage security assessment. IEEE IRons. on Power Systems, 1232–1239 (2000)
13. Trelea, I.: The particle swarm optimization algorithm: Convergence analysis and parameter selection. Inf. Process. Lett. 85(6), 317–325 (2003)
14. Zheng, Y., Ma, L., Zhang, L., Qian, I.: On the convergence analysis and parameter selection in particle swarm optimization. In: Proc. Int. Conf. Machine Learning Cybern., pp. 1802–1807 (2003)
15. Liang, J.J., Suganthan, P.N.: Dynamic Multi-Swarm Particle Swarm Optimizer. In: IEEE Swarm Intelligence Symposium, Pasadena, CA, USA, pp. 124–129 (2005)
16. El-sharkh, M.Y., El-Keib, A.A., Chen, H.: A fuzzy evolutionary programming based solution methodology for security-constrained generation maintenance scheduling. Electric Power system Research 67, 67–72 (2003)

# Co-ordinated Design of AVR-PSS Using Multi Objective Genetic Algorithm

B. Selvabala[1] and D. Devaraj[2]

[1] Lecturer, Dept. of EEE, Sri Manakula Vinayagar Engineering College,
Madagadipet, Pondicherry
[2] Research Director, Kalasalingam University, Tamilnadu

**Abstract.** Automatic Voltage Regulator (AVR) regulates the generator terminal voltage by controlling the amount of current supplied to the generator field winding by the exciter. Power system stabilizer (PSS) is installed with AVR to damp the low frequency oscillations in power system by providing a supplementary signal to the excitation system. Optimal tuning of AVR controller and PSS parameters is necessary for the satisfactory operation of the power system. When applying tuning method to obtain the optimal controller parameters individually, AVR improves the voltage regulation of the system and PSS improves the damping of the system. Simultaneous tuning of AVR and PSS is necessary to obtain better both voltage regulation and oscillation damping in the system. This paper deals with the optimal tuning of AVR controller and PSS parameters in the synchronous machine. The problem of obtaining the optimal controller parameters is formulated as an optimization problem and Multi-Objective Genetic Algorithm (MOGA) is applied to solve the optimization problem. The suitability of the proposed approach has been demonstrated through computer simulation in a Single Machine Infinite Bus (SMIB) system.

**Keywords:** Automatic Voltage Regulator, Power System Stabilizer, Multi-Objective Genetic Algorithm, Single Machine Infinite Bus system.

## 1 Introduction

Synchronous generator is equipped automatic voltage regulator and excitation system to automatically control the terminal voltage of the machine. A high-gain fast-response AVR improves the voltage regulation and improves the ability of the power system to maintain synchronism when subjected to large disturbances. The high-gain fast-response AVR action can lead to reduced damping of electromechanical modes of oscillation. The standard way of eliminating this loss of system damping is either to use transient gain reduction on the AVR or to attach a PSS to appropriate machines [1].

A PSS is directly connected to the AVR of synchronous generators and the main aim of PSS-AVR excitation control configuration is to provide damping and voltage regulation. In [2], the author has mentioned that a high-gain AVR has a detrimental effect on oscillation stability and PSS can reduce transient stability by overriding the voltage signal to the exciter. In order to avoid these issues, co-ordinated design of AVR and PSS controllers is necessary.

B.K. Panigrahi et al. (Eds.): SEMCCO 2010, LNCS 6466, pp. 481–493, 2010.
© Springer-Verlag Berlin Heidelberg 2010

Several techniques have been proposed to properly design and tune PSS–AVR schemes [3, 4], using low-order two-axis models [5] of synchronous machines. Co-ordinated controller design involves eigen value analysis which utilizes two basic tuning techniques phase compensation and root locus [6]. Phase compensation is widely used and compensates for the phase lags by providing a damping torque component. Root locus involves shifting of eigen values related to the power system modes of oscillation by shifting the poles and zeros of the stabilizer [6].

The problem of the co-ordinated design is a multimodal optimization problem. Hence, conventional optimization techniques are not suitable for such a problem. Moreover, the initialization step is crucial and affects the final dynamic response of the controlled system. From a given set of eigenvalues, different designs can be obtained by simply altering the parameters involved in the initialization step. Recently, evolutionary computation techniques such as Genetic Algorithm [7] and Particle Swarm Optimization (PSO) [8] have been applied to obtain the optimal controller parameters. El-Zonkoly [9] has proposed an Optimal tuning of lead-lag and fuzzy logic based power system stabilizers using PSO method.

When an optimization problem involves more than one objective function, it is called as a multi-objective optimization problem. A reasonable solution to a multi-objective problem is to investigate a set of solutions, each of which satisfies the objectives at an acceptable level without being dominated by any other solution. In multiobjective optimization, there may not exist a solution that is best with respect to all objectives. Instead, there are equally good, which are known as pareto optimal solutions. A pareto optimal set of solution is such that when we go from any one point to another in the set, atleast one objective function improves and at least one other worsen[10]. Neither of the solution dominates over each other and all the sets of decision variables on the pareto are equally good. A number of multiobjective evolutionary algorithms (MOEAs) has been suggested in the literature[11-15].

In this paper Multi-Objective Genetic Algorithm (MOGA) is applied to solve the optimization problem with two objectives. The effectiveness of the proposed approach has been demonstrated through computer simulation in a Single Machine Infinite Bus (SMIB) system.

## 2   Modelling of SMIB System with AVR and PSS

The general system configuration of synchronous machine connected to infinite bus system through transmission network can be represented as shown in Figure 1. The generator excitation system maintains generator voltage and controls the reactive power using an AVR. The role of AVR is to hold the terminal voltage magnitude of a synchronous generator at a specified level. However, these fast acting exciters with high gains can contribute to oscillatory instability in the power system. PSS can be added to the excitation systems to improve the oscillatory instability. The basic function of PSS is to extend the stability limit by modulating generator excitation to provide the positive damping torque to power swing modes. The power system stabilizer (PSS) generates a supplementary signal, which is added to control loop of the generating unit to produce a positive damping. A typical PSS consists of phase compensation stage, a signal washout stage and gain block. To provide damping, PSS must provide a component of electrical torque on the rotor in phase with speed deviations. PSS input signal includes generator speed, frequency and power. For any input signal, the transfer function of PSS must compensate for gain and phase characteristics of the excitation system. Figure 2 shows the thyristor excitation system including AVR and PSS.

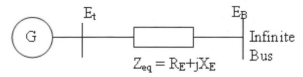

**Fig. 1.** Single Machine Infinite Bus System

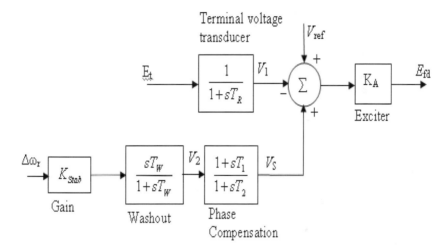

**Fig. 2.** Excitation System with AVR and PSS

The input control signal to the excitation system is the generator terminal voltage $E_t$. $E_t$ is not a state variable which is to be expressed in terms of the state variables $\Delta\omega_r, \Delta\delta, \Delta\psi_{fd}, \Delta v_1, \Delta v_2$, and $\Delta v_s$. The state space representation of the system including excitation system and AVR with PSS is given by,

$$
\begin{bmatrix}
\dot{\Delta\omega} \\
\dot{\Delta\delta} \\
\dot{\Delta\psi}_{fd} \\
\dot{\Delta v}_1 \\
\dot{\Delta v}_2 \\
\dot{\Delta v}
\end{bmatrix}
=
\begin{bmatrix}
a_{11} & a_{12} & a_{13} & 0 & 0 & 0 \\
a_{21} & 0 & 0 & 0 & 0 & 0 \\
0 & a_{32} & a_{33} & a_{34} & 0 & a_{36} \\
0 & a_{42} & a_{43} & a_{44} & 0 & 0 \\
a_{51} & a_{52} & a_{53} & 0 & a_{55} & 0 \\
a_{61} & a_{62} & a_{63} & 0 & a_{65} & a_{66}
\end{bmatrix}
\begin{bmatrix}
\Delta\omega \\
\Delta\delta \\
\Delta\psi_{fd} \\
\Delta v_1 \\
\Delta v_2 \\
\Delta v_s
\end{bmatrix}
\tag{1}
$$

where, $a_{11} = -\dfrac{K_D}{2H}$  $a_{12} = -\dfrac{K_1}{2H}$  $a_{13} = -\dfrac{K_2}{2H}$  $a_{21} = \omega_0 = 2\pi f_0$

$$a_{32} = -\frac{\omega_0 R_{fd}}{L_{fd}} m_1 L'_{ads}$$

$$a_{33} = -\frac{\omega_0 R_{fd}}{L_{fd}} \left[ 1 - \frac{L'_{ads}}{L_{fd}} + m_2 L'_{ads} \right] \qquad a_{34} = -\frac{\omega_0 R_{fd}}{L_{adu}} K_A$$

$$a_{36} = \frac{\omega_0 R_{fd}}{L_{adu}} K_A \qquad a_{42} = \frac{K_5}{T_R}$$

$$a_{43} = \frac{K_6}{T_R} \qquad a_{44} = -\frac{1}{T_R} \qquad a_{51} = K_{stab} a_{11} \qquad a_{52} = K_{stab} a_{12}$$

$$a_{53} = K_{stab} a_{13} \qquad a_{55} = -\frac{1}{T_W}$$

$$a_{61} = \frac{T_1}{T_2} a_{51} \qquad a_{62} = \frac{T_1}{T_2} a_{52} \qquad a_{63} = \frac{T_1}{T_2} a_{53} \qquad a_{65} = \frac{T_1}{T_2} a_{55} + \frac{1}{T_2}$$

$$a_{66} = -\frac{1}{T_2}$$

## 3  Problem Formulation

The co-ordinated tuning of AVR gains and Power System Stabilizer parameters is necessary to improve the damping performance of power systems with fast transient response. The task of simultaneous tuning of controller parameters is formulated as multi-objective optimization problems with minimization of the integral of time squares of the error and minimization of damping index as objectives. The objective functions are given by

$$F_1 = Min \left( \int_0^\infty t\, e^2(t)\, dt \right)$$

$$F_2 = Min \left( \sum_{i=1}^n (1 - \zeta_i) \right)$$

(2)

where, $\zeta$ is Damping ratio, DI is Damping index and n is total number of dominant Eigen values. The Eigen values are calculated based on state variables from state matrix A in the equation (1).

The above optimization problem is subjected to the following constraints:

$$K_A^{min} \leq K_A \leq K_A^{max}$$

$$K_{Stab}^{min} \leq K_{Stab} \leq K_{Stab}^{max}$$

$$T_A^{min} \leq T_A \leq T_A^{max}$$

$$T_1^{min} \leq T_1 \leq T_2^{max}$$

$$T_2^{min} \leq T_2 \leq T_2^{max}$$

$$T_W^{min} \leq T_W \leq T_W^{max}$$

$$(3)$$

Multi-Objective Genetic Algorithm is applied to the above optimization problem to search for the optimum value of the controller parameters. The detail of the proposed method is given in the next section.

## 4  Overview of Multi Objective Genetic Algorithm

Genetic algorithms [15] are search algorithms based on the mechanics of natural selection and genetics. Each chromosome represents one solution of the optimization problem. The quality of this solution is defined by the fitness function $f$ (Comparable with the object function of classic optimization methods). Genetic Algorithms has proven to be a useful approach to address a wide a variety of optimization problems. It performs well over a specific class of functions: continuous, smooth, multi-modal real–variable functions. Also, GA performs well if it has a good chance of finding the global minimum. Being a population–based approach, GA is well suited to solve multi-objective optimization problems. In this work, the multi-objective genetic algorithm proposed by Fonesca [16] is applied to solve the multi-objective controller design problem. The details of the MOGA are presented here.

In MOGA, first each solution is checked for its domination in the population. Calculate the rank of the $i^{th}$ solution as $r_i=1+ n_i$. In this way, non-dominated solutions are assigned a rank equal to one. Since no solution would dominates a non-dominated solution in a population. Once the ranking is performed, a raw fitness to a solution is assigned based on its rank. To perform this, first the ranks are sorted in ascending order. Then raw fitness is assigned to each solution by using a linear mapping function. The mapping function is chosen so as to assign fitness between N (for the best rank solution) and 1 (for the worst rank solution). Then the raw fitness is averaged to each solution of the rank which is called average fitness or assigned fitness. The average fitness to any solution i=1, …., N is given below.

$$F_i = N - \sum_{k=1}^{r_i-1} \mu(k) - 0.5(\mu(r_i) - 1)$$

In order to maintain diversity among non-dominated solutions, niching among solutions of each rank are introduced. Niche count $n_{ci}$ is calculated by the following equation:

$$nc_i = \sum_{j=1}^{\mu(r_i)} Sh(d_{ij})$$
(4)

Where $\mu(r_i)$ is the number of solutions in rank $r_i$

$$\text{Sharing function } Sh(d_{ij}) = \begin{cases} 1 - \left(\dfrac{d_{ij}}{\sigma_{share}}\right)^{\alpha} & \text{if } d_{ij} \leq \sigma_{share} \\ 0 & \text{otherwise} \end{cases}$$
(5)

Where $\sigma_{share}$ is the maximum distance between any two individuals. $\alpha$ is a scaling factor which is less than or equal to 1. $d_{ij}$ is the normalized distance between two solutions i and j.

$$d_{ij} = \left[\sum \left(\frac{f_k^{(i)} - f_k^{(j)}}{f_k^{max} - f_k^{min}}\right)^2\right]^{1/2}$$
(6)

where $f_k^{max}$ and $f_k^{min}$ are the maximum and minimum objective function value of the $k^{th}$ objective.

The shared fitness value is calculated by using $F_j' = F_j / nc_j$. Although all solutions of any particular rank have the identical fitness, the shared fitness value of a solution residing in a less crowded region has a better shared fitness. This produces a large selection pressure for poorly represented solutions in any rank. To preserve the same average fitness, scale the shared fitness as follows:

$$F_j' \leftarrow \frac{F_j \mu(r)}{\sum_{k=1}^{\mu(r)} F_k'} F_j'$$
(7)

Thus the procedure is continued until all ranks are processed. Thereafter, selection, crossover and mutation operators are applied to create a new population. The details of the genetic operators applied in this work are given below.

## 4.1 Selection

Selection is a method stochastically picks individuals from the population according to their fitness; the higher the fitness, the more chance an individual has to be selected for the next generation. There are a number of methods proposed in the literature for the selection operation. Tournament selection is used in this work. In tournament selection, "n" individuals are selected at random from the population, and the best of the "n" is inserted into the new population for further genetic processing. This procedure is repeated until the mating pool is filled. Tournaments are often held between pairs of individuals (tournament size=2), although larger tournaments can be used.

## 4.2 Crossover

The crossover operator is mainly responsible for bringing diversity in the population. Crossovers for real parameter GAs have the interesting feature of having tunable parameters that can be used to modify their exploration power. In this proposed approach each individual in the population consists of real variables. Hence BLX (Blend crossover operator) is used for real variables. Figure 4 represents the BLX-α crossover operation for the one dimensional case. In figure 3, $u^{min}$ and $u^{max}$ are the lower and upper limits respectively and I= $(u_2-u_1)$.

In the BLX-α crossover, the offspring (y) is sampled from the space [$e_1$, e2] as follows:

$$y = \begin{cases} e_1 + r \times (e_2 - e_1); \ if \ u^{min} \leq y \leq u^{max} \\ repeat \ sampling; \ otherwise \end{cases} \tag{8}$$

Where $e_1 = u_1 - \alpha \times (u_2 - u_1)$
$e_2 = u_2 + \alpha \times (u_2 - u_1)$
$r = uniform \ random \ number \in [0,1]$

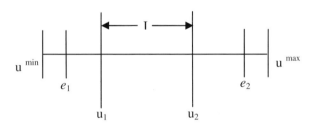

**Fig. 3.** Schematic representation of BLX- α Crossover

In a number of test problems, the investigators have observed that α = 0.5 provides good results. In this crossover operator the location of the offspring depends on the difference in parent solutions. If both parents are close to each other, the new point will also be close to the parents. On the other hand, if the parents are far from each other, the search is more like a random search. This property of a search operator allows us to constitute an adaptive search.

## 4.3 Mutation

The mutation operator is used to inject new genetic material into the population. Mutation randomly changes the new offspring. In this work, the 'Non Uniform Mutation' operator is applied to the mixed variables with some modifications. First a variable is selected from an individual randomly. If the selected variable is a real number, it is set to a uniform random number between the variable's lower and upper limits. i.e , if the selected variable is $u_k$ with the range $|u^k_{min}, u^k_{max}|$, two random numbers are generated and the result $u^1_k$ is calculated as

$$
u^1_k = \begin{cases} u_k + \left(u^k_{max} - u_k\right)\left(1 - r_1^{\left(\frac{1-p}{M}\right)^q}\right) & \text{if } r_1 \le 0.5 \\ \\ u_k - \left(u_k - u^k_{min}\right)\left(1 - r_1^{\left(\frac{1-p}{M}\right)^q}\right) & \text{if } r_1 > 0.5 \end{cases} \tag{9}
$$

where p is the generation number,
    q is a non uniform mutation parameter and
    M is the maximum generation number.

On the other hand, if the selected variable is an integer, the randomly generated floating point number is truncated to the nearest integer. After mutation, the new generation is complete and the procedure begins again with the fitness evaluation of the population.

## 5 MOGA Implementation of AVR-PSS Tuning

When applying MOGA to optimize the controller gains, two main issues need to be addressed:

    (i) Representation of the decision variables
    (ii) Fitness Function

These issues are explained in the subsequent section.

### 5.1 Representation of the Decision Variables

Each individual in the genetic population represents a candidate solution. For tuning of AVR with PSS controller, the elements of the solution consist of AVR exciter gain ($K_A$), Stabilizer gain ($K_{Stab}$), AVR exciter time constant ($T_A$), time constant of Lead compensator ($T_1$), time constant of Lag compensator ($T_2$) and washout time constant ($T_W$). These variables are represented as floating point numbers in the GA population. With this representation, an individual in the GA population for computing optimal controller parameters will look like the following:

| 198.345 | 48.452 | 0.0132 | 3.247 | 0.0501 | 0.0122 |
|---------|--------|--------|-------|--------|--------|
| $K_A$   | $K_{Stab}$ | $T_A$ | $T_1$ | $T_2$ | $T_W$ |

The use of floating point numbers and integers to represent the solution alleviates the difficulties associated with the binary-coded GA for real variables. Also with direct representation of the solutions variables the computer space required to store the population is reduced.

## 5.2  Fitness Function

The function of each individual in the population is evaluated according to its 'fitness' which is defined as the non-negative figure of merit to be maximized. It is associated mainly with the objective function. Evaluation of the individuals in the population is accomplished by calculating the objective function value for the problem using the parameter set. Here the objective is to minimize the error and damping index. The result of the objective function calculation is used to calculate the fitness value of the individual. Fitter chromosomes have higher probabilities of being selected for the next generation.

# 6  Simulation Results

The tuning of AVR-PSS parameters was tested in a typical single-machine infinite-bus system under normal and fault conditions. The software for the Multi-Objective Genetic Algorithm was written in MATLAB and executed on a PC with 2.4 MHZ and 256 MB RAM. The parameters of the excitation system are given in Table 1.

**Table 1.** Parameters of the excitation system

| $K_1 = 1.591$ | $K_2 = 1.5$ | $K_3 = 0.333$ | $K_4 = 1.8$ |
|---|---|---|---|
| $K_5 = -0.12$ | $K_6 = 0.3$ | $\omega_0 = 314$ | $T_m = 1$ |
| $T_R = 0.02$ | $T_3 = 1.91$ | $H = 3$ | $K_D = 0$ |

First, the proposed method was applied to obtain the controller parameters under normal condition. AVR exciter gain ($K_A$), Stabilizer gain ($K_{Stab}$), AVR exciter time constant ($T_A$), time constant of Lead compensator ($T_1$), time constant of Lag compensator ($T_2$) and washout time constant ($T_W$) are taken as the optimization variables. They are represented as a floating point numbers in the MOGA population. The initial population is generated randomly between the variables lower and upper limits. Tournament selection was applied to select the members of the new population. Blend crossover and non uniform mutation were applied on the selected individuals. The fitness function given by (2) is used to evaluate the fitness value of each set of controller parameters. The performance of MOGA for various value of crossover and mutation probabilities in the ranges 0.6 – 0.9 and 0.001 – 0.01 respectively was evaluated. The best results of the MOGA are obtained with the following control parameters.

Number of generations    : 75
Population size           : 50
Crossover probability     : 0.8
Mutation probability      : 0.02

It is worth mentioning that the proposed approach produces nearly 28 Pareto optimal solutions in a single run that have satisfactory diversity characteristics and span over the entire Pareto optimal front. The Pareto-optimal front curve is shown in Figure 4. Two non-dominated solutions which are the extreme points of the curve represent the minimum error and minimum damping index are given in Table 2.

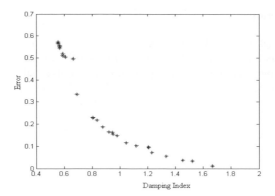

**Fig. 4.** Pareto optimal front curve

**Table 2.** Pareto optimal solutions of control variables for AVR-PSS

| Control variables | Minimum Error | Minimum Damping Index |
|---|---|---|
| $K_A$ | 237.2638 | 198.7379 |
| $K_{Stab}$ | 51.9155 | 50.1189 |
| $T_A$ | 0.0190 | 0.0202 |
| $T_W$ | 4.7560 | 4.3748 |
| $T_1$ | 0.0507 | 0.0500 |
| $T_2$ | 0.0160 | 0.0052 |

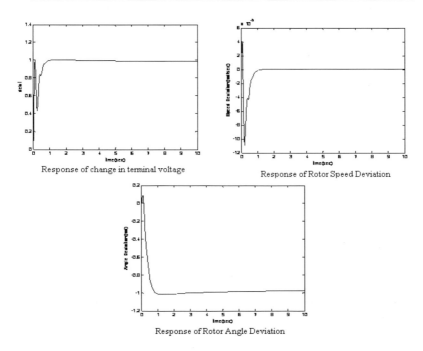

Response of change in terminal voltage

Response of Rotor Speed Deviation

Response of Rotor Angle Deviation

**Fig. 5.** Response of the system with MOGA based AVR-PSS

The system response corresponding to these two cases are given in Figure 5 and minimization of damping index is given in Figure 6. The transient parameters corresponding to the two cases are given in Table 3.

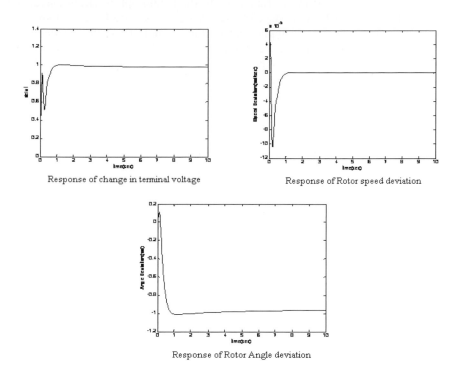

Response of change in terminal voltage

Response of Rotor speed deviation

Response of Rotor Angle deviation

**Fig. 6.** Response of the system with MOGA based AVR-PSS

**Table 3.** Transient Parameters of the System

| Parameters | Minimum Error (F₁) | | Minimum Damping Index (F₂) | |
|---|---|---|---|---|
| $T_s$ (sec) | 0.8195 | | 10 | |
| $T_r$ (sec) | 0.1070 | | 0.7064 | |
| Osh (%) | 0.0042 | | 0.004 | |
| ESS | 0.0507 | | 0.0420 | |
| Eigen Values & $\zeta$ | -59.3459 | 1.0000 | 1.0e+2 * ( -1.8527) | 1.0000 |
| | -0.2235 | 1.0000 | 1.0e+2 *( -0.0024) | 1.0000 |
| | -5.9759 | 1.0000 | 1.0e+2 *( -0.0614) | 1.0000 |
| | -8.7723 | 1.0000 | 1.0e+2*(-0.1717) | 1.0000 |
| | -19.5017 +19.1291i | 0.7139 | 1.0e+2 *( -0.1740 + 0.0178i) | 0.9948 |
| | -19.5017 -19.1291i | 0.7139 | 1.0e+2 * ( -0.1740 − 0.0178i) | 0.9948 |
| Obj F₁ | 0.5558 | | 1.6645 | |
| Obj F₂ | 0.5722 | | 0.0104 | |

Here minimization of the error and the damping index are taken as two objective functions, when designing the AVR-PSS parameters. The algorithm generates a set of optimal parameters called Pareto set corresponding to each Pareto front, which is a set of optimal results for the objective functions. In the Pareto optimal front curve, two non-dominated solutions have produced better transient response for error minimization and dynamic response for damping index minimization. From the simulation results, it is found that the proposed algorithm has resulted in minimum values of the transient parameters of the system and produce better damping index in single run under different operating conditions.

## 7  Conclusion

This paper has demonstrated the importance of co-ordinated tuning of AVR controller and Power System Stabilizer in synchronous machines. Multi-Objective Genetic Algorithm is applied for obtaining the optimal parameters of AVR gains and PSS controller parameters simultaneously. The proposed algorithm has performed well when it was used to characterize Pareto optimal front and leads to global search with fast convergence rate and a feature of robust computation. From the simulation result, it is concluded that MOGA produce better optimal solutions concurrently in a single run. Also, the proposed method has resulted in better dynamic performance as well as transient response of the system. Further, this approach is found to generate high quality solutions with more stable convergence than single objective genetic algorithms.

## 8  List of Symbols

$E_B$   : Infinite bus voltage in pu
$E_t$   : Generator terminal voltage in pu
$\omega_0$   : Rotor electrical speed in rad/sec
$\omega_r$   : Angular speed of the rotor in rad/sec
$\psi_{fd}$   : Field circuit flux linkage
$\delta_0$   : Initial rotor angle in elect. Rad
$K_D$   : Damping torque coefficient in pu torque/pu speed deviation
$K_S$   : Synchronizing torque coefficient in pu torque/rad
H    : Inertia constant in MW.s/MVA
$R_T$   : Total system resistance in pu
$R_{fd}$   : Field circuit resistance in pu
$L_{fd}$   : Field circuit reactance in pu
$X_{Tq}$   : Total q-axis reactance of the system in pu
$X_{Td}$   : Total d-axis reactance of the system in pu
$L_{adu}$ : Generator d-axis unsaturated value of mutual inductance in pu
$L_{aqu}$ : Generator q-axis unsaturated value of mutual inductance in pu
$L_{ads}$ : Generator d-axis saturated value of mutual inductance in pu
$L_{aqs}$ : Generator q-axis saturated value of mutual inductance in pu
$X_d$   : Synchronous reactance of the generator in pu
$X'_d$  : Transient reactance of the generator in pu

$K_A$ : Exciter gain
$T_W$ : Time constant of washout block in sec
$T_1, T_2$: Phase compensator time constants in sec
Osh : Overshoot (%)
Ess : Steady state error
Ts : Settling time in sec
Tr : Rising time in sec.

# References

[1] DeMello, D., Concordia, C.: Concepts of synchronous machine stability as affected by excitation control. IEEE Trans. Power App. Syst. PAS-88(2), 316–329 (1969)

[2] Kundur, P., Paserba, J., Ajjarapu, V., Andersson, G., Bose, A., Canizares, C., Hatziargyriou, N., Hill, D.: Definition and classification of power system stability. IEEE Trans. Power Syst. 19(2), 1387–1401 (2004)

[3] Machowski, J., Bialek, J., Robak, S., Bumby, J.R.: Excitation control system for use with synchronous generators. In: IEE Proceedings-Generation Transmission and Distribution, vol. 145, pp. 537–546 (1998)

[4] Mrad, F., Karaki, S., Copti, B.: An adaptive fuzzy-synchronous machine stabilizer. IEEE Trans Sys. Man Cybern, C 30, 131–137 (2000)

[5] Canay, I.M.: Modelling of alternating-current machines having multiple rotor circuits. IEEE Trans. Energy Conversion 8, 280–296 (1993)

[6] Larsen, E.V., Swann, D.A.: Applying Power System Stabilizers Part-I: General Concepts. IEEE Transactions on Power Apparatus and Systems PAS-100(6), 3017–3024 (1981)

[7] Do-Bomfim, A.L.B., Taranto, G.N., Flacao, D.M.: Simultaneous tuning of power system damping controllers using genetic algorithms. IEEE Transactions on Power Systems 15(1) (2000)

[8] EL-Zonkoly, A.M.: Optimal tuning of power systems stabilizers and AVR gains using particle swarm optimization. International Journal of Expert Systems with Applications 31(939), 551–557 (2006)

[9] El-Zonkoly, A.M., Khalil, A.A., Ahmied, N.M.: Optimal tunning of lead-lag and fuzzy logic power system stabilizers using particle swarm optimization. Expert Systems with Applications 36, 2097–2106 (2009)

[10] Coello, C.A.C., Pulido, G.T., Lechuga, M.S.: Handling multiple objectives with particle swarm optimization. IEEE Trans. on Evolutionary Computation 8(3), 256–279 (2004)

[11] Yee, A.K.Y., Ray, A.K., Rangaiah, G.P.: Multiobjective optimization of an industrial styrene reactor. Computers and Chemical Engineering 27, 111–130 (2003)

[12] Zitzler, E., Thiele, L.: Multi-objective evolutionary algorithms: a comparative case study and the strength Pareto approach. IEEE Trans. on Evolutionary Computation 3(4), 257–271 (1999)

[13] Knowles, J.D., Corne, D.W.: Approximating the nondominated front using the Pareto archive evolutionary strategy. Evolutionary Computation 8(2), 149–172 (2000)

[14] Zitler, E., Laumanns, M., Thiele, L.: SPEA2: Improving the strength Pareto evolutionary algorithm. In: Swiss Federal Institute of Technology, Lausanne, Switzerland, Tech. Rep. TIK-Rep, 103 (2001)

[15] Deb, K.: Multiobjective Optimization Using Evolutionary Algorithms. Wiley, Chichester (2001)

[16] Fonseca, C.M., Fleming, P.J.: An overview of evolutionary algorithms in multi-objective optimization. Evolutionary Computation 3(1), 1–16 (1995)

# A Genetic Algorithm Approach for the Multi-commodity, Multi-period Distribution Planning in a Supply Chain Network Design

G. Reza Nasiri*, Hamid Davoudpour, and Yaser Movahedi

Department of Industrial Engineering , Amirkabir University of Technology, Hafez Avenue,
Tehran, Iran, P.O. Box 15875-4413
Tel.: +98(21)64542760; Fax: +98(21)66413969
reza_nairi@aut.ac.ir

**Abstract.** Distribution decisions play an important role in the strategic planning of supply chain management. In order to use the most proper strategic decisions in a supply chain, decision makers should focus on the identification and management of the sources of uncertainties in the supply chain process. In this paper these conditions in a multi-period problem with demands changed over the planning horizon is considered. We develop a non-linear mixed-integer model and propose an efficient heuristic genetic based algorithm which finds the optimal facility locations/allocation, relocation times and the total cost, for the whole supply chain. To explore the viability and efficiency of the proposed model and the solution approach, various computational experiments are performed based on the real size case problems.

**Keywords:** Supply chain management, Meta-heuristics, Multi-period problem.

## 1 Introduction

In recent decades, companies increasingly see themselves as a part of a supply chain that have to compete against the other supply chains, rather than as a single firm competing against the other individual firms (Christopher, 1998). In this environment, occurrence of defect in one part of the supply chain, will affect total performance of the whole chain. On the other hand, in several researches, uncertainties in supply, processes and demands are recognized to have a major impact on the manufacturing function (Wilding, 1998). Davis (1993) believes that the real problem in managing and controlling complex networks is "the uncertainty". Uncertainty propagates throughout the network and motivates the inefficient processes and non-value adding activities. This uncertainty is expressed the questions such as: what my customers will order? How many products we should hold? And according to the order specifications, when the suppliers will deliver the requested goods? The presence of uncertainty stimulates the decision maker to create safety buffers in time, capacities and inventories to prevent bad chain performance.

---

* Corresponding author.

B.K. Panigrahi et al. (Eds.): SEMCCO 2010, LNCS 6466, pp. 494–505, 2010.
© Springer-Verlag Berlin Heidelberg 2010

This work develops a stochastic non-linear programming method for modeling the multi-period problem and capacity planning in a distribution network design. Moreover, the model incorporates optimizing the inventory policy into the facility location decisions. A Genetic Algorithm (GA) based solution approach for the distribution planning problem which is one of the NP hard problems. To investigate the performance of the proposed GA, the results obtained from solving the randomly selected problems are compared with the results obtained from LINGO software.

# 2   Problem Description and Formulation

In this research we consider a multi-period, multi-commodity location-allocation problem with stochastic customers' demands, such that demand pattern and the other parameters could change among the planning periods. We assume a two-echelon supply chain network consists of single plant, various potential warehouses and several customers with distributed demands. Location decisions are to be made for the distribution centers (DCs), which can be opened and closed more than once during the planning horizon. A decision can also be made regarding the capacity level at which each DC will operate. The single plant existing in the upper echelon can supply the DCs with every product and in every quantity that might be required. In each time period and for each product, single assignment is assumed between customers and DCs. The demand of each customer for each product in each time period is assumed to follow a Normal probability distribution. The lead time is also assumed to follow a Normal distribution.

## 2.1   Problem Formulation

Mathematical model for problem described above is formulated as follow:

**Parameters:**

| | |
|---|---|
| $I$ | Set of retailers (or customers) for $i=1, ...,m$ |
| $J$ | Set of potential distribution centers (or warehouses) for $j=1, ...,n$ |
| $K$ | Set of available capacity level for each DC for $k=1, ...,p$ |
| $L$ | Set of products, for $l=1, ...,q$ |
| $T$ | Set of planning periods, for $t=1, ..., \tau$ |
| $TC_{ijl}^t$ | Unit cost correlated with transportation one unit of product $l$ from $DC_j$ to customer $i$ in period $t$ |
| $\overline{TC}_{jl}^t$ | Unit cost correlated with transportation one unit of product $l$ from plant to customer $i$ in period $t$ |
| $LC_{jk}^t$ | Fixed location cost of $DC_j$ at $k$-th capacity level in period $t$ |
| $RC_{jk}^t$ | Fixed relocation cost of $DC_j$ at $k$-th capacity level in period $t$ |
| $Q_{jl}^t$ | Optimum order size of product $l$ in $DC_j$ in period $t$ |
| $HC_{jl}^t$ | Unit of holding cost of product $l$ in $DC_j$ during period $t$ |
| $MC_{jl}^t$ | Unit of holding cost of product $l$ in $DC_j$ in the end of period $t$ |

| | |
|---|---|
| $OC_{jl}^t$ | Fixed ordering cost in $DC_j$ for product $l$ in period $t$ |
| $SC_{jl}^t$ | Unit of shortage cost of product $l$ in $DC_j$ in the end of period $t$ |
| $s_l$ | The space needed for storage of one $l$-th product |
| $K_{jk}$ | Available capacity of $DC_j$ at level $k$ |
| $\mu_{D,il}^t$ | Mean of $i$-th customer's demand for product $l$ in period $t$ |
| $\sigma_{D,il}^{t\,2}$ | Variance of $i$-th customer's demand for product $l$ in period $t$ |
| $\mu_{L,jl}^t$ | Mean of lead time for product $l$ in $DC_j$ in period $t$ |
| $\sigma_{L,jl}^{t\,2}$ | Variance of lead time for product $l$ in $DC_j$ in period $t$ |
| $Z_{1-\alpha}$ | Value of the Standard Normal distribution |
| $D_{jl}^t$ | Average of product $l$ assigned to $DCj$ during period $t$ |
| $V_{jl}^t$ | Variance of product $l$ assigned to $DCj$ during period $t$ |

**Decision variables:**

| | |
|---|---|
| $L_{jk}^{t,t'}$ | 1, if $DC_j$ is opened at $k$-th capacity level since period $t$ and stays open until the end of period $t'$ $t$, otherwise 0. |
| $RL_{jk}^{t,t'}$ | 1, if $DCj$ is re-opened at $k$-th capacity level since period $t$ and stays open until the end of period $t'$, otherwise 0. |
| $A_{ijl}^t$ | 1, if customer $i$ for product $l$ assigned to DC $j$ during period $t$ |
| $I_{jl}^t$ | Inventory of product $l$ in $DCj$ in the end of period $t$ |
| $B_{jl}^t$ | Shortage of product $l$ in $DCj$ in the end of period $t$ |
| $N_{jl}^t$ | Number of order issued by $DCj$ for product $l$ during period $t$ |

## 2.2 Ordering and Inventory Control Policy

Assume a continuous inventory policy in any DCs/warehouses for procurement of each product in each period, shown by $(Q_{jl}^t, r_{jl}^t)$. This policy considered fixed order quantity during each period, depending on cost factors of model. $r_{jl}^t$ represents such inventory level that an order with quantity $Q_{jl}^t$ is ordered by the $DC_j$ for product $l$ in period $t$.

Thence the proposed model is a multi-period case, it is possible that any active DC has been closed then in each period, hence for avoiding miss of orders that would not being delivered until end of period, last ordered batch(es) of each DC in each period would not be ordered.

When both demand and lead time are stochastic assumed to follow a Standard Normal distribution, with a given probability $1 - \alpha$, the average inventory of each product in each DC during two consecutive orders is:

$$\frac{Q_{jl}^{t}}{2} + Z_{1-\alpha} \cdot \sqrt{\mu_{L,jl}^{t} \cdot V_{jl}^{t\,2} + D_{jl}^{t} \cdot \sigma_{L,jl}^{t\,2}} \tag{1}$$

In Eq. (1), first term represents average inventory of product $l$ at $DC_{j}$ in period $t$ and the second term denotes the safety stock must be kept at warehouse $j$. Then average holding cost during two consecutive orders is:

$$HC_{jl}^{t} \frac{Q_{jl}^{t}}{2} + Z_{1-\alpha} \cdot HC_{jl}^{t} \cdot \sqrt{\mu_{L,jl}^{t} \cdot V_{jl}^{t\,2} + D_{jl}^{t\,2} \cdot \sigma_{L,jl}^{t\,2}} \tag{2}$$

In this situation total operating cost for one order is consist of holding cost, ordering cost and transportation cost as shown below:

$$\overline{TC}_{jl}^{t} \cdot Q_{jl}^{t} + OC_{jl}^{t} + \left( \frac{HC_{jl}^{t} \times Q_{jl}^{t}}{2} + Z_{1-\alpha} \cdot HC_{jl}^{t} \cdot \sqrt{\mu_{L,jl}^{t} \cdot V_{jl}^{t\,2} + D_{jl}^{t\,2} \cdot \sigma_{L,jl}^{t\,2}} \right) \cdot \frac{Q_{jl}^{t}}{D_{jl}^{t}} \tag{3}$$

In Eq. (3), $Q_{jl}^{t} / D_{jl}^{t}$ demonstrates time between two consecutive orders, and can be shown by $T_{jl}^{t}$. Unit rate of cost correlated with ordering, holding and transportation is attained by dividing Eq. (3) by $T_{jl}^{t}$:

$$\left( \overline{TC}_{jl}^{t} + \frac{OC_{jl}^{t}}{Q_{jl}^{t}} \right) \times D_{jl}^{t} + \frac{HC_{jl}^{t} \times Q_{jl}^{t}}{2} + Z_{1-\alpha} \cdot HC_{jl}^{t} \cdot \sqrt{\mu_{L,jl}^{t} \cdot V_{jl}^{t\,2} + D_{jl}^{t\,2} \cdot \sigma_{L,jl}^{t\,2}} \tag{4}$$

By differentiating Eq. (4) in terms of $Q_{jl}^{t}$ for each DC, product and period, and replacing $Q_{jl}^{t}$ in Eq. (4), total cost of one order can be expressed as follow:

$$2OC_{jl}^{t} + (Z_{1-\alpha} \cdot HC_{jl}^{t} \cdot \sqrt{\mu_{L,jl}^{t} \cdot V_{jl}^{t\,2} + D_{jl}^{t\,2} \cdot \sigma_{L,jl}^{t\,2}}) \times \sqrt{\frac{2OC_{jl}^{t}}{D_{jl}^{t} \times HC_{jl}^{t}}} \tag{5}$$

Suppose that in each period, $N_{jl}^{t}$ order is submitted by the $DC_{j}$ for product $l$. then total cost of ordering and inventory during hole of planning horizon can be calculated.

The dynamic location-allocation problem that allows facility to open, close and re-open more than once during the planning horizon, which pursue location, allocation and inventory decisions simultaneously will be formulated as follow:

$$Min \quad \sum_{j=1}^{n}\sum_{k=1}^{p}\sum_{t=1}^{\tau}\sum_{t'=1}^{\tau}LC_{jk}^{t}\times L_{jk}^{t,t'}+\sum_{j=1}^{n}\sum_{k=1}^{p}\sum_{t=2}^{\tau}\sum_{t'=t}^{\tau}RC_{jk}^{t}\times RL_{jk}^{t,t'}$$

$$+\sum_{t=1}^{\tau}\sum_{l=1}^{q}\sum_{j=1}^{n}\sum_{i=1}^{m}(TC_{ijl}^{t}+\overline{TC}_{jl}^{t})\times\mu_{D,il}^{t}\times A_{ijl}^{t}$$

$$+\sum_{t=1}^{\tau}\sum_{j=1}^{n}\sum_{l=1}^{q}MC_{jl}^{t}\times I_{jl}^{t}+\sum_{t=1}^{\tau}\sum_{j=1}^{n}\sum_{l=1}^{q}SC_{jl}^{t}\times B_{jl}^{t}$$

$$+\sum_{t=1}^{\tau}\sum_{j=1}^{n}\sum_{l=1}^{q}N_{jl}^{t}\left\{2OC_{jl}^{t}+(Z_{1-\alpha}\cdot HC_{jl}^{t}\cdot\sqrt{\mu_{L,jl}^{t}\cdot V_{jl}^{t}{}^{2}+D_{jl}^{t}{}^{2}\cdot\sigma_{L,jl}^{t}{}^{2}})\times\sqrt{\frac{2OC_{jl}^{t}}{D_{jl}^{t}\times HC_{jl}^{t}}}\right\} \quad (6)$$

*Such that:*

$$\sum_{j=1}^{n}A_{ijl}^{t}=1 \qquad\qquad i=1,...,m;\ l=1,...,q;\ t=1,...,\tau \qquad (7)$$

$$\sum_{k=1}^{p}L_{jk}^{t,t'}\leq1 \qquad\qquad j=1,...,n;t=1,...,\tau;t'=1,...,\tau \qquad (8)$$

$$\sum_{k=1}^{p}RL_{jk}^{t,t'}\leq1 \qquad\qquad j=1,...,n;t=1,...,\tau;t'=1,...,\tau \qquad (9)$$

$$N_{jl}^{t}\times\sqrt{\frac{2OC_{jl}^{t}}{HC_{jl}^{t}\times D_{jl}^{t}}}+\mu_{L,jl}^{t}\leq T \quad j=1,...,n;l=1,...,q;\ t=1,...,\tau \qquad (10)$$

$$\sum_{l=1}^{q}D_{jl}^{t}\times s_{l}\leq k_{jk}\times(L_{jk}^{t,t'}+RL_{jk}^{t,t'}) \quad j=1,...,n;\ k=1,...,p;\ t=1,...,\tau;\ t'=t,...,\tau \ (11)$$

$$\sum_{i=1}^{m}\mu_{D,il}^{t}\times A_{ijl}^{t}=D_{jl}^{t} \qquad\qquad j=1,...,n;\ l=1,...,q;\ t=1,...,\tau \qquad (12)$$

$$\sum_{i=1}^{m}\sigma_{D,il}^{t}{}^{2}\times A_{ijl}^{t}=V_{jl}^{t} \qquad\qquad j=1,...,n;\ l=1,...,q;\ t=1,...,\tau \qquad (13)$$

$$D_{jl}^{t}-N_{jl}^{t}\times\sqrt{\frac{2D_{jl}^{t}\times OC_{jl}^{t}}{HC_{jl}^{t}}}-I_{jl}^{t}-B_{jl}^{t}=0 \quad j=1,...,n;\ l=1,...,q;\ t=1,...,\tau \ (14)$$

$$\sum_{t=1}^{a}\sum_{t'=a}^{\tau}(L_{jk}^{t,t'}+RL_{jk}^{t,t'})-A_{ijl}^{a}\geq0 \quad j=1,...,n;\ l=1,...,q;\ k=1,...,p;\ a=1,...,\tau \ (15)$$

$$\sum_{t=1}^{a-1}\sum_{t'=t}^{a-1}L_{jk}^{t,t'}-\sum_{t'=a}^{\tau}RL_{jk}^{a,t'}\geq0 \qquad\qquad j=1,...,n;k=1,...,p \qquad (16)$$

$$\sum_{t=1}^{\tau} \sum_{t'=t}^{\tau} L_{jk}^{t,t'} \leq 1 \qquad\qquad j=1,...,n; \; k=1,...,p \qquad\qquad (17)$$

$$\sum_{t=1}^{a} \sum_{t'=a}^{\tau} (L_{jk}^{t,t'} + RL_{jk}^{t,t'}) \leq 1 \qquad\qquad j=1,...,n; \; k=1,...,p; \; a=1,...,\tau \quad (18)$$

$$L_{jk}^{t,t'}, RL_{jk}^{t,t'}, A_{ijl}^{t} \in \{0,1\} \qquad i=1,...,m; \; j=1,...,n; \; k=1,...,p; \; t=1,...,\tau; \; t'=1,...,\tau \;(19)$$

$$I_{jl}^{t}, B_{jl}^{t}, N_{jl}^{t} \geq 0 \qquad\qquad j=1,...,n; \; l=1,...,q; \; t=1,...,\tau \qquad\qquad (20)$$

The objective function consists of minimization of fixed location and relocation cost, assignment and transportation cost, holding and shortage cost. Constraint (7) assures that each customer supply each product from only one DC during each period. Constraint (8) and (9) guarantee that, each DC may operate only at one capacity level during each period. Constraint (10) determines maximum number of order issued during each period by each DC for each product, such that all orders delivered before end of period. Constraint (11) ensures that capacity limitation of each active DC is regarded. Average and variance of assigned demand to each DC is determined in constraint (12) and (13). In Eq. (14) inventory balance at the end of each period is considered and hence inventory or shortage is determined. Constraint (15) assures that, at every time period a customer only can be assigned to DCs that are operational in that time period. Constraint (16) guarantees that a DC can be relocated at period "a", if it has opened earlier and is not active at the beginning of period "a". Constraint (17) states that each DC can be opened once during planning horizon, and constraint (18) imposes that in each time period, each DC may be located or relocated. Binary variables and non negative ones are introduced in constraints (19) and (20).

## 3   Proposed Genetic Algorithm

In this section, we propose a GA-based procedure for solving the presented model and describe its designed operators for the presented model.

### 3.1   Chromosome Definition

For the developed model, a two segment chromosome is proposed. Since location/allocation and relocation decisions have been integrated in our problem and each customer for each product has to be assigned only to one DC, integer encoding was used to define this situation. As shown in figure 1, the length of each chromosome equals to $n \times \tau + m \times q \times \tau$ which first section expresses location and relocation variables and the next shows assignment variables. The first section consists of $\tau$ sub-sections and genes value shows that in any period each DC in which capacity level will be opened. If a DC has zero value in each period it means that this DC is closed. Furthermore, during two consecutive periods, changing value for each warehouse means that warehouse location/relocation will be occurred. In each sub-section $m$,

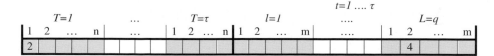

**Fig. 1.** Proposed chromosome structure

genes lied that gives value between *0* to *p* (maximum number of capacity level). Second section of chromosome determines the assignment pattern of customers to the opened DCs, in such a way, during each period every customer's product is supplied only from one DC.

Sine considered problem in the real case is very large scale, for chromosome representation we used integer string stead of binary string. This approach has a high effect in decreasing the introduced genes and algorithm efficiency.

The following notations are used to represent the GA parameters:
pop_size: population size
max_pop_size: maximum population size
free_cap: free capacity
mut_C: mutation chromosome C.

### 3.2 Generation of First Population

Considering the model constraints, the probability of a feasible chromosome in randomly population generating is very low. Thus, for achieve highest possible chance of feasibility we integrate repair procedure to the procedure of generating first population as follows:

1. *Start*
2. *pop_size==1*
3. *If* (pop_size <max_pop_size) then
4.     *Generate n\*τ random number between 0 to p*
5.     *Generate m\*q\*τ random number between 0 to m*
6.     *Determine sum of capacity, generated in first m\*τ Genes*
7.     *According to n\*τ+1 to m\*q\*τ Genes calculate sum of required storage space*
8.     *pop_size==pop_size+1*
9.     *If (Storage space<Total required capacity) then*
10.     *C⁺=DC with free capacity*
11.     *C⁻=DC with capacity shortage*
12.     *Sort C⁺ Descending and C⁻ Ascending*
13.     *Randomly select one of customers that assigned to the first DC in C⁻ and reassigned it to the first DC in C⁺*
14.     *Else go to line 3*
15. *Else go to end*
16. *Go to line 3*
17. *End.*

### 3.3  Chromosome Evaluation

To determine the fitness of generated chromosomes in each population, a one-to-one relationship must be established between chromosomes, variables and objective function of the model. Each chromosome fitness will determined with its objective function.

> *Start*
> *Input first Chromosome*
> *Determine Location, Relocation and Assignment variable according to this chromosome*
> *State optimal order size for each DC, for each product in each period*
> *Determine maximum available order for each DC*
> *Balance inventory level at each period and determine Stocks or shortage*
> *If (For each DC: required cap. <Created cap) then*
> > *Determine Fitness of desired chromosome*
> > *Read next chromosome*
>
> *Else run repair procedure*
> *End.*

If the results do not provide any feasible solutions, then the related chromosome is infeasible and should be omitted from the population. Considering the model constraints in above randomly procedure, the probability of generating feasible chromosome is very low thus in each generation the infeasible generated chromosome needs to become a feasible chromosome. For this purpose a repair procedure proposed as below:

> *Start*
> *Input Chromosome, Determine Location, Relocation and Assignment variable*
> *State total assigned Demand to each DC in each period*
> *State capacity of each the opened DC (Located or Relocated)*
> *Determine capacity Gap between available capacity and needed one*
> *If (Gap>0) then*
> > *Constitute Free_cap collection by DC with vacant capacity and Leak_cap by DC with no vacant capacity*
> > *Sort Free_cap descending and Leak_cap ascending*
> > > *Select first DC in Leak_cap and sort assigned customers descending, by their demand Determine Gap between Gap and customer demand (Gap2)*
> > > *State customer that has the least Gap2. Assigned it to the first DC at Free_cap collection*
> >
> > *Update the chromosome*
>
> *Else go to end.*
> *End.*

### 3.4  Cross over and Mutation Operators

Similar to Altiparmak et al. (2006), in a binary chromosome generated with title cross-over chromosome, a uniform cross-over operator is used. Because of specific structure of our chromosome, a two-stage mutation algorithm proposed as below. In first step, the mutated section has been determined, and in second step mutation will be performed in selected section.

```
Start
Consider chromosome C
Generate one random number between 0 and 1(rand1)
If (rand1<=mut_rate) then
        Generate another random number between 0 and 1(rand2)
    If (rand2<=0.5) then
        Select randomly two genes in the first section of the chromosome
        (G1 and G2)
        mut_C==C.
        Replace Values of G1 by G2 and G2 by G1.
    Else
        Select randomly one gene in second section of chromosome (G1)
        mut_C==C.
        Replace Values of G1 by a random number between 0 and m
        Add mut_C to population
Else go to end.
End.
```

### 3.5 Solution Reporting

Finally, if the stop conditions of the proposed algorithm are satisfied, the final chromosome and its related fitness value is determined and reported.

## 4   Computational Results

Various test problems, with different sizes are solved to evaluate the performance of the presented algorithm. The size of test problems is benchmarked by prior researches in location theory and designed test problems listed in Table 1.

For solving proposed problems, required parameters are generated randomly by uniform distribution. To capture a wide range of problem structures, twenty seven problem sets were generated randomly. The numbers of customers, potential warehouse sites and periods were varying from 40 to 75, 10 to 20, and from 3 to 5, respectively. The number of products was fixed to 2, 3 or 5 and five capacity levels were used for the capacities available to the potential warehouses (i.e., $k=5$). The proposed GA is coded with Matlab7.2 programming language and Lingo8.0 software is used to comparing the results of small-size problems. All the test problems are run on a Pentium IV, 3.4 GHz CPU with 1024 MB memory. Results are reported in Table 2.

The proposed GA runs 10 times for each problem considering following parameters: population size=100; crossover rate =0.75, mutation rate=0.2, number of generation= 500. These parameters had been determined after preliminary experiments based on the Younes (2006) approach.

**Table 1.** Test problem's size

| NO. | number of customers | number of product | number of potential DC | number of periods | number of integer variable | number of non-integer variables |
|---|---|---|---|---|---|---|
| 1 | | | | 3 | 2376 | 192 |
| 2 | 40 | 2 | 10 | 4 | 3488 | 256 |
| 3 | | | | 5 | 4840 | 320 |
| 4 | | | | 3 | 4200 | 360 |
| 5 | 40 | 3 | 10 | 4 | 6000 | 480 |
| 6 | | | | 5 | 8100 | 600 |
| 7 | | | | 3 | 6660 | 600 |
| 8 | 40 | 5 | 10 | 4 | 9280 | 800 |
| 9 | | | | 5 | 12200 | 1000 |
| 10 | | | | 3 | 5355 | 360 |
| 11 | 50 | 2 | 15 | 4 | 7740 | 480 |
| 12 | | | | 5 | 10575 | 600 |
| 13 | | | | 3 | 7650 | 540 |
| 14 | 50 | 3 | 15 | 4 | 10800 | 720 |
| 15 | | | | 5 | 14400 | 900 |
| 16 | | | | 3 | 12240 | 900 |
| 17 | 50 | 5 | 15 | 4 | 16920 | 1200 |
| 18 | | | | 5 | 22050 | 1500 |
| 19 | | | | 3 | 10140 | 480 |
| 20 | 75 | 2 | 20 | 4 | 14320 | 640 |
| 21 | | | | 5 | 19100 | 800 |
| 22 | | | | 3 | 14700 | 720 |
| 23 | 75 | 3 | 20 | 4 | 20400 | 960 |
| 24 | | | | 5 | 26700 | 1200 |
| 25 | | | | 3 | 23820 | 1200 |
| 26 | 75 | 5 | 20 | 4 | 32560 | 1600 |
| 27 | | | | 5 | 41900 | 2000 |

The results are described by providing the average and the worst values for objective function and CPU time both for the proposed GA and for the Lingo results. As it is indicated in Table 2, only for problem sets 1 to 4 and 7 feasible solution is found after running the corresponding LINGO model in 180 minutes run time. For this reason, we compare LINGO results with the proposed GA heuristic in these problems and the gap between two algorithms indicates that the results are coincidence. The results of the reported experiments in Table 2, show that the proposed heuristic, produces very good feasible solutions compared to the results generated by LINGO in significantly less CPU time. The average of CPU time for LINGO results is between 987 to 9384 seconds (only for five solved problems by Lingo), but this time for GA heuristic is between 12 to 478 seconds.

The last column of Table 2 shows that the performance of the proposed solution approach is very considerable for a wide range of problem sizes, with a mean average gap of 1.02% (from 0.0% to 3.96%) over all 270 test problems.

**Table 2.** Computational results

| No. | proposed GA | | | | Lingo | | GAP | |
|---|---|---|---|---|---|---|---|---|
| | objective function | | CPU time | | objective function | CPU time | with Lingo | with the Worst |
| | average | worst | average | worst | | | | |
| 1 | 1.8123 | 1.8123 | 12.2687 | 12.421 | 1.812279 | 987 | 0.00% | 0.00% |
| 2 | 2.5553 | 2.5553 | 12.8352 | 15.041 | 2.555258 | 1874 | 0.00% | 0.00% |
| 3 | 5.4187 | 5.4187 | 13.983 | 17.799 | 5.418706 | 3954 | 0.00% | 0.00% |
| 4 | 2.0235 | 2.0237 | 30.0572 | 35.189 | 2.0234 | 10874 | 0.01% | 0.01% |
| 5 | 2.7419 | 2.742 | 37.3119 | 41.0775 | - | - | - | 0.00% |
| 6 | 5.7139 | 5.714 | 41.8211 | 47.472 | - | - | - | 0.00% |
| 7 | 2.5997 | 2.6006 | 41.9288 | 43.826 | 2.5975 | 9384 | 0.08% | 0.04% |
| 8 | 3.2671 | 3.2791 | 52.0715 | 53.856 | - | - | - | 0.37% |
| 9 | 5.9295 | 5.9791 | 58.9439 | 60.5853 | - | - | - | 0.84% |
| 10 | 2.9523 | 2.9941 | 80.846 | 89.656 | - | - | - | 1.41% |
| 11 | 3.3339 | 3.3991 | 99.8535 | 107.7132 | - | - | - | 1.96% |
| 12 | 6.0005 | 6.0681 | 109.1255 | 130.8648 | - | - | - | 1.13% |
| 13 | 3.1624 | 3.1986 | 129.0944 | 139.2627 | - | - | - | 1.14% |
| 14 | 3.8897 | 3.9614 | 161.4958 | 188.748 | - | - | - | 1.85% |
| 15 | 6.2122 | 6.2787 | 155.8353 | 190.0475 | - | - | - | 1.07% |
| 16 | 3.26 | 3.2885 | 203.977 | 224.7154 | - | - | - | 0.87% |
| 17 | 4.3625 | 4.4353 | 255.9438 | 269.028 | - | - | - | 1.67% |
| 18 | 6.3551 | 6.5011 | 306.0428 | 320.6112 | - | - | - | 2.30% |
| 19 | 3.4693 | 3.6065 | 305.247 | 348.1044 | - | - | - | 3.96% |
| 20 | 4.7584 | 4.7801 | 237.1269 | 282.579 | - | - | - | 0.46% |
| 21 | 6.1822 | 6.3125 | 230.3784 | 252.3245 | - | - | - | 2.11% |
| 22 | 3.5629 | 3.6171 | 278.4666 | 316.1216 | - | - | - | 1.52% |
| 23 | 4.9574 | 5.0032 | 294.8646 | 327.1686 | - | - | - | 0.92% |
| 24 | 6.7686 | 6.8065 | 332.6914 | 368.8694 | - | - | - | 0.56% |
| 25 | 3.879 | 3.9229 | 397.0789 | 459.5115 | - | - | - | 1.13% |
| 26 | 5.2645 | 5.3103 | 439.2083 | 465.354 | - | - | - | 0.87% |
| 27 | 7.0963 | 7.2011 | 478.4296 | 527.8531 | - | - | - | 1.48% |

# 6  Conclusions

We have proposed a new large-scale model for designing distribution network for a two-echelon supply chain in dynamic environment. In the real world many of the input parameters are stochastic and decision making in uncertain environment must be considered in the modeling process.

This subject is considered in the proposed non-linear model and a multi-period location model with inventory decisions is described in this paper. Moreover, the proposed model provides systematic role that facilities can be activated-deactivated and reactivated during the planning horizon. Based of our literature review, we proposed a GA–based procedure for solving the presented model and compare its efficiency with Lingo results. The results for the randomly selected problems show that the performance of proposed solution approach is very considerable for a wide range of problem sizes, with a mean average gap of 1.02% with very reasonable CPU time (between 12 to 478 seconds).

# References

Altiparmak, F., Gen, M., Lin, L., Paksoy, T.: A genetic algorithm for multi-objective optimization of supply chain networks. Computers and Industrial Engineering 51, 197–216 (2006)

Christopher, M.G.: Logistics and Supply Chain Management: Strategies for Reducing Costs and Improving Services. Pitman Publishing, London (1998)

Davis, T.: Effective Supply Chain Management. Sloan Management Review, 35–46 (Summer 1993)

Wilding, R.: The Supply Chain Complexity Triangle: Uncertainty Generation in the Supply Chain. International Journal of Physical Distribution & Logistics Management 28(8), 599–616 (1998)

Younes, A.: Adapting Evolutionary Approaches for Optimization in Dynamic Environments. PhD-thesis, University of Waterloo, Waterloo, Ontario, Canada (2006)

# Particle Swarm Optimization with Watts-Strogatz Model

Zhuanghua Zhu

Economic Information Department, Shanxi Finance & Taxation College,
No.25 QianFeng South Road, Wan Bailin District, Taiyuan, 030024, P.R. China
zhuzhuanghua@sxftc.edu.cn

**Abstract.** Particle swarm optimization (PSO) is a popular swarm intelligent methodology by simulating the animal social behaviors. Recent
study shows that this type of social behaviors is a complex system, however, for most variants of PSO, all individuals lie in a fixed topology, and
conflict this natural phenomenon. Therefore, in this paper, a new variant of PSO combined with Watts-Strogatz small-world topology model,
called WSPSO, is proposed. In WSPSO, the topology is changed according to Watts-Strogatz rules within the whole evolutionary process.
Simulation results show the proposed algorithm is effective and efficient.

## 1 Introduction

Particle swarm optimization (PSO)[1][2] is a novel population-based swarm intelligent methodology. Due to the simple concepts and the ease of implementation,
it has been applied into many areas[3][4][5].

In standard particle swarm optimization, each individual is called a particle,
and flies around the search domain. Each particle manipulates four items: position, velocity, historical best positions found by itself and the entire swarm. For
standard variant of PSO, the velocity and position are updated as follows:

$$v_{jk}(t+1) = wv_{jk}(t) + c_1r_1(p_{jk}(t) - x_{jk}(t)) \tag{1}$$
$$+c_2r_2(p_{gk}(t) - x_{jk}(t))$$

$$x_{jk}(t+1) = x_{jk}(t) + v_{jk}(t+1) \tag{2}$$

where $v_{jk}(t)$ and $x_{jk}(t)$ represent the $k^{th}$ dimensional value of velocity and position vectors of particle $j$ at time $t$, respectively. $p_{jk}(t)$ means the $k^{th}$ dimensional
value of the best position vector which particle $j$ had been found, as well as $p_{gk}(t)$
denotes the corresponding dimensional value of the best position of the whole
swarm found. Inertia weight $w$, cognitive learning factor $c_1$ and social learning
factor $c_2$ are three parameters to control the size of velocity vector. $r_1$ and $r_2$
are two random numbers generated with normal distributions.

Up to date, many variants have been proposed aiming to increase the convergence speed by changing the topology. Suganthan[6] introduced a dynamic

B.K. Panigrahi et al. (Eds.): SEMCCO 2010, LNCS 6466, pp. 506–513, 2010.

neighborhood topology. He begins with an lBest topology of k=1. Therefore, the neighborhood initially consists of the particle itself. As time progresses, k is continuously increased until a gBest topology is attained. Peer[7] proposed a variant of PSO by guaranteeing the global convergence probability with one with gBest, lBest and Von Neumann topologies, respectively. HP. Mu[8] firstly proposed a new topology combined with WS small-world model, however, because the WS small-world model is determined firstly, the topology is still fixed during the iteration. With the same method, Cui et al.[9] also applied this topology to the nearest neighbor interaction PSO. In Hamdan's method[10], several neighborhoods are used simultaneously. During an iteration, each particle checks the fitness value of its new position for a star, circle and von Neumann topology. The particle then uses the topology yielding the best result. This hybrid fared well on nine continuous functions with between two and 30 dimensions. However, an increased amount of computation time must be accepted.

As we known, the animal social behaviors are complex systems, and the communications are changed dynamically. Therefore, the fixed communication topology does not describe the natural phenomenon, and will affect the performance. Therefore, in this paper, a new variant of PSO (WSPSO, in briefly) is designed, in which Watts-Strogatz small-world model is incorporated into the methodology of PSO. Different from previous hybridization, in this new variant, the topology is automated changed during the evolutionary process so that the communication topology for each particle is changed according to its performance dynamically. Simulation results show it is more effective.

The rest of paper is organized as follows. Section 2 gives a brief description for Watts-Strogatz Small-world Model. Then, the details of this new variant for particle swarm optimization is introduced in Section 3. Finally, the simulation results show the proposed algorithm can adjust the exploration and exploitation capabilities dynamically, and improve the convergence speed effectively.

## 2    Watts-Strogatz Small-World Model

Generally, the information flow in social networks is influenced by various properties[12]:

Connectivity(k): the size of the particle neighborhood;

Clustering(C): the number of neighbors of the particle which are simultaneously neighbors of each other;

Path length(L): the smallest average distance between two neighbors(strongly influenced by k and C).

According to the above analysis, Duncan J. Watts and Steven Strogatz proposed the Watts-Strogatz model in their joint 1998 Nature paper[11]. This model is a random graph generation model that produces graphs with small-world properties, including short average path lengths and high clustering.

Briefly, the Watts-Strogatz model is created as follows:

(1)Begin with a low-dimensional regular lattice;

(2)Randomly rewrite some of the links with a probability $p$;

(3)For small $p$, a mostly regular graph is produced;

(4)Small-world properties are obtained through the randomly wired links.

More details of the Watts-Strogatz model can be referred to corresponding references.

## 3    Introduction of WSPSO Algorithm

Without loss of generality, we consider the following unconstrained problem:

$$min \ f(X) \qquad X \in D \subseteq R^n \tag{3}$$

For WSPSO, because the Watts-Strogatz small-world model topology is changed dynamically during the evolutionary process. There are two problems should be considered:

(1) How to update the topology?

(2) If the topology is updated, how many iterations are needed to run PSO?

To seek the answers for the above mentioned problems, two parameters $m_1$ and $m_2$ are employed, $m_1$ is used to test how long period the topology is updated in which the PSO is applied to evolve, while $m_2$ refers to the update steps for Watts-Strogatz model.

The detailed steps of WSPSO are listed as follows.

Step1. Initializing each coordinate $x_{jk}(0)$ and $v_{jk}(0)$ sampling within $[x_{min}, x_{max}]$ and $[0, v_{max}]$, respectively, determining the historical best position by each particle and the swarm, generating the initial topology with $m_0$ edges for each particle.

Step2. Computing the fitness of each particle.

Step3. Updating the historical best positions of each particle and the swarm at time $t$;

Step4. If the current iteration $t$ is less than $p \times Generation$, goto Step 5; otherwise, goto Step 7;

Step5. If the current iteration $t$ is divisible by $m_1$, then the Watts-Strogatz update rules are applied to adjust the topology for $m_2$ steps;

Step6. Performing PSO velocity update equations (1), while symbol $p_{gk}(t)$ means the best historical position in the neighborhood of particle $k$, goto Step8;

Step7. Updating the velocity vector with equations (1);

Step8. Updating the position vector with equation (2);

Step7. If the criteria is satisfied, output the best solution; otherwise, goto step 2.

## 4    Simulation Results

Four famous benchmark functions are used to test the proposed algorithm's efficiency. They are Schwefel Problem 2.26, Ackley, and two different Penalized Functions, the global optima is 0 except Schwefel Problem 2.26 is $-418.98 \times Dimension$, while all of them are multi-model functions with many local minima.

The general information of these four benchmarks are listed as follows, more details can be seen in [13].

Schwefel Problem 2.26:

$$f_1(x) = -\sum_{j=1}^{n}(x_j \sin(\sqrt{|x_j|}))$$

where $|x_j| \leq 500.0$, and

$$f_1(x^*) = f_1(420.9687, 420.9687, ..., 420.9687)$$
$$\approx -418.98 \times Dimension$$

Ackley Function:

$$f_2(x) = -20exp(-0.2\sqrt{\frac{1}{n}\sum_{j=1}^{n}x_j^2})$$

$$-exp(\frac{1}{n}\sum_{k=1}^{n}\cos 2\pi x_k) + 20 + e$$

where $|x_j| \leq 32.0$, and

$$f_2(x^*) = f_2(0, 0, ..., 0) = 0.0$$

Penalized Function1:

$$f_3(x) = \frac{\pi}{30}\{10\sin^2(\pi y_1) + \sum_{i=1}^{n-1}(y_i - 1)^2[1 + 10\sin^2(\pi y_{i+1})]$$

$$+(y_n - 1)^2\} + \sum_{i-1}^{n}u(x_i, 10, 100, 4)$$

where $|x_j| \leq 50.0$, and

$$u(x_i, a, k, m) = \begin{cases} k(x_i - a)^m, & \text{if } x_i > a \\ 0, & \text{if } -a < x_i \leq a \\ k(-x_i - a)^m, & \text{if } x_i < -a \end{cases}$$

$$y_i = 1 + \frac{1}{4}(x_i + 1)$$

$$f_3(x^*) = f_3(1, 1, ..., 1) = 0.0$$

Penalized Function2:

$$f_4(x) = 0.1\{\sin^2(3\pi x_1) + \sum_{i=1}^{n-1}(x_i - 1)^2[1 + \sin^2(3\pi x_{i+1})]$$

$$+(x_n - 1)^2[1 + \sin^2(2\pi x_n)]\} + \sum_{i=1}^{n}u(x_i, 5, 100, 4)$$

where $|x_j| \leq 50.0$, and

$$f_4(x^*) = f_4(1, 1, ..., 1) = 0.0$$

In order to certify the efficiency,two different variants are used to compare: standard particle swarm optimization (SPSO) and modified particle swarm optimization with time-varying accelerator coefficients (TVAC)[14].

The coefficients of SPSO,TVAC and WSPSO are set as follows: the inertia weight $w$ is decreased linearly from 0.9 to 0.4. Two accelerator coefficients $c_1$ and $c_2$ are both set to 2.0 with SPSO, in TVAC and WSPSO, $c_1$ decreased from 2.5 to 0.5,while $c_2$ increased from 0.5 to 2.5. Total individual is 100, and the dimensionality is 30, 50, 100, 200 and 300, coefficient $v_{max}$ is set to the upper bound of domain. In each experiment,the simulation run 30 times, while each time the largest evolutionary generation is $50 \times Dimension$.

The first part of simulation is to decide the values of parameters $m_1$ and $m_2$. To provide a clearly choice, the Uniform Design method is employed. The Uniform design is an efficient fractional factorial design. It was proposed by Professor Fang Kai-Tai and Professor Wang Yuan in 1980. It has been successfully used in various fields such as chemistry and chemical engineering, pharmaceutics, quality engineering, system engineering, survey design, computer sciences and natural sciences. The uniform design has been recognized as an important space-filling design by the international community.

The domain of $m_1$, $m_2$ and $m_0$ are chosen from $(1, 46)$, $(50, 500)$ and $[5, 50]$, respectively, whereas $p$ is from $(0.1, 1.0]$. Total 10 sample points for each parameter are chosen uniformly from the domain, and construct a $U_{10}(10^8)$ table. Ackley function with dimension 30 is selected as an example, and the results are listed as Tab.1.

To obtain the exact parameters' values, multivariate linear regression analysis is applied , and the regression equation is

$$y = 9.7205e - 14 - 1.9087e - 15m_1 \qquad (4)$$
$$+1.5750e - 16m_2$$
$$+1.5906e - 13p$$
$$-3.5085e - 15m_0$$

It means the values of $m_1$ and $m_0$ should be the upper bounds, while $m_2$ and $p$ should be lower bounds, this setting results $7.5850e - 14$ which is less than the best solution of Tab.1. Therefore, from the $8^{th}$ setting of Tab.1, we further explore the best settings. After several tests, the final setting is: $m_1 = 36$, $m_2 = 100$, $p = 0.9$ and $m_0 = 35$.

Figure 1 to 4 illustrate the result of WSPSO compared with SPSO and TVAC. The performance of WSPSO is always superior than SPSO and TVAC in these benchmarks. Therefore, for the multi-model functions, the dynamic WS small-world topology can improve the performance significantly.

**Table 1.** Uniform Design Results for Ackley Function

| No. | $m_1$ | $m_2$ | $p$ | $m_0$ | Performance |
|---|---|---|---|---|---|
| 1 | 1 | 150 | 0.4 | 25 | 6.6021e-014 |
| 2 | 6 | 300 | 0.8 | 50 | 5.3705e-014 |
| 3 | 11 | 450 | 0.1 | 20 | 5.1336e-014 |
| 4 | 16 | 50 | 0.5 | 45 | 4.6244e-014 |
| 5 | 21 | 200 | 0.9 | 15 | 2.2861e-013 |
| 6 | 26 | 350 | 0.2 | 40 | 4.5533e-014 |
| 7 | 31 | 500 | 0.6 | 10 | 2.2909e-013 |
| 8 | 36 | 100 | 1.0 | 35 | 4.0915e-014 |
| 9 | 41 | 250 | 0.3 | 5 | 5.7376e-014 |
| 10 | 46 | 400 | 0.7 | 30 | 4.7783e-014 |

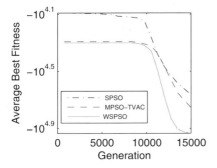

**Fig. 1.** Comparison results for Schwefel 2.26 with Dimension 300

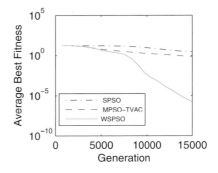

**Fig. 2.** Comparison results for Ackley with Dimension 300

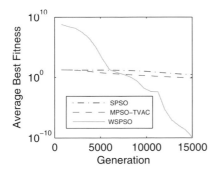

**Fig. 3.** Comparison results for Penalized Function1 with Dimension 300

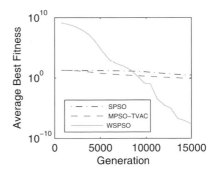

**Fig. 4.** Comparison results for Penalized Function2 with Dimension 300

# 5    Conclusion

To design the dynamical changed topology, this paper incorporates Watts-Strogatz small-world topology model into the standard particle swarm optimization to improve the escaping capability from local optimum, and proposes a new variant. The further researches are to investigate the affections of the swarm size and other topologies.

# Acknowledgement

This paper were supported by Shanxi Science Foundation for Young Scientists under Grant 2009021017-2.

# References

1. Eberhart, R.C., Kennedy, J.: A new optimizer using particle swarm theory. In: Proceedings of 6th International Symposium on Micro Machine and Human Science, pp. 39–43 (1995)
2. Kennedy, J., Eberhart, R.: Particle swarm optimization. In: Proceedings of ICNN 1995 - IEEE International Conference on Neural Networks, pp. 1942–1948. IEEE CS Press, Perth (1995)
3. Senthil Arumugam, M., Ramana Murthy, G., Loo, C.K.: On the optimal control of the steel annealing processes as a two-stage hybrid systems via PSO algorithms. International Journal of Bio-inspired Computation 1(3), 198–209 (2009)
4. Sivanandam, S.N., Visalakshi, P.: Dyanmic task scheduling with load balancing using parallel orthogonal particle swarm optimization. International Journal of Bio-inspired Computation 1(4), 276–286 (2009)
5. Chen, S., Hong, X., Luk, B.L., Harris, C.: Non-linear system identification using particle swarm optimization tuned radial basis function models. International Journal of Bio-inspired Computation 1(4), 246–258 (2009)
6. Suganthan, P.N.: Particle swarm optimiser with neighbourhood operator. In: Proceedings of the IEEE Congress on Evolutionary Computation, pp. 1958–1962. IEEE Service Center, Los Alamitos (1999)
7. Peer, E.S., van den Bergh, F., Enggelbrecht, A.P.: Using neighbourhoods with the guaranteed convergence PSO. In: Proceedings of the IEEE Swarm Intelligence Symposium, pp. 235–242. IEEE Service Center, Los Alamitos (2003)
8. Mu, H.P.: Study on particle swarm optimization based on dynamic neighborhood topology, Master Dissertation, Taiyuan University of Science and Technology (2008)
9. Cui, Z.H., Chu, Y.F., Cai, X.J.: Nearest neighbor interaction PSO based on small-world model. In: Proceedings of 10th International Conference on Intelligent Data Engineering and Automated Learning, pp. 633–640. Springer, Heidelberg (2009)
10. Hamdan, S.A.: Hybrid Particle Swarm Optimiser using multi-neighborhood topologies. INFOCOMP Journal of Computer Science 7(1), 36–44 (2008)
11. Watts, D.J., Strogatz, S.H.: Collective dynamics of 'small-world' networks. Nature 6684(393), 409–410 (1998)

12. Watts, D.J.: Small Worlds: The Dynamics of Networks Between Order and Randomness. Princeton University Press, Princeton (1999)
13. Yao, X., Liu, Y., Lin, G.M.: Evolutionary programming made faster. IEEE Transactions on Evolutionary Computation, 82–102 (1999)
14. Ratnaweera, A., Halgamuge, S.K., Watson, H.C.: Self-organizing hierarchical particle swarm opitmizer with time-varying acceleration coefficients. IEEE Transactions on Evolutionary Computation 8(3), 240–255 (2004)

# Multi-objective Evolutionary Algorithms to Solve Coverage and Lifetime Optimization Problem in Wireless Sensor Networks

Koyel Chaudhuri and Dipankar Dasgupta

Dept. of Computer Science, The University of Memphis, USA
{kchdhuri,dasgupta}@memphis.edu

**Abstract.** Multi-objective optimization problem formulations reflect pragmatic modeling of several real-life complex optimization problems. In many of them, the considered objectives are competitive with each other and emphasizing only one of them during solution generation and evolution, incurs high probability of producing one sided solution which is unacceptable with respect to other objectives. This paper investigates the concept of boundary search and also explores the application of a special evolutionary operator on a multi-objective optimization problem; Coverage and Lifetime Optimization Problem in Wireless Sensor Network (WSN). The work in this paper explores two competing objectives of WSN;network coverage and network lifetime using two efficient, robust MOEAs. It also digs into the impact of special operators in the multi-objective optimization problems of sensor node's design topology.

## 1 Introduction

Several real world decision problems involve simultaneous optimization of multiple objectives. In many multi-objective optimization problems, objectives are complex and conflicting in nature as well as their directions oppose to each other i.e. minimize cost, maximize coverage, minimum distance and many more. Genetic Algorithm is a potential meta-heuristic search which belongs to a larger class of evolutionary algorithm and it is specifically well-suited for these sorts of optimization problems. Traditional evolutionary algorithm is customized to fit into problem domains and problem specific crossover, mutation, selection, local search and boundary search operators are utilized to generate optimum solution set. A recent study [2] shows that for problems with more than ten objectives, a purely random search may perform favorably when compared with an evolutionary technique. From past researches, it has become quite evident that for single objective problems the performance of evolutionary algorithms can often be improved through the inclusion of a local search operator. The conglomeration of evolutionary algorithm with local searches are known by the names of Memetic Algorithms (MAs) [14], Hybrid Evolutionary Algorithms [3], [5], [9], and Genetic Local Search [13]. These hybrids of evolutionary and local search algorithms have been shown to provide state-of-the-art performance on

B.K. Panigrahi et al. (Eds.): SEMCCO 2010, LNCS 6466, pp. 514–522, 2010.

a wide range of hard single objective combinatorial optimization problems [11], [13], [15] and have also shown to provide a good performance on multiobjective optimization problems[6], [7], [8], [9], [10], [12].

## 2  Problem Statement: Coverage and Lifetime Optimization (CLOP) in WSN

WSNs constitute of huge number of tiny, cost-effective, power-efficient, multifunctional energy-constraint sensor nodes which can communicate over a specific distance [1]. A sensor node, in wireless sensor network is specifically capable of sensing information from surroundings and transmitting them to a High-Energy-Communication Node (HECN). The structure of the network entirely depends on node's electronic, mechanical and communication restrictions along with application-specific requirements [4]. Wireless sensor network is generally designed for getting deployed in hostile environments such as battlefield, military environment, deserts, mountainous and border areas for area monitoring, intrusion detection, environmental monitoring etc. Due to energy-constraints as well as placement of the sensor nodes, it is highly unlikely for all sensor nodes to communicate to the HECN/sink node. Because, this may shorten the lifetime of the node thereby reducing the entire lifespan of the network. The hostile environments keep no way for human intervention for battery replacement in the sensor nodes. Hence it has become the primary requirement for the sensor network design to plan the position of the sensor nodes in such a way that it maximizes the lifetime of the entire network. On the other hand, due to limited number of sensor nodes in design, the mission of covering the area as much as possible has turned out to be one more objective to fulfill. The characteristics of sensor nodes; sensing range and communication range incurs one constraint in this design model. The model needs to take care of the fact that all nodes should be connected to the network. The objective of maximizing area coverage always tends to place sensor nodes far away from the sink so as to cover maximum area whereas another objective of maximizing network lifetime will always try to place the sensor nodes around the sink/HECN so that all of them can communicate directly with it thereby reducing the network lifetime very slowly. But if any node is not in communication range of any other node in the entire network, then the information from that node will not be able to reach the base station/sink thereby making the sole purpose of the wireless sensor network lost. Therefore these issues call for simultaneous optimization of more than one non-linear design optimization while keeping connectivity constraint satisfied.

## 3  Multiobjective Evolutionary Algorithm (MOEA) to Solve CLOP

In this problem 'CLOP', two MOEAs i.e. Nondominated Sorting Genetic Algorithm (NSGA-II) and Strength Pareto Evolutionary Algorithm (SPEA-II) have been applied separately with special local search operator and their comparative analysis has been discussed.

### 3.1   Chromosome Representation

In this problem, a chromosome is made up of a set of Real values, each representing the location of sensor nodes over the hostile terrain. Location of sensor nodes refer to the $x$ and $y$ coordinates of each of the sensor node. Each of the sensor nodes are given a unique real number. The length of the chromosome is equal to the $2*$(total number of sensor nodes). In this work, we assume that the payload of the aircraft carrying sensor nodes to deploy is limited thereby making the number of available sensor nodes constant.

The deployed sensor nodes can monitor anything within $R_{Sensor}$, and where they can communicate with any other node located within $R_{COMM}$. The base station (HECN), with which every sensor must communicate (either directly or via hops maintaining the minimum path to reach the base station), is placed in anywhere in the area of interest. At the incipient stage of sensor deployment in the terrain, each sensor has the same energy in its battery for sensing and communicating the data to the base station, and in our problem, we have taken the assumption that the energy of each sensor decreases by $\frac{1}{Sensor Remaining Energy}$ unit for every data transmission through one link to next hop.

### 3.2   Objective and Fitness Measure

The two objectives of CLOP are competing with each other. Network coverage always wants to spread out network layouts, where sensors are as far apart from each other as possible in order to minimize the overlap between sensing disks. This eventually implies a large number of relay transmissions for sensors communicating directly with the base station, thereby making it highly probable for the network to fail soon due to the huge energy exploitation which will in turn make the network lifetime poor. On the contrary, in order to gain maximum lifetime, all the sensors must communicate directly to the base station, so that their energy is used only for their own data transmission, but not for transmission relaying. This implies a clustered configuration around the base station with a lot of overlap between the sensing disks, causing a poor network coverage. As mentioned above, the objective functions of the problem CLOP are the following:

- Maximum Network Coverage represented in terms of minimum sensing radius overlap:
  $MaximumCoverage = \sum_{i=1}^{n}(\Pi R_{sensor,i}^2 - ECError_i)$
  where ECError refers to Elliptical Curve Error which is represented as
  $EllipticalCurveError_i = \sum_{j=1,i\neq j}^{n} OverlappedAreas_{i,j}$
  where
  $OverlappedAreas_{i,j} = \Pi ab$
  where $a = \sqrt{b(2d-b)}$ and $b = R_{sensor} - d/2$ where $d=$ center distance between node i and j
  Finally the obtained coverage is normalized by the maximum network coverage possible which is $n\Pi R_{sensor}^2$ for $n$ number of nodes.
  Hence the final Coverage $= \frac{ObtainedMaximumCoverage}{MaximumPossibleCoverage}$

– Network Lifetime Network life time for a random deployment of sensor nodes is computed by the number of sensing cycles possible before energy of any node gets exhausted. One sensing cycle of the network is said to be complete if all the nodes are successful in transmitting message to the base station without running out of energy. Since each node spends $1/RemainingSensorEnergy$ to transmit data to 1 hop neighbor, so at every data transmission energy gets depleted for a node. The route from a node to base station is computed using Djikstra algorithm which gives the path of least energy expense. Hence number of sensing cycles depends on the deployment of sensor nodes and the order in which a node runs out of energy. The more the number of sensing cycle, the higher is the network life time.

Maximum network lifetime: $\min(\frac{T_{failure,i}}{T_{max}})$

$\forall i = 1, 2, ....., n$

Due to the nature of objectives, the layout of the sensor network always tend to spread out thereby making it highly likely for the nodes to get disconnected from the network. This speeds up the failure of the network soon. To prevent this situation, this work has introduced a constraint which takes care of the network connectivity.

### 3.3   Genetic Operators

The genetic operators used in these algorithms are all problem specifically designed to aid the MOEAs to find the optimal solutions. The crossover, mutation, selection operators along with the special operators local search and boundary search have been implemented to align with the problem. The crossover operator designed analogous to two-point crossover, once receives two parent solutions, it randomly picks two different positions of two parents to perform crossover. This operator also generates a parent feature window of random size. Later the parent features from these two windows are exchanged to form new offsprings. For mutation, it obtains the location of the sensor node selected from the solution. Afterwards it generates a random real value within the range of the terrain perimetric parameters. The generated new random real value replaces the selected sensor node coordinate which in turn mutates the solution. Local Search operator is used to fine tune the results obtained from the regular genetic search. The sole purpose of this local search operator is to find better solution in the local arena of a node.

**Boundary Search:**   Boundary Search operator plays a crucial role in solving CLOP using multi-objective evolutionary algorithm. As mentioned earlier, it has been noted that in multi-objective optimization problems, the optimal solutions reside around the boundary zone of the problems. To be more specific, the optimal solutions are normally found around the boundary wall of the constraints of the problem. Digging into the root of the concept, this work comes up with the innovative idea of designing another special operator that will aid genetic

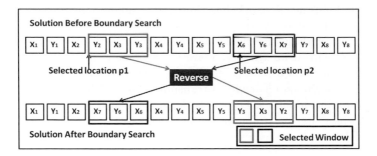

**Fig. 1.** CLOP Boundary Search

search by feeding solutions lying near the boundary. This operator is being designed under the impression as well as with the hope that it will help genetic search to find the optimal solution more effectively by feeding solutions near the boundary region. Boundary search operator works as follows: Solutions in the population set sometimes might turn out to be infeasible in spite of utilizing constraint-satisfying methodologies. This operator will come into play in this scenario; it picks up the infeasible solution (i.e. the solution which has violated any one of the constraints of the problem) and tries to find the nearest boundary of it. If the solution is found to be better with respect to fitness rather than the previous original infeasible solution, then it is fed back into the population in place of the previous one. The way boundary search operator works is as follows: Once a solution is picked up, one random position $p_1$ and $p_2$ in that solution are chosen. Then random time-frame window size $k$ (depicted in red and blue colored rectangles in Figure 1) is selected based on the positions chosen so as not to exceed the chromosome (solution) length. Thereafter, the sensor nodes coordinates in that window sizes have been picked up and kept inside two different buffers $s_1$ and $s_2$ respectively. In the next step, the sensor nodes from $s_1$ are being placed in the positions starting at $p_2$ in a reverse order and the sensor nodes from $s_2$ are also being placed in the positions starting at $p_1$ in a reverse order. The boundary search operator is shown in the Figure 1.

## 4   Experimental Results

In this problem, a problem generator has been used for producing feasible dummy data; random sensor node coordinates. This parametric problem generator is capable of producing several instances of the problem with different parameters. The parameters used in CLOP, are depicted in the Table 1. These parameters have been used in NSGA-II and SPEA-II algorithms for 10 runs of each problem instance. Figure 2 represents the solutions on pareto front while applying NSGA-II and it compares the results obtained in applying NSGA-II and hybrid approach of NSGA-II and its conglomeration with local search operator.

**Table 1.** CLOP Problem Instance Parameters

| Problem Instance | Population Size | Evaluation | Sensor Nodes |
|---|---|---|---|
| 1 | 300 | 50000 | 5 |
| 2 | 500 | 70000 | 10 |
| 3 | 1000 | 100000 | 20 |
| 4 | 2000 | 200000 | 15 |
| 5 | 3000 | 250000 | 7 |
| 6 | 4000 | 300000 | 11 |
| 7 | 5000 | 500000 | 20 |

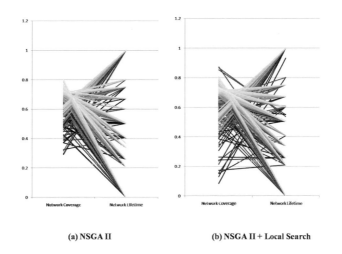

(a) NSGA II                    (b) NSGA II + Local Search

**Fig. 2.** Diversity of solutions found in the Pareto Front using a hybrid NSGA-II

It lucidly displays from the Figure 2-b that, the application of local search incorporates diversity in solutions. After NSGA-II, this problem has been experimented with another robust multi-objective evolutionary algorithm named SPEA2. Analogously, Figure 3 displays the solutions on pareto front which are obtained using SPEA2 and it also compares the results obtained by applying SPEA2 and the hybrid approach of SPEA2 and local search. It can be observed from 3 that, it comes up with substantially extreme sort of solutions with higher coverage and lower lifetime and vice versa. This algorithm turns out to be better performing over the problem rather than NSGA-II since it shows up with the solutions having both objective values high. But it is evident from the Figure 3, that this algorithm suffers from producing significant number of balanced solutions. SPEA2 also depicts that a tiny change in the sensor node placement can cause abrupt change in objective values. It is worth noticing in the Figure 3, that one solution having higher coverage (lying in the zone of 0.82) has low lifetime whereas at the same time, another solution having higher coverage in the same

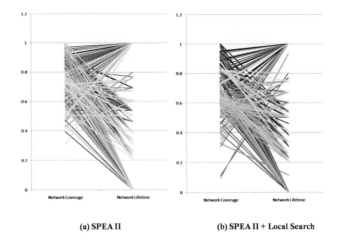

(a) SPEA II                    (b) SPEA II + Local Search

**Fig. 3.** Diversity of solutions found in the Pareto Front using a hybrid SPEA2

zone has higher lifetime too. Local search operator when applied on the SPEA2 algorithm produces even bigger diversity in the maximum coverage and also produces ceratin potential solutions where diversity of solutions can be achieved with moderate network lifetime. The objective plot of hybrid SPEA-II can be seen in the Figure 3-b. From the Figure 3-b, it is quite apparent that the local search plays a crucial role of coming up with solution diversity. Compared to the results generated by regular SPEA2, hybrid SPEA2 maintains a broad diversity of solutions. In second approach, solutions with coverage lying around the zone of 0.1 is obtained too whereas the former approach starts showing up solution with coverage lying in the zone of 0.3. This actually proves that the special operator 'Local Search' works well with the algorithm selected for the problem. It is lucidly identified from Figure 2 and 3 of two different algorithms that, the balanced solutions provide better wireless sensor network design topology rather

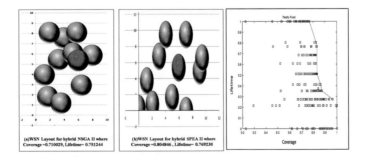

**Fig. 4.** Wireless Sensor Network node optimum deployment topology and corresponding Pareto Front

than the one-sided extreme solution. To depict the result on wireless sensor network layout, Figure 4 is displayed. Figure 4 displays the deployment of sensor nodes in the hostile terrain. It has been observed from the deployment scenarios that, some of the balanced solutions produced using hybrid NSGA-II algorithm are found to be better that the same generated by SPEA2 algorithm displayed in Figure 4-b. From the results depicted, it is clearly analyzed that NSGA-II comes up with better, feasible, acceptable, balanced solutions which is reflected in the deployment. But since SPEA2 remains able to produce extreme solutions mostly, hence the deployment, tries to plot the solutions somewhat around the base station. The pareto front obtained from the experiment with NSGA-II has been depicted in the last section of Figure 4. From the PF shown in Figure 4, it is quite comprehensible that the objective 'coverage' has been plotted against objective 'lifetime'. Pareto front shows the tarde-off between them in this figure. The red line here reflects the pareto front for maximizing objectives 'coverage' and 'lifetime'. The pareto front in Figure 4 reflects that no other solution can dominate those points which have taken part of generating pareto front.

## 5    Conclusion

In this paper, we presented two special problem specific operators amalgamated with two robust, effective and efficient multi-objective evolutionary algorithm Non-dominated Sorting Genetic Algorithm (NSGA-II) and Strength Pareto Evolutionary Algorithm (SPEA2). The proposed approach based on NSGA-II and SPEA2 have depicted to provide a broad gamut of solutions in the interior portions of the trade-off surface. The approach targets to maximize network coverage and network lifetime, therefore yields a pareto front to select balanced non-dominated solutions from. Further work is required to dig into some other special operators or other hybridization mechanisms. Moreover, implementing some domain specific genetic operators might potentially come up with further improvements in the solutions. Other than two distinct objectives considered here, several other additional components such as remote surveillance of a facility, minimization of number of available sensor nodes do exist which require further investigation. Further investigation can be made on number of objectives, several other potential MOEAs such as MOEA/D or 2LB-MOPSO algorithms and weight can be imposed on them depending upon the requirement of the application domain.

## References

1. Akyildiz, I., Su, W., Sankarasubramaniam, Y., Cayirci, E.: Wireless sensor networks: a survey. Computer networks 38(4), 393–422 (2002)
2. Corne, D., Knowles, J.: Techniques for highly multiobjective optimisation: some nondominated points are better than others. In: Proceedings of the 9th annual conference on Genetic and evolutionary computation, p. 780. ACM, New York (2007)

3. Feltl, H., Raidl, G.: An improved hybrid genetic algorithm for the generalized assignment problem. In: Proceedings of the 2004 ACM symposium on Applied computing, pp. 990–995. ACM, New York (2004)
4. Ferentinos, K., Tsiligiridis, T.: Adaptive design optimization of wireless sensor networks using genetic algorithms. Computer Networks 51(4), 1031–1051 (2007)
5. Fleurent, C., Ferland, J.: Genetic hybrids for the quadratic assignment problem. American Mathematical Society 16, 173–187 (1993)
6. Ishibuchi, H., Murata, T.: A multi-objective genetic local search algorithm and its application to flowshop scheduling. IEEE Transactions on Systems, Man, and Cybernetics–Part C: Applications and Reviews 28(3) (1998)
7. Jaszkiewicz, A.: On the performance of multiple-objective genetic local search on the 0/1 knapsack problem - a comparative experiment. IEEE Transactions on Evolutionary Computation 6(4), 402–412 (2002)
8. Knowles, J., Corne, D.: M-PAES: A memetic algorithm for multiobjective optimization. In: 2000 Congress on Evolutionary Computation 2000, Citeseer, vol. 1, pp. 325–332 (2000)
9. Knowles, J., Corne, D.: Towards landscape analyses to inform the design of a hybrid local search for the multiobjective quadratic assignment problem. Soft computing systems: design, management and applications, 271–279 (2002)
10. Knowles, J., Corne, D.: Memetic algorithms for multiobjective optimization: issues, methods and prospects. Recent advances in memetic algorithms, 313–352 (2005)
11. Krasnogor, N.: Towards robust memetic algorithms. Recent advances in memetic algorithms, 185–207 (2005)
12. Lopez-Ibanez, M., Paquete, L., Stützle, T.: Hybrid population-based algorithms for the bi-objective quadratic assignment problem. Journal of Mathematical Modelling and Algorithms 5(1), 111–137 (2006)
13. Merz, P., Freisleben, B.: A genetic local search approach to the quadratic assignment problem. In: Proceedings of the seventh international conference on genetic algorithms, Citeseer, pp. 465–472 (1997)
14. Moscato, P.: On evolution, search, optimization, genetic algorithms and martial arts: Towards memetic algorithms (Technical Report C3P 826). Caltech Concurrent Computation Program, California Institute of Technology, Pasadena, CA (1989)
15. Moscato, P.: Memetic algorithms: A short introduction. In: New ideas in optimization, p. 234. McGraw-Hill Ltd., New York (1999)

# Offline Parameter Estimation of Induction Motor Using a Meta Heuristic Algorithm

Ritwik Giri[1], Aritra Chowdhury[1], Arnob Ghosh[1],
B.K. Panigrahi[2], and Swagatam Das[1]

[1] Dept. of Electronics and Telecommunication Engg.
Jadavpur University, Kolkata 700 032, India
[2] Electrical Engg. Department, IIT-Delhi
`ritwikgiri@gmail.com`, `aritra131288@gmail.com`,
`arnob008@gmail.com`, `bijayaketan.panigrahi@gmail.com`,
`swagatamdas19@yahoo.co.in`

**Abstract.** An offline parameter estimation problem of an induction motor using a well known, efficient yet simple meta heuristic algorithm DEGL (Differential Evolution with a neighborhood based mutation scheme) has been presented in this article. Two different induction motor models such as approximate and exact models are considered. The parameter estimation methodology describes a method for estimating the steady-state equivalent circuit parameters from the motor performance characteristics, which is normally available from the manufacturer data or from tests. Differential Evolution is not completely free from the problems of slow or premature convergence, that's why the idea of a much more efficient variant of DE comes. The variant of DE used for solving this problem utilize the concept of the neighborhood of each population member. The feasibility of the proposed method is demonstrated for two different motors and it is compared with the genetic algorithm and the Particle Swarm Optimization algorithm. From the simulation results it is evident that DEGL outperforms both the algorithms (GA and PSO) in the estimation of the parameters of the induction motor.

**Keywords:** Metaheuristics, Genetic Algorithms, Particle Swarm Optimization, Differential Evolution.

## 1  Introduction

Induction machine models used for the solution of a variety of steady-state problems require equivalent circuit parameters. These parameters include the resistances and reactance representing the stator, rotor and magnetizing branches. The main problem of induction motor parameter estimation is the unavailability of manufacturer data to construct accurate models. Due to this reason, the induction motor models are not explicitly represented in various applications.

The conventional technique for estimating the induction motor parameters are based on no-load and locked-rotor tests [1]. However, these approaches cannot be implemented easily. Besides, the locked-rotor test requires that the shaft of the motor

B.K. Panigrahi et al. (Eds.): SEMCCO 2010, LNCS 6466, pp. 523–530, 2010.

be locked. In the locked-rotor condition, the frequency of the rotor is equal to the supply frequency, but under typical operations, the rotor frequency is perhaps 1–3 Hz. This incorrect rotor frequency will give misleading results for the locked-rotor test. Classical approach with linear squares has been implemented to identify machine parameters [2-3].

A simple method for determining squirrel cage induction motor parameters and problems in the determination of parameters with the two methods proposed in IEEE standard 112 was discussed [4]. The single cage rotor was modeled with a double cage rotor to predict the starting current and the torque manufacturer data, and the circuit parameters were calculated from the data of the three tests: no-load, locked rotor and over load tests. The method had the advantage of not requiring torque measurements. *Johnson and Willis* [5] and *Cirrincione et al.*[6] have applied deterministic approaches to the parameter estimation problem with some success, although with the inherent problem of convergence to a local optimum instead of the global minimum. The optimum determined by these techniques depends heavily on the initial guess of the parameter, with the possibility of a slightly different initial value causing the algorithm to converge to an entirely different solution [7-8]. Some approaches require derivative of the function, which is not always available or may be difficult to calculate. Due to these reasons, deterministic approaches often cannot find optimal solutions when dealing with non-linear systems.

In the recent years, global optimization techniques such as evolutionary algorithm [8], genetic algorithm [9-12], adaptive GA [13] and Particle Swarm Optimization (PSO) [14] have been proposed to solve the parameter estimation problems.

Differential Evolution (DE), proposed by Storn and Price [15,16], is a simple yet powerful algorithm for real parameter optimization. Recently, the DE algorithm has become quite popular in the machine intelligence and cybernetics communities. It has been shown to perform better than the GA or the PSO [14] over several numerical benchmarks. In this article an efficient variant of DE i.e. DEGL [17] has been used for induction motor parameter estimation to minimize the deviation between estimated and manufacturer data. The equivalent circuit parameters of the approximate and exact models are estimated using DEGL technique. The no-load, locked-rotor and stator resistance tests are conducted on the test machines in order to compute their parameters traditionally (classical parameter estimation method).The validity of the proposed method is tested on two motors. The results obtained using GA, PSO and classical parameter estimation methods are also provided for comparing the results with the proposed algorithm.

The rest of the paper is organized in the following way .Section 2 gives the idea of the problem and its details, section 3 illustrates the proposed algorithm briefly, section 4 presents the experimental results and finally section 5 concludes the paper and unfolds some future research works.

## 2   Problem Formulation

An induction motor can be modeled by using an approximate circuit model and an exact circuit model [18]. The parameter estimation problem is formulated as a least squares optimization problem, the objective being the minimization of deviation between the estimated and the manufacturer data. The problem formulation for the parameter estimation of two different induction motor models is described below.

## 2.1  Approximate Circuit Model Formulation

The problem formulation uses the starting torque, the maximum torque and the full load torque manufacturer data to estimate the stator resistance, the rotor resistance and the stator leakage reactance (inductance) parameters. The magnetizing reactance parameter $(X_m)$ is not considered in this model. The approximate circuit model of the induction motor is shown in Fig. 1. The objective function and associated constraints of the problem are formulated as follows:

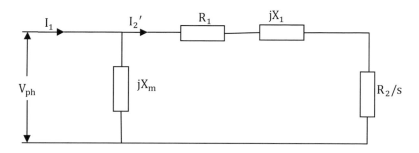

**Fig. 1.** Approximate Circuit Model

$R_2/s$ Is the variable resistance whose resistance depending on the value of slip (s).

### 2.1.1  Objective Function
Objective function is taken same as mentioned in [19]. This is defined as follows:

$$\text{Minimize } F = f_1^2 + f_2^2 + f_3^2, \tag{1}$$

Where

$$f_1 = \frac{\frac{K_t * R_2}{s*[(R_1+\frac{R_2}{s})^2 + X_1^2]} - T_{fl}(mf)}{T_{fl}(mf)}, \quad f_2 = \frac{\frac{K_t * R_2}{(R_1+R_2)^2 + X_1^2} - T_{lr}(mf)}{T_{lr}(mf)}, \quad f_3 = \frac{\frac{K_t}{2*[R_1+\sqrt{R_1^2+X_1^2}]} - T_{max}(mf)}{T_{max}(mf)}$$

$$K_t = \frac{3 * V_{ph}^2}{\omega_s}$$

Where 'mf' stands for manufacturer. $T_{fl}(mf), T_{lr}(mf)$ and $T_{max}(mf)$ are the manufacturer values of the full load torque, the locked-rotor torque and the maximum torque, respectively.

Now the constraints of this model are given below,

### 2.1.2  Constraints
- Maximum torque constraint: $\frac{T_{max}(c)-T_{max}(mf)}{T_{max}(mf)} \leq \pm 0.2$

Where $T_{max}(c)$ is the estimated maximum torque.

## 2.2 Exact Circuit Model Formulation

The problem formulation uses the starting torque, the maximum torque, the full load torque and the full load power factor manufacturer data to estimate the stator resistance, the rotor resistance, the stator leakage reactance, the rotor leakage reactance and the magnetizing leakage reactance (inductance) parameters. Equivalent circuit representing the steady-state operation of a poly-phase induction motor is shown in Fig. 2. The mathematical formulation is as follows:

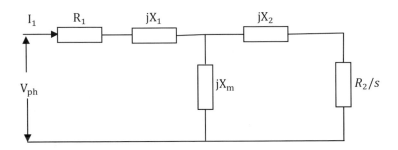

**Fig. 2.** Exact Circuit Model

$R_2/s$ is the variable resistance whose resistance depending on the value of slip (s).

### 2.2.1 Objective Function

$$\text{Minimize } F = f_1^2 + f_2^2 + f_3^2 + f_4^2, \tag{2}$$

Where

$$f_1 = \frac{\frac{K_t * R_2}{s * [(R_{th} + \frac{R_2}{s})^2 + X^2]} - T_{fl}(mf)}{T_{fl}(mf)}, \quad f_2 = \frac{\frac{K_t * R_2}{(R_{th} + R_2)^2 + X^2} - T_{lr}(mf)}{T_{lr}(mf)}, \quad f_3 = \frac{\frac{K_t}{2 * [R_{th} + \sqrt{R_{th}^2 + X^2}]} - T_{max}(mf)}{T_{max}(mf)}$$

$$f_4 = \frac{\cos\left(\tan^{-1}\left(\frac{X}{R_{th} + \frac{R_2}{s}}\right)\right) - pf_{fl}(mf)}{pf_{fl}(mf)}, \quad V_{th} = \frac{V_{ph} * X_m}{X_1 + X_m}, \quad R_{th} = \frac{R_1 * X_m}{X_1 + X_m}, \quad X_{th} = \frac{X_1 * X_m}{X_1 + X_m},$$

$$K_t = \frac{3 * V_{th}^2}{\omega_s}, \quad X = X_2 + X_{th}$$

### 2.2.2 Constraints

- Maximum torque constraint: $\frac{T_{max}(c) - T_{max}(mf)}{T_{max}(mf)} \leq \pm 0.2$

Where $T_{max}(c)$ is the estimated maximum torque.

- Efficiency balance: $\frac{P_{fl} - (I_{1fl}^2 * R_1 + I_{2fl}^2 * R_2 + P_{rot})}{P_{fl}} = \eta_{fl}(mf)$

Where $P_{fl}$ and $P_{rot}$ are the rated power and the rotational losses respectively.

# 3 DEGL Algorithm

DEGL algorithm [17] is a synergy of classical DE algorithm and local neighborhood based mutation technique. In the next section we have discussed about the modification in DEGL only. Here we have not discussed about classical DE, thus for the details of classical DE, [15] and [16] can be referred.

## 3.1 The Local and Global Neighborhood Based Mutation of DE

The DE/target-to-best/ 1 mutation scheme, in its present form, favors exploitation only, but a proper trade–off between exploration and exploitation is necessary for the efficient and effective operation. In this context we propose two kinds of neighborhood models for DE. The first one is called the *local neighborhood model*, and the second one is referred to as the *global mutation model*.

Suppose we have a DE population $P_G = [\vec{X}_{1,G}, \vec{X}_{2,G},......,\vec{X}_{NP,G}]$. Now for every vector $\vec{X}_{i,G}$ we define a neighbourhood of radius $k$ (where $k$ is a nonzero integer between 0 and $(NP-1)/2$, as the neighbourhood must be less than the population size, i.e. $2k+1 < NP$) consisting of vectors $\vec{X}_{i-k,G},......,\vec{X}_{i,G},......,\vec{X}_{i+k,G}$. We assume the vectors to be arranged in a ring topology with respect to their indices such that the two vectors $\vec{X}_{NP,G}$ and $\vec{X}_{2,G}$ are the two immediate neighbors of the vector $\vec{X}_{1,G}$. Note that the neighborhood topology is static and has been defined on the set of indices of the vectors. Although various neighborhood topologies have been defined in the literature for PSO [20] but here applying this concept of neighborhood based mutation on DE we obtained the best result assuming the simple ring topology.

For each member of the population a local donor vector is created by employing the best (fittest) vector in the neighborhood of that member and any two other vectors chosen from the same neighborhood. The model may be expressed as:

$$\vec{L}_{i,G} = \vec{X}_{best,G} + \alpha.\left(\vec{X}_{n\_best_i,G} - \vec{X}_{i,G}\right) + \beta.(\vec{X}_{p,G} - \vec{X}_{q,G}) \tag{3}$$

Where the subscript $n\_best_i$ represents the best vector in the neighborhood of $\vec{X}_{i,G}$ and $p$, $q$ is a member of $[i-k, i+k]$ with $p \neq q \neq i$. $\alpha$ and $\beta$ are the scaling factors.

Similarly the global donor vector is created as:

$$\vec{g}_{best,G} = \vec{X}_{i,G} + \alpha.(\vec{X}_{gbest,G} - \vec{X}_{i,G}) + \beta.(\vec{X}_{r_1,G} - \vec{X}_{r_2,G}) \tag{4}$$

where the subscript $g_{best,G}$ indicates the best vector in the entire population at generation $G$. $\alpha$ and $\beta$ are the scaling factors.

Now we combine the local and global donor vectors using a scalar weight $\omega \in (0,1)$ to form the actual donor vector of the proposed algorithm:

# 4 Experimental Results

The proposed DEGL algorithm has been used in estimating the different parameters of two different induction motors with capacity of 5 & 40 HP respectively using the

**Table 1.** Manufacturers' Specification of the Two Motors

| Specifications | Motor 1 | Motor 2 |
|---|---|---|
| Capacity(HP) | 5 | 40 |
| Voltage(V) | 400 | 400 |
| Current(A) | 8 | 45 |
| Frequency(Hz) | 50 | 50 |
| No. of Poles | 4 | 4 |
| Full Load Slip | 0.07 | 0.09 |
| Starting Torque[Nm] | 15 | 260 |
| Maximum Torque[Nm] | 42 | 370 |
| Starting Current(A) | 22 | 180 |
| Full Load Torque(Nm) | 25 | 190 |

**Table 2.** Comparison of Estimated Results for Motor 1

| Torque | Manufacturers Value | DEGL Model 1 Estimated Value | Error (%) | DEGL Model2 Estimated Value | Error (%) | GA Model 1 Estimated Value | Error (%) | GA Model2 Estimated Value | Error (%) | PSO Model 1 Estimated Value | Error (%) | PSO Model2 Estimated Value | Error (%) |
|---|---|---|---|---|---|---|---|---|---|---|---|---|---|
| Tst | 15 | 15.303 | 2.02 | 17.0266 | 13.51 | 17.88 | 19.2 | 16.73 | 11.53 | 15.46 | 3.07 | 17.6 | 17.36 |
| Tmx | 42 | 39.964 | -4.85 | 40.865 | 2.7 | 37.775 | -10.06 | 35.98 | -14.33 | 39.50 | -5.950 | 40.970 | -2.45 |
| Tfull | 25 | 25.6067 | 2.43 | 26.439 | 5.75 | 21.035 | -15.86 | 20.09 | -19.64 | 22.41 | -10.36 | 22.11 | -11.56 |

**Table 3.** Comparison of Estimated Results for Motor 2

| Torque | Manufacturers Value | DEGL Model 1 Estimated Value | Error (%) | DEGL Model2 Estimated Value | Error (%) | GA Model 1 Estimated Value | Error (%) | GA Model2 Estimated Value | Error (%) | PSO Model 1 Estimated Value | Error (%) | PSO Model2 Estimated Value | Error (%) |
|---|---|---|---|---|---|---|---|---|---|---|---|---|---|
| $T_{st}$ | 260 | 254.147 | -2.25 | 259.0613 | -0.36 | 150 | -42.31 | 258.7 | -0.5 | 205.8 | -20.85 | 255.55 | -1.7 |
| $T_{mx}$ | 370 | 386.4146 | 4.44 | 371.3626 | 0.37 | 315 | -14.86 | 355.48 | -3.92 | 321.07 | -13.22 | 381.63 | -3.14 |
| $T_{full}$ | 190 | 226.0764 | 18.99 | 189.9545 | -0.023 | 166.79 | -12.21 | 200.99 | -5.78 | 175.24 | -7.77 | 222.78 | 17.25 |

**Table 4.** Estimated Results by Classical Method

| Torque | Motor1 Manufacturers Value | Estimated Value | Error (%) | Motor 2 Manufacturers Value | Estimated Value | Error (%) |
|---|---|---|---|---|---|---|
| $T_{st}$ | 15 | 14.25 | -5 | 260 | 265.238 | 2.01 |
| $T_{mx}$ | 42 | 36.46 | -13.18 | 370 | 394.71 | 6.7 |
| $T_{full}$ | 25 | 27.415 | 9.66 | 190 | 178.17 | -6.22 |

**Table 5.** Estimated Parameters for Model 1 by Different Algorithms

| Parameters | Motor 1 DEGL | GA | PSO | Motor 2 DEGL | GA | PSO |
|---|---|---|---|---|---|---|
| $R_1$ | 1.21 | 5.08 | 4.37 | 1.09 | 0.023 | 0.01 |
| $R_2$ | 7.2802 | 8.2 | 6.745 | 0.9631 | 0.484 | 0.497 |
| $X_1$ | 37.2175 | 35 | 34.78 | 2.7796 | 1.72 | 1.51 |

**Table 6.** Estimated Parameters for Model 2 by Different Algorithms

| Parameters | Motor 1 | | | | Motor 2 | | | |
|---|---|---|---|---|---|---|---|---|
| | DEGL | GA | PSO | Classical | DEGL | GA | PSO | Classical |
| $R_1$ | 4.4379 | 2.79 | 1.888 | 8 | 0.8608 | 0.013 | 0.022 | 0.015 |
| $R_2$ | 6.6944 | 7.43 | 5.914 | 5.274 | 1.2342 | 0.458 | 0.454 | 0.44 |
| $X_1, X_2$ | 16.8629 | 15.8 | 15.46 | 14.81 | 1.6975 | 0.533 | 0.596 | 0.576 |
| $X_m$ | 326.8948 | 97 | 287.11 | 409.61 | 16.8175 | 12 | 12.26 | 11.57 |

two different models Approximate and Exact as mentioned in Section 2. Table 1 shows the manufacturers' specification of the two motors under consideration. The performance of DEGL has been compared with two other very well known state-of-the-art metaheuristics GA [21] and PSO [14]. As stopping criterion we have used a fixed no of iterations, $iter_{max} = 100$. To confirm the estimated results obtained by DEGL we also report the estimated circuit parameters obtained by classical parameter estimation method i.e no-load and locked-rotor tests. The three torque errors namely Starting Torque, Maximum Torque and Full-load Torque obtained by DEGL , GA  & PSO have been reported in Tables 2 & 3 for Motor 1 and Motor 2 respectively. Table 4 contains the same three torque errors obtained by classical parameter estimation method using exact circuit approximation model. The best results are marked as bold in the Tables. From these three tables 2-4 it is clearly evident that, the performance of DEGL in estimating the parameters is much better than that of GA, PSO and classical methods except few instances. The estimated approximated parameters of both the motors obtained by all the algorithms have been reported in Table 5 and 6 respectively. All the reported results obtained by DEGL and other competing algorithms have been reported after taking the mean of 50 trial runs.

## 5   Conclusion

A DEGL method-based parameter estimation of two different induction motor models has been proposed. The problem is formulated as a non-linear optimization problem. To verify the feasibility, the proposed method has been evaluated on 5 and 40HP motors and the results were compared with the GA, PSO and the classical parameter estimation method. By analyzing the results, it can be observed that the parameter estimation using DEGL method gives better results than the other techniques. DEGL method gives the minimum fitness value.  Though applied to only induction motor, this DEGL based estimation method is generally applicable to other complicated non-linear system models.

## References

[1] Say, M.G.: Alternating Current Machines. Pitman (1983)
[2] Koubaa, Y.: Recursive identification of induction motor parameters. Journal of Simulation Modeling Practice and Theory 12(5), 363–381 (2004)
[3] Stephan, J., Bodson, M., Chiasson, J.: Real time estimation of induction motor parameters. IEEE Transactions on Industry Appications 30(3), 746–759 (1994)

[4] Pedra, J., Sainz, L.: Parameter estimation of squirrel-cage induction motors without torque measurements. IEE Proceedings on Electric Power Application 153(2), 263–269 (2006)

[5] Johnson, B.K., Willis, J.R.: Tailoring induction motor analytical models to fit known motor performance characteristics and satisfy particular study needs. IEEE Transactions on Power Systems 6(3), 959–965 (1991)

[6] Cirrincione, M., Pucci, M., Cirrincione, G., Capolino, G.A.: A new experimental application of laest aquares techniques for the estimation of the induc- tion motor parameters. IEEE Transactions on Industry Applications 39(5), 1247–1256 (2003)

[7] Pillay, P., Nollan, R., Haque, T.: Application of genetic algorithms to motor parameter determination for transient torque calculations. IEEE Transactions on Industry Applications 33(5) (1997)

[8] Nangsue, P., Pillay, P., Conry, S.: Evolutionary algorithms for induction motor parameter determination. IEEE Transactionson Energy Conversion 14(3), 447–453 (1999)

[9] Bishop, R.R., Richards, G.G.: Identifying induction machine parameters using a genetic optimization algorithm. In: Proceedings on IEEE South east conference, vol. 2, pp. 476–479 (1990)

[10] Alonge, F., Dippolito, F., Ferrante, G., Raimondi, F.M.: Parameter identification of induction motor model using genetic algorithms. In: IEE Proceedings on Control Theory Applications, vol. 145(6) (1998)

[11] Rahimpour, E., Rashtchi, V., Pesaran, M.: Parameter identification of deep-bar induction motors using genetic algorithm. Electrical Engineering 89, 547–552 (2007)

[12] Orlowska Kowalska, T., Lis, J., Szabat, K.: Identification of the induction motor parameters using soft computing methods. Computation and Mathematics in Electrical and Electronics Engineering 25(1), 181–192 (2006)

[13] Abdelhadi, B., Benoudjit, A., Nait Said, N.: Identification of induction machine parameters using a adaptive genetic algorithm. Electric Power Components and Systems 32, 767–784 (2004)

[14] Eberhart, R.C., Kennedy, J.: Particle swarm optimization. In: IEEE International Conference on Neural Networks, vol. 4, pp. 1942–1947 (1995)

[15] Storn, R., Price, K.V.: Differential Evolution - a simple and efficient adaptive scheme for global optimization over continuous spaces, Technical Report TR-95-012,ICSI (1995), http://http.icsi.berkeley.edu/~storn/litera.html

[16] Storn, R., Price, K.V.: Minimizing the real functions of the ICEC 1996 contest by differential evolution. In: Proceedings of the 1996 IEEE international conference on evolutionary computation, Nagoya, Japan, pp. 842–844. IEEE Press, New York (1996)

[17] Das, S., Konar, A., Chakraborty, U.K., Abraham, A.: Differential evolution with a neighborhood based mutation operator: a comparative study. IEEE Transactions on Evolutionary Computation 13(3), 526–553 (2009)

[18] Nollan, R., Pillay, P., Haque, T.: Application of genetic algorithms to motor parameter determination. In: Proceedings of 1994 IEEE-IAS conference Denvar, pp. 47–54 (1994)

[19] Sakthivel, V.P., et al.: Multi-objective parameter estimation of induction motor using particle swarm optimization. Engineering Applications of Artificial Intelligence (2009)

[20] Mendes, R., Kennedy, J.: The fully informed Particle Swarm: simpler, maybe better. IEEE Transaction on evolutionary Computation 8(3) (2004)

[21] Eiben, A.E., et al.: Genetic algorithms with multi-parent recombination. In: PPSN III: Proceedings of the International Conference on Evolutionary Computation. The Third Conference on Parallel Problem Solving from Nature, pp. 78–87 (1994); ISBN 3-540-58484-6

# Performance Evaluation of Particle Swarm Optimization Based Active Noise Control Algorithm

Nirmal Kumar Rout[1], Debi Prasad Das[2], and Ganapati Panda[3]

[1] School of Electronics Engineering, KIIT University, Bhubaneswar, India
`routnirmal@rediffmail.com`
[2] PE&I Cell, IMMT (CSIR), Bhubaneswar, India
`debi_das_debi@yahoo.com`
[3] School of Electrical Sciences, IIT, Bhubaneswar, India
`ganapati.panda@gmail.com`

**Abstract.** Active noise control (ANC) has been used to control low-frequency acoustic noise. The ANC uses an adaptive filter algorithm and normally uses least mean square (LMS) algorithm. The gradient based LMS algorithm suffers from local minima problem. In this paper, particle swarm optimization (PSO) algorithm, which is a non-gradient but simple evolutionary computing type algorithm, is proposed for the ANC system. Detailed mathematical treatment is made and systematic computer simulation studies are carried out to evaluate the performance of the PSO based ANC algorithm.

## 1 Introduction

Active noise control (ANC) is an electroacoustic or electromechanical system which cancels an acoustic noise based on the principle of destructive interference [1]. Different types of ANC algorithms have been proposed to circumvent different issues linked with it such as nonlinear issues in [2]. In [3] genetic algorithm (GA) based algorithm is shown to be superior to the conventionally used least mean square (LMS) algorithm. Recently particle swarm optimization (PSO) has been proposed as an alternate useful and superior optimization algorithm to GA. Like GA, PSO also does not use derivative of the cost function for optimization of parameters and hence relatively free from local minima trap. The PSO is originally proposed by Kennedy *et al.* in [4] as an optimization tool. A single paper on PSO based adaptation of the weights of multilayer neural network as a nonlinear ANC algorithm has been reported in the literature [5]. In this paper, we present a systematic algorithm of the PSO based ANC system. The detailed analysis of the proposed algorithm through computer simulations would provide the merits and demerits of it. The paper is organized as follows. Section 2 describes the proposed method and deals with the advantages and the drawbacks of the PSO based ANC system. Section 3 presents the results of some computer simulations, and finally, Section 4 reports the conclusion of the findings.

## 2 Proposed Particle Swarm Optimization Based ANC System

The proposed method involves separate training and testing phase of the ANC System.

B.K. Panigrahi et al. (Eds.): SEMCCO 2010, LNCS 6466, pp. 531–536, 2010.

**A. Training Phase:** This phase employs the models of primary and the secondary paths i.e. $\hat{P}(z)$ and $\hat{S}(z)$ respectively [1]. Based on Fig. 1, a random sequence $x(n)$, treated as reference signal, is passed through the primary path model to generate $d(n)$ which is regarded as the noise signal at the canceling point. The $d(n)$ are regarded as desired signal for comparison purpose. The objective is to design a set of filter coefficient which would essentially represent the ANC. The cost function to be minimized is the square of the summation of the desired signal $d(n)$ and the output of the secondary path estimate, $\hat{d}(n)$. To apply the PSO algorithm to such an optimization problem, let us consider a set of $P$ numbers of adaptive filter coefficient as population which is represented as a set of particles as follows.

$$\mathbf{W} = \begin{bmatrix} w_1^1 & w_1^2 & \cdots & w_1^P \\ w_2^1 & w_2^2 & \cdots & w_2^P \\ \vdots & \vdots & \cdots & \vdots \\ w_N^1 & w_N^2 & \cdots & w_N^P \end{bmatrix} \tag{1}$$

Each column of the $\mathbf{W}$ in (1) is a potential initial solution and is called as a particle. As per the block diagram shown in Fig. 2, each column of $\mathbf{W}$ represents the coefficients of one of the $P$ numbers of adaptive filters which are represented as tap weights of $P$ adaptive filters. The same random inputs are fed to each of these filters which generate $y_1(n), y_2(n), ..., y_P(n)$ as outputs. These outputs are passed through the secondary path estimate $\hat{S}(z)$ to generate $\{\hat{d}_1(n), \hat{d}_2(n), ..., \hat{d}_P(n)\}$. A set of error signal $\{e_1(n), e_2(n), ..., e_P(n)\}$ is generated by combining $\{\hat{d}_1(n), \hat{d}_2(n), ..., \hat{d}_P(n)\}$ with the noise signal at the canceling point, i.e. $d(n)$. Thus the error signals generated is given by,

$$e_p(n) = d(n) + d_p(n), \tag{2}$$

where $p = 1, 2, 3, ..., P$, $n$ is the samples index of the input signal which ranges from 1 to $M$ and $M$ is the total number of samples used in each generation for training. The mean square error of each of these $P$ errors, which represents the fitness of each particle (adaptive filter) is stored in the PSO processor. The position of the $i$ th particle and its velocity in $k$ th iteration are denoted by $\mathbf{W}_i(k)$ and $\mathbf{V}_i(k)$ respectively. The $i$ th particle with smallest mean square error in the previous position is recorded and represented by the symbol $pbest_i$ (personal best) and its position is represented as $\mathbf{W}_{pbest_i}$. The index of the best $pbest_i$ among all the particles is represented by the symbol $gbest$ (global best) and its position is presented as $\mathbf{W}_{gbest}$. The particle swarm optimization algorithm updates the velocity and position of each particle towards its $\mathbf{W}_{pbest}$ and $\mathbf{W}_{gbest}$ position at each step according to the update equations (3) and (4) respectively.

$$\mathbf{V}_i(k) = \mathbf{V}_i(k-1) + r1[\mathbf{W}_{pbest_i} - \mathbf{W}_i(k)] + r2[\mathbf{W}_{gbest} - \mathbf{W}_i(k)] \qquad (3)$$

$$\mathbf{W}_i(k) = \mathbf{W}_i(k-1) + \mathbf{V}_i(k) \qquad (4)$$

Where, $r1$ and $r2$ are two random numbers in the range [0, 1]. Equation (3) calculates a new velocity for each particle (potential solution) based on its previous velocity, $\mathbf{V}_i(k-1)$ represents the particle's position at which the best fitness has been achieved, $\mathbf{W}_{pbest_i}$ the best position of each particles achieved so far among the neighbors and $\mathbf{W}_{gbest}$ denotes the global best positions among all particles. The training process is carried out until the predefined terminating condition is achieved. Even though original version of PSO is presented here, other variants of PSO such as inertia weight model, constriction coefficient model, fully informed model and the algorithms presented in [6-7] can also be applied in a similar manner.

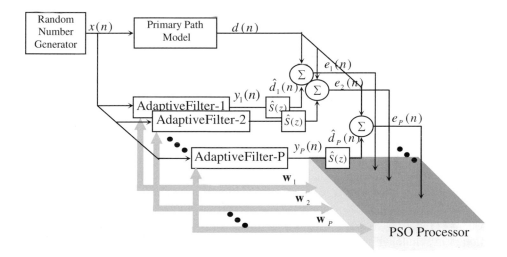

**Fig. 1.** Block diagram of proposed PSO based training of an ANC system

**B. Testing Phase:** When the ANC is in operation, i.e. during the testing phase, the actual noise signal is propagated in the primary path. The PSO tuned adaptive filter, generates anti-noise which being passed through the actual secondary path, acoustically mixes with the primary noise at the canceling point. The error signal is recorded for monitoring purpose by an error microphone. During monitoring, in case the mean and variance of the error signal is increased from the prefixed thresholds, the adaptive filter weights are updated again using PSO based learning rule.

**C. Comparison of PSO and FXLMS based ANC:** It should be remarked that filtered-X LMS (FXLMS) algorithm [1], the simplest ANC algorithm, is tuning the adaptive filter coefficients on sample-by-sample basis. However, the PSO based ANC requires an offline error minimization and the adaptive filter coefficients are updated at every generation. However, FXLMS is prone to be trapped by local minima issue as it uses gradient based optimization unlike the PSO.

**D. Comparison of PSO and GA based ANC:** Unlike PSO, the GA based ANC [3] uses a binary coded string for each weights of the adaptive filter. It involves slow convergence as it uses only one point crossover and mutation, which see very small change in individual weight update. However, in our proposed PSO based ANC system, the weights are updated using a systematic and simple update algorithm presented in (3) and (4). Hence the PSO is expected to achieve faster convergence than the GA.

## 3  Simulation Experiments

To validate the proposed PSO based algorithm for optimization of the ANC algorithm a number of simulation experiments are conducted using the primary and the secondary path models as follows: $\hat{P}(z) = z^{-5} + 0.2z^{-6} + 0.5z^{-7} - 0.9z^{-8}$ and $\hat{S}(z) = z^{-1} + 1.5z^{-2} - z^{-3}$. The primary noise signal is a randomly generated white uniform noise with zero mean.

**Experiment-1:  Effect of Population size $P$ :** To study the effect of population size on the optimization of the ANC controller, the number of generations is kept fixed as 100 and the length of the ANC adaptive filter is fixed at $N = 10$. The training algorithm is run 10000 random signals for 100 generations and the filter coefficients (here the *gbest*) are fixed for the testing phase. During testing phase, another 10000 samples of random signal is generated and the ANC is used to control the noise field. The square of the error signals averaged over 20 such experiments are computed and then plotted in semilog-$Y$ scale against iteration and is displayed in Fig. 2. The plot shows that for population size less than 40, the performance gradually decreases. However, for population size 50 and above, the mean square error remains at its lowest constant which exhibits maximum performance. Another experiment is conducted by selecting a different size of adaptive filter. In this case the adaptive filter size is $N = 20$ and it is found that even with 100 generations of training the population size needed to optimize the adaptive filter is $P = 200$.

**Experiment-2:   Effect of generation and population size for different filter length:** To study the effect of population size and the generation of training on optimization for various lengths of filter weights, a number of experiments are carried out. The condition for primary path, secondary path and the random noise source remain constant for all the experiments. It is tested in Experiment-1 that when the adaptive filter length is higher than the optimum one, it needs more population to optimize keeping the generation constant. After training the ANC controller for various population sizes like $P = 10, 20, 30, 40, 50, 100, 200$, generation count as $K=100$, 200, 300, 400 and various filter lengths $N = 10, 20, 30$, the mean of the mean square error is computed during the testing phase. This metric gives an index of the optimization performance of the algorithm and is listed in Table-1.

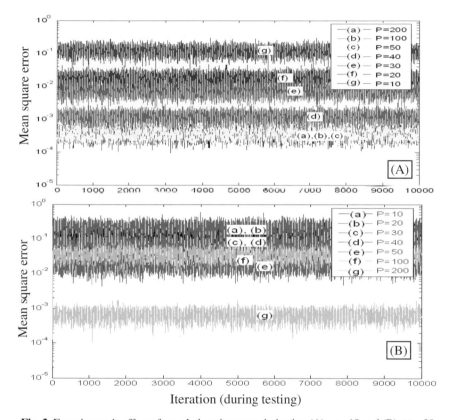

**Fig. 2.** Experiment-1: effect of population size on optimization (A) $N = 10$ and (B) $N = 20$

It shows how the increase in population sizes reduces the number of generation required for training. It also demonstrates that by increasing the length of the adaptive filter from its optimum size, the population and generation counts are required to be increased to optimize its coefficients.

**Table 1.** Effect of population and generation count on performance

| N=10 | | | | | | | |
|---|---|---|---|---|---|---|---|
| Population Count →<br>Generation count ↓ | 10 | 20 | 30 | 40 | 50 | 100 | 200 |
| 100 | 2.5250 | 0.3895 | 0.1500 | 0.0252 | 0.0077 | 0.0075 | 0.0075 |
| 200 | 4.4151 | 2.4694 | 0.5188 | 0.3534 | 0.1431 | 0.0138 | 0.0069 |
| 300 | 1.2770 | 0.0389 | 0.1820 | **0.0074** | **0.0074** | **0.0074** | **0.0074** |
| 400 | 1.2705 | 0.0387 | 0.1798 | **0.0074** | **0.0074** | **0.0074** | **0.0074** |
| N=20 | | | | | | | |
| 100 | 2.8973 | 4.4070 | 1.4754 | 0.5942 | 0.3527 | 0.7280 | 0.0134 |
| 200 | 2.6699 | 4.2124 | 1.0385 | 0.3971 | 0.1088 | 0.0260 | 0.0071 |
| 300 | 2.6416 | 4.1442 | 1.0184 | 0.3913 | 0.0784 | 0.0149 | **0.0066** |
| 400 | 2.6344 | 4.1347 | 1.0127 | 0.3865 | 0.0737 | 0.0147 | **0.0065** |
| N=30 | | | | | | | |
| 100 | 12.5586 | 6.3560 | 2.9843 | 3.3161 | 4.3892 | 0.3846 | 0.0167 |
| 200 | 12.1531 | 6.2059 | 2.6429 | 3.1853 | 4.1279 | 0.3657 | 0.0153 |
| 300 | 12.0521 | 6.1849 | 2.6129 | 2.7059 | 3.6256 | 0.3172 | 0.0145 |
| 400 | 12.0407 | 6.1793 | 2.5932 | 2.7038 | 3.6147 | 0.3059 | 0.0144 |

## 4   Conclusions

This paper presents the PSO based training of ANC algorithm with a new structure for its simulation, optimization of ANC controller and its use to control the acoustic noise. Simulation experiments are carried out to show its effectiveness. Detailed analysis is made to evaluate the effect of population and generation count of the PSO algorithm with respect to the size of the unknown adaptive filter. The proposed PSO based ANC algorithm can suitably be modified for achieving improved performance for nonlinear and multi-channel ANC systems.

## References

[1] Kuo, S.M., Morgan, D.R.: Active Noise Control Systems—Algorithms and DSP Implementations. Wiley, New York (1996)
[2] Das, D.P., Panda, G.: Active Mitigation of Nonlinear Noise Processes using a novel filtered-s LMS Algorithm. IEEE Trans. Speech and Audio Process. 12(3), 313–322 (2004)
[3] Russo, F., Sicuranza, G.L.: Accuracy and Performance Evaluation in the Genetic Optimization of Nonlinear Systems for Active Noise Control. IEEE Trans. Instrum. Meas. 56(4), 1443–1450 (2007)
[4] Kennedy, J., Eberhart, R.C.: Particle swarm optimization. In: Proc. of IEEE Int. Conf. Neural Networks, pp. 1942–1948 (1995)
[5] Modares, H., Ahmadyfard, A., Hadadzarif, M.: A PSO approach for non-linear active noise cancellation. In: Proc. the 6th WSEAS International Conference on Simulation, Modelling and Optimization, Lisbon, Portugal, pp. 492–497 (2006)
[6] Liang, J.J., Suganthan, P.N.: Dynamic Multi-Swarm Particle Swarm Optimizer. In: IEEE Swarm Intelligence Symposium, pp. 124–129 (2005)
[7] Liang, J.J., Qin, A.K., Suganthan, P.N., Baskar, S.: Comprehensive Learning Particle Swarm Optimizer for Global Optimization of Multimodal Functions. IEEE Trans. on Evolutionary Computation 10(3), 281–295 (2006)

# Solution to Non-convex Electric Power Dispatch Problem Using Seeker Optimization Algorithm

K.R. Krishnanand[1], P.K. Rout[2], B.K. Panigrahi[3], and Ankita Mohapatra[4]

[1] Multi-Disciplinary Research Cell, Siksha O Anusandhan University, Bhubaneswar, India
[2] Department of Electrical and Electronics Engineering, Institute of Technical Education and Research, Bhubaneswar, Orissa, India
[3] Department of Electrical Engineering, Indian Institute of Technology, Delhi, India
[4] Department of Electrical Engineering, CET, BPUT, Bhubaneswar, Orissa, India
krishkr09@gmail.com, pkrout_india@yahoo.com,
bkpanigrahi@ee.iitd.ac.in, ankita.cet1208@gmail.com

**Abstract.** This paper presents the application of Seeker Optimization Algorithm (SOA) to constrained economic load dispatch problem. Independent simulations were performed over separate systems with different number of generating units having constraints like prohibited operating zones and ramp rate limits. The performance is also compared with other existing similar approaches. The proposed methodology was found to be robust, fast converging and more proficient over other existing techniques.

**Keywords:** economic load dispatch, modified seeker optimization algorithm, non-convex function, prohibited operating zone, ramp rate limit, transmission losses.

## 1 Introduction

Among different issues in power system operation, economic load dispatch (ELD) problem or electric power dispatch problem constitute a major part. Essentially, ELD problem is a constrained optimization problem in power systems that have the objective of dividing the total power demand among the online participating generators economically while satisfying the various constraints. The conventional methods of solution include Lambda iteration method [1, 2], base point and participation factors method [1, 2], gradient method [1, 3], etc. For effective implementation of these methods, the mathematical formulation needs to be continuous. But a practical ELD must take ramp rate limits, prohibited operating zones and valve point loading effects into consideration to provide the completeness for the ELD problem formulation, which makes it non-convex.

Evolutionary and behavioral random search algorithms such as Genetic Algorithm (GA), Particle Swarm Optimization (PSO) [4], Improved fast Evolutionary programming algorithm [5] etc. have previously been implemented on the ELD problem at hand. Some other algorithms like binary coded GA [6], Chaotic particle swarm optimization (CPSO) [7], new particle swarm with local random search (NPSO-LRS) [8]

B.K. Panigrahi et al. (Eds.): SEMCCO 2010, LNCS 6466, pp. 537–544, 2010.
© Springer-Verlag Berlin Heidelberg 2010

and improved coordination aggregated based PSO [9] have also been successfully applied to solve the ELD problem.

This paper proposes a new optimization approach, to solve the ELD using Seeker Optimization Algorithm (SOA) [10] technique. Some interesting literatures pertaining to this proficient optimization technique can be obtained from literatures by the same authors [11, 12].

In order to establish the capability of SOA to optimize non-smooth, non-convex cost functions, this paper considers two complex thermal systems. SOA is tested on six generator and forty generator test systems. The results obtained are compared with those of GA, PSO and other promising methods. The proposed methodology emerges out to be an efficient optimization technique for solving ELD problem for various curve natures and different sized power systems.

## 2  Problem Description

The ELD problem is about minimizing the fuel cost of generating units for a specific period of operation so as to accomplish optimal generation dispatch among operating units and in return satisfying the system load demand, generator operation constraints with ramp rate limits and prohibited operating zones.

### 2.1  ELD Problem Formulation

The objective function corresponding to the production cost can be approximated to be a quadratic function of the active power outputs from the generating units. Symbolically, it is represented as

$$\text{Minimize} \quad F_t = \sum_{i=1}^{N_G} f_i(P_i) \tag{1}$$

where $f_i(P_i) = a_i P_i^2 + b_i P_i + c_i, \quad i = 1,2,3, ..., N_G \tag{2}$

is the expression for cost function corresponding to $i^{th}$ generating unit and $a_i$, $b_i$ and $c_i$ are its cost coefficients. $P_i$ is the real power output (MW) of $i^{th}$ generator corresponding to time period t. $N_G$ is the number of online generating units to be dispatched. The cost function for unit with valve point loading effect is calculated by using

$$f_i(P_i) = a_i P_i^2 + b_i P_i + c_i + \left| e_i \sin\left(f_i\left(P_i^{min} - P_i\right)\right)\right| \tag{3}$$

Where $e_i$ and $f_i$ are the cost coefficients corresponding to valve point loading effect. The constraints imposed are discussed below.

### 1)  Power Balance Constraints or Demand Constraints
This constraint is based on the principle of equilibrium between total system generation and total system loads ($P_D$) and losses ($P_L$). That is,

$$\sum_{i=1}^{N_G} P_i = P_D + P_L \tag{4}$$

where $P_L$ is obtained using B- coefficients, given by

$$P_L = \sum_{i=1}^{N_G} \sum_{j=1}^{N_G} P_i B_{ij} P_j + \sum_{i=1}^{N_G} B_{0i} P_i + B_{00}$$

(5)

## 2) The Generator Constraints

The output power of each generating unit has a lower and upper bound so that it lies in between these bounds. This constraint is represented by a pair of inequality constraints as follows.

$$P_i^{min} \leq P_i \leq P_i^{max}$$

(6)

where, $P_i^{min}$ and $P_i^{max}$ are lower and upper bounds for power outputs of the $i^{th}$ generating unit.

## 3) The Ramp Rate Limits

Under practical circumstances, ramp rate limit restricts the operating range of all the online units for adjusting the generator operation between two operating periods. The units are constrained due to these ramp rate limits as mentioned below.

If power generation increases, $\quad P_i - P_i^{t-1} \leq UR_i$    (7)

If power generation decreases, $\quad P_i^{t-1} - P_i \leq DR_i$    (8)

where $P_i^{t-1}$ is the power generation of unit i at previous hour and $UR_i$ and $DR_i$ are the upper and lower ramp rate limits respectively. The inclusion of ramp rate limits modifies the generator operation constraint (6) as follows.

$$\max(P_i^{min}, UR_i - P_i) \leq P_i \leq \min(P_i^{max}, P_i^{t-1} - DR_i)$$

(9)

## 4) Prohibited Operating Zone

The generating units may have certain zones where operation is restricted on the grounds of physical limitations of machine components or instability e.g. due to steam valve or vibration in shaft bearings. Symbolically, for a generating unit i,

$$P_i \leq \overset{n}{P}^{pz} \text{ and } P_i \geq \overset{n}{P}^{pz}$$

(10)

where $\overset{n}{P}^{pz}$ and $\overset{n}{P}^{pz}$ are the lower and upper limits of a given prohibited zone for generating unit i.

# 3  Overview of Seeker Optimization Algorithm

The seeker optimization operates on a set of potential solutions called the seekers [10]. Each seeker is a vector consisting of D number of values or dimensions. The seekers of a population can be classified into K sub-populations; with each subpopulation being considered as the neighborhood for the seeker of that subpopulation [11].

K can be any positive integer. All the optimization problems to be solved are assumed to be minimization problems.

## 3.1  Implementation of SOA

In SOA, a search direction $d(k,i,j,t)$ and a step length $\alpha(k,i,j,t)$ are computed separately for each dimension j of each seeker i belonging to each subpopulation k for each time step t, where $\alpha(k,i,j,t)>0$ and $d(k,i,j,t)$ belongs to the set $\{-1,0,1\}$.

The set denotes negative change, no change and positive change. For each seeker i ($1 \le i \le N$, N is the subpopulation size), the position update on each dimension j ($1 \le j \le D$, D is the dimension of the problem) is given by

$$x(k, i, j, t + 1) = x(k, i, j, t) + \alpha(k, i, j, t).d(k, i, j, t) \qquad (11)$$

In order to prevent premature convergence within a subpopulation, positions of the worst K-1 seekers of each subpopulation are combined with the best one in each of the other K-1 subpopulations using a uniform crossover operation.

$$x(k, n, j, t)_{worst} = x(p, j, t)_{best} \quad if \quad \Phi \le 0.5$$

$$x(k, n, j, t)_{worst} \qquad else \qquad (12)$$

where $\Phi$ is a uniform random real number within [0,1], $x(k,n,j,t)_{worst}$ is the $j^{th}$ dimension of the $n^{th}$ worst seeker belonging to $k^{th}$ subpopulation at step t, $x(p,j,t)_{best}$ is the $j^{th}$ dimension of the best seeker of the $p^{th}$ subpopulation at step t; k, p = 1,2,..., K-1 and $k \ne p$. This helps in information exchange and enhances explorative nature of the algorithm.

### 3.1.1  Determination of Search Direction

The search space may be viewed as a multiple gradient field and the empirical gradient (EG) can be found out by evaluating the response to the position change especially when the objective function is not in a differentiable form [12]. Then, the seeker can follow the EG to guide the search. The position is relatively better if it has a higher fitness value than the position compared to.

In SOA, each seeker computes the search direction based on several EGs by evaluating the current position or historical positions of one's own, or that of the neighbors, resulting in a crisp direction from combination of all directions.

An empirical direction vector called as egotistic direction at a step t is given by:

$$d(k, i, j, t)_{ego} = signum \ ( \ P(k, i, j)_{best} - x(k, i, j, t) \ ) \qquad (13)$$

where $P(k,i,j)_{best}$ denotes the $j^{th}$ dimension in the historical best position of the $i^{th}$ seeker in the $k^{th}$ subpopulation . Local altruistic direction at a step t is given by:

$$d(k, i, j, t)_{alt_{local}} = signum \ ( \ L(k, j, t)_{best} - x(k, i, j, t) \ ) \qquad (14)$$

where $L(k,j,t)_{best}$ denotes the $j^{th}$ dimension of the best seeker in the current step t belonging to the same neighborhood. Global altruistic direction is given by:

$$d(k, i, j, t)_{alt_{global}} = signum \ ( \ G(k, j)_{best} - x(k, i, j, t) \ ) \qquad (15)$$

where $G(k,j)_{best}$ denotes the $j^{th}$ dimension of the best seeker in the history of that neighborhood. Pro-active direction at a step t is given by:

$$d(k, i, j, t)_{pro} = signum \ ( \ x(k, i, j, t_1) - x(k, i, j, t_2) \ ) \tag{16}$$

where $t_1$, $t_2 \in \{t, t-1, t-2\}$ and the seeker at step $t_1$ is better than the seeker at step $t_2$. The actual search direction d(k,i,j,t) is obtained as given below.

$$d(k, i, j, t) = \begin{cases} 0 & \text{if} & \Phi \leq p^{(0)}_{(k, i, j, t)} \\ +1 & \text{if} & p^{(0)}_{(k, i, j, t)} < \Phi \leq p^{(0)}_{(k, i, j, t)} + p^{(+1)}_{(k, i, j, t)} \\ -1 & \text{if} & p^{(0)}_{(k, i, j, t)} + p^{(+1)}_{(k, i, j, t)} < \Phi \leq 1 \end{cases} \tag{17}$$

where $\Phi$ is a random number in [0,1] following the uniform distribution, $p^{(m)}_{(k,i,j,t)}$ (m $\in$ $\{-1,0,1\}$) at step t is the percentage of m in the $j^{th}$ dimension of the $i^{th}$ seeker's all four directions.

### 3.1.2  Step Length Determination

There are various methods for the variation of the step length proposed in the literature on SOA [10]. In this particular implementation, the step length variation follows a Gaussian probabilistic distribution. The algorithm shows optimistic behaviour assuming that the solutions better than the current solutions lie nearer to the current solutions. The exploitative nature of the algorithm increases towards the neighbourhood of the current solutions. This strategy facilitates the exploitative nature of SOA more for the current best solutions and gradually makes the search less exploitative for solutions with lesser quality in the given population.

## 4  Results and Discussion

The applicability and viability of the aforementioned technique for practical applications has been tested on two different power system cases. The obtained results are compared with the reported results of PSO [4], GA [4], PSO-LRS [8], NPSO-LRS [8] and CPSO [7] methods. The cases taken for our study comprises of 6 and 40 generator systems. The SOA algorithm used 30 seekers divided into 5 subpopulations, performing 1000 iterations for each run on a test system. Best results have been taken from 30 such independent runs. The following details the discussion of the results.

### 4.1  Six-Unit System

The system contains six thermal generating units. The total load demand on the system is 1263 MW. The results are compared with the elitist GA [4], PSO [4], NPSO-LRS [8], PSO-LRS [8] and CPSO [7] methods for this test system. Results obtained using the proposed SOA is listed in Table 1. In this system prohibited operating zones and ramp rate limits are taken into consideration. Parameters of all the thermal units are reported in [4]. It can be evidently seen from Table 2 that the technique provided better results compared to other reported evolutionary algorithm techniques like GA, PSO and some modified versions of PSO. It is also observed that the mean cost using the proposed approach is less than the reported minimum cost using some of other methods.

**Table 1.** Results for 6 unit system for a demand of 1263 mw

| Generator Power Output (MW) | SOA |
|---|---|
| $P_{G1}$ | 446.7217 |
| $P_{G2}$ | 173.1384 |
| $P_{G3}$ | 262.7899 |
| $P_{G4}$ | 143.4875 |
| $P_{G5}$ | 163.9215 |
| $P_{G6}$ | 85.3632 |
| Total Power Generation (MW) | 1275.4222 |
| Minimum Cost ($/hr) | 15444.1876 |
| Ploss (MW) | 12.4222 |
| Mean Cost ($/hr) | 15444.9286 |
| Standard Deviation of Cost ($/hr) | 0.0427 |

**Table 2.** Comparison of Results for 6 unit system

| Method | Minimum Cost ($/hr) | Mean Cost ($/hr) |
|---|---|---|
| GA [4] | 15459 | 15469 |
| PSO [4] | 15450 | 15454 |
| CPSO-2 [7] | 15446 | 15449 |
| PSO-LRS [8] | 15450 | 15452 |
| NPSO-LRS [8] | 15450 | 15450.5 |
| SOA | 15444.1876 | 15444.9286 |

## 4.2 Forty-Unit System

This problem involved 40 thermal units with quadratic cost function together with the effects of valve-point loading. The data for this problem are taken from [13]. In this case, the load demand expected to be determined was $P_D$= 10,500MW. Table 3 shows the best schedule obtained for the given problem by using SOA algorithm.

The mean cost for this problem is 121508.2314 ($/hr). It can be seen from the comparison Table 4 that the proposed SOA is giving better results than the other methods given in the respective literature.

**Table 3.** Best Schedule for 40 thermal unit obtained by SOA

| Generator | Power Output (MW) | Generator | Power Output (MW) |
|-----------|-------------------|-----------|-------------------|
| $P_{G1}$  | 110.8360          | $P_{G21}$ | 523.2800          |
| $P_{G2}$  | 110.8160          | $P_{G22}$ | 523.2790          |
| $P_{G3}$  | 97.4000           | $P_{G23}$ | 523.2790          |
| $P_{G4}$  | 179.7330          | $P_{G24}$ | 523.2800          |
| $P_{G5}$  | 97.0000           | $P_{G25}$ | 523.2800          |
| $P_{G6}$  | 140.0000          | $P_{G26}$ | 523.2790          |
| $P_{G7}$  | 259.6000          | $P_{G27}$ | 10.0000           |
| $P_{G8}$  | 284.6000          | $P_{G28}$ | 10.0000           |
| $P_{G9}$  | 284.6000          | $P_{G29}$ | 10.0000           |
| $P_{G10}$ | 130.0000          | $P_{G30}$ | 87.9030           |
| $P_{G11}$ | 168.8000          | $P_{G31}$ | 190.0000          |
| $P_{G12}$ | 94.0000           | $P_{G32}$ | 190.0000          |
| $P_{G13}$ | 214.7600          | $P_{G33}$ | 190.0000          |
| $P_{G14}$ | 394.2800          | $P_{G34}$ | 164.8000          |
| $P_{G15}$ | 394.2790          | $P_{G35}$ | 200.0000          |
| $P_{G16}$ | 304.5200          | $P_{G36}$ | 200.0000          |
| $P_{G17}$ | 489.2800          | $P_{G37}$ | 110.0000          |
| $P_{G18}$ | 489.2790          | $P_{G38}$ | 110.0000          |
| $P_{G19}$ | 511.2790          | $P_{G39}$ | 110.0000          |
| $P_{G20}$ | 511.2790          | $P_{G40}$ | 511.2790          |

**Table 4.** Comparison of Results for 40 Unit System

| Method | Minimum Cost ($/hr) |
|--------|---------------------|
| Anti-predatory PSO[14] | 121663.52 |
| Quantum PSO [16] | 121501.14 |
| Civilized swarm optimization [15] | 121461.67 |
| CDEMD approach [13] | 121423.4013 |
| SOA | 121420.9708 |

## 5   Conclusion

The paper has employed Seeker Optimization Algorithm on the constrained non-convex economic load dispatch problem. Practical generator operation is modeled using several non linear characteristics like ramp rate limits and prohibited operating zones. The proposed approach has produced results comparable or better than those generated by other algorithms compared and the solutions obtained have superior solution quality in satiating the objective. This capability of SOA rises from the empirical gradient calculations and the Gaussian search incorporated in it. These fundamental procedures in the SOA prevent stalling of solutions and make the algorithm more exploitative in nature. From this study, it can be concluded that the proposed algorithm can be effectively used to solve complex, non-smooth, constrained ELD problems.

# References

[1]  Wood, A.J., Wollenberg, B.F.: Power Generation Operation and Control. John Wiley & Sons, New York (1984)

[2]  Chen, C.L., Wang, S.C.: Branch and bound scheduling for thermal generating units. IEEE Trans. on Energy Conversion 8(2), 184–189 (1993)

[3]  Lee, K.Y., et al.: Fuel cost minimization for both real and reactive power dispatches. IEE Proc. C, Gener. Trsns. & distr 131(3), 85–93 (1984)

[4]  Gaing, Z.-L.: Particle swarm optimization to solving the economic dispatch considering the generator constraints. IEEE Trans. on Power Systems 18(3), 1187–1195 (2003)

[5]  Sinha, N., Chakrabarti, R., Chattopadhyay, P.K.: Evolutionary programming techniques for economic load dispatch. IEEE Trans. Evol. Comput. 7(1), 83–94 (2003)

[6]  Damousis, I.G., Bakirtzis, A.G., Dokopoulos, P.S.: Network-Constrained Economic Dispatch Using Real-Coded Genetic Algorithm. IEEE Trans. On Power Systems 18(1), 198–205 (2003)

[7]  Jiejin, C., Xiaoqian, M., Lixiang, L., Haipeng, P.: Chaotic particle swarm optimization for economic dispatch considering the generator constraints. Energy Conversion and Management 48, 645–653 (2007)

[8]  Immanuel Selvakumar, A., Thanushkodi, K.: A new particle swarm optimization Solution to nonconvex economic dispatch problems. IEEE Trans. on power systems 22(1), 42–51 (2007)

[9]  Vlachogiannis, J.G., Lee, K.Y.: Economic Load Dispatch—A Comparative Study on Heuristic Optimization Techniques With an Improved Coordinated Aggregation-Based PSO. IEEE Trans. on Power Systems 24(2), 991–1001 (2009)

[10] Dai, C., Zhu, Y., Chen, W.: Seeker optimization algorithm. In: Wang, Y., Cheung, Y.-m., Liu, H. (eds.) CIS 2006. LNCS (LNAI), vol. 4456, pp. 167–176. Springer, Heidelberg (2007)

[11] Dai, C., Chen, W., Zhub, Y., Zhang, X.: Reactive power dispatch considering voltage stability with seeker optimization algorithm. EPSR 79, 1462–1471 (2009)

[12] Dai, C., Chen, W., Zhu, Y., Zhang, X.: Seeker Optimization Algorithm for Optimal Reactive power dispatch. IEEE Transactions on Power Systems 24(3), 1218–1231 (2009)

[13] dos Santos Coelho, L., Souza, R.C.T., Mariani, V.C.: Improved differential evolution approach based on cultural algorithm and diversity measure applied to solve economic load dispatch problems. Mathematics and Computers in Simulation 79, 3136–3147 (2009)

[14] Selvakumar, A.I., Thanushkodi, K.: Anti-predatory particle swarm optimization: solution to nonconvex economic dispatch problems. Electric Power Systems Research 78(1), 2–10 (2008)

[15] Selvakumar, A.I., Thanushkodi, K.: Optimization using civilized swarm: solution to economic dispatch with multiple minima. Electric Power Systems Research 79(1), 8–16 (2009)

[16] Coelho, L.S., Mariani, V.C.: Particle swarm approach based on quantum mechanics and harmonic oscillator potential well for economic load dispatch with valve-point effects. Energy Conversion and Management 49(11), 3080–3085 (2008)

# Swarm Intelligence Algorithm for Induction Motor Field Efficiency Evaluation

V.P. Sakthivel and S. Subramanian

Department of Electrical Engineering, Faculty of Engineering and Technology,
Annamalai University, Chidambaram - 608 002, Tamilnadu, India
vp.sakthivel@yahoo.com, profdrmani@gmail.com

**Abstract.** Determining induction motor field efficiency is imperative in industries for energy conservation and cost savings. The induction motor efficiency is generally tested in a laboratories by certain methods defined in IEEE Standard – 112. But these methods cannot be used for motor efficiency evaluations in the field because it disrupts the production process of the industry. This paper proposes a swarm intelligence algorithm, Particle Swarm Optimization (PSO) for efficiency evaluation of in-service induction motor based on a modified induction motor equivalent circuit model. In this model, stray load losses are considered. The proposed efficiency evaluation method combines the PSO and the equivalent circuit method. First, the equivalent circuit parameters are estimated by minimizing the difference between measured and calculated values of stator current and input power of the motor using the PSO algorithm. Based on these parameters, the efficiency of the motor at various load points are evaluated by using the equivalent circuit method. To exemplify the performance of the PSO based efficiency estimation method, a 5 HP motor has been tested, compared with genetic algorithm (GA), torque gauge method, equivalent circuit method, slip method, current method and segregated loss method and found to be superior. Accordingly, the method will be useful for engineers who implement the energy efficiency programs to the electric motor systems in industries.

**Keywords:** Efficiency estimation, Induction motor, Equivalent circuit, Swarm intelligence algorithm.

## Nomenclature

| | |
|---|---|
| $r_1$ | stator resistance ($\Omega$) |
| $x_1$ | stator leakage reactance ($\Omega$) |
| $r_2$ | rotor resistance referred to stator ($\Omega$ ) |
| $x_2$ | rotor leakage reactance referred to stator ($\Omega$) |
| $r_m$ | core loss resistance ($\Omega$ ) |
| $x_m$ | magnetizing reactance ($\Omega$) |
| $r_{st}$ | stray loss resistance ($\Omega$ ) |
| $S$ | slip |
| $V_1$ | stator voltage (V) |

B.K. Panigrahi et al. (Eds.): SEMCCO 2010, LNCS 6466, pp. 545–558, 2010.
© Springer-Verlag Berlin Heidelberg 2010

| | |
|---|---|
| $I_1$ | stator current (A) |
| $I_2$ | rotor current (A) |
| $I_m$ | magnetizing current (A) |
| pf | power factor |
| $P_{in}$ | input power (W) |
| $P_{out}$ | output power (W) |
| $P_{fw}$ | friction and windage losses (W) |
| $\eta$ | efficiency of the motor |
| m | number of particles in the swarm |
| N | number of dimensions in a particle |
| K | pointer of iterations (generations) |
| $V_{i,n}^{k}$ | velocity of particle i at iteration k |
| W | weighting factor |
| $C_1, C_2$ | acceleration factor |
| $rand_j$ | random number between 0 and 1 |
| $X_{i,n}^{k}$ | current position of particle i at iteration k |
| $pbest_i$ | personal best of particle i |
| gbest | global best of the group |
| $W_{max}$ | final weight factor |
| $W_{min}$ | initial weight factor |
| Iter | current iteration number |
| $Iter_{max}$ | maximum iteration number |
| subscripts e and m | the estimated and measured values |

# 1 Introduction

The majority of motors in the industry are induction motors. On average, the motors are operated at 60% of its rated load and have quite low energy efficiency. Since the electric motor drive system account over 70% of industrial electricity consumption, the improvement of the motor energy usage in industry is very important to reduce the consumption of electricity. To improve the energy efficiency in industrial plants, it is essential to estimate the efficiency of the motor. The methods which do not disturb the production process, called noninvasive methods can be used for efficiency evaluation of in-service motor.

Many efficiency evaluation methods which show the differences in terms of complexity, intrusion level and accuracy have been proposed. Lu et al. have surveyed various efficiency estimation methods [1]. Among all the methods, the induction motor equivalent circuit based methods are regarded as the least intrusive methods. The IEEE Standard 112-F method is the standard equivalent circuit method [2]. It requires no-load, impedance and variable voltage tests. Besides, the stray-load loss is measured through an additional removed-rotor and reverse rotation tests. The Standard 112-F is modified by eliminating the variable voltage test [3]. However, a no-load test and a full load test both under rated voltage are still required. In addition, stator resistance measurement is also needed.

In segregated loss approach [3], the motor losses are estimated. Some of the methods in this category are quite complex and intrusive, while others rely on empirical values to estimate the losses. The shaft torque method [4] measures the shaft torque and rotor speed directly from the shaft without the need to calculate the losses. It offers the most accurate field-efficiency evaluation, but is also highly intrusive. An accurate low cost method for determining the motors efficiency has been developed [5]. In this method, the motor parameters are determined from two different motor operating points. However, it requires a rather intrusive measurement of stator resistance and stator winding temperature, which are not possible in many cases.

Evolutionary algorithms such as genetic algorithm (GA) [6-12], adaptive GA [13], evolutionary algorithm (EA) [14] and differential evolution [15] were applied for parameter identification and efficiency estimation problems. Though the GA methods have been employed successfully to solve complex non-linear optimization problems, recent research has identified some deficiencies in GA performance [16].

The PSO, first introduced by Kennedy and Eberhart is a population-based stochastic search /optimization algorithm with inherent parallelism [17]. The algorithm mimics the behaviors of individuals in a swarm to maximize the survival of the species. Recently, PSO has been used for variety of power system problems.

Simple concept, easy implementation, robustness of control parameters and computation efficiency of PSO make it an advantageous algorithm when compared with other heuristic optimization techniques [18 - 21].

In this paper, PSO algorithm is applied to in-service efficiency evaluation of an induction motor. In order to prove the efficacy of the proposed method, two different cases are considered.

## 2  Statement of the Problem

The evaluation of the motor field efficiency in this present work is based on the PSO and the equivalent circuit method. The equivalent circuit parameters can be estimated from the field test data and nameplate information by PSO algorithm instead of using no-load and locked-rotor test results. Then the efficiencies at various load points are determined by using these parameters.

A modified induction motor equivalent circuit is used in this method as shown in Fig. 1. The stray load loss is considered in the equivalent circuit by adding an equivalent resistor in the rotor circuit, whose value is derived from the assumed stray load loss suggested in IEEE Std-112. In Fig. 1(b), the parallel connection of $r_m$ and $x_m$ is transformed into a series connection. Parameters $r_m^1$ and $x_m^1$ are related to parameters $x_m$ and $r_m$ in the following way:

$$r_m^1 = \frac{r_m x_m^2}{r_m^2 + x_m^2} \tag{1}$$

$$x_m^1 = \frac{r_m^2 x_m}{r_m^2 + x_m^2} \tag{2}$$

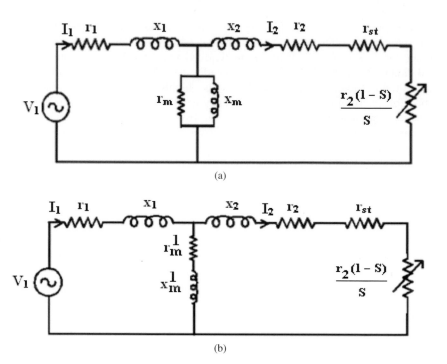

Fig. 1. Modified equivalent circuits of an induction motor

The stray load resistance is given by

$$r_{st} = \frac{0.018r_2(1-S_{fl})}{S_{fl}} \tag{3}$$

The admittance of each branch of the equivalent circuit can be calculated as follows:

$$\overline{Y_2} = \frac{1}{r_2/S + r_{st} + jx_2} \tag{4}$$

$$\overline{Y_m} = \frac{-j}{x_m} + \frac{1}{r_m} \quad \text{(for Fig. 1a)} \tag{5}$$

$$\overline{Y_m} = \frac{1}{\dfrac{1}{r_m} + jx\dfrac{1}{m}} \quad \text{(for Fig. 1b)} \tag{6}$$

$$\overline{Y_1} = \frac{1.0}{r_1 + jx_1} \tag{7}$$

The stator, rotor and magnetizing currents, power factor, input and output powers and efficiency of the motor can be calculated using the following equations.

$$I_{1e} = \left| \overline{I1} \right| = \left| \frac{V_1 Y_1 (Y_2 + Y_m)}{Y_1 + Y_2 + Y_m} \right| \tag{8}$$

$$I_{2e} = \left| \frac{\overline{V_1 Y_1 Y_2}}{Y_1 + Y_2 + Y_m} \right| \tag{9}$$

$$I_{me} = \left| \frac{\overline{V_1 Y_1}}{r_m (Y_1 + Y_2 + Y_m)} \right| \quad \text{(for Fig. 1a)} \tag{10}$$

$$I_{me} = \left| \frac{\overline{V_1 Y_1 Y_m}}{(Y_1 + Y_2 + Y_m)} \right| \quad \text{(for Fig. 1b)} \tag{11}$$

$$pf_e = \frac{\Re(\overline{I_1})}{I_{1e}} \tag{12}$$

$$P_{in\,e} = 3 \left( I_{1e}^2 r_1 + I_{2e}^2 \left( \frac{r_2}{S} + r_{st} \right) + I_{me}^2 r_m \right) \quad \text{(for Fig. 1a)} \tag{13}$$

$$P_{in\,e} = 3 \left( I_{1e}^2 r_1 + I_{2e}^2 \left( \frac{r_2}{S} + r_{st} \right) + I_{me}^2 \frac{1}{r_m} \right) \quad \text{(for Fig. 1b)} \tag{14}$$

$$P_{out\,e} = 3 I_{2e}^2 r_2 \frac{1-S}{S} - P_{fw} \tag{15}$$

$$\eta_e (\%) = \frac{P_{out\,e}}{P_{in\,e}} \times 100 \tag{16}$$

The friction and windage losses, $P_{fw}$, are taken as a constant percentage of the rated input where $P_{fw} = 1.2\%$ for 4 pole motors below 200 HP as suggested by many statistical motor efficiency estimation methods.

The objective of the PSO algorithm is to minimize the error between the measured and the estimated data. The objective function of the problem is formulated as follows:

$$\text{Min } J = \left| \frac{I_{1e}}{I_{1m}} - 1 \right|^2 + \left| \frac{P_{ine}}{P_{inm}} - 1 \right|^2 \tag{17}$$

## 3  Overview of PSO

In 1995, Kennedy and Eberhart first introduced the PSO method [17], motivated by social behavior of organisms such as fish schooling and bird flocking. PSO, as an optimization tool, provides a population based search procedure in which individuals called particles change their positions (states) with time. In a PSO system, particles fly around in a multidimensional search space. During flight, each particle adjusts its position according to its own experience, and the experience of neighboring particles, making use of the best position encountered by itself and its neighbors. The swarm direction of a particle is defined by the set of particles neighboring the particle and its history experience.

Let X and V denote the particle's position and its corresponding velocity in search space respectively. At iteration K, each particle i has its position defined by $X_i^K = [X_{i,1}, X_{i,2} .... X_{i,N}]$ and a velocity is defined as $V_i^K = [V_{i,1}, V_{i,2} ...... V_{i,N}]$ in search space N. Velocity and position of each particle in the next iteration can be calculated as

$$V_{i,n}^{k+1} = W \times V_{i,n}^{k} + C_1 \times rand_1 \times (pbest_{i,n} - X_{i,n}^{k})$$
$$+ C_2 \times rand_2 \times (gbest_n - X_{i,n}^{k}) \tag{18}$$
$$i = 1, 2 ......... m$$
$$n = 1, 2 ......... N$$

$$X_{i,n}^{k+1} = X_{i,n}^{k} + V_{i,n}^{k+1} \quad X_{min,i,n} \leq X_i^{k+1} \leq X_{max\,i,n}$$
$$= X_{min\,i,n} \quad\quad if \ X_{i,n}^{k+1} < X_{min\,i,n}$$
$$= X_{max\,i,n} \quad\quad if \ X_{i,n}^{k+1} > X_{max\,i,n} \tag{19}$$

The convergence speed of each particle could be influenced by the parameters of acceleration factors $C_1$ and $C_2$. The optimization process will modify the position slowly, if the value of $C_j$ is chosen to be very low. On the other hand, the optimization process can become unstable, if the value of $C_j$ is chosen to be very high. The first term of formula (18) the initial velocity of particle which reflects the memory behavior of particle; the second term "cognition part" which represents the private thinking of the particle itself; the third part is the "social" part which shows the particles behavior stem from the experience of other particles in the population.

The following weighting function is usually used in (18)

$$W = W_{max} - (W_{max} - W_{min}) \times Iter / Iter_{max} \tag{20}$$

The above model is called 'inertia weights approach (IWA)'. The inertia weight is employed to control the impact of the previous history of velocities on the current velocity. Thus the parameter W regulates the trade-off between the global and the local exploration abilities of the swarm. A large inertia weight facilitates exploration, while a small one tends to facilitate exploitation.

Fig. 2 shows the concept of the searching mechanism of PSO using the modified velocity and position of individual i based on Eqs. (18) and (19).

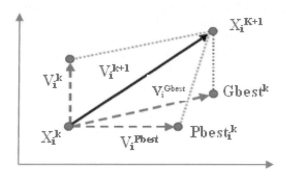

**Fig. 2.** Concept of modification of a searching point by PSO

Each particle tries to modify its position using the following information.

- the current positions,
- the current velocities,
- the distance between the current position and pbest and
- the distance between the current position and gbest.

The searching procedure for the PSO algorithm is summarized as follows.

Step 1. *Initialization:* This is to generate a group of particles (which are named individuals in the other evolutionary algorithms) which each particle is a candidate solution of the problem.

Step 2. *Evaluation:* This is to calculate the objective value of each particle.

Step 3. *Stopping criteria:* If one of the stopping criteria is satisfied, then stop, else go to step 4.

Step 4. *Updating velocities and positions:* According to the objective value, different operators are used in different algorithms to update the position of the particles, so as to search the other area in the space.

The main difference between PSO and other evolutionary algorithms is in Step 4, which is velocity and position updating.

## 4   Parameters Selection of PSO

For the implementation of PSO, several parameters are required to be specified, such as $C_1$ and $C_2$ (cognitive and social acceleration factors, respectively), inertia weights, swarm size, and stopping criteria. These parameters should be selected carefully for efficient performance of PSO. The constants $C_1$ and $C_2$ represent the weighting of the stochastic acceleration terms that pull each particle toward pbest and *gbest* positions. Low values allow particles to roam far from the target regions before being tugged back. On the other hand, high values result in abrupt movement toward, or past, target regions. Hence, the acceleration constants were often set to be 2.0 according to past experiences.

Appropriate selection of inertia weight, W, provides a balance between global and local explorations, thus requiring less iteration on average to find a sufficiently optimal solution. As originally developed, W often decreases linearly from about 0.9 to 0.4 during a run [17-20]. The parameters employed for the implementations of PSO in the present study are given in Appendix A.

## 5   PSO-Based Field Efficiency Estimation

In this paper, the efficiency evaluation of the in-service motor by a PSO algorithm is developed. The computational flowchart of the proposed method is shown in Fig. 3.

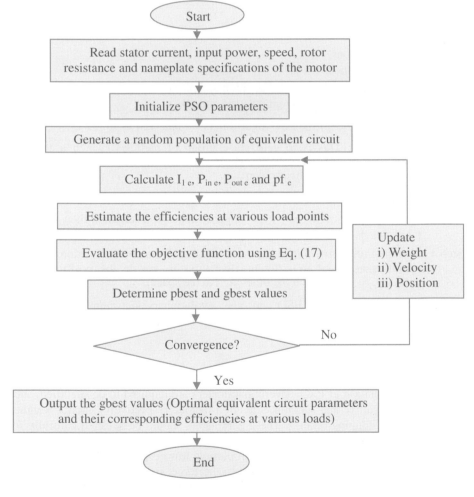

**Fig. 3.** Flowchart of the proposed method

## 6   Simulation Results and Analysis

The proposed PSO based efficiency estimation method is applied to a 5 HP three-phase cage induction motor whose specifications are given in Appendix B. The results obtained by the proposed method are compared with GA method, torque gauge method, equivalent circuit method, slip method, current method and segregated loss method. The results of the torque gauge method are given in Table 1.

In order to demonstrate the effectiveness of the PSO based efficiency estimation method, two different methods are considered. In Method 1, only fill load measured data are used for motor parameter determination and then the efficiency for each load point is evaluated. In Method 2, the measured data at each load points are used for motor parameters and efficiency estimation.

**Table 1.** Results of torque gauge method

| Motor Load | Efficiency (%) |
|------------|----------------|
| 25%        | 57.2           |
| 50%        | 67.05          |
| 75%        | 77.01          |
| 100%       | 63.81          |

**Table 2.** Model parameters obtained from equivalent circuit, GA and PSO methods

| Parameters | Equivalent circuit method | GA method | PSO method |
|------------|---------------------------|-----------|------------|
| $r_2$ (ohm) | 2.12 | 2.55 | 2.78 |
| $x_1, x_2$ (ohm) | 3.3 | 3.1 | 3.4 |
| $r_m$ (ohm) | 610.9 | 724.5 | 688.2 |
| $x_m$ (ohm) | 97.18 | 120 | 126.8 |

**Table 3.** Comparison of results of GA and PSO for Method 1 using equivalent circuit Fig. 1(a)

| Motor Load | GA | | PSO | |
|------------|----------------|-----------|----------------|-----------|
|            | Efficiency (%) | Error (%) | Efficiency (%) | Error (%) |
| 25%        | 46.46          | -10.74    | 66.08          | 8.88      |
| 50%        | 75.97          | 8.92      | 76.24          | 9.1       |
| 75%        | 87.87          | 10.86     | 69.98          | -7.03     |
| 100%       | 55.63          | -8.18     | 58.32          | -5.49     |

**Table 4.** Comparison of results of GA and PSO for Method 1 using equivalent circuit Fig. 1(b)

| Motor Load | GA | | PSO | |
|------------|----------------|-----------|----------------|-----------|
|            | Efficiency (%) | Error (%) | Efficiency (%) | Error (%) |
| 25%        | 68.48          | 11.28     | 65.51          | 8.31      |
| 50%        | 59.51          | -7.54     | 58.43          | -8.62     |
| 75%        | 86.64          | 9.63      | 69.58          | -7.43     |
| 100%       | 68.45          | 4.64      | 59.44          | -4.37     |

**Table 5.** Comparison of results of GA and PSO for Method 2 using equivalent circuit Fig. 1(a)

| Motor Load | GA | | PSO | |
|---|---|---|---|---|
| | Efficiency (%) | Error (%) | Efficiency (%) | Error (%) |
| 25% | 47.72 | -9.48 | 65.12 | 7.92 |
| 50% | 59.09 | -7.96 | 60.28 | -6.77 |
| 75% | 70.93 | -6.08 | 72.21 | -4.81 |
| 100% | 66.93 | 3.12 | 61.08 | -2.73 |

**Table 6.** Comparison of results of GA and PSO for Method 2 using equivalent circuit Fig. 1(b)

| Motor Load | GA | | PSO | |
|---|---|---|---|---|
| | Efficiency (%) | Error (%) | Efficiency (%) | Error (%) |
| 25% | 64.88 | 7.68 | 50.77 | -6.43 |
| 50% | 60.62 | -6.43 | 72.77 | 5.72 |
| 75% | 82.77 | 5.76 | 72.40 | -4.61 |
| 100% | 67.73 | 3.92 | 61.60 | -2.21 |

The equivalent circuit parameters obtained from the equivalent circuit, GA and PSO methods are presented in Table 2. The results of GA and PSO algorithms for Method 1 and 2 using equivalent circuit of Fig. 1(a) and Fig. 1(b) are presented in Tables 3 to 6. The errors of the method are defined as the percentage differences between the GA or PSO algorithm results and the torque gauge method results. From the tables, it is seen that the Method 2 produces better results than that of the Method 1.

Further, the equivalent circuit with a series connection of $r_m^1$ and $x_m^1$ gives better results than that one with parallel connection. Because $r_m^1$ value is comparable with the other parameters values of the equivalent circuit while $r_m$ is much larger.

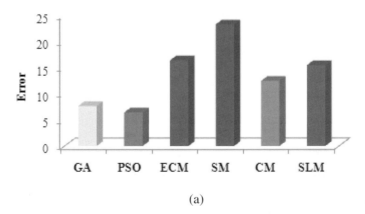

(a)

**Fig. 4.** The magnitude of errors in percentage efficiency for various methods and loads. (a) 25% load, (b) 50% load, (c) 75% load and (d) 100% load.

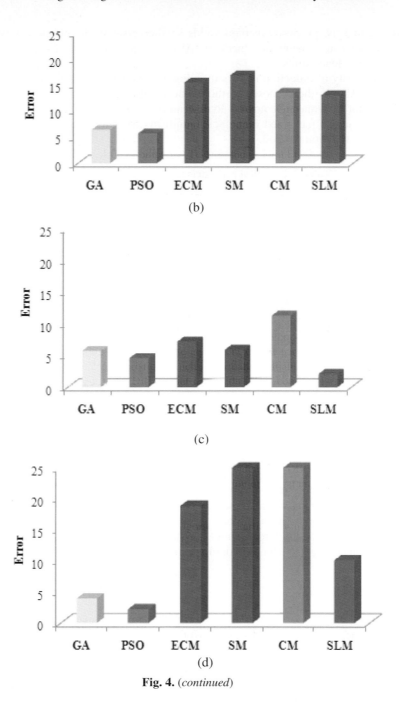

Fig. 4. (*continued*)

Fig. 4 illustrates the magnitude of errors in percentage efficiency for GA and PSO (using method 2 and Fig. 1(b)), equivalent circuit method (ECM), slip method (SM), current method (CM) and segregated loss method (SLM) at various load levels. It is observed that the proposed method yields smaller error in the efficiency evaluation than the other aforementioned methods. Also, the error is lower for full load point, than for other load points.

The majority of induction motors in industries operate at higher than 50% of their rated load. Hence, the proposed method is acceptable to estimate the field efficiency of the motor accurately at normal load conditions. A good agreement between the evaluated and the measured efficiencies confirms the superiority of the PSO based efficiency estimation method.

**Table 7.** Statistical performance of GA and PSO in 20 trials

| Objective Values | Method 1 | | Method 2 | |
|---|---|---|---|---|
| | GA | PSO | GA | PSO |
| Minimum value | 0.045 | 0.033 | 0.038 | 0.028 |
| Maximum value | 0.06 | 0.052 | 0.054 | 0.041 |
| Standard deviation | 0.0068 | 0.0054 | 0.0047 | 0.0031 |

The statistical performance of GA and PSO methods in 20 trials is presented in Table 7. As can be seen that the PSO provides lesser objective value and standard deviation than the GA. Thus the PSO based efficiency evaluation has better solution quality.

## 7   Conclusion

In this paper, a swarm intelligence algorithm based field efficiency evaluation of three-phase cage induction motor has been presented. For this purpose, the PSO algorithm and the equivalent circuit method are incorporated. The method is applied to estimate the efficiency of a 5 HP motor. The obtained results are compared with the results obtained by GA method, torque gauge method, equivalent circuit method, slip method, current method and segregated loss method.

The results show that the proposed method can evaluate the motor efficiencies with less than 2.5% errors at normal loads. Moreover, the efficiencies of the PSO method are close to those of the torque gauge methods. Thus the method will be useful for implementing energy efficiency program in industrial plants.

## Acknowledgment

The authors are grateful to the authorities of Annamalai University for providing the necessary facilities for carrying out this work.

## References

1. Lu, B., Habetler, T.G., Harley, R.G.: A Survey of Efficiency-Estimation Methods for In-Service Induction Motors. IEEE Trans. Ind. Appl. 42(4), 924–933 (2006)
2. IEEE Standard Test Procedure for Polyphase Induction Motors and Generators, IEEE Std. 112 (2004)

3. In-Plant Electric Motor Loading and Efficiency Techniques, Ontario Hydro Report TSDD – 90 – 043 (1990)
4. Hsu, J., Kueck, J., Olszewski, M., Casada, D., Otaduy, P., Tolbert, L.: Comparison of Induction Motor Field Estimation Methods. IEEE Trans. Ind. Appl. 34(1), 117–125 (1998)
5. EI-Ibiary, Y.: An Accurate Low Cost Method for Determining Electric Motor's Efficiency for the Purpose of Plant Energy Management. IEEE Trans. Industrial Applications 39(4), 1205–1210 (2003)
6. Bishop, R.R., Richards, G.G.: Identifying Induction Machine Parameters Using a Genetic Optimization Algorithm. Proc. Southeastcon. IEEE 2, 476–479 (1990)
7. Alonge, F., Dippolito, F., Ferrante, G., Raimondi, F.M.: Parameter Identification of Induction Motor Model Using Genetic Algorithms. IEE Proc. Control Theory Appl. 145(6), 587–593 (1998)
8. Pillay, P., Nollan, R., Haque, T.: Application of Genetic Algorithms to Motor Parameter Determination for Transient Torque Calculations. IEEE Trans. Ind. Appl. 33(5), 1273–1282 (1997)
9. Rahimpour, E., Rashtchi, V., Pesaran, M.: Parameter Identification of Deep-Bar Induction Motors Using Genetic Algorithm. Electrical Engineering 89, 547–552 (2007)
10. Huang, K.S., Kent, W., Wu, Q.H., Turner, D.R.: Parameter Identification for Induction Motors Using Genetic Algorithm with Improved Mathematical Model. Electric Power Components and Systems 29(3), 247–258 (2001)
11. Nollan, R., Pillay, P., Haque, T.: Application of genetic algorithms to motor parameter determination. In: Proc. of 1994 IEEE-IAS conference, Denvar, pp. 47–54 (1994)
12. Orlowska Kowalska, T., Lis, J., Szabat, K.: Identification of the Induction Motor Parameters Using Soft Computing Methods. COMPEL 25(1), 181–192 (2006)
13. Abdelhadı, B., Benoudjit, A., Nait Said, N.: Identification of Induction Machine Parameters Using an Adaptive Genetic Algorithm. Electric Power Components and Systems 32, 767–784 (2004)
14. Subramanian, S., Bhuvaneswari, R.: Evolutionary Programming Based Determination of Induction Motor Efficiency. Electric Power Components and Systems 34, 565–576 (2006)
15. Ursem, R.K., Vadstrup, P.: Parameter Identification of Induction Motors Using Differential Evolution. In: The 2993 Congress on Evolutionary Computation CEC 2003, vol. 2, pp. 790–796 (2003)
16. Fogel, D.B.: Evolutionary Computation: Toward a New Philosophy of Machine Intelligence, 2nd edn. IEEE Press, Piscataway (2000)
17. Kennedy, J., Eberhart, R.: Particle Swarm Optimization. In: Proceedings of the IEEE conference on neural networks – ICNN 1995, Perth, Australia, vol. IV, pp. 1942–1948 (1995)
18. Shi, Y., Eberhart, R.C.: Empirical Study of Particle Swarm Optimization. In: Proceedings of the IEEE International Congress Evolutionary Computation, vol. (3), pp. 101–106 (1999)
19. Eberhart, R., Kennedy, J.: A New Optimizer Using Particle Swarm Optimization. In: Proceedings of the 1995 Sixth International Symposium on Micro Machine and Human Science, pp. 39–43 (1995)
20. Eberhart, R.C., Shi, Y.: Comparing Inertia Weights and Constriction Factors in Particle Swarm Optimization. In: Proceedings of the IEEE International Congress Evolutionary Computation, vol. (1), pp. 84–88 (2000)
21. Chaturvedi, K.T., Pandit, M., Srivastava, L.: Particle Swarm Optimization with Time Varying Acceleration Coefficients for Non-Convex Economic Power Dispatch. Electrical Power and Energy Systems 31, 249–257 (2009)

# Appendix A: Parameters Used in the PSO Algorithm

| Parameter | Value |
|---|---|
| Swarm size | 20 |
| Acceleration factors $C_1$ and $C_2$ | 2 |
| Initial inertia weight ($W_{max}$) | 0.9 |
| Final inertia weight ($W_{min}$) | 0.4 |
| Maximum generations ($Iter_{max}$) | 100 |

# Appendix B: Specifications of 5 hp Motor

| Specifications | Value |
|---|---|
| Capacity | 5 HP |
| Voltage | 230 V |
| Current | 12.5 A |
| Speed | 1450 rpm |

# Artificial Bee Colony Algorithm for Transient Performance Augmentation of Grid Connected Distributed Generation

A. Chatterjee[1], S.P. Ghoshal[2], and V. Mukherjee[3]

[1] Department of Electrical Engineering, Asansol Engineering College, Asansol,
West Bengal, India
[2] Department of Electrical Engineering, National Institute of Technology, Durgapur,
West Bengal, India
[3] Department of Electrical Engineering, Indian School of Mines, Dhanbad, Jharkhand, India
nirsha_apurba@rediffmail.com, spghoshalnitdgp@gmail.com,
vivek_agamani@yahoo.com

**Abstract.** In this paper, a conventional thermal power system equipped with automatic voltage regulator, IEEE type dual input power system stabilizer (PSS) PSS3B and integral controlled automatic generation control loop is considered. A distributed generation (DG) system consisting of aqua electrolyzer, photovoltaic cells, diesel engine generator, and some other energy storage devices like flywheel energy storage system and battery energy storage system is modeled. This hybrid distributed system is connected to the grid. While integrating this DG with the onventional thermal power system, improved transient performance is noticed. Further improvement in the transient performance of this grid connected DG is observed with the usage of superconducting magnetic energy storage device. The different tunable parameters of the proposed hybrid power system model are optimized by artificial bee colony (ABC) algorithm. The optimal solutions offered by the ABC algorithm are compared with those offered by genetic algorithm (GA). It is also revealed that the optimizing performance of the ABC is better than the GA for this specific application.

**Keywords:** Artificial bee colony algorithm, distributed generation, energy storage devices, genetic algorithm, superconducting magnetic energy storage device.

## 1 Introduction

Various distributed generations (DGs) are coming into operation to fulfill the load demand. DGs not only offer reliable, economical and efficient operation of power sector, but these also offer less environmental pollution and reduce green house effect [1]. Several types of small scale generation systems can be used for DG. These may include photovoltaic (PV) cell, aqua electrolyzer (AE), fuel cell (FC), diesel engine generator (DEG) and wind turbine generator (WTG) etc. PV [2] energy has been widely utilized in small-size applications and is the most promising candidate for research and development for large-scale use, as the fabrication of less costly PV

B.K. Panigrahi et al. (Eds.): SEMCCO 2010, LNCS 6466, pp. 559–566, 2010.

devices becomes a reality. FC [3] may utilize traditional fossil fuels such as coal, petroleum, natural gas or recycled energy with hydrogen molecules such as marsh gas, methyl gas etc. Wind is an innovative, clean, and intermittent technology [4].

Flywheel energy storage system (FESS) [5] stores energy in the form of kinetic energy and may supply the same for the odd hour requirements while integrating the same with the renewable energy. The characteristic features of this device may be noted from the view points of high stored energy density, high power exchanging capability with the system, high conversion efficiency (80-90%) and pollution free operation. On the other hand, battery energy storage system (BESS) also stores energy in the form of electrical energy. It may also play an important role in the power exchange process.

The primary function of the superconducting magnetic energy storage (SMES) [6] is to insulate the network from high-frequency power fluctuations, thereby, acting as a shock absorber. The response time of the SMES, typically of the order of milliseconds, enables it to compensate for large fluctuations.

Motivated by the foraging behavior of honeybees, researchers have [7, 8] initially proposed artificial bee colony (ABC) algorithm for solving various optimization problems. ABC algorithm is easy to implement and found to be robust. The algorithm may be utilized for extracting the optimal values of the different tunable parameters of an engineering application like power system model proposed in this paper.

## 2   Proposed Hybrid Model

A single-machine infinite bus (SMIB) system [9], as shown in Fig. 1, is considered. The hybrid DG is connected to the LT bus as shown in Fig. 1. The proposed hybrid power generation scheme is depicted in Fig. 2.

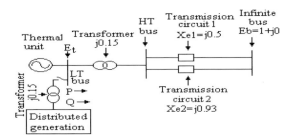

**Fig. 1.** Single-machine infinite bus system with distributed generation

### 2.1   Configuration of Conventional Thermal and DG Scheme

In the conventional power generation scheme, thermal power generator with a single stage reheat turbine is considered. A composite DG consisting of PV, AE, FC, DEG, FESS, and BESS are considered in our work. The net incremental change in mechanical power ($\Delta P_m$) is determined by the following equation

$$\Delta P_m = \Delta P_{th} + \Delta P_{deg} - \Delta P_{fess} - \Delta P_{bess} - \Delta P_{smes} + \Delta P_{pv} + \Delta P_{fc} \quad (1)$$

where $\Delta P$ represents incremental change in power, p.u. The subscript *th* represents the thermal system.

## 2.2 Configuration of Dual Input PSS

In [10], the performance of IEEE type PSS3B is found to be the best one for the studied system model. This dual input PSS configuration is considered for the present work and its block diagram representation is shown in Fig. 3.

## 2.3 Configuration of Automatic Generation Control (AGC) Loop

The area control error (ACE) consists of two parts viz. deviation in system frequency $(\Delta f)$ and deviation in tie line power exchange $(\Delta P_{tie})$. These two are related among themselves as given in (2).

$$ACE = \left(b\Delta f + \Delta P_{tie}\right) \tag{2}$$

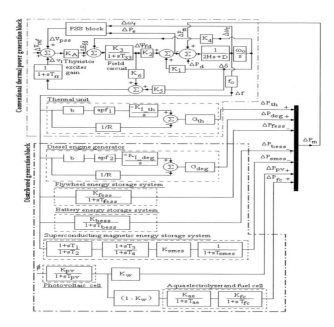

**Fig. 2.** Block diagram of the proposed hybrid power generation scheme with various DG systems (shown within dash-dotted area) along with AVR, thyristor high gain exciter and PSS block in the conventional thermal unit

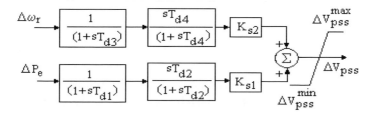

**Fig. 3.** PSS (PSS3B) block subsystem of Fig. 2

### 2.4 Configuration of SMES Loop

The input signal of SMES is $\Delta f$ while $\Delta P_{smes}$ is the active power output deviation of SMES. The structure of frequency stabilizer of SMES (Fig. 2) is based on a second order lead/lag compensator (with time constants of $T_1$-$T_4$ ). The dynamic characteristic of SMES is modeled as the first order controllers with time constant of $T_{smes}$ .

## 3 Problem Formulation

The parameters of the proposed hybrid model are to be so tuned that some degree of relative stability and damping of electromechanical modes of oscillations, minimized undershoot $(u_{sh})$, minimized overshoot $(o_{sh})$ and lesser settling time $(t_{st})$ of transient oscillations of $\Delta\omega_r$ are achieved. So, to satisfy all these requirements, two multi-objective optimization functions ( $OF_1()$ and $OF_2()$ ) as in [10] are to be minimized in succession. These two objective functions are as in (3) and (4).

$$OF_1(\ ) = OF_{11} + 10 \times OF_{12} + OF_{13} \tag{3}$$

$$OF_2(\ ) = (o_{sh} \times 10^6)^2 + (u_{sh} \times 10^6)^2 + (t_{st})^2 + (\frac{d}{dt}(\Delta\omega_r) \times 10^6)^2 \tag{4}$$

## 4 Artificial Bee Colony Algorithm

In the ABC algorithm, [7, 8, 11, 12] the colony of artificial bee consists of three groups of bees viz. employed bees, onlookers and scouts. A bee waiting on the dance area for making a decision to choose a food source is called onlooker and one going to the food source visited by it before is named as employed bee. The other kind of bee is scout bee that carries out random search for discovering new sources. In the algorithm, the first half of the colony consists of employed artificial bees and the second half constitutes the onlookers. The number of the employed bees or the onlooker bees is equal to the number of solutions in the population.

In the ABC algorithm, the position of a food source represents a possible solution to the optimization problem and the nectar amount of a food source corresponds to the quality (fitness) of the associated solution. The value of the fitness is calculated by (5).

$$fit_i = \frac{1}{1 + OF_{1_i}(\ )} \tag{5}$$

At the initialization step, the ABC generates a randomly distributed initial population $P\ (cycle = 0)$ of $np$ solutions (food source positions), where $np$ denotes the size of the population. Each solution $z_i$ where $i = 1, 2, \ldots, np$ is a $d$-dimensional vector. After the initialization, the population of the positions (solutions) is subjected to repeated cycles, $cycle = 1, 2, \ldots, \text{max\_cycles}$, of the search processes for the employed bees, the onlooker bees and scout bees. An employed bee produces a modification on the position (solution) in her memory depending on the local information (visual information) and tests the nectar amount (fitness value) of the new source (new solution). The bee memorizes the new position and forgets the old one provided that the nectar amount of the new one is higher than that of the previous one. Otherwise, she keeps the position of the previous one in her memory. After all employed bees complete the search process, they share the nectar information of the food sources and their position information with the onlooker bees on the dance area. An onlooker bee evaluates the nectar information taken from all employed bees and chooses a food source with a probability related to its nectar amount. As in the case of the employed bee, she produces a modification on the position in her memory and checks the nectar amount of the candidate source. The bee memorizes the new position and forgets the old one providing that its nectar is higher than that of the previous one.

An artificial onlooker bee chooses a food source depending on the probability ( $prob_i$ ) value associated with that food source. The value of $prob_i$ calculated by (6).

$$prob_i = \frac{fit_i}{\sum_{i=1}^{np} fit_i} \tag{6}$$

In order to produce a candidate food position from the old one in memory, the ABC uses (7).

$$v_{ij} = z_{ij} + \phi_{ij}(z_{ij} - z_{kj}) \tag{7}$$

where $k \in [1,2,.......,np]$, and $j \in [1,2,.......,d]$ are randomly chosen indices.

In the ABC, providing that a position cannot be improved further through a predetermined number of cycles, then that food source is assumed to be abandoned. The value of predetermined number of cycles is an important control parameter of the ABC algorithm, which is called *limit* for abandonment. Assume that the abandoned source is $z_i$ and $j \in [1,2,.......,d]$, then the scout discovers a new food source to be replaced with $z_i$. This operation can be modeled by (8).

$$z_i^j = z_{min}^j + rand(0,1) \times (z_{max}^j - z_{min}^j) \tag{8}$$

After each candidate source position $v_{ij}$ is produced and then evaluated by the artificial bee, its performance is compared with that of its old one. If the new food source has equal or better nectar than the old source, it is replaced with the old one in the memory. Otherwise, the old one is retained in the memory. In other words, a greedy selection mechanism is employed as the selection operation between the old and the candidate one. In a robust search process, exploration and exploitation processes must be carried out together. In the ABC algorithm, while onlookers and employed bees carry out the exploitation process in the search space, the scouts control the exploration process. The local search performance of the ABC algorithm depends on neighborhood search and greedy selection mechanisms performed by the employed and the onlooker bees. The global search performance of the algorithm depends on random search process performed by scouts and neighbor solution production mechanism performed by the employed and the onlooker bees.

## 5   Input Data and Parameters

For the ABC algorithm, *number of bees* = 50, *maximum number of allowed iteration cycles* = 1000, *run time* =50, *limit* = 40 (a control parameter in order to abandon the food source) are considered. For GA, *population size* = 50, *maximum number of allowed iteration cycles* = 1000, *crossover rate* = 100%, *probability of mutation* = 0.001, *selection ratio* $(S_r)$ = 0.3, *number of bits* = (*no. of parameters to be optimized* × 8) are considered. The simulation implemented in MATLAB 7.5 software on a PC with Dual Core 2.66GHz CPU and 1GB RAM.

## 6   Simulation Results and Discussions

The major observations of the present work are as documented below.

**(a) Performance Evaluation of SMES for Grid Connected DG:** A comparison of the system transient performances of the thermal power system and the same integrated with the DG is portrayed in Fig. 4(a) (operating conditions being *P=0.2, Q=-0.2, $X_e$=1.08, $E_t$=1.1;* all are in p.u.) for 0.01 p.u. step change in reference voltage. From this figure, it is prominent that the AGC of DG is helping in the process of transient performance stabilization. Thus, improved transient performance is noticed with the usage of DG in a grid connected thermal unit with optimized system parameters. From Fig. 4(b) it is prominent that the SMES device is helping in the process of transient performance stabilization. Thus, further improvement in the transient performance is noticed with the usage of SMES device in the grid connected DG.

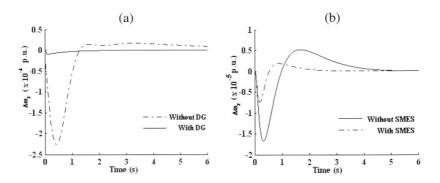

**Fig. 4.** Comparison of transient response profiles of $\Delta\omega_r$ for the proposed hybrid models (a) without DG and with DG and (b) without SMES and with SMES for 0.01 p.u. step perturbation in reference voltage

**(b) Convergence Profile:** The comparative convergence profiles of minimum $OF_1()$ values for the ABC algorithm and those of the GA are portrayed in Fig. 5 against 1% step perturbation in reference voltage for the proposed hybrid DG and

SMES integrated thermal system. The input operating conditions are $P=0.2$, $Q=-0.2$, $X_e=0.4752$, $E_t=1.1$; all are in p.u. From this figure it is clear that the $OF_1()$ values for the ABC algorithm converge faster than GA.

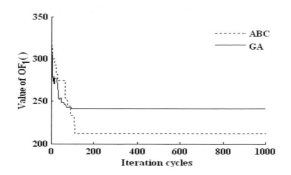

**Fig. 5.** Comparison of convergence profile of the objective function ($OF_1()$) between ABC algorithm and GA for thermal unit plus DGs and SMES

**(c) Statistical Analysis of the Results:** The values of $OF_1()$, $OF_2()$ and a statistical comparison of $OF_1()$ values for different algorithms i.e. ABC algorithm and GA after 50 trials are presented in Table 1 for the proposed hybrid DG and SMES integrated thermal system with different input perturbations. From this table it is understood that both the values of $OF_1()$, and as well as, those of $OF_2()$ are the minimum for ABC algorithm as compared to those offered by adopting GA for the proposed hybrid power system model with different input perturbations. It is clear from the statistical analysis that the ABC-based optimization technique offers promising and better results.

**Table 1.** Comparison between different optimizing algorithms of thermal unit with DG and SMES (Input operating conditions: $P = 0.2$, $Q = -0.2$, $X_e = 1.08$, $E_t = 1.1$, all are in p.u.)

| Type of perturbations | Parameter | ABC | GA |
|---|---|---|---|
| 0.01 p.u. step perturbation in reference voltage | $OF_1()$ | **203.8765** | 336.7473 |
| | $OF_2()$ ( $\times 10^7$) | **0.0013** | 1.8853 |
| | Standard deviation | **0.0639** | 3.145 |
| | t-test | **NA** | 4.587 |
| 0.01p.u. step perturbation in load torque | $OF_1()$ | **208.8271** | 226.6232 |
| | $OF_2()$ ( $\times 10^7$) | **0.1869** | 0.2907 |
| | Standard deviation | **0.5462** | 4.446 |
| | t-test | **NA** | 4.612 |

## 7 Conclusion

A proper integration of DG units with traditional generating unit is carried out for the purpose of transient stability study. DG units like PV, AE, FC, DEG, FESS and BESS are considered. The traditional unit is considered as thermal unit with single stage reheat turbine. The thermal unit is equipped with AVR, dual input PSS like PSS3B, and integral controlled AGC loop. Integral-controlled AGC loop of such an integrated hybrid module is properly tuned by using the ABC algorithm. DG is assisting in the transient stabilization process of the conventional thermal power system. With the inclusion of SMES device in the proposed DG assisted power system considerable improvement in the transient performance is noticed. The simulation results of this work reveal that the optimization performance of the ABC algorithm is better than the GA.

## References

1. Bae, I.-S., Kim, J.-O.: Reliability Evaluation of Distributed Generation based on Operation Mode. IEEE Trans. Power Syst. 22(2), 785–790 (2007)
2. Ro, K., Rahman, S.: Two-Loop Controller for Maximizing Performance of a Grid-Connected Photovoltaic-Fuel Cell Hybrid Power Plant. IEEE Trans. Energy Conver. 13(3), 276–281 (1998)
3. Kim, Y.H., Kim, S.S.: An Electrical Modeling and Fuzzy Logic Control of a Fuel Cell Generation System. IEEE Trans. Energy Conver. 14(2), 239–244 (1999)
4. Wang, P., Billinton, R.: Reliability Benefit Analysis of Adding WTG to a Distribution System. IEEE Trans. Energy Conver. 16(2), 134–139 (2001)
5. Hatziargyrio, N., Donnelly, M., Akasaki, M., et al.: Modeling New Forms of Generation and Storage. CIGRE TF.01.10, Fifth draft (2000)
6. Tripathy, S.C., Juengst, K.P.: Sampled Data Automatic Generation Control with Superconducting Magnetic Energy Storage in Power Systems. IEEE Trans. Energy Conver. 12(2), 187–192 (1997)
7. Riley, J., Greggers, U., Smith, A.D., Reynolds, D., Menzel, R.: The Flight Paths of Honeybees Recruited by the Waggle Dance. Nature 435, 205–207 (2005)
8. Karaboga, D., Basturk, B.: On the Performance of Artificial Bee Colony (ABC) Algorithm. Applied Soft. Comput. 8, 687–697 (2008)
9. Kundur, P.: Power System Stability and Control. Tata-McGraw-Hill, India (2006)
10. Ghoshal, S.P., Chatterjee, A., Mukherjee, V.: Bio-Inspired Fuzzy Logic based Tuning of Power System Stabilizer. Expert Syst. with Appl. 36(5), 9281–9292 (2009)
11. Pan, Q.-K., Tasgetiren, M.F., Suganthan, P.N., Chua, T.J.: A Discrete Artificial Bee Colony Algorithm for the Lot-Streaming Flow Shop Scheduling Problem. Informatics Sciences (in Press corrected Proof Available online January 4, 2010)
12. Akay, B., Karaboga, D.: A Modified Artificial Bee Colony Algorithm for Real-Parameter Optimization. Informatics Sciences (in Press, corrected proof available online July 27, 2010)

# Performance Comparison of Attribute Set Reduction Algorithms in Stock Price Prediction - A Case Study on Indian Stock Data

P. Bagavathi Sivakumar[1] and V.P. Mohandas[2]

[1] Assistant Professor, Department of Computer Science and Engineering, Member IEEE
[2] Professor and Chairman, Department of Electronics and Communication Engineering,
Amrita Vishwa Vidyapeetham, Ettimadai, Coimbatore – 641 105, India
pbsk@cb.amrita.edu, vp_mohandas@cb.amrita.edu

**Abstract.** Stock price prediction and stock trend prediction are the two major research problems of financial time series analysis. In this work, performance comparison of various attribute set reduction algorithms were made for short term stock price prediction. Forward selection, backward elimination, optimized selection, optimized selection based on brute force, weight guided and optimized selection based on the evolutionary principle and strategy was used. Different selection schemes and cross over types were explored. To supplement learning and modeling, support vector machine was also used in combination. The algorithms were applied on a real time Indian stock data namely CNX Nifty. The experimental study was conducted using the open source data mining tool Rapidminer. The performance was compared in terms of root mean squared error, squared error and execution time. The obtained results indicates the superiority of evolutionary algorithms and the optimize selection algorithm based on evolutionary principles outperforms others.

**Keywords:** Financial time series, Stock trend prediction, attribute set reduction algorithms, Evolutionary algorithms, Data mining, computational intelligence.

## 1 Introduction

A discrete-time signal or time series [7] is a set of observations taken sequentially in time, space or some other independent variable. Examples of time series abound in such fields as economics, business, engineering, natural sciences, medicine and social sciences. Financial time series analysis is concerned with theory and practice of asset valuation over time [8]. It is a highly empirical discipline, but like other scientific fields theory forms the foundation for making inference. There is, however, a key feature that distinguishes financial time series analysis from other time series analysis. Both financial theory and its empirical time series contain an element of uncertainty. For example, there are various definitions of asset volatility, and for a stock return series, the volatility is not directly observable [9]. Support vector machines and genetic algorithms are now widely used in time series analysis and prediction.

Genetic algorithms, the first evolutionary algorithms, have been widely studied across the world and predominantly used for optimum random search. The basic version

B.K. Panigrahi et al. (Eds.): SEMCCO 2010, LNCS 6466, pp. 567–574, 2010.

of genetic algorithm, originally proposed by Holland models the ***genetic evolution*** of a population of individuals represented by strings of binary digits. Based on this model, genetic evolutions are simulated using the operations of ***selection, crossover***, and ***mutation*** and performance is monitored using the ***fitness function*** [11].

The Feature selection or attribute set reduction is essentially a task to remove irrelevant and / or redundant features or attributes. Irrelevant features can be removed without affecting learning performance. Redundant features are a type of irrelevant feature. The distinction is that a redundant feature implies the co-presence of another feature; individually each feature is relevant, but the removal of one of them will not affect learning performance [12].

In this work, the role of various attribute set reduction algorithms are explored in stock price prediction. The research explores, given today's prices in terms of open, high, low and close values, how accurately can we predict the close price in seven days? Literature survey and related works are presented in section 2. The section 3 describes the attribute set reduction algorithms explored as part of this work. The section 4 describes the methodology used in this study.. Empirical modeling and investigations is dealt in section 5. Findings and conclusions are presented in section 6.

## 2   Literature Survey and Related Works

A case based fuzzy decision tree [1] was used to predict the stock price movement. Tiago A.E. Ferreira et al, has presented an intelligent hybrid system, composed of an artificial neural network combined with a modified genetic algorithm, for the solution of time series forecasting problems [2]. Paper [3], introduced wavelet transform and GA based SVM for forecasting share price. Genetic algorithms were used in [4], to predict the Egyptian stock market. The concepts of Genetic algorithm were applied in [5], to predict stock trading points. GA based optimized LS-SVM forecasting was explored in [13]. Kyoung-jae Kim and Ingoo Han have used genetic algorithms for the prediction of stock price index [14]. A hybrid approach of combining GA and SVM was used in [15], for the problem of bankruptcy prediction.

## 3   Attribute Set Reduction Algorithms

This section briefly describes the various attribute set reduction algorithms used in this study [10].

### 3.1   Optimized Selection (Evolutionary)

This is a genetic algorithm for feature selection. A genetic algorithm works as follows

1.  Generate an initial population consisting of population_size individuals. Each attribute is switched on with probability p_initialize
    o   For all individuals in the population Perform mutation i.e. set used attributes to unused with probability p_mutation and vice versa.
    o   Choose two individuals from the population and perform crossover with probability p_crossover. The type of crossover can be selected by crossover_type.

2. Perform selection, map all individuals to sections on a roulette wheel or any other selection scheme, whose size is proportional to the individual's fitness and draw population_size individuals at random according to their probability.
3. As long as the fitness improves, go to 2

The various selection schemes used are roulette wheel, uniform, cut, stochastic universal sampling, Boltzmann, rank, tournament and non dominated sorting. The crossover types are one point, uniform and shuffle.

## 3.2  Forward Selection

This algorithm starts with an empty selection of attributes and, in each round, it adds each unused attribute of the given set of examples. For each added attribute, the performance is estimated using inner operators, e.g. a cross-validation. Only the attribute giving the highest increase of performance is added to the selection. Then a new round is started with the modified selection. This implementation will avoid any additional memory consumption beside the memory used originally for storing the data and the memory which might be needed for applying the inner operators.

A parameter specifies when the iteration will be aborted (stopping behavior). Three different behaviors used are **without increase,** that runs as long as there is any increase in performance, **without increase of at least,** that runs as long as the increase is at least as high as specified, either relative or absolute and **without significant increase,** that stops as soon as the increase isn't significant to the specified level.

## 3.3  Backward Elimination

This algorithm starts with the full set of attributes and, in each round, it removes each remaining attribute of the given set of examples. For each removed attribute, the performance is estimated using inner operators, e.g. a cross-validation. Only the attribute giving the least decrease of performance is finally removed from the selection. Then a new round is started with the modified selection. This implementation will avoid any additional memory consumption beside the memory used originally for storing the data and the memory which might be needed for applying the inner operators.

A parameter specifies when the iteration will be aborted (stopping behavior). Three different behaviors used are **with decrease** runs as long as there is any increase in performance, **with decrease of more than,** runs as long as the decrease is less than the specified threshold, either relative or absolute and **with significant decrease,** stops as soon as the decrease is significant to the specified level.

## 3.4  Optimized Selection

This algorithm realizes the two deterministic greedy feature selection algorithms forward selection and backward elimination.

Forward Selection

1. Create an initial population with $n$ individuals where $n$ is the input example set's number of attributes. Each individual will use exactly one of the features.
2. Evaluate the attribute sets and select only the best $k$.
3. For each of the $k$ attribute sets do: If there are $j$ unused attributes, make $j$ copies of the attribute set and add exactly one of the previously unused attributes to the attribute set.
4. As long as the performance improved in the last $p$ iterations go to 2.

Backward Elimination

1. Start with an attribute set which uses all features.
2. Evaluate all attribute sets and select the best $k$.
3. For each of the $k$ attribute sets do: If there are $j$ attributes used, make $j$ copies of the attribute set and remove exactly one of the previously used attributes from the attribute set.
4. As long as the performance improved in the last $p$ iterations go to 2

### 3.5 Optimized Selection (Brute Force)

This feature selection operator selects the best attribute set by trying all possible combinations of attribute selections. It returns the example set containing the subset of attributes which produced the best performance.

### 3.6 Optimized Selection (Weight-Guided)

This operator uses input attribute weights to determine the order of features added to the feature set starting with the feature set containing only the feature with highest weight.. The algorithm stops if adding the last k features does not increase the performance or if all features were added.

## 4 Methodology

This section describes the methodology used as part of this study. At first, the four attributes, that is open, high, low and close prices of a day's price are given as input to the system. The predicted attribute is the close price after seven days. The system tries to predict what would be the closing price after seven days. The five attributes under investigation are applied to the various attribute set reduction algorithms as discussed in section 2. At this stage, a split validation operator is applied to split the set into a training and test set so that the model can be evaluated. In this study, the relative split type is used with a split ratio of 0.7 and shuffled sampling is used. Next a support vector machine learner is applied to the training set and evaluated over the test set. The performance is evaluated by root mean squared error and squared error. The data mining tool Rapidminer [10] was used to conduct this study.

## 5  Empirical Modeling and Investigations

This section deals with details of data used in this study and investigations carried out.

### 5.1  Data Used in the Study

Financial time series data used in this study is stock price index of National Stock Exchange (NSE) of India. (Source: www.nseindia.com). The data used is the open, close, low and high prices of CNX NIFTY for the period 03-11-1995 to 17-06-2009. Totally there are 3400 observations. The example set contained four regular attributes and one special attribute (trend prediction).

## 6  Findings and Conclusion

As discussed in section 3, the performances are compared in terms of root mean squared error and squared error. The following combination produced the best possible results. Optimized selection algorithm based on an evolutionary strategy marginally outperforms other algorithms. Optimized Selection (Evolutionary) algorithm, with roulette wheel selection and shuffle cross over produced an error of 149.987. Similarly, Optimized Selection (Evolutionary) algorithm, with Boltzmann selection and Uniform cross over produced an error of 150.234 and Optimized Selection (Evolutionary) algorithm, with Boltzmann selection and one point cross over produced an error of 154.371. Some other combinations were also tried out, but they did not produce any results. From the obtained results, it is clear that, it is worthwhile to try stock trend prediction rather than stock price prediction. It is widely believed that predicting the trend may be easier than predicting the exact price.

The various findings of this study are summarized in the table below.

| Algorithm | Selection Scheme | Cross over Type | Execution Time * | Root Mean Squared Error | Squared Error | Attributes selected in the model |
|---|---|---|---|---|---|---|
|  | Roulette Wheel | One point | 3.55 sec | 157.677 | 24862 + / - 66737 | Low Close |
|  |  | Uniform | 3.57 sec | 161.747 | 26162 + / - 66737 | Open Low |
|  |  | Shuffle | 4.02 sec | 149.987 | 22496 + / - 67538 | Low High Close |
|  | Uniform | One point | 3.48 sec | 154.395 | 23806 + / - 63730 | Low Close |
| Optimized |  | Uniform | 4.08 sec | 156.389 | 24457 + / - 65228 | Close |

| Selection (Evolutionary) | | Shuffle | 3.49 sec | 161.334 | 26028 +/- 73864 | High Close |
|---|---|---|---|---|---|---|
| | Cut | One point | 3.09 sec | 158.696 | 25184 +/- 72586 | Low |
| | | Uniform | 3.53 sec | 160.018 | 25605 +/- 73724 | Low Close |
| | | Shuffle | 3.34 sec | 156.732 | 24654 +/- 69519 | Low Close |
| | Boltzmann | One point | 4.01 sec | 154.371 | 23830 +/- 61984 | Open Low |
| | | Uniform | 3.43 sec | 150.234 | 22570 +/- 61162 | Low Close |
| | | Shuffle | 3.12 sec | 157.715 | 24873 +/- 67726 | Close |
| | Tournament | One point | 4.10 sec | 156.328 | 24438 +/- 63249 | Low Close |
| | | Uniform | 3.21 sec | 153.999 | 23715 +/- 63695 | High Close |
| | | Shuffle | 3.27 sec | 153.858 | 23762 +/- 60048 | Close |
| | Stopping Behavior | | | | | |
| Forward Selection | Without increase | | 7 sec | 169.833 | 28843 +/- 78403 | Low Close |
| | Without increase of at least | | 8 sec | 181.168 | 32821 +/- 86869 | High Low Open Close |
| | Without significant increase | | 5 sec | 171.699 | 29480 +/- 86164 | Low |
| Backward Elimination | With decrease | | 8 sec | 169.974 | 28891 +/- 80454 | Open High |
| | With decrease of more than | | 8 sec | 192.717 | 37139 +/- 95651 | Open |
| | With significant decrease | | 8 sec | 192.717 | 37139 +/- 95651 | Open |
| Optimized | Forward | | 7 sec | 169.833 | 28843 +/- 78403 | Low Close |

| Selection | Backward | 4 sec | 177.518 | 31512 +/- 79598 | High Low Open Close |
| Optimized Selection (Brute force) | - | 12 sec | 165.545 | 27405 +/- 74501 | Low |

* The experiments were performed on a laptop with the following configurations. Dell, Inspiron 1525, Intel® Core™2 Duo CPU, T7250 @ 2.00 GHz, 3062 MB RAM, Windows Vista Home Premium.

## Acknowledgment

The authors would like to acknowledge the role of tutorials [6], in shaping up this paper.

## References

1. Chang, P.-C., Fan, C.-Y., Yeh, C.-H., Pan, W.-L.: A hybrid system by integrating case based reasoning and fuzzy decision tree for financial time series data. In: 2008 IEEE International Conference on Fuzzy Systems (FUZZ 2008), pp. 76–82 (2008)
2. Tiago, A.E., Ferreira, G.C.V., Paulo, J.L.A.: A Hybrid Intelligent System Approach for Improving the Prediction of Real World Times Series, pp. 736–743, 0-7803-851 5-2/04/$20.00 02004, IEEE
3. Zhou, J., Bai, T., Zhang, A., Tian, J.: The Integrated Methodology of Wavelet Transform and GA based-SVM for Forecasting Share Price. In: Proceedings of the 2008 IEEE International Conference on Information and Automation Zhangjiajie, China, pp. 729–733, June 20-23 (2008)
4. Badawy, F.A.: Genetic algorithms for predicting the Egyptian stock market. In: IEEE Xplore
5. Chang, P.-C., Fan, C.-Y., Liu, C.-H.: Integrating a Piecewise Linear Representation Method and a Neural Network Model for Stock Trading Points Prediction. IEEE Transactions On Systems, Man, And Cybernetics—Part C: Applications And Reviews 39(1), 80–92 (2009)
6. http://www.neuralmarkettrends.com/
7. Bagavathi Sivakumar, P., Mohandas, V.P.: Evaluating the predictability of financial time series A case study on Sensex data. In: Sobh, T. (ed.) Innovations and Advanced Techniques in Computer and Information Sciences and Engineering, vol. XVIII (2007) ISBN: 978-1-4020-6267-4
8. Bagavathi Sivakumar, P., Mohandas, V.P.: Performance Analysis of Hybrid Forecasting models with Traditional ARIMA Models - A Case Study on Financial Time Series Data. International Journal of Computer Information Systems and Industrial Management Applications (IJCISIM) 2, 187–211 (2010), http://www.mirlabs.org/ijcisim ISSN: 2150-7988
9. Tsay, R.S.: Analysis of Financial Time Series. John Wiley & Sons, Inc., Chichester (2002)
10. http://www.rapidminer.com

11. Dobrivoje, A.K.P.: Computational Intelligence in Time Series Forecasting Theory and Engineering Applications (Advances in industrial control). Springer-Verlag London Limited (2005)
12. Liu, H., Motoda, H.: Computational methods of feature selection. Data mining and knowledge discovery series. Chapman & Hall/CRC, Boca Raton (2008)
13. Mahjoob, M.J., Abdollahzade, M., Zarringhalam, R.: GA based optimized LS-SVM forecasting of short term electricity price in competitive power markets. In: IEEE Explore, 978-1-4244-1718-6/08/$25.00 ©2008 IEEE
14. Kim, K.-J., Han, I.: Genetic algorithms approach to feature discretization in artificial neural networks for the prediction of stock price index. Expert systems with applications 19, 125–132 (2000)
15. Min, S.-H., Lee, J., Han, I.: Hybrid genetic algorithms and support vector machines for bankruptcy prediction. Expert systems with applications 31, 652–660 (2006)

# Dimensionality Reduction and Optimum Feature Selection in Designing Efficient Classifiers

A.K. Das and J. Sil

Bengal Engineering and Science University/ Department of Computer Science
and Technology, Shibpur, Howrah, India
akdas@cs.becs.ac.in, js@cs.becs.ac.in

**Abstract.** In the course of day-to-day work, huge volumes of data sets constantly grow accumulating a large number of features, but lack completeness and have relatively low information density. Dimensionality reduction and feature selection are the core issues in handling such data sets and more specifically, discovering relationships in data. Dimensionality reduction by reduct generation is an important aspect of classification where reduced attribute set has the same classification power as the entire set of attributes of an information system. In the paper, multiple reducts are generated integrating the concept of rough set theory (RST) and relational algebra operations. As a next step, the attributes of the reducts, which are relatively better associated and have stronger classification power, are selected to generate the single reduct using classical Apriori algorithm. Different classifiers are built using the single reduct and accuracies are compared to measure the effectiveness of the proposed method.

**Keywords:** Rough Set Theory, Relational Algebra, Classification, Classical Apriori Algorithm.

## 1 Introduction

Comprehensive data warehouses integrate operational data with customer, supplier and market information resulting explosion of information. Extraction of relevant attributes out of the larger set of candidate attributes is a challenging task addressed by many researchers [1-5] with an emphasis [11, 12] in pattern recognition domain to improve the classification rate by removing the influence of noise. Rough set theory (RST) [4, 5, 7], based on mathematical concept recently becomes very popular in dimensionality reduction and feature selection of large data sets. The RST approach to feature selection is used to determine a subset of features (or attributes) called "reduct" [8, 10, 13] which can predict the decision concepts and have classification capability similar to that of the entire attribute sets.

In reality, there are multiple reducts in a given information system amongst which the best performer is chosen as the final solution to the problem. But this is not always true and according to Occam's razor and minimal description length principle [18], the minimal reduct is preferred. However, Roman [20] has found that the minimal reduct is good for ideal situations where a given data set fully represents a

B.K. Panigrahi et al. (Eds.): SEMCCO 2010, LNCS 6466, pp. 575–582, 2010.

domain of interest. For real life situations and limited size data sets, other reducts might be better for prediction, selection of which is time expensive. Therefore, obtaining a best performer classifier using multiple reducts is not practical rather ensemble of different classifiers may lead to better classification accuracy. However, combining large number of classifiers increases complexity of the system. So, there must be a tradeoff between these two.

To address the issue, initially, the concept of relational algebra operations, like projection ($\Pi$) and division ($\div$) are applied on the dataset to find the indispensable set of conditional attributes called reducts [4, 5, 7]. For each conditional attribute a score is computed, which is inversely proportional to the information gain related to that attribute. Attributes are then partitioned into different groups according to their score and the group with minimum score is considered first for computing the reducts. The reducts are stored in the set RED while rest of the elements of that group are added to the group with next lower score and checked for reducts. The process is repeated for each group and finally all possible reducts are contained in set RED. It has been observed that there may be large number of reducts and as a result, classification becomes too time consuming involving large cpu time using this method [15]. So, as a next step using Apriori algorithm [6, 17] reducts are optimized to a single one, which has stronger classification power. The minimum 'support' concept has been applied on the elements of RED to obtain frequent reduct set $RED_{freq}$ ($RED_{freq} \subseteq$ RED) from which the core [4, 5, 7] attributes are selected and stored in a set CORE. Next the 'confidence' values of the remaining (non-core) attributes and their average value with respect to CORE are calculated. If the confidence of an attribute is less than the average confidence then it is treated as a redundant attribute and ignored, otherwise the attribute is added to the CORE. By repeating the above process for all non-core attributes, a single reduct is obtained in set CORE. The entire step-by-step procedure of the proposed concept is depicted in Figure 1.

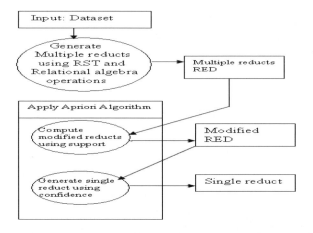

**Fig. 1.** Block Diagram of the Proposed Method

Finally, different classifiers are built using Weka tool by 10-fold cross-validation method based on the reduced attribute set obtained by proposed SRG algorithm and other existing dimensionality reduction algorithm such as Principal Component Analysis (PCA), Correlated Feature Subset (CFS) algorithm and Consistency Subset Evaluator (CSE). Accuracy of the classifiers are computed and compared to measure the effectiveness of the proposed method.

The paper is organized as follows: Section 2 describes the generation of multiple reducts. Section 3 discusses the method of single reduct generation based on Apriori concepts. Results on various benchmark datasets are described and compared in section 4. Finally, the paper is concluded in section 5.

## 2   Multiple Reduct Generation Using Rough Set Theory

An information system generally has huge dimension, consisting large number of objects and attributes, which create problem in data management. Various applications require only the relevant features for specified tasks keeping aside the irrelevant or redundant attributes.   Sets of relevant attributes establish the discernibility relation between the objects and thus preserve important information of the system by reducing dimensionality of the datasets. The minimal subset of attributes called reduct satisfies following constraint, which has the same classification power as the entire attribute set, is used instead of the entire attribute set for classification of data.

**Constraint:** *Card* ($\Pi_{\text{REDUCT, D}}$ (DS)) = Card ($\Pi_{\text{REDUCT}}$ (DS))) where, REDUCT is the set of minimal attributes.

The proposed method describes generation of all possible sets of reducts of a decision system (DS) using the concept of RST and relational algebra operations.  Let the DS contains $n$ number of conditional attributes i.e. C = {$C_1$, $C_2$,...,$C_n$}.  A score function $S(C_i)$ for attribute $C_i$ is computed using (1), which is inversely proportional to the information gain of attribute $C_i$.

$$S(C_i) = Card(\Pi_{C_i \cup D}(DS) \div \Pi_D(DS))  \tag{1}$$

where, i=1,2,...,$n$, *Card* denotes cardinality operation indicating the number of tuples in the relation and $\Pi$ is the projection operation defined in relational algebra that takes the vertical projection on DS based on the attributes in its subscript.

The attribute set C is partitioned into $g$ groups ($G_1$,$G_2$,... ,$G_g$) such that attributes with the same score values are in the same group and vice versa. It is assumed that the score of attributes in $G_i$ is less than that of $G_j$ where i < j.   Since, lower the attribute score implies higher the information gain, elements of $G_1$ are considered as the most important attributes and therefore, the possibility of occurring core attributes in $G_1$ is higher than other groups. Since, all attributes of a group are of equal score, so they are equally likely within the group. Thus, either each one individually or any possible combination of them within the group may be a subset of the final reduct therefore, each group is modified by all possible combinations of their elements (attributes).

In this approach, firstly each element of group $G_1$ are checked to see whether it would satisfy the *constraint* and if so it must be a reduct, kept in set RED. Thus all possible reducts from $G_1$ are computed. For generating other reducts, Cartesian product ($\times$) operation is applied iteratively between $G_{i-1}$ and $G_i$ and the new elements are stored in $G_i$; where i = 2, 3, …, g. The same procedure is applied on each group $G_i$

and finally multiple reducts are obtained in RED. The detailed multiple reduct generation algorithm namely MRG algorithm is in [15].

## 3   Single Reduct Formation Based on Apriori Method

Multiple reducts using MRG algorithm are analyzed by apriori method to obtain a single reduct. Given a set of reducts RED, the algorithm attempts to find subset $RED_{freq}$, the reducts of which are common to at least support threshold (min_sup) of the reducts in RED. It generates candidate attribute sets of length k from attribute sets of length k-1 and prunes the candidates with an infrequent sub pattern. Thus, apriori employs an iterative approach known as a level wise search, where attribute sets of length k are used to explore (k+1) length attribute sets. This method searches frequent attributes [6, 9] and strong rules using  (2) and (3) respectively.

*Definitions:* If A and B are two attribute sets corresponding to a reduct set RED and A => B, an association rule then

$$Support\ (A => B\ ) = P(A \cup B) = \frac{Reducts\ containing\ both\ A\ and\ B}{Total\ number\ of\ reducts\ in\ RED} \qquad (2)$$

$$Confidence\ (A => B) = P\ (B\ |\ A) = \frac{Reducts\ containing\ both\ A\ and\ B}{Total\ number\ of\ reducts\ containing\ A} \qquad (3)$$

### 3.1   Single Reduct Formation

The concept of 'Support' and 'Confidence' are used in the proposed method to obtain a set of frequent reducts and finally a single reduct. The reduct set RED obtained using MRG algorithm [15] is considered as input dataset and support (i.e., frequency) of each attribute is calculated using (2). Let $A = \{A_1, A_2, ...., A_n\}$ be the set of all attributes in RED and  each of these 1-tuple attributes are stored in an attribute set say, T i.e., T = $\{\{A_1\}, \{A_2\},....., \{A_n\}\}$. Now, frequency of each element in T is computed and T is modified by removing the elements with frequency less than a predefined threshold (i.e., '*min_sup*'), which is assumed as the minimum support among all attributes. Then 2-tuples attributes set $T_{mod}$ is formed from 1-tuple attributes set T and modified by removing the items with support less than '*min_sup*'. The procedure is repeated, until either $T_{mod}$ contains only one item or empty. If $T_{mod}$ contains one item then the set $RED_{freq}$ contains only one reduct, otherwise (*when $T_{mod}$ is empty*), the items in itemset T, obtained by previous iteration, are the final reducts and stored in $RED_{freq}$.

   As it is known that, 'Confidence' assesses the degree of certainty of the association of items, so all possible associations are formed corresponding to each itemset. In order to generate a single reduct, the proposed method is not interested to compute all the association rules, but only a subset of it is used to compute the degree of association of each non-core attributes with the core attributes. That is, the method computes the confidence of the rules of the form (CORE=> {*a*}) using equation (3), where set CORE contains the core attributes and '*a*' is the single non-core attribute. First, the core attributes (common to all reducts in $RED_{freq}$) are stored in the set

CORE, while the remaining (non-core) attributes of set $RED_{freq}$ are stored in set $A_d$. Next for each attribute 'a' present in set $A_d$, 'Confidence' of 'a' with respect to set CORE is calculated using equation (3). The minimum confidence 'min_conf' is considered, as threshold equals to the average confidence of the attributes in $A_d$. Attribute 'a' will be an element of final reduct set $RED_{single}$, provided confidence of 'a' with respect to core (i.e., CORE=> $\{a\}$) is greater than or equal to min_conf. Thus, the final reduct $RED_{single}$ is computed as: $RED_{single}$ = CORE $\cup$ $\{a \mid a \in A_d \wedge$ Confidence (CORE=> $\{a\}$) > min_conf$\}$. The SRG algorithm has been described below:

**Algorithm: Single_Reduct_Generation (SRG)**
    Input: the attributes A= $\{A_1, A_2, \ldots., A_n\}$ of the data set appear in RED.
    Output: $RED_{single}$ /* containing a single reduct*/
    Begin
        Compute the itemset , T = $\{\{A_1\}, \{A_2\}, \ldots.., \{A_n\}\}$.
        Compute frequency of each item of T in RED and let f = $\{f_1, f_2, \ldots, f_n\}$.
        Set min_sup = min$\{f_i\}$ $\forall$ i = 1, 2, …, n.
        T = T – $\{x \mid x \in T \wedge$ freq(x) < min_sup$\}$
        do$\{$
                $T_{mod}$ = T $\bowtie$ T.
                $T_{mod}$ = $T_{mod}$ – $\{x \mid x \in T_{mod} \wedge$ freq(x) < min_sup$\}$
                if $\mid T_{mod} \mid$ > 1 then T = $T_{mod}$
        $\}$ while $\mid T_{mod} \mid$ > 1.
        If $\mid T_{mod} \mid$ = 1 then $RED_{single}$ = $T_{mod}$ and return $RED_{single}$
                Else $RED_{freq}$ = T
        Let $RED_{freq}$ = $\{RED_1, RED_2, \ldots…, RED_N\}$
        Let $A_{RED}$ = $\{A_1, A_2, \ldots, A_m\}$ /*all attributes in $RED_{freq}$ */
        Compute CORE = $RED_1 \cap RED_2 \cap \ldots \cap RED_N$
        $A_d$ = $A_{RED}$ – CORE    /*rest of the attributes*/
        Sum_conf = 0
        For each a $\in$ $A_d$ do $\{$
                Compute Conf(CORE=> $\{a\}$) using (3)
                Sum_conf = Sum_conf + Conf(CORE=> $\{a\}$)
        $\}$
        Set min_conf = Sum_conf / $\mid A_d \mid$
        For each a $\in$ $A_d$ do
            If (Conf(CORE=> $\{a\}$) >= min_conf) then CORE = CORE $\cup$ $\{a\}$
        Set $RED_{single}$ = CORE
        return ( $RED_{single}$ )
    End.

## 4    Results and Discussions

The proposed method has been explained by considering the ZOO datasets of the UCI repository and the performance has been analyzed comparing with existing dimension reduction methods by considering various UCI repository data sets.

(a) In the experiment, the ZOO datasets of the UCI database is used. Using MRG algorithm discussed in section 2, multiple reducts RED is computed as RED = {{BCFHLMP}, {CDFHKLM}, {CDFHLMP}, {DEFHKLM}, {DFHKLMN}, {DFHLMNP}, {CDFJKLM}, {DFJKLMN}, {DFJLMNP}, {ACFIKLM}, {ACFILMP}, {CFHIKLM}, {CFHILMP}, {CFIJLMP}}. The distinct attributes in set RED are {A, B, C, D, E, F, H, I, J, K, L, M, N, P} and so 1-tuple attributes set T = {{A}, {B}, {C}, {D}, {E}, {F}, {H}, {I}, {J}, {K}, {L}, {M}, {N}, {P}}. Since, attributes B and E are of minimum frequency (i.e. 1) obtained using (2), so *min_sup=1*. Applying join operation iteratively on elements of T and removing the elements with 'support' less than min_sup, final frequent 7-tuple attributes are obtained which are considered as frequent reducts stored in set $RED_{freq}$, where $RED_{freq}$ ={{CDFHLMP}, {CDFLMJK}, {DEFLMKH}, {CFHLMIP}, {ACFKLMI}, {BCFLMHP}}.

To compute single reduct, core and non-core attributes are selected from $RED_{freq}$ and store in set CORE and $A_d$, where CORE ={F, L, M} and $A_d$ = {A, B, C, D, E, H, I, J, K, P}. Now for each non-core attribute a $\in$ $A_d$ confidence is calculated with respect to CORE using (3) and listed in Table 1. Since, min_conf (i.e., average confidence) = 37.14 so, the rules with consequent C, D, H, K and P are the interesting rules. Therefore, the single reduct $RED_{single}$ is obtained by adding these attributes with the core attributes F, L and M. Thus, $RED_{single}$ = {FLMCDHKP}.

**Table 1.** Confidence with respect to CORE

| non-core attributes | Association | Confidence | Interesting Rule? |
|---|---|---|---|
| A | CORE⇒A | 14.28 | No |
| B | CORE⇒B | 7.14 | No |
| C | CORE⇒C | 64.28 | Yes |
| D | CORE⇒D | 57.14 | Yes |
| E | CORE⇒E | 7.14 | No |
| H | CORE⇒H | 57.14 | Yes |
| I | CORE⇒I | 35.71 | No |
| J | CORE⇒J | 28.57 | No |
| K | CORE⇒K | 50.00 | Yes |
| P | CORE⇒P | 50.00 | Yes |
| Average | Confidence | 37.14 | |

(b) In the experiment, various datasets are collected from UCI machine learning repository [14] and 10-fold cross validations were carried out using "Weka" tool [16] to compute and compared the accuracy of the classifiers such as C4.5, Naïve Bayes and Decision Tree Learner (ID3). The results of proposed method (SRG) are compared with the results obtained using multiple reducts algorithm (MRG) in paper [15]. Table 2 shows that the average accuracy of the classifiers for the data sets are higher in case of SRG algorithm compared to MRG algorithm. Also, to analyze the performance of the proposed method, SRG algorithm is compared with other existing dimensionality reduction algorithm such as PCA, CFS and CSE by computing the

C4.5 classifier accuracy. In the paper, the number of principle components in PCA is considered equal to the number of attributes obtained by SRG algorithm. From Table 3, it is evident that the proposed method exhibits a significant improvement in the accuracy relative to the accuracy obtained using all the other methods.

**Table 2.** The Comparison of MRG and SRG algorithm

| Data sets | Using MRG algorithm | | | Using SRG algorithm | | |
|---|---|---|---|---|---|---|
| | C4.5 | Bayes | ID3 | C4.5 | Bayes | ID3 |
| Wine (objects: 178 attributes: 13 class: 3) | 94.78 | 95.01 | 93.65 | 96.78 | 97.01 | 97.80 |
| Zoo (objects: 101 attributes: 16 class: 7) | 93.17 | 90.19 | 93.29 | 95.37 | 92.75 | 94.15 |
| Hepatitis (objects: 155 attributes: 19 class: 2) | 85.55 | 83.56 | 84.70 | 88.74 | 85.60 | 86.76 |
| Average (%) | 91.16 | 89.59 | 90.55 | 93.63 | 91.79 | 92.90 |

**Table 3.** C4.5 classifier accuracy on reduced attribute set

| Dimensionality Reduction Methods | Wine data | Zoo data | Hepatitis data | Average (%) |
|---|---|---|---|---|
| PCA | 87.35 | 89.75 | 78.63 | 85.24 |
| CFS | 94.04 | 93.29 | 86.47 | 91.26 |
| CSE | 94.63 | 92.57 | 87.11 | 91.44 |
| SRG | 96.78 | 95.38 | 88.74 | 93.63 |

## 5  Conclusion

In the paper, from multiple reducts, a single reduct has been obtained, which resolves selection of approximate reducts attempted by most of the researches [18-20] in feature selection. The knowledge has been discovered generating the reducts having the features of high confidence and accurate classification power. Implementing the above approach, a single classifier is constructed, unlike other methods where multiple classifiers are constructed and combined, therefore, increasing the complexity of the system. The main demerit of Apriori algorithm is multiple scanning of the data set, resulting fall of its efficiency especially while the data set size is very large. Here, since, multiple reducts generated initially represent the data set so the data set size is very less and as a result it does not degrade the efficiency of the proposed method. On the other hand, 'support' and 'confidence' identify the most frequent and interesting attributes of the attribute set respectively. Thus the method has been developed based on only the merits of Apriori algorithm, since, the demerits do not arise in such type of applications.

# References

1. Carter, C., Hamilton, H.: Efficient attribute-oriented generalization for knowledge discovery from large databases. IEEE Trans. Knowledge and Data Engineering 10, 193–208 (1998)
2. Dong, G., Li, J.: Efficient mining of emerging patterns: Discovering trends and differences. In: Proc. 1999 Int. Conf. Knowledge Discovery and Data Mining, KDD 1999, pp. 43–52 (1999)
3. Klemettinen, M., Mannila, H., Ronkainen, P., Toivonen, H.: Finding interesting rules from large sets of discovered association rules. In: Proceedings of the 3rd International Conference on Information and Knowledge Management (CIKM 1994), pp. 401–407. ACM Press, New York (1994)
4. Pawlak, Z.: Rough set theory and its applications to data analysis. Cybernetics and systems 29, 661–688 (1998)
5. Pawlak, Z.: Rough sets – Theoritical aspects of reasoning about data, vol. 229. Kluwer Academic Publishers, Dordrecht (1991)
6. Agrawal, R., Srikant, R.: Fast Algorithm for Mining Association Rules. In: Proc. of the 20th VLDB Conference, pp. 487–499 (1994)
7. Ziarko, W.: Rough sets as a methodology for data mining. In: Rough Sets in Knowledge Discovery 1: Methodology and Applications, pp. 554–576. Physica-Verlag, Heidelberg (1998)
8. Swiniarski, W., Skowron, A.: Rough set methods in feature selection and recognition. Pattern Recog. Letters 24(6), 833–849 (2003)
9. The Apriori Algorithm (a Tutorial) Markus Hegland CMA, Australian National University John Dedman Building, Canberra ACT 0200, Australia
10. Pawlak, Z.: Drawing Conclusions from Data-The Rough Set Way. IJIS 16, 3–11 (2001)
11. Witten, I.H., Frank, E.: Data Mining:Practical Machine Learning Tools and Techniques with Java Implementations. MK (2000)
12. Han, J., Kamber, M.: Data Miningg:Concepts and Techniques. MK (2001)
13. Pawlak, Z.: Rough set. Int. J. of Computer and Information Science 11, 341–356 (1982)
14. Murphy, P., Aha, W.: UCI repository of machine learning databases (1996), http://www.ics.uci.edu/mlearn/MLRepository.html
15. Das, A.K., Sil, J.: An Efficient Classifier Design Integrating Rough Set and Graph Theory based Decision Forest. In: the 4th Indian International Conference on Artificial Intelligence (IICAI 2009), Siddaganga Institute of Technology, December 16-18, pp. 533–544, Tumkur, India (2009)
16. WEKA: Machine Learning Software, http://www.cs.waikato.ac.nz/~ml/
17. Borgelt, C.: Apriori: Finding Association Rules/ Hyperedges with the Apriori Algorithm School of Computer Science, University of Magdeburg (2004)
18. Quinlan, J.R.: The minimum description length and categorical theories. In: Proceedings 11th International Conference on Machine learning, New Brunswick, pp. 233–241. Morgan Kaufmann, San Francisco
19. Hansen, M., Yu, B.: Model selection and the principle of minimum description length. J. Am. Stat. Assoc. 96, 746–774 (2001)
20. Roman, W.S., Hargis, L.: Rough sets as a frontend as neural-networks texture classifiers. Neurocomputing 36, 85–102 (2001)

# Social Emotional Optimization Algorithm for Nonlinear Constrained Optimization Problems

Yuechun Xu[1], Zhihua Cui[1,2], and Jianchao Zeng[1]

[1] Complex System and Computational Intelligence Laboratory,
Taiyuan University of Science and Technology,
No. 66 Waliu Road, Wanbailin District, Taiyuan, Shanxi, 030024, P.R. China
[2] State Key Laboratory for Novel Software Technology,
Nanjing University, Jiangsu, 210093, P.R. China
xuyuechunwww@sina.com,
cuizhihua@gmail.com,
zengjianchao@263.net

**Abstract.** Nonlinear programming problem is one important branch in operational research, and has been successfully applied to various real-life problems. In this paper, a new approach called Social emotional optimization algorithm (SEOA) is used to solve this problem which is a new swarm intelligent technique by simulating the human behavior guided by emotion. Simulation results show that the social emotional optimization algorithm proposed in this paper is effective and efficiency for the nonlinear constrained programming problems.

## 1 Introduction

Many realistic problems cannot be adequately represented as a linear program owing to the nature of the nonlinearity of the objective function or the nonlinearity of any constraints. Therefore, nonlinear constrained optimization problem becomes a hot issue. It is an important type of problems which are widely used in the area of engineering, scientific, and operational applications. Up to date, many methods have been proposed to solve them especially for swarm intelligence optimization algorithms.

Recently, swarm intelligence algorithms have become a hot topic for nature-inspired computation family. This type of algorithms based on the swarm intelligence is a simulated evolutionary method that simulating the behaviors of social insects searching for food and building for nest, and including ant colony optimization[1][2], particle swarm optimization[3][4] and artificial fish-swarm algorithm[5].

SEOA is a novel swarm intelligent population-based optimization algorithm by simulating the human social behaviors. In SEOA methodology, each individual represents one person, while all points in the problem space constructs the social status society. In this virtual world, all individuals aim to seek the higher social status. Therefore, they will communicated through cooperation and competition to increase personal status, while the one with highest score will win and output

B.K. Panigrahi et al. (Eds.): SEMCCO 2010, LNCS 6466, pp. 583–590, 2010.

as the final solution. In this paper, SEOA is used to solve nonlinear constrained optimization algorithms.

The rest of this paper is organized as follows: The detailed description of non-linear constrained problem is given in section 2, while in section 3,the details of social emotional optimization algorithm is presented. Finally, simulation results are presented.

## 2     Nonlinear Constrained Optimization Problems

The typical nonlinear constrained optimization problems can be defined as:

$$\begin{cases} min\ f(x) \\ s.t.\quad g_i(x) \geq 0, i = 1, 2, ...m \end{cases} \tag{1}$$

where the objective function,$f(x):IR^n \rightarrow IR$, and the constraint functions, $g_i(x):IR^n \rightarrow IR$, maximization problems can be solved by multiplying the objective by -1.

The key question when dealing with this problems is how to deal with the constrains. One general constrain-handling technique is translate the constrained problem into an unconstrained one by adding a penalty function to the objective function. In other words, objective function can be re-formatted to:

$$F(x, r) = f(x) + r \sum_{i=1}^{m} \frac{1}{g_i(x)} \tag{2}$$

where $r$ is a small positive number. In this paper, $r$ sets to 0.00000000001.

## 3     Social Emotional Optimization Algorithm

In human society, all people do their work hardly to increase their society status. To obtain this object, people will try their bests to find the path so that higher rewards can be obtained from society. Inspired by this phenomenon, Cui et al.[6-8] proposed a new methodology, social emotional optimization algorithm (SEOA) in which each individual aims to increase the society status.

In SEOA methodology, each individual represents a virtual person, in each iteration, he will choice the behavior according to the corresponding emotion index. After the behavior is done, a status value will be feedback from the society to confirm whether this behavior is right or not. If this choice is right, the emotion index of himself will increase, otherwise,emotion index will decrease.

In the first step, all individuals' emotion indexes are set to 1, with this value, all individuals' emotion indexes is the largest value, therefore, they will think their behavior in this iteration is right, and choice the next behavior as follows:

$$\overrightarrow{x_j}(1) = \overrightarrow{x_j}(0) \oplus Manner_1 \tag{3}$$

while $\overrightarrow{x_j}(0)$ represents the degree of $j's$ individual in the initialization period, the corresponding fitness value is denoted as the society status value. Symbol $\oplus$

meas the operation, in this paper, we only take it as addition operation $+$. Since the belief index of $j$ is 1, the next behavior motion $Manner_1$ is determined by:

$$Manner_1 = -k_1 \cdot rand_1 \cdot \sum_{s=1}^{L}(\vec{x_s}(0) - \vec{x_j}(0)) \qquad (4)$$

while $k_1$ is a parameter used to control the size, $rand_1$ is one random number with uniform distribution. total $L$ individuals are selected whose status values are the worst to provide a reminder for individual $j$ to avoid the wrong behaviors.

In the $t$ generation, if individual $j$ do not obtain one better society status value than all previous values, the $j's$ emotional index is decreased as follows:

$$BI_j(t+1) = BI_j(t) - \Delta \qquad (5)$$

while $\Delta$ is a predefined value. In this paper, this parameter is set to 0.05, this value is coming from experimental tests. If individual $j$ is rewarded a new status value which is the best one among all iterations, then

$$BI_j(t+1) = 1.0 \qquad (6)$$

Remark: If $BI_j(t+1) < 0.0$ is occur according to Eq.(3), then $BI_j(t+1) = 0.0$.

In order to simulate the behavior of human, we define a behavior set which contains three kinds of manners $\{Manner_2, Manner_3, Manner_4\}$. Since the emotion affects the behavior behavior, the next behavior will be changed according to the following three rules:

If $BI_j(t+1) < TH_1$

$$\vec{x_j}(t+1) = \vec{x_j}(t) + Manner_2 \qquad (7)$$

If $TH_1 \leq BI_j(t+1) < TH_2$

$$\vec{x_j}(t+1) = \vec{x_j}(t) + Manner_3 \qquad (8)$$

Otherwise

$$\vec{x_j}(t+1) = \vec{x_j}(t) + Manner_4 \qquad (9)$$

Two parameters $TH_1$ and $TH_2$ are two thresholds aiming to restrict the different behavior manner. For Case 1, because the belief index is too small, individual $j$ prefers to simulate others' successful experiences. Therefore, the update equation is

$$Manner_2 = k_2 \cdot rand_2 \cdot (\overrightarrow{Status}_{best}(t) - \vec{x_j}(t)) \qquad (10)$$

while $\overrightarrow{Status}_{best}(t)$ represents the best society status degree obtained from all people previously. In other words, it is

$$\overrightarrow{Status}_{best}(t) = \arg\min_{s}\{f(\vec{x_s}(h)|1 \leq h \leq t)\} \qquad (11)$$

With the similar method, $Manner_3$ is defined

$$Manner_3 = k_3 \cdot rand_3 \cdot (\vec{x}_{j\,best}(t) - \vec{x}_j(t)) \tag{12}$$
$$+k_2 \cdot rand_2 \cdot (\overrightarrow{Status}_{best}(t) - \vec{x}_j(t))$$
$$-k_1 \cdot rand_1 \cdot \sum_{s=1}^{L}(\vec{x}_s(0) - \vec{x}_j(0))$$

while $\vec{x}_{j\,best}(t)$ denotes the best status value obtained by individual $j$ previously, and is defined by

$$\vec{x}_{j\,best}(t) = \arg\min\{f(\vec{x}_j(h)|1 \leq h \leq t)\} \tag{13}$$

For $Manner_4$, we have

$$Manner_4 = k_3 \cdot rand_3 \cdot (\vec{x}_{j\,best}(t) - \vec{x}_j(t)) \tag{14}$$
$$-k_1 \cdot rand_1 \cdot \sum_{s=1}^{L}(\vec{x}_s(0) - \vec{x}_j(0))$$

Because the phase "social cognitive optimization algorithm(SCOA)" has been used by Xie et al.[9] in 2002, we change this algorithm into social emotional optimization algorithm(SEOA) in order to avoid confusing, although they are two different algorithms.

## 4    Simulation Results

A typical nonlinear programming problem is used to test the performance of the SCOA.It is a high dimension nonlinear constrained problem which is derived from [10][11].

$$\begin{cases} max f(x) = \dfrac{|\sum_{i=1}^{n}(\cos x_i)^4 - 2\prod_{i=1}^{n}(\cos x_i)^2|}{\sqrt{\sum_{i=1}^{n} ix_i^2}} \\ s.t. \\ \prod_{i=1}^{n} x_i - 0.75 \geq 0 \\ 7.5n - \prod_{i=1}^{n} x_i \geq 0 \\ 0 \leq x_i \leq 10, i = 1, ...n \end{cases} \tag{15}$$

In order to achieve the The minimum,we can multiply the objective by -1.

**Table 1.** Results for G4

| Dim | Median | Std | Best | Worst |
|---|---|---|---|---|
| 30 | -7.3504e-001 | 1.0095e+000 | -6.0237e+000 | -4.2590e-001 |
| 50 | -6.0381e-001 | 2.1289e-001 | -1.3339e+000 | -3.6399e-001 |
| 100 | -7.5899e-001 | 4.6181e-001 | -2.9174e+000 | -3.6143e-001 |
| 150 | -8.0688e-001 | 5.3088e-001 | -2.2063e+000 | -4.9713e-001 |
| 200 | -5.8417e-001 | 4.0397e-002 | -6.4290e-001 | -4.9830e-001 |
| 250 | -6.0457e-001 | 7.5309e-002 | -7.1342e-001 | -4.9262e-001 |
| 300 | -7.3245e-001 | 3.7443e-001 | -1.7219e+000 | -5.2621e-001 |

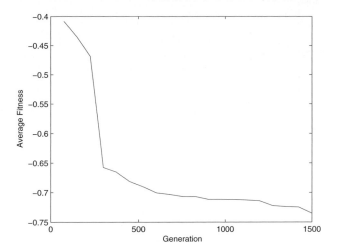

**Fig. 1.** $n = 30$

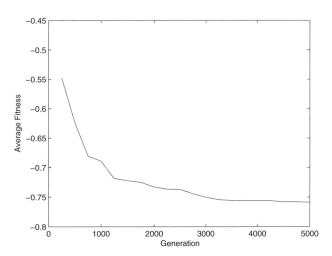

**Fig. 2.** $n = 100$

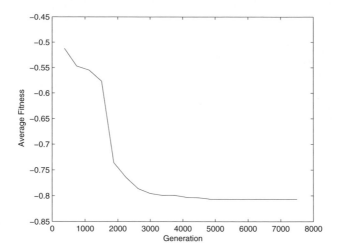

**Fig. 3.** $n = 150$

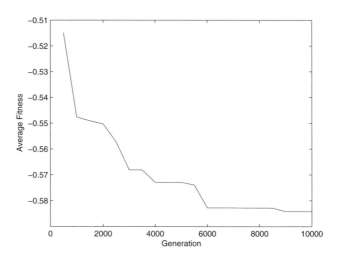

**Fig. 4.** $n = 200$

The number of population is 20, largest iteration is the $50 \times dimensions$. The simulation results are shown in Table I and Figure 1-2. The example demonstrates the efficiency, reliability and high speed of the proposed algorithm.

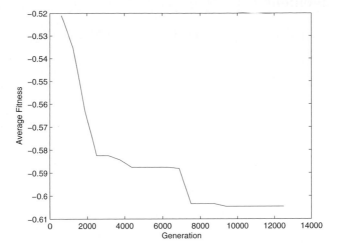

**Fig. 5.** $n = 250$

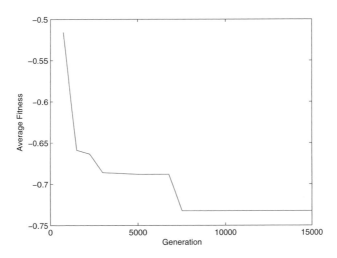

**Fig. 6.** $n = 300$

## 5   Conclusion

This paper presents a new swarm intelligent algorithm, social emotional optimization algorithm(SEOA) to solve the nonlinear constrained optimization problems. Simulation results show that SEOA is effective for this problem.

## Acknowledgement

This paper is supported by the Key Project of Chinese Ministry of Education.(No.209021).

## References

1. Dorigo, M., Maniezzo, V., Colorni, A.: The ant system: optimization by a colony of cooperating agents. IEEE Transactions on Systems, Man, and Cybernetics-Part B(S1083-4419) 26(1), 29–41 (1996)
2. Colorni, A., Dorigo, M., Maniezzo, V.: Distributed optimization by ant colonies. In: Proceedings of 1st European Conference Artificial Life, pp. 134–142. Elsevier, Pans (1991)
3. Eberhart, R.C., Kennedy, J.: A new optimizer using particle swarm theory. In: Proceedings of 6th International Symposium on Micro Machine and Human Science, pp. 39–43 (1995)
4. Kennedy, J., Eberhart, R.C.: Particle swarm optimization. In: Proceedings of ICNN 1995 - IEEE International Conference on Neural Networks, pp. 1942–1948. IEEE CS Press, Perth (1995)
5. Li, X.L., Shao, Z.J., Qian, J.X.: An optimizing method based on autonomous animats Fish-swarm algorithm. Systems Engineering Theory & Practice 22(11), 32–38 (2002)
6. Cui, Z.H., Cai, X.J.: Using Social Cognitive Optimization Algorithm to Solve Nonlinear Equations. In: Proceedings of 9th IEEE International Conference on Cognitive Informatics (ICCI 2010), July 7-9, pp. 199–203. Tsinghua University, Beijing (2010)
7. Chen, Y.J., Cui, Z.H., Zeng, J.C.: Structural Optimization of Lennard-Jones Clusters by Hybrid Social Cognitive Optimization Algorithm. In: Proceedings of $9^{th}$ IEEE International Conference on Cognitive Informatics (ICCI 2010), pp. 204–208. Tsinghua University, Beijing (2010)
8. Wei, Z.H., Cui, Z.H., Zeng, J.C.: Social Cognitive Optimization Algorithm with Reactive Power Optimization of Power System. In: Proceedings of 2nd International Conference on Computational Aspects of Social Networks, TaiYuan, China, pp. 11–14 (2010)
9. Xie, X.F., Zhang, W.J., Yang, Z.L.: Social cognitive optimization for nonlinear programming preblems. In: International Conference on Machine Learning and Cybernetics, Beijing, China, pp. 779–783 (2002)
10. Koziel, S., Michalewicz, Z.: Evolutionary Algorithms Homomorphous Mappings and Constrained Parameter Optimization. Evolutionary Computation 7(1), 19–44 (1999)
11. Runarsson, T.P., Yao, X.: Stochastic Ranking for Constrained Evolutionary Optimization. IEEE Trans. on Evolutionary Computation 4(3), 284–294 (2000)

# Multi-Objective Optimal Design of Switch Reluctance Motors Using Adaptive Genetic Algorithm

Mehran Rashidi and Farzan Rashidi

Islamic Azad University, Bandar-Abbas Branch, Bandar-Abbas, Iran

**Abstract.** In this paper a design methodology based on multi objective genetic algorithm (MOGA) is presented to design the switched reluctance motors with multiple conflicting objectives such as efficiency, power factor, full load torque, and full load current, specified dimension, weight of cooper and iron and also manufacturing cost. The optimally designed motor is compared with an industrial motor having the same ratings. Results verify that the proposed method gives better performance for the multi-objective optimization problems. The results of optimal design show the reduction in the specified dimension, weight and manufacturing cost, and the improvement in the power factor, full load torque, and efficiency of the motor. A major advantage of the method is its quite short response time in obtaining the optimal design.

**Keywords:** Switched reluctance machine, Genetic Algorithm, Multi-Objective Optimization, Optimal Design.

## 1 Introduction

A very challenging problem for today's electric machines designers is to ensure that their design is a *global optimum* one. There are many traditional optimization techniques that nearly all of them have great limitations such as:

- Some of them are only applicable to limited domains. (e.g. dynamic programming)
- Some are very unintelligent strategies and so, rarely used by themselves. (e.g. random search)
- Some are easily trapped in local optimum points. (e.g. some gradient methods)
- Some need derivatives of objective function which may be difficult or even impossible to computer for complex objective functions. (e.g. all gradient methods)
- Some obtain no overall shape of the search domain and so, they may allocate their trials evenly over the regions with low fitness and region with high fitness. (e.g. iterated search)

In comparison, the method of genetic algorithm for search and optimization has none of this limitation. It is an intelligent strategy which doesn't need the derivatives of objective function and can be set so that never trapped in local optimum points. Recently, Genetic Algorithms have been used as potent tools in design optimization

B.K. Panigrahi et al. (Eds.): SEMCCO 2010, LNCS 6466, pp. 591–598, 2010.

of electrical machinery. Unlike the standard Non-Linear Programming techniques, the Genetic Algorithms are able to find the global minimum instead of a local minimum. It does not require the use of the derivative of the function. When dealing with real measurements involving noisy data, the derivative of function is not always easily obtainable or may not even exist [1]. This fact led us to apply this method for obtaining optimum design of switch reluctance motor.

The switched reluctance motor (SRM) possesses many advantages over other motors owing to its low cost, simple rugged construction, and relatively high torque to mass ratio. These make it ideal for use in the industry, especially in the area of variable speed applications. Contrary to the conventional motors, the SRM is designed to operate in deep magnetic saturation to increase the output power density. Thus, due to the saturation effect and the variation of magnetic reluctance, all pertinent characteristics of the machine model (i.e. flux-linkage, inductance, phase torque etc.) are highly nonlinear functions of both rotor position and phase current. All this makes the task of SRM designer very complicated and time consuming [2]. In most conventional design processes a preliminary model of a SRM is approximately formed based on design guidelines and mostly designer's experiences. Performances of the generated model are evaluated by the optimization objectives. Afterwards, the dimensions of the model are altered based on these results. By repeating the process, an optimal design is developed [3]. This iteration process consumes much time and requires the great experience of designers to develop a well-optimized model. It is still difficult to globally find out an optimized solution from multi-objective problems, if many machine parameters have to be concerned. Optimization of SR motors should be realized by making trade-off between different objectives. For example, size of the machine should be small, it should be inexpensive, its efficiency and power factor should be good, etc. Taking note of these, the importance of multi objective optimization is understood in this field. In the solution of the task of optimization of SR motor, the gradient information of the objective function is troublesome and moreover the objective function is non-convex. For these reasons, the designer can profitably state the problem as a nonlinear programming problem able to deal with some or all the aforementioned difficulties and solve it with a suitable numerical optimization technique. In literature, several multiobjective approaches for the electrical machines design have been proposed. The techniques suggested in these works are mainly based on exhaustive measurement of magnetic characteristics of the SRM. All these methods address one fundamental issue, that is, given a desired torque [4].

This paper models the optimal design of a SR motor as a nonlinear multiobjective optimization problem and describes a MOGA for its solution. An example is presented for a 15hp 8/6 pole motor design, where the objective functions are the manufacturing cost, rated efficiency, power factor, cooper and iron weights, full load torque and full load current. The multiobjective genetic algorithm optimization results show that the proposed approach is viable and reliable.

## 2  Optimal Design Procedure [5]

In the solution of the task of multi objective optimization of SRM, Depending on the application, various characteristics of the motor, such as motor efficiency, overall dimensions of the motor, power factor, cost of the main components of the motor, winding hot-spot temperature rise and etc, can be chosen as constraints or as objectives. To solve the multiobjective task two things are needed: first, mathematical model of the SR motor, which can give out various characteristics such as efficiency, power factor and etc. for any set of the variable parameters (Fig. 1) and, secondly, the search algorithm which can work on the principle of multi-attribute dominance. The details of each step (mathematical modeling of the SRM, and multiobjective search algorithm) are explained in the following.

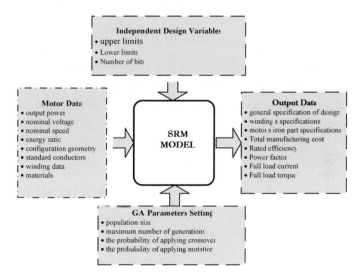

**Fig. 1.** Optimal design procedure of SRM

## 3   Mathematical Model of a Switched Reluctance Motor

To estimate the machine performance and to calculate the objective function during the optimization process for every selected design, we need mathematical model of SR motor. The SRM model used in the paper is a combination of electromagnetic, thermal and mechanical mathematical models [6], and the several other models and methods of calculation of various characteristics of SR motor which use the results of electromagnetic model. In general, the conventional machines are designed starting from the output equation. The volt-sec. relationship for a flat topped phase current $i$ is:

$$\left(L_a^s - L_u\right)i = Vt \tag{1}$$

Where $L_a^s$ is aligned saturated inductance per phase, $L_u$ is unaligned inductance per phase, $V$ is applied voltage and $t$ is time taken for the rotor to remove from the unaligned to aligned position, Also

$$t = \frac{\beta_s}{\omega_m} \tag{2}$$

Where $\beta_s$ and $\omega_m$ are stator pole arc and rotor speed, respectively. Defining,

$$\sigma = \frac{L_a^s}{L_a^u}, \quad \lambda_u = \frac{L_a^u}{L_u} \tag{3}$$

With substituting equation (3) in (1), we have:

$$V = \frac{\omega_m}{\beta_s} L_a^s i \left(1 - \frac{1}{\sigma \lambda_u}\right) \tag{4}$$

Writing the flux linkage in the aligned position as, $L_a^s i = BA_s T_{ph}$, where $A_s = \frac{DL\beta_s}{2}$ is area of the stator pole, $D$ is Bore diameter, $L$ is Axial length of the stator pole, $B$ is Flux density at the aligned position and $T_{ph}$ is Number of turns per phase. The stator current is written in terms of specific electric loading, $A_{sp}$ and is defined as,

$$i = \left(\frac{\pi D}{2T_{ph}}\right) A_{sp} \tag{5}$$

The power developed is, $P_d = K_e K_d V_i \cos\varphi$, Where $V$ and $i$ are peak values, $\varphi$ is the power factor angle, $K_d$ is the duty cycle and $K_e$ is the efficiency. The product of efficiency and power factor can be combined into a single constant as $K_{sp}$. The duty cycle can be expressed as, $K_d = \left(\frac{\theta_c}{360}\right) q p_r$, where $\theta_c$ is current conduction angle for each rising inductance profile, $q$ is number of phases, $p_r$ is number of rotor poles. With combining of equation (4) to (5), we have:

$$P = K_{ep} K_d \left(\frac{\pi^2}{120}\right)\left(1 - \frac{1}{\sigma \lambda_u}\right)(BA_{sp})D^2 Ln \tag{6}$$

Where $n$ is the rotor speed in rpm. Equation (6) can be rearranged to resemble that of the conventional output equation of ac machines and is given as,

$$P = K_{ep} K_d K_1 K_2 (BA_{sp})D^2 Ln \tag{7}$$

Where $K_1 = \frac{\pi^2}{120}$, $K_2 = 1 - \frac{1}{\sigma \lambda_u}$, and torque is expressed as,

$T_e = K_{ep} K_d K_2 K_3 (BA_{sp})D^2 L$, Where $K_3 = \frac{\pi}{4}$. It has seen that torque and power output are proportional to the product of specific electric, magnetic loading and before volume. $K_2$ is the only variable dependent on the operating point of the motor and determined by the stator phase current, magnetic characteristics of the core materials and dimensions of the motor. For a given operating point $K_2$ is a constant. Hence to assess the maximum output power of the SRM. $K_2$ needs to be calculated at the maximum stator current. For that matter the flux linkage vs. current for the aligned and unaligned position are to be estimated for various values of stator currents. For $K_d$ equal to one, the power developed is maximum for a given stator current. It is usual to find that the maximum possible duty cycle is less than one. Further, torque and power control are exercised by the variation of duty cycle similar to a chopper controlled dc motor. The speed is controlled by the frequency of the switching of the phases resembling that of a synchronous motor.

### 3.1 Independent Design Variables

The independent variables are related to the stator and rotor dimensions, the stack length, and the stator winding. It is important to underline that the outside stator diameter has not been changed in all optimizations, in order to use the same housing. In this paper, 12 parameters are selected as the design independent variables,

bore diameter ($D$), the ratio of the bore to length ($k$), stator pole arc ($\beta_s$), rotor pole arc ($\beta_r$), stator pole height ($h_s$), rotor pole height ($h_r$), air-gap in aligned position ($g$), stator yoke thickness ($d_s$), conductor's cross section diameter ($d_{con}$), maximum flux density in stator poles ($B$), width of stator winding ($b_w$), and Number of winding turns per phase ($T_{ph}$).

### 3.2 Limitations and Constraints

It is evident that designing process has some limitations and constraints. Regarding the constraints, they concern mainly the motor performance and we have chosen the following: the stator winding temperature, the rotor bars temperature, the flux density in the stator and rotor teeth, the rated slip, the starting torque, the starting current, the breakdown torque, the power factor at rated load, and the stator slot fullness. The limitations and constraints are as follows:

*A).* The Maximum Permitted Temperature: $\theta_{st} < \theta_{max}$

*B).* The Limitations of Stator and Rotor Pole:

$$\min(\beta_r, \beta_s) \geq \frac{2\pi}{qp_r}, \ (\beta_r + \beta_s) \leq \frac{2\pi}{p_r},$$

$$\beta_{s(min)} = \frac{2\pi}{qp_r}, \ \beta_{r(max)} = \frac{2\pi}{p_r}\left(1 - \frac{1}{q}\right)$$

*C).* The Minimum Desired Efficiency: $\eta > \eta_{min}$

*D).* The Limitations Subject o Width of Stator Tooth and Stator Slot Width: $W_t < W_V$, $W_t > 0.5W_V$

*E).* The Maximum and Minimum Special Electric Loading: $9000\,(A.m) < A_{sp} < 25000\,(A.m)$

*F).* The Limitation Subject to Winding Height: $h_w < h_s$

*G).* The Maximum Space for Winding: $A_w < 0.5A_P$

*H).*The minimum Desired Power factor: $\cos\varphi > (\cos\varphi)_{min}$

# 4  Simulation Results

The proposed MOGA optimization method has been successfully applied to optimize the efficiency, power factor, full load torque, full load torque, specified dimension and weight of cooper and iron of SR motor. The performance results from MOGA optimization are found to be quite satisfactory. Particular attention has to be given to choice of the GA parameters. The population size greatly affects the quality of the result and computation time. It has been observed that small populations exhibit large fluctuations both in the average and best fitness while great populations cause premature convergence. However, while with a high $P_c$ produces many new strings in the new population, deteriorating the successive generations, on the other hand, a low $P_c$ causes a contracted search that can be ineffective. In the same manner, while a high $P_m$ can compromise the convergence of the procedure, a low $P_m$ inhibits the search toward new zones. In this work, the best results are achieved with a medium population size (*N=100*), and by selecting the crossover and mutation probabilities $P_c$=0.85 and $P_m$=0. 25, respectively. The results of the industrial motor and the MOGA optimization for SR motor are given in Table 1.

**Table 1.** Comparisons of the different designs (General specification)

|  |  | *Industrial motor* | *MOGA optimization* |
|---|---|---|---|
| Output power | $P_n\,(watt)$ | 15hp | 15hp |
| Number of Poles | $P_s/P_r$ | 8/6 | 8/6 |
| Nominal Voltage | $V_n\,(volt)$ | 380 | 380 |
| Full Load Torque | $T_n\,(Nm)$ | 26 | 29.47 |
| Rotational Speed | $\omega_m\,(rpm)$ | 1500 | 1500 |
| Efficiency | $\eta\%$ | 83 | 84.4 |
| Total Loss | $P_{Loss}\,(watt)$ | 697.5 | 648.1 |
| Full Load Current | $i_{max}\,(A)$ | 10.7 | 12.2 |
| Power factor | $\cos\varphi$ | 0.837 | 0.856 |
| Total Weight | $W_{Total}\,(kg)$ | 8.077 | 7.051 |

According to Table 1, while achieving performance improvements, the weight of cooper and iron of the motor is reduced by 12%. On the other hand, the full load current and the full load torque are desirably increased by 14% and 13.3%, respectively, which are a remarkable increase. In view of the results, it is concluded that the MOGA optimization is suitable and can reach successful designs with lower

**Table 2.** Comparisons of Windings Specifications

|  |  | *Industrial motor* | *MOGA optimization* |
|---|---|---|---|
| Diameter of insulated Conductor | $d_{con(ins)}(mm)$ | 2.2 | 2.2 |
| Bore Diameter of Conductor | $d_{con}(mm)$ | 1.8 | 1.8 |
| Area of insulated Conductor Cross section | $a_{con(ins)}(mm^2)$ | 3.8 | 3.8 |
| Area of Conductor Cross section | $a_{con}(mm^2)$ | 2.543 | 2.543 |
| Number of Turns per phase | $T_{ph}$ | 136 | 100 |
| Factor of winding | $f_{wlg}$ | -- | 0.5 |
| Max. current Density | $J(a/mm^2)$ | 4 | 4.8 |
| Max Temp of Winding | $\theta_{wlg(max)}(^\circ C)$ | -- | 120 |
| Insulation class | $Ins.Class$ | F | F |
| Max permitted Temp for insulated class | $\theta_{(max-permitted)}(^\circ C)$ | -- | 155 |
| Insulation's thickness | $d_{ins}(mm)$ | -- | 1.0 |
| Copper losses | $P_{loss(cu)}(watt)$ | -- | 54.8 |
| Total Copper's Weight | $W_{cu}(kg)$ | 4.627 | 4.039 |
| Total Iron's Weight | $W_{Fe}(kg)$ | 3.450 | 3.012 |
| Saturated Aligned Inductance | $L_a^s(mH)$ | -- | 29.6 |
| Unsaturated Aligned Inductance | $L_a^u(mH)$ | -- | 149.0 |
| Unaligned Inductance | $L_u(mH)$ | -- | 25.2 |
| Width of Poles winding | $b_w(mm)$ | -- | 10 |
| Height of Pole's Winding | $h_w(mm)$ | -- | 25.5 |
| Area of Windings Cross section | $A_w(mm^2)$ | -- | 255 |
| Phase Windings Resistance | $R(\Omega)$ | 0.457 | 0.399 |

**Table 3.** Comparisons of Stator and Rotor Specifications

|  |  | *Industrial motor* | *MOGA optimization* |
|---|---|---|---|
| Rotor's Inner Radius | $R_{rt}(mm)$ | 25 | 25.4 |
| Rotor's Axial Length | $L(mm)$ | 156 | 162.2 |
| Stator Pole's Arc | $\beta_s(deg)$ | 20 | 21.6 |
| Rotor Pole's Arc | $\beta_r(deg)$ | 22 | 23.6 |
| Stator Pole's Height | $h_s(mm)$ | 30 | 29 |
| Rotor Pole's Height | $h_r(mm)$ | 24 | 26.6 |
| Thickness of Stator's Yoke | $d_s(mm)$ | 10.7 | 6.8 |
| Shaft's Radius | $R_{sh}(mm)$ | 15 | 15 |
| Aligned Air-Gap | $g(mm)$ | 0.3 | 1.0 |
| Stator's Iron Loss | $P_{Fe(s)}(watt)$ | -- | 223.7 |
| Rotor's Iron Loss | $P_{Fe(r)}(watt)$ | -- | 30 |
| Total Iron Loss | $P_{Fe}(watt)$ | -- | 254 |
| Maximum Temperature in Stator | $\theta_{s(max)}(^\circ C)$ | -- | 119 |
| Maximum Temperature in rotor | $\theta_{r(max)}(^\circ C)$ | -- | 33.2 |
| Total iron's weight | $W_{Fe}(kg)$ | 9.281 | 8.138 |
| Maximum of Flux Density in Motor | $B_{max}(Tesla)$ | -- | 1.15 |
| Thickness of Laminations | $d_{la\,min}(mm)$ | 0.35 | 0.35 |
| Class of Steel | $Steel-Class$ | M-19 | M-19 |
| Factor of Laminations | $f_{la\,min}$ | -- | 0.96 |
| Number of Laminations | $N_{la\,min}$ | -- | 445 |

cost and higher torque compared with the industrial motor while satisfying almost every constraint. Also, it was shown that MOGA optimization concludes with a good performance regarding the cost of different components and their dependencies on region, manufacturer and time.

However, it is important to notice that while the performance improved, the efficiency and the power factor of the motor increased which shows additional capabilities of the optimization process. The computation time on PENTIUM CPU, 2.66 GHz, RAM: 4GB and Hard Disc Space: 120 GB, took 94 seconds.

## 5  Conclusion

In this paper, an approach for multiobjective design optimization of the switch reluctance motor utilizing the concept of genetic algorithm has been presented. The multiobjective optimization technique based on GA has been successfully applied for the optimal design of the SRM. The computer simulation results have shown the effectiveness of the proposed method. While the total weight decreased by 12%, full load current and the full load torque increased by 14% and 13.3% respectively that shows remarkable results. The results of the example implemented in this paper confirmed excellent potential of MOGA in the tasks of optimal design.

## References

1. Cunka, M.: Design optimization of electric motors by multi-objective fuzzy genetic algorithms. Mathematical and Computational Applications 13(3), 153–163 (2008)
2. Xu, J.-X., Xu, J.-X., Zheng, Q.: Multiobjective optimization of current waveforms for switched reluctance motors by genetic algorithm. In: WCCI, vol. 2, pp. 1860–1865 (2002)
3. Owatchaiphong, S., Fuengwarodsakul, N.H.: Multi-Objective Based Optimization for Switched Reluctance Machines Using Genetic Algorithms. In: 31st Electrical Engineering Conference EECON 2008 (October 2008)
4. Sahoo, N.C., Xu, J.X., Panda, S.K.: Determination of current waveforms for torque ripple minimisation in switched reluctance motors using iterative learning: an investigation. IEEE Electric Power Application, 369–377 (1999)
5. Matveev, A.: Development of Methods, Algorithms and Software for Optimal Design of Switched Reluctance Drives, Phd thesis, Technische Universiteit Eindhoven (2006)
6. Fuengwarodsakul, N.H., Fiedler, J.O., Bauer, S.E., De Doncker, R.W.: New Methodology in Sizing and Predesign of Switched Reluctance Machines Using Normalized Flux-Linkage Diagram. In: Industry Applications Conference, vol. 4, pp. 2704–2711 (October 2005)

# Genetic Algorithm Approaches to Solve RWA Problem in WDM Optical Networks

Ravi Sankar Barpanda*, Ashok Kumar Turuk,
Bibhudatta Sahoo, and Banshidhar Majhi

Department of Computer Science & Engineering, National Institute of Technology,
Rourkela, Orissa, India
{barpandar,akturuk,bdsahu,bmajhi}@nitrkl.ac.in
http://www.nitrkl.ac.in

**Abstract.** Routing and Wavelength Assignment (RWA) problem is a classical problem in Wavelength Division Multiplexing (WDM) networks. It is reported that RWA problem is a NP-hard problem as the global optimum is not achievable in polynomial time due to the memory limitation of digital computers. We model the RWA problem as an Integer Linear Programming (ILP) problem under wavelength continuity constraint and solve it using Genetic Algorithm (GA) approach to obtain a near optimal solution.

**Keywords:** Routing and Wavelength Assignment Wavelength Division Multiplexing NP-hard Integer Linear Programming Wavelength Continuity Constraint Genetic Algorithm.

## 1 Introduction

The bandwidth demand of Internet users has been increasing rapidly due to the growth of the population of Internet users and the popularization of online applications and services that require high bandwidth, such as voice chat, video streaming, P2P file sharing, grid computing, HDTV programming and optical storage area networks[1,2]. Wavelength Division Multiplexing (WDM) is a promising technology to serve as the backbone for future Wide Area Networks (WAN) because of its capability to exploit the huge bandwidth of optical fibers [3,4,5,6,7]. WDM optical networks use lightpaths [3,4,8,9,10] to exchange information between node pairs. A lightpath is an all-optical logical connection established between a node pair. Given a set of lightpaths that need to be established, the routing problem in WDM networks consists of two subproblems that may be solved concurrently or sequentially. The first subproblem is to determine the physical links that will define each lightpath. The second subproblem is to assign a wavelength to each lightpath under wavelength continuity constraint if the network does not have wavelength conversion capability. This is

---

* This research is supported by SERC, DST, Government of India and monitored by Centre for Soft computing Research: A National Facility, ISI, Kolkata.

B.K. Panigrahi et al. (Eds.): SEMCCO 2010, LNCS 6466, pp. 599–606, 2010.

referred to as the routing and wavelength assignment (RWA) problem [10,11]. The RWA problem is typically divided into two types: static and dynamic RWA problems.In the static case, the entire set of connections is given in advance, the problem is to define lightpaths for these connection requests in an optimal way so as to minimize the network resource or to minimize the total blocking probability. Alternatively, a static RWA algorithm may attempt to set up as many of connection requests as possible given a fixed number of wavelengths. In the dynamic case, a lightpath is setup only by the time a connection request arrives and it will be released after some duration. The general objective of dynamic RWA algorithms is to minimize the total number of connections that are blocked [7,10]. The static RWA problem can be formulated as an integer linear program which is found to be NP-hard [10,12,13,14]. For large networks, randomized rounding heuristics are used to restrict the variables of the ILP to keep integral values only, thereby solving the routing sub-problem of the RWA problem. Once a route is defined to each lightpath, we assign wavelength colors to these established lightpaths under wavelength continuity constraint such that two lightpaths sharing a common fiber link must posses different wavelength colors. This is called wavelength distinct constraint. Assigning wavelength colors to lightpaths reduces to the graph coloring problem in polynomial time[10,12]. The dynamic RWA problem is more difficult to solve therefore, heuristics methods are generally employed. Heuristics exist for both the routing subproblem and the wavelength assignment subproblem [3,9,10,12].

## 2   Related Work

A literature review displays a published letter [15], where the Max-RWA model has been modified by introducing limited-range wavelength converters at the intermediate nodes. The optimization objective is to maximize the establishment of connection requests with least use of wavelength converters. The Max-RWA problem is formulated as an integer linear program and then solved using genetic algorithm.In [16], M. C. Sinclair has given a minimum cost wavelength-path routing and wavelength allocation scheme using a Genetic algorithm / Heuristic based hybrid algorithm. A cost model has been adopted which incorporates dependency on link and wavelength requirements. The hybrid algorithm uses object-oriented representation of networks and incorporates four functions: path-mutation, single-point crossover, re-route and shift-out. In addition, an operator probability adaptation mechanism is employed to improve operator productivity. In [17], Zhong Pan solved the routing sub-problem of the RWA problem using genetic algorithm. The objective was to define route to each lightpath such that the number of used wavelengths minimized to honor all the static lightpaths. The secondary targets were to minimize the total cost in setting all the lightpaths,the intermediate hops traversed by a lightpath. In [18], D. Bisbal et al. proposed a novel genetic algorithm to perform dynamic routing and wavelength assignment in wavelength routed optical networks under wavelength continuity constraint. Through simulation, they obtained a low average blocking probability associated with a connection request and a very short computation time. By controlling the evolution parameters of the genetic algorithm, a high degree of fairness among the connection requests was achieved. They also developed an extension to the proposed algorithm with the aim at providing protection to the lightpaths in the optical layer.

## 3   Work Proposed

Based on the literature review, we formulate a link based ILP to model the RWA problem as an optimization problem. Introducing additional constraints to the objective function of the formulated ILP, we establish lightpaths which are immune to signal distortion and crosstalk. A constraint on the number of intermediate hops traversed by a lightpath ensures less crosstalk accumulated by it, while in the absence of wavelength continuity constraint, a restriction on the number of wavelength converters used by a lightpath ensures less signal distortion. We add further constraints to the formulated ILP to establish lightpaths that avoid creating loops while traversing between node pairs.

## 4   ILP Formulation

The WDM network is viewed as a graph $G = (V, E)$ where $V$ is the set of routing nodes and $E$ is the set of edges in the network. Let $W$ be the set of wavelengths supported by every fiber link in the network and $K$ be the set of lightpaths to be established. The lower bound on $W$ may be stated as:

$$|W| \geq \frac{\sum_{k \in K} |k|}{|E|} \tag{1}$$

where $|k|=$ Length of a lightpath in term of all fiber links $e \in E$ traversed by it from source to destination edge node

$|E|=$ Number of fiber links in the optical network

A lightpath $k$ is identified by its source $s_k$ and destination $d_k$. The variables of concern of the formulated ILP are defined as follows:

$b_k=$ This variable is set if the $k^{th}$ lightpath is established

$b_k^w=$ This variable is set if the $k^{th}$ lightpath uses $w^{th}$ wavelength

$b_k^{w,e}=$ This variable is set if the $k^{th}$ lightpath uses $w^{th}$ wavelength on the $e^{th}$ link

Our basic objective is to minimize the congestion of the most congested link in the network thereby reducing the network load. The objective function may be stated as follows:

$$Minimize \max_{e \in E} \sum_{k \in K} \sum_{w \in W} b_k^{w,e} \tag{2}$$

The objective function subjects to the following constraints:

– **Wavelength continuity constraint:**

$$\sum_{w \in W} b_k^w \le 1; \forall k \in K \tag{3}$$

– **Wavelength distinct constraint:**

$$\sum_{k \in K} b_k^{w,e} \le 1; \forall w \in W \; and \forall e \in E \tag{4}$$

– **Demand constraint:**

$$\bigcup_{k \in K} \{\exists i \in V, \exists j \in V | \sum_{e \in \omega^-(i)} \sum_{w \in W} b_k^{w,e} - \sum_{e \in \omega^+(i)} \sum_{w \in W} b_k^{w,e} = -1$$

$$\wedge \sum_{e \in \omega^+(j)} \sum_{w \in W} b_k^{w,e} - \sum_{e \in \omega^-(j)} \sum_{w \in W} b_k^{w,e} = -1\} \le D_{ij} \tag{5}$$

where $D$ is the demand matrix and $D_{ij}$ specifies the maximum demand between node $i$ and node $j$.

– **Integer constraint:**

$$b_k, b_k^w, b_k^{w,e} \in \{0,1\} \tag{6}$$

– **Consistency constraint:**

$$b_k > b_k^w > b_k^{w,e} \tag{7}$$

– **Wavelength reservation constraint:**

$$\sum_{e \in \omega^-(v):v \in V-\{s_k,d_k\}} b_k^{w,e} - \sum_{e \in \omega^+(v):v \in V-\{s_k,d_k\}} b_k^{w,e} = 0; \forall k \in K \; and \forall w \in W \tag{8}$$

– **No looping constraint around source node:**

$$\sum_{e \in \omega^-(s_k):s_k \in V} \sum_{w \in W} b_k^{w,e} = 0; \forall k \in K \tag{9}$$

– **No looping constraint around destination node:**

$$\sum_{e \in \omega^+(d_k):d_k \in V} \sum_{w \in W} b_k^{w,e} = 0; \forall k \in K \tag{10}$$

– **No looping constraint around intermediate nodes:**

$$\sum_{e \in \omega^-(v):v \in V-\{s_k,d_k\}} \sum_{w \in W} b_k^{w,e} \le 1; \forall k \in K \tag{11}$$

$$\sum_{e \in \omega^+(v):v \in V-\{s_k,d_k\}} \sum_{w \in W} b_k^{w,e} \le 1; \forall k \in K \tag{12}$$

$$\sum_{e \in \omega^+(v):v \in V-\{s_k,d_k\}} \sum_{w \in W} b_k^{w,e} - \sum_{e \in \omega^-(v):v \in V-\{s_k,d_k\}} \sum_{w \in W} b_k^{w,e} = 0; \forall k \in K \tag{13}$$

– **Hop-Count Constraint:**

$$\sum_{e \in E} \sum_{w \in W} b_k^{w,e} \leq H \quad where \quad H = \max_{(s_k, d_k)} \{d(s_k, d_k) | \{s_k, d_k\} \in V\} + \alpha \quad (14)$$

where $d(s_k, d_k)$ is the minimum distance between a node pair $(s_k, d_k)$ and the parameter $\alpha$ depends on the heuristic used to solve the routing sub-problem of the RWA problem.

# 5    Genetic Algorithm Approach to Solve RWA Problem

Genetic Algorithms [19] are probabilistic searching algorithms based on the mechanism of biological evolution. The working of the algorithm to solve the RWA problem is described as follows.

## 5.1    The Chromosome Structure

The chromosome is coded as a path matrix $M$ of dimension $|K| \times |E|$ where every row of the matrix corresponds to a distinct lightpath $k \in K$ and every column of the matrix corresponds to a distinct link $e \in E$ . A set entry $M_{ke}$ justifies the use of $e^{th}$ link by the $k^{th}$ lightpath.

## 5.2    Initial Population

Every source node $s_k$ in the network maintains a routing table $R_{s_k}$ that collects possible routes to every other node in the network. So, $R_{s_k d_k} \subset R_{s_k}$ denotes the set of random routes from node $s_k$ to node $d_k$. By searching these routing tables, available routes for an offline request can be calculated. By selecting a random route for every offline request from the concerned routing tables, yields a chromosome. A set of chromosomes as per the given population size establishes the initial population.

## 5.3    Cost Unction

The cost function is the target function to be minimized and is used to reduce the congestion of the most congested link in the network. The cost function for implementing a single objective genetic algorithm is stated as follows:

$$C = \max_{e \in E} (\sum_{k \in K} M_{ke}) \quad (15)$$

The above cost function is modified by considering secondary objectives to implement a multi objective genetic algorithm and is stated as:

$$C = 0.80 \frac{con}{|K|} + 0.05 \frac{\max\_h\_count}{|V| - 1} + 0.05 \frac{\max\_r\_length}{d(|V| - 1)} +$$
$$0.05 \frac{tot\_fib}{|E|} + 0.05 \frac{con - l\_con}{|K|} \quad (16)$$

where,

- $con=$ Congestion of the most congested link in the network and defines the network load.
- max $\_h\_count=$ Maximum number of hops traversed by a lightpath in a chromosome.
- max $\_r\_length=$ Maximum delay of a lightpath in a chromosome.
- $l\_con=$ Congestion of the least congested link in the network.
- $tot\_fib=$ Total number of fibers used to honor all the lightpaths in a chromosome.
- $d=$Maximum delay of a link in the network.

### 5.4    Crossover

we apply single-point crossover technique for mating two selected chromosomes. A crossover point $cp$ is selected randomly such that $(0 < cp < |K|)$ . Let the partial vectors around $cp$ of each selected chromosome be swapped, rendering two new chromosomes.

### 5.5    Mutation

According to a certain mutation rate a chromosome is mutated. A random light-path $k$ is selected from the chromosome under mutation and is replaced with any random path selected from the concerned routing table $R_{s_k d_k}$.

## 6    Simulation Result

We assume that the network is static and circuit-switched. The fiber links are bidirectional. There is no limit on the number of wavelengths a fiber can carry. The parameters of interest to implement the genetic algorithm are outlined as follows:

- Population size: 4
- Maximum number of generations: 1000
- crossover probability: 0.6
- Mutation probability: 0.1

An arbitrary mesh topology network is considered for simulation; which has 6 nodes and 8 links as depicted in Fig. 1. The genetic algorithm is simulated and implemented for this network to satisfy a demand set of static lightpath requests as detailed in Table 1. Each lightpath request is availed with two random routes.

**Table 1.** Demand set of static lightpath requests

| Lightpaths | Assigned Routes |
|---|---|
| n0-n2 | n0-n1-n2<br>n0-n5-n4-n2 |
| n0-n1 | n0-n1<br>n0-n5-n1 |
| n1-n3 | n1-n2-n3<br>n1-n5-n4-n3 |
| n2-n3 | n2-n3<br>n2-n4-n3 |
| n0-n5 | n0-n5<br>n0-n1-n5 |
| n3-n4 | n3-n4<br>n3-n2-n4 |
| n3-n5 | n3-n4-n5<br>n3-n2-n4-n5 |
| n0-n4 | n0-n5-n4<br>n0-n1-n5-n4 |

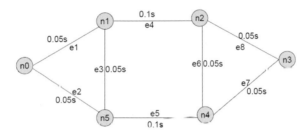

**Fig. 1.** An arbitrary mesh topology network

**Table 2.** Performance comparison between single objective and multi objective GA

| Type of GA | comparison |
|---|---|
| Single objective | The network load for establishing 8 lightpaths is: 03 |
| Multi objective | The network load for establishing 8 lightpaths is: 02<br>The difference between most congested and least congested link is: 02<br>The maximum hops traversed by a lightpath: 02<br>The number of fibers used to honor all the lightpaths: 06<br>The maximum delay of a lightpath: 0.1500 |

## 7   Conclusion

We conclude that the single objective genetic algorithm requires three wave-lengths to satisfy all the lightpath requests in the demand set while the multi objective genetic algorithm requires two wavelengths to satisfy the same set of lightpath requests. Hence, multi objective genetic algorithm performs better than single objective genetic algorithm. The performance comparison between the two types of genetic algorithms is detailed in Table 2.

# References

1. Peng, I.H.: Study of Effective Resource Allocation Schemes in WDM Networks. PhD thesis (2008) thesis.lib.ncu.edu.tw
2. Ishida, S.: A Study on Flexible, Reliable, and Scalable Wavelength-Routed Optical Networks. PhD thesis, Department of Information Networking, Graduate School of Information Science and Technology, Osaka University (February 2007)
3. Mukherjee, B.: Optical Communication Network. Mc-Graw Hill, New York (1997)
4. Ramaswami, R., Sivarajan, K., Sasaki, G.: Optical Networks: A Practical Perspective, 3rd edn. Morgan Kaufmann, San Francisco
5. Mukherjee, B.: Optical WDM Networks. Springer, Heidelberg (2006)
6. Mukherjee, B.: WDM optical networks: progress and challenges. IEEE Journal on Selected Areas in Communications 18(10), 1810–1824 (2000)
7. Ngo, S.H.: Ant-Based Mobile Agent Approach for Dynamic Routing and Wavelength Assignment in WDM Optical Networks. PhD thesis, School of Information Science, Japan Advanced Institute of Science and Technology (September 2006)
8. Chlamtac, I., Ganz, A., Karmi, G.: Lightpath Communications: An Approach to High Bandwidth Optical WAN's. IEEE Transactions on Communications 40, 1171–1182 (1992)
9. Sivaramamuthy, C., Guruswamy, M.: WDM Optical Networks- Concepts, Design and Algorithms. Prentice Hall, Englewood Cliffs (2002)
10. Zang, H., Jue, J.P., Mukherjee, B.: A Review of Routing and Wavelength Assignment Approaches for Wavelength Routed Optical WDM Networks. Optical Networks magazine 1(1), 47–60 (2000)
11. Lea, D.P.: Soft computing approaches to Routing and Wavelength Assignment in wavelength-routed optical networks. PhD thesis, North Carolina State University (2004)
12. Banerjee, D., Mukherjee, B.: A practical Approach for Routing and Wavelength Assignment in Large Wavelength-Routed Optical Networks. IEEE Journal on Selected Areas in Communications 14(5), 903–908 (1996)
13. Ramaswami, R., Sivarajan, K.N.: Design of Logical Topologies for Wavelength-Routed Optical Networks. IEEE Journal on selected areas in Communication 14(5), 840–851 (1996)
14. Michael, R.G., Johnson, D.S.: Computers and Intractability: A Guide to the Theory of NP Completeness. W. H. Freeman and Company, San Francisco (1979)
15. Qin, H., Liu, Z., Zhang, S., Wen, A.: Routing and Wavelength Assignment based on Genetic Algorithm. IEEE Communication Letters 6(10), 455–457 (2002)
16. Sinclair, M.: Operator-Probability Adaptation in a Genetic-Algorithm/Heuristic Hybrid for Optical Network Wavelength Allocation. In: IEEE International Conference on Evolutionary Computation, pp. 840–845 (1998)
17. Pan, Z.: Genetic Algorithm for Routing and Wavelength Assignment Problem in All-optical Networks. Technical report, Depatrment of Electrical and Computer Engineering, University of California, Davis (2002)
18. Bisbal, D., Miguel, I.D., Gonzalez, F., Blas, J., Aguado, J.C., Fernandez, P., Duran, J., Lopez, M.: Dynamic Routing and Wavelength Assignment in Optical Networks by means of Genetics Algorithms. Photonic Networks Communications 7(1), 43–58 (2004)
19. Goldberg, D.E.: Genetic Algorithms in Search, Optimization and Machine Learning. Addison-Wesley Publishing Company Inc., Reading (1997)

# Multi-objective Performance Optimization of Thermo-Electric Coolers Using Dimensional Structural Parameters

P.K.S. Nain[1], J.M. Giri[2], S. Sharma[3], and K. Deb[4]

[1] Department of Mechanical Engineering,
Amity School of Engineering & Technology,
Amity University, Sector 125, Noida - 201 303, India
pksnain@amity.edu
http://www.amity.edu
[2] Department of Mechanical Engineering,
Skyline Institute of Engineering & Technology,
Greater Noida - 201 306, India
jmgiri@engineer.com
http://www.skylineinstitute.com
[3] Department of Mechanical Engineering,
Noida Institute of Engineering & Technology,
Greater Noida - 201 306, India
sudhanshu.shr@gmail.com
http://www.niet.co.in
[4] Kanpur Genetic Algorithms Laboratory (KanGAL)
Department of Mechanical Engineering,
Indian Institute of Technology, Kanpur- 208 016, India
deb@iitk.ac.in
http://www.iitk.ac.in/kangal

**Abstract.** Thermo-Electric Coolers (TEC) have promising features as it is better than traditional cooling devices based on thermodynamic cycle in many ways like being noiseless, compact and environment friendly as it is free of CFC responsible for ozone layer depletion. However, TEC have poor performance in terms of Coefficient of Performance (COP) and peak value of rate at which heat is extracted from space to be cooled. Hence, it is obviously of interest to designers, that the above mentioned limitation shall be compensated by optimizing structural parameters such as area and length of thermoelectric elements such that these device operate at near optimal conditions. In present work, this problem is systematically decomposed in two segments, namely single objective optimization and multi-objective optimization. In the end, some useful insights are reported for designers about structural parameters of TEC.

**Keywords:** TEC, Practical Performance Optimization, Single Objective Optimization, Multi-Objective Optimization, NSGA-II.

## 1 Introduction

The technology of thermoelectric coolers (TEC) is different from conventional vapor-cycle based refrigerators. Thermoelectric Cooler is a solid state cooling

B.K. Panigrahi et al. (Eds.): SEMCCO 2010, LNCS 6466, pp. 607–614, 2010.

device that uses the Peltier effect through p- and n-type dissimilar semiconductor elements to convert electrical energy into a temperature gradient. Thermoelectric coolers or thermoelectric refrigerators have no refrigerant and no moving parts which make them to offer high reliability and low maintenance. Virtually no generation of electrical or acoustical noise, ecologically cleanness, any orientation and fitness for zero gravity environment applications, compact size, light weight and precise temperature control make thermoelectric coolers the device of future.

The use of thermoelectric coolers has been limited by their relative low energy conversion efficiency and ability to dissipate limited amount of heat flux. Two parameters, the maximum rate of refrigeration (ROR) and the maximum coefficient of performance (COP), are of particular interest in characterizing TEC. Generally, thermoelectric coolers operate at about 5-10% of Carnot cycle COP where as compressor based refrigerators normally operate at more than 30%. Though TEC performance is limited, new materials and improvement in design have potential to excel under raising global environmental concerns. To utilize the benefits of Thermo-Electric (TE) refrigeration globally, system level optimization is important. Though there are many conventional optimization approach as discussed by Deb [3], there are quite new methods which are becoming popular day by day. Genetic algorithm is one of these non-traditional approaches. One of the important strengths of genetic algorithms is that they can also deal with multiple objectives and can find Pareto-optimal solutions which are set of best non-dominated solutions. In the last years many multi-objective optimization algorithms have been proposed as described by Deb [2]. Non-dominated Sorting Genetic Algorithm (NSGA-II) [1] is one of most popular algorithms for multi-objective optimization.

## 2   Past Studies

TEC performance can be enhanced through designing TE materials that maximize the thermoelectric figure of merit. The non-dimensional figure of merit $(ZT)$ value of the best bulk thermoelectric materials has remained below or around one due to the difficulty to increase the electrical conductivity or Seebeck coefficient without increasing the thermal conductivity as mentioned by Rodgers [6]. Venkatasubramanian et al. [9] showed a significant increase of the figure of merit for the p-type $Bi_2Te_3/Sb_2Te_3$ super-lattice material. A non-dimensional figure of merit $(ZT)$ of approximately 2.4 at 300 K was achieved by controlling the transport of photons and electrons in the super-lattices. Harman et al. [5] has showed a $ZT$ of about 2 for n-type PbSeTe/PbTe quantum dot super-lattice structure. These material gains make a large difference in the cooling performance but problems occur due to phenomenon taking place in nanoscale because super-lattice consists of many nanosized layers. One major problem is related to electrical conductivity due to contact resistance and difficulties in predicting thermal conductivity. Ezzahri et al. [4] compared the behavior of bulk thin films of SiGe and super-lattice thin films of Si/SiGe as micro-refrigerators. They observed that though super-lattice has enhanced thermoelectric power.

# 3   Mathematical Modeling

In a TEC system, when the current is passed through the circuit, three major effects occur simultaneously. The Peltier effect is the basis for the thermoelectric cooler. When an electric current is passed through a pair of p- and n- type thermoelectric materials, a temperature gradient is established in the material. Electrons in the n-type element move opposite the direction of current flow and holes in the p-type move in the direction of current flow, both removing heat from one side of the device. Heat will flow from the hot side to the cold side through thermoelectric materials by conventional heat conduction. Also, because of the Joule effect, Heat is generated resulting from the current flow in the materials. Part of the Joulean heat will flow to each junction. It is usual to assume that one half of the Joulean heat is transferred to each junction. It is assumed that heat absorption and heat rejection occurs only at the junctions and leakage of heat to the surroundings is neglected. The p-type and n-type thermoelectric elements have same properties and Thomson effect is neglected. Under steady state conditions, the energy balance equation of TEC system can be written as:

$$Q_c = N\left[\alpha I T_c - \frac{1}{2}I^2\left(\frac{\rho L}{A} + \frac{2r_c}{A}\right) - \frac{kA(T_h - T_c)}{L}\right], \tag{1}$$

$$Q_h = N\left[\alpha I T_h + \frac{1}{2}I^2\left(\frac{\rho L}{A} + \frac{2r_c}{A}\right) - \frac{kA(T_h - T_c)}{L}\right]. \tag{2}$$

Where, $Q_c$ is rate of refrigeration (ROR) in watts and $Q_h$ is heat rejected per unit time from the hot junction. $I$ is input current of the TEC in Ampere. $\alpha$ is Seebeck coefficient in Volts/Kelvin. $T_c$ is cold side temperature in Kelvin. $N$ is number of thermoelectric elements and $k$ is thermal conductivity of material in Watt/meter-Kelvin. $A$ is area of thermoelectric elements in $m^2$. $L$ is length of thermoelectric element in meter. $\rho$ is electrical resistivity of material in Ohm-meter. $r_c$ is electrical contact resistance at junctions in Ohm-square meter. $R_{th}$ is thermal resistance of hot side heat exchanger. $T_a$ is ambient temperature in Kelvin. $T_h$ is hot side temperature in Kelvin such that the following relation is satisfied:

$$T_h = Q_h \times R_{th} + T_a, \tag{3}$$

Further, the input electrical power and coefficient of performance can be calculated using following relations.

$$P = Q_h - Q_c, \tag{4}$$

$$COP = \frac{Q_c}{P}. \tag{5}$$

The material properties are considered to be dependent on the average of hot and cold side temperatures and can be found by applying experiential formulae of Melcor Corporation, Trenton [10] which are given below.

$$\alpha = (22224 + 930.6\,T_{ave} - 0.9905\,T_{ave}^2) \times 10^{-9}, \tag{6}$$

$$\rho = (5112 + 163.4\,T_{ave} + 0.6279\,T_{ave}^2) \times 10^{-10}, \tag{7}$$

$$k = (62605 - 277.7\,T_{ave} + 0.4131\,T_{ave}^2) \times 10^{-4}. \tag{8}$$

# 4   Optimization Problem Statement and Simulation Results

The TEC system should be designed as compact as possible because the space in an electronic equipment is limited. If we know the thermal resistance of the hot side heat exchanger and the space where TEC system is to be placed, length of element and area of element can be used as variable parameters. The two very important performance parameters are rate of refrigeration (ROR) and coefficient of performance (COP) which can be optimized. The optimization of rate of refrigeration (ROR) of thermoelectric cooler is formulated as the following single objective optimization problem:

$$\text{Max ROR}$$

Subject to:
$$L_{min} \leq L \leq L_{max}$$
$$A_{min} \leq A \leq A_{max}$$

The optimization of coefficient of performance (COP) of thermoelectric cooler is formulated as the following single objective optimization problem:-

$$\text{Max COP}$$

Subject to:
$$L_{min} \leq L \leq L_{max}$$
$$A_{min} \leq A \leq A_{max}$$

In the above optimization problems, L is the length of TE elements and A is the area of TE elements. For all the cases, the cold side temperature $(T_c)$ of the TEC is set as 295 Kelvin. Ambient temperature $(T_a)$ is taken as 298.15 Kelvin (Standard Ambient Temperature and Pressure). Input current of the TEC is taken as 1 Ampere. Electrical contact resistance at junctions $r_c$ is taken as $1 \times 10^{-8}$ ohm-square meter. The total available cross sectional area for TEC device is 25 $mm^2$. The hot side temperature $(T_h)$ is initially fixed to some guess value so that the material properties can be obtained using Equations 6, 7 and 8. Employing Equations 1, 2 and 3, new value of $T_h'$ is calculated. This difference of guess and new value of $T_h$ is used to modify the guess value of $T_h$ iteratively, till it becomes negligible. The minimum and maximum limits for the length of the thermoelectric elements $(L_{min}$ and $L_{max})$ are taken as 0.1 mm and 1.0 mm respectively. The minimum and maximum limits for the area of the thermoelectric elements $(A_{min}$ and $A_{max})$ are taken as 0.3 $mm^2$ and 0.6 $mm^2$ respectively. For both single objective optimization problems, GA is run for 1000 generations with population size of 30. The probability of crossover is taken as 0.8, while that of mutation is taken as 0.33. The distribution index for crossover and mutation are taken as 10 and 50 respectively. The optimization of rate of refrigeration is done for four different values of thermal resistance of hot side heat exchanger $(R_{th})$ which are commonly used in TEC literature. These values of $R_{th}$ are 0.1 °C/W, 0.2 °C/W, 0.5 °C/W and 1.0 °C/W. Five runs were taken for single objective optimization of ROR. Table-1 presents optimum parameters for maximum ROR at best run. The Real-variable Genetic Algorithm employing SBX operator developed by Deb and Agarwal (1995) [8] is used for single objective optimization. It is clear from the Table 1 that different optimum (maximum) values of rate of refrigeration (ROR) are achieved at different values of $R_{th}$. At higher value of $R_{th}$, the value of maximum ROR drops as compared to the value of maximum ROR at lower value of $R_{th}$. Area of elements is almost constant at optimum (maximum) values of ROR for all values of $R_{th}$. It is 0.390 $mm^2$ though the permitted range of area of TE elements was 0.3 to 0.6 $mm^2$. Lengths of TE elements are different to get optimum values of ROR at different values of thermal resistance. It is observed that thermal resistance adversely affects in obtaining the optimum value of ROR. Also, higher values of length are needed to get optimum value of ROR at higher values of thermal resistance. Values of COP are not optimum during optimization of ROR. Further, with the same parameters and same GA settings five runs were held for single objective optimization of coefficient of performance (COP) for same values of thermal resistance of hot side heat exchanger $R_{th}$. Table 2 presents optimum parameters for maximum COP at best run. It is clear from the Table 2 that different optimum (maximum) values of coefficient of performance (COP) are achieved at different values of $R_{th}$. At higher value of $R_{th}$, the value of maximum COP drops as compared to the value of maximum COP at lower value of $R_{th}$. Area of elements is constant at optimum (maximum) values of COP for all values of $R_{th}$. It is 0.6 $mm^2$, while the permitted range of area of TE elements is 0.3 to 0.6 $mm^2$. So, though this variable value is hitting the upper bound and as the origin of this *active constraint* is from manufacturing technology of TE element, it has to be bore

**Table 1.** Optimum Parameters for Maximum ROR

| $R_{th}$ (°C/W) | L (mm) | A ($mm^2$) | N | Optimized ROR (W) | $T_h$ (K) | COP |
|---|---|---|---|---|---|---|
| 0.1 | 0.384029 | 0.390624 | 64 | 1.662831 | 298.168529 | 0.415271 |
| 0.2 | 0.384769 | 0.390625 | 64 | 1.661906 | 298.177368 | 0.414890 |
| 0.5 | 0.386331 | 0.390625 | 64 | 1.659125 | 298.203885 | 0.413866 |
| 1.0 | 0.387585 | 0.390625 | 64 | 1.654517 | 298.248052 | 0.412417 |

**Table 2.** Optimum Parameters for Maximum COP

| $R_{th}$ (°C/W) | L (mm) | A ($mm^2$) | N | ROR (W) | $T_h$ (K) | Optimized COP |
|---|---|---|---|---|---|---|
| 0.1 | 0.361528 | 0.6 | 41 | 1.378185 | 298.167082 | 0.828797 |
| 0.2 | 0.361943 | 0.6 | 41 | 1.377623 | 298.174471 | 0.828271 |
| 0.5 | 0.363186 | 0.6 | 41 | 1.375943 | 298.196634 | 0.826698 |
| 1.0 | 0.365248 | 0.6 | 41 | 1.373157 | 298.233556 | 0.824095 |

with till new innovation in technology is reported. Lengths of TE elements are different to get optimum values of COP at different values of thermal resistance. It is observed that thermal resistance adversely affects in obtaining the optimum value of COP. Higher values of length are needed to get optimum value of COP at higher values of thermal resistance. Values of rate of refrigeration are not optimum during optimization of COP. It can be observed from Table 1 and Table 2 which represent results of single objective optimization of ROR and single objective optimization of COP that these objectives are conflicting as optimum ROR solution does not guarantee optimum COP and vice versa. Under these circumstances, the next step is to do multi-objective optimization of COP & ROR so we can find solutions that are optimal with respect to both the objectives. Thus in multi-objective optimization approach, the task is to find the Pareto-optimal solutions. However it is difficult to prefer one solution over the other without having satisfactory higher level information. The simultaneous multi-objective optimization problem of rate of refrigeration (ROR) and coefficient of performance (COP) of thermoelectric cooler is formulated as:

$$\text{Max ROR}$$
$$\text{Max COP}$$

Subject to:
$$L_{min} \leq L \leq L_{max}$$
$$A_{min} \leq A \leq A_{max}$$

Non-dominated sorting genetic algorithm-II (NSGA-II) [1] has been used for multi-objective optimization. NSGA-II is run for 1000 generations with population size of 200. The distribution index for crossover and mutation are taken as 10 and 20 respectively. Rest of the settings are same as that of single objective optimization. Two hundred Pareto-optimal solutions are found in each case of given values of thermal resistance within two extreme values of ROR and COP. Figure 1 to 4 show the Pareto-optimal fronts found during multi-objective optimization of COP and ROR. The extreme values of ROR and COP are (1.662 W & 0.415) and (1.378 W & 0.828) at $0.1°C/W$ value of thermal resistance which are same as those obtained in single objective optimization problems discussed earlier. However, some new information is also discovered. The length of TE element now varies from 0.3906 to 0.5187 and area varies in its old range from 0.3906 to 0.6 $mm^2$. Hence NSGA-II not only captured entire Pareto-optimal front successfully but has also added new high level information about Pareto-optimal solutions. The new high level information added by NSGA-II about Pareto-optimal solutions for different settings of $R_{th}$ can be summarized as in Table 3. This new high level information added by NSGA-II is very useful to designers of TEC as they can now have complete information which will be helpful to them in decision making while designing TEC for any specific application.

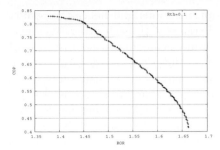

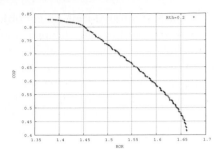

**Fig. 1.** Pareto optimal front at $R_{th} =$ 0.1°C/W

**Fig. 2.** Pareto optimal front at $R_{th} =$ 0.2°C/W

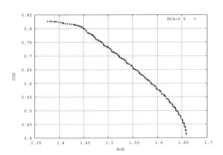

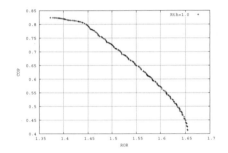

**Fig. 3.** Pareto optimal front at $R_{th} =$ 0.5°C/W

**Fig. 4.** Pareto optimal front at $R_{th} =$ 1.0°C/W

**Table 3.** Pareto-optimal solution details

| $R_{th}$ (°C/W) | $L_{min}$ (mm) | $L_{max}$ (mm) | $A_{min}$ $(mm^2)$ | $A_{max}$ $(mm^2)$ | $N_{min}$ | $N_{max}$ |
|---|---|---|---|---|---|---|
| 0.1 | 0.3615 | 0.5187 | 0.3906 | 0.6 | 41 | 64 |
| 0.2 | 0.3619 | 0.5302 | 0.3906 | 0.6 | 41 | 64 |
| 0.5 | 0.3631 | 0.5360 | 0.3906 | 0.6 | 41 | 64 |
| 1.0 | 0.3652 | 0.5385 | 0.3906 | 0.6 | 41 | 64 |

# 5    Conclusions and Scope for Future Work

In this work, the need for optimization of single stage TEC performance is discussed. A mathematical model for single stage TEC is discussed. Later, a detailed study is made by systematic investigation of two independent single objective performance optimization of single stage TEC. It is found that the optimization problems have conflicting objectives and hence is suitable for multi-objective optimization. Then results of multi-objective performance study are reported and new high level information discovered by NSGA-II is reported. The extremities at each value of thermal resistance are similar to those values which were found at optimum points during single objective optimizations and hence the results of all three optimization problems are in coherence with each other. It is also important to note that area of TE elements is almost constant to achieve optimal solutions at different values of thermal resistance while doing single objective optimization. However, it is also important to note that for maximization of COP, the area of TE element hits the upper bound and hence is restricted by the manufacturing constraint of TEC. The value of length of TE elements is varying to achieve Pareto-optimal solutions at different values of thermal resistance. At higher value of thermal resistance this value shifts towards larger values. From all the results, it is clear that structural dimensions of thermoelectric elements have significant influence on COP and ROR. While designing a TEC a designer can now choose any solution according to application dependent importance of the parameter. Designer can select the parameters as per design criteria from the Pareto-optimal solutions which give optimized values with both the objectives. The present work puts the pointer of future research for TEC in two directions. First is method to manufacture TE Elements having large area and second is technical suitability of exploring multi-stage performance optimization of TEC.

# References

1. Deb, K., Pratap, A., Agarwal, S., Meyarivan, T.: A Fast and Elitist Multi-Objective Genetic Algorithm: NSGA-II. IEEE Transactions on Evolutionary Computation 6(2), 182–197 (2002)
2. Deb, K.: Multi-Objective Optimization Using Evolutionary Algorithms, 1st edn. John Wiley & Sons, Chichester (2001)
3. Deb, K.: Optimization for Engineering Design: Algorithms & Examples. Prentice-hall of India Private Limited, New Delhi (1995)
4. Ezzahri, Y., Zeng, G., Fukutani, K., Bian, Z., Shakouri, A.: A comparison of thin film microrefrigerators based on Si/SiGe super-lattice and bulk SiGe. Microelectronics Journal 39(7), 981–991 (2008)
5. Harman, T.C., Taylor, P.J., Walsh, M.P., LaForge, B.E.: Quantum dot super-lattice thermoelectric materials and devices. Science 297(5590), 2229–2232 (2002)
6. Rodgers, P.: Silicon goes thermoelectric. Nature Nanotechnology 3, 76 (2008)
7. Rowe, D.M. (ed.): CRC handbook of thermoelectric. CRC Press LLC, USA (1995)
8. Deb, K., Agrawal, R.B.: Simulated Binary Crossover for Continuous Search Space. Complex Systems 9(2), 115–148 (1995)
9. Venkatasubramanian, R., Siivola, E., Colpitts, T., ÓQuinn, B.: Thin-film thermoelectric devices with high room-temperature figures of merit. Nature 413(6856), 597–602 (2001)
10. MELCOR Corporation, Trenton, http://www.melcor.com

# An Artificial Physics Optimization Algorithm for Multi-Objective Problems Based on Virtual Force Sorting Proceedings

Yan Wang[1,2], Jian-chao Zeng[2], and Ying Tan[2]

[1] College of Electrical and Information Engineering,
Lanzhou University of Technology,
Lanzhou, China
[2] Complex System and Computational Intelligence Laboratory,
Taiyuan University of Science and Technology,
Taiyuan, China
wy75910@163.com

**Abstract.** In order to maintain the diversity of non-dominated solutions in multi-objective optimization algorithms efficiently the authors have proposed a multi-objective artificial physics optimization algorithm based on virtual force sorting (VFMOAPO). Adopting quick-sort idea, the individuals in non-dominated solutions set were sorted by the total virtual force exerting on the other individuals. So the non-dominated solution set was pruned and the individual with the maximal sum of virtual force exerting on the other individuals was selected as the global best solution. Some benchmark functions were tested for comparing the performance of VFMOAPO with MOPSO, NSGA and SPEA. The simulation results show the algorithm is feasible and competitive.

**Keywords:** artificial physics optimization, multi-objective optimization, virtual force, quick-sort, diversity.

## 1   Introduction

With the development of heuristic optimization technology, more and more optimization algorithms simulating nature swarm intelligence have been proposed recently [1,2]. As evolutionary algorithms have been applied to solve multi-objective optimization problems successfully, more and more optimization paradigms inspired by nature system have been introduced into multi-objective area and many novel multi-objective optimization algorithms are proposed one after the other, for example, multi-objective particle swarm optimization (MOPSO) [3-5], multi-objective artificial immune optimization (MOAIO) and multi-objective estimation of distribution algorithm (MOEDA) et al.

Artificial physics optimization (APO) algorithm is a novel stochastic optimization algorithm based on swarm intelligence. Motivating by Newton's second law, the velocity and position of each individual are updated with the alteration of virtual force

B.K. Panigrahi et al. (Eds.): SEMCCO 2010, LNCS 6466, pp. 615–622, 2010.

exerted on it. So individuals move to optimal target and are convergent around the global optima [1,2]. APO algorithm is similar to PSO algorithm and it has a better global searching ability [1]. It can avoid convergence around local optima, which usually appears in PSO algorithm. Comparing with traditional evolutionary algorithm and PSO algorithm, APO has a characteristic of steady and fast convergence and at the same time it has a better robust. It has been used to solve single objective optimization problems with a good performance. However, it has not been applied to solve multi-objective optimization problems.

Usually many present literatures adopt a set called archive to store non-dominated solutions and use the information of archive set density to prune it. Then the global best solution can be selected from archive. There are several methods to acquire density information, for example, random selection, niche, hyper-grid and clustering analysis et al. It is obvious that the method of random selection has a low efficiency and a bad diversity. It is always difficult for the method of niche to determine the coefficient. The density information acquired by hyper-grid is related with the size and scale of the grid and when each grid includes a particle the method will degenerate into the method of random selection. Clustering analysis has a high computing cost. In order to overcome these drawbacks, we propose a multi-objective artificial physics optimization algorithm based on virtual force sorting (VFMOAPO). It adopts quick sorting idea to prune archive set according to sum of virtual force exerting on the other individuals and the individual with the biggest virtual force is selected as the global optimal individual.

## 2   Basic Concepts of Multi-Objective Optimization Problems

**Definition 1:** Without any loss of generality, a minimized multi-objective problem can be defined as following:

$$\min y = f(X) = (f_1(X), f_2(X), ..., f_r(X))$$
$$g_i(X) \geq 0, (i = 1, 2, ..., k)$$
$$h_i(X) = 0, (i = 1, 2, ..., l)$$

Where decision vector $X \in R^n$, objective vector $y \in R^r$ and $f_i(X), i = 1, 2, ..., r$ is objective function whereas $g_i(X) \geq 0$ and $h_i(X) \square 0$ are constrict conditions.

**Definition 2** (Pareto Optimality Set): For a general multi-objective problem, a Pareto optimality set is defined as follow:

$$P^* = \{X^*\} = \{X \in \Omega \big| \neg \exists X^{'} \in \Omega, f_j(X^{'}) \leq f_j(X),$$

$$(j = 1, 2, ..., r)\}$$

**Definition 3** (Pareto Dominance): A given vector X=($x_1,x_2,...,x_n$) is said to dominate X'=($x'_1,x'_2,...,x'_n$) if and only if

$$\forall i \in \{1, 2, ..., n\}, x_i \leq x_i^{'} \ and \ \exists i \in \{1, 2, ..., n\}, \ x_i < x_i^{'}$$

**Definition 4** (Pareto Front): The Pareto optimal solutions comprise the Pareto front.

# 3  Artificial Physics Optimization Algorithm

APO algorithm is a stochastic population-based optimization algorithm and it is mainly used to solve the optimization problems with real decision variable. In the algorithm, an individual moves to the optimum direction driven by the total virtual force from the other individuals in the search space. A population of sample searches a global optimum in the problem space driven by virtual force and each individual adjusts its own moving by its inertia and total force exerted by the other individuals [1,2]. Each individual has a mass, position and velocity. The mass of each individual corresponds to a user-defined function, which has relation with the objective function value to be optimized. An attraction-repulsion rule, the individual with better fitness attracts others with worse fitness whereas the individual with worse fitness repels others with better fitness while the individual with the best fitness attracts all the others and it is never repelled or attracted by others, is used to move individuals towards the optimality. Hence, the velocity and position of each individual are updated with the alteration of virtual force exerted on it.

In the process of force calculation, the mass of each individual should be computed firstly because it changes from iteration to iteration and the total force exerted on each individual should be computed. The mass function of individual i, the force exerted on individual i via individual j and the total force exerted on individual i via all other individuals in $k$th dimension are calculated by equation (1)-(3).

$$m_i = 1 + (f(x_{best}) - f(x_i))/(f(x_{worst}) - f(x_{best}))$$
$$i = 1, 2, ..., n$$

(1)

$$\forall i \neq j \text{ and } i \neq best$$

$$F_{ij,k} = \begin{cases} Gm_i m_j (x_{j,k} - x_{i,k}), & if (f(x_i) > f(x_j)) \\ -Gm_i m_j (x_{j,k} - x_{i,k}), & if (f(x_i) \leq f(x_j)) \end{cases}$$

(2)

$$F_{i,k} = \sum_{\substack{j=1 \\ i \neq j}}^{n} F_{ij,k} \qquad \forall i \neq best$$

(3)

Where f($x_{best}$) denotes the function value of the best individual, f($x_{worst}$) denotes the function value of the worst individual and f($x_i$) denotes the function value of individual i. The "gravitational constant" G is usually set to 10. The distance of individual j to individual i in $k$th is denoted by $x_{j,k} - x_{i,k}$ and $F_{ii,k}$=0.

The process motion uses the total force to calculate individual velocity. The velocity and position of individual i are updated by equation (4) and (5) respectively.

$$v_{i,k}(t+1) = wv_{i,k}(t) + \lambda F_{i,k} / m_i$$

(4)

$$x_{i,k}(t+1) = x_{i,k}(t) + v_{i,k}(t+1)$$

(5)

Where $v_{i,k}(t)$ and $x_{i,k}(t)$ are velocity and position of individual i in $k$th dimension at generation t. $\lambda$ is a random variable generated with uniform distributed within (0,1). W is an inertia weight and is a number within (0,1), which is usually decreased from 0.9 to 0.4 with linearity. The movement of each individual is restricted in a domain with $X_i \in [X_{min}, X_{max}]$ and $V_i \in [V_{min}, V_{max}]$.

## 4   Multi-Objective Artificial Physics Based on Virtual Force Sorting

Double-population is used in most successful multi-objective evolutionary algorithm, one is evolutionary population and the other is used to store non-dominated solutions found along the search process called archive. The best solutions set of the population is built by constructing non-dominated solutions set of present evolutionary population. We adopt the method in this algorithm. Meanwhile, we adopt random weight sum method to turn multi-objective into a total objective.

The mass of each individual in APO algorithm is not fixed and it is changed during iterative process. The larger the mass is the better is the individual [1,2]. At the same time, we can see from equation (2) that the distance between individuals is another factor impacting virtual force and the more distance between two individuals is the larger force. So if the individual i has a larger force exerting on the other individuals it is shown that individual i has a large mass or it is far from the other individuals. When its mass is large it shows that its position is good in the search space while it is far from the other individuals shows that its position is in a thin density region. In multi-objective optimization problems, pruning non-dominated solutions set is always according to density information that individuals in thin density region are kept and individuals in thick density region are pruned. Moreover, the global best solution is always selected from thin density region in order to keep a better diversity and avoid premature convergence. According the characteristic of APO algorithm we propose a multi-objective artificial physics optimization algorithm based on virtual force sorting to fit for the characteristic multi-objective optimization problems. It prunes non-dominated solutions set and selects the global best solution in terms of the force exerting on the other individuals via an individual.

In VFMOAPO algorithm inertia weight w is a coefficient to show the influence of history velocity information on present velocity of the individual. The larger w is the more strong searching ability it has while a small w is to show a better local searching ability. In order to balance the ability of global searching and local searching, w in VFMOAPO is decreased in dynamic manner during iteration process and it will stop decreasing when iterative number is up to a fixed value. The changing of w is shown in equation (6).

$$w(iter) = w_i - \frac{iter-1}{Maxit} * (w_i - w_f) \tag{6}$$

Here iter is iterative number, Maxit is the maximum iterative number and $w_i$ is initial value of w while $w_f$ is final value of w.

Another coefficient G called gravity constant is used when computing virtual force exerted on an individual in VFMOAPO algorithm. In single objective APO algorithm, usually G is a constant 10. In order to balance the ability of global searching and local searching of the algorithm we set G changing dynamic with the increasing of iterative number. In this algorithm the expression of G is shown with equation (7).

$$G(iter) = G_i - \frac{iter - 1}{Maxit} * (G_i - G_f) \tag{7}$$

Here $G_i$ and $G_f$ is initial and final value of G respectively. The initial w is always large and $G_i$ is set to a large number to balance the ability of global searching and local searching.

### 4.1 Framework of VFMOAPO Algorithm

The framework for VFMOAPO consists four parts: initialization, calculation of virtual force, sorting archive set in terms of virtual force and updating. The framework is shown in Fig. 1.

### 4.2 Initialization

In VFMOAPO we set $P$ as the evolutionary population and n individuals are produced randomly at initial. The non-dominated solution set is called *archive* set with size n and is empty at initial. The global worst fitness is used in APO algorithm and a dominated solution set $Q$ with size n is introduced here, which is empty initially. Non-dominated solutions in $P$ are put into *archive*. The individual in archive set with the minimum fitness value of random weight sum for all the objectives is selected as the global best individual because virtual force exerted on each individual is zero at initial. Meanwhile the dominated solutions in $P$ are put into $Q$ and the individual with the maximum fitness value of random weight sum for total objective in $Q$ is selected as the global worst individual. The pseudocode of initialization is shown in Fig.2.

### 4.3 Calculation of Virtual Force

The mass of individual i is computed with equation (1) and the force exerted on individual i via individual j in $k$th dimension is computed with equation (2) while total force exerted on individual i in $k$th dimension is computed with equation (3). Hence virtual force exerted on individual j via individual i in $k$th dimension is $F_{ji,k} =- F_{ij,k}$ and total force exerted on all the other individuals via individual i in $k$th dimension is $F_{i,k} = \sum_j F_{ji,k}$ and total force exerted on all the other individuals via individual i is shown with equation (8). The pseudocode of calculation of virtual force is shown in Fig.3.

$$F(i) = \sqrt{F_{i,1}^2 + F_{i,2}^2 + ... + F_{i,k}^2} \tag{8}$$

```
FunctionVFMOAPO Algorithm
MaxIt: maximum number of search
iterations
    Begin
    Initialize ( );
    For iter=1:MaxIt
        Calculate Mass with equation
(1);
        Calculate Force ( );
        Update ( );
        Sorting ( );
    End for
    Plot (archive);
    End
```

**Fig. 1.** VFMOAPO framework

```
Function Initialize Algorithm
Begin
For each individual of the population
Initialize position and velocity;
Calculate fitness value of each object;
Calculate total objective fitness value with
random weight sum;
    endfor
For each individual
If it is non-dominated individual
Put it in archive
Else
Put it in Q
Endif
Endfor
Select the individual with the minimum
fitness value in archive as the global best
fitness f(xbest);
    Select the maximum fitness value as
f(xworst);
    End
```

**Fig. 2.** Pseudocode of initialization

```
Function Calculate Force Algorithm
dim: number of total dimension
Begin
For i=1:n
For k=1:dim
  For j=i+1:n
  Calculate virtual force with
            formula (2)
  Endfor
    Calculate total force exerting
    on i in kth dimension with
    formula (3);
  Endfor
  Calculate total force exerted on
  the other individuals via i with
  formula (8);
Endfor
End
```

**Fig. 3.** Pseudocode of calculation virtual force

## 4.4 Updating

The velocity and position are updated according to equation (4) and (5). Then fitness value of each individual under every objective should be computed and store the non-dominated solutions. Then the method of random weight sum is adopted to compute the fitness values of each individual in the total objective, which is denoted as $f(x_i)$.

### 4.5  Sorting Archive with Virtual Force

Adopting quick sorting idea, it executes the quick descending order operation on *archive* in terms of the total force exerted on all the other individuals in $P$. The first individual in *archive* is the global best individual. If the number of non-dominated solutions is more than the size of *archive*, the individual with a smaller virtual force exerting on the other individuals will be pruned. The global worst solution will be found from $Q$ by means of the similar method mentioned above. Then fitness values of the global best and worst individual under the total objective denoted as *fbest* and *fworst* can be computed respectively.

## 5  Analysis to Tests

In order to test performance of VFMOAPO algorithm we choose three famous multi-objective functions to compare with three multi-objective evolutionary algorithms that are representative of the state-of –the –art: MOPSO in literature [3] and NSGA, SPEA.

In this algorithm three popular multi-objective optimization problems called ZDT1, ZDT2, ZDT3 are tested. The size of population and archive set are all 100 and w is decreased linearly from 0.9 to 0.4 according to equation (6). When iteration achieves 75% of the maximum iteration the inertia weight w stops changing. Gravity constant G is decreased linearly from 70 to 30 with equation (7). The evolutionary iteration in these tests is set to 50 (it is 5000 iteration in those compared algorithms) and as a result of that computing cost is decreased and algorithm efficient is improved. Pareto fronts found by VFMOAPO and the other three algorithms are shown in Fig.4, Fig.5 and Fig.6. The results of NSGA and SPEA are from literature [4] and the result of MOPSO is from [3].

From the figures, we can see that the found Pareto front by VFMOAPO is on the true Pareto front on the whole and it has an even diversity, especially to Pareto front of ZDT2 function, which is obviously better than that of the other algorithms. Hence comparing to those popular algorithms VFMOAPO algorithm has a better capability for multi-objective problems with convex, non-convex and discontinuous attribute.

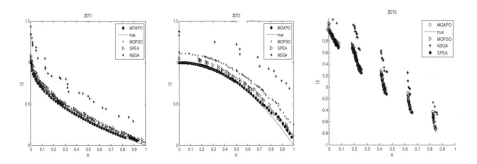

**Fig. 4.** Pareto front of ZDT1     **Fig. 5.** Pareto front of ZDT2     **Fig. 6.** Pareto front of ZDT3

# 6  Conclusions

In this paper a multi-objective artificial physics optimization algorithm based on virtual force sorting called VFMOAPO has been proposed. In this algorithm archive set and dominated solutions set of Q are pruned in terms of the total virtual force exerting on the other individuals, during which quick sorting idea has been adopted. As a result the diversity of the solutions set is improved. This algorithm has a characteristic of simple implement and little computing cost and can avoid extra computing of niche, hyper-grid and crowding distance adopted by the other algorithms to keep an even diversity. Meanwhile, comparing with MOPSO, MSGA and SPEA shows that VFMOAPO algorithm has a competitive performance.

# Acknowledgments

This paper was supported by NSFC under Grant 60975074 and Natural Science Foundation of Shanxi under Grant 2008011027-2.

# References

1. Liping, X., Jianchao, Z.: A Global Optimization Based on Physicomimetics Framework. In: The 2009 World Summit on Genetic and Evolutionary Computation (GEC 2009), Shanghai (2009)
2. Liping, X., Jianchao, Z., Zhihua, C.: Using Artificial Physics to Solve Global Optimization Problems. In: The 8th IEEE International Conference on Cognitive Informatics (ICCI 2009), Hong Kong (2009)
3. Jun-jie, Y., Jian-zhong, Z., Reng-cun, F., et al.: Multi-objective Particle Swarm Optimization Based on Adaptive Grid Algorithms. J. Journal of System Simulation. 20(21), 5843–5847 (2008) (in Chinese)
4. Test Problems and Test Data for Multiobjective Optimizers,
   http://www.tik.ee.ethz.ch/sop/download/supplementary/
   testProblemSuite/
5. Coello, C.A.C., Pulido, G.T., Lechuga, M.S.: Handling Multiple Objectives With Particle Swarm Optimization. J. IEEE Transactions on Evolutionary Computation 8(3), 256–279 (2004)

# Effective Document Clustering with Particle Swarm Optimization

Ramanji Killani[1], K. Srinivasa Rao[2], Suresh Chandra Satapathy[3],
Gunanidhi Pradhan[4], and K.R. Chandran[5]

[1] MVGR College of Engineering, Vijayanagaram, India
[2] CMR College of Engineering & Technology, Hyderabad, India
[3] ANITS, Vishakapatnam, India
[4] Govt. College of Engineering, Kalahandi, India
[5] PSG College of Technology, Coimbatore, India

**Abstract.** The paper presents a comparative analysis of K-means and PSO based clustering performances for text datasets. The dimensionality reduction techniques like Stop word removal, Brill's tagger algorithm and mean Tf-Idf are used while reducing the size of dimension for clustering. The results reveal that PSO based approaches find better solution compared to K-means due to its ability to evaluate many cluster centroids simultaneously in any given time unlike K-means.

**Keywords:** Dimensionality reduction, Clustering, PSO.

## 1 Introduction

Text mining is playing a crucial role in mining textual databases. Text Mining is a multidisciplinary field, involving information retrieval, text analysis, information extraction, clustering, categorization, visualization, database technology, machine learning and data mining [4],[10]. The applications of text mining are document clustering, document classification etc. The intention of the text document clustering is to divide the given documents into a certain number of groups and minimizing the similarities between the documents disseminated among the different groups [5]. There are well established clustering approaches called Partitional and Hierarchical [2]. Due to the high dimension of document databases it requires some form of dimensionality reduction before applying clustering approaches for effective clustering results. Dimensionality reduction is the transformation of high-dimensional data into a meaningful representation of reduced dimensionality. Ideally, the reduced representation should have a dimensionality that corresponds to the intrinsic dimensionality of the data. The intrinsic dimensionality of the data is the minimum number of parameters needed to account for the observed properties of the data [1], [6]. There are two dimensionality reduction techniques, one is Feature Transformation and the other is Feature Selection [7]. The Feature transformation will transform the high dimensional data into low dimension where as Feature Selection will selects the will only selects the specified feature in the document database.

B.K. Panigrahi et al. (Eds.): SEMCCO 2010, LNCS 6466, pp. 623–629, 2010.

In this paper we have investigated partitional clustering techniques like K-means algorithm, Particle Swarm Optimization (PSO) and hybridization of K-means and PSO for several text datasets. Due to high dimensionality of text, these clustering techniques are computationally expensive in terms of time of executions. In this paper we have used three well known dimensionality reduction techniques such as Stop-word removal, Brill's tagger rule and mean Tf-Idf.

## 2   A: Data Representation for Document Clustering

For carrying out the document matching, the document dataset is represented in Vector Space Model. Each document is represented as a vector and the document database is treated as a vector space. The documents can be represented into vectors in two phases. In the first phase the documents are scanned. This phase identifies the unique words in the document dataset and gives unique term number for each term in the document. In the second phase, the documents are represented in vectors, i.e. with their dimension and the quantity of the dimension.

A document $d$ is represented as follows, $d= \{t1, t2, t3...tn\}$ where $t1, t2...tn$ are terms.

$$d= a_1t_1+a_2t_2+...+a_nt_n \tag{1}$$

Where $a_1, a_2,...., a_n$ are frequencies of terms i.e, how many times terms $t1,t2,...,tn$ are repeated in the document.

### B: Picking Important Terms in Documents

Important terms are to be identified before applying clustering techniques. To identify important terms a measure called term-frequency and inverse document frequency (Tf-Idf) is used. The weight of term '$x$' in a document is given by the following equation [10]:

$$w_{yx} = tf_{yx} * idf_{yx} \tag{2}$$

### C: Finding Similar Documents

There are number of methods to calculate similarity between two documents such as Cosine methods, Euclidian method, Minkowski distance measure etc. In our work we have used Minkowski distance measure as it is the generalization of both Euclidian and Manhattan distance.

$$d(m_i, m_j) = \sqrt{\frac{\sum_{i=1}^{dm}(m_{ik}-m_{jk})^2}{d_m}} \tag{3}$$

where $m_i$, $m_j$ are any two document vectors, $d_m$ is the dimension of vector space and $m_{ik}$, $m_{jk}$ are weights for dimension '$k$'.

## D: Dimensionality Reduction

The major problem in text mining is the documents consist of thousands of terms i.e., the vector space dimension is really huge. So, before mining the data in text database, the dimension of the database must be reduced since it is not only difficult store the entire data into the machine but also computationally expensive.

Feature transformation and feature selection are the mostly used dimensionality reduction techniques. Some of techniques in feature transformation are principal component analysis, latent semantic indexing, and independent component analysis. Some of techniques used in feature selection are document frequency (DF), means Tf-Idf (TI) and term frequency variance.

In this paper, we have used both feature transformation and selection techniques for dimensionality reduction. Approaches like stop word removal, Brill's tagger rule and mean Tf-Idf is used for this purpose.

### i)  Stop Word Removal

Stop words are the words, which are really common in documents. For example *the, and, a* … etc are stop words which are more common in any documents. In this research work, we have taken the stop words which are used by Google search engine.

### ii)  Brill's Tagger Rule

To reduce the dimension of the text databases Brill's Tagger rule is used. Brill's Tagger rule is a feature Selection method. Ite selects the terms (words) that are having medium document frequency. Brill's Tagger rule states that the term had to appear in at least three documents and in not more than 33% document [8].

### iii)  Mean Tf-Idf Rule
Mean Tf-Idf rule selects the terms, which are having high mean tf-idf value [2],[3],[4]. In this rule, the Tf-Idf for each term in the vector space is calculated as in [2].

## 3   Clustering Algorithms

Clustering algorithms are classified into partitional clustering and hierarchical clustering. Two partitional algorithms are briefly discussed below.

### i)  K-Means Algorithm

K-Means algorithm [11] is a partitional-based clustering algorithm. It searches for the solution in local space area. K-Means algorithm divides the problem space area into partitions and searches for the solution.The algorithm take the input in matrix format. The similarity matrix consists of *Tf-Idf* values, number of clusters '$n$' and initial centroids. The output is in terms of Set of clusters, Intra-cluster distance, Inter-cluster distance. K-means has some disadvantages like the solution is completely depends upon the initial cluster centroids which are generated in random manner and it searches  for the solution in local space area and gets trapped in local optima often.

## ii)  Particle Swarm Optimization (PSO) Algorithm

PSO algorithm was originally developed by Eberheart and Kennedy in 1995[12]. PSO searches for the global optimal solution in the problem space where as K-Means searches for the local optimal solution.

PSO creates the number of particles in the solution. Each particle consists of cluster. The particles will have velocity and direction. The particles will move from one point to other in the problem space. The movement of each particle depends on the movement of the best particle which leads all the particles.

The velocity and location each particle is calculated based on the following formula

$$V_{id} = W * V_{id}$$
$$+ C_1 * rand_1 * (p_{id} - x_{id})$$
$$+ C_2 * rand_2 * (p_{gd} - x_{id})$$

(4)

$$x_{id} = x_{id} + v_{id}$$

(5)

Where $W$ denotes the inertia weight factor, $P_{id}$ is the location of the particle that experience best fitness value, $Pgd$ is the global best fitness value among all particles, C1 and C2 are constants and are known as acceleration co-efficient, $d$ denotes the dimension of the problem space, $rand_1$ and $rand_2$ are random values in the ranges of (0,1).

PSO algorithm takes the input in matrix format. The similarity matrix consists of *Tf-Idf* values, number of particles '$P$', number of cluster in each particles '$n$', initial centroids for the cluster in each particle. The output includes Set of clusters, Intra cluster distance, Inter cluster distance and fitness value of gbest particle.

The solution represented by each particle is evaluated based on the fitness of the particle. The fitness value is defined as the average distance of documents to the cluster centroid (ADDC). The fitness value of each particle is calculated by using the following formula:

$$f = \frac{\sum_{i=1}^{N_c} \dfrac{\sum_{j=1}^{P_i} d(O_i, m_{i,j})}{P_i}}{N_c}$$

(6)

Where $m_{ij}$ denotes the $j^{th}$ document vector, which belongs to cluster $i$, $O_i$ is the centroids vector of the $i^{th}$ cluster, $d(O_i, m_{ij})$ is the distance between document $m_{ij}$ and the cluster centroids $O_i$, $Pi$ stands for the number of documents, which belongs to cluster $C_i$ and $N_c$ stands for the number of clusters.

# 4  Experimental Setup and Results

This experiment is performed by using J2SE 6.0. The clusters are developed separately with K-means and PSO. In the first step we developed clustering without dimensionality reduction. PSO algorithm is executed for 10, 30, 50 iterations for each and every dataset (with no dimensionality reduction, dimension reduced by using B.T rule and stop word removal and B.T rule, stop word removal and mean Tf-Idf rule).

The three datasets are taken from Tech TC-300 repository [9]. The decriptions are given below.

1. Exp_240218_474717 consists of 185 documents and 6560 terms: data1
2. Exp_22294_25575 consists of 127 documents and 12812 terms:   data2
3. Exp_20673_269078 consists of 147 documents and 14600 terms: data3

The numbers of clusters are chosen by user based on the knowledge derived from the contents of the dataset under investigation. For all experiments we have chosen number of clusters ranging from 3 to 7. The good cluster should have minimum intra cluster and maximum inter cluster distances. Table 1 gives the comparison of cluster quality of K-means and PSO without any dimensionality reduction. Table 2 and Table 3 present the comparison with different dimensionality reduction techniques. In table 3 we have chosen 1000 dimension as the frequency for mean Tf-Idf. The results in different tables reveal that for all three datasets under investigation the optimum cluster values are settling between 6 and 7. It is clearly evident from results that K-means is trapped in local minimum due to its choosing the initial centroids. However, due to the population based nature of PSO it overcomes the demerit of K- means and often finds its optimal value. The good clusters are shown in bold face letters in the tables. The dimensionality reduction approaches have not only able to give better performance in clustering results, also could reduce the execution time.

**Table 1.** K-means and PSO with no Dimensionality Reduction (DR)

| Sl no | dataset | | # of Cluster, Avg. intra cluster,   Avg. inter cluster distance | |
|---|---|---|---|---|
| | Data set id | Size of dimension | K-means no DR | PSO no DR |
| 1 | | | 3, 9.374, 13.584 | 3, 5.004, 13.136 |
| 2 | | | 4, 8.868, 18.341 | 4, 5.478, 15.205 |
| 3 | Data1 | 185 X 6560 | 5, 7.309, 14.164 | 5, 4.446, 11.864 |
| 4 | | | 6, 9.635, 18.513 | 6, 4.180, 14.212 |
| 5 | | | 7, 6.856, 15.640 | 7, 4.786, 13.048 |
| 6 | | | 3, 7.441, 14.456 | 3, 6.468, 24.031 |
| 7 | | | 4, 8.865, 16.774 | 4, 3.268, 16.356 |
| 8 | Data2 | 127 X 12812 | 5, 6.911, 14.449 | 5, 2.543, 13.815 |
| 9 | | | 6, 7.207, 16.446 | 5, 2.400, 13.230 |
| 10 | | | 7, 6.392, 14.637 | 7, 2.005, 19.511 |
| 11 | | | 3, 8.787, 21.162 | 3, 8.027, 13.811 |
| 12 | | | 4, 8.158, 15.780 | 4, 5.024, 10.823 |
| 13 | Data3 | 147 X 14600 | 5, 5.062, 13.452 | 5, 3.551, 15.840 |
| 14 | | | 6, 5.787, 15.848 | 6, 3.839, 12.096 |
| 15 | | | 7,5.883,16.305 | 7, 2.374, 21.663 |

**Table 2.** K-means and PSO with Stop Word Removal (SWR) and Brill's tagger (BT)

| Sl no | dataset | | # of Cluster, Avg. intra cluster,  Avg. inter cluster distance | |
|---|---|---|---|---|
| | Data set id | Size of dimension | K-means with SWR and BT | PSO with SWR and BT |
| 1 | Data1 | 185 X 2096 | 3, 7.884, 15.521 | 3, 7.756, 13.505 |
| 2 | | | 4, 7.648, 15.333 | 4, 6.573, 13.479 |
| 3 | | | 5, 8.509, 19.741 | 5, 5.796, 14.026 |
| 4 | | | 6, 8.040, 16.009 | 6, 5.159, 17.024 |
| 5 | | | 7, 6.594, 16.424 | 7, 3.499, 13.083 |
| 6 | Data2 | 127 X 2134 | 3, 5.211, 18.992 | 3, 4.501, 13.122 |
| 7 | | | 4, 4.525, 21.875 | 4, 3.191, 17.918 |
| 8 | | | 5, 4.781, 19.631 | 5, 2.528, 15.444 |
| 9 | | | 6, 3.907, 20.174 | 6, 2.497, 16.990 |
| 10 | | | 7, 5.204, 20.906 | 7, 2.180, 18.106 |
| 11 | Data3 | 147 X 3003 | 3, 5.897, 23.192 | 3, 5.391, 18.965 |
| 12 | | | 4, 5.980, 22.905 | 4, 4.164, 19.219 |
| 13 | | | 5, 3.396, 24.920 | 5, 3.274, 16.814 |
| 14 | | | 6, 5.779, 24.181 | 6, 2.525, 17.803 |
| 15 | | | 7, 3.017, 22.760 | 7, 2.261, 22.172 |

**Table 3.** K-means and PSO with Stop Word Removal (SWR) and Brill's tagger (BT) and Mean Tf-Idf (MTI)

| Sl no | dataset | | # of Cluster, Avg. intra cluster,  Avg. inter cluster distance | |
|---|---|---|---|---|
| | Data set id | Size of dimension | K-means with SWR,BT,MTI | PSO with SWR,BT,MTI |
| 1 | Data1 | 185 X 1000 | 3, 7.699, 10.780 | 3, 5.562, 11.864 |
| 2 | | | 4, 6.658, 11.871 | 4, 4.082, 10.406 |
| 3 | | | 5, 5.824, 12.688 | 5, 5.222, 10.529 |
| 4 | | | 6, 5.925, 13.326 | 6, 3.868, 12.685 |
| 5 | | | 7, 5.266, 12.241 | 7, 3.753, 11.287 |
| 6 | Data2 | 127 X 1000 | 3, 6.720, 10.774 | 3,  4.044, 13.193 |
| 7 | | | 4, 4.903, 12.830 | 4, 2.625, 16.997 |
| 8 | | | 5, 4.436, 14.301 | 5, 2.286, 11.155 |
| 9 | | | 6, 4.560, 13.773 | *6, 1.876, 12.066* |
| 10 | | | 7, 3.308, 14.910 | 7, 1.729, 12.727 |
| 11 | Data3 | 147 X 1000 | 3, 4.815, 13.718 | 3, 3.754, 13.470 |
| 12 | | | 4, 5.561, 12.119 | 4, 4.998, 14.417 |
| 13 | | | 5, 5.242, 11.612 | 5, 2.811, 13.958 |
| 14 | | | 6, 4.679, 14.536 | 6, 2.414, 15.199 |
| 15 | | | 7, 3.552, 14.365 | 7, 2.947, 13.131 |

## 5  Conclusions and Further Enhancement

As the dimension of text documents is really big, so large size of main memory and high speed of machines are needed but when you reduce the dimension of data less space and minimum speed machines are sufficient to mine the document databases. When clustering databases with partitional algorithm likes K-means which finds a local optimal solution but in case of evolutionary algorithms like PSO, which finds a global optimal solution. So, by using dimensionality reduction rules and PSO in clustering document databases highly efficient solution can be obtained in a quick time. As future enhancement we would like to see some multi-objective optimization approach for clustering.

## References

1. van der Maaten, L.J.P., Postma, E.O., van den Herik, H.J.: Dimensionality Reduction a Comparative Review, Citeseer (2007)
2. Cui, X., Potok, T.E., Palathingal, P.: Document Clustering using particle swarm optimization. In: IEEE Swarm Intelligence Symposium (2005)
3. Wai-chiu, W., Ada Wai-chee, F.: Incremental Document Clustering for Web Page. In: IEEE International Conference on Information Society (2000)
4. Tan, A.-H.: Text Mining state of art and challenges. In: Zhong, N., Zhou, L. (eds.) PAKDD 1999. LNCS (LNAI), vol. 1574. Springer, Heidelberg (1999)
5. Weixin, T., Fuxi, Z.: Text document clustering based on the modifying relations. In: 2008 International Conference on Computer Science (2008)
6. Balasubramanian, M., Schwartz, E.L.: Introduction to Statistical Pattern Recognition. In: Fukanaga, K. (ed.), 2nd edn., Academic Press, San Diego (1990)
7. Parsons, L., Hague, E., Liu, H.: Subspace clustering for high dimensional data. In: Parsons, L., Haque, E., Liu, H. (eds.) ACM SIGKDD Explorations Newsletter (2004)
8. R uger, S.M., Gauch, S.E.: Feature reduction for document clustering and classification, Citeseer (2000)
9. The TechTC-300 Test Collection for Text Categorization Version: 1.0 TechTC - Technion Repository of Text Categorization Datasets Maintained by: E. Gabrilovich, gabr@cs.technion.ac.il
10. Han, J., Kamber, M.: DataMining concepts and Techniques, 2nd edn. Morgan Kaufmann publishers, San Francisco (2006)
11. MacQueen, J.B.: Some Methods for classification and Analysis of Multivariate Observations. In: Proceedings of 5th Berkeley Symposium on Mathematical Statistics and Probability, vol. 1, pp. 281–297. University of California Press (1967)
12. Kennedy, J.F., Eberhart, R.C.: Particle swarm optimization. In: Proceedings of the IEEE International conference on neural networks, Perth, Australia, vol. 4, pp. 1942–1948 (1995)

# A Hybrid Differential Invasive Weed Algorithm for Congestion Management

Aniruddha Basak[1], Siddharth Pal[1], V. Ravikumar Pandi[2],
B.K. Panigrahi[2], and Swagatam Das[1]

[1] Department of Electronics and Telecommunications,
Jadavpur University, India
[2] Department of Electrical Engineering,
IIT Delhi, India
aniruddha_ju_etce@yahoo.com, sidd_pal2002@yahoo.com,
ravikumarpandi@gmail.com, bkpanigrahi@ee.iitd.ac.in,
swagatamdas19@yahoo.co.in

**Abstract.** This work is dedicated to solve the problem of congestion management in restructured power systems. Nowadays we have open access market which pushes the power system operation to their limits for maximum economic benefits but at the same time making the system more susceptible to congestion. In this regard congestion management is absolutely vital. In this paper we try to remove congestion by generation rescheduling where the cost involved in the rescheduling process is minimized. The proposed algorithm is a hybrid of Invasive Weed Optimization (IWO) and Differential Evolution (DE). The resultant hybrid algorithm was applied on standard IEEE 30 bus system and observed to beat existing algorithms like Simple Bacterial foraging (SBF), Genetic Algorithm (GA), Invasive Weed Optimization (IWO), Differential Evolution (DE) and hybrid algorithms like Hybrid Bacterial Foraging and Differential Evolution (HBFDE) and Adaptive Bacterial Foraging with Nelder Mead (ABFNM).

**Keywords:** Invasive weed, differential evolution, congestion management, wheeling transactions, optimal power flow.

## 1 Introduction

Congestion management is of prime importance in restructured power systems mainly because of open access competitive-based electricity market which tries to derive as much economic benefits as possible. Congestion management entails all the procedures and actions that need to be followed to establish a state of operation where none of the constraints are violated.

In [1] a detailed literature survey is given which deals with congestion management in deregulated market. Alleviation of network overloads under deregulated environment based on relative distance concept is studied in [2]. Concentric relaxation approach applied to open access transmission network congestion management is considered in [3]. A procedure for minimizing the number of adjustments in preferred schedules to alleviate congestion taking contingency-constrained limits into consideration is

B.K. Panigrahi et al. (Eds.): SEMCCO 2010, LNCS 6466, pp. 630–638, 2010.
© Springer-Verlag Berlin Heidelberg 2010

explained in [4]. Deregulated power system analysis using Evolutonary programming based OPF is considered in [5]. The generation rescheduling by evolutionary programming approach is discussed in [6].

This paper proposes a new optimization approach to solve the congestion management using a hybrid Differential Invasive Weed Optimization (DIWO) algorithm. Invasive Weed algorithm was first proposed by Mehrabian and Lucas [13] and since then it has been applied to several problems. We have proposed a modified IWO and hybridized with Differential evolution [10-12] and applied the resulting hybrid algorithm to a congestion management problem. The results have been compared with other well known algorithms like Simple Bacterial Foraging [7,8], Genetic Algorithm [9], Invasive Weed Optimization (IWO) and Differential Evolution. We have also compared our results with some past works in the same field with hybrid algorithms like Hybrid Bacterial Foraging and Differential Evolution (HBFDE) [14] and Adaptive Bacterial Foraging with Nelder Mead (ABFNM) [15].

## 2   Problem Description

In a power system, the economic operation of generating utilities is always preferred. The loads are getting supply from the system through transmission network and any power transmission-related problems are well managed by the controlling authority. In the deregulated market environment, the power dispatch problem has various sub-problems varying from linear programming problems to complex nonlinear problems. The concerned problem has two parts. The first part is finding out the preferred schedule using OPF and the second part is rescheduling the generation for removing the congestion. The OPF problem is one of the different nonlinear programming sub-problems. The OPF problem is about minimizing the fuel cost of generating units for a specific period of operation so as to accomplish optimal generation dispatch among operating units and in return satisfying the system load demand, generator operation constraints, and line flow limits (security constraints).

### 2.1   Objective Function

The objective function corresponding to the production cost can be approximated to be a quadratic function of the active power outputs from the generator units. Symbolically, it is represented as

$$\text{Minimize} \quad F_t^{\text{cost}} = \sum_{i=1}^{N_G} f_i \left( P_{Gi} \right) , \tag{1}$$

where $f_i \left( P_{Gi} \right) = a_i P_{Gi}^2 + b_i P_{Gi} + c_i$ and $i = 1, 2, 3, 4, ..., N_G$. $\tag{2}$

### 2.2   Equality Constraints

$$P_{Gi} - P_{Di} - \sum_{j=1}^{n} |V_i| |V_j| |Y_{ij}| \cos \left( \theta_{ij} - \delta_i + \delta_j \right) = 0 . \tag{3}$$

$$Q_{Gi} - Q_{Di} - \sum_{j=1}^{n} |V_i| |V_j| |Y_{ij}| \sin \left( \theta_{ij} - \delta_i + \delta_j \right) = 0 . \tag{4}$$

$$P_{loss} = \sum_{k=1}^{N_L} g_k \left[ |V_i|^2 + |V_j|^2 - 2|V_i||V_j| \cos\left(\delta_i - \delta_j\right) \right]. \tag{5}$$

## 2.3  Inequality Constraints

$$P_{Gi}^{\min} \leq P_{Gi} \leq P_{Gi}^{\max} \qquad (6) \qquad\qquad Q_{Gi}^{\min} \leq Q_{Gi} \leq Q_{Gi}^{\max} \qquad (7)$$

$$V_i^{\min} \leq V_i \leq V_i^{\max} \qquad (8) \qquad\qquad S_L \leq S_L^{\max} \qquad (9)$$

## 2.4  OPF Constraints Handling

The equality and inequality constraints of the ELD problem are considered in the fitness function ( $f$ ) itself by incorporating a penalty function. Any violation is weighted and added to the congestion cost.

## 2.5  Congestion Management

The bilateral transaction between a pair of buyer bus $j$ and seller bus $i$ can be modelled as

$$P_{Gi} - P_{Dj} = 0 \tag{10}$$

The multi-lateral transaction can also be modelled as

$$\sum P_{Gi} - \sum P_{Dj} = 0 \tag{11}$$

Here in this paper rescheduling the real power generation level from the preferred schedule is considered to relieve the congestion. The incremental and decremental bidding cost are submitted by each and every generating units to SO. This bidding is useful to calculate the minimum cost necessary to remove congestion, called as congestion cost. It can be mathematically represented as

$$\text{Minimize total congestion cost} \quad T_{cc} = \sum_{i=1}^{N_g} C_i^+ \Delta P_i^+ - \sum_{i=1}^{N_g} C_i^- \Delta P_i^- \tag{12}$$

The SO always ensure the system security by making this type of rescheduling operations. In this paper, the generator rescheduling is done by hybrid differential invasive weed algorithm to minimize the congestion cost.

# 3  Proposed Hybrid Algorithm (DIWO)

In our proposed hybridization scheme the differential mutation and binomial crossover operations of Differential Evolution (DE) have been incorporated into the structure of a modified Invasive Weed Optimization (IWO) algorithm in order to achieve a far better performance than both of the ancestors. Invasive Weed Optimization (IWO) is a meta-heuristic algorithm that mimics the colonizing behavior of weeds [13]. The basic characteristic of a weed is that it grows its population entirely or predominantly in a geographically specified area which can be substantially large or small.

DE differs markedly from algorithms like Evolutionary Strategy (ES) and Evolutionary Programming (EP) in consideration of the fact that it mutates the base vectors (secondary parents) with scaled population-derived difference vectors. This leads to an automatic adaptation which significantly improves the convergence of the algorithm [12].

Main steps of the hybrid algorithm may be presented in the following way:

**A. Initialization:** A certain number of weeds are randomly spread over the entire search space ($D$ dimensional). This population at the $t$-th iteration will be termed as $X_t = \left\{ \vec{X}_{1,t}, \vec{X}_{2,t}, ..., \vec{X}_{m,t} \right\}$ .

**B. Seeds production:** Each member of the population $X_t$ is allowed to produce seeds is allowed to generate seeds according to classical IWO algorithm. Number of seeds to be generated by $\vec{X}_{i,t}$ , $i \in [1, m]$ is decided by,

$$S_i = floor\left( \frac{F_{max} - f(\vec{X}_i)}{F_{max} - F_{min}} . s_{max} \right) ,$$

(13)

where $s_{max}$ is the same as *max_seed* and *min_seed* is taken to be zero. The standard deviation, with which the seeds of each weed will be distributed in the search space, $\sigma_{i,t}$ is calculated by using,

$$\sigma_{i,t} = \begin{cases} \left( 1 + 0.5 * \dfrac{f(\vec{X}_{i,t}) - F_{median,t}}{F_{worst,t} - F_{median,t}} \right) . \sigma_t & \text{if } f(\vec{X}_{i,t}) \geq F_{median,t}, \\ \left( 1 - 0.5 * \dfrac{F_{median,t} - f(\vec{X}_{i,t})}{F_{median,t} - F_{best,t}} \right) . \sigma_t & \text{if } f(\vec{X}_{i,t}) < F_{median,t}, \end{cases}$$

(14)

where $F_{worst,iter}$ and $F_{best,iter}$ denote the worst and best fitness in the population respectively at a particular iteration.

So for each $\vec{X}_{i,t}$ we get $S_i$ seeds, generated using standard deviation $\sigma_{i,t}$. These seeds along with their parent weeds create a new intermediate population $V_t$ of size $n$. Then the mutation and crossover operation is applied on each member $\vec{V}_{i,t}$ , $i \in [1, n]$ to create another population $Z_t$ as,

$$\vec{Y}_{i,t} = \vec{V}_{\alpha_1^i,t} + F(\vec{V}_{\alpha_2^i,t} - \vec{V}_{\alpha_3^i,t}) ,$$

(15)

and $\quad z_{j,i,t} = \begin{cases} y_{j,i,t}, & \text{if } (rand(0,1] \leq p_{Cr}) \cup (j = j_{rand}) \\ v_{j,i,t}, & \text{if } rand(0,1] > p_{Cr}, \quad j \in [1, 2, .., D], \end{cases}$

(16)

where the indices $\alpha_1^i, \alpha_2^i$, and $\alpha_3^i$ are mutually exclusive integers randomly picked up from the range $[1, n]$ for each index $i$, $p_{Cr}$ is equivalent to the crossover rate Cr in DE and lies between 0 and 1, and like in (16), $j_{rand} \in [1,2,...., D]$ is a randomly chosen index, which ensures that $\vec{Z}_{i,t}$ gets at least one component from $\vec{Y}_{i,t}$.

**C. Partial Selection according to DE:** Each element in $Z$, $\vec{Z}_i$, is compared with its corresponding parent $\vec{V}_i$ and the fitter solution is chosen to survive. Using this selection procedure a population of $n$ weeds is created and this is named as $P$. So each weed in $P$ can be described by,

$$\vec{P}_i = \begin{cases} \vec{Z}_i, & \text{if } f\left(\vec{Z}_i\right) \leq f\left(\vec{V}_i\right) \\ \vec{V}_i, & \text{if } f\left(\vec{Z}_i\right) > f\left(\vec{V}_i\right) \end{cases} \tag{17}$$

**D. Final Selection of weeds:** The members of $P$ are arranged according to increasing fitness (from best to worst) and the only the first $m$ weeds are allowed to pass to the next generation.

Steps B, C, D are repeated until the maximum function evaluations are reached. From the above description of the algorithm it is clear that our algorithm is a tightly coupled hybrid algorithm and here from we will call this as Differential Invasive Weed Optimization (DIWO) algorithm.

## 4   Simulation Results

The DIWO algorithm is applied to minimize the congestion cost. We have considered several bilateral and multilateral transactions in our study. The standard IEEE 30 bus system having load demand of 283.4MW is considered for the calculation of congestion cost [16]. The line limits are taken as 115% of the standard values in all the cases studied in this paper. The algorithms are implemented in Matlab–7.8.0 programming language and the developed software code is executed on 3 GHz, 2 GBRAM Pentium IV, and IBM computer.

### 4.1   Optimal Power Flow

The preferred generation schedule corresponding to the particular load condition is obtained by running an OPF to minimize the generation cost alone. The generator outputs except the slack bus generator are considered as the variable for running OPF. The DIWO, IWO, DE, ABFNM, HBFDE, SBF and GA are used to optimize the generation cost. All the algorithms except SBF and GA give minimum generation cost values as 803.0206 $/hour. The corresponding power generation is taken as the preferred schedule (Table 2) to meet the normal load demand and the bidding cost coefficients are given in Table 1.

## 4.2  Congestion Removal

The details of bilateral and multi-lateral transactions added are given in Table 3. The addition of all these transactions as reported in Table 3 results in overloading on line numbers 10 and 23. Table 5 shows how the line flow limits are exceeded. Now using all the algorithms we try to reschedule the generators such that we don't have any congestion on line 10 and 23. The results of rescheduling are shown in Table 4. All the stochastic algorithms were allowed 30000 functional evaluations. The best cost and the other statistical results like worst, mean and standard deviation of cost over 100 runs have been reported in Table 4. We see that the lowest cost value was achieved by DIWO algorithm.

**Table 1.** Bidding Cost

| Generator number | Increment Cost | Decrement Cost | Pmin | Pmax |
|---|---|---|---|---|
| PG1 | 45 | 40 | 50 | 200 |
| PG2 | 40 | 28 | 20 | 80 |
| PG5 | 45 | 32 | 15 | 50 |
| PG8 | 40 | 38 | 10 | 35 |
| PG11 | 42 | 40 | 10 | 30 |
| PG13 | 48 | 25 | 12 | 40 |

**Table 2.** Preferred Schedule

| Generator number | DIWO | IWO | DE | ABFNM | HBFDE | SBF | GA |
|---|---|---|---|---|---|---|---|
| PG1 | 176.1979 | 176.1979 | 176.1979 | 176.19 | 176.1963 | 176.177 | 177.217 |
| PG2 | 48.7681 | 48.7696 | 48.7677 | 48.77 | 48.7265 | 48.677 | 48.471 |
| PG5 | 21.4974 | 21.4975 | 21.4979 | 21.50 | 21.4982 | 21.483 | 21.588 |
| PG8 | 22.3334 | 22.3324 | 22.3334 | 22.33 | 22.3764 | 22.288 | 21.961 |
| PG11 | 12.2536 | 12.2529 | 12.2532 | 12.25 | 12.2508 | 12.419 | 11.882 |
| PG13 | 12.0000 | 12.0000 | 12.0000 | 12.00 | 12.0000 | 12.000 | 12.000 |
| Ploss | 9.6503 | 9.6503 | 9.6503 | 9.65 | 9.648 | 9.645 | 9.719 |
| Cost $/hour | **803.0206** | **803.0206** | **803.0206** | **803.0206** | **803.0206** | 803.022 | 803.032 |

**Table 3.** Bilateral and Multilateral Transactions

| Details of Bilateral Transactions | | | Details of Multilateral Transactions | | | |
|---|---|---|---|---|---|---|
| From Bus | To Bus | Transaction Power MW | From Bus | Transaction Power MW | To Bus | Transaction Power MW |
| 14 | 22 | 17 | 18 | 20 | 08 | 15 |
| 16 | 08 | 15 | 21 | 12 | 12 | 15 |
| 17 | 24 | 15 | 03 | 26 | 25 | 10 |
| 27 | 05 | 15 | | | 20 | 18 |
| Total Power | | 62 | Total Power | | | 58 |

**Table 4.** Rescheduled Generation Values

| Generator number | DIWO | IWO | DE | HBFDE | SBF | GA | ABFNM |
|---|---|---|---|---|---|---|---|
| PG1 | 176.1975 | 176.1944 | 176.1958 | 176.1963 | 176.2390 | 176.1514 | 176.001 |
| PG2 | 48.4284 | 47.0658 | 47.0679 | 47.2473 | 47.1121 | 47.0588 | 49.1107 |
| PG5 | 21.4972 | 21.4978 | 21.4971 | 21.4982 | 21.5509 | 21.4509 | 21.5481 |
| PG8 | 24.0547 | 23.9197 | 23.9193 | 23.9247 | 23.9385 | 23.9216 | 24.0971 |
| PG11 | 13.4878 | 14.9251 | 14.9252 | 14.7468 | 14.7686 | 15.0196 | 13.6882 |
| PG13 | 12.0000 | 12.0000 | 12.0000 | 12.0000 | 12.0000 | 12.0000 | 12.00 |
| Ploss | 12.2656 | 12.2051 | 12.2052 | 12.2132 | 12.2091 | 12.2023 | 12.2710 |
| Best Cost | 130.2082 | 223.3669 | 223.3293 | 208.1798 | 217.7287 | 231.0135 | 154.5486 |
| Worst Cost | 145.2181 | 225.3312 | 225.1139 | 221.2050 | 245.9902 | 302.7994 | 161.2244 |
| Std. Cost | 3.7129 | 0.4511 | 0.2903 | 1.6274 | 7.0231 | 21.1474 | 1.555 |
| Mean Cost | **134.2963** | 224.9345 | 223.8614 | 208.6444 | 230.1797 | 257.8302 | 157.7262 |
| time/trials | 176.1204 | 173.4522 | 171.3101 | 174.6342 | 180.5659 | 188.2531 | 177.9765 |

**Table 5.** Line Flow Comparison

| Line no. | Line flow limits | Before rescheduling | DIWO | IWO | DE | HBFDE | SBF | GA | ABFNM |
|---|---|---|---|---|---|---|---|---|---|
| 10 | 36.8 | 38.45 | 36.8 | 36.799 | 36.79 | 36.795 | 36.79 | 36.789 | 36.8 |
| 23 | 18.4 | 18.566 | 18.4 | 18.4 | 18.4 | 18.4 | 18.4 | 18.3 | 18.4 |

The line flows before and after removal of congestion is clearly mentioned in Table 5. In order to show the effectiveness of the proposed algorithm with respect to traditional methods, we have assumed another transaction data with reduced multilateral transaction values and keeping the bilateral transactions values as given in Table 3. This reduced transaction dataset is given in Table 6. In Table 7 we show the rescheduled generation values for reduced transactions. Again DIWO algorithm successfully reschedules with best cost.

**Table 6.** Reduced Bilateral and Multilateral transaction details

| Details of Bilateral Transactions | | | Details of Multilateral Transactions | | | |
|---|---|---|---|---|---|---|
| From Bus | To Bus | Transaction Power MW | From Bus | Transaction Power MW | To Bus | Transaction Power MW |
| 14 | 22 | 17 | 18 | 15 | 08 | 15 |
| 16 | 08 | 15 | 21 | 12 | 12 | 12 |
| 17 | 24 | 15 | 03 | 10 | 25 | 10 |
| 27 | 05 | 15 | | | | |
| Total Power | | 62 | Total Power | | | 37 |

**Table 7.** Rescheduled generation values for reduced transactions

| Generator number | DIWO | IWO | DE | HBFDE | SBF | ABFNM | GA |
|---|---|---|---|---|---|---|---|
| PG1 | 176.1976 | 176.1990 | 176.1982 | 176.1964 | 176.2478 | 175.9096 | 176.2003 |
| PG2 | 48.7681 | 48.8118 | 48.7681 | 48.7375 | 48.8005 | 48.7645 | 48.9111 |
| PG5 | 21.4974 | 21.5027 | 21.4981 | 21.4992 | 21.6281 | 21.5396 | 21.5493 |
| PG8 | 24.1680 | 24.1114 | 24.1639 | 24.1917 | 23.8640 | 24.0574 | 23.9739 |
| PG11 | 12.2537 | 12.2623 | 12.2565 | 12.2583 | 12.3484 | 12.2534 | 12.2548 |
| PG13 | 12.0000 | 12.0000 | 12.0000 | 12.0000 | 12.0000 | 12.0000 | 12.0018 |
| Ploss | 11.4848 | 11.4871 | 11.4849 | 11.4831 | 11.4888 | 11.4683 | 11.4912 |
| Cost$/hour | **73.3824** | 73.5238 | 73.3967 | 73.4183 | 74.6373 | 73.4835 | 73.9270 |
| time/trials | 174.3419 | 172.4512 | 168.3109 | 172.8562 | 178.1134 | 175.3624 | 187.1131 |

## 5  Conclusion

This paper presents an effective implementation of a hybrid evolutionary algorithm for congestion management. We have compared the results with other standard algorithms like DE, IWO, GA and SBF and also hybrid algorithms like HBFDE and ABFNM. The proposed algorithm is shown to outperform all the existing algorithms. We believe that the proposed algorithm can be applied to real world scenarios as well because of its excellent optimizing efficiency. Future works can be based on application of this hybrid algorithm to other power system optimization problems.

## 6  List of Symbols

$a_i$, $b_i$ and $c_i$ are the cost coefficients of the $i^{th}$ generator. $C_i^+$ and $C_i^-$ are the incremental and decremental cost coefficients of the $i^{th}$ generator. $f_i\left(P_{Gi}\right)$ denotes generation cost of the $i^{th}$ generator. $F_t^{cost}$ denotes total generation cost. $g_k$ signifies the line conductance of line $k$. $N_G$ is the number of online generating units. $n$ is the number of buses in the system. $N_L$ is the number of transmission lines. $nc$ denotes number of constraints. $P_{Gi}$ and $Q_{Gi}$ are the real and reactive power injections at $i^{th}$ bus. The corresponding load demands are given by $P_{Di}$ and $Q_{Di}$. $P_{Gi}^{min}$ and $P_{Gi}^{max}$ are lower and upper bounds for real power outputs of the $i^{th}$ generating unit. $Q_{Gi}^{min}$ and $Q_{Gi}^{max}$ are lower and upper bounds for reactive power outputs of the $i^{th}$ generating unit. $\Delta P_i^+$ and $\Delta P_i^-$ are the changes in power from preferred schedule in positive or negative side at $i^{th}$ generator. $S_L$ is the power flow in $L^{th}$ transmission line. $S_L^{max}$ is the line flow capacity of $L^{th}$ transmission line. $V_i^{min}$ and $V_i^{max}$ are lower and upper bounds of the voltages. The magnitude and angle of bus admittance matrix is given as $\left|Y_{ij}\right|$ and $\theta_{ij}$ respectively. $V_i$ and $\delta_i$ are the magnitude and angle of bus voltage.

## References

1. Kumara, A., Srivastava, S.C., Singh, S.N.: Congestion management in competitive power market: a bibliographical survey. Electric Power Systems Research 76(1-3), 153–164 (2005)
2. Yesuratnam, G., Thukaram, D.: Congestion management in open access based on relative electrical distances using voltage stability criteria. Electric Power Systems Research 77(12), 1608–1618 (2007)
3. Skokljev, I., Maksimovic, V.: Congestion management utilizing concentric relaxation. Serbian Journal of Electrical Engineering 4(2), 189–206 (2007)
4. Alomoush, M.I., Shahidehpour, S.M.: Contingency-constrained congestion management with a minimum number of adjustments in preferred schedules. Electrical Power and Energy Systems 22(4), 277–290 (2000)

5. Sood, Y.R.: Evolutionary programming based optimal power flow and its validation for deregulated power system analysis. Electrical power and energy systems 29(1), 65–75 (2007)
6. Gnanadas, R., Padhy, N.P., Palanivelu, T.G.: A new method for the transmission congestion management in the restructured power market. Journal of Electrical Engineering, Electrika 9(1), 52–58 (2007)
7. Passino, K.M.: Biomimicry of bacterial foraging for distributed optimization and control. IEEE Control Systems Magazine 22, 52–67 (2002)
8. Liu, Y., Passino, K.M.: Biomimicry of social foraging bacteria for distributed optimization models, principles, and emergent behaviors. Journal of Optimization Theory and Applications 115(3), 603–628 (2002)
9. Goldberg, D.E.: Genetic Algorithms in Search. In: Optimization and Machine Learning, Addison-Wesley, Reading (1989)
10. Storn, R., Price, K.V.: Differential Evolution - a simple and efficient adaptive scheme for global optimization over continuous spaces, Technical Report TR-95-012, ICSI (1995), http://http.icsi.berkeley.edu/~storn/litera.html
11. Price, K., Storn, R., Lampinen, J.: Differential Evolution - A Practical Approach to Global Optimization. Springer, Berlin (2005)
12. Das, S., Suganthan, P.N.: Differential Evolution – a survey of the state-of-the-art. IEEE Transactions on Evolutionary Computation (accepted, 2010)
13. Mehrabian, A.R., Lucas, C.: A novel numerical optimization algorithm inspired from weed colonization. Ecological Informatics 1, 355–366 (2006)
14. Pandi, V.R., Biswas, A., Dasgupta, S., Panigrahi, B.K.: A hybrid bacterial foraging and differential evolution algorithm for congestion management. Euro Trans. Electr. Power (2009), doi:10.1002/etep.368
15. Panigrahi, B.K., Pandi, V.R.: Congestion management using adaptive bacterial foraging algorithm. Energy Convers Manage 50(5), 1202–1209 (2009)
16. Bakirtzis, A.G., Biskas, P.N., Zoumas, C.E., Petridis, V.: Optimal power flow by enhanced genetic algorithm. IEEE Transactions on Power Systems 17(2), 229–236 (2002)

# Security Constrained Optimal Power Flow with FACTS Devices Using Modified Particle Swarm Optimization

P. Somasundaram[1] and N.B. Muthuselvan[2]

[1] Assistant Professor, College of Engineering, Guindy, Anna University, Chennai
[2] Assistant Professor, SSN College of Engineering, Chennai

**Abstract.** This paper presents new computationally efficient improved Particle Swarm algorithms for solving Security Constrained Optimal Power Flow (SCOPF) in power systems with the inclusion of FACTS devices. The proposed algorithms are developed based on the combined application of Gaussian and Cauchy Probability distribution functions incorporated in Particle Swarm Optimization (PSO). The power flow algorithm with the presence of Static Var Compensator (SVC) Thyristor Controlled Series Capacitor (TCSC) and Unified Power Flow Controller (UPFC), has been formulated and solved. The proposed algorithms are tested on standard IEEE 30-bus system. The analysis using PSO and modified PSO reveals that the proposed algorithms are relatively simple, efficient, reliable and suitable for real-time applications. And these algorithms can provide accurate solution with fast convergence and have the potential to be applied to other power engineering problems.

## 1 Introduction

Conventional optimization methods [1-4] used for solving OPF problem. Methods based on successive linearization and interior point methods are popular. In the present scenario, the security and optimality of system operation have been treated simultaneously for better power system control, namely Security Constrained OPF (SCOPF) which leads to a further increase in the complexity of computation. SCOPF calculation determines the optimal control variables at a desired security level, while minimizing the generator fuel cost. With a view to reduce the computational burden, some stochastic techniques [5-8] have been developed. To reduce the computational burden, heuristic optimization methods like Evolutionary Programming (EP)[9], Simulated Annealing (SA) [10], and Genetic Algorithm (GA) [11] have been employed to overcome the drawbacks of conventional techniques. In 2002, Abido [12] Particle Swarm Optimization (PSO) which was inspired by the social behaviours of animals such as fish schooling and bird flocking. PSO approach utilizes global and local exploration. The results of his work were promising and had shown effectiveness and superiority over classical techniques and Genetic Algorithms. Also PSO algorithm is that it requires only few parameters to be tuned. In 2008, Coelho and Lee [13] employed chaotic and Gaussian function in the PSO algorithm to solve economic load dispatch problem. Inspired by this technique, the Gaussian and Cauchy probability distribution technique has been employed in the PSO to solve the SCOPF problem using FACTS devices. The proposed method was tested on IEEE 30-bus test system.

B.K. Panigrahi et al. (Eds.): SEMCCO 2010, LNCS 6466, pp. 639–647, 2010.

The simulation results reveal that the proposed PSO approaches developed using Gaussian and Cauchy distributions helps in diversifying and intensifying the search space of the particle's swarm in PSO, thus preventing premature convergence to local minima and hence improving the performance of PSO.

## 2  Problem Formulation

In the base-case the control variables are taken as real power generations, controllable voltage magnitudes, switchable shunt capacitors, transformer tap ratios, etc. The equality constraint set comprises of power flow equations corresponding to the base-case as well as the postulated contingency cases. The inequality constraints include control constraints, reactive power generation and load bus voltage magnitude constraints and MVA line flow constraints pertaining to the base-case as well as the postulated contingency cases. The next-contingency list may include the outage of one or more transmission lines, transformers, generators, synchronous compensators, etc. For the sake of simplicity only single-line outages are taken in the next-contingency list. The objective function is minimization of total fuel cost pertaining to the base case. The mathematical representation for SCOPF problem assuming a second order generator cost curves, is defined as follows,

$$f(x,u) = MinF_T = \sum_{i=2}^{NG}\left(a_i P_{gi}^2 + b_i P_{gi} + c_i\right) + a_i P_{si}^2 + b_i P_{si} + c_s \qquad (1)$$

where, $F_T$ is the total fuel cost of the generators, $P_{gi}$ is the real power output generated by the $i^{th}$ generator, $a_i$, $b_i$, $c_i$ are the fuel cost coefficients.

The equality constraints of the optimization problem are the equations defining the power flow problem. As mentioned in [1], Newton load flow polar power mismatch formulation is particularly suitable for the optimization study. The relevant equations are

$$PF(x,u) = 0 \qquad (2)$$

where $x$ is a vector of dependent variables such as slack bus power $P_{g1}$, load bus voltage $V_L$, generator reactive power output $Q_g$ and transmission line loadings output $L_F$ and $u$ is a vector of independent variables like generator voltages $V_g$, generator real power outputs $P_g$ except the slack bus power output, transformer tap settings $T$ and shunt Var compensations $Q_C$.

The power flow equations under contingency state for SCOPF is given as

$$PF^R\left(x^R, u^R\right) = 0 \qquad (3)$$

where $x^R, u^R$ are the vector of dependent and independent variables to $R^{th}$ post - contingency state.

The constraints on the dependent and independent variables are governed by their upper and lower limits as follows:

$$P_s^{\min} \le P_s \le P_s^{\max} \tag{4}$$

$$V_{g_i}^{\min} \le V_{gi} \le V_{g_i}^{A}; i = 1,2,...NG \tag{5}$$

$$Q_{g_i}^{\min} \le Q_{gi} \le Q_{g_i}^{\max}; i = 1,2,...NG \tag{6}$$

$$L_{Fi} \le L_{Fi}^{\max}; i = 1,2,...NL \tag{7}$$

$$P_{g_i}^{\min} \le P_{gi} \le P_{g_i}^{\max}; i = 1,2,...NG \tag{8}$$

$$T_i^{\min} \le T_i \le T_i^{\max}; i = 1,2,...NT \tag{9}$$

$$V_{L_i}^{\min} \le V_{Li} \le V_{L_i}^{\max}; i = 1,2,...NL \tag{10}$$

## 3  FACTS Controllers

FACTS controllers are used to enhance the system flexibility and increase system load ability. These controllers are used for enhancing dynamic performance of power system. Different FACTS devices, such as Static Var Compensator (SVC), Solid State Synchronous Compensator (STATCOM), Thyristor Controlled Series Capacitor (TCSC), Unified Power Flow Controller (UPFC) etc., are among the most potential controllers for application to power system to achieve better controllability. SVC and STATCOM essentially control the voltage of a bus in a system. TCSC essentially controls power flow over a line and UPFC controls both the bus voltage and power flow over a line.

### 3.1  Static Var Compensator (SVC)

SVC at a bus is capable of controlling the corresponding bus voltage magnitude during steady state and dynamic state. It contributes for voltage stability and has a low impact on rotor angle stability. It can exchange reactive power only with the connected bus. It consists of passive elements only. For OPF problem either power injection model or fictitious generator bus model can be used [1,2].

### 3.2  Thyristor Controlled Series Capacitor (TCSC)

TCSC is a series connected controller. Its major purpose is the increase in steady state power transfer. It can avoid sub-synchronous oscillations. It contributes mainly for rotor angle stability and indirectly controls the bus voltage. It consists of passive elements only. During steady state, TCSC can be considered as a static reactance $-jx_c$. The controllable reactance $x_c$ is directly used as the control variable in the power flow equations. Generally up to 70% compensation is allowed. For OPF problem power injection model of TCSC is used.

### 3.3  Unified Power Flow Controller (UPFC)

UPFC is a combination of STATCOM and SSSC interconnected through a d.c link. Hence it consists of two control parameters namely a voltage source inserted in series with the line and a current source connected in shunt with the line. It is capable of controlling the real and reactive power flows, as well as compensating for transient and dynamic system conditions. For OPF problem power injection model of UPFC is used [1,2].

## 4  Particle Swarm Optimization

### 4.1  Overview of PSO

The PSO method was introduced in 1995 by Kennedy and Eberhart [14]. Here individuals called as particles change their positions with time. These particles fly around in a multidimensional search space. During flight, each particle adjusts its position according to its own experience, and the experience of neighbouring particles. Let $x_i$ and $v_i$ denote the particle position and its corresponding velocity in the search space. *pbest* is the best previous position of the particle and *gbest* is the best particle among all the particles in the group. The velocity and the position for each particle is calculated by using the following formulae

$$v_i^{t+1} = k\left(w.v_i^t + \varphi_1.rand()\left(pbest - x_i^t\right) + \varphi_2.rand()\left(gbest - x_i^t\right)\right) \tag{11}$$

$$x_i^{t+1} = x_i^t + v_i^{t+1} \tag{12}$$

where $x_i$ and $v_i$ are the current position and velocity of the $i^{th}$ generation, $w$ is the inertia weight factor, $\varphi_1$ and $\varphi_2$ are acceleration constants, $rand()$ is the function that generates uniform random number in the range [0,1] and $k$ is the constriction factor introduced by Eberhart and Shi to avoid the swarm from premature convergence and to ensure stability of the system. The selection of inertia weight $w$ provides a balance between global and local explorations.

### 4.2  Gaussian and Cauchy Distribution Based PSO Model

Coelho and Krohling proposed the use of truncated Gaussian and Cauchy probability distribution to generate random numbers for the velocity updating equation of PSO. In this paper, new approaches to PSO are proposed which are based on Gaussian probability distribution $(Gd)$ and Cauchy probability distribution$(Cd)$. In this new approach, random numbers are generated using Gaussian probability function and/or Cauchy probability function in the interval [0,1].

The Gaussian distribution$(Gd)$, also called normal distribution is an important family of continuous probability distributions. Each member of the family may be defined by two parameters, location and scale: the mean and the variance respectively. A standard normal distribution has zero mean and variance of one. Hence importance of the Gaussian distribution is due in part to the central limit theorem. Since a standard Gaussian distribution has zero mean and variance of value one, it helps in a faster convergence for local search.

This work proposes new PSO approaches with combination of Gaussian distribution and Cauchy distribution function. The modification to the conventional PSO (Model 1) proceeds as follows:

**Model 2:** Here the Gaussian distribution, is used to generate random numbers in the interval [0, 1], in the Cognitive part of the particle. The modified velocity equation is given by $v_i^{t+1} = k\left(w.v_i^t + \varphi_1.Gd()\left(pbest - x_i^t\right) + \varphi_2.rand()\left(gbest - x_i^t\right)\right)$

**Model 3:** Here the Gaussian distribution Gd, is used to generate random numbers in the interval [0,1], in the Social Part of the particle. The modified velocity equation is given by $v_i^{t+1} = k\left(w.v_i^t + \varphi_1.rand()\left(pbest - x_i^t\right) + \varphi_2.Gd()\left(gbest - x_i^t\right)\right)$

**Model 4:** Here the Gaussian distribution Gd, is used to generate random numbers in the interval [0,1], in the Cognitive and Social Part. The modified velocity equation is given by $v_i^{t+1} = k\left(w.v_i^t + \varphi_1.Gd()\left(pbest - x_i^t\right) + \varphi_2.Gd()\left(gbest - x_i^t\right)\right)$

**Model 5:** Here the Cauchy distribution Cd, is used to generate random numbers in the interval [0,1], in the Cognitive Part. The modified velocity equation is given by $v_i^{t+1} = k\left(w.v_i^t + \varphi_1.Cd()\left(pbest - x_i^t\right) + \varphi_2.rand()\left(gbest - x_i^t\right)\right)$

**Model 6:** Here the Cauchy distribution Cd, is used to generate random numbers in the interval [0,1], in the Social Part The modified velocity equation is given by

$$v_i^{t+1} = k\left(w.v_i^t + \varphi_1.rand()\left(pbest - x_i^t\right) + \varphi_2.Cd()\left(gbest - x_i^t\right)\right)$$

**Model 7:** Here the Cauchy distribution Cd, is used to generate random numbers in the interval [0,1], in the Cognitive and Social Part. The modified velocity equation is given by $v_i^{t+1} = k\left(w.v_i^t + \varphi_1.Cd()\left(pbest - x_i^t\right) + \varphi_2.Cd()\left(gbest - x_i^t\right)\right)$

**Model 8:** Here the Gaussian distribution Gd, is used to generate random numbers in the interval [0,1], in the Social Part and Cauchy Distribution Cd, is used to generate random numbers in the interval [0,1] in the Cognitive Part. The modified velocity equation is given by $v_i^{t+1} = k\left(w.v_i^t + \varphi_1.Cd()\left(pbest - x_i^t\right) + \varphi_2.Gd()\left(gbest - x_i^t\right)\right)$

**Model 9:** Here the Cauchy distribution Cd, is used to generate random numbers in the interval [0,1], in the Social Part and Gaussian Distribution Gd, is used to generate random numbers in the interval [0,1] in the Cognitive Part. The modified velocity equation is given by $v_i^{t+1} = k\left(w.v_i^t + \varphi_1.Gd()\left(pbest - x_i^t\right) + \varphi_2.Cd()\left(gbest - x_i^t\right)\right)$

The above models that have been developed are implemented in the conventional PSO approach and their performances were studied.

## 5   Sample System Studies and Results

The PSO and Modified PSO algorithm for solving multi-area OPF problem with various FACTS controllers are tested on a standard IEEE 30-bus test system. The standard IEEE 30-bus test system consists of 6 generating units, 41 lines and a total demand of 283.4 MW. The optimal parameters obtained for the PSO and Modified PSO algorithms are as follows, the population size $N_p$ is 50. The initial inertia weight was set at 1.5 and the acceleration constants $\varphi_1$ and $\varphi_2$ was set at 2.05.

The SVC is located at bus 21 of IEEE 30-bus test system. Its reactive power limits are 11.2 MVAr and -2.5 MVAr with slope $X_{SL}$ as 0.02 p.u. The corresponding voltage limits are 0.9 and 1.1 p.u V. The optimal solution of IEEE 30-bus test system using the proposed algorithms with SVC is presented in Table 1. From Table 1 it is inferred that with the inclusion of SVC at bus 21 the total reactive power generations, loss and total fuel cost are reduced. Also the inclusion of SVC at bus 21 has ensured that the voltage profile of the system is well within its limits.

The TCSC is located in line 4 of IEEE 30-bus test system. The range of compensation by TCSC is 0 to 70 % of line reactance. The optimal solution of IEEE 30-bus test system using the proposed algorithms with TCSC is presented in Table 2. From Table 2 it is inferred that with the inclusion of TCSC in line 4 the active power generation of generator 1 is increased and there is a reduction of total fuel cost and loss. With the inclusion of TCSC in line 4 the power transfer capability of the line has increased, thus ensuring the enhancement of steady state stability limit of the transmission line.

The UPFC is located in line 4 of IEEE 30-bus test system. Its quadrature current limits are -1 to 1 p.u A. The magnitude and angle limits of inserted voltage are 0 to 0.1 p.u V and respectively. The optimal solutions of IEEE 30-bus test system using the proposed algorithms based single area OPF problem with UPFC in line 4 is presented in Table 3. With the inclusion of UPFC in line 4 the power transfer capability of the line has increased, thus ensuring the enhancement of steady state stability limit of the transmission line. Moreover the voltage magnitudes of all buses are higher than the base case values, thus ensuring the voltage reliability of the entire power system.

**Table 1.** Optimal Solution of IEEE 30-bus system with SVC at bus 21

| Algorithm | Model 1 | Model 2 | Model 3 | Model 4 | Model 5 | Model 6 | Model 7 | Model 8 | Model 9 |
|---|---|---|---|---|---|---|---|---|---|
| PG1 | 151.305 | 150.993 | 150.011 | 152.370 | 153.001 | 160.352 | 165.691 | 151.372 | 151.023 |
| PG2 | 56.9185 | 54.234 | 56.310 | 56.400 | 51.460 | 40.866 | 25.421 | 55.934 | 57.120 |
| PG5 | 23.2179 | 23.694 | 22.702 | 30.123 | 20.592 | 29.737 | 27.497 | 21.950 | 23.185 |
| PG8 | 29.6407 | 30.432 | 28.433 | 24.806 | 26.346 | 25.667 | 27.110 | 28.856 | 29.641 |
| PG11 | 15.8943 | 17.025 | 13.932 | 14.918 | 20.366 | 22.853 | 28.115 | 19.450 | 15.894 |
| PG13 | 14.5783 | 15.224 | 20.166 | 13.244 | 19.827 | 12.080 | 17.715 | 13.988 | 14.550 |
| Q SVC | 7.77573 | 10.1482 | 6.03788 | 7.77573 | 6.67783 | 6.03788 | 7.77573 | 6.67783 | 10.1482 |
| PG | 291.55 | 291.60 | 291.55 | 291.86 | 291.56 | 291.55 | 291.56 | 291.55 | 291.41 |
| QG | 62.3722 | 60.3306 | 63.8308 | 61.3722 | 63.2852 | 62.4318 | 61.3823 | 60.1252 | 60.2317 |
| Loss | 8.15503 | 8.30284 | 8.19323 | 8.13403 | 8.16238 | 8.11353 | 8.10303 | 8.25138 | 8.29484 |
| Fuel cost | 808.38 | 809.06 | 809.82 | 813.19 | 809.34 | 813.28 | 824.24 | 808.75 | 808.02 |
| Iterations | 50 | 50 | 50 | 50 | 50 | 50 | 50 | 50 | 50 |
| Time (sec) | 90 | 80 | 75 | 85 | 95 | 90 | 85 | 75 | 70 |

From Tables 1 to Table 3 it is inferred that for the same number of iterations the optimum values is low for Model 9 PSO algorithm than conventional PSO algorithm. Moreover the Model 9 PSO algorithm has a faster convergence than conventional PSO algorithm. Hence the Gaussian and Cauchy based PSO algorithm is simple and efficient for solving single area OPF problem with inclusion of FACTS devices like SVC and TCSC controllers.

**Table 2.** Optimal Solution of IEEE 30-bus system with TCSC in line 4

| Algorithm | Model 1 | Model 2 | Model 3 | Model 4 | Model 5 | Model 6 | Model 7 | Model 8 | Model 9 |
|---|---|---|---|---|---|---|---|---|---|
| PG1 | 153.861 | 155.726 | 155.230 | 155.831 | 156.196 | 155.605 | 151.679 | 156.444 | 156.38 |
| PG2 | 56.6043 | 54.9740 | 54.4621 | 54.5447 | 53.1302 | 54.0265 | 56.0736 | 54.6929 | 57.7051 |
| PG5 | 22.6693 | 23.0975 | 23.4713 | 23.0501 | 25.0607 | 23.7778 | 23.8075 | 24.3593 | 24.6535 |
| PG8 | 30 | 27.0975 | 27.5963 | 27.3421 | 25.8547 | 27.1813 | 29.9340 | 27.1947 | 23.1717 |
| PG11 | 15.4979 | 16.9113 | 16.4551 | 16.7528 | 14.3801 | 16.7381 | 15.1311 | 15.5184 | 17.2476 |
| PG13 | 12.4291 | 13.9964 | 14.1373 | 13.6269 | 17.0730 | 14.1762 | 14.6476 | 13.1385 | 12.0512 |
| $X_C$ | 0.02653 | 0.02572 | 0.02433 | 0.02652 | 0.02653 | 0.02552 | 0.02652 | 0.02653 | 0.02653 |
| PG | 291.062 | 291.803 | 291.352 | 291.147 | 291.695 | 291.505 | 291.273 | 291.348 | 291.209 |
| QG | 72.5579 | 72.3890 | 74.1379 | 72.1210 | 71.5562 | 74.1279 | 72.5735 | 74.5706 | 73.1882 |
| Loss | 7.66194 | 8.403 | 7.052 | 7.74739 | 8.295 | 8.105 | 7.873 | 7.94769 | 7.80942 |
| Fuel cost | 805.067 | 806.888 | 805.522 | 804.393 | 806.992 | 806.022 | 807.201 | 805.031 | 805.114 |
| Iterations | 50 | 50 | 50 | 50 | 50 | 50 | 50 | 50 | 50 |
| Time (sec) | 80 | 85 | 87 | 85 | 90 | 95 | 85 | 95 | 75 |

**Table 3.** Optimal Solution of IEEE 30-bus system with UPFC in line 4

| Algorithm | Model 1 | Model 2 | Model 3 | Model 4 | Model 5 | Model 6 | Model 7 | Model 8 | Model 9 |
|---|---|---|---|---|---|---|---|---|---|
| PG1 | 166.555 | 167.0865 | 161.0399 | 167.129 | 165.4847 | 168.0608 | 165.5537 | 168.9 | 167.15 |
| PG2 | 45.9413 | 46.5847 | 41.15867 | 46.141 | 41.7695 | 41.3833 | 45.8812 | 49.1754 | 45.13 |
| PG5 | 19.03888 | 20.4122 | 19.7796 | 20.0018 | 19.4818 | 20.7650 | 20.2236 | 21.7279 | 20.08 |
| PG8 | 25.7585 | 21.8723 | 25.2974 | 21.714 | 26.6451 | 25.0695 | 24.9898 | 20.035 | 24.075 |
| PG11 | 10.7985 | 13.0153 | 20.9055 | 13.171 | 15.0269 | 10.9553 | 11.4546 | 12.8859 | 11.7985 |
| PG13 | 18.184 | 18.4155 | 18.1982 | 18.1891 | 18.5806 | 20.6242 | 18.2889 | 13.9454 | 18.18 |
| $I_q$ | -0.113717 | -0.13586 | -0.1491 | -0.1921 | -0.1477 | -0.1487 | -0.1307 | -0.158003 | -0.1534 |
| $V_T$ | 0.0702637 | 0.0216687 | 0.0102201 | 0.06275 | 0.02715 | 0.06175 | 0.01835 | 0.0625549 | 0.0767 |
| $\Phi_T$ | -2.02493 | -2.1212 | -2.3493 | -2.0012 | -2.1073 | -2.0129 | -2.2134 | -2.2488 | -2.023 |
| PG | 286.276 | 287.3867 | 286.3793 | 286.3459 | 286.9886 | 286.8581 | 286.3918 | 286.6696 | 286.4135 |
| QG | 68.603 | 68.718 | 64.523 | 65.16 | 69.934 | 70.639 | 68.653 | 74.5706 | 67.06 |
| Fuel cost | 782.449 | 786.9002 | 789.3069 | 782.899 | 788.1119 | 787.2335 | 784.1023 | 782.3554 | 783.7282 |
| Iterations | 50 | 50 | 50 | 50 | 50 | 50 | 50 | 50 | 50 |

# 6 Conclusion

This paper presents an improved, simple, efficient and reliable particle swarm algorithms for solving multi-area OPF and SCOPF problems. The proposed algorithms were developed from basic PSO technique by an amendment in each technique using Gaussian and Cauchy distributive function for obtaining a much better convergence. This paper demonstrates with clarity, chronological development and by successful application of the proposed algorithms on standard test systems for solving OPF and SCOPF problems for interconnected power system. The results obtained from these proposed algorithms are compared. The analysis reveals that Model 9 PSO algorithm converges faster than basic PSO algorithm. All the other algorithms perform better than conventional PSO algorithm even though the particles get struck at Local minima. The proposed algorithms have the potential to be applied to other power engineering problems such as dynamic economic dispatch with several essential constraints, capacitor placement problems, optimal location of Flexible AC Transmission System (FACTS) controllers, coordination of FACTS controllers etc., since they can produce accurate optimum with fast convergence.

# References

[1] Hingorani, N.G., Gyugyi, L.: Understanding FACTS: concepts and technology of flexible AC transmission systems. The institute of Electrical and Electronics Engineers, New York (2000)
[2] Xiao, Y., Song, Y.H., Sun, Y.Z.: Power injection method and linear programming for FACTS control. In: Proceedings IEEE Power Engineering Society winter meeting, Singapore, pp. 877–884 (2000)
[3] Taranto, G.N., Pereira, M.V.F.: Representation of FACTS devices in Power System Economic Dispatch. IEEE Transactions on Power Systems 7-2, 572–576 (1992)
[4] Padhy, N.P., Abdel-Moamen, M.A.R., Trivedi, P.K., Das, H.: A Hybrid model for optimal power flow incorporating FACTS devices. IEEE Transactions on Power Systems 1, 510–515 (2001)
[5] Padhy, N.P., Abdel Moamen, M.A.: Power flow control and solutions with multiple and multi-type FACTS devices. Electric Power Systems Research 74, 341–351 (2005)
[6] Zhang, J., Yokoyama, A.: A Comparison between the UPFC and the IPFC in Optimal Power Flow Control and Power Flow Regulation. IEEE Transactions on Power Systems 06, 339–345 (2006)
[7] Zhang, Y., Zhang, Y., Chen, C.: A Noval Power Injection Model of IPFC for Power Flow Analysis Inclusive of Practical Constraints. IEEE Transactions on Power Systems 21-04, 1550–1556 (2006)
[8] Bhasaputra, P., Ongsakul, W.: Optimal placement of Mulit-Type FACTS devices by hybrid TS /SA Approach. IEEE Transactions on Power Systems 03, 375–378 (2003)
[9] Yuryevich, J., Wong, K.P.: Evolutionary programming based optimal power flow algorithm. IEEE Trans. on Power Systems 14(4), 1245–1250 (1999)
[10] Poa-Sepulveda, C.A., Pavez-Lazo, B.J.: A solution to the optimal power flow using simulated annealing. Intl. Journal on Electric Power Energy systems 25(1), 47–57 (2003)

[11] Bakirtzis, A.G., Biskas, P.N., Zoumas, C.E., Petridis, V.: Optimal power flow by enhanced genetic algorithm. IEEE Trans.on Power Systems 17(2), 229–236 (2002)
[12] Abido, M.A.: Optimal Power flow using Particle swarm optimization. Electrical and Energy Systems 24, 563–571 (2002)
[13] Coelho, L., Lee, C.S.: Solving economic load dispatch problems in power systems using chaotic and Gaussian particle swarm optimization approaches. Electric Power and Energy Systems 30, 297–307 (2008)
[14] Kennedy, J., Eberhart, R.: Particle Swarm Optimization. In: Proc. IEEE Intl. Conf. Neural Networks, vol. 4, pp. 1942–1948 (1995)

# Tuning of PID Controller Using Internal Model Control with the Filter Constant Optimized Using Bee Colony Optimization Technique

U. Sabura Banu[1] and G. Uma[2]

[1] Assistant Professor, Instrumentation and Control, BS Abdur Rahman University,Vandalur,
Chennai - 600 048, Tamil Nadu, India
sabura_banu@yahoo.co.in, sabura_banu@rediffmail.com
[2] Assistant Professor, Power Electronics, Anna University, Guindy, Chennai- 600 025

**Abstract.** The present research work presents a novel control scheme for tuning PID controllers using Internal Model control with the filter time constant optimized using Bee colony Optimization technique. PID controllers are used widely in Industrial Processes. Tuning of PID controllers is accomplished using Internal Model control scheme. IMC includes tuning of filter constant $\lambda$. Compromise is made in selecting the filter constant $\lambda$ since an increased value of $\lambda$ results in a sluggish response whereas decreased value of filter constant leads in an aggressive action. In the present work, an attempt has been made to optimize the value of the $\lambda$ by Bee colony optimization technique. Simulation results show the validity of the proposed scheme for the PID controller tuning.

**Keywords:** Internal Model Control, PID controller, Bee colony optimization, Filter constant.

## 1 Introduction

During the past decades, the process control techniques have made great advance. Numerous control methods like adaptive control, neural control, fuzzy logic control, ANFIS control are developed. Still, PID controllers are considered as the workhorse of almost all the industrial process control applications due to their structural simplicity and robust performance in a wide range of operating condition [1]. PID controller mainly depends on tuning of the gains the proportional gain, integral time and the derivative time. Tuning the PID controller gains play a major role in deciding the performance. Literature provides many tuning methodologies.

Tuning of PID parameters are based on the exact form of the process expressed by a transfer function [2-3]. Manufacturers and vendors use different tuning algorithms for designing of the PID control parameters.

Time delay degrades the performance of control system in many industrial application. That too when the time delay is very large, PID controller degrades. Smith predictor control and its improved methods [4,5] solve the control problems of time delay system. But it suffers from a sensitive problem. When there is a mismatch between the model and actual process, the closed-loop performance is also degraded.

B.K. Panigrahi et al. (Eds.): SEMCCO 2010, LNCS 6466, pp. 648–655, 2010.

So, it is used rarely in industrial application. IMC [6,7,8,9] can design controller and filter separately based on the analysis of the control system's robust stability and closed-loop performance. This design can compensate for the mismatch between actual process and model with good robustness. IMC allows a transparent controller design procedure where control quality and robustness are influenced in a direct manner. The IMC concept was conceptualized by approximating the feedback transfer function by Maclaurin's series [10-12]. Here the tuning parameter is finding the filter time constant.

Bee colony optimization technique is an attractive method which gives an optimal global search optimization for the tuning of the filter constant $\lambda$. Colonies of social insects such as ants and bees have instinct ability known as swarm intelligence [13,14]. This highly organized behavior enables the colonies of insects to solve problems beyond capability of individual members by functioning collectively and interacting primitively amongst members of the group. In a honey bee colony, this behavior allows honey bees to explore the environment in search of flower patches (food sources) and then indicate the food source to the other bees of the colony when they return to the hive. Such a colony is characterized by selforganization, adaptiveness and robustness. Seeley (1995) proposed a behavioral model of selforganization for a colony of honey bees. In the model, foraging bees visiting flower patches return to the hive with nectar as well as a profitability rating of respective patches. The collected nectar provides feedback on the current status of nectar flow into the hive. The profitability rating is a function of nectar quality, nectar bounty and distance from the hive. The feedback sets a response threshold for an enlisting signal which is known as waggle dance, the length of which is dependent on both the response threshold and the profitability rating. The waggle dance is performed on the dance floor where individual foragers can observe. The foragers can randomly select a dance to observe and follow from which they can learn the location of the flower patch and leave the hive to forage. This self-organized model enables proportionate feedback on goodness of food sources [16-20]. In the proposed research work, an attempt has been made to tuned the filter constant for IMC using Bee colony optimization technique.

## 2   Internal Model Controller Based PID Design

Internal Model Controller involves a model based procedure, where the process model is embedded in the controller. IMC involves a single tunable parameter the filter constant. Consider a linear transfer function model of the process. Figure 1 shows the block diagram of the IMC structure.

Internal Model controller involves a model based procedure, where the process model is embedded in the controller. IMC involves a single tunable parameter the filter constant. Consider a linear transfer function model of the process.

Let the process transfer function be

$$G_p(s) = \frac{y(s)}{u(s)} = \frac{K\,e^{-\theta s}}{\tau s + 1} \tag{1}$$

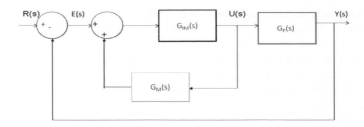

**Fig. 1.** Block diagram of the modified IMC

Applying Pade approximation for the delay term

$$e^{-\theta s} = \frac{1-\frac{\theta}{2}s}{1+\frac{\theta}{2}s} \qquad (2)$$

$$G_M(s) = \frac{y(s)}{u(s)} = \frac{K(1-\frac{\theta}{2}s)}{(\tau s+1)(1+\frac{\theta}{2}s)} \qquad (3)$$

The process model is split into inverting and non-inverting parts.

$$G_-(s) = \frac{y(s)}{u(s)} = \frac{K}{(\tau s+1)(1+\frac{\theta}{2}s)} \qquad (4)$$

$$G_+(s) = 1-\frac{\theta}{2}s$$

$G_+(s)$ leads to closed loop unstable poles, so it cannot be inverted. $G_-(s)$ alone is inverted. The Controller transfer function obtained by inverting $G_-(s)$ is hard to understand, physically unrealizable and impossible to implement exactly. For physical realizability the order of the denominator of the controller transfer function $G_{IM}(s)$ must be atleast as great as the order of the numerator requiring the inclusion of the filter transfer function.

Filter Transfer function f(s) is represented by

$$f(s) = \frac{1}{\lambda s+1} \qquad (5)$$

$$G_{IM} = \frac{f(s)}{G_-(s)} = \frac{1}{\lambda s+1} \frac{(\tau s+1)((\theta/2)s+1)}{K}$$
$$= \frac{\tau(\theta/2)s^2+(\tau+(\theta/2))s+1}{K(\lambda s+1)} \qquad (6)$$

Feedback Control is given by

$$G(s) = \frac{G_{IM}(s)}{1-G_{IM}(s)G_M(s)}$$
$$= \frac{\tau(\theta/2)s^2+(\tau+(\theta/2))s+1}{K(\lambda+(\theta/2))s} \qquad (7)$$

Comparing this with the conventional PID controller transfer function

$$G_C(s) = K_P + \frac{K_I}{s} + K_D$$

$$= \frac{K_P s + K_I + K_D s^2}{s}$$

(8)

Resulting in the controller parameter represented by

$$K_P = \frac{\tau + (\theta/2)}{K(\lambda + (\theta/2))}$$

$$K_I = \frac{1}{K(\lambda + (\theta/2))}$$

$$K_D = \frac{\tau\theta}{K(2\lambda + \theta)}$$

(9)

## 3  Bee Colony Algorithms

The challenge is to adapt the self-organization behavior of the colony for tuning the PID controller parameters.  There are two major characteristics of the bee colony in searching for food sources: Waggle dance and forage (or nector exploration).

**Waggle Dance**
A forager $f_i$ on return to the hive from nectar exporation will attempt with probability p to perform waggle dance on the dance floor with duration $D = d_i A$, where $d_i$ changes with profitability factor.  Further it will also attempt with probability $r_i$ to observe and follow a randomly selected dance. The probability $r_i$ is dynamic and also changes with profitability rating.  If a forager chooses to follow a selected dance, it will use the 'path' termed as 'preferred path' taken by the forager performing the dance to guide its direction for flower patches.  The path for a forager is a series of landmarks from a source (hive) to a destination (nectar).

For PID tuning, the profitability rating should be related to the objective function the Integral Square Error (ISE).  Let $Pf_i$ denote the profitability rating for a forager, it is given by:

$$Pf_i = 1/PI^i_{max}$$

(10)

where Performance Index, PI = ISE

$PI^i_{max}$ = Performance index generated by a forager $f_i$

## 4  Online Tuning of Filter Constant λ Using BCO

$\lambda$ is the single filter constant required for the design of the PID control using IMC technique. It is proposed to tune the filter constant optimally by Bee colony Optimization technique.  The tuned filter constant is used to design the PID controller parameter. Variation in filter constant abruptly disturbs the performance of the process. An attempt has been made to design the filter constant using Bee colony optimization technique as shown in figure 2.

Minimizing the following error criteria generates the controller parameter

$$ISE = \int_{0}^{T} \left[ r(t) - y(t) \right]^2 dt \tag{11}$$

Where:  r(t) = reference input,
        y(t) = measured variable

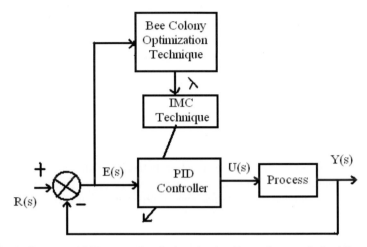

**Fig. 2.** Block diagram of PID controller designed using Bee colony optimized Internal Model Control

## 5   Case Study and Result

To verify the effectiveness of the Bee colony Optimized – Internal Model Control (BCO-IMC) tuned PID controller, two system with different $\theta/\tau$ ratio are considered. The transfer functions of the plants are as follows:

**Case I   ($\theta/\tau<1$)**

$$G(s) = \frac{2}{5s+1} e^{-0.5s} \tag{12}$$

**Case II   ($\theta/\tau>1$)**

$$G(s) = \frac{2}{5s+1} e^{-25s} \tag{13}$$

Colony Size (including Employed Bees + Onlooker bees) = 10
Maximum Cycles = 200

To prove the effectiveness of the proposed BCO-IMC based PID controller and Zeigler-Nicholas (ZN) based PID controller are also devised.  The following BCO parameters are selected for the tuning of the filter constant $\lambda$.

Error Goal = 1e-5
Limit = 100

Lower bound = 0
Upper bound = 3
Number of Runs = 3

Simulation was performed to tune the best $\lambda$ value. The $\lambda$ value generated is used to find the controller parameters $k_p$, $k_i$ and $k_d$. Table 1 shows the $\lambda$, PID parameters and ISE values for both the cases. Figures 3 shows the servo control of the proposed controller for case I. From the response, it is clear that the proposed controller is able to track the servo changes smoothly. ZN based PID controller requires fine tuning of all the parameters to get a smooth response. The rise time, settling time and the ISE indicates that the BCO-IMC based PID controller has better performance compared to that of the ZN based PID. Figure 4 shows the servo response for case II. The ZN tuning fails for the system with large $\theta/\tau$ ratio. From the response it is clear that the output oscillates and does track the step change, whereas the proposed scheme leads to a perfect tuning of the PID controller parameters leading to a good tracking control. Also the ISE value is very minimum in the case of the proposed controller based system.

**Table 1.** $\lambda$, PID parameters and ISE values for both the cases using conventional ZN,PSO & BCO

|  |  | ZN Method | PSO-IMC based PID | BCO-IMC based PID |
|---|---|---|---|---|
| Case I | $\lambda$ |  | 0.4142 | 0.3506 |
|  | $K_p$ | 9.7917 | 2.7346 | 2.9381 |
|  | $K_I$ | 8.2899 | 0.5209 | 0.5598 |
|  | $K_D$ | 1.7485 | 0.6511 | 0.6998 |
|  | ISE | 72.43 | 10.34 | 10.13 |
| Case II | $\lambda$ |  | 0.2839 | 1.6778 |
|  | $K_p$ | 3.2583 | 0.0989 | 0.0937 |
|  | $K_I$ | 0.1114 | 0.0057 | 0.0054 |
|  | $K_D$ | 15.519 | 0.3531 | 0.3347 |
|  | ISE | 39800 | 44220 | 709.5 |

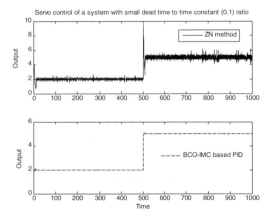

**Fig. 3.** Servo control of the BCO-IMC and ZN based PID controller for a system with $\theta/\tau=0.1$

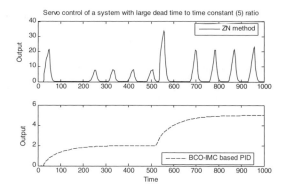

**Fig. 4.** Servo control of the BCO-IMC and ZN based PID controller for a system with θ/τ=5

# 6   Conclusion

This paper proposes a novel idea for the optimal design of the PID controller using BCO based IMC. The scheme requires tuning of a single parameter λ which in turn is used to tune the PID controller parameters. Tuning of PID controller for a system with large θ/τ cannot be accomplished using ZN tuning. In the proposed controller design, an attempt has been made to tune the PID controller parameters for the system with large θ/τ. The design, implementation and testing of BCO-IMC based PID is compared with that of the ZN based PID and the superiority of the proposed scheme is guaranteed. Also, with BCO-IMC based PID controller, improved performance index is achieved specifying faster settling time and higher robustness for any system irrespective of θ/τ ratio.

# References

1. Liu, J.K.: Advanced PID control and MATLAB simulation, 2nd edn. Publishing House of Electronics Industry (September 2004)
2. Krohling, R., Rey, J.: Design of optimal disturbance rejection PID controllers using Genetic algorithms. IEEE Transaction on Evolutionary computation 5(1) (February 2001)
3. Chwee, T.F.: Self-tuning PID controllers for dead time process. IEEE Transaction 35(1), 119–125 (1988)
4. Santacesaria, C., Scattolini, R.: Easy tuning of Smith predictor in presence of delay uncertainly. Automatica 29, 1595–1597 (1993)
5. Lee, D.K., Lee, M.Y., Sung, S.W.: Robust PID tuning for Smith presence of uncertain. J. Process Control 9(1), 79–85 (1999)
6. Hu, Q., Rangaiah, G.P.: Internal Model Control with Feedback Compensation for Uncompensation for Uncertain nonlinear Systems. International Journal of Control 74(14), 1456–1466 (2001)
7. Carcia, C.E., Morari: Internal Model Control-1: A Unifying Review and Some New Results. Ind. Eng. Chem. Proc. Des. 21, 308–323 (1982)
8. Tan, G.T., Chiu, M.-S.: A Multiple-Model Approach to Decentralized Internal Model Control Design. Chemical Engineering Science 56, 6651–6660 (2001)

9. Datta, A., Ochoa, J.: Adaptive Internal Model Control: Design and Stability Analysis. Automatica 32(2), 261–266 (1996)
10. Brosilow, C.B.: Incorporating process uncertainty and analytic design of PID controller into undergraduate process control. Computers in Engineering Education (June 1996)
11. Himer, Z.: Fuzzy control of combustion with Genetic learning automata. In: Proceedings of 16th European Simulation Symposium (2004)
12. Seborg, D.: Process Dynamics and control. John Wiley, Chichester (1989)
13. Nakrani, S., Tovey, C.: On honey bees and dynamic allocation in an internet server colony. Adaptive Behavior 12(3-4), 223–240 (2004)
14. Seeley, T.D.: The Wisdom of the Hive. Publication Harward University Press
15. Teodorovic, D., Dell'orco, M.: Bee colony optimization - A cooperative learning approach to complex transportation problems. Advanced OR and AI Methods in Transportation, 51–60 (2005)
16. Varol, H.A., Bingul, Z.: A new PID technique using ant algorithm. In: Proc. of the American Control Conference 2004, vol. 3, pp. 2154–2159 (2004)
17. Sarma, O.V.S., Rajkumar, S.M.G., Ramkumar, K.: Real time application of ants colony optimization. International Journal of Computer Applications 3(8), 1–6 (2010)
18. Karaboga, D., Akay, B.B.: Proportional-Integral-derivative controller design by using artificial bee colony, harmony sea and the bees algorithms. Journal Proceedings of the Institution of Mechanical Engineers, Part I: Journal of Systems and Control Engineering
19. Das, S., Biswas, A., Abraham, A., Dasgupta, S.: Design of fractional order $PI\lambda D\mu$ controllers with an improved differential evolution. In: Engineering Applications of Artificial Intelligence, vol. 22(2), pp. 343–350. Elsevier Science, Amsterdam (2009)
20. Chowdhury, A., Ghosh, A., Das, S., Abraham, A.: A hybrid eolutionary direct search technique for solving optimal control problems. In: Tenth International Conference of Hybrid Intelligent Systems, USA, pp. 125–30. IEEE, Los Alamitos (2010) ISBN 978-1-4244-7364-9

# An Efficient Estimation of Distribution Algorithm for Job Shop Scheduling Problem

Xiao-juan He[1,2], Jian-chao Zeng[2], Song-dong Xue[2], and Li-fang Wang[2]

[1] College of Electrical and Information Engineering, Lanzhou University of Technology,
Lanzhou 730050, China
[2] Complex System and Computational Intelligence Laboratory,
Taiyuan University of Science and Technology, Taiyuan 030024, China
hexj1993@tom.com

**Abstract.** An estimation of distribution algorithm with probability model based on permutation information of neighboring operations for job shop scheduling problem was proposed. The probability model was given using frequency information of pair-wise operations neighboring. Then the structure of optimal individual was marked and the operations of optimal individual were partitioned to some independent sub-blocks. To avoid repeating search in same area and improve search speed, each sub-block was taken as a whole to be adjusted. Also, stochastic adjustment to the operations within each sub-block was introduced to enhance the local search ability. The experimental results show that the proposed algorithm is more robust and efficient.

**Keywords:** Job Shop scheduling problem, estimation of distribution algorithm, neighboring operations, probability model.

## 1 Introduction

The Job Shop scheduling problem (JSP) is one of the well-known NP-hard combinatorial optimization problems. Many methods for JSP were proposed[1]. The traditional methods such as branch-and-bound, mixed integer programming, and linear programming were not practical because they require a large amount of computation time especially for large scale problem solving[2]. Instead, a lot of researchers put their effort into meta-heuristic and local search optimization strategies for solving JSP. Among those are priority dispatching rules, shifting bottleneck procedure, tabu search algorithm, simulated annealing method, etc[3]. Evolutionary algorithms have also been applied to JSP solving and especially genetic algorithm displays obvious superiority[4,5,6]. Recently, an evolutionary algorithm based on probability analysis, i.e., estimation of distribution algorithms (EDAs)[7,8] has became very popular. The algorithm relies on the construction and maintenance of a probability model that characterizes satisfactory solutions for a problem. Some better solutions are selected from population and are used to update the probability model iteratively. This probabilistic model is used to guide further exploration of search

B.K. Panigrahi et al. (Eds.): SEMCCO 2010, LNCS 6466, pp. 656–663, 2010.

space and realize evolution process. EDAs effectively overcomes the problem of blocks being disrupted, has shown to perform very well on a wide variety of problems. Clearly, the key of EDAs for solving JSP is a probability model constructing[9]. Because of the complexity of job shop scheduling problem, it is very difficult to build a probability model being characteristics of JSP problem. Therefore the estimation of distribution algorithms is seldom applied in this field. In this paper, a new EDAs using frequency information of multi-operations neighboring was proposed for avoiding need of complex probability model in JSP solving.

This paper is organized as follows: In Section 2, we shortly describe the basic framework of EDAs and JSP. Section 3 gives a detail description of new proposed algorithm for JSP. Section 4 discusses the experimental results and shows the efficiency of proposed algorithm. Finally, Section 5 summarizes the contribution of this paper.

## 2   Problems Description

### 2.1   Job Shop Scheduling Problem

The job shop scheduling problem can be briefly described as follows[2]. There are n jobs to be processed through m machines. Each job consists of a sequence of operations. The operations of each job must be processed in the given sequence. The processing time is fixed and known. There are several constraints on jobs and machines as follows: 1) There are precedence constraints among operations of one job and there are no precedence constraints among operations of different job; 2) Each machine can process at most one operation at a time interval, and it cannot be interrupted; and 3) At most one operation of each job can be processed at a time interval. The objective of JSP is determining the appropriate operation sequences for all jobs that minimizes makespan($C_{\max}'$).

### 2.2   Basic Framework of EDAs

EDAs has introduced a new paradigm of evolutionary computation, representing relations between the variables involved in the problem domain by building probability model. According to the complexity of probability models and different sampling methods, EDAs has a lot of different concrete realization methods. Main steps are summarized as follows:

Step 1. Generate initial population.
Step 2. Evaluate population. Constructed probability model according to the information of some better individuals selected from population.
Step 3. Generate new population sampling from the constructed model, evaluate new population.
Step 4. Update the probability model.

Repeat do the step 3and step 4 until the termination criteria is met.

# 3  EDAs for JSP

## 3.1  Encoding and Decoding Methods

The encoding method most used to solve the scheduling problem is operation-based encoding. Thus, we also apply this method in this paper. The same number denotes different operations of the same job, meaning their order of appearance in chromosome representation. The times which each job will appear in chromosome equal to the numbers of all operations of each job. For example, in a 3*3 job shop problem, a scheduling is denoted as 9 numbers, each job will appear 3 times exactly. An individual (1 3 2 2 1 3 3 2 1) is generated randomly, which denotes in turn process operations. '1'shows job1, '2'shows job2, '3'shows job3, and the 1th 1 shows the 1 operation of job 1, and the 2th 1 shows the 2 operation of job 1, and the 3th 1 shows the 3 operation of job 1, in the same way, etc. The important feature of the encoding method is that all offspring generation are feasible scheduling.

The decoding is done by priority-based way. That is, according to the order given operations in schedule and the current machine's idling state as well as the current operation's processing state, the operation that has the earliest starting time can be selected to be processed under the conditions both of the order remaining and of the other operations not being delayed.

## 3.2  Population Initialization and Fitness Evaluate

Let the set of operations $(o_{11}...o_{1m}, o_{21}...o_{2m}, ..., o_{n1}...o_{nm}) \rightarrow (o_1, o_2, ..., o_{n \times m})$ , $\pi = (\pi(1), \pi(2), ..., \pi(n \times m))$ is a integer permutation form 1 to $n \times m$. Let the population be N.. N integer sequences are randomly generated and consist of the initial population. One sequence of operations denotes one individual. Evaluate the fitness (makespan) of individuals. The less makespan be, the larger the corresponding value of fitness. Some better individuals are selected as superior population according to some proportional. Let the superior population size be D.

## 3.3  Construct and Update Probability Model

In this paper, we have constructed probability model according to the order of operations of individuals in superior population based on edge histogram[10]. Let the initial population be represented as $P(0)$ , and the initial superior population be represented as $D^0$ . The kth individual is as $x_k^0 = (\pi_k^0(1), \pi_k^0(2), ..., \pi_k^0(n \times m))$ , set $k \in D$ . The initial population is generated by uniform distribution. Through calculating the frequencies of pair-wise neighboring operations appearing in superior population $D^0$ , the probability matrix is constructed as follows:

$$P^t = \begin{bmatrix} p_{11}^t & p_{12}^t & \cdots & p_{1,n \times m}^t \\ p_{21}^t & p_{22}^t & \cdots & p_{2,n \times m}^t \\ \cdots & \cdots & \cdots & \cdots \\ p_{n \times m,1}^t & p_{n \times m,2}^t & \cdots & p_{n \times m,n \times m}^t \end{bmatrix}$$

Where t represents the iterative number, and t=1.

$$p_{ij}^{t} = (1-\alpha) \cdot \frac{1}{n \times m} + \frac{1}{D} \sum_{k=1}^{D} \delta_{ij}(x_k^0) , \quad i,j = 1,2,...n \times m \qquad (1)$$

$$\delta_{ij}(x_k^0) = \begin{cases} 1 & \pi_k^0(h) \to o_i \wedge \pi_k^0(h+1) \to o_j \\ 0 & otherelse \end{cases} \qquad (2)$$

where $h \in \{1,2,...,(n \times m-1)\}$, $\delta_{ij}(x_k^0)$ equals to 1 denotes that the neighboring operation $o_i o_j$ appear in the structure of the kth individual. Otherwise $\delta_{ij}(x_k^0)$ equals to 0. The parameter $\alpha$ is a learning rate, and $\alpha \in (0,1)$. The higher the Parameter $\alpha$ is, the greater the contribution of the previous generation population to the next generation population is, otherwise the weaker the contribution. At the same time, This statistics way can increase the probability that the pair-wise neighboring operations appearing by high frequency evolve to the next generation population.

At iteration t(t>1), The new probability matrix is built through computing the frequencies of the pair-wise neighboring operations appearing in superior population $D^t$. Updated the probability is as follows[8]:

$$p_{ij}^{t+1} = (1-\alpha) \cdot p_{ij}^{t} + \alpha \cdot \frac{1}{D} \sum_{k=1}^{D} \delta_{ij}(x_k^t) , \quad i,j = 1,2,...n \times m \qquad (3)$$

### 3.4  The Process of Block Optimization

According to the value of probability matrix, the structure of optimal individual is divided into some independent sub-blocks.

#### 3.4.1  Construct the Model of Block Structure

If there are multi-neighboring operations, their frequency appearing in superior population is higher. Then in order to avoid the multi-neighboring operations being destroyed and repeating search in same space in iterative process, these operations are connected into a whole block and take part in iterative process.

At iteration $l$, let the corresponding probability matrix be $P^l$. According to $P^l$, the model of block structure is built by dividing to the structure of optimal individual.

Here, a parameter $\partial$ is set advanced. $\partial$ means a connection condition, set $\partial \in (0,1)$. If the frequency of multi-neighboring operations appearing in superior population is bigger than the parameter $\partial$, then these neighboring operations can be connected into a block. The $\partial$ is bigger, the frequency is higher. Conversely it is lower. The main process is as follows: denotes the optimal individual as $x^* = (\pi_*^l(1), \pi_*^l(2),...,\pi_*^l(n \times m))$, and set $\pi_*^l(h) \to o_i \wedge \pi_*^l(h+1) \to o_j$.

Corresponding to the matrix $P^l$, we consider that the operation $o_i$ and $o_j$ have relativity and belong to a same sub-block if $p_{ij}$ is higher than $\partial$. Otherwise they belong to different sub-block. Then, they separately being as a whole take part in next iterative process.

If value of $\partial$ is too small, the connection condition is too easy to be met, then the multi-neighboring operations can rapidly be connected into a sub block, which will lead to the local optimum of the algorithm. Conversely, if $\partial$ is too bigger, the connection condition is difficult to be met, and the algorithm is always searching in whole space, and the search efficiency will be lowered, which can not easy to search the optimal solution. Generally empirical set $\partial \in (0.7, 0.9)$.

### 3.4.2 Generate Initial Sub-block Population

Let the number of sub-blocks be integer R. M permutations are randomly generated form 1 to R as sub-block initial population. Let initial sub-block superior population be represented by $G^0$.

### 3.4.3 Built and Update Block Probability Model

The fitness of individuals is calculated according to permutation of sub-blocks. Select the optimal individual and the sub-block superior population. Let the size of the sub-block superior population be m. At iteration t, let the sub-block superior population be $G^t$. The kth individual is denoted as $y_k^t = (\tau_k^t(1), \tau_k^t(2), ..., \tau_k^t(R))$, $k \in m$. Because the sub-blocks are independent each other, and the order among all sub-blocks can be arbitrarily exchanged, so in the $G^t$, the frequencies by which each sub-block is arranged on all positions are computed, the block model of probability is built as follows:

$$Q^t = \begin{bmatrix} q_{11}^t & q_{12}^t & \cdots & q_{1R}^t \\ q_{21}^t & q_{22}^t & \cdots & q_{2R}^t \\ \cdots & \cdots & \cdots & \cdots \\ q_{R1}^t & q_{R2}^t & \cdots & q_{RR}^t \end{bmatrix}$$

Where $q_{ij}^t$ is the probability in which the ith sub-block is arranged on the jth position. Set i, j=1,2,...R. In the iterative process, The probability is updated as follows[3]:

$$q_{ij}^{t+1} = (1-\beta).q_{ij}^t + \beta.\frac{1}{m}\sum_{k=1}^{m}\lambda_{kij}^t(y_k^t) \tag{4}$$

$$\lambda_{kij}^t = \begin{cases} 1 & \tau_k^t(i) \text{ is arranged on the jth position} \\ 0 & \text{otherwise} \end{cases} \tag{5}$$

Set $\beta \in (0,1)$, $\alpha$ and $\beta$ have the same meaning. The values of $\alpha$ and $\beta$ may be equal or not. Let $\alpha$ equal to $\beta$ in this paper.

### 3.4.4  Generate New Sub-block Population

The new sub-block population are generated by roulette wheel sampling from each column of the probability model $Q'$. The new sub-block superior population are chosen from new sub-block population, then return to step 3.4.3, the probability model $Q'$ will be updated.

The above steps from 3.4.3 to 3.4.4 are done repeatedly. When the fitness value of optimal individual remains unchanged in continual several iterative processes, two positions are randomly generated and their operations are exchanged within each sub-block, thus some new individuals will be generated. Let these new individuals and the individuals of sub block superior population be combined and then be reorder according to their fitness value, and then the new sub-block superior population is selected from them again.

## 3.5  Generate New Population

In this paper, the new population contains two portions. First portion contains N individuals which are generated by roulette wheel sampling from probability matrix $P'$. The sampling method is as follows: Randomly select a initial point(operation), $o_i$ for example, the next operation is selected from the ith row of probability matrix $P'$ by roulette wheel. If the selected next operation is $o_j$, then the next operation is selected again from the jth row of probability matrix $P'$ using roulette wheel, etc. Until all operations are selected. The other portion is the new sub-block superior population which is obtained through the process of block optimization. Let these two portion populations compose of the new population and go to 3.3.

Do repeatedly the above step from 3.3 to 3.5 until the termination criteria are met. The elitist strategy is applied to the whole iterative process for ensuring the convergence of algorithm.

In order to illustrate the performances of the proposed algorithm, no other heuristic algorithm is used in optimal process. The proposed algorithm is a blind search algorithm.

# 4  Computational Results

In this paper, we use some instances that are taken from the OR_Library as test benchmarks to test our new proposed algorithm. In these instances, FT06, FT10 and FT20 are designed by Fisher and Thompso and the others are the first instance of other type instance set. Because the proposed algorithm in this paper is a pure EDAs that doesn't hybrid other heuristic algorithms in optimal process, so the computation results are compared with pure PSO[6]. In pure PSO, the population size is 30 and the most iteration number is $10^5$. In this paper, the parameters are defined in the following: the population size is 30 and the most iteration number is 5000. Let the selected proportion of the superior population be 0.3, and set $\alpha$ =0.15and $\partial$ =0.9. When the fitness value of the best solution is not improved after the continual 5 times in iteration process, the process of block optimal is executed. After the process of block optimal iterates 5 times, return the next iterative process. Each instance is executed for 10 runs. In Table 1, Instance means the problem name. Size means the problem size. Optimum means the best known solution for the test instance. Let Min/Max/Average separately be the minimum value, maximal value and average value which are obtained in 10 iteration process of each instance.

**Table 1.** The experimental results comparison of EDAs and the PSO for JSP

| Instance | Size | Optimum | algorithm | | | | | | |
|----------|------|---------|-----------|------|---------|------|------|---------|
| | | | PSO | | | EDAs | | |
| | | | Min | Max | average | Min | Max | average |
| FT06 | 6×6 | 55 | 55 | 59 | 56.1 | 55 | 55 | 55.0 |
| FT10 | 10×10 | 930 | 985 | 1084 | 1035.6 | 937 | 937 | 937.0 |
| FT20 | 20×5 | 1165 | 1208 | 1352 | 1266.9 | 1184 | 1184 | 1184.0 |
| LA01 | 10×5 | 666 | 666 | 688 | 668.6 | 666 | 666 | 666.0 |
| LA06 | 15×5 | 926 | 926 | 926 | 926.0 | 926 | 926 | 926.0 |
| LA11 | 20×5 | 1222 | 1222 | 1222 | 1222 | 1222 | 1222 | 1222.0 |
| LA16 | 10×10 | 945 | 945 | 956 | 1035 | 945 | 946 | 945.5 |
| LA21 | 15×10 | 1046 | 1102 | 1147 | 1128.4 | 1071 | 1073 | 1071.6 |
| LA26 | 20×10 | 1218 | 1263 | 1351 | 1312.6 | 1257 | 1261 | 1257.8 |
| LA31 | 30×10 | 1784 | 1789 | 1897 | 1830.4 | 1789 | 1789 | 1789.0 |
| LA36 | 15×15 | 1268 | 1373 | 1436 | 1409.2 | 1292 | 1315 | 1312.7 |

From the result of Table 1, we can see that the values of Min, Max and Average in EDAs are all less than those in the pure PSO. This shows that EDAs has better performance than pure PSO. At the same time, the difference among Min, Max and Average in EDAs is very small. It shows that EDAs has well stability.

## 5   Conclusions

In this paper, we adopt EDAs to solve the job shop scheduling problem. The probability model is built through considering the information of neighboring operations appearing in superior population. This makes the probability model well reflect the character of job shop scheduling problem, and improves the ability of EDAs to solve job shop scheduling problem. The simulation results show that the proposed algorithm is more robust and efficient. Because the algorithm is a blind search without hybrid other heuristics search algorithm, then we test the performance of hybrid algorithm remain for future.

**Acknowledgments.** This paper is supported by The Shanxi Science Foundation for Young Scientists under Grant 2010021017-2.

# References

1. Garey, M.R., Johnson, D.S., Sethi, R.: The complexity of flowshop and jobshop scheduling. Mathematics of Operations Research 1, 117–129 (1976)
2. Blazewicz, J., Domschke, W., Pesch, E.: The job shop scheduling problem: Conventional and new solution techniques. European Journal of Operational Research 93, 1–33 (1996)
3. Binato, S., Hery, W.J., Loewenstern, D.M.: Resende M.G.C. 2002, A GRASP for job shop scheduling. In: Ribeiro, C.C., Hansen, P. (eds.) Essays and Surveys in Metaheuristics. Kluwer Academic Publishers, Dordrecht (2002)
4. Watanabe, M., Ida, K., Gen, M.: A genetic algorithm with modified crossover operator and search area adaptation for the job-shop scheduling problem. Computers &Industrial Engineering 48, 743–752 (2005)
5. Lian, Z., Jiao, B., Gu, X.: A similar particle swarm optimization algorithm for job-shop scheduling to minimize makespan. Applied Mathematics and Computation 183, 1008–1017 (2006)
6. Lin, T.-J., Horng, S.-J., Kao, T.-W., Chen, Y.-H., Run, R.-S.: An efficient job-shop scheduling algorithm based on particle swarm optimization. Expert Systems with Applications 37, 2629–2636 (2010)
7. Baluja, S.: Population-Based Incremental Learning: A Method for Integrating Genetic Search Based Function Optimization and Competitive Learning. Technical Report CMU-CS-95-163. Carnegie Mellon University, Pittsburgh (1994)
8. Pelikan, M., Goldberg, D.E., Lobo, F.: A Survey of Optimization by Building and Using Probabilistic Models. ILLiGAL Report No.99018, University of Illinois at Urbana Champaign, Illinois Genetic Algorithms Laboratory, Urbana, Illinois (1999)
9. Pelikan, M., Goldberg, D.E., Cantu-Paz, E.: BOA: the Bayesian Optimization Algorithm. In: Proceedings of the Genetic and Evolutionary Computation Conference GECCO 1999, vol. I, pp. 525–532 (1999)
10. Tsutsui, S.: Probabilistic Model-Building Genetic Algorithms in Permutation Representation Domain Using Edge Histogram. In: Guervós, J.J.M., Adamidis, P.A., Beyer, H.-G., Fernández-Villacañas, J.-L., Schwefel, H.-P. (eds.) PPSN 2002. LNCS, vol. 2439, Springer, Heidelberg (2002)

# Semantic Web Service Discovery Algorithm Based on Swarm System*

Qiu Jian-ping and Chen Lichao

School of Computer Science,
Taiyuan University of Science and Technology,
Taiyuan, Shanxi, 030024, China
choujianp@yahoo.com.cn

**Abstract.** Lacking effective web services or a chain of web services in web, a semantic web service discovery algorithm based on swarm system is proposed. Firstly, we assume that there is no central registry for services information and we use a distributed registry for storing services information. Then, in the case no single service can satisfy user request we will chain existing services to create a composite service answering user request. At last, we use VAR-GARCH (Vector Auto Regression Generalized Autoregressive Conditional Heteroskedasticity) model for service composition which incrementally gathers required services information and check them to satisfy a desired chain.

**Keywords:** Swarm System, Semantic Web, Service Discovery algorithm.

## 1 Introduction

Web services can be considered as distributed software components in the web. They are self-contained, self-describing, modular applications that can be published, located, and invoked across the Web. By using web services we can only implement our main business logic and outsource other parts from these modular applications through the web. Even If no single web service can satisfy the functionality required by the user, there should be a possibility to combine existing services together in order to fulfill the request.

Because of large number of web services in internet, it is not possible for users to know all of them to use for satisfying their requirements, so an automatic system is needed to gather services information and define an appropriate service or chain of services for satisfying user requirements. In the following sections we will represent our system which can be used for finding appropriate services based on user requests. First we will mention some related works in this field then we will explain the overall architecture of the system and introduce and explain its different parts.

## 2 Background

In this section, we discuss the previous works related to our work. These subjects are semantic web services and web service composition.

---

* Supported by project for research on learning and teaching of Taiyuan University of science and technology.

B.K. Panigrahi et al. (Eds.): SEMCCO 2010, LNCS 6466, pp. 664–671, 2010.

**Semantic Web Services.** Standard web services are described by a WSDL file which introduces service operations and how to connect to the service. WSDL contains only syntactic information and or little semantic information, so it can not be used by software agents to infer about services or to compose them.

To enable automatic reasoning in the field of web services, semantic web technologies were employed (Antoniou G). Semantic web and web services are synergistic: the semantic web transforms the web into a repository of computer readable data, while web services provide the tools for the automatic use of that data. Thus, the concept of Semantic Web Service was established. Based on concise and unambiguous semantic description frameworks for web services and related aspects, generic inference mechanisms can be developed for reasoning about semantic web services. OWL-S is the one that semantic web offers for describing web services base on OWL. OWL (web ontology language) is an extension to XML and the Resource Description Framework (RDF) enabling the creation of ontology's for any domain and the instantiation of this ontology's in the description of resources for semantic web.  A service operation in OWL-S is described by its input, output, preconditions and effects. Input and outputs are ontology classes that operation receives and returns. Preconditions are conditions on world state required prior invoking operation and effects are changes caused by operation on world state.  In this work, we use a simplified semantic model for web services which can be obtained from any semantic web services model.

**Web Service Composition.** From one perspective web service composition methods can divide into vertical and horizontal types (B.Medjahed, 2004). In vertical composition the structure of composite service is given by user as an abstract process and the system is responsible for binding abstract services to best concrete services. This binding can be according to parameters such as quality of services or other parameters. Horizontal composition method tries to obtain the chain of services suitable for user requirements from available service descriptions. Some methods in this category are related to AI planning and deductive theorem proving. The general assumption of this kinds of methods is that each Web service can be specified by its preconditions and effects in the planning context and AI planning methods can used for creating the chain (J.Rao,2004). In this paper we use a kind of VAR-GARCH algorithm for finding the chain.

# 3   Contributions

As mentioned before our goal is building a system for finding a service or chain of services. We have these assumptions in our system which makes it different from previous works:

Because of large number of services we can not assume that there is a central registry for services.

It is not required for services to belong to a special category.

The system should recognize the chain of services when it is not given by the user. The problem can be defined as below:

There is a set of available services on the Internet. Every service has a corresponding service description. There is no central registry for accessing services information. Users request the system for a certain service or chain of services. The system responds by finding a chain of services that can satisfy the user request.

Two problems are considered. The first problem is how to present services and distribute their information so that they could be stored and retrieved efficiently and the second problem is how to find the appropriate service chain. In the next section the system's overall functionality is explained and the solutions to these two problems.

## 4   System Architectures

Figure1 shows our system overall architecture. There are several conceptual parts in this architecture. The query interface allows users to request the system. The query interface passes the user request to composer part. The composer first tries to find a service that can satisfy user request using distributed registry. If does not exist such a service, it tries recursively to find a chain of services that can satisfy user request. There is no central registry in this system so the distributed registry should find services information which is distributed in different nodes. It uses VAR-GARCH algorithm to do this; the details is explained later.

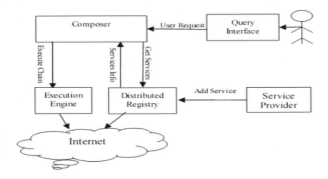

**Fig. 1.** System Overall Architecture

We have two logical types of nodes in this system which may be physically on a same node or on different nodes. We define logical node to be an application program which perform certain operation and can be physically located in one or more physical node. We consider two kinds of logical node called: service provider nodes and registry nodes. Service provider nodes are nodes which deliver services. Registry nodes are responsible for storage and retrieval of services information. Every service provider node should introduce itself to one of these registry nodes when entering the system. Registry nodes can leave and join the network in an arbitrary manner.

When a chain is found it is given to the execution engine to be executed. The execution engine carries the chain of services by performing each individual service together with necessary transformation which may be needed for connection of services. At the end the results will be returned to the user.

## 5   Creating Service Chain

The overall work of system can be seen as this:  a user gives his request as a set of inputs and a set of desired outputs, and the system should return a service or a chain of services which can receive user inputs and finally generate user requested outputs. For solving the problem we use a VAR-GARCH algorithm in which coefficients is estimated from service providers and users and uncertainty which neither the user nor the service provider can control.

VAR-GARCH algorithm (QIU Jianping, 2005)

In simplest form: $C = \mu + \xi + \varepsilon$

Where,

C = sum of three forecasts

$\mu$ = service provider's forecast

$\xi$ = user's query

$\varepsilon$ = uncertainty

The user has sources and/or experience to derive private forecast information $\xi$ which is not known to the service provider in a distributed system (information asymmetry).

However, the service provider can categorize the user into certain "types" based on prior actions of the user. Thus, the service provider updates its "forecast" of the user and may select a value of $\xi$ assumed to be represented by a normal distribution.

This introduces a random (stochastic) variable. Uncertainty is given by epsilon ($\varepsilon$) and neither the user nor the service provider can control its value.

Classic linear regression models (CLRM) have been around for a century and widely used for a variety of purposes. CLRM may be expressed as an equation for a straight line:

$$y_t = \beta_0 + \beta_1 x_t + \varepsilon_t \tag{0}$$

Where,

y = dependent variable to be modeled for forecast (for example, query of a user)

t = time period (frequency of observation, for example, t-1 may indicate prior week 1)

$\beta$ = coefficients to be estimated (based on values of y and x)

x = explanatory variable that is used to 'explain' variations in the dependent variable y.

$\varepsilon$ = random (stochastic) term

This simple technique can model multiple explanatory variables, that is, multiple x's, since the variation in y is dependent on multiple parameters. Therefore, x's may be based on underlying theoretical principles and/or practical logic. However, no matter how many x's are included, there may be an inherent randomness that cannot be explained by the model. Thus, the random term ($\varepsilon$) is included in the equation (admission of the fact that the dependent variable (y) cannot be modeled perfectly). To solve for y, a bold assumption is made that ε is characterized by a normal distribution with a mean = 0 and variance = $\sigma^2$ for all time periods (t): $\varepsilon_t \sim N(0, \sigma^2)$.

The objective of CLRM is to estimate the parameters ($\beta_0, \beta_1$) of the model (from data on y and x), depending on the sample of observations on y and x. Therefore, there can be multiple sets of ($\beta_0, \beta_1$) that can produce straight lines with varying slopes (gradient). This statistical procedure introduces two sources of error. First, taking sample data from a large number of observations inherits sampling errors. One reason for use of sample data (as practiced by the Census) may stem from lack of granular data acquisition tools. Another reason may be a lack of computing power. With low cost yet powerful microprocessors and the emergence of Grid computing, we may be increasingly better prepared to process exabytes of raw data. Second, given the multiple sets of ($\beta_0, \beta_1$) that may be estimated, the objective of CLRM is to choose that pair of ($\beta_0$, $\beta_1$) which minimizes the sum of squared residuals ($e_1^2, e_2^2, \cdots, e_n^2$). Where, $e_t$ is the random error term for the sample and $\varepsilon_t$ represents the random error term of the 'population' data. This technique is known as the principle of ordinary least squares (OLS). The sole objective of OLS is to minimize forecast errors by selecting the most suitable ($\beta_0, \beta_1$), thus ignoring the volatility of the sample.

The attractiveness of CLRM based forecasting stems from the fact that we can model cross variable linkages. The regression model is an explicit multi-variate model. Hence, forecasts are made not only on the basis of the variable's own historical data but also taking into account the historical data of other related and relevant explanatory variables, $x_1$ through $x_K$, that is, any number of x's.

With time series techniques, let us develop the concept by starting with a basic CLRM equation:

$$y_t = \beta_0 + \beta_1 x_{1t} + \beta_2 x_{2t} + \cdots + \beta_K x_{Kt} + \varepsilon_t \tag{1}$$

The effect of change in only one explanatory variable ($x_1, \cdots, x_K$) may be analyzed at a time (all else remains constant). Therefore, in building this model, the choice of x is a process decision based on the model builder's knowledge about the operation.

We start by forecasting the values of x's to obtain an unconditional forecast for y. Instead of inserting arbitrary values for future x's, we use forecasted values based on historical data. To forecast x, we fit an univariate model to x where we use past (lagged) values of x to forecast x, as given in equation 2(for $x_{1t}, \cdots, x_{Kt}$):

$$x_{1t} = \alpha_{01} + \alpha_{11}x_{1t-1} + \alpha_{12}x_{1t-2} + \cdots + \alpha_{1N_{x_{1t}}}x_{1t-N_{x_{1t}}} + \mu_{x_{1t}}$$

$$\vdots$$ 

(2)

$$x_{Kt} = \alpha_{01} + \alpha_{11}x_{kt-1} + \alpha_{12}x_{kt-2} + \cdots + \alpha_{1N_{x_{kt}}}x_{1t-N_{x_{kt}}} + \mu_{x_{kt}}$$

$$y_t = \beta_0 + \sum_{i=1}^{N_{x_1}} \alpha_{1i}x_{1t-i} + \cdots + \sum_{i=1}^{N_{x_{kt}}} \alpha_{Ki}x_{Kt-i} + \varepsilon_t .$$

(3)

$$y_t = \beta_0 + \sum_{k=1}^{K}\sum_{i=1}^{N_{x_{kt}}} \alpha_{ki}x_{kt-i} + \varepsilon_t$$

(4)

Where,

$x_{1t}$ = variable x1 at time t

$x_{Kt}$ = variable $x_K$ at time t (up to K number of x's)

$x_{1t-1}$ = value of $x_1$ at time t-1 (referred to as the lagged value by one period)

N = period up to which the lagged values of $x_{1t}$ will be used in the equation

$\mu$ = random error term

In equation 2, $\alpha_{11}, \alpha_{12}$ are coefficients of $x_{1t-1}, x_{1t-2}$ and are referred to as lagged weights. An important distinction is that instead of arbitrarily assigning weights, these coefficients are estimated using OLS technique. The error term in equation 2 represented by $\mu$ is analogous to $\varepsilon$ in equation 1. Depending on the number of x's ($x_1, \cdots, x_K$) that adequately represents the process being modeled in equation 1, there will be K number of equations (of the type equation 2) that must be estimated to forecast the x's $x_1, \cdots, x_K$) which will then be used to obtain an unconditional forecast of y. Thus, to simplify the task, we can estimate all the parameters ($\alpha, \beta$) simultaneously by re-writing equation 1, the basic CLRM equation, as equation 3 or its shortened version, as in equation 4 (above).

Equation 4 is another step toward forecasting the dependent variable (y) with greater accuracy using forecasts of x's based on historical data of x's (lagged values). But no sooner, we have moved a step ahead, it is clear that equation 4 ignores the impact on y of the past values of y itself. Consequently, a preferable model will include not only lagged values of x but also lagged values of y, as shown in equation 5 (below).

$$y_t = \beta_0 + \sum_{j=1}^{N_y} \varphi_j y_{t-j} + \sum_{k=1}^{K}\sum_{i=1}^{N_{x_{kt}}} \alpha_{ki}x_{kt-i} + \varepsilon_t$$

(5)

Present observation of a variable to its past history, for example:

$$y_t \text{ to } y_{t-1}, y_{t-2}, \cdots, y_{t-p}$$

Where, p indicates the order of the autoregressive process AR (p) or the period up to which the historical data will be used (a determination made by using other statistical tools). Thus, AR is a technique by which a variable can be regressed on its own lagged values. AR (p) is appealing to forecasters because a real-world model must link the present to the past (yet remain dynamic). MA expresses current observations of a variable in terms of current and lagged values of the random error $\varepsilon_t, \varepsilon_{t-1}, \varepsilon_{t-2}, \cdots, \varepsilon_{t-q}$ where q is the order of the moving average process MA (q). Combining AR (p) and MA (q) we get ARMA (p, q) where p and q represents the lagging order of AR and MA. Engle used this ARMA technique to model the time varying volatility and proposed the Autoregressive Conditional Heteroskedasticity model or ARCH. The 'conditional' nature of non-constant variance (Heteroskedasticity) refers to the forecasting of variance conditional upon the information set available up to a time period (t). Modeling variance in this fashion allows us to forecast the volatility of the random error term ($\varepsilon$). Using ARCH technique, the variance of the random error term ($\varepsilon_t$) in equation 5 can be expanded in terms of current and lagged values ($\varepsilon_{t-1}, \varepsilon_{t-2}, \cdots, \varepsilon_{t-q}$), as follows:

$$\sigma_t^2 = \theta_0 + \theta_1 \varepsilon_{t-1}^2 + \theta_2 \varepsilon_{t-2}^2 + \cdots + \theta_q \varepsilon_{t-q}^2$$

Where,

$\sigma_t^2$ is the variant of $\varepsilon_t$ [var($\varepsilon_t$)].

$\sigma_t^2$ (the ARCH model) by combining the existing MA(q) with an AR(p) process regresses a variable ($\sigma_t^2$) on its own (past) lagged values ($\sigma_{t-1}^2, \sigma_{t-2}^2, \cdots, \sigma_{t-p}^2$). Thus, variance of the random error term ($\varepsilon$) in a certain period ($\varepsilon_t$) depends not only on previous errors ($\varepsilon_{t-1}, \varepsilon_{t-2}, \cdots, \varepsilon_{t-q}$) but also on the lagged value of the variance ($\sigma_{t-1}, \sigma_{t-2}, \cdots, \sigma_{t-p}$). Thus, GARCH may be represented by equation 6:

$$y_t = \beta_0 + \sum_{j=1}^{N_y} \varphi_j y_{t-j} + \sum_{k=1}^{K} \sum_{i=1}^{N_{x_{kt}}} \alpha_{ki} x_{kt-i} + \varepsilon_t$$

$$\sigma_t^2 = \theta_0 + \sum_{i=1}^{q} \theta_i \varepsilon_{t-i}^2 + \sum_{j=1}^{p} \tau_j \sigma_{t-j}^2 \tag{6}$$

## 6  Conclusions

In this paper we presented a distributed registry and forecast algorithm for web services based on swarm system to answer a user request about finding web services.

By using CLRM (classic linear regression models), we offer a forecast algorithm, we introduce some random variables which neither the user nor the server provider can control its value. Such random variables which can be successively accumulated from each stage of multi-stage forecasts are reduced through the use of analytical tools that combine statistical methods with advances in time series models. Time series models can relate 'current' values of a critical variable to its past (lagged) values and to the values of current and past disturbances or random variables. Moreover, to model real world scenario, VAR-GARCH model is used to represent forecasting results which are generally influenced by interactions between decision makers.

# References

[1] Antoniou, G.V., Hamelem, F.: A semantic web primer. MIT press, Massachusetts
[2] Medjahed, B.: Semantic web enabled composition of web.services, PHD thesis, Virginia Polytechnic Institute (2004)
[3] Rao, J., Su, X.: A Survey of Automated Web Service Composition Methods. In: Cardoso, J., Sheth, A.P. (eds.) SWSWPC 2004. LNCS, vol. 3387, pp. 43–54. Springer, Heidelberg (2005)
[4] Medjahed, B.: Semantic web enabled composition of web.services, PHD thesis, Virginia Polytechnic Institute (2004)
[5] Rao, J., Su, X.: A Survey of Automated Web Service Composition Methods. In: Cardoso, J., Sheth, A.P. (eds.) SWSWPC 2004. LNCS, vol. 3387, pp. 43–54. Springer, Heidelberg (2005)
[6] Jianping, Q.: Supply chain management system based on radio frequency identification. Journal of Computer Applications 25(3), 734–736 (2005)

# Stochastic Ranking Particle Swarm Optimization for Constrained Engineering Design Problems

Samrat L. Sabat[1], Layak Ali[1], and Siba K. Udgata[2]

[1] School of Physics
[2] Department of Computer & Information Sciences
University of Hyderabad, Hyderabad 500046, India
slssp@uohyd.ernet.in, informlayak@gmail.com, udgatacs@uohyd.ernet.in

**Abstract.** This paper presents a novel hybrid algorithm by integrating particle swarm optimization with stochastic ranking for solving standard constrained engineering design problems. The proposed hybrid algorithm uses domain independent characteristics of stochastic ranking and faster convergence of particle swarm optimization. Performance comparison of the proposed algorithm with other popular techniques through comprehensive experimental investigations establishes the effectiveness and robustness of the proposed algorithm for solving engineering design problems.

**Keywords:** Constrained optimization, particle swarm optimization, stochastic ranking.

## 1 Introduction

Constrained Optimization Problems (COP) are the problems which minimizes or maximizes the objective function under certain given constraints such as inequality, equality, upper bound and lower bound. The COP can be formulated as

$$
\begin{aligned}
&Minimize \ f(\overrightarrow{x}), \overrightarrow{x} = (x_1, x_2, \ldots, x_D) \in S \\
&subject \ to: \quad g_i(\overrightarrow{x}) \leq 0, i = 1, 2, \ldots, q \\
&\qquad h_i(\overrightarrow{x}) = 0, i = q+1, q+2, \ldots, m \\
&\qquad l_i \leq x_i \leq u_i, i = 1, 2, \ldots, D
\end{aligned}
\tag{1}
$$

Where $f$ is the objective function, $g_i$, and $h_i$ are the number of inequality and equality constraints respectively. The values $l_i$ and $u_i$ for $1 \leq i \leq D$ are the lower and upper bounds defining the search space S.

Constraint-handling techniques are mainly based on three different methods i.e.,repair method, tournament selection method and penalty method [9,3]. Efficient handling of constraints is a major challenge for evolutionary algorithm (EA) and swarm intelligence (SI) methods in COP. The repair method applies certain operators on the obtained solutions to move an infeasible solution closer

B.K. Panigrahi et al. (Eds.): SEMCCO 2010, LNCS 6466, pp. 672–679, 2010.

to the feasible solution space. In tournament selection method, an individual has to satisfy all constraints before evaluating the objective function. The penalty function is a most common approach for handling constraints. In this method, a penalty factor is used in the objective function to transform the constrained optimization problem to unconstrained optimization problem. Although it is simple, selection of penalty factor is an important issue. The optimum value of penalty factor maintains a proper balance between objective function and penalty function. As penalty factor is mostly problem-dependent it is difficult to decide the optimum value apriori. Stochastic ranking (SR) technique has been proposed [13] to maintain the required balance between objective function and penalty function. This SR technique uses stochastic bubble-sort algorithm to rank the individuals for generating offsprings for the next generation.

Particle Swarm Optimization (PSO) is a population-based SI technique that simulates the social behavior of a group of simple individuals i.e. bird flock or fish school [4]. Based on the collective intelligence, the swarm adjusts its flying direction and search for a global optimum solution. PSO has shown a good performance in solving nonlinear unconstrained optimization problems [11,12]. However the basic PSO, like other evolutionary algorithms, lacks an explicit mechanism to handle constraints which are common in science and engineering optimization problems. A good comparison of different techniques for solving constrained optimization benchmark function along with ensamble of constraint handling techniques can be found in [8]. This paper proposes a stochastic ranking PSO (SRPSO) technique integrating PSO to handle constraints and solve complex constrained engineering design problems [3,10].

This paper is organized as follows. Section 2 briefs about the stochastic ranking technique. Section 3 introduces the basic particle swarm optimization. Section 4 describes the proposed constrained particle swarm optimization technique. Simulation and experimental setup for solving five well-known engineering design problems along with results and discussions are discussed in Section 5 followed by conclusions in Section 6.

## 2   Stochastic Ranking

The constrained optimization problem of equation (1) can be transformed into unconstrained optimization problem with the introduction of penalty factor as

$$\psi(x) = f(x) + r_k \phi(g_i(x); i = 1, 2, \ldots, m) \tag{2}$$

where $\phi \geq 0$ is a real valued function that imposes a penalty. The penalty on each constraint is imposed by the penalty factor $r_k$. Although the above penalty function method works well for certain constrained optimization problems, but selection of penalty factor $r_k$ remains to be a challenge. If the penalty factor is chosen to be too small, an infeasible solution may not be penalized enough (underpenalization), leading to a final infeasible solution. If the penalty factor is too large, a feasible solution is very likely to be found (overpenalization), but could be of very poor quality. Thus underpenalization and overpenalization are not efficient for handling constraints. The optimum value of penalty factor need to be selected for proper balance between objective function and penalty function. To address the problem of underpenalization and overpenalization the stochastic ranking technique has been proposed [13].

The stochastic ranking technique uses a simple bubble-sort algorithm to rank the individuals for producing offsprings for next generation. In stochastic ranking, a probability $P_f$ is introduced to rank individuals. $P_f$ is used to compare the objective function in infeasible regions of the search space. Generally two adjacent individuals are used for comparison. If both are in feasible space, the individual with smaller objective values will be of higher rank. If both adjacent individuals are in infeasible space, the individual with smaller objective value will occupy the higher rank with a probability $P_f$. Similarly all individuals are ranked by comparing adjacent individuals. If one particle is in feasible space and the other one is in infeasible space, then the particle in feasible space awarded with higher rank.

## 3    Particle Swarm Optimization: PSO

PSO is one of the popular SI technique being used for optimization [4]. It utilizes the searching capability of the swarm that arises from the interaction of the simple individuals [4]. Each individual (particle) in the swarm represents a potential solution. Every particle remembers its current position and the best position found so far called personal best (*pbest*). The best solution among the whole swarm is called global best (*gbest*). The location of this particle is communicated to all particles and hence the flying trajectory of the particles is recalculated based on the swarm's *gbest* t and its own *pbest* value as

$$V = V + c_1 * \varepsilon_1 * (pbest - X) + c_2 * \varepsilon_2 * (gbest - X)$$
$$X = X + V$$

where $X$ and $V$ are position and velocity, $c_1$ and $c_2$ are cognitive and social component respectively. $\varepsilon_i$ are independent random variables uniformly distributed in the range $[0, 1]$.

## 4    Stochastic Ranking Particle Swarm Optimization: (SRPSO)

Many studies have been done for solving constrained optimization problems using EA [3,13,2] and PSO [15,14]. PSO shows better performance on unconstrained optimization problems and is also popular for its fast convergence [12,11]. However, PSO neither explicitly nor implicitly has the mechanism to handle constraints. Due to the faster convergence of PSO and effectiveness of stochastic ranking for constraint handling, SRPSO is proposed in this paper as an integration of both stochastic ranking and PSO. Algorithm 1 shows detail implementation steps of proposed SRPSO algorithm. All the $NP$ number

---

**Algorithm 1.** SRPSO

---

**Initialization**

Initialize the swarm of size NP:

Initialize position $'X'$ and velocity $'V'$ in $D$ -dimensional search range $(X_{max}, X_{min})$.

Initialize $c_1 = 1.479, c_2 = 1.479$.

Evaluate the fitness of all particles (NP).

Set the current position as *pbest* of each particle and best pbest value as *gbest*.

**Optimize**

**for** $t \leftarrow 1, Maxgen$ **do**

Update velocity and position of each particle as

$$V_{i,d}^{t+1} = V_{i,d}^t + c_1 * rand_1 * (pbest_{i,d}^t - X_{i,d}^t) + c_2 * rand_2 * (gbest_d^t - X_{i,d}^t) \quad (3)$$

$$X_{i,d}^{t+1} = X_{i,d}^t + V_{i,d}^{t+1} \quad (4)$$

Rank the individuals according to Stochastic Ranking.

Select the highest ranked $\mu$ particles.

Generate NP particles from $\mu$ individuals.

Evaluate fitness of each particle.

Update *pbest*: If current fitness dominates the previous then set current position as *pbest* else retain previous *pbest*.

Update *gbest*: If best of all current *pbest* dominates the previous *gbest* then set current best *pbest* as *gbest* else retain previous *gbest*.

**end for** $t$

continue optimizing until stopping criteria or exceeding maximum iteration

**Report results**

**Terminate**

---

of particles in the population are initialized randomly in the search space. The objective function $f(x)$ and penalty function $\phi(g(x))$ of all $NP$ particles are evaluated. Based on constraint violations, particles are categorized as feasible and infeasible, and are ranked using a simple bubble-sort principle. The balance between underpenalization and overpenalization is achieved by setting the probability $P_f$ to less than $\frac{1}{2}$ [13]. The $P_f$ is used to compare particles in infeasible regions of the search space. If both are in feasible space, the individual with smaller objective values will be of higher rank. If both adjacent individuals are in infeasible space, the individual with smaller objective value will occupy the higher rank with a probability $P_f$. Similarly all individuals are ranked by comparing adjacent individuals. If one particle is in feasible space and the other one is in infeasible space, then the particle in feasible space awarded with higher rank. The highest ranked particle will be global best *gbest* for the current generation and is compared with *gbest* of previous generation. The *gbest* for next generation is determined with minimum objective value of the above two. The personal best *pbest* of the particles are also decided based on the similar stochastic ranking procedure. The highest ranked $\mu$ individuals out of $NP$ are selected for the next generation ($\mu$ is set as $\frac{NP}{7}$). In the next generation $NP$ particles are regenerated again from highest-ranked $\mu$ particles. The learning rate and mean step sizes are set as in [13] and in our experiment $P_f$ is set to 0.45.

# 5   Simulation Results and Discussions

The simulations are carried out using a standard PC with specifications of Pentium Core2Duo, 2GHz with 2GB RAM. Algorithm is coded in Matlab 7.2 in Windows-XP platform. The SRPSO with population size of 100 is executed for 30 independent runs on each function. We have set $c_1$, $c_2$ to be 1.479 and $P_f = 0.45$. The performance of proposed SRPSO algorithm is evaluated for five engineering design problems 1) Welded beam design problem, 2) Pressure vessel design problem, 3) Three-bar truss design problem 4) Speed reducer design problem and 5) Himmelblau Nonlinear problem [3,10].

## 5.1   Engineering Design Problems

The complete design solutions obtained by proposed SRPSO on five engineering design problems are tabulated in Table 1. The first column of Table 1 show different algorithm used for comparison for the design problems. This table also summarizes the statistical results i.e., best, mean, worst, and standard deviation obtained for each design problem. The robustness of the algorithm is tested as a measure of standard deviation on the solutions over 30 independent runs and is also tabulated in Table 1.

**Welded beam design problem**
This problem aims to minimize the cost of beam subject to constraints on shear stress, bending stress, bucking load, and the end deflection. Four continuous design variables are the thickness of the beam, width of the bean, length of the weld, and the weld thickness. The best feasible solution found by SRPSO is $f$ (0.22104332, 5.8282757, 6.6883208, 0.22104332)= 1.7248665802025513. This problem has also been solved in the recent past [6,10,1,5,16,7,17]. A comparison of simulation result statistics is presented in Table 1. The proposed SRPSO gives better performance with regard to quality of solution (mean of all runs), fastness (number of function evaluations), and robustness in terms of standard deviation as compared to other standard and recent reported approaches.

**Pressure vessel design problem**
This problem aims to minimize the fabrication cost of cylindrical pressure vessel subjects to constraints on thickness of pressure vessel, thickness of the head, inner radius of the vessel and length of the vessel. The best solution obtained by SRPSO is $f(0.80866029, 0.3997212, 41.899497, 180.39996)$=5886.1983537314236. This solution is far better than all the existing schemes interms of all considered statistical parameters. It also demonstrates the superiority of proposed SRPSO algorithm for finding the global minima as compared to other techniques with regard to number of function evaluations.

**Speed reducer design problem**
In this constrained optimization problem, the weight of speed reducer is to be minimized subject to constraints on bending stress of the gear teeth, surface stress, transverse deflections of the shafts, and stresses in the shafts. As shown

**Table 1.** Comparison of engineering design problem results of SRPSO with other state-of-the-art

|  | best | mean | worst | std | FES |
|---|---|---|---|---|---|
| WELDED BEAM [10] | | | | | |
| SRPSO | 1.72486658 | 1.72489934 | 1.72542212 | 1.12e-6 | 20,000 |
| CDE [6] | 1.733461 | 1.768158 | 1.824105 | 2.2e-02 | 240,000 |
| Ray and Liew [10] | 2.3854347 | 3.0025883 | 6.3996785 | 9.6e-01 | 33,095 |
| NM-PSO [16] | 1.724717 | 1.726373 | 1.733339 | 0.3e-02 | 200,000 |
| CPSO [5] | 1.728024 | 1.748831 | 1.782143 | 0.129e-01 | 80.000 |
| IHS [7] | 1.7248 | NA | NA | NA | 65,300 |
| DSS-MDE[17] | 2.3809 | 2.38095 | 2.38095 | 2.1e-10 | 24,000 |
| PRESSURE VESSEL [3] | | | | | |
| SRPSO | 5886.1984 | 5942.8353 | 6315.0147 | 80.4459 | 20,000 |
| CDE [6] | 6059.7340 | 6085.2303 | 6371.0455 | 4.3e+01 | 240,000 |
| GQPSO[1] | 6059.7208 | 6440.3786 | 7544.4925 | 448.4711 | NA |
| CPSO [5] | 6061.0777 | 6147.1332 | 6363.8041 | 86.4545 | 200,000 |
| NM-PSO [16] | 5930.3137 | 5946.7901 | 5960.0557 | 9.16 | 80,000 |
| IHS [7] | 7197.730 | NA | NA | NA | 100,000 |
| THREE-BAR STRUSS [10] | | | | | |
| SRPSO | 263.895844 | 263.897780 | 263.907955 | 3.02e-03 | 20,000 |
| Ray and Liew [10] | 263.89584654 | 263.90335672 | 263.96975638 | 1.3e-02 | 17,610 |
| DSS-MDE [17] | 263.89584 | 263.89584 | 263.89584 | 9.2e-7 | 15000 |
| SPEED REDUCER [10] | | | | | |
| SRPSO | 2506.942407 | 2756.525088 | 2947.825502 | 91.766319 | 20,000 |
| Ray and Liew [10] | 2994.744241 | 3001.758264 | 3009.964736 | 4.0 | 54,456 |
| IHS [7] | 2994.4 | NA | NA | NA | 20,000 |
| DSS-MDE[17] | 2994.47106 | 2994.47106 | 2994.47106 | 3.5e-12 | 30000 |
| HIMMELBLAU [3] | | | | | |
| SRPSO | -31025.554042 | -31019.990288 | -31005.091619 | 5.990052 | 20,000 |
| CPSO [5] | -31025.600 | NA | NA | NA | NA |
| IHS [7] | -31025.565 | NA | NA | NA | 20,100 |

in Table 1, the best solution obtained by SRPSO is $f(2.7540737, 0.72184566, 17.571564, 7.8446617, 7.7938804, 3.2070532, 5.1558205 )$ =2506.9424074072431 in comparison to the available methods for this problem. The total number of evaluations is 20,000 in SRPSO, while 54,456 number of evaluations in Ray and Liew [10]. Although the proposed method gives better solution but the standard deviation is quite high.

**Three-bar truss design problem**
This problem deals with the design of a three-bar truss structure where the volume is to minimized subject to stress constraints. The best feasible solution found by SRPSO is $f(0.7887701, 0.40799905 )$=263.8958, matches with the reported best-known result for this problem. A comparison of results presented in Table 1 shows that SRPSO outperforms Ray et al., and Zhang et al. [10,17] , in terms of quality of solution and robustness.

**Himmelblau Nonlinear problem**
The best feasible solution found for this problem by SRPSO is $f$ (78, 33.049666, 27.133319,45, 44.776691) = -31025.554041580137. The obtained objective function value is comparable and even better than then existing methods.

To summarize the result statistics reported in Table(1), the proposed SRPSO algorithm has substantial capability to handle various constrained engineering optimization problems efficiently with regard to quality of solution, robustness and fastness.

## 6   Conclusions

In this paper, a new Stochastic Ranking based Particle Swarm Optimization algorithm (SRPSO) is proposed for solving constrained engineering design problems. This method improves the search capacity by integrating stochastic ranking technique with PSO. This technique is able to find competitive results on five standard engineering design problems. The simulation results conclude that the SRPSO is superior in terms of various performance evaluation criteria such as mean, best , worst and standard deviation. The computation cost represented by the number of function evaluations of SRPSO is less than other existing techniques reported in literature. Thus, SRPSO technique can be used as a good alternative for solving constrained engineering design problems.

## References

1. Coelho, L.S.: Gaussian quantum-behaved particle swarm optimization approaches for constrained engineering design problems. Expert Systems with Applications 37(2), 1676–1683 (2010)
2. Coello, C., Carlos, A.: Use of a self-adaptive penalty approach for engineering optimization problems. Comput. Ind. 41(2), 113–127 (2000)
3. Coello, C., Carlos, A.: Theoretical and numerical constraint-handling techniques used with evolutionary algorithms: A survey of the state of the art. Comput. Meth. Appl. Mech. Eng. 191, 1245–1287 (2002)
4. Eberhart, R., Kenedy, J.: Particle swarm optimization. In: Proceedings of IEEE Int. Conference on Neural Networks, Piscataway, NJ, pp. 1114–1121 (November 1995)
5. He, Q., Wang, L.: An effective co-evolutionary particle swarm optimization for constrained engineering design problems. Engineering Applications of Artificial Intelligence 20(1), 89–99 (2007)
6. Huang, F.Z., Wang, L., He, Q.: An effective co-evolutionary differential evolution for constrained optimization. Applied Mathematics and Computation 186(1), 340–356 (2007)
7. Jaberipour, M., Khorram, E.: Two improved harmony search algorithms for solving engineering optimization problems. Communications in Nonlinear Science and Numerical Simulation 15(11), 3316–3331 (2010)
8. Mallipeddi, R., Suganthan, P.: Ensemble of constraint handling techniques. IEEE Transactions on Evolutionary Computation 14(4), 561–579 (2010)
9. Michalewicz, Z., Schoenauer, M.: Evolutionary algorithms for constrained parameter optimization problems. Journal of Evolutionary Computation 4(1), 1–32 (1996)
10. Ray, T., Liew, K.M.: Society and civilization: an optimization algorithm based on the simulation of social behavior. IEEE Transactions on Evolutionary Computation 7(4), 386–396 (2003)

11. Sabat, S.L., Ali, L.: The hyperspherical acceleration effect particle swarm optimizer. Appl. Soft. Computing 9(13), 906–917 (2008)
12. Sabat, S.L., Ali, L., Udgata, S.K.: Adaptive accelerated exploration particle swarm optimizer for global multimodal functions. In: World Congress on Nature and Biologically Inspired Computing, Coimbatore, India, pp. 654–659 (December 2009)
13. Runarsson, T.P., Yao, X.: Stochastic ranking for constrained evolutionary optimization. IEEE Trans. Evol. Comput. 4(3), 284–294 (2000)
14. Takahama, T., Sakai, S.: Solving constrained optimization problems by the $\epsilon$ constrained particle swarm optimizer with adaptive velocity limit control. In: IEEE Congress on Evolution Computation, Vancouver, BC, Canada, pp. 308–315 (July 2006)
15. Yang, B., Chen, Y., Zhao, Z., Han, Q.: A master-slave particle swarm optimization algorithm for solving constrained optimization problems. In: 6th Congress on Intelligent Control and Automation, Dalian, pp. 3208–3212 (2006)
16. Zahara, E., Kao, Y.-T.: Hybrid nelder-mead simplex search and particle swarm optimization for constrained engineering design problems. Expert Systems with Applications 36(2, Part 2), 3880–3886 (2009)
17. Zhang, M., Luo, W., Wang, X.: Differential evolution with dynamic stochastic selection for constrained optimization. Information Sciences 178(15), 3043–3074 (2008)

# A New Improved Particle Swarm Optimization Technique for Daily Economic Generation Scheduling of Cascaded Hydrothermal Systems

K.K. Mandal[*], B. Tudu, and N. Chakraborty

Jadavpur University,
Department of Power Engineering,
Kolkata-700098, India
Tel.: 91-33-23355813; Fax: 91-33-23357254
kkm567@yahoo.co.in

**Abstract.** Optimum scheduling of hydrothermal plants is an important task for economic operation of power systems. Many evolutionary techniques such as particle swarm optimization, differential evolution have been applied to solve these problems and found to perform in a better way in comparison with conventional optimization methods. But often these methods converge to a suboptimal solution prematurely. This paper presents a new improved particle swarm optimization technique called self-organizing hierarchical particle swarm optimization technique with time-varying acceleration coefficients (SOHPSO_TVAC) for solving daily economic generation scheduling of hydrothermal systems to avoid premature convergence. The performance of the proposed method is demonstrated on a sample test system comprising of cascaded reservoirs. The results obtained by the proposed methods are compared with other methods. The results show that the proposed technique is capable of producing comparable results.

**Keywords:** Hydrothermal Systems, cascaded reservoirs, self-organizing hierarchical particle swarm optimization with time-varying acceleration coefficients (SOHPSO_TVAC).

## 1 Introduction

The optimum scheduling of hydrothermal plants is one of the important planning task in power system operation. The main objective is to allocate generations of hydroelectric and thermal plants in such a way so as to minimize the total operation cost of the systems subjected to a variety of constraints. With the insignificant operating cost of hydroelectric plants, the problem of minimizing the operational cost of a hydrothermal system essentially reduces to that of minimizing the fuel cost for thermal plants under the various constraints on the hydraulic and power system network.

---

[*] Corresponding author.

B.K. Panigrahi et al. (Eds.): SEMCCO 2010, LNCS 6466, pp. 680–688, 2010.

The main constraints include the cascaded nature of the hydraulic network, the time coupling effect of the hydro sub problem where the water inflow of an earlier time interval affects the discharge capability at a later period of time, the varying hourly reservoir inflows, the physical limitations on the reservoir storage and turbine flow rate, the varying system load demand and the loading limits of both thermal and hydro plants.

Many methods have been applied to solve this problem. Some of these solution methods include dynamic programming [Chang et al. 1990], genetic algorithm [Gil et al. 2003] simulated annealing technique [Wong and Wong 1994], hybrid differential evolution technique [Lakshminarasimman and Subramanian 2008], mixed- integer quadratic programming method [Catalao et al. 2010] etc.

Particle swarm optimization (PSO) happens to be a comparatively new combinatorial metaheuristic technique which is based on the social metaphor of bird flocking or fish schooling [Kennedy and Eberhart 1995]. The PSO technique has been applied to various fields of power system optimization. Park et al. presented a method for solving economic dispatch with non-smooth cost functions [Park et al 2005]. Yu et al. used particle swarm optimization technique to solve short-term hydrothermal scheduling problem [Yu et al. 2007] with an equivalent thermal unit having smooth cost functions.

A novel parameter automation strategy called self-organizing hierarchical particle swarm optimization technique with time-varying acceleration coefficients (SOHPSO_TVAC) is applied in this paper for the hydrothermal scheduling to address the problem of premature convergence. In this case, the particle velocities are reinitialized whenever the population stagnates at local optima during the search. A relatively high value of the cognitive component results in excessive wandering of particles while a higher value of the social component causes premature convergence of particles. Hence, time-varying acceleration coefficients (TVAC) [Ratnaweera et al. 2004] are employed to strike a proper balance between the cognitive and social component during the search. The proposed approach was tested on a simple test system. The results have been compared with other evolutionary methods and found to be superior.

## 2   Problem Formulation

As the fuel cost of hydroelectric plants is insignificant in comparison with that of thermal power plants, the objective is to minimize the fuel cost of thermal power plants, while making use of the availability of hydro-resources as much as possible. The objective function and associated constraints are described as follows:

Minimize

$$F\left(P_{sit}\right)=\sum_{t=1}^{T}\sum_{i=1}^{N_s}\left[f_{it}\left(P_{sit}\right)\right] \tag{1}$$

where $F\left(P_{sit}\right)$ is the total fuel cost, $T$ is the number of time interval for scheduling horizon, $N_s$ is the number of thermal plants and $P_{sit}$ is the power generation by the $i$ th thermal plants at time t.

Conventionally, the fuel cost curve for any unit can be represented by segments of quadratic functions of the active power output of the generator and can be expressed as

$$f_{it}(P_{sit}) = a_{si} + b_{si}P_{sit} + c_{si}P_{sit}^2 \qquad (2)$$

where, $a_{si}, b_{si}, c_{si}$ : fuel cost coefficients of the $i$th thermal unit.

The above objective function described by (1) is to be minimized subject to a variety of constraints as follows:

(i) Demand constraints

The total power generated must balance the power demand plus losses, at each time interval over the entire scheduling period

$$\sum_{i=1}^{N_s} P_{sit} + \sum_{j=1}^{N_h} P_{hjt} - P_{Dt} - P_{Lt} = 0 \qquad (3)$$

where $P_{hjt}$ is the power generation of $j$ th hydro generating unit at time $t$, $P_{Dt}$ is power demand at time $t$ and $P_{Lt}$ is total transmission loss at the corresponding time.

The hydropower generation is a function of water discharge rate and reservoir storage volume, which can be described by (4) as follow:

$$P_{hjt} = C_{1j}V_{hjt}^2 + C_{2j}Q_{hjt}^2 + C_{3j}V_{hjt}Q_{hjt} + C_{4j}V_{hjt} + C_{5j}Q_{hjt} + C_{6j} \qquad (4)$$

where $C_{1j}, C_{2j}, C_{3j}, C_{4j}, C_{5j}, C_{6j}$ are power generation coefficients of $j$ th hydro generating unit, $V_{hjt}$ is the storage volume of $j$ th reservoir at time $t$ and $Q_{hjt}$ is water discharge rate of $j$ th reservoir at time $t$.

(ii) Power generation constraints

$$P_{si}^{\min} \le P_{sit} \le P_{si}^{\max} \qquad (5)$$

$$P_{hj}^{\min} \le P_{hjt} \le P_{hj}^{\max} \qquad (6)$$

where $P_{si}^{\min}$ and $P_{si}^{\max}$ are the minimum and maximum power generation by $i$-th thermal generating unit, $P_{hj}^{\min}$ and $P_{hj}^{\max}$ are the minimum and maximum power generation by the $j$-th hydro generating unit respectively.

(iii) Water dynamic balance

$$V_{hjt} = V_{hj,t-1} + I_{hjt} - Q_{hjt} - S_{hjt} + \sum_{m=1}^{R_{uj}} \left( Q_{hm,t-\tau_{mj}} + S_{hm,t-\tau_{mj}} \right) \qquad (7)$$

where $I_{hjt}$ is natural inflow of $j$-th hydro reservoir at time t, $S_{hjt}$ is spillage discharge rate of $j$-th hydro generating unit at time $t$, $\tau_{mj}$ is the water transport delay from reservoir $m$ to $j$ and $R_{uj}$ is the number of upstream hydro generating plants immediately above the $j$ th reservoir.

(iv) Reservoir storage volume constraints

$$V_{hj}^{\min} \leq V_{hjt} \leq V_{hj}^{\max} \tag{8}$$

where $V_{hj}^{\min}, V_{hj}^{\max}$ are the minimum and maximum storage volume of $j$ th reservoir.

(v)   Water discharge rate limit

$$Q_{hj}^{\min} \leq Q_{hjt} \leq Q_{hj}^{\max} \tag{9}$$

where $Q_{hj}^{\min}$ and $Q_{hj}^{\max}$ are the minimum and maximum water discharge rate of the $j$-th reservoir respectively.

## 3   Overview of Some PSO Strategies

### 3.1   Classical PSO

The Particle Swarm Optimization (PSO) is one of the recent developments in the category of heuristic optimization technique.   Kennedy and Eberhart [Kennedy and Eberhart 1995] originally developed the PSO concept based on the behavior of individuals (i.e. particles or agents) of a swarm or group.

Let in a physical $d$-dimensional search space, the position and velocity of the $i$ th particle (i.e. $i$ th individual in the population of particles) be represented as the vectors $X_i = (x_{i1}, x_{i2}, ...., x_{id})$   and   $V_i = (v_{i1}, v_{i2}, ...., v_{id})$ respectively. The previous best position   of   the   $i$ th   particle   is   recorded   and   represented as $pbest_i = (pbest_{i1}, pbest_{i2}, ...., pbest_{id})$. The index of the best particle among all the particles in the group is represented by the $gbest_d$. The modified velocity and position of each particle can be calculated using the current velocity and the distance from $pbest_{id}$ to $gbest_d$ as shown in the following formulas:

$$V_{id}^{k+1} = w * V_{id}^k + c_1 * rand(\ ) * \left(pbest_{id} - X_{id}^k\right) + c_2 * rand(\ ) * \left(gbest_d - X_{id}^k\right)$$
$$i = 1, 2, ............., N_p, \qquad d = 1, 2, ............., N_g \tag{10}$$

where $N_p$ is the number of particles in a swarm or group, $N_g$ is number of members or elements in a  particle, $N_g$ is the number of members or elements in a  particle, $V_{id}^k$ is the velocity of individual $i$ at iteration $k$, $w$ is the weight parameter or swarm inertia, $c_1$ , $c_2$  is the acceleration constant and $rand(\ )$ is uniform random number in the range [ 0 1]. The updated velocity can be used to change the position of each particle in the swarm as depicted in (11) as:

$$X_{id}^{k+1} = X_{id}^{k} + V_{id}^{k+1} \tag{11}$$

## 3.2  Concept of Time-Varying Acceleration Coefficients (TVAC)

It is observed from (10) that the search toward the optimum solution is heavily dependent on the two stochastic acceleration components (i.e. the cognitive component and the social component). Thus, it is very important to control these two components properly in order to get optimum solution efficiently and accurately.  Kennedy and Eberhart [Kennedy and Eberhart 1995] reported that a relatively higher value of the cognitive component, compared with the social component, results in excessive roaming of individuals through a larger search space. On the other hand, a relatively high value of the social component may lead particles to rush toward a local optimum prematurely.

   In general, for any population-based optimization method like PSO, it is always desired to encourage the individuals to wander through the entire search space, during the initial part of the search, without clustering around local optima. In contrast, during the latter stages, it is desirable to enhance convergence towards the global optima so that optimum solution can be achieved efficiently. For this, the concept of parameter automation strategy called Time Varying acceleration Coefficients (TVAC) had been introduced [Ratnaweera et al. 2004]. The main purpose of this concept is to enhance the global search capability during the early part of the optimization process and to promote the particles to converge toward the global optimum at the end of the search.  In TVAC, this can be achieved by changing the acceleration coefficients with time. The concept of time varying acceleration coefficients (TVAC) can be introduced mathematically as follows [Ratnaweera et al. 2004].

$$C_1 = \left(C_{1f} - C_{1i}\right)\frac{iter}{iter_{\max}} + C_{1i} \tag{12}$$

$$C_2 = \left(C_{2f} - C_{2i}\right)\frac{iter}{iter_{\max}} + C_{2i} \tag{13}$$

where $C_{1i}, C_{1f}, C_{2i}, C_{2f}$ are constants representing initial and final values of cognitive and social acceleration factors respectively.

## 3.3  Self-Organizing Hierarchical PSO with TVAC (SOHPSO_TVAC)

It is seen that the classical PSO is either based on a constant inertia weight factor or a linearly varying inertia weight factor.  In SOHPSO_TVAC, the previous velocity term in (10) is kept at zero. It is observed that in the absence of previous velocity term the particles rapidly rush towards a local optimum solution and then stagnate due to the lack of momentum. To overcome this difficulty, the modulus of velocity vector of a particle is reinitialized with a random velocity (called reinitialization velocity) whenever it stagnates in the search space. When a particle is stagnated, it's *pbest* remains unchanged over a large number of iterations. When more particles are stagnated, the *gbest* also remains unchanged and the PSO algorithm converges to a local minimum prematurely. The necessary momentum is imparted to the particles by reinitialization of velocity vector with a random velocity. The above method can be implemented as follows [Ratnaweera et al. 2004]:

$$V_{id}^{k+1} = \left( \left( C_{1f} - C_{1i} \right) \frac{iter}{iter_{\max}} + C_{1i} \right) \times rand_1 \times \left( pbest_{id} - X_{id}^k \right)$$

$$+ \left( \left( C_{2f} - C_{2i} \right) \frac{iter}{iter_{\max}} + C_{2i} \right) \times rand_2 \times \left( gbest_d - X_{id}^k \right) \qquad (14)$$

If $V_{id} = 0$ and $rand_3 \langle 0.5$ then

$$V_{id} = rand_4 \times V_{d\max} \text{ else } V_{id} = -rand_5 \times V_{d\max} \qquad (15)$$

The variables $rand_3$, $rand_4$ and $rand_5$ are numbers generated randomly between 0 and 1. A time varying reinitialization strategy is used to overcome the difficulties of selecting appropriate reinitialization velocities.

## 4   Simulation Results

The proposed algorithm was implemented using in house Matlab code on 3.0 MHz, 2.0 GB RAM PC. It was applied on a sample test systems to obtain the simulation results.

**Table 1.** Hourly discharge ($\times 10^4 m^3$) using SOHPSO_TVAC

| Hour | $Q_{h1}$ | $Q_{h2}$ | $Q_{h3}$ | $Q_{h4}$ |
|------|----------|----------|----------|----------|
| 1 | 13.8283 | 14.4910 | 24.2658 | 15.2399 |
| 2 | 12.6601 | 9.2900 | 24.9872 | 17.2769 |
| 3 | 5.9466 | 6.6413 | 22.9332 | 13.6824 |
| 4 | 13.3810 | 14.3373 | 29.3514 | 18.3014 |
| 5 | 8.2904 | 6.0950 | 28.7873 | 16.5410 |
| 6 | 11.8885 | 11.9559 | 28.6013 | 14.0943 |
| 7 | 12.6919 | 6.2446 | 15.9601 | 18.0801 |
| 8 | 9.3017 | 8.6030 | 19.3372 | 14.6328 |
| 9 | 11.3282 | 8.9676 | 14.8883 | 13.0162 |
| 10 | 10.9708 | 7.6717 | 16.7851 | 16.4236 |
| 11 | 9.4602 | 13.9516 | 15.3201 | 18.9266 |
| 12 | 11.1395 | 14.0177 | 14.0084 | 13.1561 |
| 13 | 14.5317 | 9.4261 | 14.0798 | 17.8119 |
| 14 | 7.9011 | 8.9554 | 18.0524 | 16.6606 |
| 15 | 8.3188 | 10.2877 | 24.4559 | 15.5128 |
| 16 | 9.8519 | 7.3214 | 13.7804 | 13.0263 |
| 17 | 6.6072 | 12.1301 | 22.8774 | 14.1860 |
| 18 | 11.8547 | 6.4092 | 10.0867 | 16.8845 |
| 19 | 12.9146 | 13.9743 | 13.8062 | 15.9441 |
| 20 | 12.5296 | 12.0523 | 19.1564 | 19.4293 |
| 21 | 8.9751 | 14.7372 | 17.1883 | 15.3933 |
| 22 | 8.3536 | 11.6243 | 29.4380 | 17.6711 |
| 23 | 13.9647 | 8.6715 | 15.8585 | 16.2179 |
| 24 | 9.7047 | 13.2850 | 14.4794 | 19.7077 |

The proposed method has been applied to a test system consisting of four cascaded hydro units and an equivalent thermal plant [Yu et al. 2007]. The scheduling period has been kept to 24 hours with one hour time interval. The water transport delay between connected reservoirs is also considered. The load demand, hydro unit power generation coefficients, reservoir inflows, reservoir limits, the generation limits, cost coefficients of thermal unit and other data are taken from [Yu et al. 2007].

**Table 2.** Hydrothermal generation (MW) using SOHPSO_TVAC

| Hour | $P_{h1}$ | $P_{h2}$ | $P_{h3}$ | $P_{h4}$ | $P_{s1}$ |
|------|----------|----------|----------|----------|----------|
| 1 | 97.4547 | 87.6571 | 21.8256 | 230.3377 | 932.7249 |
| 2 | 93.5193 | 64.7935 | 23.6970 | 229.6978 | 978.2924 |
| 3 | 58.4330 | 78.5222 | 57.6787 | 210.2464 | 955.1197 |
| 4 | 94.1196 | 83.3466 | 0.0000 | 198.7914 | 913.7424 |
| 5 | 92.6744 | 72.8456 | 0.0000 | 220.9078 | 903.5722 |
| 6 | 86.4760 | 74.3160 | 0.0000 | 191.6303 | 1057.5777 |
| 7 | 85.4516 | 41.7571 | 43.1969 | 229.6711 | 1249.9233 |
| 8 | 72.1956 | 55.8172 | 34.0058 | 219.9818 | 1617.9996 |
| 9 | 79.3600 | 76.5117 | 49.5002 | 232.1563 | 1802.4718 |
| 10 | 77.5266 | 48.6986 | 46.1335 | 266.1956 | 1681.4457 |
| 11 | 72.0148 | 74.7016 | 50.6196 | 283.0959 | 1749.5681 |
| 12 | 79.5559 | 70.6179 | 53.8710 | 237.5837 | 1868.3715 |
| 13 | 83.9767 | 50.1964 | 55.1515 | 278.0854 | 1762.5900 |
| 14 | 63.1928 | 46.7289 | 51.5653 | 268.6745 | 1769.8385 |
| 15 | 67.5760 | 52.7787 | 24.7423 | 258.2166 | 1726.6864 |
| 16 | 76.1820 | 36.8627 | 60.4846 | 234.3241 | 1662.1466 |
| 17 | 58.5041 | 58.7856 | 45.1654 | 246.2596 | 1721.2853 |
| 18 | 84.1886 | 27.4923 | 58.0117 | 272.4697 | 1697.8377 |
| 19 | 83.9924 | 57.9884 | 62.2518 | 272.4128 | 1763.3546 |
| 20 | 79.5395 | 46.5762 | 55.1625 | 295.3375 | 1803.3843 |
| 21 | 64.5494 | 47.7753 | 60.4145 | 268.9274 | 1798.3334 |
| 22 | 60.4338 | 35.1203 | 64.1562 | 281.8141 | 1678.4756 |
| 23 | 74.3806 | 41.0008 | 63.0802 | 276.4471 | 1395.0913 |
| 24 | 62.6654 | 35.5388 | 64.6617 | 294.0484 | 1133.0857 |

**Table 3.** Comparison of Cost and Computation time   using SOHPSO_TVAC

| Method | GCPSO | LWPSO | MHDE | MDE | Proposed SOHPSO_TVAC |
|--------|-------|-------|------|-----|----------------------|
| Cost ($) | 927288.00 | 925383.80 | 921893.94 | 922555.44 | 922018.24 |
| CPU Time (sec) | 182.4 | 82.9 | 8 | 45 | 6.65 |

The performance of PSO algorithm is quite sensitive to the various parameter settings. Tuning of parameters is essential in all PSO based methods. Based on empirical studies on a number of mathematical benchmark functions [Ratnaweera et al. 2004] it has been reported the best range of variation as 2.5–0.5 for $C_1$ and 0.5–2.5 for $C_2$. We experimented with the same range and the best results were obtained for $2.5 - 1.2$ for $C_1$ and $0.8 - 2.5$ for $C_2$ out of 50 trial runs. The optimization is done with a randomly initialized population of 50 swarms. The maximum iteration was set at 500.

Table 1 shows the optimal water discharge obtained by the proposed method. The optimal hydrothermal generation schedule along with demand for 24 hours is shown in Table 2. The proposed method converges to the optimal solution in 6.65 seconds. The optimal cost is found to be $ 922018.24.

The results of the proposed method are compared with the results obtained by various versions of particle swarm optimization (PSO) techniques and genetic algorithm [Yu et al. 2007], modified hybrid differential evolution [Lakshminarasimman and Subramanian 2008] and are shown in Table 3. It is clearly seen that the proposed method based SOHPSO_TVAC yields comparable results.

## 5  Conclusions

Optimum scheduling of hydrothermal plants generation is of great importance to electric utilities. In this paper, a novel algorithm called self-organizing hierarchical particle swarm optimization technique with time-varying acceleration coefficients (SOHPSO_TVAC) for solving daily economic generation scheduling of hydrothermal systems to avoid premature convergence has been proposed and successfully applied to solve daily hydrothermal scheduling problem. The results obtained by the proposed method have been compared with other evolutionary algorithms like improved PSO and modified hybrid differential evolution (MHDE). It is found that proposed method SOHPSO_TVAC can produce comparable results.

## References

Catalão, J.P.S., Pousinho, H.M.I., Mendes, V.M.F.: Scheduling of head-dependent cascaded hydro systems: Mixed-integer quadratic programming approach. Energy Conversion & Management 51, 524–530 (2010)

Chang, S., Chen, C., Fong, I., Luh, P.B.: Hydroelectric generation scheduling with an ef-fective differential dynamic programming. IEEE Trans. PWRS 5(3), 737–743 (1990)

Gil, E., Bustos, J., Rudnick, H.: Short-Term Hydrothermal Generation Scheduling Model Using a Genetic Algorithm. IEEE Transaction on Power Systems 18(4), 1256–1264 (2003)

Jiekang, W., Jianquan, Z., Guotong, C., Hongliang, Z.: A Hybrid Method for Optimal Scheduling of Short-Term Electric Power Generation of Cascaded Hydroelectric Plants Based on Particle Swarm Optimization and Chance-Constrained Programming. IEEE Transaction on Power Systems 23(4), 1570–1579 (2008)

Lakshminarasimman, L., Subramanian, S.: A modified hybrid differential evolution for short-term scheduling of hydrothermal power systems with cascaded reservoirs. Energy Conversion & Management 49, 2513–2521 (2008)

Park, J.B., Lee, K.S., Shin, J.R., Lee, K.Y.: A Particle swarm optimization for solving the economic dispatch with non-smooth cost functions. IEEE Transaction on Power Systems 20(1), 34–42 (2005)

Ratnaweera, A., Halgamuge, S.K., Watson, H.C.: Self-organizing hierarchical particle swarm optimizer with time-varying acceleration coefficients. IEEE Trans. Evol. Comput. 8(3), 240–255 (2004)

Wong, K.P., Wong, Y.W.: Short-term hydrothermal scheduling part 1: simulated annealing approach. In: IEE Proceedings Generation, Transmission and Distribution, vol. 141(5), pp. 497–501 (1994)

Yu, B., Xiaohui Yuan, X., Wang, J.: Short-term hydro-thermal scheduling using particle swarm optimization method. Energy Conversion & Management 48, 1902–1908 (2007)

Kennedy, J., Eberhart, R.: Particle swarm optimization. In: Proc. IEEE Conf. Neural Networks (ICNN 1995), vol. IV, pp. 1942–1948 (1995)

# Improved Real Quantum Evolutionary Algorithm for Optimum Economic Load Dispatch with Non-convex Loads

Nidul Sinha, Kaustabh Moni Hazarika, Shantanu Paul,
Himanshu Shekhar, and Amrita Karmakar

Department of Electrical Engineering, NIT, Silchar, Assam, India-788010
nidulsinha@hotmail.com

**Abstract.** An algorithm based on improved real quantum evolutionary algorithm (IRQEA) was developed to solve the problem of highly non-linear economic load dispatch problem with valve point loading. The performance of the proposed algorithm is evaluated on a test case of 15 units. The performance of the algorithm is compared with floating point genetic algorithm (FPGA) and real quantum evolutionary algorithm (RQEA). Results demonstrate that the performance of the IRQEA algorithm is far better than FPGA and RQEA algorithms in terms of convergence rate and solution quality.

**Keywords:** Real Quantum Evolutionary Algorithm, Floating point Genetic Algorithm, Economic Load dispatch.

## 1 Introduction

Operation, monitoring and control of power system in an optimal manner is a major challenge for power system utility operators. Economic load dispatch is the indispensable part in optimal operation of power system. Economic load dispatch (ELD) is the allocation of load amongst the committed generating units in an optimal manner subject to satisfaction of the constraints. Most of the conventional classical dispatch algorithms, like lambda-iteration method, base point and participation factors method, and the gradient method [1], [2] are gradient based methods and hence, find difficulty in finding optimal solution for non-convex problems. Before applying these algorithms the non-convex functions are approximated as quadratic ones which may result into suboptimal solutions. This may cause huge loss of revenue over time. And most of the modern practical thermal units do have highly non-linear input-output characteristics because of valve point loadings prohibiting operating zones etc resulting in multiple local minima in the cost function. The solution of multi-modal optimization problems like ELD demands for solution methods, which have no restrictions on the shape of the fuel cost curves. Though enumerative method like dynamic programming (DP) [1] is capable of solving ELD problems with inherently nonlinear and discontinuous cost curves but proves to suffer from intensive mathematical computations and memory requirement. With nonlinear and non-differentiable objective functions, modern heuristic search approaches are the methods of choice. The best known of these are

B.K. Panigrahi et al. (Eds.): SEMCCO 2010, LNCS 6466, pp. 689–700, 2010.
© Springer-Verlag Berlin Heidelberg 2010

genetic algorithm (GA) [3]-[11], evolutionary strategy (ES) [12], [13], evolutionary programming (EP) [13]-[21], simulated annealing (SA) [3], [22], particle swarm optimization (PSO) [23]-[25], and differential evolution (DE) [26]-[27]. At the heart of every direct search method is a strategy that creates new solutions and some criterion to accept or reject the new solutions. While doing this all basic direct search methods use some greedy criteria. One of the greedy criteria is to accept a new solution if and only if it reduces the value of the objective function (in case of minimization) and the other may be forcing to create more new solutions nearer to already found better solutions. Although the greedy decision process converges fairly fast, it runs the risk of getting trapped in a local minimum. Inherently all parallel search techniques like genetic and evolutionary algorithms have some built-in safeguards like exploration to forestall misconvergence. Simulated annealing [3], [22] is though reported to have performed better in solving non-linear ELD problems, however, it suffers from the difficulty in determining an appropriate annealing schedule, else the solution achieved may still be a locally optimal one. More and more research efforts are directed towards use of heuristic algorithms like GA, ES and EP etc., which are based on the simulated evolutionary process of natural selection and genetics. EAs are more flexible and robust than conventional calculus based methods. Due to its high potential for global optimization, GA has received great attention in solving ELD problems. Walters and Sheble [4] reported a GA model that employed units' output as the encoded parameter of chromosome to solve an ELD problem with valve-point discontinuities. To enhance the performance of GA, Yalcinoz et al. [10] have proposed the real-coded representation scheme, arithmetic crossover, mutation, and elitism in the GA to solve more efficiently the ELD problem, and it can obtain a high-quality solution with less computation time.

Recent addition in EAs is Quantum evolutionary algorithms (QEAs). QEAs have been reported to be very efficient to optimize functions with binary parameters [27]. The advantageous features of the QEA is that, unlike the other EAs, it can work with small population sizes without getting stuck in local minima and without converging prematurely because of loss of diversity. The immense representation power of the qubits enables the use of a single qubit string to represent the entire search space without compromising the quality of solution [30]. This reduces the computational burden and enables in finding the solution of large-sized problems. QEAs are very recent and have not yet been attempted exhaustively for power system problems. In the same lines, principles of quantum computing (QC) have been embedded in various stochastic search techniques such as particle-swarm optimization [31].However, binary QEA is not suitable for many of the real-world problems, in general, and power systems problems, in particular. ELD is optimization of real-parameter functions. Using binary numbers to represent the parameters forces a trade-off between accuracy of representation and string lengths. Hence, Babu et al [33] proposed a real parameters based QEA (RQEA) which optimizes the real-valued functions. To enable the dealings of real parameters, new quantum operators have been designed to generate solution strings with real parameters. RQEA is reported to have performed better than binary QEAs specifically for real valued non-convex optimization problems. However, in their work, new solutions are created only in one randomly chosen direction of search space using one of the two probabilities. To improve the search capability of the algorithm it is proposed create solutions  in both directions using both the probabilities.

Hence, in this paper, an improved version of RQEA is presented and applied to ELD problem. Results obtained on several examples using proposed technique are compared with floating point genetic algorithm (FPGA) and RQEA.

The rest of the paper is organized as follows. Section 2 describes the problem formulation of ELD prolem. Section 3 describes the RQEA and the proposed IRQEA technique. Section 4 presents the experimentation results and discussions about the performance of the algorithms. Conclusions are drawn in Section 5.

## 2   ELD Problem Formulation

Economic load dispatch (ELD) problem is to obtain optimal allocation of load amongst the committed generating units so as to minimize the operating cost while satisfying various systems and unit-level equality and inequality constraints.

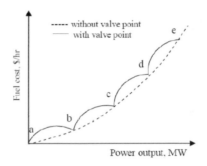

**Fig. 1.** The quadratic cost function with valve point loading

Mathematically, ELD can be represented as follows:

$$F_C = Minimize(F_{PG})  \tag{1}$$

Here, $F_{PG}$ is the total Rs/h fuel cost and is given by:

$$F_{PG} = \sum_{i=1}^{Ng} (a_i P_{g_i}^2 + b_i P_{g_i} + d_i + \left| e_i \sin(f_i (P_{gmin_i} - P_{g_i})) \right|)  \tag{2}$$

where Ng is the total number of generating units, $a_i$, $b_i, d_i, e_i, f_i$ the fuel cost coefficients of $i_{th}$ generator, Pgi and Pgmin,i are the real power outputs of $i_{th}$ generator in MW and its minimum limit, respectively, and PG is the vector of real power outputs of all generators. Fig. 1 depicts the cost function used in the study.

A solution of ELD, thus found, must satisfy the equality and inequality constraints which are as follows.

**Power balance constraint.** The total MW generation from all the generators must be equal to the sum of power demand (PD) and real power loss (P_{loss}) in the transmission lines. This is mathematically expressed as

$$\sum_{i=1}^{N_g} \mathrm{P}_{\mathrm{g}_i} = P_D + P_{loss} \tag{3}$$

**Generator capacity constraint.** Real power generation of each unit should lie between minimum and maximum limit:

$$\mathrm{Pgmin}_i \le \mathrm{Pg}_i \le \mathrm{Pgmax}_i, \quad \forall_i \,, \; i = 1,2, \dots \mathrm{Ng} \tag{4}$$

The generating units with multi-valve steam turbines exhibit a greater variation in the fuel cost functions. The valve-point effects introduce ripples in the heat rate curves.

Now the fitness function which is the sum of production cost and penalty for constraint violation can be calculated for each individual of the parent population as

$$FIT_l = F_c + \sum_{z=1}^{N_c} PF_z \tag{5}$$

and   penalty function, $PF_z = \lambda_z \; X \; [VIOL_z]^2$
$\lambda_z$ = penalty multiplier, $VIOL_z$ = Violation
$N_c$ = Number of constraints.

## 3   Real Parameter QEA (RQEA)

The binary QEA is good to optimize functions with binary parameters. However, requirement of handling real parameters dictates that RQEA has to be designed differently [27].

The main features of RQEA are as follows.

- RQEA uses qubit representation that has a better characteristic of population diversity. This enables the use of smaller population with corresponding reduction in computational effort just as in the case of QEA.
- Unlike QEA, which uses the concept of observing qubit strings to generate candidate feasible solutions, RQEA uses special quantum evolution operators to generate the candidate solution strings that comprise real parameters. The operator has to strike a balance between adequate exploration and full exploitation.
- Like QEA, RQEA also uses quantum rotation gate for updating the qubit strings.
- Migration between families of solutions, which are produced from different qubit strings, is employed in RQEA which helps in improving the convergence and the quality of solution strings.

These features along with the inherent representational power of qubits and search power of quantum operators make RQEA a powerful, flexible and robust algorithm for solving highly non-linear real-parameter optimization problems. One straight forward approach to make RQEA flexible enough to handle real parameters is to provide multiple qubits for encoding each parameter and then regarding the binary string generated by collapsing the qubits as representing a real number between 0 and 1.

RQEA has a more sophisticated approach to generate real-numbered candidate solution strings during the search process.

A set of Np qubit strings, $Q_i^t$, i=1, 2,...,Np, is maintained as in QEA in $t^{th}$ iteration. Correspondingly, another set of Np strings each of Ng real numbers, $P_i^t$, i=1, 2, . . . , Np, is maintained. Each Qi also has Ng qubits, each of which is initialized with 0.707. Similarly, value of each element of Pi, i=1, 2,..., Np, is initialized with a random number between the minimum and maximum values allowed for the parameter. Each pair consisting $Q_i^t$ and $P_i^t$ represent the $i^{th}$ family in $t^{th}$ iteration.

For $i^{th}$ family, Nc solution strings, $p_{ij}^t$, j ¼ 1, 2, . . . , Nc, are generated using $Q_i^t$, $P_i^t$ and $P_{BEST}^t$ where $P_{BEST}^t$ is the solution string with best fitness found so far. This process is described later in this section. The fitness of each of the strings, $p_{ij}^t$ is evaluated after ensuring constraint compliance.

Two neighborhood operators, neighborhood operator 1(NO1) and neighborhood operator 2 (NO2) are used to generate the Nc neighborhood solution strings, and the best out of these, $c_i^t$, is determined for each family i. If $c_i^t$ is better than $P_i^t$, it replaces $P_i^t$ to become $P_i^{t+1}$. The best out of all $P_i^{t+1}$s, i = 1, 2, . . . , Np, replaces $P_{BEST}^t$ to become $P_{BEST}^{t+1}$ if it is found better.

## A. *Evolving qubit*
Evolving a qubit implies that state of the qubit, which is a superposition of state 0 and 1, is shifted to a new superposition state. This change in probability magnitudes $|\alpha|^2$ and $|\beta|^2$ with change in state is transformed into real-valued parameters in the problem space by two neighborhood operators, NO1 and NO2.

## B. *Neighborhood operator 1 (NO1) for IRQEA*
Given in the $t^{th}$ iteration, Np qubit strings Qi ( $\forall$ i , i=1, 2, ..., Np ), each having Ng elements, NO1 generates solution strings $p_{ij}^t$ ( $\forall$ j, j =1, 2, ..., Nc ), each having Ng elements. This is done for particular i, j as follows:

An array $R_{ij}$ is created with Ng elements generated at random such that every element in $R_{ij}$ is either -1 or +1.

Let $\rho_{ijk}$ be the $k^{th}$ element in $R_{ij}$. Then $\theta_{ijk}^t$ is given by

$$\theta_{ijk}^t = \theta_{ijk}^{t-1} + \rho_{ijk} * \delta \qquad (6)$$

Where $\delta$ is the alteration in angle and $\theta_{ijk}^t$ is the rotated angle which is given as $\tan^{-1}\left(\beta_{ijk}/\alpha_{ijk}\right)$. $\delta$ is randomly chosen in the range $\left[0,\theta_{ijk}^{t-1}\right]$ if $\rho_{ijk}$ =-1 and in the range $\left[\theta_{ijk}^{t-1}, \Pi / 2\right]$ if $\rho_{ijk}$ =+1.

The new probability amplitudes, $\alpha_{ijk}^t$ and $\beta_{ijk}^t$, are calculated using rotation gate as:

$$\begin{bmatrix} \alpha_{ijk}^t \\ \beta_{ijk}^{t-1} \end{bmatrix} = \begin{bmatrix} \cos\delta & \sin\delta \\ -\sin\delta & \cos\delta \end{bmatrix} \begin{bmatrix} \alpha_{ijk}^{t-1} \\ \beta_{ijk}^{t-1} \end{bmatrix} \qquad (7)$$

These probabilities are then transformed to solution space to determine individual element as

$$C1^t_{ijk} = (\alpha^t_{ijk})^2 (P_{k\,max} - P_{k\,min}) + P_{k\,min} \qquad (8)$$

$$C2^t_{ijk} = (\beta^t_{ijk})^2 (P_{k\,max} - P_{k\,min}) + P_{k\,min} \qquad (9)$$

where $P_{k\,max}$ and $P_{k\,min}$ are the maximum and minimum allowable values for $P_k\,\forall k$ .

### C. Neighbourhood operator 2 (NO2 for IRQEA)

NO2 works just as NO1 except that it generates a point between Pb and $P_{BEST}$ and is primarily utilized to exploit search space. The NO2 determines the $C1^t_{ijk}$ & $C2^t_{ijk}$ using equation (8) & (9) such that,

$$C1^t_{ijk} = (\alpha^t_{ijk})^2 (P_{k\,max} - P_{k\,min}) + P_{k\,min}$$

& $\qquad C2^t_{ijk} = (\beta^t_{ijk})^2 (P_{k\,max} - P_{k\,min}) + P_{k\,min}$ ,

where

$$P_{k\,max} = \max imum(P_{BESTik}, C^t_{ik})$$

$$P_{k\,min} = \min imum(P_{BESTik}, C^t_{ik})$$

Here, $C^t_i$ is the best child of $i^{th}$ family in $t^{th}$ iteration.

The rationale for two neighbourhood operators is:

- NO1 has a greater tendency for exploration in the sense that solutions generated for a given string could be quite different from the given string.
- NO2 has a greater tendency towards exploitation because, as the algorithm progresses, the values of Pj would converge towards $P_{BESTj}$ .

The desired property of search by any evolutionary algorithm is that exploration should gradually yield to exploitation. Thus, the two operators are used with the frequency of NO1 taken high to start with and increasing the proportion of NO2 as the search progresses. The neighbourhood operators thus generate new feasible solution strings directly from the existing strings. This approach removes all disadvantages of binary representation of real numbers and, at the same time, balances exploration and exploitation in the sense that it adopts the 'step-size' from large initially to progressively smaller size.

### D. Updating qubit string

In the updating process, the individual states of all the qubits in Q are modified so that the probability of generating a solution string which is similar to the current best solution is increased in each of the subsequent iterations.

Premature convergence indicates the identicalness of solutions in population and is prevalent in most of the population-based search techniques. In QEA, the diversity in population is decided by the qubit string.

When a qubit has $\alpha$ and β as 0.707, diversity is the highest. The diversity is least when the value is near the extremes, that is, 0 or 1.

E. *Migration*

Two levels of migration are incorporated, local and global. In local migration, one randomly chosen $P^t$ is used to update some $Q_i^t$. In global migration, $P_{BEST}$ is used to update

$$Q_i^t \ \forall \ i \ , \ i = 1, 2, \ ..., \ Np \ .$$

# 4 Numerical Tests

The performance of the proposed algorithms are experimented on the test case of 15 units. The programs are developed in Matlab command line and results are obtained on a Pentium IV PC, 2.4 GHz 500 MB RAM.

Table 1 shows the units data for the test case under study.

Floating point GA (FPGA) features used:

   (i)  Heuristic crossover
   (ii)  Non-uniform mutation
   (iii) Normalized geometric select function

The GA optimization toolbox GAOT in Matlab proposed by C.R. Houck et al. [11] is used

Tuned parameters for the FPGA algorithm:
Population Size = 60
Maximum Iterations = 400

**Table 1.** Units data for the test case (15 units case) with load 2650MW (with valve point loadings)

| $P_i$ | Output Limits | | Fuel Coefficients | | | | |
|---|---|---|---|---|---|---|---|
| | Min | Max | a | b | c | e | f |
| 1 | 15 | 55 | 323.79 | 12.41 | 0.004447 | 120 | 0.077 |
| 2 | 150 | 455 | 574.54 | 10.22 | 0.000183 | 300 | 0.035 |
| 3 | 20 | 130 | 374.59 | 8.8 | 0.001126 | 120 | 0.077 |
| 4 | 20 | 130 | 374.59 | 8.8 | 0.001126 | 120 | 0.077 |
| 5 | 150 | 470 | 461.37 | 10.4 | 0.000205 | 300 | 0.035 |
| 6 | 135 | 460 | 630.14 | 10.1 | 0.000301 | 300 | 0.035 |
| 7 | 135 | 465 | 548.2 | 9.87 | 0.000364 | 300 | 0.035 |
| 8 | 60 | 300 | 227.09 | 11.5 | 0.000338 | 200 | 0.042 |
| 9 | 25 | 162 | 173.72 | 11.21 | 0.000807 | 120 | 0.077 |
| 10 | 20 | 160 | 175.95 | 10.72 | 0.001203 | 120 | 0.077 |
| 11 | 20 | 80 | 186.86 | 11.21 | 0.003586 | 120 | 0.077 |
| 12 | 20 | 80 | 230.27 | 9.9 | 0.005513 | 120 | 0.077 |
| 13 | 25 | 85 | 225.28 | 13.12 | 0.000371 | 120 | 0.077 |
| 14 | 15 | 55 | 309.03 | 12.12 | 0.001929 | 120 | 0.077 |
| 15 | 150 | 455 | 671.03 | 10.07 | 0.000299 | 300 | 0.035 |

Penalty multiplier = 100.

Parameters for RQEA:

Penalty Constant ($\lambda$) = 10

Number of iterations = 100

Number of chromosomes (num) = 60

Number of generators (numVars) = 15

Number of solution strings, Nc = 4.

**Table 2.** Frequency of the use of NO1 and NO2

| Stage of search | Proportion of NO1 (%) | Proportion of NO2 (%) |
|---|---|---|
| First one-fifth iterations | 90 | 10 |
| Second one-fifth iterations | 70 | 30 |
| Third one-fifth iterations | 50 | 50 |
| Fourth one-fifth iterations | 30 | 70 |
| Last one-fifth iterations | 10 | 90 |

Table 2 shows the frequency of the use of NO1 and NO2 during the entire evolution process.

The convergence characteristics of the FPGA, RQEA and IRQEA algorithms are shown in Fig.2 for the test case. Investigation of the figure reveals that IRQEA converges faster than FPGA or RQEA while RQEA converges faster than FPGA. Performance of the proposed IRQEA in terms of convergence rate is the best amongst three algorithms.

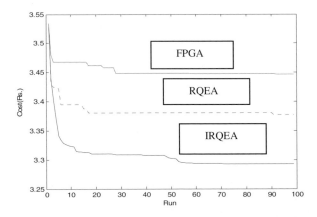

**Fig. 2.** The convergence nature of FPGA, RQEA and IRQEA algorithms on the test case

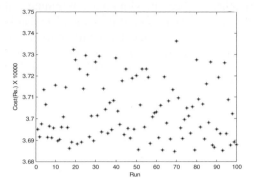

**Fig. 3.** Statistical results of 100 runs with different initial populations with FPGA

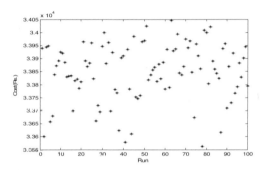

**Fig. 4.** Statistical results of 100 runs with different initial populations with RQEA

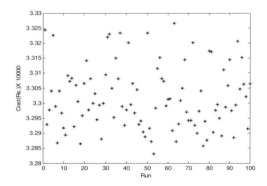

**Fig. 5.** Statistical results of 100 runs with different initial populations with IRQEA

To investigate the effects of initial trial solutions all three algorithms were run with 100 different initial trial solutions and the performance is reported in table 3. The average cost achieved in all the runs with each of the algorithm shows the capability of the algorithm in escaping local minima and find the better global solutions. Also, the lower value in the difference between maximum and minimum values further demonstrates better performance. It can be observed from the table that IRQEA achieved the least average cost amongst three and the least difference between maximum and minimum values. The performance of RQEA algorithm is better than FPGA. Figs. 3, 4 and 5 show the statistical results of 100 runs with FPGA, RQEA and IRQEA algorithyms respectively.

**Table 3.** Statistical test results of 100 runs with different initial solutions (with non-smooth cost curves) for the test case

| Method | Average cost (Rs.) | Maximum cost (Rs,) | Minimum cost (Rs.) |
|--------|--------|--------|--------|
| FPGA | 37032.32 | 37363.22 | 36849.41 |
| RQEA | 33849.42 | 34047.23 | 33563.41 |
| IRQEA | 33018.01 | 33265.11 | 32831.66 |

## 5  Conclusion

Algorithms based on FPGA, RQEA and IRQEA are developed in Matlab command line. Their performances are tested on a test case of 15 units for non-convex economic load dispatch problems with valve point loading effects. Experimental results reveal that all the algorithms are competent to provide better quality solutions. However, RQEA is found to perform better than FPGA and IRQEA has outperformed the other two algorithms. IRQEA exhibited the highest capability of converging to better quality solutions with higher convergence rate. Hence, IRQEA is recommended for solution of highly nonlinear ELD problems in power system

## References

1. Liang, Z.-X., Glover, J.D.: A zoom feature for a dynamic programming solution to economic dispatch including transmission losses. IEEE Trans. on Power Systems 7(2), 544–549 (1992)
2. Wood, A.J., Wollenberg, B.F.: Power Generation, Operation and Control, 2nd edn. Wiley, New York (1996)
3. Wong, K.P., Wong, Y.W.: Thermal generator scheduling using hybrid genetic/simulated annealing approach. IEE Proc. Part-C 142(4), 372–380 (1995)
4. Walter, D.C., Sheble, G.B.: Genetic algorithm solution of economic dispatch with valve point loading. IEEE Trans. on Power Systems 8(3), 1325–1332 (1993)
5. Bakirtzis, A., Petridis, V., Kazarlis, S.: Genetic algorithm solution to the economic dispatch problem. IEE Proc. Part-D 141(4), 377–382 (1994)
6. Sheble, G.B., Brittig, K.: Refined genetic algorithm — Economic dispatch example. IEEE Trans. on. Power Systems 10, 117–124 (1995)

7. Chen, P.H., Chang, H.C.: Large-scale economic dispatch by genetic algorithm. IEEE Trans. on Power Systems 10(4), 1919–1926 (1995)
8. Fogel, D.B.: A comparison of evolutionary programming and genetic algorithms on selected constrained optimization problems. Simulation, 397–404 (June 1995)
9. Goldberg, D.E.: Genetic Algorithms in Search, Optimization and Machine Learning. Addison Wesley, MA (1989)
10. Yalcionoz, T., Altun, H., Uzam, M.: Economic dispatch solution using a genetic algorithm based on arithmetic crossover. In: Proc. Power Tech. Conf. IEEE, Portugal (September 2001)
11. Houck, C.R., Joines, J.A., Kay, M.G.: A genetic algorithm for function optimization: A Matlab implementation. Technical Report NCSU-IE TR 95-09, North Carolina State University (1995)
12. Bäck, T., Schwefel, H.P.: An overview of evolutionary algorithms for parameter optimization. Evolutionary Computation 1(1), 1–23 (1993)
13. Fogel, D.B.: Evolutionary Computation: Toward a New Philosophy of Machine Intelligence. IEEE Press, Piscataway (1995)
14. Fogel, D.B.: An introduction to simulated evolutionary optimization. IEEE Trans. on Neural Networks 5(1), 3–14 (1994)
15. Chellapilla, K.: Combining mutation operators in evolutionary programming. IEEE Trans. on Evolutionary Computation 2(3), 91–96 (1998)
16. Wolpert, D.H., Macready, W.G.: No free lunch theorems for optimization. IEEE Trans. on Evolutionary Computation 1(1), 67–82 (1997)
17. Yang, H.T., Yang, P.C., Huang, C.L.: Evolutionary programming based economic dispatch for units with non-smooth fuel cost functions. IEEE Trans. on Power Systems 11(1), 112–118 (1996)
18. Yao, X., Liu, Y., Lin, G.: Evolutionary programming made faster. IEEE Trans. Evolutionary Computation 3, 82–102 (1999)
19. Sinha, N., Chakrabarti, R., Chattopadhyay, P.K.: Evolutionary programming techniques for economic load dispatch. IEEE Trans. on Evolutionary Computation 7(1), 83–94 (2003)
20. Sinha, N., Chakrabarti, R., Chattopadhyay, P.K.: Fast Evolutionary programming techniques for short-term hydrothermal scheduling. IEEE Trans. on Power Systems 18(1), 214–220 (2003)
21. Yao, X., Liu, Y.: "Fast evolutionary programming. In: Fogel, L.J., Bäck, T., Angeline, P.J. (eds.) Proc. 5th Annu.Conf. Evolutionary Programming, Cambridge, MA, pp. 451–460 (1996)
22. Wong, K.P., Fung, C.C.: Simulated annealing based economic dispatch algorithm. IEE Proc. Part-C 140(6), 544–550 (1992)
23. Kennedy, J., Eberhart, R.: Particle Swarm Optimization. In: Proceedings of IEEE International Conference on Neural Networks, Perth, Australia, vol. IV, pp. 1942–1948 (1995)
24. Park, J.-B., Lee, K.-S., Shin, J.-R., Lee, K.Y.: A particle swarm optimization for economic dispatch with non-smooth cost Functions. IEEE Trans. on Power Systems 20(1), 34–42 (2005)
25. El-Gallad, A., El-Hawary, M., Sallam, A., Kalas, A.: Particle swarm optimizer for constrained economic dispatch with prohibited operating zones. In: Proc. IEEE Canadian Conf. on Electrical and Computer Engineering, pp. 78–81 (2002)
26. Storn, R.: System design by constraint adaptation and differential evolution. IEEE Trans. on Evolutionary Computation 3(1), 22–34 (1999)
27. Han, K., Kim, J.: Quantum-inspired evolutionary algorithm for a class of combinatorial optimization. IEEE transactions on evolutionary computation 6(6) (December 2002)

28. Alfares, F., Alfares, M.S., Esat, I.I.: Quantum-Inspired Evolution Algorithm: Experimental Analysis. Presented at Sixth International Conference on Adaptive Computing in Design and Manufacture, Bristol, UK, pp. 377–389 (2004)
29. Rieffel, E., Polak, W.: An introduction to quantum computing for non-physicists, arxive.org, quantph/9809016 v2 (January 2000)
30. Han, K.H., Kim, J.H.: On the analysis of the quantum-inspired evolutionary algorithm with a single individual. In: 2006 IEEE Congress on Evolutionary Computation, Vancouver, BC, Canada, July 16-21 (2006)
31. Yang, S., Wang, M., Jiao, L.: 'A quantum particle swarm optimization'. In: Proc., IEEE Congress on Evolutionary Computation, CEC 2004, vol. 1, pp. 320–324 (2004)
32. Wang, Y., Feng, X.-Y., Huang, Y.-X., Pu, D.-B., Zhou, W.-G., Liang, Y.-C., Zhou, C.-G.: A novel quantum swarm evolutionary algorithmand its applications. Neurocomputing 70, 633–640 (2007)
33. Sailesh Babu, G.S., Das, D.B., Patvardhan, C.: Real-parameter quantum evolutionary algorithm for economic load dispatch. IET Gener. Transm. Distrib. 2(1), 22–31 (2008)

# Linear Array Geometry Synthesis with Minimum Side Lobe Level and Null Control Using Dynamic Multi-Swarm Particle Swarm Optimizer with Local Search

Pradipta Ghosh and Hamim Zafar

Dept. of Electronics and Telecommunication Engg. Jadavpur University,
Kolkata 700 032, India
pghosh1990@gmail.com, hmm.zafar@gmail.com

**Abstract.** Linear antenna array design is one of the most important electromagnetic optimization problems of current interest. This paper describes the synthesis method of linear array geometry with minimum side lobe level and null control by the Dynamic Multi-Swarm Particle Swarm Optimizer with Local Search (DMSPSO) which optimizes the spacing between the elements of the linear array to produce a radiation pattern with minimum side lobe level and null placement control. The results of the DMSPSO algorithm have been shown to meet or beat the results obtained using other state-of-the-art metaheuristics like the Genetic Algorithm (GA),General Particle Swarm Optimization (PSO), Memetic Algorithms (MA), and Tabu Search (TS) in a statistically meaningful way. Three design examples are presented that illustrate the use of the DMSPSO algorithm, and the optimization goal in each example is easily achieved.

**Keywords:** Antenna array, null control, Dynamic Multi-Swarm Particle Swarm optimization, side lobe suppression, and metaheuristics.

## 1 Introduction

Antenna arrays play an important role in detecting and processing signals arriving from different directions. The goal in antenna array geometry synthesis is to determine the physical layout of the array that produces a radiation pattern that is closest to the desired pattern. Many synthesis methods are concerned with suppressing the Side Lobe Level (SLL) while preserving the gain of the main beam. Other methods deal with the null control to reduce the effects of interference and jamming. For the linear array geometry, this can be done by designing the spacing between the elements, while keeping a uniform excitation over the array aperture. The computational drawbacks of existing numerical methods have forced the researchers all over the world to rely on metaheuristic algorithms founded on simulations of some natural phenomena to solve antenna problems. These algorithms use an objective function, optimization of which leads to the side lobe suppression and null control [2] .In recent past, the computational cost is reduced almost dramatically. Following this

B.K. Panigrahi et al. (Eds.): SEMCCO 2010, LNCS 6466, pp. 701–708, 2010.

tradition. In this paper, DMSPSO is to optimize the spacing between the elements of the linear array to produce a radiation pattern with minimum SLL and null placement control. Three numerical instantiations of the design problems have been used to illustrate the application of the algorithm. Comparison with the results obtained with other best known metaheuristics like GA, PSO, TS, MA etc. reflect the superiority of DMSPSO in a statistically significant fashion. The rest of the paper is organized in the following way. A formulation of the array pattern synthesis as an optimization task has been discussed in Section 2. Section 3 provides a Comprehensive overview of the PSO algorithm. Section 4 provides a Comprehensive overview of the DMSPSO algorithm [1]. Experimental settings have been discussed and the results have been presented in Section 5. Section 6 finally concludes the paper and unfolds a few future research issues.

## 2   Formulation of the Design Problem

An antenna array is a configuration of individual radiating elements that are arranged in space and can be used to produce a directional radiation pattern. For a linear antenna array, let us assume that we have $2N$ isotropic radiators placed symmetrically along the $x$-axis.

The array geometry is shown in Figure 1.

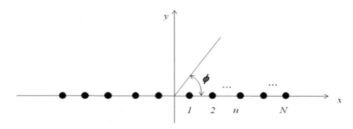

**Fig. 1.** Geometry of the 2N- element symmetric linear array placed along the x-axis

The array factor in the azimuth plane can be written as,

$$AF(\phi) = 2. \sum_{n=1}^{N} I_n.\cos[k.x_n.\cos(\phi) + \varphi_n]. \tag{1}$$

Where k is the wave number, and $I_n, \varphi_n$, and $x_n$ are, respectively excitation magnitude, phase and location of the $n$th element. If we further assume a uniform excitation of amplitude and phase (that is $I_n = 1$ and $\varphi_n = 0$ for all elements), the array factor can be further simplified as:

$$AF(\phi) = 2. \sum_{n=1}^{N} \cos[k.x_n.\cos(\phi)] \tag{2}$$

Now the statement of the problem, addressed here, simply reduces to: apply the DMSPSO algorithm to find the locations $x_n$ of the array elements that will result in an array beam with minimum SLL and, if desired, nulls at specific directions. For side lobe suppression, the objective function is:

$$f_1 = \sum_i \frac{1}{\Delta \phi_i} \int_{\phi_{li}}^{\phi_{ui}} |AF(\phi)|.d\phi \tag{3}$$

And for null control we use:

$$f_2 = \sum_k |AF(\phi_k)|^2 \tag{4}$$

To minimize both of them we use a sum of (3) and (4) as our combined objective function of the DMSPSO algorithm. So to achieve this goal, the following function is used to evaluate the fitness:

$$Fitness = \sum_i \frac{1}{\Delta \phi_i} \int_{\phi_{li}}^{\phi_{ui}} |AF(\phi)^2| d\phi + \sum_k AF(\phi_k)^2 \tag{5}$$

Where $[\phi_{ui}, \phi_{li}]$s are the spatial regions in which the SLL is suppressed, $\Delta \phi = \phi_{ui} - \phi_{li}$ represents the bandwidth to suppress and $\phi_k$'s are the directions of the nulls. Our main motive is to make the antenna very directive in nature. For this reason we have to reduce the side lobes as much as possible. There are two techniques in evaluating the contribution of side lobes in radiation pattern. We can consider that each side lobe is situated between two nulls and their contributions in fitness are evaluated separately. Otherwise, we can consider entire beam pattern except main lobe as side lobe and take the null directions separately in fitness concern. We have to prevent widening of the main beam's width while achieving the side lobe suppression and nulls' design. This is done basically by considering the contribution of main lobe as a separate fitness function.

## 3 An Overview of PSO Algorithm

The PSO algorithm is an evolutionary algorithm capable of solving difficult multidimensional optimization problems in various fields. Since its introduction in 1995 by Kennedy and Eberhart [4], the PSO has gained an increasing popularity as an efficient alternative to GA and SA in solving optimization design problems in antenna arrays. As an evolutionary algorithm, the PSO algorithm depends on the social interaction between independent agents, here called particles, during their search for the optimum solution using the concept of fitness. After defining the solution space and the fitness function, the PSO algorithm starts by randomly initializing the position and velocity of each particle in the swarm. PSO is initialized with a population of random solutions (i.e., particles) flown through a hyper dimensional search space. Each particle in PSO has an adaptable velocity. Moreover, each particle has a memory remembering the best position of the search space that has ever been visited. Particles have the tendency to fly towards a better search area over the course of the search process. Thus their movement is an aggregated acceleration towards its best previously visited position and towards the best individual of a particle neighborhood.

All the information needed by the PSO algorithm is contained in X (Position matrix), V (Velocity matrix), P (Personal best position matrix) and G (Global best position). The velocity matrix is updated according to [4], [5]

$$v_{mn}^t = wv_{mn}^{t-1} + c_1 U_{n1}^t (p_{mn}^t - x_{mn}^{t-1}) + c_2 U_{n2}^t (g_n^t - x_{mn}^{t-1}) \tag{6}$$

Where the superscripts t and t-1 refer to the time index of the current and the previous iterations, $U_{n1}$ and $U_{n2}$ are two uniformly distributed random numbers in the interval [0,1] and these random numbers are different for each of the n components of the particle's velocity vector. The parameters $c_1$ and $c_2$ specify the relative weight of the personal best position versus the global best position. They are called *acceleration constants*. The parameter **w** is a number, called the *"inertial weight"*, in the range [0, 1], and it specifies the weight by which the particle's current velocity depends on its previous velocity and how far the particle is from its personal best and global best positions.

The position matrix is updated at each iteration according to

$$X^t = X^{t-1} + V^t \tag{7}$$

In each iteration of the algorithm, the particle's position vector that resulted in the best fitness is chosen as the global best position vector, and this information is passed to all other particles to use in adjusting their velocity and position vectors accordingly.

## 4   An Overview of DMSPSO Algorithm

The dynamic multi-swarm particle swarm optimizer is constructed based on the local version of PSO with a new neighborhood topology. PSO with small neighborhoods performs better on complex problems. Hence, In order to slow down the population's convergence velocity and increase diversity and achieve better results on multimodal problems, in the DMS-PSO, small neighborhoods are used. The population is divided into small sized swarms. Each swarm uses its own members to search for better area in the search space. Since the small sized swarms are searching using their own best historical information, they are easy to converge to a local optimum because of PSO's convergence property. In order to avoid it we must allow information exchange among the swarms. And in the information exchange schedule, we want to keep more information including the good ones and the not so good ones to add the varieties of the particles and achieve larger diversity. So a randomized regrouping schedule is introduced to make the particles have a dynamic changing neighborhood structures. Every R generations, the population is regrouped randomly and starts searching using a new configuration of small swarms. Here R is called *regrouping period*. In this way, the information obtained by each swarm is exchanged among the swarms. With the randomly regrouping schedule, particles from different swarms are grouped in a new configuration so that each small swarms search space is enlarged and better solutions are possible to be found by the new small swarms. This procedure is shown in Figure 2.

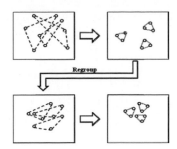

**Fig. 2.** DMS-PSO's Search

In this paper, we introduce two concepts to modify the DMS-PSO for seeking better performance. In order to alleviate this weakness and give a better search in the better local areas, a local search is added into DMS-PSO:

1) Every $L$ generations, sort the groups according to their fitness value and refine the *lbest* of the best 25% groups using the Quasi-Newton method.
2) In the end of the search, the best solution achieved so far is refined using Quasi-Newton method .Combining with the local search schedule, the DMS-PSO is modified to DMS-PSO with local search (DMS-L-PSO).

## 5  Experimental Results

Here we have used DMSPSO for linear antenna design. The results have been compared with that of Genetic Algorithm (GA), Tabu Search Algorithm (TSA), Memetic Algorithm (MA) and Particle Swarm Optimization (PSO). For DMSPSO we used the following parametric setup for all the design examples considered here: $N_p$ = no of particles = 30, I = no of iteration = 2000, $c_1 = c_2$=1.494, $w$ = 0.793. Once set, no further hand tuning has been allowed for any of the parameter. For the competitor algorithms PSO, GA, MA, and TSA, we used the best possible parametric setup. In the first example DMSPSO, GA, TSA, PSO, and MA were used to design 12 element array for minimum SLL in bands $[0°,82°]$ and $[98°,180°]$ and no null direction. Figure 3 shows the Gain versus Azimuth Angle plot. Table 4 shows the geometry of the linear array normalized to $\lambda/2$. Table 1 shows the mean objective function values and standard deviations as obtained for the different optimization technique.

A non-parametric statistical test called *Wilcoxon's rank sum test* [6] for independent samples is conducted at the 5% significance level.

**Table 1.** Statistical values pertaining to example 1

| ALGORITHM | DMS | GA | TSA | PSO | MA |
|---|---|---|---|---|---|
| Mean obj. func. value | **0.00898** | 0.009061 | 0.011219 | 0.010843 | 0.009196 |
| Std. Dev | **0.000141** | 0.000681 | 0.000712 | 0.000319 | 0.000521 |
| *P*-values | NA | 2.2917e-10 | 1.3493e-11 | 3.9034e-13 | 1.3493e-16 |

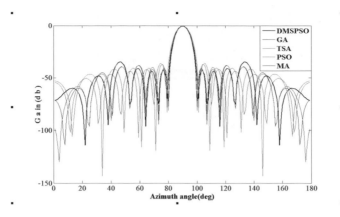

**Fig. 3.** Normalized patterns for 12 element array (example 1)

The second example has minimum SLL in bands $[0°,82°]$ and $[98°,180°]$ and null direction in $81°$ and $99°$. The array pattern from the DMSPSO algorithm is shown in Figure 4, along with patterns obtained using other competitive metaheuristics.

From Figure 3 it is evident that DMSPSO has minimized SLL to the greatest extent and has a low gain value at the null directions as well.

The P-values show that the difference between the mean objective function values obtained with DMSPSO and any other competitive algorithm is statistically significant.

In the third example, 26 element arrays has been designed for minimum SLL in bands $[0°,80°]$ and $[100°,180°]$ and with nulls at $12°$, $60°$, $120°$ and $168°$.

Figure 5 show that DMSPSO has successfully minimized both the side lobe level and in the required null directions.

Tables 3 and 6 present similar results as Tables 1 and 4 but now for design example 3. Table 3 shows that DMSPSO can yield statistically significantly better final accuracy than all its competitors. Figure 5 indicates that not only does DMSPSO yield the most accurate results for nearly the design problem, but it does so consuming the least amount of computational time. Note that we omitted the convergence graph for the first two design problems in order to save space and also in consideration of the fact that these graphs show a similar trend.

**Table 2.** Statistical values pertaining to example 2

| ALGORITHM | DMS | GA | TSA | PSO | MA |
|---|---|---|---|---|---|
| Mean obj. func. value | **0.0193** | 0.023662 | 0.021898 | 0.026755 | 0.021630 |
| Std. Dev | **0.001033** | 0.001201 | 0.001109 | 0.001613 | 0.001331 |
| *P*-values | **NA** | 6.1304e-12 | 5.5647e-12 | 9.6808e-15 | 8.0040e-14 |

**Table 3.** Statistical values pertaining to example 3

| ALGORITHM | DMS | GA | TSA | PSO | MA |
|---|---|---|---|---|---|
| Mean obj. func. value | **0.0155** | 0.050279 | 0.061428 | 0.048131 | 0.027195 |
| Std. Dev | **0.001430** | 0.003163 | 0.008221 | 0.003331 | 0.001109 |
| *P*-values | **NA** | 5.5647e-12 | 9.6808e-15 | 4.0040e-13 | 6.1304e-12 |

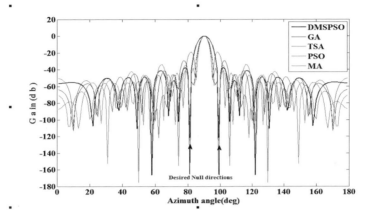

**Fig. 4.** Normalized patterns for 22 element array (example 2)

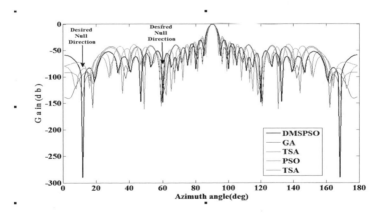

**Fig. 5.** Normalized patterns for 26 element array (example 3)

**Table 4.** Geometry of the 12 element linear array normalized with respect to $\lambda/2$ (median Solution of 50 runs)

| DMSPSO | ±0.4939 | ±1.1579 | ±2.2620 | ±3.0264 | ±4.3651 | ±5.8311 |
|---|---|---|---|---|---|---|
| GA | ±0.506812 | ±1.261121 | ±2.288589 | ±3.191000 | ±4.561101 | ±5.999814 |
| TSA | ±0.388182 | ±1.258812 | ±2.107651 | ±3.052561 | ±4.188121 | ±5.450781 |
| PSO | ±0.247040 | ±1.310992 | ±1.936749 | ±2.971791 | ±3.927218 | ±5.180897 |
| MA | ±0.481956 | ±1.278123 | ±2.288123 | ±3.235781 | ±4.602561 | ±5.999021 |

**Table 5.** Geometry of the 22 element linear array normalized with respect to $\lambda/2$ (median solution of 50 runs)

| DMSPSO | ±0.2192 | ±0.8695 | ±1.6173 | ±1.8142 | ±2.5762 | ±3.1445 | ±3.6477 | ±4.4561 | ±5.1962 | ±6.1716 | ±7.0915 |
|--------|---------|---------|---------|---------|---------|---------|---------|---------|---------|---------|---------|
| GA  | ±0.0002 | ±1.061 | ±1.486 | ±2.419 | ±3.386 | ±4.285 | ±5.407 | ±6.846 | ±8.042 | ±9.136 | ±10.398 |
| TSA | ±0.6982 | ±1.071 | ±2.485 | ±2.541 | ±4.148 | ±5.479 | ±6.480 | ±7.573 | ±8.714 | ±10.211 | ±11.64 |
| PSO | ±0.3006 | ±1.177 | ±1.855 | ±2.685 | ±3.524 | ±4.428 | ±5.468 | ±6.580 | ±7.953 | ±9.552 | ±11.00 |
| MA  | ±0.8113 | ±2.273 | ±3.157 | ±3.948 | ±4.770 | ±5.411 | ±6.432 | ±6.934 | ±7.896 | ±8.712 | ±10.124 |

**Table 6.** Geometry of the 26 element linear array normalized with respect to $\lambda/2$ (median Solution of 50 runs)

| DMSPSO | ±0.2758 | ±1.3622 | ±1.9908 | ±2.9325 | ±3.6961 | ±4.5679 | ±5.5225 | ±6.4848 | ±7.3669 | ±8.1894 | ±9.1213 | ±10.0872 | ±11.2330 |
|--------|---------|---------|---------|---------|---------|---------|---------|---------|---------|---------|---------|----------|----------|
| GA  | ±0.4242 | ±0.8472 | ±1.579 | ±2.468 | ±2.993 | ±4.391 | ±4.629 | ±5.640 | ±6.399 | ±7.791 | ±8.795 | ±9.974 | ±11.38 |
| TSA | ±0.5311 | ±1.491 | ±2.468 | ±3.445 | ±4.524 | ±5.501 | ±6.491 | ±7.268 | ±8.498 | ±9.514 | ±10.27 | ±11.44 | ±12.42 |
| PSO | ±0.5798 | ±1.741 | ±2.806 | ±3.923 | ±4.885 | ±5.939 | ±7.100 | ±8.137 | ±9.171 | ±9.956 | ±10.75 | ±11.82 | ±13.00 |
| MA  | ±0.4521 | ±0.8512 | ±1.606 | ±2.497 | ±3.019 | ±4.397 | ±4.629 | ±5.687 | ±6.399 | ±7.792 | ±8.796 | ±9.976 | ±11.40 |

# 6 Conclusion

This paper illustrated the use of the DMS-PSO algorithm in the synthesis of linear array geometry for the purpose of suppressed side lobes and null placement in certain directions. DMS-PSO was successfully used to optimize the locations of array elements to exhibit an array pattern with either suppressed side lobes, null placement in certain directions, or both. In each of these cases, the DMS-PSO algorithm easily achieved the optimization goal, beating four other state-of-the-art optimization techniques in a statistically significant fashion. Future research may focus on achieving more control of the array pattern by using the DMS-PSO algorithm to optimize, not only the location, but also the excitation amplitude and phase of each element in the array, and exploring other array geometries. As a metaheuristic algorithm, DMS-PSO will most likely be an increasingly attractive alternative, in the electromagnetic and antennas community, to other evolutionary algorithms such as GAs and other PSOs. It can also be easily implemented and has less time complexity.

# References

[1] Liang, J.J., Suganthan, P.N.: Dynamic Multi-Swarm Particle Swarm Optimizer with Local Search. In: CEC 2005 (2005)
[2] Khodier, M.M., Christodoulou, C.G.: Linear array geometry synthesis with minimum side lobe level and null control using particle swarm optimization. IEEE Transactions on Antennas and Propagation 53(8) (August 2005)
[3] Godara, L.C. (ed.): Handbook of Antennas in Wireless Communications. CRC, Boca Raton (2002)
[4] Kennedy, J., Eberhart, R.C.: Particle swarm optimization. In: Proc. IEEE Conf. Neural Networks IV, Piscataway, NJ (1995)
[5] Eberhart, R.C., Shi, Y.: Particle swarm optimization: developments, applications and resources. In: Proc. 2001 Congr. Evolutionary Computation, vol. 1 (2001)
[6] Wilcoxon, F.: Individual comparisons by ranking methods. Biometrics Bulletin 1, 80–83 (1945)

# Constraint Handling in Transmission Network Expansion Planning

R. Mallipeddi[1], Ashu Verma[2], P.N. Suganthan[1], B.K. Panigrahi[3], and P.R. Bijwe[3]

[1] School of Electrical and Electronic Engineering,
Nanyang Technological University, Singapore 639798
[2] Department of Energy and Environment,
The Energy and Resources Institute (TERI) University, Delhi, India
[3] Department of Electrical Engineering,
Indian Institute of Technology, Delhi, India
mallipeddi.ram@gmail.com, ashu.verma@teri.res.in,
epnsugan@ntu.edu.sg, bkpanigrahi@ee.iitd.ac.in,
prbijwe@ee.iitd.ac.in

**Abstract.** Transmission network expansion planning (TNEP) is a very important and complex problem in power system. Recently, the use of metaheuristic techniques to solve TNEP is gaining more importance due to their effectiveness in handling the inequality constraints and discrete values over the conventional gradient based methods. Evolutionary algorithms (EAs) generally perform unconstrained search and require some additional mechanism to handle constraints. In EA literature, various constraint handling techniques have been proposed. However, to solve TNEP the penalty function approach is commonly used while the other constraint handling methods are untested. In this paper, we evaluate the performance of different constraint handling methods like Superiority of Feasible Solutions (SF), Self adaptive Penalty (SP), $\mathcal{E}$-Constraint (EC), Stochastic Ranking (SR) and the ensemble of constraint handling techniques (ECHT) on TNEP. The potential of different constraint handling methods and their ensemble is evaluated using an IEEE 24 bus system with and without security constraints.

**Keywords:** Transmission network expansion planning, differential Evolution, security constraints, optimization, constraint handling.

## 1 Introduction

Transmission network expansion planning (TNEP) [1] deals with finding out the least cost expansion of new lines such that the cost of expansion plan is minimum and no power system constraints are violated during the planning horizon. The TNEP problem is a mixed integer, non linear, non convex optimization problem. Also, the number of options to be analyzed is very large and increases exponentially with the size of the system. Hence, more robust and efficient techniques are required for

B.K. Panigrahi et al. (Eds.): SEMCCO 2010, LNCS 6466, pp. 709–717, 2010.
© Springer-Verlag Berlin Heidelberg 2010

TNEP. Metaheuristic techniques are known for their computational rigorousness and ability to find global optimum solution.

Metaheuristic techniques such as Genetic Algorithm (GA) [2-4], Simulated Annealing (SA) [5], Tabu Search (TS) [6-7], greedy randomized adaptive search procedure (GRASP) [8], particle swarm optimization [9], Improved Harmony Search (IHS) [10] have been used to solve the TNEP problem because of their superior performance compared to conventional methods in finding better optimal solution. Evolutionary algorithms (EAs) always perform unconstrained search. Thus solving constrained optimization problems, they require additional mechanisms to handle constraints. In the literature, several constraint handling techniques have been proposed to be used with the EAs [11].

In constrained optimization, discarding the infeasible individuals in the process of evolution may result in the loss of potential information, due to which probabilistic search methods such as EAs may be trapped in the local minima in discontinuous search spaces. Thus, a constrained optimization problem can better solved by the effective usage of the potential information present in the infeasible individuals. Therefore, different techniques have been developed to exploit the information in infeasible individuals. Michalewicz and Schoenauer [12] grouped the methods for handling constraints within EAs into four categories: preserving feasibility of solutions [13], penalty functions, make a separation between feasible and infeasible solutions, and hybrid methods. According to the no free lunch theorem [14], no single state-of-the-art constraint handling technique can outperform all others on every problem. Hence, solving a particular constrained problem requires numerous trial-and-error runs to choose a suitable constraint handling technique and to fine tune the associated parameters. In [15] an ensemble of constraint handling techniques (ECHT) was proposed as an efficient alternative to the trial-and-error based search for the best constraint handling technique with its best parameters for a given problem.

Real world problems such as TNEP, involve hard constraints, the satisfaction of which is essential for the stable and secure operation of the system. In TNEP literature, to handle the constraints, penalty function approach is widely used in conjunction with EAs. In penalty function approach, each constraint violation is multiplied by a penalty coefficient and added to the objective function to obtain a fitness value. The choice of penalty coefficients is problem dependant. Hence choosing the appropriate penalty values for different constraints is necessary, the failure in which leads to a degraded performance by the algorithm. The appropriate selection of the penalty coefficients requires a tedious trial and error procedure as [16]: 1) small penalty coefficients over explore the infeasible region delaying the process of finding feasible solutions and may prematurely converge to an infeasible solution, 2) large penalty coefficients may not explore the infeasible region properly, thus resulting in premature convergence. The tedious process of choosing a suitable penalty parameter can be avoided by using different constraint handling techniques present in the EC literature, which are untested in the field of power engineering. In this paper, using DE as the basic search algorithm, we have evaluated the performance of different constraint handling methods such as Superiority of Feasible

Solutions (SF), Self adaptive Penalty (SP), $\mathcal{E}$ - Constraint (EC), Stochastic Ranking (SR) and ECHT for TNEP with and without security constraints.

## 2  Transmission Network Expansion Planning

In this section the formulation of TNEP problem is discussed. System security is an important aspect and must be considered in a TNEP problem. The *N-1* contingency analysis looks at the system state after a single line outage. A comprehensive model for TNEP with security constraints is presented in [17], which is used as a base for formulating TNEP with security constraints in this paper. The TNEP with security constraints, can be stated as follows [10],

$$\min \ v = \sum_{l \in \Omega} c_l n_l \tag{1}$$

s.t.
$$S \ f^k + g \ = d \tag{2}$$

$$f_l^k - \gamma_l \left( n_l^0 + n_l \right)(\Delta \theta_l^k) = 0, \text{for } l \in 1,2.........., nl \ \& \ l \neq k \tag{3}$$

$$f_l^k - \gamma_l \left( n_l^0 + n_l - 1 \right)(\Delta \theta_l^k) = 0, \text{for } l{=}k, \tag{4}$$

$$\left| f_l^k \right| \le \left( n_l^0 + n_l \right) \overline{f_l} \ , \text{for } l \in 1,2.........., nl \ \& \ l \neq k \tag{5}$$

$$\left| f_l^k \right| \le \left( n_l^0 + n_l - 1 \right) \overline{f_l} \ , \ \text{for } l{=}k, \tag{6}$$

$$0 \le n_l \le \overline{n_l} \tag{7}$$

$f_l^k$ and $\theta_l^k$ are unbounded,
$n_l \ge 0$, and integer, for $l \in 1,2.........., nl \ \& \ l \neq k$, $\quad (n_l + n_l^0 - 1) \ge 0$, and integer, for $l = k$
$l \in \Omega$, and $k{=}0,1,........................, NC$,
where, $k = 0$, represents the base case without any line outage.

$S$ : branch-node incidence transposed matrix of the power system, $C_l$: cost of $l^{th}$ line, $g$: generation vector, $d$: demand vector, $f^k$ :vector with elements $f_l^k$, $\gamma_l$ : susceptance of the circuit that can be added to $l^{th}$ right-of-way, $n_l$ : the number of circuits added in $l^{th}$ right-of-way, $n_l^0$ : number of circuits in the base case, $\Delta \theta_l^k$ : phase angle difference in $l^{th}$ right-of way when $k^{th}$ line is out, $f_l^k$ : total real power flow by the circuit in $l^{th}$ right-of-way  when $k^{th}$ line is out, $\overline{f_l}$ : maximum allowed real power flow in the circuit in $l^{th}$ right-of-way, $\overline{n_l}$ : maximum number of circuits that can be added in $l^{th}$ right-of-way, $\Omega$ :set of all right-of-ways, $nl$: total number of lines in the circuit, $NC$: number of credible contingencies (taken as equal to $nl$ in the present case).

The objective of TNEP is to find the set of transmission lines to be constructed such that the cost of expansion plan is minimum, satisfying the constraint on real power flow in the lines of the network, for base case and *N-1* contingency cases. In the above formulation, constraint (2) represents the power balance at each node.

Constraint (3) and (4) are the real power flow equations in DC network. Constraint (5) and (6) represents the line real power flow constraint. Constraint (7) represents the restriction on the construction of lines per corridor (R.O.W).

**Note:** *The transmission network expansion planning without security constraints is a special case of TNEP with security constraints with k=0.*

## 3   Constraint Handling in Evolutionary Algorithms

A constrained optimization problem with $n$ parameters to be optimized is usually written as a nonlinear programming problem of the following form [18]:

$$\text{Minimize: } f(X), \quad X = (x_1, x_2, \ldots, x_n) \text{ and } X \in S_r \tag{8}$$

$$\text{subject to: } \begin{matrix} g_i(X) \leq 0, & i = 1, \ldots, p \\ h_j(X) = 0, & j = p+1, \ldots, m \end{matrix} \tag{9}$$

where, $f$ need not to be continuous but it must be bounded.

$S_r$ is the whole search space

$p$ is the number of inequality constraints

$(m - p)$ is the number of equality constraints

The equality constraints in equation (9) can be transformed into inequality form and can be combined with other inequality constraints as

$$G_i(X) = \begin{cases} \max\{g_i(X), 0\} & i = 1, \ldots p. \\ \max\{| h_i(X)| - \delta, 0\} & i = p+1, \ldots, m \end{cases} \tag{10}$$

Where, $\delta$ is a tolerance parameter for the equality constraints. Therefore, the objective is to minimize the fitness function $f(X)$ such that the optimal solution obtained satisfies all the inequality constraints $G_i(X)$. The overall constraint violation for an infeasible individual is a weighted mean of all the constraints, which is expressed as:

$$v(X) = \frac{\sum_{i=1}^{m} w_i(G_i(X))}{\sum_{i=1}^{m} w_i} \tag{11}$$

Where, $w_i \left(= 1/G_{\max_i}\right)$ is a weight parameter, $G_{\max_i}$ is the maximum violation of constraint $G_i(X)$ obtained so far. Here, $w_i$ is set as $1/G_{\max_i}$ which varies during the evolution in order to balance the contribution of every constraint in the problem irrespective of their differing numerical ranges.

A brief overview of the most commonly used constraint handling techniques in the EA literature and their ensemble is described in [15]. The flow chart of the ECHTDE algorithm is presented in Fig 1.

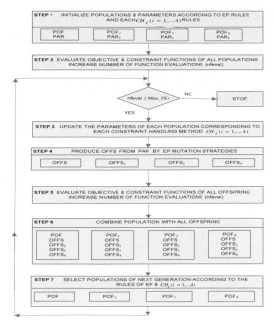

**Fig. 1.** Flowchart of ECHTDE (CH: Constraint Handling Method, POP: Population, PAR: Parameters, OFF: Offspring, Max_FEs: Maximum number of function evaluations)

## 4 Results

In this paper an IEEE 24 bus standard test system is used as a case study. The IEEE 24 bus system consists of 24 buses, 41 candidate circuits and 8550 MW of total demand. A maximum of three lines per corridor can be added. The initial network can be found in [19, 20]. The electrical data and generation/load data have been taken for Plans $G_1$- $G_4$ of [20].

DE is used as the basic search algorithm and the algorithms evaluated are

1. Superiority of feasible solutions with DE (SFDE)
2. Self-adaptive penalty with DE (SPDE)
3. Epsilon constraint with DE (ECDE)
4. Stochastic ranking (SRDE)

The constraint handling methods SF and SP do not have any parameters. The parameters used by EC are set to: $T_c = 0.2T_{max}$, $C_p = 5$. $C_p$ and $T_c$ are the control parameters of EC while $T_{max}$ is the maximum number of iterations. The probability parameter $P_f$, corresponding to SR is linearly decreased from an initial value of 0.475 to 0.025 in the final generation [15].

*The DE parameter settings used are*

Population size = 50, Scale factor (F) = 05, Crossover rate (CR) = 0.3, Maximum number of function evaluations used = 100000 (TNEP without security constraints), 2000000 (TNEP with security constraints).

## 4.1 TNEP without Security Constraints

The results for TNEP without security constraints for the four cases $G_1$-$G_4$ with different constraint methods and their ensemble are given in the Tables 1-4. From the results presented below it can be observed that no individual constraint handling method is superior on all the plans ($G_1$ –$G_4$). It can also be observed that the performance of ECHTDE is consistent on all the plans.

**Table 1.** Results for TNEP without security constraints for generation plan $G_1$

| Plan ($G_1$) | SFDE | SPDE | SRDE | ECDE | ECHTDE |
|---|---|---|---|---|---|
| No of trails in without constraint violation | 50 | 50 | 42 | 50 | 50 |
| Min Cost | 406 | 390 | 439 | 390 | 390 |
| Max Cost | 511 | 497 | 696 | 502 | 479 |
| Mean | 451.22 | 438.66 | 545.56 | 442.66 | 393.34 |
| std | 27.9294 | 28.0136 | 59.5278 | 29.1194 | 13.03779 |

**Table 2.** Results for TNEP without security constraints for generation plan $G_2$

| Plan ($G_2$) | SFDE | SPDE | SRDE | ECDE | ECHTDE |
|---|---|---|---|---|---|
| No of trails in without constraint violation | 50 | 50 | 50 | 50 | 50 |
| Min Cost | 336 | 336 | 336 | 336 | 336 |
| Max Cost | 352 | 367 | 498 | 352 | 356 |
| Mean | 341.64 | 346.42 | 383.82 | 342.02 | 337.76 |
| std | 5.9307 | 7.6880 | 26.7219 | 6.042 | 5.3702 |

**Table 3.** Results for TNEP without security constraints for generation plan $G_3$

| Plan ($G_3$) | SFDE | SPDE | SRDE | ECDE | ECHTDE |
|---|---|---|---|---|---|
| No of trails in without constraint violation | 50 | 50 | 50 | 50 | 50 |
| Min Cost | 220 | 220 | 230 | 220 | 220 |
| Max Cost | 257 | 268 | 308 | 254 | 257 |
| Mean | 238.38 | 229.90 | 278.18 | 236.56 | 241.06 |
| std | 11.2357 | 10.1141 | 16.6692 | 12.2638 | 10.6223 |

**Table 4.** Results for TNEP without security constraints for generation plan $G_4$

| Plan ($G_4$) | SFDE | SPDE | SRDE | ECDE | ECHTDE |
|---|---|---|---|---|---|
| No of trails in without constraint violation | 50 | 50 | 50 | 50 | 50 |
| Min Cost | 292 | 292 | 292 | 292 | 292 |
| Max Cost | 299 | 304 | 311 | 300 | 300 |
| Mean | 293.40 | 299.00 | 301.62 | 294.36 | 298.40 |
| std | 1.6903 | 2.7921 | 4.1201 | 2.6323 | 2.4244 |

## 4.2 TNEP with Security Constraints

The results for TNEP with security constraints for the four cases $G_1$-$G_4$ with different constraint methods and their ensemble are given in the Tables 5-8. From the results presented below it can be observed that no individual constraint handling method is superior on all the plans ($G_1$ –$G_4$). It can also be observed that the performance of ECHTDE is consistent on all the plans. It can be seen from the results that on all the plans ($G_1$-$G_4$), the number of trails in which ECHTDE is able to find feasible solutions is more than individual constraint handling techniques.

**Table 5.** Results for TNEP with security constraints for generation plan $G_1$

| Plan ($G_1$) | SFDE | SPDE | SRDE | ECDE | ECHTDE |
|---|---|---|---|---|---|
| No of trails in without constraint violation | 4 | 3 | 0 | 8 | 44 |
| Min Cost | 1119 | 1225 | - | 1058 | 917 |
| Max Cost | 1331 | 1283 | - | 13310 | 1285 |
| Mean | 1252.3 | 1251.0 | - | 1230.3 | 1081.4 |
| std | 92.5 | 29.5 | - | 100.1 | 94.6 |

**Table 6.** Results for TNEP with security constraints for generation plan $G_2$

| Plan ($G_2$) | SFDE | SPDE | SRDE | ECDE | ECHTDE |
|---|---|---|---|---|---|
| No of trails in without constraint violation | 45 | 36 | 0 | 40 | 49 |
| Min Cost | 1000 | 1017 | - | 1017 | 974 |
| Max Cost | 1371 | 1285 | - | 1378 | 1361 |
| Mean | 1093 | 1122.2 | - | 1110.1 | 1019.2 |
| std | 72.4 | 74.7 | - | 93.4 | 65.8 |

**Table 7.** Results for TNEP with security constraints for generation plan $G_3$

| Plan ($G_3$) | SFDE | SPDE | SRDE | ECDE | ECHTDE |
|---|---|---|---|---|---|
| No of trails in without constraint violation | 50 | 47 | 0 | 50 | 50 |
| Min Cost | 948 | 920 | - | 959 | 870 |
| Max Cost | 1210 | 1253 | - | 1169 | 1174 |
| Mean | 1079 | 1106.6 | - | 1066 | 1051.5 |
| std | 49.9 | 65.5 | - | 50.0 | 58.0 |

**Table 8.** Results for TNEP with security constraints for generation plan $G_4$

| Plan ($G_4$) | SFDE | SPDE | SRDE | ECDE | ECHTDE |
|---|---|---|---|---|---|
| No of trails in without constraint violation | 50 | 50 | 0 | 50 | 50 |
| Min Cost | 959 | 989 | - | 963 | 961 |
| Max Cost | 1108 | 1262 | - | 1087 | 1141 |
| Mean | 1031.4 | 1071.1 | - | 1013.6 | 1020.5 |
| std | 32.8 | 32.8 | - | 27.0 | 33.8 |

## 5   Conclusions

In this paper we evaluated the performance of different constraint handling methods using DE have been investigated for transmission network expansion planning without and without security constraints. Results for IEEE 24 bus systems confirm the potential of proposed ECHTDE algorithm. The performance of ECHTDE is consistent and better than individual constraint handling techniques.

## References

[1] Garver, L.L.: Transmission network estimation using linear programming. IEEE Transactions on PAS 89(7), 1688–1697 (2007)
[2] da Silva, E.L., Gil, H.A., Areiza, J.M.: Transmission network expansion planning under an improved genetic algorithm. IEEE Transactions on Power Syst. 15(3), 1168–1175 (2000)
[3] Escobar, A.H., Gallego, R.A., Romero, R.: Multistage and Coordinated planning of the expansion of transmission systems. IEEE Transactions on Power Syst. 19(2), 735–744 (2004)
[4] Romero, R., Rider, M.J., de Silva, I.J.: A Metaheuristic to solve the Transmission Expansion Planning. IEEE Transactions on Power Syst. 22(4), 2289–2291 (2007)

[5] Romero, R., Gallego, R.A., Monticelli, A.: Transmission network expansion planning by Simulated Annealing'. IEEE Transactions on Power Syst. 11(1), 364–369 (1990)

[6] Gallego, R.A., Romero, R., Monticelli, A.J.: Tabu search algorithm for network synthesis. IEEE Transactions on Power Syst. 15(2), 490–495 (2002)

[7] de Silva, E.L., Oliveira, G.C., Binato, S.: Transmission network expansion planning under a tabu search approach. IEEE Transactions on Power Syst. 16(1), 62–68 (2001)

[8] Binato, S., de Oliveira, G.C., de Araújo, J.L.: A greedy randomized adaptive search procedure for transmission expansion planning. IEEE Transactions on Power Syst. 16(2), 247–253 (2001)

[9] Jin, Y.X., Cheng, H.Z., Yan, Y.J., Zhang, L.: New discrete particle swarm optimization and its application in transmission network expansion planning. Electric power system research 77, 227–233 (2007)

[10] Verma, A., Panigrahi, B.K., Bijwe, P.R.: Harmony Search algorithm for transmission network expansion planning. IET Generation, Transmission and Distribution 4(6), 663–673 (2010)

[11] Coello, C.A.: Theoretical and Numerical Constraint-handling Techniques used with Evolutionary Algorithms: A Survey of the state of the art. Computer Methods in Applied Mechanics and Engineering 191, 1245–1287 (2002)

[12] Michalewicz, Z., Schoenauer, M.: Evolutionary Algorithms for Constrained parameter Optimization Problems. Evolutionary Computation 4, 1–32 (1996)

[13] Koziel, S., Michalewicz, Z.: Evolutionary Algorithms, Homomorphous Mappings, and Constrained Parameter Optimization. Evolutionary Computation 7, 19–44 (1999)

[14] Wolpert, D.H., Macready, W.G.: No Free Lunch Theorems for Optimization. IEEE Transactions on Evolutionary Computation 1, 67–82 (1997)

[15] Mallipeddi, R., Suganthan, P.N.: Ensemble of Constraint Handling Techniques. IEEE Transactions on Evolutionary Computation (2010)

[16] Michalewicz, Z., Fogel, D.B.: How to solve it: Modern Heuristics. Springer, Berlin (2000)

[17] de Silva, I., Rider, M.J., Romero, R., Garcia, A.V., Murari, C.A.: Transmission network expansion planning with security constraints. In: IEE Proc. Gener. Transm. Distrib., vol. 152(6), pp. 828–836 (2005)

[18] Qin, K., Huang, V.L., Suganthan, P.N.: Differential evolution algorithm with strategy adaptation for global numerical optimization. IEEE Transactions on Evolutionary Computation 13, 398–417 (2009)

[19] Fang, R., Hill, D.J.: A new strategy for transmission expansion in competitive electricity markets. IEEE Trans. Power Syst. 18(1), 374–380 (2003)

[20] Romero, R., Rocha, C., Mantovani, J.R.S., Sánchez, I.G.: Constructive heuristic algorithm for the DC model in network transmission expansion planning. IEE Proc. Gener. Transm. Distrib. 152(2), 277–282 (2005)

# A Novel Multi-objective Formulation for Hydrothermal Power Scheduling Based on Reservoir End Volume Relaxation

Aniruddha Basak[1], Siddharth Pal[1], V. Ravikumar Pandi[2], B.K. Panigrahi[2], M.K. Mallick[3], and Ankita Mohapatra[4]

[1] Department of Electronics and Telecommunications,Jadavpur University, India
[2] Department of Electrical Engineering,IIT Delhi, India
[3] ITER, Siksha ,O' Anusandhan University, Bhubaneswar, Orissa, India
[4] CET, BPUT, Bhubaneswar, Orissa, India
aniruddha_ju_etce@yahoo.com, sidd_pal2002@yahoo.com,
ravikumarpandi@gmail.com, bkpanigrahi@ee.iitd.ac.in,
mk_mallick2004@yahoo.com, ankita.cet1208@gmail.com

**Abstract.** The paper presents a new multi-objective approach to determine the optimal power generation for short term hydrothermal scheduling. Generation cost is considered as one objective. Novelty of the paper lies in choosing the second objective. Instead of introducing a hard constraint on the reservoir end volume we have reasoned that allowing it to relax makes better solutions feasible. The degree of relaxation is kept as the second objective. We have tested our approach on a multi-reservoir cascaded hydrothermal system with four hydro and one thermal plant. We have solved the optimization problem using a decomposition based MOEA called MOEA/D-DE.

**Keywords:** Hydrothermal scheduling, multi-objective, evolutionary computation, decomposition, differential evolution.

## 1   Introduction

Short-term hydrothermal scheduling is a difficult constrained optimization problem which has attracted the attention of many researchers over the years. The principal requirement is to determine the power that will be delivered by the hydro and thermal generators over the entire scheduling horizon maintaining all the equality and inequality constraints associated with the modeling of the hydrothermal plant.

Over the years, researchers have focused their energies on making simplifying assumptions to make the hydrothermal scheduling problem more solvable. The problem has been tackled with classical methods [1,2]. Most of the classical methods suffer from computational overburden because of the huge dimensionalty of the real world problem. Moreover the nonlinearity of some of the constraints make the optimization problem more intractable for them to solve. In the recent past, stochastic search algorithms like simulated annealing(SA)[3], genetic algorithm(GA)[4], particle swarm optimization [5] have reported to perform much better than the other

B.K. Panigrahi et al. (Eds.): SEMCCO 2010, LNCS 6466, pp. 718–726, 2010.
© Springer-Verlag Berlin Heidelberg 2010

conventional techniques. Hydrothermal scheduling has also been visualized as a multi objective problem[6-7]. In those works the principal objectives were- (1) Cost,(2) NOx Emission,(3)SO$_2$ Emission and (4) CO$_2$ Emission. In our work we consider a whole new objective to make the hydrothermal scheduling more cost effective.

In this study, we employ a decomposition-based MOEA, called MOEA/D-DE [8], that ranked first among 13 state-of-the-art MOEAs in the unconstrained MOEA competition held under the IEEE Congress on Evolutionary Computation (CEC) 2009 [9]. MOEA/D-DE uses Differential Evolution (DE) [10,11] as its main search strategy and decomposes an MO problem into a number of scalar optimization sub-problems to optimize them simultaneously. Each sub-problem is optimized by only using information from its several neighboring sub-problems and this feature considerably reduces the computational complexity of the algorithm.

This paper is divided into 5 sections. In the second section we describe the hydrothermal scheduling problem. In section 3 we briefly describe the multi objective algorithm that will be used for our study. Section 4 presents the simulation results and we conclude the paper in Section 5.

## 2   Problem Description

We perform short-term hydrothermal scheduling to minimize the total thermal cost such that the load demands can be met in the intervals of the generation scheduling horizon. The above objective is minimized satisfying all the associated equality and inequality constraints.

We will first describe the constraints associated with the modeling of the particular problem.

*A. Inequality Constraints*

**Thermal generator constraints:** The operating limit of the thermal generator has upper and lower bound given by $P_T^{\max}$ and $P_T^{\min}$ respectively.

$$P_T^{\min} \leq P_{Tj} \leq P_T^{\max} \tag{1}$$

Where, $P_{Tj}$ is the power generation of thermal unit at interval $j$.

**Hydro generator constraints:** The operating limit of hydro plant must lie in between its upper and lower bound given by $P_{Hi}^{\max}$ and $P_{Hi}^{\min}$ respectively.

$$P_{Hi}^{\min} \leq P_{Hij} \leq P_{Hi}^{\max} \tag{2}$$

Where $P_{Hij}$ is the power generated by the $i$th hydro unit in the $j$th scheduling interval.

**Reservoir capacity constraint:** The operating volume of the reservoir storage must lie in between the maximum and minimum capacity limits given by $V_i^{\max}$ and $V_i^{\min}$ respectively.

$$V_i^{\min} \leq V_{ij} \leq V_i^{\max} \tag{3}$$

Where, $V_{ij}$ is the volume of water stored in the $i$th reservoir in the $j$th scheduling interval.

**Water discharge constraint:** The water discharge rate of turbine must be within the maximum and minimum operating limits given by $Q_i^{max}$ and $Q_i^{min}$ respectively.

$$Q_i^{min} \leq Q_{ij} \leq Q_i^{max} \tag{4}$$

Where, $Q_{ij}$ is the water discharge rate of the $i$th hydro unit in the $j$th scheduling interval.

*B. Equality Constraints*

**Power Demand constraints:** This constraint stems from the concept that the total power generated from the thermal and hydro plants must meet the demand power and supply the power losses as well for every scheduling interval $j$.

$$P_{Tj} + \sum_{i=1}^{n} P_{Hij} = P_{Dj} + P_{lossj} , \text{ for } j=1,2,...,m. \tag{5}$$

Where $P_{Tj}$, $P_{Dj}$ and $P_{lossj}$ are the generated thermal power, demand power and loss power in the $j$th scheduling instant respectively. $P_{Hij}$ is the power generated by the $i$th hydro unit in the $j$th scheduling interval.

**Hydraulic continuity constraint:** The storage reservoir volume limits are expressed in terms of the initial volume as in equation 6.

$$V_{i(j+1)} = V_{ij} + \sum_{u=1}^{R_u} \left[ Q_{u(j-\tau)} + s_{u(j-\tau)} \right] - Q_{i(j+1)} - s_{i(j+1)} + r_{i(j+1)} , \text{ for } j=1,2,3,..,m. \tag{6}$$

where $\tau$ is the water delay time between reservoir $i$ and its upstream $u$ at interval $j$ and $R_u$ is the set of upstream units directly above hydroplant $i$. Inflow rate into the storage reservoir of $i$th hydro plant at interval $j$ is denoted by $r_{ij}$ and $s_{ij}$ represents the spillage of $i$th reservoir in interval $j$.

**Hydro Power Generation:** The hydro power generated by $i$th hydro unit in the $j$th scheduling interval is assumed to be a function of discharge rate and storage volume. The exact dependence is given in equation 7.

$$P_{Hij} = c_{1i} V_{ij}^2 + c_{2i} Q_{ij}^2 + c_{3i} \left( V_{ij} Q_{ij} \right) + c_{4i} V_{ij} + c_{5i} Q_{ij} + c_{6i} \tag{7}$$

The above equation shows the high nonlinear dependence of $P_{Hij}$ where $c_{1i}, c_{2i}, c_{3i}, c_{4i}, c_{5i}$ and $c_{6i}$ are the coefficients.

*C. Objectives*

The first objective is to minimize the fuel cost for running the thermal system required to meet the load demand in a given scheduling horizon. It is denoted by $F$ and the expression is given below,

$$\text{minimize } F = \sum_{j=1}^{m} f_j \left( P_{Tj} \right) \tag{8}$$

where $m$ is the number of scheduling intervals and $f_j \left( P_{Tj} \right)$ is the fuel cost during the $j$th scheduling interval.

The fuel cost function of the thermal unit is,

$$f_j \left( P_{Tj} \right) = 5000 + 19.2 P_{Tj} + 0.002 P_{Tj}^2 \tag{9}$$

In many hydrothermal scheduling papers the final volume of the reservoir were made to meet a certain desired value. This is a rather hard constraint which can be relaxed. Relaxation of this constraint and allowing certain deviation from the desired final volume can lead to significant savings in terms of fuel cost. The second objective is the deviation of the reservoir end volume from the desired value. The expression is given in equation 10.

$$\text{minimize } percent\ allowance = \max_{i} \left[ \frac{\left( \left| V_{i(m+1)} - V_{i(desired)} \right| \right)}{V_{i(desired)}} \right] \times 100 . \tag{10}$$

The index $i$ represents the $i$th hydro plant. Since we might have several hydro plants we consider the objective to be the maximum percentage deviation from the desired final volume among all the hydro plants.

## 3   The MOEA/D-DE Algorithm- An Outline

Due to the multiple criteria nature of most real-world problems, Multi-objective Optimization (MO) problems are ubiquitous, particularly throughout engineering applications. As the name indicates, multi-objective optimization problems involve multiple objectives, which should be optimized simultaneously and that often are in conflict with each other. This results in a group of alternative solutions which must be considered equivalent in the absence of information concerning the relevance of the others. The concepts of *dominance* and *Pareto-optimality* have been discussed in [12,13].

Multi-objective evolutionary algorithm based on decomposition was first introduced by Zhang and Li in 2007 and extended with DE-based reproduction operators in [8]. Instead of using non-domination sorting for different objectives, the MOEA/D algorithm decomposes a multi-objective optimization problem into a number of single objective optimization sub-problems by using weights vectors $\lambda$ and optimizes them simultaneously. Each sub-problem is optimized by sharing information between its neighboring sub-problems with similar weight values.   MOEA/D uses Tchebycheff decomposition approach   to convert the problem of approximating the PF into a number of scalar optimization problems. Let $\vec{\lambda}^1, ..., \vec{\lambda}^N$ be a set of evenly spread weight vectors and $\vec{Y}^* = \left( y_1^*, y_2^*, ..., y_M^* \right)$ be a reference point i.e. for minimization problem, $y_i^* = \min\{f_i(\vec{X}) \mid \vec{X} \in \Omega\}$ for each $i = 1, 2\ldots M$. Then the problem of approximation of the PF can be decomposed into $N$ scalar optimization subproblems by Tchebycheff approach and the objective function of the $j$-th subproblem is:

$$g^{te}(\vec{X} \mid \vec{\lambda}^j, \vec{Y}^*) = \max_{1 \le i \le M}\left\{\lambda_i^j \left| f_i(x) - y_i^* \right|\right\},$$ (11)

where $\vec{\lambda}^j = (\lambda_1^j, \ldots, \lambda_M^j)^T$, $j = 1, \ldots, N$ is a weight vector i.e. $\lambda_i^j \ge 0$ for all $i = 1$,

2, ..., $m$ and $\sum_{i=1}^{m} \lambda_i^j = 1$. MOEA/D minimizes all these $N$ objective functions simultaneously in a single run. Neighborhood relations among these single objective subproblems are defined based on the distances among their weight vectors. Each subproblem is then optimized by using information mainly from its neighboring subproblems. In MOEA/D, the concept of neighborhood, based on similarity between weight vectors with respect to Euclidean distances, is used to update the solution. The neighborhood of the $i$-th subproblem consists of all the subproblems with the weight vectors from the neighborhood of $\vec{\lambda}^i$.

At each generation, the MOEA/D maintains following variables:

A population ($\vec{X}^1, \ldots, \vec{X}^N$) with size $N$, where $\vec{X}_i$ is the current solution to the $i$-th subproblem.

The fitness values of each population corresponding to a specific subproblem.

The reference point $\vec{Y}^* = \left(y_1^*, y_2^*, \ldots, y_M^*\right)$, where $y_i^*$ is the best value found so far for objective $i$.

An external population (EP), which is used to store non-dominated solutions found during the search.

The MOEA/D-DE algorithm is schematically presented in Table 1.

**Table 1.** The MOEA/D-DE algorithm

| 1. *Initialization* | Initialize the External Population (EP) |
|---|---|
| | Compute the Euclidean distances between any two weight vectors and find out the $T$ closest weight vectors to each weight vector where $T$ is the neighborhood size. |
| | Randomly generate an initial population $\vec{x}^1, \ldots, \vec{x}^N$ and evaluate the fitness values. |
| | Initialize the reference points by a problem-specific method. |
| 2. *Update* | Reproduction: reproduce the offspring $\vec{U}_i$ corresponding to parent $\vec{X}_i$ by DE/rand/1/bin scheme (Page 37 – 42, [29]). |
| | $u_{i,j} = x_{r_1^i,j} + F.(x_{r_2^i,j} - x_{r_3^i,j})$, with probability $Cr$ |
| | $= x_{j,i}$, with probability $1 - Cr$ |

**Table 1.** (*continued*)

| | | |
|---|---|---|
| | | Repair: Repair the solution if $\vec{U}$ is out of the boundary and the value is reset to be    a randomly selected value inside the boundary. |
| | | Update of reference points, if the fitness value of $\vec{U}$ is better than the reference point. |
| | | Update the neighboring solutions, if the fitness value of $\vec{U}$ is better. |
| | | Update of EP by removing all the vectors that are dominated by $\vec{U}$ and add $\vec{U}$ to EP if no vector in EP dominates it. |
| 3.     Stopping Criteria | | If stopping criteria is satisfied, then stop and output EP. Otherwise, go to Step 2 |

## 4   Results and Discussions

The simulations have been carried out on a test system given in Ref.[4]. It consists of an equivalent thermal power plant and a multichain cascade of four hydro power plants. The scheduling horizon is 1 day with 24 time intervals of 1 hour each. The data of the test system is considered here are the same as in Ref. [4]. While running MOEA/D-DE, in all cases, for the DE operator we took $F = 0.5$, $CR - 1$, distribution index $\eta = 20$, and the mutation rate $p_m = \frac{1}{D}$ as per [8]. The constraints were handled by means of a penalty function. In other words the constraint violations were added to the objective function after multiplying it with a huge factor (1e4). In what follows we report the best results obtained from a set of 25 independent runs of the algorithm where each run was continued up to $3 \times 10^5$ Function Evaluations (FEs). Figure 1 shows that with no allowed deviation in final volume of reservoir the operating cost is $9.276 \times 10^5$ whereas with 25% allowed deviation the operating cost is $9.185 \times 10^5$. The general trend is that with

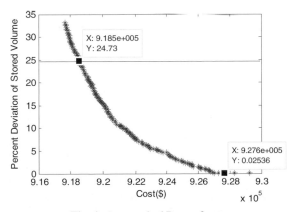

**Fig. 1.** Approached Pareto front

greater relaxation or allowance we get lesser and lesser cost. The plant operator can decide on the allowed deviation and choose a solution from the approached pareto front. Here we assume that 25% deviation is allowable.

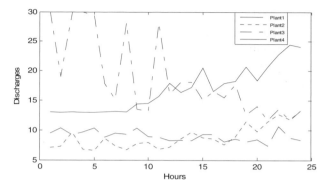

**Fig. 2.** Hydro Plant Discharges

**Table 2.** Hydro plant power outputs and Thermal Generations

| Hour | Hydro Power Generations(MW) | | | | Thermal Generations(MW) |
|---|---|---|---|---|---|
| | Plant 1 | Plant 2 | Plant 3 | Plant 4 | |
| 1 | 83.8879 | 56.6581 | 0 | 200.2905 | 1029.164 |
| 2 | 87.1468 | 58.3181 | 37.7749 | 187.7724 | 1018.988 |
| 3 | 81.4502 | 71.2176 | 0 | 174.1879 | 1033.144 |
| 4 | 82.6271 | 56.1130 | 0 | 156.6651 | 994.595 |
| 5 | 83.7497 | 56.0120 | 0 | 178.6369 | 971.602 |
| 6 | 75.9365 | 67.7454 | 29.5834 | 186.2994 | 1050.435 |
| 7 | 78.4745 | 59.3875 | 39.0478 | 206.5013 | 1266.589 |
| 8 | 77.6081 | 54.9899 | 0 | 223.5372 | 1643.865 |
| 9 | 82.0195 | 61.7697 | 39.7141 | 250.6335 | 1805.863 |
| 10 | 76.4220 | 63.5345 | 41.7854 | 255.2367 | 1883.021 |
| 11 | 77.2314 | 57.6321 | 0 | 264.9034 | 1830.233 |
| 12 | 74.7697 | 60.5091 | 33.4570 | 291.6751 | 1849.589 |
| 13 | 75.9366 | 68.6139 | 28.2050 | 277.1772 | 1780.067 |
| 14 | 76.7098 | 74.4623 | 27.8982 | 279.9981 | 1740.932 |
| 15 | 83.4986 | 69.4568 | 38.3788 | 309.2615 | 1629.404 |
| 16 | 83.4390 | 68.1146 | 35.8471 | 281.5973 | 1601.002 |
| 17 | 76.2318 | 62.2454 | 40.6233 | 292.2718 | 1658.628 |
| 18 | 79.2795 | 68.2818 | 35.3072 | 294.7695 | 1662.362 |
| 19 | 76.2097 | 76.6642 | 46.9638 | 303.9107 | 1736.252 |
| 20 | 77.5508 | 68.2542 | 46.8977 | 287.8655 | 1799.432 |
| 21 | 70.5654 | 73.6472 | 50.1431 | 296.0326 | 1749.612 |
| 22 | 87.6457 | 75.1404 | 52.2221 | 299.4040 | 1605.588 |
| 23 | 78.2192 | 69.2793 | 53.9734 | 289.4135 | 1359.115 |
| 24 | 77.0638 | 69.3397 | 56.3168 | 275.0983 | 1112.181 |
| Total Cost of Thermal Generation($) | | | | | 918543.11 |

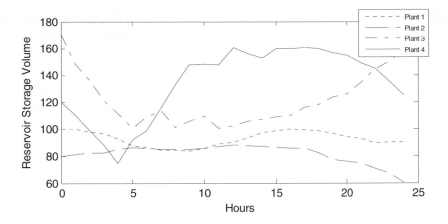

**Fig. 3.** Hydro Reservoir Storage Volume

All the results correspond to 25% deviation in storage volume from end desired volume. The plant operator can fix any value of allowed deviation. Then from the approached pareto curve he can take the solution which shows the maximum deviation less than or equal to the allowed value. This solution will naturally have the best possible cost value. In Figure 2 we show the hourly plant discharges. In Table 2 we show the hydro plant and thermal plant power outputs. In Figure 3 we show the hourly reservoir storage volumes. In Table 3 we show the desired end volume of the reservoirs and the deviations produced by the solution. Since the maximum deviation is 24.73%, this figured as the 2$^{nd}$ objective value. However the average deviation is only 13.82%.

**Table 3.** Reservoir End Volume

|  | Desired End Volume | Actual End Volume | % Deviation |
|---|---|---|---|
| Plant 1 | 120 | 90.32 | 24.73% |
| Plant 2 | 70 | 60.62 | 13.40% |
| Plant 3 | 170 | 159.26 | 6.32% |
| Plant 4 | 140 | 124.82 | 10.84% |

## 5   Conclusion

This is the first time a study of this kind has been carried out. It has been observed that by slight relaxation of the reservoir end volume we are achieving saving in thermal generation cost. This phenomenon is observed because relaxation of a rather hard constraint like this makes better solutions possible. We believe that this work has practical value as well and can be taken up by the hydrothermal plant operators.

# References

[1] Turgeon, A.: Optimal operation of multi reservoir power systems with stochastic inflows. Water Resources Research 16(2), 275–283 (1980)
[2] Chang, S., Chen, C., Fong, I., Luh, P.B.: Hydroelectric generation scheduling with an effective differential dynamic programming. IEEE Trans. PWRS 5(3), 737–743 (1990)
[3] Wong, K.P., Wong, Y.W.: Short term hydrothermal scheduling: Part 1. Simulated annealing approach. IEE Proc. C 141, 497–501 (1994)
[4] Orero, S.O., Irving, M.R.: A genetic algorithm modeling framework and solution technique for short-term optimal hydrothermal scheduling. IEEE Trans. Power Syst. 13, 501–518 (1998)
[5] Hota, P.K., Barisal, A.K., Chakrabarti, R.: An improved PSO technique for short-term optimal hydrothermal scheduling. Electric Power Systems Research 79, 1047–1053 (2009)
[6] Dhillion, J.S., Parti, S.C., Kothari, D.P.: Fuzzy decision-making in stochastic multi objective short-term hydrothermal scheduling. In: IEEE Proc. Generator Transmission Distribution, vol. 149(2), pp. 191–200 (March 2002)
[7] El-Hawary, M.E., Ravindranath, K.M.: Combining loss and cost objectives in daily hydro thermal economic scheduling. IEEE Trans. Power Syst. 6(3), 1106–1112 (1991)
[8] Li, H., Zhang, Q.: Multiobjective Optimization Problems with Complicated Pareto Sets, MOEA/D and NSGA-II. IEEE Trans. on Evolutionary Computation 12(2), 284–302 (2009)
[9] Zhang, Q., Zhou, A., Zhao, S.Z., Suganthan, P.N., Liu, W., Tiwari, S.: Multiobjective Optimization Test Instances for the CEC 2009 Special Session and Competition, Technical Report CES-887, University of Essex and Nanyang Technological University (2008)
[10] Storn, R., Price, K.: Differential evolution – A simple and efficient heuristic for global optimization over continuous spaces. Journal of Global Optimization 11(4), 341–359 (1997)
[11] Price, K., Storn, R., Lampinen, J.: Differential Evolution - A Practical Approach to Global Optimization. Springer, Berlin (2005)
[12] Abraham, A., Jain, L.C., Goldberg, R. (eds.): Evolutionary Multiobjective Optimization: Theoretical Advances and Applications. Springer, London (2005)
[13] Coello Coello, C.A., Lamont, G.B., Van Veldhuizen, D.A.: Evolutionary Algorithms for Solving Multi-Objective Problems. Springer, Heidelberg (2007)

# Particle Swarm Optimization and Varying Chemotactic Step-Size Bacterial Foraging Optimization Algorithms Based Dynamic Economic Dispatch with Non-smooth Fuel Cost Functions

P. Praveena, K. Vaisakh[*], and S. Rama Mohana Rao

Department of Electrical Engineering, AU College of Engineering,
Andhra University, Visakhapatnam-530003, AP, India
nambaripraveena@yahoo.co.in,
vaisakh_k@yahoo.co.in,
ramu_sanchana@yahoo.com

**Abstract.** The Dynamic economic dispatch (DED) problem is an optimization problem with an objective to determine the optimal combination of power outputs for all generating units over a certain period of time in order to minimize the total fuel cost while satisfying dynamic operational constraints and load demand in each interval. Recently social foraging behavior of Escherichia coli bacteria has been explored to develop a novel algorithm for distributed optimization and control. The Bacterial Foraging Optimization Algorithm (BFOA) is currently gaining popularity in the community of researchers, for its effectiveness in solving certain difficult real-world optimization problems. This article comes up with a hybrid approach involving Particle Swarm Optimization (PSO) and BFO algorithms with varying chemo tactic step size for solving the DED problem of generating units considering valve-point effects. The proposed hybrid algorithm has been extensively compared with those methods reported in the literature. The new method is shown to be statistically significantly better on two test systems consisting of five and ten generating units.

**Keywords:** Dynamic economic dispatch, ramp rate limits, Bacterial Foraging, chemo-tactic step size, particle swarm optimization.

## 1 Introduction

Dynamic economic dispatch (DED), which is a major operational decision, is used to determine the optimal generation schedule of on-line generators, so as to meet the predicted load demand over certain period of time at minimum operating cost under various system and operational constraints. Recently, SA [1], hybrid EP-SQP [2], DGPSO [3] and hybrid PSO-SQP [4] methods are proposed to solve dynamic

---

[*] Corresponding author.

B.K. Panigrahi et al. (Eds.): SEMCCO 2010, LNCS 6466, pp. 727–738, 2010.
© Springer-Verlag Berlin Heidelberg 2010

economic dispatch problem with non-smooth fuel cost functions. These hybrid methods utilize local searching property of SQP along with stochastic optimization techniques to determine the optimal solution of DED problem.

In the DED problem the operational decision at hour $t$ may affect the operational decision at a later hour due to the dynamic constraint known as ramp rate constraint. The power system with binding ramp-rate limits must be properly modeled in production simulation. The DED is not only the most accurate formulation of the economic dispatch problem but also the most difficult dynamic optimization problem. DED problems are modeled with convex cost functions [5]–[7]. Accurate modeling of DED problem will be improved when the valve point loadings of the steam turbines in the generating units are taken into account [8]-[10]. Various mathematical programming methods and optimization techniques have been employed for solving DED problems. Traditional methods when used to solve DED problem, suffer from myopia for nonlinear, discontinuous search spaces, leading them to a less desirable performance and these methods often use approximations to limit complexity.

The Bacterial Foraging Optimization Algorithm (BFOA) is currently gaining popularity in the community of researchers, for its effectiveness in solving certain difficult real-world optimization problems. This article comes up with a hybrid approach involving Particle Swarm Optimization (PSO) and BFOA algorithm for solving the DED problem of generating units considering valve-point effects. The chemo-tactic step size is varied in the direction of tumble and swim. The varying step size leads to reach the global solutions quickly. The proposed hybrid algorithm has been extensively compared with those methods reported in the literature on two test systems consisting of five and ten generating units.

The paper is organized as follows. The formulation of the DED problem is explained in section 2. Section 3 and section 4 gives overview of BFOA, PSO and BSO (Bacterial swarm optimization) algorithm. Section 5 presents the simulation results and discussions of various test case scenarios.

## 2   Dynamic Economic Dispatch Problem Formulation

The classic DED problem minimizes the following incremental cost function associated to dispatchable units

$$Min \quad F = \sum_{t=1}^{T}\sum_{i=1}^{N} F_{it}(P_{it}) \quad (\$) \tag{1}$$

where F is the total generating cost over the whole dispatch period, T is the number of intervals in the scheduled horizon, N is the number of generating units, and $F_{it}(P_{it})$ is the fuel cost in terms of its real power output $P_{it}$ at time t. Taking into account of the valve-point effects, the fuel cost function of $i^{th}$ thermal generating unit is expressed as the sum of a quadratic and a sinusoidal function in the following form

$$F_{it}(P_{it}) = a_i P_{it}^2 + b_i P_{it} + c_i + \left| e_i \sin(f_i(P_{i\min} - P_{it})) \right| \tag{2}$$

where $a_i$, $b_i$ and $c_i$ are cost coefficients, $e_i$ and $f_i$ are constants from the valve point effect of the $i^{th}$ generating unit, and $P_i$ is the power output of the $i^{th}$ unit in megawatts.

The minimization of the generation cost is subjected to the following equality and inequality constraints:

## 2.1 Real Power Balance Constraint

$$\sum_{i=1}^{N} P_{it} - P_{Dt} - P_{Lt} = 0 \tag{3}$$

where t = 1, 2, ..., T. $P_{Dt}$ is the total power demand at time t and $P_{Lt}$ is the transmission power loss at time t in megawatts. $P_{Lt}$ is calculated using the B-Matrix loss coefficients and the general form of the loss formula using B-coefficients is

$$P_{Lt} = \sum_{i=1}^{N}\sum_{j=1}^{N} P_{it} B_{ij} P_{jt} \tag{4}$$

## 2.2 Real Power Generation Limit

$$P_{i\min} \le P_{it} \le P_{i\max} \tag{5}$$

where $P_{i\min}$ is the minimum limit, and $P_{i\max}$ is the maximum limit of real power of the $i^{th}$ unit in megawatts.

## 2.3 Generating Unit Ramp Rate Limits

$$P_{it} - P_{i(t-1)} \le UR_i, \quad i = 1,2,3....., N$$
$$P_{i(t-1)} - P_{it} \le DR_i \tag{6}$$

where $UR_i$ and $DR_i$ are the ramp-up and ramp-down limits of $i^{th}$ unit in megawatts. Thus the constraint of (6) due to the ramp rate constraints is modified as

$$\max(P_{i\min}, P_{i(t-1)} - DR_i) \le P_{it} \le \min(P_{i\max}, P_{i(t-1)} + UR_i) \tag{7}$$

such that

$$P_{it,\min} = \max(P_{i\min}, P_{i(t-1)} - DR_i)$$
$$P_{it,\max} = \min(P_{i\max}, P_{i(t-1)} + UR_i) \tag{8}$$

## 3   Overview of PSO-BFA

Bacterial Foraging Optimization Algorithm (BFOA) was proposed by K.M.Passino based on the foraging strategies of the E. Coli bacterium cells in 2001[11]. Until date there have been a few successful applications of the said algorithm in optimal control engineering, harmonic estimation [12], transmission loss reduction [13], machine learning [14] and so on. Experimentation with several benchmark functions reveal that BFOA possesses a poor convergence behavior over multi-modal and rough fitness landscapes as compared to other naturally inspired optimization techniques like the Genetic Algorithm (GA) [15] Particle Swarm Optimization (PSO) [16] and Differential Evolution (DE)[17]. Its performance is also heavily affected with the growth of search space dimensionality. In 2007, Kim et al. proposed a hybrid approach involving GA and BFOA for function optimization [18]. The proposed algorithm outperformed both GA and BFOA over a few numerical benchmarks and a practical PID tuner design problem.

In this paper, varying step size BFOA is synergistically coupled with the PSO. The later is a very popular optimization algorithm these days and it draws inspiration from the group behavior of a bird flock or school of fish etc. The proposed algorithm performs local search through the chemo-tactic movement operation of BFOA whereas the global search over the entire search space is accomplished by a PSO operator. In this way it balances between exploration and exploitation enjoying best of both the worlds. Therefore, the proposed algorithm, referred to as Bacterial Swarm Optimization (BSO).

## 4   The Bacterial Swarm Optimization Algorithm

The classic DED problem minimizes the following incremental cost function associated to dispatchable units Particle swarm optimization (PSO) [16] is a stochastic optimization technique that draws inspiration from the behavior of a flock of birds or the collective intelligence of a group of social insects with limited individual capabilities. It is similar to other evolutionary computation techniques like Genetic Algorithm (GA) and Evolutionary Programming (EP) in that PSO also initializes a population of individuals randomly. These individuals are known as particles and have positions and velocities. Each particle adjusts its velocity dynamically corresponding to its flying experiences and its neighbors. The velocity of the particle is updated to new position according to its modified velocity. The best evaluation function (fitness) is evaluated for the entire run and is stored in $gbest$. The velocity of $i^{th}$ particle is represented as $V_i = (V_{i1}, V_{i2}, .... V_{ij})$. Hence the modified velocity of each particle can be calculated using the information.

  a.   The current velocity
  b.   The distance between the current position and $pbest$.
  c.   The distance between the current position and $gbest$.

$$V_{ij}(it+1) = w * V_{ij}(it) + C_1 * rand_1 * (pbest_{ij} - x_{ij}(it))$$
$$+ C_2 * rand_2 * (gbest_i - x_{ij}(it)) \tag{9}$$

where

$rand_1$, $rand_2$ = uniform random values in the range [0, 1]

$x_{ij}(it)$ = current position of the $i^{th}$ particle in $j^{th}$ dimension at iteration $it$.

$V_{ij}(it)$ = velocity of the $i^{th}$ particle in $j^{th}$ dimension at iteration $it$

The BFOA is on the other hand is based upon search and optimal foraging decision making capabilities of the E.Coli bacteria [21]-[25]. The coordinates of a bacterium here represent an individual solution of the optimization problem. Such a set of trial solutions converges towards the optimal solution following the foraging group dynamics of the bacteria population. Chemo-tactic movement is continued until a bacterium goes in the direction of positive nutrient gradient (i. e. increasing fitness). After a certain number of complete swims the best half of the population undergoes reproduction, eliminating the rest of the population. In order to escape local optima, an elimination-dispersion event is carried out where, some bacteria are liquidated at random with a very small probability and the new replacements are initialized at random locations of the search space. A detailed description of the complete algorithm can be traced in [11].

In this hybrid approach, after undergoing a chemo-tactic step, each bacterium also gets mutated by a PSO operator. In this phase, the bacterium is stochastically attracted towards the globally best position found so far in the entire population at current time and also towards its previous heading direction. In what follows we briefly outline the new BSO algorithm step by step.

**Step 1:** Initializing parameters

1a.

$S$ = The number of bacteria in the population.

$N_C$ = The number of chemo-tactic steps.

$N_{re}$ = The number of reproduction steps.

$N_{ed}$ = The number of elimination-dispersal events.

$N_S$ = Swimming length is the maximum number of steps taken by each
bacterium when it moves from low nutrient area to high nutrient area.

$P_{ed}$ = Probability of elimination and dispersal

$C$ = size of the step taken in the random direction specified by the tumble.

$w$ = The inertia weight.

$P(t, j, k, l, m)$ = Position vector of $j^{th}$ unit in $t^{th}$ hour, $k^{th}$ bacterial
Population, $l^{th}$ reproduction and $m^{th}$ elimination-dispersal, where
$l = 1,2,....,N_{re}$ and $m = 1,2,....,N_{ed}$

$V(t, j, k)$ = Velocity vector of the $j^{th}$ unit in $t^{th}$ hour and $k^{th}$ bacterial
      population.

$pbest$ = The best previous position of $k^{th}$ particles.

$gbest$ = The index of the best particle among all particles in the group.

$CR$    = The Cross over probability

$C_1, C_2$ = Acceleration constants

rand, Rand = Random value in the range [0,1]

1b. Randomly initialize positions $P(t, j, k, l, m)$ and velocities $V(t, j, k)$ in $t^{th}$
hour for $j^{th}$ unit, $k^{th}$ bacterial population, $l^{th}$ reproduction $(l = 1)$ and
$m^{th}$ elimination-dispersal ($m = 1$).

**Step 2:** Starting of the elimination-dispersal loop $(m = m + 1)$.

**Step 3:** Starting of the reproduction loop $(l = l + 1)$.

**Step 4:** Starting of the chemo-tactic loop $(iter = iter + 1)$.

**Step 5:** For each bacterium $(k = k + 1)$.

**Step 6:** Compute fitness function $JF(k, l, m)$ and cost function $J(k, l, m)$ , let

$$JFlast = JF(k, l, m) \tag{10}$$

where

$$JF = 1/(J + penality\ function) \tag{11}$$

$$penality\ function = \begin{cases} k_c \left| (P_k - P_k^{\lim}) \right| \\ 0 \end{cases} \tag{12}$$

$k_c$ is a constant value

**Step 7:** Move to new position

7a.    Compute

$$C(k) = rand + k_d \tag{13}$$

$$P(t, j, k, l, m) = P(t, j, k, l, m) + C(k) * Delta(t, j, k) \tag{14}$$

*where Delta$(t, j, k) = V(t, j, k)$ for $k = 1,2,3....S$*

7b.  Handle constraints

          I.      generation limit

          II.     ramp rate limit

After every new power generation of all the generator units the above discussed constraints should be handled in order to maintain their boundaries. For example if the sum of generation of all units does not satisfy the load demand of that interval. It should be repaired such that it satisfies the load demand of that hour. Similarly if the generation does not satisfy the ramp-rate limits then repair them as in equation (7) and this equation can also be represented as

$$if \ P_{it} > P_{it,\max} \quad then \quad P_{it} = P_{it,\max}$$
$$if \ P_{it} < P_{it,\min} \quad then \quad P_{it} = P_{it,\min}$$

(15)

**Step 8:** swimming

8a. swim-count=0

8b. while (swim-count<Ns) and $JF(k,l,m) > JFlast$

   i.   swim-count = swim-count + 1

   ii.  $JFlast = JF(k,l,m)$

   iii. $P(t,j,k,l,m) = P(t,j,k,l,m) + C(k) * Delta(t,j,k)$

   iv. Handle constraints

     a.   generation limit

     b.   ramp rate limit

   v. Compute JF and J

**Step 9:** Update best location *pbest* and *gbest*

**Step 10:**

10a. Compute new velocity

$$V(t,j,k) = w * V(t,j,k) + C_1 * rand * (pbestP(t,j,k) - P(t,j,k,l,m))$$
$$+ C_2 * rand * (gbestP(t,j) - P(t,j,k,l,m))$$

(16)

10b. $Delta = V$

**Step 11:** If $k < S$ then go to step5

**Step 12:** If $iter < N_c$ then go to step4

**Step 13:** Reproduction operations

13a. *JFhealth* is the measure of particles with good fitness (good fitness means higher fitness and lower cost)

$$JFhealth(k) = pbestJF(k,l,m)$$

(17)

13b. Sort bacteria in the order of ascending fit. The weaker $S_r = S/2$ bacteria die and the rest $S_r$ best bacteria each split into two bacteria which are placed at the same location.

13c. If $l < N_{re}$ then go to step3 to start the next generation in the chemo-tactic loop else go to step14.

**Step 14:** Elimination-dispersal operation

14a. For k=1, 2, 3……, S a random number is generated and if it is less than or equal to $P_{ed}$ than that bacterium is dispersed to a new random location else it remains at its original location.

14b. If m<Ned then go to step2 otherwise stop.

In the original bacterial foraging algorithm C indicate a basic chemo-tactic step size (chemo-tactic step size is the lengths of steps taken during runs). This value should be greater than zero. The normal choice for this step size is 0.1. It is taken in the tumble and swimming operations so that it moves in a direction specified by them and helps in reduction of cost. The chemo-tactic step size in this paper is proposed to vary in the range (0.1, 2) by using the relation

$$C(k) = rand + k_d$$

Usually the $k_d$ is a constant, its value is a number between 0.1 and 0.9; rand (0, 1) is a uniformly distributed random number within the range [0, 1]. For every chemo-tactic step in the tumble and swimming operation the step size value taken in this paper lead to fine reduction in cost.

## 5   Simulation Results and Discussion

A PSO and BFA algorithm for the DED problem described above has been applied to five-unit and ten-unit systems with non-smooth fuel cost function to demonstrate the performance of the proposed method. The simulations were carried out on a PC with Pentium IV 3.1-GHZ processor. The software is developed using the MATLAB 7.1. Number of trials has been conducted with changes in the size of population, number of generations, and number of trials per iteration in order to obtain the best values to achieve the overall minimum cost of generation. The best solution obtained through the proposed method is compared to those reported in the recent literature. The parameters chosen for this system are $N_c = 500$, $N_{ed}$=2, $N_{re}$=4, $N_s$=4, S=120 and $P_{ed}$=0.2.

### 5.1   5–Unit System Results

The cost coefficients, generation limits, load demand in each interval and ramp-rate limits of five-unit sample system with valve-point loading are taken from Ref. [1]. The scheduling time horizon is one day divided into 24 intervals. The transmission losses are calculated using B-coefficient loss formula. The sum of total generating power in each interval satisfies the load demand plus transmission losses. Best scheduling for 5-unit system is represented in Table 1. The minimum cost for the 5-unit system of the proposed method in $/24h is 43195.54 and the time taken for chemo-tactic step is 2.48 seconds. The optimal cost of the proposed method is compared with that of improved DE [19] method, Adaptive Paticle Swarm Optimization APSO [20], Simulated Annealing SA [1] methods is given in Table 2.

**Table 1.** Best scheduling of 5-unit system

| Unit Hour | 1 (MW) | 2 (MW) | 3 (MW) | 4 (MW) | 5 (MW) | Loss | Cost($/h) |
|---|---|---|---|---|---|---|---|
| 1 | 10.0000 | 20.0007 | 30.0000 | 124.4053 | 229.5116 | 3.9176 | 1226.9 |
| 2 | 19.1067 | 20.0053 | 30.0000 | 140.7245 | 229.5207 | 4.3572 | 1417.6 |
| 3 | 10.0000 | 20.0005 | 30.0000 | 190.7245 | 229.5162 | 5.2413 | 1493.9 |
| 4 | 10.0001 | 20.0001 | 66.8627 | 209.8158 | 229.5194 | 6.1981 | 1662.3 |
| 5 | 10.0000 | 23.7281 | 91.6163 | 209.8158 | 229.5194 | 6.6796 | 1704.1 |
| 6 | 10.0173 | 53.7281 | 112.6739 | 209.8158 | 229.5198 | 7.7550 | 1815.5 |
| 7 | 10.0001 | 72.2691 | 112.6173 | 209.8158 | 229.5182 | 8.2205 | 1840.9 |
| 8 | 19.2691 | 91.6679 | 112.6734 | 209.8158 | 229.5192 | 8.9455 | 1860.3 |
| 9 | 49.2691 | 98.5422 | 112.6841 | 209.8416 | 229.5225 | 9.8596 | 1977.2 |
| 10 | 63.6902 | 98.5384 | 112.6716 | 209.8158 | 229.5181 | 10.2341 | 1996.5 |
| 11 | 74.9989 | 103.6879 | 112.6749 | 209.8158 | 229.5200 | 10.6975 | 2035.2 |
| 12 | 74.9999 | 124.3330 | 112.6734 | 209.8158 | 229.5196 | 11.3417 | 2178.0 |
| 13 | 63.6882 | 98.5390 | 112.6734 | 209.8158 | 229.5176 | 10.2341 | 1996.5 |
| 14 | 49.3330 | 98.5248 | 112.6663 | 209.8158 | 229.5195 | 9.8594 | 1977.0 |
| 15 | 47.1871 | 98.5398 | 112.6735 | 174.9126 | 229.5196 | 8.8326 | 2061.1 |
| 16 | 21.3888 | 98.5399 | 112.6754 | 124.9126 | 229.5187 | 7.0354 | 1653.5 |
| 17 | 10.0001 | 87.5246 | 112.6011 | 124.8908 | 229.5175 | 6.5341 | 1615.8 |
| 18 | 10.0000 | 98.5398 | 112.6735 | 165.0127 | 229.5196 | 7.7456 | 1852.9 |
| 19 | 12.4330 | 98.5426 | 112.6754 | 209.8163 | 229.5198 | 8.9872 | 1795.5 |
| 20 | 42.4315 | 119.8776 | 112.6818 | 209.8158 | 229.5200 | 10.3267 | 2114.2 |
| 21 | 39.0552 | 98.5399 | 112.6735 | 209.8158 | 229.5196 | 9.6040 | 1943.4 |
| 22 | 10.0000 | 98.5398 | 112.6658 | 161.9442 | 229.5196 | 7.6694 | 1842.8 |
| 23 | 10.0000 | 95.9758 | 72.6658 | 124.8598 | 229.5178 | 6.0193 | 1657.0 |
| 24 | 10.0000 | 70.7856 | 32.6658 | 124.9079 | 229.5186 | 4.8779 | 1477.3 |

**Table 2.** Cost comparison results for 5-unit system

| Method | SA [1] | IDE [19] | APSO [20] | BSO |
|---|---|---|---|---|
| Total Fuel Cost($/24h) | 47356 | 45800 | 44678 | 43195.54 |

## 5.2 10-Unit System Results

In this example, the DED problem of the 10-unit system is solved by the proposed method by neglecting transmission losses in order to compare the results of the proposed PSO-BFOA method with hybrid methods such as Hybrid EP-SQP [2], IDE [19], Hybrid PSO-SQP [4], Deterministically guided PSO [3] algorithms reported in literature. The load demand of the system was divided by 24 intervals. The system data for ten-unit sample system is taken from the [2]. Transmission losses have been ignored for the sake of comparison of results with those reported in literature. The optimum scheduling of generating units for 24 hours using proposed method is given in Tables 3. The time taken for a chemo-tactic step is 3.85 seconds.

Cost convergence characteristics for three best trials (10-unit system) are shown in Figures 1 respectively and observed that trial 3 converges with global cost as represented in Table 4.

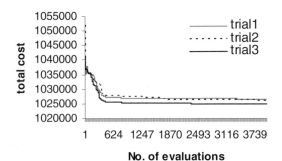

**No. of evaluations**

**Fig. 1.** Cost convergence characteristics for different trials (10-unit system)

**Table 3.** Best scheduling of 10-unit system

| Unit | 1 | 2 | 3 | 4 | 5 | 6 | 7 | 8 | 9 | 10 |
|------|---|---|---|---|---|---|---|---|---|----|
| Hour | (MW) | (MW) | (MW) | (MW) | (MW) | (MW) | (MW) | (MW) | (MW) | (MW) |
| 1 | 150.0000 | 135.0000 | 206.0000 | 60.0000 | 73.0000 | 160.0000 | 130.0000 | 47.0000 | 20.0000 | 55.0000 |
| 2 | 150.0000 | 135.0000 | 280.0000 | 60.0000 | 73.0000 | 160.0000 | 130.0000 | 47.0000 | 20.0000 | 55.0000 |
| 3 | 230.0000 | 143.0000 | 340.0000 | 60.0000 | 73.0000 | 160.0000 | 130.0000 | 47.0000 | 20.0000 | 55.0000 |
| 4 | 298.7335 | 222.2665 | 340.0000 | 60.0000 | 73.0000 | 160.0000 | 130.0000 | 47.0000 | 20.0000 | 55.0000 |
| 5 | 365.4671 | 229.5329 | 340.0000 | 60.0000 | 73.0000 | 160.0000 | 130.0000 | 47.0000 | 20.0000 | 55.0000 |
| 6 | 383.4671 | 309.5329 | 340.0000 | 60.0000 | 123.0000 | 160.0000 | 130.0000 | 47.0000 | 20.0000 | 55.0000 |
| 7 | 456.4968 | 316.7994 | 333.8372 | 60.0000 | 122.8666 | 160.0000 | 130.0000 | 47.0000 | 20.0000 | 55.0000 |
| 8 | 394.4675 | 396.7994 | 340.0000 | 60.0000 | 172.7331 | 160.0000 | 130.0000 | 47.0000 | 20.0000 | 55.0000 |
| 9 | 379.8726 | 460.0000 | 340.0000 | 110.0000 | 222.1274 | 160.0000 | 130.0000 | 47.0000 | 20.0000 | 55.0000 |
| 10 | 456.4968 | 460.0000 | 340.0000 | 150.9035 | 222.5997 | 160.0000 | 130.0000 | 77.0000 | 20.0000 | 55.0000 |
| 11 | 456.4968 | 460.0000 | 340.0000 | 196.1911 | 243.0000 | 160.0000 | 130.0000 | 85.3121 | 20.0000 | 55.0000 |
| 12 | 456.4969 | 460.0000 | 340.0000 | 240.1910 | 243.0000 | 160.0000 | 130.0000 | 115.3121 | 20.0000 | 55.0000 |
| 13 | 456.4968 | 460.0000 | 292.4005 | 190.1910 | 222.5996 | 160.0000 | 130.0000 | 85.3121 | 20.0000 | 55.0000 |
| 14 | 379.8726 | 396.7994 | 340.0000 | 164.4162 | 222.5996 | 160.0000 | 130.0000 | 55.3121 | 20.0000 | 55.0000 |
| 15 | 303.2484 | 391.8515 | 325.8998 | 120.4006 | 222.5997 | 160.0000 | 130.0000 | 47.0000 | 20.0000 | 55.0000 |
| 16 | 303.2484 | 311.8515 | 283.7664 | 70.4006 | 172.7331 | 160.0000 | 130.0000 | 47.0000 | 20.0000 | 55.0000 |
| 17 | 226.6242 | 309.5329 | 299.1098 | 60.0000 | 172.7331 | 160.0000 | 130.0000 | 47.0000 | 20.0000 | 55.0000 |
| 18 | 303.2484 | 316.2476 | 340.0000 | 83.7709 | 172.7331 | 160.0000 | 130.0000 | 47.0000 | 20.0000 | 55.0000 |
| 19 | 379.8726 | 396.2476 | 340.0000 | 75.1467 | 172.7331 | 160.0000 | 130.0000 | 47.0000 | 20.0000 | 55.0000 |
| 20 | 456.4968 | 460.0000 | 340.0000 | 120.8384 | 222.6647 | 160.0000 | 130.0000 | 77.0000 | 50.0000 | 55.0000 |
| 21 | 456.4968 | 460.0000 | 300.7063 | 110.0671 | 184.7297 | 160.0000 | 130.0000 | 47.0000 | 20.0000 | 55.0000 |
| 22 | 379.8726 | 382.6208 | 220.7063 | 60.0671 | 172.7331 | 160.0000 | 130.0000 | 47.0000 | 20.0000 | 55.0000 |
| 23 | 303.2484 | 302.6208 | 168.8159 | 60.0000 | 122.8650 | 122.4498 | 130.0000 | 47.0000 | 20.0000 | 55.0000 |
| 24 | 226.6242 | 222.6208 | 139.8884 | 60.0000 | 122.8665 | 160.0000 | 130.0000 | 47.0000 | 20.0000 | 55.0000 |

**Table 4.** Cost comparison results for 10-unit system

| Method | Hybrid EP-SQP [2] | DGPSO [3] | Hybrid PSO-SQP [4] | IDE [19] | BSO |
|---|---|---|---|---|---|
| Fuel Cost ($/24h) | 1031746 | 1028835 | 1027334 | 1026269 | 1024945 |

## 6  Conclusion

The paper has presented a PSO and BFA algorithm by combining the PSO based mutation operator with bacterial chemo-tactic for determination of optimal solution for DED problem with the generator constraints. The presented scheme attempts to make a judicious use of exploration and exploitation abilities of the search space and therefore likely to avoid false and premature convergence. The feasibility of the proposed method was demonstrated with five and ten-unit sample systems. The test results reveals that the optimal dispatch solution obtained through the BSO lead to less operating cost than that found by other methods, which shows the capability of the algorithm to determine the global or near global solution for DED problem. The proposed approach outperforms SA, hybrid EP-SQP, DGPSO and PSO-SQP methods.

## References

1. Panigrahi, C.K., Chattopadhyay, P.K., Chakrabarti, R.N., Basu, M.: Simulated annealing technique for dynamic economic dispatch. Electric Power Components and Systems 34(5), 577–586 (2006)
2. Attaviriyanupap, D., Kita, H., Tanaka, E., Hasegawa, J.: A hybrid EP and SQP for dynamic economic dispatch with nonsmooth incremental fuel cost function. IEEE Trans. Power Syst. 17(2), 411–416 (2002)
3. Aruldoss Albert Victoire, T., Ebenezer Jeyakumar, A.: Deterministically guided PSO for dynamic dispatch considering valve-point effect. Elect. Power Syst. Res. 73(3), 313–322 (2005)
4. Aruldoss Albert Victoire, T., Ebenezer Jeyakumar, A.: Reserve constrained dynamic dispatch of units with valve-point effects. IEEE Trans. Power Syst. 20(3), 1273–1282 (2005)
5. Granelli, G.P., Marannino, P., Montagna, M., Silvestri, A.: Fast and efficient gradient projection algorithm for dynamic generation dispatching. Proc. Inst. Elect. Eng., Gener. Transm. Distrib. 136(5), 295–302 (1989)
6. Li, F., Morgan, R., Williams, D.: Hybrid genetic approaches to ramping rate constrained dynamic economic dispatch. Elect. Power Syst. Res. 43(2), 97–103 (1997)
7. Han, X.S., Gooi, H.B., Daniel, Kirschen, S.: Dynamic economic dispatch: feasible and optimal solutions. IEEE Trans. Power Syst. 16(1), 22–28 (2001)
8. Walters, D.C., Sheble, G.B.: Genetic algorithm solution of economic dispatch with valve point loadings. IEEE Trans. Power Syst. 8(3), 1325–1331 (1993)
9. Jayaprakash, K., Jeyakumar, D.N., Raghunathan, T.: Evolutionary programming techniques for different kinds of economic dispatch problems. Elect. Power Syst. Res. 73(2), 169–176 (2005)
10. Gaing, Z.-L.: Particle swarm optimization to solving the economic dispatch considering the generator constraints. IEEE Trans. Power Syst. 18(3), 1187–1195 (2003)

11. Passino, K.M.: Biomimicry of Bacterial Foraging for Distributed Optimization and Control. IEEE Control Systems Magazine, 52–67 (2002)
12. Mishra, S.: A hybrid least square-fuzzy bacterial foraging strategy for harmonic estimation. IEEE Trans. on Evolutionary Computation 9(1), 61–73 (2005)
13. Tripathy, M., Mishra, S., Lai, L.L., Zhang, Q.P.: Transmission Loss Reduction Based on FACTS and Bacteria Foraging Algorithm. In: PPSN, pp. 222–231 (2006)
14. Kim, D.H., Cho, C.H.: Bacterial Foraging Based Neural Network Fuzzy Learning. In: IICAI 2005, pp. 2030–2036 (2005)
15. Holland, J.H.: Adaptation in Natural and Artificial Systems. University of Michigan Press, Ann Harbor (1975)
16. Kennedy, J., Eberhart, R.: Particle swarm optimization. In: IEEE International Conference on Neural Networks, pp. 1942–1948 (1995)
17. Storn, R., Price, K.: Differential evolution – A Simple and Efficient Heuristic for Global Optimization over Continuous Spaces. Journal of Global Optimization 11(4), 341–359 (1997)
18. Kim, D.H., Abraham, A., Cho, J.H.: A hybrid genetic algorithm and bacterial foraging approach for global optimization. Information Sciences 177(18), 3918–3937 (2007)
19. Balamurugan, R., Subramanian, S.: An Improved Differential Evolution Based Dynamic Economic Dispatch with Nonsmooth Fuel Cost Function. Journal of Electrical Systems 3-3, 151–160 (2007)
20. Panigrahi, B.K., Ravikumar Pandi, V., Das, S.: Adaptive Particle Swarm Optimization approach for static and dynamic economic load dispatch. Energy Conversion and Management 49, 1407–1415 (2008)
21. Dasgupta, S., Das, S., Abraham, A., Biswas, A.: Adaptive computational chemotaxis in bacterial foraging optimization: an analysis. IEEE Transactions on Evolutionary Computing 13(4), 919–941 (2009)
22. Das, S., Dasgupta, S., Biswas, A., Abraham, A., Konar, A.: On stability of chemotactic dynamics in bacterial foraging optimization algorithm. IEEE Transactions on SMC, Part – A 39(3), 670–679 (2009)
23. Biswas, A., Dasgupta, S., Das, S., Abraham, A.: Dynamics of reproduction in artificial bacterial foraging system: modeling and stability analysis. Theoretical Computer Science 411(21), 2127–2139 (2010)
24. Biswas, A., Dasgupta, S., Das, S., Abraham, A.: Analysis of the reproduction operator in an artificial bacterial foraging System. Applied Mathematics and Computation 215(9), 3343–3355 (2010)
25. Biswas, A., Dasgupta, S., Das, S., Abraham, A.: Synergy of PSO and bacterial foraging optimization: a comparative study on numerical benchmarks. In: Corchado, E., et al. (eds.) Second International Symposium on Hybrid Artificial Intelligent Systems (HAIS 2007). Innovations in Hybrid Intelligent Systems, Advances in Soft computing Series, ASC, vol. 44, pp. 255–263. Springer, Germany (2007)

# Hydro-thermal Commitment Scheduling by Tabu Search Method with Cooling-Banking Constraints

Nimain Charan Nayak[1] and C. Christober Asir Rajan[2]

[1] Research Scholar, Department of EEE, Sathyabama University, Chennai – 600 119
[2] Associate Professor, Department of EEE, Pondicherry Engg College, Pondicherry – 605 014
ncneee@rediffmail.com, asir_70@pec.edu

**Abstract.** This paper presents a new approach for developing an algorithm for solving the Unit Commitment Problem (UCP) in a Hydro-thermal power system. Unit Commitment is a nonlinear optimization problem to determine the minimum cost turn on/off schedule of the generating units in a power system by satisfying both the forecasted load demand and various operating constraints of the generating units. The effectiveness of the proposed hybrid algorithm is proved by the numerical results shown comparing the generation cost solutions and computation time obtained by using Tabu Search Algorithm with other methods like Evolutionary Programming and Dynamic Programming in reaching proper unit commitment.

**Keywords:** Unit Commitment, Dynamic Programming, Tabu Search.

## 1 Introduction

Unit Commitment Problem (UCP) is a non-linear combinatorial optimization problem, which is used in power systems to properly schedule the on/off status of all the generating units in the system. The ultimate goal is to determine the minimum cost turn ON and turn OFF of power generating units to meet the load demand in addition to satisfying various operating constraints of the generating units. For large power systems the problem of unit commitment has generally been difficult to solve because of the complex and uncertain nature of the problem. The operating constraints of the generating units make the problem highly non-linear to solve. There are other problems of inconsistency that affect the overall economic operation of the power station. The exact solution of UCP can be obtained by a complete enumeration of all feasible combination of generating units which would be a huge task. The growth in the demand for electricity forced to introduce many power systems like steam, hydro, nuclear, thermal, tidal and so on. The interconnection of different power systems reduces the cost of generation required to meet the power demand. When the size of the power systems is larger, it is essential to interconnect them to operate the systems economically. Thermal and hydro power systems are often interconnected to meet the demand. The thermal system unit commitment and hydro power generation are to be determined to meet the demand at each hour. The hydro plant reduces the load applied to the thermal system thereby reducing the number of units required to meet the demand with remaining units under shut down. This reduces the fuel cost of

B.K. Panigrahi et al. (Eds.): SEMCCO 2010, LNCS 6466, pp. 739–752, 2010.
© Springer-Verlag Berlin Heidelberg 2010

the thermal power system and in turn reduces the total operating cost [9]. The real practical barrier is solving UCP is the high dimensionality of the possible solution space. Research endeavors have been focused on developing efficient algorithms that can be applied to large power systems and have less memory and computation time requirements. A number of numerical optimization techniques have been employed to solve the complicated UCP. The different categories being used to solve UCP include Classical methods like the Dynamic Programming (DP), the Lagrangian Relaxation (LR), the Fuzzy Logic Approach (FLA), the Tabu Search Method (TSM), the Genetic Algorithm (GA), and the Evolutionary Programming (EP). The major limitations of the numerical techniques are inability to handle problem dimensions, large computation time, more memory space and complexity in programming.

The proposed two-stage method [1] has smaller computational requirements than that of the Simulated Annealing algorithm. The optimal generation from hydro and thermal resources is computed simultaneously in the two stage algorithm; there is no need for assuming constant operation of some reservoirs as in the Simulated Annealing method. No discretization of state and control variables is needed in the proposed method. The required storage as well as computing time in the proposed method is reduced as compared to those in the successive-approximations algorithm. The proposed LR-DP method [2] is efficiently and effectively implemented to solve the UC problem. The proposed LR total production costs over the scheduled time horizon are less than conventional methods especially for the larger number of generating units. The proposed MILP model allows to accurately represent most of the hydroelectric system characteristics, and turns out to be computationally solvable for a planning horizon of one week, proving the high efficiency of modern MILP software tools, both in terms of solution accuracy and computing time [3]. Complex hydraulic chains or additional constrains can be easily modeled and/or added. In our studies [4], reductions in the overall CPU time to solve the problem depended on the case, with a minimum reduction of two times as compared to the classical Multi Stage Benders Decomposition approach and four times as compared to the single linear program approach.

This work [5] builds a fuzzy rule base with the use of the area control error and rate of change of the error. The simulation results show that the proposed fuzzy logic based controller yields improved control performance than the dual mode controller. TS [6] is a powerful, general-purpose stochastic optimization technique, which can theoretically converge asymptotically to a global optimum solution with probability one. But it will take much time to reach the near-global minimum. GA [7], using new specialized operators, have demonstrated excellent performance in dealing with this kind of problem, obtaining near-optimal solutions in reasonable times and without sacrificing the realism of the electric and economic models. Developed algorithms provide optimal unit commitment and also optimal MW values for energy, spinning reserve and non-spin. Results [8] show that with quadratic thermal cost and without prohibited discharge zones, all EP-based algorithms converge faster during initial stages while Fast EP and Classical EP slow down in the latter stages compared to Improved Fast EP. Improved Fast EP performs the best amongst the three in solving this problem in terms of execution time, minimum cost, and mean cost.Solving the UCP by a single optimization algorithm is ineffective and time consuming. Hence, we are proposing a UCP solving approach based on TSM with cooling and banking constraints which provides an effective scheduling with minimum cost. An IEEE test system consisting of 4 hydro generating units and 10 thermal generating units has been considered as a case study and the results obtained are compared with different tabu list and sizes and with the trial solutions.

## 2 Problem Formulation

The main objective of UCP is to determine the on/off status of the generating units in a power system by meeting the load demand at a minimum operating cost in addition to satisfying the constraints (1) of the generating units. The problem formulation [31] includes the quadratic cost characteristics, startup cost of thermal power system and operating constraints of thermal and hydro generating units. The power generation cost for thermal power system is given in (1a).

$$F_{s,it}(P_{s,it}) = A_i + B_i P_{s,it} + C_i P_{s,it}^2 \quad (Rs/hr) \tag{1a}$$

where,

$A_i, B_i, C_i$ - The Cost Function parameters of unit $i$ (Rs/hr, Rs/MWhr, Rs/MW²hr).

$F_{s,it}(P_{s,it})$ - The generation cost of unit $i$ at time $t$ (Rs/hr).

$P_{s,it}$ - The output power from unit $i$ at time $t$ (MW).

The overall objective function [9] of UCP that is to be minimized is given in (1b)

$$F_T = \sum_{t=1}^{T} \sum_{i=1}^{N} (F_{it}(P_{it})U_{it} + S_i V_{it}) \quad (Rs/hr) \tag{1b}$$

where,

$U_{it}$ – Unit $i$ status at hour $t$

$V_{it}$ – Unit $i$ start up/shut down status at time $t$

$F_T$ – Total operating cost over the schedule horizon (Rs/hr)

$S_{it}$ – Startup cost of unit $i$ at time $t$ (Rs).

### 2.1 Constraints

#### 2.1.1 Load Power Balance Constraint
The real power generated by thermal and hydro generating units must be sufficient enough to meet the load demand and must satisfy the equation

$$\sum_{i=1}^{N} P_{s,it} + \sum_{j=1}^{M} P_{h,it} = P_{D,i} + P_{L,i} \quad 1 \le t \le T \tag{2}$$

#### 2.1.2 Spinning Reserve Constraint
Spinning reserve is the total amount of generation available from all units synchronized on the system minus the present load plus the losses being supplied. The

reserve is usually expressed as a percentage of forecasted load demand. Spinning reserve is necessary to prevent drop in system frequency and also to meet the loss of most heavily loaded unit in the power system.

$$\sum_{i=1}^{N} P_{max,i} U_{it} \geq (P_{D,i} + R_t) \qquad 1 \leq t \leq T \tag{3}$$

### 2.1.3  Thermal Constraints

A thermal unit undergoes gradual temperature changes and this increases the time period required to bring the unit online. This time restriction imposes various constraints on generating unit. Some of the constraints are minimum up/down time constraint and crew constraints.

*Minimum Up time*
If the units are already running there will be a minimum time before which the units cannot be turned OFF and the constraint is given in (4).

$$T_{on,i} \geq T_{up,i} \tag{4}$$

*Minimum Down time*
If the units are already OFF there will be a minimum time before which they cannot be turned ON and the constraint is given in (5).

$$T_{off,i} \geq T_{down,i} \tag{5}$$

### 2.1.4  Must Run Units

Some units in the power system are given must run status in order to provide voltage support for the network.

### 2.1.5  Unit Capacity Limits

The power generated by the thermal unit must lie within the maximum and minimum power capacity of the unit.

$$P_{s,i}^{min} \leq P_{s,i} \leq P_{s,i}^{max} \tag{6}$$

### 2.1.6  Hydro Plant Generation Limits

The power generated by the hydro units must be within the maximum and minimum power capacity of the unit [3,9].

$$P_{h,i}^{min} \leq P_{h,i} \leq P_{h,i}^{max} \tag{7}$$

### 2.1.7  Hydraulic Network Constraints

1)  Physical limitations on reservoir storage volumes and discharge rates.

$$V_{h,i}^{min} \leq V_{h,i} \leq V_{h,i}^{max} \tag{8}$$

$$Q_{h,i}{}^{\min} \le Q_{h,i} \le Q_{h,i}{}^{\max} \tag{9}$$

2)  The initial volume and the final volume that is to be retained at the end of scheduling period.

$$V_{h,it}{}^{t=0} = V_{h,i}{}^{begin} \tag{10}$$

$$V_{h,it}{}^{t=T} = V_{h,i}{}^{end} \tag{11}$$

The Continuity equation for hydro reservoir network is given in (12).

$$V_h(i,t) = V_h(i,t-1) + I_h(i,t) - S_h(i,t) - Q_h(i,t) -$$
$$\sum_{m=1}^{Ru} [Q_h(m,t-\Gamma(i,m)) + S_h(m,t-\Gamma(i,m))] \tag{12}$$

### 2.1.8  Hydro Plant Unit Power Generation Characteristics

The hydro power generated is related to the reservoir characteristics as well as water discharge rates. Hydro power output is a function of the volume of the reservoir and discharge rate. The equation representing the hydro power generation characteristics is given in (13).

$$P_h(i,t) = C_{1,i}V_h(i,t)^2 + C_{2,i}Q_h(i,t)^2 +$$
$$C_{3,i}[V_h(i,t)Q_h(i,t)]C_{4,i}V_h(i,t) + C_{5,i}Q_h(i,t) + C_{6,i} \tag{13}$$

## 3  Tabu Search

### 3.1  Overview

Tabu Search [17-19] utilizes the technique of extended neighborhood search which has been applied to many complicated optimization problems. It is an iterative procedure that searches for a set of feasible solutions in the possible solution space to reach a better solution. Tabu Search provides a means for eliminating the problem of entrapment in local optima by employing a short term memory structure of recently visited solutions. The procedure will shift the direction of the algorithm on the next move during the local optimal condition which may ultimately lead to a better solution. The main two components of Tabu Search algorithm are the Tabu List Restrictions and Aspiration Level of the solution associated with these restrictions. The following sections explain the above mentioned components of TSA.

### 3.2  Tabu List Restrictions

The Tabu Search approach for solving UCP is to overcome the problem of local optimality by the strategy of forbidding certain moves that deteriorates the quality of the solution. The purpose of assigning tabu status to certain moves is to prevent cycling which reduces the processor time and also enhances the quality of the solution.

TS introduce the tabu list (TL) to control the change of the attributes. The objective of the tabu list is to avoid short term solution candidates circulating in the solution search space. The tabu list works as a temporary memory that stores attributes during some iterations. The attributes stored in the tabu list are fixed while other attributes are changeable for finding a better solution. Once a new attribute enter the tabu list the older attribute is released from the list. The tabu list length is the parameter that controls the TS performance [4-6].

The TL is designed to ensure elimination of cycles of length equal to the TL size. The TL sizes that provide good solution depend on the size of the problem. For smaller size lists the number of cycles occurring is more. For large size lists the quality of the solution may deteriorate due to the elimination of too many moves. Hence the best size lies in between these extremes. The best size can be found by repeated execution of the tabu search program with different TL sizes [17].

### 3.3  Aspiration Level

TL stores the solutions that are likely to provide local optima by assigning tabu status to the solutions. But all the solutions in the TL that owns tabu status may not be local optimal solutions. Hence tabu status can be overruled if certain conditions are met expressed in the form of Aspiration Level (AL).If appropriate aspiration criterion is satisfied the tabu status of the solution can be overruled. Hence AL is designed to override tabu status if a move is good enough. Different forms of AL can be used. But the proposed algorithm associates AL with the objective function of the solution obtained during a move. If the tabued move yields a solution with better objective function than the one obtained in the previous move then AL can be used to override the tabu status. AL is used to add flexibility in the tabu search by directing the search towards attractive moves that lead to a better solution [17].

### 3.4  Termination of the Algorithm

The algorithm can be terminated at any time if it satisfies certain conditions. There may be several possible conditions for termination of the algorithm. But the best conditions are selected by the quality of the solution obtained after termination. In this algorithm two possible conditions for termination have been applied. The algorithm will be terminated if the following conditions are satisfied:

- given number of iterations have been performed (or)
- the operating cost repeats successively for certain number of iterations.

### 3.5  General Tabu Search Algorithm

The TSA is applied for solving many combinatorial optimization problems. The iterative algorithm starts with the formation of an initial feasible random solution. Then a move is performed to this initial solution to obtain neighbors to this solution. A move to the neighbor is performed if it is not present in TL or in case of being in

TL it passes the AL test. During this search process the best solution is always updated and stored in a variable until the iteration is stopped.

The following notation is used to describe the general TSA algorithm [17] for solving combinatorial optimization problems.

$X$    :    the set of feasible solutions for a given problem
$x$    :    current solution, $x \in X$
$x''$   :    best solution reached
$x'$   :    best solution among a sample of trial solutions
$E(x)$ :   objective function of solution $x$
$N(x)$ :   set of neighborhood of $x \in X$ (trial solutions)
$S(x)$ :   sample of neighborhood of $x$; $S(x) \in N(x)$
$SS(x)$:  sorted sample in ascending order according to their   objective functions, $E(x)$
TL  :  tabu list  and   AL  :   aspiration level

The steps of general TSA are as follows:

1. Set TL as empty and AL as zero.
2. Set iteration counter K=0. Select an initial solution $x \in X$ and set $x'' = x$.
3. Generate randomly a set of trial solutions $S(x) \in N(x)$ (neighbor to the current solution $x$) and sort them in an ascending order, to obtain $SS(x)$. Let $x'$ be the best trial solution in the sorted set $SS(x)$ (the first in the sorted set).
4. If $E(x) > E(x')$, go to Step 4, else set the best solution $x'' = x'$ and go to Step 4.
5. Perform the tabu test. If $x'$ is not in TL, then accept it as a current solution, set $x = x'$ and update the TL and AL and go to Step 7, else go to Step 5.
6. Perform the AL test. If satisfied, then override the tabu state, set $x = x'$, update the AL and go to Step 7, else go to Step 6.
7. If the end of $SS(x)$ is reached, go to Step 7, otherwise, let $x'$ be the next solution in $SS(x)$ and go to Step 4.
8. Perform the termination test. If the stopping criterion is satisfied then stop, else set K=K+1 and go to step 2.

## 4  Tabu Search Algorithm For UCP

### 4.1  TSA for Solving UCP

The variables used for solving the UCP are the unit status variables U and V which are binary digits either 0 or 1 and the unit output power variable P. The following are the steps of tabu search algorithm for solving the unit commitment problem in hydro-thermal power system. The complete flowchart for solving UCP is shown in Fig. 1.

1. Get the thermal and hydro power system data and load pattern for a day.
2. Calculate the water discharge rates and hence the hydro power output.

3.  Calculate the thermal system load $P_{dt}$ by subtracting the hydro power $P_{dh}$ from the total demand $P_d$.
    $P_{dt} = P_d - P_{dh}$
4.  Initialize all variables *(U, V, P)* to zero and set the iteration counter K=0.
5.  Generate randomly an initial current feasible solution *($U_i^0$, Vi0)*.
6.  Calculate the total operating cost, $F_i^0$ for this solution.
7.  Set the global best solution equal to the current solution, *($U_B$, VB)* = *($U_i^0$, Vi0)*, $F_B = F_i$.
8.  Find a set of trial solutions $S(U_i^K, V_i^K)$ that are neighbors to the current solution *($U_i^K, V_i^K$)* with objective values $F^K(S)$ and sort them in an ascending order. Let $SF^K(S)$ be the sorted values. Let *($U_b^K, V_b^K$)* be the best trial solution in the Set, with an objective value $F_b$.
9.  If $F_b \geq F_B$ go to Step 10, else update the global best solution, set *($U_B, V_B$)* = *($U_b^K, V_b^K$)* and go to Step 10.
10. If the trial solution *($U_b^K, V_b^K$)* is NOT in the TL, then update the TL, the AL and the current solution; set *($U_i^K, V_i^K$)* = *($U_b^K, V_b^K$)*, $F_i^K = F_b$ and go to Step 13, else go to Step 11.
11. If the AL test is NOT satisfied go to Step 12 else, override the tabu state, set *($U_i^K, V_i^K$)* = *($U_b^K, V_b^K$)* update the AL and go to Step 13.
12. If the end of the $SF^K(S)$ is reached go to Step 13, otherwise let *($U_b^K, V_b^K$)* be the next solution in the $SF^K(S)$ and go to Step 10.
13. Stop if the termination criterion is satisfied, else set K=K+1 and go to Step 8.
14. For the units, which are in the off states, calculate the cost for both cooling and banking.
15. Compare the cooling and banking costs, if banking cost is lesser than cooling, bank the unit.
16. Print the optimum schedule.

## 4.2  Generation of a Neighbor

Generating a neighbor to the current solution is the important section of the tabu search algorithm [17]. The neighbors created must be feasible to meet the demand and also span as much of the problem solution space as possible. The better is the neighbor created the better will be the final solution. Hence a lot of future work is required in this area to develop a randomly feasible neighbor to the current solution. The additional contribution in this paper is the proposal and implementation of new rules to improve the speed of formation of neighbor and its quality. The new rules implemented to obtain the neighbors to the current solution are described in the following steps. The same rules can be used to create the initial feasible current solution.

1.  Consider a unit $i$ and generate randomly a time $t$, $t \sim UD(1,T)$ and get the status of the unit at $t$.
2.  If the unit $i$ at hour $t$ is ON, then go to Step 3 for switching it OFF around this time $t$. If the unit $i$ at hour $t$ is OFF then go to Step 4 for switching it ON around this time $t$.

3. Switching the unit $i$ from ON to OFF:
   a) Move backward and forward in time from the hour $t$ to find the length of the ON period of the unit $i$. Let the number of ON periods be $n$.
   b) Note down the time $t1$ and $t2$ which are the first and last hours at which the unit is ON.
   c) If the time $t$ obtained randomly is an odd number, then generate an odd number $L \sim UD(1,n)$ and switch OFF all the units starting from $t1$ till $t1+L-1$ hour is reached.
   d) If the time $t$ obtained randomly is an even number, then generate an even number $L \sim UD(1,n)$ and switch OFF all the units starting

4. Switching the unit $i$ from OFF to ON:
   a) Move backward and forward in time from the hour $t$ to find the length of the OFF period of the unit $i$. Let the number of OFF periods be $n$.
   b) Note down the time $t1$ and $t2$ which are the first and last hours at which the unit is OFF.
   c) If the time $t$ obtained randomly is an odd number, then generate an odd number $L \sim UD(1,n)$ and switch ON all the units starting from $t1$ till $t1+L-1$ hour is reached.
   d) If the time $t$ obtained randomly is an even number, then generate an even number $L \sim UD(1,n)$ and switch ON all the units starting from $t1$ till $t1+L-1$ hour is reached.

5. Check if the obtained neighbor meets the load demand. If it meets the demand, then the obtained neighbor is feasible, otherwise repeat the above steps to obtain the feasible neighbor to the current solution.

## 4.3 Formation of Tabu List

The TL is the main component of tabu search technique [17]. It uses short term memory structure to store forbidden moves and prevents the cycling of the forbidden solutions which reduces the processor time. The TL eliminates the cycles of length 'Z' where 'Z' is the size of the tabu list. The TL can store the 'Z' entries of the entire solution matrices. But this requires large amount of memory space and increases the execution time of the algorithm. Hence it is worth proposing different techniques for formation of TL types that utilizes less memory and stores attributes that are most appropriate in representing the solution nature.

In the implementation of different TL types in this paper, a separate TL for each generating unit is created and is called Generating Unit TL (GUTL). Each GUTL has dimensions of Z X L, where L is the recorded attributes length. In this technique, the number of TLs required is equal to the number of generating units. The second technique uses a single TL for the whole solution. Two different techniques to form TL are described in the following section.

## 4.4 Different Types of Tabu List

The two proposed techniques for the formation of TL types are as follows:

**Technique 1**

This technique uses only one TL for the whole solution. This reduces the space occupied by the TL. Here each entry records the objective function values of the trial solutions generated. Whenever a new objective value is obtained, it is compared with the available values in TL. If the new objective value is found minimum, then its corresponding solution is taken as the current solution and next iteration is performed. If it is not found minimum, then it is stored in TL and the minimum objective value solution in TL is taken as the current solution and next iteration is performed.

**Technique 2**

In this technique, each GUTL contains one dimensional array of 'Z' entries. Each entry records the number of ON periods for the respective unit. This technique represents the solution nature in the most appropriate and easy way. In this technique the assumption is that two solutions with same number of ON periods will have the same operating cost irrespective of their status at different hours in the scheduled horizon.

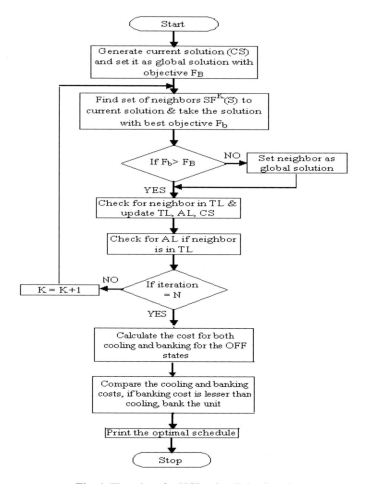

**Fig. 1.** Flowchart for UCP using Tabu Search

# 5   Case Study

An IEEE test system consisting of 4 hydro generating units and 10 thermal generating units has been considered as a case study. A time period of 24 hours is considered and the unit commitment problem is solved for these 10 units power system. The required inputs for solving the UCP are tabulated below. The IEEE thermal test system is shown in Table 1, hydro discharge coefficients, reservoir volumes and discharge limits and inflows to the reservoir are shown in Tables 2, 3 and 4. The daily load pattern considered is shown in Table 5. The operating cost comparison of TS with DP and LR is shown in Tables 6, 7, 8 and 9. The Cost convergence graphs of TS for different iterations are shown in Figures 2 and 3.

**Table 1.** IEEE thermal test system

| Unit | Pmax (MW) | Pmin (MW) | A ($/h) | B ($/MWh) | C ($/MW²h) | Startup Cost ($) | Tup & Tdown (h) |
|------|-----------|-----------|---------|-----------|------------|------------------|------------------|
| 1  | 455 | 150 | 1000 | 16.19 | 0.00048 | 4500 | 8 |
| 2  | 455 | 150 | 970  | 17.26 | 0.00031 | 5000 | 8 |
| 3  | 130 | 20  | 700  | 16.6  | 0.002   | 550  | 5 |
| 4  | 130 | 20  | 680  | 16.5  | 0.00211 | 560  | 5 |
| 5  | 162 | 25  | 450  | 19.7  | 0.00398 | 900  | 6 |
| 6  | 80  | 20  | 370  | 22.26 | 0.00712 | 170  | 3 |
| 7  | 85  | 25  | 480  | 27.74 | 0.00079 | 260  | 3 |
| 8  | 55  | 10  | 660  | 25.92 | 0.00413 | 30   | 1 |
| 9  | 55  | 10  | 665  | 27.27 | 0.00222 | 30   | 1 |
| 10 | 55  | 10  | 670  | 27.79 | 0.00173 | 30   | 1 |

**Table 2.** Hydro discharge coefficients

| UNIT | $C_1$ | $C_2$ | $C_3$ | $C_4$ | $C_5$ | $C_6$ |
|------|-------|-------|-------|-------|-------|-------|
| 1 | -0.0042 | -0.42  | 0.03  | 0.9  | 10  | 50 |
| 2 | -0.004  | -0.3   | 0.015 | 1.14 | 9.5 | 70 |
| 3 | -0.0016 | -0.125 | 0.014 | 0.55 | 5.5 | 40 |
| 4 | -0.003  | -0.31  | 0.027 | 1.14 | 14  | 90 |

**Table 3.** Reservoir volume & discharge limits (x $10^4$ m$^3$)

| Unit | Vmin | Vmax | Vini | Vend | Qmin | Qmax | Pmin | Pmax |
|------|------|------|------|------|------|------|------|------|
| 1 | 0 | 200 | 100 | 100 | 0 | 30 | 0 | 500 |
| 2 | 0 | 200 | 100 | 100 | 0 | 30 | 0 | 500 |
| 3 | 0 | 350 | 150 | 150 | 0 | 40 | 0 | 500 |
| 4 | 0 | 350 | 150 | 150 | 0 | 40 | 0 | 500 |

**Table 4.** Inflows to the reservoir (x $10^4$ m$^3$)

| UNIT | 1 | 2 | 3 | 4 | 5 | 6 | 7 | 8 |
|------|----|----|------|------|------|------|------|------|
| 1 | 12 | 12 | 11.8 | 11.7 | 11.7 | 11.6 | 11.5 | 11.4 |
| 2 | 6  | 6  | 6.5  | 6.7  | 6.8  | 6.9  | 7    | 7.2  |
| 3 | 3  | 4  | 5    | 6    | 7    | 8    | 8.8  | 8.9  |
| 4 | 3  | 2  | 2    | 0    | 0    | 0    | 0    | 0    |

**Table 5.** Load pattern for 24 hours

| PERIOD (h) | LOAD (MW) | PERIOD (h) | LOAD (MW) |
|---|---|---|---|
| 1 | 1400 | 13 | 2075 |
| 2 | 1450 | 14 | 2000 |
| 3 | 1350 | 15 | 1900 |
| 4 | 1650 | 16 | 1750 |
| 5 | 1700 | 17 | 1800 |
| 6 | 2000 | 18 | 1900 |
| 7 | 1850 | 19 | 1950 |
| 8 | 1900 | 20 | 2100 |
| 9 | 2000 | 21 | 2050 |
| 10 | 1400 | 22 | 1800 |
| 11 | 2100 | 23 | 1600 |
| 12 | 2150 | 24 | 1500 |

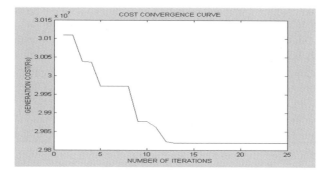

**Fig. 2.** Cost convergence characteristics for 25 iterations with TL size=10

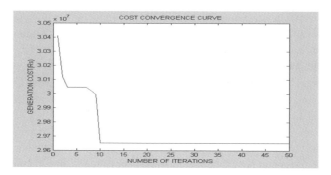

**Fig. 3.** Cost convergence characteristics for 50 iterations with TL size=10

**Table 6.** Production cost for different techniques

| Techniques Used | Iterations | Production Cost (Rs) | Computation Time (Sec) |
|---|---|---|---|
| DP | - | 3,27,74,013 | 83.90 |
| LR | - | 3,06,56,586 | 73.65 |
| TS (without Cooling & Banking) | 25 | 2,98,19,243 | 18.07 |
| TS (without Cooling & Banking) | 50 | 2,96,51,741 | 18.00 |
| TS(With Cooling & Banking) | 25 | 2,98,01,102 | 17.91 |
| TS(With Cooling & Banking) | 50 | 2,96,43,612 | 17.02 |

**Table 7.** Comparison of costs for different TL Types

| Technique No. | 1 | 2 |
|---|---|---|
| Cost (Rs) | 2,96,51,741 | 2,98,84,529 |

**Table 8.** Comparison of costs for different TL size

| TL size | 5 | 10 | 15 | 20 |
|---|---|---|---|---|
| Cost (Rs) | 3,00,92,462 | 2,96,51,741 | 2,99,90,843 | 3,01,71,755 |

**Table 9.** Cost for different trial solutions formed

| Number of trail solutions formed | 5 | 10 | 14 | 20 |
|---|---|---|---|---|
| Cost (Rs) | 3,00,54,542 | 3,00,24,486 | 2,96,51,741 | 3,02,13,153 |

# 6 Conclusions

UCP is solved using the tabu search method with cooling and banking constraints. The results obtained during the execution of the program clearly provide the following observations. The better final solution of UCP is mainly influenced by the initial current feasible solution. If the current solution provides a better objective function then the final solution obtained reaches the global optimum solution with probability very close to one. The time of execution taken by TSA with cooling and banking constraints to solve UCP is equal to 25 % of the time of execution taken by TS without cooling and banking. The size of the TL also influences the quality of the final solution obtained. The better solutions are obtained for the tabu list size of 10. The percentage of escape from the local optima for the proposed algorithm is almost reaching 70%. From the two types of TL proposed, better solutions are obtained in the case of Technique 1. The size of the TL does not affect the time of execution of the program but it is limited by the deterioration in the quality of the solution obtained.

In this paper a new algorithm with cooling and banking constraints for solving the unit commitment problem in a hydro-thermal power system is proposed. The TS is characterized by its ability to escape from the local optima by employing short term memory structure. The TS also has a strategy called AL which directs the search towards attractive moves leading to a better ultimate solution. Different techniques for constructing tabu list have been proposed and tested which provided good solutions. The effectiveness of the algorithm is proved by considering an IEEE thermal and hydro test system. The results obtained from the proposed algorithm are better than the results obtained from the other methods tried. The Tabu Search algorithm can be used as a powerful tool for solving many combinatorial optimization problems. Even better solutions can be obtained by employing sophisticated procedures in the formation of trial solution and tabu list. Thus the ability of tabu search method to escape local optima with reduced computation time proves the strength of the algorithm.

# References

[1] Ferrero, R.W., Rivera, J.F., Shahidehpour, S.M.: A Dynamic Programming Two-Stage Algorithm For Long-Term Hydrothermal Scheduling Of Multi reservoir Systems. IEEE Transactions on Power System 13(4), 1534–1540 (1998)
[2] Benhamida, F.: A Hybrid Lagrangian Relaxation – Dynamic Programming Solution to the Unit Commitment Problem. Journal of Electrical Engineering 9(4), 31–40 (2009)
[3] Borghetti, A., D'Ambrosio, C., Lodi, A., Martello, S.: An MILP Approach for Short-Term Hydro Scheduling and Unit Commitment with Head-Dependent Reservoir. IEEE Transactions on Power Systems 23(3), 1115–1124 (2008)
[4] dos Santos, T.N., Diniz, A.L.: A New Multi period Stage Definition for the Multistage Benders Decomposition Approach Applied to Hydrothermal Scheduling. IEEE Transactions on Power Systems 24(3), 1383–1392 (2009)
[5] Srinivasa Rao, C., Siva Nagaraju, S., Sangameswara Raju, P.: Automatic generation control of TCPS based hydrothermal system under open market scenario: A fuzzy logic approach. International Journal of Electrical Power and Energy Systems 31(1), 315–322 (2009)
[6] Mantawy, A.H., Abdel-Magid, Y.L., Selim, S.Z.: A Unit Commitment by Tabu Search. IEE Proc. Generation, Transmission and Distribution 145(1), 56–64 (1998)
[7] Gil, E., Bustos, J., Rudnick, H.: Short-Term Hydrothermal Generation Scheduling Model Using a Genetic Algorithm. IEEE Transactions on Power Systems 18(4), 1256–1264 (2003)
[8] Sinha, N., Chakrabarti, R., Chattopadhyay, P.K.: Fast Evolutionary Programming Techniques for Short-Term Hydrothermal Scheduling. IEEE Transactions on Power Systems 18(1), 214–220 (2003)
[9] Wood, A.J., Wollenbergm, B.F.: Power Generation, Operation and Control. John Wiley & Sons Ltd., Chichester (1984)

# Author Index

Abhaikumar, V.   46
Abraham, Ajith   54
Agarwal, Sanchit   286
Aggarwal, Nupur   38
Agrawal, Sanjay   351
Ali, Layak   155, 672
Arvind, M.   270

Babu, A. Vinaya   278
Bajaj, Ruchika   230
Banati, Hema   305
Bansal, Jagdish Chand   460
Banu, U. Sabura   648
Barpanda, Ravi Sankar   599
Basak, Aniruddha   254, 630, 718
Baskar, S.   79, 171
Bedi, Punam   230
Bhargava, Rohit   305
Bhattacharjee, Anup Kumar   432
Bijwe, P.R.   709
Biswal, Bibhuti Bhusan   111
Bouvry, Pascal   54

Cai, Zhaoquan   222, 338
Chaganti, Vinaykumar   278
Chakraborty, N.   680
Chandra, Satish   286
Chandran, K.R.   623
Chatterjee, A.   559
Chaudhuri, Koyel   514
Chauhan, Nikunj   38
Chauhan, Pinkcy   139
Chintalapati, Janaki   270
Chowdhury, Aritra   62, 87, 523
Cui, Zhihua   389, 583

Das, A.K.   575
Das, Debi Prasad   531
Das, Swagatam   1, 62, 87, 119, 206,
    254, 322, 416, 523, 630
Dasgupta, Dipankar   514
Davoudpouri, Hamid   494
Deb, Kalyanmoy   182, 330, 607
Deep, Kusum   139, 460
Dehuri, S.   370

Deng, Guang-Feng   238
Devaraj, D.   481
Devi, S.   322
Dheeba, J.   404
Dileep, M.   370
Divya, V.   46

Fernández-Martínez, Juan Luis   147

García-Gonzalo, Esperanza   147
Ghose, D.   11
Ghosh, Arnob   62, 87, 523
Ghosh, Pradipta   701
Ghosh, Saurav   119
Ghoshal, Sakti Prasad   432, 559
Giri, J.M.   607
Giri, Ritwik   11, 62, 87, 523
Goel, Preeti   214
Gouthanan, Pushpan   19
Gunjan, Kumar   206
Gupta, H.M.   246
Gupta, Shivam   182

Hanmandlu, Madasu   246
Hanuman, A. Sai   278
Hao, Zhi-Feng   190, 222, 262, 296, 338
Hashemi, Ali B.   129
Hazarika, Kaustabh Moni   689
He, Xiao-juan   656
Huang, Han   190, 222, 262, 338

Islam, Sk..Minhazul   119

Jadhav, D.G.   322
Jatoth, Ravi Kumar   380
Jeyakumar, G.   29, 95
Jian-ping, Qiu   664
Joe Amali, S. Miruna   79
Jothi Swaroopan, N.M.   468

Kachroudi, Sofiene   314
Kamosi, Masoud   129
Kant, Ajay   286
Karmakar, Amrita   689
Killani, Ramanji   623

Krishnanand, K.R.   537
Kumar, Amioy   246
Kumar, Naik Manoj   362
Kumar, Pravesh   103

Li, Benqing   190
Li, Haozhe   190
Li, Xueqiang   262, 338
Lichao, Chen   664
Lim, Meng Hiot   198
Lin, Woo-Tsong   238
Ling, Shaohu   190
Lohokare, M.R.   322

Mahapatra, S.S.   396
Maity, Sayan   206
Majhi, Banshidhar   599
Mallick, M.K.   718
Mallipeddi, Rammohan   71, 709
Manda, Kalyani   278
Mandal, Durbadal   432
Mandal, K.K.   680
Mangala, N.   270
Mehta, Shikha   305
Meybodi, M.R.   129
Mini, S.   424
Mishra, Debadutta   111
Mohandas, V.P.   567
Mohapatra, Ankita   537, 718
Movahedi, Yaser   494
Mukherjee, V.   559
Muthuselvan, N.B.   639

Nain, P.K.S.   607
Nasiri, G. Reza   494
Nayak, Nimain Charan   739

Ohdar, R.K.   396
Ong, Yew Soon   198

Padmavathi, S.   448
Pal, Siddharth K.   230, 254, 630, 718
Panda, B.S.   214
Panda, Ganapati   531
Panda, Rutuparna   351
Panda, Sumanta   111
Pandi, V. Ravikumar   630, 718
Panigrahi, B.K.   322, 523, 537, 630,
    709, 718
Pant, Millie   54, 103, 139

Pattnaik, S.S.   322
Paul, Shantanu   689
Ponnambalam, S.G.   440
Pradhan, Gunanidhi   623
Praveena, P.   727
Priyanka, S.   270

Qu, Bo Yang   19

Rajan, C. Christober Asir   739
Raju, S.   46
Rama Mohana Rao, S.   727
Rao, B. Tirumala   370
Rao, K. Srinivasa   623
Rashidi, Farzan   591
Rashidi, Mehran   591
Rathi, Amit   163
Ravi, V.   38
Reddy, Gogulamudi Anudeep   380
Rout, Nirmal Kumar   531
Rout, P.K.   537
Roy, Subhrajit   119
Rutuparna, Panda   362

Sabat, Samrat L.   155, 424, 672
Sachdeva, Bhuvan   305
Sahoo, Bibhudatta   599
Sakthivel, V.P.   545
Sarkar, Soham   416
Sasikumar, T.   448
Satapathy, Suresh Chandra   278, 623
Sathyabama, B.   46
Selvabala, B.   481
Selvi, Tamil   404
Shalinie, S. Mercy   448
Shanmugavelayutham, C.   95
Sharma, Arnesh   286
Sharma, S.   607
Shekhar, Himanshu   689
Shi, Zhongzhi   389
Sil, J.   575
Sinha, Nidul   689
Sivakumar, P. Bagavathi   567
Somasundaram, P.   468, 639
Someshwar, B.C.   448
Song, Li Qin   198
Sood, Anoop Kumar   396
Srivastava, Soumil   330
Subramanian, S.   545

Sue-Ann, Goh     440
Suganthan, Ponnuthurai Nagaratnam
    1, 19, 71, 709

Tan, Ying     615
Thangaraj, Radha     54
Thangavelu, S.     344
Tudu, B.     680
Turuk, Ashok Kumar     599

Udgata, Siba K.     155, 424, 672
Uma, G.     648

Vaisakh, K.     727
Valadi, Jayaraman     270
Velayutham, C. Shunmuga     29, 344
Verma, Ashu     709

Vijay, Ritu     163
Vindhya, A.     370

Wang, Li-fang     656
Wang, Yan     615
Willjuice Iruthayarajan, M.     171

Xu, Yuechun     583
Xue, Song-dong     656

Zafar, Hamim     701
Zeng, Jian-chao     389, 583, 615, 656
Zhang, Yu Shan     296
Zhao, Shi-Zheng     1
Zhu, Yifan     222
Zhu, Zhuanghua     506

Printing: Mercedes-Druck, Berlin
Binding: Stein+Lehmann, Berlin